Classics Series

Gower's Principles of Modern Company Law

Paul L. Davies QC (hon), FBA
Allen & Overy Professor of Corporate Law Emeritus
Senior Research Fellow
Harris Manchester College
University of Oxford

Sarah Worthington QC (hon), FBA
Downing Professor of the Laws of England and Fellow of Trinity College
University of Cambridge

with a contribution from

Dr. Eva Micheler
Reader in Law
London School of Economics and Political Science
Ao Universitätsprofessor
Wirtschaftsuniversität Wien

SWEET & MAXWELL

THOMSON REUTERS

First Edition   1954
Tenth Edition   2016

Published in 2016 by Thomson Reuters (Professional) UK Limited, trading as Sweet &
Maxwell. Registered in England & Wales, Company No.1679046. Registered Office and
address for service: 5 Canada Square, Canary Wharf, London, E14 5AQ.

For further information on our products and services, visit *www.sweetandmaxwell.co.uk*

Typeset by Letterpart Limited, Caterham on the Hill, Surrey, CR3 5XL.

Printed and bound by CPI Group (UK) Ltd, Croydon, CR0 4YY.

No natural forests were destroyed to make this product: only farmed timber was used and
re-planted.

A CIP catalogue record of this book is available from the British Library.

ISBN: 978-0-414-05626-8

Preface

In addition to the general updating which a book of this scope requires for a new edition, there have been three drivers of change in the corporate law area since the ninth edition of 2012. First, the Supreme Court has continued to be active in the area of core corporate law, unusually so by historical standards. Even the old chestnut, piercing the veil, has given the Justices something to chew on in *VTB Capital Plc v Nutritek International Corp* [2013] UKSC 5 and *Petrodel Resources Ltd v Prest* [2013] UKSC 34. These decisions confirm the limited scope of that doctrine in English law, whilst demonstrating the availability of alternative techniques for handling the underlying problem. Re-assertion of orthodoxy was also the main thrust of *Eclairs Group Ltd v JKX Oil and Gas Plc* [2015] UKSC 71 on directors' use of powers for an improper purpose, though dicta in the case generate some uncertainties for the future. The Supreme Court's latest and perhaps conclusive statement on the availability of proprietary remedies for breach of fiduciary duty is to be found in *FHR European Ventures LLP v Mankarious (No.2)* [2014] UKSC 45. Finally, in *Bilta (UK) Ltd v Nazir* [2015] UKSC 23 the Court began the process of bringing order out of the chaos left by its previous decision in *Stone & Rolls Ltd v Moore Stephens* [2009] UKSC 39 concerning the availability of the illegality defence where the company has been used as a vehicle for fraud by its only directors and shareholders.

On the domestic legislative front, life has been quiet since the passing of the Companies Act 2006, but the Small Business, Enterprise and Employment Act 2015 has had a significant impact in some particular areas of company law, despite the lack of any explicit reference to companies in the title. The requirement for the revelation of controlling positions in all companies aims to make it less easy for companies to be used to hide criminal or otherwise objectionable activities. One might say that this is using the law in an attempt to limit the 'negative externalities' of the corporate form. It is thus quite different from the beneficial ownership disclosures long required (and at a much lower level) in relation publicly traded companies, which are motivated by more traditional company and market concerns. Consequently, we deal with the new disclosure rules in Ch.2, whilst leaving the established 'major shareholdings' rules in Ch.26. In addition, the 2015 Act underlines government's view that the promotion of small businesses and enterprise requires enhanced creditor protection in relation to limited companies, in this case through reforms both t the procedures for disqualifying directors (Ch.10) and to those for recoveri compensation from directors who engage in wrongful trading (Ch.9). Legislat

v

reversal of the courts' (at least initial) unwillingness to apply directors' duties to shadow directors goes in the same direction.

Finally, the shape of the substantive reforms resulting from the financial crisis of 2007–9, which were inchoate at the time of the previous edition, have now become clearer. Not surprisingly, given the nature of the crisis, the reforms have focussed on banks and other financial institutions rather than on companies across the board. Nevertheless, the reform of financial markets has had an impact on the rules governing access by companies to the capital markets and their obligations once admitted, as discussed in Part 6 of the book. This is an area where EU law frequently takes the lead and a significant change here has been the Community's increasing use of Regulations, rather than Directives, to effect the reforms, with a consequent change in the balance between EU and domestic rules in implementing the changes. At the time of writing the future shape of this body of rules is subject to considerable political uncertainty.

We would like to thank very warmly Professor Eva Micheler of the London School of Economics and Political Science for updating Ch.27 on Transfer of Shares, for which she has taken responsibility over a number of editions.

Sarah Worthington would like to thank Michael Lok for his significant research assistance in the updating of particular parts of this edition; that he managed to provide this help while also conducting an increasingly busy and successful practice in Hong Kong is testament to his energy and organisation.

We have sought to state the law as at the end of February 2016, although some references to later material have been possible.

PLD, SEW

June 2016

Table of Abbreviations

AADB	Accounting and Actuarial Discipline Board
ADR	American Depositary Receipt
AGM	Annual General Meeting
AIM	Alternative Investment Market
AMP	Accepted Market Practice
APB	Auditing Practices Board
ARC	Accounting Regulatory Committee
ARD	Accounting Reference Date
ARP	Accounting Reference Period
ASB	Accounting Standards Board
BERR	Department for Business, Enterprise & Regulatory Reform
BIS	Department for Business Innovation & Skills
BoT	Board of Trade
BR	Business Review
CA	Companies Act
CARD	Consolidated Admissions Requirements Directive
CDDA	Company Directors Disqualification Act 1986
CEO	Chief Executive Officer
CESR	Committee of European Securities Regulators
CfD	Contract for Differences
CFO	Chief Financial Officer
CGC	UK Corporate Governance Code
CIB	Companies Investigation Branch (of BERR)
CIC	Community Interest Company
CIO	Charitable Incorporated Organisation
CJA	Criminal Justice Act 1993
CLR	Company Law Review
CPR	Civil Procedure Rules
CRR	Capital Redemption Reserve

DB	Defined Benefit (pension scheme)
DC	Defined Contribution (pension scheme)
DEPP	Decision Procedure and Penalties Manual (of FCA)
DTI	Department of Trade and Industry
DTR	Disclosure and Transparency Rule (of FCA)
DR	Directors' Report
DRR	Directors' Remuneration Report
EBLR	European Business Law Review
EBOR	European Business Organization Law Review
ECJ	European Court of Justice
ECtHR	European Court of Human Rights
EEA	European Economic Area
EEIG	European Economic Interest Grouping
EFRAG	European Financial Reporting Advisory Group
EG	Enforcement Guide (of FCA)
ESMA	European Securities and Markets Authority
ESV	Enlightened Shareholder Value
FCA	Financial Conduct Authority
FRC	Financial Reporting Council
FRRP	Financial Reporting Review Panel
FRS	Financial Reporting Standard
FRSEE	Financial Reporting Standard for Smaller Entities
FSA	Financial Services Authority
FSAP	Financial Services Action Plan (of the EC Commission)
FSMA	Financial Services and Markets Act 2000
GAAP	Generally Accepted Accounting Principles
GEFIM	Gilt-edged and Fixed-Interest Markets
GP	General Principle (of the Code on Takeovers and Mergers)
HKCFAR	Hong Kong Court of Final Appeal Reports
HLG	High Level Group of Company Law Experts
IA	Insolvency Act
IAASB	International Auditing and Assurance Standards Board
IAS	International Accounting Standards
IASB	International Accounting Standards Board
IFRS	International Financial Reporting Standards

IPO	Initial Public Offering
ISA	International Standard on Auditing
JCLS	Journal of Corporate Law Studies
KPI	Key Performance Indicators
LLP	Limited Liability Partnership
LP	Limited Partnership
LR	Listing Rules
LSE	London Stock Exchange
Ltd	Limited
Ltip	Long-term incentive plan
MAD	Market Abuse Directive (Directive 2003/6/EC)
MAR	Market Abuse Regulation (Regulation (EU) No.596/2014)
MIFID	Directive on Markets in Financial Instruments
MTF	Multilateral Trading Facility
MO	Management Organ (of an SE)
Nasdaq	National Association of Securities Dealers Automated Quotation System (a US stock exchange)
NED	Non-Executive Director
OEIC	Open-ended Investment Company
OFR	Operating and Financial Review
OR	Official Receiver
OSOV	One Share One Vote
OTC	Over the counter
PCP	Permissible Capital Payment
PD	Prospectus Directive (Directive 2003/71/EC)
PIE	Public Interest Entity
PIP	Primary Information Provider
PLC	Public Limited Company
POB	Public Oversight Board
PR	Prospectus Rules (of FCA)
PSC	People with Significant Control
PSM	Professional Securities Market
PUSU	"Put Up or Shut Up"
PIE	Public Interest Entity
RINGA	Relevant Information not Generally Available
RIS	Regulated Information Service
RS	Reporting Standard or Statement

RSB	Recognised Statutory Body
SBEEA 2015	Small Business, Enterprise and Employment Act 2015
SCE	European Cooperative Society
SE	Societas Europaea or European Company
SME	Small or Medium-sized Enterprise
SNB	Special Negotiating Body (of employee representatives)
SO	Supervisory Organ (of an SE)
SPV	Special Purpose Vehicle
SR	Strategic Report
SS	Secretary of State
SSAP	Statement of Standard Accounting Practice
TD	Transparency Directive (Directive 2004/109/EC)
UCITS	Undertakings for Collective Investment in Transferable Securities
UCTA	Unfair Contract Terms Act
USR	Uncertificated Securities Regulations
UKLA	United Kingdom Listing Authority

Documents from the Company Law Review and the Government Response to it

Completing	CLR, *Completing the Structure,* URN 00/1335, November 2000
Developing	CLR, *Developing the Framework*, URN 00/656, March 2000
Final Report	CLR, *Final Report*, 2 vols, URN 01/943, July 2001
Formation	CLR, *Company Formation and Capital Maintenance*, URN 99/1145, October 1999
Maintenance	CLR, *Capital Maintenance: Other Issues*, URN 00/880, June 2000
Modernising	*Modernising Company Law*, Cm 5553, 2 vols, July 2002
Overseas Companies	CLR, *Reforming the Law Concerning Oversea Companies*, URN 99/1146, October 1999
Strategic	CLR, *The Strategic Framework*, URN 99/654, February 1999

TABLE OF CONTENTS

PART 1
Introductory

1. TYPES AND FUNCTIONS OF COMPANIES

4. FORMATION PROCEDURES

PART 2
Separate Legal Personality and Limited Liability

7. CORPORATE ACTIONS

10. DISQUALIFICATION OF DIRECTORS

11. LEGAL CAPITAL, MINIMUM CAPITAL AND VERIFICATION

12. DIVIDENDS AND DISTRIBUTIONS

13. CAPITAL MAINTENANCE

PART 3
Corporate Governance: The Board and Shareholders

14. THE BOARD

15. SHAREHOLDER DECISION-MAKING

16. DIRECTORS' DUTIES

17. THE DERIVATIVE CLAIM AND PERSONAL ACTIONS AGAINST DIRECTORS

PART 4
Corporate Governance—Majority and Minority Shareholders

19. CONTROLLING MEMBERS' VOTING

20. UNFAIR PREJUDICE

PART 5
Accounts and Audit

21. ANNUAL ACCOUNTS AND REPORTS

22. AUDITS AND AUDITORS

PART 6
Equity Finance

23. THE NATURE AND CLASSIFICATION OF SHARES

24. SHARE ISSUES: GENERAL RULES

25. PUBLIC OFFERS OF SHARES

26. CONTINUING OBLIGATIONS AND DISCLOSURE OF INFORMATION TO THE MARKET

PART 7
Debt Finance

31. DEBTS AND DEBT SECURITIES

32. COMPANY CHARGES

PART 8
Insolvency and its Consequences

33. WINDING UP, DISSOLUTION AND RESTORATION

TABLE OF CASES

TABLE OF STATUTES

TABLE OF STATUTORY INSTRUMENTS

TABLE OF EUROPEAN MATERIAL

TABLE OF TAKEOVERS CODE

PART 1

INTRODUCTORY

The company, incorporated under the successive Companies Acts, is a dominant institution in our society, and all the more so with increasing government or public sector retreat from a number of areas in which previously it had been a monopoly or near-monopoly provider of services or, less often, of goods. Yet, the role of the Companies Act company is not easy to describe with accuracy. Even in the area of profit-making business activity, where it is a major force, it has no exclusive position and faces competition, at least in relation to smaller businesses, from other legal forms, such as the partnership or the sole trader (if the latter is a legal form at all). Moreover, the company is not just a vehicle for making profits: it can be, and is increasingly, used in the not-for-profit sector, i.e. where the aim of the undertaking is either not to make profits or, if it is, not to distribute them to the members of the company. And finally, the Companies Act company is not the only type of company; companies may also be created by Act of Parliament or royal charter, although this happens rather rarely.

The dominance of Companies Act companies arises largely because this is a highly flexible vehicle for carrying on business, whether for profit or not-for-profit. Of course, the question inevitably arises whether the proposed activity should be carried on through a company or another legal form, but none of these other legal forms is used across so many types and scales of activity as is the corporate form. In other words, the company has many competitors in the shape of other legal vehicles for carrying on business, but it is perhaps not much of an exaggeration to say that for all these other vehicles their primary competitor is the company. Companies are used as business vehicles from the smallest, one-person business to the largest, multi-national undertaking. The characteristics of the corporate form which give it such flexibility obviously deserve to be studied.

Of course, business today is often a multi-national activity. British companies may carry on activities in other states, and companies from other jurisdictions may carry on business in the UK. The right of British companies to carry on business in other Member States of the EU, whether directly or through a subsidiary company, and the right of companies from other Member States to do so in the UK (their "freedom of establishment"), are obviously matters of legitimate concern for the EU. However, globalisation means that the international dimension of British company law is not restricted to the EU, nor, indeed, has it ever been.

In this part we shall try to analyse the function of the modern company and its structure, discuss its advantages and disadvantages, see how it is created and introduce the international element of British company law.

CHAPTER 1

TYPES AND FUNCTIONS OF COMPANIES

USES TO WHICH THE COMPANY MAY BE PUT

Although company law is a well-recognised subject in the legal curriculum and   **1–1**
forms the subject of a voluminous literature, its exact scope is not obvious since
"the word company has no strictly legal meaning".[1] Explicitly or implicitly, many
courses on "company law" solve the problem of defining the scope of the subject
by concentrating on those companies created by registration under the Companies
Acts. That will be true of this book. Since there are more than three million such
companies in the UK today, in practical and pragmatic terms this is a sensible
solution, for clearly the law applying to such companies is a matter of major
concern to many people. However, to state that a book is going to deal,

---

[1] Per Buckley J in *Re Stanley* [1906] 1 Ch. 131 at 134.

principally, with companies formed under particular Acts of Parliament does not convey much by way of understanding what role such companies perform in society.

The term "company" implies an association of a number of people for some common object or objects. The purposes for which men and women may wish to associate are multifarious, ranging from those as basic as marriage and mutual protection against the elements to those as sophisticated as the objects of the Confederation of British Industry or a political party. However, in common parlance the word "company" is normally reserved for those associated for economic purposes, i.e. to carry on a business for gain.[2] But it would be wrong to say that company law is concerned only with those associations which people use to carry on business for gain—and for two reasons. First, companies are not the only legal vehicles which people may use in order to associate for gainful business. Secondly, companies incorporated under the Companies Acts may be used for carrying on not-for-profit businesses, or for purposes which can be only doubtfully characterised as businesses at all. We will look at each of these matters in turn.

Business vehicles: companies and partnerships (limited and unlimited)

Partnership Act 1890 and Companies Act 2006

1–2 English law provides two main types of organisation for those who wish to associate in order to carry on business for gain: partnerships and companies. Historically, the word "company" was colloquially applied to both,[3] but the modern lawyer regards companies and company law as distinct from partnerships and partnership law. Partnership law, which is now largely codified in the Partnership Act 1890, is based on the law of agency, each partner becoming an agent of the others,[4] and it therefore affords a suitable framework for an association of a small body of persons having trust and confidence in each other. A more complicated form of association, with a large and fluctuating membership, requires a more elaborate organisation which ideally should confer corporate personality on the association: that is, it should recognise that it constitutes a distinct legal person, subject to legal duties and entitled to legal rights separate from those of its members. This the modern company can provide easily and cheaply by permitting incorporation under a general Act of Parliament, the current such Act being the Companies Act of 2006.

1–3 This might seem to imply that the difference between partnerships and companies is that the former is used to carry on small businesses and the latter large ones (or, better, that the former is used by a small number of people to carry on a business and the latter by a large number). The mid-Victorian legislature was, it seems,

---

[2] But not universally; we still talk about an infantry company, a livery company and the "glorious company of the Apostles".

[3] So that it was common for partners to carry on business in the name of "—& Company".

[4] Partnership Act 1890 s.5.

animated by some such idea.[5] Partnership numbers were capped by statute, and incorporation was compulsory for larger numbers of people associating themselves for business purposes. Thus, s.716(1) of the Companies Act 1985, re-enacting a provision first introduced by the Joint Stock Companies Act 1844 (which in fact set the limit slightly higher at 25), provided that, in principle, an association of 20 or more persons formed for the purpose of carrying on a business for gain must be formed as a company[6] (and so not as a partnership); whilst the Limited Liability Act 1855 required companies with limited liability to have at least 25 members.[7] However, the Joint Stock Companies Act 1856 quickly reduced the minimum number to seven for companies,[8] and the decision of the House of Lords at the end of the nineteenth century in *Salomon v Salomon*[9] in effect allowed the incorporation of a company with a single member, the other six being bare nominees for the seventh. This judicial decision preceded by nearly a century the adoption of EC Directive 89/667,[10] which required private companies formally to be capable of being formed with a single member. The 2006 Act extended this facility to public companies.[11] As for the maximum limit for partnerships, this too has been eliminated over the past two decades, thus, the 2006 Companies Act contains no equivalent to s.716 of the 1985 Act.

But this eventual collapse of the Victorian segregation of the two business forms does not mean that they are equally well adapted to different sizes of business. In fact, it is clear that where a large and fluctuating number of members is involved, the company has distinct advantages as an organisational form. This is because the company has built into it a distinction between the members of the company (usually shareholders) and the management of the company (vested in a board of directors). Although this division can be replicated within a partnership, it has to be distinctly chosen by the partners, since the default rule is the less practical universal participation in management.[12]

Limited Liability Partnerships Act 2000

On the other hand, where a small number of persons intend to set up a business and all to be involved in running it, the distinction made by company law between shareholders and directors often becomes a nuisance, for they are the

1–4

---

[5] Though the legislature seems to have been influenced in this view more by problems of civil procedure in relation to large partnerships than by the idea that the partnership itself was inappropriate for large numbers of joint venturers. See Law Commission and Scottish Law Commission, *Joint Consultation Paper on Partnership Law* (London, 2000), paras 5.51–5.61.

[6] It could be formed as a registered company or as a statutory or chartered one (see below, para.1–26) or indeed as an Open-Ended Investment Company under the Financial Services and Markets Act 2000 (see below, para.1–31). If it was formed as a partnership it would be automatically dissolved for illegality: Partnership Act 1890 s.34.

[7] And contained other provisions designed to restrict limited liability to relatively substantial companies, such as that each of the 25 members had to have subscribed for shares with a nominal value of at least £10, of which 20 per cent had to be paid up.

[8] And removed the capital requirements of the 1855 Act.

[9] *Salomon v Salomon* [1897] A.C. 22. See below, paras 2–1 et seq.

[10] EC Directive 89/667 [1989] O.J. L395/40.

[11] 2006 Act s.7(1)—which is not confined to private companies.

[12] Partnership Act 1890 s.24(5).

same (or nearly the same) people. The internal machinery imposed by company law often appears impossibly cumbersome in such cases. Despite the amendments made in recent years to meet the needs of small companies,[13] the practical problems have proved troubling. As a result, the Limited Liability Partnerships Act 2000 now provides a useful hybrid legal vehicle. Although a hybrid, the limited liability partnership ("LLP") is much nearer to a company than to a partnership, and to that extent the title of the Act is misleading. The LLP is governed by company law principles, often adapted to its particular needs, rather than by partnership law principles, except in two crucial respects. Like companies, the LLP has separate legal personality and the partners have limited liability. Unlike companies, however, are taxation rules (the members are taxed as if they were partners) and the internal decision-making machinery, where the division between members and directors is abandoned, and the members have the same freedom as in a partnership to decide on their internal decision-making structures.[14] The LLP has proved a reasonably attractive legal form, especially for professional businesses.[15]

Limited Partnership Act 1907

1–5   The Limited Liability Partnerships Act 2000 is to be sharply distinguished from the confusingly similarly named, but much earlier, Limited Partnership Act 1907. The limited partnership is a true partnership, which is governed by the 1890 Partnership Act and the common law of partnership, except insofar as is necessary to give effect to its particular features.[16] These special features are that some (but not all) the partners of a limited partnership have limited liability,[17] and that, in return, they are prohibited from taking part in the management of the partnership business and do not have power to bind the partnership as against outsiders, and certain information about the limited partnership has to be publicly filed (in fact, with the registrar of companies).[18] From 1 October 2009, limited partnerships have had to indicate this feature in their names by the addition of the words "limited partnership" or "LP".[19] The 1907 Act in effect provides for the existence of a "sleeping partner", often someone who contributes assets to the partnership and therefore wishes to become a member of the partnership in order to safeguard his or her investment and obtain an appropriate return on it, but who does not want to be involved in its business. There were more than 33,000 limited

---

[13] Discussed throughout this book, but especially in Ch.15.

[14] For more detail see G. Morse et al (eds), *Palmer's Limited Liability Partnership Law*, 2nd edn (London: Sweet & Maxwell, 2011). The Limited Liability Partnerships (Application of Companies Act 2006) Regulations 2009/1804 repeals and replaces much of SI 2001/1090. It, plus SI 2009/1833, SI 2008/1911, SI 2008/1912, and SI 2008/1913, applies parts of the CA 2006 to LLPs.

[15] Almost 60,000 were on the register at the end of 2014/15 (though there were over 3.3 million private companies registered at the same date): BIS/Companies House, *Statistical Tables on Companies Registration Activities 2014/15*, p.6.

[16] 1907 Act s.7.

[17] 1907 Act s.4(2) requires that there must be at least one general partner who is liable for the debts and obligations of the firm.

[18] 1907 Act ss.6 and 8.

[19] Legislative Reform (Limited Partnership) Order 2009/1940 inserting ss.8A and 8B into the Limited Partnership Act 1907.

partnerships in existence in 2015.[20] Although a small number compared with the private company, the number has been growing in recent years, because of the attraction of the limited partnership in certain specialised fields of commercial activity.[21] For the purposes of this book, however, there is a gulf between, on the one hand, the registered company and the limited liability partnership, which are both in essence creatures of company law, and, on the other, the partnership and the limited partnership, which are creatures of partnership law.

Non-business vehicles: charitable, community interest and limited by guarantee companies

Not-for-profit companies

As noted earlier, the statement that company law is the law relating to associations formed with a view to carrying on business for gain is inaccurate; there is no requirement in the Companies Act or elsewhere that use of a registered company should be limited to such purposes.[22] In practice, a company may be not-for-profit in a strong sense, in that a provision in its constitution prohibits the distribution of profits to the members of the company, either by way of dividend or in a winding up. Or it may be so in the weak sense of not being run in order to make a profit, though it may from time to time do so and it may then distribute these profits to its members. "Not-for-profit" is not a term of art in British company law, in the way it is in the laws of many states of the US.

1–6

Not-for-profit companies may pursue purposes which are charitable in a legal sense (in which case the company will be subject to the charities legislation as well as the companies legislation)[23] or which are public interest purposes which do not fall within the rather narrow legal definition of charitable purposes.[24] Alternatively, the purpose of the company may be to promote a private interest, but that private interest may not be making a profit. A typical example is the use by the tenants of a block of flats of a company to hold the freehold title to the block or to see to the care and maintenance of the common parts of the block. These are clearly purely private purposes, but the tenants will fund the company,

1–7

---

[20] BIS/Companies House, *Statistical Tables on Companies Registration Activities 2014/15*, p.6. However, it is not clear how many of them are active: the 1907 Act requires limited partnerships to register but provides no mechanism for de-registration.

[21] Notably, venture capital or private equity investment funds, where the investors can be limited partners distinct from the managers of the fund who are general partners; and in property investment, where tax-exempt investors may wish to be excluded from any management role. See the Law Commissions, *Limited Partnerships Act 1907: A Joint Consultation Paper* (2001), Pt I.

[22] Unlike both the partnership and the LLP where the intention (if not the actuality) of carrying on the business for profit is part of the definition of these legal vehicles, and indeed an unincorporated association meeting this test is a partnership, without the need for any formalities to make it so: Partnership Act 1890 s.1(1); Limited Liability Partnerships Act 2000 s.2(1).

[23] There is no obligation for bodies which pursue charitable objects to incorporate, though they increasingly do so today in order to obtain the benefits of limited liability, since such organisations are increasingly carrying more financial risk.

[24] An adaptation of the corporate form especially designed for those pursuing public interest goals which are not charitable is the Community Interest Company (CIC): see below, para.1–12.

usually through service charges, simply to the level needed so that it can discharge its obligations and would be surprised, even indignant, if the company made a significant profit on its activities.

Company limited by guarantee

1–8   The Companies Acts have long provided a particular form of the company which may be regarded as particularly suitable for companies which carry on a not-for-profit activity. This is the company "limited by guarantee", as opposed to the company "limited by shares",[25] the latter being the form normally used for profit-making activities and by far the more common one. The Companies Act does not permit a company to be created in which the members are free from any liability whatsoever, but, as an alternative to limiting their contribution to the amount payable on their shares,[26] it enables them to agree that in the event of liquidation they will, if required, subscribe an agreed amount.[27] The guarantee company is widely used by charitable and quasi-charitable organisations (such as schools, colleges and the "Friends" of museums and picture galleries) since incorporation with limited liability is often more convenient and less risky than a trust.[28] However, a division of such an undertaking into shares is unnecessary, since no sharing of profits is contemplated, and the creators of the company may regard membership of the company divorced from shareholding as a more appropriate expression of the objectives of the company.

1–9   It might be thought that a company limited by guarantee imposes a more limited financial obligation upon the members than one limited by shares, since the members of a guarantee company do not have to put any money into the concern when it is set up, as they normally would have to if they subscribed for shares. The members of a guarantee company are under no liability so long as the company remains a going concern; they are liable, to the extent of their guarantees, only if the company is wound up and a contribution is needed to enable its debts to be paid. But since the par value of shares can be set at a very low level (perhaps one penny)[29] and a member of a company limited by shares is obliged to buy only one share, it is doubtful whether this financial argument carries much weight in the choice between companies limited by shares and by guarantee. In fact, the level of the guarantee is usually also set at a nominal level, so the financing aspects of not-for-profit companies probably play little part in a person's decision whether to apply for membership. For this reason, companies limited by shares can be and are in fact used for non-profit purposes. For example, in the case of the service company mentioned above, often each tenant will have one share in the company.[30]

---

[25] 2006 Act s.3(1).

[26] It is not possible to create a hybrid form (i.e. a company limited by guarantee but also with a share capital), although prior to 1980 it was: s.5.

[27] 2006 Act s.3(3).

[28] There were some 40,000 guarantee companies in existence in 1998: CLR, Developing, para.9.12.

[29] See para.11–3.

[30] This may be convenient if the members are not to have exactly identical obligations, for example, where the obligation to contribute to the costs of the company is related to the size of the flats. In that case different contribution obligations can be attached to each share.

A more important advantage of the guarantee company would seem to be the fact that admission to, and resignation from, membership are easier than in a share company. Upon resignation from a share company, the member's share has to be allocated elsewhere, either back to the company or to a new member, and on admission of a new member a new share may have to be created, unless another member is resigning at exactly the same time. The issuance, transfer and repurchase of shares are all matters which are regulated by the Companies Act in the interests of creditors,[31] and these provisions may make the transfer of membership in not-for-profit companies cumbersome. Where, however, membership is not attached to shares, joining and leaving can be as easy as in any club or association, i.e. normally, joining is simply a matter of agreement between company and prospective member and leaving is a matter of unilateral decision by the member, perhaps subject to certain conditions relating to notice or discharge of obligations owed to the company.[32]

1–10

Company limited by shares

A guarantee company is, however, unsuitable where the primary object is to carry on a business for profit and to divide that profit among the members. Just as a partnership agreement will need to prescribe the shares of the partners, so will a company's constitution need to define the shares of its members, and if these shares are to be transferable it will be convenient for them to be expressed in comparatively small denominations. The members who subscribe for the shares will be under a duty to pay the company for them in money or money's worth, and the company is accordingly said to be "limited by shares", that is to say, the members' liability to contribute towards the company's debts is limited to the nominal value of the shares for which they have subscribed, and once the shares have been "paid up" (i.e. paid for) the members are under no further liability.[33] A fundamental distinction between this type of company and the guarantee company is that the law assumes that in a company limited by shares its working capital will be, to some extent at any rate, contributed by the members; their contributions float the company on its launching and are not a mere life-belt to which creditors may cling when the company sinks, which is how the guarantee company might be viewed. However, as we shall see,[34] since the Companies Act lays down no minimum capital requirement for private companies, the contribution of the shareholders to the initial financing of the company limited by shares may be exiguous.

1–11

---

[31] See below, Chs 11 and 12.

[32] Where membership changes are expected to be relatively rare and where a new member will always be available to replace the leaving one, as with the service company formed by the leaseholders of a block of flats, this potential disadvantage of the share company will not show itself.

[33] 2006 Act s.3(2) and more clearly in s.74(2)(d) of the Insolvency Act 1986, discussed further in paras 8–1 to 8–4.

[34] See below, Ch.11.

Community Interest Company ("CIC")

1–12 Despite the long availability of the guarantee company for non-profit purposes, it does have a limitation in terms of its financing. Since there are no shares to be sold, the guarantee company must either operate on the basis that it needs no long-term working capital (many clubs can exist simply on their subscription income) or it must raise that capital by way of debt (i.e. loans to it). Partly for this reason, in Pt 2 of the Companies (Audit, Investigations and Community Enterprise) Act 2004 the Government created a new type of company,[35] known as the Community Interest Company, to which the 2006 Act provisions apply subject to the modifications made in the 2004 Act.[36] Such a company can be either a company limited by shares or by guarantee, its purposes are limited to pursuit of community interests,[37] distributions to the members of the company and the payment of interest on debentures are subject to a cap and its assets otherwise "locked in",[38] and, investors having less incentive to exercise control over the company because their potential rewards are limited, a Regulator of Community Interest Companies is given potentially extensive powers of intervention in the CIC's affairs.[39] Registration as a CIC is not compatible with charitable status[40] and does not attract the tax relief afforded to charities, and so it is not clear how attractive the CIC would be where the community purposes were also charitable (which, however, they might well not be).[41]

The advantages of the modern corporate form

1–13 So far, we have established two negative, and therefore not wholly helpful, propositions. First, the company form is not limited to the association of large numbers of people in the carrying on of a business, but can be used by small numbers, even by the individual entrepreneur. Secondly, the company form is not confined to the carrying on of a profit-making activity. However, a positive proposition has also emerged. This is that the comparative advantage of the company (as against, for example, the partnership or the trust) does indeed lie in the association of large numbers of people for the carrying on of large-scale business. This is for two reasons.

The first is more obvious. Company law, by insisting upon the central role of directors in the running of the company, permits a large and fluctuating body of members (the shareholders) to delegate oversight of the company's business to a small and committed group of persons (the directors). As important, however, is that over the years successive Companies Acts and the common law have

---

[35] 2004 Act s.26(1). A company may be formed as a CIC or later convert into one.

[36] 2006 Act s.6(2). Also see SI 2009/1942 amending SI 2005/1788.

[37] 2004 Act s.35.

[38] 2004 Act ss.30–31.

[39] 2004 Act ss.41–51—subject to an appeal to an Appeal Officer (s.28).

[40] 2004 Act s.26(3).

[41] As at the end of 2015 some 10,639 CICs had been registered. See Regulator of Community Interest Companies Annual Report 2014/2015, p.38.

developed a set of rules for regulating the relationship between shareholders and directors when authority is delegated to the directors in this way.[42]

Secondly, and less obviously, by providing for the creation of separate legal personality, limited liability and transferable shares, company law makes it possible to isolate business risks within the business vehicle (thus insulating the shareholders), and facilitates the raising of risk capital from the public for the financing of corporate ventures. Raising funds by the sale of shares often gives companies greater flexibility than in the case of debt finance, and is therefore a crucial element in financing all businesses except those where the risk of failure is very low.[43] Although there are other ways of isolating risk and financing enterprises, none is both as simple and as flexible as the company.

This analysis is borne out by the statistics classifying businesses by their legal type. These show that of businesses in the private sector of the economy in 2015 employing more than 250 employees, 6,860 were organised as companies and only 55 as partnerships (and five as sole traders). On the other hand, of those with fewer than five employees, 1,232,210 were companies (75 per cent of all companies), 160,905 were partnerships (69 per cent), and 425,175 were sole traders (87 per cent).[44] This shows not only, as one would expect, that there are many more small businesses than large businesses, but also, and more relevant from our point of view, that among large businesses the company form predominates, whilst in small businesses it faces a distinct challenge from the partnership and from those who make no formal distinction between their personal and business lives (the sole trader).

1–14

From a functional viewpoint it could be said that today there are three distinct types of company:

1–15

1. Companies formed for purposes other than the profit of their members, i.e. those formed for social, charitable or quasi-charitable purposes. In this case incorporation is merely a more modern and convenient substitute for the trust.
2. Companies formed to enable a single trader or a small body of partners to carry on a business. In these companies, incorporation is a device for personifying the business and, normally, divorcing its liability from that of its members despite the fact that the members retain control and share the profits. In this case, the company is often a substitute for a partnership.
3. Companies formed in order to enable the investing public to share in the profits of an enterprise without taking any part in its management. In this last type, which is economically (but not numerically) by far the most important, the company is again a device analogous to the trust, but this time it is designed to facilitate the raising and putting to use of capital by enabling a large number of owners to participate in endeavours too large for any of them individually, and to entrust management of the endeavour to a small number of expert managers.

---

[42] See below, Pt 3.
[43] See below, Pts 6 and 7.
[44] Office for National Statistics, *UK Business: Activity, Size and Location 2015.*

1–16 However, this threefold categorisation needs to be treated with caution. First, there may be hybrid companies or companies which in a particular moment of their growth straddle the second and third categories. For example, a company which was formerly controlled wholly by the members of a particular family may have begun to bring in one or two outside financiers (sometimes called "business angels") in order to expand the business and these outsiders will naturally have wanted a share in the control of the company. At a later date, the family members may have retired from active management of the company and may have brought in professional managers to run the company (to whom shares have been allocated), but the family members may still be the predominant shareholders.

Secondly, even if a company is squarely within the third category and has a large number of shareholders, from whom the directors constitute a distinct body, there may be great variations in extent to which the shareholdings are dispersed and the ease with which those shares can be traded. At one end of the scale is a company listed on the London Stock Exchange[45] with many thousands of shareholders who are able to trade their shares with other investors with great ease; whilst at the other end is a company which does in fact have several hundred shareholders, many of whom are perhaps its employees, but which has never made a formal offer of its shares to the public and whose shares may not be traded on a public exchange.

DIFFERENT TYPES OF REGISTERED COMPANIES

1–17 It follows from what has just been said that the range of functions that may be performed by a company formed by registration under the Companies Acts is extremely wide. Yet, they are all subject to a single Act, today that of 2006. Is this sensible? Would it be better to have different legislation for different types of company, or can sufficient differentiation among different sorts of companies be achieved within a single Act? Let us look at this matter with reference to five possible divisions among companies, the first three of which have long been recognised in British law, the fourth of which is not formally so recognised but is in practice catered for to some extent, and the fifth of which can be said to have become recognised in recent years.

Public and private companies

1–18 A division commonly found in the company laws of many states is that between public and private companies, the former being those which are permitted to offer their securities (whether shares or marketable debt securities[46]) to the public[47] (though they may not in fact have done so) and the latter being those which are

---

[45] See below, Ch.25.

[46] See below, Ch.31.

[47] 2006 Act s.755. Further, s.74 of the FSMA 2000 and its associated regulations prevent a private company from having its securities listed on an exchange. See below, para.25–15. The largest IPO (Initial Public Offering) on the London Stock Exchange was completed in May 2011 by Glencore International Plc. The company raised $10 billion at admission, but the 2014 NYSE listing of Alibaba Holdings Group more than doubled that.

not so permitted. The distinction is embedded in the Companies Act, and suffixes, which are a mandatory part of a company's name, distinguish private ("limited" or "Ltd") from public ("public limited company" or "Plc") companies.[48] The distinction is important not just for the obvious one that companies which do not offer their shares to the public need not be concerned with the rules governing this process, which today are set out largely in the Financial Services and Markets Act 2000 ("FSMA") and not in the Companies Act.[49] Rather, whether a company is public or private is taken more generally as an indication of the social and economic importance of the company, so that the public company is more tightly regulated than the private company in a number of ways which do not directly concern the offering of shares to the public.

However, unlike many continental European countries, there is no separate legislation for public and private companies. The approach of the single Act seems to be feasible because, although British public companies are more highly regulated than private companies, the British legislation has always had less ambitious regulatory goals for public companies than our continental counterparts. Thus, for example, the German *Aktiengesetz*, applying to public companies, divides the board of directors into two bodies, the supervisory board and the management board, and deals in some detail with the allocation of functions between them and the method of appointment of their members.[50] By contrast, the British Act says very little about what the board is to do or how its members are to be appointed,[51] and certainly does not require the creation of separate supervisory and management boards.[52] These matters are left to be decided by each company itself in its constitution. Consequently, different sizes and types of company can adjust these matters to suit their own particular situation, whereas in Germany to relieve private companies of the demands of the *Aktiengesetz* has been seen to require the enactment of a separate and more flexible statute for private companies (the *GmbHGesetz*).

1–19

Moreover, where a distinction is needed between the level of regulation to be applied to public and private companies, that can readily be embedded in a single Act. The risk with a singleAct, however, is that too little thought will be given to explicitly applying or disapplying the relevant rules, and as a consequence public companies may be under-regulated or private ones over-regulated. To address this issue, the Company Law Review[53] considered the then current rules applying to private companies to see which were excessive and could therefore be eliminated entirely or applied only in a modified form. It also advocated re-ordering the

1–20

---

[48] 2006 Act ss.58 and 59. Companies registered in Wales may use the Welsh equivalents. See below, Ch.4.

[49] See below, Ch.25.

[50] Other legislation requires the mandatory presence of employee representatives on the boards of large public companies, but this applies also to the boards of large private companies.

[51] Though it does contain an important provision, s.303, enabling an ordinary majority of the shareholders to remove any director at any time. See Ch.14.

[52] Typically, there is only a single board in British companies, but there is nothing in the legislation to stop them establishing a separate "management board" below the main board, and this is sometimes done. On the division within a single board between executive and non-executive directors, see paras 14–75 to 14–76.

[53] See para.3–3.

Companies Act provisions so as to make it more transparent which applied to private companies.[54] The Companies Act 2006 embodies this approach.

1–21   The choice between a public and a private company is one for the incorporators themselves or, after incorporation, for the shareholders.[55] The default rule is that the company is private unless the parties state otherwise,[56] and an overwhelming proportion of companies on the companies register are private ones. As of 2015, only about 7,500 companies on the register in Great Britain were public (down from 9,200 in 2009), whilst the total number of registered companies was over three million.[57]

This is a big change from the position which obtained when the notion of the private company was introduced by the Companies (Consolidation) Act 1908. The view then was that, because a private company was exempted from some of the publicity provisions of the Act, access to that status should be restricted. A company could qualify as private only if it (a) limited its membership to 50; (b) restricted the right to transfer shares; and (c) prohibited any invitation to the public of its shares. Only (c) has survived into the modern law as a requirement for private status.[58]

Officially listed and other publicly traded companies

1–22   Although public companies may offer their shares to the public, some choose not to. And even if they do, those shares may or may not be subsequently traded on a public share exchange, such as the London Stock Exchange. Offering shares to the public and arranging for those shares to be traded on a public market are two separate things, although the public's willingness to buy the shares offered is likely to be increased if the shares can later be traded on a public market. This is because a public market makes it much easier for a shareholder to sell shares to another investor, or to purchase more shares in the company, should that be desired. Consequently, public offerings of shares and the introduction of those shares to trading on a public market often go together.[59]

1–23   By and large, the companies legislation makes very few differentiations according to whether a public company's shares have actually been offered to the public or are in fact publicly traded, and the 2006 Act makes fewer than its predecessor. However, a company taking either of these steps will find itself

---

[54] Final Report I, Ch.2. Particular CLR proposals are noted at appropriate points in the book, but an illustration of the recommendations noted here was the removal of the prohibition on a company giving financial assistance for the acquisition of its shares from private companies. See paras 13–44 et seq.

[55] A company originally incorporated as private may, subject to certain safeguards, transform itself into a public one, or vice versa. See paras 4–39 et seq.

[56] 2006 Act s.4(2)(a).

[57] BIS/Companies House, *Statistical Tables on Companies Registration Activities 2014/15*, p.8. The total number of companies on the register has been increasing quite rapidly, whilst the number of public companies gently declined over the same period. Now fewer that one in 400 companies is a public one.

[58] Private companies are in fact very likely to restrict the transfer of shares (see Ch.27) and to have fewer than 50 members, but these are no longer necessary incidents of being private.

[59] These processes are discussed in Ch.25.

subject to the Financial Services and Markets Act 2000 and to rules made under it by the Financial Conduct Authority ("FCA"),[60] as well as to an increasing number of Community laws. This regulation, naturally, is mainly concerned with the issues thrown up by public offers and public trading—these are discussed later in the book—but it is important to note at this stage a curiosity of the British approach. This is that admission to a public market may bring with it obligations for the company of a recognisably "company law" type, obligations which could have been included in the Act but are not. This is particularly true of certain parts of the "Listing Rules" made by the FCA. A company seeking to have its shares traded on the Main Market (whether Premium or Standard Listing)[61] of the London Stock Exchange must first have them admitted to the "Official List" of securities, a list maintained by the FCA, acting in its capacity as the UK Listing Authority ("UKLA").[62] Although a main purpose of this regulation is to secure proper disclosure of information about the company at the time its shares are offered to the public,[63] the UKLA is also empowered to impose on listed companies rules governing their conduct thereafter.[64] Such listing rules relate mainly to the orderly conduct of the public share market, but they also contain rules regulating the internal affairs of companies, which thus supplement the provisions of the Companies Act and the common law relating to companies.[65] In particular, the Listing Rules contain provisions on related party transactions[66] and significant transactions[67] which supplement the statutory rules on directors' and controlling shareholders' conflicts of interest, set a limit on the constitutional division of powers within companies,[68] and provide the legal anchor for the UK Corporate Governance Code.

This last is probably the best-known example of such a "supplementary" Listing Rule. Companies subject to the Listing Rules must indicate to their shareholders each year how far they have complied with the UK Corporate Governance Code

1–24

---

[60] On 1 April 2013, the former Financial Services Authority was replaced by the Financial Conduct Authority (responsible for policing the City and the banking system), and a new Prudential Regulatory Authority (responsible for carrying out the prudential regulation of financial firms, including banks, investment banks, building societies and insurance companies), with all other responsibilities being assumed by the Bank of England and its Financial Policy Committee.

[61] The Listing Regime is divided into two segments, giving UK and overseas issuers the same choice of Listing Regimes. These are either Premium or Standard, with Premium Listing requiring adherence to more stringent standards (including for overseas companies), including "comply or explain" against the UK Corporate Governance Code, and the requirement to offer pre-emption rights. Standard Listing requires adherence to the lower EU minimum standards, including compliance with the EU Company Reporting Directive which requires companies, amongst other things, to provide a corporate governance statement and to describe their internal control and risk management systems' main features.

[62] FSMA 2000 Pt VI.

[63] See below, Ch.25.

[64] FSMA 2000 s.96.

[65] Companies whose shares are traded on secondary markets, such as the Alternative Investment Market, may also be subject to exchange rules which perform a similar function, but the rules of secondary markets are less demanding than the Listing Rules which apply to the Main Market/Official List.

[66] LR 11.

[67] LR 10.

[68] See paras 14–18, 16–77 and 19–2 on these matters.

(a Code drafted by the Financial Reporting Council[69] and attached to the Listing Rules) and to explain areas of non-compliance.[70] This Code deals with the composition and functions of the board of directors. In short, the fact of listing is being used to identify a small group of very important British and overseas companies to which additional company law obligations are attached.[71]

1–25 The identification of publicly traded companies as a separate group for company law purposes has become increasingly important in recent years and it is unlikely that the importance of this category will diminish in the future. However, it is not obvious that the additional regulation of such companies should be confined to listed companies on the Main Market and not extend to those whose shares are traded on "secondary" markets, such as the Alternative Investment Market ("AIM").[72] Nor is it obvious that such additional regulation should be embodied in the Listing Rules rather than the Companies Act.

1–26 Because of the importance, even in core company law matters, of a company having its securities traded on a public market, an ambiguity has arisen about the term "public company". For the company lawyer it normally still means a company which for the purposes of the Companies Act is public, not private, as discussed in the previous section. For the capital markets lawyer, that is not enough to make a company public: it must also have offered its shares to the public and/or have made a public market available for the trading of the shares. The ambiguity can be avoided by using the term "publicly traded" to refer to the latter type of company.

Limited and unlimited companies

1–27 We have already considered how the liability of members may be either limited by shares or limited by guarantee.[73] Since limited liability is the advantage which is often said to drive entrepreneurs' decisions to incorporate, it is notable that the Act also provides a category of private company where members' liability is unlimited. Such an unlimited company may have a share capital (in order to provide working capital and to measure each member's rights in the company), but that capital no longer acts as a limit on liability.[74] It is not surprising that few unlimited companies are formed,[75] and it has never been suggested that there should be separate legislation for such companies. Nevertheless, the current law does take the view that some regulation otherwise applicable to companies registered under the Act need not be applied to unlimited companies. This is true

---

[69] See below, para.3–9.

[70] LR 9.8.6 and 9.8.7. See further below, para.14–69.

[71] There are some 1,500 British companies listed on the Exchange. However, most of the Listing Rules apply to all companies with primary listings, no matter where incorporated.

[72] The CLR thought the Combined Code (the predecessor to the UK Corporate Governance Code), for example, should apply to all quoted companies: Completing, para.4.44.

[73] See above, paras 1–8 and 1–9.

[74] 2006 Act s.3(4). However, only a private company can be unlimited; a public company must be limited by shares or guarantee: s.4(2).

[75] BIS/Companies House, *Statistical Tables on Companies Registration Activities 2014/15*, p.8 indicates that in 2015 there were fewer than 5,000 on the register.

in particular of the obligation to publish the company's accounts[76] (since creditors of such companies can rely on the credit of the shareholders), and the prohibition on a company acquiring its own shares[77] (again a potential threat only to creditors who are confined to the company's assets for the satisfaction of their claims). Consequently, the unlimited company may be attractive for those shareholders who are willing to stand behind their company and for whom the advantages of privacy or flexibility of capital structure are important.

Classification according to size: large, medium and micro companies

Classification based on size does not differentiate technical legal categories, although the Companies Act recognises the different needs of different sizes of company. At one end of the scale is the listed company, at the other is the very small company where the directors and the shareholders are the same people and where the size of the business carried on is also small. The Company Law Review reported research which indicated that 65 per cent of active companies have a turnover of less than £250,000, 70 per cent have only two shareholders and 90 per cent fewer than five shareholders.[78] However, the Review came out against separate legislation for companies whose directors and shareholders were identical and whose businesses were small in size (sometimes called "micro" companies) on the grounds that it would be undesirable to create a regulatory barrier to expansion, which might occur if a company became subject to different rules when its directors and shareholders ceased to be identical.[79] For the same reason, it was opposed to a distinct regime for micro companies even within a single Act.[80] Instead, it applied most of its reforms to private companies as a whole, but some of them were crafted as default rules drafted with micro companies particularly in mind, and it was expected that private companies of a larger size would opt out of them. The advantage of such an approach is that the legal regime does not formally cease to be applicable to a particular small company as it expands, though it is likely to find the regime less convenient and thus to opt out of it. The Companies Act 2006 adopts this approach. Those who want a corporate form which gives still more flexibility than the private company provides, especially in relation to internal decision-making structure, must go to the Limited Liability Partnership.[81]

1–28

---

[76] 2006 Act s.448. See para.21–35. Unlimited companies must still produce accounts for their members.
[77] 2006 Act s.658. See para.13–2.
[78] Developing, paras 6.8–6.9.
[79] Strategic Framework, Ch.5.2.
[80] Developing, Ch.6; Final Report I, para.2.7.
[81] See above, para.1–4.

Classification according to activity: for-profit and not-for-profit companies

1–29   The term "not-for-profit company" is not formally used in the legislation. As we have already seen, these activities are typically run though companies limited by guarantee, which may prove suitable for carrying on a not-for-profit business but are not regulated in fundamentally different ways from a company limited by shares.[82] The same is true of the community interest company ("CIC"), created in 2004.[83] A CIC is either a company limited by shares or limited by guarantee and formed under the Companies Act 2006, but the Companies (Audit, Investigations and Community Enterprise) Act 2004 provides a set of rules which those forming a CIC can adopt and which are designed to meet the needs of an entity whose aims are to promote the interests of the community or a section of it rather than to make a private profit for its members.[84]

1–30   Those not-for-profit companies which are also charities[85] are presently subject to the burden of double regulation, under the Companies Act and the charities legislation.[86] Consequently, there is an argument that a special form of charitable company should be created and made subject to a single regulatory regime, namely, that for charities. This has been done, but on an optional basis.[87] The Charities Act 2006 has introduced the Charitable Incorporated Organisation ("CIO") for England and Wales. A CIO is a corporate form available to companies whose purposes are charitable, and is designed for their particular needs. However, unlike a CIC, a CIO is not registered by the Registrar of Companies under the Companies Act 2006 but by the Charity Commissioners under the Charities Act 2011. Nevertheless, much of the law applicable to CIOs will be familiar to a general company lawyer and some of the decisions on the companies legislation will be capable of being read across to the rules governing the CIO.[88]

UNREGISTERED COMPANIES AND OTHER FORMS OF INCORPORATION

Statutory and chartered companies

1–31   Beyond the different types of companies registered under the Companies Act, there are alternative forms of incorporation which are available for the carrying on of business, including large-scale businesses, namely by special Act of Parliament or by means of a charter granted by the Crown, either under the Royal Prerogative or under powers conferred upon the Crown by statute to grant

---

[82] See above, para.1–8.

[83] See above, para.1–12.

[84] Profitable trading will be a condition for the company's survival but that profit will be devoted mainly to the promotion of the community objectives.

[85] For the categorisation of not-for-profit companies see above, para.1–7.

[86] Charities Act 2011 in England and Wales; Charities and Trustee Investment (Scotland) Act 2005. The regulation of charities is a devolved matter.

[87] Developing, paras 9.7–9.40; Completing, paras 9.2–9.7; Final Report I, paras 4.63–4.67.

[88] Charities Act 2011 Pt 11.

charters of incorporation.[89] In 2015, there were 43 companies in existence formed under special Acts and 850 incorporated by Royal Charter.[90]

In the past, statutory incorporation by private Acts of public utilities, such as railway, gas, water and electricity undertakings, was comparatively common since the undertakings would require powers and monopolistic rights which needed a special legislative grant. During the nineteenth century, therefore, public general Acts[91] were passed providing standard clauses which could be deemed to be incorporated into the private Acts unless expressly excluded. As a result of post-war nationalisation measures, most of these statutory companies were taken over by public boards or corporations set up by public Acts (but many, if not most, of them have now been "privatised" and become registered companies). These boards and corporations fall outside the scope of this book. But some statutory companies remain and others may be formed. The statute under which they are formed need not incorporate them but today this is invariably done.

As for companies chartered by the Crown, such a charter normally confers corporate personality, but, as it was regarded as dubious policy for the Crown to confer a full charter of incorporation on an ordinary trading concern, it was empowered by the Trading Companies Act 1834 and the Chartered Companies Act 1837 to confer by letters patent all or any of the privileges of incorporation without actually granting a charter. Today an ordinary trading concern would not contemplate trying to obtain a Royal Charter, for incorporation under the Companies Acts would be far quicker and cheaper. In practice, therefore, this method of incorporation is used only by organisations formed for charitable, or quasi-charitable, objects, such as learned and artistic societies, schools and colleges, which want the greater prestige that a charter is thought to confer.

However, there is an important regulatory policy issue arising out of the fact that statutory and "letters patent" companies are not created by registration under the Companies Act. Unless express provision is made to the contrary, the provisions of the Companies Act will not apply to such companies. This may give such "unregistered" companies an unfair competitive advantage as against companies formed by registration under the Act, and may mean that those dealing with such companies are inadequately protected. This problem was addressed, but only partially solved, by s.1043 of the 2006 Act, which applies some, but not all, of the provisions of the Act to unregistered companies, being "bodies incorporated in and having a principal place of business in the United Kingdom",[92] unless they

1–32

---

[89] Under many ad hoc statutes the Crown has been given power to grant charters in cases falling outside its prerogative powers. Moreover, by the Chartered Companies Acts 1837 and 1884, the prerogative was extended by empowering the Crown to grant charters for a limited period and to extend them. Thus the BBC Charter was for 10 years and has been prolonged from time to time.

[90] BIS/Companies House, *Statistical Tables on Companies Registration Activities 2014/15*, p.8.

[91] The Companies Clauses Acts 1845–1889. These Acts, containing the general corporate powers and duties, were supplemented in the case of particular utilities by various other "Clauses Acts", e.g. the Lands Clauses Consolidation and Railways Clauses Consolidation Acts 1845, the Electric Lighting (Clauses) Act 1899, and numerous Waterworks Clauses Acts, and Gasworks Clauses Acts.

[92] This is an interesting nod on the part of British law towards the "real seat" theory of incorporation (see below, paras 6–2 et seq.), for this section does not apply to a British unregistered company which does not have a place of business in the UK. By contrast, a company registered under the Companies Act will be governed by that Act even if it conducts the whole of its business outside the UK.

are incorporated by or under a general public Act of Parliament.[93] In addition, unregistered companies falling within the section must have been formed for the purpose of carrying on a business for gain.[94] In other words, the problems of unfair competition and inadequate protection were not perceived as arising in relation to not-for-profit companies, which, as we have seen, constitute the main type of company created by the Crown.

The section provides that those parts of the Act which apply to unregistered companies are to be set out in regulations,[95] and any charter, enactment or other instrument (e.g. letters patent) constituting the company is subordinated to those parts of the Act which are thereby made applicable.[96] The main areas of regulation so applied are those relating to accounts and audit, corporate capacity and directors' authority, company investigations and fraudulent trading. This leaves out some large and important parts of the Act, such as those dealing with the removal of directors, fair dealing by directors, distribution of profits and assets, registration of charges, arrangement and reconstructions and takeover offers, and unfair prejudice.

1–33   An alternative policy embodied in the Act towards unregistered companies is to encourage them to register under the Act and thus become subject to its provisions in full. This encouragement is provided by enabling them to register under the Companies Act without having to form a new company and wind up the old one, although sometimes registration under the Act is a step in a plan designed to produce the winding-up of the company once it has registered. The method of doing this is dealt with in Pt 33 Ch.1 of the Act. As far as statutory and letters patent companies are concerned, a basic distinction is drawn between those which are "joint stock companies" (essentially those with a share capital)[97] and those which are not. Only the former may make use of this special registration process and must register as a company limited by shares and not as an unlimited or guarantee company.[98] The details of the effect of registration, provisions for the automatic vesting of property, savings for existing liabilities and rights and similar matters are dealt with in regulations.[99]

---

[93] 2006 Act s.1043(1)(a). This would include the Companies Act itself but also, for example, the Co-operative and Community Benefit Societies Act 2014. See below, paras 1–35 and 1–36.

[94] 2006 Act s.1043(1)(b). Open-ended investment companies are also excluded (s.1043(1)(d)) as are other unregistered companies specifically excluded by direction of the Secretary of State (s.1043(1)(c)).

[95] 2006 Act s.1043(2), (3). These are the Unregistered Companies Regulations 2009 (SI 2009/2436).

[96] 2006 Act s.1043(4).

[97] See 2006 Act s.1041.

[98] See 2006 Act s.1040(4), qualifying the broader provisions of s.1040(3).

[99] 2006 Act s.1042. See the Companies (Companies Authorised to Register) Regulations 2009 (SI 2009/2437), which not only applies the relevant parts of the Companies Act 2006, but also the Companies (Cross-Border Mergers) Regulations 2007 (SI 2007/2974). This Part of the Act also allows for the registration of the few remaining "deed of settlement" companies, a private law form of quasi-incorporation which was invented to avoid the costs of statutory or royal incorporation and which was overtaken by the introduction of formation by registration under a general Act in the middle of the nineteenth century. For details, see the sixth edition of this book at pp.29–31.

Building societies, friendly societies and co-operatives

Although the Victorian legislature devoted considerable efforts to the elaboration of what we today call companies legislation in order to facilitate the carrying on of large-scale business, it did not confine its efforts to this legislation. Even in the area of commercial activities, the legislature was aware that the company form, despite its flexibility, would not suit all types of business, especially where the members of the organisation were intended to have a different relationship with it than shareholders with a company.

1–34

Some of these other forms of incorporation were confined to specific activities, such as the building societies,[100] whose principal purpose is to make loans secured on residential property. The building society is an incorporated body, very similar to a company—which is why it has been easy for many of them in recent years to "demutualise" by converting themselves into registered companies—but its members are those who deposit money with it or borrow from it rather than those who invest risk capital in it.

A less striking example is the friendly societies legislation,[101] which until recently contemplated only the formation of unincorporated bodies, but now permits incorporation of bodies whose purposes must include the provision on a mutual basis of insurance against loss of income arising out of sickness, unemployment or retirement. The friendly society constituted, if you like, a self-help response to the perils of ordinary life before the rise of the welfare state from the beginning of the twentieth century, and still such societies have a role to play in the areas neglected by the state system.

However, probably the most important of the "non-company" incorporated bodies were those created under the old Industrial and Provident Societies Acts, and now the Co-operative and Community Benefit Societies Act 2014,[102] which provide, inter alia, for the incorporation of co-operative societies, which can be deployed in a wide range of commercial settings. Membership and financial rights are accorded to people in co-operatives usually on the basis of the extent to which they have participated in the business of the society, whether as customers (as in retail co-operatives), producers (for example, agricultural co-operatives) or as employees (worker co-operatives). There were over 10,100 industrial and

1–35

---

[100] The current legislation is the Building Societies Acts 1986–1997, but it can trace its origins to an Act of 1874.

[101] Currently, the Friendly Societies Act 1992, but that legislation can be traced as far back as the Friendly Societies Act 1793.

[102] The legislation is traceable back to the middle of the nineteenth century.

provident societies in existence in 2015,[103] and they are of importance in some limited areas of commercial activity.[104] All these entities are outside the scope of this book.[105]

Open-ended investment companies

1–36   The Victorian penchant for devising corporate vehicles for specialised purposes was revived in 1996 with the creation of the Open-Ended Investment Company. It is perhaps an indication of the changes in the nature of the UK economy over the previous 150 years that, this time, the specialised purpose was that of "collective investment". Broadly, collective investment means the coming together of a number of investors, often a large number of relatively small investors, who pool their resources for the purposes of achieving better returns on their investments. Those investments will typically be the purchase of corporate securities, though the range of investments is not confined to these. This better return, it is hoped, will result partly from the greater size of the fund to be invested and partly from the employment of specialised management to discharge the investment task.[106]

Both the trust (in the shape of "unit trusts", which can trace their origin back to the 1860s) and the registered company (in the shape of the "investment company") have long been used for this purpose. In the case of an investment company the investor buys shares in a company whose resources are allocated to the purchase of investments. However, as we have noted already in relation to guarantee companies,[107] a company limited by shares suffers from the disadvantage that the repurchase of shares by the company is not freely available. An investor who wishes to dispose of his or her investment in the company will normally have to sell the shares to another investor, but the market price of the shares, depending on supply and demand, may well be less than the value of the underlying investments held by the company which the share represents. These difficulties can be avoided by the use of the unit trust, which is free to make a standing offer to buy back units from investors at a price which fully reflects the value of assets held in the trust. However, in the 1990s the trust came to be regarded as an English peculiarity which might not fare well in international competition with continental European and US investment funds, organised on a corporate basis.

The Government's response was the creation of a corporate vehicle which had the same freedom as the trust to repay to investors the value of the shares held, the value being calculated on a similar basis. Thus, s.262 of the Financial

---

[103] BIS/Companies House, *Statistical Tables on Companies Registration Activities 2014/15*, p.8. The registration function had been delegated, somewhat bizarrely, to the Financial Services Authority. Since the Co-operative and Community Benefit Societies Act 2014 came into force, the registration function has now been transferred to the Financial Conduct Authority.

[104] For a fascinating comparative attempt to explain the successes and failures of the co-operatives, see H. Hansmann, *The Ownership of Enterprise* (USA: Harvard University Press, 1996).

[105] As is the trade union, that other expression of the Victorian genius for collective self-help, but with whose legal status the legislature encountered much more difficulty.

[106] The legal definition of a "collective investment scheme" is to be found in s.235 of the FSMA 2000.

[107] See above, para.1–8.

Services and Markets Act 2000 (the current governing legislation) permits the Treasury to make regulations for the creation of corporate bodies to be known as open-ended investment companies ("OEIC"), and an essential ingredient of the definition of an OEIC is that it provides to investors in it an expectation that they shall be able to realise their investment within a reasonable period and on the basis of a value calculated mainly by reference to the value of the property held within the scheme by the company.[108] This power has been exercised in regulations,[109] which require the OEIC to provide that its shareholders be entitled either to have their shares redeemed or repurchased by the OEIC upon request at a price related to the value of the scheme property or to sell their shares on a public exchange at the same price.[110] In general, the Regulations are a combination of provisions drawn from the Companies Act 1985[111] (but without the crucial general principle to be found in the companies legislation that a company limited by shares cannot acquire its own shares)[112] and from the Financial Services and Markets Act concerning the authorisation of those wishing to engage in investment business.[113]

EUROPEAN UNION FORMS OF INCORPORATION

European Economic Interest Grouping

Legislation creating corporate bodies remains mainly a matter for the Member States of the EU, but there are now two forms of incorporation provided by EU law. Both are concerned to promote cross-border co-operation among companies formed in different Member States; both are in consequence rather specialised forms of incorporation; both are implemented by Regulations, which are therefore directly applicable in the Member States (though in both cases supplementary national legislation is required); but the two differ in most other respects. The European Economic Interest Grouping ("EEIG") is based on the model of the French *groupement d'intérêt économique* ("GIE"), and is designed to enable existing business undertakings in different Member States to form an autonomous body to provide common services ancillary to the primary activities of its members. Any profits it makes belong to its members and they are jointly and severally responsible for its liabilities. In addition, the members of the EEIG, acting as a body, may take "any decision for the purpose of achieving the objects of the grouping".[114] Although the managers of the EEIG also constitute an organ of the Grouping and may bind it as against third parties, it is clear that the Regulation does not insist upon the delegation of management authority from the

1–37

---

[108] FSMA 2000 s.236(3).
[109] Open-Ended Investment Company Regulations (SI 2001/1228), as amended by SI 2005/923, SI 2009/553 and SI 2011/3049.
[110] SI 2001/1228 reg.15(11).
[111] Pt III of the Regulations.
[112] See para.13–2.
[113] Pt II of the Regulations.
[114] Council Regulation 2137/85 [1985] O.J. L199/1 art.16.

members to the managers. For this reason and because of the lack of limited liability for the members, the EEIG is as much like a partnership as like a company.

1–38   The basic requirements for the formation of an EEIG are simply the conclusion of a written contract between the members and registration at a registry in the Member State where it is to have its principal establishment. The members must be at least two in number and may be companies incorporated under national laws, partnerships or natural persons, but at least two of the members must carry on their principal activities in different Member States.[115] The Regulation[116] confers upon the EEIG full legal capacity, though whether it is afforded corporate personality is left to national law,[117] which is also left with considerable scope to supplement the mandatory provisions of the Regulation. The UK supplemented the EC Regulations by the European Economic Interest Grouping Regulations 1989[118] which nominate the Companies Registrar as the registering authority. A number of the sections of the Companies Act 2006[119] and the Insolvency Act[120] are applied to an EEIG as if it were a company registered under the Companies Act and it may be wound up as an unregistered company under Pt V of the Insolvency Act.[121]

1–39   The ancillary nature of the EEIG is illustrated by the restrictions placed upon it by art.3 of the EU Regulation. The general principle is that the EEIG's activities "shall be related to the economic activities of its members and must not be more than ancillary to those activities". The latter part of the restriction, in particular, is then supplemented by prohibitions on the EEIG (a) exercising management over its members' activities or those of another undertaking; (b) holding shares in a member company; (c) employing more than 500 workers[122]; or (d) being a member of another EEIG. Given the above, it was always likely that the take-up of the EEIG in Britain would not be high. That has turned out to be the case, though the number of EEIGs with principal establishment in Great Britain has grown steadily from 23 in 1991 to 279 in 2015.[123] The EEIG will receive little further discussion in this book.

---

[115] Council Regulation 2137/85 [1985] O.J. L199/1 art.4.

[116] Council Regulation 2137/85 [1985] O.J. L199/1.

[117] In the case of EEIGs with their principal establishment in Great Britain corporate personality is conferred by the European Economic Interest Grouping Regulations 1989 (SI 1989/638) reg.3, as amended by SI 2009/2399 which updates the regulations to accommodate the Companies Act 2006.

[118] See previous note.

[119] SI 1989/638 reg.18 and Sch.4.

[120] SI 1989/638 reg.19.

[121] In which case the provisions of the Company Directors Disqualification Act 1986 (see below, Ch.10) apply: reg.20.

[122] This restriction seems to have been motivated in part to avoid the EEIG being used by German companies to avoid domestic worker participation legislation, which bites at the 500 employee level.

[123] BIS/Companies House, *Statistical Tables on Companies Registration Activities 2014/15*, p.8.

The European Company (societas europaea or "SE")

The European Company,[124] by contrast, is not intended for ancillary activities but rather to facilitate the cross-border mergers of companies and their mainstream activities, something which the creation of a single market within the EU has promoted. Of course, a cross-border merger does not necessarily need a European Company. An English company could merge with a French company, so as to produce a resulting company which was either English or French (or indeed registered in some third state), though in fact such an exercise has been difficult to carry out in the past, but should be facilitated by the Cross-Border Mergers Directive.[125] Alternatively, the English or French company can offer to buy the shares of the other company (a process known as a takeover offer).[126] If the offer is accepted by the shareholders of the offeree company, that company becomes a subsidiary of the offeror company, but the important point for present purposes is that, in a takeover, there is no need for structural changes to the pre-existing companies: the two companies continue as before after the takeover, albeit with different shareholders in the target company (and perhaps also in the bidder). In this way, the English or French company could build up a string of subsidiary companies operating in as many Member States of the EU as was desired.

1–40

What can the European Company add to this situation? Its advantages from a company law perspective are mainly psychological. In the situation described at the end of the previous paragraph, the English (or French) company had built up a group structure which operated effectively throughout the EU, but the lead or head company in the group was clearly identified as English (or French, as the case might be). It is argued that a cross-border group might be more acceptable to those who work in or with it if it could be formed under a EU type of incorporation, which was not identified with any particular Member State,[127] and there might even be some saving of transaction costs if all the existing national subsidiaries could be folded into a single SE. Thus, the English and French companies, when they originally merge, might choose to do so by forming an SE, to replace the existing French and English companies. In addition or instead, the controllers of the group might choose to roll their various national subsidiaries into an SE, whether the top company in the group continued to be an English company or a French company or was a newly formed SE.

1–41

This was the vision of the original proponents of the SE, put forward as long ago as 1959.[128] By the time the SE was adopted by the EU (in 2001[129]) and came into

1–42

---

[124] There is also a statute for a European Co-operative Society (SCE) (Council Regulation 1435/2003 [2003] O.J. L207/1) and an accompanying directive on the involvement of employees (Directive 2003/72/EC [2003] O.J. L207/25). They have been transposed domestically by the European Cooperative Society Regulations 2006/2078. These are not discussed further in this book.

[125] Directive 2005/56/EC. See Ch.29, below.

[126] See below, Ch.28.

[127] It is easy to overstate the force of this psychological argument: there is no guarantee that the shareholdings or management of a SE will be spread equally across the Member States in which it operates.

[128] By Professor P. Sanders of the University of Rotterdam, though the French claim co-paternity.

[129] Council Regulation 2157/2001/EC [2001] O.J. L294/1, and the accompanying Directive on worker involvement (Council Directive 2001/86/EC [2001] O.J. L294/22). The European Company

force (in October 2004), however, this vision had been crucially compromised. Essential to the concept of an EU form of incorporation, divorced from the law of the Member States, is the notion that the SE law should provide a comprehensive code of company law rules for the SE. However, the adopted version of the SE not only fails to regulate adjacent legal areas such as taxation, competition law, intellectual property and insolvency,[130] even within core company law the SE law relies heavily on the national laws of the Member States.[131] The provisions specified at EU level for the SE come near to detailed regulation in only four areas: formation, transfer of the registered office of the SE,[132] board structure and employee involvement.[133] In the latter two areas the rules applying to any particular SE will vary according to the choice made by the SE itself, any agreement made between the SE and the employee representatives or to the national origins of the companies forming the SE. Outside these four areas, the SE is to be governed by the law relating to public companies in the jurisdiction in which it is registered.[134] Thus, it seems that there will be at least as many different SEs as there are Member States of the EU. This fact is emphasised by the absence of an EU registry for the SE. The SE has to be registered in one of the Member States of the EU. Since the SE is to be embedded in the domestic law of the state of registration, this is obviously the correct technical rule, but it does make clear the fact that, for example, a German-registered SE will look rather different from a British-registered one.[135]

1–43 What the SE law achieves is only partial harmonisation of the company law applying to that body.[136] In fact, since those forming an SE apparently have a free choice of the state in which they register their SE—it does not have to be one of the states in which existing businesses operate—the SE rules may promote a certain competition among the Member States to make their rules transposing the SE, and by extension their national company laws, attractive to businesses. However, it should be noted that the requirement to have registered and head offices in the same state will constitute a brake on such competition.[137]

1–44 Unlike a domestic company, the SE can be formed only by existing companies[138] and not by natural persons. In line with its cross-border objectives, those existing companies must already have a cross-border presence. The four methods of

---

must use the abbreviation SE as either a prefix or suffix to its name and in the future other types of entity will not be able to avail themselves of this acronym: Regulation art.11.

[130] Reg.2157/2001 art.63 and Preamble 20.

[131] See SI 2009/2400 making the necessary changes to apply Companies Act 2006, and SIs 2009/2401 and 2009/2402 on employee involvement in Northern Ireland and Great Britain.

[132] See para.6–27.

[133] This is the matter dealt with in the accompanying Directive. See below, Ch.14.

[134] Articles 9(1)(c)(ii) and 10 of reg.2157/2001. It seems that this happens automatically, by force of the Regulation, without the Member State having to provide for it or to identify the applicable parts of the domestic law. For this reason the European Company statute, as adopted, is relatively short (70 articles in the Regulation and 17 in the Directive), whereas the 1975 proposal contained 284 articles.

[135] It has been unkindly remarked that the SE proposal started as a "sausage" and ended up as a "sausage skin".

[136] K.J. Hopt, "The European Company under the Nice Compromise: Major Breakthrough or Small Coin for Europe?" [2000] Euredia 465.

[137] See paras 6–17 et seq.

[138] And sometimes analogous legal entities.

formation are: merger, formation of a holding SE, formation of a subsidiary SE and transformation.[139] The merger route is confined to public companies[140] (which in this context includes an SE) and to certain types of merger.[141] The companies must have registered and head offices in the EU and at least two of them must be incorporated in different Member States. A holding SE can be formed by public or private companies if at least two of them are incorporated in different Member States or for two years have had a subsidiary or branch in another Member State. The SE in this case results from a form of share-for-share takeover offer, made by the new SE to the shareholders of the founding companies. A subsidiary SE may be formed by a similar set of companies, in this case by the forming companies subscribing for the shares of the SE. The most tightly regulated form of incorporation of the SE is that of transformation: a public company which for at least two years has had a subsidiary company governed by the law of another Member State may convert itself into an SE. The Regulation also provides for the conversion back of an SE into a public company governed wholly by domestic law.[142] It will be clear from this that the SE is a form of incorporation not available to companies incorporated outside the EU.

Since the SE is so much part of domestic law, the rules applying to SEs registered in Great Britain will be referred to from time to time in this book. However, the take-up of this legal form has been rather limited. Throughout the EU as a whole only some 60 SEs had been formed as of early 2007 and only 12 of these had operations and employees (as opposed to being shelf companies).[143] There were three SEs registered in the UK, but all without operations and employees.

1–45

Despite these discouraging figures the Commission has committed itself to producing an equivalent form of EU incorporation specifically designed for small- and medium-sized private enterprises, the "Societas Privata Europaea" or SPE,[144] and, more recently, on a single-member private company, the "Societas Unius Personae" or SUP.[145]

1–46

---

[139] Reg.2157/2001 art.2 and ss.2–4. In addition, an established SE can set up further SEs as subsidiaries: art.3(2).

[140] Including, of course, their equivalents in other Member States.

[141] Merger by acquisition and merger by formation of a new company: see para.29–12.

[142] Reg.2157/2001 art.66.

[143] Please see *http://www.seeurope-network.org/homepages/seeurope/secompanies.html#established* [Accessed 11 April 2016]. The legality of forming shelf SEs has been contested on the grounds that there will have been no negotiations with the employee representatives over employee involvement.

[144] For further details, see *http://www.europeanprivatecompany.eu/home/* [Accessed 31 January 2016]. Proposal for a Council Regulation on the Statute for a European private company, COM(2008) 396/3 of 25 June 2008; European Parliament legislative resolution of 10 March 2009 on the proposal for a Council Regulation on the Statute for a European private company (COM(2008)0396 – C6-0283/2008 – 2008/0130(CNS)).

[145] Please see *http://www.consilium.europa.eu/en/press/press-releases/2015/05/28-29-compet-single-member-private-companies/* [Accessed 11 April 2016].

CONCLUSION

1–47   After a period of stability in the variety of legal forms on offer to those who wish to incorporate their businesses—before 2000 the last significant innovation had been the introduction of the private company at the beginning of the twentieth century—at least four significant new forms of incorporation have been made available in less than a decade: the limited liability partnership, the community interest company, the charitable incorporated organisation and the European Company (or societas europaea). These innovations reflect different driving forces at the policy level. The LLP was a response to the desire of large partnerships to find a form of incorporation with limited liability in an increasingly litigious world, but which nevertheless provided the tax advantages and internal management flexibility traditionally associated with the ordinary partnership. The CIC reflected the Government's desire to encourage the deployment of entrepreneurial skills towards the solution of social problems; and the CIO a desire to involve private bodies in the delivery of welfare state objectives. The SE reflected the goal of the European Commission and Community more generally to deepen the single European market by promoting cross-border mergers. Of the three, only the last produced an innovation in the core areas of company law, but, so far, its up-take, as we have noted, has been limited.

CHAPTER 2

ADVANTAGES AND DISADVANTAGES OF INCORPORATION

LEGAL ENTITY DISTINCT FROM ITS MEMBERS

As already emphasised, the fundamental attribute of corporate personality—from which indeed all the other consequences flow—is that the corporation is a legal entity distinct from its members. Hence it is capable of enjoying rights and of being subject to duties which are not the same as those enjoyed or borne by its members. In other words, it has "legal personality" and is often described as an *artificial person* in contrast with a human being, a *natural person*.[1]

2–1

As we have seen, corporate personality became an attribute of the normal joint stock company only at a comparatively late stage in its development, and it was not until *Salomon v Salomon*[2] at the end of the nineteenth century that its implications were fully grasped even by the courts. The details of this justly celebrated case merit attention.

Salomon had carried on a prosperous business as a leather merchant for many years. In 1892, he decided to convert his business into a limited company, and for this purpose Salomon & Co Ltd was formed with Salomon, his wife and five of his children as members, and Salomon as managing director. The company purchased Salomon's business as a going concern for £39,000—"a sum which represented the sanguine expectations of a fond owner rather than anything that can be called a businesslike or reasonable estimate of value".[3] The price was

2–2

---

[1] A company, even if it has only one member, is a "corporation aggregate" as opposed to the somewhat anomalous "corporation sole" in which an office, e.g. that of a bishop, is personified.

[2] *Salomon v Salomon* [1897] A.C. 22 HL.

[3] *Salomon v Salomon* [1897] A.C. 22 HL at 49, per Lord Macnaghten.

satisfied by £10,000 in debentures, conferring a charge over all the company's assets; £20,000 in fully paid £1 shares; and the balance in cash. The result was that Salomon held 20,001 of the 20,007 shares issued, and each of the remaining six shares was held by a member of his family, apparently as a nominee for him. The company almost immediately ran into difficulties and only a year later the then holder of the debentures appointed a receiver and the company went into liquidation. Its assets were sufficient to discharge the debentures but nothing was left for the unsecured creditors.

2–3   In these circumstances Vaughan Williams J and a strong Court of Appeal held that the whole incorporation transaction was contrary to the true intent of the Companies Act and that the company was a mere sham, and an alias, agent, trustee or nominee for Salomon, who remained the real proprietor of the business. As such he was liable to indemnify the company against its trading debts. But the House of Lords unanimously reversed this decision. They held that the company had been validly formed, since the Act merely required seven members holding at least one share each. It said nothing about their being independent, or that they should take a substantial interest in the undertaking, or that they should have a mind and will of their own, or that there should be anything like a balance of power in the constitution of the company. Hence the business belonged to the company and not to Salomon, and Salomon was *its* agent. In the blunt words of Lord Halsbury LC[4]:

> "Either the limited company was a legal entity or it was not. If it was, the business belonged to it and not to Mr Salomon. If it was not, there was no person and no thing to be an agent at all; and it is impossible to say at the same time that there is a company and there is not."

Or, as Lord Macnaghten put it[5]:

> "The company is at law a different person altogether from the subscribers…; and, though it may be that after incorporation the business is precisely the same as it was before, and the same persons are managers, and the same hands receive the profits, the company is not in law the agent of the subscribers or trustee for them. Nor are the subscribers, as members, liable in any shape or form, except to the extent and in the manner provided by the Act."[6]

2–4   The *Salomon* case established that (a) provided the formalities of the Act are complied with, a company will be validly incorporated, even if it is only a "one person" company; and (b) the courts will be reluctant to treat a shareholder as personally liable for the debts of the company by "piercing the corporate veil".[7] Whereas acceptance of the former argument would have involved denying the separate legal personality of the company, the second could have been upheld without that consequence, though it would have involved undermining the concomitant of separate legal personality, i.e. limited liability (see below).

---

[4] *Salomon v Salomon* [1897] A.C. 22 HL at 31.

[5] *Salomon v Salomon* [1897] A.C. 22 HL at 51.

[6] For an early statutory recognition of the same principle, see the House of Commons (Disqualification) Act 1782, which disqualified those holding Government contracts from election to Parliament but expressly provided (s.3) that the prohibition did not extend to members of incorporated companies holding such contracts.

[7] See further Ch.8.

The objection of the unsecured creditors in this case was based on the overvaluation of the business which was sold to the company in exchange for shares and debentures in it. In the case of a public company today, the business would be the subject of an independent valuation so far as it was used to pay up shares,[8] but in the case of a private company, or even of debentures issued by a public company, the main protection of unsecured creditors lies in disclosure of the company's financial position.[9] Unlike some countries, English law has developed no significant doctrine whereby loans to a company by its major shareholders are treated as equity. Even today, the best the unsecured creditors could hope for is that a floating charge securing a debenture might be at least partially invalidated if there was either a successful petition for a winding-up or an administration order within two years of the creation of the charge.[10] In this case, Salomon was able to give himself protection against the downside risks of his business by taking a position as secured creditor through the debentures, whilst taking the full benefit of any upside gains through his (in effect) 100 per cent shareholding.[11]

2–5

Of course, this decision does not mean that a promoter can with impunity defraud the company which he forms, or swindle his existing creditors. In the *Salomon* case it was argued that the company was entitled to rescind the sale of the business in view of its wilful overvaluation by Salomon. But the House held that there was no basis for rescission on the facts, since all the shareholders were fully conversant with what was being done and had effectively affirmed the deal. Had Salomon concealed the profit from his fellow shareholders, the position would have been different.[12] Nor was there any fraud on Salomon's pre-incorporation creditors, all of whom were paid off in full out of the purchase price. Otherwise, they or Salomon's trustee in bankruptcy might have been entitled to upset the sale.[13]

2–6

In any event, since the *Salomon* case, the complete separation of the company and its members has never been doubted. The decision opened up new vistas to company lawyers and the world of commerce. Not only did it finally establish the legality of the "one-person" company (long before EC law required this) and showed that incorporation was as readily available to the small private partnership and sole trader as to the large public company, but it also revealed

2–7

---

[8] See para.11–13. However, since Salomon was the only beneficial shareholder, it really mattered little to him whether he was issued with 20,000 or 10 shares in exchange for the business, for the value of the shares in aggregate (no matter how many or how few), would be the same, i.e. they represent the economic value (if any) of the business. However, independent valuation might protect creditors from being misled about the value of the assets contributed to the company, and also enable any new shareholders to ensure their relative financial inputs were reflected in the relative size of their shareholding.

[9] See below, Ch.21.

[10] Insolvency Act 1986 s.245. See para.32–14.

[11] But, in this particular case, Salomon seems to have been one of the victims rather than the villain of the piece for he had mortgaged his debentures and used the money to try to support the tottering company. However, the result would have been the same if he had not, and even if he had been the only creditor to receive anything from the business, which was "his" in fact though not in law.

[12] See para.5–2 and paras 5–23 et seq.

[13] Under what are now ss.423–425 of the Insolvency Act 1986.

that it was possible for a trader not merely to limit his liability to the money which he put into the enterprise but even to avoid any serious risk to the major part of that by subscribing for secured debentures rather than shares. This result at the time seemed shocking, and the decision was much criticised.[14] A partial justification for it is that the public deal with a limited company at their peril and know, or should know, what to expect.[15] In particular a search of the company's file at Companies House should reveal its latest annual accounts and whether there are any charges on the company's assets.[16]

2–8   Nonetheless, the doctrine of separate corporate personality is what underpins much of the success of companies as effective business structures, and its inviolability was further reinforced in *Prest v Petrodel*,[17] where the Supreme Court affirmed the importance of the doctrine and indicated that the courts may only "pierce the corporate veil" in exceptionally limited circumstances.[18]

LIMITED LIABILITY

2–9   It follows from the fact that a corporation is a separate person that its members are not as such liable for its debts.[19] Hence, in the absence of express provision to the contrary, the members will be completely free from any personal liability for the company's debts. The rule of non-liability also applies to obligations other than debts: the company is liable and not the member.

2–10   However, the principle applies only so long as we concentrate on the position of members as such, and remains true, once the company ceases to be a going concern, only subject to the particular terms of the shareholding—then, members may be required to make contributions to the company's assets if their shares were issued on that basis. Something more should be said about each of these qualifications on limited liability.

2–11   First, members who become involved in the management of the company's business, for example as directors, will find that separate legal personality does

---

[14] See, e.g. O. Kahn-Freund, "Some Reflections on Company Law Reform" in (1944) 7 M.L.R. 54 (a thought-provoking article still well worth study) in which it is described as a "calamitous decision". For a more positive assessment see D. Goddard, "Corporate Personality—Limited Recourse and its Limits" in R. Grantham and C. Rickett (eds) *Corporate Personality in the Twentieth Century* (Oxford: Hart Publishing, 1998). On the rationales for limited liability, see para.8–1.

[15] Although there are undoubtedly many who think that "Ltd" is an indication of size and stability (which "Plc" may be but "Ltd" certainly is not) rather than a warning of limited access to assets (i.e. access confined to the company's assets, however few, with no access to the shareholders').

[16] And in the House of Lords no sympathy was wasted on those who do not search the registers: "A creditor who will not take the trouble to use the means which the statute provides for enabling him to protect himself must bear the consequences of his own negligence": [1897] A.C. 22 at 40, per Lord Watson.

[17] *Prest v Petrodel* [2013] UKSC 34.

[18] See Ch.8; and note also *Antonio Gramsci Shipping Corp v Aivars Lembergs* [2013] EWCA Civ 730.

[19] This sentence was quoted and relied on by Kerr LJ in *Rayner (Mincing Lane) Ltd v Department of Trade* [1989] Ch.72 at 176 as an accurate statement of English law although, as he pointed out, it is not accurate in relation to most Civil Law countries—including Scotland so far as partnerships are concerned—or to international law: ibid. at 176–183.

not necessarily protect them from personal liability. Although acting on behalf of the company, they may have done things which have made them personally liable to the company or to outsiders. The most obvious example is that of a tort committed in the course of directorial duties. The extent to which those acting on behalf of companies are personally liable for their acts to third parties depends on the operation of the doctrines of agency and rules such as assumption of responsibility in tort law and identification in criminal law. These are matters discussed in Ch.7.

Secondly, although the doctrine of separate legal personality normally shields members (as such) from personal liability so long as the company is a going concern, it does not necessarily extend further. If a company enters insolvent liquidation, the question becomes whether the liquidator acting on behalf of the company can seek contributions from its members so as to bring the company's assets up to the level needed to meet the claims of the company's creditors. In the case of an unlimited company,[20] s.74 of the Insolvency Act does indeed impose on the members such an obligation to contribute to the assets of the company. In the case of companies limited by shares or by guarantee,[21] however, that obligation is limited (hence, by transfer, the term "limited company") and is not, as it is with unlimited companies, open-ended.

2–12

   In the case of a company limited by shares, each member is liable to contribute when called upon to do so the full nominal value of the shares held insofar as this has not already been paid by the shareholder or any prior holder of those shares (which it normally will have been). In the case of a guarantee company, each member is liable to contribute a specified amount (normally small) to the assets of the company in the event of its being wound up while a member, or within one year after ceasing to be a member. In effect the member, without being directly liable to the company's creditors, is in both cases a limited guarantor of the company. When, therefore, obligations are incurred on behalf of a limited company, the company is liable and not the members, though in the case of a guarantee company or of partly paid shares the company may ultimately be able to recover a contribution from the members towards the discharge of its obligations. However, in the typical case of a company limited by shares with fully paid shares in issue, no further liability will arise for the member in the absence of specific statutory provision to the contrary, which provisions are rare.[22]

By contrast, an unincorporated association, not being a legal person, cannot itself be liable, and obligations entered into on its behalf can bind only the actual officials who purport to act on its behalf, or the individual members if the officials have actual or apparent authority to bind them. In either event the persons bound will be liable to the full extent of their property unless they expressly or impliedly restrict their responsibility to the extent of the funds of the association, as the officials may well do. Hence the extent to which the member will be liable depends on the terms of the contract of association. In the case of a

2–13

---

[20] See above, para.1–27.
[21] See above, paras 1–8 and 1–11.
[22] See Ch.9.

club, and presumably most learned and scientific societies, there will generally be implied a term that the members are not personally liable for obligations incurred on behalf of the club.

2–14 And the position is different again for members of a partnership, being an association carrying on business for gain. Each partner is an agent of all the others, and acts done by any one partner in "carrying on in the normal way business of the kind carried on by the firm" bind all the partners.[23] Only if the creditor knows of the limitation placed on the partner's authority will the other members escape liability.[24] Moreover, an attempt to restrict the partners' liability to partnership funds by a provision to that effect in the partnership agreement will be ineffective even if known to the creditors[25]; the partners can restrict their financial liability, in respect of acts otherwise authorised, only by an express agreement to that effect with the creditor concerned.[26] This explains the pressure, which bore fruit in 2000, for the creation of an incorporated legal entity with the internal flexibility of a partnership but the advantage of limited liability, i.e. the limited liability partnership.[27]

2–15 The overall result of the broad recognition by the courts of the separate legal entity of the company and of the limited liability of its members is to produce at first sight a legal regime which is very unfavourable to potential creditors of companies, a situation which they have naturally sought to readjust by contract in their favour, so far as is in their power. For large lenders, especially banks, there are a number of possibilities, to be used separately or cumulatively. Apart from the obvious commercial response of charging higher interest rates on loans to bodies whose members have limited liability, such lenders may seek to leap over the barrier created by the law of limited liability by exacting as the price of the loan to the company personal guarantees of its repayment from the managers or shareholders of the company, guarantees which may be secured on the personal assets of the individuals concerned. Instead of or in addition to obtaining personal security by contracting around limited liability, large lenders may seek to improve the priority of their claims by taking security against the *company's* assets. As we shall see later on in this chapter, chancery practitioners in the nineteenth century were quick to respond to this need by creating the flexible and all-embracing instrument of the floating charge to supplement the traditional fixed charge mechanisms which were already available.

However, these self-help remedies may not be practicable for trade creditors or employees[28] and, even in the case of large lenders, there is a strong danger that, when things begin to go wrong, the controllers of the company will take risks with the company's capital which were not within the contemplation of the

---

[23] Partnership Act 1890 s.5. This applies equally to Scotland thus largely negativing the consequence of recognising the Scottish firm as a separate person.

[24] Partnership Act 1890 ss.5 and 8.

[25] *Re Sea, Fire and Life Insurance Co* (1854) 3 De G.M. & G. 459.

[26] *Hallett v Dowdall* (1852) 21 L.J.Q.B. 98.

[27] Limited Liability Partnerships Act 2000. See para.1–4.

[28] Unless and to the extent that they have a statutory preference, unsecured creditors are in the worst possible world. Limited liability normally stops them suing the shareholders or directors, whilst the fixed and floating charges of the big lenders often soak up all the available assets of the company.

parties when the loan was arranged. For these reasons, although the legislature has not overturned *Salomon v Salomon* and, indeed, under the influence of EU law,[29] the one-person company is now expressly recognised by domestic law, the Companies and Insolvency Acts are full of provisions whose purpose cannot be completely understood except against the background of limited liability. In particular, the extensive publicity and disclosure obligations placed upon limited liability companies,[30] the provisions relating to wrongful trading,[31] and the expanded provisions on the disqualification of directors, especially on grounds of unfitness,[32] must all be seen in this light.

PROPERTY

One obvious advantage of corporate personality is that it enables the property of the association to be more clearly distinguished from that of its members. In an unincorporated society, the property of the association is the joint property of the members. The rights of the members to that property differ from their rights to their separate property, since the joint property must be dealt with according to the rules of the society and no individual member can claim any particular asset. By virtue of the trust the obvious complications can be minimised but not completely eradicated. And the complications cause particular difficulty in the case of a trading partnership both as regards the true nature of the interests of the partners[33] and as regards claims of creditors.[34] By contrast, on incorporation, the corporate property belongs to the company, and members have no direct proprietary rights to it but merely to their "shares" in the undertaking.[35] A change in the membership, which causes inevitable dislocation to a partnership firm, leaves the company unconcerned; the shares may be transferred, but the company's property will be untouched and no realisation or splitting up of its property will be necessary, as it will on a change in the constitution of a partnership firm.

2–16

Identification of the company's property is not the only advantage; corporate personality also enables that property to be segregated from the members' personal assets. Thus, the claims of the business creditors will be against the property of the company and the claims of the members' personal creditors

2–17

---

[29] See Council Directive 89/667 on single-member private limited liability companies [1989] O.J. L395, 12 December 1989.

[30] See below, Ch.21, but note s.448 whereby the directors of unlimited liability companies are not normally required to deliver accounts and reports to the registrar for general publication.

[31] See para.9–6.

[32] See Ch.10.

[33] See Partnership Act 1890 ss.20–22; *Re Fuller's Contract* [1933] Ch. 652.

[34] Partnership Act 1890 s.23, and the Insolvent Partnerships Order 1994 (SI 1994/2421), as amended.

[35] "Shareholders are not, in the eye of the law, part owners of the undertaking. The undertaking is something different from the totality of the shareholdings": per Evershed LJ in *Short v Treasury Commissioners* [1948] 1 K.B. 116, 122 CA; affirmed [1948] A.C. 534 HL.

against the property of the member. Neither set of creditors is in competition with the other; and each has to monitor the disposition only of the assets against which its claims lie.[36]

SUING AND BEING SUED

2–18   Closely allied to questions of property are those relating to legal actions. The difficulties in the way of suing, or being sued by, an unincorporated association have long bedevilled English law.[37] The problem is obviously of the greatest practical importance in connection with trading bodies, and in fact has now been solved in the case of partnerships by allowing a partnership to sue or be sued in the firm's name. Hence, there is now no difficulty so far as the pure mechanics of suit are concerned—although there may still be complications in enforcing the judgment.

In the case of other unincorporated bodies (such as clubs and learned societies) not subject to special statutory provisions, the problems of suit are still serious. Sometimes its committee or other agents may be personally liable or authorised to sue. Otherwise, the only course is a "representative action" whereby, under certain conditions, one or more persons may sue or be sued on behalf of all the interested parties.[38] But resort to this procedure is available only subject to compliance with a number of somewhat ill-defined conditions, and the law, which has been inadequately explored, is obscure and difficult. The result is apt to be embarrassing to the society when it wishes to enforce its rights (or, more properly, those of its members) though it has compensating advantages when it wishes to evade its duties.[39]

Needless to say, none of these difficulties arises when an incorporated company is suing or being sued: the company as a legal person can take action to enforce its legal rights and can be sued for breach of its legal duties.

PERPETUAL SUCCESSION

2–19   One of the obvious advantages of an artificial person is that it is not susceptible to "the thousand natural shocks that flesh is heir to". It cannot become incapacitated by illness, mental or physical, and it has not (or need not have) an allotted span of life.[40] This is not to say that the death or incapacity of its human members may

---

[36] R. Kraakman and H. Hansmann, "The Essential Role of Organizational Law" (2000) 110 Yale L.J. 387.

[37] As we saw above (para.1–3) this problem seems to have lain behind the former restriction of the number of partners to a maximum of 20.

[38] CPR 19.6, permitting representative actions. The provision is strictly interpreted: *Emerald Supplies Ltd v British Airways Plc* [2010] EWCA Civ 1284.

[39] "An unincorporated association has certain advantages when litigation is desired against them": per Scrutton LJ in *Bloom v National Federation of Discharged Soldiers* (1918) 35 T.L.R. 50, 51 CA.

[40] Insolvency Act 1986 s.84(1)(a) envisages that the period of the company's duration may be fixed in the articles, but this is rarely done in practice and, even if it were, the company would not automatically expire on the expiration of the term; the section provides that expiration of the term is a ground on which the members by ordinary resolution may wind the company up voluntarily. It is otherwise with chartered companies: see para.1–31, fn.89.

not cause the company considerable embarrassment; obviously it will if all the directors die or are imprisoned, or if there are too few surviving members to hold a valid meeting, or if the bulk of the members or directors become enemy aliens.[41] But these vicissitudes of the flesh have no direct effect on the disembodied company.[42] The death of a member leaves the company unmoved; members may come and go but the company can go on forever.[43] The insanity of the managing director will not be calamitous to the company provided that he is removed promptly; he may be the company's brains, but lobectomy is a simpler operation than on a natural person.

Once again, the disadvantages in the case of an unincorporated society can be minimised by the use of a trust. If the property of the association is vested in a small body of trustees, the death, disability or retirement of an individual member, other than one of the trustees, need not cause much trouble. But, of course, the trustees, if natural persons, will themselves need replacing at fairly frequent intervals and the need for constant appointment of new trustees is a nuisance if nothing worse. Indeed, it may be said that the trust never functioned at its simplest until it was able to enlist the aid of its own child, the incorporated company, to act as a trust corporation with perpetual succession. **2–20**

Moreover, the trust can obviate difficulties easily only when a member, or his estate, has, under the constitution of the association, no right to be paid a share of the assets on death or retirement, which, of course, is the position with the normal club or learned society. But on the retirement or death of a partner, the default rule is that the partnership is automatically dissolved, so far at any rate as the departing partner is concerned,[44] and he or his estate will be entitled to be paid his share. The resulting dislocation of the firm's business can be reduced by special clauses in the articles of partnership, providing for a formula for valuation of his share and for deferred payment, but cannot be eradicated altogether.[45]

With an incorporated company these problems do not arise. Although the member or his estate is not generally entitled to be paid out by the company, if the member (or a personal representative, trustee in bankruptcy, or receiver) wishes to realise the value of the shares, these can be sold, whereupon the purchaser will, on entry **2–21**

---

[41] cf. *Daimler Co v Continental Tyre and Rubber Co* [1916] 2 A.C. 307 HL.

[42] As Greer LJ said in *Stepney Corporation v Osofsky* [1937] 3 All E.R. 289 at 291 CA: a corporate body has "no soul to be saved or body to be kicked". This epigram is believed to be of considerable antiquity. G. Williams, *Criminal Law: The General Part*, 2nd edn (London: Steven & Sons), p.856, has traced it back to Lord Thurlow and an earlier variation to Coke, cf. the decree of Pope Innocent IV forbidding the excommunication of corporations because, having neither minds nor souls, they could not sin: see C.T. Carr, *The General Principles of the Law of Corporations* (Cambridge: CUP, 1905), p.73. In *Rolloswin Investments Ltd v Chromolit Portugal SARL* [1970] 1 W.L.R. 912 it was held that since a company was incapable of public worship it was not a "person" within the meaning of the Sunday Observance Act 1677 so that a contract made by it on a Sunday was not void (the court was unaware that before the case was heard the Act had been repealed by the Statute Law (Repeals) Act 1969).

[43] During the Second World War all the members of one private company, while in general meeting, were killed by a bomb. But the company survived; not even a nuclear bomb could have destroyed it. And see the Australian case of *Re Noel Tedman Holding Pty Ltd* (1967) Qd.R. 561 Qd Sup Ct where the only two members were killed in a road accident.

[44] And, in the absence of contrary agreement, as regards all the partners: Partnership Act 1890 s.33.

[45] Also see below, para.2–23.

in the share register, become a member in place of the former holder. This is not always as easy as it sounds, however. The seller might not be able to find a purchaser at all, especially one who meets any restrictions which might be imposed on transfer,[46] and the other members might not have sufficient free capital to purchase the shares. Now, therefore, but subject to stringent conditions, purchase by the company is allowed,[47] as it has long been under the laws of many other countries.

2–22
The continuing existence of a company, irrespective of changes in its membership or its management, is helpful in other directions also. When an individual sells a business to another, difficult questions may arise regarding the performance of existing contracts by the new proprietor,[48] the assignment of rights of a personal nature,[49] and the validity of agreements made with customers ignorant of the change of proprietorship.[50] Similar problems may arise on a change in the constitution of a partnership.[51] Where the business is incorporated and the sale is merely of the shares, none of these difficulties arises. The company remains the proprietor of the business, performs the existing contracts and retains the benefits of them, and enters into future agreements. The difficulties attending vicarious performance, assignments and mistaken identity do not arise.

2–23
Although a company may shift control of its business by means of a transfer of its shares to new investors, it does not follow that it will always choose this method of effecting the change of control. The directors or shareholders of the company could decide instead to sell the underlying business of the company to the new investors, who, perhaps, may form their own company in order to take the new business. In this case, the transferring company (rather than its shareholders) will be left holding the consideration received on the sale of its business. This method is particularly likely to be attractive to the transferring company if it is divesting itself of control of only part of its business (though even then a transfer of control by sale of shares may be possible if the relevant part of the business is held in a separate group subsidiary company). When a company disposes of the whole or part of its business (as opposed to the shareholders deciding to transfer their shares), the difficulties mentioned in the previous paragraph in relation to the sale of a business by an unincorporated entity arise in relation to companies as well. To sum up, a company,[52] unlike an unincorporated body, has the option to shift

---

[46] For an unsuccessful attempt to use the unfair prejudice provisions to secure the return to the shareholder's estates of the capital represented by his shares see *Re A Company* [1983] Ch. 178; and see also the explanation of this case in *Re A Company* [1986] B.C.L.C. 382 (para.20–8).

[47] See para.13–17.

[48] *Robson v Drummond* (1831) 2 B. & Ad. 303; cf. *British Waggon Co v Lea* (1880) 5 Q.B.D. 149.

[49] *Griffith v Tower Publishing Co* [1897] 1 Ch. 21 (publishing agreement held not assignable); *Kemp v Baerselman* [1906] 2 K.B. 604 CA (agreement not assignable if question of one party's obligation depends on the other's "personal requirements"), cf. *Tolhurst v Associated Portland Cement* [1902] 2 K.B. 660 CA.

[50] *Boulton v Jones* (1857) 2 H. & N. 564.

[51] See *Brace v Calder* [1895] 2 Q.B. 253 CA where the retirement of two partners was held to operate as the wrongful dismissal of a manager. And see also Partnership Act 1890 s.18. In practice such difficulties are often avoided by an implied novation.

[52] Of course, even in relation to companies this proposition applies only to companies limited by shares and not to guarantee companies.

control by means of a transfer of shares, but it may choose instead to dispose of the underlying business (or even just of the assets used in the business).

TRANSFERABLE SHARES

Incorporation, with the resulting separation of the business (owned by the company) from the shares (owned by its members), greatly facilitates the transfer of the members' interests. Without this formal incorporation of the business enterprise, approximately the same ends can be achieved through the device of the trust coupled with an agreement for transferability in the deed of settlement. But in this case, even after transfer, the member will remain liable for the firm's debts incurred during the time when he or she was a member.[53] This ongoing liability (i.e. the absence of limited liability associated with companies) means that opportunities to transfer are, in practice, much restricted.

2–24

A partner has a proprietary interest which can be assigned (subject to the terms of the partnership deed), but the assignment does not operate to divest the partner of status or liability as a partner; it merely affords the assignee the right to receive whatever the firm distributes in respect of the assigning partner's share.[54] The assignee can be admitted into partnership in the place of the assignor only if the other partners agree[55] and the assignor will not be relieved of any existing liabilities as a partner unless the creditors agree, expressly or impliedly, to the release.[56]

With an incorporated company, freedom to transfer members' interests, both legally and practically, can be readily attained. The company can be incorporated with its liability limited by shares, and these shares constitute items of property which are freely transferable in the absence of express provision to the contrary, and in such a way that the transferor drops out[57] and the transferee steps into his shoes.

2–25

Even in an incorporated company, the power to transfer may, of course, be subject to restrictions. In a private company some form of restriction was formerly essential in order to comply with the then current statutory definition; although this is no longer a statutory requirement, it is still a desirable provision if such a company is to retain its character as an incorporated private partnership. In practice, these restrictions are usually so stringent as to make transferability largely illusory. Nor is there any legal objection arising out of the Companies Act to restrictions in the case of a public company, although such restrictions, except as regards partly paid shares, are unusual, and are prohibited by the Listing Rules if the shares are to be marketed on the Stock Exchange.[58] But there is this

2–26

---

[53] This assumes the member was, as a member, personally liable; this is not always the case. See above, para.2–7.

[54] Partnership Act 1890 s.31.

[55] Partnership Act 1890 s.24(7).

[56] Partnership Act 1890 s.17(2) and (3).

[57] Companies Act 2006 s.544. Subject only to a possible liability under ss.74 and 76 of the Insolvency Act 1986 if liquidation follows within a year and the shares were not fully paid up or were redeemed or purchased out of capital. On the latter see para.13–18.

[58] See para.25–15.

fundamental difference: in a partnership, transferability depends on express agreement and is subject to legal and practical limitations, whereas in a company it exists to the fullest extent in the absence of express restriction. The partnership relationship is essentially personal, and where a private company is, functionally, an incorporated partnership, the same approach is maintained.[59] On the other hand, the relationship between members of a public company is essentially impersonal and financial and hence there is usually no reason to restrict changes in membership.

MANAGEMENT UNDER A BOARD STRUCTURE

2–27   A further important feature of company law is that it provides a structure for the pursuit of larger and riskier endeavours by allowing many people to participate, via the purchase of shares, and separating that participation from the management of the company, which is delegated to a smaller and expert group of people who partly constitute and who are partly supervised by a board of directors. This separation of what is conventionally, but controversially, termed "ownership" of the company (i.e. shareholding) from its "control" (i.e. management) is a feature of large companies and it is therefore important that the organisational law governing companies should deal with its consequences. By contrast, as with transferable shares, this is not a feature of small companies, where "owners" and "managers" are often identical people, or substantially so. Then, as noted in Ch.1,[60] the corporate machinery for separating these roles may be more of a hindrance than a help, but it is crucial in the efficient functioning of large companies.

2–28   The legal implications of this development were first explored in the US by A.A. Berle and G.C. Means in *The Modern Corporation and Private Property*,[61] which drew attention to the revolutionary change thus brought about in our traditional conceptions of the nature of property. Today, the great bulk of large enterprise, at least in the US and the UK, is in the hands not of individual entrepreneurs but of large public companies in which many individuals have property rights as shareholders in the enterprise to which they have directly or indirectly contributed capital. After home ownership, direct or indirect[62] investment in companies probably constitutes the most important single item of property for most people, and yet whether this property brings profit to its "owners" no longer depends on their energy and initiative but on that of the management from which they are divorced. The modern shareholder in a public company has ceased to be a quasi-partner and has become instead simply a supplier of capital. If a person invests in the older forms of private property, such as a farm or a shop, he or she becomes tied to that property and the business endeavour. The modern public

---

[59] In recent years the courts have shown a welcome tendency to recognise this functional reality in applying the legal rules to such incorporated partnerships: see especially *Ebrahimi v Westbourne Galleries Ltd* [1973] A.C. 360 HL. See below, Ch.20.

[60] See above, para.1–28 and below, Ch.15.

[61] New York, 1933, reprinted in 1968 with a new preface.

[62] For most people the investment is indirect, perhaps even not conscious, as in the case of contributions to occupational pension schemes.

company provides a new type of property in which the relationship between the "owner" and the business plays little part; and indeed the owner can realise the wealth represented by the property whenever needed, by selling shares, and therefore without removing the business property from the enterprise which requires it indefinitely. "The separation of ownership from management and control in the corporate system has performed this essential step in securing liquidity."[63]

Even when, as is increasingly the case, shareholding in large companies is concentrated in the hands of institutional shareholders, such as pension funds and insurance companies, which do have a more significant potential for intervention in management than individual shareholders, such participation is discontinuous or episodic and usually precipitated by some crisis in the company's affairs rather than a day-to-day way of managing the company.[64]

Despite the fact that the board, and especially the "managing director" or the "chief executive officer", is the driving force behind the operation of the large company, the British Companies Act, unlike its continental counterparts, says very little about the board of directors. The Act insists there be directors, but only two are required in the case of a public company and, in the case of a private company, one will do.[65] Many sections of the Act impose administrative burdens on the directors or assume in some other way the existence of a board of directors, but the composition, structure and functions of the board are left to a very high degree to companies to decide themselves, through their articles of association[66] or through mere corporate practice. In the case of listed companies, however, this private ordering by companies themselves has become significantly qualified by the development in the last 18 years of the UK Corporate Governance Code and its predecessors.[67]

2–29

In the face of this "hands off" approach on the part of the Act, can the claim be made good that British company law provides machinery, except in the most rudimentary way, whereby the separation of ownership and control can flourish? The most obvious answer to this question consists in pointing to the duties created originally by the common law, but now restated in the Act, which aim to require the directors to exercise the powers conferred upon them competently and loyally in the interests of the company, which is normally to be seen as the interests of the shareholders.[68] Thus, one may say that the approach of company law to the regulation of the separation of ownership from control is to allow companies maximum freedom to decide on the division of powers between shareholders and board and on the functions of the board, but then to concentrate on the regulation of the way the board discharges the powers conferred upon it, whatever they may be. How successfully this is done is the topic of later chapters. All we need note here is the importance of the fact that in large companies there

2–30

---

[63] See above, fn.61 at p.284.
[64] See P. Davies, "Institutional Investors in the United Kingdom" in D. Prentice and P. Holland (eds), *Contemporary Issues in Corporate Governance* (Oxford: Oxford University Press, 1993).
[65] Companies Act 2006 s.154.
[66] See below, Ch.14.
[67] See para.14–69.
[68] See below, Ch.16.

are two decision-making bodies, shareholders in general meeting and the board of directors, and that in terms of management functions the board is invariably the more important organ.

BORROWING

2–31 So far we have considered only the advantages or disadvantages which flow inevitably or naturally from the fact of incorporation. But incorporation also has important consequences in respect of borrowing and taxation.

2–32 At first sight one might suppose that a sole trader, or partners, being personally liable, would find it easier than a company to raise money by borrowing. In practice, however, this is not so, since a company is often able to grant a more effective charge to secure the proposed indebtedness. The ingenuity of equity practitioners led to the evolution of an unusual but highly beneficial type of security known as the floating charge; i.e. a charge which "floats" over all the assets of the company falling within a generic description, but without preventing the chargor from disposing of those assets in the usual course of business, at least until something occurs to cause the charge to become crystallised or fixed. This type of charge is particularly suitable when a business has no fixed assets, such as land, which can be included in a normal security, but carries a large and valuable stock-in-trade. Since this stock needs to be turned over in the course of business, a fixed charge is impracticable because the consent of the chargee would be needed every time anything was sold, and a new charge would have to be entered into whenever anything was bought. A floating charge obviates these difficulties; it enables the stock to be turned over, but (if defined widely enough) attaches to whatever it is converted into and to whatever new stock is acquired.

In theory, there is no reason why such charges should not be granted by sole traders and ordinary partnerships as well as by incorporated companies (and now, LLPs). But two pieces of legislation have effectively precluded that. The first was the "reputed ownership" provision in the bankruptcy legislation relating to individuals.[69] This provision never applied to the winding-up of companies, and has now been repealed for individuals by the Insolvency Act 1986.[70] The second, which still remains, is that the charge, insofar as it relates to chattels, would be a bill of sale within the meaning of the Bills of Sale Acts 1878 and 1882, which apply only to individuals and not to companies.[71] Hence it would need to be registered in the Bills of Sale Registry,[72] and, what is more important, as a mortgage bill it would need to be in the statutory form,[73] which involves

---

[69] Bankruptcy Act 1914 s.38(1)(c).

[70] This reform was a result of the Cork Committee (1982) Cmnd. 8558, Ch.23. Its repeal had been recommended in the Report of the Blagden Committee 25 years earlier: (1957) Cmnd.221.

[71] This was always accepted in relation to mortgages in the light of s.17 of the 1882 Act. It was later held, after an exhaustive review of the conflicting authorities, that both Acts apply only to individuals: *Slavenburg's Bank v International Natural Resources Ltd* [1980] 1 W.L.R. 1076.

[72] For some reason registration of a bill of sale against a tradesman destroys his credit, whereas registration of a debenture against a company does not. This can only be explained on the basis that the former is exceptional, whereas the latter is usual and familiarity has bred contempt.

[73] 1882 Act s.9. Nor could it cover future goods: see ss.5 and 6(2), ibid allows a limited power of replacement but not anything as fluid as a floating charge.

specifying the chattels in detail in a schedule. Compliance with the latter requirement is obviously impossible, since in a floating charge the chattels are, by definition, indeterminate and fluctuating.

When, belatedly, we eventually get round to reforming, as many common law countries have done, our antiquated law relating to security interests in movables, we shall be able to repeal the Bills of Sale Acts and thus make it practicable for unincorporated firms to borrow on the security of floating charges,[74] or some comparable form of security on the lines of that provided by art.9 of the American Uniform Commercial code. In the meantime, use of this advantageous form of security is in practice restricted to bodies corporate. By virtue of it the lender can obtain an effective security on "all the undertaking and assets of the company both present and future" either alone or in conjunction with a fixed charge on its land.[75] By so doing the lender can place himself in a far stronger position than if merely the personal security of the individual trader supported the loan. It therefore happens not infrequently that a business is converted into a company solely in order to enable further capital to be raised by borrowing. And sometimes, as the *Salomon* case[76] shows, a trader by "selling" his business to a company which he has formed can give himself priority over his future creditors by taking a debenture, secured by a floating charge, for the purchase price.[77]

2–33

TAXATION

Once a company reaches a certain size, the attraction of limited liability is likely to outweigh all other considerations when business people are considering in what form to carry on their activities. Investors are unlikely to be willing to put money into a company where their liability is not limited, especially if they are to have no or little control over the running of the company. However, with small businesses, where it is feasible to give all the investors a say in management, it is likely that tax considerations will play a major part in determining whether the business will be set up in corporate form or as a partnership, especially as in such cases where, as we have seen, limited liability may not be available in practice vis-à-vis large lenders.[78] This is not the place to examine the tax considerations which may cut one way or another at different times on this issue. What should be noted, however, is that in the case of small companies, the investors' return on

2–34

---

[74] Farmers can already do so under the Agricultural Credits Act 1928 which permits individuals to grant to banks floating charges over farming stock and agricultural assets and excludes the application of the former reputed ownership provision and the Bills of Sale Acts: see ss.5 and 8(1), (2) and (4). Farming stock and agricultural assets are more readily distinguishable from a farmer's other assets (than, say, the stock of an antique dealer who lives over his shop) thus meeting the difficulty referred to in the text.

[75] The implications of floating charges are discussed more fully below, in Ch.32.

[76] *Salomon v Salomon* [1897] A.C. 22 HL.

[77] The ability of the fixed and floating chargeholder to "scoop the pool" of the company's assets has now been restricted, after long debate, by the Enterprise Act 2002, which requires "a prescribed part" of the company's assets to be kept available for the unsecured creditors. See below, Ch.32.

[78] As noted, in the case of professional businesses the rules of the governing professional body may require the partnership form, though in fact many professional bodies have become more flexible on this issue in recent years.

their capital may take the form of the payment of directors' fees rather than dividends, so that participation in the management of the company may be the means for the investor both to safeguard the investment and to earn a return on it.[79]

FORMALITIES AND EXPENSE

2–35 Turning from advantages to costs, incorporation is necessarily attended with formalities, loss of privacy (see below) and expense greater than that which would normally apply to a sole trader or partnership. A sole trader already exists. A partnership arises out of the facts of a relationship, and does not need a formal agreement provided the parties are carrying on a business in common with a view of profit.[80] An unincorporated firm can conduct its affairs without any formality and publicity beyond that which may be prescribed by the regulations (if any) applying to the particular type of business. If the business is carried on under a name different from the true name of the sole trader or those of all the partners, it will have to comply with the provisions on business names (as would a company trading under a pseudonym)[81] but these are not onerous. The business, unless it is insolvent, can eventually be wound up equally cheaply, privately and informally. An incorporated company, on the other hand, necessarily involves formalities, publicity and expenses at its birth, throughout its active life, and on its final dissolution.

2–36 The costs of formation, at least of a private company (and most companies are formed as private even if they become public later in life), are very low, however. A competent incorporation agent should be able to set up a basic company for less than £200. British law does not require a private company, unlike a public one, to have a minimum share capital.[82] Consequently, the incorporators can borrow what money they need to set the company up and do not need to sink their own money into it, which, indeed, they may not have. However, the combination of no minimum capital and limited liability could be an invitation to trading at the expense of the creditors, and so British law, even if it has no ex ante minimum capital requirement, has developed significant ex post controls on those who behave in this way after the company has been formed.[83]

2–37 Once the company is set up, there are also ongoing formalities and reporting requirements to meet. These ensure a degree of transparency that is not demanded of sole traders or partnerships. At the least, the documents on the public record remain accurate (so, for example, changes to the company's directors, and to its constitution must be filed[84]), and the state of the company business must be made

---

[79] See Ch.20.
[80] Partnership Act 1890 s.1(1). Typically there is an agreement, but this can be written on a half-sheet of notepaper or be an informal oral agreement.
[81] See para.4–20.
[82] See para.11–8.
[83] See Chs 9 and 10.
[84] See paras 3–20 et seq.

visible, at least to some extent, to those who might deal with the company in the future—so security granted over the company's assets should be registered,[85] and annual accounts may need to be filed.[86]

Finally, we have noted at a number of points in this chapter that the requirement of two separate decision-making organs, shareholders' meeting and board of directors, may seem over-elaborate for small companies, though something has now been done to alleviate this problem without, however, going to the extent of permitting small companies to adopt a single decision-making body.[87]

2–38

PUBLICITY

The company's affairs

As already noted, the costs of incorporation also come with the much greater publicity required of a company as against a partnership, since the former is required, but the latter is not, to make their annual accounts available publicly through filing at Companies House.[88] Until recently, small companies were required, in addition, to produce accounts in what was an over-elaborate format and to have those accounts audited, but these requirements have now been relaxed.[89]

2–39

The company's members and directors

Further, since a company can only act through the individuals behind the company—principally its board of directors, but also its members in general meeting—it is probably not surprising that there should be public registers of both the directors and the members, with more details required of the former (although now increasingly limited by concerns of privacy and personal safety).[90]

2–40

Disclosure of a company's members was never especially reliable, however, for the simple reason that s.126 prohibits trusts of any sort from being entered on the register of members. This means that the "real" owners of shares are not necessarily discoverable, even when the (disclosed) legal owner must comply absolutely with their directions on voting and distribution of the economic benefits of the shareholding. This is now the subject of significant change, as outlined below.

2–41

---

[85] See para.32–26.

[86] See Chs 21 and 22.

[87] See Ch.15.

[88] Public filing is seen to be a quid pro quo of limited liability. Thus, unlimited companies are not required to file their accounts publicly (s.441) whereas the limited liability partnership (above, para.1–4) is subject to the publicity regime applied to companies: Limited Liability Partnerships Regulations 2001 (SI 2001/1090) Pt II.

[89] See Chs 21 and 22.

[90] Companies Act 2006 Pt 10 Ch.1 (directors) and Pt 8 Ch.2 (members); and below, Chs 14 and 24 respectively.

"People with significant control"—the PSC Register

2–42   From 2016, almost all companies will be required to keep, open to the public, a register of "people with significant control", called the company's PSC Register (ss.790C(10), 790M).[91] This does not require the company to disclose every beneficial interest in its shareholdings, but it does require disclosure of every person (human or corporate) who is able to exert "significant influence or control" over the company's business, with that phrase defined in the Act, amplified by Regulations,[92] and then supplemented by formal statutory Guidance[93]—all seen as necessary, given the potential breadth of the definition.

2–43   The government's objectives in implementing these reforms on transparency in corporate control is to ensure that the "UK is, and is seen to be, an open and trusted place to invest and do business. Knowing who ultimately owns and controls our companies will contribute to that objective"; and, in addition, to "deter and disrupt the misuse of companies,[94] and identify and sanction those responsible when illegal activity does take place".[95]

2–44   To these ends, the company must keep a register of people "with significant control over the company" (s.790M(1)). Interestingly, the information is not to be removed from the Register until 10 years after the person ceases to have such control (s.790U(1)). A person is deemed to have such control (i.e. to be a PSC) if they meet at least one of the following five conditions:

(i)   directly or indirectly hold more than 25 per cent of the nominal share capital; or

(ii)   directly or indirectly control more than 25 per cent of the votes at general meetings; or

---

[91] The mechanics for achieving this objective are rather intricate. SBEEA 2015 inserts a substantial new Pt 21A (ss.790A–790ZG) and Sch.1A into the Companies Act 2006, and that is supplemented by Regulations and formal statutory Guidance. The new rules will apply to all UK companies, except those subject to the disclosure requirements of DTR 5 (e.g. LSE main market and AIM companies) (s.790C(7)), and legal entities with voting shares admitted to trading on a regulated market in an EEA state other than the UK, or in Japan, the USA, Switzerland and Israel (s.790C(7) and (draft) Regulations). This is because these companies are already required to make details of major shareholdings public. The provisions will also apply to LLPs and UK registered Societas Europaea (on the latter, see also art.9 of Regulation 2157/2001 EC of 8 October 2001). Generally, see *https://www.gov.uk/government/uploads/system/uploads/attachment_data/file/486520/BIS-15-622-register-of-people-with-significant-control-consultation-response.pdf* [Accessed 29 January 2016]. The EU has also introduced similar measures in the Fourth Money Laundering Directive (EU 2015/849) which came into force on 25 June 2015 and must be implemented by all Members States by 26 June 2017.

[92] The Register of People with Significant Control Regulations 2016 (SI 2016/339): *http://www.legislation.gov.uk/uksi/2016/339/pdfs/uksi_20160339_en.pdf* [Accessed 29 May 2016].

[93] For the current (April 2016) Statutory Guidance, see *https://www.gov.uk/government/uploads/system/uploads/attachment_data/file/523120/PSC_statutory_guidance_companies.pdf* [Accessed 29 May 2016].

[94] For money laundering, tax evasion, corruption, terrorist financing, etc.

[95] BIS, *The Register of People with Significant Control (PSC Register)* (October 2014), as stated in the Foreword: *https://www.gov.uk/government/uploads/system/uploads/attachment_data/file/395478/bis-14-1145-the-register-of-people-with-significant-control-psc-register-register-final-1.pdf* [Accessed 29 January 2016].

(iii) directly or indirectly are able to control the appointment or removal of a majority of the board; or

(iv) actually exercise, or have the right to exercise, significant influence or control over the company; or

(v) actually exercise or have the right to exercise significant influence or control over any trust or firm (which is not a legal entity) which has significant control (under one of the four conditions above) over the company.

Both the Act, the Regulations and the formal statutory Guidance contain detailed provisions relating to the interpretation of these five conditions.[96]

The real breadth in the disclosure rules is embraced by the expression "significant influence or control". The statutory Guidance indicates that influence and control are alternatives, and that neither needs to be in fact exercised by the PSC, nor exercised by the PSC with a view to its own economic benefit. "Control" indicates that the PSC is able to direct the company's activities, while "influence" indicates that the PSC can ensure (in fact, rather than as a matter of legal right) that the company generally adopts the activities which the PSC desires.[97] As illustrations of the latter, the Guidance suggests that such influence could arise because the PSC owns intellectual property, or was the company's founder, or is indeed a shadow director.[98] If interests are held jointly, then the above tests are to be applied to each person as if each joint holder held the entire interest (Sch.1A regs 11, 12). The intended breadth is clear—the goal is to identify exactly who is pulling the strings behind the corporate veil.[99]

Of course, this definition is so wide that it embraces those whose control or influence is far from sinister, and whose identity ought not to be necessarily revealed as a PSC. Thus the Guidance excludes parties who merely have the ability to exercise the usual veto rights given to all members to protect their personal interests (e.g. in amending the constitution, preventing share dilution, limiting corporate borrowing, or winding up the company). Similarly exempted are parties such as the company's professional advisers, third party suppliers etc., liquidators, the company's own managing director, and any non-executive directors with a casting vote.[100]

These inclusions and exclusions amply demonstrate the tightrope being walked in articulating a satisfactory and workable definition of PSCs.

Even with a watertight definition of a PSC, the next difficulty is how the company is to collect the information it is required to register. The company has a duty to gather the necessary information and keep it up to date (ss.790D, 790E), and the requested parties a corresponding duty to supply the information and keep it up to date (ss.790G, 790H), with the company and every officer or other party in default otherwise held to have committed an offence (s.790F, 790I and

2–45

---

[96] See the sources cited in earlier footnotes.

[97] But with this expressly being wider than the definition of a "shadow director" of the company. As to the latter, see para.16–9.

[98] See para.16–9.

[99] See Guidance, Section 1.

[100] See Guidance, paras 4.2–4.6.

Sch.1B). The company's arm is strengthened, in that failure by an individual or legal entity to respond to the company's enquiries will give the company the ability (without a court order) to disenfranchise, and impose other restrictions on, any shares held by the individual.[101] The risk of misinformation is not insignificant, and the company is required to confirm all the details before they are registered (s.790M), although quite how this is to be done is not clear. In addition, given the possible risks associated with disclosing these details of significant corporate "control or influence", there are extensive provisions on protecting both information and individuals from relevant disclosures (s.790ZF, Sch.1A Ch.5).

2–46 Once the details have been gathered, the company must make its own PSC Register open to inspection by the public without charge (ss.790N, 790O),[102] or alternatively it may elect to have the register kept by Companies House for this purpose (s.790W). Access to the Register is not unrestricted, however. Those seeking inspection must provide their name, address and the purpose for which they seek access (ss.790O(4), with it being an offence to knowingly or recklessly mislead in this regard, or to pass on the information so gleaned to other parties—s.790R). It is easy to see that without this restriction, access might be abused, but at this distance it is difficult to predict quite which purposes the courts might regard as proper, other than searches by government agencies seeking evidence of identity when pursuing suspected illicit activities. We will see these "proper purpose" restrictions in operation in other contexts where access to registers is sought,[103] however, and here too the company is given a time-limited right to apply to court to seek an order that it need not make the requested disclosure (s.790P).

2–47 These provisions may seem unremarkable to those who are unfamiliar with the history of companies in the UK, but they represent one of the more radical departures from the status quo seen for some time.[104] No doubt they reflect the reality that companies can be used for evil as well as good, and the corporate form has to date provided an effective shield of anonymity behind which those in real control can hide. Perhaps these days there is in any event greater recognition that, even when the corporate activities are all for the good, companies wield such power and influence (over 95 per cent of businesses are run through companies) that it is perhaps as well to have some means of knowing who really lies behind the corporate structure.

CONCLUSION

2–48 The balance of advantage and disadvantage in relation to incorporation no doubt varies from one business context to another, at least as far as small firms are concerned; for large trading organisations, the arguments in favour of

---

[101] The details are in the Regulations: see fn.91, above.
[102] The information on the PSC Register will also need to be confirmed to Companies House at least every 12 months and will be held by it on a publically searchable database.
[103] See para.19–11.
[104] By comparison, other disclosure rules are considered in detail in Ch.26.

incorporation are normally conclusive. This may reflect the firms' respective needs for expert centralised management and capital to finance their operations. For large firms the division between board and shareholders, transferable shares and the conferment of limited liability on the shareholders are helpful for the raising of capital. As for the large firm which does not have a large capital requirement, such as large professional firms, these have happily traded as partnerships in the past and were, indeed, often required to do so by the rules of the relevant profession, most of which have now been relaxed. Unlimited liability was seen as a badge of professional respectability. However, the threat of crippling damages awards for professional negligence led the accountancy profession in particular to press for an appropriate form of limited liability vehicle for the conduct of their businesses. As we saw in Ch.1,[105] this led to the creation of the limited liability partnership, which combines the limited liability of the company with the flat internal hierarchy of the partnership. However, where the large firm means also a need for a large amount of risk capital, the corporate form predominates.

The main policy issue, therefore, has been how far small firms should have easy access to the corporate form. Ever since the decision in *Salomon v Salomon*,[106] English law has leant in favour of not restricting access, and the Company Law Review endorsed that approach.[107] As we shall see in Pt 2, the issue is essentially about the access of small business to limited liability, since that feature of incorporation has a major potential impact on third parties who deal with the company, whilst separate legal personality, management under a board structure and transferable shares seem either benign, as far as third parties are concerned, or of concern only to those within the company.

---

[105] See above, para.1–4.
[106] See above, para.2–1.
[107] Developing, paras 9.61–9.71.

CHAPTER 3

SOURCES OF COMPANY LAW AND THE COMPANY'S CONSTITUTION

SOURCES

As far as domestic companies are concerned, the immediate sources of the rules **3–1**
applicable to them, and the hierarchy of those sources, are the ones familiar to
students of other bodies of law. They are: primary legislation, secondary
legislation, rule-making by legislatively recognised bodies, the common law of
companies, and the company's own constitution (in particular, its articles of
association). Of these, the last may perhaps appear unfamiliar, but students of
contract law are used to idea that the rules applicable in any particular situation
are as likely to be found in the terms of the parties' agreement as in legislative or
common law rules, and students of trade union law or of the law of other types of
association know that the particular association's rule-book is an important
source of law, at least for its members. As to the third category, legislation may
delegate to bodies outside the legislature the power to make rules relevant to
companies. These bodies may themselves be agencies created by statute or they
may be pre-existing bodies which the legislature recognises for the purposes of
rule-making.

Finally, and standing outside the above hierarchy but with links to it, there
may be examples of "self-regulation" where the relevant rules have no legislative
or common law foundation, but are nevertheless observed in practice, as a result
of non-legal pressures, including the threat that government might intervene with
legislation if the self-regulatory rules were not obeyed. Historically, the leading
example of this phenomenon in our area was the City Panel on Takeovers and
Mergers, and the Code it administers, but these were put on a statutory basis by
the Companies Act 2006, implementing the Community Directive on takeovers,

though its non-statutory methods of working have survived to a considerable extent.[1] Thus, self-regulation is a less obvious feature of company law than it used to be.

3–2   Whatever the source of the rule, one should also note that its content may be located on a spectrum running from "hard" to "soft". At the "hard" end, the obligation may be imposed by the rule without giving those to whom it applies any choice as to whether they comply with it (a "mandatory" rule). Moving along the spectrum, the rule may permit those to whom it prima facie applies to modify or remove the obligation. Such rules, conventionally called "default rules", are in fact quite common in company law. What is the function of such a rule, given that the parties themselves are apparently free to deprive it of regulatory force? Where the obligees can easily remove the obligation, the rule may nevertheless have the important function of relieving parties of the task of working out the best rule for themselves. In formulating the default rule, the legislature will have tried to identify the rule which most parties in the relevant situation would devise for themselves. Only if the particular parties want something different from that normally adopted will they have to go through the process of altering the rule. Thus, a number of provisions in the Act on shareholder meetings apply only "subject to any provision in the company's articles".[2] Since it is relatively easy for companies to make different provisions in their articles upon formation of the company or later, these provisions may be regarded as a pure type of default rule.

In other cases the procedure for amending the position produced by the default rule may be more demanding and the regulatory objectives of such a rule may also be more sophisticated. For example, many rules relating to the duties of directors may be disapplied by the shareholders, by majority vote, either before or after the breach of duty.[3] The purpose of such a rule may be to induce the directors to bargain with the shareholders over the handling of conduct which would otherwise be in breach of duty. This rule contains a more demanding procedure because those upon whom the obligation is imposed (the directors) need to obtain the consent of another group of people within the company (the shareholders) for the modification of the rule, and are thus forced to disclose to the shareholders their actual or potential wrongdoing. Such a rule may be useful where the rule-maker cannot predict what the result should be in a particular class of case (otherwise it could use a mandatory rule) nor does it think it wise to leave it to the directors themselves to modify the rule (because of their conflict of interest).

Finally, the procedure for amending the rule may be so demanding that in practice little use is made of it. In such a case, it is doubtful whether the rule should be regarded as in substance a default rule. This may be true of the example given in the previous paragraph. Thus, if the only way in which directors can secure shareholder modification of the default rule is to call a meeting of the shareholders to discuss each case of breach of duty as it arises, then in a large company they may regard such a procedure as so cumbersome and unpredictable

---

[1] See below, Ch.28.
[2] See below, Ch.15.
[3] See below, Ch.16.

that they treat the default rule as in fact mandatory.[4] Whether they then choose to comply with it or to break the rule and hide the breach is a different question.

At the "soft" end of the spectrum are "rules" which are in fact only recommendations or exhortations. No sanction is attached to the breach of the rule. Each obligee decides for itself whether and how far to comply with the recommendation. A possible way of injecting some bite into recommendations is to put them on a "comply or explain basis". In this situation, the only formal obligation imposed by the rule is to explain publicly how far the recommendations have been complied with and the reasons for any areas of non-compliance. Such disclosure meets all the formal obligations of the rule, even if it shows that the recommendations have not been complied with at all, but publicity may generate extra-legal pressures on the company to comply (or to comply more fully) with the recommendations. The primary example of such a mechanism in British company law is the UK Corporate Governance Code,[5] in relation to which a "comply or explain" obligation is imposed.

Primary legislation

The principal legislative source of rules is the Companies Act 2006, the latest in a line of Acts produced as the original legislation of the mid-nineteenth century has been reformed periodically. This latest effort involved the most comprehensive review of the area since company law's inception, and the resulting legislation is said to be the longest ever to be passed by Parliament.

3–3

The process began in 1998 with the then Secretary of State commissioning an independent review of company law.[6] This Company Law Review ("CLR") was carried out with the support of DTI civil servants, a Project Director, a permanent Steering Group[7] and Consultative Committee, and a series of ad hoc Working Groups.[8] The Steering Group produced a number of consultative documents, some very large, and a two-volume final report. In its Final Report it declared its aims to have been to produce a company law that was "primarily enabling or facilitative" and to "strip out regulation that is no longer necessary". This would not mean an absence of statutory law, for the framework of company law "should provide the necessary safeguards to allow people to deal with and invest in companies with confidence".[9]

The immediate response of the Government was enthusiastic, but developments were rather slow.[10] A Bill was finally introduced into Parliament in November 2005, received Royal Assent a year later, and was then phased in over

---

[4] For an insightful discussion of default rules see S. Deakin and A. Hughes, "Economic Efficiency and the Proceduralisation of Company Law" (1999) 3 C.F.I.L.R. 169.

[5] See below, Ch.14.

[6] DTI, *Company Law Reform: Modern Company Law for a Competitive Economy* (1998).

[7] The editors of this edition were involved, Paul Davies substantially, as a member of the Steering Group from March 1999, and Sarah Worthington to a limited degree, as a member of one of the Working Groups. Comments on the Review in this book should be read in the light of that fact.

[8] See Final Report II, Annex E for details.

[9] Final Report I, para.9.

[10] See *Modernising Company Law*, Cm. 5553, July 2002—also in two volumes; and then *Company Law Reform*, Cm. 6456, March 2005.

a period of time, ending on 1 October 2009. The result is an Act of some 1,300 sections and 16 Schedules. This may seem an odd result for a legislative process aimed to be facilitative. Two points can be made in mitigation of its length. First, enabling legislation is not to be confused with the absence of statutory law: often confining law narrowly takes more statutory words than a sweeping prohibition. Secondly, the Act is drafted in a lengthy way, paradoxically to make it more user-friendly. Few people read an Act from beginning to end. What they need to be able to do is to find quickly the provisions relevant to their problem. Setting out the provisions in a disaggregated form (for example, separate provisions for public and private companies on a particular topic, even if the provisions are similar) is helpful in that regard.

3–4   Other legislation is also important. Provisions relating to the insolvency of companies were hived off into an Insolvency Act of 1986, which also contains provisions dealing with the period before the company enters insolvency and intended to protect creditors in that period.[11] In the same year, a Financial Services Act (now replaced by the Financial Services and Markets Act 2000) took over the provisions relating to the public offering and listing of shares, and the 2000 Act has been modified subsequently to take account of the burgeoning EU law in this area.[12] These two examples illustrate perennial problems of classification. Should rules on the insolvency of companies go in a company law consolidation or an insolvency law consolidation; equally, should rules on share issues by companies go in a company law consolidation or a capital markets or securities law consolidation? There are arguments both ways, but it is the case that, functionally, important parts of the law relating to companies are not to be found in Acts which contain the word "company" in their title.[13]

Secondary legislation

3–5   One major difficulty attending legislation as long as the Companies Act is that a major commitment of parliamentary time by the- Government is required to get such legislation onto the statute books. Once there, ministers are likely to take the view that company law has had its turn for some while and will be reluctant to devote additional parliamentary time to proposals for its further reform. This can be a distinct disadvantage for those parts of the Act which relate to matters where the technical or economic context is changing rapidly and fairly frequent updating of the legislation would be desirable. One solution to this problem is greater use of subordinate legislation, amending primary legislation but for which the process of parliamentary scrutiny is much reduced and which therefore is

---

[11] See Ch.9.
[12] See para.6–14 and Chs 25 and 26.
[13] Other important examples of separate legislation are the Bribery Act 2010 (applying not just to corporate businesses—see paras 7–46 and 16–107) and the Company Directors Disqualification Act 1986 (see below, Ch.10), which at least has the word "Company" in its title and seems to have become a separate Act because it consolidates provisions previously found partly in the Companies Acts and partly in the Insolvency Act.

much less time-consuming.[14] The 2006 Act contains important examples of this technique in particular areas, for example, companies' accounts[15] or share capital,[16] both areas likely to be affected by changes occurring outside the UK (whether at EU or broader international levels) to which it was desirable for the Government to be able to respond quickly. The CLR proposed a general power to use secondary legislation to amend the Act, but this was dropped after opposition from Parliament.[17]

It is also the case that the EU obligations of the UK in relation to company law may be implemented by secondary legislation under general powers conferred by the European Communities Act 1972, which powers are not confined to the company law area. However, it is not absolutely clear how far this power extends beyond the minimum necessary to transpose, for example, a Directive into domestic law.

Although quicker to implement than primary legislation, secondary legislation suffers from two defects. The first is that the rules are subject to less democratic scrutiny than an Act of Parliament. For this reason, the Company Law Review, whilst proposing greater use of secondary legislation, also recommended that "the basic principles and architecture of the new framework would be set out in primary legislation".[18] The second is that secondary legislation may not be as expert as rules produced by rule-makers closer to the regulated, despite the conscientious consultation process in which the relevant Department engages before making secondary rules. This second defect can be overcome by delegation of law-making powers to a more expert body than the Department.

3–6

Delegated rule-making

The Financial Conduct Authority

A primary example of delegation beyond central government in the current law is the rule-making power conferred upon the Financial Conduct Authority ("FCA"). The FCA makes three types of rules which are of particular interest to us. First, it took over from the Stock Exchange the long-standing and originally self-regulatory task of laying down Listing Rules ("LR") for companies whose securities have been entered onto the "official list".[19] In exercising this function, it is referred to as the UK Listing Authority ("UKLA"). Some of the EU obligations of the UK are implemented through the LR, but, as we have noted in Ch.1, they have also been used to promote purely domestic policies and thus to

3–7

---

[14] Instead of three readings and a committee stage in each House of Parliament over several months, as in the case of an Act, there will be only a single short debate, and in the case of subordinate legislation subject to "negative resolution", there will not even be a debate unless MPs take the necessary steps to initiate one. See Companies Act 2006 ss.1288–1292.

[15] 2006 Act s.468.

[16] 2006 Act s.657.

[17] Final Report I, paras 5.7 and 5.10 and Modernising, I, p.9. Some power to reform by statutory instrument is now given to Government across legislation generally by the Legislative and Regulatory Reform Act 2006.

[18] Final Report I, para.5.4.

[19] For the meaning of this term see para.25–5.

introduce for listed companies an additional set of core rules that are not applied to non-listed companies. It has also introduced further sets of rules—Prospectus Rules ("PR") and Disclosure and Transparency Rules ("DTR"). These are heavily driven by the need to transpose EU law in the UK, however, the transposition has had the further impact of shifting some topics from the companies legislation to the FCA's rules.[20] Here it is interesting that Parliament has proceeded with transposition not primarily by way of direct amendment of the FSMA, but by giving the FCA extended rule-making powers. Finally, it was required in the FSMA to produce a Code of Market Conduct ("MAR") to flesh out the meaning of the statutory prohibition on market abuse, which we consider in Ch.30.

3–8   In short, the FCA has power to issue elaborate sets of rules, without the need for formal approval by either Parliament or a Governmental Department.[21] The public interest is protected, however, by the statutory requirement to publish a statement of policy on the imposition of sanctions for breaches of the Rules.[22] Thus, although the FCA is a private company formed under the Companies Act, in fact a company limited by guarantee,[23] and is financed by a levy on those who engage in financial services business, it has extensive public functions and is itself subject to controls thought to be appropriate to a public body.

Financial Reporting Council

3–9   The second area where delegated rule-making is to be found on a substantial scale in the present law is in relation to corporate governance, accounting standards, the accuracy of accounts, auditing standards and the regulation of auditors and accountants. This is an area where the Financial Reporting Council ("FRC") and its various subsidiaries are immensely important. Their functions were much enhanced as a result of reforms implemented in the UK in the wake of the Enron and related scandals in the US,[24] and the impact of their rule-making has grown further as a result of the 2008 financial crisis. These functions are analysed in Chs 21 and 22, and that analysis need not be anticipated here. What needs to be noted, however, is that, like the FCA, the FRC acquires its powers by way of delegation from the Secretary of State (who can therefore re-allocate them).[25] Like the FCA, the FRC and its subsidiaries are companies limited by guarantee, but its directors are appointed by the Secretary of State, so that the FRC, although more expert than a Government Department (and partly financed by those it regulates), is tied into the governmental machinery.

---

[20] Mainly the rules on disclosure on interests in shares on the part of directors and "major" shareholders. See Ch.26.

[21] As ss.73A and 119 of FSMA 2000 contemplate.

[22] FSMA 2000 ss.93–94.

[23] See above, para.1–8.

[24] The main legislative expression of these reforms was the Companies (Audit, Investigation and Community Enterprise) Act 2004, some parts of which have survived the 2006 Act.

[25] 2006 Act ss.457 and 1217 and Sch.10.

Common law

In spite of the bulk of the Companies Act and its satellite legislation, it does not contain a code of company law. The British Companies Acts have never aspired to lay down all the rules which sustain the core features of company law, as identified in the previous chapter. However, the 2006 Act goes further in that regard than previous Acts. The Law Commissions recommended that there should be a statutory statement of the common law duties of directors (though not of the remedies for breach)[26] and the English Law Commission that the law relating to the enforcement of those duties should be both reformed and stated in legislative form.[27] Both these sets of recommendations were broadly endorsed by the Company Law Review, and were included in the 2006 Act, thus effecting a major extension of statutory company law.[28]

Although these reforms significantly altered the balance between statute law and common law in company law, they may have a much less pronounced effect upon the role of the judges in developing company law. So far as directors' duties are concerned, although the statutory statement largely replaces the existing common law and equitable rules, it is drafted as a relatively "high level" statement. Consequently, the pre-existing case law will remain relevant where the statement simply repeats, rather than reforms, the common law; and recourse throughout the statement to broad standards, rather than precise rules, means the judges will have an important role in developing and applying the standards, just as they have had in respect of those standards which were embodied in statute from the beginning.[29] Indeed, in performing this task, s.170(4) of the 2006 Act specifically, and uniquely for a UK statute, requires that "[t]he general duties shall be interpreted and applied in the same way as common law rules or equitable principles, and regard shall be had to the corresponding common law rules and equitable principles in interpreting and applying the general duties". As to the enforcement of these statutory directors' duties, the reform creates a greater judicial discretion to allow or refuse derivative actions, so that the judges are, if anything, more important under the Act than the prior common law.

Review and reform

It is clear that company law consists of a complex and diverse body of rules. Keeping this law under review is now, in the main, the task of the Department of Business, Innovation and Skills ("BIS"),[30] which is the Government Department currently responsible for company and insolvency law, among many other matters. As for financial services law, including public offerings of securities and

3–10

3–11

---

[26] *Company Directors: Regulating Conflicts of Interest and Formulating a Statement of Duties*, Cm. 4436, 1999.
[27] *Shareholder Remedies*, Cm. 3769, 1997.
[28] See below, Chs 16 and 17.
[29] For example, the unfair prejudice provisions, discussed in Ch.20.
[30] Its predecessors were the Department for Business, Enterprise and Regulatory Reform ("BERR"), and, before that, the Department of Trade and Industry ("DTI"), responsible for the CLR.

their listing, the Treasury is the leading source of policy. As noted above, in recent years the Law Commissions (English and Scottish) have also played an important part in company law reform.

The Company Law Review, carried out by the DTI and referred to above, may be seen as the latest in a series of reviews of company law carried out by the various predecessors of BIS since the introduction of incorporation by registration in the middle of the nineteenth century. Its method of operation was rather different from that of its predecessors, however. They had consisted of small committees of enquiry which took formal evidence but did not engage in widespread consultation; they also tended to concentrate on particular aspects of the subject thought to need reform, rather than upon a comprehensive review. The two most recent Committee reports of this older type which are still important for an understanding of the current law are the Jenkins[31] and Cohen[32] Committee reports (so referred to after the names of their chairmen).

3–12 In the long term, however, the CLR was unconvinced that ad hoc, periodic, comprehensive reviews of the type it had undertaken were the best way forward, because they depend so heavily upon governmental commitment to devote the necessary resources to the exercise. It recommended instead that a standing Company Law and Reporting Commission should have the remit of keeping company law under review and reporting annually to the Secretary of State its views on where, if anywhere, reform was needed. In addition, the Secretary of State would be obliged to consult the Commission on proposed secondary legislation.[33] In this way, it was hoped, company law reform would become a continuing and expert process, so that less weight would need to be placed on ad hoc, across-the-board reviews. This proposal was, however, rejected by the Government,[34] so the ad hoc approach remains the order of the day.

THE COMPANY'S CONSTITUTION

The significance of the constitution

3–13 A remarkable feature of British company law is the extent to which it leaves regulation of the internal affairs of a company to the company itself through rules laid down in its constitution, in particular in its articles of association (which prescribe the regulations for the company[35]). In fact, the principle is that the articles may deal with any matter which is not, or to the extent that it is not, regulated through any of the sources mentioned above. This is not stated explicitly in the Act, but is rather an assumption upon which the Act is drafted, too obvious to be worth stating. However, the crucial point is not just the formal relationship between the articles and the other sources of company law, especially the Act, but the extent to which substantive matters, central to the company's operation, are left to be regulated by the articles. Examples of important matters

---

[31] Report of the Company Law Committee, Cmnd. 1749, 1962.
[32] Report of the Committee on Company Law Amendment, Cmnd. 6659, 1945.
[33] Final Report I, para.5.22.
[34] Modernising, I, pp.48–49.
[35] 2006 Act s.18.

which are regulated mainly by the articles are the division of powers between the shareholders and the board of directors, and the composition, structure and operation of the board of directors.[36] Many jurisdictions regulate these matters through their companies legislation, rather than the company's constitution, and this is true of systems as otherwise different as those of Germany and the US.[37]

In the American case, it is true, the legislation often uses default rules, which can be changed by appropriate provisions in the company's constitution, so that, where this is the case, the shareholders can ultimately adopt the set of rules they want, as is the case in Britain. For example, para.8.01 of the Model Business Corporation Act gives a broad management power to the board of a US company, but allows the shareholders, in the constitution or by shareholder agreement, to cut down that provision if they wish and allocate decisions to themselves; whereas the directors of a British company have management powers only to the extent that they are given to the board by the articles (as, normally, they are, and the default model articles for all companies are in this form[38]). The ultimate practical division of powers between board and shareholders, in similar types of company, may thus be equivalent in the two countries despite their different starting points.

The German and, even, the American approach can be said to be based on the principle that the allocation of powers to the organs of the company is the result of a legislative act, even if, within limits, the shareholders may alter the initial legislative allocation. By contrast, since the shareholders control the constitution (see below), the British approach can be said to represent the view that the shareholders constitute the ultimate source of managerial authority within the company and that the directors obtain their powers by a process of delegation from the shareholders, albeit a delegation of a formal type which, so long as it lasts, may make the directors the central decision-making body on behalf of the company.[39] In each of these jurisdictions, however, the practical allocation of power ultimately depends on the ease with which the default rules may be overridden.[40] If the shareholders agree to override the default rules at the time the company is formed, the barriers are often relatively low. On the other hand, if they only decide later that the legislative default rules (in the US) or the model articles (in the UK) should be amended, then the process is inevitably more complicated: issues of who is entitled to propose the necessary resolutions and call the necessary meetings (the directors or a shareholder), and what level of voting support is necessary to adopt the change (a simple majority or some sort of super majority) will, in practice, determine the ease with which changes can be effected.

---

[36] Although, for listed companies, the UK Corporate Governance Code now trespasses upon the autonomy of the company, at least in the sense that it requires "comply or explain" conformity with defined best practices. See below, Ch.14.

[37] See for Germany the *Aktiengesetz*, Pt Four, subdivisions One and Two, and for the US, the Model Business Corporation Act, Ch.8.

[38] See SI 2008/3229 Sch.3, the model articles for public companies, art.3: "Subject to the articles, the directors are responsible for the management of the company's business, for which purpose they may exercise all the powers of the company". The model article for private companies limited by shares is in similar terms.

[39] See below, Ch.14.

[40] See above, para.3–2.

Model articles of association

3–14   In the British scheme it is essential that a company have articles, and this is reflected in the provisions in the Act authorising the Secretary of State to promulgate model articles of association for companies of different types[41] and giving those statutory models default status.[42] This power is long standing, and from time to time lettered "tables" of model articles were issued under it, with those for companies limited by shares being invariably "Table A". Many companies still exist whose articles are based on the Table A of 1985 or the earlier one of 1948 or, conceivably, even earlier versions. The current statutory models are contained in the Companies (Model Articles) Regulations 2008/3229, and are applicable to companies incorporated on or after 1 October 2009. These new models are no longer denoted by lettered tables, and in addition, following the CLR,[43] there are now separate model articles for private and public companies limited by shares (previously Table A articles applied to both), and also for companies limited by guarantee.[44] Given the range of companies falling under the companies legislation, it is surprising that a single model set of articles for companies limited by shares was thought for so long to be adequate.[45]

3–15   When a limited company is formed, it will be treated as having adopted the relevant model articles, except to the extent that it chooses to have different articles, either in whole or in part.[46] This means that those registering the company could say nothing, in which case the model will apply in full.[47] At the other extreme, they could expressly exclude the model entirely and adopt a set of articles which contains very different provisions. Typically, however, companies adopt an intermediate position, registering articles which adopt the default model subject to a list of specific amendments. Section 20(1)(b) suggests that choice may be expressed implicitly, by adopting articles which in one or more respects are inconsistent with the model, and then the model will apply to govern matters not dealt with by the company, i.e. the model performs a gap-filling role in such a case. This does mean that the full articles of the company can be established only through the laborious process of taking the model articles and applying the specified changes to it, which hardly amounts to a transparent exposition of the company's regulations. Any different approach—despite the requirement that the articles "must be contained in a single document"[48]—would, however, lose the crucial gap-filling role of the model articles mandated by s.20(1)(b).

---

[41] 2006 Act s.19.

[42] 2006 Act s.20.

[43] Final Report II, Ch.17.

[44] The model for private companies limited by shares is in Sch.1, and that for public companies in Sch.3. The model for private companies limited by guarantee is in Sch.2.

[45] Probably the facility of company formation agents in developing their own standard model articles for different classes of company met much of the need in practice.

[46] 2006 Act s.20(1). This presumption applies whatever the type of limited company. By contrast, s.8(2) of CA 1985 created a default only in the case of companies limited by shares.

[47] 2006 Act s.20(1)(a)—unless there is no model prescribed, in which case it must register articles of association: s.18(2).

[48] 2006 Act s.18(3)(a).

The version of the model which is implied into the company's articles (unless excluded) is that which existed when the company was formed. The subsequent promulgation of a revised version of the model will not affect companies already registered, but only those registered in the future.[49] Hence the fact, noted above, that there are many companies in existence for whom the relevant model is Table A of 1948. For the practitioner, therefore, the replacement of one model by another is not a reason to forget the learning about former models.

Under the British structure the company cannot work effectively without fairly elaborate articles, and the models aim to supply that need for those who do not wish, or cannot afford, to work out their own internal regulations.

What constitutes the constitution?

Unlike its predecessors, the 2006 Act defines the company's constitution. The term includes the articles of association but is not limited to them. Also included are "any resolutions or agreements to which Chapter 3 [of Pt 3] applies".[50] Chapter 3 applies to special resolutions of the shareholders (whether passed as such or by virtue of unanimous agreement among the members)[51]; any resolution or agreement of a class of members binding all the members of the class (for example, a resolution varying class rights)[52]; any unanimous resolution or agreement adopted by the members of a class provided that it would not otherwise be binding on them unless passed by a particular majority or in a particular manner; and any other resolution or agreement to which the chapter applies by virtue of any enactment.[53] In practice, the most important category is special resolutions of the shareholders. Given its much reduced legal status, it is not surprising that the memorandum of association no longer features as part of the company's constitution.[54]

3–16

As might be expected, shareholder agreements, considered below, are not generally regarded as part of the company's constitution; but that rule has one important exception, noted in passing here.[55]

3–17

The legal status of the constitution

The common law tends to classify the rule-books of associations, whether they are clubs, trade unions, friendly societies or other, as contractual in nature. The articles of association are no exception to this principle, though in this case the classification is done by the Act. Section 33 of the Act provides that "the provisions of the company's constitution bind the company and its members to the same extent as if there were covenants on the part of the company and of each

3–18

---

[49] 2006 Act s.20(2).
[50] 2006 Act s.17.
[51] See paras 15–15 and 15–44.
[52] See Ch.19. This could be an ordinary resolution of the class, if it binds all the members of the class.
[53] 2006 Act s.29.
[54] For the residual function of the memorandum, see para.4–5.
[55] They are included as part of the constitution for the purposes of s.40: see s.40(3)(b) and para.7–14.

member to observe it". The wording of this important section can be traced back, with variations, to the original Act of 1844.[56] What is clear, however, is that the articles constitute a rather particular form of contract, and the peculiarities of that contract need to be noted here.

(i)   The parties to the contract

3–19   It is clear from the express statutory wording of s.33 that the articles constitute a contract between the company and each member. It is thus a multi-party contract, like many other contracts found in the commercial world, and is enforceable by any one party against any other. This feature is commonly used when there is breach or threatened breach of articles which confer on members a right of pre-emption (or first refusal) when another member wishes to sell his shares,[57] or impose a duty on the remaining members or the directors to buy the shares of a retiring member (a less common provision).[58] What makes this contract different, as we shall see, is that not all of its provisions will be enforced in the courts.[59]

(ii)   The contract as a public document

3–20   Although the articles of association have a contractual status, they are clearly more than a private bargain among the company and its members. The company's articles become a public document at the moment of formation, either because the relevant model articles, themselves a public document, will apply or because the company supplies to the registrar for public registration its own articles which amend or even fully replace the statutory model.[60] Publicity of the company's constitution has always been a requirement of British company law, and since 1968 is in any event a requirement of EU company law.[61] Thus, those who deal with the company have a legitimate expectation that the registered articles represent an accurate statement of the company's internal regulations.

3–21   Because of this special feature, the courts have concluded that standard contract law should apply to the articles only with certain qualifications. In particular, the courts are reluctant to apply to the statutory contract any contract law doctrines

---

[56] The current provision makes explicit the fact that the company too is bound by the rules (important in giving members rights against the company). Practitioners had long treated earlier versions of the articles as binding between member and company despite the statutory wording making no reference to the company, although on the basis of only a first instance authority: *Hickman v Kent or Romney Marsh Sheepbreeders Association* [1915] 1 Ch. 881. The treatment of the articles as a deed has also been removed from the current section, thus removing the consequence that a debt owed by the member to the company was a "specialty" debt, with its special limitation period, rather than an ordinary one. Contrast s.14(2) of CA 1985 and s.33(2) of CA 2006; and cf. *Re Compania de Electridad de Buenos Aires* [1980] Ch. 146 at 187.

[57] *Borland's Trustee v Steel* [1901] 1 Ch. 279 (member seeking declaration that rights of pre-emption in articles were valid); cf. *Lyle & Scott v Scott's Trustees* [1959] A.C. 763 HL; and see para.27–7.

[58] *Rayfield v Hands* [1960] Ch. 1, where Vaisey J was prepared to make an order in effect for specific performance.

[59] See below, paras 3–23 to 3–30.

[60] 2006 Act ss.9(5)(b) and 14.

[61] Directive 68/151/EEC [1968] O.J. 41 art.2(1)(b).

which might result in the articles being held to have a content substantially different from that which someone reading the registered documents would have understood them to have.

Thus, the Court of Appeal has held that articles cannot later be rectified to give effect to what the incorporators actually intended but failed to embody in the registered document, since the reader of the registered documents could have no way of guessing that any error had been made in transposing the incorporators' agreement into the document.[62]

Equally, that Court has refused to imply terms into the statutory contract from extrinsic evidence of surrounding circumstances where that evidence would probably not be known to third parties who would thus have no basis for anticipating that any such implication was appropriate.[63]

Further, in this case Steyn LJ was of the view that for the same reasons the statutory contract "was not defeasible on the grounds of misrepresentation, common law mistake, mistake in equity, undue influence or duress".[64]

These decisions by the courts on the meaning of the company's constitutional documents support the policy underlying the statutory provision on the conclusiveness of the certificate of incorporation.[65] Both conduce to protection of third parties by enabling the third party to rely on what he or she finds upon a search of the public registry.[66]

However, the policy behind these cases is somewhat undermined by those decisions which have allowed the doctrine of informal, unanimous shareholder consent to be applied to changes to the company's constitution. Under this doctrine, which is discussed further in Ch.15, decisions taken informally by shareholders will nevertheless be effective, if taken unanimously. Although the Act requires informal resolutions altering the articles to be communicated to the Registrar,[67] the informality alone means this is unlikely to happen, and then the registered constitution will no longer reflect the actual set of articles.[68] Failure to

3–22

---

[62] *Scott v Frank F. Scott (London) Ltd* [1940] Ch. 794 CA.

[63] *Bratton Seymour Service Co Ltd v Oxborough* [1992] B.C.L.C. 693 CA. In this case the majority were in effect seeking to avoid the prohibition on alterations to the constitution without individual shareholder consent which have the effect of increasing the shareholder's financial liability to the company (see s.25 and below, para.19–1). See also *Towcester Racecourse Co Ltd v Racecourse Association Ltd* [2003] 1 B.C.L.C. 260, where, in any event, the judge regarded the suggested implied terms as inconsistent with the express terms of the articles. But contrast *AG v Belize Telecom* [2009] B.C.C. 433, where the extrinsic evidence was known to the third parties. See also *Re Coroin Ltd* [2011] EWHC 3466 (Ch) (affirmed [2012] B.C.C. 575), where the court was prepared to admit the shareholder agreement pursuant to which the articles were adopted as extrinsic evidence.

[64] *Bratton Seymour Service Co Ltd v Oxborough* [1992] B.C.L.C. 693 at 698 CA. On the other hand, investor protection was not inconsistent with the implication of terms based on the construction of the language used in the articles, for here the basis of the implication was available to those who read the company's constitution.

[65] See below, para.4–7.

[66] A further and important restriction on the remedies available in respect of breaches of the corporate constitution, namely the supposed rule that damages were not available to a shareholder in an action against his company so long as he remained a member, seems to have been removed by what is now s.655, originally inserted by the 1989 Act.

[67] 2006 Act ss.29 and 30. And see below, para.15–15.

[68] *Cane v Jones* [1980] 1 W.L.R. 1451; *Re Home Treat Ltd* [1991] B.C.L.C. 705.

inform the registrar is a criminal offence and may attract civil penalties, but the validity of the alteration appears not to be affected by non-compliance.[69]

(iii)   Limits to the provisions which can be enforced: only rights "as a member"

3–23   The standard answer to the question, at common law, of who can enforce a contract is: the parties to the contract.[70] Since it is members who are party to the contract with the company, it follows that non-members cannot enforce the contract, even if they are intimately involved with the company, for example, as directors. Suppose, however, a person is both a member of the company and one of its directors. Can he or she enforce rights conferred by the articles, even if that right is conferred upon the claimant in his or her capacity as director of the company? The answer appears to be in the negative. The decisions have constantly affirmed that the section confers contractual effect on a provision in the articles only in so far as it affords rights on a member "qua member", or as a member.[71] As Astbury J said in the *Hickman* case[72]:

> "An outsider to whom rights purport to be given by the articles in his capacity as such outsider, whether he is or subsequently becomes a member, cannot sue on those articles, treating them as contracts between himself and the company, to enforce those rights."

The same applies to the contract between the members inter se.[73]

On the wording of the section it would be difficult to interpret it as creating a contract with anyone other than the company and the members. Furthermore, there is perhaps sense in restricting the ambit of the section to matters concerning the affairs of the company, although the Act itself is not explicitly worded restrictively. The question is whether it is justified to restrict the statutory wording still further, so that it applies only to matters concerning a member in his capacity of member.[74] As a consequence of this interpretation, a promoter, who becomes a member, cannot enforce a provision that the company shall reimburse the expenses he or she incurred[75] nor a solicitor, who becomes a member, a provision that he or she shall be the company's solicitor.[76] More important, this approach to the section apparently prevents a member who is also a director or other officer of the company from enforcing any rights purporting to be conferred

---

[69] 2006 Act ss.26 and 27.

[70] The Contracts (Rights of Third Parties) Act 1999 does not apply to the company's constitution: s.6(2) of that Act.

[71] While this restriction on the types of *rights* which can be enforced is well-supported by precedent (even if difficult to explain), it is less clear whether the restriction also limits enforcement to those provisions which impose *obligations on a member* "as a member". It seems not: see *Rayfield v Hands* [1960] Ch. 1, where the provision concerned the liabilities of members qua directors; and *Lion Mutual Marine Insurance v Tucker* (1883) 12 Q.B.D. 176 CA, where the provision concerned the liabilities of members qua insurers.

[72] *Hickman v Kent or Romney Marsh Sheepbreeders' Association* [1915] 1 Ch. 881 at 897.

[73] *London Sack & Bag Co v Dixon & Lugton* [1943] 2 All E.R. 763 CA.

[74] The *Hickman* case may reflect the high regard in which the courts then held the doctrine of privity of contract.

[75] *Re English & Colonial Produce Co* [1906] 2 Ch. 435.

[76] *Eley v Positive Life Association* (1876) 1 Ex. D. 88 CA.

by the articles on directors or officers. Only if he or she has a separate contract, extraneous to the articles, will the director have contractual rights and obligations vis-à-vis the company or fellow members. For this reason, executive directors will be careful to enter into service contracts with their company (into which it is entirely permissible to incorporate provisions from the articles of association)[77] in order to safeguard their remuneration, and non-executive directors would be well advised to do so also.[78]

It is somewhat anomalous to treat directors as "outsiders" since for most purposes the law treats them as the paradigm "insiders" (which members, as such, are not) and they will breach their fiduciary duties and duties of care if they do not act in accordance with the company's constitution.[79] It also produces some strange results. *Hickman*'s case concerned a provision in the articles stating that any dispute between the company and a member should be referred to arbitration and this was enforced as a contract. But in the later case of *Beattie v Beattie Ltd*,[80] where there was a similar provision, the Court of Appeal, relying on the dictum in *Hickman*, held that a dispute between a company and a director (who was a member) was not subject to the provision because the dispute was admittedly in relation to the director qua director. In the still later case of *Rayfield v Hands*,[81] the articles of a private company provided that a member intending to transfer his shares should give notice to the directors "who will take the said shares equally between them at a fair value". A member gave notice but the directors refused to buy. Vaisey J felt able to hold that the provision was concerned with the relationship between the member and the directors as members and ordered them to buy.[82]

3–24

However, academic argument has been made to the effect that the *Hickman* principle can be side-stepped, in most or all cases, by the identification of an appropriate membership right. In 1957, Lord Wedderburn, in his seminal article on *Foss v Harbottle*,[83] pointed out that, in *Quinn & Axtens Ltd v Salmon*,[84] the Court of Appeal and the House of Lords allowed a managing director, suing as a member, to obtain an injunction restraining the company from completing transactions entered into in breach of the company's articles which provided that the consent of the two managing directors was required in relation to such

3–25

---

[77] Relatively little is needed for the court to conclude that the articles have been incorporated into the service contract, but there must be something: see *Globalink Telecommunications Ltd v Wilmbury Ltd* [2003] 1 B.C.L.C. 145.

[78] On directors' contracts see Ch.14.

[79] 2006 Act s.171. See paras 16–24 et seq.

[80] *Beattie v Beattie Ltd* [1938] Ch. 708 CA.

[81] *Rayfield v Hands* [1960] Ch. 1.

[82] What he would have held had one of the directors not been a member is unclear.

[83] See "Shareholders' Rights and the Rule in *Foss v Harbottle*" in [1957] C.L.J. 193, especially at 210–215. See also Beck in (1974) 22 Can.B.R. 157 at 190–193.

[84] *Quinn & Axtens Ltd v Salmon* [1909] 1 Ch. 311 CA; affirmed [1909] A.C. 442 HL. For subsequent dicta in support of this view see, e.g. *Re Harmer Ltd* [1959] 1 W.L.R. 62 at 85 and 89 CA; *Re Richmond Gate Property Co* [1965] 1 W.L.R. 335 (see (1965) 28 M.L.R. 347 and (1966) 29 M.L.R. 608 at 612); *Hogg v Cramphorn* [1967] Ch. 254; *Bamford v Bamford* [1970] Ch. 212; *Re Sherbourn Park Residents Co Ltd* (1986) 2 B.C.C. 99 at 528; *Breckland Group Holdings v London & Suffolk Properties* [1989] B.C.L.C. 100 (see (1989) 52 M.L.R. 401 at 407–408); *Guinness Plc v Saunders* [1990] 2 A.C. 663 HL; *Wise v USDAW* [1996] I.C.R. 691 at 702.

transactions. This, in effect, showed that a member had a membership right to require the company to act in accordance with its articles, which right could be enforced by the member even though the result was indirectly to protect a right which was afforded to him as director. If this is correct, the supposed principle, that there is a statutory contract between the company and its members only in respect of matters affecting members qua members, is effectively outflanked—and, if so, whether it can then still apply to the statutory contact between members inter se seems debatable.[85]

3–26   Despite the criticisms which can be levelled against the *Hickman* principle, when the Company Law Review consulted on the question of whether this aspect of the Act required reform,[86] a positive response was not forthcoming and the recommendation from the CLR was accordingly to leave the law as it is.[87] Perhaps this indicates that, although the *Hickman* principle may not be wholly desirable, the costs of contracting around it are not high. Consequently, practice has accommodated itself to the rule. On the other hand, when the common law of privity of contract was reformed, it is perhaps easier to understand why there was no pressure to change the current rule to one which would permit *non*-members to enforce rights in their favour contained in the articles.[88]

(iv)   Further limits to the provisions which can be enforced: not mere procedural irregularities

3–27   Although the Company Law Review was content to let the "member qua member" aspect of the statutory contract remain undisturbed, the same cannot be said of a related aspect of the contract with which we must deal. Even though a member sues as a member and even though he or she sues to enforce a provision in the articles which appears to confer a right on the member, he or she may nevertheless be defeated by the argument that the provision does not confer a personal right on the member but creates only an obligation on the company, breach of which constitutes "a mere internal irregularity" on the company's part. The consequence of the categorisation of the breach of the articles as an internal irregularity is that the decision whether to sue to enforce the provision is a matter for the shareholders collectively, whereas personal rights, not surprisingly, can be enforced by individual shareholders.

The issue has tended to arise particularly in relation to those provisions dealing with the convening and conduct of meetings of shareholders or the selection of members of the board. These are areas where there are statutory provisions, but they are of a limited nature and much is left to be regulated in the company's articles.[89] If, for example, the chairman of a shareholders' meeting acts in breach of the provisions of the articles governing meetings, is that an

---

[85] For subsequent academic discussion of the principle, see Goldberg in (1972) 33 M.L.R. 362; Prentice in (1980) 1 Co. Law 179; Gregory in (1981) 44 M.L.R. 526; Goldberg (replying) in (1985) 48 M.L.R. 121; Drury in [1989] C.L.J. 219; and Worthington, (2000) 116 L.Q.R. 638.
[86] Formation, paras 2.6–2.8.
[87] Completing, paras 5.66–5.67.
[88] See above, fn.70.
[89] See Chs 14 and 15, below.

infringement of the shareholders' personal rights or a mere internal irregularity? There are a number of decisions of the courts over the past 150 years putting such breaches in one category or the other, but it is difficult to discern the principled basis on which the classification was carried out. The importance, if not the nature, of the distinction is shown by two ultimately irreconcilable cases from the 1870s, *MacDougall v Gardiner*[90] and *Pender v Lushington*.[91] In the former the decision of the chairman of the shareholders' meeting wrongfully (i.e. in breach of the articles) to refuse a request for a poll was held to be an internal irregularity, whilst in the latter the refusal of a chairman to recognise the votes attached to shares held by nominee shareholders was held to infringe their personal rights. Each decision has spawned a line of equally irreconcilable authorities. In truth, there is a conflict here between proper recognition of the contractual nature of the company's constitution and the traditional policy of non-interference by the courts in the internal affairs of companies.

As Smith has suggested,[92] ultimately the only satisfactory solution is to choose which policy is to have priority. Moreover, it is surely clear today that it ought to be the former. It can hardly be argued in modern law that it is an example of excessive interference by the courts to hold a company (or any other association) to the procedures which it itself has adopted in its constitution for its internal decision-making (until such time as it decides to change those internal rules according to the procedures set down for that to occur).[93] Indeed, it might even be suggested that effective protection of this procedural entitlement of members is basic to any satisfactory system of company law.[94]   **3–28**

Part of the confusion may have arisen because of a failure to appreciate that the same situation may give rise to wrongs both by and against the company, and the individual shareholder's position will vary according to which wrong he seeks to redress. Thus, the chairman of a shareholders' meeting who breaches the relevant provisions of the articles may both put the company in breach of its contract with the members and him- or herself be in breach of duty to the company for not observing the provisions. An analogy is provided by the decision in *Taylor v NUM (Derbyshire Area)*.[95] The plaintiff successfully sued his trade union[96] in a personal capacity to obtain an injunction restraining the officials of the union from continuing a strike which it was a breach of the union's rule-book (in fact,   **3–29**

---

[90] *MacDougall v Gardiner* (1875) 1 Ch.D. 13.

[91] *Pender v Lushington* (1877) 6 Ch.D. 70.

[92] R.J. Smith, "Minority Shareholders and Corporate Irregularities" (1978) M.L.R. 147.

[93] This argument would lack force only if, as is *not* usually the case for companies or, indeed, most associations, the procedure for amending the rules on how decisions are to be taken was the same as the one for taking substantive decisions.

[94] Such a statement would surely be regarded as uncontroversial if made in relation to trade union law. cf. O. Kahn-Freund, *Kahn-Freund's Labour and the Law*, 3rd edn (Stevens, 1983), pp.286 et seq. The courts do not lack techniques for dealing with members whose complaints are purely "technical", i.e. where it is clear that the same result would have been arrived at even if the proper procedure had been followed: *Harben v Phillips* [1974] 1 W.L.R. 638.

[95] *Taylor v NUM (Derbyshire Area)* [1985] B.C.L.C. 237. For the application of the distinction between personal and derivative actions to companies in an ultra vires context, see *Moseley v Koffyfontein Mines* [1911] 1 Ch. 73 CA.

[96] To which this distinction between personal rights and mere internal irregularities also applies.

beyond its capacity) to conduct, but failed in his claim for an order requiring the same officials to restore to the union the funds already expended on the strike, because he did not have standing to bring a derivative action on behalf of the union.[97] The same analysis may often be applicable to breaches of the articles.[98] In other words, the company may be regarded as breaching its contract with the member if it seeks to act upon a resolution improperly passed and should be restrainable by the member, but for the loss (say the wasted costs of organising the meeting) caused to the company by the chair of the meeting in not conducting it in accordance with the company's regulations, the company is the proper plaintiff.[99]

3–30   An alternative line of attack on the above decisions might be provided by the general membership right, postulated by Professor Wedderburn and noted above, to have the affairs of the company conducted in accordance with the articles, for that right was also put forward by him as a personal right. Consequently, this general right, if recognised by the courts or the legislature, would defeat both the "outsider right" argument and the "mere internal irregularity" argument against shareholder enforcement of the articles of association. After some hesitation, the Company Law Review decided to take a bold approach which amounted, in effect, to the acceptance of Professor Wedderburn's argument, at least on the matter of the range of provisions enforceable by the member as member. All duties imposed in favour of members under the constitution should be enforceable by individual shareholders.[100] In principle, if the company acted in breach of such duties, then the member would be able to bring an action to enforce the company's rule-book. Or the member would be able to sue another member if the obligation was laid by the articles on that member. This would not mean that every breach of the articles by a corporate officer would entitle each shareholder to sue the company for damages. Damages would be an available remedy only if the shareholder personally[101] had suffered loss as a result of the breach. In the case of a breach of procedure in the conduct of a meeting, a remedy other than damages might well be more appropriate, for example, an injunction preventing the company from acting on an improperly passed resolution. In other cases no remedy at all might be ordered. If the breach of procedure had been purely technical and it was clear that the resolution would have been passed even if the correct procedure had been followed, the court should not grant any remedy at all and might even award costs against the complainant shareholder. This proposal was subject to one qualification: it would be possible for the shareholders to opt, by an appropriate provision included therein, for some or all of the articles not to be enforceable. In such a case, the relevant articles would not

---

[97] See Ch.17 for a discussion of derivative actions in relation to companies.

[98] But note *Devlin v Slough Estates Ltd* [1983] B.C.L.C. 497, refusing to recognise that the particular article in question, relating to the preparation of the company's accounts, conferred a right upon individual shareholders (as contrasted with "the company").

[99] There is some suggestion in the language used in *MacDougall v Gardiner* and *Pender v Lushington* (see above, fnn.90 and 91), respectively, that the decisions are to be explained on the basis that the two courts simply fastened on two different legal aspects of a single situation.

[100] Completing, para.5.73; Final Report I, paras 7.34–7.40.

[101] On the crucial distinction between corporate and individual loss, see para.17–34.

be enforceable as a contract,[102] even if they would be under the current law. Thus, general contractual enforcement of the articles would be the default rule, and in any case it should be clear which articles were enforceable and which not.

However, the 2006 Act does not take up this proposal and so the uncertainties of the case law, discussed above, remain.

(v)   Altering the contract

It is crucial that the articles, as part of the constitution of an ongoing organisation, be capable of amendment from time to time. Section 21 expressly provides that "a company may amend its articles by special resolution".[103] Thus, a member enters into a contract on terms which are alterable by the other party (the company, acting through the shareholders collectively),[104] rather in the same way as a member of a club agrees to be bound by the club rules as validly altered from time to time by the members as a whole, or a worker agrees to be employed on the terms of a collective agreement as varied from time to time by the employer and trade union. That a majority of the members should normally be able to alter the articles by following a prescribed procedure and thus alter for the future the contractual rights and obligations of individual shareholders is hardly surprising. It reflects the fact that the company is an association and that some process of collective decision-making is needed, in relation to its constitution, if it is to be able to adapt to changing circumstances in the business environment. The alternative would be constitutional change only with the consent of each individual shareholder, which would be very difficult to obtain in many cases and which would give unscrupulous individuals golden opportunities for disruptive behaviour.

3–31

On the other hand, the ability of the majority to bind the minority through decisions which alter the articles of the company creates the potential for opportunistic behaviour on the part of the majority towards the minority. As we shall see in Chs 19 and 20, company law has developed some general standards which address this problem, which arises in all situations where the majority may bind the minority, whether the matter at issue is an amendment to the articles or not.

3–32

Here we need note only two particular restrictions on the majority's power to alter the articles. One is highly precise. The consent of the individual member is required if he or she is to be bound by an alteration which requires members to subscribe for further shares in the company or which increases liability to contribute to the company's share capital or pay money to the company.[105]

---

[102] Though they could still be used as the basis for an unfair prejudice remedy: see Ch.20, below. That remedy today is probably the mechanism by which complaints of breaches of the articles are most often litigated.

[103] Changes in the articles must be notified to the registrar: s.26. In the case of charitable companies the power to amend the articles is subject to the requirement of the charities legislation operating in the three UK jurisdictions: s.21(2), (3).

[104] *Shuttleworth v Cox Bros & Co (Maidenhead) Ltd* [1927] 2 K.B. 9 at 26 CA, per Atkin LJ; *Malleson v National Insurance and Guarantee Corp* [1894] 1 Ch. 200 at 205, per North J.

[105] 2006 Act s.25(1).

The other restriction is of a procedural nature and enables the shareholders to contract around the principle of majority rule for alteration of the articles. The normal rule is that the company cannot contract out of its power to alter the articles.[106] However, s.22 enables the shareholders to "entrench" provisions of the company's constitution, i.e. to make them capable of amendment or repeal "only if conditions are met, or procedures complied with, that are more restrictive than those applicable in the case of a special resolution."[107] Those additional restrictions may not make the articles completely unalterable[108]—probably a wise provision, because even a member who insists on such a provision may subsequently change his or her mind. However, amendment or repeal could be made conditional on the consent of a particular member or a higher percentage of the members than a special resolution requires. Entrenched status can be conferred upon provisions in the articles either upon the formation of the company or subsequently, but in the latter case only with the unanimous consent of the members.[109] The registrar must be given notice of the adoption of entrenchment provisions and of their removal[110]; and the company must certify compliance with the entrenchment provisions whenever it alters its articles.[111] Thus, the principle that the constitution of the company can be altered by a three-quarters majority of the members can in fact be set aside by using the entrenchment provisions, though for most companies it would be unwise to do so on a significant scale.[112]

SHAREHOLDER AGREEMENTS

3–33   The freedom of the shareholders to fashion the company's constitution facilitates the input of a significant element of "private ordering" into the rules governing the company, but the articles of association are not the only method whereby the shareholders can generate their own rules for the governance of their affairs. An alternative method is an agreement, concluded among some or all the shareholders, but existing outside and separate from the articles and to which the company itself may or may not be a party. Such an agreement is not normally treated as part of the constitution of the company, though it may have an effect which is rather similar to a provision in the articles, and so there are exceptions to this general rule.[113]

---

[106] On the impact of this principle on contracts outside the articles, see paras 19–25 et seq.

[107] Under the prior law, entrenchment could be achieved by placing the provision in the memorandum of association and subjecting it to restrictive alteration conditions—and the prior law did seem to permit making a provision unalterable in any circumstances (other than a court order). See CA 1985 s.17(2)(b). The new scheme follows that proposed by the CLR: Formation, para.2.27.

[108] 2006 Act s.22(3)(a) expressly provides that entrenchment cannot prevent alteration by agreement of all the members.

[109] 2006 Act s.22(2). On formation all the subscribers in effect agree to the contents of the articles and subsequent members join on the basis of what those articles provide.

[110] 2006 Act s.23.

[111] 2006 Act s.24.

[112] The entrenchment provisions can be overridden by a court order: s.22(3)(b), (4). See, for example, ss.899–901 and Ch.29.

[113] Shareholder agreements are included within the meaning of the constitution of the company for the purposes of s.40: see s.40(3)(b) and para.7–14.

The main advantages of the shareholder agreement over the articles are that the agreement is a private document which does not have to be registered at Companies House and that it derives its contractual force from the normal principles of contract law and not from the Act, so that the limitations discussed above on the statutory contract do not to apply to shareholder agreements.

3–34

The main disadvantages are that the shareholder agreement does not automatically bind new members of the company, as the articles do.[114] A new member of the company will not be bound by the agreement unless that person assents to it and so the shareholder agreement may not continue to bind all the members. Securing the assent of new members may or may not be easy to bring about. Nor does the Act provide an overriding mechanism for majority alteration to the shareholder agreement. The parties to that agreement may provide such a mechanism, but if they do not do so, then, under normal contractual rules, the consent of each party to the agreement would be necessary to effect a change. In addition, the protection provided by such an agreement may be more limited than supposed, since remedies for breach may be restricted to damages rather than an order for specific performance, and indeed the company cannot agree to be bound in matters which are contrary to the Companies Act. In short, a shareholder agreement displays both the advantages and disadvantages of private contracting.

3–35

We discuss shareholder agreements and other methods of protecting minority shareholders, such as the issue of shares with special rights attached to them, in Ch.19.

THE EUROPEAN COMPANY

As far as the European Company is concerned, a hierarchy of sources of rules is set out in the European Company Statute.[115] The primary source of rules for the SE is EU law, as one would expect, in the shape of the European Company Statute, which applies directly in the Member States without the need for transposition, which a Directive requires.[116] The second source of law for the SE is its own statutes (or constitution or articles of association, as we might term them), but only to the extent that the Regulation expressly permits the SE through its statutes to regulate a particular matter. In fact, some highly significant choices are expressly given by the Regulation to the SE, to be made through its statutes, for example, the choice between a one-tier and a two-tier board.[117] However, as we noted in Ch.1,[118] the European Regulation does not aim to provide a comprehensive code of company law for the SE. Much is referred to the law of the state in which the SE is registered, and so domestic law becomes an important

3–36

---

[114] 2006 Act s.33(1) says that the articles bind the company and the members, meaning those who at any one time are the members of the company.

[115] Council Regulation 2157/2001/EC art.9.

[116] However, since the provisions on worker involvement in the SE are contained in a Directive, which needs transposition, the Regulation applies in the Member States only together with the national provisions transposing the Directive. For the UK see European Public Limited-Liability Company Regulations (SI 2004/2326) Pt 3 (hereafter European Company Regulations).

[117] Regulation 2157/2001/EC art.38. See further below, para.14–64.

[118] See above, para.1–40.

source of rules for the SE. The Regulation contemplates two types of domestic law as being relevant. The third source is thus domestic law passed specifically in order to embed the Regulation in the domestic company law or to exercise choices conferred by the SE Statute on the Member States in relation to the SE.[119] For example, Member States may, but need not, lay down rules about the maximum and minimum number of members of a one-tier board (if the SE chooses this system of governance)[120] or a Member State may reduce below 10 per cent the figure for the proportion of shareholders who are entitled to insist that an item be added to the agenda of a meeting of the SE's shareholders.[121]

However, the more important domestic (and fourth) source of rules for the SE is likely to be the rules applying to public companies in the jurisdiction of registration. These rules will apply to the SE automatically and without the need for special national implementing legislation. Often, the SE Statute says in relation to a particular subject-matter that these domestic rules shall apply (for example, in relation to the legal capital of the SE),[122] but this is declared generally to be the principle in relation to matters not governed, or to the extent not governed, by the regulation itself.[123] Thus, much of the law governing domestic public companies limited by shares will apply to the SE. Indeed, the main interest of the SE as a legal form can be said to lie in those relatively limited areas where the domestic rules are trumped by rules emanating from EU law and the EU rules are significantly different from those which domestic law applies to its public companies,[124] and it is on those aspects that the later chapters in this book will concentrate. An obvious example is the requirement for the domestic legislature to make a two-tier board model of governance available for the SE to take up, if it so wishes.

The final source of rules for the SE under the regulation brings the statutes of the SE back into the picture once again. They are a source of law "in the same way as for a public limited-liability formed in accordance with the law of the Member State in which the SE has its registered office".[125] As we have seen, the domestic law makes the articles a major source for the rules governing the internal affairs of the public company, and this will be the case also for the SE, except to the extent that the regulation itself has occupied ground which the domestic company law leaves to the articles of association. This will probably mean that the statutes of a British-registered SE will be an important source of rules, but a less important source than for a domestic public company, because Title III of the regulation governs the structure of the European Company (board of directors and shareholders' meeting) more extensively than does the Companies Act or the common law in relation to a domestic company.

---

[119] See the European Company Regulations Pt 4 (exercising options) and Pts 2 and 5–7 doing various types of "embedding".

[120] SE Statute art.43(2).

[121] SE Statute art.56.

[122] SE Statute art.5.

[123] SE Statute arts 9(1)(c) and 10.

[124] Of course, some of the mandatory rules to be found in the Regulation may in fact track the domestic rules with perhaps minor changes.

[125] Reg.2157/2001/EC art.9(1)(c)(iii).

However, the EU rules relating to the SE are not to be found wholly in the regulation. The crucial issue of employee involvement in the SE[126] is dealt with at EU level by a Directive.[127] Directives do require transposition into domestic law. Moreover, if the Directive is properly transposed, the domestic law becomes the source of obligation in the national legal system, not the Directive. Consequently, the employee involvement Directive, despite the importance of its subject-matter, has no greater impact on the sources of domestic company law than do any of the many other EC Directives which have played a part in shaping modern British company law,[128] and so it need not be considered further here.

---

[126] See further below, Ch.14.

[127] Directive 2002/14/EC [2002] O.J. L80/29.

[128] Discussed generally in Ch.6.

CHAPTER 4

FORMATION PROCEDURES

FORMATION OF DIFFERENT TYPES OF COMPANY

4–1   As noted earlier,[1] there are three basic types of domestic incorporated company—statutory, chartered and registered—and the formation rules vary fundamentally as between each type. The last class, the class of registered companies, includes both companies registered by the Registrar of Companies under the Companies Act 2006 and Charitable Incorporated Organisations ("CIOs") registered by the Charity Commissioners under the Charities Act 2011.[2] In this chapter the focus is on companies registered under the Companies Act, for these are overwhelmingly the most common and important types of companies. Recall that this category includes public companies (limited by shares) and private companies (whether limited by shares, by guarantee, or unlimited), and also the special corporate forms (community interest companies ("CICs", limited by shares or by guarantee),[3] and European Companies ("SEs")[4]). Formation of these registered companies is briefly compared with the less common alternatives.

Statutory companies

4–2   These are formed by the passing of a Private Act of Parliament, especially where an enterprise is required for public purposes or requires special powers (e.g. to compulsorily purchase land for public utilities). The procedure is that generally applicable to Private Bill legislation. In practice the work is monopolised by a few firms of solicitors who specialise as parliamentary agents and by a handful of counsel at the parliamentary bar. The numbers of such Acts and supporting specialist practitioners are dwindling, given the move first to nationalisation and now to privatisation, both of which are achieved under Public Acts.

Chartered companies

4–3   The creation of new chartered trading companies is now unlikely, but the grant of charters to charitable or public bodies is not uncommon. The procedure in such cases is for the promoters of the body to petition the Crown (through the office of

---

[1] See above, paras 1–17 and 1–31.

[2] See above, para.1–29, and recall that the CIO status is optional; companies which are charitable may, alternatively, be registered under the Companies Act (with all that entails) and be obliged, in addition, to comply with the Charities Act. In addition, specific types of association must be registered under specific Acts: see Building Societies Act 1986, Friendly Societies Act 1992 and Co-operative and Community Benefit Societies Act 2014.

[3] See above, para.1–12.

[4] See above, para.1–40. The European Company ("SE"), introduced in 2004, is formed under the relevant EU Regulation, as supplemented by domestic law, but with Companies House acting as the registration body for SEs registered in Great Britain. Note, however, that the European Company cannot be formed by natural persons but only by existing companies (or analogous bodies) in the ways specified in the Regulation: merger, joint subsidiary, joint holding company, transformation. Recall also the separate avenues for alternative forms of incorporation under the European Economic Interest Grouping Regulations 1989 (SI 1989/638) and the European Public Limited Liability Company Regulations 2004 (SI 2004/2326).

the Lord President of the Council) praying for the grant of a charter, a draft of which is normally annexed to the petition. If the petition is granted the promoters and their successors then become:

> "one body corporate and politic by the name of—and by that name shall and may sue or be sued plead and be impleaded in all courts whether of law or equity…and shall have perpetual succession and a common seal."

Sometimes a charter will be granted to the members of an existing guarantee company registered under the Companies Acts in which event the assets of the company will be transferred to the new chartered body and the company wound up unless the Registrar can be persuaded to exercise his power to strike it off the register, thus avoiding the expense of a formal liquidation.[5]

Registered companies

Today, the vast majority of companies, whatever their objects, are formed by registration under the Companies Act 2006 Pt 2. The rest of this chapter is concerned with that registration process, the decisions which have to be made to implement it, and its immediate consequences.

4–4

The Act allocates specific functions to the Registrar of Companies and to the Secretary of State, with such powers typically exercised by their authorised delegates.[6] For example, most of the powers described in this chapter are exercised by Companies House, which is an executive agency of the Department of Business, Innovation and Skills ("BIS").

For ease of explanation, those forming a company (the "promoters") are referred to as if they were natural persons, though this need not be the case: an existing company is equally capably of forming a new company. Indeed, this is common practice, since all but the smallest businesses are carried on by corporate groups rather than single companies.[7]

---

[5] See below, Ch.33.

[6] Contracting Out (Functions in Relation to the Registration of Companies) Order 1995 (SI 1995/1013) made under the Deregulation and Contracting Out Act 1994.

[7] The establishment of a corporate group does not necessarily require the creation of a new company, however. A group may also be formed if the original company acquires the shares of an existing company, as it would likely do if the company is expanding by acquiring an established business rather than by setting up its own new business from scratch.

FORMING A COMPANY BY REGISTRATION

Registration documents

4–5   In order to form a registered company,[8] the promoters must deliver certain documents to the Registrar of Companies and pay a registration fee.[9] Listing these documents helps identify the various decisions which promoters must take even earlier, before registration is possible. In addition, and perhaps surprisingly, the Companies Act is explicit that a company cannot be formed for unlawful purposes.[10] The documents which must be registered are:

(i)   A memorandum of association in prescribed form indicating that those whose names are subscribed to the memorandum wish to form a company and become its initial members.[11]

(ii)   An application for registration, stating[12]:

    (a)   The company's proposed name.[13]

    (b)   Whether the company's registered office is to be in England and Wales, Wales, Scotland or Northern Ireland,[14] and its address.[15]

    (c)   Whether the liability of the members is to be limited and, if so, whether by shares or guarantee.[16] In the latter case a statement of guarantee must be part of the application[17] and that must state the amount which each member of the company agrees to contribute to the company on its winding up[18] and it must contain the names and

---

[8] This describes the requirements under the Companies Act 2006. A "company" includes companies registered under earlier Acts going back to 1856, even though the registration requirements have changed over time: s.1(1).

[9] Registrar of Companies (Fees) (Companies, Overseas Companies and Limited Liability Partnerships) Regulations (SI 2012/1907) Sch.1 para.8 (ranging from £13–£30 for electronic registration, and £40–£100 for non-electronic registration). Registrations are now overwhelmingly electronic.

[10] 2006 Act s.7(2): "A company may not be formed for an unlawful purpose". This is interpreted as banning both purposes which are criminal and those which are regarded as contrary to public policy: *R. v Registrar of Joint Stock Companies* [1931] 2 K.B. 197 CA; *R. v Registrar of Companies, Ex p. HM's Attorney-General* [1991] B.C.L.C. 476. In the light of the decision in *Yuen Kun Yeu v Attorney-General of Hong Kong* [1988] A.C. 175 PC, it seems clear that a member of the public subsequently defrauded by the company could not successfully sue the Registrar on the ground that he was negligent in registering the company (or, in the case of a public company, issuing the trading certificate).

[11] 2006 Act ss.7(1), 8 and 16(2). By contrast to this basic document, the memorandum of a company registered before 1 October 2009 (an "old style memorandum") was a radically different important constitutional document, the provisions of which are now treated as provisions of the company's articles (s.28).

[12] 2006 Act s.9.

[13] 2006 Act s.9(2)(a), and see below, paras 4–13 to 4–21.

[14] 2006 Act s.9(2)(b). This place of registration will define the company's domicile, and a company cannot unilaterally abandon this domicile and adopt a new one (as a natural person can): *Carl Zeiss Siftung v Rayner and Keeler Ltd (No.3)* [1970] Ch. 506, 544.

[15] 2006 Act s.9(5)(a).

[16] 2006 Act s.9(2)(c), and see below, paras 4–10 to 4–11.

[17] 2006 Act s.9(4)(b).

[18] 2006 Act s.11.

addresses of each of the subscribers to the memorandum (who, of course, become its first members).[19]

In the case of a company having a share capital[20] a statement of capital and initial shareholdings must be part of the application.[21] This must give particulars of the nominal value of and amount paid up on the shares taken by the subscribers on formation (both in aggregate and individually).[22]

(d) Whether the company is to be public or private.[23]

(e) A statement of the proposed officers of the company,[24] meaning its first directors and secretary (if any[25]), and containing a statement by the subscribers that each person named has consented to act.[26]

(f) A statement of initial significant control,[27] meaning particulars of persons or legal entities who are considered to exercise significant control over the company on incorporation.[28] This includes persons or legal entities holding 25 per cent of the shares or voting rights in the company, those who have the right to appoint or remove a majority of the board of directors, and those who have the right to exercise, or actually exercise, significant influence or control over the company.[29]

(iii) A copy of the proposed articles of association, to the extent that these are not supplied by the default model articles.[30]

(iv) A statement of compliance, which the Registrar may accept as sufficient evidence that the requirements of the Act have been complied with.[31]

Only if the company is to be a community interest company will something more be required. First, in order to meet the restrictions which the 2004 Act places on such companies, especially in relation to the distribution of assets, the company's articles must include the provisions set out in the appropriate Schedule to the

4–6

---

[19] Companies (Registration) Regulations 2008/3014 (hereafter "Registration Regulations") reg.3.

[20] If the company has a share capital, it will normally be limited by shares but not necessarily so. This would not be the case with an unlimited company having a share capital.

[21] 2006 Act s.9(4)(a).

[22] 2006 Act s.10 and the Registration Regulations reg.3. The company's power to issue shares of various classes will be set out, of course, in the articles of association. See Ch.24 for the rules governing the exercise of this power.

[23] 2006 Act s.9(2)(d).

[24] 2006 Act s.9(4)(c).

[25] A private company need not have a secretary (s.270), but a public company must (s.271).

[26] 2006 Act s.12. The Act has abolished the requirement for a private company to have a secretary and so all that will probably be provided is the name of the first directors of the company. This is the first expression of an obligation which will continue throughout the company's life periodically to inform the Registrar about these matters: see para.14–23.

[27] 2006 Act s.9(4)(d). This provision was introduced as part of the reforms under SBEEA 2015 to improve transparency around who owns and controls UK businesses. See above, paras 2–42 et seq.

[28] As defined in Pt 1 of Sch.1A. See s.12A, s.790M, s.790C, s.890K, Pt 1 of Sch.1A.

[29] This condition is potentially broad. See above, para.2–44.

[30] 2006 Act ss.9(5)(b) and 20, and see below at para.4–32.

[31] 2006 Act s.13.

Community Interest Company Regulations 2005.[32] Further, the company may only be registered as a CIC if the Regulator accepts that its objectives constitute the furtherance of a community interest. The promoters must provide the Registrar with a "community interest statement", being a document signed by each person who is to be a first director of the company declaring that the company will carry on its activities in order to benefit the community and indicating how the company's activities will benefit the community.[33] Only if the Regulator concludes that the community interest test is met will the Registrar register the company as a CIC.[34] This test is rather open-ended—"a company satisfies the community interest test if a reasonable person might consider that its activities are being carried on for the benefit of the community"[35]—and so there may be some scope for debate about its application and for appeals from the Regulator to the Appeal Officer.[36]

Certificate of incorporation

4–7 In itself none of this is very demanding, although it disguises a number of crucial decisions that the promoters must take, as described below. If Companies House is satisfied that the registration requirements have been met, then it must register the company,[37] allocate the company a "registered number",[38] and provide the company with a certificate of incorporation[39] which is conclusive evidence that the requirements of the Act have been met and that the company is duly registered under the Act.[40] This is so even if the registration had been procured by fraud.[41]

4–8 The effect of incorporation is that "the subscribers to the memorandum, together with such other persons as may from time to time become members of the company, are a body corporate by the name stated in the certificate of incorporation".[42] Further, the subscribers to the memorandum become the holders of the shares specified in the statement of capital and the directors and secretary (if any) named in the statement of proposed officers are appointed to their offices.[43]

---

[32] Community Interest Company Regulations 2005 (SI 2005/1788). And for CIOs, see above, para.1–30.

[33] Community Interest Company Regulations 2005 (SI 2005/1788) regs 2 and 11. Note the decision not to require an "objects clause" in the company's constitution for this purpose. See further para.7–29.

[34] Companies (Audit, Investigations and Community Enterprise) Act 2004 s.36(3)–(6).

[35] 2004 Act s.35(2).

[36] The Regulations give some further guidance (see regs 1–3), notably by excluding political activities.

[37] 2006 Act s.14.

[38] 2006 Act s.1066.

[39] 2006 Act s.15—signed by the registrar and authenticated by the registrar's official seal (s.15(3)).

[40] 2006 Act s.15(4).

[41] *Bank of Beirut SAL v Prince El-Hashemite* [2015] 3 W.L.R. 875.

[42] 2006 Act s.16(2)—thus making clear the company's nature as an incorporated association.

[43] 2006 Act s.16(5),(6).

Challenging the issue of a certificate of incorporation is difficult, as discussed below.[44]

Purchase of a shelf-company

The majority of new companies are formed by specialist company formation experts.[45] Historically, these agents ran their businesses by registering large numbers of companies and holding them ready to sell "off the shelf" to promoters who wanted to incorporate rapidly. The agents themselves (and persons associated with them) were the original subscribers, first members and officers of the company, and the promoters then simply purchased the shares, voted in new officers, changed the company name and registered office, and reported all these amendments to Companies House. Now, however, with electronic registration, company formation agents can meet promoters' specific requests very quickly and directly without the use of shelf companies.

4–9

CHOICE OF TYPE OF REGISTERED COMPANY

One of the earliest decisions taken by the promoters is resolving which of the several types of registered company they wish to form, since this will certainly affect the contents of the documents required to be registered.

4–10

First, they must choose between a limited and an unlimited company.[46] Both are fully liable to their creditors; the distinction refers to the extent of the members' liability (to their company, not directly to their company's creditors[47]) to meet the company's liability for its debts. In an unlimited company, the members will ultimately be personally liable (jointly, severally and to an unlimited extent) for the company's debts in the event of the company's formal liquidation. For this reason promoters are likely to steer away from this form, especially if the company intends to trade. If the company is merely to hold land or investments, however, then the absence of limited liability may not matter and may confer certain advantages, for example, as regards returning capital[48] to the members and avoiding the need for public disclosure of the company's financial position[49]; the absence of limited liability may also render the company more acceptable in certain circles (for example, the turf).

If the promoters decide upon a limited company, they must then make up their minds whether it is to be limited by shares or by guarantee. As already

---

[44] See below, para.4–34.

[45] Developing, para.11.32, estimating they are responsible for approximately 60 per cent of registrations.

[46] An alternative, which in practice was very rarely adopted, was a limited company with unlimited liability on the part of the directors (s.306 of CA 1985) but the 2006 Act no longer provides for this.

[47] *Oakes v Turquand and Harding* (1867) L.R. 2 H.L. 325; Insolvency Act 1986 s.74.

[48] The prohibition against a company acquiring its own shares applies only to limited companies (s.658(1) and Ch.13).

[49] An unlimited company is not required to file its annual accounts and reports (and so make them publicly available): s.448 and Ch.21.

explained,[50] this is largely determined by the purpose for which the company has been formed, and only if it is to be a non-profit-making concern are they likely to form a guarantee company, which is especially suited to a body of that type.

4–11   Overlapping these distinctions, but closely bound up with them, is the further point of whether or not the company should have a share capital. If, as is most probable, the company is to be limited by shares this question does not arise. Likewise, if it is to be limited by guarantee.[51] But if the company is unlimited it may or may not have its capital divided into shares. Once more, the decision is dependent on the company's purpose: if the company is intended to make and distribute profits, share capital will be appropriate.

    The promoters will further have to make up their minds whether the company is to be public or private. As noted earlier,[52] public and private companies essentially fulfil different economic purposes: the former to raise capital from the public to run the corporate enterprise, the latter to confer a separate legal personality on the business of a single trader or a partnership. Once again, therefore, the choice will in practice be clear-cut, and normally it will be to form a private company. The incorporators may have the ultimate ambition of "going public", but rarely will they be in a position to do so immediately. If, however, they are, then the company will have to be a company limited by shares, the certificate of incorporation will have to state that it is to be a public company, special requirements as to its registration will have to be complied with,[53] and it must comply with prescribed minimum capital requirements.[54] Any other type of company will, perforce, be a private company.

4–12   Finally, and again cutting across the above distinctions, is the question of whether the company's objectives are to be restricted to charitable purposes so as to make it a charitable company.[55] Moreover, since 2004 it has been possible for a limited company to be formed as a "community interest company" under the provisions of Pt 2 of the Companies (Audit, Investigations and Community Enterprise) Act 2004. Such companies must have the pursuit of a community interest as their objective (but need not be legal charities) and their articles must contain restrictions on the payment of dividends and, generally, on the transfer of corporate assets other than for full consideration.[56]

---

[50] See Ch.1, above.

[51] Since the coming into force of the Companies Act 1980 no further companies limited by guarantee and having a share capital can be formed: s.5.

[52] See Ch.1, above.

[53] 2006 Act s.4(2).

[54] A public company must have a nominal value of allotted share capital not less than the statutory "authorised minimum" (s.761), currently £50,000 or its prescribed euro equivalent (s.763), denominated in sterling or euros but not both (s.765), at least one-quarter of which must be paid up before the company starts trading (s.586).

[55] See para.1–30.

[56] 2004 Act ss.30 and 32 and the Community Interest Company Regulations 2005 (SI 2005/1788) regs 7–11.

In practice, the vast majority of companies formed are private companies limited by shares which are neither charitable nor community interest companies.[57]

CHOICE OF COMPANY NAME

The incorporators must decide on a suitable name.[58] This identifies the artificial person,[59] describes its status as a limited public or private company,[60] and over time becomes the name associated with the reputation and goodwill of the company. Given the importance of a company's name, there are rules governing the choice of names (including their length[61]), their mandatory publicity,[62] their protection from abuse, and their alteration.[63]

4–13

Warning the public about limited liability or other status

If the company is a limited company, its name must end with the prescribed warning suffix—"limited" (or "Ltd") if it is a private company, or "public limited company" (or "Plc") if it is a public one.[64] The purpose of this requirement is to warn a person dealing with the company that it is a body with limited liability, though whether it is very effective in this regard is another matter.

4–14

---

[57] According to Companies House, *Statistical Release: Companies Register Activities 2014/15* p.8, as of 31 March 2015, private limited companies account for over 96 per cent of all the corporate bodies on the register.

[58] The application for registration must state the company's proposed name: s.9(2)(a).

[59] Though less so now that the Registrar has to allot each company a registered number (s.1066) which it has to state on its business letters and order forms: s.82(1)(a) and regulations made thereunder.

[60] See below, para.4–14.

[61] Under the 2006 Act, largely for reasons of convenience of the Companies House computer system, a limit has been set on the number of characters of which a company's name may consist (no more than 160) and permitted characters have been prescribed as well as matters relating to the format of the name: s.57 and the Company, Limited Liability Partnership and Business (Names and Trading Disclosures) Regulations (SI 2015/17) reg.2. The DTI consultation document (DTI, *Implementation of the Companies Act 2006: Consultation Document*, February 2007), para.2.38, revealed that the longest registered name at that time had 159 characters. Like the famously long Welsh place name, Llanfairpwllgwyngyllgogerychwyrndrobwllllantysiliogogogoch, it is more a description than a name.

[62] The Secretary of State has power to require companies to give appropriate publicity to their names at their places of business and on business correspondence and related documentation: s.82(2)(a). The name must also be on the company's seal: s.45.

[63] Each described below in paras 4–14 et seq.

[64] 2006 Act ss.58–59. In the case of a Welsh company (i.e. one which is registered on the basis that its registered office is to be in Wales—see s.88(1) and below, para.4–14) the Welsh equivalents ("cyfyngedig" (or "cyf") or "cwmni cyfyngedig cyhoeddus" (or "ccc")) may (not must) be used instead. Similarly, in the case of a community interest company that term (or its abbreviation "cic") must be used as the suffix, if it is a private company, and "community interest public limited company" (abbreviated to "community interest plc") in the case of a public company: 2004 Act s.33. The Welsh equivalents are "cwmni buddiant cymunedol" (cbc) and "cwmni buddiant cymunedol cyhoeddus cyfyngedig" ("cwmni buddiant cymunedol ccc"). And the name of an SE must begin or end with "SE", and no company or firm formed on or after 8 October 2004 may use that abbreviation otherwise in its name: Regulation 2157/2001 art.11.

In addition, the name must not include, except at the end, any use of "public limited company", "community interest company" or "community interest public limited company" or their abbreviations or Welsh equivalents; and the company may not use "limited" or "unlimited" (or their abbreviations or Welsh equivalents) anywhere in the name, unless the company is in fact a limited or unlimited company.[65] This is done primarily to prevent any blurring of the warnings implied by "Ltd" or "Plc".[66]

4–15   The Act provides some narrow exemptions to the above rules requiring a private limited company to have "limited" at the end of its name.[67] Charitable companies are exempted from the requirement.[68] The Names Regulations are slightly wider, exempting a company limited by guarantee and engaged in "the promotion of commerce, art, science, education, religion, charity or any profession", the articles of which require its income to be devoted to the promotion of these objects, forbid the payment of dividends or any return of capital to members and require its assets on a winding-up to be transferred to a body with like objects or to a charity.[69] In effect, the exemption is available to charitable companies or those with public interest objectives which cannot be used as vehicles for making a profit for their members. Finally, certain companies are exempted under the "grandfather" provision applying to companies which were exempted from the requirement under earlier rules.[70]

Prohibition on illegal or offensive names

4–16   More important than what the name must contain is what it must not. Certain expressions are banned. If, in the opinion of the Secretary of State, the name is such that its use would constitute a criminal offence or be "offensive", it cannot be adopted.[71]

---

[65] 2006 Act s.65(1) and the Company, Limited Liability Partnership and Business (Names and Trading Disclosures) Regulations (SI 2015/17) regs 4–6. Nor may the company use the terms "open ended investment company", "investment company with variable capital" or "limited liability partnership" (or their abbreviations or Welsh equivalents).

[66] However, the inclusion of "unlimited" (for which, incidentally, there is no authorised abbreviation) would presumably prevent a moneylender from incorporating as "Unlimited Loans Ltd".

[67] 2006 Act s.60.

[68] 2006 Act s.60(1)(a).

[69] 2006 Act s.60(1)(b) and the Company, Limited Liability Partnership and Business (Names and Trading Disclosures) Regulations (SI 2015/17) reg.3. The Department had originally proposed to confine the exemption to statutory regulators established as companies (for example, the Financial Services Authority) on the grounds that the community interest company form catered for other companies for which exemption was appropriate, but it changed its mind after consultation. See DTI, *Implementation of the Companies Act 2006: Consultation Document*, February 2007, para.2.47; BERR, *Government Response to consultation on Companies Act 2006: Company and Business Names*, para.2.8 (URN 07/1244/GR).

[70] 2006 Act ss.60(1)(c) and 61, 62.

[71] 2006 Act s.53. An example of the use of a particular name being a criminal offence would be where the name holds out the company as carrying on a business which requires a licence or authorisation (for example, as a bank) which the company does not have.

Names requiring special approval

Certain names may be adopted only with the express approval of the Secretary of State. These are names which would be likely to give the impression that the company is connected in any way with the Government, a local authority or other specified public authority.[72] Further regulations specify other sensitive words or expressions for which approval is required; the current regulations list approximately 130 such words.[73] In both cases, the Secretary of State is empowered to require the person asking for permission to seek comments from the government department or other body which is thought to have an interest in the matter and, in particular, to ask that body whether it objects and, if so, why.[74] The relevant regulations generally specify the body which has to be invited to object.[75] When a request is made, the application for registration must contain a statement that the body has been asked and a copy of any response.[76]

4–17

Prohibition on using a name already allocated

The name must not be the same as any name already on the Registrar's index of names.[77] This is likely to present the severest obstacle because there are over two million names on that index. It is an index not just of names of companies incorporated under the 2006 or earlier Companies Acts but also of unregistered companies, overseas companies which have registered particulars in the UK, limited liability partnerships, limited partnerships, European Economic Interest Groupings registered in the UK, open-ended investment companies and registered societies under the Co-operative and Community Benefit Societies Act 2014.[78] Certain differences are to be disregarded when judging whether a name is the same and certain expressions are to be treated as the same,[79] thus expanding the scope of the prohibition. Hence a Smith, Jones, Brown or Davies who has

4–18

---

[72] 2006 Act s.54 and the Company, Limited Liability Partnership and Business (Names and Trading Disclosures) Regulations 2015/17.

[73] 2006 Act s.55 and the Company, Limited Liability Partnership and Business Names (Sensitive Words and Expressions) Regulations 2014/3140.

[74] 2006 Act s.56.

[75] e.g. if the name includes "Charitable" or "Charity", the Charity Commission or Office of the Scottish Charity Regulator must be asked; if "Dental" or "Dentistry", the General Dental Council; and if "Windsor" (because of its royal associations), the Ministry of Justice, the Welsh Assembly Government or the Scottish Executive.

[76] 2006 Act s.56(3).

[77] 2006 Act s.66.

[78] 2006 Act s.1099.

[79] 2006 Act s.66(3) and the Company, Limited Liability Partnership and Business (Names and Trading Disclosures) Regulations (SI 2015/17) reg.7 and Schs 2 and 3. For example, the words "company" and "cwmni" appearing at the end of the name are to be disregarded in judging whether the name is the same (so that if the only difference between the names is this one, they will be held to be the same) and "@" and "at" are to be treated as the same.

carried on an unincorporated business under his or her name may have difficulty in finding an available way of continuing to use that name on incorporating the business.[80]

There is, however, power to permit registration of a name that would otherwise be prohibited where the company seeking registration is part of the same group as the body already registered with the same name and the body already registered agrees to the registration of the new company.[81] Because of the requirement that the two bodies with the same name be part of the same group, the risk of confusion of the public is reduced[82] and the consent required of the body already registered serves to protect its interests.

Restrictions on use of a defunct company's name—phoenix companies

4–19   The restrictions just noted do not prevent a company adopting the name of a defunct company. However, a person who was a director or shadow director of a company that went into insolvent liquidation must not be a director of or take part in the management of a company with the same or a similar name for the next five years.[83] Breach of this prohibition attracts both civil and criminal liability.

Use of a business name other than the corporate name

4–20   Both companies and individuals may conduct their businesses under their corporate or individual names.[84] They may also adopt "business names" (or "trading names"), but the choice of such names, whether by companies or individuals, is now subject to broadly all the same restrictions and permissions as corporate names.[85] In relation to the business name, however, the convenient administrative sanction of refusing to register a company with a non-compliant name is not available, since unincorporated businesses do not need to be registered in order to carry on business. Consequently, contravention of the rules on business names is made a criminal offence.[86] In addition, the unincorporated business will have to observe the provisions of Ch.2 of Pt 41, regarding disclosure of the identity of the proprietors, which are the equivalent of the

---

[80] Those with less common surnames can often surmount this difficulty by, for example, inserting an appropriate place-name: e.g. Gower (Hampstead) Ltd.

[81] 2006 Act s.66(4) and Company, Limited Liability Partnership and Business (Names and Trading Disclosures) Regulations (SI 2015/17) reg.8. If the body already registered subsequently withdraws its consent, that will not affect the registration of the company.

[82] Though surely not eliminated, for example, where one of the two companies with the same name is a well capitalised parent company and the other an undercapitalised subsidiary.

[83] Insolvency Act 1986 s.216; and see below, paras 9–16 et seq.

[84] Corporate names are subject to all the restrictions noted here. An individual (or a partnership) can trade under the individual's (or individuals') own names: s.1192(2) and (3).

[85] 2006 Act Pt 41 (ss.1192–1199) (previously governed by the Business Names Act 1985).

[86] See ss.1193(4), 1194(3), 1197(5), 1198(2) and 1207.

trading disclosure rules applied to companies.[87] However, there is nothing in Pt 41 which empowers the Secretary of State or an adjudicator to direct the change of a business name because it is the same as, or too like, the name of an existing business, corporate or incorporate.

It will, therefore, be apparent that it may be difficult to find a name acceptable to both the incorporators and the Registrar and Secretary of State. But until it is achieved, it will be impossible to complete the documents required to obtain registration and unsafe to order the stationery which the company will need once it is registered. We have never introduced a system, comparable to that in some other common law countries, whereby a name can be reserved for a prescribed period. Prior to 1981, however, it was possible and usual to write to the Registrar submitting a name (or two or three alternative names) and asking if it was available. If the reply was affirmative it was usually safe to proceed so long as one did so promptly. Now, however, the incorporators or their professional advisers have to search the index[88] and make up their own minds. **4–21**

MANDATORY AND ELECTIVE NAME CHANGES

Even if the promoters do secure registration of their company under a particular name they cannot be certain that they will not be forced to change it. The Secretary of State has power to direct the company to change its name in certain circumstances. Alternatively, a name change may be required following a successful application to the company names adjudicator or to the courts (in a passing off action), arguing that the chosen name either exploits or damages the goodwill or reputation of another business. Finally, the company may, of course, choose to change its own name. **4–22**

Requirements to change a name

The Secretary of State may require a company to change its name if the company is no longer exempted from the requirement to include "limited" in its name[89]; or if the name harmfully misleads the public as to the company's activities[90]; or if the company provided misleading information or gave unfulfilled undertakings in **4–23**

---

[87] 2006 Act Ch.2 of Pt 41. The same civil sanction is applied as in the case of companies: s.1206 and para.9–3. The disclosure provisions of Ch.2 of Pt 41 apply only to individuals and partnerships (s.1200), because s.82 (trading disclosure) performs the same function for companies.

[88] And, ideally, also the Register of Trade Marks to ensure that the name proposed is not someone's registered trade mark.

[89] 2006 Act s.64. There is no time limit for giving such a direction.

[90] 2006 Act s.76. There is no time limit for giving such a direction. The company may appeal to court within three weeks of the direction, but otherwise must comply with the direction (or the court order) within six weeks: s.76(3)–(5). For example, in *Association of Certified Public Accountants of Britain v Secretary of State for Trade and Industry* [1998] 1 W.L.R. 164 the court confirmed the direction for a name change, identifying the harm as persuading the public to pay more for the services of members by giving a misleading impression of their qualifications because of the word "Certified". In general, however, little use is made of this power; undoubtedly the names of many companies give totally misleading indications of the nature of their activities but this, on its own, has apparently not been thought "likely to cause harm to the public".

order to be registered with the chosen name[91]; or if the name is "the same as, or in the opinion of the Secretary of State, too like[92]…a name appearing at the time of registration in the registrar's index of company names…or which should have appeared in that index at the time".[93]

This last option enables the correction of errors made in complying with the non-discretionary prohibition on using a name that is the same as an existing company name[94] (either because the name had not then been entered on the index or because the fact that it was the same as that of the new company had escaped detection). More interestingly, and unlike the other provisions, it also gives the Secretary of State a slightly broader discretion to direct a name change where the company has not simply breached the non-discretionary rules on names, but has a name that, while not the "same as" an existing company name, is "too like", and therefore might cause confusion in the minds of the public.[95] The existing company does not have to prove likely damage to its business goodwill, as is required in a passing off action (see below), but this statutory route is only open for 12 months. After that, it might be thought that the new company, too, is likely to have acquired goodwill in its name and will suffer loss if it is later required to change it, so the complainant should then be put to the more stringent tests of a passing off action.

4–24   Note, however, that the power given to the Secretary of State is to direct the company to act to change its name, not to direct the Registrar to amend the register.[96] The company may change its name by special resolution or by other procedures specified in its articles[97] (or by resolution of the directors if the direction relates to the exemption from using the word "limited"[98]). In every case, the company and each of its officers commits an offence if the Secretary of State's direction is not complied with.

Passing off actions

4–25   The directed name changes just noted deal with a company's failure to comply with the statutory requirements in relation to company names (with the added discretion in relation to names which are "too like" existing names). But the complaint is more typically that the chosen name meets all these statutory requirements, but is deceptively similar to an existing company's name, with both

---

[91] 2006 Act s.75. A direction may given up to five years after registration: s.75(2)(a).

[92] For a case where the names were not thought "too like" although they were sufficiently alike to have caused a petitioning creditor to obtain a winding up order against the wrong company with damaging consequences to it, see *Re Calmex Ltd* [1989] 1 All E.R. 485.

[93] 2006 Act s.67. Any direction must be given within 12 months of registration: s.68(2)(a).

[94] 2006 Act s.66.

[95] Although an interlocutory application in a passing off action may provide speedier relief: *Glaxo Plc v Glaxowellcome Ltd* [1996] F.S.R. 388.

[96] See *Halifax Plc v Halifax Repossessions Ltd* [2004] 2 B.C.L.C. 455 CA, a case dealing with an action for trade mark infringement, but the wording of all these statutory provisions indicates the same constraints will apply.

[97] 2006 Act s.77(1) and see below, para.4–30.

[98] 2006 Act s.64(3).

companies carrying on the same of type of business (broadly defined[99]), so that the newer company is, in effect, cashing in on the reputation of the first and appropriating its goodwill and connection. The claim in such circumstances is for the tort of passing off. The newer company will be liable in damages and may be restrained by injunction. The practical effect of such an injunction is that the offending company must either change its name[100] or dissolve itself.[101] Intention to pass off is irrelevant.[102] A similar claim can be advanced for use of another's registered trade mark.[103]

More recently, the courts have also been alert to pre-emptive strikes, whereby entrepreneurs register companies with names which existing traders or famous people may want to use in the future, and then demand inflated sums for the sale of these registered companies to the named individuals. The wrong is seen as an abuse of the registration process,[104] or the creation of potential instruments of fraud[105] (being names which can be used for passing off, although this is rarely the objective of the initial registrant).

4–26

Company names adjudicators

A passing-off action requires the claimant company to demonstrate that the new company's choice of name presents a serious threat to the claimant's business. The Company Law Review, which thought the law on names broadly satisfactory, was attracted by the idea that there should be a new statutory basis for ordering a name change, namely, that the registration constituted an abuse of the registration process (along the lines of the expanded tort claim, noted above).[106]

The Act sets up a new procedure whereby a person (including another company) may apply to a company names adjudicator,[107] apparently at any time, for an order that a company's name must be changed because it is either the same as a name associated with the applicant and in which the applicant has goodwill or it is sufficiently similar to such a name that its use in the UK would be likely to mislead by suggesting a connection between the respondent company and the

4–27

---

[99] See *Burge v Haycock* [2001] EWCA Civ 900; [2002] R.P.C. 28 on the breadth of the interests protected.

[100] The company must change its name itself; the court cannot order the Registrar to change the company's name. Similarly, see (above) para.4–24, and (below) para.4–28.

[101] See, e.g. *Tussaud v Tussaud* (1890) 44 Ch.D. 678 (an injunction was ordered preventing a member of the Tussaud family from registering Louis Tussaud Ltd to carry on a waxworks show, although the court would not restrain an individual from trading under his or her own surname); *Panhard et Levassor v Panhard Levassor Motor Co* [1901] 2 Ch. 513; *Exxon Corp v Exxon Insurance Consultants International Ltd* [1982] Ch. 119.

[102] *British Diabetic Association v Diabetic Society Ltd* [1995] 4 All E.R. 812.

[103] *Baume and Co Ltd v AH Moore Ltd* [1958] R.P.C. 226; *Parker-Knoll Ltd v Knoll International Ltd* [1962] R.P.C. 243.

[104] *Glaxo Plc v Glaxowellcome Ltd* [1996] F.S.R. 388; *Direct Line Group Ltd v Direct Line Estate Agency Ltd* [1997] F.S.R. 374.

[105] *British Telecommunications Plc v One In A Million Ltd* [1999] 1 W.L.R. 903 (which concerned registration of an internet domain name, not a company name, but the principle is the same).

[106] Completing, para.8.30.

[107] Appointed by the Secretary of State: s.70.

applicant.[108] The mechanism thus aids the applicant in protecting its goodwill in a name. If either condition is made out, then the applicant will succeed unless the respondent company can bring itself within one of five categories.[109]

The first is that its name was registered before the commencement of the activities upon which the applicant relies to show goodwill. This does not necessarily mean the respondent has to have been registered first. For example, the applicant may have been registered first but may have remained dormant until after the respondent was registered, and in such a case the respondent would be able to bring itself within this category.

The second is that the respondent company is operating under the name, or has formerly operated under it and is now dormant, or is proposing to operate under it and has incurred substantial start-up costs. This is an important defence for the respondent because it means that operating under the name (or even incurring substantial costs in preparation for so doing) protects the respondent (subject to the qualification set out below) against the requirement to change its name.

Thirdly, the respondent shows that the name was registered in the ordinary course of a company formation business and is available for sale to the applicant on the standard terms of that business. In this case the applicant can solve its problem by simply buying the respondent company for a modest sum.

The fourth category is that the respondent acted in good faith and the fifth that the interests of the applicant have not been affected to any significant extent. In the first three cases, however, the applicant will succeed in any event if it shows that the respondent's main purpose was to obtain money or other benefits from the applicant or to prevent the applicant from registering the name.[110] Thus, beginning to operate will not protect the respondent from the applicant's challenge if the main purpose of the respondent's activity was to extort a large sum of money from the applicant in exchange for giving up its rights to the name.

4–28   If the adjudicator upholds the complaint, an order must be made requiring the respondent to change its name to an acceptable one and to take all steps within its power to achieve that end, including not forming another company with a similar offending name.[111] The adjudicator's order may be enforced in the same way as an order of the High Court (or decree of the Court of Session)[112] and, if the name is not changed by the respondent within the specified time, the adjudicator can effect the change.[113] There is an appeal to a court from the adjudicator's decision.[114]

---

[108] 2006 Act s.69(1).

[109] 2006 Act s.69(4).

[110] 2006 Act s.69(5).

[111] 2006 Act s.73(1). Although the company is the primary respondent, the applicant may make its directors or members respondents as well (s.69(3)), which will be important for the range of persons caught by the adjudicator's order.

[112] 2006 Act s.73(3)—including therefore by way of an order for contempt of court.

[113] 2006 Act s.73(4). Thus avoiding the problem which arose in *Halifax Plc v Halifax Repossessions Ltd* [2004] 2 B.C.L.C. 455 CA, where, after a successful trade mark infringement and passing-off action, the court was held to have no power of its own motion to alter the defendant company's name but only to order the shareholders to secure such a change.

[114] 2006 Act s.74.

Even if the applicant fails under this statutory procedure, a common law claim in passing off remains open. Indeed, the statutory defences effectively demarcate the circumstances in which the additional hurdles imposed in advancing a successful common law claim are seen as warranted (see especially the second and fourth defences, which exempt from the statutory procedure occasions which do not of themselves suggest the respondent is abusing the registration process, but which may nevertheless fall foul of the tort of passing off).

4–29

Company's election to change its name

As noted earlier, a company may, in general, change its name by special resolution or by other procedures specified in its articles.[115] If the change also reflects a change in the company's status (from private to public, for example), then additional rules apply, as described below.[116]

4–30

Effect of a name change

On a change of name, whether voluntarily or because of a direction,[117] the Registrar must be notified and will enter the new name on the register in place of the old and issue an amended certificate of incorporation.[118] The change is effective from the date on which that certificate is issued.[119] But the company remains the same corporate body and the change does not affect any of its rights or obligations or render defective any legal proceedings by or against it.[120]

4–31

CHOICE OF APPROPRIATE ARTICLES

The next decisions relate to the company's constitution, especially the company's articles of association. As noted in the previous chapter, the company's articles are especially important because they, not the general law, provide many of the rules governing the internal operation of the company. The legislature has provided model versions,[121] and the promoters must determine the extent to which the appropriate model is ousted or adopted (whether explicitly or by default).[122] Company formation agents normally have their own standard forms, which formally exclude the model altogether, though these standard forms are themselves typically developed from the statutory model and its predecessors. The other extreme, the option of not registering any articles and relying entirely

4–32

---

[115] 2006 Act s.77(1) and see below, para.4–31.

[116] See paras 4–39 et seq.

[117] 2006 Act s.77.

[118] 2006 Act s.80.

[119] 2006 Act s.81(1).

[120] 2006 Act s.81(2),(3). Hence contracts entered into prematurely under the new name will not be pre-incorporation contracts on which the individual who acted will be personally liable (see paras 5–24 et seq.).

[121] See above, para.3–14.

[122] See above, para.3–15.

on the model,[123] is rarely chosen because most companies will wish to define their own rules. For example, the model articles for private companies limited by shares give the directors a discretion to refuse to register share transfers,[124] but the incorporators are likely to want more elaborate provisions, such as ones requiring the shares to be offered to existing shareholders if a member wishes to sell.

4–33   A significant change under the 2006 Act was the downgrading to a vestigial role of the memorandum of association, which, under the procedures introduced in the early days of modern company law, had contained the most important information about the company and had, originally, been largely unalterable after the registration of the company.[125] Under the 2006 Act the memorandum, which must still be delivered to the Registrar as a necessary step in the formation process,[126] simply has to state that the subscribers to it (of whom there need only be one)[127] wish to form a company under the Act and agree to become members of the company upon its formation and, in the case of a company having a share capital, agree to take at least one share each.[128] The memorandum has to be authenticated by each subscriber,[129] the Registrar being empowered to specify the method of authentication, but not in such a way as to impede electronic delivery of the memorandum (and the other registration documents) to the Registrar.[130]

CHALLENGING THE CERTIFICATE OF INCORPORATION

4–34   The functions of the Registrar in deciding whether or not to register the company are administrative, rather than judicial, but a refusal to register can be challenged by judicial review, albeit with scant hope of success.[131] Normally, the registration of a company cannot be challenged because of the conclusive effect of the certificate. This, happily, has rendered English company law virtually immune from the problems arising from defectively incorporated companies which have plagued the US and many continental countries.[132] But the decided cases on

---

[123] 2006 Act s.9(5)(b).

[124] Companies (Model Articles) Regulations 2008 Sch.1 art.26.

[125] The CLR had recommended that the memorandum be abolished entirely (Final Report I, para.9.4) but this was thought in some quarters, oddly, to raise the question of whether it was intended to alter the nature of the company as an incorporated association. Hence, apparently, the vestigial role for the memorandum.

[126] 2006 Act s.9(1).

[127] 2006 Act s.7(1).

[128] 2006 Act s.8(1). 2006 Act s.112(1) deems the subscribers to have agreed to become members of the company and provides that, upon registration of the company, they do become members of it.

[129] 2006 Act s.8. Bizarrely, for such a simple document, the memorandum is required to be in the prescribed form, and very straightforward forms are prescribed for companies with and without share capital respectively, in Schs 1 and 2 to the Registration Regulations.

[130] 2006 Act s.1068(3),(5).

[131] R. v Registrar of Joint Stock Companies [1931] 2 K.B. 197 CA where an application for mandamus to order the Registrar to register a company formed for the sale in England of tickets in the Irish Hospital Lottery was rejected on the ground that the Registrar had rightly concluded that such sales were illegal in England.

[132] See R. Drury, "Nullity of Companies in English Law" (1985) 48 M.L.R. 644. The First Company Law Directive contains three Articles dealing with nullity.

s.15(4) (or its predecessors under earlier Acts), and the review of them by the Court of Appeal[133] in a case concerning the then comparable provision relating to a certificate of registration of a charge on a company's property, show that this immunity is not complete.

Since s.15 and its predecessors in earlier Companies Acts are not expressed to bind the Crown, the Attorney-General can apply to the court and may obtain certiorari to quash the registration.[134] This was successfully done in *R. v Registrar of Companies, Ex p. HM's Attorney-General*,[135] where a prostitute had succeeded in incorporating her business under the name of "Lindi St Claire (Personal Services) Ltd" (the Registrar having rejected her first preference of "Prostitutes Ltd" or "Hookers Ltd" and shown no enthusiasm for "Lindi St Claire (French Lessons) Ltd") and, with scrupulous frankness, she specified its primary object in the constitution as being "to carry on the business of prostitution".[136] The court, on judicial review at the instance of the Attorney-General, quashed the registration on the ground that the stated business was unlawful as contrary to public policy.[137] It is unlikely, however, that the Attorney-General (or any other Crown servant) will take action unless public policy is thought to be involved and will not do so if all that has occurred is a technical breach of the formalities of incorporation.

4–35

Nevertheless, there is one other situation in which the certificate does not seem to be conclusive of valid incorporation. This results from what is now s.10(3) of the Trade Union and Labour Relations (Consolidation) Act 1992 (repeating similar provisions in earlier Acts) which declares that the registration of a trade union under the Companies Acts shall be void. In the past, parties other than the Crown have been held entitled to rely on this; for example, as a defence to a claim by a registered company whose objects make it a trade union. The reported cases[138] related to earlier versions of what is now s.15(4), which were less comprehensive and which were not thought to cover substantive matters but only ministerial acts leading to registration.[139] Hence, it seems doubtful that they would be followed

4–36

---

[133] *R. v Registrar of Companies, Ex p. Central Bank of India* [1986] Q.B. 1114 CA. Reversing the decision at first instance, the Court of Appeal held that, even on judicial review, the effect of s.98(2) of the Companies Act 1948, under which the certificate of registration of a charge was "conclusive evidence that the requirements as to registration have been satisfied", was to make evidence of non-compliance inadmissible, thus precluding the court from quashing the registration.

[134] *Bowman v Secular Society* [1917] A.C. 406 HL where, however certiorari was denied as the Society's purposes were held not to be unlawful.

[135] *R. v Registrar of Companies, Ex p. HM's Attorney-General* [1991] B.C.L.C. 476.

[136] Had she been less frank, for example by stating the primary object as "to carry on the business of masseuses and to provide related services", she would probably have got away with it.

[137] Notwithstanding that, as she indignantly protested, she paid income tax on her earnings. Since prostitution can be carried on without necessarily committing any criminal offence and since she continued, without incorporation, to practise her profession (for which she has become a well-known spokeswoman), some may think that this was an example of the "unruly horse" of public policy unseating its judicial riders.

[138] *Edinburgh & District Water Manufacturers Association v Jenkinson* (1903) 5 Sessions Cases 1159; *British Association of Glass Bottle Manufacturers v Nettlefold* (1911) 27 T.L.R. 527 (where, however, the company was held not to be a trade union).

[139] *British Association of Glass Bottle Manufacturers*, fn.138 above, at 529.

today. However, the researches of Mr Drury[140] have unearthed a more recent example of a company's removal from the register because its objects made it a trade union. The company in question was one formed by junior hospital doctors to represent their interests. It was later realised that its objects made it a trade union within the statutory definition. The Department of Trade took the view that the labour law provision overrode what is now s.15(4) of the Companies Act and accordingly the Registrar removed the company from the register for "void registration".[141] This, apparently, was done without any court order[142] and without challenge by the doctors. Presumably this action by the Registrar could be regarded as having been taken on behalf of the Crown and as the correction of a mistake which he, or one of his predecessors, had made and therefore as rectifiable.[143]

4–37 Hence, it now seems probable, but not certain, that in no circumstances can anyone other than the Crown plead the nullity of a registered company unless and until it has been removed from the register as a result of action by or on behalf of the Crown. Removal as a result of that action is tantamount to a declaration that it never existed as a corporate body. This is not likely to be a satisfactory outcome if it has in fact been carrying on business under the guise of what both its members and its creditors believed to be a registered company; it should be wound up[144] rather than declared never to have existed.[145]

COMMENCEMENT OF BUSINESS

4–38 From the date of registration mentioned in the certificate of incorporation, the company, if it is a private company, becomes "capable of exercising all the functions of an incorporated company".[146] However, it may choose not to do so. Indeed, in the case of a shelf company it is inherent in the arrangement that the company will remain dormant and begin trading only some time after registration. In the case of a public company, there is in any event a further legal obstacle to its beginning trading. It needs to obtain a further certificate from the Registrar (a "trading certificate") certifying that the amount of its allotted share capital is not less than the required minimum.[147] Without it, the public company must not do business or exercise any borrowing powers unless it has re-registered

---

[140] Drury, "Nullity of Companies in English Law" (1985) 48 M.L.R. 644 at 649–650.

[141] See *Companies in 1976*, Table 10.

[142] Notwithstanding that the First Company Law Directive provides by art.11.1(a) that "Nullity must be ordered by a decision of a court of law".

[143] But, presumably, unless the company agreed, he could not take this action unless the incorporation was void (as in the case of a trade union or where the purposes were unlawful), rather than voidable (which would seem to be the case where, for example, registration had been secured by fraudulent misrepresentations).

[144] But as what? As a registered company, which it ostensibly is? Or as an unregistered company under Pt V of the Insolvency Act 1986?

[145] As the First Directive appears to envisage: see art.12.2.

[146] 2006 Act s.16(3).

[147] 2006 Act s.761. This is discussed further at para.11–8. In the more usual case where original registration was as a private company but it later converts to a public one, similar requirements will first have to be met, but there is no suspension of business during the process of conversion.

as a private company. The certificate of trading is "conclusive evidence that the company is entitled to do business and exercise any borrowing powers".[148] However, by analogy with the decisions referred to above in relation to the certificate of incorporation, it appears that, as this section is not expressed to bind the Crown, the Registrar's decision could be quashed on judicial review at the instance of the Attorney-General. This, in contrast with quashing registration, would not have the undesirable effect of nullifying the incorporation. A more likely course, however, would be for the Secretary of State, if he had grounds for suspecting that the share capital had not been properly allotted, to institute an investigation[149] and, if his suspicions proved well-founded, petition the court to wind up the company under ss.124 or 124A of the Insolvency Act.

RE-REGISTRATION OF AN EXISTING COMPANY

A company may, at some stage, wish to convert itself into a company of a different type. In most cases it may do this without the expense of effecting a complete re-organisation of the types referred to in Ch.29, below, and without having to form a brand new company. The circumstances and methods whereby conversions may be achieved are now collected together in Pt 7 of the Act (although, as not every possible option is covered, some conversions may have to be done in two steps).

4–39

(i) Private company becoming public

Under ss.90–96 a private company limited by shares can become re-registered as a public company, by passing a special resolution that it should be so re-registered, satisfying three conditions and then making application to the Registrar.[150] The three conditions all relate to the legal capital rules which apply in a much more onerous way to public than to private companies. In brief they are, first, that the nominal value of the company's allotted share capital must be not less than the authorised minimum (currently £50,000) and the associated rules as to the payment for those shares must have been met.[151] Secondly, the company must produce unqualified recent accounts which show, as certified by the auditor, that its net assets (assets less liabilities) are not less than the aggregate of its called-up share capital and undistributable reserves.[152] Although there is no precisely equivalent rule applying to public companies on formation, this will be the factual situation before a company formed as public begins to trade.[153] Thirdly, if the company allots shares in the period after the accounts just mentioned were drawn up and before the special resolution is passed and those

4–40

---

[148] 2006 Act s.763(4).
[149] See Ch.18.
[150] 2006 Act s.90(1).
[151] 2006 Act s.91. See Ch.11, below.
[152] 2006 Act s.92. Note that this is not a rule about minimum capital but about the relationship between the company's net assets and the legal capital it has chosen to raise.
[153] All that s.831 provides is that a public company which is not in this position cannot make a distribution to its members.

shares were issued wholly or partly other than for cash, then the rules applicable to non-cash consideration received by a public company have been complied with.[154]

If the Registrar is satisfied on the above matters on the basis of the documents the company is required to include in its application to re-register,[155] then the company shall be re-registered as a public company, with an amended certificate of incorporation,[156] the alterations in the articles take effect, and the company becomes a public company.[157] In effect, the certificate is a combined certificate of incorporation and trading certificate which would have been needed had the company been initially registered as a public company.

Since it is more common for a public company to be formed by conversion from private status than by direct formation as a public company, the above rules are of some importance.

If the private company which wishes to convert to a public one is an unlimited company it will have to become limited, that being one of the essential elements of the definition of a public company. This it is enabled to do in the conversion operation—and rather more simply than if it first re-registered as limited under (iv) below, and subsequently re-registered as a public company. It merely has to add to the special resolution the necessary changes to its articles.[158]

(ii) Public company becoming private limited company

4–41   To convert from public to private (an operation which must not be confused with ceasing to have securities traded on a public market, which does not necessarily involve any change in the company's status under the Act, or with "privatisation" in the sense of de-nationalisation) is comparatively simple unless there is disagreement among the members. The company can convert to a private company limited by shares or by guarantee[159] by passing a special resolution making the necessary alterations in its name and its articles and applying, in the prescribed form, to the Registrar.[160] But special safeguards are prescribed since loss of public status may have adverse consequences for the members, especially as regards their ability to dispose of their shares. Hence, members who have not consented to, or voted in favour of, the resolution can, within 28 days of the resolution, apply to the court for the cancellation of the resolution if they can muster the support of:

---

[154] 2006 Act s.93. In addition, the rules requiring independent valuation of transfers of non-cash assets to a public company in the "initial period" (see para.11–16) apply to a company re-registered as public, but with the members of the company being substituted for the subscribers to the memorandum as the persons in respect of whom the rule applies (see s.603(a) and para.5–3). These rules apply after re-registration and so are not a condition of it.

[155] 2006 Act s.94 (including a statement of proposed secretary, if the company does not already have one, which, as a private company, it was not required to: ss.94(1)(b) and 95).

[156] Which is conclusive evidence that the requirements have been met: s.96(5). On "conclusiveness", see paras 4–34 et seq., above.

[157] 2006 Act s.96.

[158] 2006 Act s.90(4).

[159] For obvious reasons it cannot, by this simple process, convert to an unlimited company: s.97(1).

[160] 2006 Act s.97.

(a)   holders of not less than 5 per cent in nominal value of the company's share
      capital or any class of it; or

(b)   if the company is not limited by shares,[161] not less than 5 per cent of the
      members; or

(c)   not less than 50 members.[162]

The Registrar must not issue a new certificate of incorporation until the 28 days
have expired without an application having been made or, if it has been made,
until it has been withdrawn or dismissed and a copy of the court order delivered
to the Registrar.[163] The court has broad powers to cancel or confirm the
resolution, on such terms and conditions as it thinks fit, including ordering the
company to purchase the shares of any members.[164] Thus, the court may grant
dissenting shareholders an exit right rather than require them to accept the
company's change of status. Unless the court cancels the resolution, the Registrar
issues a new certificate of incorporation with the usual conclusive consequences.[165]

A public company will have to re-register as a private company if, under s.648,[166]   **4–42**
the court makes an order confirming the reduction of its capital which has the
effect of reducing the nominal amount of its allotted share capital below "the
authorised minimum". In such circumstances that order will not be registered and
come into effect (unless the court otherwise directs) until the company is
re-registered as a private company.[167] The court may (and, in practice will)
authorise this to be done through an expedited procedure without the need to
resort to the provisions just discussed. Instead of the company having to pass a
special resolution, the court will specify in the order the alterations to be made in
the articles and, on application in the prescribed form the Registrar will issue the
new certificate of incorporation. In this case there can be no application to the
court by dissenting members since the company has no option but to become
private.

(iii)   Private or public limited company becoming unlimited

The conversion which presents the greatest dangers to the members is, obviously,   **4–43**
that from a limited company to an unlimited one. Nevertheless, it is not
completely banned since the members may legitimately conclude that forfeiting
the advantages of limited liability is worthwhile, as enabling them to operate with

---

[161] The category (b) of objectors is somewhat puzzling since, until the Registrar issues a new
certificate, the company remains a public company which it could not be unless it had a share capital.
Presumably (b) is to cater for an "old public company" which has still not re-registered under the
transitional provisions, now in the Companies Consolidation (Consequential Provisions) Act 1985
ss.1–9. As there can now be few, if any, such companies that have not re-registered under the
transitional provisions either as Plcs or as private companies, this book ignores them.
[162] 2006 Act s.98.
[163] 2006 Act s.97(2).
[164] 2006 Act s.98(3)–(6).
[165] 2006 Act s.101.
[166] See para.13–34, below.
[167] 2006 Act ss.650–651.

much the same flexibility (particularly as regards withdrawal of their capital) and privacy of their financial affairs as a partnership, while yet retaining all the advantages of corporate personality other than limited liability. Hence, the Act provides that a limited company may re-register as an unlimited company if *all* the members agree.[168] The one condition which must be met is that the private company has not previously been re-registered as limited,[169] or the public company has not previously been re-registered as either limited or unlimited.[170] As with other conversions, an application, in the prescribed form, has to be lodged with the Registrar, together with supporting documents.[171] Those documents must contain a statement by the directors of the company that the persons by or on whose behalf the application form is authenticated constitute the whole of the membership of the company and that, in the case of authentication through an agent, the directors have taken all reasonable steps to satisfy themselves that the agent was authorised to act on behalf of the member.[172] The Registrar then issues a new certificate of incorporation with the usual conclusive effect.[173]

Ban on vacillation between limited and unlimited

4–44   What a company is not permitted to do is to chop and change more than once between limited and unlimited. Once a limited company has been re-registered as unlimited it cannot again re-register as a public company[174] or as a private limited company.[175] Once an unlimited company has been re-registered as a limited company, it cannot be re-registered as an unlimited company, whether it was immediately before the second attempted re-registration a private[176] or a public[177] limited company. There is, however, no ban on switching back and forth between private limited company and public limited company status.

(iv)   Unlimited company becoming a private limited company

4–45   In this, the converse of case (iii), it is not the members who need special safeguards but the creditors. Surprisingly, however, under the provisions under which this conversion is effected the only protection afforded them is that the new suffix, "Ltd", to the company's name should alert them to the fact that it has become a limited company. Their real protection is afforded by what is now s.77 of the Insolvency Act 1986. The effect of this is that those who were members of the company at the time of its re-registration remain potentially liable in respect of its debts and liabilities contracted prior thereto if winding up commences

---

[168] 2006 Act s.102(1)(a) for private companies and s.109(1)(a) for public companies.
[169] 2006 Act s.102(2).
[170] 2006 Act s.109(2).
[171] 2006 Act s.102(1)(c) and s.109(1)(c) for private and public companies respectively.
[172] 2006 Act s.103(4) and s.110(4).
[173] 2006 Act s.104 and s.111.
[174] 2006 Act s.90(2)(e).
[175] 2006 Act s.105(2).
[176] 2006 Act s.102(2).
[177] 2006 Act s.109(2).

within three years of the re-registration. The Act permits re-registration as a private limited company, whether limited by shares or by guarantee, so long as the company has not previously been re-registered as limited. As far as the members are concerned the crucial requirement is the passing of a special resolution stating which of these the company is to be and making the necessary alterations to its name and articles.[178]

(v)   Becoming or ceasing to be a community interest company

A limited company, whether limited by shares or guarantee and whether public or private, may convert to a community interest company.[179] This step requires a special resolution of the members, making the probably quite extensive changes to its constitution which are necessary for this purpose,[180] and the approval of the Regulator of Community Interest Companies, who needs to be satisfied that the company satisfies the community interest test.[181] However, a CIC cannot simply revert to not being a CIC. Unless it opts to be dissolved, the CIC's choices are limited to becoming a charity or a registered society.[182] Otherwise, the constraints on distributions to members by a CIC could be easily avoided by shedding that status.

4–46

CONCLUSION

Despite the potential problems caused by the company names rules, the process of registration of a company in the UK is both speedy and cheap. The rules on changing company status are not complex either, despite their detail, although they are probably used on a large scale only for transfer from private limited to public limited status and vice versa.

4–47

---

[178] 2006 Act s.105.
[179] 2006 Act s.37 of the Companies (Audit, Investigations and Community Enterprise) Act 2004. Being limited is a necessary part of the definition of a CIC: s.26. However, if the company wishing to convert to CIC status is unlimited, it can first become limited under (iv) above. More important in this respect is the prohibition on a CIC re-registering as an unlimited company: s.52(1).
[180] See paras 1–7 and 1–10.
[181] 2006 Act s.38(2).
[182] 2006 Act s.53.

CHAPTER 5

PRE-INCORPORATION AND INITIAL CORPORATE CONTRACTING

INTRODUCTION

In the earlier chapters we examined the advantages of incorporation, the **5–1** processes for achieving that status, and the various sources of rules regulating the corporate form once created.[1] And in later chapters we look in detail at the law as it applies to companies, paying particular attention to the sources of a company's capital and the various constraints on its use,[2] as well as the legal constraints on the powers exercised by the company's management, especially by its directors.[3] All these various legal rules are designed to ensure that the company is run as a success, thus enabling the company's shareholders, creditors and other stakeholders to prosper.

    Extensive though these rules are, they leave a window of time which is potentially unregulated. This is the period during which individuals with good ideas for a new business set to work on creating a company and bringing it into existence ready to do business. This may seem a relatively unimportant time in the scheme of things, especially now that buying a company off the shelf makes the process so quick.[4] But two particular problems are common. The first is the intuitive concern with the probity of transactions between the newly formed company buying assets, for example, from the very people who set the company up and determine its first steps. The risk is that these deals overly advantage the originators, or "promoters", at the expense of the company and those persuaded to become its members. Secondly, there is the practical problem of how a

---

[1] See Chs 1–4.
[2] See Chs 11–13, 24–25, 31.
[3] See especially Ch.16, but also Chs 15 and 19.
[4] See para.4–9, and here using "off the shelf" to refer to the modern direct electronic registration, including by promoters themselves.

company not yet in existence can enter into contracts which bind the company once it is formed. In agency terms, this is a case where the principal is not "undisclosed" (indeed, its expected genesis is usually made clear), but is "non-existent" at the time of the deal. This too may seem an unlikely problem, but it is sometimes (although increasingly rarely) simply the case that a time-sensitive opportunity presents itself before the company can be formed, and yet those involved do not want to be personally liable; they want—for all the reasons we have already considered—to have the deal pursued under a corporate umbrella.

We take each problem in turn. They raise quite different issues, the first dealt with primarily by the common law, the second by a combination of the common law and statute.

"PROMOTERS" AND THEIR DEALINGS WITH THE COMPANY

Meaning of "promoter"

5–2   Much of the current law on promoters emerged in the nineteenth century, when there were no restrictions on inviting the public to subscribe for shares in newly formed companies, and the caricature "company promoter" was an individual of dubious repute who made it his profession to form bogus companies and foist them off on a gullible public, to the latter's detriment and his own profit. But even in those days a much more typical example was the village grocer who converted his business into a limited company.[5] The motivations of each might be different, and the grocer less likely than the professional to abuse his position since he can be expected to remain the majority shareholder in his company, whereas the promoter, if a shareholder at all, usually intends to off-load his holdings onto others as soon as possible. But both create, or help to create, the company, and seek to sell it something, whether it be their services or a business. Both are well-placed to take advantage of their position by obtaining a recompense grossly in excess of the true value of what they are selling.[6] For that reason it has long been held that both should be subjected to rather onerous common law and equitable duties, given the power that they wield over the company. The parallels with the rules applying to directors of companies already in existence will be clear when we come to consider those rules.[7]

5–3   But who should be subject to such tough rules? Both the professional promoter and the village grocer are promoters to the fullest extent, in that each "undertakes to form a company with reference to a given project, and to set it going and takes the necessary steps to accomplish that purpose".[8] But a person who has taken a much less active and dominating role may also be a promoter. Indeed, the potential activities of promoters are so varied that no comprehensive definition has ever been formulated, beyond confining it to activities related to bringing a

---

[5] Or a bootmaker: see the discussion of *Salomon v Salomon & Co Ltd* [1897] A.C. 22 HL, at paras 2–1 et seq.

[6] e.g. *Re Darby* [1911] 1 K.B. 95.

[7] See below, Ch.16.

[8] Per Cockburn CJ in *Twycross v Grant* (1877) 2 C.P.D. 469 at 541 CA.

company into existence.[9] The expression may, for example, cover any individual or company that arranges for someone to become a director, places shares, or negotiates preliminary agreements.[10] Nor need he or she necessarily be associated with the initial formation of the company; one who subsequently helps to arrange the "floating off" of its capital (in the manner explained in Ch.25) will equally be regarded as a promoter.[11] On the other hand, those who act in a purely ministerial capacity, such as solicitors and accountants, will not be classified as promoters merely because they undertake their normal professional duties[12]; although they may if, for example, they have agreed to become directors or to find others who will.[13]

Who constitutes a promoter in any particular case is therefore a question of fact,[14] and the promoter's role continues until the particular functions of promotion come to an end.[15] The expression has never been clearly defined either judicially[16] or legislatively, despite the fact that it is frequently used both in decisions and statutes; this vagueness is apt to be embarrassing when legislation requires promoters to be named or transactions with them to be disclosed.[17]

5–4

In many ways the risks of promotion are now lower. In private companies the rules very easily merge with those applying to corporate directors, since in this context the promoter usually becomes, and was always intended to become, a director of the newly formed company. And, as far as public companies are concerned, these days, promoters cannot simply invite the public to subscribe for shares in any proposed new venture: only a public company can invite the public to subscribe for shares, and before a public company is listed on the Main Market of the Stock Exchange or quoted on the Alternative Investment Market, it must be able to show some track record. Consequently, here too the duties of the promoters are often swallowed up in such cases in those of the directors.[18] But corporate promotion continues, even if on a smaller scale, and indeed more

5–5

---

[9] *Whaley Bridge Calico Printing Co v Green* (1880) 5 Q.B.D. 109 at 111 (Bowen J).

[10] cf. *Bagnall v Carlton* (1877) 6 Ch.D. 371 CA; *Emma Silver Mining Co v Grant* (1879) 11 Ch.D. 918 CA; *Whaley Bridge Calico Printing Co v Green* (1880) 5 Q.B.D. 109; *Lydney & Wigpool Iron Ore Co v Bird* (1886) 33 Ch.D. 85 CA; *Mann v Edinburgh Northern Tramways Co* [1893] A.C. 69 HL; *Jubilee Cotton Mills v Lewis* [1924] A.C. 958 HL; and cases cited below.

[11] *Lagunas Nitrate Co v Lagunas Syndicate* [1899] 2 Ch. 392 at 428 CA.

[12] *Re Great Wheal Polgooth Co* (1883) 53 L.J. Ch. 42; *Houghton v Saunders* [2015] 2 N.Z.L.R. 74.

[13] *Lydney & Wigpool Iron Ore Co v Bird* (1886) 33 Ch.D. 85 CA; *Bagnall v Carlton* (1877) 6 Ch.D. 371 CA.

[14] See J.H. Gross (1970) 86 L.Q.R. 493.

[15] As they will when the directors are appointed and take over the management: per Cockburn CJ in *Twycross v Grant* (1877) 2 C.P.D. 469 at 541 CA.

[16] For attempts, in addition to Cockburn CJ's description (above), see those of Lindley J in *Emma Silver Mining Co v Lewis* (1879) 4 C.P.D. 396 at 407; and of Bowen J in *Whaley Bridge Calico Printing Co v Green* (1880) 5 Q.B.D. 109 at 111.

[17] e.g. under s.762(1)(c) (in relation to obtaining a trading certificate: see para.4–38, above). EU law seems to prefer the term "founders" which is not really any clearer: Commission Regulation 809/2004 of 29 April 2004 (the Prospectus Regulation) Annex I, para.14.1.

[18] As pointed out in Ch.25, the handling of public issues is now virtually monopolised by investment bankers whose activities are highly regulated, often by reference to standards set these days by EU law.

recently there has been an increase in public offers of unlisted shares, including shares in new start-up ventures, so the law on promoters may become increasingly important again.

Duties of promoters

5–6 The problems which must be dealt with are clear. Promoters are in a particularly advantaged position to sell their own assets or services to the company at an inflated price; to mislead likely investors into buying shares in the new company; and, once that is done, perhaps to induce the company to confirm that all is proper, and any breach might be waived.

(a) Statutory rules

5–7 The early Companies Acts contained no provisions regarding the liabilities of promoters, and current legislation remains largely silent on the subject, merely imposing liability for untrue statements in listing particulars or prospectuses to which they are parties.[19] Since these rules apply only to public offers and not to company formations unaccompanied by a public offer or the introduction of the securities to a public market, discussion of them is postponed to Ch.25.

5–8 There are also statutory rules relating to sales of assets to public companies. Article 11 of the Second Company Law Directive was intended to ensure that, when a public company acquired a substantial non-cash asset[20] from its promoters within two years of its entitlement to commence business, an independent valuation of that asset and approval by the company in general meeting should be required. But, as we shall see,[21] as implemented by the UK this applies only to acquisitions from the subscribers to the memorandum, who need not be the true promoters and generally are not. However, when a private company re-registers as a public one (a more common occurrence than initial formation as a public company) a similar requirement applies to such acquisitions from anyone who was a member on the date of re-registration,[22] and that may well catch a promoter. This, therefore, affords an additional statutory protection against the risk that promoters will seek to off-load their property to the company at an inflated price, but one which can be avoided by the promoters ceasing to be members prior to the re-registration.

5–9 Finally, if the promoter exchanges his or her own assets for shares, then there are also statutory rules designed to prevent issues of shares at a discount. But these

---

[19] FSMA 2000 s.90 (see para.25–32). But note s.90(8) which makes it clear that in respect of the duty of disclosure a promoter is in no worse position than any other person responsible for the prospectus.
[20] One for which the consideration paid by the company was equal to one-tenth or more of the company's issued share capital.
[21] 2006 Act s.598. See para.11–17, below.
[22] 2006 Act s.603(a).

too are focused on public companies rather than private ones, where it is largely left to the common law and equitable rules to regulate the problem.[23]

(b)   Common law and equitable rules

Thus, in the main, promoters' duties have been developed by the courts. Promoters are of course subject to the general law on fraud, misrepresentation, negligence, unjust enrichment, and so on, and in the right context these duties can be important. But their most significant duties are equitable. In a series of cases in the last quarter of the nineteenth century, the courts were alert to the possibilities of abuse inherent in the promoter's position, and thus determined that promoters stand in a fiduciary position towards the company,[24] with all the duties of disclosure and accounting which that implies. These fiduciary restrictions profoundly affect three particular contexts: unless promoters obtain the fully informed consent of the company, they cannot enter into any sale or purchase transactions with the company (the conflict between their personal interest in the transaction and their duty to obtain the best price for the company is obvious), or be remunerated, or take commissions from third parties (absent consent, these both constitute secret profits). These fiduciary duties have not been restated in the 2006 Act, as directors' fiduciary duties have been,[25] and so they remain regulated by the common law. However, the two sets of rules are likely to continue to influence each other, and the detail of promoters' duties and their application can be gleaned from the analogous cases concerning directors.[26]

5–10

(c)   Full disclosure and consent

The main difficulty with promoters' fiduciary duties has been deciding how to effect proper disclosure to, and obtain approval from, the company—the company being an artificial entity. As we will see later, the powers of the company are generally exercised by the board of directors or (where that is not possible or where otherwise agreed) by the shareholders in general meeting.[27] But adopting either option typically raises a very real practical problem: voting may in either case be dominated by the promoter, thus allowing the promoter to be judge in his or her own cause. That does not seem right, and here, as elsewhere, the courts have struggled towards an effective solution to the problem.[28]

5–11

---

[23] See below, paras 11–15 et seq.; and 2006 Act ss.593 et seq. Contrast that with the situation in *Salomon v Salomon & Co Ltd* [1897] A.C. 22 HL, discussed at paras 2–5 et seq.

[24] *Erlanger v New Sombrero Phosphate Co* (1878) 3 App.Cas. 1218 HL 1236 (Lord Cairns). Since the duty is owed to the company, any action against the promoters must be taken by the company, not by its members: *Foss v Harbottle* (1843) 2 Hare 461, 489.

[25] See Ch.16, below. Since promoters can adopt very different roles, their particular duties and liabilities require close examination of the facts: *Lydney and Wigpool Iron Ore Co v Bird* (1886) 33 Ch.D. 85, 93; *Ladywell Mining Co v Brookes* (1887) 35 Ch.D. 400, 407 and 411, per Cotton LJ.

[26] See Ch.16.

[27] See paras 14–1 et seq.

[28] See paras 16–117 et seq. (directors), 19–4 et seq. (shareholders) and 31–30 et seq. (bondholders).

5–12   The first leading case on the subject, *Erlanger v New Sombrero Phosphate Co,*[29] suggested that it was the promoter's duty to ensure that the company had an independent board of directors and to make full disclosure to it. In that case Lord Cairns said[30] that the promoters of a company:

> "stand undoubtedly in a fiduciary position. They have in their hands the creation and moulding of the company; they have the power of defining how, and when, and in what shape, and under what supervision, it shall start into existence and begin to act as a trading corporation . . . I do not say that the owner of property may not promote and form a joint stock company and then sell his property to it, but I do say that if he does he is bound to take care that he sells it to the company through the medium of a board of directors who can and do exercise an independent and intelligent judgment on the transaction."

5–13   Such a decision would undoubtedly be effective, but will anything less suffice? An entirely independent board would be impossible in the case of most private and many public companies, and since *Salomon v Salomon*[31] it has never been doubted that the fully informed consent of the members would be equally effective. In that famous case it was held that the liquidator of the company could not complain of the sale to it at an obvious over-valuation of Mr Salomon's business, all the members having acquiesced therein. Note, however, that in this case the shareholders' consent was unanimous, and so it might be thought irrelevant that Salomon himself held the overwhelming majority of the shares: all who could agree on the company's behalf had done so; there was no dissent. But could Salomon have carried such a vote against a unanimously opposed independent minority? Logic suggests not, yet the cases pull both ways.[32] Even the older cases saw the problem. This was evident in the speeches of the House of Lords in the second great landmark case in the development of this branch of the law, *Gluckstein v Barnes.*[33] That case made it clear that a promoter could not escape liability by disclosing to a few cronies who constituted the company's initial members, when it was the intention immediately to float off the company to the public or to induce some other dupes to purchase the shares. "It is too absurd", said Lord Halsbury with his usual bluntness:

> "to suggest that a disclosure to the parties to this transaction is a disclosure to the company. They were there by the terms of the agreement to do the work of the syndicate, that is to say, to cheat the shareholders; and this, forsooth, is to be treated as a disclosure to the company, when they were really there to hoodwink the shareholders."

The modern trend is in the same direction, and would seem to favour denying Salomon—or any other director or promoter—the right to be the person whose

---

[29] *Erlanger v New Sombrero Phosphate Co* (1878) 3 App.Cas. 1218 HL.
[30] *Erlanger v New Sombrero Phosphate Co* (1878) 3 App.Cas. 1218 at 1236 HL.
[31] *Salomon v Salomon & Co Ltd* [1897] A.C. 22 HL: see para.2–1, above. Also see *Lagunas Nitrate Co v Lagunas Syndicate* [1899] 2 Ch. 392 at 426 CA (Lindley MR).
[32] Contrast two cases on directors, admittedly in different contexts, but both involving breaches of fiduciary duty: *North-West Transportation v Beatty* (1887) 12 App.Cas. 589 PC; and *Cook v Deeks* [1916] 1 A.C. 554 PC.
[33] *Gluckstein v Barnes* [1900] A.C. 240 at 247 HL.

own votes determine the outcome of the company's decision when the question in issue is forgiveness or waiver of his own wrongs to the company.[34]

Finally, still on disclosure and consent, a number of older cases have suggested that a promoter cannot effectively contract out of his or her fiduciary duties simply by inserting a clause in the articles whereby the company and the subscribers agree to waive their rights.[35] This is clearly right if the articles purport to exclude fiduciary duties entirely, or even to consent in advance to their general waiver during the period of promotion.[36] On the other hand, if the articles provide full disclosure of the terms of a material transaction with one of the promoters, and new subscribers join the company on the basis that they confirm their consent to that arrangement, then there seems no reason at all, on general principles, why this should not meet the demands of full disclosure and informed, and indeed unanimous, consent.

5–14

Remedies for breach of promoters' duties

There are various remedies available against promoters, but the most common is for breach of their fiduciary duties: the company (to whom these duties are owed) brings proceedings for recovery of any secret profits which the promoter has made, or for rescission of contracts it has with the promoter.[37]

5–15

A promoter, being a fiduciary, is not entitled to make a secret profit. Although the promoter's profit is most likely to derive from an over-priced sale of the promoter's property to the newly formed company (as to which, see below), if a profit has been made on some ancillary transaction there is no doubt that this too may be recovered. The classic illustrations are typically bribes or secret commissions paid by third parties to the promoters for the benefit of particular privileges in future engagements with the company. But there are more complex cases too, as in *Gluckstein v Barnes*[38] itself.[39] In that case a syndicate had been formed for the purpose of buying and reselling Olympia, then owned by a company in liquidation. The syndicate first bought up at low prices certain charges on the property and then bought the freehold itself for £140,000. They then promoted a company of which they were the directors, and to it they sold the freehold for £180,000, which was raised by a public issue of shares and debentures. In the prospectus the profit of £40,000 was disclosed. But in the meantime the promoters had had the charges on the property repaid by the

5–16

---

[34] See fn.28, above. Also see S. Worthington, "Corporate Governance: Remedying and Ratifying Directors' Breaches" (2000) 116 L.Q.R. 638, since the concerns are equally applicable.

[35] *Gluckstein v Barnes* [1900] A.C. 240 HL; *Omnium Electric Palaces v Baines* [1914] 1 Ch. 322 at 347, per Sargant J. Such "waiver" clauses used to be common, apparently, and, except as regards actual misrepresentations (on which see Misrepresentation Act 1967 s.3), there is still no statutory prohibition of them: s.232 (invalidating exemption clauses) applies only to directors.

[36] *Armitage v Nurse* [1998] Ch. 241 CA.

[37] Note the critical comments in *Bentinck v Fenn* (1887) L.R. 12 App.Cas. 652 HL, where the (unsuccessful) action was pursued—inappropriately is the suggestion—by a contributor.

[38] *Gluckstein v Barnes* [1900] A.C. 240 HL. And see *Jubilee Cotton Mills v Lewis* [1924] A.C. 958 HL.

[39] See below, paras 16–86 et seq. for the analogous rules in relation to directors.

liquidator out of the £140,000 original sale price, and had thereby made a further profit of £20,000. This was not disclosed in the prospectus, though reference was made there to a contract, close scrutiny of which might have revealed that some profit had been made. Four years later the new company went into liquidation and it was held that the promoters must account to the company for this secret profit of £20,000. Alternatively, the same facts may permit the company to sue the promoter for damages for fraud (deceit),[40] or perhaps for misrepresentation.[41]

5–17   Far more common, however, is the scenario where the promoter sells his or her property to the company without proper disclosure, and the company may then rescind the contract. Rescission must be exercised on normal contractual principles[42]; that is to say, the company must have done nothing to show an intention to ratify the agreement after finding out about the non-disclosure[43] and restitutio in integrum must still be possible.[44] The restitutio requirement means the company must be in a position to return the property,[45] prima facie in its original state (although it is immaterial if it is no longer of the same value[46]) although the courts' wide discretion to order financial adjustments when directing rescission means the rule now operates as much less of an impediment.[47]

5–18   If rescission of the contract between company and promoter is no longer possible (because of delay, affirmation or inability to effect restitutio), the alternative remedy of an account of profits, designed to strip the defaulting fiduciary of the profits of the breach, is not generally allowed.[48] In principle, the court could of course assess the market value of the asset at the date of sale and on that basis force the promoter to account, but this, it has been argued, would be to make a

---

[40] *Whaley Bridge Calico Printing Co v Green* (1879) 5 Q.B.D. 109, a successful action to recover secret profits, with Bowen J noting at 110–111 that the company could alternatively have succeeded in an action for fraud.

[41] See below, para.5–20.

[42] S. Worthington, "The Proprietary Consequences of Rescission" (2002) Restitution Law Review 28–68.

[43] *Lagunas Nitrate Co v Lagunas Syndicate* [1899] 2 Ch. 392 CA. Here again "the company" must mean the members or an independent board; clearly ratification by puppet directors cannot be effective.

[44] *Re Leeds & Hanley Theatre of Varieties* [1902] 2 Ch. 809 CA; *Steedman v Frigidaire Corp* [1933] 1 D.L.R. 161 PC; *Dominion Royalty Corp v Goffatt* [1935] 1 D.L.R. 780 Ont CA; affirmed [1935] 4 D.L.R. 736 CanSC.

[45] And, even then, note the dicta in *Smith New Court Securities v Scrimgeour Vickers (Asset Management) Ltd* [1977] A.C. 254, 262 (Lord Browne-Wilkinson) suggesting that if the law denied rescission where shares had been on-sold on the market by the claimant, but an equivalent parcel could be repurchased for return to the defendant, then the law needed review. However, the orthodox position is, and as yet remains, that rescission is not available if the original asset cannot be returned: *Re Cape Breton Co* (1885) 29 Ch.D. 795 CA; affirmed sub nom. *Cavendish Bentinck v Fenn* (1887) 12 App. Cas. 652 HL; *Ladywell Mining Co v Brookes* (1887) 35 Ch.D. 400 CA.

[46] *Armstrong v Jackson* [1917] 2 K.B. 822.

[47] *Erlanger v New Sombrero Phosphate Co* (1878) 3 App. Cas. 1218 HL; *Spence v Crawford* [1939] 3 All E.R. 271 HL.

[48] *Re Ambrose Lake Tin Co* (1880) 14 Ch.D. 390 CA; *Re Cape Breton Co* (1885) 29 Ch.D. 795 CA; affirmed sub nom. *Cavendish Bentinck v Fenn* (1887) 12 App. Cas. 652 HL; *Ladywell Mining Co v Brookes* (1887) 35 Ch.D. 400 CA; *Lady Forrest (Murchison) Gold Mine* [1901] 1 Ch. 582; *Burland v Earle* [1902] A.C. 83 PC; *Jacobus Marler Estates v Marler* (1913) 85 L.J.P.C. 167n.; *Cook v Deeks* [1916] 1 A.C. 554 at 563, 564 PC; *Robinson v Randfontein Estates* [1921] A.D. 168 S.Afr.S.C.App.Div.; *P & O Steam Nav Co v Johnson* (1938) 60 C.L.R. 189 Aust. HC.

new contract for the parties.[49] The only exception, it seems, and a rare one at that,[50] arises where the very specific duties owed by the promoter at the time of the initial purchase make it possible to say that this original purchase by the promoter was, at least in equity, a purchase for the company[51]; then the re-sale by the promoter to the company is nugatory, and the company can accordingly recover the difference between the two prices as a simple secret profit made by the promoter.[52]

This restricted view of when an account of profits is available can clearly work an injustice if restitutio in integrum has become impossible, and the company then seems to have no remedy against its defaulting promoter. In practice, the courts have avoided this injustice by upholding other remedies against the promoter, either finding that the promoter was fraudulent, and accordingly liable for damages in a common law action for deceit,[53] or negligent in allowing the company to purchase at an excessive price,[54] the damages being the difference between the market value and the contract price. It is not possible to reach these same ends using the Misrepresentation Act 1967,[55] since the court's discretionary jurisdiction to award damages in lieu of rescission for innocent or negligent misrepresentations inducing a contract[56] does not, it seems, exist unless rescission is available at the time the court exercises the discretion.[57]

5–19

The company is not, however, the only party able to bring claims against the promoters. As already noted, promoter may be liable to those who have acquired securities of the company in reliance on misstatements in listing particulars or prospectuses to which the promoter was a party. The remedies available against him are the same as those against the officers of the company or others responsible for the listing particulars or prospectuses and are dealt with in Ch.25. In addition, other participants may have claims at common law.[58]

5–20

---

[49] *Re Cape Breton Co* (1885) 29 Ch.D. 795 CA.

[50] See especially *Omnium Electric Palaces v Baines* [1914] 1 Ch. 332 CA; and also [1914] 1 Ch. 332 at 347, per Sargant J. Also see *Re Ambrose Lake Tin & Copper Mining Co, Ex p. Moss* (1880) LR 14 Ch.D. 390 CA.

[51] cf. *Cook v Deeks* [1916] 1 A.C. 554 PC. There seems to be no objection in principle to the establishment of a trust in favour of an unformed company—for there can certainly be a trust in favour of an unborn child. By contrast, there cannot be an agency relationship with an unformed principal, so this approach cannot alleviate the problem of pre-incorporation contracts dealt with below at paras 5–4 et seq.

[52] See Lord Parker's clear explanation in *Jacobus Marler Estates Ltd v Marler* (1913) 85 L.J.P.C. 167n. Also see above, para.5–10.

[53] *Re Olympia Ltd* [1898] 2 Ch. 153; affirmed sub nom. *Gluckstein v Barnes* [1900] A.C. 240 at 247 HL; *Re Leeds and Hanley Theatre of Varieties* [1902] 2 Ch. 809 CA (and perhaps Vaughan Williams LJ takes an even wider view of when damages are available, at 825).

[54] Note the restrictions described by Lord Parker in *Jacobus Marler Estates v Marler* (1913) 85 L.J.P.C. 167n at 168.

[55] Misrepresentation Act 1967 s.2(1) and s.2(2), allowing damages to be awarded in lieu of rescission.

[56] And the mere non-disclosure of the amount of the promoter's profit is not misrepresentation; *Lady Forrest (Murchison) Gold Mine* [1901] 1 Ch. 582; *Jacobus Marler Estates Ltd v Marler* (1913) 85 L.J.P.C. 167n.

[57] *Salt v Stratstone Specialist Ltd* [2015] EWCA Civ 745.

[58] See above, para.5–10.

Remuneration of promoters

5–21   A promoter is not entitled to recover any remuneration for his services from the company unless there is a valid contract to that end between promoter and company. Indeed, older cases have suggested that without such a contract the promoter is not even entitled to recover preliminary expenses or the registration fees,[59] but whether these decisions would survive modern unjust enrichment analysis is perhaps moot. In this respect the promoter is at the mercy of the directors of the company. Until the company is formed it cannot enter into a valid contract[60] and the promoter therefore has to expend the money without any guarantee of repayment. In practice, however, recovery of preliminary expenses and registration fees does not normally present any difficulty. The directors will normally be empowered to pay them and will do so. It may well be, however, that the promoter will not be content merely to recover his expenses; certainly a professional promoter will expect to be handsomely remunerated. Nor is this unreasonable. As Lord Hatherley said,[61] "The services of a promoter are very peculiar; great skill, energy and ingenuity may be employed in constructing a plan and in bringing it out to the best advantages". Hence it is perfectly proper for the promoter to be rewarded, provided, as we have seen, that there is full disclosure to the company of the rewards to be obtained.

5–22   The reward may take many forms. The promoter may purchase an undertaking and promote a company to repurchase it at a profit, or the undertaking may be sold directly by the former owner to the new company, the promoter receiving a commission from the vendor. A once-popular device was for the company's capital structure to provide for a special class of deferred or founders' shares which would be issued credited as fully paid in consideration of the promoter's services.[62] Such shares would normally provide for the lion's share of the profits available for dividend after the preference and ordinary shares had been paid a dividend of a fixed amount. This had the advantage that the promoter advertised his or her apparent confidence in the business by retaining a stake in it; but all too often the stake (which probably cost the promoter nothing anyway) was merely window-dressing. And if, in fact, the company proved an outstanding success the promoter might do better than all the other shareholders put together. Today, when the trend is towards simplicity of capital structures, founders' shares are out of favour and, in general, those old companies which originally had them have got rid of them on a reconstruction.[63] A more likely alternative is for the promoter

---

[59] *Re English and Colonial Produce Co* [1906] 2 Ch. 435 CA; *Re National Motor Mail Coach Co* [1908] 2 Ch. 515 CA.

[60] See below.

[61] In *Touche v Metropolitan Ry Warehousing Co* (1871) L.R. 6 Ch. App. 671 at 676.

[62] The promoter should obtain a contract with the company prior to rendering the services, for past services are not valuable consideration: *Re Eddystone Marine Insurance, Re* [1893] 3 Ch. 9 CA. Hence if the services are rendered before the company was formed the promoter will have to pay for the shares. Moreover, in the case of a public company, an undertaking to perform work or supply services will no longer be valid payment: s.585(1) and see para.11–15. But provided the shares are given a very low nominal value this may not be a serious snag.

[63] There have been many interesting battles between holders of founders' shares and the other members. If the holdings of founders' shares are widely dispersed there is obviously a risk of block

to be given warrants or options entitling him or her to subscribe for shares at a particular price (e.g. that at which they were issued to the public) within a specified time. If the shares have meanwhile gone to a premium this will obviously be a valuable right.

PRELIMINARY CONTRACTS ENTERED INTO BY PROMOTERS

Until the company has been incorporated it cannot contract or do any other act. Nor, once incorporated, can it become liable on or entitled under contracts purporting to be made on its behalf prior to incorporation,[64] for ratification is not possible when the ostensible principal did not exist at the time when the contract was originally entered into.[65] Hence, preliminary arrangements will either have to be left to mere "gentlemen's agreements" or the promoters will have to undertake personal liability. Which of these courses will be adopted depends largely on the demands of the other party. If our village grocer is converting his business into a private company of which he is to be managing director and majority shareholder he will obviously not be concerned to have a binding agreement with anyone. In such a case a draft sale agreement will be drawn up and the main object of the company will be to acquire the business as a going concern "and for this purpose to enter into an agreement in the terms of a draft already prepared and for the purpose of identification signed by…". When the incorporation is complete the seller will ensure that the agreement is executed and completed.

5–23

If, however, promoters are arranging for the company to take over someone else's business, the seller certainly, and the promoters probably, will wish to have a binding agreement immediately. In this event the sale agreement will be made between the vendor and the promoters, and it will be provided that the personal liability of the promoters is to cease when the company in process of formation is incorporated and enters into an agreement in similar terms.

COMPANIES' PRE-INCORPORATION CONTRACTS

If the law described in the previous section is not appreciated, then difficulties can easily arise: promoters may purport to cause the as yet unformed company to enter into transactions with third parties. As already noted, these contracts cannot bind the non-existent entity, and the company, once formed, cannot ratify or adopt the contract.[66] Prior to statutory amendments driven by the UK's entry into the EU, the legal position as between the promoter and the third party seemed to

5–24

being acquired on behalf of the other classes in the hope of outvoting the remaining founders' shareholders at a class meeting to approve a reconstruction. To safeguard their position, in a number of cases the founders' shareholders formed a special company and vested all the founders' shares in it, thus ensuring that they were voted solidly at any meeting.

[64] See below.

[65] Contrast the position when a public company enters into transactions after its registration but before the issue of a trading certificate (see para.11–8) or when a company changes its name (above, para.4–23).

[66] Unless it enters into a new contract. This, of course, does not mean that, in the absence of a new contract, the company or the other party can accept the delivery of the goods or payment without being under any obligation.

depend on the terminology employed. If the contract was entered into by the promoter and signed "for and on behalf of XY Co Ltd" then, according to the early case of *Kelner v Baxter*,[67] the promoter would be personally liable. But if, as is much more likely, the promoter signed the proposed name of the company, adding his own to authenticate it (e.g. XY Co Ltd, AB Director) then, according to *Newborne v Sensolid (Great Britain) Ltd*,[68] there was no contract at all. This was hardly satisfactory.

5–25   The statutory rule took a clear if rather dramatic stand. The relevant provision is now CA 2006 s.51, which reads:

> "(1) A contract which purports to be made by or on behalf of a company at a time when the company has not been formed, has effect, subject to any agreement to the contrary, as one made with the person purporting to act for the company or as agent for it, and he is personally liable on the contract accordingly."

The obvious aim of the provision is to increase security of transactions for third parties by avoiding the consequences of the contract with the company being a nullity. The provision imposes contractual liability on the promoter, and applies even if the new company is never formed.[69] To avoid the promoter's personal liability under the statute, the third party must explicitly agree to forego the protection—consent cannot be deduced simply from details of the contract which, interpreted widely, would be inconsistent with the promoter accepting personal liability, such as the promoter signing as agent for the company.[70]

5–26   The presence of the statutory provision has had an effect on the courts' perception of the common law in this area. In *Phonogram Ltd v Lane*, Oliver LJ said that the "narrow distinction" drawn in *Kelner v Baxter* and the *Newborne* case did not represent the true common law position, which was simply: "does the contract purport to be one which is directly between the supposed principal and the other party, or does it purport to be one between the agent himself—albeit acting for a supposed principal—and the other party?"[71] This question is to be answered by looking at the whole of the contract and not just at the formula used beneath the

---

[67] *Kelner v Baxter* (1866) L.R. 2 C.P. 174. See also *Natal Land Co v Pauline Syndicate* [1904] A.C. 120 PC.

[68] *Newborne v Sensolid (Great Britain) Ltd* [1954] 1 Q.B. 45 CA. In that case it was the promoter who attempted to enforce the agreement but it appears that the decision would have been the same if the other party had attempted to enforce it, as was so held in *Black v Smallwood* [1966] A.L.R. 744 Aust. HC: see also *Hawkes Bay Milk Corp Ltd v Watson* [1974] 1 N.Z.L.R. 218; cf. *Marblestone Industries Ltd v Fairchild* [1975] 1 N.Z.L.R. 529. The promoter should, it seems, be liable for breach of implied warranty of authority: *Royal Bank of Canada v Starr* (1985) 31 B.L.R. 124.

[69] *Phonogram Ltd v Lane* [1982] 1 Q.B. 938 CA.

[70] *Phonogram Ltd v Lane* [1982] 1 Q.B. 938 CA; *Royal Mail Estates Ltd v Maples Teesdale* [2015] EWHC 1890 (Ch). See, however, the decision of the First-tier Tribunal (Tax Chamber), obiter, in *Hepburn v Revenue and Customs Commissioners* [2013] UKFTT 455, where an agreement to the contrary was inferred from conduct of the parties, including the tendering of invoices to the company instead of the promoter. This approach goes against the trend of earlier cases, and appears doubtful.

[71] *Phonogram Ltd v Lane* [1982] 1 Q.B. 938 at 945 CA. This approach was applied by the Court of Appeal in *Cotronic (UK) Ltd v Dezonie* [1991] B.C.L.C. 721; and in *Badgerhill Properties Ltd v Cottrell* [1991] B.C.L.C. 805.

signature. If after such an examination the latter is found to be the case, the promoter would be personally liable at common law, no matter how he signed the document.

On this analysis the difference between s.51 and the common law is narrowed, but not eliminated. At common law, if the parties intend to contract with the non-existent company, the result will be a nullity and the third party protected only to the extent that the law of restitution provides protection. Under the statute, a contract which purports to be made with the company will trigger the liability of the promoter, unless the third party agrees to give up the protection. In other words, the common law approaches the question of the third party's contractual rights against the promoter as a matter of the parties' intentions, with no presumption either way, whereas the statute creates a presumption in favour of the promoter being contractually liable. The common law is still important in those cases which fall outside the scope of the statute.[72]

5–27

Despite the improvements which the statute has effected, there are still some problems with its operation. First, perhaps as a consequence of the legislature's concern with the promotion of third-party protection, the section did not make it clear whether the promoter acquires a right under the statute to enforce the contract, as well as the risk of being subjected to contractual obligations. It was submitted in earlier editions of this book that normal principles of contractual mutuality should lead to this latter result and this conclusion has been confirmed by the Court of Appeal.[73]

5–28

Secondly, the section bites only when the contract "purports" to be made on behalf of a company which has not been formed. Thus, where the parties thought the company existed, though it had in fact been struck off the register, the Court of Appeal held that their contract was not at the time one which purported to be made on behalf of the company of the same name which was hurriedly incorporated when the parties later discovered their mistake.[74] The contract in truth purported to be made on behalf of the company which had been struck off, clearly not a company of which it could be said it "has not been formed". Ensnared in this conundrum, the claimant failed. Thus, the section has not been construed as protecting third parties in all situations where they in fact attempt to contract with non-existent companies, but only in those situations where the contract identifies a specific company as the purported contracting party and where that company is one which has not been formed.[75]

---

[72] See below, para.5–28, for identification of such cases.

[73] *Braymist Ltd v Wise Finance Co Ltd* [2002] Ch. 273 CA. However, since this means a contract purportedly made by the company may be enforced by its agent (the promoter), the third party may be able to resist enforcement where the identity of the counterparty is important. See also *Royal Mail Estates Ltd v Maple Teesdale* [2015] EWHC 1890 (Ch) (appeal pending), where the court held that an express agreement that the benefit of the contract was personal to the company did not exclude the effect of the equivalent of s.51 of the Companies Act 2006, such that the agent may still be liable on the pre-incorporation contract.

[74] In *Cotronic (UK) Ltd v Dezonie* [1991] B.C.L.C. 721.

[75] See also *Badgerhill Properties Ltd v Cottrell* [1991] B.C.L.C. 805. On the other hand, it is submitted that the decision in *Oshkosh B'Gosh Inc v Dan Marbel Inc Ltd* [1989] B.C.L.C. 507 CA,

Thirdly, and undoubtedly the most serious,[76] the reforms have done nothing to make it simpler for companies to "assume" or adopt the rights and obligations of a pre-incorporation transaction. While one can understand that the Directive preferred to leave that to each Member State, the UK has not got round to doing anything about it. Many common law countries have recognised, either by judge-made law or by statute, that a company when formed can effectively elect to adopt pre-incorporation transactions purporting to be made on its behalf without the need for a formal novation, and that the liability of the promoter ceases when the company adopts it. In 1962, the Jenkins Committee recommended this reform but it still has not happened.[77] At present the only way in which the company can adopt the contract is by entering into a post-incorporation agreement in the same terms. Even if the company does so, that will not relieve the promoters of personal liability (at any rate while the new agreement remains executory)[78] unless they are parties to the new agreement, which expressly relieves them of liability under the pre-incorporation agreement. The need for all this is frequently overlooked. This may not matter much if all those concerned remain able and willing to perform their obligations under the pre-incorporation agreement. But it can be calamitous if one or more of them becomes insolvent or wants to withdraw because changes in market conditions have made the transactions disadvantageous to him or them.

As pre-incorporation transactions are inevitable features of every new incorporation, it ought to be made as easy as possible to achieve what the parties intend (or would have intended if they had realised that the company was not yet incorporated and had understood the legal consequences). In this case, if not generally, the legal technicality that ratification dates back to the date of the transaction so that it is not effective unless, at that time, the ratifying person existed and had capacity to enter into the transaction, should not apply.

CONCLUSION

5–29   If this chapter reveals any surprises, it is that, despite all the ambitions to simplify the law relating to companies and streamline its operation, especially for small businesses, there remains this relatively untouched territory—but nevertheless territory which must inevitably be navigated by every single company in its transition from pre-incorporation to post-incorporation. Across this territory it is

---

that s.51 does not apply to a company which trades under its new name before completing the statutory formalities for change of name, is correct, since a change of name does not involve re-incorporation. See para.4–23.

[76] Also serious from the point of view of the harmonising objectives of the First Directive was the decision of Harman J in *Rover International Ltd v Cannon Film Sales Ltd* [1987] B.C.L.C. 540, that s.36C (now s.51) does not apply to companies incorporated outside Great Britain, a view from which the Court of Appeal did not dissent ([1988] B.C.L.C. 710). But this is now altered by reg.6 of the Overseas Companies (Execution of Documents and Registration of Charges) Regulations 2009 (SI 2009/1917).

[77] The CLR, curiously, left this issue untouched.

[78] If the new contract has been fully performed by the company, after incorporation, and by the other party, that clearly will end any liability under the pre-incorporation contract.

largely, although not entirely, left to the common law to regulate the activities of the company's promoters, and their engagements with the company and with third parties.

CHAPTER 6

OVERSEAS COMPANIES, EU LAW AND CORPORATE MOBILITY

This chapter discusses three main issues. First, how far are companies   **6–1**
incorporated outside the UK subject to British company law if they carry on
business within the UK? Secondly, to what extent does the freedom of companies
within the EU to carry on business across borders suggest that the EU should take
action to harmonise the company laws of the Member States? Thirdly, what is the
extent of the freedom companies have to choose the country in which their
registered office is located or subsequently to move it to another jurisdiction? The
third issue is closely related to the second. The effect of a change of the
jurisdiction in which the registered office is located is a change in the company
law to which the company is subject from the transferor jurisdiction's law to that
of the transferee jurisdiction. Free movement of a company's registered office is a
necessary but not a sufficient condition for competition among the Member
States in the provision of company laws which companies find attractive. If such
competition develops, that may lead to convergence among the company laws of
the Member States, even if there is no harmonisation of company law at EU level.
In other words convergence of Member States' company laws may result from
"top-down" harmonisation by the EU or from "bottom up" competition among
the Member States (or, of course, from a mixture of the two processes). The first

issue is also linked to the second, since it raises the question of whether the UK is happy to allow the internal relations of companies operating in the UK to be determined by foreign law.

OVERSEAS COMPANIES

6–2 British law might have refused to recognise companies not incorporated in one of the UK jurisdictions,[1] thus putting in jeopardy the validity in those jurisdictions of transactions entered into by non-UK incorporated companies and in effect requiring companies which wished to carry on business in the UK to do so through a British subsidiary. In fact, British law has never adopted such an approach. As Lord Wright said in 1933: "English courts have long since recognised as juristic persons corporations established by foreign law in virtue of the fact of their creation and continuance under and by that law".[2] Indeed, as we shall see below, to adopt a different rule today would be a breach of the Treaty on the Functioning of the European Union ("TFEU"). Thus, as a general rule,[3] a company incorporated outside the UK, whether within the EU or not, need not form a British subsidiary company in order to do business in the UK. It may trade through an agency or branch in this country or, indeed, simply contract with someone in the UK without establishing any form of presence in this country.[4] Of course, when a company incorporated elsewhere intends to carry on a substantial business in the UK, it is likely to form a British subsidiary in order to do so. This might be regarded as a sign of commitment to the British economy, and it also allows the foreign parent company to ring-fence its British operations by putting them in a separate subsidiary with limited liability.[5] The point, however, is that the foreign company is not obliged to take this route; it can do business here in its own right, if it so wishes.

This long-standing stance of British law towards foreign companies conducting business in the UK means that it is broadly content to leave the regulation of the internal affairs of such companies to the law of the jurisdiction in which they have their registered office, even though those dealing with it may not be aware of its jurisdictional location and the implications of this fact for its governing company law. To combat this risk a requirement is imposed on overseas companies with a significant presence in the UK, to make public disclosures which match those of required of domestic companies.

---

[1] See Ch.1 for a discussion of the various forms of incorporation available in Great Britain.

[2] [1933] A.C. 289 at 297 HL.

[3] In particular industries a company operating in the UK may be required to do so through a British subsidiary. Thus, banks from (non-EU) countries with a poor record of banking supervision were reported to have been required by the FSA (predecessor to the FCA) to withdraw from the business of taking retail deposits in the UK, unless they incorporated their branches as subsidiaries, which would be required to have their own capital: *Financial Times*, 25 June 2002, p.2. However, such national requirements must not infringe EU law on freedom of establishment. See Case C-221/89, *Factortame* [1991] E.C.R. I-3905.

[4] For example, where the contract is concluded over the telephone or the internet by someone in the UK with a company established in another country.

[5] See Ch.8, below. In the future the multinational parent might put all its European operations (perhaps of a particular type) into an SE—see above, para.1-40—and the SE might or might not be registered in the UK.

The rules on disclosure by foreign companies are to be found in Pt 34 of the Act **6–3** and regulations made under it. This Part is entitled "overseas companies",[6] a term that might be thought to conjure up a picture of companies formed in some distant and exotic location, as they sometimes are, though in fact it may be only the Straits of Dover or the Irish Sea which separate the country of incorporation from the UK. An overseas company is simply "a company incorporated outside the United Kingdom".[7] The regulatory objectives of this Part are relatively modest. They are principally to ensure that there is available in the UK some basic information about a company incorporated elsewhere which has established a presence in this country from which it does business. That information is, essentially, the information a British company would have to provide on incorporation[8] or as part of its annual financial returns,[9] plus some information relating to those who represent the overseas company in the UK. However, some provisions go beyond disclosure.

Immediately prior to the 2006 Act this was an area of law which, despite its modest objectives, was overly complicated, because there were two sets of provisions, each containing slightly different disclosure requirements, for overseas companies. This arose in part because the Act does not attempt to regulate all overseas companies which do business in the UK (for example, over the internet) but only those which have some sort of base in the UK. However, two different connecting factors emerged as ways of defining that base. One was the result of the UK's implementation of the Eleventh Company Law Directive[10] which used the concept of a "branch" to define the connection which an overseas company needed to have with the UK to fall within the overseas companies rules. The other connecting factor was the traditional domestic one, based on the company having a "place of business" in the UK. Even this might not have been problematic if both connecting factors had been linked to the same set of disclosure requirements. However, the two connecting factors were linked to slightly different disclosure requirements, so that companies could not simply proceed on the basis that they did not need to decide whether they operated a branch or a place of business. Rather, they had to decide between the two, in order to determine which disclosure regime applied.[11] Although it was clear that a company subject to both regimes must comply with the EU rules if they were more demanding than the domestic ones (which was generally the case), companies might be far from clear whether the EU regime applied to them or only the domestic one.[12]

---

[6] Before 2006 the even more quaint term "oversea" company was used.

[7] 2006 Act s.1044. This means that Channel Island and Isle of Man companies are "overseas" companies as well.

[8] See above, Ch.4.

[9] See below, Ch.21.

[10] Directive 89/666/EEC [1989] O.J. L395/36.

[11] The situation seems to have arisen because the then Government was unwilling to allocate parliamentary time for primary legislation on overseas companies (which would have allowed for the integration of the two regimes) but decided instead to implement the Eleventh Directive by secondary legislation under the European Communities Act 1972.

[12] In this connection it is important to note that the Eleventh Directive applies, not only to EU companies setting up branches in the UK, but to all foreign companies so doing. Thus, its scope was parallel to that of the traditional domestic law.

The CLR recommended,[13] and the Government accepted and eventually implemented,[14] the re-establishment of a single regime. This is based on a single set of disclosure requirements, derived from the Eleventh Directive, but using a multi-pronged connecting factor. The Overseas Companies Regulations 2009[15] are expressed to apply whenever an overseas company opens an "establishment" in the UK; but "establishment" is defined to mean a branch within the meaning of the Eleventh Directive or a place of business which is not a branch.[16] Thus, either a branch or a place of business will trigger the operation of the provisions relating to overseas companies, but the crucial point is that the disclosure rules will not now vary according to whether the "establishment" test is met on the basis of a branch or a place of business.[17]

Establishment: branch and place of business

6–4   The terms "branch" and "place of business" obviously overlap to a large extent, but it seems that both at the top and at the bottom of the spectrum a place of business may exist even though a branch does not. To take the bottom end, this situation may arise because, it seems, activities ancillary to a company's business may constitute a place of business but not a branch. It is difficult to be absolutely certain about this, because the Eleventh Directive does not define a "branch" whilst the Regulations do not define a "place of business", but it seems to be the case. It has been said in case law that establishing a place of business, as opposed to merely doing business, in this country requires "a degree of permanence or recognisability as being a location of the company's business".[18] However, it is not fatal to the establishment of a place of business that the activities carried on there are only subsidiary to the company's main business, which is carried on outside the UK, or are not a substantial part of the company's overall business.[19] As to the meaning of a branch some clues may be derivable from the EU legislation referring to bank branches.[20] This does contain a definition of a bank branch, from which some guidance may be obtainable. That definition refers to a place of business through which the bank "conducts directly some or all of the operations inherent in the business".[21] So it may be that purely ancillary activities, such as warehousing or data processing, do not constitute the

---

[13] Oversea Companies (1999) and Final Report I, paras 11.21–11.33.

[14] Modernising Company Law, 2002, Cm 5553–1, para.6.17. The havering around the implementation of this policy in the Act itself was described in the 8th edn of this book at pp.122–123.

[15] Overseas Companies Regulations 2009 (SI 2009/1801), as amended.

[16] SI 2009/1801 regs 2, 3, 30 and 68.

[17] However, the trading disclosures requirements apply on an even broader basis: see para.6–6.

[18] [1986] 1 W.L.R. 180 at 184. See also [1990] B.C.L.C. 546.

[19] *South India Shipping Corp v Export-Import Bank of Korea* [1985] 1 W.L.R. 585 CA; *Actiesselskabat Dampskib "Hercules" v Grand Trunk Pacific Railway Co* [1912] 1 K.B. 222 CA. Registration in the UK of an establishment in order to carry on business involves the creation of a place of business, even if business has not yet commenced at the establishment: *Teekay Tankers Ltd v STX Offshore & Shipping Co* [2015] 2 B.C.L.C. 210. However, the business must be the business of the company, not of its agent or subsidiary: *Rakusens Ltd v Baser Ambalaj Plastik Sanayi Ticaret AS* [2002] 1 B.C.L.C. 104 CA; *Matchnet Plc v William Blair & Co LLC* [2003] 2 B.C.L.C. 195.

[20] This EU legislation is not otherwise dealt with here.

[21] See, for example, Directive 94/19/EC on deposit guarantee schemes, art.1(5).

establishment of a branch though they could amount to a place of business. To like effect is the definition of a branch adopted by the Court of Justice for the purposes of the Brussels Convention: a branch has the appearance of permanency and is physically equipped to negotiate business with third parties directly.[22] At the other end of the spectrum, a company incorporated outside the UK but which has its head office here,[23] clearly has a place of business in the UK, but it might be argued that this is not a branch, since a branch supposes that the head office is elsewhere.[24]

Disclosure obligations

The Act and the Overseas Companies Regulations impose disclosure require-   **6–5**
ments on an overseas company having an establishment in the UK in all phases of its life. An overseas company which opens an establishment must file with the Registrar within one month information relating to both itself and the establishment.[25] Subsequent alterations in the registered particulars must also be notified.[26] Failure to do so constitutes a criminal offence on the part of both company and any officer or agent of the company who knowingly and wilfully authorises or permits the default,[27] but, apparently, does not affect the validity of transactions the company may enter into through its unregistered operation. There is no need in a book of this nature to go into the detail of what is required, but it should be noted that the requirements are more limited where the company is incorporated in an EEA Member State than where this is not so.[28] This reflects the approach of the Eleventh Directive.[29] Overall, the policy can be said to be to put the person dealing with the overseas company through its establishment in a similar informational position as would obtain if the company were one incorporated under the Act.

---

[22] Case 33/78 *Etablissements Somafer v Saar-Ferngas* [1978] E.C.R. 2183.

[23] In principle, British law accepts such an arrangement, though not all European countries do: see paras 6–17 et seq., below.

[24] However, in the *Centros* case (Case C-212/97 [1999] E.C.R. I-1459) the CJEU seems to have treated as a branch, for the purposes of art.49 TFEU, the British company's place of business in Denmark, even though it carried on no business anywhere else, including the UK, which was simply its place of incorporation. Putting the matter the other way around, this might suggest that the British head-office of a company incorporated elsewhere would also be a "branch" for the purposes of the Eleventh Directive.

[25] 2006 Act s.1046 and the Overseas Companies Regulations 2009 Pt 2. The information about the company must include a certified copy of its constitution (reg.8(1)). The residential addresses of directors or permanent representatives are subject to the same protective provisions as in the case of UK-incorporate companies: Pt 4. Although the disclosure obligation applies in principle each time the overseas company opens an establishment in the UK (reg.4(2)), the company need not repeat the company-specific information each time, but simply cross-refer to it (reg.5). This applies even though the establishments are in different UK jurisdictions.

[26] 2009 Regs Pt 3.

[27] 2009 Regs regs 11 and 17.

[28] 2009 Regs reg.6.

[29] cf. arts 2 and 8 of the Eleventh Directive. The theory, presumably, is that the more extensive information about the company is available from the national registries of EU Member States, under the provisions of the First Directive.

A crucial concern of those who deal with overseas companies is how to serve legal documents on the company. The particulars relating to the establishment must give the name and service address of every person resident in the UK authorised to accept service on behalf of the company or a statement that there is no such person.[30] In addition, the information must state the extent of the powers of the directors of the overseas company to represent the company in dealings and in legal proceedings[31] and give a list of those authorised to represent the company as a permanent representative of the company in respect of the branch.[32]

6–6 On-going disclosure requirements fall into two categories. First, the "trading disclosure" rules which apply to domestic companies[33] are adapted so as to apply to overseas companies "carrying on business in the United Kingdom".[34] These rules are, rightly, not confined to those overseas companies which have an establishment in the UK, though doing business "in" the UK is not defined. The aim of the rules is to provide third parties with certain information at the point at which they deal—or are likely to deal—with overseas companies. Thus, the company must display its name and country of incorporation at every location at which it carries on business[35]; its name on its business letters and a wide range of analogous documents[36]; and, where it has an establishment in the UK, a range of further information on these documents.[37] There are penalties for non-compliance,[38] but non-compliance also carries civil consequences on the same basis as that applied to domestic companies.[39]

Secondly, annual reporting requirements are applied to overseas companies, but, in this case, only if they have an establishment in the UK.[40] These requirements vary according to whether the overseas company is required by the law of the country in which it is incorporated (its "parent" law) to prepare, have audited and to disclose annual accounts. If it is,[41] the overseas company

---

[30] 2006 Act ss.1056 and 1139(2)(a). In *Teekay Tankers Ltd v STX Offshore & Shipping Co* [2015] 2 B.C.L.C. 210 the judge confirmed the traditional view that, despite the apparently narrower wording of reg.7(1)(e), the service did not have to concern the business of the establishment (as opposed to the business of the company more generally). If there is no such person or if the registered person refuses to accept service, then service can be effected at any place of business in the UK (s.1139(2)(b)).

[31] 2009 Regs reg.6(1)(e).

[32] 2009 Regs reg.7(1)(f). Part 4 of the regs applies provisions equivalent to those operating in relation to domestic companies for the protection of directors' residential addresses from public disclosure. See para.14–23.

[33] See para.9–20.

[34] 2006 Act s.1051 and 2009 Regs Pt 7.

[35] 2009 Regs regs 60–61 (and at the service address of every person authorised to accept service on behalf of the company in respect of the branch).

[36] 2009 Regs reg.62.

[37] 2009 Regs reg.63.

[38] 2009 Regs reg.67.

[39] 2009 Regs reg.66. For a discussion of those civil consequences, see para.9–20.

[40] 2006 Act s.1049 and 2009 Regs Pt 5. Unlimited overseas companies are exempted (as domestic ones are) from this obligation, and special rules (not considered here) apply to credit or financial institutions (Pt 6).

[41] If the overseas company is incorporated in an EEA state, it falls within this category even if it is exempted by its parent law from the requirements to have its accounts audited or to deliver them (reg.31(1)(b)). Such exemptions are controlled by the relevant EU law, which is discussed in Ch.21.

discharges its disclosure obligations by delivering to the Registrar a copy of the accounting documents prepared in accordance with the parent law.[42] The "accounting documents" include not only the accounts themselves (including the consolidated accounts, if relevant) and auditors' report but also the directors' report.[43] The company has the relatively generous period of three months from the date the documents were first disclosed under the parent law to file them with the Registrar.[44] If it is not so required, the overseas company is subject to a version of the accounting and filing requirements applied to domestic companies.[45] In addition to the option, available to domestic companies, to file accounts in accordance with International Accounting Standards, the overseas company may choose to prepare its accounts in accordance with its parent law.[46] However, the accounts of companies in this second category are not subject to an audit requirement. Despite the absence of an audit requirement, the obligation to produce annual accounts is clearly a burdensome one for overseas companies which are not required by their parent law to do so—though there must now be few countries in the world which do not require their companies to produce annual financial statements.

Finally, if an overseas company closes an establishment in the UK, it must give notice to the Registrar.[47] As to the overseas company itself, it must give information to the Registrar if it is wound up or becomes subject to insolvency proceedings.[48]

The Act lays down a general rule that documents delivered to the Registrar must be in English.[49] However, the company's memorandum or articles of association may be delivered in another language, provided they are accompanied by a certified translation into English.[50]

Execution of documents and names

Although the overseas companies provisions are primarily concerned with disclosure, there are two sets of further provisions going beyond this. One set is largely facultative. It applies, with appropriate modifications, the domestic rules

6–7

---

[42] The most recent accounting documents have to be included with the initial return to the Registrar (reg.9(1),(2)). Thereafter, Pt 5 applies (reg.32(5)). The accounts delivered to the Registrar must identify the legislation under which the accounts have been prepared, which GAAP has been used, if any; and whether they have been audited and, if so, according to which Generally Accepted Auditing Standards (reg.33).

[43] 2009 Regs reg.31(2). The auditors' report is not required if the company is exempted from audit.

[44] 2009 Regs reg.34.

[45] 2009 Regs Pt 5 Ch.3. See Ch.21 below. This is a considerable improvement on the previous law which applied to overseas companies in such cases a modification of an out-dated set of accounting rules based on the 1948 Act.

[46] 2006 Act s.395, as applied to overseas companies by reg.38. This assumes, of course, that the parent law does not *require* preparation, audit and filing of the accounts of the overseas company, in which case it will fall within the first category of companies.

[47] 2006 Act s.1058 and reg.77—transfer of an establishment from one jurisdiction of the UK to another counts as the closure of one establishment and the opening of another.

[48] 2006 Act s.1053(2) and 2009 Regs Pt 8.

[49] 2006 Act s.1103(1).

[50] 2006 Act s.1105 and the Registrar of Companies and Applications for Striking Off Regulations 2009 reg.7.

about execution of documents and seals to overseas companies, whether or not that company has an establishment in the UK or even whether or not it can be said to do business "in" the UK.[51] The second set applies to company names and is regulatory in intent.[52] An overseas company is required to register, on creation, the name of its establishment in the UK. That name may be its corporate name or the name under which it proposes to carry on business in the UK (its alternative name).[53] In principle, the domestic rules on company names[54] are applied to the overseas company's registered name.[55] Despite apparent contravention of the domestic policy, however, an overseas company which is registered in an EEA Member State is exempt from the domestic name controls over its corporate name, except those relating to permitted characters in a corporate name.[56] The Eleventh Directive does not provide for controls on the choice of name by overseas companies and the virtual non-application of such controls to the corporate names of EEA companies seems to have been the result of a fear that to impose them would infringe the freedom of establishment rules of the EU.[57]

Other mandatory provisions

6–8   In the final analysis, Pt 34 applies the equivalent of only a small part of the British Act to overseas companies and, as we have seen, where the home state requires the production of public, audited accounts, even Pt 34 relies on the rules of the state of incorporation rather than on the rules of the British Act. Some further protection for third parties, based on British law, may apply as a result of provisions in the Insolvency Act 1986. Thus, the rules restricting the re-use by successor companies of the name of a company which has gone into insolvent liquidation[58] apply to overseas companies. This is achieved by use of the formula that the relevant sections of the 1986 Act apply also to companies "which may be wound up under Part V of this Act".[59] Part V of the 1986 Act permits the court in certain circumstances compulsorily to wind up an unregistered company, the

---

[51] 2006 Act s.1045 and the Overseas Companies (Execution of Documents and Registration of Documents) Regulation 2009/1917 Pt 2

[52] The rules on company charges created by overseas companies (s.1052) are also regulatory and are considered in paras 32–28 et seq. They were reduced in scope in 2011.

[53] 2006 Act ss.1047(1),(2) and 1048—and it may alter its alternative name and toggle between its corporate and alternative names.

[54] See paras 4–13 et seq.

[55] 2006 Act s.1047(4),(5)—and to any alteration of the registered name.

[56] 2006 Act s.1047(3),(5). These controls are set out in s.57 and regulations made thereunder.

[57] Case C-167/01 *Kamer van Koophandel en Fabrieken voor Amsterdam v Inspire Art Ltd* [2003] E.C.R. I-10155, where the ECJ struck down Dutch "pseudo-foreign company" requirements applied to an overseas (in fact, British) company which went beyond the Eleventh Directive. However, the Court recognised the possibility of justification which, one would have thought, would have been applicable in principle to the domestic name requirements, on the grounds of third-party protection, not involving a disproportionate cost to the company. However, this conclusion cannot be firmly arrived at without knowing the nature and extent of the name controls applied in the Member State of incorporation. The approach of the Act simply side-steps these difficulties.

[58] See below, para.9–16.

[59] IA 1986 ss.216(8) and 217(6).

definition of which is broad enough to include overseas companies.[60] To fall within Pt V the overseas company need not have an established place of business in Great Britain nor, indeed, any assets here at the time the application for winding up is made.[61] The courts have also accepted that the jurisdiction to wind up unregistered companies brings into play certain other sections of the Insolvency Act, even though those sections do not in terms apply to "Part V" companies.[62] These include the important provisions relating to fraudulent and wrongful trading.[63] Important though these provisions may be, they apply only to companies which are have been placed in an insolvency procedure in the UK, which in the case of an overseas company may well not happen.[64] Finally, the Company Directors Disqualification Act 1986[65] also applies to a company incorporated outside Great Britain if it is a company capable of being wound up under the Insolvency Act 1986.[66]

COMPANY LAW AT EU LEVEL

Harmonisation

The underlying policy of Pt 34 of the Act is to rely on the company law of the state of incorporation when a foreign company does business in the UK. When the European Economic Community was founded in the middle of the 1950s, a very different approach was taken in the Treaty of Rome. It was expected that, in the Community, companies based in one Member State would penetrate more readily the economies of other Member States, without necessarily establishing subsidiaries in those States. It was decided that this was acceptable only if accompanied by a programme for the mandatory harmonisation by the

6–9

---

[60] IA 1986 s.220 ("any company", except, of course, those incorporated under the British companies legislation). See *Re Paramount Airways Ltd* [1993] Ch. 223 at 240 CA. Voluntary winding-up of an unregistered company, however, is not permitted: s.221(4).

[61] *Stocznia Gdanska SA v Latreefers Inc (No.2)* [2001] 2 B.C.L.C. 116 CA. However, the company must have some connection with Great Britain and there must be some good reason for winding it up here.

[62] See previous note.

[63] See *Stocznia Gdanska SA v Latreefers Inc (No.2)* [2001] 2 B.C.L.C. 116 CA; and IA 1986 ss.213 and 214. See also Ch.9, below. It seems likely that the application of ss.213 and 214 to EU companies does not infringe the Treaty provisions relating to freedom of establishment. See Case C-594/14, *Kornhaas v Dithmar* [2016] B.C.C. 116 and below fn.135.

[64] In the case of insolvent companies with the centre of their main interests in another EU Member State, Council Regulation (EU) 2015/848 on insolvency proceedings ([2015] O.J. L141/19) favours the opening of insolvency proceedings in that other Member State.

[65] See Ch.10.

[66] IA 1986 s.22(2). See also *Re Seagull Manufacturing Co Ltd (No.2)* [1994] 1 B.C.L.C. 273—Act applicable to foreigners outside the jurisdiction and to conduct which occurred outside the jurisdiction, though presumably only in relation to a company falling within the Act. In the case of undischarged bankrupts the connecting factor is instead whether the company has an established place of business in Great Britain.

Community of the company laws of the Member States.[67] In other words, in the minds of the drafters of the original EC Treaty, freedom of establishment for companies and harmonisation of company laws in the EU were closely linked. Consequently, what is today art.50(2)(g) TFEU provides that the Council of Ministers by qualified majority vote, on a proposal from the European Commission and with the consent of the European Parliament,[68] may adopt Directives[69] which aim to protect the interests of members "and others"[70] by "co-ordinating to the necessary extent the safeguards which…are required by Member States of companies and firms . . .with a view to making such safeguards equivalent throughout the Union". Thus, reliance on other Member States' company laws was to be accompanied by EU legislation which made those laws "equivalent", at least in certain respects.

The proposed programme for extensive mandatory harmonisation, from the top down, of Member States' domestic company laws got off to an impressive start, but by the middle 1990s, if not earlier, it had run out of steam, with only part of the proposed programme of "company law directives" enacted. This may have been because the theory linking freedom of establishment with a need for harmonised company law was never satisfactorily articulated. There was little empirical evidence that "members and others" were suffering in the EU's single market from the lack of harmonised company laws. There was also the criticism that, once a policy had been embodied in EU company law, it was more difficult to change it than in the case of domestic legislation, at least for the majority of Member States. In other words, the EU legislative process was more "sticky" than national ones.

6–10   In any event, for harmonisation to be fully successful, (a) there must exist a common best rule for all the Members States; (b) the EU Commission, which has a monopoly on the initiation of Community legislation, must be able to identify it; and (c) the participants in the Community's legislative process must accept the common rule. None of these characteristics was ever completely in place. The structure of shareholding (dispersed or concentrated) differs across the Member States, at least in relation to large companies, so that the dominant problem in some jurisdictions is the relationship between management and shareholders as a class and in other jurisdictions that between controlling and non-controlling shareholders. In some Member States board level representation of employees is an important part of the domestic industrial relations system, whilst in others it is

---

[67] See J. Wouters, "European Company Law: *Quo Vadis?*" (2000) 37 C.M.L.R. 257 at 269; and G. Wolff, "The Commission's Programme for Company Law Harmonisation" in M. Andenas and S. Kenyon-Slade (eds), *EC Financial Market Regulation and Company Law* (London, 1993), p.22. This position was adopted in particular by France.

[68] Under the "ordinary" legislative procedure of the EU: art.294 TFEU.

[69] Directives are binding on the Member States as to the principles to be embodied in national legislation but give the states some flexibility in the transposition of the Directive into national law: art.288 TFEU. Article 50 does not provide for the adoption of Regulations, which are directly applicable in the Member States.

[70] This includes creditors and, probably, employees. Basing the Directive on employee involvement in the SE (see above, para.1–40) on what is now art.50 was controversial and it was eventually adopted on the basis of what is now art.352 TFEU, which requires unanimity. However, the controversy was as much about whether the SE rules could be regarded as a harmonising measure as about the subject-matter of the Directive.

not. Both features made the identification of a single common rule very difficult in the most sensitive areas of company law. As to the EU Commission, it never had the time or the resources to develop the highly sophisticated comparative law analysis which legislating for an ever-growing block of countries requires. Finally, since the adoption of legislation requires a supermajority vote of the Member States, there is plenty of scope for the states to defend national interests, normally by watering down the proposals put forward by the EU Commission. It may be difficult to say whether the resistance of a Member States is driven by the fact that the EU Commission has proposed an inefficient rule for that state or by pressure from incumbent national interests which will lose out if the efficient rule is adopted.

Nevertheless, some parts of the proposed programme of company law directives were enacted by the middle of the 1990s. This period saw the adoption of the First (safeguards for third parties),[71] Second (formation of public companies and the maintenance and alteration of capital),[72] Third (mergers of public companies),[73] Fourth (accounts),[74] Sixth (division of public companies),[75] Seventh (group accounts),[76] Eighth (audits),[77] Eleventh (branches)[78] and Twelfth (single-member companies) Directives,[79] though they were not adopted in that precise order. Subsequently, there have been significant directives on takeovers, cross-border mergers and shareholders' rights (though, significantly, the twenty-first century directives are no longer allocated a number in an overall proposed programme of directives). However, the Directives are not equally important for the UK. Some of them did not significantly alter the existing national law, because the EU rule reflected existing national law or because Member States were given a range of options in implementing the Directive and could choose to preserve the status quo or because the subject-matter of the Directive was not important in the UK.[80] As far as the UK is concerned, the most important Directives have been the First (which triggered a review of the common law rules on ultra vires and agency as they applied to companies)[81]; the Second (which led to a tightening of the rules on dividend distributions and legal capital generally)[82]; and the Fourth (which led to a re-thinking of the relationship between the law and accountancy practice).[83] Of lesser impact were the Eighth on

6–11

---

[71] Council Directive 68/151 [1968] O.J. 68.
[72] Council Directive 77/91 [1977] O.J. L26/1.
[73] Council Directive 78/855 [1978] O.J. L295/36.
[74] Council Directive 78/660 [1978] O.J. L222/11.
[75] Council Directive 82/891 [1982] O.J. L378/47.
[76] Council Directive 83/349 [1983] O.J. L193/1.
[77] Council Directive 84/253 [1984] O.J. L126/20.
[78] Council Directive 89/666 [1989] O.J. L395/36.
[79] Council Directive 89/667 [1989] O.J. L395/40.
[80] For similar reasons, the overall significance of the EU company law directives has been questioned: L. Enriques, "EC Company Law Directives and Regulations: How Trivial Are They?" (2006) 27 University of Pennsylvania Journal of International Economic Law 1.
[81] See para.7–29, below.
[82] See Chs 11–13, below.
[83] See Ch.21, below. The Seventh on group accounts was less important since domestic law already recognised the principle of group accounting.

audits[84] and the Eleventh on branches.[85] Apart from the Second, which froze the law on legal capital in an unideal position, the impact of the Directives on UK company law has been beneficial overall.

By contrast, some proposals were never adopted by the Community legislature because it proved difficult to obtain the necessary level of Member State support for the more controversial proposed harmonisation measures. This was true, in particular, of the proposed Fifth Directive which dealt with two sensitive topics upon which Member States are pretty equally split: should the board be a one-tier structure (as is the practice in the UK) or a two-tier one, consisting of separate supervisory and management boards, and, even more controversial, should employee representation on the board (whether one-tier or two-tier) be mandatory?[86] The Fifth Directive was never adopted. For many years, the issue of mandatory employee representation also held up agreement on the European Company (see below) and on a Directive on cross-border mergers, and the issue was resolved there only by abandoning any significant commitment to uniformity, or even equivalence, of rules on employee representation. Instead, the matter is regulated, mainly though not exclusively, according to the model required by the law of the state from which the merging company with the highest level of representation comes.[87] Equally controversial has been the draft Ninth Directive on corporate groups, where the majority of states deal with group problems through general mechanisms of company law, whereas Germany has developed a separate regime for addressing issues of minority shareholder and creditor protection in group situations.

A new approach and subsidiarity

6–12 Such was the state of uncertainty into which the company law harmonisation programme had fallen by the end of the twentieth century that, at the end of 2001, the Commission appointed a High Level Group of Experts with the brief of providing "recommendations for a modern regulatory European company law framework". The HLG's Final Report[88] proposed a "distinct shift" in the approach of the EU to company law. Instead of the emphasis being, as hitherto, on the protection of members and creditors, the focus in future should be on what the Group saw as the "primary purpose" of company law: "to provide a legal framework for those who wish to undertake business activities efficiently, in a way they consider to be best suited to attain success".[89] Although the proper protection of members and creditors was an element of an efficient system of company law, those protections themselves should be subject to a test of

---

[84] See Ch.22, below, but the Eighth was revised in 2006 (Directive 2006/43/EC [2006] O.J. L157/87) and the second version was more significant.

[85] See para.6–2, above.

[86] See Ch.14, below.

[87] See paras 14–67 and 29–20, below.

[88] *Final Report of the High Level Group of Company Law Experts on a Modern Regulatory Framework of Company Law in Europe*, Brussels, 4 November 2002.

[89] Final Report, Ch.II.1.

efficiency. The Commission responded to the Group's Report in 2003 by producing a company law Action Plan which largely accepted the Group's recommendations.[90]

What were the main features of the new approach? First, the role of the EU in the area of company law became a more modest, though still significant, one. So long as the EU's task was viewed as one of harmonising Member States' company laws so as to produce equivalent protections across the Member States, no serious question could be raised about the central role of the EU in this process and the whole of company law was in principle open to EU regulation. By definition, harmonisation of national systems (if it is to be achieved by legislative fiat) is something which only EU law can guarantee and national laws cannot.[91] However, once the goal is put in terms of identifying an efficient framework for company law, the issue of subsidiarity[92] is clearly raised. It is not obvious that the EU, in principle, is better equipped to identify an efficient system of company law than the Member States, especially as national contexts differ substantially. An important implication of this new approach therefore was that the EU should concentrate, as far as new Directives were concerned, on those areas of company law where it has an especial legislative advantage, principally in relation to cross-border corporate issues.[93] The most significant Directives adopted in the company law area since the adoption of the Action Plan have fitted this pattern: the Cross-Border Mergers Directive (2005)[94] and the Directive on Shareholder Rights (2007).[95] However, it should be noted, in relation to the latter, that although the driving concern of the Commission was the difficulties facing a shareholder in Member State A wishing to exercise voting rights in a company incorporated and listed in Member State B, the Directive approaches this issue by conferring minimum rights on all shareholders in companies whose shares are traded on a regulated market. It is the limitation of the Directive to companies with publicly traded shares which really indicates the cross-border impetus of the Directive.

EU forms of incorporation

An alternative approach to harmonisation is for the EU itself to provide the corporate vehicle for businesses to adopt rather than for this to be a purely national competence. Unlike with the harmonisation of national company laws, there is no specific Treaty power for the EU to engage in this activity, and so proposals had to be put forward under the "gap-filling" powers in the Treaty,

6–13

---

[90] Communication from the Commission to the Council and the European Parliament, COM(2003) 284, 21 May 2003.

[91] On harmonisation "from the bottom up" see below para.6–25.

[92] Article 5 TFEU. Where both the EU and the Member States have competence, the EU should take action "only if and insofar as the objectives of the proposed action cannot be sufficiently achieved by the Member States and can therefore, by reason of the scale or effects of the proposed action, be better achieved by the Community".

[93] See above, fn.90, Ch.II.1.

[94] Directive 2005/56/EC [2005] O.J. L310/1. See Ch.29, below.

[95] Directive 2007/36/EC [2007] O.J. L184/17. See Ch.21, below.

which require unanimous Member State consent.[96] This necessarily made progress difficult. After many years the EU achieved success with the creation of an optional form of EU incorporation, the European Company ("SE"),[97] designed essentially for large companies and aimed at providing a mechanism for the cross-border amalgamation of public companies. The proposals had been beset by the same two problems as afflicted the Fifth Directive proposal (above). These problems were solved by giving the SE a choice between one-tier and two-tier board structures and by making employee representation mandatory for the SE only if one of the founding companies was already subject to such requirements under its national law. More generally, the law applicable to the SE depends heavily on the company law of the state in which it is registered, so that the degree of uniformity achieved is limited. However, it may have helped in securing adoption that the SE, unlike the Fifth Directive, did not require changes in national law but made available to national companies, if they wished to use it, a form of EU re-incorporation. Those supporting the SE proposal hoped it would encourage cross-border mergers (the founding companies are normally required to be in different Member States), either at top company level or within corporate groups. In fact, there is little evidence that the SE has been used extensively for this purpose—or, indeed, extensively used at all except in a few Member States.[98] Nevertheless, it has clearly not been an outright failure.[99]

The EU was emboldened by the adoption of the SE later to propose a European Private Company ("SPE") form of EU incorporation. This, however, is in effect a disguised harmonisation measure (it was to be available to individuals and had only a weak cross-border requirement). It constituted in fact a direct challenge to national regimes for private companies and it ran into predictable opposition from some of the Member States and was abandoned by the EU.[100] The effect of this defeat was to push the EU into producing a reduced but hybrid proposal for Single Person Company ("SUP"—*societas unius personae*). This is based on art.50 TFEU, where only a qualified majority vote of the Member States is required, and indeed it is formally an addition to the Twelfth Directive mentioned above,[101] but it requires Member States in effect to introduce a new

---

[96] Article 308, TFEU. In Case C-436/03 *Parliament v Council of the European Union* [2006] E.C.R. I-3733 the CJEU confirmed that proposals for EU forms of incorporation could not be brought forward under art.50 TFEU because they were not harmonisation measures.

[97] Council Regulation (EC) No 2157/2001 on the Statute for a European Company [2001] O.J. L294/1 and the accompanying Directive on employee involvement in the SE (Council Directive 2001/86/EC [2001] O.J. L294/22). See para.1–40.

[98] H. Eidenmuller, A. Engert and L. Hornuf, "Incorporating under European Law: The Societas Europaea as a Vehicle for Legal Arbitrage" (2009) 10 European Business Organization Law Review 1.

[99] As at the end of March 2015 there were 44 SEs registered in the UK, though that was decline of about 20 over the end March 2014 and 2013 figures: Companies House, *Company Registration Activity in the United Kingdom 2014-2015*, Table E3.

[100] [2014] O.J. C154/03. See P. Davies, *The European Private Company (SPE): Uniformity, Flexibility, Competition and the Persistence of National Laws* (Oxford Legal Studies Research Paper No.11/2011; ECGI—Law Working Paper No.154/2010. Available at SSRN: *http://ssrn.com/abstract= 1622293* [Accessed 28 April 2016]).

[101] See para.6–11, above.

form of incorporation into their national laws and to give that form of incorporation a common EU name (the "SUP").[102]

The single financial market and company law

An even more important conclusion which was drawn from taking subsidiarity **6–14** seriously was that the creation of a single financial market in Europe was a more appropriate area for EU activity than a harmonised company law. The integration of national capital markets was seen as a crucial aspect of the construction of the Single Market, more so than company law harmonisation, which was, so to speak, the price for freedom of establishment (also an essential feature of the Single Market) rather than a direct contributor to the Single Market. One consequence of the focus on securities law was to favour the adoption of some Directives which had been regarded previously as examples of the company law harmonisation process—the line between company and securities law being inexact. Thus, a Directive on takeover bids[103] was adopted in 2004, which had originally been proposed as the Thirteenth Directive in the company law series, but it eventually emerged without that formal designation. Equally, rules on disclosure of financial information by companies, a traditional area of company law when viewed through the lens of shareholder protection, could be re-packaged in a securities market context and presented as investor protection measures.

However, the focus of the EU on the single capital market did not just operate as a way of taking forward what might be regarded as "really" company law initiatives. Most financial market measures at EU level were aimed mainly at companies in their capacity as fund raisers on public markets. Clear examples were the Directives dealing with initial process of raising capital through public offers and the admission of securities to trading on public markets; subsequent disclosure to the market by issuers and, to some extent, their shareholders; and ensuring the non-distorted functioning of securities and other markets. The first two sets of Directives are discussed in more detail in Chs 25 and 26, below, and the third in Ch.30. All that need be noted here is that the first area (public offers and admission to trading) became a focus of EU action as long ago as the 1970s, so that for some time the company law and securities law programmes of the EU proceeded in parallel. However, a major change of gear occurred with the adoption in 1999 of a Financial Services Action Plan ("FSAP"),[104] which led to a significant level of legislative activity in the succeeding years and to the production, in particular, of Directives on prospectuses,[105] on disclosure by issuers (the Transparency Directive),[106] and on market manipulation (the Market Abuse Directive).[107] Not surprisingly, after the financial crisis of 2007 onwards,

---

[102] At the time of writing the Directive had not been adopted.
[103] Directive 2004/25/EC [2004] O.J. L142/12. See Ch.28, below.
[104] Financial Services, *Implementing the Framework for Financial Markets: Action Plan*, COM (1999) 232, 11 May 1999.
[105] Directive 2003/71/EC [2003] O.J. L345/64.
[106] Directive 2004/109/EC [2004] O.J. L390/38.
[107] Directive 2003/6/EC [2003] O.J. L96/16.

an intensification of regulation in this area occurred. A number of the earlier Directives were re-cast in a stronger form. In addition, in many cases the new EU instruments emerged as Regulations rather than Directives, since the available legal base for financial market legislation (art.114 TFEU) permitted the EU to adopt "measures" (not just Directives) "for the approximation of the provisions laid down...in Member States which have as their object the establishment and functioning of the internal market".

The FSAP was accompanied by a further innovation in legislative procedure at EU level, known as the "Lamfalussy" procedure for the regulation of European securities markets.[108] Under this approach the EU Directive or Regulation will sometimes contain only the principles of the legislation and the detail is laid down subsequently by the Commission, after consultation with (now) the European Securities Markets Authority, but without the need to go through the full EU legislative process.[109] The Commission has two broad types of secondary legislative powers: a narrower power relating to "technical standards" and a broader power relating to "delegated acts".[110] In both cases power to issue secondary legislation must be specifically conferred on the Commission by the parent Directive or Regulation. Where the Commission acts, the parent Directives and Regulations have to be read along with various implementing instruments (Directives or Regulations) issued by the Commission, which constitute a very significant part of the legislative process.

Corporate governance

6–15   A further implication of the new approach recommended by the High Level Group was that EU law-making, where this was required, should be less reliant on detailed Directives of the traditional type and make more use of Recommendations[111] and of instruments which imposed disclosure requirements rather than substantive rules.[112] This approach was initially particularly apparent in the sensitive area of corporate governance. Thus, the topics of board composition[113] and directors' remuneration[114] have been dealt with at EU level in this way—indeed through Commission rather than EU recommendations—with the recommendations again confined to publicly traded companies. Further, the EU rules on corporate governance codes take the form of a comply or explain obligation (as indeed is typical of national corporate governance codes) but with

---

[108] See the *Final Report of the Committee of Wise Men on the Regulation of European Securities Markets*, Brussels, February 2001.

[109] In EU jargon the subsequent procedure for law-making by the Commission is known as "comitology".

[110] Articles 290 and 291 TFEU.

[111] "Recommendations shall have no binding force": art.288 TFEU.

[112] See HLG, above, fn.88, Ch.II.2 and 3.

[113] Commission Recommendation 2005/162/EC on the role of non-executive or supervisory directors of listed companies and on committees of the (supervisory) board, [2005] O.J. L52/51, supplemented by the recommendation of 2009 mentioned in the following note.

[114] Commission Recommendation 2004/913/EEC fostering an appropriate regime for the remuneration of directors of listed companies [2004] O.J. L385/55, supplemented by Commission Recommendation C(2009) 3177, 30 April 2009.

the content of the code being determined, not by the EU, but by national-level bodies.[115] However, nothing is stable in the battle over law-making between central and national levels. At the time of writing agreement is likely at EU level on an expansion of the Shareholder Rights Directive,[116] which will substantially extend the mandatory EU rules in the area of corporate governance, so that they are as much concerned with constraining shareholder behaviour as giving shareholders' rights.

Reform of the existing directives

Some minor steps have also been taken to address the point about the "stickiness" of EU legislation. In fact, the Commission moved on this front ahead of the High Level Group's Report. It adopted in 1996 the Simpler Legislation for the Single Market ("SLIM") initiative. This was a general initiative, not confined to company law, but several of the initial company law directives have been amended through the SLIM process, albeit with only modest results.[117] In 2015 the Commission proposed to "codify" in a single document the core company law Directives on the basis that this would make access to them easier.[118]

6–16

CORPORATE MOBILITY

Corporate mobility can mean a number of things, perhaps most obviously the question of what constraints exist on a company's freedom to move its *head* office from one jurisdiction to another, something it may want to do in order to obtain the benefit of a more favourable tax regime. However, for the purposes of this chapter corporate mobility refers to the constraints on the freedom of a company to choose the jurisdictional location of its *registered* office and, having made an initial choice, to move it to another legal jurisdiction, without at the same time having to locate its head office or any other aspect of its operations in the jurisdiction of registration or to move them on a subsequent change of jurisdiction. This is a significant question because, under the British conflicts of law rules and those of most other jurisdictions, the company law applicable to a company is determined by the jurisdictional location of its registered office. If a company can freely choose its initial jurisdiction for incorporation and subsequently alter it, it is in a position to choose and subsequently alter the company law to which it is subject. However, that freedom will be constrained if its exercise imposes requirements on the location of its operational activities.

6–17

---

[115] See art.46A of the Fourth Directive, inserted by Directive 2006/46/EC art.1(7).

[116] Above fn.95.

[117] See Directive 2003/58/EC [2003] O.J. L221/13 (amending the First Directive); Directive 2006/68/EC [2006] O.J. L264/32 (amending the Second Directive); Directives 2007/63/EC [2007] O.J. L300/47 and Directive 2009/109/EC [2009] O.J. L259/14 (amending the Third and Sixth Directives); and Directive 2009/49/EC [2009] O.J. L164/42 amending the Fourth and Seventh Directives. Others of the initial directives have been substantially expanded over the years, notably the audit and accounts directives, so that they now have a broader scope than when adopted.

[118] Proposal for a Directive relating to certain aspects of company law (codification) (COM/2015/ 0616 final).

If we assume that entrepreneurs are free to choose and subsequently alter the law applicable to their company, then the scene is set, potentially, for regulatory competition among states as they seek to offer the law which is most attractive to companies and for regulatory arbitrage by companies as they move to the jurisdiction which offers the law which they favour. Corporate mobility does not in itself ensure regulatory competition by states and regulatory arbitrage by companies. Regulatory competition also requires that states conceive it to be in their interests to attract incorporations and regulatory arbitrage requires that companies perceive that the advantages of choosing the most favourable law outweigh any potential disadvantages. Without corporate mobility, however, regulatory competition will be weakened.

Nor does it follow that the result of competition would be that companies (or companies of a particular type) incorporate overwhelmingly in a particular state. This is certainly what has happened in the US where regulatory competition has led a large proportion of publicly traded companies to incorporate in the state of Delaware. It might be, instead, that states all bring their company laws in line with the model which companies prefer (in order not to lose incorporations) so that what competition produces is not migration of companies but convergence of states' company laws. In this perspective, the power to transfer the registered office would put some pressure on those responsible for company law in a particular jurisdiction to ensure that it remained attractive to businesses. The CLR thought this was the correct approach in principle: "In general, it is desirable that businesses should remain in Great Britain because it is attractive for them to do so, and not because company law in some sense locks them in".[119] If Member States reacted in this way to competition, then the result might be characterised as harmonisation of company laws "from the bottom up" rather than "from the top down", as under the EU's original programme of company law Directives, discussed in para.6–9. Alternatively, competition might lead not to harmonisation on a single model but to a form of "specialisation" in which different Member States offer somewhat different corporate laws, each adapted to the dominant form of business organisation to be found in their jurisdiction. Whatever the precise result, it would be the operation of competitive pressures rather than legislative fiat which determined the nature and extent of the harmonisation process.[120]

As we shall see below, whilst corporate mobility has long been freely available in the US, in the EU that is not (or not yet) fully the case. Some jurisdictions (such as the UK ones) have long made the choice of company law on initial incorporation available and as a result of decisions of the Court of Justice of the European Union ("CJEU"), interpreting the Treaty provisions on freedom of establishment, this principle now applies throughout the EU. Freedom subsequently to alter the applicable company law by moving the registered office, however, is much less securely available—even for UK-incorporated companies or foreign-incorporated companies which wish to move into a British jurisdiction.

---

[119] Completing, para.11.55.
[120] For an extended analysis of the issues discussed in this paragraph see J. Armour, "Who Should Make Corporate Law? EC Legislation versus Regulatory Competition" (2005) 58 *Current Legal Problems* 369.

We begin with a brief discussion of the purely domestic rules on corporate mobility before moving onto the more challenging question of how far they have been modified by EU law.

Domestic rules

As we have seen in para.6–2, British law recognises the existence of companies **6–18** validly formed under the law of a foreign jurisdiction when they carry on business in the UK. This principle is applied even if the company carries on no business in its state of incorporation but operates entirely in the UK—and it was always intended by its founders that it should do so. So, the British rule of recognition of a foreign company is simply its valid incorporation elsewhere (the "incorporation rule"). Thus, at the point of initial incorporation of a company, the founders have a free choice of the applicable company law. As far as British law is concerned, they may choose any jurisdiction for incorporation and then carry on business entirely in the UK. The alternative recognition rule, used by some Member States of the EU, is the "real seat" rule, which requires the registered office to be in the same jurisdiction as the company's headquarters (or place of central management). Such a state would refuse to incorporate a company whose central management is not present in that state. Even more important, this state might well refuse to recognise the existence of a company validly incorporated in another jurisdiction under that jurisdiction's rules, but carrying out no or only insignificant activities there, thus putting its contracts and property in jeopardy in the state where it operates.

If a company incorporated in a foreign jurisdiction, but operating in the UK, wishes to move its registered office to another foreign jurisdiction, that is a matter for the jurisdictions involved. If the foreign jurisdictions allow this to happen, British law will recognise the result. However, British law is directly engaged if a company registered in one of the UK jurisdictions wishes to move its registered office to a foreign jurisdiction—or if a company registered in a foreign jurisdiction wishes to move its registered office to the one of the UK jurisdictions. Curiously, in contrast with its liberal stance at the point of incorporation, British law provides no simple mechanism whereby a company may make such a move, even as between the British jurisdictions. When the founders apply to register a company in the UK, they must state in which of the three UK jurisdictions its registered office is to be situated: England and Wales, Scotland or Northern Ireland.[121] There is no simple mechanism provided whereby the registered office can be changed subsequently from the jurisdiction of incorporation to another.[122] Thus, a company which is formed with its registered office in England and Wales cannot decide by resolution to transfer its registered office to Scotland, still less to some other Member State of the EU or to a state

---

[121] 2006 Act s.9(2)(b).

[122] The facility for companies whose registered office is in fact in Wales to alter the statement so as to toggle between "Wales" and "England and Wales" does not involve a change of legal jurisdiction. The change has an impact on the availability or otherwise on the use of Welsh in the company's official documents and in communications with Companies House. See s.88.

outside the EU.[123] Nor will it accept an incoming company on the basis of a simple resolution of its shareholders to move the registered office to the UK.

6–19   However, it is possible to produce indirectly a transfer of registered office into or out of the UK. The transferring company might go into (solvent) liquidation in its current jurisdiction and in that process transfer its assets to a company incorporated in the new jurisdiction, but the tax consequences of such a way of proceeding make that course of action unattractive. Within the UK the company might use a scheme of arrangement to effect a merger with another company located in the new jurisdiction.[124] Or the transferring company might make use of the EU's cross-border merger Directive to move its registered office into or out of the UK.[125] But a simple transfer of the registered office is not a technique which is made available. On the other hand, these alternative mechanisms contain a reasonably high level of protection for shareholders, creditors and perhaps other interests. These protections are built into the scheme of arrangement and cross-border merger mechanisms. When the liquidation mechanism is used, the assets of the company are valued at the time of transfer and that value is paid by the new company to the former owner, thus protecting both existing shareholders and existing creditors. The transferring company's creditors are protected because the transferring company will receive the proceeds of the sale against which they can assert their claims, and the liquidation gives the shareholders of the transferring company an exit route from the company and some assurance that the transferring company's assets have been properly valued.

However, it is difficult to believe that adequate protection for members and creditors could not be provided through a set of rules applying to a simple transfer of the registered office. The Company Law Review proposed such a scheme for exit from a UK jurisdiction,[126] which was based on that laid down in the European Company Statute.[127] The SE is empowered to move its registered office from one EU State to another (albeit provided it moves its head office as well, which was not a feature of the CLR's proposals). Moreover, the CLR proposals envisaged the possibility of transfer of the registered office outside the EU and also within the UK (which is not a matter for EU regulation). The basis of the proposal was that transfer in principle should be permitted (i.e. the opposite of the present law) but subject to adequate safeguards for shareholders and creditors. The main elements of protection for members would be the requirement that the board draw up a detailed proposal about the transfer, that the proposal should require approval by special resolution of the shareholders (thus requiring a three-quarters majority approval) and that dissenting members should have the power to apply to the court which might order such relief as it thought appropriate. Thus, for shareholders, the protective techniques invoked were disclosure, supermajority approval and court control. For the protection of

---

[123] Since British law adopts the incorporation theory, a UK company may freely move its headquarters out of the UK without imperiling the validity of its incorporation in the UK in the eyes of British law. This is useful for companies which wish to retain British company law but does not address the issue of companies which wish to change the applicable company law.

[124] On schemes of arrangement see Ch.29.

[125] Cross-border mergers are discussed below at para.6–27.

[126] Completing, paras 11.54–11.70 and Final Report I, Ch.14.

[127] Reg.2157/2001/EC art.8.

creditors, it was additionally proposed that the directors would have to declare the company to be solvent and able to pay its debts as they fell due for the 12 months after emigration, the creditors would have the right to apply to the court to challenge the proposal and the company would have to accept service in the UK even after emigration in respect of claims arising from commitments incurred before emigration.[128]

Transfer would have been permitted, on compliance with these rules, to any EU or EEA Member State, but transfer to a non-EU state would be dependent upon the Secretary of State having approved that state for this purpose, the criteria for approval being related mainly to levels of creditor protection, especially for creditors resident outside the state. Finally, for transfer within the UK a less detailed proposal would need to be developed by the board and the right of dissenting shareholders to apply to the court would be removed. The full range of creditor protections, however, would apply since there are significant differences in security and property law between the three jurisdictions.[129] However, the Government rejected the CLR's proposals for international migration, on grounds of feared loss of tax revenues.[130]

EU law: initial incorporation

We now turn to the question of how far the above rules have been modified by EU law. Corporate mobility is an area where EU law has had a significant impact, but, unusually for company law, law developed by the CJEU rather than the EU legislature has been the driver of reform to date. The court has proceeded mainly on the basis of its interpretation of the freedom of establishment provisions of the Treaty. Article 49 TFEU prohibits restrictions on the freedom of establishment of nationals of one Member State in the territory of another Member State and adds that such prohibition also applies "to restrictions on the setting up of agencies, branches or subsidiaries".[131] Just to make things absolutely clear, art.54 TFEU requires companies "formed in accordance with the law of a Member State and having their registered office, central administration or principal place of business within the Community" to be treated in the same way as natural persons who are nationals of a Member State. The EU has from time to time mooted the adoption of a directive dealing with corporate mobility and it may be that, after a period of not being interested in the topic, it is about to return to the EU's agenda.[132] There

6–20

---

[128] If the company, after emigration, maintained a place of business in the UK it would become subject to the information provision rules for overseas companies (above); if not, it would in any event have to file with Companies House contact details relating to its new jurisdiction.

[129] Immigration would also be permitted but there the regulatory burden would fall mainly on the former state of registration. The British requirements would parallel those for a domestic company which re-registers: Final Report I, para.14.12 and above, paras 4–20 et seq.

[130] Modernising, pp.54–55.

[131] The right of a company established in another Member State to set up an agency, branch or subsidiary in Great Britain is normally referred to as the right of "secondary establishment". The right of a company to transfer its registered office to another Member State is referred to as the right of "primary establishment" and is dealt with at paras 6–22 et seq., below.

[132] The Commission has a long-standing proposal for a Fourteenth Directive in the company law harmonisation series on the transfer of the registered office, on which work has been intermittent. It ceased most recently in 2007 (Commission Staff Working Document, *Impact Assessment on the*

is a strong case for a Directive, since the CJEU has not been able to resolve all the issues surrounding corporate mobility. To put it briefly, the Court has established freedom for the founders to choose the applicable corporate law at the point of incorporation but has not yet established fully corporate mobility thereafter. Since UK domestic law already provided choice of law at the point of incorporation, the impact of the Court's rulings to date has been to benefit founders who wanted to operate in other Member States of the EU through companies incorporated in one of the UK jurisdictions where that other Member State applied the "real seat" theory or in some way qualified its application of the "incorporation" theory.

6–21   The first proposition which seems to have emerged from the CJEU's decisions is that a company validly established under the law of Member State A must be recognised by Member State B, even if B would not recognise the company as validly established under its own rules. This is also the domestic UK rule. As understood in the UK, its "incorporation rule" turns on valid incorporation in another Member State but it does not seek to evaluate the incorporation rules set by that state.[133] Consequently, if B is a real seat state, the rules about the location of operational activities would have to be respected for incorporation to take place in B and, in consequence, for British law to recognise the incorporation.

6–22   The starting point for the Court's development of the law was its decision in the *Centros* case.[134] In *Centros*, the Court held that Denmark had infringed a company's freedom of establishment, when that company was incorporated in England, but carried on all its business in Denmark and the Danish authorities refused to register its Danish operations as a branch. It was clear that the British incorporation had been effected in order to avoid the Danish minimum capital requirements. However, the Danish position was perhaps weakened by the fact that the Danish authorities admitted that the branch would have been registered, if the company had carried on some business in the UK, even though its main business was in Denmark, Denmark being an incorporation rule state. This reduced the force of the argument that the minimum capital rules were a necessary protection for Danish creditors. More important was the decision in *Inspire Art*,[135] also involving an incorporation theory state, the Netherlands. Dutch law thus had no difficulty about recognising the existence of a company incorporated in another Member State (again the UK) and so did not refuse to register its branch. However, Dutch law did apply to "pseudo-foreign" companies (i.e. those incorporated elsewhere but for the purpose of doing business wholly in the Netherlands) certain rules of Dutch law, notably its minimum capital rules. The CJEU held that creditor protection did not justify the imposition of

---

Directive on the cross-border transfer of registered office, SEC (2007) 1707, 12 December 2007). However, in 2013 the Commission again consulted on the topic.

[133] See the quotation from Lord Wright, above para.6–2.

[134] Case C-212/97 *Centros Ltd v Erhverus-og Selkabsstyrelsen* [1999] E.C.R. I-1459. For an earlier and under-appreciated decision going in the same direction see Case 79/85 *Segers v Bestuur Bedrijfsvereniging voor Bank-en Verzekeringswezen, Groothandel en Vrije Beroepen* [1986] E.C.R. 2375.

[135] *Kamer van Koophandel en Fabrieken voor Amsterdam v Inspire Art Ltd* [2003] E.C.R. I-10155. However, the state where the main centre of operations is located is free to apply its insolvency law to a company registered elsewhere, since such provisions do not infringe freedom of establishment: Case C-594/14, *Kornhaas v Dithmar* [2016] B.C.C. 116.

requirements additional to those imposed by the state of incorporation: creditors were sufficiently protected by the fact that the company in question did not hold itself out as a Dutch company but as one governed by English law.

These two decisions had a substantial impact in practice. Entrepreneurs from other Member States, not intending to do business in the UK, may choose to incorporate in the UK in order to avoid minimum capital requirements and expensive formation formalities in their home jurisdictions; and this produced the expected response in the shape of other Member States seeking to reduce or remove their minimum capital requirements for private companies.[136] This was a clear case of corporate mobility leading to regulatory arbitrage by companies to which the Member States affected responded by harmonising their laws on or towards the British model, at least in the narrow area of legal capital and, perhaps, formation procedures.

6–23

A particularly interesting aspect of the *Inspire Art* decision was the implication that the Eleventh Directive on branches[137] determined the maximum level of regulation a Member State was permitted to impose on companies incorporated in other Member States—subject, however, to one important exception. Restrictions of freedom of establishment by national legislatures are permitted, provided they meet the "*Gebhard* test",[138] that is, they are non-discriminatory, pursue a legitimate objective in the public interest, are appropriate to ensuring the attainment of that objective and do not go beyond what is necessary to attain it. This is the general formula used by the Court to determine the extent to which Member States may constrain the fundamental free movement provisions of the Treaty. The test, it can be seen, sets out very general standards and it is not clear how much freedom it gives to Member States to impose national rules on pseudo-foreign companies. Would it be lawful, for example, for the German legislature to require a pseudo-foreign company to abide by its domestic rules on mandatory representation for workers on the boards of large companies?

EU law: subsequent re-incorporation

The Court of Justice has not had to decide squarely a case involving post-incorporation transfer of the registered seat alone. All the litigation to date has involved companies which transferred their headquarters or central administration to another jurisdiction and either did not want to change the applicable law or wished to change the applicable law at the same time as moving the headquarters. Some transfer cases can be disposed of under the proposition identified above about B recognising valid incorporations in A. In *Uberseering*[139]

6–24

---

[136] See M. Becht, C. Mayer and H. Wagner, "Where Do Firms Incorporate? Deregulation and the Costs of Entry" (2008) 14 *Journal of Corporate Finance* 241; W. Bratton, J. McCahery and E. Vermeulen, "How Does Corporate Law Mobility Affect Lawmaking? A Comparative Analysis" (2009) 57 American Journal of Comparative Law 347.

[137] Above, para.6–3.

[138] Case C-55/94 *Reinhard Gebhard v Consiglio dell'Ordine degli Avvocati e Procuratori di Milano* [1995] E.C.R. I-4165.

[139] Case C-208/00 *Uberseering BV v Nordic Construction Company Baumanagement GmbH* [2002] E.C.R. I-9919.

a company transferred its centre of administration from an incorporation theory state (in this case the Netherlands) to a real seat theory state (in this case Germany). The German courts refused to recognise the company's legal personality and so it could not sue to enforce its contractual rights in a German court. The CJEU held that this was an infringement of the Dutch company's freedom of establishment. Since the company was still validly incorporated under Dutch law, German law was obliged to recognise its existence, even though the company did not meet the standards for incorporation under German law.[140] Although not a case about transfer of the registered office, *Uberseering* does establish the proposition that, provided a company acts in compliance with the rules of its state of incorporation, it has a EU law, right to transfer its headquarters to another state within the EU. For UK courts, the significance of the proposition is limited, since in a UK jurisdiction transfer of the headquarters would not cast doubt on the validity of the incorporation in the UK. The importance of the proposition is that the state receiving the headquarters must continue to recognise the validity of the UK incorporation.[141]

However, it is unclear whether the first proposition relates solely to compliance with company law rules of the state of incorporation. UK company law places no obstacles in front of transfer of the headquarters but what about tax law? An early decision of the European Court suggested that the transferring state had considerable freedom in this regard. In *Daily Mail*[142] an English-incorporated company wished to transfer its central administration outside the UK, whilst keeping its registered office in the UK, but was discouraged from doing so by a swingeing domestic tax demand. The domestic restrictions were upheld. Although some doubt on the validity of exit taxes under the Treaty provisions on freedom of establishment was generated in cases subsequent to *Daily Mail*,[143] that decision has not been overruled.

6–25   The second proposition which has emerged from the cases and which does have significance for a company seek to transfer its registered office is that the Member State's incorporation rules, whatever they may be, must be applied in an equal fashion to domestic and foreign companies. However, implicit in this proposition is acceptance that the state of current incorporation remains in control of its rules for valid incorporation—subject to any relevant EU Directives. In particular, if it is a real seat state, the Treaty provisions on freedom of establishment do not require it to abandon those rules. This illustrated by the decision in *Cartesio*.[144] Like *Uberseering*, this was a case where the company transferred its headquarters (from Hungary to Italy) and did not want to change its applicable law. Unlike *Uberseering*, the question for the Court was the validity

---

[140] "The requirement of reincorporation of the same company in Germany is tantamount to outright negation of freedom of establishment" (at 81).

[141] If the transferring state is a real seat state, then of course moving the headquarters to another state does cast doubt on the validity of the company's incorporation in the transferring state and EU law does not seek to alter that result. See *Cartesio*, below.

[142] Case C-81/87 *Daily Mail and General Trust* [1988] E.C.R. 5483.

[143] Case C-9/02 *Hughes de Lasteyrie du Saillant v Ministère de l'Economie, des Finances et de l'Industrie* [2004] E.C.R. I-2409; Case C-196/04 *Cadbury Schweppes Plc v Commissioners of Inland Revenue* [2006] E.C.R. I-4585.

[144] Case C-210/06 *Cartesio Oktató és Szolgáltató bt* [2008] E.C.R. I-964.

of the company's continued incorporation in the transferring state (Hungary), not its recognition in the transferee state. Also, unlike in *Uberseering*, the transfer of the headquarters out of Hungary did affect the validity of its continued incorporation in Hungary, whose officials refused to continue the company's registration in that state. The Court (Grand Chamber) upheld the Hungarian decision, on the grounds that the determination of the factors required for the validity or continued validity of incorporation in a Member State was a matter for that state, not for EU law.[145] However, the court did go out of its way to address the situation which was not before it, i.e. where the company wishes to transfer its registered office in order to change the applicable law. Here, by contrast, the Courts approach was different. The *Cartesio* facts were to be "distinguished from the situation where a company governed by the law of one Member State moves to another Member State with an attendant change as regards the national law applicable, since in the latter situation the company is converted into a form of company which is governed by the law of the Member State to which it has moved". Here the Court's view was that the national legislation of the transferor state was not justified "by requiring the winding up or liquidation of the company, in preventing that company from converting itself into a company governed by the law of the other Member State, to the extent that it is permitted under that law to do so".[146]

In *Vale*[147] the situation arose which was in many ways the converse of the situation in *Cartesio*. In *Vale* an Italian company de-registered in Italy with a view to transferring both its registered office and its business to Hungary, but the Hungarian authorities refused to effect the transfer, on the grounds that the domestic re-incorporation provisions did not apply to foreign-incorporated companies. The Court held that this refusal was a breach of arts 49 and 54 TFEU. The core of the reasoning was as follows. Hungarian law did have provisions which allowed domestic businesses to convert from one form of incorporation to another (without loss of legal personality), just as UK law allows provides for conversion from a private to a public company and vice versa, for example. It appears that in this case *Vale* proposed to re-incorporate in Hungary as the same type of company as it had been in Italy. Nevertheless, the Court held that the exclusion of a cross-border re-incorporation from the domestic conversion provisions was in principle discrimination against foreign companies. This meant that the national authorities would have to adapt the domestic procedural rules to deal with the situation of re-incorporation by a foreign company. In particular, the Hungarian authorities would have to take account of the documentation issued by the Italian authorities in the course of the Italian de-registration proceedings. On the other hand, there appears in the judgment to be no infringement of the

6–26

---

[145] "Thus a Member State has the power to define both the connecting factor required of a company if it is to be regarded as incorporated under the law of that Member State and, as such, capable of enjoying the right of establishment, and that required if the company is to be able subsequently to maintain that status. That power includes the possibility for that Member State not to permit a company governed by its law to retain that status if the company intends to reorganise itself in another Member State by moving its seat to the territory of the latter, thereby breaking the connecting factor required under the national law of the Member State of incorporation" (at 110).

[146] See at 111–112.

[147] Case C-378/10 *VALE Epitesi kft* [2013] 1 W.L.R. 294.

principle of national control of incorporation requirements. If the Italian company had proposed not to transfer its headquarters to Hungary and this was a requirement for incorporation in Hungary (for all companies), the Hungarian authorities would have been entitled to refuse registration.

On the other hand, these decisions can be said to have implications for domestic law. The fact that the Court in *Vale* required domestic re-incorporation provisions to be adapted for use by companies incorporated in another Member State suggest the UK should introduce some simple transferring in procedure. Since the UK is an incorporation rule state, there would be no need for the transferring-in company to move its operations to the UK at the same time as it moved its registered office. Some Member States, for example, Spain[148] do permit a transfer in of the registered office, but many, including the UK, do not. Equally, the dictum in *Cartesio* suggests the UK should have some simple procedure for transferring out the registered office.

EU law: alternative transfer mechanisms

6–27   There are other mechanisms available to a company which wishes to change its applicable law. The obvious alternative technique—though it is rather more costly—is to form a subsidiary in the new jurisdiction and merge the existing company into it. Unlike for the transfer of a registered office, EU law does now provide a mechanism for a cross-border merger.[149] This is potentially significant. For example, in the US the standard mechanism for transferring incorporation to the state of Delaware is the merger of the existing company into a Delaware corporation. However, the crucial point to be made here is that the company resulting from the merger (whether a new company or an existing one) must be validly incorporated in the new jurisdiction and the Directive, following the policy of the CJEU, leaves criteria for valid incorporation to be determined by the member states.[150] Consequently, a real seat state may continue to insist that, for valid incorporation in that state, the headquarters of the resulting company be located in that state. This reduces the attraction of the merger mechanism if what the company seeks to achieve is a simple change in the applicable law—unless it is prepared to incur the potentially substantial additional costs of moving the company's headquarters to the jurisdiction of the resulting company. By contrast, the cross-border merger directive does facilitate the choice by a company of the law of an incorporation rule state.

A further mechanism which EU law makes available is the European Company ("SE").[151] The companies which found an SE may choose any Member State in which to incorporate the new entity, whether or not any of the founding companies operated in that jurisdiction.[152] Furthermore, the SE does benefit from a EU mechanism for the simple transfer of its registered office to another

---

[148] See art.94 of the Ley 3/2009 de Modificaciones estructurales de las sociedades mercantiles (LME) and art.309 of the Reglamento del Registro Mercantil (RRM).

[149] The UK transposing rules are discussed in Ch.29, below.

[150] Directive 4.1(b) and Recital (3).

[151] See para.6–13, above.

[152] SE Reg art.7

Member State after formation.[153] However, the SE is currently required to have its headquarters in the same jurisdiction as its registered office,[154] thus reducing its attractiveness as a mechanism for changing the applicable company law alone. If this ceases to be the case, the state of registration must take steps to require the SE either to move its head office back to the state of registration or to move its registered office to the State where its head office now is; failing either of these things, the state of registration must have the SE wound up.[155] The SE Regulation required the Commission to report on the functioning of the SE statute after five years of operation and in particular on the appropriateness of maintaining this requirement,[156] but no reform resulted from the report.[157] Even if this restriction were removed, the costs of establishing a SE simply for the purposes of changing the applicable law might deter significant use of this mechanism.

Finally, and most obviously, the EU might act to require all Member States to amend their laws so as to provide to all companies a simple mechanism for the transfer of their registered office. Thus, the law of the state of current incorporation would have to permit the transfer of the registered office to transferee state and the law of the transferee state would have to permit re-incorporation, in both cases without the company in question being wound up, but subject to appropriate safeguards for minority shareholders, creditors and employees. But the EU appears reluctant to grapple with this issue.[158]

Conclusion

The changes in the rules governing corporate freedom to move the registered office have produced regulatory competition at the level of company formation. Whether providing an equivalent level of corporate freedom at the stage of re-incorporation would generate the same level of regulatory competition among states and regulatory arbitrage by companies is much less clear. Even if a convenient legal mechanism for transfer were provided, would states compete for re-incorporations and would companies wish to transfer their registered offices? The particular revenue gains from reincorporation which the state of Delaware obtains in the US are simply not available in the EU, though there may be other incentives for states to attract re-incorporations.[159] As for the companies themselves, the incentives for mature companies to change jurisdictions will be very different from those operating at the time of initial incorporation of small

6–28

---

[153] SE Reg art.8. See para.6–19, above, for some of the details of this process.

[154] SE Reg art.7.

[155] SE Reg art.64, implemented by the Insolvency Act 1986 s.124B.

[156] SE Reg art.69(a).

[157] The Commission's report might be said to favour the arguments for removing the restriction, but the Commission did not positively recommend this course of action: *Report from the Commission ... on the application of Council Regulation 2157/2001 on the Statute for a European Company (SE)*, SEC(2010) 1391, 17 November 2010, 4.2.

[158] See fn.132, above.

[159] J. Armour, "Who Should Make Corporate Law? EC Legislation versus Regulatory Competition" (2005) 58 *Current Legal Problems* 369. Whilst not disputing that the revenue-raising incentives operating on the state of Delaware have no counterpart in the case of the UK, he sees the incentive as located with the "magic circle" law firms based in London, which would pressurise the government to provide laws which encourage re-incorporations.

companies. They may not wish to litigate their corporate law matters in a jurisdiction with which they are not otherwise connected or, alternatively, have the courts of their headquarters jurisdiction apply a foreign law with which those courts may be unfamiliar.

However, it is not clear that there is a strong argument against permitting freedom to transfer the registered office by way of re-incorporation. On the contrary, if Member States, when reforming corporate law, are influenced mainly by a desire to provide efficient company law to their "own" companies rather than to attract re-incorporations of foreign companies, then this suggests that no element of "corporate dumping" is involved when a company does decide to move to the law of another Member State. Equally, if companies weigh all the relevant factors before deciding to re-incorporate, this suggests that the choice which is ultimately made will be the appropriate one.

6–29   The contrary argument to those put forward in favour of regulatory competition, and which constitutes the basis of the real seat theory, is that to allow a company to choose a jurisdiction for incorporation, even though it carries on no substantial economic activities in that state or perhaps even no economic activities at all, weakens the power of the state where those activities are carried on to impose mandatory rules on companies for the benefit of members, creditors or employees. If a company does not like the rules of the state where it has based its operations, it will simply choose the law of another Member State for its incorporation.[160] What will then ensue is a "race to the bottom" among the Member States of the EU as they compete to provide company laws which companies find attractive.

Although these fears are not fanciful, they can be exaggerated and may even be misplaced. First, as a result of the EU's initial company law harmonisation programme (discussed above in this chapter), there are minimum standards in place below which no Member State's company law can go. Secondly, and most importantly, competition does not necessarily result in a reduction of protection. In the case of financial markets, competition among stock exchanges for investors' funds has led to a raising of standards, especially in areas such as insider dealing, market abuse and corporate governance. The crucial question is who decides on the distribution of the good (in this case, the incorporation decision) for which the competition exists. In the US, where incorporations are a matter for each state, where the incorporation theory prevails and where a high proportion of public companies choose to incorporate in Delaware, even though their businesses may have no connection with Delaware, the argument that this situation has produced a race to the bottom seems to be based on the proposition that re-incorporations are in practice the result of a board decision, so that Delaware has a strong incentive to produce a corporate law which is too favourable to management and which provides too little protection for

---

[160] Of course, this is an existing risk for incorporation theory states whose company law contains some feature which incorporators do not like and which some other available jurisdiction does not insist on. See the *Kamer van Koophandel en Fabrieken voor Amsterdam v Inspire Art Ltd* [2003] E.C.R. I-10155. Real seat theory states seek to protect themselves against competitive pressures through a private international law rule, whereas incorporation theory states will have to use some other technique to address the threat, such as a "pseudo-foreign" company statute.

shareholders and creditors.[161] One way of addressing this problem is not to make the re-incorporation decision a purely managerial one. It is relatively easy to build into the re-incorporation decision a substantial role for shareholders, creditors and employees, as the cross-border mergers Directive does. Moreover, in the case of listed companies, it is probably the rules and mechanisms of the exchange which are more important for the protection of shareholders than the provisions of company law as such.

CONCLUSION

British company law has traditionally adopted a welcoming stance towards companies incorporated elsewhere. This is shown both by the limited extent to which it applies the provisions of the British Act to such companies and its acceptance of incorporation as the connecting factor in its private international law rules. However, it is much less open to transfers by British companies of the registered office to other jurisdictions or the simple transfer in of the registered office by companies already incorporated in other jurisdictions (as opposed to their conduct of business in the UK). However, to a substantial extent, it has preferred the goals of maximising freedom of movement and promoting a degree of competition among jurisdictions as against ensuring that those dealing with foreign companies do so on the basis of a framework of law with which they are familiar. Within the EU these two objectives have been reconciled to some degree through the programme for the harmonisation of company laws, though that initiative never achieved all its promoters wished and expected of it. However, free movement and jurisdictional competition cannot be achieved by one state alone, since the migrating company is dependent also on the laws of the country to which or from which it moves. For this reason, corporate migration is undoubtedly a proper subject for the attention of the EU legislator, or failing that, of the Court of Justice of the European Union.

6–30

---

[161] It is much controverted whether the Delaware law maximises managerial freedom or shareholder value. For a convenient short account of the, now very large, literature, see R. Romano, *The Foundations of Corporate Law* (New York: Oxford University Press, 1993), pp.87–99.

PART 2

SEPARATE LEGAL PERSONALITY AND LIMITED LIABILITY

We saw in Pt 1 that the separate legal personality of the company is a necessary feature of the creation of a company and that limited liability, although optional, is overwhelmingly chosen by those who incorporate a company. Having created an artificial person, the law has to decide how that person acts and knows. This can be done only by attributing the acts and knowledge of natural persons to the company in appropriate situations. The delineation of those situations has proved to be a taxing exercise, mainly because the rules of attribution need to vary from one area of liability to another. There is no reason to suppose that the rules should be the same in relation to, for example, contractual and criminal liability—and in fact every reason to suppose that they should not be. The first chapter in this part analyses the rules of attribution.

The remainder of this part deals with limited liability. Opinions continue to differ on the question of whether limited liability is a natural consequence of separate legal personality or a perversion of the ordinary and proper state of affairs. Nevertheless, it is clear that British company law is firmly committed to the principle and that it is only rarely that the common law will set that principle aside. Statute law has shown some greater willingness to do so in recent years (or to disqualify directors from acting through the corporate form in the future), where limited liability has been abused. These innovations have had an important impact on small companies, where the interposition of a company between the entrepreneur and his or her creditors can seem, on occasion, artificial.

The traditional response of company law to the risks of limited liability, however, has been not to set that principle aside but rather to lay down rules on "legal capital", which in British law turn out to be mainly rules restricting the freedom of the controllers of companies to move assets out of the company when this might prejudice the company's creditors. By contrast, British law has traditionally shown little interests in rules on minimum capital. Legal capital is an area where the British rules have been particularly influenced by EU law in the shape of the Second Company Law Directive. Again, opinions differ on the efficacy of legal capital rules in protecting creditors and on whether the statutory rules, mentioned in the previous paragraph, are a better solution to the problem, though increasingly penetrating criticisms of the concept of legal capital in general, and of the Second Directive in particular, have been advanced in recent years.

[148]

CHAPTER 7

CORPORATE ACTIONS

INTRODUCTION

One consequence of the abstract nature of a company as a legal person is that   7–1
inevitably decisions for, and actions by, it have to be taken by natural persons.
Decisions on its behalf may be taken either (a) by its primary decision-making
bodies (the board of directors or the members collectively); or (b) by officers
(including individual directors), agents or employees of the company. Acts done
on its behalf will perforce be by (b). Similar problems of attribution arise where
the question is simply whether the company "knew" about a certain fact or
situation. The question is whether the decision taken, act done or knowledge held
by the natural persons can properly be attributed to the company. There clearly
needs to be some linkage between the natural persons in question and the
company for the company's legal position to be regarded as having been altered.
Much of this chapter is about identifying the linkages that the law has accepted
and those it has rejected. Those connections are clearly easier to identify where
the board or shareholders as a body have purported to act as the company, but
corporate life would be difficult or inappropriately regulated if the company's
legal position could be affected only by actions of the board or the shareholders
collectively. On the one hand, a large company would find contracting a

cumbersome activity if all contracts, even relatively minor ones, had to be approved by the board or the shareholders collectively. On the other, it would be surprising if a company could escape all tortious or criminal liability where the wrongful act was authorised or committed by a senior manager who was neither a director nor a shareholder.

In this chapter we are concerned with the answers to these questions primarily in two contexts. The first is where the company purports to enter into a contract with an outside third party. If a company could not acquire and enforce contractual rights and subject itself effectively to contractual duties, it would find the carrying on of its business a very difficult matter. This is obviously true of companies with a commercial purpose, but the statement is true of all companies which need to deal with third parties. The company would find it difficult to plan its future in the absence of enforceable contractual rights, and, in the absence of contractual duties enforceable against the company, counterparties would be unwilling to contract with companies or would routinely require guarantees from individuals of the company's obligations. What is required is a simple and straightforward set of rules whereby the company can contract through the actions of individuals, for the benefit of both companies and third parties.[1] The law has developed two principal approaches to providing those rules. Where the company contracts through the decision-making bodies established in its articles of association (board of directors, shareholders collectively), the solution is provided by organisational law and is straightforward. The company is bound because its constitutionally established decision-making bodies have committed it to the contract. Where, however, the contract is entered into on the company's behalf other than by these bodies, some further set of rules is required. There was no need to develop a company-specific set of overall rules to achieve this goal. The common law of agency, applying to non-corporate as well as corporate principals and their agents, furnished the bed-rock structure. However, as we shall also see, agency and organisational rules have had to be tweaked in order to deal with some particular features of corporate structure and doctrine.

7–2   The second situation is where the individual acting on behalf of the company commits a wrongful act. Is the company liable in this situation? This question arises principally in the criminal law and in tort, though it exists in other areas, such as wrongdoing in equity. The company may seem to have an obvious interest in not being liable for the wrongdoing of those connected with it. However, on a more sophisticated view it is doubtful whether this is true. If companies, some of which are powerful economic actors and all of which contribute to the functioning of the economy, are seen to be free of liability for the wrongful acts of those acting for them, then there is likely to be increased

---

[1] At least this is the "ex ante" position, i.e. before any contracting has taken place. Ex post, i.e. once a "contract" has been made and has been broken, one or other party may have an interest in arguing that the agreement was never effective as a contract. Ex ante, however, where neither company nor counterparty will know whether it will wish to enforce or avoid the agreement, it is suggested that both will be in favour of rules facilitating contracting.

political pressure for rules which reduce the freedom of action of companies.[2] From the point of view of the efficient enforcement of the law, it can be argued, further, that corporate liability gives those in control of the company a strong incentive to constrain wrongful action on the part of those acting on its behalf and so corporate liability contributes to law enforcement—an argument that has appealed to the legislature in recent years.

With wrongdoing it is again appropriate to hold the company liable where the constitutional decision-making bodes of the company have committed the wrong. Normally, this means the company is liable because board or shareholders collectively have authorised the wrongdoing, though in the case of a company with only a single shareholder or director, that person might actually commit the wrongful act. Beyond those bodies, general doctrines of the common law again provided a second basis for corporate liability, without the need to establish a company-specific set of rules. In the law of tort, the doctrine of vicarious liability is available to provide a framework of corporate liability and proved to be capable of dealing with most cases of corporate principals as it did with non-corporate ones. In criminal law and some cases of non-criminal liability, however, vicarious liability has proved controversial, at least in relation to serious crimes, whether the person sought to be made vicarious liable was a company or not. Here the law developed a third layer of rules for those areas where vicarious liability did not "work" in relation to companies.

This third layer of rules, like the first, is company-specific, in the sense that they require consideration of how a particular liability rule relates to the processes whereby decisions are taken and implemented within companies. Sometimes, these rules were made by the legislature, sometimes by the courts. Thus, from the beginning of the twentieth century the courts developed the notion of corporate "direct" liability, whereby the actions and states of mind of the person connected with the company were attributed to the company so as to make it a wrongdoer. Unlike with vicarious liability, where only the liability of the connected person was visited on the company and the company itself was not a wrongdoer, with direct liability the company itself becomes a wrongdoer.[3] As we shall see below, the courts had difficulty in establishing the boundaries of direct liability and it has only recently begun to be developed in a satisfactory way. Legislative interventions to create direct liability have been uncommon. The principal example is the Corporate Manslaughter and Corporate Homicide Act 2007, which imposes criminal liability for this serious crime in circumstances where the notion of common law direct liability proved inadequate.

Overall, therefore, the broad answer to this fundamental question—how does a company decide, act or know?—is provided through a tripartite hierarchy of rules. At the top are the rules setting up the constitutional structure of the

7–3

---

[2] An analogy is provided by the application in the nineteenth century of the ultra vires doctrine to companies (see para.7–29, below). In this case the externality which drove the application of this restriction seems to have been fear of the negative impact of limited liability on the position of creditors.

[3] *Jetivia SA v Bilta (UK) Ltd* [2015] 1 B.C.L.C. 443 at [70] (Lord Sumption) and [186] & [203] (Lords Toulson and Hodge). Thus, although Lord Sumption disagreed with the approach of the other judges to the disposition of this case, both accepted this distinction between vicarious and direct liability.

company and its decision-making bodies, i.e. its articles of association; then general doctrines of the common law such as agency and vicarious liability; and at the bottom, where neither of these approaches is available, statutory or common law rules attributing liability specifically to companies in some cases. The top and bottom layers in this tripartite division involve analysis of issues peculiar to companies (or at least corporations). The middle (and practically very important layer) consists of general common law doctrines, which are not company-specific, though their application to companies raises some difficulties which do not arise where companies are not involved. Following the terminology developed by Lord Hoffmann in *Meridian Global Funds Management Asia Ltd v Securities Commission*[4] the first layer can be referred to as company law's "primary rules of attribution" because of their location in the constitution of the company; the second as its "general rules of attribution"—general because they apply also to principals who are not companies but natural persons; and the third as its "special rules of attribution" because their function is to provide for corporate liability in situations where such liability is thought to be appropriate but neither of the first two approaches to attribution is capable of achieving that result. The residual and ill-defined function of the third approach no doubt explains why definition of its scope has proved so controversial, both in the courts and the legislature.

CONTRACTUAL RIGHTS AND LIABILITIES

7–4   As noted above, decisions can be taken by or on behalf of a company to enter into a contract or other transaction with a third party in two ways, either by the decision-making bodies established under the Companies Act by the company's articles of association (i.e. its board of directors or the shareholders acting collectively) or by persons (who may include individual directors) acting as its agents. Where the board or the shareholders collectively act, they constitute the company, i.e. they act *as* the company. They are not its agents. For the same reason, they will not be personally liable on any resulting contract, which will exist only between the third party and the company. Where the company contracts through an agent, the law of agency, as we shall see, produces a similar result in the standard case, i.e. that the contract exists only between the third party and the company. Despite the similarity of the results in the two cases, we need to examine them separately because the rules applicable in the two situations are not identical. We will begin with corporate contracting through the directors or shareholders collectively[5] and then move on to contracting through agents.

---

[4] *Meridian Global Funds Management Asia Ltd v Securities Commission* [1995] 2 A.C. 500 at 506 PC. In the nineteenth century the courts did often categorise the board as the agent of the company, but this view seems not to have survived the early twentieth century re-characterisation of the articles as a constitution, dividing the powers of the company between the shareholders collectively and the board. See para.14–6 and the use by the Act of the term "constitution" to refer to the articles of association (s.17). For a discussion of this development whereby the board came to be seen as acting as the company rather than on its behalf, see Lord Walker of Gestingthorpe NPJ in *Moulin Global Eyecare Trading Ltd v Comr of Inland Revenue* [2014] 3 HKC 32 HKCFA at [61]–[64].
[5] The directors or shareholders may operate not by making a contractual offer to or accepting an offer made to them by a third party but by approving the agreement in principle and by authorising

Although there is a good deal of similarity in the law applicable in the two situations, it is suggested that the complexity of the applicable law can better be understood by dividing the subject-matter up as proposed. It is also necessary to set out the common law agency rules, partly because they explain the form of the modern rules on contracting via the board and partly because they still largely determine legal outcomes where third parties contract other than through the board or the shareholders collectively.

Contracting through the board or the shareholders collectively

Where the articles confer management powers on the board or the shareholders collectively and the board or shareholders, in the exercise of those management powers, enter into contracts with third parties, the conclusion that an effective contract results is straightforward. If the law rejected this proposition, corporate contracting would become an unwarrantably complicated matter. Where the board or the shareholders collectively contract, the question of how authority to contract was conferred upon them is easily answered: it is to be found in the company's constitution, principally its articles. The difficulty which has exercised both the courts and the legislature since the early years of modern corporate law is how to deal with situations where either board or shareholders go beyond the powers conferred upon them by the articles. As we have seen in Ch.3, it is rare for the board and the shareholders each to have unrestricted and equivalent management powers—though it seems that the constitutional arrangements of the company could be set up in this way. Normally, the articles of association divide up the management powers of the company between the shareholders and the directors, giving the greater part to the directors. Thus, it is possible that a third party will contract with the company via the board in an area where the board cannot act or where the board's powers are restricted. The same issue may also arise in relation to contracting through the shareholders collectively. Third parties probably expect the shareholders' powers under the articles to commit the company to contracts to be limited, but, by contrast, they normally expect that the board will have wide management powers. Consequently, they are likely to be surprised if, after apparently contracting with the company through the board, they are met with the argument that the board did not have power to bind the company.[6]

7–5

---

someone else to contract on behalf of the company when all the details have been settled. So, board involvement in the contracting process does not necessarily mean that the board contracts as the company; instead an agent may contract on the company's behalf acting within the authority conferred by the board. Where the company contracts directly, its decision needs to be manifested in some way to the counterparty. Until the last quarter of the nineteenth century, the company executed a contract by having its seal attached to a written contract by a person authorised to attach it, and that procedure is still available (s.43). Now the contract may be executed by a company without a seal, normally by the signatures of two directors or of a director and the secretary or of one director whose signature is attested by a witness (s.44) and a company need no longer have a common seal (s.45). If, however, the company wishes to execute the contract as a deed, rather than a simple contract, the rules are somewhat more constraining: ss.44 and 46 (these sections do not apply in Scotland). For benevolent interpretation of s.44 see *Williams v Redcard Ltd* [2011] 2 B.C.L.C. 350 CA.

[6] Thus, even in relation to private companies, the model articles confer responsibility for the management of the company on the board and provide that "for which purpose they may exercise all

In any event, an immediate question thus arises: is the contract binding on the company if the board (or shareholders) act outside the powers conferred upon them by the articles of association? From the point of view of the shareholders as a whole in the case of a board decision or the non-assenting shareholders in the case of a shareholder decision to contract, there is an argument that the constitutional arrangements of the company should be paramount. Either the articles are followed or the company should not be contractually committed (until such time as the articles are altered). Overall, the development of the law in recent times has been in the opposite direction, i.e. towards preserving third parties' reasonable expectations that the body purporting to contract as the company had power to do so, even if that power was restricted by the articles. Given the primacy of the board in relation to the allocation of management powers under the articles of most companies, this policy was implemented in relation to board contracting, and it is upon board contracting that we will concentrate below. The modern view is thus away from the notion that restrictions in the company's articles on the contracting powers of the board are something with which third parties are expected to familiarise themselves.[7] However, this is not the position from which company law started out.

Constructive notice and the rule in Turquand's case

7–6   As the law developed in the nineteenth century the answer to the question whether the company was bound by a transaction entered into by the board (or shareholders)[8] outside their powers as laid down in the articles was perceived to turn principally on whether the third party knew (or ought to have known) that the board were acting outside their authority. If the third party knew the board had so acted, then the transaction was not binding on the company unless the company chose to ratify it.[9] Thus, the security of the third party's transaction depended on the will of the company in such a case. The view was taken that the third party, knowing of the board's lack of authority, had no legitimate claim to hold the company to the contract against the company's wishes.

---

the powers of the company" (Model Articles for private companies, art.3). By implication the powers of the shareholders do not extend to management, except to the extent that the articles of a particular company (or, of course, the Act) explicitly confer management powers upon them. Under the model articles a major qualification to art.3 is to be found in art.4 which gives the shareholders a reserve power of intervention: the shareholders at any time by special resolution may instruct the directors what action to take or refrain from taking in a specific situation.

[7] This approach clearly favours third parties and reduces the transaction costs associated with corporate contracting. But it does not turn the allocation of management powers in the articles into a dead letter. The directors may still be liable to the company for acting in breach of the articles (a liability expressly preserved by s.40(5) of the Act and then identified by s.171—see paras 7–15 and 7–24, below). The directors may thus be liable to make good to the company any loss it suffers as a result of unauthorised contracting and, in the unlikely event the shareholders get wind of proposed unauthorised contracting, they might be able to secure an injunction against the directors to restrain it.
[8] In the nineteenth century the question arose really only in relation to the board because the shareholders' powers were then regarded as unlimited (except by the objects clause). See para.14–6, below.
[9] On ratification see para.7–27.

This potentially defensible position was rendered completely indefensible, however, by the doctrine of constructive notice, which deprived the third party of the security of the transaction, even though that party had no actual knowledge of the board's want of authority and no practical means of finding it out, other than a detailed study of the company's constitution. The rule developed by the courts in the nineteenth century was that anyone dealing with a company registered under the companies legislation was deemed to have notice of its "public documents", a term which certainly included its articles, which are required to be filed at Companies House.[10] By developing this rule the courts substantially enhanced the restrictive impact of provisions in the articles limiting the board's authority. By treating third parties as knowing that which they would have known had they read and understood the articles, the courts in many cases deprived the third party of a plausible claim to a reliance interest which the law should protect. The company might choose to ratify the contract but was not bound to do so, so that the third party's contractual rights and duties rested on the company's decision.

However, the nineteenth century position was not quite as harsh as the above paragraph suggests. It was modified by the so-called "rule in *Turquand's* case"[11]—sometimes referred to as the "indoor management rule". This rule had the effect that, in some cases, the third party could assume that the directors had authority to act, even if a fair reading of the articles might lead a third party to make further enquiries. In *Turquand*[12] itself security for a loan had been given by a company through its directors, but the articles provided that the directors could borrow only such sums as were authorised by the shareholders in general meeting and the requisite authority had not been given. Jervis CJ said that a third party reading the company's articles would discover "not a prohibition on borrowing, but a permission to do so under certain conditions. Finding that the authority might have been made complete by a resolution, he would have a right to infer the fact of a resolution authorising that which on the face of the document appeared to be legitimately done". This was a benign interpretation of the constructive notice doctrine, since the courts might have said that the constructive notice of the articles put the third party on notice to enquire whether the shareholders had in fact given the requisite authority. It should be noted this benign removal of the duty to make further enquiries must apply, a fortiori, to a third party who has actually read the articles.

In *Mohoney v East Holyford Mining Co*,[13] the *Turquand* doctrine was approved and applied by the House of Lords in an even more difficult case. Here, a bank had honoured the company's cheques, signed by two of three named directors, after having received from the company's secretary a copy of a board resolution giving cheque-signing powers to the three directors, to which their signatures had been appended. Unfortunately, neither "secretary" nor "directors"

7–7

---

[10] *Ernest v Nicholls* (1857) 6 H.L.C. 401 HL: "If [third parties] do not choose to acquaint themselves with the powers of the directors, it is their own fault and if they give credit to any unauthorized persons they must be contented to look to them only", per Lord Wensleydale.

[11] *Royal British Bank v Turquand* (1856) 6 E. & B. 327 Exch.Ch.

[12] The account in the text of the facts has been somewhat altered to relate the holding to a modern company.

[13] *Mohoney v East Holyford Mining Co* (1875) L.R. 7 H.L. 869.

had been appointed but had simply acted as such. Nevertheless, the bank successfully resisted an action for the repayment of the money. Provided nothing appeared which was contrary to the articles, the bank was entitled to assume that the apparent directors had been properly appointed. This protection for third parties was partially re-affirmed by statute which originally provided[14] that the acts of a director were valid "notwithstanding any defect that may afterwards be discovered in his appointment or qualification". However, in *Morris v Kanssen*[15] the House of Lords held that the section applied only when there had been a defective appointment and not where there has been "no appointment" at all. In the light of this, s.161 of the 2006 Act provides a somewhat expanded protection, applying not only in the case of the subsequently discovered defect in the appointment but also where the director is disqualified from holding office, has ceased to hold office,[16] is not entitled to vote on the matter in question or (which was already part of the statutory protection) the appointment was in breach of the requirement that appointments of directors be voted on individually.[17] However, the section does not render valid the acts of a person who acts as director without ever purportedly having been appointed. In this situation the decision in *Mahoney* continues to provide protection.[18] The *Kanssen* case also establishes that the protection of what is now s.161 does not apply to a third party who actually knows of the facts giving rise to the invalidity of the director's appointment.[19]

7–8   Although immensely important in keeping the doctrine of constructive notice within some sort of bounds, the indoor management rule has significant limitations. First, it does not protect the third party if the constitution simply provides that a particular type of contract cannot be entered into by board at all. To vary the facts of *Turquand* slightly, if the articles had provided that loans above a certain amount could not be contracted for by the directors at all (i.e. third parties must contract with the shareholders in such cases), the rule would not have protected a lender whose contract was approved by the board alone, even if the restriction on the board's powers was an unusual one.[20]

---

[14] See, for example, s.285 of the 1985 Act.

[15] *Morris v Kanssen* [1946] A.C. 459; applied in *Re New Cedos Engineering Co Ltd* [1994] 1 B.C.L.C. 797, a case decided in 1975.

[16] This was the issue in *Morris v Kanssen* itself, where an originally valid appointment had expired without being renewed and this was treated as "no appointment at all" when the director continued to act as such.

[17] The extensions result from the incorporation into the Act of provisions previously found in art.92 of Table A, the current model articles containing no provisions of this type. On the requirement for voting individually, see para.14–25.

[18] It may be wondered how the shareholders are protected against the actions of rogues unconnected with the company who manage to persuade a third party that they are the directors of the company and can contract with him. In *Mahoney* it was an important part of the reasoning that the shareholders had acquiesced in the activities of the de facto directors.

[19] See also *Channel Collieries Trust Ltd v Dover etc Light Railway Co* [1914] 2 Ch. 506; and *British Asbestos Co Ltd v Boyd* [1903] 2 Ch. 439.

[20] *Irvine v Union Bank of Australia* (1877) 2 App. Cas. 366 PC extended this proposition. The directors' authority to borrow was limited to a certain amount unless a "special vote" of the shareholders had enlarged their powers. If there had been such a special vote, it would have been required to be notified to the Registrar of companies and be made publicly available in the same way as the articles. The court refused to apply *Turquand* on the ground that inspection of the company's registered documents would have revealed whether the directors' powers had been enlarged or not.

Secondly, and perhaps more important, the *Turquand* rule does not apply if the third party has been put on notice or on enquiry as to the board's lack of authority. Obviously, this exception cannot arise simply out of the third party's constructive or even actual notice of the company's constitution, for that would be entirely to negate the indoor management rule. Something else is required. In the leading case on this point, *B. Liggett (Liverpool) Ltd v Barclays Bank*,[21] where the third party bank had actual knowledge of the articles, the question was whether the bank was entitled to assume that the appointment of a third director had been properly made. Such appointment required the consent of both existing directors. The letter informing the bank of the appointment was signed by only one existing director (L). The other existing director (M) had for a long time made it clear to the bank that it should not meet cheques which were not signed by himself, in line with the articles' requirement for two signatory directors, because he thought that L was improperly withdrawing money from the company's account. Nevertheless, after the "appointment" of the third director by L, the bank met cheques which carried the signatures of L and the purported third director. The prior dealing between M and the bank as to the signing of company cheques was the "something else" which put the bank on enquiry to establish whether M had in fact consented to the appointment of the third director; the bank was not entitled to assume such consent.

Statutory protection for third parties dealing with the board

Despite the qualifications to the constructive notice doctrine which the indoor management rule had introduced, from the point of view of third parties the resulting state of the law was unattractive. No third party could safely refrain from reading and analysing the company's articles before contracting with it, for fear of finding a ban or restriction on the board's contracting powers which could not be removed by some internal corporate procedure. In modern times the policy view has been taken that commerce will be promoted by relieving third parties from the need to check the company's constitutional documents before engaging with the company's board. The company is free to limit the authority of the board, but the constitution is no longer seen as an obviously appropriate way to communicate such limitations to third parties. Other and more direct methods must be employed. In line with this policy, the legislature moved to enact statutory provisions which extended the protection afforded to third parties by the indoor management rule. The reforms were introduced in 1972,[22] revised in 1989, and the current version is s.40 of the 2006 Act.[23]

7–9

Subsection (1) of s.40 provides:

This suggests that *Turquand* is limited to cases where the necessary shareholders' resolution is one that does not need registration in the public registry.

[21] *B. Liggett (Liverpool) Ltd v Barclays Bank* [1928] 1 K.B. 48. For a more modern example see *Wrexham Associated Football Club Ltd v Crucialmove Ltd* [2007] B.C.C. 139 CA.

[22] Somewhat surprisingly in s.9 of the European Communities Act of that year. It was required upon the UK's entry into the EU to comply with the First Company Law Directive. Without this stimulus it is very unclear when this sensible reform would have been introduced.

[23] Section 40 does not apply to a charitable company, except in the cases set out in s.42, principally where T (i) is unaware the company is a charity; or (ii) gives full consideration in the transaction and

"(1) In favour of a person dealing with a company in good faith, the power of the directors to bind the company, or authorise others to do so, shall be deemed to be free of any limitations under the company's constitution."

This provision overtakes the indoor management rule because it simply removes all limitations on the powers of the board to contract for the company which the articles impose, whether those limitations are removable by shareholder resolution or are absolute. It effectively repeals the constructive notice rule within the scope of application of the section. But the section is subject to some limitations.

(a) "In favour of a person dealing with a company in good faith"

7–10 This phrase makes it clear that the section is for the benefit of third parties, not the company. The company cannot rely on it to make the contract binding as against a third party where the agent lacked authority and the third party seeks to escape from the contract. However, this point is not as important as it might seem, since the company can often make the contract binding on itself and the third party by ratifying it (see para.7–27 below). More important, these words demonstrate that not all third parties are to benefit from the section. Only "good faith" third parties will do so. But other provisions make it clear that "bad faith" is going to be difficult to establish. Section 40(2) provides a three-tiered set of protections for third parties. First, it provides that a person dealing with the company "is not bound to enquire as to any limitation on the powers of the directors to bind the company or authorise others to do so".[24] This sets aside the "put on enquiry" qualification to the indoor management rule. The fact that circumstances indicated that there might be some limitation on the directors' authority in the articles and the third party failed to follow this up will not now by itself put the third party in the "bad faith" category.

Secondly, the third party is presumed to have acted in good faith, unless the contrary is proved, so that the burden of proof falls on the company rather than the third party.[25] Thirdly, and most startling, the section provides that the third party is not to be regarded as acting in bad faith "by reason only of his knowing that an act is beyond the powers of the directors under the company's constitution". This appears to contemplate that a person dealing with directors with actual knowledge that they are exceeding their powers will not necessarily be found to be in bad faith. The section does not provide, of course, that actual knowledge cannot be an ingredient in the establishment of bad faith, but it does prohibit the simple equation of knowledge and bad faith. As Nourse J said of the same phrase in s.9 of the European Communities Act 1972:

---

is unaware of the directors' lack of authority. In addition, ratification of an unauthorised act requires the consent of the charity commissioners. For Scotland see s.112 of the Companies Act 1989 which makes similar provisions.

[24] 2006 Act s.40(2)(b)(i).

[25] 2006 Act s.40(2)(b)(ii).

"What it comes to is that a person who deals with a company in circumstances where he ought anyway to know that the company has no power to enter into the transaction will not necessarily act in good faith. Sometimes, perhaps often, he will not. And a fortiori where he actually knows."[26]

However, this dictum does not help enormously in working out when a third party with knowledge will be deemed to lack good faith. One might think that only little need to be added to knowledge of lack of authority to produce bad faith.[27]

(b) "Dealing with a company"

Subsection (2) gives help in the interpretation of dealing. It provides: 7–11

"(2) For this purpose—
(a)   a person 'deals with' a company if he is a party to any transaction or other act to which the company is a party."

A person deals with the company so long as he is a party to a transaction (e.g. a contract) or an act (e.g. a payment of money) to which the company is also a party. Despite this, the courts remain reluctant to bring gratuitous transactions with the meaning of the subsection.[28]

(c) Persons

Section 40 seems to apply quite generally to "persons" dealing with the company   7–12
in good faith. However, there is an obvious policy question about whether corporate insiders (especially directors) should be permitted to take advantage of the section when they deal with the company. Are they truly third parties or should they be treated as persons in relation to whom the principle that they should know and understand the limitations contained in the company's constitution is a perfectly reasonable and practicable one? The issue had already arisen at common law in relation to the question of whether corporate insiders could benefit from the indoor management rule. In *Morris v Kanssen*[29] the claimant seeking to rely on the *Turquand* rule had assumed the functions of a director of the company at the time of the disputed transaction. The House of

---

[26] *Barclays Bank Ltd v TOSG Trust Fund Ltd* [1984] B.C.L.C. 1 at 18.
[27] In *Ford v Polymer Vision Ltd* [2009] 2 B.C.L.C. 160 the judge was prepared to send to trial the issue of the third party's good faith where the disputed transaction was so one-sided against the company as to raise the question whether the claimant knew or ought to have known the directors were acting in breach of duty in entering into it. Note that the breach of duty was not the directors' failure to observe the articles; to allow bad faith to be established on the basis of breach of that duty would completely undermine the section.
[28] *EIC Services Ltd v Phipps* [2004] 2 B.C.L.C 589 CA at [35], excluding an issue of bonus shares on the grounds that the subsection requires either a bilateral transaction or an act to which both company and third person are parties and which is binding on the company, if s.40 is to apply; and *Re Hampton Capital Ltd* [2016] 1 B.C.L.C. 374, excluding restitutionary claim for money misappropriated from the company. See also *International Sales and Agencies Ltd v Marcus* [1982] 3 All E.R. 551 at 560, but decided on different wording.
[29] *Morris v Kanssen* [1946] A.C. 459 (para.7–7, above). See also *Howard v Patent Ivory Manufacturing Co* (1888) 38 Ch. D. 156.

Lords held that, as he was thus under a duty to see that the company's articles were complied with, it would be inconsistent to allow him to take the benefit of the rule. However, in *Hely-Hutchinson v Brayhead Ltd*[30] Roskill J interpreted the exclusion more narrowly: a director was an "insider" only if the transaction with the company was so intimately connected with his position as a director as to make it impossible for him not to be treated as knowing of the limitations on the powers of the officers through whom he dealt.

However, in relation to s.40, the legislature seemed to have answered the question in s.41. Where the company enters into a transaction which exceeds a limitation on the powers of the directors under the company's constitution and the other parties to the transaction include a director of the company or its holding company or a person connected with such a director,[31] the transaction, far from being enforceable against the company, is voidable at the instance of the company.[32] Furthermore, whether or not the transaction is avoided, such parties *and* any director who authorised the transaction on behalf of the company are liable to account to the company for any gains made and to indemnify the company against any loss resulting from the transaction.[33] Thus, the company might seek to stay with the contract (perhaps because it is too late to obtain a substitute performance elsewhere) but sue the director acting outside the articles for damages (for example, where at the time of contracting the substitute consideration was available at a lower price). The transaction ceases to be voidable in any of the four events[34] set out in subs.(4) but this, in principle, does not affect the company's other remedies.[35] The section does not affect the operation of s.40 in relation to any party to the transaction other than a director or a person with whom the director is connected but where that other party is protected by s.40 and the director is not, the court may make such order affirming, severing or setting aside the transaction on such terms as appear to be just.[36]

Despite the presence of s.41, a majority of the Court of Appeal (Robert Walker LJ, as he then was, dissenting on this point) held in *Smith v Henniker-Major*[37] that s.40 was not available to the director, at least on the facts of that case, where the director dealing with the company was also chairman of the company (and therefore under an obligation to see that its constitution was properly applied) and was responsible for the error in the transaction with himself (a rare legal recognition of the importance of the chairman of the board). The point may seem an arcane one, since the director in that case clearly fell within what is now s.41, but it has some importance, because a transaction within s.40, but caught by s.41,

---

[30] *Hely-Hutchinson v Brayhead Ltd* [1968] 1 Q.B. 549.

[31] 2006 Act s.41(2), (7)(b). The meaning of "connected person" is discussed in para.16–71.

[32] 2006 Act s.41(2).

[33] 2006 Act s.41(3). There is a defence for non-director defendants (i.e. connected persons who are not directors) if they can show they did not know the directors were exceeding their powers: s.41(5).

[34] (a) restitutio in integrum is no longer possible; (b) the company has been indemnified; (c) rights of a bona fide purchaser for value (other than a party to the transaction) would be affected; or (d) the transaction is affirmed by the company.

[35] But note that actual indemnification is one of the situations in which the transaction ceases to be voidable: s.41(4)(b).

[36] 2006 Act s.40(6). See *Re Torvale Group Ltd* [1999] 2 B.C.L.C. 605.

[37] *Smith v Henniker-Major* [2002] 2 B.C.L.C. 655 CA.

is binding unless set aside by the company, whereas, if the transaction is outside s.40 and governed by the common law, it will not be binding on the company unless ratified by it. In other words, s.41 is more favourable to third parties than the common law. It is submitted that the reasons given by Robert Walker LJ are the more convincing, i.e. that, in the light of the fact that the legislature has expressly addressed the issue of corporate insiders in s.41, there is no need for the courts to give the word "person" an unnaturally limited meaning in s.40.[38] In short, it is submitted that corporate insiders, dealing with the company in good faith, are within s.40 but that the protection they obtain is that laid down in s.41.[39]

(d) The directors

The section removes limitations in the company's constitution on the powers of directors to bind the company or to authorise others to do so.[40] Thus, a person who deals with the company through its shareholders in general meeting obtains no benefit from the section, for example, where the company's constitution provides that the shareholders cannot commit the company to a particular type of contract without the approval of X, who might be a shareholder of the company, a director or neither. Here, the limitation in the constitution relates to the power of the shareholders, not the directors, to bind the company. So, those who deal with the shareholders are still subject to the perils of the common law, including constructive notice as modified by the indoor management rule.

7–13

Of course, it is unusual for third parties to deal with companies through the shareholders as a body, and hardly feasible except in the case of small companies. Even where the third party deals with the directors, all may not be plain sailing. Suppose that the board has purported to act on behalf of the company but is for some reason unable to act, for example, because it is inquorate. Will the third party still have the protection of the section? It was held at first instance under the previous version of the section that the third party was not then protected: if there were not enough members of the board present under its rules to constitute a meeting of the board, the directors could not be said to have done anything.[41] However, s.40, by substituting the word "directors" for the phrase "board of directors" in the provision quoted in the previous paragraph, seems designed to settle this point in the third party's favour. If the directors collectively have decided to contract, it does not matter that their decision does not constitute a valid board decision. Nevertheless, the underlying problem remains. It can hardly

---

[38] For the same reason it is submitted that the dicta in *EIC Services v Phipps* [2004] 2 B.C.L.C. at [37] CA to the effect that even shareholders are not intended to be protected by s.40, should not be followed. Since Parliament dealt with the position of directors in s.41, it is unlikely it would not have dealt with that of shareholders, if it had wished to qualify the protection conferred on them by s.40.

[39] It is true that s.41(1) preserves "any rule of law by which the transaction may be called in question" but the *Smith* decision proceeded on the basis of an interpretation of s.40, not by application of an independent rule of law.

[40] The significance of the extension of the section to those authorised by the directors is discussed in para.7–25.

[41] *Smith v Henniker-Major & Co* [2002] B.C.C. 544, upheld on appeal ([2002] 2 B.C.L.C. 655 CA), but with only Carnwath LJ fully supporting the judge's reasoning on this point and Robert Walker LJ taking the contrary view. In other words, in the latter's view the quorum requirement is to be treated as one of the limitations in the company's constitution which the section is designed to override.

be the case that third parties, dealing with persons with no connection with the company, can claim the benefit of s.40 on the grounds that the failure of those persons to be elected directors by the company is a "limitation under the company's constitution" which third parties are entitled to ignore, provided they are good faith third parties. As has been said, the "irreducible minimum" for s.40 to operate must be "a genuine decision taken by a person or persons who can on substantial grounds claim to be the board of directors acting as such".[42]

(e) Any limitation under the company's constitution

7–14 The company's constitution includes its articles of association, which constitute, in fact, the principal element of the constitution.[43] The standard definition of the constitution in the Act extends further to special and other supermajority resolutions and their equivalents.[44] But for the purposes of s.40 the constitution includes in addition ordinary resolutions of the company or a class of shareholders and agreements among the members of the company or any class of them.[45] In short, the constitution here means any formal rules laid down by the shareholders generally (or any class of them) for the conduct of the company's affairs, whether taking the form of the adoption or alteration of the company's articles or not.

(f) The internal effects of lack of authority

7–15 As the opening words of s.40 make clear, the purpose of the section is to protect good faith third parties dealing with the company. Its aim is not to alter the internal effect of directors' actions taken without authority, except insofar as such amendment is needed to protect third parties. Consequently, the Act preserves individual shareholders' powers to bring an action to restrain the directors from doing an act to which would be in excess of their powers.[46] Such relief cannot be granted, however, if it would impede the fulfilment of the company's legal obligations to the third party. The provision thus operates in the narrow window where the directors are proposing to exceed their powers, but have not yet done so, or have exceeded their powers without creating a legally binding obligation on the company (e.g. creating a contractual option in the company's favour). Further, s.40(5) preserves the liability of directors "and any other person" who causes the company to contract in breach of limitations contained in its constitution. That liability may arise under s.171, requiring directors "to act in accordance with the company's constitution".[47] Likewise, it seems likely that the section does not affect the liability of a third party to return property or its value

---

[42] *Smith v Henniker-Major & Co* [2002] 2 B.C.L.C. 655 at [41], per Robert Walker LJ. Under the current law the word "directors" should be substituted for "board of directors".
[43] 2006 Act s.17(a).
[44] 2006 Act s.29.
[45] 2006 Act s.40(3).
[46] 2006 Act s.40(4).
[47] See para.16–24. "Constitution" of the purposes of s.171 is defined in s.257. The "other person" might be someone who assists the director in the breach of duty.

to the company as a constructive trustee, where corporate property is received knowing (to the appropriate extent) that its transfer is in breach of directors' duties.[48]

Contracting through agents

The second situation we need to consider is where the company contracts through an agent acting on its behalf. As we have noted above, it would be highly inconvenient for companies and their counterparties if all contracts required board or shareholder approval. A low-cost mechanism is needed whereby individual managers within the scope of their duties can contract with third parties on behalf of the company. In some cases the company may wish to confer contracting authority even on outsiders. That mechanism is provided by the law of agency, which is based on the notion of authority. Under agency law a person, the principal (P), who authorises another, the agent (A), to contract on his or her behalf with a third party (T) will be bound by the contract which results from A's successful negotiations with T. The resulting contract will exist between P and T. A will not be a party to it and will normally owe no duties to T in relation to the contract.[49] Thus, if the company (P) authorises a manager (A) to contract with third parties in a particular area of the company's activities, that manager will be able to bring about contracts between the company and third parties without the need for specific board consent for each contract.

7–16

The first and obvious question is, how does a corporate P confer authority upon a managerial A? It is conceivable that the articles will confer power upon a particular person to contract on the company's behalf, just as the articles normally confer broad managerial powers on the board. However, such provisions in the articles are rare. The articles are altered only infrequently and through a procedure requiring shareholder consent,[50] whilst the allocation of contracting powers across the company's managerial hierarchy may require frequent adjustment. More commonly, therefore, corporate agents are authorised through a process of delegation and sub-delegation of managerial powers by the board. The board will typically appoint the company's senior managers with wide managerial powers, which will explicitly or implicitly include powers to contract with third parties on the company's behalf. Those managers may appoint more junior managers with authority to contract within the scope of their functions. And so on. The result is a highly flexible system for the distribution of contracting powers across the company. In companies with large businesses contracting authority can be widely dispersed; in small businesses the articles may allocate all contracting powers to the board or even to the shareholders; and all manner of other patterns of contracting authority can be created.

---

[48] *International Sales and Agencies Ltd v Marcus* [1982] 3 All E.R. 651; *Re Hampton Capital Ltd* [2016] 1 B.C.L.C. 374.

[49] The classic exception to this statement is where A does not disclose to T the fact of the agency (the "undisclosed principal" case). On discovering the truth, T can choose to continue to hold A to the contract or to treat the contract as one with P.

[50] See para.3–31, above.

7–17   The system works smoothly so long as A in fact has authority to contract. Legal dispute arises when A acts beyond the authority conferred or the purported A was never given any authority. The question arises whether the agreement negotiated by A with T purportedly on behalf of P has resulted in a binding contract between P and T. The underlying policy questions are the same as with board contracting. Is priority to be given to the company's allocation of contracting authority (implying the company is not bound if A has exceeded the authority conferred by P or simply has no authority) or are T's reasonable expectations that A had authority to be protected (implying that *in some cases* T should be able to enforce the agreement against P despite A's lack of authority)? A principal function of the law of agency is in fact to protect the reasonable expectations of T. However, identifying the appropriate balance between T and P is not easy. There are two principal questions to be answered. First, assuming ignorance on the part of T of A's lack of authority, was it reasonable for T to suppose that the unauthorised A did in fact have authority to enter into the contract in question on behalf of the company? Second, if T knew or could have found out about A's lack of authority, does that deprive T of the protection that a positive answer to the first question would have conferred upon T?

The first question does not arise in relation to board contracting—or rather the answer to it is very straightforward—because s.40 in effect embodies the proposition that it is reasonable for good faith third parties to assume that the contracting powers of board are unlimited. Formally, s.40 removes in favour of good faith T only limitations on the board's powers which are contained in the company's constitution. Once these are taken out of the picture, however, it is difficult to see what other restrictions on the board's powers might be set up against T, since the board's managerial powers are derived from the constitution.[51] However, there is no basis for making an assumption of unlimited contracting powers in relation to sub-board agents, and to do so would deprive the board of all control over the allocation of contracting power within the company. Thus, the first question to be answered is, assuming T's ignorance of the lack of authority, on what basis is T entitled to treat (sub-board) A as authorised to contract, even though A had no actual authority to enter into the contract in question? Then follows the second question, which we have examined above in relation to board contracting. Even if the contract would be binding on P in the absence of T's knowledge of the absence of actual authority, should the opposite answer be given if T knew or had the means of finding out about A's lack of authority? The answers to these questions are provided by the common law of agency, though, as we shall see, there is some debate about the relevance of s.40 to sub-board agents.

---

[51] An example might be thought to be where the shareholders have exercised their art.4 powers (above, para.7–14) to direct the board by special resolution not to exercise a power that art.3 prima facie confers on the board. However, the definition of the company's constitution (s.17) includes special resolutions (s.29). Of course, the board's managerial powers might be limited by a mandatory rule of company law (as was previously the case with the ultra vires doctrine) but such restrictions are rare.

Agency principles

Since this is not a book on the law of agency, for our purposes we can concisely state the main features of its rules of attribution in relation to contracts as follows. P is bound by the transactions on its behalf by A if the latter acted within either: **7–18**

(a) the actual scope of the authority conferred upon them by P prior to the transaction or by subsequent ratification; or
(b) the apparent (or ostensible) scope of their authority.

As far as (a) is concerned, this captures the process of delegation and sub-delegation referred to above. All that needs be added is that actual authority may be conferred expressly or impliedly. Authority to perform acts which are reasonably incidental to the proper performance of an agent's duties will be implied unless expressly excluded,[52] so that actual authority to contract may be inferred in appropriate cases from the allocation of managerial tasks to a person where no explicit reference to contracting is made. In addition, where A on previous occasions has been allowed by P to exceed the actual authority originally conferred, A may thereby have acquired actual authority to continue so to act.

As far as (b) is concerned, this is the crucial concept which agency law uses to hold P liable even in the absence of A's actual authority, in order to protect the legitimate interests of T. Apparent authority consists of (i) the authority which a person in A's position and in the type of business concerned can reasonably be expected by T to have; and (ii) the authority which the particular A has been held out to T by P as having. The line between apparent authority and implied actual authority may thus seem a fine one, but the establishment of actual authority focuses on the relationship between the P and A, whilst apparent authority focuses on the relationship between the P and T.[53]

The doctrine of ostensible or apparent authority attempts to hold a balance   **7–19**
between the interests of the company and of the third party. On the one hand, a company should not normally be liable for the acts of persons whom it has not authorised to act on its behalf. As a qualification to that starting point, however, it will be reasonable to hold the company to the acts of an unauthorised agent if the company has in some way misled the third party into thinking the person is so authorised. It follows from this that A cannot confer ostensible authority on

---

[52] *Hely-Hutchinson v Brayhead Ltd* [1968] Q.B. 549 CA, per Lord Denning.

[53] See previous note. Suppose a person has just been appointed to a position within a company, to which certain powers are normally attached, but the powers granted in the particular case have been unusually restricted by the appointer and that restriction has not been communicated to third parties. The person appointed would not have implied actual authority to act within the restricted area, but might well have apparent authority to do so. See *Hopkins v T L Dallas Group Ltd* [2005] 1 B.C.L.C. 543—fraud of agent took his actions outside the scope of his implied actual authority but not his apparent authority. Equally, where A has been permitted by P to act in excess of formal authority in the past, A might acquire implied actual authority, even though persons in A's position do not normally have that authority and P had not signalled the extension to T.

himself by representing that he has actual authority.[54] That can be conferred only by conduct of the company, acting through a primary decision-making body or an agent of the company, such as a managing director, with actual authority to make representations as to the extent of the authority of the company's officers or agents. The position rather is that, if the company has made such representations on which the third party has acted in good faith, the company will be estopped from setting up the truth of the relationship between the company and the agent as a ground of non-liability.[55]

Establishing the ostensible authority of corporate agents

7–20 The application of these general principles of the law of agency to establish a corporate agent's actual or apparent authority is a fact-dependent exercise, focusing on the P/A or P/T relationship, as the case may be. Nevertheless, certain broad lines of approach have emerged. Individual non-executive directors have no managerial responsibility unless the board specifically delegates it to them, and the courts have accordingly been restrictive in their approach to the apparent authority of such directors.[56] Even they, however, may be assumed to have some individual ministerial authority, for example, to authorise the use of the company's seal.[57] By contrast, if the person acting for the company is its chief executive officer or managing director, then, unless there are suspicious circumstances, or the transaction is of such magnitude as to imply the need for board approval, that person may safely be assumed to be authorised. In practice, that person will probably have actual authority[58] but, even if not, he or she will have ostensible authority and his or her acts will bind the company.[59] Moreover, it is not uncommon for the board of directors to allow one of their number to assume the position of managing director even though never formally appointed to that position and in these circumstances the courts have treated that person as having the actual authority of a managing director.[60]

7–21 Much the same applies to other executive directors, except that, if the descriptions of their posts suggest particular areas of responsibility ("finance director", "sales director" or the like), they cannot be assumed to have authority

---

[54] *Armagas Ltd v Mundogas SA* [1986] A.C. 717 HL; *Hudson Bay Apparel Brands LLC v Umbro International Ltd* [2011] 1 B.C.L.C. 259 CA.

[55] Contrary to what was thought at one time, this is so even if the officer or agent has forged what purported to be a document signed or sealed on behalf of the company: *Uxbridge Building Society v Pickard* [1939] 2 K.B. 248 CA; explaining dicta in *Ruben v Great Fingall Consolidated* [1906] A.C. 439 HL; *Kreditbank Cassel v Schenkers* [1927] 1 K.B. 826 CA; *South London Greyhound Racecourses v Wake* [1931] 1 Ch.496; *Lovett v Carson Country Homes Ltd* [2009] 2 B.C.L.C. 196.

[56] *Rama Corp v Proved Tin & General Investments Ltd* [1952] 2 Q.B. 147.

[57] cf. Model articles for public companies, art.81. On the seal see fn.5, above.

[58] *Hely-Hutchinson v Brayhead Ltd* [1968] 1 Q.B. 549 CA.

[59] *Freeman & Lockyer v Buckhurst Park Properties Ltd* [1964] 2 Q.B. 480 CA, especially the judgment of Diplock LJ at 506. However, within a corporate group a senior executive of a subsidiary cannot be assumed to have authority to bind the parent, though such authority may be established on the facts of the case: *Hudson Bay Apparel Brands LLC v Umbro International Ltd* [2011] 1 B.C.L.C. 259 CA.

[60] See, e.g. *Biggerstaff v Rowatt's Wharf Ltd* [1896] 2 Ch.93 CA; *Clay Hill Brick Co v Rawlings* [1938] 4 All E.R. 100; *Freeman & Lockyer v Buckhurst Park Properties Ltd* [1964] 2 Q.B. 480 CA.

outside those areas. Some decisions have even suggested that a non-executive chairman of the board has, as such, individual authority equating with that of a managing director.[61] But why the right to take the chair should imply a right to manage out of the chair is difficult to understand and the proposition has been doubted.[62] This is not to deny that the chair of the board has important corporate governance responsibilities[63] but rather to question whether those responsibilities involve contracting on behalf of the company. Nor is it to deny that a company might appoint someone to a chairman post with executive responsibilities, though the corporate governance rules frown on the cumulation of the positions of chief executive and chair of the board.[64]

A third party may deal with an officer or employee below the level of director. For many years, the courts showed a marked reluctance to recognise any ostensible authority even of a manager.[65] But this has now changed and it may be taken that a manager, even if actual authority is lacking, will generally have ostensible authority to undertake everyday transactions relating to the branch of business which he or she is managing (though probably not if they are really major transactions)[66] and that the secretary will similarly have such authority in relation to administrative matters.[67] Indeed, almost every employee of a trading company must surely have apparent authority to bind the company in some transactions, though the extent of that authority may be very limited. For example, people behind the counter in a department store clearly have ostensible authority to sell the goods on display for cash and at the marked prices. Whether their apparent authority extends beyond that (for example, to take goods back if the customer returns them) we shall probably never know, for it is unlikely to be litigated—at any rate against the customer.[68]

7–22

In all the above cases the question has been whether the agent had actual or apparent authority to *contract* on behalf of the company. In a relatively recent line of cases, however, the question has arisen whether the company is bound if the

7–23

---

[61] *B.T.H. v Federated European Bank* [1932] 2 K.B. 176 CA; *Clay Hill Brick Co v Rawlings* [1938] 4 All E.R. 100.

[62] In *Hely-Hutchinson v Brayhead* [1968] 1 Q.B. 549 CA, per Roskill J at first instance at 560D, and per Lord Wilberforce at 586G.

[63] See para.14–75, below.

[64] See para.14–75, below.

[65] *Houghton & Co v Nothard, Lowe & Wills* [1927] 1 K.B. 246 CA; affirmed on other grounds [1928] A.C. 1 HL; *Kreditbank Cassel v Schenkers* [1927] 1 K.B. 826 CA; *South London Greyhound Racecourses v Wake* [1931] 1 Ch. 496; see also the observations of Willmer LJ in *Freeman & Lockyer v Buckhurst Park Properties Ltd* [1964] 2 Q.B. at 494.

[66] See *Armagas Ltd v Mundogas SA* [1986] A.C. 717 HL. There an employee who bore the title of "Vice-president (Transportation) and Chartering Manager" was held not to have authority to bind his company to charter back a vessel which it was selling. But there were complicating factors in that case for the employee was colluding with an agent of the other party in a dishonest arrangement and did not purport to have any general authority to bind the company but merely alleged that he had obtained actual authority for that particular transaction. *MCI WorldCom International Inc v Primus Telecommunications Inc* [2004] 1 B.C.L.C. 42—in-house lawyer negotiating a contract did not have apparent authority to give undertakings as to the future financial soundness of a parent company.

[67] *Panorama Developments Ltd v Fidelis Furnishing Fabrics Ltd* [1971] 2 Q.B. 711 CA. How far, if at all, the secretary's ostensible authority extends to the commercial side of the company's affairs is still unclear; see, per Salmon LJ at 718.

[68] The issue might arise in litigation between salesperson and employer.

agent has authority, not to contract, but to make representations on behalf of the company about whether another person with actual authority to contract has committed the company to the contract. Can the company be bound on the basis of such a representation, even if that representation is false? In *First Energy (UK) Ltd v Hungarian International Bank Ltd*[69] a senior manager was held to have ostensible authority to communicate to a third party head office approval of a loan application, even though he did not have authority to contract on the bank's behalf, as the third party knew, and the head office had not in fact approved the loan. Once the third party had accepted the "offer" communicated by the manager, it could sue the bank on the resulting contract. Again, it has been held that a company can be bound as a result of a representation, made by an agent with ostensible authority to make it, to the effect that another agent of the company was authorised to contract with the third party on behalf of the company. When the third party purported to contract with the company through the second agent, the company was bound, even though neither first nor second agent had actual or ostensible authority to enter into the contract in question.[70] This new line of authority advances the security of third parties' transactions but is capable, unless closely confined to the facts of particular cases, of extending companies' liability for unauthorised contracts and of undermining the proposition that an agent cannot create apparent authority for himself through his own assertions.[71]

Knowledge

7–24   We now turn to the second question identified in para.7–17, above. Even if A has apparent authority, it can be argued that T has no legitimate claim to protection if T knows or ought to have known that the agent was not actually authorised. Under the agency rules the balance shifts decisively in favour of P, if T knew A did not have actual authority to contract. The law will also deprive T of the benefit of the doctrine of apparent authority if T was put on enquiry as to whether A was acting within the scope of authority. Thus, in one case, where T had contracted with a single director rather than with the board as a whole, that director was held not to have created a contract with the company because the contracts were abnormal in relation to the business of the company (implying no apparent authority) and because the circumstances were such as to raise questions about whether A was acting properly (T put on enquiry).[72]

In addition, at common law T may also be deprived of transactional security on the basis of constructive notice of the constitution, as discussed above in relation to board contracting,[73] i.e. where A has entered into a contract in breach of a provision in the articles limiting A's authority—even though T has not read

---

[69] *First Energy (UK) Ltd v Hungarian International Bank Ltd* [1993] B.C.L.C. 1409 CA. See also *The Raffaella* [1985] 2 Lloyd's Rep. 36.

[70] *ING Re (UK) Ltd v R&V Versicherung AG* [2007] 1 B.C.L.C. 108.

[71] See the reservations expressed by the Singapore Court of Appeal in *Skandinaviska Enskilda Banken AB (Publ), Singapore Branch v Asia Pacific Breweries (Singapore) Pte Ltd* [2011] SGCA 22.

[72] *Hopkins v T L Dallas Group Ltd* [2005] 1 B.C.L.C. 543.

[73] See para.7–6.

the articles. The rule in *Turquand's Case* modifies the constructive notice doctrine to some extent, as we have seem, but otherwise the constructive notice doctrine (as modified by *Turquand*) continues to operate at common law. It may well be that this issue is less important in relation to sub-board agents, because the restrictions on their authority are less likely to be found in the company's articles and more likely to be contained in the internal decision whereby authority was delegated to the agent. Since the constructive notice doctrine does not catch such internal restrictions, which will not show up in the company's file in the public registry, T is less exposed to the risk of constructive knowledge. Yet, it is not impossible to think of cases where the articles might be relevant to sub-board agents' contracting powers. Take our stock example. Suppose there is a provision in the articles requiring shareholder approval for contracts above a certain value. If this is couched as a prohibition on anyone other than the shareholders contracting, the constructive notice doctrine will defeat T contracting via a sub-board agent. If, to vary the situation slightly, sub-board agents are permitted to contract for high-value contracts provided they have obtained the prior approval of the shareholders, then the indoor management rule will probably save T.

Thus, given the importance of knowledge in the law of agency, there is some incentive for T dealing with sub-board agents to try and bring themselves within s.40, even though that section applies only to limitations on authority located in the company's constitution. The advantages T may seek are from s.40 are, in relation to constitutional limitations, (i) escape from the doctrine of constructive notice; (ii) where T has some knowledge, not being put under a duty to enquire; and (iii) again where T has some knowledge, benefitting from the wide definition of good faith in the section. There are two situations where this question may arise. First, assume T contracts with a single director (in the case of a company having multiple directors) rather than the board. Can T invoke s.40 in relation to authority limitations in the articles? Before 2006 the answer was clearly in the negative because the section referred to "the power of the board of directors" whilst now it refers to "the power of the directors" to bind the company. We have suggested in para.7–13, above a reason why this change was made. That reason suggests the change was intended to extend the section only to cases of the directors acting collectively (but, for some procedural reason, not as a board) rather than to cases of contracts with individual directors, which the wording is not apt to cover. Even if s.40 can be extended, it should be noticed that s.40 does not operate so as to confer ostensible authority on a single director but only to allow T potentially to rely on such ostensible authority as the director has despite T's actual or constructive knowledge. The ostensible authority of the single director has to be established as a prior step in the argument on the basis of the principles discussed in para.7–20, above.

Secondly, the section protects from limitations in the articles not only the power of the directors to bind the company but also their power "to authorise others to do so".[74] Thus, if the articles state that only the shareholders can enter

7–25

---

[74] 2006 Act s.40(1). It is clear that the section creates no presumption that A has been authorised by the board to contract. Only if A has been so authorised will the exclusion of limitations in the articles on the board's powers to authorise be removed in favour of a good faith T. See *Wrexham Associated*

into high-value contracts, a good faith T can rely as against the company on an agreement made either by the board or by someone who has been specifically authorised by the board to enter into high-value contracts. It is not clear whether s.40 goes beyond this base case. First, does it apply only where the board gives express actual authority to T or does it capture situations of implied actual authority as well?[75] In other words, must the board authorisation expressly say that A may enter into high value contracts or is it enough to appoint A to a managerial position incidental to which is entering into high-value contracts? Second, must A have been appointed by the directors or is it enough that A was appointed by a senior manager who was appointed by the directors and whose functions include the appointment of junior managers? The underlying question is whether the extension in s.40 to "authorising others" was intended to cover only situations where the board approves the contract in principle but delegates the actual contracting decision to a manager or whether the extension is designed to exempt the management hierarchy as a whole from the restrictions in the articles on their contracting power. It seems likely that, if Parliament had intended the broader result, it would have used clearer words. Overall, therefore, it seems that A's authority to bind the company, where A is not the board of directors or an apparent board, will be determined overwhelmingly by the common law of agency coupled with constructive notice of the company's public documents as modified by *Turquand*.[76]

Knowledge of the constitution as an aid to third parties?

7–26 So far, we have considered knowledge (actual or constructive) of the company's constitution as something negative from T's point of view, as something which could deprive T of the security of the transaction with the company. Can T rely on knowledge of the articles as a building block in a claim against the company? As far as constructive knowledge of the constitution is concerned, the courts have held that the fact that T was deemed to have notice of the contents of the articles did not mean that T could rely on something in those documents to estop the company from denying the ostensible authority of an officer of the company who would not otherwise have had authority of the relevant type. Constructive notice was a negative doctrine curtailing what might otherwise be the apparent scope of the authority and not a positive doctrine increasing it.[77] The position might be different, however, if T had actual knowledge of the articles and had relied on some provision in them. Even here, however, what is clear is that mere knowledge that the board of directors might have delegated authority to a particular person does not estop the company from denying that it has done so. It

---

Football Club Ltd v Crucialmove Ltd [2008] 1 B.C.L.C. 508 CA at [47]. But see fn.5 above on why it might be convenient for the board to act in this way.

[75] For this distinction see para.7–18.

[76] The Companies Act 1989 contained a provision (inserted as s.711A into the Companies Act 1985) which would have abolished generally the doctrine of constructive notice arising from the public filing of corporate documents. However, the section was never brought into force and the Companies Act 2006 contains no equivalent provision.

[77] Any doubt on this point was finally dispelled by the Court of Appeal in *Freeman & Lockyer v Buckhurst Park Properties Ltd* [1964] 2 Q.B., especially Diplock LJ at 504.

would be necessary for T also to establish that "the conduct of the board, in the light of that knowledge, would be understood by a reasonable man as a representation that the agent had authority to enter into the contract sought to be enforced".[78] Thus, actual knowledge of the articles coupled with conduct of the board might be enough to generate apparent authority, but there seems to be no reported case in which that has occurred. If estoppel is to arise in these circumstances, it will generally be because of conduct by the company's primary decision-making bodies and not because of any provision in its articles.[79]

Ratification

We have already noted that the legal effect of lack of actual or ostensible authority on the agent's part is that the transaction is not binding on the company unless it is ratified by the company. The company thus has an option to take up the transaction or to treat it as not binding on it. Determining who has the power to ratify the transaction is a matter for the company's constitution. There is no requirement in the Act, as there is for breaches of directors' duties, that ratification must be by the shareholders,[80] though it appears the shareholders will usually be able to ratify unauthorised actions of the board or sub-board agents.[81] Normally, it is a matter of finding who, under the company's constitution, has actual authority to enter into the transaction and securing their approval of it. In addition, it is not necessary that ratification should take the form of an express decision to approve the transaction. Ratification can be implied from conduct[82] and the conduct may amount to ratification if the company has knowledge of the essentials of what the agent has done, even if it did not know that the agent had acted without authority.[83] If there is ratification, it has retrospective effect, i.e. it renders the transaction with the company binding on it as from the time it was entered into by the agent. It is sometimes difficult to distinguish a subsequent ratification (which is a unilateral act of the company) from the entering into by the company and the third party of a new transaction which replaces the one

7–27

---

[78] per Diplock LJ in *Freeman & Lockyer v Buckhurst Park Properties* [1964] 2 Q.B. 508. See also Atkin LJ in *Kreditbank Cassel v Schenkers* [1927] 1 K.B. 826 CA at 844.

[79] *Mercantile Bank of India v Chartered Bank of India* [1937] 1 All E.R. 231 is sometimes misunderstood in this regard. The headnote is misleading in suggesting that it was the fact that the articles expressly empowered the board to delegate by powers of attorney that brought about the estoppel. It was the actual exercise of that power by the board that did so. The only relevance of the articles (of which third parties were deemed to have notice) was that they did not preclude the grant of such powers of attorney.

[80] See para.16–117, below.

[81] *Grant v United Kingdom Switchback Railway Co* (1888) 40 Ch.D. 135 CA. If ratification would involve a breach of the articles *by the shareholders*, then shareholder approval, it seems, would need to be by a majority equivalent to that for a change in the articles.

[82] *Re Mawcon Ltd* [1969] 1 W.L.R. 78.

[83] *ING Re (UK) Ltd v R&V Versicherung AG* [2007] 1 B.C.L.C. 108.

entered into by the agent without authority.[84] There is also a time limit on the ratification process in the sense that ratification will not be permitted if it would unfairly prejudice a third party.[85]

Overall

7–28   A third party dealing with the company through its board of directors has a higher level of security of transaction than a person dealing with the company otherwise. In the former case, the primary rules of attribution start from the position that the board has power to bind the company—subject to the articles—and s.40 goes on to protect a good faith third party (widely defined) from attack based on limitations contained in the articles. By contrast, where T deals with an agent, A's authority to bind the company needs to be established under the standard agency rules and s.40 offers less (probably much less) protection against attacks based on limitations contained in the articles, throwing T in some cases back onto the indoor management rule. This may not be an inappropriate result. The standard division of powers within a company is one which allocates general management powers to the board.[86] So, the third party's expectations as to the security of the transaction will be particularly high when that person deals with the company through the board. The primary rules of attribution and s.40 recognise this. By contrast, where the company contracts through an agent, it has a legitimate claim to be able to limit the scope of its agents' authority, just as a natural person can. Otherwise, the directors would lose a significant method of controlling the conduct of the company's business and boards would either have to run the risk of acquiring contractual obligations through unauthorised means or devote a disproportionate amount of board time to the contracting process. T can have no legitimate expectation that the board would routinely delegate all its powers to any particular person. However, even in this case, the interests of the third party are by no means neglected. The general rules of attribution—agency rules—will protect the third party who has acted reasonably but been misled by the company as to the authority of the corporate agent, just as they do when P is not a company.

The ultra vires doctrine and the objects clause

7–29   Before finishing our consideration of corporate contracting, we need briefly to consider the ultra vires doctrine and its relationship with a particular clause often found in the articles, namely, the objects clause. Although the ultra vires doctrine caused a lot of anxiety to third parties during its history,[87] that is no longer the case because the third party is protected against its effects by s.39 of the Act, whether the third party has acted in good faith or not. The objects clause defines the capacity of the company, i.e. it states what the company is legally capable of

---

[84] This was the point upon which the "ratification" failed in *Smith v Henniker-Major* [2002] 2 B.C.L.C. 655.

[85] See the discussion ibid. and *The Borvigilant* [2003] 2 All E.R. (Comm) 736 CA.

[86] See para.14–3, below.

[87] For a brief history of the ultra vires doctrine and its reform in 1972 and again in 1989 see the fifth edition of this book (London: Sweet & Maxwell, 1992) at pp.166 et seq.

doing, whether it acts through its board or via the shareholders collectively or through an agent. A company was required by the early legislation to include a statement of its objects in its memorandum of association and from that the courts deduced that the company did not have legal capacity to act outside its objects. Any such action was in principle void. This was normally referred to as the ultra vires doctrine.[88] It had a major and adverse impact on the security of third parties' transactions with the company. Not even ratification was available in relation to ultra vires acts. So, it is not surprising that the doctrine was the object of reform; what is surprising is that reform took so long.

There is no longer a provision in the Act requiring a company to set out its objects.[89] Unless it chooses otherwise, the company's objects will be unrestricted, i.e. it will have unlimited capacity.[90] Even if a company chooses to adopt restrictions on its capacity (which will appear today necessarily in the articles rather than the memorandum of association),[91] those restrictions will not affect the validity of the acts of the company: s.39(1) provides that "the validity of an act done by a company shall not be called into question on the ground of lack of capacity by reason of anything in the company's constitution". Thus, the ultra vires doctrine, so far as it is based on the company's objects clause,[92] no longer threatens the security of third parties' transactions.[93] A company may also amend or remove its object clause by the same means as it can use for altering its articles,[94] except in the case of charitable companies.[95]

---

[88] Ultra vires is a Latin expression which lawyers and civil servants use to describe acts undertaken beyond (ultra) the legal powers (vires) of those who have purported to undertake them. In this sense its application extends over a far wider area than company law. For example, those advising a minister on proposed subordinate legislation will have to ask themselves whether the enabling primary legislation confers vires to make the desired regulations.

[89] This is based on an interpretation of art.2(b) of the Second Directive (Directive 2012/30/EU) as requiring the company's articles to state its objects (if it has them) but not as requiring the company to have objects.

[90] 2006 Act s.31(1).

[91] See para.4–33, above.

[92] For the possible deployment of the ultra vires doctrine from other doctrinal bases see para.12–9, below.

[93] 2006 Act s.39 does not attempt to deal with the internal aspects of the ultra vires doctrine, thus underlining that these are matters to be dealt with according to the ordinary rules on directors' duties or the enforcement of the articles as between shareholder and company. A particularly complex issue of this sort is addressed in s.247, concerning gratuitous payments by directors to employees where a company is closing down or transferring a business. In *Parke v Daily News* [1962] Ch. 927 such payments were held to be ultra vires the company. That issue is no longer relevant and the matter is large dealt with in the section as one of directors' duties. However, interestingly the section does mandatorily extend the powers of the directors to make such payments, even if the company's constitution does not confer such powers. However, there are strict controls over the exercise of the power in the interests of the shareholders and other creditors of the company.

[94] This provision applies equally to companies in existence when this reform was introduced by the Companies Act 2006 and which necessarily had objects clauses in their memorandum of association. Objects clauses set out in the memorandums of existing companies are to be treated as provisions in the articles, by virtue of s.28(1), and as such will benefit from s.39 and also from the new alteration/removal regime.

[95] 2006 Act s.31 preserves the operation of ss.197 and 198 of the Charities Act 2011, applying in England and Wales. The broad effect of that section is that where a charity is a company, no alteration which has the effect of the body ceasing to be a charity will affect the application of any of its existing property unless it bought it for full consideration in money or money's worth. In other words,

Nevertheless, many existing companies will continue to have objects clauses and some newly created ones may choose to adopt them. The central point is that, whilst the ultra vires doctrine is dead as a restriction on the capacity of the company, objects clauses continue to limit the authority of the board, the shareholders collectively or any of its agents to bind the company, in the same way as any other provision in the articles. The objects clause is part of the company's constitution and the rules discussed above, including s.40 of the Act, apply to it accordingly. Equally, a director may be liable to the company for exceeding the limits in the objects clause, as with any other authority limitation in the articles. Indeed, it is precisely because the rules on authority hold the balance between the interests of the company and of third parties in what is now regarded as the appropriate way that it was possible for s.39 to be cast in such blunt terms.

Tort and Crime

7–30   We have suggested above that both companies and their potential counterparties benefit from rules which facilitate contracting between them. The rules discussed in the first part of this chapter are designed to effect such facilitation. Since the purpose of the rules is to produce a contract between P and T, it is wholly acceptable that in the normal case those who act as or on behalf of the company do not acquire any liability under the contract. Whether the company contracts via its constitutional bodies or via an agent, we have seen that this is the result which is normally achieved. If the company contracts through the board, the directors do not become parties to the contract. If the company acts through an agent, once negotiations are successfully concluded between A and T, A drops out of the picture, becoming neither a party to the contract nor personally liable under it, unless A chooses to accept liability under it (something that may not be entirely easy to determine).[96] Perhaps surprisingly, this rule also applies where a contract with P fails to come into existence because of A's lack of authority.[97] Here, however, A may be liable to the third party on a "warranty of authority" for the loss suffered by T through the failure of the contracting process, if the agent has misrepresented the extent of his authority, no matter how innocently.[98]

In the situations we discuss in the second part of this chapter, however, the non-liability of the person acting as or on behalf of the company cannot be the typical outcome. These are situations of wrongdoing and it would be odd if the addition of corporate liability removed liability from the individual. Thus, whereas with contracting it is necessary to explain instances where those contracting as or on behalf of the company become liable, with wrongdoing the

---

although the company is not prevented from changing its objects (so long as it obtains the prior written consent of the Charity Commission) in such a way that they cease to be exclusively for charity, its existing property obtained by donations continues to be held for charitable purposes only. In effect, the company will be in an analogous position to an individual trustee of a charitable trust; part of its property will be held for charitable purposes only and part of it not. And, presumably, it will have to segregate the former. Scotland and Northern Ireland have separate legislation on this point.

[96] For a discussion of this issue in the context of pre-incorporation contracts, see para.5–25, above, where, however, the default position is that A is liable.

[97] *Lewis v Nicholson and Parker* (1852) 18 Q.B. 503.

[98] *Collen v Wright* (1857) 8 E. & B. 647.

situation is the other way around: explanation is needed if the addition of corporate liability appears to remove liability from the individual.[99] If responsibility for wrongdoing is attributed to the company on the basis of vicarious liability, the outcome is in accordance with this postulate. It will be the case that both agent/employee and company are liable. The liability of the agent is attributed to the company but not the wrongful acts of the agent. The agent remains a wrongdoer; indeed, if the agent does not, vicarious liability cannot arise.[100] Where, however, the basis of the principal's liability is not vicarious liability, the question will arise whether the company is liable but not the agent. Sometimes, perhaps often, they will both be liable but sometimes not.

Tortious liability

Vicarious liability

Actions against the company in tort (and for other forms of civil liability) are overwhelmingly based on the vicarious liability of the company for the wrongs of its agents and employees, so that both employee/agent and company are liable. Nevertheless, the mere fact of being an employee or agent of the company is not enough to generate liability in tort for the company in relation to torts committed by those agents or employees. There must be some connection between the company's activities and the acts of the tortfeasor if the company is to be held liable as well. Defining the nature of this link may be said to constitute the central problem within the doctrine of vicarious liability. Over the years, the nature of the link has been broadened by the courts. From an early date, the courts were unwilling to confine the scope of the company's (or any principal's) vicarious liability to those actions actually authorised by the company. Thus, it has been clear for some time that a company or other employer does not escape vicarious liability simply because the agent has done an act which the agent or employee has been prohibited from doing or even because the agent has done a deliberate act for his own benefit which has prejudiced the employer.[101] This led to the famous (but unclear) dichotomy between doing an unauthorised act (no vicarious liability) and doing an authorised act in an unauthorised way (vicarious liability). In its more recent decisions on the doctrine,[102] the House of Lords/Supreme

7–31

---

[99] Campbell and Armour, (2003) 62 Cambridge L.J. 290.

[100] See *Jetivia SA v Bilta (UK) Ltd* [2015] 1 B.C.L.C. 443. "Such vicarious liability is indirect liability; it does not involve the attribution of the employee's act to the company. It entails holding that the employee has committed a breach of a tortious duty owed by himself, and that the company as his employer is additionally answerable for the employee's tortious act or omission", per Lords Toulson and Hodge at [186].

[101] *Lloyd v Grace, Smith & Co* [1912] A.C. 716 HL (fraud on client by solicitors' clerk); *Morris v CW Martin & Sons Ltd* [1966] 1 Q.B. 716 CA (theft by employee of customer's coat).

[102] *Lister v Hesley Hall Ltd* [2001] 2 All E.R. 769 HL (sexual abuse of children in a care home by the staff employed to look after them); *Dubai Aluminium Company Ltd v Salaam* [2003] 1 B.C.L.C. 32 HL (firm vicariously liable for knowing assistance by a solicitor partner in a breach of trust); *Mohamud v WM Morrison Supermarkets Plc* [2016] UKSC 11 (assault by employee on a customer for reasons personal to the employee). At the same time, the range of "employee like" relationships which may give rise to vicarious liability of the government has been expanded: *Cox v Ministry of Justice* [2016] UKSC 10 (vicarious liability for acts of a prisoner).

Court moved beyond that distinction and imposed vicarious liability when there was a sufficiently close connection between the wrongful acts of the agents or employees and the activities which those persons were employed to undertake. The fact that the wrongful acts were clearly unauthorised and not for the employer's benefit did not prevent the imposition of liability, if this test was satisfied.

At a general level, the doctrines of a "sufficiently close connection" in tort and of ostensible authority in the law of agency perform a similar role, i.e. the protection of the legitimate interests of third parties coming into contact with businesses. However, they are by no means identical doctrines: ostensible authority turns on a holding out by the principal of the agent to the third party,[103] whereas vicarious liability does not depend upon what the third party understood to be the agent's connection with the company—the third party may not even know of it at the time the tort was committed—but upon an objective assessment of the relationship between the agent's actions and the company's activities. In other words, the focus in the case of vicarious liability is on the relationship between the employee or agent and the company, not on the relationship between the company and the third party. The approach is more like that used by the courts to identify the actual authority of agents,[104] but the tort test is much broader since it may lead to liability in tort for acts which were clearly unauthorised and, indeed, may have been expressly forbidden.

Assumption of responsibility

7–32   However, difficult problems can arise when the law of tort and the law of contract come together to regulate the process of contracting. Suppose an agent acting for a company makes negligent statements about the promised contractual performance during the contracting process. If the third party subsequently sues in contract, only the company will be liable; if the third party sues in tort, the maker of the statement might be thought to be primarily liable and the company liable only vicariously. The company will be liable on either theory, but the choice of claim will be important if the company is not available to be sued (for example, because it is insolvent). The issue is particularly important in small companies, for example, where the shareholder, director and main employee are the same person. If the suit is in contract, the personal assets of the shareholder/director will be protected; if in tort, they will not be.

After some uncertainty, the House of Lords[105] avoided that adverse result for the one-person company[106] by holding that a person who makes negligent misstatements whilst contracting on behalf of a company does not assume personal responsibility for the truth of the statements made, assumption of responsibility being a necessary ingredient for liability in the tort of negligent misstatement. Responsibility is to be treated as assumed (in the usual case) only

---

[103] See above, para.7–18.

[104] See above, para.7–18.

[105] *Williams v Natural Life Health Foods* [1998] 1 W.L.R. 830 HL.

[106] The decision applies, of course, to all sizes of company, but it is suggested that the one-person company was the difficult case. With large companies, it will be even more difficult to find that the agent assumes personal responsibility.

on behalf of the company. Thus, it is the company which has committed the tort (by making the false statement through the agent) rather than the agent; the company's liability is thus direct, not vicarious.[107] As the court made clear, this approach applies not only to negligent misstatements but also to cases of negligent delivery of services due under a contract, where again contractual and tortious duties coincide. However, two points should be noted about the scope of this decision. First, it is a statement only of the starting point for the courts' analysis. A director or other agent of the company may on the facts be treated as having assumed personal responsibility for the negligent misstatement or the negligent provision of services.[108] Moreover, the test for assumption of personal responsibility is not the subjective one of what the agent believed to be the case; rather the test is objective, something along the lines of whether it was reasonable for the third party to conclude that the director or other agent had accepted personal responsibility.[109] The principle of *Williams* may thus apply in different ways to different types of business.[110]

Secondly, the result in *Williams* was achieved, not by applying any special doctrine of company law, but by relying on the requirement for an assumption of responsibility as a necessary ingredient of liability under the tort of negligence in relation to the misstatements. It follows that a director or other agent will not escape liability where assumption of responsibility is not a necessary ingredient for tortious liability, for example, in deceit.[111] Thus, as far as tortious liability is concerned, the personal liability of directors of companies is crucially dependent upon the common law of tort rather than upon any provisions in the Companies Act or even the common law of companies. A negligent director will escape liability in tort only on the basis of rules which apply also to all agents.

Fraud

At one stage, it seems to have been thought that a company could not be held vicariously liable for fraudulent conduct on the part of an employee or agent, at

7–33

---

[107] The decision is not explicit on whether the company was liable in the tort of negligent misstatement, but it is submitted that it was in that case where the maker of the statement was clearly its "directing mind and will". However, since the court was apparently laying down a general approach, it may be better to view the analysis as being that the assumption of responsibility by any agent acting within his authority is attributed to the company.

[108] Thus, *Fairline Shipping Corp v Adamson* [1975] Q.B. 180 is now to be seen as a case where the director did personally assume responsibility for the performance of the services which the company had contracted to provide, despite the rather thin evidence of such an assumption. See also para.28–64, below, for the application of this principle to statements made by target boards in takeover bids.

[109] *Williams v Natural Life Health Foods* [1998] 1 W.L.R. 830 HL.

[110] Thus, the courts have been reluctant to exempt from personal responsibility agents who are professionally qualified. See *Merrett v Babb* [2001] Q.B. 1174 CA (surveyor employed by a partnership); *Phelps v Hillingdon LBC* [2001] 2 A.C. 619 HL (educational psychologist employed by LEA). These cases, especially the first, may contribute to the debate whether the *Williams* principle will be applied by the courts to LLPs (see para.1–4, above). It is submitted that it will but perhaps not with the same benefits for agents of LLPs running professional businesses as it provides for non-professional businesses.

[111] *Standard Chartered Bank v Pakistan National Shipping Corp (No.2)* [2003] 1 A.C. 959 HL; *Contex Drouzhba Ltd v Wiseman* [2008] 1 B.C.L.C. 631 CA.

least where the fraud was directed at benefiting the agent rather than the company.[112] However, the clear view today is that such cases are to be explained on the basis that the agent or employee was acting outside the scope of their authority when carrying out the fraud and that, had this not been the case, the company or principal would have been liable for the fraud.[113] As far as corporate liability towards third parties is concerned, the tort of deceit and other torts based on fraudulent conduct are thus to be treated in the same way as other torts. There is no special exclusionary rule for such conduct. It is still necessary, of course, to show that the individual was acting in the course of his or her employment when committing the fraud, but the introduction of the "sufficiently close connection" test for establishing this relationship has also made this task easier for the claimant. Indeed, the denial of a special exclusionary rule for fraud and the introduction of the "sufficiently close connection" test for determining the scope of employment both point in the same direction: the company or other employer carries (and thus has an incentive to control) the risks to third parties generated by fraud within its business activities, even if some of the risks in question harm the company as well.[114]

Recovery by the company from the agent

7–34   Even if the third party successfully sues the company in tort, the company may be able to recover from the agent at least some of the amount it has to pay to the third party. In all cases of vicarious liability, agent and company are joint tortfeasors,[115] and so the company can claim a contribution from the agent towards the damages payable to the third party. Since the company is a wholly innocent party, that contribution will usually be a complete one, i.e. an indemnity.[116] Of course, there may be good non-legal reasons for reluctance on the part of an employer to seek a contribution from an employee. Equally, where the employee has acted in a way required by the employer in the discharge of his duties, the employee may have a claim for an indemnity against the employer, so that the employer's contribution claim would be barred for circularity. However, this will not be the case where commission of the tortious act constituted a breach of duty or of the contract of employment on the part of the agent or employee.[117]

---

[112] See in particular *Ruben v Great Fingall Consolidated* [1906] A.C. 439 HL.

[113] *Uxbridge Permanent Benefit Building Society v Pickard* [1939] 2 K.B. 248 CA; *Armagas Ltd v Mundogas SA* [1986] 1 A.C. 717 HL; *Credit Lyonnais Bank Nederland NV v Export Credit Guarantee Department* [2000] 1 A.C. 486 HL; and see the cases cited in fn.101 above.

[114] Note, however, the reluctance of the Singapore Court of Appeal, even under the "sufficiently close connection" test, to hold the company vicarious liable for the self-interested fraud of a manager which the third party was in a better position to discover than the company: *Skandinaviska Enskilda Banken AB (Publ), SingaporeBranch v Asia Pacific Breweries (Singapore) Pte Ltd* [2011] SGCA 22.

[115] *New Zealand Guardian Trust Co Ltd v Brooks* [1995] 1 W.L.R. 96 PC.

[116] Civil Liability (Contribution) Act 1978 s.1; *Lister v Romford Ice and Cold Storage Co* [1965] A.C. 555 HL.

[117] The duties of directors are discussed in Ch.16. For non-director managers the conduct might be a breach of their contracts of employment. See M.R. Freedland, *The Personal Employment Contract* (Oxford: OUP, 2003), pp.146–147.

Liability of non-involved directors

So far, we have discussed the respective liabilities in tort to third parties of the company's agents (who may be its directors or who may be, and often are, more junior members of the organisation) and the company, on the assumption that the agent is a tortfeasor. However, the question has been raised in a number of cases of whether a director of a company, who is not the tortfeasor, can be liable in tort to a third party simply by virtue of his directorship of the company. Many of the cases concern tortious acts consisting of infringements by the company's agents of another person's intellectual property rights, such as patents or copyright. It seems clear that, in principle, the answer is in the negative, even if the tortfeasors are other directors of the company. As long ago as 1878, Fry J said in a case of fraudulent misrepresentation[118] that two classes of person could be responsible for the fraud (the agent who actually made the fraudulent misrepresentations and the principal on the basis of vicarious liability) but that "one agent is not responsible for the acts of another agent". This principle has been confirmed in a number of subsequent cases.[119] It supports the proposition that involvement in the management of the company does not lead to personal liability, unless the director or manager himself commits a wrong.

7–35

Accessory liability

However, there is an important qualification to be made to the statement of Fry J. If a director, whilst not committing the tort him- or herself, authorises or procures the commission of the tortious act by someone else, whether that act constitutes deceit or some other tort, there will be liability on the part of the director as a joint tortfeasor with the person who commits the tort. This liability arises under the normal rules applying to accessory liability in the law of tort, but it is an important extension of tort liability in the company context. Given the managerial role of directors in companies' affairs, they are more likely to procure the commission of tortious acts than to commit those acts themselves. It is not necessary that that the director authorising or procuring the tortious acts should realise their tortious nature or display any other particular mental element in relation to the acts, unless this is a requirement of the tort being so authorised or procured.[120]

7–36

The rules about accessory liability for directors who procure tortious acts, together with the vicarious liability of the company for unauthorised and forbidden acts sufficiently connected with the company's business, provide a strong incentive for directors to acquaint themselves with, and to secure

---

[118] *Cargill v Bower* (1878) 10 Ch.D. 502 at 513–514.

[119] *Rainham Chemical Works Ltd v Belvedere Fish Guano Co Ltd* [1921] 2 A.C. 465 HL; *Performing Right Society Ltd v Ciryl Theatrical Syndicate Ltd* [1924] 1 K.B. 1 CA; *British Thomson-Houston Co Ltd v Stirling Accessories Ltd* [1924] 2 Ch. 33.

[120] *C Evans & Sons Ltd v Spritebrand Ltd* [1985] 1 W.L.R. 317 CA; *Mancetter Developments Ltd v Garmanson Ltd* [1986] Q.B. 1212 CA; *MCA Records Inc v Charly Records Ltd* [2003] 1 B.C.L.C. 93 CA; *Koninklijke Philips Electronics N V v Princo Digital Disc GmbH* [2004] 2 B.C.L.C. 50; cf. *White Horse Distilleries Ltd v Gregson Associates Ltd* [1984] R.P.C. 61.

observance by the company's agents of, the tort rules which impinge upon the company's business. Nevertheless, the principle of personal liability is still controversial in some quarters.[121]

Direct liability

7–37   Overwhelmingly, the tortious liability of companies is approached by the courts through the doctrine of vicarious liability, i.e. the company, like any other person, is liable for torts committed by an agent or employee, provided that person's torts have a sufficiently close connection with the business of the company. As with contractual liability, however, the company can also be liable on the grounds that its constitutional bodies (board or shareholders collectively) have committed a tort. In this case, the company's liability is direct,[122] not vicarious. Normally, this will be on the basis that the constitutional bodies have authorised the tort and, unlike with contracting by the board, the directors will also normally be tortiously liable for authorising the wrongdoing.[123] Given the width of the doctrine of vicarious liability, it is rarely necessary to consider, in a claim by a third party against the company,[124] whether the company is liable directly or vicariously. However, in some cases of statutory civil liability, the drafting of the statute does make it important to establish whether the company's liability is direct or vicarious, because the statute excludes vicarious liability. The courts have also concluded that the same issue may arise in some areas of civil liability at common law where vicarious liability is not available.[125] But above all, the issue has arisen in relation to the criminal liability of companies, for in criminal law vicarious liability is treated with some reserve, since it is a form of strict liability, whether applied to companies or other principals. We will therefore treat these instances together in the next section where we deal with criminal liability. As we shall see, the central question is how far liability should be imposed beyond the actions of the company's constitutional bodies.

---

[121] See the attempt by Nourse J in the *White Horse* case (see previous note) to restrict the director's personal liability to those situations where he acted "deliberately or recklessly and so as to make [the tortious conduct] his own, as distinct from the act or conduct of the company". This approach seems to have been motivated by a desire to preserve the benefits of limited liability, especially in a one-person company. In other words, Nourse J proposed a general "assumption of responsibility" test (for all torts) in the case of tortious conduct authorised by the directors. See also *MCA Records* (see previous note) where the court drew a distinction between control exercised through the constitutional organs of the company (e.g. voting at board meetings—not attracting tortious liability) and control exercised otherwise (potentially attracting tortious liability).

[122] *Jetivia SA v Bilta (UK) Ltd* [2015] 1 B.C.L.C. 443 at [187].

[123] See above para.7–36.

[124] The point may become important where the company sues the director to recover the loss suffered (see para.16–111) or a third party for failing to discover the directors' wrongdoing (see para.22–41).

[125] *El Ajou v Dollar Land Holdings Plc* [1994] 1 B.C.L.C. 464 CA; *Royal Brunei Airlines Bhd Shd v Tan* [1995] 2 A.C. 378 PC.

Criminal liability

As we have just seen, vicarious liability provides the bedrock upon which companies are held liable in tort. In criminal law, by contrast, vicarious liability is regarded with suspicion in relation to serious crimes involving mens rea. Consequently criminal law has had to place greater reliance on the direct liability of the company. On this approach, the acts and state of mind of officers or employees are treated at those of the company. However, the criminal law has had great difficulty in determining the criteria for direct liability. If they are broadly set, there will be little difference from the company's point of view between vicarious and direct liability; if narrowly set, companies will often escape criminal punishment.

7–38

Regulatory offences

In the case of regulatory offences based on strict liability, it will be relatively easy to convince the court that Parliament intended to attribute the acts of even junior persons in the business to the company.[126] In an important decision the Court of Appeal was prepared to go further and apply this approach in the case of a hybrid offence, where the strict liability was qualified by a "reasonably practical" defence.[127] In this case, it was not a defence for the company that the senior management had taken all reasonable care to avoid a breach of the statutory duty; it was necessary that those actually in charge of the dangerous operation should have done so. Where liability is imposed, then on usual principles the fact that the employees were acting contrary to their instructions does not necessarily provide the company with a defence.[128]

7–39

Identification

Outside the area of regulatory offences, the traditional approach has been to impose liability on the company only on the basis of an "identification" doctrine. This doctrine has its origins in the area of statutory civil liability and was only later transferred to the criminal law. The classic formulation is to be found in *Lennard's Carrying Co Ltd v Asiatic Petroleum Co Ltd*,[129] concerning corporate civil liability under the merchant shipping legislation which required a finding of "actual fault or privity" on the part of the company. This formulation was taken to exclude vicarious liability as a technique for holding the company liable. There, Lord Haldane based identification on the concept of a person "who is really the directing mind and will of the corporation, the very ego and centre of the

7–40

---

[126] This step was taken at an early stage. See *Moussell Brothers Ltd v London & North Western Railway Co* [1917] 2 K.B. 836.

[127] *R. v British Steel Plc* [1995] I.C.R. 586 CA. The doctrine used to achieve this result was that the company had a "non-delegable duty" to produce a safe workplace. This case only opens up the potential for imposing liability for hybrid offences. Whether a particular statute does so is again a matter of construction.

[128] *Re Supply of Ready Mixed Concrete (No.2)* [1995] 1 A.C. 456 HL.

[129] *Lennard's Carrying Co Ltd v Asiatic Petroleum Co Ltd* [1915] A.C. 705 HL. See also *The Truculent* [1952] P. 1; *The Lady Gwendolen* [1965] P. 294 CA.

personality of the corporation".[130] This was both an anthropomorphic and limited concept of attribution. Lord Haldane extended the directing mind and will concept beyond the constitutional bodies of the company only to include persons given the equivalent of board powers by the articles or by the general meeting.[131]

In the period immediately after the Second World War the same idea was applied in the criminal law and its use was eventually approved and clarified by the House of Lords in 1972 in the case of *Tesco Supermarkets Ltd v Nattrass*.[132] Their lordships took a similar view of what constituted the directing mind and will as in the earlier case, except that they added persons to whom the board had delegated its functions.[133] Of course, the concept is needed only in circumstances in which the formulation of the offence is thought to rule out the attribution to the company of the acts and state of mind of persons not falling within the "directing mind and will" concept. Where the crime is more broadly formulated, the company can be held liable on the basis of what those other employees thought and did, as Tesco itself discovered in a later case.[134]

The third area where the directing mind and will theory was accepted was accessory liability for breach of fiduciary duty. This was a more surprising development since, for the purpose of civil litigation by third parties against companies, the actions and states of mind of agents are normally attributed to the principal, so that the "directing mind and will concept" need not be deployed. However, in *El Ajou v Dollar Land Holdings Plc*,[135] the knowledge of a director who had responsibility for a particular category of transactions on the company's behalf was attributed to the company for the purposes of making the company liable for knowing receipt of the proceeds of a fraud. It has been disputed academically whether this result could have been achieved on the basis of normal agency principles and that criticism has received some judicial support.[136]

Beyond "directing mind and will"

7–41   However, the position reached in the *Nattrass* case in the early 1970s did not prove stable, for two reasons. First, the line between regulatory offences where

---

[130] *Lennard's Carrying Co Ltd v Asiatic Petroleum Co Ltd* [1915] A.C. 705 at 713. Lord Haldane's dictum was probably influenced by the clear distinction drawn between agents and organs in German company law, Haldane having studied in his youth in Germany.

[131] In the case itself the defendant company was held liable on the basis of the actions of the managing director of another company which managed the ship on behalf of the defendant company, but this was on the basis that the defendant company had failed to reveal the nature of the manager's relationship with the defendant company.

[132] *Tesco Supermarkets Ltd v Nattrass* [1972] A.C. 153. The earlier cases included *DPP v Kent & Sussex Contractors Ltd* [1944] K.B. 146; *R. v ICR Haulage Ltd* [1944] K.B. 551 CCA; *Moore v Bresler* [1944] 2 All E.R. 515; and *Bolton (Engineering) Co Ltd v Graham & Sons* [1957] 1 Q.B. 159—in some of which a very broad interpretation was given to the concept of the directing mind and will.

[133] Since the individual whose acts were in question was a lowly employee in the case, the judges did not have to explore in detail what board delegation meant: was delegation of board powers enough (as Lord Diplock suggested) or did the board need to delegate in addition its responsibility for a certain area of the company's business (as Lord Reid indicated)?

[134] *Tesco Stores Ltd v Brent LBC* [1993] 1 W.L.R. 1037 DC.

[135] *El Ajou v Dollar Land Holdings Plc* [1994] 1 B.C.L.C. 464 CA.

[136] Watts, (2000) 116 L.Q.R. at 529. See *Jetivia SA v Bilta (UK) Ltd* [2015] 1 B.C.L.C. 443 at [197].

the liability of the company could readily be inferred and other crimes where the much more restrictive identification doctrine held sway proved difficult to draw.[137] Secondly, the use of a concept—the "directing mind and will"—which has its origins in relation to natural person provided very little guidance about the function and scope of this concept in relation to an abstract person such as a company.[138] Consequently, the definition of who counted as the directing mind and will of the company continued to be uncertain. A partial breakthrough came in *Meridian Global Funds Management Asia Ltd v Securities Commission*,[139] a case involving administrative penalties for breaches of securities legislation. Lord Hoffmann sought to take an approach based on analysis of the rule in question rather than on the company's internal decision-making. Where statutory liability was imposed on a company, then, where the company's constitutional bodies had not acted and the doctrine of vicarious liability was not available for some reason, the question was who, for the purposes of the statute, was to be treated as the company. Whilst Lord Haldane's phrase might have suited the statute and the corporate structure he had to deal with, it did not define the correct overall approach. "The question is one of construction rather than metaphysics." The true question in each case was who, as a matter of construction of the statute in question, or presumably other rule of law,[140] is to be regarded as "the company" for the purpose of the identification rule. In appropriate cases, that might be a person who was less elevated in the corporate structure than those Lord Haldane had in mind. In *Meridian* itself, where the question was whether the company was in breach of the New Zealand laws requiring disclosure of substantial shareholdings knowingly held by an investor,[141] the relevant persons were held to be two senior investment managers who were not members of the company's board. Given the purpose of the statute—speedy disclosure of shareholdings—it was appropriate to treat those in charge of dealing in the markets on behalf of the company as its "controllers" in this respect.

Welcome and more straightforward though the new approach is, it inevitably still leaves uncertainty as to who will be regarded as the relevant person within the corporate hierarchy for the purposes of the identification rule in any particular case. According to the statute, this might range from almost any agent or employee of the company acting within the scope of his or her authority to only those holding senior management positions, perhaps in some cases only the board itself. Since, however, a precise answer to the question of whose acts and knowledge are to be attributed to the company depends ex hypothesi on an

---

[137] See in particular the decision of the CA in *Tesco Stores Ltd v Brent LBC* [1993] 2 All E.R. 718 CA, not following the earlier *Tesco* case (previous note). See also Law Commission, *Criminal Liability in Regulatory Contexts*, Consultation Paper 195, 2010, paras 5.45–5.83.

[138] Ferran, (2011) 127 L.Q.R. 239.

[139] *Meridian Global Funds Management Asia Ltd v Securities Commission* [1995] 2 A.C. 500 at 509. The case is noted by Sealy, [1995] C.L.J. 507; Wells, (1995) 14 I.B.F.L. 42; and Yeung, [1977] C.F.I.L.R. 67.

[140] See *El Ajou v Dollar Land Holdings Plc* [1994] 2 All E.R. 685 CA, where the Court of Appeal, including Hoffmann LJ, as he then was, applied a similar approach to the question of whether a company was in equity in knowing receipt of trust property. See also *Lebon v Aqua Salt Co Ltd* [2009] 1 B.C.L.C. 540 PC—same approach used to determine whether a director's knowledge is to be attributed to the company under Mauritian law.

[141] For the equivalent British rules see Ch.26, below.

analysis of the context of the particular rule with which the court is dealing, it is doubtful whether more certainty can be provided at a general level.[142] In this respect it is helpful that these "special" rules of attribution are needed only where the "primary" and "general" rules of attribution are unavailable.[143]

Criminal liability of directors

7–42   Is a director exposed to criminal liability where he or she has not committed the criminal act for which the company is vicariously or directly liable? In principle, the answer is in the negative, but criminal liability on the director may arise in some cases. The common law normally treats as guilty of the offence those who counsel or procure the commission of that offence, for example, by a company. They are liable for the principal offence as well as those who actually commit it, just as tort law treats persons as joint tortfeasors in such cases.[144] This common law liability will arise even in relation to statutory offences, unless the statute excludes it. Further, many statutes expressly impose a somewhat similar liability expressly upon directors and managers where they consent to or connive at the commission of an offence by the company.[145] Under this rule the director or manager can be criminally liable personally where he or she is fully aware of or approves the corporate criminal offence, even though that awareness or approval do not encourage or assist the commission of the offence by the company. The imposition of criminal liability in this situation puts strong pressure on directors and managers to intervene and prevent wrongdoing within the company when they are aware of it.

Liability for the principal offence is also imposed under another common statutory formula which, however, goes considerably beyond consent or connivance. Under this second statutory formula liability is imposed when neglect by a director or manager has contributed to the commission of the offence by the company.[146] Here, a causal link between the neglect by the director and the commission of the offence by the company must be shown (an element not required under the "consent or connivance" formula) but the director or manager is made liable for the principal offence without necessarily being subjectively aware of the wrongdoing within the company. The Law Commission has suggested that it is unfair to impose liability upon the director for the principal offence in this second case, if the offence requires proof of fault or conviction carries a high stigma. However, the Commission did accept that it is appropriate

---

[142] Despite the uncertainty, the Law Commission (above fn.137, paras 5.103–5.110) has commended this approach to the courts in all cases where the statute does not itself deal with the issue of corporate liability. On this approach the identification doctrine, at least in its classic form, would be just one possible result of the exercise of statutory construction. For an example of the traps inherent in this approach see *St Regis Paper Co Ltd v R.* [2011] EWCA Crim 2527.

[143] See para.7–3 for a description of these terms.

[144] See para.7–36, above.

[145] The standard formulation covers "a director, manager, secretary or similar officer", those who purport to act as such, and the members of the company if its affairs are conducted by the members and the member had a membership function. See e.g. Fraud Act 2006 s.12.

[146] An example is s.400 of the Financial Services and Markets Act 2000—which imposes consent or connivance liability as well.

in some circumstances to impose a separate liability for negligently failing to prevent the commission of an offence by the company.[147]

Finally, the director (or manager) might be civilly liable to the company for the loss suffered by it as a result of the commission of an offence, on the grounds that permitting or causing the company to commit the offence was a breach of duty or breach of contract by the director as against the company.[148]

Corporate manslaughter

The *Meridian* approach to corporate liability may come to dominate the issue in relation to statutory crimes. However, the Court of Appeal refused to adopt it in respect of the common law crime of manslaughter by gross negligence. Accordingly, for this important common law crime a company could be convicted only if an identifiable human being could be shown to have committed that crime and that individual met the strict test for the identification of that person with the company (i.e. the "directing mind and will" test).[149] Consequently, in respect of this important crime it was difficult to secure the conviction of other than small companies when serious fatalities occurred in the course of the company's business. The gross negligence required could rarely be located sufficiently high up in the corporate hierarchy. As long ago as 1996, the Law Commission proposed a solution to this difficulty in its recommendation that a company should be criminally liable if management failure was a cause of a person's death, without the need to show that any human being was guilty of manslaughter or, indeed, any other crime.[150] On this approach the company could be liable criminally even though none of those whose actions were attributed to it was criminally liable. The focus would be on the quality of the operating systems deployed by the company rather than the guilt of individuals.

7–43

After a remarkably tortuous legislative passage, extending over a number of years, the Corporate Manslaughter and Corporate Homicide Act 2007[151] eventually reached the statute book. It creates an offence for companies[152] to cause a person's death as a result of the way its activities are organised or managed where that organisation or management amounts to a gross breach of a duty owed by the company to the deceased. The new statutory offence replaces the common law as far as companies are concerned.[153] The requirement for a

---

[147] Above fn.137, paras 7.41–7.52. This would avoid the stigma associated with conviction for the principal offence, e.g. where the company has been convicted of an offence involving dishonesty. See further para.7–46, below.

[148] *Safeway Stores Ltd v Twigger* [2010] 2 B.C.L.C. 106; reversed ([2011] 2 All E.R. 841 CA) on the grounds that it would be inconsistent with the purpose of the particular statute imposing liability on the company that the company should recover its loss from the directors.

[149] *Re Attorney-General's Reference (No.2 of 1999)* [2000] Q.B. 796 CA.

[150] Law Commission, *Legislating the Criminal Code: Involuntary Manslaughter*, Law Com. No.237, H.C. 171, 1996.

[151] The offence is corporate manslaughter in England, Wales and Northern Ireland; corporate homicide in Scotland.

[152] And for other corporate bodies, which need not concern us here, though the question of how far public sector bodies should be the brought within the scope of the Act was one of the most contentious in Parliament.

[153] 2007 Act s.20.

gross breach of duty owed to the deceased[154] reflects the common law of manslaughter by gross negligence. From the point of view of the above discussion the crucial point is that no individual has to be identified whose acts constitute the offence of manslaughter and whose acts and knowledge can then be attributed to the company. The company can be convicted on its organisational failings alone, irrespective of the guilt of any individual person. However, some rule has to be provided to identify the persons whose organisational failings are attributed to the company. Here, the notion that the company should be found guilty only for failings at a senior level is retained in the provision that corporate guilt arises "only if the way in which its activities are managed or organised by its senior management is a substantial element in the breach".[155] If the failings are wholly at subordinate level, the company will not be guilty. However, significant failings at lower levels are bound to raise the question of whether the senior levels of management should have picked up these lower level failings.

Sanctions

7–44 If the company is found guilty under the Act, it is liable to an unlimited fine.[156] How is this supposed to further the deterrent aims of the criminal law, either in the case of corporate manslaughter or more generally? The financial penalty falls on the shareholders rather than on the senior management whose failings led to the criminal offence.[157] It may be that this will encourage the shareholders to take action which is adverse to the interests of the directors (e.g. removing them) or put pressure on them to avoid repetitions of the offence. Whether the imposition of a penalty on the company will have such effects will depend in part on the nature of the shareholder/management relations in the company. It is perhaps least likely to operate in this way in large companies for which the 2007 Act was particularly designed. Greater pressure on the shareholders to take action might arise if the consequence of a criminal conviction were the exclusion of the company from a certain area of business, but this raises even more strongly the question of the rationale for imposing a penalty on shareholders for managerial wrongdoing.

A greater deterrent impact may result from the reputational harm the management will likely suffer if the company is found guilty of corporate manslaughter whilst they were in charge of it. In this respect, the court's power to order the company to give publicity to the fact of its conviction may be

---

[154] The existence of the duty is a question of law for the judge (s.2(5)); whether the breach of the duty is "gross" a question for the jury (s.8). The duty in question must be a duty under the law of negligence falling into one of the categories listed in s.2, though these categories are widely defined.

[155] 2007 Act s.1(3).

[156] 2007 Act s.1(6).

[157] The fine reduces the value of the shareholders' equity. The share price fall may further reflect the reputational harm suffered by the company as a result of the crime. However, not all crimes reduce the willingness of customers to deal with companies nor show that the directors were acting contrary to the interests of the shareholders. Possibly even the reverse can be true. See J. Armour, C. Mayer and A. Polo, "Regulatory Sanctions and Reputational Damage in Financial Markets", Oxford Legal Studies Research Paper No 62/2010; ECGI—Finance Working Paper No.300/2010. Available at SSRN: *http://ssrn.com/abstract=1678028* [Accessed 21 March 2016].

helpful.[158] At one stage it had been mooted that convictions would be required to be reported in the company's Operating and Financial Review.[159] Although neither the 2007 Act nor the provisions governing the Business Review (which replaced the OFR) in terms require this, such publication could be required as part of a court's publicity order.

The court has a further power—which may operate more directly on the management of the company—to order a convicted company to take steps, not only to remedy the breach and any matter resulting from it which were a cause of the death, but also "any deficiency, as regards health and safety matters, in the organisation's policies, systems or practices of which the relevant breach appears to the court to be an indication". The application for the order may be made only by the prosecution, which must consult the relevant enforcement authority (for example, the Health and Safety Executive) about what should be asked for. The order will set a time limit for the specified steps to be taken and may require the company to provide evidence to the relevant enforcement authority that those steps have been taken.[160] However, the enforcement authority is given no greater monitoring role in relation to the management of the company than this, though it may think it appropriate to use its general inspection powers more vigorously in relation to a company which has been convicted of corporate manslaughter than one which has not.

Personal liability under the 2007 Act

Since the deterrent effect of the sanction turns on its impact on the management of the company, one may wonder whether the criminal liability of the company is something of a side-show, unlike in tort law where the compensatory goals of tort law are advanced by corporate liability. One might further wonder whether the crucial issue rather is the personal criminal liability of the directors or other senior managers, as discussed in para.7–42, above, rather than the liability of the company. Thus, it is not surprising that, during the passage of the 2007 Act, there was an intensive debate about whether penalties—whether by way of criminal sanctions or by way of disqualification—should be imposed on those members of the senior management of the company who were to blame for the organisational failings. In this debate, the wheel thus came full circle: under the directing mind and will doctrine the crimes of individual managers make the company liable; now the question was how far corporate crime should make individual managers liable. The Government resisted strongly any moves in this direction. The 2007 Act creates corporate offences only and excludes criminal liability even in relation to the counselling and procuring of the offence, though disqualification is possible.[161]

7–45

---

[158] 2007 Act s.10. Non-compliance with a publicity order is itself a criminal offence.
[159] See below, para.21–24.
[160] 2007 Act s.9.
[161] 2007 Act s.18. Conviction for an indictable offence in connection with the management of the company is a basis for disqualification, as is, even without conviction, unfitness to be involved in the management of a company. See Ch.10.

Failure to prevent criminal acts

7–46   The Corporate Manslaughter and Corporate Homicide Act creates strong incentives for companies to organise their businesses so as not impose risks of serious harm on their employees and outsiders. Criminal liability for failure to address risks within the organisation could be imposed on a wider basis. It appears to be becoming attractive to the legislature to impose such liability where the risk in question is the risk of a criminal act being committed within the organisation, presumably on the basis that the senior management of the company are better at discouraging criminal acts within it than are the ordinary law enforcement bodies. A significant step was taken in the Bribery Act 2010. This Act not only updates and extends the substantive offence of bribery, but it also imposes (in ss.7 and 8) criminal liability on companies for failing to prevent bribery by a person associated with the company. In addition, s.14 imposes on "senior officers" (not just directors) of the company "consent or connivance" liability (see para.7–42, above) in respect of the failure. The associated person could be simply an employee or agent of the company. The liability arises only if the associated person was intending to obtain a business advantage for the company. More important, it is a defence for the company that it has in place adequate procedures designed to prevent bribery by employees and agents. In essence, the threat of criminal liability is used to induce companies to put in place adequate internal controls over bribery. This incentive rationale for imposing criminal liability for failure to prevent crime could be used extensively in relation to crime committed within the scope of a company's business. In its *Anti-Corruption Plan*[162] the government stated that it "will therefore examine the case for a new offence of corporate failure to prevent economic crime and look at the rules on establishing corporate criminal liability more widely".

Litigation by the company

7–47   We have been concerned in this part of the chapter with how a company becomes liable in respect of wrongdoing when the wrongful acts and states of mind must necessarily have been those of natural persons. Our core case has been an action by the third party against the company. But we have noticed at various points that the company itself might sue in respect of the wrongdoing, either against those whose acts or states of mind made it liable or against third parties (in the case of companies, typically its auditors) who ought to have discovered the wrongdoing and notified it to the company. We discuss these claims in other chapters, notably Ch.16 (actions against directors) and Ch.22 (auditors). All we need note here is that the rules on attribution which apply in actions by third parties are not the same as those which apply in the case of actions against the third party by the company. If they did, the company's action might be blocked on the grounds of consent or illegality. It is now recognised, in both civil[163] and criminal[164] law, that

---

[162] HM Government, December 2014, Action 36.

[163] *Jetivia SA v Bilta (UK) Ltd* [2015] 1 B.C.L.C. 443 at [7].

[164] *Attorney-General's Reference (No.2 of 1982)* [1984] Q.B. 624 CA; *R. v Phillipou* (1989) 89 Cr. App. R. 290 CA; *R. v Rozeik* [1996] B.C.C. 271 CA.

to block the company's action against the director on the grounds that the company was is some sense party to the illegality would be to undermine the duties owed by directors to their companies and that, except for rare cases, this is not the law. The position of the auditor is less clearly settled, though it is moving in the same direction.

CONCLUSION

As we observed at the beginning of this chapter, since the company is a separate but abstract legal person, it can act only through natural legal persons. From this trite proposition a complex body of law has emerged to determine which people in which circumstances can be regarded as having acted as or on behalf of the company. Nevertheless, some lines on the map are clear. In relation to contracting the modern tendency has been to promote the security of third parties' transactions by reducing the impact of restrictions in the company's constitution upon the effectiveness of the contracting process. As far as directors are concerned, the operation of the rules of agency normally means they are not liable or entitled on the resulting contracts, but only the company is. By contrast, in the area of tort and crime the personal liability of those acting on behalf of the company is the normal rule. The tendency has been to extend somewhat corporate liability in tort and crime in recent years, through expansion of the scope of vicarious liability, downgrading the "directing mind and will" test and statutory interventions in the area of criminal liability.

7–48

CHAPTER 8

LIMITED LIABILITY AND LIFTING THE VEIL

THE RATIONALE FOR LIMITED LIABILITY

The company laws of all economically advanced countries make available **8–1**
corporate vehicles through which businesses can be carried on with the benefit of
limited liability for their members. For shareholders this means that their liability
for the company's debts is limited to the amount they have paid or have agreed to
pay to the company for its shares. For most shareholders this means that, once the
shares have been paid for, whether they were acquired directly from the company
or from an existing shareholder, the worst fate that can befall them if the
company becomes insolvent is that they lose the entire value of their investment.[1]
However, their other assets—their homes, pension funds, domestic goods—will
be unaffected by the collapse of the company in which they have invested. To put
the matter from the creditors' perspective, their claims are limited to the assets of
the company and cannot be asserted against the shareholders' assets. This can be
regarded as a strong rule because, if the opposite economic development occurs
and the company is highly successful, the shareholders are likely to receive all the
residual benefit of that success, once the creditors have been satisfied, either
through dividends or the capital appreciation of their shares.[2] So, there is an
apparent asymmetry in the risks and rewards which are allocated to shareholders:
they benefit, through limited liability, from a cap of their down-side risk, whereas
the chance of up-side gain is unlimited.

    Why does the law treat shareholders in this favourable way? During the battle
for legislative acceptance of the principle of limited liability in the middle of the

---

[1] Section 3 of the 2006 Act gives the shareholders/incorporators the option of limiting shareholders'
liability in two ways via provisions in the articles: either to the amount, if any, unpaid on the shares
(company limited by shares) or to the (usually nominal) amount the members agree to contribute in a
winding up (company limited by guarantee—a much less popular choice). Section 3 is reinforced by
the Insolvency Act 1986 s.74. In the absence of choice, the liability of the shareholders is unlimited.
[2] Insolvency Act 1986 s.107.

nineteenth century,[3] the argument which seems to have weighed most heavily with the legislator was that limited liability would facilitate the investment by members of the public, who were not professional investors, of their surplus funds in the many large capital projects which companies were being set up to carry out at that time, in particular the construction of a national network of railways. Members of the public, whose primary activity and expertise did not lie with the running of companies, would be much less likely to be willing to buy shares in such companies, if the full range of their personal assets were to be put at risk. They might be prepared to become lenders of money to such companies, but it was the flexibility of risk capital through shares which those companies sought.[4] The shareholders might earn a big return if the company's project was successful, but equally, at least in the case of ordinary shares, the company would be free to pay them nothing or very little, if the project achieved only modest success, whereas debt holders would normally be entitled to their fixed return by way of interest and repayment of capital, no matter whether the project was successful, provided the company stayed out of insolvency.

Halpern, Trebilcock and Turnbull[5] have pointed out that limited liability, in addition, facilitates the operation of public securities markets, because it relieves the investor of the need to be concerned about the personal wealth of fellow investors. Under a rule whereby the shareholders were jointly and severally liable for a company's debts, my shares would be more valuable to me if the wealth of my fellow investors increased (because I would be less likely to have to pay more than the proportion of the company's debts which my shares constituted of the company's total share capital), and vice versa if the wealth of my fellow shareholders decreased. So limited liability facilitates the trading of the company's shares at a uniform price on the public exchanges and reduces shareholders' monitoring costs. This adverse effect of unlimited liability could be mitigated, of course, by making the shareholders liable only on a proportionate basis (i.e. liability on the part of each investor only for his or her "share" of the company's debts).[6]

Further, limited liability encourages equity investment by those of modest means by facilitating diversification of investment across a number of companies in different sectors and perhaps countries, thus reducing the investor's company-specific and country-specific risks. Under a regime of unlimited liability, investors would be incentivised to monitor closely the companies in which they were invested and this would push them towards reducing the range of their investments in order to reduce monitoring costs.

8–2 The above arguments in favour of limited liability are stronger in relation to companies which have offered their shares to the public, but are less persuasive for companies which have not and do not plan to do so, i.e. for all private companies (which constitute the overwhelming number of companies on the

---

[3] For an account, see the sixth edition of this book at pp.40–46.

[4] The distinction between equity and debt is discussed further in para.31–2, below.

[5] "An Economic Analysis of Limited Liability" (1980) 30 University of Toronto L.J. 117.

[6] Though the current rule of insolvency law, if limited liability does not apply, is joint and several liability: IA 1986 s.74(1).

register)[7] and even for some public companies. Yet, as we saw in Ch.2, a great deal of effort was expended on the part of practitioners in the second half of the nineteenth century in securing the extension of limited liability to all companies, including the smallest, a goal achieved when the House of Lords handed down its decision in *Salomon v Salomon*,[8] and the legislature decided not to reverse that decision. That decision has remained controversial,[9] but so entrenched in our law is the principle of limited liability for all companies, large or small, that arguments for the reversal of *Salomon* have made no progress with policy-makers.

During the Company Law Review at the turn of the last century, the argument was made that the flexibility of organisational rules, which those running small businesses seek, should be provided outside company law, through a new and optional organisational form with unlimited liability, whilst those who seek limited liability should have to accept the burdens of company law, which indeed might well be somewhat enhanced, especially in relation to minimum capital requirements.[10] The Company Law Review, anxious not to place barriers in the way of the organic growth of small companies and to encourage entrepreneur-ship, rejected the arguments for a separate form of incorporation and a reduction in the availability of limited liability for small businesses,[11] and in fact, under the banner "Think Small First", proposed some further deregulation of company law as it applies to small companies.[12] Moreover, as we saw in Ch.1,[13] the Government later did provide a separate and highly flexible form of business organisation through the limited liability partnership, introduced by the Limited Liability Partnership Act of 2000, but crucially attached limited liability to it. Indeed, the main object of the reform was to make a partnership-like form available but with the benefit of limited liability.

The rationales for limited liability, identified above, are more persuasive, perhaps even assume, that the shareholders are natural persons. However, very many businesses are today carried on through a group of holding and subsidiary companies rather than through a single company.[14] This raises the question of whether the doctrine of limited liability should apply only as between the holding (or parent) company and its shareholders or also within the group, i.e. between the holding company and the subsidiaries and among the subsidiary companies. Whether or not the parent benefits from limited liability as against its subsidiaries, the shareholders of the parent cannot lose more than the value of their investment provided the parent is subject to the doctrine. In fact, the doctrine does apply within groups, a conclusion which the courts have arrived at without any deep consideration of the matter as an inevitable consequence of the

---

[7] See above, Ch.1.

[8] *Salomon v Salomon & Co Ltd* [1897] A.C. 22; above, para.2–1.

[9] In (1944) 7 M.L.R. 54, Otto Kahn-Freund described it as "calamitous".

[10] This case has been put in its most attractive form by A. Hicks, R. Drury and J. Smallcombe, *Alternative Company Structures for the Small Business*, ACCA Research Report 42 (1995). On minimum capital requirements see Ch.11, below.

[11] Strategic Framework, Ch.5.2.

[12] Final Report I, Ch.2.

[13] See above, para.1–4.

[14] See further below at paras 8–11 and 9–21.

doctrine of separate legal personality. This could be justified on the grounds that it encourages investment by "outside" investors in the subsidiaries (as opposed to the parent), but this argument does not carry weight in relation to wholly-owned subsidiaries, which are the norm in the UK.

8–3   The rationales for limited liability so far identified equate the societal benefit of limited liability with the greater ease with which companies can raise risk capital. From the creditors' point of view, however, limited liability seems unattractive as it confines their claims to the company's assets. It might be argued that this does not matter because creditors, as well, have limited liability: their downside exposure is capped at the amount they are owed by the company.[15] Unlike shareholders, however, creditors' upside potential is meagre: their claim on the company does not normally increase if the company does well—though the probability of actually receiving that claim may improve. However, limited liability may in fact decrease the probability of repayment to creditors. Shareholders with their asymmetrical awards may fail to constrain management engaged in taking reckless risks, thus increasing the probability of corporate failure. In response, creditors may monitor management more closely, thus increasing the costs of providing credit. So, creditors might prefer unlimited liability for shareholders because that would throw the additional monitoring costs onto the shareholders. From the point of view of corporate finance, however, it may not matter where those costs are allocated, provided that the costs of effective monitoring are roughly the same in the two cases.

However, a rationale for limited liability has been advanced which takes as its starting point the monitoring incentives of creditors and provides a general justification for limited liability precisely on the grounds that it *reduces* the costs of creditor monitoring (and not only in relation to free-standing, publicly traded companies). This is the "asset partitioning" rationale.[16] What limited liability facilitates, together with the concept of separate legal personality, is the segregation of collections of assets between investors and the company, in the case of a single company, or as among different companies in corporate groups. Although the doctrines are normally presented as hindering the enforcement of claims by corporate creditors, it can be argued that they work to their benefit. Just as limited liability prevents creditors of a company from asserting their claims against the shareholders' assets, so also the doctrine of the company as a separate legal person prevents the creditors of a shareholder from asserting their claims against the company's assets. Within a group the same argument applies in relation to the creditors of subsidiary and of the parent company (or a fellow subsidiary). In other words, a creditor of the company does not have to face

---

[15] It is possible to conceive of the law imposing liability upon a lender, beyond loss of the amount of the loan or deposit, if the borrower becomes insolvent, but since the lender has limited access to the up-side benefit of corporate success, such a rule would be likely to choke off the supply of debt to companies. Debt investors are usually seeking relatively modest returns for relatively modest risk. However, "lender liability" is imposed if the lender involves itself in the running of the company to the extent of becoming a "shadow" director (see para.9–7), but this is precisely because the lender has moved out of that limited role and involved itself in the central management of the company.

[16] H. Hansmann and R. Kraakman, "The Essential Role of Organizational Law" (2000) 110 Yale L.J. 387; H. Hansmann, R. Kraakman and R. Squire, "Law and the Rise of the Firm" (2005–6) 119 Harvard L.R. 1335.

competition from the shareholder's creditors, just as the corporate creditor does not compete with the creditors of the shareholder. Each set of creditors is thus safe in confining their monitoring efforts to the company's or the shareholder's assets, as the case may be, and creditors may be expected to specialise in these different forms of monitoring. Overall, creditors' monitoring costs can be expected to be reduced under a system of asset partitioning. More generally, whilst the shareholder will not normally be pushed into bankruptcy by the failure of the company in which they have invested, because they lose only their investment, so equally the creditors of the shareholders will not be able to seize the company's assets to satisfy their claims. This is likely to be of overall benefit to society because it protects the integrity of the assets which the company has assembled to conduct its business and the benefits the company generates, not only for its investors, but also for others by way of employment and tax payments. This rationale for asset partitioning is as powerful within groups as between the parent and its shareholders.

An alternative or supplementary way of looking at limited liability emphasises **8–4** that it is not a mandatory rule. Limited liability is, it might be said, a default rule and those who do not like it can contract out of it. The incorporators themselves may opt out of limited liability across-the-board, by forming an unlimited liability company—though this occurs but rarely.[17] Alternatively, particular creditors may contract with the company and its shareholders on the basis that both will be liable on the obligations undertaken. Where the rationales for limited liability are most in question, in relation to groups and small companies, it is in fact common for some creditors to contract out of limited liability. Those setting up small companies, into which they are not willing to inject a significant amount of share capital, will usually find that a bank will not lend money to the company unless the shareholders give a personal guarantee of the loan to the company.[18] In this way, the personal assets of the shareholders become available to the bank if there is default on the loan; the bank is not confined to the assets of the company. Equally, those dealing with an undercapitalised company in a group of companies may obtain a guarantee from the parent company[19] or, less securely, the parent company may issue a "letter of comfort" to the subsidiary's auditors, allowing them to certify the subsidiary's accounts on a going concern basis, or to a third party contemplating contracting with the company.[20] The implication of the contractual approach might be thought to be that there is no need for the law to control limited liability for it lies in the hands of those contracting with the company to protect their interests themselves. In the case of large or frequent creditors this is very often true. But not all creditors can adjust their contractual relations with the company so as to reflect the riskiness of their situation and for

---

[17] See para.1–27, above.
[18] cf. the facts of *Regal (Hastings) Ltd v Gulliver* [1942] 1 All E.R. 378 HL, one of the leading cases on directors' fiduciary duties, but where the underlying problem arose out of the third party's request for a personal guarantee which the directors were unwilling to give.
[19] See *Re Polly Peck International Plc (In Administration)* [1996] 2 All E.R. 433 (involving a single purpose finance vehicle which had no substantial assets of its own).
[20] *Re Augustus Barnett & Son Ltd* [1986] B.C.L.C. 170; *Kleinwort Benson Ltd v Malaysia Mining Corp Bhd* [1989] 1 W.L.R. 379 CA (letter of comfort not intended in this case to create legal relations).

such "non-adjusting" creditors, notably tort victims, the default rule of the law is a crucial determinant of the legal position.[21]

Finally, sight should not be lost of the argument that the incentives to take risks, associated with the asymmetric position of the shareholders, has a positive value. The purpose of commercial companies is to embark on risky ventures. A company dominated by risk-averse creditors might not add much to the store of social wealth because they would put pressure on the management to avoid risk.

LEGAL RESPONSES TO LIMITED LIABILITY

8–5   Of course, the supporters of limited liability do not deny that there is a role for company law beyond the adoption of the principle of limited liability. There are two potential roles for company law to fulfil given the establishment of a doctrine of limited liability. First, it might be able to promote creditor monitoring (i.e. self-help on the part of the creditors); secondly, it might be able to protect creditors against the opportunistic conduct on the part of shareholders or directors to which the doctrine of limited liability exposes them, for example, when they move assets out of the company just before the creditor assets its claim against the company. Monitoring by creditors can operate effectively only if creditors have the tools available to them to implement supervision. As we shall see at many points in this Part, a crucial legal tool for creditors is simply the law of contract, for example, terms inserted into loan contracts, rather than company law. However, the focus in this Part is on the contribution which company law makes to the promotion of creditor monitoring beyond what creditors can achieve for themselves via contract. Company law provides standardised rules more cheaply than creditors can do through contract. However, contract allows the rules to be adjusted to the specific situation of each company and creditor and facilitates re-negotiation of the rules as circumstances change. Consequently, the role for the law here is subordinate to contract. In relation to the second role, company law might be better able than contract to protect creditors against opportunistic behaviour by directors or shareholders because of the more powerful enforcement mechanisms and remedies it has at its disposal. Here, the potential role for standardised rules is somewhat larger.

Before we turn to company law, however, it is worth pointing out that the major contribution of statutory law to creditor protection is not provided by company law at all but by insolvency law (which we discuss, but in outline only, in Ch.33, below). When the company becomes insolvent, the directors responsible to the shareholders are replaced by an insolvency practitioner responsible to the creditors. At this point, the law facilitates creditors' access to the corporate assets in order that those assets can be best deployed so as to meet their claims.

---

[21] It has been suggested that limited liability should not apply to involuntary creditors: H. Hansmann and R. Kraakman, "Towards Unlimited Shareholder Liability for Corporate Torts" (1991) 100 Yale L.J. 1879.

Disclosure of information

The techniques available to the law to achieve these two goals are various. We **8–6**
discuss them in this Part of the book. Perhaps the most obvious response of the
law is to require publicity for the fact that corporate creditors' claims are confined
to the assets of the company, since knowledge of that fact is an essential
pre-requisite for any effective self-help action on the part of creditors. The
legislature has always made it an essential condition of the recognition of
corporate personality with limited liability that it should be accompanied by wide
publicity, starting with disclosure that the company has limited liability through
mandatory attachment of the suffix "ltd" or "plc" to the company's name.[22]
Although third parties dealing with the company will normally have no right of
resort against its members, they are nevertheless entitled to see who those
members are, what shares they hold and who holds the beneficial interests in
those shares, if substantial, so that they can know who is in ultimate control of the
company. They are also entitled to see who its officers are (so that they know
with whom to deal), what its constitution is (so that they know what the company
may do and how it may do it), and what its capital is and how it has been obtained
(so that they know whether to trust it). And unless it is an unlimited company
they are also entitled to see its accounts, or at least a modified version of
them—again in order to know whether to trust it. The exemption of the unlimited
company from the obligation to file accounts with the Registrar[23] is a particularly
strong illustration of the link between publicity and limited liability.

Normally, however, third parties are neither bound nor entitled to look behind
such information as the law provides shall be made public; in addition to the veil
of incorporation, there is something in the nature of a curtain formed by the
company's public file in the companies registry (or with the regulator of the stock
exchange), and what goes on behind it is concealed from the public gaze.[24] But
sometimes this curtain also may be raised. For example, inspectors may be
appointed to investigate the company's affairs,[25] in which case they will have the
widest inquisitorial powers; indeed they may even be appointed for the purpose
of going behind the company's registers to ascertain who are its true owners.

LIFTING THE VEIL

Disclosure is a fundamental regulatory tool, but its effectiveness depends upon **8–7**
how well those receiving the information can make use of it. At the opposite end
of the spectrum, the law might tackle the limited liability principle head-on and
make the shareholders liable for the debts and other obligations of the company
in certain cases, so that the need for creditors to monitor is substantially reduced.

---

[22] Which we discussed above at para.4–14.

[23] 2006 Act s.448. On the general disclosure requirements see in particular paras 2-39 et seq., 4-5, 11-11 and 26-9 et seq., and Ch.21.

[24] As we saw in the previous chapter, this may sometimes benefit the third party: the limitation of the outsider's knowledge to what is stated in the constitution is the foundation of the rule in *Royal British Bank v Turquand* (1856) 6 E. & B. 327 Exch.Ch.

[25] See para.18–11, below. However, routine requirements for the disclosure of beneficial ownership make investigations on this ground less common today. See paras 2-42 and 26-14.

This may happen as a result of judicial creativity or explicit legislative policy. Legislative breaches of the doctrine of limited liability tend to be few and targeted. We discuss the principal examples of this targeted approach in the following chapter. Judicial breaches are potentially wide-ranging, under the doctrine of "lifting the corporate veil". As the phrase suggests, the discussion in these cases tends to revolve around the applicability of the doctrine of the separate legal personality of the company rather than that of limited liability. The point is that, if the separate legal personality of the company is ignored, there is no scope for the doctrine of limited liability, because nothing now stands between the creditors and the shareholders. There are in fact very few cases where the courts have concluded that the wording and policy of the statute require the separate legal personality of the company to be ignored so that personal liability can be imposed on shareholders. However, ignoring the separate legal personality of the company may operate the other way around, that is, permit those holding entitlements against the shareholder to enforce those entitlements against the company, thus undermining the asset partitioning function of company law. As we shall see below, more of these cases can be found. In particular, the courts are willing to constrain shareholders' use of the corporate form to escape pre-existing liabilities.

Under statute or contract

8–8   When analysing the judicial decisions on lifting the veil, it is crucial to distinguish between those situations where the court is applying the terms of a statute (other than the legislation relating to companies) or, less often, a contract, from those where, as a matter of common law, the veil is lifted. The reason is that the justification for lifting the veil in the former group of cases is to be found in the wording of the statute or the contract. As we have noted, it is perfectly in line with the doctrine of limited liability that parties should contract out of it and so there is nothing remarkable in the courts' deciding that this has occurred in a particular case, provided the parties' intention has been accurately identified. Equally, Parliament is free to decide that the policy of a particular statute requires that the doctrine of limited liability needs to be overruled, though it is doubtless the case that if Parliament took this step routinely, one would begin to have doubts about its commitment to the doctrine of limited liability.

In looking at the statutory cases, it is also crucial to distinguish between those cases where the courts decide that the separate legal personality of the company should be disregarded and those where, in consequence of this disregard, the additional consequence follows that the shareholders are made liable for the company's debts or other obligations or the company for the shareholders' obligations. Only in these latter cases is the doctrine of limited liability set aside. Typically, as a result of ignoring the separate legal personality of the company, some legal issue other than the limited liability of the shareholders is determined in a way which is different from the way in which it would have been determined, had the separate legal personality been maintained. Thus, in *Re FG (Films) Ltd*[26]

---

[26] *Re FG (Films) Ltd* [1953] 1 W.L.R. 483.

a US company had incorporated a shell company in Britain for the purposes of claiming a declaration that a film it produced was British. The result of the failure by the courts to uphold the separation between the British and US companies was that the film was not classified as British, so that the subsidiary could not claim a subsidy which was contingent on the film being British, but the parent's liability for the debts of its subsidiary was simply not an issue in the case. In some cases, in fact, ignoring the separate legal personality of the company has been for the benefit of its shareholders.[27]

One statutory provision which does bring the company's liability home to its controllers is that which empowers the courts to make a "non-party costs order" against corporate controllers in favour of a successful party in litigation. This can be used where the controllers of the company (normally the persons who are both the shareholders and directors of the company) have used the company as a vehicle for litigation without considering whether the company had an independent to make interest in the litigation and knowing that it would be unable to meet the costs of failure.[28] Although important in practice, in principle this statutory provision needs little comment, since it clearly implements a policy that liability for costs should fall on the person in whose interests the litigation is being conducted.

In deciding whether to lift the veil in statutory cases, the courts are guided by their understanding of the statute in question, and so the decision arrived at is likely to vary from statute to statute. Nevertheless, it is difficult to avoid the conclusion that the courts are slow to find that the statutory wording has clearly overridden the separate legal personality doctrine. Thus, in *Prest v Petrodel Resources Ltd*[29] the Supreme Court refused to hold that the Matrimonial Causes Act 1973 permitted the court routinely to treat an asset owned by the company as the asset of its sole controlling shareholder simply because it would further the policy of that Act. The court achieved justice in that case by the alternative reasoning that, on the facts of the case, the property was held by the company on trust for the sole shareholder. A general doctrine of the law of equity thus did the work of an expansive interpretation of the wording of a statute.

Another example of a refusal to lift the veil, to the benefit of the employee/shareholder, is afforded by *Lee v Lee's Air Farming Ltd*.[30] There Lee, for the purpose of carrying on his business of aerial top-dressing, had formed a company of which he beneficially owned all the shares and was sole "governing director". He was also appointed chief pilot. Pursuant to the company's statutory

8–9

---

[27] *Trebanog Working Men's Club and Institute Ltd v MacDonald* [1940] K.B. 576 (incorporated club treated in the same way as an unincorporated one for the purposes of an exemption from the liquor licence rules); *DHN Food Distributors Ltd v Tower Hamlets LBC* [1976] 1 W.L.R. 852 CA (ignoring separate legal entity of subsidiary permitted parent to claim compensation under the planning legislation); *Smith Stone & Knight Ltd v Birmingham Corp* [1939] 4 All E.R. 116 (*ditto*); but cf. *Woolfson v Strathclyde Regional Council*, 1978 S.L.T. 159 HL (*DHN* not followed in a case on similar facts).

[28] Senior Courts Act 1981 s.51(3) and CPR 48.2(1). For recent examples see *Systemcare (UK) Ltd v Services Design Technology Ltd* [2012] 1 B.C.L.C. 14 CA; *Raleigh UK Ltd v Mail Order Cycles Ltd* [2011] B.C.C. 508; *Europeans Ltd v HMRC* [2011] B.C.C. 527.

[29] *Prest v Petrodel Resources Ltd* [2013] UKSC 34.

[30] *Lee v Lee's Air Farming Ltd* [1961] A.C. 12 PC.

obligations he caused the company to insure against liability to pay compensation under the Workmen's Compensation Act. He was killed in a flying accident. The Court of Appeal of New Zealand held that his widow was not entitled to compensation from the company (i.e. from their insurers) since Lee could not be regarded as a "worker" within the meaning of the Act. But the Privy Council reversed that decision, holding that Lee and his company were distinct legal entities which had entered into contractual relationships under which he became, qua chief pilot, an employee of the company. In his capacity of governing director he could, on behalf of the company, give himself orders in his other capacity of pilot, and hence the relationship between himself, as pilot, and the company was that of servant and master. In effect the magic of corporate personality enabled him to be master and servant at the same time and to get all the advantages of both (and of limited liability). No doubt the court was influenced by the fact that Lee had acted in pursuance of a purported statutory obligation and had in fact paid the necessary contributions over a period of time, thus forgoing the opportunity of making alternative insurance arrangements. More recent cases in Britain have accepted that in principle a person who is a 100 per cent shareholder in a company may enter into a valid contract of employment with that company, even though that person also appears, in effect, on the other side of the employer/employee relationship, so that the control element, normally inherent in the employment contract, is missing.[31]

At common law

8–10   Challenges to the doctrines of separate legal personality and limited liability at common law tend to raise more fundamental questions, because they are formulated on the basis of general reasons for not applying them, such as fraud, the company being a "sham" or "façade", that the company is the agent of the shareholder, that the companies are part of a "single economic unit" or even that the "interests of justice" require this result. However, the courts seem, if anything, more reluctant to accept such general arguments against the doctrines than arguments based on particular statutes or the terms of particular contracts. The decision of the House of Lords in *Salomon v A Salomon and Co Ltd*,[32] where the court refused to hold the sole owner of the company's shares liable for its debts, has stood the test of time. The leading modern case is *Adams v Cape Industries Plc*.[33] That case raised the issues in a sharp fashion. It concerned liability within a group of companies and the purpose of the claim was to circumvent the separate legal personality of the subsidiary in order to make the parent liable for the obligations of the subsidiary towards involuntary tort victims. Thus, the case encapsulated two features—internal group liability and involuntary creditors—where limited liability is most questionable. The facts of the case were somewhat complicated but for present purposes it suffices to say that what the Court had ultimately to determine was whether judgments obtained

---

[31] *Neufeld v Secretary of State for Business, Enterprise and Regulatory Reform* [2009] 2 B.C.L.C. 273 CA.

[32] *Salomon v A Salomon and Co Ltd* [1897] A.C. 22; see para.2–1, above.

[33] *Adams v Cape Industries Plc* [1990] Ch. 433, Scott J and CA (pet. dis. [1990] 2 W.L.R. 786 HL).

in the US against Cape, an English registered company whose business was mining asbestos in South Africa and marketing it worldwide, would be recognised and enforced by the English courts. In the absence of submission to the foreign jurisdiction on the part of Cape, this depended on whether Cape could be said to have been "present" in the US. On the facts, the answer to that question turned on whether Cape could be said to be present in the US through its wholly owned subsidiaries or through a company (CPC) with which it had close business links. The court rejected all the arguments by which it was sought to make Cape liable.[34]

The "single economic unit" argument

The first of these, described as the "single economic unit argument", proceeded **8–11** as follows: Admittedly there is no general principle that all companies in a group of companies are to be regarded as one; on the contrary, the fundamental principle is unquestionably that "each company in a group of companies is a separate legal entity possessed of separate rights and liabilities".[35] Nevertheless, it was argued that, where the group companies are operated as a single unit for business purposes, the court will ignore the distinction between them, treating them as one. For this proposition a number of authorities were cited, but the court distinguished them all as turning on the interpretation of particular statutory or contractual provisions.[36] After reviewing these authorities the Court in *Cape* expressed some sympathy with the claimants' submissions and agreed that:

> "To the layman at least the distinction between the case where a company trades itself in a foreign country and the case where it trades in a foreign country through a subsidiary, whose activities it has power to control, may seem a slender one."[37]

---

[34] Note, however, the alternative legal approach to the problem, by-passing the separate legal personality issue by postulating a duty owed in tort by the parent company directly to the asbestos victims (the employees of the subsidiary): *Connelly v RTZ Corp Plc* [1998] A.C. 854 HL; *Lubbe v Cape Plc* [2000] 1 W.L.R. 1545 HL; *Chandler v Cape Plc* [2012] EWCA Civ 525. Doctrinally, this approach leaves the separate legal personality and limited liability concepts intact within groups but in fact imposes liability on the parent towards tort victims of subsidiaries. Whether a duty of care will be imposed on the parent turns on the degree of control exercised by the parent over the relevant activities of the subsidiary. If developed extensively, the tort doctrine could in practice remove limited liability within groups in relation to tort victims, not necessarily a matter of regret since limited liability is most questionable in relation to non-adjusting creditors. However, to date the courts have been cautious: for the parent company simply to appoint the directors of the subsidiary will not attract liability to the parent nor will running the subsidiaries as a division of the parent, if the separate legal personalities of the companies are respected: *Thompson v The Renwick Group Plc* [2014] 2 B.C.L.C 97 CA.

[35] *Adams v Cape Industries Plc* [1990] Ch. 433 at 532; quoting Roskill LJ in *The Albazero* [1977] A.C. 744 CA and HL at 807.

[36] *The Roberta* (1937) 58 L.L.R. 159; *Holdsworth & Co v Caddies* [1955] 1 W.L.R 352 HL; *Scottish Co-operative Wholesale Society Ltd v Meyer* [1959] A.C. 324 HL (Sc.); *DHN Food Distributors Ltd v Tower Hamlets LBC* [1976] 1 W.L.R. 852 CA (probably the strongest case in the tort victims' favour, because it was strongly arguable that the court there did not base itself on the particular statutory provision but on a more general approach founded on the idea of single economic entity); *Revlon Inc v Cripp & Lee Ltd* [1980] F.S.R. 85; and the Opinion of the Advocate General in Cases 6 and 7/73 [1974] E.C.R. 223.

[37] *Adams v Cape Industries Plc* [1990] Ch. 433 at 536B.

It seems, therefore, that in aid of interpretation (of statute or contract) the court may have regard to the economic realities in relation to the companies concerned. But that now seems to be the extent to which the "single economic unit" argument can succeed.

Façade or sham

8–12   In *Cape* the court accepted that "there is one well-recognised exception to the rule prohibiting the piercing of the 'corporate veil'".[38] This exception today is generally expressed (and was in *Cape*) as permitting disregard of the company when the corporate structure is a "mere façade concealing the true facts"— "façade"[39] or "sham" having replaced an assortment of epithets[40] which judges have employed in earlier cases. The difficulty is to know what precisely may make a company a "mere façade".

In general, the court felt that it was "left with rather sparse guidance as to the principles which should guide the court in determining whether or not the arrangements of a corporate group involve a façade…" but, unfortunately, it declined to "attempt a comprehensive definition of those principles".[41] It did, however, decide that one of Cape's wholly owned subsidiaries (AMC incorporated in Liechtenstein) was a façade in the relevant sense. Scott J had found as a fact that arrangements made in 1979 regarding AMC and other companies concerned in the marketing of Cape's asbestos "were part of one composite arrangement designed to enable Cape asbestos to continue to be sold into the United States while reducing, if not eliminating, the appearance of any involvement therein of Cape or its subsidiaries".[42] What seems to have been regarded as decisive was the fact that AMC was not only a wholly owned subsidiary of Cape but also no more than a corporate name which Cape or its subsidiaries used on invoices.[43] However, the implications of that were not pursued because all the court was concerned with was whether Cape could be regarded as present in the US and "on the judge's undisputed findings AMC was not in reality carrying on any business in the United States",[44] and therefore could not cause Cape to be regarded as present there. Presumably, however, those who, as a result of the invoices, thought they were dealing with AMC would, if AMC failed to perform the contract, have been able to sue Cape.

What mattered in relation to establishing that Cape was present in the US was whether another company, CPC, incorporated and carrying on business in the US, was a façade. Despite the fact that CPC was a party to the same arrangement as

---

[38] *Adams v Cape Industries Plc* [1990] Ch. 433 at 539.

[39] Used, clearly, in its secondary meaning (the primary one being "the face of a building"), i.e. "an outward appearance or front, especially a deceptive one".

[40] Such as "device", "creature", "stratagem", "mask", "puppet" and even (see *Re Bugle Press* [1961] Ch.270 at 288 CA) "a little hut".

[41] *Adams v Cape Industries Plc* [1990] Ch. 433 at 543D.

[42] *Adams v Cape Industries Plc* [1990] Ch. 433 at 478F; approved by the Court of Appeal at 541G–H, 544A and B.

[43] *Adams v Cape Industries Plc* [1990] Ch. 433 at 479E and 543E. If the motives of those setting up the companies are dishonest, that will make it easier for the court to conclude that the company is a sham: *Kensington International Ltd v Republic of the Congo* [2006] 2 B.C.L.C. 296.

[44] *Adams v Cape Industries Plc* [1990] Ch. 433 at 543G.

AMC and that it probably had been incorporated at Cape's expense, that did not in itself make it a mere façade. On the facts the court was satisfied that it was an independent corporation, wholly owned by its chief executive and carrying on its own business in the States and not the business of Cape or its subsidiaries. Moreover the court declared[45] that it did not accept that:

> "as a matter of law the court is entitled to lift the corporate veil as against a defendant company which is the member of a corporate group, merely because the corporate structure has been used so as to ensure that the legal liability (if any) in respect of particular future activities of the group (and correspondingly the risk of enforcement of that liability) will fall on another member of the group rather than the defendant company. Whether or not this is desirable, the right to use a corporate structure in this manner is inherent in our corporate law."[46]

The agency and trust arguments

A company having power to act as an agent (most companies) may do so as agent **8–13** for its parent company or indeed for all or any of its individual members if it or they authorise it to do so. If so, the parent company or the members will be bound by the acts of its agent so long as those acts are within the actual or apparent scope of the authority.[47] But there is no presumption of any such agency relationship between company and even a controlling shareholder and, in the absence of an express agreement between the parties,[48] it will be very difficult to establish one. In *Cape* the attempt to do so failed.[49] While it was clear that CPC rendered services to Cape and in some cases acted as its agent in relation to particular transactions, that did not suffice to satisfy the conditions which the Court had held to be necessary if Cape was to be regarded as "present" in the US. The same analysis can be applied to the argument that a company holds its assets on trust for its shareholders. This is not the normal case, even if the shares are held by a single shareholder, but on the facts of a particular case a trust may be found.[50]

The interests of justice

Although the interests of justice may provide the policy impetus for creating **8–14** exceptions to the doctrines of separate legal personality and limited liability, as an exception in itself it suffers from the defect of being inherently vague and providing to neither courts nor those engaged in business any clear guidance as to

---

[45] *Adams v Cape Industries Plc* [1990] Ch. 433t 544D, E.
[46] Hence Cape's wholly owned American subsidiary NAAC which, prior to its winding up, had performed a similar role to that undertaken thereafter by CPC had equally to be regarded as a separate entity: see at 538.
[47] See Ch.7, above.
[48] As in *Southern v Watson* [1940] 3 All E.R. 439 CA, where, on the conversion of a business into a private company, the sale agreement provided that the company should fulfil existing contracts of the business as agents of the sellers, and in *Rainham Chemical Works v Belvedere* [1921] 2 A.C. 465 HL where the agreement provided that the newly formed company should take possession of land as agent of its vendor promoters.
[49] Both in relation to CPC (at 547–549) and to its predecessor, NAAC (fn.46, above) despite the fact that it had been Cape's wholly owned subsidiary (at 545–547).
[50] As in *Prest v Petrodel Resources Ltd* [2013] UKSC 34; para.8–8, above.

when the normal company law rules should be displaced. Consequently, it is difficult to find cases in which "the interests of justice" have represented more than simply a way of referring to the grounds identified above in which the veil of incorporation has been pierced.[51]

Impropriety

8–15   In a number of recent cases the courts have considered the principle that the corporate veil can be set aside on the grounds that the company has been used in order to avoid the impact of a legal obligation or an order of the court. The impact of ignoring the separate legal personality of the company in such cases is usually to allow the holder of a legal entitlement against a shareholder to enforce it against the company, thus cutting against the asset partitioning which separate legal personality and limited liability together bring about.[52] In *Prest v Petrodel Resources Ltd*[53] Lord Sumption engaged in an heroic effort to identify the situations where this would be justified. On his approach, ignoring the separate personality of the company would be justified only where the corporate form had been adopted in order to evade an existing legal obligation. In that case the argument failed because the companies had been established and had carried on business long before the legal obligation in question had come into being.

He put forward as examples of his principle the decisions in *Gilford Motor Co Ltd v Horn*[54] and *Jones v Lipman*.[55] In the former a director of a company sought to avoid a personal post-employment competition restraint by setting up the rival business through a company which he controlled, rather than carrying it on directly. The important point about the decision was that the court extended the injunction to the company as well as to Horne himself. Again, in *Jones v Lipman* a defendant sought to avoid a decree of specific performance against himself by conveying the land subject to the order to a company he owned. The order was enforced against the company. In both cases, however, the result could be explained without recourse to the doctrine of lifting the veil, on the basis that the knowledge of the sole shareholder was to be imputed to the company. By contrast, ignoring the separate personality of the company in order to create a liability on the shareholder which would not otherwise exist was impermissible. So, in the Supreme Court's slightly earlier decision, *VTB Capital Plc v Nutritek International Corp*,[56] the court refused to ignore the legal personality of the company where the purpose of so doing was to make the controlling shareholders liable on a contract which the company had entered into. To do so would be to

---

[51] See the rejection of this ground in *Cape* at 536.
[52] See para.8–3, above.
[53] Above fn.29. See also *Yukong Line Ltd of Korea v Rendsburg Investments Corp of Liberia (No.2)* [1998] 1 W.L.R. 294. The majority seem to have agreed with Lord Sumption's analysis, but Lords Mance and Walker declined to commit themselves to such a rigid view, thus preserving the potential for a wider role for the doctrine in the future.
[54] *Gilford Motor Co Ltd v Horn* [1933] Ch. 935 CA.
[55] *Jones v Lipman* [1962] 1 W.L.R. 832.
[56] *VTB Capital Plc v Nutritek International Corp* [2013] UKSC 5.

create a liability on the shareholders which had not previously existed rather than to ensure that the shareholders could not avoid an existing liability by use of the corporate form.

Lord Sumption distinguished this "evasion" principle from what he identified as the "concealment" principle. Combatting concealment did not involve ignoring the separate legal personality of the company. Rather, "the interposition of a company or perhaps several companies so as to conceal the identity of the real actors will not deter the courts from identifying them, assuming that their identity is legally relevant. In these cases the court is not disregarding the 'façade', but only looking behind it to discover the facts which the corporate structure is concealing". An example was *Gencor ACP Ltd v Dalby*,[57] where a director had diverted money in breach of fiduciary duty to a company controlled by him which received it as his nominee. The order against the director could be upheld on the concealment principle and the order against the company on the grounds that the shareholder's knowledge about the tainted source of the funds was to be attributed to it.

8–16

Impropriety, thus, has a very narrow meaning: adopting the corporate form deliberately to avoid a liability which either has arisen or is imminent. It does not embrace designing the corporate structures so as to minimise the impact of future liabilities on the firm's business. After all, in *Cape* itself the company was aware of the risk of negligence liability which was inherent in its activities and took steps to quarantine the impact of such liability within certain of the group companies. The court took the view that, far from being improper, this was an entirely legitimate use of the group corporate structure.[58] However, even this limited doctrine is more than some think is appropriate. In the *VTB* case counsel for the defendants argued vigorously to the Supreme Court that the doctrine of ignoring the legal personality of the company does not exist at all in English law. In the *Prest* case the Supreme Court seem to have been convinced, in Lord Sumption's words, that a limited exception to the separate legal personality doctrine "is necessary if the law is not to be disarmed in the face of abuse".[59]

CONCLUSION

The doctrine of lifting the veil plays a small role in British company law, once one moves outside the area of particular contracts or statutes. Even where the case for applying the doctrine may seem strong, as in the undercapitalised one-person company, which may or may not be part of a larger corporate group, the courts are unlikely to do so. As Staughton LJ remarked in *Atlas Maritime Co SA v Avalon Maritime Ltd, The Coral Rose*[60]:

8–17

> "The creation or purchase of a subsidiary company with minimal liability, which will operate with the parent's funds and on the parent's directions but not expose the parent to liability, may not seem to some the most honest way of trading. But it is extremely common in the

---

[57] *Gencor ACP Ltd v Dalby* [2000] 2 B.C.L.C. 734.
[58] See above, para.8–12.
[59] *Prest v Petrodel Resources Ltd* [2013] UKSC 34 at [27].
[60] *Atlas Maritime Co SA v Avalon Maritime Ltd, The Coral Rose* [1991] 4 All E.R. 769 at 779.

international shipping industry and perhaps elsewhere. To hold that it creates an agency relationship between the subsidiary and the parent would be revolutionary doctrine."

This is in contrast to the law in the US where the veil is lifted more readily.[61] However, even in the US it seems the courts have never lifted the veil so as to remove limited liability in the case of a public company and will not do so as a matter of routine in private companies.[62] Probably, the most significant addition to the grounds for lifting the veil which US law adds to the categories recognised by British law is that of inadequate capitalisation. As we shall see in the next chapter, British law has approached that problem through the statutory doctrine of wrongful trading rather than through lifting the veil. Indeed, at a more general level, the approach of British law to regulation of the abuse of limited liability is a combination of facilitating self-help and statutory constraints. The common law doctrine of piercing the veil is a technique available to the courts but it has not been developed in such a way as to be the central legal strategy for addressing abuses of limited liability. Instead, the burden of action has fallen on the legislature, which has developed certain targeted rules to impose liability on shareholders or directors of companies in the case of abuse of limited liability, which we turn to in the next chapter.

---

[61] See P. Blumberg, *The Multinational Challenge to Corporate Law* (Oxford: Oxford University Press, 1993), especially Pt II.

[62] See R. Thompson, "Piercing the Corporate Veil: An Empirical Study" (1991) 76 Cornell L.J. 1036. On these points the findings of Dr Charles Mitchell in a study of English cases do not differ ("Lifting the Corporate Veil in the English Courts: an Empirical Study" (1999) 3 C.F.I.L.R. 15). "No case was found in which the English courts have even been asked to fix the shareholders of a public company with liability for its obligations." (pp.21–22) On the various factors influencing veil lifting in private companies, see p.22 (Table 4), but in no case was it routine.

CHAPTER 9

PERSONAL LIABILITY FOR ABUSES OF LIMITED LIABILITY

From the beginnings of modern company law in the middle of the nineteenth century, the legislature has been ready, in a small number of cases, to remove the shield of limited liability and impose responsibility for the company's obligations on the shareholders personally. More often it imposed the liability on the directors of the company. Some of the examples which survived into modern law were surprising, because the sanction of personal liability seemed disproportionate to the importance of the rules which the sanctions upheld. A good example was the imposition of personal liability on the remaining shareholder where the number of members was reduced below two, a provision not repeated in the 2006 Act.[1] This rule was the final remnant of a legislative policy which attached significance to the number of members of a company as a protection for those who dealt with it. The Limited Liability Act 1855 applied only to companies with at least 25 members, and as late as 1980 public companies had to have at least seven members. But this policy was effectively undermined by the decision in *Salomon*'s case[2] in 1897, allowing nominee shareholders (e.g. those holding shares as bare trustees for another person) to count towards the required statutory number.

9–1

In fact, in modern law it is extremely difficult to find examples of the companies legislation imposing personal liability on shareholders in order to combat opportunistic behaviour encouraged by the doctrine of limited liability. The target

9–2

---

[1] Companies Act 1985 s.24—a provision applying initially to all companies but from 1992 only to public companies since private companies were then empowered to have a single member. This is now the position for public companies as well: CA 2006 s.7.
[2] *Salomon v Salomon* [1897] A.C. 22. See above, para.2–1.

of the anti-abuse legislation is rather those in charge of the company's central management, i.e. typically its directors. Directors, responsive to shareholder interests, are much more likely to be in a position to initiate such action on the company's part than the shareholders, because of the concentration of power and authority in the board.[3] Shareholders are not excluded from such liability if they involve themselves in the central management of the company (for example, as "shadow" directors) or in the conduct which the law wishes to prohibit. But they are not liable personally simply because they are shareholders.

PREMATURE TRADING

9–3   A public limited company, newly incorporated as such, must not "do business or exercise any borrowing powers" until it has obtained, from the Registrar of Companies, a certificate that it has complied with the provisions of the Act relating to the raising of the prescribed minimum share capital or until it has re-registered as a private company.[4] The link between this provision and the doctrine of limited liability is that requiring a company to hold assets to a certain value when it is formed is arguably a protection for those whose claims are confined to the assets of the company, though it is highly doubtful whether the actual minimum capital rule found in the Companies Act operates to confer any such protection.[5] If the company enters into any transaction in contravention of this provision, not only are the company and its officers in default liable to fines,[6] but if the company fails to comply with its obligations in relation to the transaction within 21 days of being called upon to do so, the directors of the company are jointly and severally liable to indemnify the counterparty in respect of any loss or damage suffered by reason of the company's failure to comply.[7]

Whether this is a true example of lifting the veil is questionable; technically it does not make the directors liable for the company's debts but rather requires the directors to indemnify creditors for any loss suffered as a result of the company's default in complying with the section. But the effect is much the same. The section, however, is unlikely to be invoked often since it is unusual for companies to be formed initially as public ones. Usually, companies are formed as private companies and later convert through re-registration to public status. If this way of proceeding is adopted, however, obtaining the required minimum share capital is made a pre-condition to re-registration[8] and so trading as a public company without the authorised minimum is avoided in that way.

---

[3] See para.14–3, below.
[4] See s.761 and para.11–8, below.
[5] See below para.11–9.
[6] 2006 Act s.767(1),(2).
[7] 2006 Act s.767(3). The validity of the transaction, however, is not affected.
[8] 2006 Act ss.90 and 91.

FRAUDULENT AND WRONGFUL TRADING

Of far greater practical importance are the provisions on fraudulent trading. These **9–4** provisions recognise that the separate entity and limited liability doctrines generate an incentive for company controllers to defraud creditors, knowing that the creditors' claims are limited to the company's assets. The fraudulent trading provisions aim to redress the balance. They come in both a criminal[9] and a civil liability form. Section 993 (constituting the single-section Pt 29 of the Act) creates a specific, but widely defined, criminal offence of carrying on the business of a company with intent to defraud the creditors[10] of the company or of any other person or for any other fraudulent purpose. Every person knowingly party to the carrying on of the business in this manner commits a criminal offence. So, here the personal scope of the criminal liability is defined by reference to being party to the fraud. Shareholders may be included in this class but are not liable simply as shareholders. The civil liability is imposed by ss.213 and 246ZA of the Insolvency Act 1986.[11] These sections are analysed further below but, in essence, they operate on the basis of the same test for liability as does the criminal provision.

Abuse in the shape of hiding behind limited liability to effect fraud is easy to identify as something the law should address, as the long-standing provisions against fraudulent trading indicate. More significant are the provisions on wrongful trading, added initially in the 1980s. These seek to address the risk, when the company is in the vicinity of insolvency, but has not yet entered a formal insolvency procedure, that the directors will take excessive risks with the business of the company, in the hope of escaping from its financial troubles, but knowing that, if the gamble is unsuccessful, limited liability will place most or all of the additional losses on the creditors. If such action is taken deliberately, it will probably fall within the fraudulent trading provisions. The wrongful trading provisions of the Insolvency Act give directors, contemplating this strategy—but without fraud or at least provable fraud—an incentive to accord greater consideration to the interests of the creditors. The creditors are highly exposed to the downside risk of the strategy whilst the benefits of it, if they occur, will accrue overwhelmingly to the shareholders. This can been seen most clearly if, at the time the strategy is adopted, the company's assets are just enough to meet its liabilities, but no more, so that, if the company then stopped trading and were wound up, the creditors would be repaid but the shareholders would receive nothing. If the directors continue trading, the shareholders will be no worse off, but have a chance (perhaps a small one) of being much better off, whilst the

---

[9] Fraud is a general criminal offence, of course, but it has been regarded as less confusing for juries to face them with a single charge of fraudulent trading rather than with numerous charges of individual acts of fraud: see *R. v Kemp* [1988] Q.B. 645 CA. (pet. dis. [1988] 1 W.L.R. 846 HL). The legislature thought so well of the offence that it enacted in s.9 of the Fraud Act 2006 a similar offence in respect of those businesses carried on by persons falling outside the scope of s.993, including sole traders. This shows that the absence of limited liability is not a guarantee of the absence of fraud.

[10] The section embraces fraud on future, as well as present, creditors: *R. v Smith* [1996] 2 B.C.L.C. 109 CA.

[11] The shift of the civil liability provision out of the companies legislation and into the insolvency legislation occurred as a result of the recommendations of the Cork Committee on Insolvency Law (Cmnd. 8558 (1981), Ch.44).

creditors will be no better off but have a chance (perhaps a large one) of being much worse off. Whilst continuing to trade is not necessarily against the interests of the creditors, doing so in a risky way in likely to be, whilst potentially benefitting shareholders. The wrongful trading provisions attempt to re-set the incentives of the directors by making them personally liable for the increased liabilities of the company if the gamble fails and the court adjudges the directors to have acted negligently. Again, it is to be noted that the persons potentially made liable are the controllers of the company (directors and shadow directors) rather than its shareholders. The latter will fall within the scope of the provisions only if they fall within the category of a "shadow director" (see below). However, it is directors responsive to the interests of the shareholders who are most likely to fall foul of s.214.

The importance attached by the legislature to the provisions on fraudulent and wrongful was demonstrated by their reform in 2015. Previously, they had applied only when the company was in insolvent liquidation but they were extended to companies in administration,[12] a significant change since administration often precedes, or even eliminates the need for, liquidation.[13] The 2015 reforms also made it easier for liquidators and administrators to obtain financing for litigation to enforce these liabilities, as is discussed below.

Civil liability for fraudulent trading

9–5   The Insolvency Act mimics for the purposes of civil liability the criteria laid down in s.993 of the Companies Act for criminal liability, i.e. that the business of a company was carried on with intent to defraud the creditors of the company or of any other person or for any other fraudulent purpose. However, ss.213 and 246ZA require in addition that the company be in the course of administration or winding up (which the criminal section does not) before the liability can be enforced.[14] Assuming this to be the case, the court, on the application of the administrator or liquidator, may declare the persons who were knowingly parties to carrying on[15] the business of the company in this way "liable to make such contributions (if any) to the company's assets as the court thinks proper."[16] Since the company in winding up will be in need of such a contribution only where its assets are insufficient to meet its liabilities, this is in effect an indirect way of making the persons in question liable for the company's debts (to at least some

---

[12] Insolvency Act 1986 ss.246ZA and ZB, inserted by s.117 of the Small Business and Enterprise Act 2015.

[13] For a discussion of the role of administration see paras 32–43 et seq, below.

[14] The fraudulent trading will have occurred before the company went into administration or liquidation. In fact, there is no limit in the section on the prior period which may be scrutinised for evidence of fraudulent trading. The company being in liquidation or administration is simply a condition for the claim being brought. However, the longer-lived the fraudulent scheme, the less likely it is the early creditors will have suffered a loss. So, older fraud is likely to be less relevant to the setting of the amount of the contribution: see para.9–8, below.

[15] A business may be regarded as "carried on" notwithstanding that the company has ceased active trading: *Re Sarflax Ltd* [1979] Ch. 592.

[16] 1986 Act ss.213(2)/246ZA(2).

degree).[17] As with criminal liability, the persons liable are those party to carrying on the business of the company in the fraudulent way; they need have no other connection with the company, i.e. they do not need to be directors of or shareholders in the company—though they often will be.[18] It is enough to establish liability that only one creditor was defrauded and in a single transaction.[19] However, in the case of a one-off fraud there is a risk that the court will not be able to conclude that the business of the company was carried on for fraudulent purposes, in which case liability will not arise.[20]

Given the wide personal scope of the sections, banks and parent companies (third parties) have at times felt inhibited from providing finance to ailing companies, fearing that they may thereby fall foul of these provisions as persons knowingly party to the fraud. It is sometimes said that their fears are unfounded so long as they play no active role in running the company with fraudulent intent.[21] However, the extent of the exposure of a third party company to liability under the sections will depend in part on what rule of attribution is used to determine the extent of the knowledge the third party company possesses of the activities within the fraudulently run company. In *Re Bank of Credit and Commerce International SA (No.15)*[22] the Court of Appeal rejected the proposition that only the knowledge of the board of the third party was to be attributed to it. Here, the court attributed to the defendant company the knowledge of a senior manager who had been given authority by the board to set the terms of transactions with the company whose business was being carried on fraudulently and to which fraud the manager had turned a blind eye. Thus, as was already clear and as this case illustrates, a third party can fall within the sections

---

[17] Unlike the situation before 1985, it is no longer possible to impose liability under ss.213 and 246ZA in respect of particular debts or in favour of particular creditors: cf. *Re Cyona Distributors Ltd* [1967] Ch. 889 CA.

[18] And it is no bar to inclusion within the section that the activities in question occurred abroad: *Jetivia SA v Bilta (UK) Ltd* [2015] 1 B.C.L.C. 443 SC. This is on the basis that the winding up of a company incorporated in the UK has effect, as far as domestic law is concerned, in relation to all the assets of the company, no matter where situated. This reasoning would seem equally applicable to liability for wrongful trading under ss.214/246ZB of the Act.

[19] *Re Cooper Chemicals Ltd* [1978] Ch. 262 (only one creditor defrauded). Indeed, for criminal liability to arise it is not clear that it is necessary for any person actually to be defrauded provided that the business of the company was carried on with intent to defraud (*R. v Kemp* [1988] Q.B. 645 CA—only potential creditors defrauded).

[20] *Morphitis v Bernasconi* [2003] 2 B.C.L.C. 53 CA. The defrauded person will have remedies under the general law of fraud.

[21] In *Re Maidstone Building Provisions Ltd* [1971] 1 W.L.R. 1085 an attempt to obtain a declaration against the company's secretary, who was also a partner in its auditors' firm, failed because, although he had given financial advice and had not attempted to prevent the company from trading, he had not taken "positive steps in the carrying on of the company's business in a fraudulent manner". In *Re Augustus Barnett & Son Ltd* [1986] B.C.L.C. 170 an attempt against its parent company (Rumasa) failed on the same ground.

[22] *Re Bank of Credit and Commerce International SA (No.15)* [2005] 2 B.C.L.C. 328 CA, following the lead given in *Meridian Global Funds Management Asia Ltd v Securities Commission* [1995] 2 A.C. 500 PC (above, at para.7–41). This step was facilitated by the separation of the criminal and civil liability for fraudulent trading, so that there is no implication from this decision that the same attribution rule would be applied if criminal liability were in question: at [107] and [129].

if it participates, with knowledge,[23] in the fraudulent activity of a company, even though that party could not be said to have taken a controlling role within the company.[24] Overall, therefore, these rules encourage third parties, whose dealings with a company might assist the fraudulent running of that company's business, to have in place internal controls designed to identify at an early stage and to deal with situations where relevant employees of the third party have knowledge of the fraudulent activities. In this way the third party may hope to avoid the risk that it will be liable to contribute under the sections.[25]

As to whether those conducting business are doing so fraudulently, it has been said that what has to be shown is "actual dishonesty involving, according to current notions of fair trading among commercial men, real moral blame".[26] That may be inferred if "a company continues to carry on business and to incur debts at a time when there is, to the knowledge of the directors, no reasonable prospect of the creditors ever receiving payment of those debts",[27] but it cannot be inferred merely because they ought to have realised there was no prospect of repayment. It was this need to prove subjective moral blame that led the Jenkins Committee in 1962 vainly to recommend the introduction of a remedy for "reckless trading"[28] and the Cork Committee, 20 years later,[29] successfully to promote it under the name of "wrongful trading".

---

[23] The required degree of knowledge is "blind eye" knowledge, i.e. "a decision to avoid obtaining confirmation of facts in whose existence the individual has good reason to believe" (*Re Bank of Credit and Commerce International SA (No.15)* [2005] 2 B.C.L.C. 328 CA at [14] quoting Lord Scott in *Manifest Shipping Co Ltd v Uni-Polaris Shipping Co Ltd* [2003] 1 A.C. 469 at [116]). See also *Re Bank of Credit and Commerce International SA (No.14)* [2004] 2 B.C.L.C. 236.

[24] In *Re Gerald Cooper Chemicals Ltd* [1978] Ch. 262 it was held that a declaration could be made against a creditor who refrained from pressing for repayment knowing that the business was being carried on in fraud of creditors and who accepted part payment out of money which he knew had been obtained by that fraud. *Gerald Cooper Chemicals* was followed in *Re Bank of Credit and Commerce International SA (No.14)* [2001] 1 B.C.L.C. 263.

[25] In *Re Bank of Credit and Commerce International SA (No.15)* [2005] 2 B.C.L.C. 328 CA it was left open whether the third party's liability could not be more simply and widely established on the basis of the third party's vicarious liability for breaches of s.213 by its employees. See *Dubai Aluminium Co Ltd v Salaam* [2003] 2 A.C. 366 HL and para.7–31. This approach would strength the incentives of third parties to control participation by their employees in the fraudulent conduct of the company's business.

[26] *Re Patrick Lyon Ltd* [1933] Ch. 786 at 790, 791.

[27] *Re William C Leitch Ltd* [1932] 2 Ch. 71 at 77, per Maugham J. See also *R. v Grantham* [1984] Q.B. 675 CA, where the court upheld a direction to the jury that they might convict of fraudulent trading a person who had taken an active part in running the business if they were satisfied that he had helped to obtain credit knowing that there was no good reason for thinking that funds would become available to pay the debts when they became due or shortly thereafter. That dishonesty may be inferred in these cases does not mean, of course, that it can never be established in other cases: *Aktieselskabet Dansk Skibsfinansiering v Brothers* [2001] 2 B.C.L.C. 324 HKCFA.

[28] Cmnd. 1749, para.503(b).

[29] Above fn.11. For the argument that the Cork Committee overestimated the potential role of the wrongful trading provisions, partly because existing Companies and Insolvency Act provisions already cover much of the ground, partly because defendants financially able to meet the liability are likely to be few, see R. Williams, "What can we expect to gain from reforming the insolvent trading remedy?" (2015) 78 M.L.R. 55.

Wrongful trading

Sections 214 and 246ZB empower the court to make a declaration similar to that **9–6** under ss.213 and 246ZA where the company has gone into *insolvent* administration or liquidation. An insolvent is distinguished from a solvent procedure on a balance-sheet test, i.e. were the assets of the company sufficient to meet its liabilities and the costs of the procedure at the point the company entered into it.[30] The basis for imposing the obligation to contribute is that the director (or shadow director) knew, or ought to have concluded, at some point *before* the administration or winding-up, that there was no reasonable prospect that the company would avoid going into insolvent administration or liquidation.[31] A declaration will then be made unless the court is satisfied that the person concerned thereafter took every step with a view to minimising the potential loss to the company's creditors as he ought to have taken, on the assumption that he knew there was no reasonable prospect of avoiding insolvency.[32] In judging what facts the director ought to have known or ascertained, what conclusions the director should have drawn and what steps should have been taken, the director is to be assumed to be a reasonably diligent person having both the general knowledge, skill and experience to be expected of a person carrying out the director's functions in relation to the company[33] and the general knowledge, skill and experience that the director in fact has.[34] This formulation heavily influenced the general duty of care now imposed on directors by s.174 of the Companies Act 2006[35]. The wrongful trading provisions, s.174 of the 2006 Act and the director disqualification provisions (discussed in the following chapter) constitute the three main areas where sanctions are imposed on directors for negligent discharge of their duties. In the case of ss.214/246ZB, however, the beneficiaries of the duty to take care are the creditors rather than the shareholders, whom s.174 of the 2006 Act protects.

Section 214 poses two questions which have to be answered, both on an objective basis. Should the director have realised there was no reasonable prospect of the company avoiding insolvent liquidation and, once that stage has been reached, did the director take all the steps he or she ought to have taken to minimise the loss to the company's creditors, especially, no doubt, by seeking to have the company cease trading? Both these judgments will depend heavily on the facts of particular cases: what sort of company was involved, what were the

---

[30] 1986 Act ss.214(6)/246ZB(6). Section 213 formally applies in any winding up (solvent or insolvent) but in practice it is needed only in insolvent winding up.

[31] 1986 Act ss.214(2)/246ZB(2). It appears it is sufficient that the directors should have anticipated, for example, insolvent liquidation but the company ends up in insolvent administration.

[32] 1986 Act ss.214(3)/246ZB(3). The burden of proof on knowledge is on the claimant, on "every step" on the directors: *Brook v Masters* [2015] B.C.C. 661.

[33] This includes functions entrusted to the director even if the director has not carried them out: ss.214(5)/246ZB(5). If the director has failed the objective test he or she cannot be excused by the court, under Companies Act 2006 s.1157, on the ground that the director has acted honestly and reasonably: *Re Produce Marketing Consortium Ltd* [1989] 1 W.L.R. 745.

[34] 1986 Act ss.214(4)/246ZB(4).

[35] Below, para.16–15.

functions assigned to or discharged by the director in question, what outside advice was taken and what was its content?[36]

Shadow directors

9–7   Section 214 applies to shadow directors as well as to directors, i.e. a person, other than a professional adviser, in accordance with whose directions or instructions the directors of a company are accustomed to act.[37] This considerably widens the class of persons against whom a declaration can be made, though not as widely as under s.213 which brings in any person who is party to the fraudulent trading (see above). The shadow director definition catches only the person who influences at least a certain category of board decisions on a continuing basis.[38] The two potential defendants of greatest interest are, once again, banks and parent companies. As far as the former are concerned, the courts have so far taken a cautious line, initially on the grounds that the definition of a shadow director required that the board cede its management autonomy to the alleged shadow director. This was not regarded as occurring as a result of the bank taking steps to protect itself, provided the company retained the power to decide whether to accept the restrictions put forward by the bank, even though the company might be thought to have no other practicable alternative.[39]

In relation to parent companies, such a degree of cession of autonomy by the subsidiary may be more easily found, but much will still depend upon how exactly intra-group relationships are established. The degree of control exercised by parent companies may vary from detailed day-to-day control to virtual independence for the subsidiary's board, with many variations in between. It would seem that the establishment of business guidelines within which the subsidiary has to operate would not make the parent inevitably a shadow director of the subsidiary.[40] However, the Court of Appeal has rejected the proposition that it is necessary for the board to cast itself in a subservient role or surrender its discretion in order for the alleged shadow director to be found to be such, thus casting doubt on the "cessation of autonomy" test and potentially broadening the scope of shadow director liability.[41] It is important to note that the shadow director definition in s.251 of the Insolvency Act does not exclude parent

---

[36] The directors are likely to be treated with a particular lack of sympathy by the court if they have not abided by the statutory requirements for keeping themselves abreast of the company's financial position: *Re Produce Marketing Consortium Ltd (No.2)* [1989] B.C.L.C. 520 at 550, which requirements Knox J referred to as the "minimum standards". See Oditah, [1990] L.M.C.L.O. 205; and Prentice, (1990) 10 O.J.L.S. 265.

[37] Insolvency Act 1986 s.251.

[38] *Secretary of State for Trade and Industry v Becker* [2003] 1 B.C.L.C. 565; *Secretary of State for Trade and Industry v Deverell* [2000] 2 B.C.L.C. 133 CA.

[39] *Re Hydrodan (Corby) Ltd* [1994] 2 B.C.L.C. 180; *Re PFTZM Ltd* [1995] B.C.C. 280; cf. *Re A Company Ex p. Copp* [1989] B.C.L.C. 13.

[40] In *Re Hydrodan (Corby) Ltd* [1994] 2 B.C.L.C. 180 the judge was prepared to treat the indirect parent as a shadow director of a company, but that was because the directors of the company in question were corporate bodies and so must have received their instructions from elsewhere. Even here, the *directors* of the indirect parent were held not to be shadow directors.

[41] *Secretary of State for Trade and Industry v Deverell* [2000] 2 B.C.L.C. 133 CA, where the precise definition of "shadow director" was determinative of the appeal. The court also decided that the central question was whether the board in fact did what the alleged shadow directors proposed and not

companies, in contrast to the exclusion in s.251 of the Companies Act which provides that a parent company is not to be considered a shadow director "by reason only that the directors of the subsidiary are accustomed to act in accordance with [the parent's] directions or instructions". It would thus seem that, so long as the subsidiary is a going concern, the parent company may impose a common policy on the group companies without being in danger of infringing their general duties in relation to the subsidiary. Once insolvency threatens the subsidiary, however, the interests of its creditors take priority over the interests of the parent and the group policy.[42] When ss.214/246ZB are triggered, they will apply to the actions of the boards of both the subsidiary and the parent company (provided the latter falls within the definition of a shadow director).

The declaration

Section 215 contains certain procedural provisions common to both fraudulent and wrongful trading. Those provisions are to have effect notwithstanding that the person concerned may be criminally liable.[43] The court may direct that the liability of any person against whom the declaration is made shall be a charge on any debt due from the company to that person or on any mortgage or charge in that person's favour on assets of the company. This enables the company to set off what it owes to the director against what the director is declared liable to contribute to the company, which may prove valuable in the bankruptcy of the director.[44] In addition, s.215[45] provides that the court may direct that the whole or any part of a debt, and interest thereon, owed by the company to a person against whom a declaration is made, shall be postponed to all other debts, and interest thereon, owed by the company. Thus, even if, for example, the court makes only a small contribution order, which the director is able to meet, the director may suffer a further financial loss by having his or her debts due from the company subordinated to those of the company's other creditors, a potentially important provision since the company ex hypothesi is insolvent.

9–8

The central question, however, is the amount of the contribution, a matter with which s.215 does not deal. The fraudulent and wrongful trading provisions simply say that the amount of the contribution shall be "as the court thinks proper".[46] It is now established that contribution orders in relation to both wrongful and fraudulent trading are intended to be compensatory in relation to the company.[47] The outer boundaries of the contribution are thus set by the

---

whether those proposals were couched as directors or instruction or mere "advice"; nor was it necessary to prove the subjective expectations of the alleged shadow director and directors as to whether the advice would be followed.

[42] For the general duties see Ch.16, below.

[43] 1986 Act s.215(5), applied to administrations by s.246ZC.

[44] Including any assignees from that person (other than a good faith assignee for value without notice): IA 1986 s.215(2) and (3).

[45] 1986 Act s.215(4).

[46] 1986 Act ss.213(2)/246ZA(2) and 214(1)/246ZB(1).

[47] See *Re Produce Marketing Consortium Ltd* [1989] 1 W.L.R. 745, for wrongful trading and *Morphitis v Bernasconi* [2003] 2 B.C.L.C. 53 CA, for fraudulent trading, the latter reversing the previous understanding in relation to fraudulent trading where a penal element was thought appropriate in some cases.

amount by which the company's assets have been depleted by the director's conduct. Thus, the trading provisions will not replace the Insolvency Act rules on preferences, which deal with the situation where the company improperly pays one creditor ahead of another. As far as the company is concerned, a preference is balance-sheet neutral: assets are certainly paid out to the preferred creditor but the company's liabilities are reduced to the same extent, so that overall the company is no worse off. Preference rules are apt to deal with the improper distribution of assets among creditors; trading rules with situations where the creditors as a class are disadvantaged by the directors' actions.

Within the parameter of the overall loss to the company, the court has a discretion to fix the amount to be paid as it thinks proper. The assessment is to be made against each defendant individually rather than on some basis of collective responsibility.[48] Despite this method of calculating the upper limit on the contribution, the contribution from the directors is to the assets of the company generally and not for the particular benefit of those who became creditors of the company during the period of wrongful or fraudulent trading. Consequently, pre-wrongful trading creditors may actually benefit from the wrongful trading,[49] a somewhat ironic result but one driven, presumably, by a desire for simplicity.

Impact of the wrongful trading provisions

9–9 The wrongful trading provisions are capable of playing a central role in re-orienting the duties of directors as the company's insolvency becomes overwhelmingly likely. However, the drafters of the wrongful trading provisions were careful not to specify the precise action directors are required to take to meet its requirements. Instead, the provisions lay down a standard to which the director must conform in order to avoid liability, i.e. "to take every step with a view to minimising the potential loss to the company's creditors as (assuming him to have known that there was no reasonable prospect that the company would avoid going into insolvent liquidation or entering insolvent administration) he ought to have taken".[50] A central question is whether the section requires the directors, in all cases where there is no reasonable prospect of avoiding insolvent liquidation, to cause the company to cease trading and put the company into an insolvency procedure. Certainly, one of the commonest forms of wrongful trading is to keep the company's business on foot even after the accounts or other management information have clearly revealed that the company is in a chronically loss-making position.[51] However, there are good reasons for not requiring this response across the board. In the interests of both creditors (higher recovery of their debts) and of shareholders and other stakeholders (such as

---

[48] See the dicta of Park J in *Re Continental Assurance Co of London Plc (No.4)* [2007] 2 B.C.L.C. 287 at [382]–[390] (s.214); and *Re Overnight Ltd* [2010] 2 B.C.L.C. 186 (s.213). The defendants' liability may, but need not, be put on the basis of joint and several liability.

[49] Assume a pre-wrongful trading position of assets 50, liabilities 100, so creditors paid 50p in the pound. Assume wrongful trading which increases liabilities to 150 and a contribution which raises assets to 100. Creditors now receive 66p in the pound (assuming no transaction costs).

[50] 1986 Act s.214(3).

[51] See *Re Produce Marketing Consortium Ltd* [1989] 1 W.L.R. 745; *Re Brian D. Pierson (Contractors) Ltd* [2001] 1 B.C.L.C. 275.

employees) it may well be better if the company can be turned around or its business disposed of in some other way, which an immediate cessation of trading might jeopardise.

The courts can adjust the section to the needs of the "rescue culture" either by postponing the point at which they conclude the directors ought to have realised the company had no reasonable prospect of avoiding insolvency or by taking a broad view of the appropriate actions of the directors once that point is reached. An example of the first approach can be seen in *Re The Rod Gunner Organisation Ltd*,[52] where the court refused to find "no reasonable prospect" for a period of six months after the company became unable to meet its debts as they fell due, on the grounds that the directors reasonably thought an outside investor was going to come in with substantial funding (though that analysis no longer held once it became clear that the investor would not live up to the directors' expectations of him). Similarly, in *Re Continental Assurance Co of London Plc (No.4)*,[53] where a substantial insurance company had suffered unexpected losses, the court refused to find "no reasonable prospect" during a period of some six months in which the directors commissioned a report as to the company's solvency and decided to continue trading on the basis of the report received, until it later became clear that the company was in fact insolvent. Park J was very aware of the dangers of judging the directors' conduct on the basis of hindsight, and he remarked pithily in relation to the general issue that "ceasing to trade and liquidating too soon can be stigmatised as the cowards' way out". Once the point of "no reasonable prospect" is reached, however, the section appears to shift the risk of continued trading onto the directors. If the continued trading reduces the company's net deficiency, no contribution will be required of them. But in the opposite case they will be exposed.[54]

However, any analysis of the impact of the wrongful trading provisions also requires an assessment of the effectiveness of its enforcement. In contrast to litigation under the disqualification provisions discussed in the next chapter, where the public purse pays for the cases and there has been a high level of activity, litigation about wrongful trading seems to have been sparse and certainly there are few reported cases. As we have seen, the Act places the initiation of litigation in the hands of the liquidator or administrator ("office holders"), who does not have access to any public funds to support any litigation it is proposed to bring. Assuming the insolvent company does have some realisable assets, the office holder may contemplate using those to fund the litigation in the hope of swelling the ultimate amount available for distribution to the creditors. However,

9–10

---

[52] *Re The Rod Gunner Organisation Ltd* [2004] 1 B.C.L.C 110. Similarly, *Roberts v Frohlich* [2011] 2 B.C.L.C. 501.

[53] *Re Continental Assurance Co of London Plc (No.4)* [2007] 2 B.C.L.C. 287. See also *Re Sherborne Associates Ltd* [1995] B.C.C. 40, in which the judge held that the liquidator had to identify and then stick to a particular date by which it was argued the directors should have realised the company had no reasonable prospect of avoiding insolvent liquidation. Contrast *Singla v Hedman* [2010] 2 B.C.L.C. 61: causing a company without any secure financing to begin contracting for production was a breach of s.214.

[54] *Grant v Rails* [2016] B.C.C. 293, where Snowden J held that continued trading in favourable conditions did not afford the directors a defence under the "every step" provision because new creditors would be worse off, i.e. "every step" was equated with every creditor.

even if the office holder can secure solicitors who will take the case on a conditional fee basis—not always possible—the litigation is likely to involve some costs (for example, for the insurance to meet the other side's costs if the litigation is unsuccessful), and so the office holder is likely to be unwilling to risk the company's already inadequate assets on litigation unless there is a very strong chance of success.[55] The office holder might conceivably seek funding for the litigation from a floating charge holder, but there is little incentive for such a creditor to provide funding, for the proceeds of fraudulent and wrongful trading claims go to benefit the unsecured creditors, not the holders of a floating charge.[56]

The obvious step for the office holder to take, faced with this uncertainty, is either to sell the claim to a third party or to obtain funding for the claim by assigning some part of the fruits of the litigation to a third party. A third party whose business consists of buying or funding such claims is in a position to take a more adventurous view of which claims may be litigated, because it spreads its risks across a number of such claims, unlike the office holder who has only "one shot" on behalf of the unsecured creditors of any particular company. However, until the reforms of 2015 the office holder could not sell the wrongful trading claim under the general power to dispose of the company's assets, because the right to claim under the section is vested in the office holder personally, not in the company.[57] The 2015 reforms sensibly cut through this difficulty by giving the office holder an express statutory right to assign a wrongful or fraudulent trading claim (or the proceeds of such an action).[58] However, the rule that the proceeds of such an action are not the property of the company is retained.[59] This means that the proceeds are not swept up by the holders of any floating charge the company has issued, but rather remain available for the benefit of the unsecured creditors.

COMMON LAW DUTIES IN RELATION TO CREDITORS

9–11 The wrongful trading reforms of the mid-1980s, discussed in the previous section, create a statutory duty of care on the part of directors towards creditors at the point when insolvency seems unavoidable. Despite this statutory reform, the common law has not entirely neglected the interests of creditors at this point in

---

[55] The issue that the costs of the s.214 litigation might not count as costs of the liquidation was determined in favour of the liquidator by an amendment to r.4.218 of the Insolvency Rules 1986/1925, made in 2002 and by s.176ZA of the IA 1986, inserted by s.1282 of the Companies Act 2006, which gives liquidation expenses priority over both preferential debts and assets secured by a floating charge (subject to exceptions to prevent abuse), overruling the result of *Buchler v Talbot* [2004] 2 A.C. 298 HL. Thus, the disincentive to liquidator litigation arising from the risk of the liquidator being left to bear the litigation costs personally has been considerably reduced, if not eliminated.

[56] *Re Yagerphone Ltd* [1935] 1 Ch. 395.

[57] A liquidator or administer who sought to avoid this rule by assigning the fruits of the litigation rather than the claim itself would find it difficult to give the funder sufficient control of the litigation. See *Grovewood Holdings Plc v James Capel & Co Ltd* [1995] Ch. 80; *Re Oasis Merchandising Services Ltd (In Liquidation)* [1998] Ch. 170 CA; *Ruttle Plant Ltd v Secretary of State for the Environment, Food and Rural Affairs (No.3)* [2009] 1 All E.R. 448; *Rawnsley v Weatherall Green & Smith North Ltd* [2010] 1 B.C.L.C. 658.

[58] 1986 Act s.246ZD.

[59] 1986 Act s.176ZD.

the company's life-cycle and we analyse that development in this section. Although the statutory codification of the duties of directors in s.172 of the Companies Act 2006[60] does not in terms list creditors among those to whose interests the directors must have regard when promoting the success of the company, nevertheless it does recognise and preserve this common law development. Section 172(3) provides that the duty the section creates "has effect subject to any enactment or rule of law requiring directors, in certain circumstances, to consider or act in the interests of the creditors of the company". This removes any doubt that might otherwise have existed about whether the wrongful trading rules had been in any way qualified or reduced as a result of the enactment of s.172, but this provision also preserves ("or rule of law") the common law developments.[61]

Starting in Australia in the 1970s,[62] the notion of a common law duty upon directors to take account of the interests of creditors as insolvency approaches has been widely accepted throughout the common-law world. The principle was adopted by the Court of Appeal in *West Mercia Safetywear v Dodd*.[63] As with most significant common-law developments in their relatively early stages, there was and still remains considerable uncertainty about the conceptual boundaries of this doctrine. There are still uncertainties about when the duty bites, about its content, the remedies available and, to a lesser extent, the mechanisms for enforcing it. On the answer to these questions turns the broader issue of what, if anything, the common law duty adds to the statutory wrongful trading remedy.

9–12

Only the most imprecise indications have been given by the courts as to when the duty is triggered, except that there appears to be general acceptance that the duty can bite in advance of the company being insolvent.[64] In *Brady v Brady*, Nourse LJ said that the interests of the company were really the interests of the creditors when the company was "doubtfully solvent",[65] whilst in *Nicholson v Permakraft (NZ) Ltd*[66] the judge conceivably was prepared to go a bit further by suggesting the duty was triggered by "a course of action which would jeopardise solvency". In any event, while it is clear that the common law duty, like the statutory one, may apply before the company is insolvent, it is unclear whether the common law applies at a pre-insolvency point which is earlier than under the statutory test of

9–13

---

[60] See para.16–16, below.
[61] The CLR in fact proposed that the wrongful trading duty should be embodied in the statutory statement of directors' duties (CLR, Final 1, p.348 (Principle 9)), but the Government rejected this proposal on the grounds that decoupling the substantive provisions at present in s.214 from the remedies available under the 1986 Insolvency Act would be "incongruous" (*Modernising Company Law*, Cm. 5533-I, July 2002, para.3.12). Had this step been taken, the common law duties would have been wrapped up into the statutory statement as well (CLR, Final I, para.3.17).
[62] *Walker v Wimborne* (1976) 137 C.L.R. 1.
[63] *West Mercia Safetywear v Dodd* [1988] B.C.L.C. 250 CA. In this case the payment by the insolvent company to a particular creditor involved both a breach of fiduciary duty by the director and also a fraudulent preference (being motivated by a desire to protect the director from liability under a personal guarantee to the creditor).
[64] Even then it is often unclear whether the court is using a balance sheet definition of insolvency (liabilities exceed assets) or a cash-flow approach (company does not have enough cash to pay its debts as they fall due).
[65] *Brady v Brady* [1988] B.C.L.C. 20, 40 CA.
[66] *Nicholson v Permakraft (NZ) Ltd* [1985] 1 N.Z.L.R. 242.

"no reasonable prospect of avoiding insolvent liquidation or administration". This question is not made any easier to answer by the fact that the statutory test itself carries a penumbra of uncertainty (when does the reasonable prospect finally disappear?).

9–14   Assuming the duty has been triggered, how does it require directors to behave? There are some indications in the early cases[67] that the duty is akin to the duty of care under the statute. It is a duty to protect the creditors from further harm rather than a duty to promote the interests of the creditors in a more general sense. For example, the directors of a financially troubled company might adopt a course of action designed to advance the interests of the shareholders, provided it did not increase the riskiness of the creditors' claims on the company.[68] However, the most recent cases treat the common law duty as a fiduciary duty, by analogy with the core directors' duty set out in s.172(1).[69] At first glance, this seems disadvantageous to creditors since it is well established that this core duty is a subjective one, i.e. the directors must act in what they consider (not what a court would consider) to be the best way to further creditor interests. By contrast, as we have seen, under the statutory duty of care the minimum standard of care is set objectively.[70] Thus, the directors appear to have greater freedom of action under the fiduciary approach. However, the contrast may be more apparent than real, at least in the typical case. These are cases where the court finds that the directors acted without considering the creditors' interests at all. The failure itself may constitute a breach of duty or at least open the way for the court to apply the objective test of whether a reasonable director would have acted in the same way as the directors in the instant case.[71]

Where directors do seek to fulfil their fiduciary duty to creditors, there are uncertainties about what is required of them. In some cases the interests of the creditors are described as "paramount", implying that creditor interests are to be the sole concern of the directors, once the duty has been triggered.[72] Other cases do not adopt this approach or even reject it,[73] suggesting that directors may pursue the interests of the shareholders as well as of the creditors once the duty is triggered. Probably, the required action turns on the financial condition of the company. Where the company is hopelessly insolvent or the decision facing the directors, if taken a particular way, will put the company into that position, only the creditors' interests should be considered by the directors. If the company is in financial difficulties of a less serious sort, there may be scope for taking action to

---

[67] For example, *Re Welfab Engineers Ltd* [1990] B.C.L.C. 833.

[68] Thus, the directors might continue the trading of an unprofitable but balance sheet solvent company, in the hope of returning to profitability, without altering the risk profile of the company's business, even though the creditors' interests would most obviously be advanced by liquidating the company now and allowing them to crystallise their claims against the company's assets.

[69] See para.16–37, below for a discussion of this duty.

[70] See para.9–6.

[71] *Re HLC Environmental Projects Ltd* [2014] B.C.C. 337 at [92]. The reasonable director approach is based on *Charterbridge Corp Ltd v Lloyds Bank Ltd* [1970] Ch. 62 (see para.16–42, below).

[72] *Colin Gwyer and Associates Ltd v London Wharf (Limehouse) Ltd* [2003] 2 B.C.L.C. 153 at [74]; *Re HLC Environmental Projects Ltd* [2014] B.C.C. 337.

[73] *Bell Group Ltd (In Liquidation) v Westpac Banking Corp (No.9)* [2008] WASC 239 at [4436]; *Ultraframe (UK) Ltd v Fielding* [2005] EWHC 1638 (Ch).

promote shareholder interests whilst still protecting creditors.[74] In this sense the creditors' interests are always "paramount" (they must always be protected) but, depending on the company's financial position, they may not have to be the exclusive focus of directorial action.

This analysis may be particularly important when the duty is triggered significantly in advance of insolvency, so that, whilst the risk of future insolvency has increased substantially to the detriment of the creditors, the shareholders still have some equity in the business. Where the directors seek to keep the company going rather than, as is typical in the decided cases, extract assets from it, there is some scope for action which advances both shareholder and creditor interests, provided the duty is not one to maximise the welfare of the creditors. After all, even from a purely creditor point of view, continued trading is not necessarily contrary to their interests. As Scott VC recognised in *Facia Footwear Ltd v Hinchliffe*[75] "a continuation of trading might mean a reduction in the dividend eventually payable to creditors but it represented the creditors' only chance of full payment. It is, therefore, not in the least obvious that in continuing to trade the directors were ignoring the interests of the creditors".

The remedies available for breach of fiduciary duty are superior to those for breach of the duty of care. Both will provide recompense for loss (equitable compensation, damages respectively), but if assets extracted from the company have ended up in the hands of the directors, as will often be the case, the fiduciary claim may give the company a proprietary and not just a personal claim for their return.[76] As the previous sentence implies, the creditor-regarding duty, like the other duties of directors, is owed to the company and is therefore enforceable by the company alone, not by individual creditors.[77] As Gummow J said in the Australian High Court, "the result is that there is a duty of imperfect obligation owed to creditors, one which the creditors cannot enforce save to the extent that the company acts on its own motion or through a liquidator".[78] Typically, enforcement will be by the liquidator, as with enforcement of the wrongful trading duty. However, in principle the company or a shareholder suing derivatively could seek to enforce breaches of the duty outside insolvency. This could conceivably occur where the former creditors of the company have taken control of it via a debt for equity swap as a means of avoiding its liquidation. The main disadvantage of the common law duty being owed to the company, not to

9–15

---

[74] See fn.68.

[75] *Facia Footwear Ltd v Hinchliffe* [1998] 1 B.C.L.C. 218 (an application for summary judgment). For a similar approach to wrongful trading see above, para.9–9.

[76] See para.16–112, below.

[77] *Yukong Line Ltd of Korea v Rendsburg Investments Corp of Liberia (The Rialto)* [1998] 1 W.L.R. 294; *Kuwait Asia Bank EC v National Mutual Life Nominees Ltd* [1991] 1 A.C. 187, 217 (Lord Templeman); *Spies v R* [2000] HCA 43; [2000] 201 C.L.R. 603 Aust HC. In this respect the dictum of Lord Templeman in *Winkworth v Edward Baron Development Co Ltd* [1986] 1 W.L.R. 1512 at 1517 goes too far. But in the same vein see the decision of the Supreme Court of Canada, *Peoples Department Stores v Wise* [2004] 3 S.C.R. 461, adopting the notion of direct duties to individual creditors (criticised by Stéphane Rousseau, correctly it is submitted, on the basis that the case involved a reversal of "a fundamental principle of corporate law": "Directors' Duty of Care after *Peoples*: Would it be Wise to Start Worrying about Liability?" (2005) 41 *Canadian Business Law Journal* at 225).

[78] *Sycotex Pty Ltd v Baseler* (1994) 122 A.L.R. 531, 550.

individual creditors—and it is a significant one—is that its proceeds would appear not to go primarily to the unsecured creditors, but are typically caught by any security interests the company has granted. As we have seen, this result is avoided under the wrongful trading provisions.[79]

However, breach of the creditor-facing duty may avail litigants who bring personal actions against the company or its directors, because the breach of duty displaces an answer to the claim which the defendants would otherwise have. Thus, in *Colin Gwyer and Associates Ltd v London Wharf (Limehouse) Ltd*[80] a shareholder challenge to the validity of a board resolution succeeded because the breach of the creditor duty was held to disqualify the director from being counted towards the quorum required under the articles. Recognition of creditors' interests in advance of insolvency may also have an impact on litigation brought against directors for breaches of their non-creditor duties. Such breaches cannot be ratified by the shareholders in the vicinity of insolvency because they are no longer the ones primarily interested in the value of the company's assets.[81]

PHOENIX COMPANIES AND THE ABUSE OF COMPANY NAMES

9–16   The Company Law Review described the "Phoenix company" problem in the following terms:

> "The 'phoenix' problem results from the continuance of a failed company by those responsible for that failure, using the vehicle of a new company. The new company, often trading under the same or similar name, uses the old company's assets, often acquired at an undervalue, and exploits its goodwill and business opportunities. Meanwhile, the creditors of the old company are left to prove their debts against a valueless shell and the management conceal their previous failure from the public."[82]

However, it also went on to point out that the actions just described are not necessarily improper. They will be so where their purpose is to deprive the creditors of the first company of the value of that company's assets by transferring them at an undervalue to the second company; or where the purpose of the actions is to mislead the creditors of the second company by disguising the lack of success of the business when it was carried on by the first company. In other cases, however, such purposes may be lacking, The failure of the first company may be for reasons outside the control of its directors and, further, "the only way to continue an otherwise viable business and their own and their employees' ability to earn their livelihood may be for them to do so in a new vehicle using the assets and trading style of the original company".[83] Thus, the

---

[79] See para.9–10, above. Indeed, there is a broader question here of what the duty to the creditors means when there are several classes of creditor. Junior creditors, who are "out of the money" at the time of the relevant decision, may, like shareholders, have an interest in taking on very risky projects, because only in that way have they any hope of recovering anything. Senior creditors, by contrast, may be better off by stopping trading at once.

[80] Above fn.72.

[81] *Kinsela v Russell Kinsela Pty Ltd* [1986] 4 N.S.W.L.R. 722.

[82] Final Report I, para.15.55.

[83] Final Report I, para.15.56. The facts giving rise to the application to use a similar name in *Re Lightning Electrical Contractors Ltd* [1996] 2 B.C.L.C. 302 might be thought to be an example of

regulation of the Phoenix company is not an easy matter: too light a regulation may permit abuses to continue; too heavy a regulation may lead to the cessation of otherwise viable businesses.

The prohibition

As will be clear, the Phoenix problem needs to be tackled from two angles. One is the transfer of the assets of the first company at an undervalue to a new company controlled by the same persons. Since the claims of the creditors are confined, at least in principle, to the assets of the first company, this is a problem generated by limited liability. Within company law, the regulation of such an event is primarily the function of ss.190 et seq. (substantial property transactions with directors), which we discuss in Ch.16. Here the CLR recommended reforms but they were not taken up in the Companies Act 2006.[84] So, the law continues as before. The second angle is the re-use of the first company's name by the second company. This is perhaps the converse abuse of limited liability. The company against which the creditors' claims lie is in this case the second company, but it appears to be a more credit-worthy operation than it really is, because it appears at first glance to be the first company, whose demise is concealed.[85] In this case, substantial reform, involving the imposition of personal liability for the debts of the second company, was brought about by s.216 of the Insolvency Act 1986. It proceeds by laying down a broad prohibition about the re-use of the first company's name or a name similar to it (to which prohibition both criminal and civil sanctions are attached) and then providing certain exceptions to it. Its primary objective seems to be to prevent the creditors of the new company from being misled about the history of the company with which they are dealing. The prohibition is attached to the directors and shadow directors of the first company and is triggered if the first company goes into insolvent liquidation.

9–17

In somewhat more detail, s.216 of the Insolvency Act makes it an offence (of strict liability)[86] for anyone, who was a director or shadow director of the first company at any time during the 12 months preceding its going into insolvent liquidation, to be in any way concerned (except with the leave of the court or in such circumstances as may be prescribed) during the next five years in the

9–18

---

this: the administrative receivership of a medium-sized company was brought about by the failure of two large client companies to pay the money due from them; the successor company's use of the similar name was supported by the receivers since it enable them to maximise the value of the first company's assets.

[84] CLR, Final Report I, paras 15.65–15.72. The problem with the existing law is perhaps demonstrated by the background facts of *Secretary of State for Trade and Industry v Becker* [2003] 1 B.C.L.C. 565.

[85] If misleading the creditors as to the creditworthiness of the second business is the rationale of the section, it is perhaps understandable that the prohibition extends even to the carrying on of the second business in non-corporate form (i.e. potentially without limited liability): (s.216(3)(c)). However, no personal liability is imposed in this case, presumably on the basis that it is unnecessary: s.217(1). In many cases the defendant will be liable as partner or sole trader, but it is conceivable that a person could "directly or indirectly be concerned or take part in the carrying-on" of a non-corporate business without attracting personal liability as a partner or sole trader, so that the absence of personal liability under s.217 is important.

[86] *R. v Cole* [1998] 2 B.C.L.C. 234 CA.

formation or management of a company, or business, with a name by which the original company was known or one so similar as to suggest an association with that company (known as a "prohibited name"). The prohibited name may be the first company's name or a name under which that company carried on business; and the prohibition applies to both the second company's corporate and trading names.[87] Whether the similarity of names is made out is to be judged by the court by reference to the circumstances in which the companies with the allegedly similar names operate, and so it is a highly fact-specific determination.[88] It is clear that no person needs to have been misled by the prohibited act; it is enough to show that the names had a tendency to mislead.[89] Finally, it should be noted that the prohibition applies whether or not the first element of the classic "Phoenix" syndrome is present, i.e. the transfer of assets from first to second company. The syndrome may have provided the rationale for the legislation but the section is not formally tied to it and has a life of its own separate from the Phoenix rationale.[90]

In addition to the criminal offence, s.217 makes a person acting in breach of s.216 personally liable, jointly and severally with the new company and any other person so liable, for the debts and other liabilities of the new company incurred while he or she was concerned in its management in breach of s.216.[91] In this case, therefore, the defendant is personally liable in relation to a specific set of debts rather than liable, as under the fraudulent and wrongful trading provisions, to make a general contribution to the assets of the company in order to help meet the claims of all its creditors. This somewhat different approach follows on from the fact that the liability arises under s.216 towards the creditors of the second company and arises whether or not the second company is in insolvent liquidation or, indeed, any particular form of financial difficulty, although it typically will be. Also liable is anyone involved in the second company's management who acts or is willing to act on the instructions given by a person whom he knows, at that time, to be in breach of s.216.[92] Use of s.217 seems

---

[87] 1986 Act s.216(6)—an important extension, for otherwise the prohibition could be easily avoided by the transferee company's registered name being quite dissimilar from the transferor company's but by the transferee then carrying on business under a similar name. See *R. (Griffin) v Richmond Magistrates Court* [2008] EWHC 84 (Admin). The CLR found that this was a practice used effectively to avoid the impact of the provisions, even though ostensibly caught by them.

[88] *First Independent Factors and Finance Ltd v Mountford* [2008] 2 B.C.L.C. 297.

[89] *Ricketts v Ad Valorem Factors Ltd* [2004] 1 B.C.L.C. 1 CA; *Revenue and Customs Commissioners v Walsh* [2005] 2 B.C.L.C. 455, though in the former case there was a disagreement among the judges as to whether the facts needed only to "suggest" an association or give rise to a probability that members of the public would associate the two companies.

[90] *Ricketts v Ad Valorem Factors Ltd* [2004] 1 B.C.L.C. 1 CA.

[91] 1986 Act s.217. That the liability is restricted to debts incurred by the company in the period during which the person was in breach of s.216 (and did not extend to all the debts incurred whilst that person was a director of the company) was accepted by Arden LJ in *ESS Productions Ltd v Sully* [2005] 2 B.C.L.C. 547 at [75]. See also *Glasgow City Council v Craig* [2009] 1 B.C.L.C. 742: liability confined to the debts of that part of the business which was carried on under the prohibited name.

[92] Though such a person does not commit a criminal offence. For the purpose of both ss.216 and 217, "company" includes any company which may be wound up under Pt V of the Insolvency Act, i.e. virtually any company or association: s.220.

somewhat higher than the use of the wrongful trading provisions.[93] This may be because s.217 can be triggered by a wider range of claimants than the wrongful trading provisions, i.e. individual creditors rather than just the liquidator or administrator. Not only does this rule generate more potential claimants but the restrictions on the assignment of claims which have affected liquidators in the past do not apply to third-party creditors.[94]

Exceptions

The policy behind the provisions is perhaps most clearly revealed in the three prescribed cases, set out in the Insolvency Rules,[95] where liability is not imposed. The first, and probably most important, of the cases is where a successor company purchases the whole of the insolvent company's business from an insolvency practitioner acting for the transferor company (thus reducing the risk of a sale at undervalue) and gives notice of the name the successor company intends to use to all the creditors of the insolvent company. The Court of Appeal held that this exception is available only where the directors of the insolvent company were not already directors of or involved in the management of the successor company at the time the notice was given, on the grounds that the warning function (see below) of the rules would otherwise be undermined.[96] This ruling caused difficulty in two situations. First, where the successor company (with common directors) bought the business from a company which, although insolvent, was not in liquidation, but, for example, in administration, it was common for the successor company to give the requisite notice in case, not in itself unlikely, the first company should go into liquidation after the administration. Secondly, and more limited, this first case, as originally drafted, would not apply if the directors were already directors of the successor company at the time notice was given, even if at that time the successor company was not known by a prohibited name (though it subsequently acquired one). In 2007 the Insolvency Rules were amended so as to extend the first exception to these two situations.[97]

Overall, the first case might be thought to suggest that the aim of the section is partly the protection of the creditors of the insolvent company. This is because the insertion of the insolvency practitioner is intended to ensure that the sale by the insolvent company is not at an undervalue and the notice to the creditors of that company ensures that they are not misled into thinking that they may assert their claims against the new company.[98] However, if the requirements of this case are

9–19

---

[93] The CLR reported that the Official Receiver was aware of 134 cases of breaches of s.216 in 1999/2000, which led to 118 warning letters and nine convictions, but these figures apparently relate only to criminal liability under the section: Completing, para.13.105.

[94] *First Independent Factors and Finance Ltd v Mountford* [2008] 2 B.C.L.C. 297—claim brought by debt factor which had acquired the claims from two trade creditors at a discount. cf. fn.57 above.

[95] Insolvency Rules (SI 1986/1925), rr.4.228 to 4.230; and the Insolvency (Scotland) Rules (SI 1986/1915), rr.4.78 to 4.82.

[96] *First Independent Factors and Finance Ltd v Churchill* [2007] 1 B.C.L.C. 293 CA.

[97] The Insolvency (Amendment) Rules 2007 (SI 2007/1974).

[98] See *Penrose v Secretary of State for Trade and Industry* [1996] 1 W.L.R. 482. In the *Churchill* case (fn.96, above) the Court of Appeal put the function of the notice rather differently: it was to help

not met, the liability of the directors is not to the creditors of the insolvent company but to those of the successor company, as indicated above. Nor is the successor company itself, which simply falls outside s.216, liable for the debts of the insolvent company. The CLR considered, but rejected, a proposal that the liability of the successor company and those acting in breach of s.216 should be extended to the creditors of the insolvent company, but rejected it.[99] So, the extent of the protection afforded by s.216 to the creditors of the insolvent first company is limited.

The third case[100] excepts from s.216 the situation where the "new" company has been known by the prohibited name for the whole of the 12 months ending with the liquidation of the first company.[101] The purpose of this provision is, in particular, to permit the transfer of businesses within an existing group of companies. The risk of the creditors being misled, although it exists, is not in this case the result of action taken after the liquidation of the original company but of decisions taken in advance of the liquidation by a period of at least one year—a period thought to be enough to prevent opportunistic use of this exception.[102] This exception has been given a broad interpretation by the courts: it is not necessary to show that the company was known during the 12-month period by the prohibited name it had at the time the debt arose (provided it was known during that period by one or more prohibited names) or that it used the prohibited name in relation to the whole of its business.[103]

MISDESCRIPTION OF THE COMPANY AND TRADING DISCLOSURES

9–20   This is an area of creditor protection where personal liability is no longer imposed after the 2006 Act, but the underlying disclosure obligation still exists in the current legislation. The notion is that a company should be required fully to disclose its name when transacting so that a creditor who wishes to carry out a search of the company's records in Companies House (or elsewhere) is put in a position to do so. By what was s.349(4) of the Companies Act 1985, if the correct and full name of the company did not appear on cheques and related instruments or orders for goods signed by an officer (or even an employee) of the company,

---

creditors of the first company make an informed assessment of the risks of extending credit to the successor company, i.e. the focus was on protection of the creditors of the successor company. This approach seems more consistent with the drafting of the section. On the other hand, it is not then clear why the notice has to be given before the directors of the first company become involved with the successor company: it should be enough if notice is given before creditors of the first company extend credit to the successor company.

[99] Final Report I, para.15.62.

[100] The second case (r.4.229) is ancillary to the provision permitting a person to act in breach of s.216 if the court gives permission. The second case permits a director, who applies for leave within seven days of the first company going into liquidation, to continue to act in breach of s.216 for a period of six weeks or until the court disposes of the application for leave, whichever is the shorter.

[101] Rule 4.230—and has not been a dormant company. Otherwise, a shelf company could be formed purely for the purpose of triggering this exception.

[102] Though cf. *Morphitis v Bernasconi* [2003] 2 B.C.L.C. 53 CA: scheme to avoid s.216 by the directors resigning from the company at least a year before it was liquidated.

[103] *ESS Production Ltd v Sully* [2005] 2 B.C.L.C. 547 CA.

the signatory would be personally liable to pay if the company did not.[104] It made no difference that the third party concerned had not been misled by the description. The requirement to state the company's name correctly on cheques, etc. is only one of a number of disclosure requirements imposed by the legislation on companies in relation to those who deal or might deal with them (known as "trading disclosures"), but it was the only one in relation to which personal liability was imposed. Those requirements are re-stated in Ch.6 of Pt 5 of the 2006 Act, where the Secretary of State is given power to make regulations requiring the company to give specified information, not only in "specified descriptions of documents or communications" but also in specified locations (such as the company's place of business or its website) or to those who deal with the company.[105]

Although the sanction of personal liability has been removed for failure to state the company's name correctly on cheques, etc. such a failure is not devoid of civil consequences, though they are now visited wholly on the company.[106] Moreover, these civil consequences now apply to any breaches of the trading disclosure requirements, whether involving the misstatement of the company's name on a cheque, etc. or some other failure to conform to them.[107] Where a company seeks to enforce a right arising out of a contract made in the course of business and the company was in breach of the disclosure requirements at the time, the court is required to dismiss the company's claim if the defendant shows that he or she has a claim against the company which the defendant is unable to pursue because of the company's breach of the disclosure requirements or that he or she has suffered a financial loss by reason of the company's breach. Even in these two cases, the court may permit the company's claim to continue if it thinks it just and equitable to do so.[108] Thus, not only are the civil consequences of misdescriptions confined to the company but the company will bear them only where the misdescription has caused harm to the defendant and, even then, the court may permit the company's claim to proceed (for example, where the harm to the defendant was out of proportion to the harm the company might suffer by being denied its contractual rights and the defendant's loss could be taken into account in calculating the company's damages).

Overall, the thrust of the disclosure rules is now on fostering self-help on the part of those dealing with the company,[109] rather than with providing them with

---

[104] See *Atkins v Wardle* (1889) 5 T.L.R. 734 CA; *Scottish & Newcastle Breweries Ltd v Blair*, 1967 S.L.T. 72; *Civil Service Co-operative Society v Chapman* [1914] 30 T.L.R. 679; *British Airways Board v Parish* [1979] 2 Lloyd's Rep. 361.

[105] 2006 Act s.82(1) and the Company Limited Liability Partnership (Names and Trading Disclosure) Regulations 2015 (SI 2015/17) Pt 6.

[106] This is a more radical response than that recommended by the CLR which would have kept personal liability but on a narrower basis: Final Report I, paras 11.55–11.57.

[107] This is new: previously, other than as provided by s.349(4), the sanctions for breach of the disclosure requirements were only criminal. However, the civil liability imposed by s.83 is modelled on that imposed by s.5 of the Business Names Act 1985 which already applied to companies trading other than under their corporate name. The criminal sanctions are retained in s.84 of the 2006 Act.

[108] 2006 Act s.83(1),(2). The restriction does not apply if the company seeks to enforce its contractual rights in proceedings brought by another person (for example, by way of counter-claim): s.83(3).

[109] Hence the importance of disclosure of the company's name, not only in correspondence, but on its website and at any place of business: Trading Regulations, regs 4 and 6(2).

an additional avenue of civil redress against company officers or employees, and on making the company liable only where those dealing with it have suffered harm as a result of the misdescription.

COMPANY GROUPS

Limited liability

9–21 The final area for consideration is the operation of the doctrine of limited liability within groups of companies. Even relatively modest businesses often operate through groups of companies and large businesses invariably do so, and so the issue is one of great practical importance. Where the companies in the group are wholly owned, directly or indirectly, by the parent, only the rationale of asset partitioning[110] provides a reason for the extension of limited liability to intra-group relations, since the raising of equity capital and the trading of shares on public exchanges could occur effectively with limited liability confined to the shareholders of the parent company. Where the subsidiary is only partly owned by the parent, and in particular where the "outside" shares are traded on a public market, the other rationales for limited liability also apply within groups.[111] British law does in fact apply the doctrine of limited liability to intra-group shareholders as much as to extra-group shareholders and, as we saw in the previous chapter,[112] the courts will not pierce the veil within a group of companies simply on the grounds that the group constitutes a single economic entity. However, from time to time there have been proposals for statutory provisions to modify the veil within groups, both at EU level and domestically, but, so far, without result.

How might creditors of a subsidiary be disadvantaged as a result of the company becoming, or being, a member of a group of companies? In general the answer is because, at least in a group with an integrated business strategy,[113] business decisions may be taken on the basis of maximising the wealth of the group as a whole (which usually means the value of the parent company), rather than of the particular subsidiary of which the claimant is a creditor. This phenomenon may show itself in a variety of ways. Three examples may be given. Most obviously, the parent may instruct the board of the subsidiary to do something which is not in the best interests of the subsidiary, because that decision will maximise the benefits of the group. Secondly, the parent may allocate new business opportunities to the subsidiary which can maximise the benefit for the group, even though another subsidiary could develop the

---

[110] The rationales for limited liability are discussed at paras 8–1 et seq.

[111] This situation is not usual, but is certainly not unknown, in the UK: "Governance concerns rise after London IPOs", *Financial Times*, 16 June 2011.

[112] At para.8–11, above.

[113] This does not include all groups of companies: in conglomerate groups (i.e. groups of diversified businesses) the advantages of common ownership may well reside in something other than the imposition of a single business strategy (for example, access to sources of finance or managerial expertise).

opportunity effectively, if less profitably. Finally, if a subsidiary falls into insolvency, the parent may refrain from rescuing it, even though the group has sufficient funds to do so.

It is far from clear that the actions described above in the second and third examples do, or ought to, involve any illegality on the part of those involved. Unless the business opportunity had been generated by a particular subsidiary,[114] it is not clear that it has, or ought to have, any claim to take all the opportunities arising within the group which it could effectively develop. Nor is it obvious that the descent into insolvency of a properly capitalised subsidiary which has fully disclosed the risks of its business should be allowed to threaten the economic viability of the remainder of the group's operations. In short, the overruling of limited liability within corporate groups is likely to require sophisticated and nuanced regulation if it is to make sense in policy terms.

The strongest case for intervention is the first: directions to the subsidiary to act in a way which is disadvantageous to it (and its creditors and outside shareholders) in order to benefit the parent (and its creditors and shareholders). Egregious cases of this type are already caught by existing British law, for example, the application of the rules against fraudulent trading to all those party to it and of wrongful trading to shadow directors, both of which extensions may bring in parent companies, at least in some circumstances.[115] These are examples of the overall domestic approach to group problems, i.e. the extension of general creditor-protection rules to deal with the particular situation of group creditors. An alternative approach would be the development of distinct rules for corporate groups. This alternative approach is to be found in German law dealing with public companies which contains a separate section dealing with the issue of creditor and minority shareholder protection within groups,[116] though even these provisions do not purport to deal comprehensively with group issues but focus predominantly on the first example of disadvantageous behaviour given above. Even within Germany, however, these provisions are not thought to work effectively.[117]

The German statutory regulation of public companies provides two models of regulation, one of which is contractual and thus optional. Under the optional provision, in exchange for undertaking an obligation to indemnify the subsidiary

9–22

---

[114] On "corporate opportunities" see para.16–86, below.

[115] For an example of the use of the strategy of disqualifying directors (discussed in the following chapter) see *Re Genosyis Technology Management Ltd* [2007] 1 B.C.L.C. 208—directors disqualified for causing debts due to subsidiary to be paid to parent company.

[116] *Aktiengesetz*, Book Three.

[117] For a discussion of German "*Konzernrecht*", see K.J. Hopt, "Legal Elements and Policy Decisions in Regulating Groups of Companies" in C.M. Schmitthoff and F. Wooldridge (eds), *Groups of Companies* (London: Sweet & Maxwell, 1991), p.81; H. Wiedemann, "The German Experience with the Law of Affiliated Enterprise", in K.J. Hopt (ed.), *Groups of Companies in European Laws, Legal and Economic Analyses on Multinational Enterprises*, Vol. II (Walter de Gruyter, 1982) 21. For a comparative perspective, see Forum Europaeum Corporate Group Law, "Corporate Group Law for Europe" (2000) 1 European Business Organization Law Review 165; and V. Priskich, "Corporate Groups: Current Proposals for Reform in Australia and the United Kingdom and a Comparative Analysis of the Regime in Germany" in (2002) 4 I.C.C.L.J. 37; and K.J. Hopt, "Groups of Companies" in J. Gordon and G. Ringe (eds), *Oxford Handbook of Corporate Law and Governance* (OUP, online ed, 2015).

for its annual net losses incurred during the term of the agreement, the parent acquires the right to instruct the subsidiary to act in the interests of the group rather than its own best interests. This option has been taken up only by a small number of companies, presumably because the incentive to do so (i.e. protection from the potential liabilities for ignoring the separate legal personality of the subsidiary) is too small. The Company Law Review proposed something similar: in exchange for a guarantee by the parent of the liabilities of its subsidiary, the subsidiary would be freed from the obligation to publish separate accounts, thus reducing the costs of running the group.[118] However, the proposal was not proceeded with, partly because it was again thought that the incentive provided was not large enough to induce a substantial take-up of the option and, partly and conversely, because there were fears about loss of information about subsidiary companies if the option were taken up, especially where the subsidiary was the main British operating company of a foreign parent.[119]

The second strand of the German statutory regime is mandatory and applies to de facto groups. The core provision[120] is that the parent is liable for the damage to the subsidiary if the parent causes the subsidiary to enter into a disadvantageous transaction, unless, within the fiscal year, the parent has compensated the subsidiary for the loss or agreed to do so. The provision has proved less effective than expected seemingly because of difficulties of proof, both in relation to identifying particular disadvantageous transactions (where there is a continuous course of dealing between parent and subsidiary) and to identifying the loss caused by those transactions. This weakness of the de facto group regime undermines also the contractual group rules, since it is escape from the former which could provide a major incentive for companies to enter into the optional regime.[121]

9–23 Nevertheless, the German model, which has been followed within the EU only by Portugal and Croatia, was used by the European Commission in its preliminary consideration of a draft Ninth Company Law Directive on groups in the early 1980s. However, so remote from the traditions of the other Member States was this idea that the draft was never adopted by the full Commission. The Report of the High Level Group of Company Law Experts,[122] whilst not proposing a revival of the Ninth Directive, did propose that Member States should be required to introduce into their company laws the principle that the management of the parent company should be entitled to pursue the interests of the group, even if a

---

[118] Completing, Ch.10. On parent and subsidiary company reporting requirements see immediately below.

[119] Final Report I, paras 8.23–8.28. Nevertheless, a variant of the idea (exemption from audit but not from producing accounts in exchange for a guarantee from the parent) has been implemented in UK law: see para.22-7.

[120] *Aktiengesetz*, s.317.

[121] A possible partial solution, which the German courts have used for private companies (GmbH), would be to use the contractual group model under which exercise of influence to disadvantageous ends would make the parent liable for all the subsidiary's losses, whether they could be related to a particular disadvantageous contract or not.

[122] Brussels, 4 November 2002, Ch.V. See above, para.6–12. For more detailed consideration of the options, see Forum Europaeum, above fn.117. The proposal was made again—this time for an EU Recommendation—in the *Report of the Reflection Group on the Future of EU Company Law*, Brussels April 2011, Ch.4.

particular transaction was to the disadvantage of a particular subsidiary, provided that, over time, there was a fair balance of burdens and advantages for the subsidiary.[123] The modalities of the incorporation of this principle into national law would be for each Member State to decide. The Report thus put as much stress on the need for group management to be able to run a coherent group policy as it did on the protection of creditors and minority shareholders in the subsidiary. In fact, British law has a somewhat similar approach, but applies it to the directors of the subsidiary, not the parent.[124] The directors of a subsidiary ought to consider whether it is in the interests of the subsidiary to follow instructions from the parent—though it is likely that the subsidiary directors, who will often be employees of the parent, do not in fact go through this exercise. It may well be in the interests of the subsidiary to do what the parent requires, for example, where the business of the subsidiary is dependent on inputs from other group companies.

The High Level Group also proposed greater disclosure of information about the group, both of a financial and, more important, of a non-financial kind, relating, in particular, to control relations within the group and the types of dependency created. Although the latter proposal has achieved some legislative result in the Takeovers Directive,[125] proposals for action beyond disclosure have not been taken up at EU level.

Finally, in some jurisdictions, part of the solution to the group problem, especially in the case of the third example given above, is to be found in insolvency law, where the court may be given a discretion in certain circumstances to bring a solvent group company into the insolvency of another group company.[126] The High Level Group also supported this principle.

Ignoring separate legal personality

If it is rare for British law to ignore the principle of limited liability within groups, it would be completely wrong to conclude that the law is not prepared to override the separate legal personality of companies within groups where this does not involve any infringement of the principle of limited liability. There are many instances in which domestic company law takes account of group structures, though these instances tend to be rather ad hoc, rather than the result of the application of a single general principle.

Perhaps the best known example is in the area of financial reporting. It has long been recognised that, in relation to financial disclosure, the group phenomenon cannot be ignored if a "true and fair" view of the overall position of the company is to be presented, and that accordingly when one company (the

9–24

---

[123] This is often referred to as the *Rozenblum* doctrine, after the name of the French case (*Bulletin criminel* 1985 No.54) in which the principle was articulated.

[124] See further para.16–47, below. The potential liability of the parent company as a shadow director of the subsidiary is largely excluded by s.251(3) of the CA 2006, unless the subsidiary is in the vicinity of insolvency.

[125] See para.28–25.

[126] On New Zealand law and Australian proposals, see R.P. Austin, "Corporate Groups" in R. Grantham and C. Rickett (eds), *Corporate Personality in the Twentieth Century* (Oxford: Hart Publishing, 1998), especially at pp.84–87.

parent or holding company) controls others (the subsidiary and sub-subsidiary companies) the parent company must present group financial statements as well as its own individual statements, thus avoiding the misleading impression which the latter alone might give.[127] The subordinate companies in the group must also produce individual accounts. This is discussed more fully in Ch.21.

The Companies Acts have also long used the concept of the parent-subsidiary relationship in areas other than that of financial disclosure. Clearly if one is to ban or control certain types of transaction between a company and its directors it is essential to ensure that this cannot be easily evaded by effecting the transactions with or through another company in the group. Hence many of the sections in Ch.4 of Pt 10 (Transactions with Directors Requiring Approval of Members) contain such anti-avoidance provisions.[128] Similarly, the prohibition on financial assistance for the purchase of a company's own shares extends to financial assistance by any of its subsidiaries.[129]

In non-legal and much legal discourse, the expressions "parent" and "holding" company are used interchangeably. Until the Companies Act 1989, UK company legislation used the latter, but the EU Company Law Directives use the former, which seems preferable, since "holding" suggests that the sole function of the parent is to control the operations of subsidiaries whereas it too may well be undertaking one or more of the trading activities of the group. Now, in the Act, the two terms have slightly different meanings, the definition of a "parent" company being broader than that of a "holding" company; and the term "parent" company being used in relation to company accounts and that of "holding" company elsewhere where the Act recognises group situations.[130] This came about because, when the Seventh Directive compelled a change in the definition for the purposes of accounts, it was represented that to apply the whole of the extended definition to other cases would introduce an unreasonable degree of uncertainty.[131] Hence it was decided to adopt a narrower definition in the non-accounts area, albeit one based on the EU definition. While it is a pity that it was thought necessary to have different definitions for what is essentially the same concept, there is no doubt that both are considerable improvements on the previous definition[132] since they recognise that what counts is "control" and not majority shareholding which, because of non-voting shares or weighted voting, will not necessarily afford control.

Under s.1159 the definition of "holding" and "subsidiary" company now is:

"A company is a 'subsidiary' of another company, its 'holding company', if that other company

---

[127] To take a simplified example: if a parent company A has two wholly-owned subsidiaries, B and C, and in a financial year B makes a loss of £100,000 while C makes a distributable profit of £10,000 all of which it pays to A by way of dividend, the individual accounts of A (assuming it has broken even) will show a profit of £10,000 whereas in fact the group has made a loss of £90,000.

[128] See para.16–70, below.

[129] See para.13–47.

[130] "Parent company" is defined in s.1162 and Sch.7 (see para.21–10) and "holding company" in s.1159 and Sch.6.

[131] For purposes of consolidation a measure of uncertainty is acceptable because, when in doubt, one can play safe and consolidate.

[132] 1948 Act s.154. Under the former s.154(10)(a)(ii) holding more than half in nominal value of a company's equity share capital (voting or non-voting) made it a subsidiary.

(a)   holds a majority of the voting rights in it, or

(b)   is a member of it and has the right to appoint or remove a majority of its board of directors, or

(c)   is a member of it and controls alone, pursuant to an agreement with other members, a majority of the voting rights in it.

or if it is a subsidiary of a company which is itself a subsidiary of that other company."[133]

CONCLUSION

Since the Cork Committee[134] reported in 1982, statutory willingness to impose liability towards creditors on the directors of companies which abuse the mechanism of limited liability has significantly increased. Both the wrongful trading provisions and those dealing with the re-use of corporate names were a response to primarily small company problems. Together with the provisions on the disqualification of directors,[135] also aimed primarily at small companies, they may be said to constitute the legislature's preferred alternative to compulsory minimum capital requirements[136] for dealing with the abuses of limited liability in small companies. These provisions, however, are not formally limited to small companies; and the wrongful trading provisions, through the use of the idea of shadow directors, are capable also of catching abuses outside small companies, in particular within corporate groups. However, the issue of limited liability within groups has not received the same degree of legislative attention. Like the judges, whose decisions on lifting the veil we examined in the previous chapter, the legislature has touched on limited liability within groups only gingerly, whilst showing itself perfectly able to recognise group structures in other areas of company law.

9–25

---

[133] Unfortunately, this relatively simple definition requires additional refinement to make it work (which is contained in Sch.6 to the Act) and, as *Enviroco Ltd v Farstad Supply A/S* [2011] 2 B.C.L.C. 165, SC demonstrated, that refinement was not itself sufficiently refined because it failed to take full account of the definition of a "member" in s.112 of the Act.

[134] See above fn.11.

[135] Discussed in the next chapter.

[136] See para.11–8, below.

CHAPTER 10

DISQUALIFICATION OF DIRECTORS

In the previous chapter we examined the provisions which, at the instigation of those in charge of the insolvency of a company, may lead to the imposition of a financial liability on directors and shadow directors who, in the period preceding the insolvency, engaged in conduct which exploited the vulnerabilities of creditors and caused a diminution in the company's assets. The Cork Committee, which recommended this reform in 1982, went further, however, and argued that "proper safeguards for the public" required that wrongful trading be supplemented by provisions which ensure that "those whose conduct has shown them to be unfitted to manage the affairs of a company with limited liability shall, for a specified period, be prohibited from doing so".[1] In particular, they thought the law should "severely penalise those who abuse the privilege of limited liability by operating behind one-man, insufficiently capitalised companies".[2] This recommendation is now embodied in the Company Directors Disqualification Act 1986,[3] as later amended. Like the wrongful trading provisions, the central provisions of the Act (disqualification on grounds of "unfitness") apply to shadow directors as well as directors.[4] The law was here to be used in general deterrence mode, for the protection of future creditors of companies as a whole, rather than to seek compensation for existing creditors. However, under the Small

10–1

---

[1] Report of the Review Committee on Insolvency Law and Practice, Cmnd. 8558 (1982), para.1808.

[2] Cmnd. 8558, para.1815.

[3] This is still the principal legislation and references in this chapter to sections will be to that Act, as amended, unless otherwise indicated.

[4] 1986 Act ss.6(3C), 8(1).

Business and Enterprise Act 2015 a compensation power was grafted onto the disqualification provisions, thus holding out some prospect that the provisions will aid in addition the creditors of the company whose directors have been disqualified.

A further significant feature of the Act is that initiation of disqualification action lies exclusively in the hands of the public authorities in the case of the most commonly used provisions, i.e. where disqualification is based on "unfitness".[5] Initiation of the disqualification process is assigned to the Secretary of State ("SS") (i.e. the relevant government minister), though the minister may delegate that function, and normally does, to the Insolvency Service, a government agency.[6] The SS also has exclusive control over the initiation of the new compensation provisions.[7] Outside the area of unfitness, the liquidator or any past member or creditor may apply for a disqualification order,[8] but it is unclear that they will have any great incentive to do so, because the benefits of disqualification accrue to future creditors. In other words, the forward looking disqualification process and its initiation by the public authorities are linked features of the legislation. When compensation was grafted onto the legislation in 2015, the opportunity might have been taken to open up the range of potential initiators, but it was not.

The introduction of a compensation mechanism was not the only significant reform after 1986. In particular, reforms in the Insolvency Act 2000 introduced the notion of an out-of-court "disqualification undertaking" in cases of unfitness to supplement the "disqualification order", which only a court can make.[9] In addition, the 2015 Act[10] made reforms aimed at taking into account the cross-border environment in which many companies now operate but which national prudential rules often ignore. These changes make it possible for conduct of the director in relation to overseas companies (i.e. companies incorporated outside Great Britain)[11] to be taken into account in appropriate circumstances by the court or SS when considering disqualification. However, powers already contained in Pt 40 of the Companies Act 2006[12] have not been used to date. These empower the SS to make regulations so that a person disqualified in a foreign jurisdiction would or could be prohibited from acting in relation to a company incorporated in Great Britain. New s.5A (see para.10–12, below) gets close to this principle, but is based on conviction abroad for a serious offence, not disqualification abroad. The attraction of the more general principle clearly

---

[5] 1986 Act ss.6 and 8.
[6] 1986 Act s.7.
[7] 1986 Act s.15A(1).
[8] 1986 Act s.16.
[9] 1986 Act ss.1 and 1A. See further below, para.10–2.
[10] For the policy behind the 2015 Act in the disqualification area see BIS, *Transparency & Trust: Enhancing the Transparency of UK Company Ownership and Increasing Trust in UK Business: Government Response*, April 2014 (BIS/14/672) Ch.5–9.
[11] 1986 Act s.22(2A). The reference is to "Great Britain" rather than the "United Kingdom" because Northern Ireland has separate disqualification legislation—The Company Directors Disqualification (Northern Ireland) Order 2002—though its scope is similar.
[12] 2006 Act s.1184.

depends upon the equivalence of the foreign jurisdictions' disqualification provisions to those in the UK. It is an issue in which the EU is likely to show interest.

In addition to the general ground of unfitness, there are a number of more specific cases in which disqualification can be imposed on persons. Although these persons are typically directors or shadow directors of companies, these disqualification provision apply more broadly in some cases. The specific instances can best be analysed as falling within the following categories:

(a)   commission of a serious offence, usually involving dishonesty, in connection with the management of a company;

(b)   being found liable to make a contribution to the assets of the company on grounds of fraudulent or wrongful trading;

(c)   failure to comply with the provisions of the companies or insolvency legislation relating to the filing of documents with the Registrar.

Finally, there is a long-standing provision in the companies legislation which disqualifies an undischarged bankrupt from being involved in the management of companies, to which was added in 2002 the notion of "bankruptcy restriction orders".

DISQUALIFICATION ORDERS AND UNDERTAKINGS

The power to disqualify has generated a high level of activity. In the years 1997–1998 to 2000–2001 between 1,250 and 1,500 directors were disqualified each year by court order and in 2001–2002, when disqualification undertakings were introduced, the total of orders and undertakings was nearly 2,000.[13] Since then, the total of orders and undertakings has fluctuated within a slowly declining pattern. In 2014/15 there was a total of 1,227 (899 undertakings and 328 court orders)—about 4 per cent of the total number of directors of failed companies in that year. Over 80 per cent of the orders and undertakings were on grounds of unfitness.[14] Thus, the Act has been the basis of a considerable activity on the part of the public authorities. The rationale behind the introduction of undertakings in unfitness cases by the Insolvency Act 2000 was the fact that, under the previous legislation, even where the public authorities and the director could reach agreement on how the provisions of the Act should apply in the particular case, it was necessary to go to court to obtain an order and it was doubtful whether the court could simply accept, and rubber-stamp, the agreement between them.[15] The amended Act permits the SS and the director to reach an agreement out-of-court on a disqualification undertaking, which will restrict the director's future activities in the same way as a disqualification order, but without the need for a

10–2

---

[13]   DTI, *Companies in 2001–2002* (2002), Table D1.

[14]   Companies House, *Statistical Tables on Companies Registration Activities 2014–2015*, Table D1.

[15]   Though the courts had developed a summary procedure for dealing with non-contested cases: *Re Carecraft Construction Co Ltd* [1994] 1 W.L.R. 172; and Practice Direction [1999] B.C.C. 717. The summary procedure has effectively been overtaken by the out-of-court undertaking, though in principle it is still available.

court hearing.[16] The director can always trigger a court hearing by refusing to agree terms for an undertaking, though he or she will normally be liable for the SS's costs, as well as his or her own costs, if the court makes an order. Alternatively, a director who has accepted an undertaking may subsequently apply to the court, apparently at any time, for the period of the disqualification to be reduced or for the undertaking to cease to apply.[17] This is equivalent to the power which the court has under the Insolvency Rules to review, vary or rescind disqualification orders.[18] Although the power is broadly framed, the courts are likely to find it appropriate to alter the undertaking for the future (the court has no power to declare that it ought not to have been made) only in limited circumstances. In particular, it would be likely to undermine the undertaking procedure if directors, having entered into an undertaking, were able freely to invoke the section.[19]

Scope of disqualification orders and undertakings

10–3   The scope of the disqualification order or undertaking is obviously a crucial matter in the design of the legislation. It would be too limited for such an order to prohibit a person from acting only as director of a company, since there are many ways of controlling a company's management without being a director of the company. A way forward might have been to extend the prohibition to being a shadow director of a company but the Act in fact avoids the difficulties of that definition and takes an even broader approach. The prohibition imposed by a disqualification order or undertaking extends to "in any way, directly or indirectly, be[ing] concerned or tak[ing] part in the promotion, formation or management of a company".[20] The courts have taken a broad approach to what being concerned or taking part in the management of a company may embrace.[21] In addition, the disqualified person is prohibited from acting as an insolvency practitioner.[22] Finally, the disqualified person is denied access to limited liability

---

[16] 1986 Act ss.1 and 1A.

[17] 1986 Act s.8A. This is separate from the director's power to apply to the court for leave to act notwithstanding the undertaking, a power which applies also to orders: s.17. See below, para.10–3.

[18] Insolvency Rule r.7.47(1).

[19] *Re INS Realisations Ltd* [2006] 2 B.C.L.C. 239—director not normally able to use the section to challenge the facts on which the undertaking was premised, but in the particular circumstances of that case the power was used to cause the undertaking to cease to operate. See also *Re Morija Plc* [2008] 2 B.C.L.C. 313.

[20] 1986 Act ss.1(1) and 1A(1). If a court makes a disqualification order, it must cover all the activities set out in the statute, but the court could give the disqualified director limited leave to act despite the order. See *Re Gower Enterprises (No.2)* [1995] 2 B.C.L.C. 201; and *Re Seagull Manufacturing Co Ltd* [1996] 1 B.C.L.C. 51 and below.

[21] Management of a company is thought to require involvement in the general management and policy of the company and not just the holding of any post labelled managerial, though in small companies it may not be possible to distinguish between policy-setting and day-to-day management: *R. v Campbell* (1983) 78 Cr. App. R. 95 CA (acting as a management consultant); *Drew v HM Advocate*, 1996 S.L.T. 1062; *Re Market Wizard Systems (UK) Ltd* [1998] 2 B.C.L.C. 282.

[22] 1986 Act ss.1(1)(b) and 1A(1)(b).

through some corporate form other than a registered company, such as a limited liability partnership, a building society or an incorporated friendly society.[23]

Adherence to a disqualification order or undertaking is secured by criminal penalties[24] and, probably much more important, by personal liability for the debts and other liabilities of the company incurred during the time the disqualified person was involved in its management in breach of the order or undertaking.[25] This demonstrates that it is misuse of the facility of limited liability which lies at the heart of disqualification orders. Personal liability is also extended to any other person involved in the management of the company who knowingly acts on the instructions of a disqualified person.[26] Indeed, entrusting the management of a company to someone known to be disqualified might well be a basis for disqualifying the entrusting director on grounds of unfitness.[27]

The temporal scope of the disqualification order is also important in assessing its rigour. The approach of the Act is to set maxima and then to leave the actual disqualification period to be fixed in the order or undertaking. The maxima vary from one disqualification ground to another, the longest being in the case of disqualification on grounds of unfitness, where it is set at 15 years.[28] There is also a minimum period of two years in the case of unfitness in relation to insolvent companies.[29] After some lack of clarity in the cases the Court of Appeal has opted for setting the actual period of disqualification on grounds of unfitness by assessing how far below the conduct expected of a director the respondent fell.[30] In *Re Sevenoaks Stationers (Retail) Ltd*[31] the Court of Appeal divided the 2–15 year period for unfitness disqualification into three brackets, reflecting different levels of seriousness, though it cannot be said that it drew the dividing line between them very clearly.[32]

---

[23] 1986 Act ss.22A–C and E–F and the Limited Liability Partnership Regulations 2001 (SI 2001/1090), reg.4(2). The disqualified director is also prohibited from acting as the trustee of a charitable trust, whether that trust is incorporated or not: Charities Act 2011 ss.178 et seq., though the charity commissioners may give leave to act.

[24] 1986 Act ss.13 and 14. The equivalent offence in relation to acting when bankrupt has been held to be one of strict liability (*R. v Brockley* (1993) 92 Cr. App. R. 385 CA) and the arguments used to support that conclusion would seem equally applicable to the offence of acting when disqualified.

[25] 1986 Act s.15(1)(a).

[26] 1986 Act s.15(1)(b). The various people made personally liable by s.15 are jointly and severally liable with each other and with the company and any others who are for any reason personally liable: s.15(2).

[27] See *Re Moorgate Metals Ltd* [1995] 1 B.C.L.C. 503.

[28] 1986 Act ss.6(4) and 8(4).

[29] 1986 Act s.1A(2) applies the minima to undertakings as well.

[30] *Re Grayan Building Services Ltd* [1995] Ch. 241 CA. In this case the Court of Appeal held that the respondent could not reduce the period of disqualification by showing that, despite past shortcomings, he was unlikely to offend again. Such evidence, however, could be taken into account on an application for leave. See also *Re Westmid Packing Services Ltd* [1998] 2 All E.R. 124 at 131–132 CA.

[31] *Re Sevenoaks Stationers (Retail) Ltd* [1991] Ch. 164 at 176 CA.

[32] The court distinguished between a top bracket of over ten years for "particularly serious" cases; a middle bracket of six to ten years for serious cases "which do not merit the top bracket"; and a minimum bracket for "not very serious" cases. See also *Re Westmid Packing Services Ltd* [1998] 2 All E.R. 124 CA: fixing of length of disqualification to be done on the basis of "common sense")—ibid. at 132.

The prohibition (except that part of it which relates to acting as an insolvency practitioner) may be relaxed by the court, which may give leave to the disqualified person to act in a particular case. In the case of disqualification on grounds of unfitness under s.6, it is the practice to consider such applications at the same time as the disqualification order is made (in those, now minority, cases in which the disqualification is imposed by the court).[33] The leave granted, which obviously must not be so wide as to undermine the purposes of the Act,[34] often relates to other companies of which the applicant is already a director, which are trading successfully and whose future success is thought to be dependent on the continued involvement of the applicant. Often the leave is made conditional upon other steps being taken to protect the public, such as the appointment of an independent director to the board.[35] Overall, what the court has to do is to balance the need to protect the public, especially future creditors, as demonstrated by the conduct which has rendered the director unfit, with the interest of the director or other persons dependent on the company in relation to which leave is sought in the director having access to trading with limited liability.[36]

Compensation

10–4   The compensation provisions introduced in 2015 mean that the disqualification process may have significance for present as well as future creditors. The provisions apply to all classes of disqualification order or undertaking, provided that the company has become insolvent, the conduct for which the person was disqualified caused loss to one or more creditors and the disqualified person was at any time a director of it.[37] This appears to mean that only present or former directors may be subject to compensation orders (not shadow directors, for example) but that the conduct leading to the disqualification need not be conduct as a director (it might be conduct as a shadow director provided that person was at some point a director of the company). The initiation of the compensation procedure lies in the hands of the SS, by way of application to the court or acceptance of a compensation undertaking, who has two years from the initial disqualification order or undertaking to seek to add compensation to it—though

---

[33] *Secretary of State for Trade and Industry v Worth* [1994] 2 B.C.L.C. 113 CA, which indeed puts the applicant under some costs pressure to apply then, if his application is based on circumstances existing at the time of the order. If disqualification is by undertaking, a separate application for leave will, of course, be necessary. Leave cannot be given by the Secretary of State, only by the court.

[34] *Secretary of State for Trade and Industry v Barnett* [1998] 2 B.C.L.C. 64; *Re Britannia Homes Centres Ltd* [2001] 2 B.C.L.C. 63: leave refused where director with history of insolvencies wished to incorporate a new and wholly-owned company to carry on trading in same line of business.

[35] *Re Cargo Agency Ltd* [1992] B.C.L.C. 686; *Re Chartmore Ltd* [1990] B.C.L.C. 673; *Re Clenaware Systems Ltd* [2014] 1 B.C.L.C. 447. The practice has been followed in Scotland despite doubts whether the power to give leave confers upon the courts the power to specify conditions: *Secretary of State for Trade and Industry v Palfreman* [1995] 2 B.C.L.C. 301. If the conditions attached by the court are not strictly complied with, the director is in breach of the disqualification order and so exposed to personal liability: *Re Brian Sheridan Cars Ltd* [1996] 1 B.C.L.C. 327.

[36] *Re Barings Plc (No.3)* [2000] 1 W.L.R. 634; *Re Tech Textiles* [1998] 1 B.C.L.C. 259.

[37] 1986 Act s.15A(3)(4), insolvency being defined so as to include insolvent liquidation, administration and administrative receivership.

both may be dealt with at the same time.[38] In effect, the company's creditors piggy-back on the efforts of the public authorities to enforce the disqualification provisions. But the creditors have no independent right of action. The utility of the new compensation provisions thus depends on the SS's willingness to use them. Where there is clear loss to creditors and an available mechanism for distributing the compensation, there is no reason why the SS (or, rather, the Insolvency Service on his behalf) should not use them.[39] But a pre-condition of use of the compensation power is the existence of a disqualification order or undertaking. The Insolvency Service has power to seek these on grounds of unfitness—the most widely deployed ground—only where it regards this course of action as being "in the public interest".[40] It is unclear whether the Service will regard simple loss to creditors as a ground for seeking disqualification and then compensation. The amount of the compensation is not specified precisely, but is to be fixed (by the court or SS) having regard "in particular" to the amount of the loss caused, the nature of the conduct which led to the loss and any recompense already made.[41] This suggests that the loss suffered as a result of the director's conduct sets the outer boundary of the compensation to be awarded and, within that, the seriousness of the conduct will be crucial.

DISQUALIFICATION ON GROUNDS OF UNFITNESS

There are in fact two mechanisms in the 1986 Act for obtaining disqualification on unfitness grounds, the initiative in both cases lying with the SS. Under ss.6 and 7 the SS may apply to the court to have a director[42] or shadow director[43] of an insolvent[44] company disqualified where the SS thinks it is expedient in the public interest to do so.[45] Instead, the SS may accept a disqualification undertaking from the director in such circumstances.[46] Secondly, under s.8 the SS may apply to the court or accept an undertaking in relation to a similar range of

10–5

---

[38] 1986 Act s.15A(5).

[39] 1986 Act s.15B(2) provides that the compensation may be ordered in favour of the Secretary of State for distribution among the specified creditors (whoever they may be) or, as with wrongful trading awards, take the form of a contribution to the assets of the company. It is implicit in the second case that the company is in the hands of an insolvency practitioner. It is likely that the Insolvency Service will favour the latter method of distribution, if only because it avoids the costs of undertaking this task.

[40] 1986 Act s.7(1)(2A).

[41] 1986 Act s.15B(3).

[42] Including a de facto director (s.22(4)), i.e. a person who acts as a director even though he has not been validly appointed as a director or even though there has been no attempt at all to appoint him as director: *Re Kaytech International Plc* [1999] 2 B.C.L.C. 351 CA.

[43] 1986 Act s.22(5). On the meaning of "shadow director" see the previous chapter at para.9–7 and, below, Ch.16 at para.16–8.

[44] A company is insolvent if it goes into liquidation with insufficient assets to meet its liabilities, if an administration order has been made in relation to the company or if an administrative receiver is appointed: s.6(2). Thus, the disqualification provisions, unlike the wrongful trading provisions, are not confined to companies which go into insolvent liquidation. The court is specifically given power to look at the director's conduct post-insolvency. Sections 21A–C apply the Act to the specialised mechanisms for bank insolvencies and administrations.

[45] 1986 Act s.7(1).

[46] 1986 Act s.7(2A).

people, whether the company is insolvent or not, if he or she decides it is in the public interest to do so.[47] Under s.6 disqualification is mandatory for a minimum period of two years, if unfitness is found; the maximum period is 15 years under both sets of provisions.[48] Thus, although in the wake of the Cork Report business opposition fought off the idea of automatic disqualification in the case of directors of insolvent companies, the Government managed to avoid leaving the issue entirely to the discretion of the courts.[49]

Once the company has become insolvent, the director is liable to have the whole of his or her conduct as director of that company scrutinised for evidence of unfitness. Unlike the wrongful trading provisions considered in the previous chapter, that scrutiny is not confined to the director's conduct in the period immediately before the insolvency. Moreover, ss.6(2) and 8(2) include within the scrutiny the director's conduct of other companies where that person was a director or shadow director. These other companies may not have fallen into insolvency and there need be no particular business or other link between the "lead" company and the other companies in order for the director's conduct in relation to them to be taken into account.[50] In short, once the unfitness provisions are triggered, the scrutiny is capable of reaching out into the whole of the activities of the directors of that company in their capacity as directors.[51] In an important extension made by the 2015 Act these additional companies include companies incorporated outside Great Britain, so that geography no longer confines the court's examination—though evidential difficulties may do so.[52]

10–6 Despite the fact that ss.6–8 apply to shadow directors, in 2015 the disqualification provisions were extended to other "influencers" of directors' "unfit" conduct. This means that a disqualification order may be made against or a disqualification undertaking accepted from a person in accordance with whose directions or instructions the director has acted.[53] These additional provisions are ancillary in the sense that they may be invoked, in the case of an order against the influencer,[54] only if there is a disqualification order or an undertaking on grounds of unfitness in place against the director. In the case of an undertaking given by the influencer, one or other of those two situations must exist or the SS must be satisfied that an undertaking could be accepted from the director.[55] In many cases the influencer will be a shadow director and so can be tackled directly under ss.6–8. But the extension does not depend, as with a shadow director, on the board as a whole being accustomed to act in accordance with the non-director's

---

[47] Until 2015 this power was exercisable only on the basis of information obtained via official investigation into the company (under a variety of powers). The s.8 power was previously rarely used; it remains to be seen whether the reform will change that.

[48] 1986 Act s.6(1)(4), 8(4) and 1A(2).

[49] See A. Hicks, "Disqualification of Directors—Forty Years On" [1988] J.B.L. 27 at 35 and 38–40.

[50] *Secretary of State for Trade and Industry v Ivens* [1997] 2 B.C.L.C. 334 CA. However, it would seem that a director cannot be disqualified on the basis of his conduct of the non-lead companies alone.

[51] And, indeed, post-insolvency activities: s.6(2).

[52] The court may look at the conduct in relation to "one or more other companies or overseas companies": ss.6(1)(b),(1A) and 8(2),(2B).

[53] 1986 Act ss.8ZA(2), 8ZD(3).

[54] 1986 Act ss.8ZA(1), 8ZD(1).

[55] 1986 Act ss.8ZC(1), 8ZE(1).

directions or instruction. The focus is on the relationship between the influencer and the person disqualified. Nor does the person disqualified need to be accustomed to act as the influencer wishes, provided the conduct forming the basis of the underlying conduct was in fact influenced in the required way. The extension seems to have been part of a general policy which was being promoted in the run up to the 2015 Act of making transparent where control of companies lies and bringing responsibility home to the real controllers.[56]

The role of the Insolvency Service

When recommending what is now s.6, the Cork Committee[57] said that its aim was to "replace by a far more rigorous system the present ineffective provisions". The effectiveness in practice of s.6 can be said to depend upon two matters. The first is the assiduity of the Insolvency Service, to which the SS normally delegates disqualification powers, in enforcing the provisions of the Act; and the second is the courts' approach to s.6, especially their interpretation of the central concept of unfitness and how they set the period of disqualification.

10–7

In order to maximise the chances of applications being made, the Cork Committee[58] recommended that applications by liquidators or, with leave, other creditors should be permitted, and so confining applications to the SS was regarded at the time of the passage of the Insolvency Act 1986 as a retrograde step. There are two reasons why the Insolvency Service might not prove effective. The first is lack of information about directors' conduct, especially when the company is being wound up voluntarily, so that the Official Receiver is not involved.[59] This is addressed by the imposition of a requirement on liquidators, administrators and receivers to report to the SS on the conduct of directors and shadow directors of companies for whose affairs they are responsible though the quality of the information provided is not always high.[60] In 2015 the obligation was strengthened to require a report of relevant information in all cases and not only where the office holder believed there had been a breach of s.6.[61] Secondly, there was doubt about the quantity and quality of the resources the government would devote to the enforcement of the legislation. Although the early efforts of the Insolvency Service were criticised,[62] the enforcement effort is now substantial, as we have noted, though only a small

---

[56] BIS Ch.4 ("Opaque corporate control through irresponsible 'front' directors").

[57] See above, fn.1 at para.1809.

[58] See above, fn.1 at para.1818.

[59] In Scotland, where there are no Official Receivers, even compulsory liquidations are handled by insolvency practitioners and the potential scope of the problem is accordingly greater.

[60] See S. Wheeler, "Directors' Disqualification: Insolvency Practitioners and the Decision-making Process" (1995) 15 L.S. 283. Moreover, the statutory scheme does not bite if the company is simply struck off the register (see below, paras 33–35 et seq.) without going through any of these procedures.

[61] 1986 Act s.7A and SI 2016/180. The obligation is to provide any information about conduct which may help the Insolvency Service decide whether to implement disqualification proceedings. Previously, this information was to be provided by the insolvency practitioner only if the Service asked for it. The request power now exists in relation to all persons other than the insolvency practitioners (s.7(4)).

[62] National Audit Office, *The Insolvency Service Executive Agency: Company Director Disqualification* (1993) H.C. 907.

percentage of the directors of failed companies are disqualified. Nevertheless, it is clear that the Service still experiences difficulties in commencing applications within the two-year period originally permitted by the statute[63] and in prosecuting them with sufficient vigour to avoid striking out on grounds of delay or infringement of the director's human rights (i.e. the right to have one's civil rights and obligations determined within a reasonable time, as required by art.6(1) of the European Convention on Human Rights).[64] The response of the legislature in 2015 was to extend the period for commencing proceedings to three years—though this does not help, but rather exacerbates, the human rights issue.

There is an additional risk that the human rights of directors will be threatened by the disparity between the state resources available to the Insolvency Service and those available to the director, who, in the case of a small company, may be virtually bankrupt. In particular, there is a danger that the impoverished director will give a disqualification undertaking because he or she cannot afford the costs of a full-scale court examination of the issues. So far, these issues have been addressed rather little in litigation, though appreciation of the situation may lie behind the courts' unwillingness to impose too high a level of competence on directors under the disqualification provisions.[65] As far as the European Convention on Human Rights is concerned, both the domestic courts and the European Court of Human Rights seem agreed that disqualification proceedings are civil in nature, not criminal, so that a lower, but not negligible, standard of fairness is required in conducting them.[66] In particular, the domestic courts have concluded that the Human Rights Convention does not require the automatic exclusion of evidence against the director which was obtained from him or her under statutory powers of compulsion.[67] However, the exclusion of such evidence has been achieved in fact, as a matter of interpretation of the domestic law, in the case of the statutory provisions most likely to be of use to the Insolvency Service. Under ss.235 and 236 of the Insolvency Act 1986 the liquidator of a company and the Official Receiver are empowered to require answers to questions which they put to directors of companies in insolvent liquidation and to require the

---

[63] 1986 Act s.7(2). The court may give leave to commence the application out of time, though the Secretary of State must show a good reason for any extension: *Re Copecrest Ltd* [1994] 2 B.C.L.C. 284 CA; *Re Instant Access Properties Ltd* [2012] 1 B.C.L.C. 710.

[64] *Re Manlon Trading Ltd* [1996] Ch. 136; *Davies v UK* [2006] 2 B.C.L.C. 351 ECtHR (a case decided in 2002); *Eastaway v UK* [2006] 2 B.C.L.C. 361 ECtHR. However, in the last of these cases the Court of Appeal refused to set aside the disqualification agreement entered into by the director under the *Carecraft* procedure (above, fn.15), even though the ECtHR had held the proceedings to have taken too long: *Eastaway v Secretary of State for Trade and Industry* [2007] B.C.C. 550. The National Audit Office, above, fn.62 para.18; found that the Insolvency Service in most cases took nearly the full two-year period permitted to bring an application and that up to a further four years might elapse before a disqualification order was made, during which period the director was free to carry on business with limited liability.

[65] See para.10–10, below and the extra-judicial remarks of Lord Hoffmann, Fourth Annual Leonard Sainer Lecture in (1997) Company Lawyer 194.

[66] *R. v Secretary of State for Trade and Industry Ex p. McCormick* [1998] B.C.C. 379 CA; *DC v United Kingdom* [2000] B.C.C. 710 ECtHR.

[67] *Official Receiver v Stern* [2000] 1 W.L.R. 2230 CA. Contrast the decision in *Saunders v United Kingdom* [1998] 1 B.C.L.C. 362 ECtHR.

production of documents, but the Court of Appeal has held that these provisions cannot be used for the purpose of supporting disqualification applications.[68]

The role of the court

Turning to the role of the courts, some guidance is given in Sch.1 on how the courts (and indeed the SS) should approach disqualification determinations. The Schedule was revised in 2015 so as to set out the relevant matters at a higher level of generality than previously, so as to emphasise the width of the courts' investigation. The applicability of the Schedule was also widened since it now applies to all disqualification decisions, not just to the determination of unfitness.[69] In all cases the court must take into account the extent to which the company was in breach of legislative requirements (not necessarily just the requirements of the companies legislation), the defendant's responsibility for the company[70] becoming insolvent, the loss actually or potentially caused by the defendant's conduct and the frequency with which a director has engaged in conduct caught by the Schedule. Where the defendant is a director—the standard case—the court must have regard to the director's breach of fiduciary duties or other duties applying specifically to directors.

10–8

Breach of commercial morality

It is possible to divide the cases in which the courts have found unfitness into two rough categories: probity and competence.[71] However, it must be remembered that the concept of unfitness is open-ended, so that it cannot be claimed that all potential, or even actual, disqualification applications can be forced into one or other of these categories. Further, in the nature of things, many disqualification cases display aspects from both categories. Nevertheless, it is thought that identifying the two categories is a useful starting point.

10–9

The first category, breach of commercial morality,[72] has at its centre the idea of conducting a business at the expense of its creditors. A leading example, though only an example, of such conduct is the Phoenix company described by the Cork Committee in terms of a person who sets up an undercapitalised company, allows it to become insolvent, forms a new company (often with assets purchased at a discount from the liquidator of the old company), carries on trading much as before, and repeats the process perhaps several times, leaving

---

[68] *Re Pantmaenog Timber Co Ltd* [2001] 4 All E.R. 588 CA.

[69] 1986 Act s.12C (replacing the former s.9).

[70] This includes not just the "lead" company but all other companies, including overseas ones, brought in under s.6(1)(b).

[71] "Those who trade under the regime of limited liability and who avail themselves of the privileges of that regime must accept the standards of probity and competence to which the law requires company directors to conform" (per Neill LJ in *Re Grayan Building Services Ltd* [1995] Ch. 241 CA).

[72] Of course, simple fraud will be a basis for disqualification. As a proposition of substantive law this is straightforward; the complications are procedural. See *Secretary of State v Doffmann (No.2)* [2011] 2 B.C.L.C. 541.

behind him each time a trail of unpaid creditors.[73] More generally, the courts have been alert to find unfitness where the directors have apparently attempted to trade on the backs of the company's creditors.[74] It was thought at one time that particular obloquy attached to directors who attempted to trade out their difficulties by using as working capital in the business monies owed to the Crown by way of income tax, national insurance contributions or VAT, on the grounds that the Crown was an involuntary creditor. Although that view has been rejected by the Court of Appeal, the same court has affirmed that, in relation to any creditor, paying only those creditors who pressed for payment and taking advantage of those creditors who did not, in order to provide the working capital which the company needed, is a clear example of unfitness.[75] If the directors of the financially troubled company are at the same time paying themselves salaries which are out of proportion to the company's trading success (or lack of it) or making disguised distributions to themselves of corporate assets, the likelihood of a disqualification order being made is only increased.[76]

Recklessness and incompetence

10–10   In the previous section the cases considered highlighted opportunistic behaviour by directors towards the creditors of the company by failing to pay the creditors whilst continuing trading. The cases considered in this section focus more generally on the recklessness or incompetence of the directors' conduct of the business. They may pay the creditors the money due to them, as long as the company is able to do so, but the directors may be regarded as responsible for bringing about the situation where the company ultimately has to default on its commitments because of the way they have chosen to run it. In many cases, of course, both aspects of unfitness can be found.

The early cases put liability on the basis of recklessness,[77] but more recently it has been said that "incompetence or negligence to a very marked degree"[78] would be enough. The danger which the courts have to avoid in this area is that of treating any business venture which collapses as evidence of negligence. To do so would be to discourage the taking of commercial risks, which must be the life-blood of corporate activity. However, creating a space for proper risk-taking is no longer thought to require relieving directors of all objective standards of

---

[73] Cork Committee, para.1813. For the operation of the rule forbidding re-use of corporate names in this situation, see Ch.9, above. For examples in the disqualification case law, see *Re Travel Mondial (UK) Ltd* [1991] B.C.L.C. 120; *Re Linvale Ltd* [1993] B.C.L.C. 654; *Re Swift 736 Ltd* [1993] B.C.L.C. 1.

[74] *Re Keypak Homecare Ltd* [1990] B.C.L.C. 440.

[75] *Re Sevenoaks Stationers (Retail) Ltd* [1991] Ch. 164 CA; *Secretary of State for Trade and Industry v McTighe (No.2)* [1996] 2 B.C.L.C. 477 CA.

[76] *Re Synthetic Technology Ltd* [1993] B.C.C. 549; *Secretary of State v Van Hengel* [1995] 1 B.C.L.C. 545; *Secretary of State for Business Innovation and Skills v Doffman (No.2)* [2011] 2 B.C.L.C. 541.

[77] *Re Stanford Services Ltd* [1987] B.C.L.C. 607.

[78] *Re Sevenoaks Stationers (Retail) Ltd* [1991] Ch. 164 CA at 184.

conduct. In *Re Barings Plc (No.5)*[79] the Court of Appeal gave guidance on what constitutes a high degree of incompetence in the common situation of the directors having properly delegated functions to lower levels of management. Provided the articles of association permit such delegation, as they inevitably will in large organisations, delegation in itself is not evidence of unfitness. However, the responsible director may be found to be unfit if there is put in place no system for supervising the discharge of the delegated function or if the director in question is not able to understand the information produced by the supervisory system. In other words, in large organisations directors must ensure there are in place adequate internal systems for monitoring risk and failure to do so may be grounds for disqualification.

However, the proposition that directors "have a continuing duty to acquire and maintain a sufficient knowledge and understanding of the company's business to enable them properly to discharge their duties as directors"[80] applies not just to duties delegated to sub-board level but also to reliance by directors on their board colleagues to take responsibility for particular functions and duties. Although such reliance is again in principle acceptable, so that there can be a division of functions on the board, most obviously between executive and non-executive directors, all directors must maintain a minimum level of knowledge and understanding about the business so that important problems can be identified and dealt with before they bring the company down. Thus, in *Re Richborough Furniture Ltd*[81] a director was disqualified for three years, on the basis of "lack of experience, knowledge and understanding. She did not have enough experience or knowledge to know what she should do in the face of the problems of pressing creditors, escalating Crown debts and lack of capital. It seems that she was not sufficiently skilful as regards the accounts functions to see that the records were inadequate." Disqualification of incompetent directors has thus become a crucial tool in the enforcement of directors' standards of competence, perhaps more so than actions for breach of the director's general duty of care,[82] which must be funded by private litigants. The two areas of law will no doubt continue to influence each other.

In this area, particular importance is attached by the courts to failure by directors **10–11** to file annual returns or, in future, confirmation statements, produce audited accounts and to keep proper accounting records.[83] These are the practical expressions of a more general view that all directors must keep themselves au fait with the financial position of their company and make sure that it complies with

---

[79] *Re Barings Plc (No.5)* [2000] 1 B.C.L.C. 523 CA. The case involved the insolvency of an old and respected merchant bank brought about by the huge losses generated by the unauthorised trading activities of a junior employee whose activities were neither well understood nor effectively monitored by his superiors.

[80] *Re Barings Plc (No.5)* [2000] 1 B.C.L.C. 523 at 536. See also *Re Westmid Packing Services Ltd* [1998] 2 All E.R. 124; and *Re Vintage Hallmark Plc* [2007] 1 B.C.L.C. 788.

[81] *Re Richborough Furniture Ltd* [1996] 1 B.C.L.C. 507.

[82] See para.16–15.

[83] These may be ingredients in a finding of unfitness, even though, as we see below, para.10–14, non-compliance with the reporting requirements of the legislation is a separate ground of disqualification, albeit only for up to five years. For further discussion of what is required in this area see Ch.21.

the reporting requirements of the companies legislation, for otherwise they cannot know what corrective action, if any, needs to be taken.[84] Although this duty may fall with particular emphasis on those responsible for the financial side of the company, all directors must keep themselves informed about the company's basic financial position.[85] On the other hand, seeking and acting on competent outside advice when financial difficulties arise will be an indication of competence, even if the plan recommended does not pay off and the company eventually collapses.[86] It should also be remembered that, in the disqualification area, the courts have required a "marked degree" of negligence[87] before declaring a director unfit. There is a contrast here with wrongful trading and the standard of care under the directors' general duties[88] where there is no suggestion that a low standard of care is to be applied to directors.[89] It is suggested that this contrast is explained by the fact that a disqualification order can often have the effect of depriving the director of his livelihood and that, once unfitness is found, a two-year disqualification is mandatory.

DISQUALIFICATION ON GROUNDS OTHER THAN UNFITNESS

Serious offences

10–12 The remaining provisions of the 1986 Act permit, but do not require, the court to disqualify a director, on various grounds. With one exception, disqualification here is based on a court order. Disqualification by means of undertaking is not generally available. These other grounds of disqualification will be dealt with briefly, partly because they have not generated as much controversy as the unfitness ground. Disqualifications under s.2 (disqualification on conviction of an indictable offence) apparently constitute the second most common source (after unfitness) for disqualification orders.[90]

---

[84] *Re Firedart Ltd* [1994] 2 B.C.L.C. 340; *Re New Generation Engineers Ltd* [1993] B.C.L.C. 435.

[85] *Re City Investment Centres Ltd* [1992] B.C.L.C. 956; *Secretary of State v Van Hengel* [1995] 1 B.C.L.C. 545; *Re Majestic Recording Studios Ltd* [1989] B.C.L.C. 1; *Re Continental Assurance Co of London Plc* [1977] 1 B.C.L.C. 48; *Re Kaytech International Plc* [1999] 2 B.C.L.C. 351 CA.

[86] *Re Douglas Construction Services Ltd* [1988] B.C.L.C. 397. Conversely, ignoring a plan produced by outside accountants is likely to be characterised as "obstinately and unjustifiably backing [the director's] own assessment of the company's business": *Re GSAR Realisations Ltd* [1993] B.C.L.C. 409.

[87] See above, fn.78.

[88] See para.9–6, above, and para.16–16, below.

[89] Of course, keeping an insolvent company going can be grounds for disqualification for being unfit but only in strong cases. See, for example, *Re Living Images Ltd* [1996] 1 B.C.L.C. 348, where the directors were aware of the company's parlous condition and keeping it going was described as "a gamble at long odds" and "the taking of unwarranted risks with creditors' money", so that there was a lack of probity involved and not just negligence. cf. the refusal to make a disqualification order in *Re Dawson Print Group Ltd* [1987] B.C.L.C. 601; *Re Bath Glass Ltd* [1988] B.C.L.C. 329; *Re CU Fittings Ltd* [1989] B.C.L.C. 556; and *Secretary of State v Gash* [1997] 1 B.C.L.C. 341.

[90] A. Hicks, *Disqualification of Directors: No Hiding Place for the Unfit?* (ACCA Research Report 59, 1998), p.35, found that in 1996 about one quarter of those at that time disqualified were in that position as a result of a s.2 disqualification. The proportion has probably fallen since then, with the rise of unfitness disqualifications, especially via undertakings. The Companies House figures (above,

In relation to serious offences, there are two routes to a disqualification order, depending upon whether the person concerned has actually been convicted of an offence. If there has been a conviction, a disqualification order may be made against a person, whether a director or not, who has committed an indictable offence in connection with the promotion, formation, management, liquidation or striking off of a company or in connection with the receivership or management of its property.[91] Usually, the disqualification will be ordered by the court by which the person is convicted and at the time of his or her conviction. However, if the convicting court does not consider the issue, the SS or the liquidator or any past or present creditor or member of the company in relation to which the offence was committed may apply to any court having jurisdiction to wind up the company to impose the disqualification.[92] Here, too, the courts have taken a wide view of what "in connection with the management of the company" means in this context.[93] Where a person has been convicted of an equivalent offence outside Great Britain the SS may seek a disqualification order from the High Court or Court of Session or accept an undertaking from that person.[94]

Where there has not been a conviction, but the company is being wound up, then if it appears that a person has been guilty of the offence of fraudulent trading[95] or has been guilty as an officer[96] of the company of any fraud in relation to it or any breach of duty as an officer, then the court having jurisdiction to wind up the company may impose a disqualification order.[97]

Disqualification in connection with civil liability for fraudulent or wrongful trading

In addition to the array of civil orders which the court may make under ss.213 **10–13** and 214 of the Insolvency Act 1986 when it finds fraudulent or wrongful trading,[98] s.10 of the Disqualification Act adds the power to make a disqualification order. The court may act here on its own motion, that is, whether or not an application is made to it by anyone for an order to be made. Since there

---

fn.14) do not distinguish among disqualifications on any of the grounds laid down in ss.2–5 of the Act, but indicate that in 2014/15 217 out of 1227 disqualifications took place under ss.2–5.
[91] 1986 Act s.2.
[92] 1986 Act s.16(2). If the criminal court does consider the matter and decide not to impose disqualification, it is an abuse of process to pursue the same issue before a civil court: *Secretary of State v Weston* [2014] B.C.C. 581. However, the courts have permitted disqualification orders to be pursued in such cases under other grounds for disqualification contained in the Act: *Secretary of State v Rayna* [2001] 2 B.C.L.C. 48; *Re Denis Hilton Ltd* [2002] 1 B.C.L.C. 302.
[93] *R. v Goodman* [1994] 1 B.C.L.C. 349 CA (insider dealing by a director in the shares of his company); *R. v Georgiou* (1988) 4 B.C.C. 625; *R. v Ward, The Times*, 10 April 1997 (conspiracy to defraud by creating a false market in shares during a takeover bid); *R. v Creggy* [2008] 1 B.C.L.C. 625 CA (facilitating criminal activity by third parties).
[94] 1986 Act s.5A introduced in 2015.
[95] See para.9–5.
[96] Also included are the usual cast of liquidators, receivers and administrative receivers and also shadow directors: s.4(1)(b) and (2).
[97] 1986 Act s.4, upon application by those listed in s.16(2). It is unclear whether the breach of duty referred to must involve the commission of a criminal offence, but the use of the word "guilty" suggests so.
[98] See para.9–8.

are only low levels to litigation to recover contributions in cases of fraudulent and wrongful trading, the number of disqualifications is also low.[99]

Failure to comply with reporting requirements

10–14   Again, there are separate provisions according to whether the person to be disqualified has been convicted or not. If he or she has been convicted of a summary offence in connection with a failure to file a document with or give notice of a fact to the Registrar, then the convicting court may disqualify that person if in the previous five years he has had at least three convictions (including the current one) or default orders against him for non-compliance with the reporting requirements of the Companies and Insolvency Acts.[100] If the current conviction is on indictment, then the provisions of s.2 (above) apply, but, where the current conviction is summary, the fact that the earlier convictions were on indictment does not prevent the convicting summary court from taking them into account.[101]

Where there has been no conviction, the SS and the others mentioned in s.16(2)[102] may apply to the court having jurisdiction to wind up the companies in question for disqualification orders to be made on the grounds that the respondent has been "persistently in default" in complying with the reporting requirements of the Companies and Insolvency Acts.[103] The "three convictions or defaults in five years" rule applies here too, but without prejudice to proof of persistent default in any other manner.[104] Since the offences involved in these sections may be only summary ones, the maximum period of disqualification is limited to five, instead of the usual 15, years. Nevertheless, the fact that these provisions are in the Act at all is a testimony to the importance attached recently to timely filing of accounts and other documents. However, the improvement recorded in this area may be due more to the introduction of late filing penalties than the disqualification orders.

REGISTER OF DISQUALIFICATION ORDERS

10–15   Crucial to the effective operation of the disqualification machinery is that publicity should be given the names of those who have been disqualified. Thus, the Act requires the SS to create such a register of orders and undertakings, which register is open to public inspection.[105] The register is also to contain details of any leave given to a disqualified person to act despite the disqualification. However, either because of doubts about the accuracy of the register or to relieve

---

[99] No disqualification order was made under s.10 in the period 2010–2015 (Companies House, above, fn.14) though it is possible that disqualification in relation to fraudulent trading was imposed in a few cases under s.4.

[100] 1986 Act s.5.

[101] Contrast the wording of subs.(1) and (2) of s.5.

[102] See above, text attached to fn.92.

[103] 1986 Act s.3.

[104] 1986 Act s.3(2).

[105] 1986 Act s.18 and the Companies (Disqualification Orders) Regulations 2009 (SI 2009/2471).

the Registrar of the need to check it, the 2006 Act contains a power for the SS to make regulations about the returns which companies have to make to the Registrar about the appointment of directors and secretaries. The regulations may require the return to contain the statement in relation to a disqualified person that the leave of the court to act has been obtained.[106]

BANKRUPTS

The prohibition on undischarged bankrupts acting as directors or being involved **10–16** in the management of companies can be traced back to the Companies Act 1928. Although bankruptcy does not necessarily connote any wrongdoing, the policy against permitting those who have been so spectacularly unsuccessful in the management of their own finances taking charge of other people's money is so self-evident that it has not proved controversial. The prohibition is now contained in s.11 of the 1986 Act, which makes so acting a criminal offence,[107] and the main point of interest about it for present purposes is that it is an automatic disqualification, not dependent upon the making of a disqualification order by the court. In 2002 the prohibition was extended to include acting in breach of a bankruptcy restriction order or undertaking, themselves creations of the legislative reforms of that year.[108] Bankruptcy restriction orders and undertakings, clearly modelled to some extent on directors' disqualification orders and undertakings, put restrictions on a former bankrupt's activities after discharge from bankruptcy, in general an earlier event than had previously been the case.

However, the disqualification is not absolute, because the bankrupt or previous bankrupt may apply to the court for leave to act in the management of a company, other than as an insolvency practitioner.[109] In other words, the statute really reverses the burden of taking action, by placing it upon the bankrupt to show that he or she may be safely involved in the management of companies rather than upon the state to demonstrate to a court that the bankrupt ought not to be allowed to act.

OTHER CASES

Disqualification has become a popular legislative technique in recent years. The **10–17** 1986 Act itself applies to those in charge of other corporate bodies as if they were companies formed under the Companies Acts, such as building societies, incorporated friendly societies, NHS foundation trusts, registered societies and

---

[106] CA 2006 s.1189. At the time of writing no regulations have been made.
[107] Acting in breach of the prohibition also attracts personal liability for the company's debts (s.15—though this may not be of much utility in relation to bankrupts) and could, apparently, give rise to the making of a disqualification order under s.2 (above, para.10–9): *R. v Young* [1990] B.C.C. 549 CA).
[108] These changes were effected by Sch.20 to the Enterprise Act 2002, introducing a new Sch.4A into the Insolvency Act 1986.
[109] IA1986 ss.11(1) and 390(4)(a).

charitable incorporated organisations.[110] Another extension is to apply disqualification to the directors of companies for breaches of provisions other than company law rules. Thus, ss.9A–9E make provision for disqualification orders and undertakings in relation to directors (and shadow directors) of companies which have broken competition law where a court or regulator is of the opinion that the director is in consequence unfit to be involved in the management of a company. Finally, breaches of sector-specific rules, such as in the banking sector, could form the basis for disqualification, for example, on grounds of unfitness, but the Government stopped short of giving sectoral regulators disqualification powers under the 1986 Act: instead, they have to operate through the Insolvency Service. Of course, sector-specific legislation may give sectoral regulators disqualification powers in relation to the areas of economic activity they regulate, as is the case with financial regulators—but such provisions are outside the scope of this chapter.

CONCLUSION

10–18 For many years the disqualification provisions of the successive Companies Acts seemed to make little impact. Important in principle as a technique for dealing with corporate wrongdoing of one sort or another, especially on the part of directors, the practical consequences of the provisions were limited. The combination of the substantive reforms recommended by the Cork Committee and of acceptance by Government that the promotion of small, and not-so-small, businesses needed to be accompanied by action to raise the standards of directors' behaviour and to protect the public from the scheming and the incompetent, brought the disqualification provisions to the fore. Further, as we have seen in Ch.7,[111] controversy about whether directors whose companies are convicted of the proposed new corporate killing offence should be disqualified from acting in connection with businesses delayed progress on that reform proposal, though in the end the legislation did not make use of the disqualification technique. As to disqualification orders in company law, judged by the level of disqualification orders and undertakings, the provisions now have a substantial impact. An independent survey[112] found a widespread consensus that the provisions performed a useful role and should be retained, although they were certainly capable of improvement, especially at the level of securing compliance with the disqualification orders made.[113]

However, it would be wrong to see disqualification as solely a response to abuses of limited liability within small companies. There is some evidence that

---

[110] 1986 Act ss.22A–C, E–F.

[111] See above, para.7–45.

[112] By A. Hicks; see fn.90, above. The report makes a number of interesting and thought-provoking suggestions for reform. For a more sceptical account see R. Williams, "Disqualifying Directors: a Remedy Worse than the Disease?" (2007) 7 J.C.L.S. 213.

[113] *Companies in 2005–2006* (above, fn.13) reveals that some 90 prosecutions for breach of disqualification orders or of the prohibition on bankrupts acting as directors were launched in that year, producing 81 convictions. More recent statistics appear not to be available. It is difficult to know whether this relatively modest total indicates a high level of compliance with the disqualifications or a low level of detection of breaches.

the public authorities use disqualification to inflict reputational harm on directors of companies which have failed in circumstances giving rise to public condemnation and where no other remedy is readily available. We noted above the disqualification of directors of Barings Bank which collapsed as a result of failure to identify and prevent large foreign exchange bets being placed by a junior trader.[114] Another example is the disqualification undertakings, offered by the four directors of MG Rover Group Ltd after its well-publicised collapse, and accepted by the SS. The company had gone into administration in April 2005, owing creditors nearly £1.3 billion, causing many employees to lose their jobs and ending large-scale, British-owned car manufacturing. In this case, the ground work for the disqualification had been provided through a lengthy and expensive public investigation into the collapse of the company.[115] The removal of the investigation pre-condition to the use of s.8 by the SS may increase this use of the provision in the future.

---

[114] See above, fn.79.
[115] Department of Business Innovation and Skills, Press Release, 9 May 2011.

CHAPTER 11

LEGAL CAPITAL, MINIMUM CAPITAL AND VERIFICATION

MEANING OF CAPITAL

In the previous two chapters we saw how the law applies sanctions to the **11–1**
controllers of companies who abuse the facility of limited liability. In particular,
personal liability for the company's obligations and disqualification from being
involved in the management of a company in the future are techniques used by
the law in these cases. Both are ex post techniques, i.e. the sanctions are applied
after the event, normally after the company has fallen into insolvency. Sanctions
are applied on the basis, most often, that the court has concluded that the
controllers have infringed some broad and general standard laid down for the
assessment of their conduct, for example, engaging in "wrongful" trading or
displaying "unfit" conduct. In this chapter and the next two, by contrast, we
consider ex ante approaches to controlling abuse of limited liability, i.e. the rules,
generally of a precise and detailed character, which apply before the company is
in insolvency or even in the region of insolvency. Given that creditors' claims are
confined to the assets of the company, the techniques now discussed seek to
ensure that the shareholders contribute to or maintain in the company an
appropriate level of assets for the benefit of creditors. A good level of
shareholder-contributed assets, it can be argued, will both reduce the chances of
the company falling into insolvency and increase the likely size of the pay-out to
creditors if insolvency does occur. This idea can be given expression in a number
of ways, which will be explored in these chapters.

The traditional protective mechanism of company law in this area, which is as
old as limited liability itself, involves laying down rules about the raising and

maintenance of "capital". "Capital" is a word of many meanings,[1] but in company law it is used in a very restricted sense. It connotes the value of the assets contributed to the company by those who subscribe for its shares. By and large, the value of what the company receives from investors in exchange for its shares constitutes its capital.[2] One talks about the value of what is received, rather than the assets themselves, because those assets will change form in the course of the business activities of the company. If the company receives cash in exchange for its shares, the directors will turn that cash into other types of asset in order to promote its business: indeed, if they did not, they would probably be in breach of duty. So, the focus is on using the number in the company's accounts which indicates the value of what was received by the company in the exchange for the shares to constrain the actions of the company in various ways, in UK law principally to constrain the company's freedom to make distributions to its shareholders.

The value of the assets which the company receives in exchange for its shares (its legal capital) will normally be less than the total value of the company's assets. Even where the company has not yet begun to trade, it may have raised money in ways other than share issues. For example, it may have borrowed money from a bank or a group of banks, which loan contributes to the company's cash assets. The value of such loans does not count towards its legal capital, however. This is because the aim of the capital rules is to protect creditors as a class and only assets contributed by shareholders do this effectively.[3] The cash provided by the lender will be exactly counterbalanced by an increase on the liabilities side of the company's balance sheet, so that the creditors as a whole are no better off. Once a company has begun trading and if it has done so profitably, it will have assets which represent the profits. These, too, do not count as part of the company's legal capital: they may have been earned, at least in part, by deploying the shareholders' contributions to the business but the profits were not contributed by the shareholders. Nevertheless, the totality of the surplus of assets over the liabilities is a very important accounting concept and is often referred to as "the shareholders' equity" or the company's "net asset value". The law distinguishes between the company's "net asset value" and the value of the assets contributed by the shareholders (its legal capital). Broadly, the company is free to distribute to the shareholders the difference between the net asset value and the legal capital value—provided that is a positive number! By contrast, therefore, if the company trades unsuccessfully, it may run through any profits made in

---

[1] cf. Capital punishment, capital letter, capital ship, capital city, capital of a pillar, capital and labour, capital and income, and "capital!".

[2] In *Kellar v Williams* [2000] 2 B.C.L.C. 390, the Privy Council accepted that it was possible for an investor to make a capital contribution to a company, other than in exchange for the purchase of shares, in which case the contribution is to be treated in the same way as a share premium (see below, para.11–8). Such a procedure is very unusual, of course, since the contributor is left substantially in the dark as to what he or she is getting in exchange for the contribution. However, one can see that an existing shareholder in a company wholly controlled by him might act in this way. The difficulty is to distinguish between such a capital contribution and a loan to the company.

[3] Of course, a contribution made by a creditor may in fact benefit other creditors, for example, a loan made to a company just before insolvency may mean the creditors as a class obtain a larger percentage pay out than if the loan had not been made, but that benefit to the earlier creditors is paid for by the later lender.

previous years and begin to eat into the value of the assets contributed by its shareholders. In this situation its net asset value may fall below the value of its legal capital, and no distribution is permitted to be made. In short, the value of the assets contributed by the shareholders is not a measure of the company's net worth, which may be higher or lower than the legal capital figure at any one time and only by chance will the two figures be the same.

An alternative use of the legal capital figure is to use it to identify the amount the **11-2** shareholders must contribute to the company's assets before it is permitted to begin trading. Such rules are called minimum or initial capital rules. British law has never made much use of this concept. Minimum capital has been required of public companies, since the implementation in the UK of the Second European Company Law Directive of 1977,[4] but private companies are not subject to the rule and, historically, apart from a short period in the early years of modern company law in the middle of the nineteenth century, British law has not attached importance to minimum capital requirements for any class of company.

However, and contrary to what is sometimes thought, British law currently does make use of legal capital to constrain to a significant extent distributions to shareholders. On this approach the law leaves companies wholly or substantially free to decide their own level of legal capital, but attaches legal consequences to the amount of legal capital the company in fact chooses to raise. This second policy has been central to British company law since its origins and remains so. From the early days the courts have laid down that, given limited liability, "it is clearly against the intention of the legislature that any portion of the capital should be returned to the shareholders without the statutory conditions being complied with".[5] The rule against the return of capital to shareholders is elaborated in a three main ways. First, as noted, the value of the company's legal capital is used as a yardstick to measure the amount of a company's assets which may be returned to the shareholders by way of a dividend or other form of distribution. We consider this aspect of the "no return" policy in Ch.12. All modern jurisdictions place constraints on distributions to shareholders but it is controversial whether such rules should be based on the concept of legal capital, as the British ones currently are. Secondly, the repurchase or redemption of its shares by the company may occur only through tightly controlled procedures which aim to maintain the value of the company's legal capital. Thirdly, the company may reduce the value of its legal capital in its accounts only through procedures which are designed to protect the interests of the creditors. The second and third manifestations of the "no return" policy are considered in Ch.13, together with the rules prohibiting a company from giving financial assistance to a person in connection with the acquisition by that person of its shares. The second and third sets of rules are normally lumped together under the heading of "capital maintenance", though it is debatable whether the financial assistance rules are linked to the notion of legal capital.

---

[4] Council Directive 77/91/EC [1977] O.J. L26/1 (now replaced by Directive 2012/30/EU [2012] O.J. L315/74, to which version the references in this chapter relate). See para.6–11.
[5] *Re Exchange Banking Co, Flitcroft's Case* (1882) 21 Ch. D. 519, per Jessel MR.

In this chapter we elaborate some of the basic elements of the concept of legal capital and consider in particular the role of the minimum or initial legal capital rule.

NOMINAL VALUE AND SHARE PREMIUMS

Nominal value

11–3   We have talked so far about legal capital being the amount that the company receives from those who subscribe for its shares. Very broadly, this is true, but the law arrives at this result in a surprisingly complex way. This is because the law distinguishes between the "nominal" value of the share and any amount received above the nominal or "par" value, which is referred to as the "premium". The Act stipulates that shares in a limited company "must each have a fixed nominal value" and that an allotment of shares not meeting this requirement is void.[6] In other words a monetary value needs to be attached to the company's shares. In consequence, one talks of the company having issued a certain number of "£1 shares" or "10p shares" and so on. The par value is a doubtfully useful concept because it does not normally indicate the price at which the share is likely to be issued to investors; still less the price at which the share is likely to trade in the market after issue. The only linkage between the nominal value of the share and the price the subscriber pays for it is the rule that a share may not be issued at less than its nominal value[7]—often referred to as the "no discount" rule.[8] However, the company, whilst being obliged to attach a nominal value to the share, maintains full control over its level. This freedom, coupled with the "no discount" rule, gives the company an incentive to keep the nominal value of the share low in relation to its issue price. The lower the nominal value, the less likely the company is to find itself in the situation, either now or in the future, where investors will be prepared to buy its shares only at less than their nominal value.

If a further tranche of shares already in issue is offered to the public, then the par value is likely to be even less related to the purchase price. Suppose a company has initially issued shares at par, has traded successfully, re-invested the profits and seeks capital for further expansion. The second tranche of shares will naturally be issued at a price higher than par; otherwise, the second set of shareholders would obtain a disproportionately large interest in the company. In effect, they would be obtaining an interest in the profits earned in the past without having contributed any of the capital which was used to earn them. The situation can be rectified by setting the share price on the second issue so that it reflects the total value of the shareholders' interest in the company. In the case of publicly traded companies, this will be what market price of the share reflects.

---

[6] 2006 Act s.542(1),(2). This implements the requirements of the Second Directive, although the requirement of a nominal value was not introduced into UK law by that Directive.

[7] 2006 Act s.580.

[8] Note, however, the discount here is to the nominal value of the share, not to its market value, which is the issue addressed by the pre-emption rules. See para.24–6.

The CLR contemplated abolishing par value for private companies,[9] but eventually resiled from the proposal. The Second Directive was thought to require the retention of par value, or something very much like it,[10] for public companies, and the transitional difficulties likely to arise when a company moved from private to public were thought to militate against this reform.[11] So, unless and until the Second Directive is amended on this point, par values will remain part of the law.

No issue of shares at a discount

For investors the nominal value requirement is potentially misleading because it tells them nothing about the market price of the share or its value measured in any other way. Does the rule, which was established by the courts in the nineteenth century,[12] that shares must not be issued at a discount to their nominal par value act as a protection for creditors? The common law rule is now stated in the Act,[13] which specifically provides that, if the shares should be so issued, the allottee is liable to pay to the company the amount of the discount with interest.[14] This provision is of some value to creditors, but of only limited value, given the company's control over the setting of the nominal value. The creditor is probably more interested in the actual price at which the share was issued and in the total value of the consideration received by the company from its share issue. In fact, it could be argued that the rule against discounts to nominal value harms creditors, at least where the company nears insolvency. Suppose that, because of the unsuccessful trading of the company, its shares are in fact trading on the market at less than par. The company needs to raise new capital. No sensible investor will pay more than the market price for the shares and yet the Act seems to prevent the company from recognising the economic reality of its situation in the pricing of

11-4

---

[9] Strategic, paras 5.4.26–5.4.33. The Gedge Committee, Cmd. 9112, had recommended as long ago as 1954 that no-par equity shares should be introduced and the Jenkins Committee (Cmnd. 1749, 1962, paras 32–34) recommended this reform in relation to all classes of share. The reform has been widely introduced in common law jurisdictions elsewhere, but now seems unlikely to be introduced here unless the Second Directive is amended on this point. Introduction of no-par shares would require some matters to be expressed differently or regulated differently in the contract of issue. For example, the dividend on a preference share is normally expressed as a percentage of its nominal value (but could as easily be expressed as so many pence per share) and surplus assets are distributed on a winding in accordance with nominal values, so that a different formula would have to be adopted. See *Birch v Cropper* (1889) 14 App. Cas. 525.

[10] The Directive (art.8) refers to "accountable par" as a permitted alternative to "nominal value" (but without defining it). The concept appears to be that one takes the total consideration raised through the issue of shares and divides it by the number of shares in issue at any time. Two consequences follow: the shares do not have a fixed nominal value (because the accountable par would change on a new share issue at a different price) but a par value does exist at all times; and the company has no freedom to set the nominal value: it is simply the result of an arithmetical exercise. See Bank of England, *Practical Issues Arising From the Euro*, Issue 8, June 1998, Ch.6 at paras 24–28.

[11] Completing, para.7.3.

[12] Finally in *Ooregum Gold Mining Co v Roper* [1892] A.C. 125 HL.

[13] 2006 Act s.580(1).

[14] 2006 Act s.580(2).

any new issue, which may help it back to solvency.[15] Yet, in this situation creditors will benefit if the legal capital of the company is increased, no matter how little the company receives for any one of its shares. Any contribution from shareholders increases the amount available to satisfy the claims of the creditors.

In fact, there are a number of ways around this problem, though it cannot be guaranteed that in every situation one will be available. For example, a new class of share may be created with a lower par value but otherwise with rights substantially the same as the existing shares. This new class of share can be issued without infringing the prohibition on issuing shares at a discount. Nevertheless, as noted, the risk that the par value rule will hamper the company in the future gives companies some incentive to fix low par values initially and to raise most of the consideration for the shares by way of premium, so that the par value displays an even more remote relationship to the issue price than it might otherwise do.

11–5   It might be argued that the rule is better understood as a protection for the shareholders. The rule, it might be said, was intended to protect existing shareholders from directors who proposed to devalue (or "dilute") the existing shareholders' interest in the company by issuing shares to new shareholders too cheaply. However, dilution arises only if the shares are issued to new investors at a price which is lower than the current market price of the shares, so that the "no shares at a discount" rule is not well adapted to shareholder protection either. It will be under-protective of shareholders where the market price is above nominal value and over-protective where it is below. Indeed, what is surprising from a shareholders' perspective is that there is no precise statutory obligation laid on the company to issue shares at a premium, where the market will bear one.[16] This is probably because the company may have a number of good reasons to contract on the basis that the share will be issued at less than its full market price.[17] However, the directors' duty to promote the success of the company for the benefit of its members[18] will normally require the directors to issue shares at the best obtainable price; otherwise the company will be overpaying for its capital, just as it would be if it bought raw materials at above market price.[19]

---

[15] See the facts of *Ooregum Gold Mining Co v Roper* [1892] A.C. 125 HL where the "no discount" rule enabled the existing shareholders to act in a wholly opportunistic way towards an investor who was willing to inject new money into the company at market value (but less than the nominal value) of the shares at a time when the existing shareholders were unwilling to advance further capital.

[16] *Hilder v Dexter* [1902] A.C. 474 HL. The argument was there rejected that failing to obtain the premium amounted to the payment of a commission, contrary to what is now s.552 (see below). The decision was undoubtedly right on its facts, since the right to purchase further shares at par was an explicit part of the contract under which the investor had originally become a shareholder in a corporate rescue.

[17] See the previous note and directors' share option schemes, the essence of which is that the director has the right to subscribe in the future for shares in the company at today's share price.

[18] See para.16–64.

[19] "If the share stands at a premium, the directors *prima facie* owe a duty to the company to obtain for it the full value which they are able to get. It is true that it is within their powers under the Companies Acts to issue it at par, even in such a case, but their duty to the company is not to do so unless for good reason." (per Lord Wright in *Lowry v Consolidated African Selection Trust Ltd* [1940] A.C. 648, 679.) See also *Shearer v Bercain Ltd* [1980] 3 All E.R. 295: "Those who have practised in the field of company law for any length of time will have spent many hours convincing directors that it is wholly

The share premium

It is clear that the amount received by the company by way of the nominal value **11–6** of the shares issued constitutes part of its legal capital. The amount (often much more significant) received by way of premium is today treated in much the same way. Prior to 1948, when companies issued shares at a premium, the value of the premium was treated differently from the par value. Legal capital was regarded as determined by the nominal or par value of the shares; if they had been issued at a price above par the excess was not "capital" and, indeed, constituted part of the distributable surplus which the company, if it wished, could return to the shareholders by way of dividend.[20] This was, of course, a ridiculous rule, except on the basis that it might be an indirect way of subverting the capital-based distribution rules. If the price paid for the shares was £100,000, the amount received by the company was also £100,000 (assuming no transaction costs) and it should make no difference to the analysis whether the £100,000 was obtained by issuing 100,000 £1 shares at par or by issuing 100,000 1p shares at £1 (i.e. at a premium of 99p per share). In either case, the issue price (£1 in both cases) determined the amount raised by the company, whilst the par value, set by the company, is a figure determined in order to give the company maximum flexibility under the Act.[21] This situation was changed, however, by the 1948 Act. The rule, now stated in s.610 of the 2006 Act, is that a sum equal to the aggregate amount or value of the premiums shall be transferred to a "share premium account" which, in general, has to be treated as if it were part of the paid-up share capital. However, the Act does not fully assimilate share capital and the share premium. It is still necessary to refer expressly to both, and for the company, in its annual accounts and reports, to distinguish between the share capital account and the share premium account. What, if it were not for arbitrary par values, would be a single item—capital—has to be treated as two distinct items, albeit for most purposes treated identically.

However, share capital and share premium are not treated as wholly identical, **11–7** though the 2006 Act has narrowed some of the differences between them. Section 610 provides two "exceptions" and two "reliefs" for the share premium account which do not apply to the capital account. The first exception is that a company may apply the share premium account in paying up bonus shares.[22] A bonus share is a share issued to the existing shareholders, without requiring any payment from

---

wrong for them to issue to themselves and their friends shares at par when they command a premium, however great the company's need for capital may be." (per Walton J). See also *Re Sunrise Radio* [2010] 1 B.C.L.C. 367.

[20] *Drown v Gaumont British Corp* [1937] Ch. 402. See C. Napier and C. Noke, "Premiums and Pre-acquisition Profits" (1991) 54 M.L.R. 810.

[21] In some cases, the nominal value of the share has a more substantial significance. The dividend entitlement of a preference share is normally set as a percentage of the nominal value of the share, so that choosing a low nominal value for a preference share might imply a high percentage dividend. To produce the equivalent of a 10 per cent dividend on a £1 share, the dividend entitlement on a 1p share would have to be 1000 per cent! In general with preference shares, given their bond-like characteristics (see para.23–7), the nominal value will be set much closer to the issue price, since the nominal value will also determine what the preference shareholder receives in a reduction of capital or liquidation, at least if the holder has no right to participate in surplus assets.

[22] 2006 Act s.610(3).

them, but is paid for, in this case, by reducing the share premium account.[23] Since the effect of this transaction is to reduce the share premium account but to increase the share capital account by an equivalent amount, it is wholly unobjectionable from the creditors' point of view,[24] and it is hardly an exception to the main rule laid down by s.610. It would, of course, be impossible thus to apply share capital account but to apply share premium account in this way is unobjectionable since the only effect is to convert it, or a part of it, to share capital proper. The second exception is that the share premium account may be applied in writing off the expenses of or the commissions paid on the issue of the shares which generated the premiums.[25] This is a real exception, but now is a relatively minor contrast with share capital. Within limits, share capital may also be used to pay commission.[26] Although the rule in relation to the share premium account is somewhat more broadly phrased than that relating to the capital account, the share premium rule is now tighter than it was previously.[27]

More important (and more interesting) are the "reliefs". Section 610 (as did its predecessors) expressly applies to issues at a premium "whether for cash or otherwise". The result of this was held to be that if, say, on a merger one Company (A) acquired the shares of another (B) in consideration of an issue of A's own shares and the value of B's shares exceeded the nominal value of those issued by A, a share premium account had to be established in respect of the excess.[28] The result of this was that B's undistributed profits formerly available for distribution by way of dividend ceased to be distributable. This caused something of a furore in commercial circles. However, in 1980 the question was again litigated and the earlier decision fully upheld.[29] In consequence, "merger relief" was introduced in the Companies Act 1981. The general effect of the merger relief provisions[30] is that the premium does not have to be transferred to the share premium account when, pursuant to a merger arrangement, one company has acquired at least 90 per cent of *each*[31] class of equity shares[32] of another in exchange for an allotment of its equity shares at a premium.

---

[23] The bonus issue could also be funded by distributable profits. See below at para.11–20.

[24] The issuance of a bonus share has little impact on the shareholders either in the normal case. The shareholder now has more shares, but since the value of the company is not increased by this exercise, the market price of each share in the expanded class will fall. Sometimes bonus shares are issued precisely to achieve this result because it is thought that the market value of the share has become so large that it is an obstacle to trading them. See *EIC Services Ltd v Phipps* [2004] 2 B.C.L.C. 589 CA, where the (botched) bonus issue was aimed at reducing the trading price of the shares. A similar result can be obtained by effecting a "stock split" under s.618, an exercise which is possible no matter whether the company has a share premium account of any size.

[25] 2006 Act s.610(2).

[26] 2006 Act s.553 and see below, para.11–14.

[27] Under the 1985 Act the share premiums account could be written off against a wider range of share issue expenses which, in particular, did not necessarily have to have been incurred in relation to the shares generating the premiums.

[28] *Head & Co Ltd v Ropner Holdings Ltd* [1952] Ch. 124.

[29] *Shearer v Bercain Ltd* [1980] 3 All E.R. 295.

[30] 2006 Act ss.612–613.

[31] 2006 Act s.613(3).

[32] Which will include preference shares if they have a right to participate in either dividends or surplus on a winding up beyond a fixed amount: ss.616(1) and 548.

The Act also modifies (rather than removes) the requirement for a transfer to the share premium account in certain cases of reconstruction within a group of companies.[33] The relief applies in the case of issues at a premium by a wholly-owned subsidiary in consideration of a transfer to it of non-cash assets from another company in the group comprising the holding company and its wholly-owned subsidiaries. In this case the company issuing the shares is permitted to value the assets received, not by reference to their market value, but by reference to the cost of their acquisition by the transferor company or their value in the books of the transferor company. In this way, the value of the assets received in exchange for the shares will often be understated, but, to the extent that this understated value in fact exceeds the nominal value of the shares issued, the excess must still be transferred to the share premium account.[34] If this relief is available on the facts of a particular case, the more extensive merger relief is not.[35]

Finally, the Secretary of State is empowered by s.614 to make regulations providing further relief in relation to premiums other than cash premiums or for modifying the reliefs in the Act (but has not done so).

MINIMUM CAPITAL

With the above preliminaries, we can turn to an analysis of the minimum capital rule. As we have noted, as a result of the Second Directive,[36] a minimum capital requirement was introduced for public companies. Section 761 requires that the *nominal* value of the company's allotted share capital meet a certain minimum level That was set at the derisory level (for a public company) of £50,000 (or, currently, €57,100),[37] though that is double the amount required by the Directive.[38] Moreover, that £50,000 (or assets of equivalent value) does not have to be handed over to the company at the time of issue of the shares. It is enough, as with all share issues by public companies, that one quarter of the nominal value of the shares be paid at the time of issue.[39] The rest may remain unpaid, though of course subject to being called up by the company at a later date or in its liquidation. Nevertheless, the minimum capital requirement puts a little pressure on public companies not to issue shares at a hefty premium (because the premium does not count towards the required minimum). However, the Act retains its traditional aversion to minimum capital requirements in respect of private companies, where none is imposed. This is said to have been a major factor behind the incorporation in England of companies from other EU countries which applied minimum capital requirements to their equivalents of private companies.[40]

11–8

---

[33] 2006 Act s.611.

[34] 2006 Act s.611(2)–(5), defining the "minimum premium value".

[35] 2006 Act s.612(4).

[36] See above, fn.4, art.6.

[37] 2006 Act s.763 and the Companies (Authorised Minimum) Regulations 2009 (SI 2009/2425) reg.2.

[38] Second Directive art.6: €25,000.

[39] 2006 Act s.586.

[40] See M. Becht, C. Mayer and H.F. Wagner, "Where do Firms Incorporate? Deregulation and the Cost of Entry" (2008) 14 *Journal of Corporate Finance* 241.

In the relatively unusual case of a company being formed directly as a public company, the minimum capital requirement operates, not as a condition of its formation, but as a condition of its commencing business.[41] In order to commence business (or to exercise any borrowing powers—an important addition) it must apply to the Registrar for a "trading certificate"[42] (in addition to the formation certificate which it will already have obtained); and the condition for the issuance of a trading certificate is that the nominal value of the company's allotted share capital must be not less than the required or "authorised" minimum.[43] The company is under some pressure to obtain the trading certificate, because if it does not do so within a year from incorporation, it may be wound up by the Court and the Secretary of State may petition for that to happen.[44] A public company which trades or borrows without a certificate is liable to a fine, as is any officer of the company (including therefore its directors) who is in default.[45] However, the interests of third parties are properly protected in this case. Transactions entered into by the company in such a case are valid, and further, if the company fails to comply with its obligations, the directors of the company are jointly and severally liable to indemnify third parties in respect of any loss or damage suffered.[46] Thus, personal liability of the directors, criminal and civil, operates to give them a strong incentive not to trade without a trading certificate.

In the more usual case of a company becoming public upon conversion from private status, the requirement that the company's allotted capital be not less than the authorised minimum operates as a condition for the re-registration of the private company as a public one.[47]

If the nominal value of the company's allotted share capital meets the authorised minimum, on either of the occasions described above, it will normally remain at that level thereafter. This is because the nominal value of the shares does not change, no matter how much the value of the company may decline. However, in relatively rare cases the nominal value of the company's allotted capital might subsequently fall below the authorised minimum. There is no general provision in the Act dealing with this eventuality. Rather, provision is made on an ad hoc basis. Thus, if under the reduction of capital procedure[48] the

---

[41] 2006 Act s.761.

[42] The form of the application, containing a statement of compliance on the part of the company, is set out in s.762. It is not demanding and the Registrar may accept the company's statement of compliance as sufficient evidence of the matters stated in it, and the Registrar must issue the certificate if satisfied the minimum capital requirements are met: s.765(2). The trading certificate, once issued, is conclusive evidence that the company is entitled to commence business: s.761(4). However, by analogy with the decisions referred to in para.4–35 in relation to the certificate of incorporation, it appears that, as this section is not expressed to bind the Crown, the Registrar's decision could be quashed on judicial review at the instance of the Attorney-General.

[43] 2006 Act s.761(2). A company's capital may be stated in euros in which case s.763 deals with the fixing of the equivalent prescribed euro amount. Where a company has some share capital denominated in pounds and some in euros, the company's application for a certificate must be made by reference to the sterling capital or to the euro capital alone and not by reference to a mixture of the two types of capital: s.765.

[44] Insolvency Act 1986 ss.122(1)(b) and 124(4)(a).

[45] 2006 Act s.767(1),(2).

[46] 2006 Act s.767(3),(4).

[47] 2006 Act ss.90(1)(b), (2)(b) and 91(1)(a).

[48] See Ch.13.

company's capital is reduced below the authorised minimum, the normal requirement is that the company must re-register as a private company before the reduction of capital order is finalised.[49] Further, the Secretary of State has power to alter the authorised minimum by regulation (subject to affirmative resolution).[50] Were that alteration to be in an upward direction, the Secretary of State also has the power to require existing public companies to bring their nominal values into line with the new authorised minimum or to re-register as a private company.[51]

Objections to the minimum capital requirement

There are two objections which can be made to minimum capital rules. First, company laws normally set only one (as in the UK) or a small number of minimum capital rules (for example, one for private and another for public companies), but in fact, to be effective, the minimum capital requirement ought to be related to the riskiness of the business which the company undertakes. General minimum capital requirements tend either to be too low effectively to protect creditors (as in the case of the current British requirement) or too high, in which case they reduce competition (by discouraging new entrants into the field) whilst over-protecting creditors. However, adjusting capital requirements to the riskiness of the company's business would be a complex and continuing activity, as is shown by the special regulation necessary to implement such a principle in those industries, for example banking and insurance, where capital adequacy requirements are taken seriously (and also where "capital" means net asset value, not "legal" capital). Thus, it is not surprising that the approach of company laws to minimum capital requirements is relatively crude; and in practice in developed economies tends towards the "too low" end of the spectrum, thus conferring no substantial protection on creditors but conceivably discouraging the incorporation of companies.

If, therefore, the minimum capital requirement has no claim to be a genuine assessment of the amount of risk capital the company needs to survive the vicissitudes of its business, could it nevertheless be justified as a "cushion" of assets provided by the shareholders for the protection of the creditors? This is also a difficult argument to sustain. The creditors need the protection of an asset cushion when the company begins to trade unprofitably. A minimum capital requirement imposed at the time the company commences trading does not guarantee any particular level of assets being available for the creditors at this later date or when the company goes into an insolvency procedure. For example, a minimum capital requirement of, say, £3,000 for a private company, even if paid in cash, could soon be returned quite legitimately to the incorporators by

11–9

---

[49] 2006 Act.650(2). The court may order otherwise. Section 651 provides an expedited procedure for re-registering as a private company in such cases. See also s.662(2)(b), dealing with the consequences of a forced cancellation by a public company of its own shares.
[50] 2006 Act s.764(1),(4).
[51] 2006 Act s.764(3)—no doubt through an expedited procedure.

means of salary payments for services rendered to the company[52] or it could be satisfied by the contribution to the company by the incorporators of a depreciating asset, such as a second-hand car. Thus, minimum capital rules are likely to be ineffective beyond a very short initial period unless coupled with rules which require the directors to take action if the net value of the company's actual assets declines below the value of its legal capital.

The Act does in fact contain a rule which requires action on the part of the company if its net asset value falls below a certain proportion of its legal capital. However, this rule is not linked to the minimum capital requirement and would therefore survive even if the authorised minimum were abolished. Nor does the rule specify the substantive action the company should take in this situation. Section 656 requires a public company to convene an extraordinary meeting of the shareholders if the net value of its assets falls below one half of its called-up share capital, which may be, and typically will be, far in excess of the authorised minimum.[53] The section does not require the shareholders or the directors to take any particular action in this situation (for example, cause the company to cease trading or raise further capital from the shareholders).[54] This section seems not to be very important in practice, probably because, before it becomes operative, large lenders will have exercised rights under their loan contracts to replace the failing management or otherwise to redress the situation[55] or the wrongful trading provisions[56] will have required the directors to take corrective action. Consequently, it can be argued that, at the initial stage, the minimum capital requirement is too low to confer substantial protection on creditors and that subsequent adverse developments in the company's trading ability are dealt with through mechanisms other than those which focus on the minimum capital.[57]

DISCLOSURE AND VERIFICATION

11–10   Whether or not a legal system imposes a minimum capital requirement, there are obvious arguments in favour of requiring the company to disclose the amount it has raised by way of the issuance of its shares and providing some assurance that the amounts stated in the capital accounts are accurate. This information will facilitate creditor self-help, i.e. making it easier for creditors to decide whether to lend to the company and on what terms. The extent of the facilitation should not be over-estimated. It will perhaps be useful at the point of issuance of the shares, but the creditor is really interested in the company's overall net asset position

---

[52] As we shall see below at para.12–9, directors' remuneration would not normally be caught by the rules controlling distributions by companies.

[53] 2006 Act s.547 makes it clear that called up share capital includes capital payments to be made in the future if those future payment dates are laid out in the company's articles, the terms of allotment of the shares or other arrangements for the payment of the shares. This section implements domestically art.19 of the Second Directive. Article 19 refers to the company's "subscribed" capital, which probably means the nominal value of the issued share capital, thus reducing the impact of the rule.

[54] As is the case in some continental European jurisdictions.

[55] See paras 31–26 et seq.

[56] See paras 9–6 et seq.

[57] See Chs 9 and 10, above.

which, as the company trades, is likely to be more and more divorced from its legal capital figure.[58] Thus, the creditor is likely to pay more attention to the verification of the company's assets and liabilities as a whole, not just the amounts raised through share issues; and that assurance is provided, to the extent that it is, through the company's annual financial statements and their audit.[59] In addition, those who are shareholders at the time the shares are issued will have an interest in knowing and verifying the amounts raised through share issues, in order to be satisfied that new shareholders are not being admitted to the company too cheaply.[60]

UK company law has developed over time a number of rules which address the above policies, and they were substantially added to when the Second Directive was implemented in the UK.

Initial statement and return of allotments

When a company is formed, assuming it is limited by shares, the application for registration must contain a statement of capital and initial shareholdings. This requires disclosure of information relating to the totality of the shares to be taken by the subscribers and to their individual subscriptions. In particular, the number of shares, their aggregate nominal amount, the amounts, if any, to be left unpaid and the prescribed rights attached to the shares must be disclosed.[61] In practice, the answer will often be one £1 share taken by each of two people, upon which nothing is paid up, the two people being employees of a company formation business, which has created a shelf private company. When more serious amounts of shares are issued at a later date, similar information has to be given to the Registrar of companies via a "return of allotments".[62] Thus, data about those to whom shares of various classes have been issued,[63] the amounts paid for the shares and the main rights and obligations attached to those shares is public information, but this is a disclosure provision, not a provision which regulates the amount or type of share the company issues. Although it is a criminal offence knowingly or recklessly to deliver a false statement to the Registrar,[64] these provisions do not otherwise provide verification of the information delivered.

11–11

---

[58] Above, para.11–1.

[59] See Chs 21 and 22.

[60] Above, para.11–5.

[61] 2006 Act s.10. Prescribed are details of the right to vote, to receive a distribution either by way of dividend or capital, and provisions about redemption: Companies (Shares and Share Capital) Order 2009/388 art.2.

[62] 2006 Act s.555 and see para.23–6.

[63] As we see in para.26–18, those who take the shares may be nominees for others who have the financial interest in them, but this is perhaps of less moment to the creditors whose main interest is in the amount of shares issued, rather than data about their holders. Since the shareholders' liability is limited, it does not matter to the creditors whether the shareholders are rich or poor, at least once the shares are fully paid up.

[64] 2006 Act s.1112.

Abolition of authorised capital

11–12   The 2006 Act did away with the former concept of "authorised capital", as recommended by the CLR.[65] This was a concept which sounded important but which fulfilled no identifiable creditor-protection role. Under the old law, a company with a share capital (unless it was an unlimited company) was required to state in its memorandum "the amount of the share capital with which [it] proposes to be registered and the division of that share capital into shares of a fixed amount".[66] Until the authorised capital was allotted, i.e. an investor agreed to take some shares in exchange for a consideration provided to the company, the authorised capital in no way increased the company's assets. The company's authorised capital might have been 10 million shares of £1 each, but if only two of those shares had been issued, say at par, then its legal capital was £2. If anything, authorised capital served to confuse the potential investor.

In fact, the requirement for authorised capital had more to do with relations between directors and shareholders than with creditor relations. The directors could not issue more than the amount of the company's authorised capital without returning to the shareholders for approval of an increase in the authorised amount.[67] However, if the authorised capital was set at a high level, as it normally was, this was not a significant constraint on the directors. Shareholder control of share issues is now effected by other sections of the Act and shareholders, if they wish, can put stronger controls in the company's constitution, so that authorised capital is not needed for the protection of shareholders either.[68]

Consideration received upon issue

11–13   We next turn to the rules which focus on the quality and even the reality of the consideration received by a company upon the issuance of its shares, whether the shares are issued to satisfy the minimum capital requirement or not and irrespective of whether that consideration is referable to the nominal value of the share or the premium payable. Before 1980 the domestic rules in this area were exiguous, but they were strengthened as a result of the Second Directive, which, however, was somewhat relaxed in 2006.[69] As a result, there is a marked divergence between the rules applying to all companies and to public companies only.

---

[65] Modernising, para.6.5.
[66] 1985 Act s.2(5)(a).
[67] 1985 Act s.121.
[68] See Ch.24.
[69] A set of relaxations to the original version of the Second Directive was made by Directive 2006/68/EC ([2006] O.J. L264/32). However, in relation to the issues discussed below the Government took the view that the permitted relaxations were so minor and so hedged about with qualifications that it was not worth taking them up: DTI, *Implementation of the Companies Act 2006: A Consultation Document*, February 2007, para.6.23.

Rules applying to all companies

We should first note that the law does not require that the consideration promised **11–14** for the shares be immediately due to the company. There is thus a distinction between paid-up capital and uncalled capital, the former being, for example, the amount paid on allotment and the latter the amount payable when the company calls upon the shareholder for the payment in accordance with the terms of the allotment.[70] Long-term uncalled capital could be a valuable indication of creditworthiness since, in effect, it affords a personal guarantee by the members, but it is doubtful whether it is extensively used in private companies.[71]

A potentially important creditor protection rule restricts the use of capital to pay commissions etc. Payment by way of commissions, brokerage or the like to any person in consideration for subscribing or agreeing to subscribe is prohibited,[72] even if the shares are issued at a premium, except to the limited extent to which they are explicitly permitted. Without this rule, the amount actually received by the company from an investor in exchange for its shares might be substantially less than appears. However, the Act permits commission for subscribing for shares (or procuring others to do so) to be paid out of capital provided it is limited to 10 per cent of the issue price and is authorised by the articles (which may set a lower percentage).[73] It would be logical if this restriction on the payment of commission did not apply to payments out of distributable profits, since creditors have no claim to limit what the company does with such funds. This is what s.552 appears to say, since it provides that a company "must not apply any of its shares or capital money" in the payment of commissions etc.[74] However, the section no longer attempts to do that which earlier drafts of the statute attempted, i.e. to make clear the consequences of infringing the prohibition. Those drafts provided that, if there were an agreement to pay commission, etc. in breach of the prohibition, the agreement was to be void; if the payment had been made, the amount of the inducement was to be recoverable, either from the person to whom it was paid or any third party who knew of the circumstance constituting the contravention and benefited from it.[75] A court could deduce these consequences from the prohibition contained in the current section.

---

[70] 2006 Act s.547 defines called-up capital so as to include that amount represented by calls which have been made, whether or not they have been met, and the amount payable under the articles or the terms of allotment on a specified future date, even though that date has not arrived.

[71] Or, indeed, by public ones. As the CLR proposed, the Act no longer contains provisions which permit a company to determine by special resolution that any part of its capital which has not been called up shall be incapable of being called up except in a winding up.

[72] 2006 Act s.552.

[73] 2006 Act s.553. Section 552(3) also permits the payment of "such brokerage as has previously been lawful"—an obscure and potentially wide permission. On the use of the share premium account to pay commissions, etc. see above, para.11–7.

[74] Of course, for a company to make such a payment, even out of distributable profits, might infringe the prohibition on a company giving financial assistance towards the purchase of its own shares, but the latter rule no longer applies to private companies: see para.13–55, below.

[75] *Modernising Company Law—Draft Clauses*, Cm 5553-II, July 2002, cl.28.

Payment does not have to be in cash; it can instead be made in kind[76] and very frequently is in private companies.[77] But, except in relation to public companies, it seems that the parties' valuation of the non-cash consideration will be accepted as conclusive[78] unless its inadequacy appears on the face of the transaction[79] or there is evidence of bad faith.[80] Hence on an issue for a non-cash consideration it is possible to some degree to "water" the shares by agreeing to accept payment in property which is worth less than the value of the shares.

Public companies

11–15   Shares allotted by a public company must be paid up (in cash or in kind) at least as to one quarter of their nominal value and the whole of any premium due.[81] If this does not occur, the share is nevertheless to be treated as if this had happened and the allottee is liable to pay the company that amount, with interest. This provision reduces the company's and creditors' exposure to the continuing solvency of its shareholders, although it is relatively uncommon for companies not to require full payment upon allotment. Where the company does want to stagger the payments for the shares, this rule creates a disincentive to setting the nominal value of the shares well below the issue price,[82] because the whole of the premium must be paid up on allotment.

The remaining rules for public companies concern the regulation of non-cash issues, but before turning to them it is important to note the width of the definition of "cash consideration" in s.583(3), for these rules do not apply where the consideration is cash, as defined. The section includes within the definition of "cash consideration" an undertaking to pay cash to the company in the future, thus putting the company at risk of the insolvency of the shareholder, but also the reducing the disincentive mentioned at the end of the previous paragraph.[83] Also treated as cash is the release of a liability of the company for a liquidated sum.[84] The latter is a useful provision in facilitating equity for debt swaps whereby the creditors of an insolvent company forgo their claims as debtors against the company in exchange for the issue to them of equity shares. The company is

---

[76] 2006 Act s.582(1) restates the general rule that "shares allotted by a company may be paid-up in money or money's worth (including goodwill and know-how)" but this is followed by exceptions and qualifications relating to public companies only. Again, bonus shares are specifically allowed.

[77] For example, when the proprietor of a business incorporates it by transferring the undertaking to a newly formed company in consideration of an allotment of its shares.

[78] *Re Wragg* [1897] 1 Ch. 796 CA; *Park Business Interiors Ltd v Park* [1992] B.C.L.C. 1034.

[79] *Re White Star Line* [1938] Ch. 458.

[80] *Tintin Exploration Syndicate v Sandys* (1947) 177 L.T. 412.

[81] 2006 Act s.586.

[82] See para.11–3, above.

[83] 2006 Act s.583(3)(d). There is no apparent limit on the future date which may be fixed for the actual payment, for the five-year limit in s.587 (see below) applies only to non-cash payments, but the undertaking must be one given to the company in consideration of the allotment of the shares: *System Controls Plc v Munro Corporation Plc* [1990] B.C.C. 386. And the "cash" must be given to the company, not a third person: s.583(5).

[84] 2006 Act.583(3)(c). So, if the company owes the investor a sum of money, the release by the investor of the company from that obligation in exchange for the shares amounts to the provision of a cash consideration for them: *EIC Services Ltd v Phipps* [2004] 2 B.C.L.C. 589 at [36] to [52] (Neuberger J).

thereby released from an often crippling burden of interest payments and the removal of the debt may even produce by itself a surplus of assets over liabilities. This will be to the immediate benefit of the shareholders and non-converting creditors, though if the company prospers in the future, the original shareholders will naturally find that their equity interest has been extensively diluted. It seems that no infringement of the rule forbidding issuing shares at a discount to par value occurs where the face value of the debt is taken for the purposes of paying up the new shares, even though the market value of the debt at the time of the swap was less than its face value because of the debtor's insolvency.[85]

A public company may not accept, in payment for its shares or any premium on them, an undertaking by any person that he or another will do work or perform services for the company or any other person.[86] If it should do so, the holder of the shares[87] at the time they are treated as paid up (wholly or partly) by the services is liable to pay the company an amount equal to the nominal value of the shares plus the premium or such part of that amount as has been treated as paid up by the undertaking.[88] Nor may the company allot shares as fully or partly paid-up if the consideration is *any* sort of undertaking to provide a non-cash consideration which need not be performed until after five years from the date of the allotment.[89] If the undertaking should have been performed within five years but is not, payment in cash then becomes due immediately.[90] And (though this is of minimal importance) shares taken by a subscriber to the memorandum of association in pursuance of his undertaking in the memorandum must be paid for in cash.[91]

Valuation of non-cash consideration

Finally, the possibility of "share-watering" by placing an inflated value on the non-cash consideration is tackled in the case of public companies by requiring that consideration to be independently valued. Under Ch.6 of Pt 17 a public company may not allot shares as fully or partly paid-up (as to their nominal value or any premium) otherwise than in cash unless:—(i) the consideration has been valued in accordance with the provisions of the Part; (ii) a report is made to the company during the six months immediately preceding the allotment; and (iii) a copy is sent to the proposed allottee.[92] To this there are exceptions in relation to

11–16

---

[85] *Re Mercantile Trading Co, Schroeder's Case, Re* (1871) L.R. 11 Eq. 13; *Pro-Image Studios v Commonwealth Bank of Australia* (1990–1991) 4 A.C.S.R. 586, though it should be noted that in this case both the debt and the consideration for the new shares were immediately payable. Independent valuation of the debt is not required because its release constitutes a cash consideration.

[86] 2006 Act s.585. But this section (nor s.587 below) does not prevent the company from enforcing the undertaking: s.591. If a private company wishes to convert to a Plc such undertakings must first be performed or discharged: s.91(1)(d).

[87] Including the holder of the beneficial interest under a bare trust: s.585(3).

[88] 2006 Act s.585(2).

[89] 2006 Act s.587(1). If contravened the consequences are similar to those for contravention of s.585, except that the liability falls on the allottee: s.587(2). If a contract of allotment does not offend s.587(1) but is later varied so as to produce this consequence, the variation is void: s.587(3).

[90] 2006 Act s.587(4). And see s.91(1)(d) regarding a private company converting to a Plc.

[91] s2006 Act s.584.

[92] 2006 Act s.593(1).

bonus issues[93] and in relation to most types of takeovers and mergers.[94] But, in other cases, if the allottee has not received the copy of the valuation report or there is some other contravention of the Part, which he knew, or ought to have known, amounted to a contravention, once again he or she is liable to pay in cash with interest.[95] These provisions clearly protect existing shareholders as well as creditors.

However, if the correct valuation steps are taken, there is no statutory prohibition on the company issuing shares in a transaction which puts a higher valuation on the non-cash consideration than has emerged in the valuation process. In that situation the directors might well be in breach of their fiduciary duties[96] and the subscriber would be in a poor position to assert that he or she was unaware of this.

The valuation has to be made by a person "qualified to be appointed, or continue to be, an auditor of the company"[97] and that person must meet statutory tests of independence from the company.[98] The expert has a right, similar to that of an auditor, to require from officers of the company the information and explanations required to produce the valuation.[99] The expert may, however, arrange for and accept a valuation from another person who appears to him to have the requisite experience and knowledge and who is not an employee or officer of any company in the group.[100] In practice, therefore, the report will be by the company's auditor supported by another professional valuation of any real property or other consideration which the auditor does not feel competent to value on his own. The report has to go into considerable detail[101] and must support the conclusion that the aggregate of the cash and non-cash consideration is not less than the nominal value and the premium.[102]

A private company proposing to convert to a public one cannot evade these valuation requirements by allotting shares for a non-cash consideration shortly before it re-registers as a public one. In such a case, the Registrar cannot entertain the application to re-register unless the consideration has been valued and reported on in accordance with the above provisions.[103]

11–17   This relatively straightforward mandatory valuation procedure, imposed where a public company issues shares for a non-cash consideration, is extended by the Act to a category of cases where the company acquires a non-cash asset in exchange

---

[93] 2006 Act s.593(2).

[94] 2006 Act ss.594–595. The rules of the Act, the Takeover Panel or the FCA will normally ensure that there has been professional assessment of value in such cases.

[95] 2006 Act s.593(3). As is a subsequent holder unless he is or claims through a purchaser for value without notice: s.605(1),(3). See *Re Bradford Investments* [1991] B.C.L.C. 224.

[96] See para.11–5.

[97] 2006 Act ss.596(1) and 1150. For these qualifications, see Ch.22, below.

[98] 2006 Act ss.1151–1152.

[99] 2006 Act s.1153. Knowingly or recklessly making a false statement under the section is a criminal offence: s.1153(2)–(4). Unlike the auditor's right, the independent expert's does not extend to employees of the company. See para.22–30.

[100] 2006 Act s.1150(2).

[101] 2006 Act s.596(3)–(5).

[102] 2006 Act s.586(3)(d).

[103] 2006 Act s.93.

for something other than the issuance of shares.[104] This extension applies only during the period of two years after the company has been issued with a trading certificate[105]; only to agreements on the part of the company to acquire non-cash assets from anyone who was a subscriber to the memorandum on the company's formation or a member of it on its conversion to a public company[106]; and only where the consideration to be provided by the company is at least equal to one tenth of its issued share capital. This provision is aimed at a purchase by the company of property from the promoters of the company at an excessive price, though it seems relatively easy to avoid by simply not becoming a member of the company until just after either of the two dates which trigger the mandatory valuation rule. Again, these controls protect both creditors and "outside" shareholders, but a significant feature of the extended rule is that it places greater emphasis on the protection of the shareholders through the imposition of the additional requirement that the shareholders approve of the proposed trans-action.[107]

The valuation requirements, especially on a small issue of shares, are potentially time-consuming and expensive. However, they are required by the Second Directive.[108] In 2006 the Directive was amended so as to permit certain assets to be valued without an independent expert's report.[109] Although the Act contains a power for the Secretary of State to make regulations to modify the independent valuation requirements,[110] the Government did not propose to take up the options offered by the amendment to the Directive, on the grounds it was not clear the amendments did relax the provisions of the Directive and, in any event, they would not simplify the legislation.[111]

Further provisions as to sanctions

The above provisions, both those relating to all companies and those applying to public companies alone, impose civil liability on the allottee (normally) towards the company, as we have seen. However, by the time the company comes to enforce that liability, it is not unlikely that the shares will be in the hands of someone else. The general policy of the Act is to impose liability jointly and severally with the allottee on the subsequent holder[112] of the shares, but subject to a major defence.[113] Following normal equitable principles, that defence is that the holder is a purchaser for value in good faith (i.e. without actual knowledge of the contravention concerned) of the securities or someone who derives title from

11–18

---

[104] 2006 Act s.598.
[105] 2006 Act.598(2)—the "initial period". For the requirement for a public company to obtain a trading certificate see above, para.11–4.
[106] 2006 Act ss.598(1)(a) and 603.
[107] 2006 Act ss.599(1)(c) and 601.
[108] Second Directive arts 10 et seq.
[109] Now arts 11 and 12.
[110] 2006 Art s.657(1).
[111] DTI, above, fn.69, para.6.23.
[112] "Holder" is defined to include not just the registered holder of the share but also a person who has the unconditional right to be included in the company's register of members or to have a transfer of the share executed in his favour: ss.588(3) and 605(4). See Ch.27, below.
[113] 2006 Act ss.588 and 605.

such a purchaser.[114] Consequently, if the shares have been traded in the normal way on a public market, the current holder will not be liable. On the other hand, a donee of the shares would be jointly and severally liable.

The liability which the above provisions impose on the allottee or the current holder of the shares is potentially substantial, in respect of what might be only a technical breach of the statute, for example, the allottee has not been sent a copy of the valuer's report, though the allottee is in fact aware of its contents. Even where there has been a more than technical breach, the liability imposed may be penal. For example, a failure to have non-cash assets valued makes the allottee liable to pay the whole of the consideration due for the shares in cash with interest,[115] without any account being taken of the actual value of the non-cash assets transferred. Consequently, the court has the power to grant relief against liability to make a payment to the company in most cases,[116] but that power to grant relief is limited.[117] In particular, the court must have regard to two "overriding principles", namely:

(a)   that a company which has allotted shares should receive money or money's worth at least equal in value to the aggregate of the nominal value of those shares and the value of the premium or, if the case so requires, so much of that aggregate as is treated as paid-up[118]; and

(b)   that when the company would, if the court did not grant exemption, have more than one remedy against a particular person it should be for the company to decide which remedy it should remain entitled to pursue.[119]

Share capital and choice of currency

11–19   The Act requires the minimum capital requirement for public companies to be satisfied by shares denominated in either pounds sterling or euros, presumably for some sort of verification reason.[120] However, apart from this, the company has considerable freedom to denominate shares in such currency as it wishes. It has never been doubted that this was possible in relation to the share premium account (and other capital reserves) but the issue was debated in relation to the share capital account until it was decided in favour of giving the company this

---

[114] 2006 Act ss.588(2) and 605(3). The requirement for "actual notice" is favourable to the subsequent holder. On the possible meanings of "actual knowledge" see *Eagle Trust Plc v SBC Securities Ltd* [1991] B.C.L.C. 438.

[115] 2006 Act s.593(3).

[116] There is no relief power in relation to the allottee in the case of issuance of shares at a discount or breach of the paying-up requirements: s.589(1).

[117] 2006 Act ss.589 and 606.

[118] The importance of which is demonstrated in *Re Bradford Investments Plc (No.2)* [1991] B.C.L.C. 688; cf. *Re Ossory Estates Plc* (1988) 4 B.C.C. 461.

[119] 2006 Act ss.589(5) and 606(4). For other matters which the court should take into account, see ss.589(3),(4) and 606(2),(3). When proceedings are brought by one person (e.g. a holder of the shares) against another (e.g. the original allottee) for a contribution in respect of liability the court may adjust the extent (if any) of the contribution having regard to their respective culpability in relation to that liability: ss.589(6) and 606(5). And see s.606(6) for exemption from liability under s.604(3)(b).

[120] 2006 Act s.765(1).

freedom in *Re Scandinavian Bank*.[121] The Act now puts the point beyond doubt.[122] Moreover, the Act adds to this freedom by providing a simple procedure for re-denominating share capital from one currency to another (into or out of sterling or from one non-sterling currency to another), including the re-denomination of the shares used to satisfy the minimum capital requirement when trading began. Formerly, this could be achieved only by the cumbersome and potentially expensive procedure of a reduction of capital and an issue of new shares in the desired currency.[123] Now any limited[124] company, subject to contrary provision in its articles, may re-denominate its shares by ordinary resolution of the members.[125] Such re-denomination does not affect the currency in which dividends are required to be paid by the company or calls on shares smet by the shareholder.[126]

Such re-denomination, which must be carried out at prevailing rates of exchange,[127] could produce new nominal values of a rather awkward kind, for example, $2.24. The company may respond in two ways: by capitalising distributable reserves so as to increase the nominal values to a more acceptable level, for which no special statutory permission is needed,[128] or by reducing the nominal values so as to achieve the same result, which the statute permits without the need to follow the full reduction of capital procedure. All that is required is a special resolution of the members, provided the decision is taken within three months of the re-denomination resolution and does not reduce the company's share capital by more than 10 per cent.[129] Further, the amount of the reduction must be carried to a "re-denomination reserve" which is a new undistributable reserve created by the Act.[130] It is also conceivable that the reduction following re-denomination could produce the result that neither the euro nor the sterling requirements for the authorised minimum capital of a public company is met, in which case the company will have to re-register as a private company.[131]

---

[121] *Re Scandinavian Bank* [1988] Ch. 87. Of course, until the rules on share capital were brought into line with those on share premium, the company was not in a position to exercise freedom of choice in relation to currency.

[122] 2006 Act s.542(3): shares "may be denominated in any currency and different classes of shares may be denominated in different currencies" (subject, of course, to s.765, above, fn.120).

[123] As happened in *Re Scandinavian Bank* [1988] Ch. 87. For the reduction of capital procedure see para.13–30.

[124] Unlimited companies had the freedom already.

[125] 2006 Act s.622(1). The section requires the actual conversion to take place within 28 days of the adoption of the resolution (s.622(5),(6)).

[126] 2006 Act s.624(1). Other rights and obligations of members under the constitution or the terms of issue of the shares are also expressly preserved.

[127] 2006 Act s.622(3).

[128] On capitalisation issues see below, para.11–20.

[129] 2006 Act s.626. Thus, in the example in the text, the company would not be able to use this procedure to reduce the nominal value to $2, but it would be able to if the unreduced nominal value were $2.20. There must also be notification to the Registrar: s.627.

[130] 2006 Act s.628. For the significance of this for the payment of dividends see para.12–2.

[131] 2006 Act s.766 and the Companies (Authorised Minimum) Regulations 2008/729 reg.5. A speedy method of re-registration is provided.

CAPITALISATION ISSUES

11–20   The net worth of a business will fluctuate from time to time according to whether the company makes profits and ploughs them back or suffers losses. But a company's legal capital, i.e. the issued share capital plus share premium account (if any) does not automatically fluctuate to reflect this. It remains unaltered until increased by a further issue of shares, which must be made in conformity with the rules dealt with above, or reduced in accordance with the rules dealt with in Ch.13. If, however, the company has made profits and not distributed them as dividends, a necessary consequence of the static nature of its capital accounts is that its net asset value will exceed its legal capital. This is not necessarily something either company or shareholders need worry about—in fact, they should welcome the profits—but an accounting device is needed to bring the company's books back into balance. This is to be found by including a (notional) liability on the balance sheet in order to balance the "assets" and "liabilities". This is normally described as a "reserve", an expression which may confuse those unaccustomed to accounting practice since it may suggest (falsely) that the company has set aside an actual earmarked fund to meet some potential or actual liability. The crucial point is that this reserve is a distributable reserve, unlike the capital accounts, i.e. the company can distribute assets to its shareholders up to the value in the reserve, and keep its books in balance by reducing the reserve accordingly.

Should a profit-rich company wish to bring its legal capital more into line with its net worth, it can do so by making a "bonus" or "capitalisation" issue[132] to its shareholders. The former expression is likely to be used by the company when communicating with its shareholders (in the hope that they will think that they are being treated generously by being given something for nothing) and the latter when communicating with the workforce (which might otherwise demand a bonus in the form of increased wages). In fact, such an issue is merely a means of capitalising reserves by using them to pay-up shares newly issued to the shareholders.[133] We have already noted one form of bonus issue, where the shares are paid up out of the share premium account, which is accordingly reduced to the extent of the nominal value of the bonus shares, whilst the share capital account is correspondingly increased. Here, however, the bonus shares are paid up out of the distributable profits reserve. For example, suppose that before the issue the net asset value (taking book values) of the company was £2 million and

---

[132] The two expressions mean the same thing and, indeed, so does a third ("scrip" issue) which is sometimes used.

[133] Technically, there is a two-stage process. First, the undivided profits of the company are capitalised and then there is the appropriation to each member who would have been entitled to a distribution of the profits by way of dividend of the amount needed to pay up as fully paid the shares to be issued. See *Topham v Charles Topham Group Ltd* [2003] 1 B.C.L.C. 123, especially at 139–141, where the failure of a parent company to carry out the first step (because its accounts in fact showed no distributable profits, though its subsidiary did have such profits) meant that the issue of the bonus shares was ineffective to create any right in the shareholders to receive the shares. cf. *Re Cleveland Trust* [1991] B.C.L.C. 424, where the company's accounts erroneously showed a distributable profit (in fact the profit so shown was repayable to a subsidiary) and the issue of the bonus shares was held to have been effective, as far as the statute was concerned, but rendered void by the common law doctrine of common mistake.

the issued capital one million shares of £1 each. The shares, on book values, will be worth £2 each.[134] The company then makes a one-for-one bonus issue paid up out of the distributable profits reserve. The immediate effect on a shareholder is that for each former £1 share worth £2 he or she will now have two £1 shares each worth £1.[135] However, a more significant change has occurred, which may have implications for the future. The formerly distributable profit can no longer be distributed because it has been converted into share capital. The company is thus signalling a need to have greater permanent risk capital than might previously have been understood to be the case. Further, it is likely to stop short of capitalising undistributed reserves to an extent which would impair its freedom to pursue an appropriate dividend policy in the future. Thus, a bonus share paid up out of distributable reserves is a potentially more significant event than an issue of bonus shares paid up from the share premium account, where the decrease in one undistributable account is balanced by the increase in another.

CONCLUSION

The requirement that a public company have a minimum allotted capital when it begins trading is of doubtful utility to creditors, given the low level at which it is set. Protections of creditors which take as their base the nominal value of the share (notably the rule against issues at a discount to nominal value) are also of doubtful utility, given the company's freedom to set the nominal value of the share, and may even be harmful to their interests in certain circumstances. The rules designed to ensure that a company receives assets of a value equal to the price at which it has issued the shares are more useful to creditors and also promote equal treatment of different groups of members holding the same class of share. However, such rules do not depend for their effectiveness on a concept of legal capital. Such rules could equally well be formulated and enforced even if there were no legal capital rules. The main claim that the legal capital rules have to remain part of our company law must rest, therefore, on their role in constraining the payment of distributions to the members of the company to which we turn next.

11–21

---

[134] This does not mean that listed shares will be quoted at that price: that will depend on many other factors, including in particular the expected future profits and dividends. And the book values, of fixed assets in particular, may not reflect their present values.

[135] The *quoted* price is not likely to fall by a half because it is to be expected that the company will seek to maintain approximately the same level of dividend per share as before the issue.

CHAPTER 12

DIVIDENDS AND DISTRIBUTIONS

THE BASIC RULES

The rules on legal capital, discussed in the previous chapter, have their main impact on companies through their role in setting the maximum amount payable by way of dividend or other form of distribution to shareholders. Whether the company chooses to make the maximum distribution permitted by the distribution rules is, in most circumstances, a matter for it. Where a company has substantial distributable profits, it will often not pay them all out to the shareholders but will keep some for re-investment. The legal rules have their bite where the company does in fact hold enough cash to pay a dividend but the rules to be discussed in this chapter prevent a distribution at the level the company would otherwise desire.

12–1

The distributions rules discussed in this chapter are aimed at protecting creditors. This will be our main focus. However, there may also be shareholder/board conflicts over the level of distributions, managers perhaps preferring to re-invest surplus cash in the business, the shareholders preferring cash in hand.[1] The respective roles of the board and the shareholders in determining the level of dividend are left to be determined in the articles of association (subject, of course, to the constraints imposed by the creditor protection rules). The model articles for private and public companies limited by

---

[1] Theoretically, it is far from clear that there is a real conflict here. If management retains earnings to invest in good projects, which the market evaluates appropriately, then the company's share price will rise and a shareholder seeking income can sell part of the (now more valuable) shareholding. So, the issue is simply the form of the income: dividend or capital gain. But investors may not trust managers to make good investment decisions or may have different time-frames from the managers for realisation of their investments.

shares require both a recommendation from the board and shareholder approval for a dividend, but with the shareholders not permitted to approve a level of dividend above that recommended by the directors.[2] In effect, this is a mutual veto arrangement.[3] If the articles, unusually, say absolutely nothing about the mechanism for determining dividends, then on normal principles that decision would rest with the shareholders alone. There is no apparent reason why the articles should not give the dividend decision entirely to the directors, though it is rare to do so (except in relation to interim dividends). It is thought that it would require very clear words to produce that result, i.e. the court would be unlikely to deduce exclusive director control over dividends from a general grant of management powers to the board, since dividends are as much an investment as a management matter.

Public and private companies

12–2   Turning to creditor protection, the inter-relationship between the legal capital rules and the rules on distributions appears most clearly in the rule applicable to public companies only and set out in s.831 of the Act.[4] It applies a balance-sheet test for the legality of a distribution. It is unlawful for a company to make a distribution if its net assets (assets minus liabilities) are (or would be after the distribution) less than its called up share capital and undistributable reserves.[5] Its undistributable reserves include its share premium account.[6] Thus, to take a simple example, a company which has issued as fully paid up 200 £1 shares at an issue price of £1.50 will have a share capital of £200 and a value of £100 in its share premium account. Consequently, for such a company it will not be enough to permit a distribution of, say, 10p per share that it has positive net assets of £20, so that it can pay the dividend and still have assets in balance with its liabilities. Instead, it must have positive net assets of £320 before it pays the dividend. The legal capital rules thus lead to greater conservatism in the payment of dividends than would a "bare" net assets test for the legality of dividend payment. One can also see from this example the significance of the share premium account being classified as an undistributable reserve in domestic law.[7] If, as before 1948, the share premium account were a distributable reserve, the company would need to have positive net assets of only £220 before it made the dividend payment. And had the company chosen to set the par value at 10p (but still issued the shares at the same price, generating a premium of £1.40 per share), it would have needed positive net assets of only £40 before it made the dividend payment.

---

[2] Model articles for private companies art.30; for public companies art.70. But directors may unilaterally declare interim dividends. Dividends must be declared pro rata, which is an important protection for minority shareholders. See further Ch.19.

[3] Of course, the shareholders' general governance rights (e.g. to remove directors) may make the board responsive to the shareholders' interests in relation to dividends, or capital market pressures may produce a similar result.

[4] The rule is derived from art.15(1)(a) of the Second Directive (77/91/EEC).

[5] 2006 Act s.831(1),(2).

[6] 2006 Act s.831(4)(a). On the share premium account see para.11–6.

[7] 2006 Act s.610 and para.11–6.

Undistributable reserves include more than the share premium account. Also added is the "capital redemption reserve" which we shall consider in the following chapter.[8] That is created when a company re-purchases or redeems its shares, and it simply replaces the reduction in the share capital account which the re-purchase or redemption brings about. In other words, the capital redemption reserve operates so as to hold legal capital constant in this situation but it does not increase it. Further, there is added any other undistributable reserve created by an enactment other than Pt 23 of the Act (Disbributions).[9] The company itself may also add restrictions in its articles by creating an undistributable reserve.[10] There is one final item in the list of undistributable reserves which, however, is best examined after looking at the distribution rule which applies to all companies.

The general rule, applying to companies public or private, is set out in s.830[11] and states that a company may "make a distribution only out of profits available for the purpose". It then defines "profits available for the purpose" as the company's "accumulated realised profits, so far as not previously utilised by distribution or capitalisation, less its accumulated, realised losses, so far as not previously written off in a reduction or reorganisation of capital duly made".[12] This second rule, unlike the first one, seems focused on the company's profit and loss account, rather than its balance sheet. The thrust of the rule is on two points. First, the company needs to assess its accumulated profits and losses over the years to determine whether, at the point a dividend is under consideration, there are profits to support it. Thus, what are sometimes called "nimble dividends" are not permitted, i.e. the paying of dividends out of profits earned in a particular year, even though in previous years the company has made losses, which have not been replaced.[13] More fully, the company must subtract from the profits it has made over the years any amounts already paid out by way of dividend or any profits which have been capitalised,[14] but it may also deduct from its losses it has made over the years any amount properly written off through a reduction or reorganisation of capital.[15] If the company's aggregate profits over the years exceed its aggregate losses over the years, it may make a distribution under this rule to the extent of the surplus profit, subject, however, to one further—and crucial—qualification.

12–3

The second feature of s.830 is that it applies to only "realised" profits and "realised" losses. "Unrealised" profits and losses are left out of account in the

---

[8] Below, para.13–11.

[9] An example of an undistributable reserve created elsewhere in the Act is the re-denomination reserve created by s.620 of the Act. See para.11–19. This operates in the same way as the CRR.

[10] Which was the cause of the problems in *Re Cleveland Trust Plc* [1991] B.C.L.C. 424 where the company's constitution provided that certain realised profits "shall be dealt with as capital surpluses not available for the payment of dividends", which provision, however, was overlooked.

[11] Derived from art.15(1)(c) of the Directive.

[12] 2006 Act s.830(2). With one exception, the Act does not distinguish between trading profits and capital profits, such as that made on the ad hoc disposal of the company's head office, and both are distributable. In the case of investment companies, however, only revenue profits are in principle distributable: ss.832–835.

[13] This reverses the common law: *Lee v Neuchatel Asphalte Co* (1889) 41 Ch.D. 1 CA; *Ammonia Soda Co v Chamberlain* [1918] 1 Ch. 266 CA.

[14] See para.11–20.

[15] See Ch.13.

calculation required by s.830.[16] "Realised" profits and losses are not defined in the Act which delegates the solution to accounting practice.[17] In fact, the precise line between the two is a matter of some controversy,[18] but for present purposes it is perhaps enough to give two clear examples, one on each side of the line. Suppose a company has a piece of real property which it acquired some years ago for £1 million. Because of inflation in asset prices, the property is now worth £5 million. If the company sells the property at its current valuation, receiving £5 million in cash in exchange, it will report a profit of £4 million (assuming no taxes or transaction costs) which it may distribute in whole to its shareholders (assuming it has no accumulated realised losses from the past which it must set against the profit). If, however, the company simply re-values the property in its books at £5 million (but does not dispose of it), which is something it might do in order to demonstrate that a takeover bidder was offering too low a price for the company or because it has adopted accounting principles which systematically deal with its assets and liabilities on a "mark to market" basis, it has recorded simply an unrealised profit.[19] Since the property will be reflected in the balance sheet at this higher value, under historic cost accounting a counterbalancing entry is needed, which will probably take the form of a "revaluation reserve".[20] The same principles apply to losses: only realised losses count against the amount of distributable profit.

12–4   What is the interrelationship between the two rules laid down in ss.830 and 831? Since the former applies to all companies and the latter to public companies alone, the latter presumably prevents certain amounts contributing towards a distribution by a public company which would count in the case of a private company distribution. The general rule focusses on successive profit and loss accounts and the public company rule on the current state of the balance sheet.

---

[16] This again reverses the English common law rule which allowed unrealised profits on fixed assets to be distributed: *Dimbula Valley (Ceylon) Tea Co Ltd v Laurie* [1961] Ch. 353. Scots law took a stricter view: *Westburn Sugar Refineries v IRC*, 1960 S.L.T. 297.

[17] 2006 Act s.853(4): they are "such profits or losses of the company as fall to be treated as realised in accordance with principles generally accepted at the time when the accounts are prepared". However, s.841 does lay down that provisions in the accounts (other than revaluation provisions) should be treated as realised losses (for example, depreciation provisions); s.844 requires development costs to be treated as a realised loss, even if stated as an asset in the accounts; and s.843 makes provisions about the realised gains and losses of long-term insurance businesses.

[18] See CLR, *Capital Maintenance: Other Issues*, paras 62–66; ICAEW, *Guidance on the Determination of Realised Profits and Losses in the Context of Distributions under the Companies Act 2006*, Tech 01/09.

[19] If, however, the re-valued asset is later distributed *in specie* to its shareholders (a perfectly possible, if not common, course of action, because distributions do not have to be in cash) the amount of the unrealised profit is treated as a realised profit for the purpose of determining the legality of the distribution: s.846. The purpose of this provision is to make it possible for the company to distribute assets at book value, even if the value to be found in the company's accounts represents a revaluation of the assets. See further below at para.12–11. The provision was driven initially by a perceived need to facilitate de-mergers, in which assets or shares held by a company might be distributed to its shareholders.

[20] Which is a undistributable reserve unless it represents realised gains: Fourth Directive (78/660/EEC) art.33(2)(c). Where assets are valued on a "mark to market" basis, there will be no revaluation reserve, but the valuation will not add to distributable profits unless the asset is readily convertible into cash (as with gilts or treasury bills).

The profit and loss account records the company's financial success (or lack of it) over a period of a year, the balance sheet its assets and liabilities at the end of the year.[21] Although the profit or loss in a particular year inevitably feeds into the balance sheet at the end of the year, the crucial difference between the two tests appears to be that the public company test incorporates legal capital into its constraints on distributions. The general rule, by contrast, requires only cumulative profits to support a distribution. A public company, therefore, must have both cumulative profits of the requisite size and, after the distribution, net assets on its balance sheet at least equivalent to its legal capital and undistributable reserves.

The further difference between ss.831 and 830 appears to be that the latter takes no account of unrealised losses. Under the test for all companies, a company with an accumulated positive balance of realised profits and losses may lawfully distribute them, even if it is carrying extensive unrealised losses (though it may be a breach of directors' duty or imprudent to do so). In the case of public companies the unrealised losses must be taken into account when establishing the amount available for distribution, except to the extent that the unrealised losses are covered by unrealised gains.[22]

IDENTIFYING THE AMOUNT AVAILABLE FOR DISTRIBUTION

It is apparent from the foregoing that, in determining whether distributions can be made in accordance with the statutory rules, what counts in most cases are the relevant figures in the company's accounts. This may seem an obvious way to proceed: companies are normally required by the Act to produce accounts annually and, except for small companies, to have them audited, thus providing a degree of verification; and the declaration of a dividend is normally one of the decisions for the annual general meeting of the shareholders, at which the accounts will be considered as well. At least for public companies, use of the accounts is mandated by the Second Directive in respect of the net asset restriction in s.831[23] and it probably also applies—though this is less clear from the wording of the Directive—to the accumulated net profits rule of s.830. Certainly, the Directive has been interpreted by the drafters in the UK as requiring both tests to be applied by reference to the numbers in the accounts, and that approach has been applied to private companies as well.

12–5

The statute calls the accounts which are to be used for assessing the legality of the distribution the "relevant" accounts. Since dividends are paid by individual, not groups of, companies, it is the individual accounts of the paying company, not the group accounts, which are the relevant ones.[24] Beyond that, the general rule is

---

[21] See further, Ch.21 below.

[22] 2006 Act s.831(4)(c). "This means that, in calculating the amount available for distributions, a public company must reduce the amount of its net realised profits available for distribution by the amount of its net unrealised losses" (ICAEW, above fn.18, at 2.31).

[23] See art.17(1) but cf. art.17(3).

[24] 2006 Act s.836(2). For an example of the problems that ignoring this point can cause see *Inn Spirit Ltd v Burns* [2002] 2 B.C.L.C. 780.

easy to state: the most recent statutory accounts should be used.[25] When that is so, the distribution is lawful so long as it is justified by reference to those accounts and the accounts have been properly prepared in accordance with the Act, or have been properly prepared subject only to matters not material for determining whether the distribution would be lawful.[26] These accounts must have been duly audited, if subject to audit, and, if the auditors' report is qualified, the auditors must also state in writing whether the respect in which the report was qualified is material in determining whether the distribution would be lawful. This statement must have been laid before the company in general meeting, or sent to the members where no meeting is held.[27]

Interim and initial accounts

12–6   In two cases, however, special accounts will be needed. The first is where the distribution would contravene the statutory distribution rules if reference were made only to the last annual accounts. In that event the company may be able to justify the distribution by reference to additional "interim accounts".[28] The second is where it is proposed to declare a dividend during the company's first accounting period or before any accounts have been presented in respect of that period.[29] In that event it will have to prepare "initial accounts". Initial accounts enable the company to make a distribution before its first set of financial statements is produced. Interim accounts allow the company to take advantage of an improvement in its financial position since the previous statutory accounts were produced. This might occur, for example, when a realised profit had been made on the sale of fixed assets after the date of the last annual accounts and the company wanted to distribute part or all of it to its shareholders without waiting for the next annual accounts. It could also occur if the net trading profits in the current year are seen to be running at a rate considerably higher than formerly and the directors wished to give the shareholders early concrete evidence of this

---

[25] 2006 Act s.836(2).

[26] 2006 Act s.837(2). If the directors knew or ought to have known of a serious defect in the company's accounts, they will not be "properly prepared" nor give a true and fair view, so that any distribution by the company will be unlawful: *Re Cleveland Trust Plc* [1991] B.C.L.C. 424. This may also be the case if the directors are non-negligently ignorant of the defect, but they might then seek to protect themselves against liability by invoking s.1157 (see para.12–13, below).

[27] 2006 Act s.837(3),(4). The auditor's statement may be made whether or not a distribution is proposed at the time when the statement is made and may refer to all or any types of distribution; it will then suffice to validate any distributions of the types covered by the statement: s.837(5). This rule also applies if the directors choose to have an audit, although not obliged to do so. The need for the auditors' statement where the accounts are qualified is frequently overlooked and the resulting distribution will be unlawful: *Precision Dippings Ltd v Precision Dippings Marketing Ltd* [1986] Ch. 447 CA; *BDS Roof-Bond Ltd v Douglas* [2000] 1 B.C.L.C. 401.

[28] 2006 Act s.836(2)(a).

[29] 2006 Act s.836(2)(b).

by paying an immediate dividend. In both these examples the previous year's accounts might well not justify the payment and would have to be supplemented by interim accounts.[30]

Interim dividends

The term "interim accounts", although now well established in the Act, is potentially confusing because it might lead one to suppose that such accounts are needed whenever it is proposed to declare interim (which are very common) or special dividends, in addition to the normal dividend for the year. That is not so. So long as the company has duly complied with its obligations under the Act in respect of its annual accounts for the previous year, it can, in the current year, pay interim or other special dividends in addition to the final dividend for the year so long as these dividends are supported by those accounts.[31] It is only when the last annual accounts would not justify a proposed payment that it is necessary to prepare interim accounts. Normally, however, it will not be necessary to prepare interim accounts merely because the company pays quarterly or half-yearly interim dividends, in anticipation of the final dividend for the year, to be declared by the company when that year's accounts are presented. The previous year's accounts are used to support the interim dividends. The articles normally provide for interim dividends to be paid on the authority of the directors alone, there not being any regularly scheduled meeting of the shareholders to which the matter could be put.[32]

12–7

Adverse developments subsequent to the accounts

The need for interim accounts arises out of possible improvements in the company's financial position which may have occurred since the last statutory accounts were drawn up. What, however, about the opposite situation, where the company's financial position has deteriorated since the statutory accounts were drawn up? If the directors have discovered that the relevant accounts were so seriously inaccurate that they did not in fact give a true and fair view of the state of the company's affairs and its profits or losses at the time the accounts were signed, they clearly should not recommend a dividend, and should withdraw any recommendation they have made; for the dividend, if paid, would be unlawful on the part of the company.[33] If, however, the relevant accounts truly reflected the position as at their date but there has occurred some financial calamity thereafter, payment of the dividend would not, seemingly, be unlawful under the statute. However, as we have seen, a directors' recommendation as to the level of the

12–8

---

[30] The requirements for interim and initial accounts are set out in ss.838 and 839. They are onerous for public companies, though interim accounts need not be audited. Listed companies probably meet the statutory requirements routinely since they are subject to the FCA's requirements for regular half-year financial statements. See para.26–3.

[31] 2006 Act s.840.

[32] As do the model articles for both public (art.70) and private (art.30) companies.

[33] *Re Cleveland Trust Plc* [1991] B.C.L.C. 424. See fn.26, above. And the accounts should be revised; there are now statutory provisions for this: see para.21–31.

dividend is, normally, an essential part of the dividend-setting process. Consequently, the fiduciary duties of directors (discussed in Ch.16) are relevant to this particular decision of the board, as to any other. Payment in such circumstances might constitute a breach of the directors' fiduciary duties—for example, to promote the success of the company—or an act of wrongful trading.[34] The Company Law Review recommended[35] that the statute itself should provide that subsequent losses, of which the company was aware at the time of taking the decision to declare a dividend, should be deducted from the distributable profits shown in the relevant accounts, so that it would be unlawful for the company to make a distribution above that amount. However, this has not been implemented, and so the law on directors' duties fills the gap. One significant difference between the two approaches is that a distribution not permitted by the statutory distribution rules is an unlawful act of the company, which the shareholders cannot ratify, whereas they can in principle ratify a breach of duty by the directors—and may well want to if the breach consists in the payment of a dividend.[36]

A related and more general issue is that, under modern developments in accounting, there is an increasing emphasis on using current market valuations, rather than historic ones, in the accounts. Such an approach can produce considerable volatility in companies' profits from year to year.[37] Even if no particular calamity has struck the company but "mark to market" accounting policies produce volatility in the company's reported profits, the directors' fiduciary duties would require them to take that fact into account in setting the level of dividend.[38]

However, it is possible that a failure to take post-accounts events into consideration when making a distribution would constitute, not simply a breach of duty on the part of the directors, but an unlawful act on the part of the company. This is because, despite the statutory restrictions on distributions, the Act preserves "any rule of law" restricting dividends.[39] Thus, the common law rule prohibiting the return of capital to shareholders[40] continues in force in relation to distributions. In principle, this is odd, since there is some uncertainty about the scope of the common law principle and to have it running in the background of the precise statutory rules creates a legal risk for companies which is difficult to justify.[41] Nevertheless, in the particular situation under discussion, it may have a useful role to play. Since the common law rule applies on the basis of the financial position of the company at the time the distribution is declared, it

---

[34] See above, para.9–6.

[35] Maintenance, para.38.

[36] If the company is in the vicinity of insolvency, the creditors' interests are dominant within directors' duties and the shareholders may not be allowed to ratify a breach. See further para.9–15.

[37] See J. Rickford, "Reforming Capital" (2004) 15 E.B.L.R. 1, especially Ch.4 dealing with pension scheme deficits.

[38] ICAEW, above fn.18, paras 2.3–2.5.

[39] 2006 Act s.851(1)—unless otherwise expressly provided, as discussed in para.12–11.

[40] *Trevor v Whitworth* (1887) 12 App. Cas. 409 HL.

[41] After some havering, the CLR proposed to reverse the position that the common law and statutory regimes operate in tandem and to make the statute the exclusive source of rules in this area (see Formation, para.3.66; Maintenance, Pt II; Completing, para.7.21), but this proposal was not taken up in the Act.

would be breached if company made a distribution on the basis of profits shown in the accounts which had been dissipated by the time the directors came to declare the dividend.[42]

DISGUISED DISTRIBUTIONS

The above rules apply to "distributions" by companies. Beyond making it clear that a distribution need not be in cash and that the definition is intended to be extensive, the statutory definition is not very helpful: "every description of distribution of a company's assets to its members, whether in cash or otherwise".[43] No doubt, this is sufficient to catch the most common form of distribution, the yearly or semi-yearly payment of a dividend by a company to its shareholders, usually in cash but sometimes with the alternative of subscribing for additional shares in the company. The statutory definition is clearly intended to go beyond that simple situation, by its reference to non-cash dividends, but how far? Does it catch what are sometimes referred to as "disguised distributions", i.e. transactions between a company and a shareholder on other than an arm's length basis, so that value is transferred from the company to the shareholder? In many cases, the implementation of such a transaction will be a breach of duty on the part of the directors who authorised it, but, if the distribution rules apply, the transaction will be an unlawful one (sometimes referred to as an "ultra vires" transaction)[44] on the part of the company as well.

12–9

Many, though not all, of the relatively few cases on disguised distributions have been decided on the basis of the common law rule, so it perhaps best to begin by setting it out. In *Ridge Securities Ltd v Inland Revenue Commissioners*[45] Pennycuick J said:

> "A company can only lawfully deal with its assets in furtherance of its objects. The corporators may take assets out of the company by way of dividend, or, with the leave of the court, by way of reduction of capital, or in a winding-up. They may of course acquire them for full

---

[42] See *Peter Buchanan Ltd v McVey* [1955] A.C. 516 at 521–522, a decision of the High Court of Justice of Eire.

[43] 2006 Act s.829(1). Certain transactions are specifically exempted from the term: an issuance of bonus shares (for the reasons given at para.11–20); transactions regulated elsewhere in the Act (reductions of capital and redemption or re-purchase of shares (see the following chapter)); and distributions on a winding up (regulated by the Insolvency Act 1986): s.829(2). The exclusion of bonus shares permits companies to capitalise unrealised (and thus undistributable) profits, assuming they have power in the articles so to do.

[44] This is a different use of the term "ultra vires" from the one we examined in para.7–29. There it meant a transaction outside the company's own objects clause; here it means a transaction not permitted by general company law. The directors' duties implications of self-dealing transactions are considered in paras 16–54 et seq.

[45] *Ridge Securities Ltd v Inland Revenue Commissioners* [1964] 1 W.L.R. 479, 495; approved by Lord Walker in *Progress Property Co Ltd v Moorgarth Group Ltd* [2010] UKSC 55 at [1]. The relatively small number of cases on disguised dividends is probably to be explained on the grounds that the greatest temptation to make such payments is in the period immediately prior to insolvency when specific provisions of the Insolvency Act 1986 (especially ss.238 and 242—transactions at an undervalue—and 239 and 243—preferences) may be easier to use.

consideration. They cannot take assets out of the company by way of voluntary distribution, however described, and if they attempt to do so, the distribution is ultra vires the company."[46]

This passage suggests that the common law rule is broader than the statutory provisions on distributions, for it indicates that any return of corporate assets to the shareholders, which is not justified by a statutory provision or the pursuit of the company's objects, will be unlawful, even if the company has distributable profits. However, if there are distributable profits the statutory provisions discussed above provide a mechanism for making a distribution which does not breach the common law rule. Consequently, if there are no distributable profits, both the statutory and common law rules will be broken, but the common law rule will catch any improper return of assets to the shareholders whether that return is classified as a distribution or not.

12–10   The core element of a disguised contribution is that it is a transaction between the company and a shareholder which does not purport to be a distribution but which contains a transfer of value to the shareholder[47] because of a discrepancy between the value provided to the company by the shareholder and the greater value provided to the shareholder by the company. It is not necessary that the transaction be a sham to be characterised as a disguised distribution: it is the imbalance in the considerations that is the focus of the courts' concerns. The two main issues arising are: (i) how rigorously will the courts examine the discrepancy in the values provided to and by the company; and (ii) what is the relevance of the good faith or otherwise of the parties to the transaction? As we shall see, these questions are to some degree interlinked.

In some cases the discrepancy is obvious, not necessarily because the value transferred to the shareholder is large but because the shareholder provides nothing or virtually nothing to the company in exchange for the value transferred.[48] These may be thought of as virtually gratuitous transactions. Outside gratuitous transactions, the courts are clearly reluctant to be put in a position where they may have to scrutinise routinely the exchange of values in commercial transactions between shareholders and their companies. In *Progress Property Co Ltd v Moorgarth Group Ltd*[49] Lord Walker stated that the parties should have a "margin of appreciation" in relation to the assessment of the value of what was transferred under the contract, at least where the transaction was

---

[46] See also *MacPherson v European Strategic Bureau Ltd* [2000] 2 B.C.L.C. 683 CA. "In my view, to enter into an arrangement which seeks to achieve a distribution of assets, as if on a winding up, without making proper provision for creditors is, itself, a breach of the duties which directors owe to the company; alternatively, it is ultra vires the company" (per Chadwick LJ); and *Barclays Bank Plc v British and Commonwealth Holdings Plc* [1996] B.C.L.C. 1 (replacement of obligation of an insolvent company to redeem shares by an obligation to pay damages of like amount in respect of the failure to redeem would have been ultra vires if it had not been approved by the court as part of a statutory scheme of arrangement—see Ch.29).

[47] Normally, that shareholder is a controlling shareholder (i.e. the controller is extracting value from the company to the detriment of the non-controlling shareholders or the company's creditors) but the other party to the transaction may be all the shareholders in the company. See *Clydebank Football Club Ltd v Steedman*, 2002 S.L.T. 109.

[48] See *Re Halt Garage (1964) Ltd* [1982] 3 All E.R. 1016—payment of remuneration where no services rendered held to be a disguised return of capital; *Ridge Securities Ltd v IRC* [1964] 1 W.L.R. 479—payment of interest "grotesquely out of proportion" to the amount lent.

[49] *Progress Property Co Ltd v Moorgarth Group Ltd* [2010] UKSC 55 at [31]–[33].

entered into in good faith. In other words, it would be necessary to show a very large discrepancy between the values provided and received by the company in such a case for the disguised contribution rule to be triggered.

However, it is clear that good faith will not take the parties to the transaction outside the scope of the disguised distribution rule altogether. In *Re Halt Garage (1964) Ltd*[50] the shareholder and the company (in effect the same person, as is often the situation in these cases) had acted entirely honestly, having been misled by professional advice. However, the company had paid for services which in effect had never been received and the amount paid had to be accounted for to the company (now in liquidation). This case might be distinguished as in effect a gratuitous transaction. Certainly, in *Aveling Barford Ltd v Perion Ltd*,[51] which was not a gratuitous transaction but a case of a transfer of corporate property to a controlling shareholder at a considerable undervalue, Hoffmann J put some emphasis on the fact that the parties (again in effect a single controlling shareholder) knew and intended the sale to be at an undervalue. In *Progress Property Co Ltd v Moorgarth Group Ltd*[52] Lord Walker thought that sometimes the parties' subjective intentions would be relevant and sometimes they would not, but he did agree that an apparent distribution disguised as an arm's length commercial transaction was the "paradigm case" where subjective intentions were relevant.

> "If the conclusion is that it was a genuine arm's length transaction then it will stand, even if it may, with hindsight, appear to have been a bad bargain [for the company]. If it was an improper attempt to extract value by the pretence of an arm's length sale, it will be held unlawful. But either conclusion will depend on a realistic assessment of all the relevant facts, not simply a retrospective valuation exercise in isolation from all other inquiries."[53]

It may be that a question which it will often be helpful to ask is whether the company would have been willing to enter into the same transaction with a non-shareholder. In *Aveling Barford* the answer was clearly "no", whereas in *Progress Property*, where an honest mistake was made as the existence of a liability between the parties, the answer was "yes" (i.e. the company would not have altered the contractual price if the purchaser had been a non-shareholder, assuming a similar mistake about the liability existed). If the company would not have been willing to enter into the transaction on the same terms with a non-shareholder, it will be caught by the common law rule, but may of course be justified in one of the ways mention by Pennycuick J. Thus, a gratuitous payment to a shareholder will almost always be caught the common law rule, but would be capable of being justified as a distribution by a company with distributable profits.

---

[50] *Re Halt Garage (1964) Ltd* [1982] 3 All E.R. 1016.

[51] *Aveling Barford Ltd v Perion Ltd* [1989] B.C.L.C. 626.

[52] *Progress Property Co Ltd v Moorgarth Group Ltd* [2010] UKSC 55 at [27]–[31].

[53] *Progress Property Co Ltd v Moorgarth Group Ltd* [2010] UKSC 55 at [29]. This relatively relaxed approach may have been encouraged by the specific statutory controls which exist over substantial property transactions with directors. See paras 16–123 et seq.

Intra-group transfers

12–11 In *Aveling Barford Ltd v Perion Ltd*[54] the company, which was solvent (in the sense that it could pay its debts as they fell due) but had accumulated heavy losses, and so was not in a position to meet the general rule requiring distributions only out of accumulated profits, transferred to another company, controlled by the same person as was its controlling shareholder, an important asset at an undervalue as compared with its current market value.[55] The decision that the transfer was unlawful caused considerable alarm in commercial circles about the legality of intra-group transfers of assets, which are, of course, a common occurrence as a result of the carrying on of business through groups of companies.[56] Such transfers are usually effected on the basis of the value of the asset as stated in the transferring company's accounts (its "book" value), which may not reflect the current market price of the asset.[57] Advice was given that the common law rule might strike down a transaction where a company transferred an asset at book value to another group company, if the asset was in fact worth more than its book value, possibly even where the transferring company had distributable reserves (which was not the case in *Aveling Barford* itself).

The 2006 Act deals with this problem by laying down rules about distributions in kind which apply to both the statutory restrictions on distributions and any other rule of law restricting distributions.[58] The core new provision[59] applies where the transferring company has profits available for distribution.[60] Where this is not the case, the common law will continue to apply unamended, with the apparent requirement that the asset would have to be transferred at market value to be sure of avoiding the risk of infringing the common law rules on distributions. Given the risk of opportunism on the part of controlling shareholders where the company has no distributable profits, this restriction in the new section is probably wise. Assuming distributable profits, the amount of the distribution is assessed under the section at zero, provided the consideration received for the asset is at least equivalent to its book value, and otherwise is restricted to the amount by which the book value exceeds the consideration.[61] If, by contrast, the consideration received upon the transfer of the asset exceeds its book value, the distributable profits of the transferring company are increased by

---

[54] *Aveling Barford Ltd v Perion Ltd* [1989] B.C.L.C. 626.

[55] The fact that the payment was made to a company controlled by its main shareholder rather than to the shareholder directly was regarded as "irrelevant".

[56] The nature of the reaction to the decision is set out by the CLR in Maintenance, Pt II.

[57] Since accounts are often, even today, constructed on a "historical" basis, an asset is likely to be shown in the company's balance sheet at the price paid for it (or perhaps less, if it has been depreciated), rather than at its current market value, which might be higher.

[58] 2006 Act s.851(2)—thus embracing not only the common law rules but also rules contained in a statute other than the Act (unless that Act overrides the Act explicitly or by necessary implication).

[59] 2006 Act s.846 (above, fn.19) is also added to the common law rules.

[60] 2006 Act s.845(1)—the amount of the distributable profits needs to be enough to cover any discrepancy between the contract price and the book value but does not need to cover the gap between the contract price and the market value. So, for a transfer at book value, distributable profits of £1 will do.

[61] 2006 Act s.845(2).

the amount of the excess.[62] Of course, the rules relating to directors' fiduciary duties[63] are unaffected by these changes.

CONSEQUENCES OF UNLAWFUL DISTRIBUTIONS

Recovery from members

No criminal sanctions are provided in the Act in respect of distributions which it renders unlawful, but something (though precious little) is said about the civil consequences. This is done by s.847 which provides that, when a distribution[64] is made to a member which the member knows, or has reasonable grounds for believing, is made in contravention (in whole or in part) of the statutory distribution rules, that person is liable to repay it or, if the distribution was otherwise than in cash, its value.[65] Thus, by virtue of this section, the payment, though "unlawful", is neither void nor voidable but can nevertheless be recovered from any recipient of it who knew or ought to have known that it was unlawful.

12–12

This provision has been interpreted to mean that there is liability to repay the dividend if the recipient knows it has not been paid out of distributable profits, even if that person is unaware that such distributions are illegal.[66] The section is thus potentially wide-ranging in its impact on shareholders if this limited definition of what has to be known is coupled with a broad approach to what "knowledge" consists of. This raises the question of whether "reasonable grounds for believing" means that a shareholder is treated as knowing those facts which would have been discovered through proper enquiries (constructive knowledge) or only those to which the recipient turned a blind eye.[67] On the former approach it might be argued that a shareholder who had received the annual reports should be treated as knowing, for example, that the company had no distributable profits or that the auditor had not included the required statement in the case of a

---

[62] 2006 Act s.845(3).

[63] On the duties of directors in self-dealing transactions, see paras 16–54 et seq., below.

[64] Other than a distribution which constitutes financial assistance for the acquisition of the company's own shares given in breach of the Act (see para.13–44, below) or any payment made in respect of the redemption or purchase of shares in the company (para.13–7): s.847(4).

[65] 2006 Act s.847(2).

[66] *It's A Wrap (UK) Ltd v Gala* [2006] 2 B.C.L.C. 634 CA, a case which illustrates the arbitrary nature of many of the legal capital rules. The defendants, who ran a small business which was unsuccessful, paid themselves a modest remuneration, which they could have received entirely lawfully as salary under their service contracts with the company or as directors' fees. See para.11–9, above. However, they were diverted from this course of action by advice that it would be more tax efficient for the remuneration to be paid by way of dividend.

[67] Arden and Chadwick LJJ were divided on this issue in *It's A Wrap (UK) Ltd v Gala* [2006] 2 B.C.L.C. 634 CA —the point not being relevant to the decision in that case. The former is a more natural reading of the language of the section and conforms to the approach of the common law (see below), whilst the latter is a more natural reading of the language of the Directive (an irregularity of which the recipient "could not in view of the circumstances have been unaware"), which the section implements in the UK.

qualified report,[68] even if he or she had not in fact read them, and that such knowledge is all that is required to trigger the repayment obligation.[69]

However, this section does not constitute the only basis on which a claim for repayment of dividend can be made against a shareholder. The company may claim repayment at common law.[70] This is on the basis that the payment of an unlawful dividend amounts to a misapplication by the directors of corporate property and where "the transferee of the assets has knowledge of the facts rendering the disposition ultra vires, that party is under a duty to restore those assets to the company because he is deemed to hold them as constructive trustee".[71] The common law claim, which may or may not be broader than the statutory claim in terms of its definition of knowledge,[72] operates by making the recipient a constructive trustee of the distribution.[73]

Recovery from directors

12–13   The statute provides for no specific remedy against the directors, who authorised the unlawful distribution, but here again the common law provides a remedy.[74] It has been clear since the decision in *Flitcroft*'s case[75] in the nineteenth century that directors who cause the company to pay unlawful dividends are under a duty to restore to the company the value of the assets wrongfully paid away. In *Bairstow v Queens Moat Houses Plc*[76] the principle was applied to hold directors liable where the accounts failed to give a true and fair view[77] of the company's financial situation as a result of accounting irregularities of which the directors were aware. This rule applies whether the distribution was unlawful under the statutory rules (as in *Bairstow*) or by virtue of the common law (as in *Flitcroft's* case). The principle that the directors should restore the value of corporate assets unlawfully paid away is potentially a much broader one than the claim that a

---

[68]   Above, para.12–5 and see *Precision Dippings Ltd v Precison Dippings Marketing Ltd* [1986] Ch. 447.

[69]   It seems fanciful to suppose that any court would hold that a small shareholder in a listed company should study the relevant accounts and the documents accompanying them and read them with an understanding of the Act to check that their dividends are lawfully payable, no matter how much that court may be committed to the doctrine that ignorance of the law is no excuse. In relation to an institutional investor, however, or a "business angel" who has invested in a start-up company, the proposition is not so fanciful.

[70]   This basis of claim is specifically preserved by s.847(3).

[71]   *Rolled Steel Products (Holdings) Ltd v British Steel Corp* [1986] Ch. 246, 303–304, per Browne-Wilkinson LJ. Not surprisingly, the principle applies equally where the transferee is the director receiving the dividend as shareholder: see *Allied Carpets Plc v Nethercott* [2001] B.C.C. 81; following the earlier case of *Precision Dippings Ltd v Precison Dippings Marketing Ltd* [1986] Ch. 447. Indeed, a director of the company or of another group company is the person in respect of whom the knowledge requirements can most easily be met.

[72]   Constructive knowledge appears to suffice for liability at common law: see *Rolled Steel Products (Holdings) Ltd v British Steel Corp* [1986] Ch. 246 at 297–298, per Slade LJ.

[73]   See further at para.16–106, below.

[74]   If the director is a recipient shareholder, then, of course, he or she may be liable in that way. See fn.71.

[75]   *Re Exchange Banking Co* (1882) 21 Ch.D. 519 CA.

[76]   *Bairstow v Queens Moat Houses Plc* [2001] 2 B.C.L.C. 531 CA.

[77]   On the meaning of this phrase see para.21–14.

shareholder should return to the company dividends improperly paid to that shareholder. The director might have received no dividends him- or herself and yet be liable, in principle, to restore the whole of the amount wrongfully paid out of the company's assets. However, in *Bairstow* the court showed little interest in confining the scope of the directors' liability. The principle in *Flitcroft*'s case, the court held, was not limited to companies which were insolvent at the time of the claim against the director (where the directors' payment would go to benefit the creditors) but applied also to solvent companies, so that the directors might end up putting the company in funds whereby it could pay the dividend all over again.[78]

A long debated issue is whether the directors' liability to restore the value of the distribution is a strict one or is based on fault, requiring dishonesty or at least negligence. In *Re Paycheck Services 3 Ltd*[79] Rimer LJ thought obiter that the liability was strict, but subject to the court's discretion to grant relief under s.1157 of the Act, where the director had acted "honestly and reasonably".[80] On appeal to the Supreme Court this view was endorsed, again obiter, by three of the justices.[81] Reliance on court discretion to grant relief is obviously less attractive to a director than a fault requirement for initial liability.

It follows from the principle that the director is liable to restore to the company the assets wrongfully paid away that the amount of that liability is not limited to the loss suffered by the company as a result of the wrongful payment.[82] If, for example, the distribution was not supported by proper set of accounts, the directors are in principle liable to restore the whole of it, even if a properly drawn set would have allowed some lower level of distribution to be made or even the level of distribution which was actually made. However, this last point has been somewhat qualified in subsequent cases. Where there is a properly drawn set of accounts in existence which justify a distribution up to a particular level but the

12–14

---

[78] The so-called "windfall" objection to the principle of repayment. The objection works, of course, only if the directors have the resources to repay the dividend and if the company could lawfully pay out the money restored by the directors, for example, if properly drawn accounts would reveal a distributable surplus. The court did leave open the possibility that the repaying directors could claim an equitable contribution from the shareholders who had received the improper dividend with notice of the facts.

[79] *Re Paycheck Services 3 Ltd* [2009] 2 B.C.L.C. 309 at [81]–[85] CA. There are two competing lines of authority on the point, as laid out in the judgment in this case.

[80] See para.16–125, below. If the company's claim is brought, as it often is, by a liquidator acting under s.212 of the Insolvency Act 1986 the court has a power to order an account of such amount "as the court thinks just". It is unclear whether this discretion adds to what is available to the court under s.1157 of the Companies Act 2006. See the debate among the judges in *Re Paycheck Services 3 Ltd* [2009] 2 B.C.L.C. 309 CA.

[81] *Re Paycheck Services 3 Ltd* [2011] 1 B.C.L.C. 141 at [45]–[47] (Lord Hope); [124] (Lord Walker); and [146] (Lord Clarke).

[82] *Bairstow v Queens Moat Houses Plc* [2001] 2 B.C.L.C. 531 at 548–550 CA; distinguishing *Target Holdings v Redferns* [1996] A.C. 421 HL. Hence, the risk of a windfall to the company if the directors restore the assets. See fn.78, above. See also *Inn Spirit Ltd v Burns* [2002] 2 B.C.L.C. 780, where a subsidiary had paid a dividend directly to the shareholders of the parent company and the court refused to entertain the question of whether the same amount of dividend could have reached the shareholders' pockets by way of a distribution to the parent and then a distribution by the parent.

company exceeds that level, it seems that the requirement to make "a distribution out of profits available for the purpose" means that the directors act improperly only to the extent of the excess.[83]

The upshot of these rules is that directors who make improper distributions are more likely to be held liable to compensate the company than the shareholders, who receive them, to restore them to the company. If directors cannot meet the requirements of s.1157, it is probably right that they are liable to the company for the full amount of the unlawful dividend, since the dividend rules, being tied to the accounting numbers, are not difficult to comply with. Although recovery of small amounts of dividend from numerous shareholders is probably not practicable, it is not clear that recovery should be confined to those who receive the dividend with knowledge of its unlawfulness where this practical objection does not apply.[84]

Finally, one should not forget the possibility of an action by the company against its auditors if it can be shown that their negligence led the directors to approve a defective set of accounts.[85]

REFORM

12–15   This chapter has shown that that British law has developed a complex set of rules for the purpose of setting the maximum level of dividend (or other distribution) payable by a company in respect of a particular financial period. Those rules take as their central idea that, for public companies, a distribution should be made only if, after it has been made, the company will retain assets whose value exceeds its liabilities by the amount of the company's legal capital. It is not enough that, post the distribution, the company's assets should equal its liabilities. As it has been put, the requirement is that the assets should exceed the liabilities by a "margin" and that margin is set by the amount of the company's legal capital.[86] It is clearly a sensible measure of creditor protection that a company should be subject to constraints on its freedom to transfer assets to shareholders by way of a distribution (for which it receives nothing tangible in return). There would be little point in giving the creditors priority over the members in a winding up if there were no limits on the company's freedom to return assets to members whilst it is a going concern, and the rules of insolvency law, operating only in the vicinity of insolvency, can be argued not to fill the whole of this regulatory need. The question, however, is whether basing those constraints around the notion of legal capital is the most appropriate technique.

It is sometimes said that the centrality of legal capital in the distribution rules is the result of the Second Directive. This is only partly true. British law adopted the notion of distribution rules based on legal capital at a very early stage of its

---

[83] *Re Marini Ltd* [2004] B.C.C. 172.

[84] For an attractive argument that shareholders should always be liable to repay the dividend, subject to a defence of change of position, see J. Payne, "Unjust Enrichment, Trusts and Recipient Liability for Unlawful Dividends" (2003) 119 L.Q.R. 583.

[85] See para.22–36, below.

[86] J. Rickford, "Reforming Capital: Report of the Interdisciplinary Group on Capital Maintenance" [2004] E.B.L.R. 1, 51.

development in the nineteenth century.[87] And it was in 1948, before the EU was created and long before the UK joined it, that domestic law adopted the position that the share premium must be treated in virtually the same way as the nominal value of the share for the purposes of legal capital rules,[88] probably the single most important step in making the distribution rules an effective constraint on companies. Whilst the Second Directive undoubtedly did tighten the previously applicable distribution rules, for example, by ruling out "nimble" dividends,[89] it did not introduce a fundamentally new approach into domestic law. The inflexibility of the Second Directive relates rather to fundamental reform of the distribution rules. As far as public companies are concerned, it is not possible for the UK to move away radically from the test of positive net assets plus a margin represented by legal capital for the legality of dividends, without a reform at EU level.[90] Without reform of the public company rules, there is little demand for reform of the rules for private companies, since s.831 does not apply to them anyway.[91] Reform at EU level, of course, could take the form either of the adoption by EU law of a test for distributions no longer based on legal capital or of a decision that the setting of distribution rules is a matter for the Member States, in which the EU has no or only a limited interest.[92]

The central issues

Whether reform takes place primarily at EU or at domestic level, the question still remains of the strength of the case for reform. There are really three questions which need to be considered, which can only be sketched out here. First, do the current rules provide creditor protection effectively? There are reasons to think that they do not, for the reason that many, perhaps all, classes of creditor do not rely on them. Sophisticated (i.e. large-scale and repeat) creditors, such as banks, place their trust in the terms of their loan contracts, which deal with many risks other than excessive distributions.[93] Trade creditors use other protective techniques, such as retention-of-title clauses or simply not becoming heavily exposed to a single debtor. Finally, involuntary creditors (notably tort victims)

12–16

---

[87] See, for example, *Flitcroft's Case, Re Exchange Banking Co* (1882) 21 Ch. D. 519 CA.

[88] Above, para.11–6.

[89] Above, para.12–3.

[90] Arguably, this statement is subject to the strong qualification that the Second Directive does not require the share premium to be treated as part of legal capital, in which case the impact of the current distribution rules could be heavily reduced by reducing the margin to the amount of the nominal value of the shares. A legal capital test for distributions would be left in place but it would be largely ineffective. See above, para.11–6. On the pros and cons of such an approach see J. Rickford, "Reforming Capital: Report of the Interdisciplinary Group on Capital Maintenance" [2004] E.B.L.R. 1, 51 at 70 et seq.

[91] The one area where "private companies only" reform has occured is in relation to financial assistance (see para.13–55, below), but the financial assistance rules are not a necessary consequence of distribution rules based on legal capital.

[92] The Commission carried out a feasibility study on alternatives to the current capital maintenance regime, but concluded that reform of the Directive was unnecessary. See KPMG, *Feasibility Study on an alternative to the capital maintenance regime established by the Second Company Law Directive*, Berlin, 2008. For a critique of the KPMG approach see K. Fuchs, "The Regulation of Companies' Capital in the European Union: What is the Current State of Affairs?" (2011) 22 E.B.L.R. 237.

[93] See para.31–24, below.

necessarily do not rely on the company's balance sheet and really need a guarantee that their claims will be met, which the legal capital rules do not provide (though they may help) but compulsory insurance would—and does in some cases.[94] In other words, it is not at all easy to identify the beneficiaries of the current rules or, therefore, those who would be harmed if those rules were substantially amended.[95]

Secondly, however, it might be argued that, although the distribution rules may not do much good, they cause little harm and so should be left in place to pick up those cases where self-help or mandatory insurance, for one reason or another, do not deal with the problem. This approach would be acceptable if it were clear that the current distribution rules carry with them no costs—or at least fewer costs than benefits. The second question therefore relates to the costs of the current distribution rules. The argument that the current rules do carry considerable costs was vigorously propounded in the Rickford Report.[96] At the centre of its argument was a change in the role of the company accounts to which, as we have seen, the present distribution rules are tightly linked. The trend from historic cost accounting to reporting on the basis of current values for assets and liabilities, associated with the adoption of International Financial Reporting Standards,[97] is designed to make the accounts more helpful for shareholders and investors, but can be argued to have distorted the creditor protection function of the accounts. Reported profits have become more volatile, whilst retention of the "realised profits" rule for distributions[98] does not permit the company to take advantage of the upward fluctuations in asset values when considering distributions.

Even so, the case for reform is still not made out unless a workable alternative test for the legality of distributions can be advanced. As it happens, there is considerable comparative experience with alternative tests, since the US jurisdictions abandoned legal capital a long time ago and so have had to devise alternative tests, and some Commonwealth countries, notably New Zealand, have taken the same step. The Rickford Report, which gives an account of alternatives, recommended an approach based on a solvency test.[99] This is not an entirely new technique even in domestic law, where it is used in certain limited areas.[100] However, its adoption as the test for the legality of distributions would be novel. In essence, the directors would have to form a judgment about what level of dividend the company could appropriately pay, without endangering its solvency.

---

[94] The most pressing classes of claim (from road accident victims and employees) are subject to mandatory insurance, which, suggestively, is required to be taken out by all those engaged in the relevant activity, whether they operate with limited liability or not.

[95] See J. Armour, "Share Capital and Creditor Protection: Efficient Rules for a Modern Company Law" (2000) 63 M.L.R. 355; and "Legal Capital: An Outdated Concept" (2006) 7 E.B.O.R. 5; and the slightly more optimistic conclusions of D. Kershaw, "The Decline of Legal Capital: An Exploration of the Consequences of Board Solvency-based Capital Reductions" in D. Prentice and A. Reisberg (eds), *Corporate Finance Law in the UK and EU* (Oxford: Oxford University Press, 2011) Ch.2.

[96] Above, fn.86, especially Chs 3 and 4.

[97] See para.21–18, below.

[98] Above, para.12–3.

[99] Above, fn.86, Ch.5. For counter-argument see W. Schön, "Comment: Balance Sheet Tests or Solvency Tests—or Both?" (2006) 7 E.B.O.R. 181.

[100] For the operation of such a scheme in relation to reductions of capital out of court by private companies, see para.13–40, below.

The directors already take a similar decision when deciding, within the limits set by the distribution rules, what level of distribution it is appropriate to make to shareholders and how much to keep in the company for investment in future projects. Under the reform proposal the role of the directors' judgment would be expanded to embrace creditors' as well as shareholders' interests.

Since company law is structured so as to require the directors to put the shareholders' interests first, so long as the company is a going concern, the obvious risk with this proposal is that the directors will undervalue the interests of the creditors and overvalue those of the shareholders when taking this new or expanded decision. At present, the rule-based distribution test gives directors no discretion about the maximum which is distributable; under the reform proposal that issue would become a matter of the directors' judgment about the impact of the proposed distribution on the company's ability in the future to meet its debts as they fall due. In order to counteract a pro-shareholder bias the directors would be required to certify (through a public "solvency statement") that the proposed distribution would not affect the company's ability to meet its debts, either immediately or for a period after the distribution (probably one year). Sanctions (probably both criminal and civil) would be attached to directors whose statement was made negligently. Of course, the threat such liability might cause directors to be cautious in their dividend decisions, in which case the alleged pro-shareholder bias of the solvency test would be counteracted, but it might also make directors unenthusiastic about the proposed reform.[101]

---

[101] That there is personal liability for directors even under the current rules is clear (above, para.12–13) but directors might consider a rule-based system as easier to comply with than one based on a standard.

CHAPTER 13

CAPITAL MAINTENANCE

In the previous chapter we analysed at some length the rules limiting the maximum amount a company may make by way of a distribution to its shareholders. There are two clear ways in which a company might seek to circumvent this rule. First, instead of making a distribution (for example, paying a dividend) to its shareholders, it could offer to buy back some of the shares held by them. In this way the company would be returning assets to its shareholders (or some of them), as would occur in a distribution, and so the interests of the creditors would be engaged in such a move. However, the distribution rules would not apply on the basis that this exercise was not a gratuitous transaction (assuming shares repurchased at market price). In addition, the company would be reducing the amount standing in its share capital and, possibly, share premium accounts through the repurchases. By returning assets to its shareholders in this way a public company would be making it easier to carry out a regular distribution to shareholders in the future. The reduction of the amounts in the capital accounts would lessen the impact of the distribution rule discussed in the previous chapter, i.e. that after the distribution the company should have net assets at least equal to its capital. Perhaps it is not surprising that, for both these

13–1

reasons, the nineteenth century view was that a company could not acquire its own shares. However, a less draconian approach—close to that eventually adopted in the modern reforms—would have been to subject the acquisition, by analogy, to the distribution rule.

Secondly, a public company could seek directly to reduce the amounts standing in its share capital and other capital accounts, thus facilitating distributions, either immediately after the reduction or in the future. This might seem to be a straightforward and unlawful manipulation by the company of its accounts. Having insisted on the creation of capital accounts in the first place and having imposed a distribution rule by reference to the balance sheet, how could the law permit the company to adjust downwards the amounts stated in those accounts? The answer, of course, is that the company is permitted no such general freedom. However, there are circumstances in which it might be in the interests of all involved—shareholders and creditors alike—to permit a reduction of the amounts stated in the capital accounts. This might be so even in the case of a private company, for example, to avoid the rule about not issuing shares at a discount to nominal value (see para.11–4, above). The law thus provided from an early stage a procedure by which the capital figures might be reduced, whilst protecting shareholder and creditor interests, and in the 2006 reforms an additional and more flexible procedure was added for use by private companies.

We look first at acquisitions by a company of its shares, then at the capital reduction procedure and finally turn to the matter of a company giving financial assistance for the purchase of its own shares. This third issue seems only tangentially related to the issue of legal capital, though it has traditionally been so regarded, and so we take it last.

ACQUISITIONS OF OWN SHARES

The general prohibition

13–2   It was held by the House of Lords in the nineteenth century that a company could not acquire its own shares, even though there was an express power to do so in its memorandum, since this would result in a reduction of capital.[1] Assuming that on acquisition by the company the shares were cancelled and nothing put in their place this would necessarily reduce the capital yardstick represented by issued share capital and it could also be regarded as objectionable as a diversion of the company's assets to the shareholders whose shares were acquired, possibly in circumstances in which an ordinary dividend could not be paid because of the rules discussed in the previous chapter. Today, however, acquisitions by companies of shares held by their investors are common. Acquisitions may occur because the company is able to meet its investment needs from internally generated profit and so has less need of externally provided equity finance, or because it wishes to give investors who no longer rate the company an attractive opportunity to exit it, whilst retaining those shareholders who think the

---

[1] *Trevor v Whitworth* (1887) 12 App. Cas. 409 HL. Since at this stage in the development of UK company law, there was no distinction between public and private companies, the rule necessarily applied to all companies incorporated under the Acts.

company's prospects are good. Thus, the story of the law's development is from prohibition of acquisition to specification of circumstances in which acquisition by a company of its own shares is allowed. As we shall see, the Act now legitimises two forms of acquisition: redemption and re-purchase.

The 2006 Act begins by confirming the common law rule that a limited company "shall not acquire its own shares whether by purchase, subscription or otherwise".[2] If it purports to do so, the company and every officer in default is liable to a fine and the purported acquisition is void.[3] In addition, a public company is prohibited from taking a lien or charge over its own shares (that is also treated as void), except to cover the unpaid liability on a partly paid share.[4] Moreover, this central prohibition is buttressed by two further statutory restrictions.

Acquisition through a nominee

First, the prohibition could be avoided in certain cases if the company acquired the shares through a nominee rather than directly. Accordingly, in such a case the shares are treated as held by the nominee on its own account and the company is regarded as having no beneficial interest in them.[5] Further, if the nominee does not meet the financial obligations attached to the shares, then that liability will fall on the other subscribers to the memorandum (where the nominee is a subscriber) and in the other cases it will fall on the directors of the company at the time the shares were issued to or acquired by the nominee.[6] In both cases it is a joint and several liability.

However, this liability rule is applied only when the nominee for the company acquires the shares as a subscriber to its memorandum, where the shares are issued by the company to the nominee, or when the nominee acquires the shares partly paid from a third person.[7] It does not apply if the nominee acquires fully paid shares from a third party, even if the nominee does so with funds provided by the company.[8] This suggests that the rationale of the nominee rules is to ensure that the company receives the full price of the shares it issues, which price the company will necessarily have received before the nominee's acquisition of the shares in the case of the acquisition of fully paid shares by a nominee from an existing holder. Furthermore, where shares are acquired by a nominee for the company rather than by the company directly, the shares remain in the hands of the nominee (i.e. are not cancelled) so that the company's capital accounts remain

13–3

---

[2] 2006 Act s.658(1)—the exemption of unlimited companies from this prohibition shows the connection between the rule and creditor protection.

[3] 2006 Act s.658(2).

[4] 2006 Act s.670. There are also exceptions for companies whose ordinary business includes the lending of money and the charge is part of that business, and for charges taken by a private company before it re-registered as public.

[5] 2006 Act s.660(2). In effect, the nominee arrangement is unwound by the law.

[6] 2006 Act.661(2), but the court has the power to relieve a director or subscriber who has acted honestly and reasonably from the whole or part of the liability: s.661(3)–(4).

[7] 2006 Act s.660.

[8] Though the financial assistance rules, below, para.13–44, may apply.

unaffected. This also helps to explain why the general prohibition applies, by contrast, to direct acquisition by the company of even fully paid shares in the company.

Company may not be a member of its holding company

13–4 Secondly, the prohibition on acquisition of own shares is supplemented by s.136 which provides that a company cannot be a member of its holding company, either directly or through a nominee,[9] and any allotment or transfer of shares in the holding company from an existing shareholder in the parent to the subsidiary or its nominee is void. Section 136 is aimed at preventing the de facto reduction of capital which would result from a subsidiary company acquiring shares in its holding company. The holding company, through its subsidiary, would be returning assets to the selling shareholder.[10] Nevertheless, s.136 does not apply where the subsidiary, at the time of acquisition of the shares in the holding company, is not a subsidiary of it, but later becomes so, for example, as a result of a takeover.[11] The upshot of the exception is that the resources of the holding company may be expended in buying (in effect) its own shares (i.e. when it completes the takeover), but it has been held, nevertheless, that this result cannot be prevented by relying on the general prohibition on a company acquiring its own shares (s.658) rather than s.136.[12] Presumably the desire to permit a useful commercial transaction was thought, in this instance, to outweigh the policy behind the prohibition on the acquisition of own shares.

Specific exceptions to the general prohibition

13–5 This apparently comprehensive set of prohibitions is, however, subject to a number of exceptions. Thus, a company may acquire its own shares by way of gift[13] or by way of forfeiture for non-payment of calls.[14] In the latter case, however, a public company must cancel the shares and reduce its capital account accordingly if the shares are not disposed of within three years of the forfeiture.[15] Both these exceptions are of long-standing. In 1983 there was added a further complex set of rules to deal with possible problems faced by public companies in relation to shares acquired by the trustees of a company's employee share scheme

---

[9] 2006 Act s.144.

[10] However, if such a transaction were permitted, the parent's legal capital account would not be reduced by the fact that one of its members is a subsidiary—any more than in the case of shares held by a nominee—so that it would not become easier for the parent to make distributions.

[11] 2006 Act s.137(1)(b), (c). The company may not exercise the voting rights attached to the shares, once it becomes a subsidiary (s.137(4)), but this does little to help creditors.

[12] *Acatos & Hutchinson Plc v Watson* [1995] 1 B.C.L.C. 218. Technically, the basis of the decision was that the bidder was acquiring the shares of the its new subsidiary, not its own shares.

[13] 2006 Act s.659(1)—"otherwise than for valuable consideration". This was held to be permissible at common law in *Re Castiglione's Will Trust* [1958] Ch. 549, where the acquisition was through a nominee, but the Act permits direct acquisition in such a case.

[14] 2006 Act s.659(2)(c).

[15] 2006 Act s.662(1)(a),(2),(3)(a).

or pension scheme.[16] These do not need to be further analysed in a work of this kind. There are also scattered throughout the Act provisions which permit the court to order that a company acquire shares from a shareholder, as a remedy for some wrong which has been done to that shareholder. The best known example is a compulsory purchase order made by the court under the unfair prejudice provisions, considered in Ch.20.[17] Finally, an acquisition of shares by the company under a reduction of capital carried out under the provisions discussed below is exempted from the prohibition.[18]

Where a public company is permitted to acquire its own shares, whether directly or through a nominee, then so long as it holds those shares (i.e. does not cancel or dispose of them) and decides to show those shares as an asset in its balance sheet, an amount equal to the value of the shares must be transferred out of profits available for dividend to an undistributable reserve.[19] In effect, the amount available for distribution will be reduced by the value of the purchase. Thus, suppose a public company acquires through a nominee fully paid shares from a third party, providing the nominee with the funds to effect the purchase. The company's net asset value will remain the same, the reduction in cash being offset by the value of the shares acquired. However, by virtue of the requirement to create an undistributable reserve, the amount of the profit available for distribution will be reduced, thus protecting creditors.[20] To put the matter another way, the purchase of the shares is treated as a distribution to the shareholder whose shares the nominee acquired.

13–6

REDEMPTION AND RE-PURCHASE

Introduction

However, the developments in the modern law which most directly qualify the "no acquisition" principle are those which specify the conditions under which a company may redeem or re-purchase its own shares. In these cases the legislature has taken the view that the transactions could be structured in such a way as not to endanger the interests of creditors and that the nineteenth century prohibition was over-inclusive in its reach.

13–7

Redeemable shares are shares which are issued on the basis that they are to be or may be redeemed (i.e. bought back) at a later date by the company. The terms of issue may be that the shares will be redeemed at a certain point or that they may be, and in the latter case the option to redeem may be allocated to the

---

[16] These problems were originally tackled by the Companies (Beneficial Interests) Act 1983: see now the 2006 Act ss.671–676. The acquisition of such shares is likely to be financed by the company and the company may have a residuary beneficial interest in them which, under these provisions, may be disregarded.

[17] 2006 Act s.659(2)(b), which also lists three other situations where the court may order the purchase of shares, i.e. under ss.98, 721(6) and 759.

[18] 2006 Act s.659(2)(a).

[19] 2006 Act s.669.

[20] This result will be achieved as a result of the requirement in s.831 that a public company may make a distribution only to the extent that its net assets (unchanged in this example) exceed its legal capital and undistributable reserves (increased in the example by the value of the share purchase).

shareholder or the company or both. The process of redemption is thus different from the process of re-purchase, where the Act, under certain conditions, permits the company to re-purchase shares, something which would otherwise be unlawful. With re-purchase, however, there is no obligation upon the company to make an offer to re-purchase or, if one is made, upon the shareholder to accept it. The redemption arrangement, by contrast, will always create some rights or duties to redeem or be redeemed.

Redeemable shares thus involve an element of planning of its financial structure by a company, because the terms of the redemption have to be set at the time of issue. As compared with non-redeemable shares, the holder of a right to have the shares redeemed is not locked into the company and able to dispose of the shares only to an investor who is prepared to buy them at the prevailing market prices. An investor may welcome the right to exit the company at a particular period in the future on terms set out in advance. Such an arrangement makes the redeemable share a hybrid between debt and equity, the debt holder also being someone who normally has a repayment right at an identifiable point in the future and on pre-set terms. Equally, the company may wish to issue redeemable shares over which it has a redemption right, perhaps as an alternative to standard preference shares which can normally also be squeezed out through a reduction of capital.[21]

However, the freedom of the company and the shareholder to agree upon a re-purchase of shares is more useful than the redemption procedure, precisely because it does not involve commitment in advance. It is a mechanism which can be resorted to as occasions arise, whilst the occasions when it is desirable to redeem some of the company's shares may be difficult to identify in advance. It is true that the re-purchase provisions do not create a mechanism whereby the shareholder can be compelled to sell the shares back to the company or whereby the company can be compelled to buy them, but there are many instances where company and shareholder interests are aligned so that the repurchase is likely to go ahead in those cases, if the law permits it, as it now does. The company may wish to return unwanted equity capital to the shareholders, either because it has no need at all for the financing represented by the shares repurchased or because it wishes to replace that financing with an alternative, such as debt. More questionably, the incumbent board may wish to buy out a group of shareholders who are causing trouble for the incumbent management—a process referred to in the US literature as "greenmail", presumably after the colour of the dollar bill. As we shall see, there are features of the re-purchase mechanism aimed at combating such opportunism. As for the shareholders, some may welcome the chance to exit the company at an attractive price, whilst those remaining may hope that the company's earnings per share will increase when some of the shareholders are paid off, if indeed it was the case that the capital returned to them was not earning a high reward or if it can be replaced by a cheaper form of financing.

---

[21] See para.19–35.

Some history

Redeemable shares have been permissible since the Companies Act 1929. **13–8** However, prior to the 1981 Companies Act, only preference shares could be issued as redeemable.[22] Now, however, as s.684 provides, a company may issue shares of any class which are to be redeemed or are liable to be redeemed, whether at the option of the company or the shareholder. However, the 1929 Act made the crucial breakthrough because it introduced a method whereby redemption could take place without prejudicing the interests of creditors and this method was adopted again when, also in 1981, companies were empowered to re-purchase their own shares, whether or not they were issued as redeemable.[23] This method has two crucial creditor-protection features, which are discussed further below. First, the shares may be redeemed or re-purchased only out of distributable profits or (in most cases) out of the proceeds of a fresh issue of shares made for the purposes of the redemption or re-purchase. Insofar as distributable profits (as defined in the previous chapter) are used to fund the redemptions or re-purchases, the creditors have no cause to complain, since the company could have used them to fund dividends instead. Secondly, as far as the capital accounts are concerned, the capital created by the fresh issue will replace the capital removed by the redemption or re-purchase and so the level of protection afforded to the creditors through the capital accounts will be the same. In addition, provided it is disclosed that redemption or re-purchase of existing shares is the reason for the fresh issue, creditors will not be misled into thinking that the company is issuing shares in order permanently to raise the amounts stated in its capital accounts. However, the impact of a purchase on the company's capital accounts remains to be dealt with if the redemption or re-purchase is funded out of distributable profits. Once the shares are re-purchased the amount stated in the company's capital accounts will be reduced, thus lowering the level of creditor protection. This problem was met by requiring the company to establish an undistributable reserve of an amount equal to the capital reduction when the redemption or re-purchase was funded out of distributable profits. This is known as the "capital redemption reserve" ("CRR").

General restrictions on redeemable shares and on repurchases

Redeemable shares may not be issued unless the company has also issued shares **13–9** which are not redeemable.[24] This provision eliminates the risk of the company ending up with no members if and when all the redeemable shares are redeemed.[25] However, the Act makes no stipulation as to the number or value of

---

[22] Perhaps because they were already capable of being squeezed out through the reduction procedure (see para.19–35, below) and the redemption mechanism allowed the parties to contract about the handling of this process.

[23] The crucial policy document was *The Purchase by a Company of its own Shares* (DTI, 1980, Cmnd. 7944).

[24] 2006 Act s.684(4).

[25] Moreover, after issue, the non-redeemable shares cannot be re-purchased so as to produce the result that the company has only redeemable or treasury shares in issue: s.690(2). Nor may a private company reduce its share capital through the solvency statement regime so as to produce the result

the non-redeemable shares which are required to have been issued, and so the main form of equity financing for the company could be via redeemable shares. Somewhat similarly, a re-purchase cannot be made if the result would be that there were no longer any members of the company holding non-redeemable shares or only treasury shares remained.[26]

In the case of a public company redeemable shares may not be issued unless the company is authorised in its articles to do so and, in the case of a private company, the articles may exclude or restrict the issue of redeemable shares.[27] Thus, the default rule is in favour of the private company having the power to issue redeemable shares and against it in the case of public companies. This requirement is additional to the provisions discussed in Ch.24 which, in some cases, require the directors to seek the authorisation of the shareholders before they take advantage of the power to issue any type of share. The default rule addresses the logically prior question of whether the company has power to issue redeemable shares at all. Nevertheless, both sets of rules create a requirement for shareholder consent. The main difference between them appears to be that, in the case of a public company, authority to issue shares can be given to the directors by ordinary resolution.[28] By contrast, a provision in the articles conferring power on the company to issue redeemable shares must either be there from the beginning, and thus be consented to by all the subscribers to the memorandum, or be introduced at a later date by special resolution of the members altering the articles. This higher level of shareholder consent might be thought to be justified by the drain on the company's cash resources that redemption is likely to entail, thus reducing the cash available to pay dividends to the other shareholders or to invest in projects for the benefit of the shareholders as a whole.

A company may purchase its own shares (including redeemable shares),[29] subject to any restriction or prohibition in the company's articles.[30] Thus, the default rule for both public and private companies is that the company does have power to re-purchase its shares. The contrast with the default rule for public companies in relation to redeemable shares (no power to do so) can be explained by the greater protection for shareholders which exists in relation to the actual implementation of the re-purchase, as we shall see below.[31]

13–10   Concern about the impact of the redemption on the non-redeemable shareholders also lies behind a long-running debate concerning the setting of the terms of the redemption. Under the 1985 Act, in order to protect the shareholders whose shares were not to be redeemed (and indeed the offerees of the redeemable shares), the terms and manner of the redemption were required to be set out in the

---

that it has only redeemable shares in issue: s.641(2). In the case of the court-centred reduction, the court could permit such a reduction but, presumably, would be unlikely to do so.

[26] 2006 Act s.690(2). On treasury shares, see below para.13–24.

[27] 2006 Act s.684.

[28] 2006 Act s.551 and see para.24–4.

[29] Thus enabling the company to "redeem" them prior to a date fixed in the terms and conditions if it can reach agreement with the holder.

[30] 2006 Act s.690. A purported re-purchase in breach of the articles would be void, because the company would no longer be protected from the operation of s.658(2) (above, para.13–2); cf. *Hague v Nam Tai Electronics Inc* [2007] 2 B.C.L.C. 194 PC.

[31] See paras 13–19 et seq.—though that protection was somewhat reduced in 2013.

company's articles, so that all would know the position.[32] However, this was thought to be an inflexible requirement and the rule now embodied in the Act is somewhat more flexible.[33] Fixing the terms in the articles remains the default rule,[34] but, provided either the articles or an ordinary resolution of the company permit it, the directors may fix the terms and conditions of the redemption.[35] Protection for the shareholders is maintained by the requirement that the directors, if they set the terms, must do so before the shares are allotted and the company's statement of capital provided to the Registrar must include the terms of the redemption.[36]

The Act contains two further relevant provisions, one restrictive, the other facultative. First, redeemable shares may not be redeemed until they are fully paid[37]; and the same rule is applied to re-purchases.[38] This avoids the acquisition wiping out the personal liability of the holders in respect of uncalled capital. Secondly, the terms of redemption may provide that, by agreement between company and shareholder, the amount due is to be paid on a date later than the redemption date[39]; whereas the requirement that the shares be paid for on re-purchase is unqualified.[40]

Once the acquisition is effected, the Registrar must be informed in the usual way and supplied with details of the transaction.[41]

Creditor protection: all companies

The core of the nineteenth century objection to redemption and re-purchase of shares was creditor protection. Therefore, the crucial step in permitting these transactions was producing a solution to the creditor protection issue. That solution, as now embedded in the 2006 Act, consists of two sets of rules: one applying to all companies and a set of relaxations which only private companies can take advantage of. We will look first at the rules applying to all companies and then at the private company relaxations.

13–11

The general solution to the creditor protection issue consisted, as noted, of providing that shares could be redeemed or re-purchased only out of distributable profits or out of the proceeds of a fresh issue of shares made for the purpose of the redemption or re-purchase.[42] Any premium payable on redemption or

---

[32] 1985 Act s.160(3).

[33] Though not as flexible as the CLR's recommendation, which would have given the directors an unconditional power to set the terms of the redemption: Final Report I, para.4.5.

[34] 2006 Act s.685(4).

[35] 2006 Act.685(1),(2).

[36] 2006 Act s.685(3).

[37] 2006 Act ss.686(1).

[38] 2006 Act s.691(1).

[39] 2006 Act s.686(2)—otherwise the shares must be paid for on redemption: s.686(3).

[40] 2006 Act s.691(2)—except in relation to a private company purchasing shares pursuant to an employee share scheme. For the problems to which this lack of flexibility can give rise see *Peña v Dale* [2004] 2 B.C.L.C. 508; *Kinlan v Crimmin* [2007] 2 B.C.L.C. 67 (though in the latter case the judge managed to avoid requiring the shareholder to return to the company the money received by resort to the defence of a good faith change of position).

[41] 2006 Act ss.689 (redemption) and 707 (re-purchase).

[42] 2006 Act ss.687(2) and 692(2).

re-purchase must be paid out of distributable profits alone, unless the redeemed or re-purchased shares were issued initially at a premium, in which case the redemption premium may be paid out of the proceeds of a new issue, up to the amount of the premium received on issue or the value of the company's current share premium account, whichever is the less.[43] This rather complicated rule ensures that the money received on the new issue of shares is paid out only to the extent that it reflects the reduction in the capital accounts arising out of the redemption or re-purchase. If more is needed to redeem the shares, the excess must be provided out of distributable profits.[44]

Once the shares have been redeemed, they are treated as cancelled and the amount of the company's issued share capital is diminished by the nominal value of the shares redeemed.[45] The company may also cancel its repurchased shares. In these cases the company must create an (undistributable) CRR. The amount of this reserve is equivalent to the amount by which the company's issued share capital is diminished by a purchase wholly out of profits[46] or, where the redemption is financed partly by the proceeds of a new issue and partly by distributable profits, the amount by which the proceeds of the new issue fall short of the amount paid on redemption or re-purchase.[47] However, since 2003 the company has had the option not to cancel shares which have been re-purchased but instead to hold them "in treasury", usually for later re-issue. (Treasury shares are considered further at paras 13–24 et seq., below.) This is a significant difference between the redemption and re-purchase procedures. Where shares are held in treasury, the creation of a CRR is unnecessary, because the company's capital accounts are not altered.

Private companies: redemption or purchase out of capital

13–12   In relation to both redemptions and re-purchases of shares, special concessions are made to private companies. It is thought often to be impossible for a private company to redeem or purchase its own shares unless it could do so out of capital and without having to incur the expense of a formal reduction of capital with the court's consent. There might not be sufficient distributable profits, and there might be no available takers for a fresh issue of shares. The whole concept of

---

[43] 2006 Act ss.687(3), (4) and 692(2)(b), (3).

[44] To see this, let us suppose that, immediately before the re-purchase, a public company has net assets exactly equivalent to its then legal capital. Thus, it has distributable profits of zero. It raises money by issuing 100 new shares at par at £2 per share. Its share capital account will increase by £200. It uses the money to re-purchase 100 £1 shares at a premium of £1, the shares having been originally issued at par. After cancellation of the re-purchased shares, the company's share capital will be reduced by £100 (the nominal value of the shares). However, by raising the finance for the re-purchase in the way indicated, the company has brought about a net increase in its legal capital of £100 (the increase arising out of the new issue (£200) less the nominal value of the shares re-purchased and cancelled (£100)). It cannot distribute the amount needed to finance the redemption premium without reducing its net assets below the (newly increased) capital yardstick. It must thus finance the premium on re-purchase out of distributable profits or not pay a redemption premium at all.

[45] 2006 Act s.688.

[46] 2006 Act s.733(2).

[47] 2006 Act s.733(3).

raising and maintaining capital is, in relation to such companies, of somewhat dubious value. Hence it was decided that, subject to safeguards, they should be empowered to redeem or buy without maintaining the former capital yardstick. In particular, the aim was to permit entrepreneurs to withdraw assets from their company to fund their retirement rather than by selling control to a larger competitor.

There are in fact now two concessions. The first, introduced in 2013 and applying to repurchases only, simply allows a private company to spend in any financial year up to (the lower of) £15,000 or 5 per cent of the nominal value of its share capital on re-purchases. There are no additional formalities to be met, provided only that the company is authorised by its articles to take this action.[48] This provision is clearly crafted with small-scale but potentially frequent re-purchases in mind, probably linked to employee share schemes, rather than one-shot retirement exercises.

The second set of provisions, which date back to 1981, are now contained in Ch.5 of Pt 18 of the Act. They have been retained even though there has now been provided to private companies a non-court based method of reducing capital.[49] These rules apply to redemptions as well as repurchases, but, to shorten exposition, the rules are stated here in relation to re-purchases.[50] **13–13**

Section 709 provides that, subject to what follows, a private company, unless restricted or prohibited by its articles from so doing, may make a payment in respect of the purchase of its shares otherwise than out of its distributable profits or the proceeds of a fresh issue of shares. Such a payment is termed a payment "out of capital".[51] This is a very wide definition and may explain why it was thought there might be some cases where re-purchase "out of capital" would be available, whereas a reduction of capital would not. Suppose a company wishes to acquire shares for a price above their nominal value but has no share premium or capital redemption reserve. No matter how much the share capital account is reduced, this will not free up a sufficient amount of assets to be distributed so as to meet the redemption premium. Assuming, however, that the company has sufficient cash, it may be able to engage in re-purchase by making a payment "out of capital" under s.709. This section helpfully says that a payment other than out of distributable profits or the proceeds of a fresh issue is a payment out of capital (and so in principle permitted) "whether or not it would be regarded apart from this section as a payment out of capital". Provided the company has the necessary cash and follows the provisions of this part of the Act, that is all it needs to be concerned with.[52]

The extent of any such payment out of capital is restricted, however, to what is described as "the permissible capital payment" ("PCP").[53] In brief, the rule is that any distributable profits and any proceeds of fresh issue made for the purpose of the re-purchase must first be used before resort may be had to a payment out of

---

[48] 2006 Act s.692(1ZA).
[49] See para.13–39, below.
[50] 2006 Act s.709(1).
[51] 2006 Act s.709(2).
[52] HL Debs, Grand Committee, Tenth Day, 20 March 2006, cols.31–32.
[53] 2006 Act s.710.

capital. The rules for determining distributable profits are those considered in the previous chapter in relation to dividends, but there are certain amendments,[54] perhaps the most important of which is that the accounts by reference to which the profits are calculated must be prepared within a period of three months ending with the date of the statutory declaration which the directors are required to make.[55]

The principal protective techniques used in the Chapter in respect of the PCP are, in the case of creditors and shareholders, the requirement for a solvency statement from the directors; in the case of shareholders, the requirement for approval of the proposed re-purchase by special resolution; and, in both cases, the availability of a right of objection to the court.

Directors' statement

13–14 As far as the solvency statement is concerned, the requirements of the Act are similar to those applied in the case of a solvency statement upon a reduction of capital out of court by a private company, including the requirement for the directors to take into account contingent and prospective liabilities.[56] However, they are not the same. In particular, the directors are apparently unable to make the required forward-looking statement in the case of a purchase out of capital, if they intend to wind the company up within 12 months of the proposed payment.[57] And the forward-looking statement, applying to the immediately following year, is required to be a little fuller. The form of the required statement is that, having regard to the "the amount and character of the financial resources" which will be available to the company in the directors' view, the directors have formed the opinion that the company will be able to carry on business as a going concern throughout that year (and accordingly will be able to pay its debts as they fall due).[58] The emphasis is thus on an opinion which envisages a continuing business, not just the ability of the company to pay its debts.[59] Perhaps because of these differences the statement required on a purchase is termed a "directors' statement" in the Act, whilst the term "solvency statement" is reserved for the statement required of directors under the out-of-court reduction procedure, though both statements are, substantively, statements about the solvency of the company.

---

[54] 2006 Act s.711.

[55] 2006 Act s.712(6),(7). The available profits so determined have then to be treated as reduced by any lawful distributions made by the company since the date of the accounts and before the date of the statutory declaration: s.712(3),(4).

[56] 2006 Act s.714(4). On the requirements for a capital reduction see para.13–40, below.

[57] Presumably on the grounds that a re-purchase to enable the founding entrepreneur to retire is in those circumstances unnecessary: the withdrawal can take place as part of the winding up. Section 714(3)(b) requires the statement to say that the directors' opinion is that the company will be able to carry on business as a going concern in the following year "having regard to their intentions with respect to the management of the company during the year", so that they could not honestly make the required statement if they contemplated a winding up.

[58] 2006 Act s.714(3)(b).

[59] As to the opinion about the current position, that relates to the position "immediately following" the date on which the PCP is proposed to be made (s.714(3)(a)) rather than the date of the statement (cf. s.643(1)(a)), so that it requires a small degree of foresight.

The Act applies to the directors' statement the same criminal liability for negligence as is applied to the solvency statement.[60] There is also a limited statutory civil liability in negligence to the company if the company goes into winding up within one year of the payment being made to the shareholder.[61] However, a major difference with the solvency statement is that the directors' statement needs to be accompanied by a report from the company's auditors stating their opinion that the amount of the PCP has been properly calculated and that they are not aware of any matters, after inquiry into the company's affairs, which renders the directors' statement unreasonable in all the circumstances.[62]

Shareholder resolution

The solvency statement can be said to protect both the creditors of the company and the shareholders who will remain in the company after the re-purchase. An additional protection for the shareholders is the special resolution which is required to be passed within a week of the directors' statement and on the basis of prior disclosure to the members of the directors' statement and auditors' report.[63] In this case it is explicitly provided that the resolution is ineffective if these requirements are not complied with.[64] Further, the resolution will not be effective to authorise the purchase out of capital if the shares to which the resolution relates vote on the resolution and their votes were necessary to secure its adoption.[65]

13–15

Appeal to the court

The final protective device (for both creditors and dissenting members) is court scrutiny. The Act entitles any member of the company, who has not consented to or voted for the resolution, and any creditor of the company, to apply to the court for the cancellation of the resolution, provided this action is taken within five weeks of the passing of the resolution.[66] The court is given the widest powers. For example, it can cancel the resolution, confirm it, or make such orders as it thinks expedient for the purchase of dissentient members' shares or for the protection of creditors, and may make ancillary orders for the reduction of the company's capital.[67]

13–16

---

[60] 2006 Act s.715 cf. s.643(4) (see below, para.13–41).

[61] Insolvency Act 1986 s.76. See fn.73, below.

[62] 2006 Act s.714(6). The less demanding "solvency statement" approach is used for payments out of capital for purchases under an employee share scheme (s.720A).

[63] 2006 Act s.718(1),(2)—the method of disclosure varying according to whether a written resolution or a resolution at a meeting is contemplated.

[64] 2006 Act s.718(3), cf. s.642(4) applying to solvency statements, where the validity of the resolution is expressly preserved (see para.13–42, below) and reliance is placed instead on criminal sanctions to produce compliance with the disclosure obligation: s.644(7).

[65] 2006 Act s.717, cf. s.695.

[66] 2006 Act s.721(1),(2). The shareholder should know about the resolution but the creditor may not. Consequently, s.719 requires publicity to be given to the resolution, within one week of its adoption, giving the relevant details, including the amount of the PCP and naming a place where the directors' and auditors' reports may be consulted.

[67] 2006 Act s.721(3)–(7).

Legal capital consequences

13–17   If there is no court objection, the PCP must be made between five and seven weeks after the adoption of the resolution.[68] Upon the re-purchase of the shares, the company's share capital account will be reduced accordingly, but, because this is a permitted payment out of capital, there will be no need to transfer a corresponding amount to the CRR, as would happen in the case of a purchase out of distributable profits.[69] A transfer to CRR will be needed only to the extent that distributable profits have been used in part to fund the purchase of the shares.[70] Where the PCP is greater than the nominal value of the purchased shares (i.e. they are being purchased at a premium), the company is given permission to reduce its CRR, share premium account and its revaluation reserve accordingly.[71] In other words, the company's capital yardstick will in all probability be reduced to the extent of the PCP.[72] This is, after all, the object of the exercise. Overall, indeed, the effect of the foregoing provisions is that a private company may be able to make a return to one or more of its members which will exhaust its accumulated profits available for dividend and reduce both its assets and its capital yardstick.

13–18   As far as the Companies Act is concerned, this is the end of the procedure. However, the Insolvency Act contains a limited mechanism for unscrambling the acquisition. If the company goes into liquidation within one year of the payment being made to the shareholder, that person is liable to return to the company the amount of the payment out of capital, to the extent that this is needed to meet any deficiency of the company's assets in relation to its liabilities.[73]

Protection for shareholders

13–19   We now turn to how the law handles intra-shareholder conflicts arising in redemptions and re-purchases generally (i.e. beyond the specific shareholder protection put in place for acquisitions out of capital). This is particularly needed for re-purchases. Redemptions, if not out of capital, tend not to raise issues for shareholders because the terms of the redemption are set out at the time of issue of the shares. By contrast, it is clear that re-purchases have implications for the relations of shareholders among themselves. Controlling shareholders—or shareholders whom the management wish to see exit the company—may be given the opportunity to sell their shares when other shareholders are excluded, or may be given the opportunity to sell on more favourable terms. The Act contains some provisions aimed at controlling such abuses. These protections vary

---

[68] 2006 Act s.723.

[69] See para.13–12 above. Since this is a private company procedure, there is no question of the company holding the shares in treasury. See para.13–24.

[70] 2006 Act s.734(4).

[71] 2006 Act s.734(3). Section 734(4) deals with the complication where the purchase is partly by way of PCP and partly by way of the proceeds of a fresh issue.

[72] But note the example given above in para.13–13 where the PCP is greater than the company's CRR and share premium account.

[73] Insolvency Act 1986 s.76. The directors of the company who signed the statement are jointly and severally liable with the shareholders unless the director can show reasonable grounds for the opinion set out therein.

according to whether the purchase is to be an "off-market" or a "market" purchase. The essential distinction between the two situations is whether the purchase takes place on a "recognised investment exchange", i.e. one authorised by the Financial Conduct Authority.[74] In broad terms this means that it is a market purchase if it takes place on the main market of the London Stock Exchange or on the Alternative Investment Market.[75] Market purchases create fewer risks of abuse since the offer will be a public one and the purchases will be effected at an objectively determined market price. If there is no market, the opportunities for favouritism are much greater.

Off-market purchases

Under s.694 an off-market purchase can be made only in pursuance of a contract the terms of which have been authorised by a resolution of the shareholders before it is entered into.[76] Until 2013 a special resolution was required, but now an ordinary one will suffice.[77] The contract so approved may take the form of a "contingent purchase contract", i.e. one where the company's obligation or entitlement to purchase shares is subject to a contingency which may arise sometime in the future.[78] Contingent purchase contracts may be particularly useful because they enable the company to bind or entitle itself to purchase the shares of a director or employee upon termination of employment, or, as an alternative to the creation of a new class of redeemable shares, to meet the requirements of a potential investor in an unquoted company who wants assurance that he or she will be able to find a purchaser if the investor needs to realise his investment.[79] The authorisation can subsequently be varied, revoked or renewed by a like resolution.[80]

13–20

In the case of a public company the authorising resolution must specify a date on which it is to expire and that date must not be later than five years after the passing of the resolution,[81] so that directors may not subsequently act on a "stale" authority, but no such rule applies to private companies.[82] Moreover, on any such resolution, whether of a public or private company, a member, holding shares to

---

[74] 2006 Act s.693(2),(5). See para.25–8, below.

[75] However, even if the trade takes place on a RIE it will not count as a market purchase if the market authorities have given only restricted permission for trading in the shares: s.693(3)(b).

[76] The contract may be entered into before approval, but in that case no shares may be purchased in pursuance of it before approval is obtained: s.694(2)(b). Under s.693A the requirements discussed in this section are somewhat modified in connection with purchases under an employee share scheme, but these variations are ignored here.

[77] The Government's reasons for downgrading minority protection were not particularly persuasive: below, fn.82 at para.25 ("sufficient other safeguards" but none as effective).

[78] 2006 Act s.694(3).

[79] There is the potential small disadvantage to the contingent purchase contract that the consideration for the contract or any variation of it must be provided out of distributable profits (s.705). However, the actual acquisition of the shares may be funded in accordance with the rules discussed in para.13–11.

[80] 2006 Act s.694(4).

[81] 2006 Act s.694(5). Until 2009 the period was 18 months.

[82] BIS, *Implementation of Nuttall Review – Recommendation V: Government response to consultation* February 2013, para.22, interprets s.694 as meaning that a private company cannot give advance approval at all but it is far from clear that this is what the section says.

which the resolution relates, may not exercise the voting rights of those shares[83] and if the resolution would not have been passed but for those votes the resolution is ineffective.[84] This is an interesting example of the exclusion of interested shareholders from voting on resolutions in which they have a personal financial interest—a rule which normally does not apply at common law.[85] The resolution is also ineffective unless a copy of the contract or a memorandum of its terms is available for inspection by members, and in the case of a resolution passed at a meeting it must be available at the company's registered office for not less than 15 days before it is held.[86] The same requirements apply on a resolution to approve any variation of the contract[87] or to an agreement whereby the company releases its rights under the contract,[88] since both variation and release provide opportunities for favourable treatment of insiders just as the initial off-market contract does.

Essentially, the shareholder protection technique deployed in the case of an off-market purchase is the requirement for approval by the shareholders in advance of the terms of the re-purchase contract with the potential sellers excluded from voting.

Market purchases

13–21   Under s.701 a company (necessarily a public one) cannot make a market purchase of its own shares unless the making of such purchases has first been authorised by ordinary resolution of the company in general meeting.[89] Those whose shares are to be purchased are not excluded from voting, for the very good reason that, with a market purchase, their identities will not be known in advance. For the same reason, the shareholders are asked to approve in this case, not a contract (even a contingent one) for the purchase of the shares of specified members, but an authorisation to the company (in practice, its directors) to go into the market in the future and acquire its shares on certain terms. The authorisation may be general or limited to shares of any particular class or description and may be conditional or unconditional[90] but it must specify the

---

[83] Or, on a written resolution, vote any shares held: s.695(2).

[84] 2006 Act s.695 which also provides (a) that it applies whether the vote is on a poll or by a show of hands; (b) that, notwithstanding any provision in the company's articles, any member may demand a poll; and (c) that a vote and a demand for a poll by a member's proxy is treated as a vote and demand by the member.

[85] See also s.239 for the exclusion of shareholders from voting on the ratification of their own wrongdoing as directors (para.16–193).

[86] 2006 Act s.696. In the case of a written resolution the information is sent to the members at or before the copy of the proposed resolution: s.696(2)(a). In either case the names of members holding shares to which the contract relates must be disclosed. These rights, being for the benefit of the shareholders, may be waived by their unanimous agreement: *Kinlan v Crummin* [2007] 2 B.C.L.C. 67; and see para.15–8.

[87] 2006 Act ss.697–699.

[88] 2006 Act s.700.

[89] As in the case of off-market purchases, the authority may be varied, revoked or renewed by a like resolution: s.701(4).

[90] 2006 Act s.701(2).

maximum number of shares to be acquired, the maximum and minimum prices,[91] and a date on which it is to expire, which must not be later than five years after the passing of the resolution.[92] Thus, the potential for a re-purchase resolution to create uncertainty about the appropriate market price of the share is reduced. Moreover, a copy of the resolution required by the section has to be sent to the Registrar within 15 days,[93] so that the market is formally aware of the company's intentions or at least its powers. Thus, the directors are given a re-purchase authority but one which is exercisable only within the specified limits as to price, amount and timing.

Companies with a premium listing

In the case of a re-purchase effected by a company with a premium listing on the Main Market of the London Stock Exchange, the Listing Rules add a further and significant set of rules relating to the exercise by the company of the authority conferred upon it under the statutory provisions, whether the re-purchase is on- or off-market. In order to provide some degree of equality of treatment of shareholders in relation to substantial market re-purchases, which might affect the balance of power within the company, the Listing Rules require re-purchases of more than 15 per cent of a class of the company's equity shares[94] to be by way of a tender offer to all shareholders of the class (i.e. to be on-market) or, alternatively, that the full terms of the re-purchase have been "specifically" approved by the shareholders.[95] A standard tender offer is an offer open to all the shareholders of the class on the same terms for a period of at least seven days, capable of being accepted by the shareholders pro rata with their existing holdings, and setting a fixed or maximum price for the purchase.[96] Thus, in a fixed price tender a shareholder holding 2 per cent of the class may sell shares to the company up to the amount of 2 per cent of the shares the company acquires through the tender process. Where the tender is at a maximum (but not a fixed) price, the shareholder has to indicate the price at which it is prepared to sell its shares to the company (a price not exceeding the maximum set by the company) and the company will implement the tender by accepting the lowest-priced offers first and continue up the price curve until it has fulfilled its tender. Even where the purchase is of less than 15 per cent, the company must either use the tender offer procedure or limit the price it is offering to not more than 5 per cent above

13–22

---

[91] 2006 Act s.701(3). The resolution may specify a particular sum or a non-discretionary formula for calculating the price (for example, by reference to the market price of the shares): s.701(7).

[92] 2006 Act s.701(5). Again, 18 months until 2009. But the purchase may be completed after the expiry date if the contract to buy was made before that date and the authorisation permitted the company to make a contract which would or might be executed after that date: s.701(6).

[93] 2006 Act s.701(8), applying Ch.3 of Pt 3 of the Act to this ordinary resolution.

[94] This includes preference shares which are participating in either dividend or distributions on a winding up: LR, Glossary Definition, "equity share capital".

[95] LR 12.4.2.

[96] LR, Glossary Definition, "tender offer".

the market price of the shares over the five days preceding the purchase.[97] This limits the possibilities for favoured shareholders to sell their shares to the company at an above-market price.

Listing Rules also require the prior consent of any class of listed securities convertible or exchangeable into equity shares of the class to which the re-purchase proposal relates, unless the terms of issue of the security provided that the company may re-purchase the relevant equity shares.[98] Thus, in principle, the holders of convertible bonds will need to consent (by special resolution in a separate meeting) to a re-purchase of the equity shares into which the bonds are convertible. Further, where an off-market transaction is contemplated, the Listing Rules apply their rules concerning related-party transactions.[99] These exclude from voting on the resolution a wider range of persons than would the statute, because the statute excludes only those whose shares are to be re-purchased, whereas the Listing Rules also exclude their associates.[100] Finally, the FCA's Rules not surprisingly address market issues, such as the need for the market to be informed immediately of all the stages of a share re-purchase, from proposal to results[101]; and the need to avoid insider trading by excluding, subject to exceptions, re-purchases during prohibited trading periods.[102] In addition, the Investment Association guidelines[103] propose that companies should always act by special resolution even if the statute permits an ordinary resolution, so that listed companies, or at least those with large institutional shareholdings, will tend to follow this path, even if the statute does not formally require it.

Payments otherwise than by way of the price

13–23   It is conceivable that a company might pay money to a shareholder, not as the price for the shares purchased, but, for example, by way of consideration for:

(a)   acquiring any right (for example an option) to purchase under a contingent purchase contract;

(b)   the variation of any off-market contract; or

(c)   the release of any of the company's obligations under any off-market or market contract.[104]

---

[97] LR 12.4.1. If a higher limit is permitted under the market stabilisation rules (see para.30–37), that will replace the 5 per cent figure.

[98] LR 12.4.7–8.

[99] LR 12.3.1. The rule will catch on-market transactions as well if there was an understanding at the time of the resolution to repurchase that a particular related party would be able to take up the offer.

[100] LR 11.1.7(4)(b). "Associate" is defined widely in LR, Glossary Definition, "associate".

[101] LR 12.4.4–6. In addition the legislation requires ex post disclosure of the shares purchased in the directors' annual report: SI 2008/410 Sch.7 Pt 2.

[102] LR 12.2.1. The specific protections against liability for market abuse in the course of share buy-backs are dealt with in para.30–44, below.

[103] Investment Association, *Share Capital Management Guidelines*, 2014, 1.3.1.

[104] These difficulties do not arise in relation to redemptions. Nor does the issue of payment for a variation arise in relation to a market contract since these cannot be varied.

Although such payments are not strictly part of the purchase price,[105] none of them is normal expenditure in the course of the company's business but rather constitute a distribution to members, and the payment would not have been made but for the fact that the company was minded to agree to purchase its shares. Such payments ought therefore to be treated, so far as practicable, in the same way as the purchase price. It is highly unlikely that a company would contemplate making a new issue of shares for the purpose of financing any such payment.[106] Hence, as a matter of creditor protection, the Act provides that they must be paid for out of distributable profits only. If this is contravened, in cases (a) and (b) above, purchases are not lawful, and in case (c) the release is void.[107]

Treasury shares

The question of whether a company can itself hold the shares it acquires is another issue that arises only in relation to re-purchases of shares, since a cancellation rule is imposed in the case of redemptions.[108] Re-purchases of treasury shares were not permitted under the original reforms of 1981, but the subsequent history has been one of progressive liberalisation. In 1998, the Government began consultation over the proposition that companies should be able to retain re-purchased shares and re-issue them, as required.[109] The main argument in favour of this reform was that it would permit companies to raise capital in small lots but at a full market price by re-selling the re-purchased shares as and when it was thought fit to do so. The argument against was that the freedom to re-sell would give boards of directors opportunities to engage in the manipulation of the company's share price, i.e. an argument based on investor protection rather than creditor protection. In 2001, the Government issued a further consultation document which accepted the idea in principle, but only for companies whose shares were traded on a public market, and consulted on further issues related to its implementation.[110] The manipulation danger was thought to be addressed by the separate provisions, contained in the FSMA 2000, dealing with market abuse,[111] and by the restriction on the amount of the treasury shares to 10 per cent of any class (as then required by the Second Directive).

13–24

---

[105] Though, in case (a), the division of the total price between that paid for the option and that paid on its exercise may be arbitrary.

[106] Which, in case (a) and perhaps (b), would be made some time before any actual purchase and which in cases (a) and (c) might never be made at all.

[107] 2006 Act s.705.

[108] 2006 Act s.688(a).

[109] See DTI, *Share Buybacks*, URN 98/713 (1998).

[110] DTI, *Treasury Shares*, URN 01/500 (2001).

[111] FSMA 2000 Pt VIII, especially s.118 and the Financial Services and Markets Act 2000 (Prescribed Markets and Qualifying Investments) Order 2001 (SI 2001/996). See Ch.30. Note also that a company cannot assign its rights under a contract to re-purchase shares (s.704), whether the shares are to be held in treasury or not, and this rule reduces the company's ability to trade in its own shares.

13–25 These proposals were implemented in 2003[112] and Ch.6 of Pt 18 of the 2006 Act re-stated them without substantive change. In 2009, however, following amendments to the Second Directive, the 10 per cent limit was removed.[113] Under the 2003 reforms only "qualifying shares"[114] could be re-purchased. These were publicly traded shares. In 2013, however, the restriction to qualifying shares was removed from the legislation,[115] so that all shares subject to re-purchase may be held in treasury and all companies may hold treasury shares (the previous approach having necessarily excluded private companies from holding shares in treasury).

The principal restriction today on holding treasury shares is that their re-purchase must have been financed out of distributable profits, even in the case of a private company.[116] This limitation seems to have been imposed because it was thought that there would be little demand for re-purchases out of new issues. This approach also simplifies the legal capital issues. Deployment of distributable profits has no impact on the company's capital accounts. Moreover, no balancing transfer to the capital redemption reserve is required where the re-purchased shares are not cancelled.

Sale of treasury shares

13–26 The underlying rationale of the treasury share scheme is achieved by the provision that treasury shares may at any subsequent time be sold by the company for cash.[117] When this happens, there is a sale by the company of existing shares, not an allotment of new shares. Consequently, the rules requiring shareholder authorisation of directors to allot shares do not apply,[118] thus facilitating speedy action by the directors. The same argument could be advanced in relation to pre-emption rights for shareholders on allotment, but the Act artificially extends the statutory concept of allotment so as to make pre-emption rights applicable on sales of ordinary shares held in treasury.[119] Although shareholders can waive pre-emption rights in advance, the fact that treasury shares are in principle subject to these rights is another example of the attachment of institutional shareholders to pre-emption rights.[120]

Where the proceeds of the sale are equal to or less than the purchase price paid by the company, the money received by the company is to be treated as a realised

---

[112] By the Companies (Acquisition of Own Shares) (Treasury Shares) Regulations 2003 (SI 2003/1116) and the No.2 Regulations (SI 2003/3031). See G. Morse, "The Introduction of Treasury Shares into English Law and Practice" [2004] J.B.L. 303.

[113] This was achieved through the repeal of s.725.

[114] 2006 Act s.724(1),(2), as originally enacted.

[115] 2006 Act s.741(1),(2), as amended.

[116] 2006 Act s.724(1)(b).

[117] 2006 Act s.727(1)(a). Cash is widely defined in s.727(2). There is one minor restriction: where a company has been the subject of a successful takeover offer (which included the treasury shares) and the bidder is using the statutory squeeze-out procedure, the treasury shares can be sold only to the bidder: s.727(4) and see para.28–69, below.

[118] See para.24–4, below.

[119] 2006 Act s.560(3).

[120] See para.24–14, below.

profit and so potentially distributable by the company.[121] Since the shares will have been acquired out of distributable profits, which were thereby diminished, there can be no creditor-protection objection to the proceeds of the sale being treated as a realised profit. Any excess of the price received by the company over that paid by it, however, must be transferred to the share premium account.[122] This again seems correct. The increase in the price of the shares presumably represents an increase in the value of the company since the shares were purchased, so that the portion of the price obtained on re-sale which represents that increase in value should be treated as legal capital, just as the premium received by the company on the initial issue of shares would be so treated.[123]

Alternatively, the company may transfer treasury shares to meet the requirements of an employees' share scheme.[124] Or it may do what it could have done when it originally acquired the shares, i.e. cancel them.[125] In this latter case its share capital account must be reduced by the amount of the nominal value of the shares cancelled and an equivalent amount transferred to the capital redemption reserve.[126] In the usual way the company has to inform the Registrar when it disposes of the shares (in either of the permitted ways) or cancels them, giving the necessary particulars.[127]

Whilst the shares are in treasury

Whilst the shares are still held by the company, it may not exercise any of the rights attached to them (notably the right to vote) and any such purported exercise is void,[128] so that the directors cannot strengthen their position in the general meeting of the company through the use of the treasury shares. Nor may a dividend be paid or any other distribution be made on the treasury shares.[129] However, the company may receive (fully paid) bonus shares in respect of the treasury shares, for otherwise the proportion of the equity represented by the treasury shares would decline. The bonus shares so allotted are to be treated as treasury shares purchased by the company at the time they were allotted.[130] On a subsequent sale of the bonus shares their purchase price is to be treated as nil, so that the full amount received for them must be transferred to the share premium account.[131] This seems correct, since the purpose of issuing bonus shares is to

13–27

---

[121] 2006 Act s.731(2).

[122] 2006 Act s.731(3). On the share premium account see para.11–6.

[123] Of course, what is transferred to the share premium account is the excess above the nominal value of the share (see para.11–6), whereas what is being transferred here is the excess above the purchase price.

[124] 2006 Act s.727(1)(b).

[125] 2006 Act s.729. It may be obliged to cancel them if the shares cease to be "qualifying shares": s.729(2),(3).

[126] 2006 Act ss.729(4) and 733(4). The directors may do this without following the reduction of capital procedure: s.729(5).

[127] 2006 Act ss.728 and 730.

[128] 2006 Act s.726(1),(2).

[129] 2006 Act s.726(3)—including a distribution on a winding up.

[130] 2006 Act s.726(4)(a),(5). On capitalisation issues see para.11–20.

[131] 2006 Act.731(4)(b).

capitalise profits and so the sale price of the bonus shares needs to be added to the company's capital accounts and not be treated as a realised profit.[132]

Failure by the company to perform

13–28 So far, we have assumed that the company has discharged its obligation to redeem shares under the terms of their issue or to re-purchase shares as a result of a contract entered into with the shareholder. Normally, this will be the case but it is conceivable that the company will not fulfil its obligations. This may occur because the company decides to break the contract or because it cannot lawfully perform it since, for example, the new issue of shares has not raised the proceeds expected and the company has inadequate available profits.[133] What are the remedies of a shareholder if the company does not perform the contract to redeem or purchase his shares? Section 735 provides that the company is not liable in damages in respect of any failure on its part to redeem or purchase.[134] It was thought that damages were not an appropriate remedy; it would result in the seller retaining his shares in, and membership of, the company and yet recovering damages (paid perhaps out of capital) from the company.[135] Any other right of the shareholder to sue the company is expressly preserved, but, even then, it is provided that the court shall not grant an order for specific performance (perhaps a more appropriate discretionary remedy) "if the company shows that it is unable to meet the costs of redeeming or purchasing the shares in question out of distributable profits".[136] Apart from this, the section gives no indication of what "other rights" the shareholder might have. There is little doubt that these would include the right to sue for an injunction restraining the company from making a distribution of profits which would have the effect of making it unlawful for the company to perform its contract.

However, the ban on the recovery of damages can be circumvented by using an indirect procedure to this end. In *British & Commonwealth Holdings Plc v Barclays Bank Plc*[137] a consortium of banks had promised to take the shares from the shareholder if the company could not redeem them and the company had promised to indemnify the banks in respect of actions by it which made it impossible for it to redeem. It was held that the section did not prevent the banks suing the company on its promises, even though the aim of the whole scheme was to ensure that the shareholder would be able to redeem even if the company had

---

[132] By the same token, the value treasury shares acquired by purchase will be reduced by the bonus issue, thus reducing the amount of realised profit arising on their re-sale.

[133] The company could, presumably, protect itself from being in breach by expressly providing in the contract that the purchase is conditional upon its having the needed proceeds or sufficient profits.

[134] 2006 Act s.735(2).

[135] In any event, the section does not protect the company against paying damages in all cases as a result of its failure to redeem. See *British & Commonwealth Holdings Plc v Barclays Bank Plc* [1996] 1 W.L.R. 1 CA, below.

[136] 2006 Act s.735(2),(3). This ignores the possibility that it has adequate proceeds of a fresh issue but has nevertheless decided to break the contract. Surely the seller should then be entitled to specific performance?

[137] *British & Commonwealth Holdings Plc v Barclays Bank Plc* [1996] 1 W.L.R. 1 CA. The case also raises issues about financial assistance which are discussed at para.13–49, below.

no distributable reserves. The case strongly suggests, but does not finally decide, that s.735 is concerned only with the range of remedies available to the shareholder rather than with ensuring that a company never in effect redeems shares out of capital.

A second issue which arises is the position if the company goes into liquidation before the shares have been redeemed or re-purchased. The Act provides that the terms of redemption or purchase may be enforced against the company in winding up,[138] but subject to the restriction on specific performance noted above. However, the shareholder will gain little or nothing by enforcing the contract if the winding up is an insolvent liquidation since the member is a deferred creditor. Any claim in respect of the purchase price is postponed to the claims of all other creditors—and, indeed, to those of other shareholders whose shares carry rights (whether as to capital or income) which are preferred to the rights as to capital of the shares to be redeemed or purchased.[139] Moreover, even this limited right may not be enforced in liquidation if the terms of redemption or purchase provided for performance to take place at a date later than that of the commencement of the winding-up; or if during the period beginning with the date when redemption or purchase was to take place and ending with the commencement of the winding-up, the company did not have distributable profits equal in value to the redemption or purchase price.[140] In this case it appears the member is treated in the winding-up as if there were no obligation on the company to redeem or purchase the shares and as if he or she were still a member of the company.

Conclusion

Even if one takes the view that legal capital is a central doctrine of company law, the above discussion has shown that it is relatively easy to reconcile it with the acquisition by a company of its own shares, provided certain conditions are met. In particular, acquisitions out of distributable profits, coupled with an appropriate adjustment to the company's capital accounts, present no threat to the integrity of the doctrine of legal capital. We should note, however, that the facility for a private company to purchase shares out of capital, provided the decision is supported by what is, in effect, a solvency statement, is a legislative move towards the adoption of an alternative to legal capital as the primary protection mechanism for creditors. In the case of re-purchases, where the directors have a greater discretion than in the case of redemptions, shareholder agency problems emerge as an issue which has to be faced, but a combination of the standard techniques of disclosure and shareholder approval, plus in appropriate cases, reliance on the functioning of a public market, ought to be sufficient to address those problems as well.

13–29

---

[138] 2006 Act s.735(4). Hence in respect of these shares the seller will cease to be a member or "contributory" and will become a creditor in respect of the price.

[139] 2006 Act s.735(6). In a solvent liquidation the shareholder may be worse off than if shares had not been redeemed or purchased, if the share gave a right to participate in surplus assets but the purchase or redemption price did not reflect the value of this right.

[140] 2006 Act s.735(5).

REDUCTION OF CAPITAL

Why are reductions of capital allowed?

13–30 Acquisition by a company of its shares through redemption or re-purchase is akin to a distribution to shareholders, discussed in the previous chapter, to the extent that assets are returned by the company to its shareholders. Unlike a distribution, which is a gratuitous disposition by the company, in a redemption or re-purchase the company receives shares in exchange for the assets. However, if the shares are immediately cancelled, the acquisition has a largely gratuitous character; and the cancellation generates a reduction in the company's legal capital yardstick. Only if the re-purchased shares are held in treasury does the company obtain value for the price paid, to the extent that the re-purchased shares can be sold again to investors.

A reduction of capital, by contrast, does not necessarily involve a return of assets to shareholders, though it may pave the way for such action, either immediately or in the future. What is reduced in a reduction of capital are the amounts stated in the company's capital accounts.[141] The initial puzzle is why the company should be permitted by the law to take this step at all. Having built a creditor-protecting distribution rule, which turns on the numbers in the company's balance sheet, and especially those in its capital accounts, why should the law allow the company to reduce those numbers so as to facilitate a distribution to shareholders, either immediately or in the future? More generally, the creditors might conceivably rely on the numbers stated in the capital accounts as an indication of its creditworthiness, that is, as indicating the level of the shareholders' commitment to the company. In principle, the company cannot reduce its capital, but the law has long recognised that it is legitimate to do so in some circumstances, subject to safeguards to protect creditors and to deal with intra-shareholder conflicts, especially conflicts among different classes of shareholder.

13–31 The following are examples of situations where a reduction of the numbers in the capital accounts might be thought to be legitimate. Suppose the company has traded unsuccessfully, so that its net asset value (assets less liabilities) is less than its legal capital. However, the company has found a new investor who is prepared to inject funds into the company so that it can try an alternative business plan. In return, however, the new investor wants to make sure that any profits made in the future can be paid out immediately and that he or she obtains the fair share of those profits. Thus, the investor requires that, before the issue of new shares is made, the value of the company's legal capital accounts is reduced to reflect the value of the existing shareholders' equity in the company. In short, the new investor does not want his investment to fund the past losses of the company nor that existing shareholders should participate in future profits except to the extent that their investments have survived the company's previous trading misfortunes. Both these aims can be achieved if the company's legal capital is reduced to the

---

[141] 2006 Act s.641, introducing the reduction procedures, in terms applies only to the share capital account, but the share premium account and capital redemption reserve are treated as share capital for the purposes of the reduction procedure: ss.610(4) and 733(6).

level of its current net asset value.[142] For example, if the company's net asset value is half its legal capital, the shares having all been issued at par, equilibrium could be achieved by reducing the nominal value of the existing shares by half. The new investor would then obtain twice the number of shares—again assuming issuance at par—when the new money is injected compared to the pre-reduction situation. This ensures fairness as between old and new investors as well as allowing future profits to be distributed immediately they are earned. There is no particular reason for the creditors to object to this procedure: any contribution by the new investor to the assets of the company improves their position because their claims on the company's assets have priority over those of the shareholders (old and new).

A situation at the opposite end of the spectrum is where the company has more equity capital than it needs and wishes to reduce its capital by repaying the holders of a particular class of share. Here, the reduction of capital is indeed accompanied by a return of assets to the shareholders. One might say that the return of assets to the shareholders is the driving force behind the transaction and the reduction of capital is the consequent adjustment to the balance sheet which is necessary to reflect what has been done. Here, reduction of capital appears as a functional substitute for a redemption or re-purchase of shares, as discussed in the previous section of this chapter. However, there is one significant difference. The outcome of the reduction procedure is a decision which is binding on all the shareholders in question. This may also be the case in a redemption (depending on how the terms of issue were drafted), but it is not the case in a re-purchase where, as we have seen, the statutory procedure simply makes it lawful for company and shareholder to agree to the re-purchase.[143] In this example, since assets are being returned to shareholders, the interests of creditors can be said to be engaged, whilst the decision as to which shareholders are to be squeezed out of the company and on what terms may provide fertile ground for intra-shareholder conflicts. **13–32**

The statutory procedures

For many years successive Companies Acts have provided a procedure through which the reduction can be effected and the claims of shareholders and creditors that the proposed reduction is adverse to their interests can be evaluated and protection provided, if it is due.[144] Before the passage of the 2006 Act there was **13–33**

---

[142] There are other techniques which could be used to achieve the same result, such as issuance at par of a new class of share to the new investor where the new class has a lower par value than and priority as to dividends over the existing shares, but issuing shares of the same class after a reduction may reduce the risk of intra-shareholder disputes in the future.

[143] See para.13–7, above.

[144] Reduction of capital is to be distinguished from the situation where the company simply divides its share capital into shares of a smaller nominal value or consolidates them into shares of a larger nominal value, but where the aggregate nominal value of the shares (and thus the company's share capital) remains the same, though there is a smaller or a larger number of shares representing that aggregate. These steps present no creditor protection issues and the matter is one for the shareholders alone (s.618). However, there are potential issues of intra-shareholder conflict with divisions: see *Greenhalgh v Arderne Cinemas* [1946] 1 All E.R. 512 CA; and para.19–18, below.

only one procedure. The general principle was that a company might reduce its capital if the proposal was adopted by a special resolution of the shareholders and confirmed by the court. However, a private company rarely needed to resort to that procedure. The main situation in which a private company may wish to reduce capital is when it needs to buy out a retiring member of the company or to return to the personal representatives of a deceased member his share of the capital, but has insufficient profits available for dividend to enable it to do so except out of capital. As we have seen above,[145] when companies were empowered to purchase their own shares, special concessions were made to private companies to enable them to do so out of capital and without the need for a formal reduction. This provided a substitute for capital reduction which met the needs of private companies in many cases.[146] However, the 2006 Act introduced an alternative procedure for the reduction of capital by private companies, for which court confirmation is not needed, but it left in place the special rules enabling private companies to re-purchase shares out of capital. In the case of public companies, the 2006 Act left the previous law unchanged.

Whichever procedure is used, the Act provides that a company may reduce its share capital "in any way"[147] but it then sets out three typical situations, which are important because of their different implications for creditor protection. The three situations are: (a) by reducing or extinguishing the amount of any uncalled liability on its shares[148]; (b) by cancelling any paid-up share capital "which is lost or unrepresented by available assets"[149]; (c) by paying off any paid-up share capital which is in excess of the company's wants.[150] Situations (b) and (c) are exemplified by the examples discussed in paras 13–31 and 13–32. In situation (a), which arises only where the company has issued shares as not fully paid up, a shareholder's liability to the company is terminated and so the interests of the creditors are engaged, as are the interests of the shareholders whose commitments to the company are fully paid up.[151]

---

[145] Above at para.13–13.

[146] 2006 Act s.617(5) makes it clear that a repurchase or redemption of shares in accordance with the Act does not fall foul of the prohibition on altering share capital contained in that section.

[147] 2006 Act s.641(3).

[148] 2006 Act s.641(4)(a)—in the unlikely event of its having uncalled capital.

[149] 2006 Act s.641(4)(b)(i). Technically share capital (a notional liability) cannot be "lost" (see Ch.11, above) but may well be "unrepresented by available assets". However, this does not seem to have bothered the courts which have interpreted "lost" to mean that the value of the company's net assets has fallen below the amount of its capital (i.e. its issued share capital, and, if any, its share premium account and capital redemption reserve) and that this "loss" is likely to be permanent.

[150] 2006 Act s.641(4)(b)(ii).

[151] Where there is a reduction of capital by means of extinguishing uncalled capital, it is normal accounting practice to create a reserve to reflect the reduction. Section 654 says the reserve is to be undistributable, but allows the Secretary of State to specify cases where the prohibition does not apply. Making ample use of this power reg.3 of the Companies (Reduction of Share Capital) Order 2008/1915 says the reserve is to be treated as a realised profit under both procedures, unless the court order, the company's articles or a company resolution specify otherwise.

Procedure applying to all companies

Under the procedure applying to all companies a reduction of capital requires a special resolution of the members and confirmation by the court.[152] It is the requirement for court approval which is supposed to provide the necessary protection for creditors (as well as for minority shareholders insofar as the supermajority vote requirement does not achieve that end). The obtaining of shareholder consent is most likely to raise tricky issues where there is more than one class of share and the reduction does not affect all the classes rateably. If the rights of a class of shareholders are affected by the reduction proposal, the separate consent of that class will be required under the "class rights" provisions discussed in paras 19–13 et seq.[153] In particular, companies have often wanted to cancel the shares issued to preference shareholders, whose entitlement to a fixed preference dividend has moved out of line with interest rates in the market, so that the contribution of those shareholders can be re-financed more cheaply. The courts have held that mere cancellation of preference shares does not infringe their rights, provided the preference shareholders are treated in accordance with the rights they would have on a winding up of the company.[154] Thus, the question becomes whether the reduction of the preference shares meets this test. Although the court probably has discretion to approve a reduction of shares which infringes class rights and which has not secured the consent of that class, it is highly unlikely to do so.[155] Where there is only one class of share, the minority's protections are less extensive,[156] though they do have the chance to oppose the confirmation of the reduction by the court under the reduction procedure.

13–34

Creditor objection

Creditor protection is provided solely through the mechanism of court confirmation of the reduction proposal.[157] The practical pressure generated by the procedure used to be towards making the company discharge or secure all the creditors' claims outstanding at the time of the reduction before application was made to the court for confirmation. These were the remedies the court could order

13–35

---

[152] 2006 Act s.641(1)(b). The previous requirement that the company have power under its articles to reduce its capital has been removed.

[153] The issue of how to identify of the rights of preference shareholders is discussed in Ch.23.

[154] The proposition that the preference shareholders are treated in breach of their rights by cancellation of their shares and deprivation of a favourable dividend entitlement was decisively rejected by the Court of Appeal in *Re Chatterly-Whitfield Collieries* [1948] 2 All E.R.593, so that the issue has become whether the terms of the reduction are in accordance with the rights which they would have on a winding up. The effect of the decision was to make preference shares in effect redeemable by the company, even if not formally issued as redeemable, provided the company could satisfy the requirements of the reduction procedure. It is to be noted that a reduction in order to replace preference shares with a cheaper form of financing does not clearly fall within any of the three categories specified in s.641(4) but it does fall within s.641(3)—reduction "in any way": *Re Hunting Plc* [2005] 2 B.C.L.C. 211.

[155] 2006 Act s.645 in terms requires only a resolution of the company, not of the class in question.

[156] These possibilities are also discussed in Ch.19.

[157] 2006 Act s.645(1).

in favour of an objecting creditor.[158] In order to avoid the difficulty of identifying every one of a fluctuating body of trade creditors, companies often felt obliged to short-circuit the objection procedure and arrange for a sufficient sum to be deposited with or guaranteed by a bank or insurance company to meet the claims of all the unsecured creditors before applying for court confirmation. The Company Law Review ("CLR") thought that the interests of creditors were thus often over-protected, because creditors obtained either payment of or security for their previously unsecured debts, whether or not their chances of repayment had been adversely affected by the repayment of capital.[159] However, its proposal for reform did not make its way into the Act. Nevertheless, the story did not end there. In 2006 the European Union amended the Second Directive's provisions on reduction of capital[160] so as to make them less protective of creditors. The Government's initial reaction was not to take advantage of this new flexibility,[161] but after consultation changed its mind.[162] The reduction of capital provisions of the 2006 Act were then amended by statutory instrument[163] so as to make the procedure less protective of creditors, thus achieving, albeit by slightly different wording, the policy recommended by the CLR.

The crucial change is that it is no longer the case that every creditor is entitled to object to the reduction of capital who, at the relevant date, has a debt or claim which would be admissible in proof were the company being wound up.[164] Under the prior law this was the position where the reduction fell within cases (a) or (c) above (para.13–33) or analogous cases.[165] Now, in order to obtain a right of objection the creditor, upon whom the burden of proof lies, must demonstrate not only the existence of situations (a) or (c) and an admissible debt or claim but, in addition, "a real likelihood that the reduction would result in the company being unable to discharge the debt or claim when it fell due".[166] The list of objecting creditors will, in future, thus consist of those who have demonstrated that their claim is subject to real risk of non-payment if the reduction goes ahead, so that the pressure on the company to settle the claims of all creditors should be mitigated, if not eliminated.

---

[158] 2006 Act s.648(2).

[159] Strategic, para.5.4.5.

[160] Directive 2006/68/EC amending art.32 of Directive 77/91/EEC (now art.36 of the 2012 version of that Directive).

[161] DTI, *Implementation of the Companies Act 2006*, February 2007, Ch.6.

[162] *The Government response to the consultation on the implementation of amendments to the 2nd Company Law Directive*, 28 October 2007.

[163] The Companies (Share Capital and Acquisition by Company of Own Shares) Regulations 2009 (SI 2009/2022) reg.3. The Secretary of State has power under s.657 to amend a number of the elements in Pt 17 of the Act, in addition to the usual powers under s.2 of the European Communities Act 1972.

[164] Not all claims a creditor might make in the future are provable: see *Re Liberty International Plc* [2010] 2 B.C.L.C. 665 (debtor liable only if a third party exercises a discretion so as to impose the liability).

[165] See s.645(2). The court has a dispensing power under s.645(4), but this was rarely used against creditors whose claims had not been secured. In case (b) there is no right of objection, unless the court so orders: s.645(4).

[166] 2006 Act s.646(1)(b). That likelihood, "beyond the merely possible, but short of the probable", will be more difficult to demonstrate the further into the future the debt falls due: *Re Liberty International* [2010] 2 B.C.L.C. 665 at [19]–[20].

Confirmation by the court

In principle, the court is required to settle a list of creditors and to do so as far as possible without requiring an application from a creditor to be included on the list.[167] However, this rarely happens.[168] In the past this was because creditors were repaid or secured before confirmation was sought, as indicated above. It would be an unwanted side-wind of the introduction of the "real likelihood" test if court consideration of the claims of objecting creditors became routine. In fact, the court has power to order that the creditor objection procedure shall not apply in a particular case.[169] Under the new test companies are likely to rely on evidence about their business prospects over the next few years as grounds for dispensing with the objection procedure. This is a form of non-statutory solvency certification. To date the courts have been disposed to accept such evidence as grounds for disapplication, stressing in particular that the test is whether the reduction of capital creates a "real risk" of non-payment for the creditor, so that the creditor's continued exposure to the general risks of the company's business is not as such permissible ground for objection.[170]

13–36

Even if there are no objecting creditors or their objections have been dealt with, it appears that the court must still have regard to creditor interests when deciding whether to confirm the reduction "on such terms and conditions as it thinks fit". This is shown by the case law concerning reductions of capital because that capital was not represented by available assets (i.e. case (b) above). Here, there is no right of objection for creditors, unless the court so orders.[171] Nevertheless, the courts might regard the interests of creditors in such a case as requiring protection at the confirmation stage. A standard situation falling within case (b) is where a company is required to write down the value of an asset in its accounts (for example, a loan which the company now thinks is unlikely to be re-paid), thus extinguishing its distributable profits. It then wishes to reduce its share capital (and probably its share premium account) so as to permit the distribution of future profits. However, a variation on this theme is where, on the facts, it is possible (and foreseeable at the time of the write-down) that the asset may recover in value. In that case the court may impose a condition that any amount recovered in the future should be put in an undistributable reserve. However, it seems that this will be required only if needed to protect the creditors existing at the time of the write-down[172] and that future creditors are regarded as sufficiently protected by the publicity requirements for the reduction of capital (below).

---

[167] 2006 Act s.646(2)(3).

[168] In *Re Royal Scottish Assurance Plc,* 2011 S.L.T. 264 Lord Glennie stated that this had not been done, in either Scotland or England, since 1949.

[169] 2006 Act s.645(2)—this was the formal basis on which the prior practice avoided the creditor objection procedure. Under s.645(3) the court may also order that the procedure shall not apply to particular class or classes of creditor because of "the special circumstances of the case".

[170] Re *Vodafone Group Plc* [2014] 2 B.C.L.C. 422; *Re Sportech Plc,* 2012 S.L.T. 895; *Re Royal Scottish Assurance Plc,* 2011 S.L.T. 264.

[171] 2006 Act s.645(4).

[172] *Re Grosvenor Press Plc* [1985] B.C.L.C. 286; cf. *Re Jupiter House Investments (Cambridge) Ltd* [1985] B.C.L.C. 222.

13-37   The court may make ad hoc publicity requirements part of its order confirming the reduction, including the requirement that, for a specified period, the company include the words "and reduced" in its name.[173] In addition, the company must deliver a copy of the court order and a statement of its capital,[174] as now reduced, to the Registrar, who must register and certify them[175]; the registration must be publicised; and the reduction takes effect only upon registration.[176] It is conceivable that the reduction in capital would mean that the company no longer met the minimum capital requirements for a public company, in which case it must re-register as a private company before the Registrar will register the reduction (unless the court orders otherwise).[177]

13-38   Minority shareholders as well may seek—or the court may provide—protection at the confirmation stage, even if the requirements for shareholder meetings have been met before application to the court. The two main requirements for shareholder protection which the court will insist on are that the reduction treat the shareholders equitably and that the reduction proposal be properly explained to the shareholders who approved it. It is established that the court must be satisfied on these matters, even if the petition for confirmation is unopposed, as it often will be.[178] However, before a conclusion of inequitable treatment is reached, a significant risk to those shareholders arising out of the reduction must be identified. Thus, in *Re Ransomes Plc*[179] a substantial reduction in share premium account was permitted over the objections of preference shareholders, in order to permit a distribution to the ordinary shareholders, on the grounds that the preference shareholders' entitlements to dividend and return of capital (non-participating in both cases) were not put at risk by the proposed distribution. Even after the proposed distribution, the company would have assets and projected profits well in excess of what was required to meet the preference shareholders' entitlements. In other words, the protection for both creditors and shareholders now revolves around the same general notion: their objections will be plausible if the reduction is likely significantly to harm their entitlements. The apparently strict procedural requirements of proper explanation have been

---

[173] 2006 Act s.648(3)(4).

[174] Equivalent to that required on an allotment of shares.

[175] The certificate constitutes "conclusive evidence" that the statutory reduction requirements have been complied with and that the company's share capital is as stated in the statement of capital: s.649(6).

[176] 2006 Act s.649. There is more flexibility about the effective date where the reduction is part of a scheme of arrangement because that is normally upon delivery of the order to the Registrar, a matter under the control of the company (see Ch.29 and CLR, Final Report, para.13.11): s.649(3)(a).

[177] 2006 Act s.650. An expedited re-registration procedure, which dispenses with shareholder authorisation, may be used if the court authorises it (s.651). The basis for this provision is presumably the shareholder authorisation which was a necessary step in the reduction procedure.

[178] *Re Ransomes Plc* [1999] 2 B.C.L.C. 591, 602 CA.

[179] *Re Ransomes Plc* [1999] 1 B.C.L.C. 775 (affirmed on appeal; see previous note). See also *Re Ratners Group Plc* [1988] B.C.L.C. 685; and *Re Thorn EMI Plc* (1988) 4 B.C.C. 698 (reduction of share premium account to write off goodwill arising out of the same transaction as generated the premium).

somewhat qualified by the adoption of a "no difference" rider, i.e. the court may forgive procedural inadequacies if convinced that following the correct procedure would have led to the same result.[180]

Procedure available to private companies only

The provisions for reduction of capital without court confirmation apply only to private companies. These were introduced in 2006 to mitigate the delay and cost involved in court confirmation. The CLR wished to make this procedure available to public companies as well, but with the rider, needed to meet the requirements of the Second Directive, that creditors entitled to object to the reduction could invoke the court to veto or modify the reduction.[181] In place of court confirmation reliance would be put on a solvency statement made by the directors. For both types of company the procedure with court confirmation (above) would be kept as an alternative, because it allows directors to avoid the potential liabilities arising out of the solvency statement.[182] However, in the event the Act makes the procedure of reduction without court approval available to private companies only (which retain the option of using the court-based procedure).[183]

13–39

Solvency statement

Under the procedure available to private companies only, a special resolution of the shareholders is still required,[184] as discussed above, with the need to hold separate meetings of each class of shares whose rights are varied by the proposed reduction. However, the resolution of the members is to be supported by a solvency statement from the directors rather than confirmed by the court. The essence of the solvency statement is that to some degree it transfers responsibility for the reduction from the court to the directors of the company. This is a gain for the company in terms of speed and cost, but a potential risk for the directors, in so far as personal liability attaches to their approval of the solvency statement.[185] The solvency statement, which must accompany the resolution, is not an entirely novel device in British company law. It was required as part of the (now repealed) "whitewash" procedure available to private companies wishing to give financial assistance for the purchase of their own shares.[186] Something similar is also to be

13–40

---

[180] See previous note—a hypothetical and sometimes difficult judgment, which the courts should use sparingly.

[181] Company Formation and Capital Maintenance, para.3.27. However, in the absence of creditor objection, court involvement would not be necessary.

[182] Completing, para.7.9.

[183] DTI, *Company Law Reform*, Cm. 6456, para.4.8 rejected the application of the alternative procedure to public companies. It was thought that the possibility of creditor objection and thus court involvement would lead public companies to opt for the court-confirmation route, though it is not clear that this is a strong argument against making the option available to public companies.

[184] 2006 Act s.641(1)(a).

[185] Under the court procedure, liability (for example, in negligence) could attach to the directors for proposing the reduction, but they would be protected to a considerable extent against such liability in practice by the subsequent examination of the scheme by the court.

[186] Companies Act 1985 s.155. The financial assistance rules no longer apply to private companies: see below, para.13–55.

found in the rules governing share re-purchases by private companies from capital.[187] However, unlike the re-purchase statement, the solvency statement on a reduction of capital is not required to be audited.

The solvency statement is a statement by each director of the company, who must each sign it.[188] Each director asserts in it that he or she has formed an opinion on two matters. The first relates to the company's current financial position at the time the statement is made and is to the effect that "there is no ground on which the company could be found unable to pay (or otherwise discharge) its debts".[189] The second relates to the future and covers a period of one year after the date of the statement. The second opinion comes in two alternative forms.[190] If it is intended to commence the winding up of the company within a year,[191] then the required opinion is that the company will be able to pay or otherwise discharge its debts within 12 months of the winding up. In any other case, it is that the company will able to pay (or discharge) its debts as they fall due within the 12 months after the date of the statement. The required opinion relates only to the payment or discharge of debts (i.e. claims on the company to pay a liquidated sum). However, the directors are required to take into account contingent and prospective liabilities when forming their opinions.[192] The obligation to take into account prospective liabilities is hardly surprising, since these are liabilities which will certainly become due in the future (though it may not be clear precisely when). Contingent liabilities are those which may arise in the future because of an existing legal obligation or state of affairs. In other words, directors have to take account of contingent and prospective liabilities which may become debts payable by the company and imperil its ability to pay its debts, either at the date of the statement or, more likely, as they fall due over the 12-month period required to be considered under the second opinion.[193]

13–41   The transfer of responsibility to the directors is most graphically illustrated by the provision in the Act that it is a criminal offence for a director to make a solvency statement without having reasonable grounds for the opinions expressed in it—unless the solvency statement is not delivered to the Registrar, so that the reduction does not take effect.[194] This criminalises purely negligent conduct on the part of the director, an unusual step, for the Act normally confines criminal

---

[187] See above, para.13–14.
[188] 2006 Act s.643(1),(3) and the Companies (Reduction of Share Capital) Order 2008/1915 reg.2. Although the section does not extend to shadow directors, the term "director" does include de facto directors: see s.250. In *Re In A Flap Envelope Co Ltd* [2004] 1 B.C.L.C. 64, a case arising under the financial assistance whitewash procedure, a director who resigned for part of a day in order that the statement could be signed by his replacement, was held to be a de facto director during this period and thus liable to make the statement required under those provisions.
[189] 2006 Act s.643(1)(a).
[190] 2006 Act s.643(1)(b).
[191] So that the reduction of capital is a prelude to a winding up, as in *Scottish Insurance Corp Ltd v Wilsons and Clyde Coal Co Ltd* [1949] A.C. 462 HL.
[192] 2006 Act s.643(2).
[193] The language of s.643 reflects to some considerable degree the language to be found in s.123(1)(e) of the Insolvency Act, on which see R. Goode, *Principles of Corporate Insolvency Law*, Student Edn (London: Sweet & Maxwell, 2005) paras 4–15 to 4–23 and 4–28 to 4–29.
[194] 2006 Act s.643(4). The offence is punishable by imprisonment, whether tried summarily or on indictment: s.643(5).

sanctions to knowing or reckless misstatements. The greater liability imposed by the Act is an indication of the importance attached by the legislature to the accuracy of the solvency statement. The Act is silent on the civil liabilities of the directors for making an inaccurate solvency statement. The CLR had recommended that there should be an express civil liability on the directors to pay up the capital reduced,[195] but this suggestion is not taken up in the Act. However, it seems clear, at least where the reduction involves a return of assets to the shareholders, that the directors could be liable to the company for the loss suffered on the grounds that they are in breach of their general duties to the company; and that those who receive the assets with knowledge of the breach, whether directors or shareholders, would be liable to restore them to the company, under the principles discussed in relation to unlawful dividends.[196] It is further arguable that the reduction is ineffective where the directors have not made a solvency statement in accordance with the requirements of the Act, in particular where they do not have reasonable grounds for the opinions expressed in it.[197] In this case, the recipients could be said to be liable to return the company's assets, whether they know of the breach or not, subject only to defences such as change of position.[198]

A copy of the solvency statement must be provided to the members voting on the **13–42** reduction resolution (in different ways according to whether the vote is at a meeting or by written resolution),[199] but it is expressly provided that failure to observe these requirements does not affect the validity of the resolution passed.[200] The solvency statement must precede the date on which the resolution is passed by no more than 15 days and, if this is not the case, it appears the resolution cannot be said to be supported by a solvency statement. Thus, if the date for passing the resolution slips for one reason or another, the directors will be required to review and re-issue their solvency statement. After the passing of the resolution, the company has a further 15 days to file the copy of the resolution and the solvency statement and a current statement of the company's capital with the Registrar.[201] It is only with the registration of these documents by the Registrar (thus making them publicly available) that the reduction is effective.[202] Failure to deliver the documents to the Registrar on time does not affect the validity of the resolution but it does constitute an offence on the part of every officer of the company in default.[203]

---

[195] *Company Formation and Capital Maintenance*, para.3.35.

[196] See para.12–12. However, the specific statutory rules on distributions will not be relevant since a reduction of capital in cases (a) and (c) does not amount to a distribution for the purposes of Pt 23 (s.829(2)(b)) and in case (b) no assets are returned to the shareholders.

[197] If a solvency statement is not made in accordance with s.643, the resolution for the reduction of capital appears not to be "supported by a solvency statement" as s.642(1) requires and no other provision of the Act explicitly saves the resolution from this defect.

[198] cf. *MacPherson v European Strategic Bureau Ltd* [2000] 2 B.C.L.C. 683 CA.

[199] 2006 Act s.642(2),(3). On these different methods of shareholder decision-making see Ch.15.

[200] 2006 Act s.642(4). However, it is an offence on the part of every officer in default to fail to comply with this requirement: s.644(7)–(8), but liability is restricted to a fine.

[201] 2006 Act s.644(1),(2) and the Shares Regulations reg.10.

[202] 2006 Act s.644(3),(4).

[203] 2006 Act s.644(6),(7).

Reduction, distributions and re-purchase

13–43 Provided a private company observes the requirements of the Act, especially the requirement laid upon the directors to have reasonable grounds for the beliefs stated in the solvency statement, it is provided with an inexpensive and quick method of reducing its capital. It is arguable that, in consequence, the test for the legality of a distribution by such a company is a solvency test. Although the cumulative profits test, discussed in Ch.12, still applies to private companies, the impact of that rule can be mitigated by reducing the company's capital to write off losses, provided the solvency test (and other requirements of the private company procedure) are met. However, it may be that this step does not generate profits for a distribution even after the company's capital has been reduced, even to near vanishing point. Consequently, in this case the net accumulated profits rule will still operate as a binding constraint on distributions, especially if the private company was only thinly capitalised in the first place.[204]

The simplified procedure for reduction of capital without court approval also constitutes a functional substitute for a re-purchase or redemption out of capital, as discussed above.[205] Which will prove more popular where both mechanisms are available? Re-purchase out of capital has the virtue of familiarity and may continue to be used quite widely, at least initially, but the procedure for reduction out of court seems simpler and cheaper. No auditors' report is required on the directors' solvency statement, no special accounts have to be prepared[206] and there is no right of objection to the court on the part of creditors or non-approving members.

FINANCIAL ASSISTANCE

Rationale and history of the rule

13–44 Section 678 prohibits a public company (or its subsidiary) from giving financial assistance to a person for the acquisition by that person of the company's shares, whether the assistance is given in advance of or after the acquisition. The history of this rule does not constitute one of the most glorious episodes in British company law. The rationale for its introduction was under-articulated; it has proved capable of rending unlawful what seem from any perspective to be perfectly innocuous transactions; and it has proved resistant to a reformulation which would avoid these problems. The CLR eventually decided that, for private companies, the only way forward was to take them out of the scope of the rule altogether, which reform proposal was implemented in the 2006 Act. The CLR also proposed a series of amendments to the rule as it applies to public companies,[207] but most of these were not implemented in the 2006 Act. The

---

[204] For a discussion of the general test applying to distributions by private companies see para.12–3.

[205] See para.13–13.

[206] Though the directors can hardly make the required statement unless they have at least up-to-date management accounts.

[207] *Company Formation and Capital Maintenance*, paras 3.42 and 3.43. These proposals were derived in the main from proposals for reform made earlier by the DTI itself.

Government took the view that the Second Directive prevented significant changes to the rule as it applies to public companies.[208] Since then, the Second Directive itself has been amended,[209] but the Government regarded the relaxations introduced as not significant[210] and pinned its hopes on a more radical reform of the Directive in the future (which, however, seems unlikely to occur).

The rule against financial assistance for acquisitions of the company's shares was not developed by the nineteenth century judges as part of the capital maintenance regime. Rather, it was a statutory reform introduced in the 1929 Act as a result of the recommendations of the Greene Committee.[211] Although conventionally dealt with, as in this work, under the heading of legal capital, it is clear that in formal terms financial assistance may have no impact on the company's legal capital. If a company lends £100,000 to someone to purchase its shares from another investor and that person does not act as a nominee for the company but acquires the shares beneficially, the company's share capital, share premium account and capital redemption reserve will not be in any way altered by that loan or the subsequent purchase of the shares. The Greene Committee seems to have thought that financial assistance offended against the spirit, if not the letter, of the rule in *Trevor v Whitworth* (company prohibited from acquiring its own shares),[212] but the Jenkins Committee commented that, had the ban "been designed merely to extend that rule, we should have felt some doubt whether it was worth retaining".[213]

Nor does financial assistance necessarily reduce the company's net asset position. If in the above example the borrower is fully able to repay the loan, the company is simply replacing one asset (cash) with another (the rights under the loan) and possibly the latter will earn the company a higher rate of return. For obvious reasons, there is no general principle of creditor protection in company law which prohibits the company from altering the risk characteristics of its assets,[214] and so it is by no means clear that the rule against financial assistance be justified on that ground.

In fact, the Greene Committee seems to have been heavily, perhaps inappropri- **13–45** ately, influenced by the use of financial assistance in schemes which it disapproved of for more general reasons. The Committee thought, in particular, that it was abusive to finance a takeover by a loan and immediately repay it by raiding the coffers of the cash-rich company which is taken over or to use the assets of the new subsidiary as security for the takeover loan.[215] Now that highly

---

[208] DTI, *Company Law Reform*, Cm. 6456, March 2005, paras 42–43.

[209] Now arts 25 and 26 of the current version of the Second Directive (Directive 2012/30/EU).

[210] DTI, *Implementation of Companies Act 2006: A Consultative Document*, February 2007, para.6–26.

[211] Cmnd. 2657 (1926).

[212] See fn.1, above.

[213] Cmnd. 1749 (1962), para.173. Of course, if the shares are held by the person to whom the assistance is given, not beneficially, but as a nominee for the company, then the provisions discussed above at para.13–3 will apply (so that the financial assistance rules are not necessary to address the nominee situation).

[214] Lenders may impose such constraints by contract, of course. See para.31–24.

[215] On variations on this theme see *Selangor United Rubber Estates v Cradock (No.3)* [1968] 1 W.L.R. 1555; *Karak Rubber Co v Burden (No.2)* [1972] 1 W.L.R. 602; and *Wallersteiner v Moir* [1974] 1 W.L.R. 991 CA (pet. dis.) [1975] 1 W.L.R. 1093 HL.

leveraged takeovers are a common event, this worry looks somewhat overdone. More to the point, as it has operated in recent years, the financial assistance rule has not proved a major hindrance to such takeovers. In particular, the legislation has for some time permitted a payment of cash from the new subsidiary to the parent provided it is made by way of lawful dividend.[216] This suggests that, at least under the current law, the objection is not to the use of the subsidiary's cash balances to repay the loan but rather that the aim is to allow repayment only in a way which protects both creditors (by requiring the dividend to be paid in accordance with the distribution rules)[217] and minority shareholders, since dividends are paid pro rata to the proportion of the share capital held.[218] In other words, the financial assistance prohibition does not express a policy about desirable and undesirable takeovers but more general concerns about creditor and minority shareholder protection. However, the financial assistance rule seems too broad to be supported on a simple creditor or minority shareholder rationale, as the above example of a loan to purchase shares suggests. For example, if the loan were for some purpose other than the purchase of shares, the rule would not bite, yet the borrower might be less able to repay the loan than the borrower for the share purchase.

13–46   However, the Greene Committee's recommendations were enacted as s.45 of the 1929 Act, which was re-enacted with amendments as s.54 of the 1948 Act. Section 45 immediately revealed the difficulties involved in drafting a prohibition that was properly targeted on the perceived abuses. That section, despite its relative brevity, became notorious as unintelligible and liable to penalise innocent transactions while failing to deter guilty ones. The Jenkins Committee[219] suggested an alternative approach very similar to that eventually adopted in 1981 in relation to private companies, but at the time no action was taken on that suggestion and, when the Second Company Law Directive was adopted, it became impracticable in relation to public companies.[220]

However, in 1980 two reported cases[221] caused considerable alarm in commercial and legal circles, suggesting, as they did, that the scope of the section was even wider, and the risk of wholly unobjectionable transactions being shot down even greater, than had formerly been thought. Hence it was decided that something had to be done about it in the 1981 Act which was then in preparation. Probably more midnight oil was burnt on this subject than on all the rest of that Act, and the resulting elaborate provisions were certainly some improvement on s.54. However, they still did not produce the holy grail of a precisely targeted prohibition and, after the controversy generated by the House of Lords decision in *Brady v Brady*,[222] the Government made proposals for the further relaxation of

---

[216] 2006 Act s.681(2).
[217] See paras 12–1 and 12–2.
[218] See para.19–2.
[219] Cmnd. 1749 (1962) paras 170–186.
[220] See art.23 of Directive 77/91 [1977] O.J. L26/1.
[221] *Belmont Finance Corp v Williams Furniture Ltd (No.2)* [1980] 1 All E.R. 393 CA; *Armour Hick Northern Ltd v Whitehouse* [1980] 1 W.L.R. 1520.
[222] *Brady v Brady* [1989] A.C. 755 HL.

the provisions.[223] However, before these proposals could be implemented, the CLR was established, with the results described above. In the meantime, the difficulty of producing a targeted formula continued to be demonstrated in litigation, for example, in the decision of the Court of Appeal in *Chaston v SWP Group Ltd*[224] in 2002.

The prohibition

Section 678 distinguishes between assistance given prior to the acquisition and that given afterwards.[225] Its subs.(1) says that, subject to exceptions:

13–47

> "where a person[226] is acquiring or is proposing to acquire[227] shares in a public company, it is not lawful for that company, or a company that is a subsidiary of that company,[228] to give financial assistance directly or indirectly[229] for the purpose of that acquisition before or at the same time as the acquisition takes place."

Subsection (3) provides that, subject to the same exceptions, when a person has acquired shares in a company and any liability has been incurred (by that or any other person) for that purpose, it is not lawful for the company or any of its subsidiaries to give financial assistance, directly or indirectly, for the purpose of reducing or discharging that liability, if at the time the assistance was given the company in which the shares were acquired was a public company. Thus, if A (probably a bank) lends B (a bidder) £1 million to enable B (an acquisition vehicle) to make a takeover of a target company and C (probably B's parent company) guarantees repayment, it will be unlawful for any financial assistance to be given by the target, when taken over, to B or C towards the discharge of their obligations to A. However, since private companies are now excluded from the rule, it is important to know whether the target whose shares were acquired

---

[223] DTI, *Company Law Reform: Proposals for Reform of Sections 151–158 of the Companies Act 1985* (1993); DTI, *Consultation Paper on Financial Assistance* (November 1996).

[224] *Chaston v SWP Group Ltd* [2003] 1 B.C.L.C. 675, helpfully considered by E. Ferran, "Corporate Transactions and Financial Assistance: Shifting Policy Perceptions but Static Law" (2004) 63 C.L.J. 225.

[225] On the other hand, the drafters seem to have thought of financial assistance, whether given before or after the event, as a one-off transaction. For the difficulties involved in calculating the impact of the assistance on the company's net assets where the assistance is continuing, see *Parlett v Guppys (Bridport) Ltd* [1996] 2 B.C.L.C. 34 CA.

[226] The Government's interpretation of the section is that the person must be someone other than the company itself: HC Debs, Standing Committee D, 20 July 2006, cols. 856–857 (Vera Baird).

[227] In contrast with s.54 of the 1948 Act, which used the expression "purchase or subscription", this section refers to "acquire" or "acquisition" thus extending the ambit of the section to non-cash subscriptions and exchanges.

[228] The sections do not apply to financial assistance by a holding company for the acquisition of shares in its subsidiary; in such a case there is less likelihood of prejudice to other shareholders or to creditors. The subsidiary must be a "company" within the meaning of the Act (see s.1) so that foreign subsidiaries are not caught by the prohibition. This was the view taken previously: see *Arab Bank Plc v Merchantile Holdings Ltd* [1994] Ch. 755.

[229] A charge given by a company to secure a loan to the company which both lender and company knew was to be on-lent to the purchaser of a company's shares to finance the purchase constitutes indirect financial assistance: *Re Hill and Tylor Ltd* [2005] 1 B.C.L.C. 41; *Central and Eastern Trust Co v Irving Oil Ltd* (1980) 110 D.L.R. (3d) 257 Sup Ct. Can.

and which is now giving the financial assistance is a public company at the time the assistance is given by it. Thus, in this example, if the target company were a public company, it could nevertheless give financial assistance after the acquisition, provided it had by then been re-registered as a private company. This step is commonly taken in private equity buy-outs.

13–48   Section 683 provides that a reference to a person incurring a liability includes:

> "his changing his financial position by making an agreement or arrangement (whether enforceable or unenforceable and whether made on his own account or with any other person)[230] or by any other means"

It adds that reference to a company giving financial assistance to reduce or discharge a liability incurred for the purposes of acquiring shares includes giving assistance for the purpose of wholly or partly restoring the financial position of the person concerned to what it was before the acquisition. This results in an enormous extension of the normal meaning of "liability" and seems to mean that, before a company can give any financial assistance to *any* person (whether or not the acquirer), it must assess his overall financial position before and after the acquisition[231] and if, afterwards, it has deteriorated, must refrain from any form of financial assistance which is not covered by one of the exceptions—at any rate if there is a causal connection between the deterioration and the acquisition.

The scope of the prohibition depends crucially on what is meant by "financial assistance". Section 677 apparently defines financial assistance, but in fact fails to do so. It defines the types of financial assistance falling within the Act, without defining what "financial" assistance is—as opposed to other forms of assistance. Given that limitation, however, the section widely defines the types of financial assistance which are covered. In addition to such obvious assistance as gifts, loans, guarantees, releases, waivers and indemnities,[232] the definition includes any other agreement under which the obligations of the company giving the assistance are to be fulfilled before the obligations of another party to the agreement,[233] and the novation of a loan or of other agreement; or the assignment of rights under it. If the financial assistance is of one or more of these types, it is irrelevant whether or not the net assets of the company providing it are reduced by reason of the assistance.[234]

However, this is not all. The list of types of financial assistance concludes with "any other financial assistance given by a company, the net assets[235] of which are thereby reduced to a material extent, or which has no net assets". The effect of

---

[230] The words "or with any other person" are somewhat puzzling; one would have expected "or that of any other person". Can there be an agreement or arrangement which is not made with some other person? And, if there can, would it not be covered by "or by any other means"?

[231] The difficulty of doing this after a takeover is mind-boggling.

[232] 2006 Act s.677(1)(a)–(c)—other than an indemnity given in respect of the indemnifier's own neglect or default.

[233] e.g. where a company which is a diamond merchant sells a diamond to a dealer for £100,000, payment to be 12 months hence, the intention being that the dealer will sell the diamond at a profit or borrow on its security thus putting him in funds to acquire shares in the company.

[234] In some cases (e.g. gifts) they will be; in others (e.g. loans or guarantees) they may or may not.

[235] Defined as "the aggregate of the company's assets, less the aggregate of its liabilities" and "liabilities" includes any provision for anticipated losses or charges: s.677(2).

this is that, even if the financial assistance does not fall within the specific types that the drafter was able to foresee, it will nevertheless be unlawful if the company has no net assets or if the consequence of the assistance is to reduce its net assets "to a material extent". Only in this last case, and where the company has net assets, does it seem to be a requirement of the definition of financial assistance that the company giving it should suffer a financial detriment. Clearly "materiality" is to be determined to some extent by the relationship between the value of the assistance and the value of the net assets: assistance worth £50 would reduce the net assets materially if they were only £100 but immaterially if they were £1 million. But how far is that to be taken? A company with net assets of £billions might regard a reduction of £1 million as immaterial, but it seems unlikely that judges (most of whom are not accustomed to disposing of £millions) would so regard it. At the other end of the scale, it was held in *Chaston*[236] that an expenditure of £20,000 by a subsidiary, whose net assets were only £100,000, was material, even though the assistance was in relation to the purchase of the shares of the parent at a price of some £2.5 million.[237]

As noted, however, assistance will not be unlawful unless it is "financial". Merely giving information (even financial information) is not financial assistance.[238] Moreover, even if financial, the assistance must fall within the admittedly wide definition if it is to be unlawful. In other words, the definition of the types of financial assistance which fall within the Act seems intended to be exhaustive. Thus, timely repayment of a debt due, even if done in order to assist the creditor in the purchase of the debtor's shares, would not seem to be caught,[239] but it might be if the debt were paid early because it could then be said to have an element of gift in it.[240]

13–49

Finally, the impugned transaction must actually be capable of assisting the acquirer to obtain the shares. In *British & Commonwealth Holdings Plc v Barclays Bank Plc*,[241] the promises, made by the company to banks which could be required to acquire the shares from the shareholder if the company did not redeem them, were regarded as an "inducement" to the shareholder to acquire the redeemable shares in the first place but not as financial assistance to it to do so.

---

[236] Above, fn.224.

[237] If the assistance had been provided by the parent, as it could well have been, no question of financial assistance would probably have arisen.

[238] But reimbursement of the costs of digesting and assessing the information could be, as in *Chaston*. Nor is assistance financial if it consists of the parent instructing its subsidiary to pay money to the vendor of the shares, where no financial asset leaves the parent and the assistance provided by the (foreign incorporated) subsidiary is lawful: *AMG Global Nominees (Private) Ltd v Africa Resources Ltd* [2009] 1 B.C.L.C. 281 CA. This is a surprising decision and the CA's reliance on the *Arab Bank* case (above, fn.228) seems misplaced, since the issue there was the legality of the assistance provided by the subsidiary and not, as in *AMG*, the assistance provided by the parent.

[239] cf. *MT Realisations Ltd v Digital Equipment Co Ltd* [2003] 2 B.C.L.C 117 CA—enforcement of security rights was recovery of a legal entitlement rather than the receipt of financial assistance.

[240] See *Plaut v Steiner* (1988) 5 B.C.C. 352, but note also the insistence by the Court of Appeal in *British & Commonwealth Holdings Plc v Burclays Bank Plc* [1996] 1 W.L.R. 1 CA that the terms used in the definition must be given their technical meaning (in this case in relation to the meaning of an "indemnity").

[241] Above, para.13–28.

However, in *Chaston*[242] this decision was explained on the basis that the company did not expect to have to meet its obligations at the time the promises were made and it was held that there was no general rule that an inducement could not constitute financial assistance. In *Chaston* the subsidiary of the target had paid for an accountant's report on the target, which was an inducement to the potential bidder to make the offer, but it was also financial assistance in the sense that it reduced the costs the potential bidder incurred in investigating the worth of the target.

Chaston is another example of the financial assistance prohibition striking down an entirely innocuous transaction. The company (or rather its subsidiary) spent a modest amount of money to further a sale of the company to a purchaser—a sale which was clearly in the shareholders' interests (as the subsequent litigation showed) and which carried no additional risks (probably the opposite) for its creditors. For this exemplary business decision the directors of the company were found to be in breach of their fiduciary duties to the company (by providing the unlawful financial assistance) and held personally liable to restore the amount of the assistance to the company, i.e. to the purchaser, which sued as assignee of the subsidiary's claim.[243]

The exceptions

Specific exceptions

13–50 The Act provides a number of exceptions to the prohibitions. Some are unconditional, i.e. always excepted. They include allotment of bonus shares, lawful distributions, anything done in accordance with a court order, reductions of capital or redemptions or purchases of shares under the provisions discussed above, and anything done under the reconstruction provisions discussed in Ch.29.[244] Others are conditional. In the case of a public company the conditional exemptions apply only to certain types of financial assistance, which are thought to be harmless, for example, where lending money is part of the ordinary business of the company and the financial assistance is provided within that business or the assistance is provided in connection with an employees' share scheme.[245] Even then, the exemption applies only if the company's net assets are not thereby reduced or, if reduced, the reduction is financed out of distributable profits.[246]

13–51 The interesting point about the conditional exceptions for public companies is that they do link the financial assistance rules to the underlying policy of creditor

---

[242] Above, fn.224.

[243] In *Anglo Petroleum Ltd v TFB (Mortgages) Ltd* [2007] B.C.C 407, a differently constituted CA took a more commercially robust line, notably in rejecting the argument that any payment by a company which "smoothed the path to the acquisition" of its shares constituted financial assistance.

[244] 2006 Act.681. There is no express exemption for the expenses of share issues (for example, commissions—see para.11–14), but there clearly should be.

[245] 2006 Act s.682(2). There is also a conditional exception for financial assistance given in connection with private company acquisitions, but this is of such importance that it is treated separately in para.13–55 below.

[246] 2006 Act s.682(1). Distributable profits are defined in s.683(1), which essentially tracks the rules governing distributions.

protection. If there is no reduction in net assets or, even if there is, the creditors cannot legitimately complain because the reduction is financed out of distributable profits, the conditional exceptions apply. Article 25 of the Second Directive, in its current version[247] no longer contains a prohibition on financial assistance but allows (but does not oblige) Member States to permit financial assistance, subject to certain conditions. One of these is that the financial assistance should be financed out of distributable profits if it involves a reduction of net assets. It is thus open to the UK government to remove the financial assistance prohibition generally—not just in the specific cases mentioned above—where the assistance is financed from distributable profits. This would establish a firm link between the prohibition and the capital maintenance rules. However, the government has not chosen to take this step, because of the additional conditions set out in art.25, which would also need to be met as part of such a reform and which were regarded as onerous.[248] In particular, it would be necessary to impose liability upon the directors if the assistance were not provided "under fair market conditions", to require the company to carry out due diligence on the creditworthiness of the person receiving the assistance, and to make the assistance subject to a special resolution of the shareholders, acting upon a report from the directors.

General exceptions

As things stand, however, the main and most debated exception to the prohibition is to be found in s.678 itself. This was intended to allay the fears aroused by two decisions in 1980.[249] The section relates to the purposes for which the financial assistance was given. It is a necessary pre-condition for liability under s.678 that the financial assistance should have been given for the purpose of the acquisition of the shares. In some cases the company will be able to show that, although the financial assistance was given in connection with an acquisition of shares, it was not given for that purpose.[250] However, the exceptions come into play where that cannot be shown, i.e. where the purpose of the financial assistance was to facilitate the acquisition of shares. Under s.678(2) the prohibition on a company from giving financial assistance before or at the time of the acquisition nevertheless does not apply if:

13–52

(a)   the company's principal purpose in giving the assistance is not to give it for the purpose of any such acquisition; or

(b)   if the giving of the assistance for that purpose is only an incidental part of some larger purpose of the company; and the assistance is given in good faith in the interests of the company.

---

[247] Directive 2012/30/EU [2012] O.J. L315/74

[248] Above, fn.210, para.6.23. For trenchant criticism of the limited scope of the reforms to art.23, see E. Ferran, "Simplification of European Company Law on Financial Assistance" (2005) 6 E.B.O.L.R. 93.

[249] *Belmont Finance Corp v Williams Furniture Ltd (No.2)* [1980] 1 All E.R. 393 CA; *Armour Hick Northern Ltd v Whitehouse* [1980] 1 W.L.R. 1520.

[250] *Dymont v Boyden* [2005] 1 B.C.L.C. 163 CA.

Subsection (4) provides similarly that the prohibition does not apply to assistance given subsequently to the acquisition if:

(a)   the company's principal purpose in giving the assistance is not to reduce or discharge any liability incurred by a person for the purpose of the acquisition of shares in the company or its holding company; or

(b)   the reduction or discharge of any such liability is only an incidental part of some larger purpose of the company; and the assistance is given in good faith in the interests of the company.

13–53   On the meaning of these difficult subsections there is an authoritative ruling from the House of Lords in the case of *Brady v Brady*,[251] a case remarkable both because of the extent of the judicial disagreement to which it gave rise and because it was ultimately decided on a ground not argued in the lower courts. It related to prosperous family businesses, principally concerned with haulage and soft drinks. The businesses were run and owned in equal shares by two brothers, Jack and Bob Brady, and their respective families, through a parent company, T. Brady & Co Ltd (Brady's), and a number of subsidiary and associated companies. Unfortunately Jack and Bob fell out, resulting in a complete deadlock. It was clear that unless something could be agreed amicably, Brady's would have to be wound-up—which was the last thing that anyone wanted. It was therefore agreed that the group should be reorganised, sole control of the haulage business being taken by Jack and that of the drinks business by Bob. As the respective values of the two businesses were not precisely equal, this involved various intra-group transfers of assets and shareholdings which became increasingly complicated as the negotiations proceeded. It suffices to say that, in the eventual agreement, one of the companies had acquired shares in Brady's and the liability to pay for them thus incurred was to be discharged by a transfer to it of assets of Brady's. Bob, however, contended that further valuation adjustments were needed and refused to proceed further unless they were made. Jack then started proceedings for specific performance which Bob defended on various grounds among which was that it would require Brady's to give unlawful financial assistance.

It was conceded that the transfer of assets would be unlawful financial assistance unless, in the circumstances, the prohibition was disapplied by what is now s.678(4). On the face of it one might have thought that the circumstances afforded a classic illustration of the sort of situation that the above provisions were intended to legitimate. At first instance, that view prevailed. In the Court of Appeal,[252] however, while all three judges thought that the conditions relating to

---

[251] *Brady v Brady* [1989] A.C. 755 HL. This case is an illustration (of which *Charterhouse Investment Trust v Tempest Diesels Ltd* ([1987] B.C.L.C. 1) is another) of how, all too often, parties agree in principle to a simple arrangement which on the face of it raises no question of unlawful financial assistance but then refer it to their respective advisers who, in their anxiety to obtain the maximum fiscal and other advantages for their respective clients, introduce complicated refinements which arguably cause it to fall foul of the prohibition on financial assistance. In the *Charterhouse* case, where the former s.54 applied, Hoffmann J, by exercising commonsense in interpreting the meaning of "financial assistance", was able to avoid striking down an obviously unobjectionable arrangement. But the elaborate definition of that expression in the present Act leaves less scope for commonsense.

[252] *Brady v Brady* [1988] B.C.L.C. 20 CA.

"purpose" were satisfied, the majority thought that those relating to "good faith in the interests of the company" were not. In contrast, in the House of Lords it was held unanimously that the good faith requirements were complied with but that the purpose ones were not. Hence the contemplated transfer would be unlawful financial assistance if carried out in the way proposed.

Lord Oliver, in a speech concurred in by the other Law Lords, subjected the purpose requirements to detailed analysis.[253] He pointed out that "purpose" had to be distinguished from "reason" or "motive" (which would almost always be different and wider) and that the purpose requirements contemplated alternative situations. The first is where the company has a principal and a subsidiary purpose: the question then is whether the principal purpose is to assist or relieve the acquirer or is for some other corporate purpose. The second situation is where the financial assistance is not for any purpose other than to help the acquirer but is merely incidental to some larger corporate purpose.[254] As regards the first alternative, he accepted that an example might be where the principal purpose was to enable the company to obtain from the person assisted a supply of some product which the company needed for its business.[255] As regards the second, he offered no example, merely saying that he had "not found the concept of larger purpose easy to grasp" but that:

> "if the paragraph is to be given any meaning that does not provide a blank cheque for avoiding the effective application of [the prohibition] in every case, the concept must be narrower than that for which the appellants contend."[256]

The trial judge, and O'Connor LJ in the Court of Appeal,[257] had thought that the larger purpose was to resolve the deadlock and its inevitable consequences; and Croom-Johnson LJ[258] had found it in the need to reorganise the whole group. But if either could be so regarded, it would follow that, if the board of a company concluded in good faith that the only way that a company could survive was for it to be taken over, it could lawfully provide financial assistance to the bidder—the very "mischief" that the legislation was designed to prevent. The logic is, of course, impeccable. But the result seems to reduce the purpose exceptions to very narrow limits indeed and to make one wonder whether the midnight oil burnt on the drafting of the two subsections had achieved anything worthwhile.

13–54

The transaction was in fact saved by application of the special provisions then applying to private companies (now repealed). However, the (eventually) successful outcome in that particular case did not get rid of the awkward issues

---

[253] *Brady v Brady* [1989] A.C. 755 at 778. Agreeing with O'Connor LJ in the Court of Appeal ([1988] B.C.L.C. 20 at 25) he described the paragraph, with commendable restraint, as "not altogether easy to construe".

[254] The layout of ss.678(2) and (4) now reflects this analysis more clearly than did the previous legislation.

[255] A situation envisaged by Buckley LJ in his judgment in the *Belmont Finance* case [1980] 1 All E.R. at 402, as giving rise to doubts under the former s.54 of the 1948 Act.

[256] *Brady v Brady* [1989] A.C. 755 at 779.

[257] *Brady v Brady* [1988] B.C.L.C. 20 at 26.

[258] *Brady v Brady* [1988] B.C.L.C. 20 at 32.

raised by it. The DTI[259] floated the ideas of substituting "predominant reason" for "principal purpose" or relying solely on the test of good faith in the interests of the company. The CLR supported the first of these suggestions.[260] However, these suggestions do nothing to address the arguments put forward in the House of Lords in favour of giving the purpose requirements a strict interpretation, if the prohibition is to remain a meaningful restriction. In any event, the 2006 Act retains the established wording.

Exemption for private companies

13–55   In the reforms of 1981 a more relaxed regime for private companies was introduced, allowing assistance if this did not involve a reduction of the company's net assets or if the financial assistance was given out of distributable profits.[261] The effect of this provision was to tie the financial assistance rule more clearly to the creditor protection concerns of the rules applying to distributions.[262] The 2006 Act went further and removed the financial assistance prohibition from private companies, as the CLR recommended. Section 678 applies only to financial assistance given to a person who is proposing to acquire shares in a public company or, in relation to an acquisition which has occurred, where the company whose shares have been acquired is at the time of the assistance a public company. Consequently, where a public company is taken over and then re-registered as a private company, it may give financial assistance by way of reducing or discharging the liabilities of the (new) parent incurred for the purpose of the acquisition.[263] The limitation in s.678 thus focusses on the private status of the company whose shares are subject to the acquisition. Consequently, if a private subsidiary gives financial assistance for the purchase of the shares of its public parent, as in the *Chaston* case,[264] that situation will still be caught by the prohibition. Moreover, the prohibition is extended by s.679 to catch financial assistance given by a public company towards the acquisition of shares in its private holding company—an unusual but not impossible situation.[265] In this case the status of the provider of the assistance as a public company subsidiary is enough to trigger the rule.

---

[259] *Company Law Reform: Proposals for Reform of Sections 151–158 of the Companies Act 1985* (1993).

[260] Completing, para.7.14.

[261] 1985 Act s.155(2). As we have seen, the Directive now adopts this criterion as one of the conditions under which financial assistance may be permitted (above, para.13–51).

[262] See Ch.12.

[263] Of course, the directors of the (new) subsidiary will need to continue to comply with their fiduciary duties to their company.

[264] Above, fn.224.

[265] 2006 Act s.679. An example might be where a target public company in a takeover is re-registered as a private company (to avoid the ban on its giving financial assistance to its new parent) but still has subsidiary companies which are public companies. Section 679 prevents the subsidiaries giving financial assistance to their immediate parent (unless an exception applies). At least this is what s.679(3) appears to say.

Civil remedies for breach of the prohibition

The only sanctions prescribed by the Act for breaches of the prohibition are **13–56** fining the company[266] and fining or imprisoning (or both) its officers in default.[267] More important are the consequences in civil law resulting from the fact that the transaction is unlawful. Unfortunately, precisely what these consequences are has vexed the courts both of England and of other countries which have adopted comparable provisions and it is a pity that the current Act did not attempt to clarify the position.[268]

What has caused the courts to make heavy weather of this is the somewhat curious wording of the prohibition down the years. Since the object of the section is to protect the company and its members and creditors, one would have expected it to say that it is not lawful for any person who has acquired or is proposing to acquire shares of a company to receive financial assistance from the company or any of its subsidiaries. That would have pointed the courts in the right direction to work out the consequences. But instead it declares that it is unlawful for the company to give the assistance, and follows that by imposing criminal sanctions on the company and (the one thing that makes good sense) on the officers of the company who are in default. This could be taken to imply (and was so taken by Roxburgh J in *Victor Battery Co Ltd v Curry's Ltd*)[269] that the object of the prohibition was not to protect the company but to punish it and its officers by imposing fines. This calamitous decision continued to be accepted in England, and was cited with apparent approval by Cross J (subsequently a Law Lord) 20 years later,[270] though rejected by the Australian Courts whose decisions helped those in England eventually to see the light. The decision has now been disapproved or not followed in a series of cases[271] and is accepted to be heretical.

Freed from the fetters of that heresy the courts have since given the section real **13–57** teeth and it is submitted that the following propositions can now be regarded as reasonably well established:

---

[266] Since the prohibition is intended to protect the company and its members and creditors it is difficult to conceive of a more inappropriate sanction than to reduce the company's net assets (still further than the unlawful financial assistance may have done) by fining the company. The CLR had proposed that the criminal sanction on the company be removed: Formation, para.343(d).

[267] 2006 Act s.680.

[268] The remedies for an unlawful distribution are specifically excluded from the area of unlawful financial assistance: s.847(4)(a).

[269] *Victor Battery Co Ltd v Curry's Ltd* [1946] Ch. 242.

[270] *Curtis's Furnishing Stores Ltd v Freedman* [1966] 1 W.L.R. 1219. But he ignored it in *South Western Mineral Water Co Ltd v Ashmore* [1967] 1 W.L.R. 1110.

[271] *Selangor United Rubber Estate Ltd v Cradock (No.3)* [1968] 1 W.L.R. 1555; *Heald v O'Connor* [1971] 1 W.L.R. 497; and Lord Denning MR in *Wallersteiner v Moir* [1974] 1 W.L.R. at 1014H–1015A. The modern view helped Millett J to conclude in *Arab Bank Plc v Mercantile Holdings Ltd* [1994] Ch. 71 that the legislation applies to assistance provided by a subsidiary of an English company only where the subsidiary is not a foreign company, on the grounds that the protection of the shareholders and creditors of a company is a matter for the law of the place of incorporation. By the same token, the giving of assistance by the English subsidiary of a foreign parent ought to be regulated by the Act, though it is by no means clear that it is.

(a)   An agreement to provide unlawful financial assistance, being unlawful, is unenforceable by either party to it. This proposition is undoubted and authority for it is the decision of the House of Lords in *Brady v Brady*.[272] However, if the contract could be performed legally (i.e. without giving unlawful financial assistance), but unlawful financial assistance is in fact provided, then the legality of the contract depends on whether the other party to it was party to a common design to act unlawfully.[273]

(b)   However, the illegality of the financial assistance given or provided by the company normally does not taint other connected transactions, such as the agreement by the person assisted to acquire the shares. It would be absurd if, for example, a takeover bidder which had been given financial assistance by the target company, or by a subsidiary of the company, could escape from the liability to perform purchase contracts which it had entered into with the shareholders of the target. Clearly, it cannot.

(c)   This, however, is subject to a qualification if the obligation to acquire the shares and the obligation to provide financial assistance form part of a single composite transaction. The obvious example of this would be an arrangement in which someone agreed to subscribe for shares in a company (or its holding company) in consideration of which the company agreed to give him some form of financial assistance. In such a case the position apparently depends on whether the terms relating to the acquisition of shares can be severed from those relating to the unlawful financial assistance. If they can, those relating to the acquisition can be enforced. If they cannot, the whole agreement is void. The authorities supporting this proposition are the decisions of Cross J in *South Western Mineral Water Co Ltd v Ashmore*[274] and of the Privy Council in *Carney v Herbert*.[275] In essence, the facts of both were that shares of a company were to be acquired and payment of the purchase price was to be secured by a charge on the assets of, in the former case, that company and, in the latter, its subsidiary. The agreed security was, of course, unlawful financial assistance. In the former case, the shares had not been transferred or the charge executed; in the latter, they had. In the former it was held that unless the sellers were prepared to dispense with the charge (which they were not) the whole agreement was void and that the parties must be restored to their positions prior to the agreement. In the latter it was held that the unlawful charge could be severed from the sale of the shares and that the sellers were entitled to sue the purchaser for the price. Despite the different results, the Privy Council judgment, delivered by Lord Brightman, cited with approval

---

[272] *Brady v Brady* [1989] A.C. 755. See also *Re Hill and Tyler Ltd* [2005] 1 B.C.L.C. 41.
[273] *Anglo Petroleum Ltd v TFB (Mortgages) Ltd* [2007] B.C.C. 407 CA: a contract to lend money to a company where the contract did not require the sum advanced to be used to provide unlawful financial assistance but where the lender knew the money lent was to be used to repay monies due to the company's former parent from the purchaser of the company's shares from the former parent. The CA thought there was no public policy in forcing the lender to investigate whether the proposed use of the loan would constitute unlawful financial assistance and so held the contract of loan enforceable (though this view was, strictly, obiter).
[274] *South Western Mineral Water Co Ltd v Ashmore* [1967] 1 W.L.R. 1110.
[275] *Carney v Herbert* [1985] A.C. 301 PC, on appeal from the Sup. Ct. of N.S.W.

the decision of Cross J in the earlier case. In both cases a fair result seems to have been arrived at and certainly one preferable to that for which the assisted purchaser contended in *Carney*, namely that he should be entitled to retain the shares without having to pay for them.[276] It is therefore to be hoped that even in a single composite transaction the courts will permit severance or order restitutio in integrum unless there are strong reasons of public policy[277] why the whole transaction should be treated as unlawful so as to preclude the court from offering any assistance to any party to it.

(d)   If the company has actually given the unlawful financial assistance, that transaction will be void. The practical effect of that depends on the nature of the financial assistance. If it is a mortgage, guarantee or indemnity or the like, the party to whom it was given cannot sue the company upon it.[278] It is that party who suffers,[279] and the company, so long as it realises in time that the transaction is void, need do nothing but defend any hopeless action that may be brought against it. If, however, the unlawful assistance was a completed gift or loan, the company will need to take action if it is to recover what it has lost. And a long line of cases has established that, in most circumstances, this it will be able to do.[280] Its claim may be based on misfeasance, when recovery is sought from the directors or other officers of the company, or on restitution, conspiracy, or constructive trust, when the claim is against them or those to whom the unlawful assistance has passed or who have otherwise actively participated in the unlawful transaction. The most popular basis seems to be constructive trust, the argument being that the directors committed the equivalent of a breach of trust when they caused the company's assets to be used for the unlawful purpose and the recipients became constructive trustees thereof. The constructive trust is discussed further in Ch.16, below.

(e)   In the light of propositions (a)–(d) it would also seem to follow that if the unlawful assistance given by the company is a loan secured by a mortgage or charge on the borrower's property[281] then, so long as the company has rights of recovery from the borrower under proposition (d), it should be able to do so by realising its security. This would certainly be so if the mortgage or charge could be severed from the unlawful loan—which,

---

[276] Yet Lord Brightman seemed to think that this would be the consequence if severance was not possible: see [1985] A.C. at 309.

[277] In support of this caveat, see [1985] A.C. at 313 and 317.

[278] See the cases discussed under (c) and *Heald v O'Connor* [1971] 1 W.L.R. 497, where the unlawful assistance was a mortgage on the property of the company whose shares were being acquired, the purchaser guaranteeing the payment of sums due under the mortgage. The mortgage was unlawful. Hence the purchaser escaped liability on the guarantee (though that was lawful) since no payments were lawfully due under the mortgage. It would have been different had the guarantee been an indemnity.

[279] Since the mortgage is illegal and void (not merely voidable) presumably a bona fide purchaser of it without notice could not enforce it either.

[280] *Steen v Law* [1964] A.C. 287 PC; *Selangor United Rubber Estates v Cradock (No.3)* [1968] 1 W.L.R. 1555; *Karak Rubber Co v Burden (No.2)* [1972] 1 W.L.R. 602; *Wallersteiner v Moir* [1974] 1 W.L.R. 991 CA; *Belmont Finance Corp v Williams Furniture Ltd (No.2)* [1980] 1 All E.R. 393 CA; *Smith v Croft (No.2)* [1988] Ch. 114; *Agip (Africa) Ltd v Jackson* [1991] Ch. 547 CA.

[281] Unless the company is a public company and the charge is on shares in it, for then the charge may be void under s.670: see above, para.13–2.

however, might be regarded as impossible since the consideration given for the mortgage or charge *was* the unlawful loan. But, since the effect of the recent case law is to recognise that the object of the prohibition, despite its wording, is to protect the company, the courts ought not to boggle at the conclusion that the security given to the company can be realised to recover what is due to it by the borrower.

(f)   The above points all go to the validity of the financial assistance transaction and transactions associated with it. In addition, the directors who cause the company to give the unlawful finance assistance may be found to have been in breach of their duties to the company and the company is not prevented from enforcing those duties against the directors (normally to recover any loss suffered) by virtue of the fact that the company's act in providing the assistance was unlawful.[282]

13–58   It will therefore be seen that we have come a long way from the time when it was believed that the only likely sanctions were derisory fines on the company and its officers in default. These developments have caused the banking community some alarm, for there is no doubt that banks could find themselves caught out—as indeed they have been in the past.[283] The fact that money passing in the relevant transactions is likely to do so through banking channels inevitably exposes banks to risks.[284] The government proposed, in consequence, that transactions in breach of the prohibition should no longer be void for that reason alone,[285] but the Act did not take up this proposal.

CONCLUSION

13–59   The elaborate rules on preservation of legal capital, discussed in this chapter, can be justified only if the role of legal capital in controlling distributions by companies is regarded as a valuable one. This was discussed in Ch.12. If the concept of legal capital were removed from the distribution rules, the Act could be simplified substantially by largely removing the rules on reduction of capital—or at least by confining them to their shareholder protection aspects— and simplifying those on the redemption and re-purchase of shares. Creditor protection would then turn on other concepts. The financial assistance rules, by contrast, are a candidate for reform even if the concept of legal capital is maintained, since they have no necessary connection with that doctrine in their

---

[282] *Steen v Law* [1964] A.C. 287; *Selangor United Rubber Estates v Cradock (No.3)* [1968] 1 W.L.R. 1555; *Chaston v SWP Group Plc* [2003] 1 B.C.L.C. 675 CA. The same principle is applied to actions the company may have against third parties who are implicated in the provision of the financial assistance: *Belmont Finance Corp Ltd v Williams Furniture Ltd* [1979] Ch. 250 CA.

[283] See, for example, *Selangor United Rubber Estates v Cradock (No.3)* [1968] 1 W.L.R. 1555; *Karak Rubber Co v Burden (No.2)* [1972] 1 W.L.R. 602.

[284] But they are afforded special protection since the prohibition does not invalidate a loan "where the lending of money is part of the ordinary business of the company" and the loan is "in the ordinary course of its business": s.682(2)(a). This recognises that it would be absurd if, on a public issue of shares by one of the major High Street banks, its branches had to refuse to honour applicants' cheques if they were customers who had been granted overdrafts.

[285] DTI, *Consultation Paper on Financial Assistance* (1996), para.14.

current form. Further, the other goals which the financial assistance rules might be thought to promote are, these days, probably better targeted by other provisions with less potential for disruption of innocuous transactions. For example, where a target company in a takeover lends money to, or indemnifies against loss, known sympathisers who buy its shares or where, on a share-for-share offer, either or both of the target and predator companies do so to maintain or enhance the quoted price of their own shares, such practices are now regulated by the provisions on market abuse or by the rules of the Takeover Panel.[286] Again, in the case of abuses in the period prior to insolvency the provisions on wrongful trading may be better targeted.[287] Progress on either front, however, requires changes to EU law in the shape of the Second Directive, since that Directive is still committed to legal capital as a required element in the test for distributions by public companies and its relaxation in 2006 of the financial assistance rules did not go far enough to encourage significant domestic reform.

---

[286] See Chs 28 and 30, below. This example is particularly pertinent since the Greene Committee (above fn.211 at para.30) specifically mentioned the undesirability of a company "trafficking in its own shares" are a justification for the prohibition on financial assistance.

[287] See Ch.9, above.

PART 3

CORPORATE GOVERNANCE: THE BOARD AND SHAREHOLDERS

Over recent decades, corporate governance has been a highly fashionable topic in company law and has generated an enormous literature.[1] The subject came to prominence in the US with the work leading to the publication of the American Law Institute's *Principles of Corporate Governance* in 1994 and in the UK the topic is associated above all with the Cadbury Committee Report of 1992 and its associated Code of Best Practice,[2] which has provided a focal point for the subsequent spread of corporate governance codes throughout Europe.[3] Best practice is now subject to constant review.[4]

However, one could say that corporate governance, whether recognised under that name or not, is a topic which is as old as the large company. The fact which the corporate governance debate takes as its starting point is the appearance, in large companies, of a group of senior managers who are separate and distinct from the shareholders. There are good reasons why, in economically large companies with large groups of shareholders, the functions of investment and

---

[1] It is too vast to cite, but for a representative sample of this work at its highest level see K.J. Hopt et al. (eds), *Comparative Corporate Governance* (Oxford: Clarendon Press, 1998); K.J. Hopt et al. (eds), *Corporate Governance in Context* (Oxford: OUP, 2005). And placing this endeavor in context, see B.R. Cheffins, "The History of Corporate Governance" in M. Wright et al. (eds), *The Oxford Handbook of Corporate Governance* (Oxford: OUP, 2013), 46; and "The Rise of Corporate Governance in the U.K.: When and Why" (2015) C.L.P. 387.

[2] *Report of the Committee on the Financial Aspects of Corporate Governance* (1992). See further below, paras 14–69 et seq.

[3] Such codes have become a standard feature in continental Europe: see Weil, Gotshal and Manges (on behalf of the European Commission), *Comparative Study of Corporate Governance Codes Relevant to the European Union and its Members* (January 2002). For an index of codes, see *http://www.ecgi.org/codes/all_codes.php* [Accessed 23 April 2016].

[4] See the BIS consultation, *A Long Term Focus for Corporate Britain* (2010) *http://www.bis.gov.uk/ Consultations/a-long-term-focus-for-corporate-britain* [Accessed 23 April 2016], and subsequent outcomes discussed below. Indeed, best practice now extends to shareholder intervention, especially for institutional shareholders: see FRC, *The UK Stewardship Code* (2012) *https://www.frc.org.uk/Our-Work/Publications/Corporate-Governance/UK-Stewardship-Code-September-2012.pdf* [Accessed 23 April 2016], below at para.15–30. For a list of all present and past consultations on the topic of corporate governance, see *https://www.gov.uk/government/policies/corporate-governance* [Accessed 23 April 2016].

management should be carried out by separate, though possibly overlapping, groups of people. Where there are large numbers of shareholders, taking management decisions through the shareholders, meeting would be impossibly cumbersome. Further, where the company's capital needs have led to a public offering of its shares, there is no reason to suppose that those who buy the shares have the necessary expertise or commitment to run a large business organisation, and this is likely to be just as true of professional fund managers as it is of individual members of the public. In such a situation, the emergence of a specialist cadre of corporate managers is a natural development, managers who do not simply do as the shareholders say but who develop and implement corporate strategy on their own responsibility. In order for such managers to exercise these functions, it is necessary that a very broad set of discretionary powers be conferred upon them. In some jurisdictions this is done through the companies legislation itself, but in the UK this result is achieved by the practice of including provisions in the company's articles of association giving the board of directors extensive power to manage the company's business and to exercise the company's powers.

Thus arises the central issue of the corporate governance debate, which is the accountability of the senior management of the company for the extensive powers vested in them. Since the historical development was, or is perceived to have been, one of a movement from a situation in which shareholders were both investors and managers to one in which management became a separate function from that of investment, it is natural to think of the accountability issue as being one of the accountability of the managers to the shareholders. This is the tradition in British company law, tempered only by the qualification, which we noted at several points in Pt 2 and will see again in Pt 3, that, as the company nears insolvency, accountability to the creditors is as important as, and even replaces, accountability to the shareholders. However, the separation out of management as a distinct function creates the possibility of imposing lines of accountability on management towards other groups who have a long-term interest in the company (usually referred to as "stakeholders"). One group of such stakeholders, the employees, has become the beneficiary of the accountability rules of corporate law (mainly through board representation) in about half of the Member States of the EU.[5] Though once proposed by an official committee for the UK,[6] board representation is not an idea which has taken root within British company law, though traces of it can be found. In its detailed examination of company law, the Company Law Review did not find sufficient support for the stakeholder model to justify a major shift in the accountability rules,[7] and so it concentrated its efforts on promoting a modernised and inclusive version of the tradition of

---

[5] Final Report on the Group of Experts on European Systems of Worker Involvement (Davignon Report), Brussels, 1997, Table I. The split seems to have remained largely the same even after the enlargement of the Community: N. Kluge and M. Stollt, *Board-level Representation in the EU-25* (Brussels, European Trade Union Institute, 2004). The proportion of countries with board level employee-representation is greater if those with representation only in public sector companies are taken into account.

[6] *Report of the Committee of Inquiry on Industrial Democracy*, Cmnd. 6706 (1975) (the "Bullock Report").

[7] Strategic, Ch.5.1; Developing, Ch.2.

accountability to shareholders.[8] That "enlightened shareholder value" approach found its way into the Companies Act 2006.

Some ("managerialists") have even gone so far as to argue that elaborate accountability structures are not necessary because management will function so as to adjudicate neutrally and impartially among the competing claims of the various stakeholder groups on the company. This vision, however, ignores the fact that management itself is an important stakeholder group and it is difficult to see why, in the absence of accountability rules, managers would not give in to the temptation to overvalue their own claims on the company and undervalue those of other groups, for example, in the setting of their own remuneration. However, the managerialists make a better point when they argue that the accountability rules will be self-defeating if they operate so as to prevent or discourage managers from discharging effectively the tasks which the institution of centralised management entrusts to them. In other words, the accountability rules, no matter to whom the accountability lies, must not be so restrictive as to stifle the entrepreneurial talents of the managers, which talents constitute the rationale for conferring the wide discretion upon them in the first place.

Since the emergence of specialised management is not a phenomenon of just the last 20 years—large companies with such managements can be traced back at least as far as the late nineteenth century—it is not surprising that company law has always contained some mechanisms whereby the accountability issue can be addressed. The very requirement that a company appoint directors[9] provides a rudimentary mechanism for accountability. Unlike a partnership, where all the partners are prima facie entitled to participate in the management of the partnership,[10] in a company the requirement for directors presupposes that directors will play an important role, at least in large companies. In short, the default rule in partnerships is management by the partners; in companies, it is management by the directors. However, since British company law, unlike the corporate governance codes, says little or nothing about the structure and composition of the board of directors, the board's position in company law is deeply ambiguous. The board is the point of contact between the shareholders as a group and the senior management of the company, but whether, in any particular company or in companies generally, it acts predominantly as a monitor of the management on behalf of the shareholders or mechanism through which the managers promote their control of the company is a matter for empirical investigation—and the situation may vary from company to company and from time to time. As we shall see in the following chapter, in order to reduce the likelihood of boards acting purely as instruments of management domination, modern corporate governance codes have been concerned to restrict the proportion of board seats held by the managers of the company by requiring the presence of a proportion of "non-executive" directors on the board.

Despite the ambiguous role of the board, it constitutes a convenient focus for the legislature and the courts when developing rules to constrain the exercise by

---

[8] Final Report, Ch.3. For what this might entail, see paras 16–37 et seq., below.

[9] 2006 Act s.154 (at least two for public companies and one for private companies).

[10] Partnership Act 1890 s.24(5); LLP Regulations 2001 reg.7(3). However, the partners are free to create, by agreement, delegation structures akin to those found in companies, and in large partnerships normally do so.

management of the discretion vested in them. Whether the board monitors management or does the managing itself (or does a bit of each), imposition of accountability rules on the board should have an impact, directly or indirectly, on the way the management function is discharged. The underlying aim of the law may be control of the management function, but the subjects of the legal rules are the directors. The issue of how far those controls extend to managers who are not directors is, as we shall see, controversial. By the same token, when the articles delegate a wide discretion from the shareholders, they do so by conferring power, not on the company's managers as such, but on the board of directors. The rules conferring the powers and the rules constraining the exercise of the powers focus on the board rather than on the senior management as a whole. Thus, although the corporate governance debate starts from the functional differentiation between investment and management, company law operates by regulating the actions, not of managers in general, but of the board of directors.

In this Part we look at three sets of rules which the courts, the legislature and business bodies have created to constrain the exercise by directors individually and the board collectively of the discretion vested in them. The first set concerns the extent to which the shareholders have the power to appoint or, more importantly, remove the directors of the company. How easy is it, for example, for the shareholders to remove directors who exercise their powers in a way of which the shareholders disapprove? The second concerns the structure and composition of the board of directors, matters upon which the Companies Acts and the common law have traditionally had little to say, but which are a central focus for the corporate governance codes. Should the board be structured in such a way as to facilitate control over the managers of the company by the board? Thirdly, we consider a set of rules which the common law and the legislature have spent much effort in elaborating, from the very beginnings of modern company law in the first half of the nineteenth century. This is the law of "directors' duties" and, as important, the law relating to the enforcement of those duties. These duties operate directly upon the directors so as to control the ways in which they exercise their discretion. When these duties are breached, the decision which the directors have taken may be ineffective or at least capable of being set aside, or the director may have to compensate the company for any harm it has suffered, or account to the company for profits made from the breach of duty, or some other remedy may be available.

Although the rules discussed in this Part are a central part of company law and the subject of public controversy, it is important to stress that the problem they aim to deal with is premised upon a distinction between those who are shareholders in the company and those who are its directors. In the case of economically small companies—being the majority of companies on the register—this situation does not obtain because the shareholders and the directors are the same people. For such companies, the rules analysed in this Part are of less significance. It would be wrong to say that they are of no significance, because those who are the owner/controllers of a small company may fall out with one another and one faction may be tempted to act in a way which is in breach of their duties as directors, for example, by diverting corporate opportunities away from the jointly-owned company to another controlled wholly by themselves. However, even when there is a falling out among the owner-controllers, the situation is probably better analysed as a conflict between one group of shareholder/directors and another group, rather than a conflict between shareholders on the one hand and directors on the other. We discuss this issue further in Pt 4 of the book.

Finally, even when one is dealing with an economically large company with shareholders who are distinct from the managers, the complexity of the problems thrown up by the shareholder/director relationship depends significantly upon the structure of the company's shareholdings, in particular on whether they are concentrated or dispersed. Where there is concentrated shareholding (for example, one shareholder who holds a block of shares which gives him or her de facto control of the company), there will normally be little difficulty in that shareholder ensuring that the directors do as the shareholder wishes. The more problematic issue is likely to be whether the controlling shareholder takes appropriate account of the interests of the non-controlling shareholders. In this case, again, the potential conflict is one between controlling and non-controlling shareholders rather than between shareholders and directors, although again some aspects of directors' duties, for example, those concerning related-party transactions, may be relevant here. However, block-holder control of economically large companies is relatively uncommon in the UK, where a more dispersed pattern of shareholding still prevails, notwithstanding the increasing power of institutional investors. Consequently, the issue of shareholder and director relationships is a crucial one.

CHAPTER 14

THE BOARD

THE ROLE OF THE BOARD

The board of directors is the most important decision-making body within the   **14–1**
company. The first Principle of the UK Corporate Governance Code[1] states:
"Every company should be headed by an effective board, which is collectively
responsible for the success of the company", The Supporting Principles to this
main principle add the following explanation about the role of the board:

---

[1] Financial Reporting Council, *UK Corporate Governance Code*, September 2014 (and similarly the
draft April 2016 version).

"The board should set the company's strategic aims, ensure that the necessary financial and human resources are in place for the company to meet its objectives and review management performance. The board should set the company's values and standards and ensure that its obligations to its shareholders and others are understood and met."

Even after making allowances for the fact that the UK Corporate Governance Code applies formally only to companies with a Premium Listing of equity shares on the London Stock Exchange,[2] and that in small companies things may appear very differently, this is a formidable specification for the board's role.

14-2   However, it would be difficult to glean any similar understanding of the importance of the board from a reading of the Companies Act. Although s.154 requires all public companies to have two directors and private companies one,[3] it leaves the determination of the role of the board very largely to the company's constitution, which is, of course, under the control of the shareholders. Unlike in many, perhaps most, other jurisdictions, the division of powers as between board and the shareholders is a matter for private ordering by the members of the company rather than something to be specified mandatorily in the companies legislation. This may reflect the partnership origins of British company law (under partnership law the partners are given a very broad freedom to arrange the internal affairs of the partnership as they wish) and it certainly facilitates the use of a single Act to regulate all manner and sizes of company. Jurisdictions which specify the role of the board for large companies in legislation often have a separate statute for smaller companies which gives the members in the latter class of company a freedom nearer to that enjoyed by the members of a British company.[4] It is also a point of some theoretical (even ideological) importance: the directors' authority is derived from the shareholders through a process of delegation via the articles and not from a separate and free-standing grant of authority from the State. This helps to underline the shareholder-centred nature of British company law.

The default provision in the model articles

14-3   Since the division of powers between board and shareholders is a matter for the articles (subject to a limited range of matters where the statute requires the participation of the shareholders in the decisions, discussed below), it is difficult to generalise about the patterns of division found in practice. However, some

---

[2] For the meaning of "Premium Listing" see below at paras 25–6 and 25–15.

[3] After the 2006 Act at least one of those directors must be a natural person (s.155)—as opposed to a corporate director—in order to improve the enforceability of directors' obligations. The requirement however will be expanded so as to require all company directors to be natural persons, subject to certain yet-to-be-defined exceptions, as a result of s.87 of the Small Business, Enterprise and Employment Act 2015, *https://www.gov.uk/government/news/the-small-business-enterprise-and-employment-bill-is-coming* [Accessed 28 April 2016]. The Act also contains a mechanism for dealing with the situation where the company does not comply with ss.154 or 155. The Secretary of State may issue a direction to the company, specifying the action the company must take and failure to comply with the Secretary of State's direction constitutes a criminal offence on the part of the company and any officer in default, including a shadow director: s.156.

[4] Contrast, for example, Pt 4, Divisions One and Two of the German *Aktiengesetz* for large companies and of the statute for the *Gesellschaft mit beschränkter Haftung* (private company).

limited help can be gained from the model sets of articles which apply unless excluded by the incorporators in a particular case.[5] For both public and private companies, the default provision is the same, and it is one which gives substantial authority to the board: "Subject to the articles, the directors are responsible for the management of the company's business, for which purpose they may exercise all the powers of the company".[6] This follows quite closely the provision found in earlier sets of model articles.

It is perhaps surprising that the model article for public companies refers to "management" quite generally, since it is clear that, in a large company, the totality of its management is something quite beyond the grasp of even the most talented set of directors. The provision of the UK Corporate Governance Code, quoted above, is more realistic for large companies when it gives the board the functions of setting the corporate strategy and reviewing management performance, thus indicating that the task of executive management is otherwise not for it but rather for the full-time senior employees of the company. This approach causes no formal difficulty for the model set of articles, since the model gives the board a wide power of delegation of the powers conferred upon them by the articles "to such person to such an extent and on such terms and conditions as they think fit".[7] Thus, delegation of powers by the board to the senior management of the company is provided for in the model articles. The point rather is that the strategy followed in the model set of articles for public companies of a broad grant of management power to the board which is then permitted a wide power of delegation does not tell one what pattern of division of function is in fact adopted in large companies between the board and senior (and, indeed, other) management.[8] On that, the UK Corporate Governance Code may be a better guide.

Turning to private companies, here discharge of the full management function by the board is often in fact possible, but it is equally possible in small companies for the shareholders to play a larger role in decision-making than in large companies. Often in such companies important shareholders who are not also directors will expect to have such a role. In quasi-partnership companies in particular the incorporators may wish to reproduce the rule which would apply if the entity were a partnership rather than a company. This rule is that "any differences arising as to ordinary matters connected with the partnership business may be decided by a majority of the partners, but no change may be made in the nature of the partnership business without the consent of all existing partners".[9] Such a desire again creates no formal problem for the model articles, since the grant of management authority to the board is "subject to the articles". It is thus possible for the articles to provide that certain types of decision shall either not be given to the board at all or shall be subject to the shareholders' consent (even

14–4

---

[5] See para.3–14.

[6] Article 3 of the model articles in each case.

[7] Article 5 of the model articles for public companies. The same provision is included for private companies limited by shares: art.5.

[8] Exercise of the delegation power also raises questions of compliance by directors with their general duties, notably in relation to the degree of supervision they should maintain over delegated functions. See paras 16–16 and 16–33, below.

[9] Partnership Act 1890 s.24(8).

though such consent is not required by the Act). Again, however, the model articles provide no hint as to the ways in which or the extent to which this power is in fact used in small companies to move away from the default rule.

Thus, in both public and private companies (though for different reasons) the model articles provide only a starting point in determining the role of the board which may be modified substantially through either board decisions to delegate authority to management (in public companies) or modifications of the articles in the case of private companies so as to confer decision-making authority on the shareholders. One may wonder how useful such a default provision is, but the truth is that the variations from the default are so many and so varied (depending on the circumstances of the particular company) that it is impossible to identify a better default provision.

The power of the board—the legal effect of the articles

The board and shareholders

14–5   It is not possible to make general statements about the typical division of authority between shareholders and the board and management, because that is, in the main, open to being tailored to suit the individual company in question. But it is possible, nevertheless, to analyse the legal effect of the articles. That has changed over time, with an evolution in the answer being given to the key question of whether the effect of the delegation of authority in the articles to the directors was simply to confer authority on the directors or also, at the same time, to restrict the authority of the shareholders in general meeting to take decisions in the delegated area. Was the relationship between company and shareholders simply one of principal and agent[10] or did the articles effect something in the nature of a constitutional division of powers as between the shareholders in general meeting and the board? At one level, this was simply a matter of choosing the appropriate default rule. A principal conferring authority on an agent does not normally restrict its own authority to act, but there is no reason why the principal should not contract on the basis that the agent has authority to the exclusion of the principal. Equally, a constitution normally divides up authority among the various relevant bodies, but there is no legal reason why a constitution should not confer concurrent competence on two or more bodies. However, the choice between these two legal analyses did affect very strongly the way in which the courts approached the interpretation of provisions in the articles of particular companies.

14–6   Until the end of the nineteenth century, it was generally assumed that the general meeting was the supreme organ of the company and the board of directors was merely an agent of the company subject to the control of the company in general meeting. It followed that the shareholders could at any time by ordinary resolution give the directors binding instructions as to how they were to exercise

---

[10] i.e. in legal terms. It is clear that, in terms of the functional analysis of economists, directors are agents and shareholders principals because the former have the factual power to affect the well-being of the latter. But this does not mean the authority of the directors is conferred upon them in such a way as to make them the legal agents of the shareholders.

their management powers. Thus, in *Isle of Wight Railway v Tahourdin*,[11] the court refused the directors of a statutory company an injunction to restrain the holding of a general meeting, one purpose of which was to appoint a committee to reorganise the management of the company.

In 1906, however, the Court of Appeal in *Automatic Self-Cleansing Filter Syndicate Co v Cuninghame*,[12] made it clear that in registered companies the division of powers between the board and the company in general meeting depended entirely on the construction of the articles of association and that, where powers had been vested in the board, the general meeting could not interfere with their exercise. The articles were held to constitute a contract by which the members had agreed that "the directors and the directors alone shall manage".[13] Hence the directors were entitled to refuse to carry out a sale agreement adopted by ordinary resolution in general meeting where that decision fell within the management powers conferred upon the board. *Tahourdin's* case was distinguished on the ground that the wording of s.90 of the Companies Clauses Act 1845 was different—though that section does not in fact seem to have been relied on in the earlier case.

The new approach did not secure immediate acceptance,[14] but since *Quin & Axtens v Salmon*[15] it has been generally accepted that where the relevant articles are in the normal form, as exemplified by successive model sets of articles, the general meeting cannot interfere with a decision of the directors unless they are acting contrary to the provisions of the Act or the articles.[16]

In *Shaw & Sons (Salford) Ltd v Shaw*,[17] in which a resolution of the general meeting disapproving the commencement of an action by the directors was held to be a nullity, the modern doctrine was expressed by Greer LJ as follows[18]:

"A company is an entity distinct alike from its shareholders and its directors. Some of its powers may, according to its articles, be exercised by directors, certain other powers may be reserved for the shareholders in general meeting. If powers of management are vested in the directors, they and they alone can exercise these powers. The only way in which the general body of the shareholders can control the exercise of the powers vested by the articles in the directors is by altering their articles, or, if opportunity arises under the articles, by refusing to re-elect the directors of whose actions they disapprove.[19] They cannot themselves usurp the powers which by the articles are vested in the directors any more than the directors can usurp the powers vested by the articles in the general body of shareholders."

---

[11] *Isle of Wight Railway v Tahourdin* (1883) 25 Ch.D. 320 CA, esp. at 329.

[12] *Automatic Self-Cleansing Filter Syndicate Co v Cuninghame* [1906] 2 Ch. 34 CA.

[13] per Cozens-Hardy LJ at 44. Also see *Gramophone & Typewriter Ltd v Stanley* [1908] 2 K.B. 89 CA; see especially, per Fletcher Moulton LJ at 98, and per Buckley LJ at 105–106 (despite the fact that the then current edition of his book took the opposite view).

[14] *Marshall's Valve Gear Co v Manning Wardle & Co* [1909] 1 Ch. 267.

[15] *Quin & Axtens v Salmon* [1909] 1 Ch. 311 CA; [1909] A.C. 442 HL.

[16] But for contrary views, see G. Goldberg in (1970) 33 M.L.R. 177; M. Blackman in (1975) 92 S.A.L.J. 286; and G. Sullivan in (1977) 93 L.Q.R. 569.

[17] *Shaw & Sons (Salford) Ltd v Shaw* [1935] 2 K.B. 113 CA. See also *Rose v McGivern* [1998] 2 B.C.L.C. at 604.

[18] *Shaw & Sons (Salford) Ltd v Shaw* [1935] 2 K.B. 113 at 134 CA.

[19] They can now remove the directors by ordinary resolution: s.168, below.

And, in *Scott v Scott*[20] it was held, on the same grounds, that resolutions of a general meeting, which might be interpreted either as directions to pay an interim dividend or as instructions to make loans, were nullities. In either event the relevant powers had been delegated to the directors, and until those powers were taken away by an amendment of the articles the members in general meeting could not interfere with their exercise. As Lord Clauson[21] rightly said, "the professional view as to the control of the company in general meeting over the actions of directors has, over a period of years, undoubtedly varied".[22]

14–7　From 1985 onwards the model set of articles sought to make the position clear, for those companies adopting them, on the lines indicated in the above cases. Thus, in the current model sets of articles for both private and public companies, the grant of authority to the board is qualified by the phrase "subject to the articles" and there is now a specific article dealing with the "members' reserve power".[23] This makes it clear that the members may by special resolution (i.e. as would be needed to change the articles) instruct the directors "to take, or refrain from taking, specified action". By implication, any instruction given by the shareholders by ordinary majority to the board within the area of authority delegated to the directors is not binding on the directors.

14–8　To some considerable extent, however, this development of the case law has been overtaken by a change made to the statute in 1948 when the power, presently in s.168, was introduced, giving the shareholders the ability to remove directors at any time by ordinary resolution (as discussed below). Thus, at the very moment when the new interpretation became fully accepted in the case law, the legislature changed the rules so as to give shareholders a removal power exercisable by ordinary majority. Although a removal power is different from a power to give instructions, the two overlap to a considerable extent, for the disgruntled shareholders can say, in effect, to the directors: if you choose not to follow our views, we will by ordinary majority seek to remove you from office. That can be a powerful inducement to the directors to follow the line of action preferred by the shareholders.

---

[20] *Scott v Scott* [1943] 1 All E.R. 582. See also *Black White and Grey Cabs Ltd v Fox* [1969] N.Z.L.R. 824 NZCA; where the cases were reviewed, as they were by Plowman J at first instance in *Bamford v Bamford* [1970] Ch. 212 CA.

[21] *Scott v Scott* [1943] 1 All E.R. 582 at 585D. Lord Clauson was sitting as a judge of the Chancery Division.

[22] This is clearly seen if the judgments in the above cases are compared with that in *Foss v Harbottle* (1843) 2 Hare 461; see below, para.17–4. The modern view was reiterated at first instance in *Breckland Group Holdings Ltd v London and Suffolk Properties Ltd* [1989] B.C.L.C. 100, noted by K. Wedderburn in (1989) 52 M.L.R. 401; and L. Sealy in [1989] C.L.J. 26.

[23] Article 4 in each case. However, the special resolution altering the articles or giving instructions to the directors does not have the effect of invalidating anything done by the directors before the passing of the resolution: art.4(2). If the directors have merely resolved to take course X before the shareholders resolve by special resolution to take contradictory course Y, then presumably the shareholder resolution constitutes a binding instruction to the directors not to implement their prior resolution. However, if in implementation of their prior resolution the directors have contracted on behalf of the company with a third party, that third-party contract would remain binding on the company. If extensive powers of direction are exercised by the shareholders, it is conceivable that they might come to be regarded as de facto or shadow directors of the company. See para.16–8, below.

The board and senior management

The directors' power of delegation to senior management has not given rise to **14–9** any equivalent debate as to its legal effects. This has a number of explanations. Partly it is because that power of delegation is broadly drafted (see above) and includes an express power to "revoke any delegation in whole or part, or alter its terms and conditions". As well, managers, unlike shareholders, have no formal place in the company's legal structure.[24] Finally, the initial division of power is not set out in the articles, so any subsequent alteration does not require an alteration of the articles; rather, when delegating, the board exercises a power conferred upon it by the articles, and in practice powers will be delegated on the basis that the delegation continues only at the pleasure of the board. The board can normally revoke its grant of authority as readily as it made it. However, although alteration or revocation of authority by the board may be effective, as we shall see below it may also constitute a breach (perhaps even a de facto termination) of the service contract entered into by the company with the manager, giving rise to claims for compensation on the part of the manager against the company, sometimes of a substantial character.

Nevertheless, in practice such delegation is of enormous importance in large **14–10** companies. In particular, there is normally a very large grant of managerial power to the most senior of the company's managers, who will invariably be a member of the board of directors as well. Such a person was traditionally known in British parlance as the "managing director" but now more often, following US terminology, as the "chief executive officer" ("CEO"), is the driving force behind the formulation and implementation of the company's strategy. Of increasing importance as well is the "chief financial officer" ("CFO"). As we shall see below, the major motivation behind the development of the UK Corporate Governance Code was the desire to place the CEO within a framework of accountability to the board, a problem created, but not solved, by use of the extensive delegation power contained in the articles.

Default and confirmation powers of the general meeting

Despite what has been said above about the powers of the board and their impact **14–11** on the powers of the shareholders, it seems that, if for some reason the board cannot exercise the powers vested in them, the general meeting may do so. On this ground, action by the general meeting has been held effective where there was a deadlock on the board[25]; where there were no directors[26]; where an

---

[24] Unless the "manager" can be classified as a shadow or de facto director: see para.16–8. Contrast the position in other jurisdictions, such as Australia, where the general statutory duties apply not only to directors but also to "officers".

[25] *Baron v Potter* [1914] 1 Ch. 895. Contrast situations in which a board cannot do what the majority of the directors want because of the opposition of a minority acting within its powers under the articles: see, e.g. *Quin & Axtens v Salmon* [1909] A.C. 442 HL; and the decision of Harman J in *Breckland Group Holdings v London & Suffolk Properties* [1989] B.C.L.C. 100.

[26] *Alexander Ward & Co v Samyang Navigation Co* [1975] 1 W.L.R. 673 HLSc, per Lord Hailsham at 679 citing the corresponding passage from the 3rd edn of this book.

effective quorum could not be obtained[27]; or the directors were disqualified from voting.[28] These exceptions are convenient, but difficult to reconcile in principle with the strict theory of a division of powers. Their exact limits are not entirely clear. However, there seems good sense in the proposition that the shareholders may take the substantive decision only where the articles do not give them some effective way of reconstituting the board so as to remove the impediment to board decision-making.[29]

14–12 In addition, if the directors have purported to exercise powers reserved to the company in general meeting, their action can be effectively ratified by the company in general meeting. And for the purpose of ratifying past actions of the board, as opposed to conferring powers on the board for the future, it is not necessary to pass a special resolution altering the article; normally an ordinary resolution will suffice.[30]

14–13 Finally, it is generally assumed that it is perfectly in order for the board of directors, if it so wishes, to refer any matter to the general meeting either to ratify what the board has done or to enable a general meeting to decide on action to be taken. It is quite clear, as was affirmed by the Court of Appeal in *Bamford v Bamford*,[31] that an act of the directors which is voidable because, for example, it is in breach of their fiduciary duties, can be ratified by the company in general meeting if (and all the conditions are important) the act is within the powers of the company and the meeting acts with full knowledge and without oppression of the minority. It is, perhaps, less clear whether the board, without taking a decision on a matter within its powers, can initially refer it to the general meeting for a decision there. In an elaborate discussion at first instance in the *Bamford* case,[32] Plowman J had held that the general meeting then had power to act under residual powers, but he suggested that this might depend on the terms of the articles of the company concerned. The Court of Appeal considered that this question was irrelevant to the issue before them and expressed no view on it. It seems absurd if the directors are forced to take a decision and then to ask the general meeting to whitewash them, but perhaps the safest course is for them to resolve on action "subject to ratification by the company in general meeting". Alternatively, asking the general meeting to decide might be regarded as a delegation by the board of their powers on the particular issue (back) to the shareholders.

14–14 In short, the shareholders have power to act, despite provisions in the articles apparently conferring exclusive authority on the directors: they can take, or participate in the taking of, a corporate decision if the board is unable to exercise its powers, if the board's decision is in some way defective or, perhaps, if they are invited by the board to participate in the decision.

---

[27] *Foster v Foster* [1916] 1 Ch. 532.
[28] *Irvine v Union Bank of Australia* (1877) 2 App. Cas. 366 PC.
[29] *Massey v Wales* (2003) 57 N.S.W.L.R. 718 NSWCA.
[30] *Grant v UK Switchback Rys* (1888) 40 Ch.D. 135 CA.
[31] *Bamford v Bamford* [1970] Ch.D. 135 CA.
[32] *Bamford v Bamford* [1970] Ch.D. 135 CA.

Unanimous consent of the shareholders

Established case law indicates that the shareholders may bind the company by unanimous agreement—"unanimous" here meaning all the shareholders entitled to vote, not just all those who turn up at a meeting. The main function of this common law rule, which is discussed below,[33] is to permit shareholders in small companies to take the decisions allocated to them without the need to hold a meeting (for example, by circulating a resolution, to which they individually indicate their consent) or without observing all the formalities (for example, as to notice) which shareholder meetings entail, though this common-law facility has now been overtaken in the normal case by more extensive statutory provisions.

14–15

However, there are also dicta in the cases which suggest that the unanimous consent of the shareholders binds the company, even on matters which the constitution allocates to the board.[34] Nevertheless, none of the decided cases clearly present the situation of the shareholders unanimously taking a decision which had been allocated by the constitution to the board. The nearest case is *Re Express Engineering Works Ltd,*[35] where the decision in question was the purchase of certain property and thus would clearly have fallen within the clause conferring general management powers on the board, but in fact all the directors were disqualified from acting on the purchase, and so the shareholders could be said to have had default powers to take this decision, under the principle discussed above.

14–16

The Company Law Review proposed that the unanimous consent rule should be codified and that this should be done on the basis that "the members of the company may, by unanimous agreement, bind or empower the company, regardless of any limitation in its constitution".[36] However, the Government decided against codification, though the new companies legislation preserves the common law rule,[37] so that it appears that the question of whether the unanimous consent rule operates within or outside the constitutional division of powers produced by the articles will be left for the courts to decide.[38]

As to the merits of allowing the shareholders unanimously to depart from the constitution, the requirement of unanimity means that there is no issue of the protection of minority shareholders, which was one of the factors which weighed with the courts when they introduced the doctrine that shareholders, by ordinary resolution, could not give directors instructions on matters within their

14–17

---

[33] Ch.15.

[34] See, for example, *Salomon v Salomon & Co Ltd* [1897] A.C. 22 at 57, per Lord Davey.

[35] *Re Express Engineering Works Ltd* [1920] 1 Ch. 466 CA. To similar effect is *Euro Brokers Holdings Ltd v Monecor (London) Ltd* [2003] 1 B.C.L.C. 506 CA, where the decision in question (under a shareholders' agreement) required a resolution of the board but unanimous shareholder agreement was treated as a substitute. Again, however, the board was disabled from acting and so the case could be seen as one in which the shareholders had a default power to act.

[36] Final Report I, para.7.17. The Report states that this is how the rule is recognised at common law, though this may rather overstate things.

[37] Modernising, paras 2.31–2.35; CA 2006 s.281(4).

[38] Of course, the model articles make this issue irrelevant (other than in avoiding the formalities of a special resolution), since they impose a lower threshold, empowering the shareholders to direct the directors by special resolution (art.4).

competence. Allowing unanimous shareholder consent to override the articles would further emphasise the primacy of shareholders as against the directors. Shareholders would be able to tell the directors what to do, even within the area of competence granted by the articles to the board, provided only they acted unanimously. As against this, however, even if it is conceded that the shareholders acting unanimously are competent to act, the shareholders are not subject to the same duties as directors, so the risk is then that stakeholders other than the shareholders, perhaps especially the creditors, will not be protected from adverse corporate decisions in the same way that they are when those decisions are taken by the board. Of course, since the shareholders have statutory power to dismiss directors, as discussed below, this theoretical conflict seems quite unlikely to emerge in practice.

The mandatory involvement of shareholders in corporate decisions

14–18   Despite the flexibility which British company law gives the company to divide decision-making powers between shareholders and the board, there are a number of situations where the legislation requires shareholder approval of the board's decision (and sometimes even permits the shareholders to initiate a decision). The main category of such cases is where decision is likely to have an impact upon the shareholders' legal or contractual rights, even if the practical impact of that change on the member in a particular case is small (as with many changes to the articles). Without giving an exhaustive list of such situations, the following can be said to constitute the main examples of this policy:

- alterations to the company's articles[39];
- alteration of the type of company, for example, from public to private or vice versa[40];
- decisions to issue shares[41] or to disapply pre-emption rights on issuance[42];
- decisions to reduce share capital, re-purchase shares; redeem or re-purchase shares out of capital in the case of private companies or give financial assistance in the case of private companies[43];
- alterations to the class rights attached to shares[44];
- adoption of schemes of arrangement[45];
- decisions to wind the company up voluntarily.[46]

All these provisions place limits on the extent to which the articles may authorise the board to proceed solely on its own initiative. They probably reflect the view that shareholder interests are potentially involved in such decisions, that

---

[39] As discussed in Ch.3, above. The adoption of the initial constitution is also an act of the shareholders, since the incorporators become members of the company: above, para.4–5.
[40] Discussed in Ch.4, above.
[41] 2006 Act s.549 (below, Ch.24).
[42] 2006 Act ss.569 et seq. (below, Ch.24).
[43] All these matters are discussed in Ch.12, above.
[44] 2006 Act ss.630 et seq., discussed below in Ch.19.
[45] 2006 Act ss.895 et seq., discussed below in Ch.29.
[46] Insolvency Act 1986 s.84.

shareholders are probably as well-equipped to take the decisions as the board, and that they are not decisions which occur frequently in the life of the company, but, beyond that, the provisions do not contribute directly to the development of good corporate governance.

There are, however, four further cases where contributing directly to good corporate governance underpins the requirement of shareholder approval of: **14–19**

- the appointment of the company's auditors[47];
- certain transactions entered into by directors or their associates with their company[48];
- ratification of the taking by directors of corporate opportunities[49];
- defensive measures to be taken once a takeover offer is imminent—a requirement contained in the rules of the City Code on Takeovers and Mergers, with those rules now having statutory force.[50]

The first of these requirements is designed to promote the independence of the company's auditors from its management (though it is far from clear that it always successful in doing so) and the others deal with conflicts of interest between the director and his or her company.

Finally, the Listing Rules, which apply to Premium Listed companies quoted on the London Stock Exchange, introduce a third basis for shareholder approval, namely the size of the transaction. Under those Rules, significant transactions (both acquisitions and disposals) which meet the test of being either "Class 1" transactions or "reverse takeovers" require shareholder approval. In brief, the Class 1 criteria are met if any one of four financial ratios which compare the size of the transaction with the size of the company is 25 per cent or more; and an acquisition is a reverse takeover if any of the ratios is 100 per cent or more, or if the transaction would result in a fundamental change in the company's business, board composition or voting control. The financial ratios relate to the company's gross assets, profits, consideration and gross capital.[51] The thought behind the provisions seems to be that a big transaction is as much like an investment decision as a management decision, and so the shareholders are to be involved in the taking of the decision, along with the management. This ground for insisting on shareholder involvement in a decision has no counterpart in the Act. **14–20**

The mandatory functions of the directors

Just as the Act requires shareholders to be involved in some corporate decisions, so, scattered throughout the Act, are functions which are imposed on the directors of companies and which therefore may not be given to the shareholders. It would **14–21**

---

[47] 2006 Act Pt 16, Ch.2, discussed below at paras 22–7 et seq.
[48] 2006 Act Pt 10, Ch.3, discussed below at paras 16–67 et seq.
[49] Discussed below at paras 16–117 et seq. See also the mandatory role of shareholders on board remuneration: below at paras 14–30 et seq.
[50] See paras 28–20 et seq.
[51] LR 10. The FCA has the power to dispense from the strict application of this rule.

be too tedious to list them all. What needs to be noted, however, is that they relate to two main areas of corporate life, the production of the annual accounts and reports and the regular administration of the company, in particular its communications with Companies House. Thus, the directors are under a duty to prepare accounts and reports each year; having done that, to approve them and to send copies to the Registrar; and, in most cases, to lay them before the shareholders in general meeting.[52] What these statutory provisions do not purport to do is to stipulate the division of decision-making about the company's business activities as between the shareholders in general meeting, the board and the management. That is left for stipulation in or under the company's constitution. The statutory provisions relate essentially to the administrative obligations of the company.

14–22 One further point should be made about these obligations. In many cases, the obligation is laid not only on the director, but upon any "officer" of the company, and the sanction for non-compliance, normally a minor criminal sanction, is laid on any "officer who is in default". Examples are where the company fails to carry out its third task with respect to the annual accounts, i.e. fails to send a copy to every shareholder,[53] or where the company fails to keep an accurate record of its members.[54] The Act defines "officer"[55] as including "a director, manager or secretary" and now goes on to add "any person who is to be treated as an officer of the company for the purposes of the provision in question". These are thus cases where the Act imposes liabilities on sub-board managers. This is sensible in principle, given that such administrative tasks are likely to be delegated to levels of management below the board.[56] The CLR recommended that the definition of manager should be restricted normally to a person who "under the immediate authority of a director or secretary is charged with managerial functions which include the relevant function"[57] but this limitation has not been adopted. The CLR also recommended that, for all those covered by the definition of officer, i.e. including directors, default should be taken to have occurred only where the person had authorised, actively participated in, knowingly permitted or knowingly failed to take active steps to prevent the action in question, and this recommendation is reflected in the Act.[58]

---

[52] 2006 Act Pt 16, discussed further in Ch.21, below.

[53] 2006 Act s.425.

[54] 2006 Act s.113.

[55] 2006 Act s.1121. Where the director or officer is itself a company, there is no liability unless one of the latter's officers is in default, in which case he or she is criminally liable as well as the corporate officer or director: s.1122.

[56] To some extent the statute is following the lead given by the decision in *Meridian Global Funds Management Asia Ltd v Securities Commission* [1995] 2 A.C. 500 PC. The CLR reported that, under the previous law, the uncertainty as to who was a manager meant that prosecution of sub-board managers was rarely attempted: Final Report, Ch.14, fn.296.

[57] Final Report, para.15.54, though for particular offences it would be possible to cast the net wider. It would not be necessary for such a manager to be employed by the company, as where the particular administrative function had been out-sourced to an independent organisation.

[58] 2006 Act s.1121(3).

APPOINTMENT OF DIRECTORS

The Act itself says little about the means of appointing the directors, leaving this **14–23** to the articles of association. Its main concern is to give publicity to those who are appointed rather than to regulate the appointment process. On initial registration, the company must send to the Registrar of Companies particulars of the first directors[59] and a statement that they have consented to act. Thereafter the company must send particulars of any changes, with corresponding statements that any new directors consent to act.[60] The company must also maintain a register giving particulars of its directors.[61] Both registers are open to inspection by members of the public and so the public can obtain information about who the directors are either from Companies House or from the company's registered office. This is a crucial provision, enabling people to know who controls what might otherwise appear to be faceless companies and facilitating the enforcement of the obligations to which directors are subject, whether by creditors, the public authorities or others.

However, as a result of the threats, or actual infliction, of violence by protestors on the persons or property of the directors of companies carrying on lawful activities to which the protestors objected, the scope of the information on the public registers has been reduced. No longer does the company's public register have to contain the director's usual residential address but only a service address (which might be the company's registered address), though the company must maintain a register of the directors' residential addresses which is not open to public inspection. Moreover, the company is prohibited from disclosing, except in limited circumstances, the residential address of a director or former director.[62] Equally, whilst the company must give to the Registrar the information which is contained in both its public and non-public registers, the Registrar must omit this "protected information" from the Registrar's public register and not otherwise disclose it, except in limited circumstances.[63]

As far as appointment is concerned, and contrary to popular belief, the Act **14–24** requires neither that directors be elected by the shareholders in general meeting nor that they submit themselves periodically to re-election by the shareholders. This may often be the case, though it is far from universal practice, but, if it is, it is a consequence of the provisions of the company's articles, not of the Act's

---

[59] 2006 Act s.12.

[60] 2006 Act s.167.

[61] 2006 Act ss.162 et seq.

[62] 2006 Act ss.163, 165 and 241. The company, on the application of a member, liquidator or creditor or other person with a sufficient interest, may be ordered by the court to disclose the residential address if there is evidence that service of documents at the service address is ineffective or it is necessary or expedient to do so in connection with the enforcement of a court order: s.244.

[63] 2006 Act ss.240 and 242. The Registrar may use protected information for the purposes of disclosure to a public authority specified in regulations or, again subject to regulations, a credit reference agency, for otherwise the company might not be able to obtain credit: s.243 and the Companies (Disclosure of Address) Regulations 2009 (SI 2009/214). Further, the Registrar may put the director's address on the public record if communications sent to the director by the Registrar remain unanswered or there is evidence that service of documents at the director's service address is ineffective. The director and the company must be consulted before this step is taken. If it is, the company must alter its public record as well: ss.245 and 246.

requirements. Equally, there is nothing to prevent articles providing that directors can be appointed by a particular class of shareholders, rather than the shareholders as a whole, by debenture holders or, indeed by third parties. In the case of community interest companies s.45 of the Companies (Audit, Investigations and Community Enterprise) Act 2004 explicitly empowers the Regulator of CICs to appoint a director of a CIC and for that person not to be removable by the company. In fact, the articles of public companies normally provide for retirement of board members by rotation on a three-year cycle and for the filling of the vacancies at each annual general meeting.[64]

14–25   The Act provides that each appointment in a public company shall be voted on individually[65] unless the meetings shall agree *nem. con.* that two or more shall be included in a single resolution. However, there are often provisions in the company's articles (as to notice to be given by shareholders to the company of their proposed candidates, etc.) which make it difficult for shareholders, if they are so minded, to put up candidates against the board's nominees. So, the crucial decisions for the shareholders in public companies are normally whether to accept the board's nominees for election at the annual general meeting and whether subsequently to exercise their removal rights, as discussed below.

14–26   Unless the articles so provide, directors need not be members of the company. At one time it was customary so to provide,[66] but now the possibility of a complete separation of shareholders and directors is recognised and the model articles no longer provide for a share qualification. Of course, it is common for directors of public companies to become shareholders, often in a major way, under a share-option or other incentive scheme (discussed below), but even in these cases being a shareholder is not a formal condition of being a director.

14–27   As to age requirements, the law has undergone a complete reversal in recent years. The Cohen Committee tried to ensure that directors should normally retire when they attained the age of 70,[67] but as finally enacted this provision was so riddled with exceptions that it proved to have little impact. It no longer appears in the Companies Act, as recommended by the CLR.[68] However, the 2006 Act introduced a minimum age requirement of 16, apparently because of evidence that appointment of young directors was being used in order to exploit their immunity from prosecution or the unwillingness of public authorities to prosecute young persons.[69] Any such appointment is void, though the person appointed remains subject to the duties of directors under the Act.[70] This may mean that the

---

[64] Model public company articles, art.21. The model for private companies makes no such provision. The board also has power to appoint directors (arts 17 (private) and 20 (public))—this is a useful power for filling vacancies arising unexpectedly between annual general meetings—and again, directors of public companies appointed by the board come up for re-election at the next AGM (art.21), with private companies having no equivalent.

[65] 2006 Act s.160. This is designed to prevent the members being faced with the alternative of either accepting or rejecting the whole of a slate of nominees.

[66] Companies Act 1929 Table A art.66.

[67] Cmnd. 6659, para.131.

[68] Completing, paras 4.42–4.43.

[69] 2006 Act s.157.

[70] 2006 Act s.157(4),(5). Existing under-age directors ceased to be directors on the section coming into force (s.159(2)).

company will no longer be in compliance with the requirements as to the minimum number of directors and thus be open to a direction from the Secretary of State as to the action it must take to remedy this situation.[71] However, the Secretary of State has power to make regulations permitting the appointment of classes of person under the age of 16, which regulations may make different provisions for different parts of the UK.[72] Other than this, no positive qualifications are required of directors—though, as we saw in Ch.10, they may be disqualified on the ground of misconduct or unfitness.

Sometimes the articles entitle a director to appoint an alternate director to act for him at any board meeting that he is unable to attend. The extent of the alternate's powers and the answer to such questions as whether he is entitled to remuneration from the company or from the director appointing him will then depend on the terms of the relevant article.[73]   **14–28**

Finally, it should be noted that not everyone who is a called a director is a director in the terms of the Act and some people who are not called directors are directors in terms of the Act. The law does nothing to control the growing and potentially misleading practice of giving employees the title of director, even though they perform none of the central management functions of a director and are thus not directors under the Act. On the other hand, a person who is a director, as meant by the Act, need not be so called, for the term director, as used in the legislation, includes any person occupying the position of director, by whatever name called,[74] and directors of some guarantee companies are still called "governors" or the like.   **14–29**

REMUNERATION OF DIRECTORS

The remuneration of directors comes from two sources: fees paid to them for acting as directors and, in the case of executive directors, money and other benefits receivable under the service contract entered into by them as managers with the company. The latter is by far the greater source of income of the executive directors of companies, especially of large companies, and it has been and continues to be a source of controversy and increasing regulatory and indeed legislative action in recent years.[75] Reflecting the trust origins of the company, a   **14–30**

---

[71] See above, fn.3.

[72] 2006 Act s.158. This particular aspect of the regulation-making power is necessary because, under devolution, the age of criminal responsibility could vary within the UK.

[73] See the model articles for public companies, arts 13 and 25–27, which go far to clarify the alternate's position. The model articles for private companies make no provision for alternates.

[74] 2006 Act s.250.

[75] See the work of High Pay Centre, an independent non-party think tank established specifically to monitor pay at the top of the income distribution which emanated from a year-long independent review: High Pay Commission (now High Pay Centre), *Cheques with Balances: Why tackling high pay is in the national interest* (Final Report, 22 November 2011) *http://highpaycentre.org/files/ Cheques_with_Balances.pdf* [Accessed 27 April 2016]; the government consultation on the issue: *BIS Discussion Paper: Executive Remuneration http://www.bis.gov.uk/Consultations/executive-remuneration-discussion-paper* [Accessed 27 April 2016] which resulted in a series of reforms through both primary and secondary legislation applicable to quoted companies; and the review produced by the Hay Group on the current state of play: *What's your next move? Executive reward:*

director is not entitled to a fee for acting as such, unless the articles or a resolution of the company makes provision for such payments, as they invariably will. By contrast, a person who provides additional services as a manager to the company, even if also a director, is entitled to reasonable remuneration on a quantum meruit basis for services actually accepted by the company, even in the absence of a contract, although the two situations may not be easy to distinguish.[76] In practice, these difficulties rarely arise, since the company will have express power under its articles to remunerate directors and employ managers and an explicit contract is made in both cases.

14–31   In either case, a director dealing with the company as to fees and remuneration is in a stark position of conflict of interest, and the traditional common law rule in such a case was that the sanction of the shareholders was needed for the agreement between director and company.[77] However, directors found this rule inconvenient and, for more than a century, it has been common to provide in the articles that the board shall have power to set directors' remuneration as executives, though the director whose remuneration is at issue is not usually permitted to vote on the matter.[78] The current model article applies this rule also to directors' fees, even though under the 1985 model articles the default rule was that fees required shareholder approval.[79]

14–32   Setting remuneration in this way is a classic case where the risk of "mutual back scratching" arises: directors may not scrutinise too closely the remuneration of a fellow director in the expectation of similar treatment in return when their cases are considered. The increase in the levels of executive remuneration has been a matter of considerable public controversy in recent years, not simply because of the growing gap between executive salaries and the average incomes of others in society, but also because of the unsatisfactory negotiating process through which executive salaries are set under the typical form of articles. If directors, directly or indirectly, sit on both sides of the table when their remuneration is determined, then the results cannot be justified as emerging from a market process. Since this defect may characterise pay-setting in most companies with large shareholder bodies, it amounts to an example of a market failure, which justifies regulatory intervention.

---

review of the year 2011 (Hay Group) *http://www.haygroup.com/downloads/uk/Whats_your_next_ move.pdf* [Accessed 27 April 2016]. Also see the 2015 government report: *https://www.gov.uk/ government/publications/2010-to-2015-government-policy-corporate-accountability/2010-to-2015- government-policy-corporate-accountability* [Accessed 27 April 2016].

[76] *Craven-Ellis v Canons Ltd* [1936] 2 K.B. 403 CA, cf. *Re Richmond Gate Property Co Ltd* [1965] 1 W.L.R. 335, which is probably based on a misunderstanding of the earlier case. See also *Diamandis v Wills* [2015] EWHC 312 and less directly, the decision of the Supreme Court in *Benedetti v Sawiris* [2013] UKSC 50; [2014] A.C. 938 on the general interaction between contract and a claim in restitution for quantum meruit.

[77] See paras 16–63 et seq.

[78] Model articles for public companies, arts 13 and 23 (a widely expressed power). Similar provisions are to be found for private companies (arts 14, 19). For the problems which arise if the company seeks to fix the terms of executive remuneration without complying with its articles, see *Guinness v Saunders* [1990] 2 A.C. 662 HL; *UK Safety Group Ltd v Hearne* [1998] 2 B.C.L.C. 208; and below, para.16–24.

[79] Table A, art.82.

What sort of regulation, however, should be adopted? The courts have been unwilling to scrutinise directors' remuneration decisions on grounds of excess or waste, refusing even to prescribe that pay must be set by reference to market rates, provided the decision on remuneration is a genuine one and not an attempt, for example, to make distributions to shareholders/directors where there are no distributable profits.[80] This is probably a wise decision on the part of the courts, which might otherwise find themselves saddled with developing a general policy about the remuneration of directors of large companies. Neither has the legislature shown any enthusiasm to grasp the nettle of determining, substantively, what the level, or rate of increase, of directors' pay should be.

In this situation of abstention from settling the substantive issue, attention focuses on the procedure within the company for the setting of directors' remuneration. Several options are available, some now mandatory at least for larger companies.

Composition of the remuneration committee

One strategy is further to exclude executive directors from the process of remuneration setting, so that, not only is the individual executive whose remuneration is at issue forbidden from voting on the decision, but executive directors are side-lined in the remuneration-setting process. Under this strategy, remuneration decisions are allocated principally to a committee of the board consisting of non-executive directors. We examine this strategy further when we look more generally at the role of non-executive directors later in this chapter.[81] The doubts about it relate principally to the question of how independent even non-executive directors are when it comes to the setting of executive remuneration. Nevertheless, this approach is favoured by the UK Corporate Governance Code for Premium Listed companies,[82] with associated calls for greater board diversity although not for the more controversial inclusion on remuneration committees of employee or shareholder appointees who are not board members. It also warns the committee to ensure that pay rates are not simply ratchetted up without any necessary correlation with improved performance.[83]

14–33

---

[80] *Re Halt Garage (1964) Ltd* [1982] 3 All E.R. 1016. This case involved a decision by shareholders as to the remuneration to be paid to themselves as directors. It seems likely that the same principle would be applied to a directors' decision, except that the directors would also have to meet their core duty of loyalty (see below at paras 16–52 and 16–84). In the context of unfair prejudice petitions (that is, in cases of disputes between shareholders) the courts have struck out more boldly and have been willing to assess whether the remuneration paid to the controllers as directors was appropriate: see below at para.20–10.

[81] See below, para.14–75.

[82] Principle D.2.1, and note the 2014 (and draft 2016) version of D.2.4.

[83] Principle D.1.

Mandatory shareholder approval of certain aspects of the remuneration package

General

14–34   A further, and perhaps complementary, strategy is to revive the common law principle of shareholder approval of directors' contracts.[84] There has been an increasing regulatory and legislative creep back to this earlier position. We shall see later in this chapter that the companies legislation has reintroduced the principle of shareholder approval in relation to certain termination payments. In addition, focussing on larger companies, shareholder approval is required under the Listing Rules for certain share option schemes and other long-term incentive plans ("ltips") for directors of companies admitted to Premium Listing on the London Stock Exchange.[85] And, most recently, shareholder approval of the company's general remuneration policy (plus an advisory vote on its implementation) is required for all quoted companies.

Long-term incentive pay schemes

14–35   Under a share option scheme a director is given the right to subscribe at some time in the future (normally after a period of years) for shares in the company and to pay for them (the "exercise price") the price which the shares had at the time the option was granted. The theory is that the director is thus incentivised to increase the price of the shares over the intervening period for the benefit of the shareholders. In order to meet the obvious objection that the increase in the stock price may have little to do with the efforts of the directors, ltips substitute some other form of incentive to be provided by the company in place of the shares.

14–36   Given these concerns about the alignment, or misalignment, of incentives, the payment of performance-related remuneration to executive directors (it is less typically paid to non-executive directors[86]) is now regarded with far more caution than it was only a few years ago, and instead simpler and more transparent pay structures are favoured.[87] The UK Corporate Governance Code in its Main Principle on remuneration now includes the statement: "Executive directors' remuneration should be designed to promote the long-term success of the

---

[84] Though one should note the argument of Professors Cheffins and Thomas that such approval is more likely to be effective in relation to sudden leaps in executive pay in a particular company than in controlling a steady, general upward drift in pay across all companies: "Should Shareholders Have a Greater Say over Executive Pay? Learning from US Experience" (2001) 1 J.C.L.S. 277.

[85] LR 9.4.

[86] Principle D.1.3.

[87] See High Pay Commission (now High Pay Centre), *Cheques with Balances: Why tackling high pay is in the national interest* (Final Report, 22 November 2011) *http://highpaycentre.org/files/Cheques_with_Balances.pdf* [Accessed 27 April 2016]; and more recently, an attack by the High Pay Centre on performance-related remuneration: High Pay Centre, *No Routine Riches: Reforms to Performance-Related Pay* (13 May 2015) *http://highpaycentre.org/files/No_Routine_Riches_FINAL.pdf* [Accessed 19 April 2016]; and *The Metrics Re-Loaded: Examining Executive Remuneration Performance Measures* (10 June 2015) *http://highpaycentre.org/files/Metrics_Reloaded.pdf* [Accessed 27 April 2016].

company. Performance-related elements should be transparent, stretching and rigorously".[88] And, further, that "[p]erformance conditions, including non-financial metrics where appropriate, should be relevant, stretching and designed to promote the long-term success of the company. Remuneration incentives should be compatible with risk policies and systems. Upper limits should be set and disclosed".[89] Moreover, packages should be sensitive to pay and employment conditions elsewhere within the group, especially in relation to rates of increase in salary; and, finally, and by way of rejecting the popular argument of global competition driving up pay, that companies should of course benchmark against their peers, but not in a way that leads to an upward ratchet without any improved performance.[90]

Originally because the granting of share options could dilute the position of the other shareholders, the LR made the introduction of such a scheme subject to shareholder approval.[91] The principle was later extended to other forms of ltip and it now provides a convenient mechanism for the shareholders to express concerns about whether, for example, the performance criteria attached to the ltip are "challenging". However, because obtaining shareholder approval is time-consuming and leaves the director in doubt as to what ltip the remuneration package will include, the company is given permission to dispense with shareholder approval where the option scheme or other ltip is "established specifically to facilitate, in unusual circumstances, the recruitment or retention of the relevant individual". This permission is subject to disclosure in the company's next annual report of the principal terms of the scheme and the reasons why the circumstances in question were viewed as unusual.[92]

14–37

Mandatory and advisory shareholder votes on remuneration policy and implementation

This ltip intervention, just described, might have been regarded as the tip of the iceberg. Growing public sentiment against escalating remuneration packages and perceived "payments for failure" (discussed below, whereby poorly performing managers are nevertheless contractually entitled to handsome rewards on their departure) inevitably prompted renewed consideration of whether shareholders should have a binding vote on some or all aspects of general remuneration policy

14–38

---

[88] Principle D.1.
[89] Sch.A.
[90] Principle D.1. and Sch.A.
[91] It should be noted that the statutory pre-emption rights of shareholders (see below at para.24–6) might lead to a similar requirement for shareholder approval, but the statutory rights (a) do not apply to an allotment of securities under an employees' share scheme (s.566), which might include a scheme for executive directors; and (b) can be disapplied in advance by shareholder vote (ss.569–571), whereas the rights under the LR may not be. It should also be noted that the LR do not require shareholder approval for share option schemes or other long-term incentive plans which are open to all or substantially all the company's employees (provided that the employees are not coterminous with the directors), presumably on the grounds that the wide scope of the scheme is protection against directorial self-interest: LR 9.4.2.
[92] LR 9.4.2–3.

or particular remuneration agreements.[93] The policy tension is evident: regulation of remuneration packages is fraught with difficulties, practical, policy-based and political; and rewards for failure are of course undesirable, but corporate ventures are inherently risky, and not every risky venture will succeed however good the management—in those circumstances, termination payments are unfairly condemned as rewards for failure. This concern is evident in the increasingly explicit focus in the CGC on possible "claw-backs", with the 2014 version now providing explicitly that performance-related schemes "should include provisions that would enable the company to recover sums paid or withhold the payment of any sum, and specify the circumstances in which it would be appropriate to do so".[94]

14–39   Given this climate, and the selective intervention adopted by the Listing Rules and the CGC, increased Government intervention was inevitable. This has happened in stages, beginning with simple disclosure rules in 2002. The current legislation, introduced in 2013, requires that (a) directors of quoted companies produce an annual remuneration report in prescribed form[95] (as discussed below); and (b) that shareholders be given a triennial binding vote on the company's "remuneration policy", as laid out in that report; and (c) an annual advisory vote on its implementation.[96] Moreover, the directors cannot lightly escape their obligations to put these matters to the vote. Subject to very limited defences, s.440 makes it a criminal offence on the part of every officer in default (but, rightly, not on the part of the company) to fail to give the necessary notices of meetings or put the required resolutions to the vote (as described in ss.439 and 439A, and discussed below).[97]

By way of evidence of a public vote of confidence in this model as being an attractive regime for regulating directors' remuneration in large companies, it is possible to look to the ongoing negotiations towards a reformed EU Shareholder Rights Directive.[98] This might be read as indicating the EU-wide appeal of UK models, especially the UK Corporate Governance and Stewardship Codes,[99] but of particular relevance here is the EU proposal for a shareholder "say on pay" which largely follows the existing UK model.

---

[93] See *BIS Discussion Paper: Executive Remuneration http://www.bis.gov.uk/Consultations/executive-remuneration-discussion-paper* [Accessed 27 April 2016], and *Discussion paper: summary of responses* (ibid), indicating the problems with binding votes, although the possibility remains live.
[94] Principle D.1.1.
[95] 2006 Act s.420 et seq., noting especially ss.421(2A) and 422A.
[96] 2006 Act ss.439 and 439A.
[97] Finally, it is noteworthy that the FCA has in place four Remuneration Codes tailored to different types of firm, each directed at enhancing awareness of risk and ensuring that risk is better managed and better aligned with individual reward: see *https://www.the-fca.org.uk/remuneration* [Accessed 27 April 2016].
[98] Please see *http://ec.europa.eu/internal_market/company/docs/modern/cgp/shrd/140409-shrd_en.pdf* [Accessed 27 April 2016], proposing amendments to the existing Shareholder Rights Directive (Directive 2007/36/EC) and Directive 2013/34/EU. On issues relating to corporate governance reporting ("comply or explain"), the UK (through the FRC) has responded to the Commission on its progress in implementing those recommendations: *https://www.frc.org.uk/News-and-Events/FRC-Press/Press/2015/July/UK-responds-to-European-Commission-s-Recommendatio.aspx* [Accessed 19 April 2016].
[99] On the UK Stewardship Code, see para.15–30.

The definition of a quoted company is wider than companies incorporated in the **14–40** UK and subject to the Listing Rules. The statute also embraces British-incorporated companies if they have been included in the official list of any Member State of the European Economic Area or if their securities have been admitted to trading on the New York Stock Exchange or Nasdaq.[100] The purpose of this broader definition is to remove any incentive for British companies to escape the new requirements by listing their securities elsewhere than in London. The Secretary of State has the power to alter the definition of a quoted company by regulation,[101] which, presumably, he might do if admission to trading on an exchange other than those mentioned above were to become a practical possibility for British companies.

The crucial innovation in the current version of the legislation is not mere **14–41** disclosure, since much of the information was already required to be disclosed under the LR.[102] It is the requirement for a triennial[103] binding vote of the shareholders on the company's remuneration policy (s.439A), and an advisory vote on its implementation (s.439). The remuneration policy must both describe and justify: it must set out how the company proposes to pay directors, including every element of the remuneration package, and how the chosen approach supports the company's long-term strategy and performance. In addition, the policy must set out the company's approach to recruitment and loss of office payments. Once a remuneration policy has been approved, a company may only make remuneration and loss of office payments as permitted within the limits of the policy, unless the payment has been approved by a separate shareholder resolution. Failure to pass the remuneration policy would effectively block the company's right to pay its directors. Any arrangements made contrary to approved policy are void (s.226E(1)),[104] and any payments received by the director are held on trust for the company (ss.226E(2) and (3)). In addition, any director who authorised such a payment is jointly and severally liable to indemnify the company for loss, unless the director is shown to have acted honestly and reasonably in the circumstances (ss.226E(2), (3) and (5)).

Shareholders also have an annual advisory vote on the implementation report, **14–42** which sets out how the approved pay policy has been implemented, including a single figure for the total pay directors received that year (with this designed to allow shareholders to make ready comparisons year-on-year, and between companies). In this case, however, an adverse vote does not affect director's entitlements,[105] although the failure will trigger the need for the company to put the remuneration policy to shareholders the following year. But failure to pass the report would inevitably have significant practical effect because of likely market

---

[100] 2006 Act s.385.

[101] 2006 Act s.385(4)–(6).

[102] For the current requirements see LR 9.8.8.

[103] Or more frequently if the policy changes, even in a minor way.

[104] The very limited transition exception is that legal obligations made before the legislation introducing these reforms was published on 27 June 2012 and which have not been amended or renewed since, will not be subject to the restrictions in 2006 Act Ch.4A: Enterprise and Regulatory Reform Act 2013 s.82.

[105] 2006 Act s.439(5). The director and company could agree of course that some item of the remuneration package should be so conditional.

reaction, so perhaps the real benefit of the annual advisory vote is that it gives the shareholders a further guaranteed opportunity to express their views on the directors' remuneration, which, without s.439, they would be able to do only if they requisitioned a resolution to be added to the agenda of the accounts meeting or requisitioned an extraordinary meeting of the shareholders, neither of which is necessarily easy to arrange.[106]

14–43   In all of this, "remuneration" is defined very broadly: it includes any form of payment or other benefit made to or otherwise conferred on a person in return for them holding, agreeing to hold or having held office as a director of the company (or any other role in connection with the management of the affairs of the company or its subsidiaries whilst a director of the company) (s.226A). The restrictions on remuneration payments therefore apply to payments such as those which might be made to new directors to buy-out existing remuneration entitlements at their existing company. The restrictions on payments for loss of office extend to amounts paid to settle statutory or contractual claims arising in connection with a director's loss of office. In each case, therefore, unless the remuneration policy contemplates such remuneration payments or payments for loss of office, they must be separately approved by the shareholders (although where other legislation or a court requires a payment to be made, the Act will not prevent the company from paying it).

General disclosure: the directors' remuneration report

14–44   Public disclosure—transparency—is commonly used to support effective market control, especially in areas where targeted regulation is difficult. The disclosure obligations imposed on companies in relation to the remuneration of their directors vary according to whether the company is a "small company" (ss.381–384), an unquoted company, or a "quoted company" (s.385). Section 412 gives the Secretary of State power to make provision by regulations requiring information about directors' remuneration to be given in notes to a company's annual accounts. Predictably the most onerous rules are imposed on quoted companies, and we start with those. The necessary information must be provided in the directors' remuneration report ("DRR"), with its contents now prescribed in enormous detail by the Secretary of State in regulations.[107] The regulations divide the remuneration report into two parts: one, which is not subject to audit, relates to the company's remuneration policy, and another, which is subject to audit, concerns payments actually made to directors in the financial year in question.[108] The approach to legislative requirement for the disclosure of remuneration policy in the DDR is interesting: it requires the board to justify, rather than simply report, the company's remuneration arrangements[109]; but it does that in a very

---

[106] See paras 15–48 et seq.
[107] Large and Medium-Sized Companies and Groups (Accounts and Reports) Regulations 2008 (SI 2008/410) Sch.8, as amended by the Large and Medium-Sized Companies and Groups (Accounts and Reports) (Amendment) Regulations 2013 (SI 2013/1981) Sch.8.
[108] See Large and Medium-sized Companies and Groups (Accounts and Reports) (Amendment) Regulations 2013 (SI 2013/1981) Sch.8 Pt 5.
[109] SI 2013/1981 Pts 4 and 6.

detailed way, requiring the company to provide standardised information, often in tabular form, by which the policy might be assessed, including details of specific remuneration components and the objectives sought to be achieved by their inclusion, with illustrative workings of the ramifications for current directors over time. In addition, details are required explaining the way in which the company's overall pay policy has been derived, and how the views of shareholders have been accommodated.

The audited part of the remuneration report concerns payments actually made to persons who served as directors during the financial year. The ambition is to require companies to provide reports in a standardised way so that shareholders can compare remuneration outcomes in a variety of ways, whether between directors, across different years, and with other companies. To that end, this part of the report requires the company to list its directors by name and provide in a tabular display the "single total remuneration figure" for each of them, along with its component parts (as prescribed and defined in the regulations, and including the total amount of salary and fees, all taxable benefits, all money or other assets received by way of performance bonus, and all pension benefits). Any sums subject to claw back must be noted, and previous year comparisons of all elements must be provided.[110] All that must be audited. In addition, the implementation report must also provide performance graphs and tables which set out a number of matters, including the percentage change in the remuneration of the chief executive officer over his term in office, comparing that with the percentage change in employee pay (with provisions for considering corporate groups as a whole)[111]; the total company spend, and the relative spend on remuneration and distributions to shareholders. Other options, such as the mandatory disclosure of top-to-bottom pay differentials, appear now to be seen as uninformative and therefore as potentially counter-productive[112]; and the mandatory capping of executive pay has never attracted serious support. Finally, the report must contain statements of how the directors' remuneration policy of the company will be implemented in the next financial year; the consideration given by directors to the matter of remuneration; and a statement of the detailed result of the voting on any resolutions in respect of the directors' remuneration report or policy at the last general meeting of the company. To further improve transparency, from 1 October 2013, whenever a director leaves office, companies will need to publish a statement setting out what payments the director has received or may receive in future. This statement must be published as soon as reasonably practicable. All of this provides an enormous amount of detail, not just to shareholders, and it is difficult to say how it will be used, or by whom.

14–45

---

[110] See Large and Medium-sized Companies and Groups (Accounts and Reports) (Amendment) Regulations 2013 (SI 2013/1981) Sch.8.

[111] This represents an obvious attempt to persuade directors and shareholders to focus on the issue of widening pay dispersal within companies, with the multiples by which executive directors' remuneration exceeds the average remuneration of employees increasing dramatically.

[112] The mooted mandatory disclosure of the ratio between top executive salaries and the mean or median salaries in the company seems generally to be regarded as too dependent on the size of the company, the nature of its business, and its geographical spread to provide helpful data for cross-company comparisons.

14–46   Even unquoted companies cannot remain entirely silent on the subject of directors' remuneration. The matters about which information may be required include gains on the exercise of share options; benefits receivable under long-term incentive schemes; compensation for loss of office (as defined in s.215); contributions and benefits receivable with respect to past services; and consideration receivable by third parties for making available the services of a director (s.412(2)). The information must also include benefits receivable by a person "connected with" a director, or by a body corporate "controlled by" a director (s.412(4), and see ss.254 and 255 for interpretation of these terms). However, the relevant rules do not require a binding shareholder vote on policy, and there is no equivalent of the detailed implementation report. All that is required is the disclosure of aggregate remuneration only, or, where the data is further broken down, does not require recipients to be identified by name.[113] A small company can omit this information from the accounts it files at Companies House.

14–47   In an extension of the usual role of the auditor, if the auditor concludes that the information required, of either a quoted or unquoted company, in relation to directors' remuneration has not been provided, then a statement giving the required particulars must be contained in the auditor's report, so far as the auditor is reasonably able to provide it.[114] This is presumably thought to be a more effective remedy than fining the directors for failure to produce proper accounts and reports, though that sanction is available as well.

REMOVAL OF DIRECTORS

14–48   Accountability of the directors to the shareholders is obviously enhanced if shareholders can influence directly the choice of those who sit on the board. As we have seen above, company law does little to enhance shareholders' control over the appointment process, which is regulated predominantly by the company's articles of association. As far as company law is concerned, it would not be a breach of any mandatory rule for the articles to provide that none of the directors should be required to stand for re-election and that the existing directors, again without shareholder sanction, should choose any replacements for directors who resigned or were removed. In other words, shareholders could be wholly written out of the appointment process. In practice such extreme cases are rare, though for reasons that reflect market rather than legal constraints: large companies might find it difficult to sell their shares to institutional investors on the basis of such articles. This fact of life is reflected in the CGC whose "best

---

[113] Large and Medium-Sized Companies and Groups (Accounts and Reports) Regulations 2008 (SI 2008/410) Sch.5 para.1 requires the disclosure of aggregate remuneration (a rule applied to quoted companies as well), para.2 of the amount paid to the highest paid director (but without naming that person) if the aggregate remuneration exceeds £200,000, and paras 3–5, the aggregates paid by way of early retirement benefits, compensation for loss of office and to third parties by way of directors' services.

[114] 2006 Act s.498(4). On the role of the auditor see Ch.22.

practice" provision is that "all directors should be submitted for re-election at regular intervals, subject to continued satisfactory performance".[115]

Shareholders' statutory termination rights

When we turn to the removal of directors, however, we find that the legal rules are entirely different, although this has been the case only for the past half century or so. Until 1948, the power of the shareholders to remove directors depended, as with their appointment powers, on the provisions of the articles of association. However, under what is now s.168 of the Companies Act 2006, a director can be removed by ordinary resolution of the shareholders at any time. This expressly applies notwithstanding anything to the contrary in any agreement between the company and the director.[116] The articles may provide additional grounds for the removal of directors, the most common being a request from fellow directors.[117]

14–49

In comparative terms, this is a very strong provision. It means that the notion of a term of office for a director has little meaning. The articles may in fact provide that directors shall be appointed for three years at a time and things may be carefully arranged so that no more than one third of the board comes up for election in any one year,[118] but these provisions cannot be relied upon because the shareholders may intervene at any time to secure a removal. It means also that there is little point in the board securing the appointment of a director over the vigorous opposition of the shareholders, since this may simply provoke them to remove those of whom they disapprove. Finally, as we have already noted,[119] there is now a certain policy tension between the common law decisions, discussed above, which prevent the shareholders from giving directions by ordinary resolution to directors on matters within their exclusive competence, and the statutory provisions permitting the removal of directors at any time by ordinary resolution. In practice, presumably, the latter overshadows the former:

---

[115] CGC, Main Principle B.7. Even as late as 1985 the model set of articles (Table A) provided that "a managing director and a director holding any other executive office shall not be subject to retirement by rotation" (art.84). The current set of model articles for public companies contains no such provision (that for private companies contains no provision for regular re-election at all, whether for executive or non-executive directors).

[116] 2006 Act s.168(1). The previous version of the section (s.303 of the 1985 Act) also explicitly overrode anything to the contrary in the articles. This is not repeated in s.168, presumably on the grounds that it was unnecessary so to provide. The statute will override the articles, unless otherwise provided in the statute, although one would have thought that the same was true of a private agreement. In the case of a community interest company the Regulator is empowered to remove a director at any time, but not apparently so as to give the director a claim for compensation against the company. Instead, the director can appeal to the court against the Regulator's decision, apparently with the effect of reinstating the director if the appeal is successful: Companies (Audit, Investigations and Community Enterprise) Act 2004 s.46.

[117] The current model articles for public and private companies do not include such a provision, but see *Bersel Manufacturing Co Ltd v Berry* [1968] 2 All E.R. 552 HL (power of life directors to terminate the appointment of ordinary directors); *Lee v Chou Wen Hsien* [1984] 1 W.L.R. 1201 PC (power of majority of directors to require a director to resign).

[118] Such arrangements are what in the US are referred to as "staggered boards".

[119] See above, paras 14–5 et seq.

directors may commit no legal wrong if they refuse to obey such instructions, but they will be aware that disobedience may trigger their removal from office.

14–50 There are two principal qualifications to the powers contained in s.168 which need to be noted: first, the courts have authorised provisions in the articles which provide an indirect way around the section, at least in relation to private companies; and the section itself preserves certain rights for directors upon removal, notably their right to compensation for breach of contract.

Weighted voting rights

14–51 On the first, it has been held by the House of Lords in *Bushell v Faith*[120] that the object of the section can be frustrated by a provision in the articles attaching increased votes to a director's shares on a resolution to remove him, thus enabling him always to defeat such a resolution. This apparently indefensible decision can perhaps be justified on the ground that in a small private company[121] which is, in effect, an incorporated partnership, or in a joint-venture company it is not unreasonable that each "partner" should, as under partnership law, be entitled to participate in the management of the firm in the absence of his agreement to the contrary and to protect himself against removal by his fellow partners. Moreover, it has been recognised that the removal of a director in the case of such "quasi-partnerships" (as they have come to be called) may so strike at the essential underlying obligations of the members to each other as to justify a remedy on grounds of unfair prejudice or even the compulsory winding-up of the company on the ground that it is "just and equitable" to do so.[122] Nevertheless, the decision was much criticised[123] but has not been reversed in subsequent legislation. In effect, for private companies s.168 is only the default rule.

Director's procedural rights on termination

14–52 Even where the articles contain no provisions as to weighted voting rights, the successful operation of the section requires some pretty stringent conditions to be

---

[120] *Bushell v Faith* [1970] A.C. 1099 HL. The shares in a private company were held equally by three directors and the articles provided that in the event of a resolution to remove any director the shares held by that director should carry three times their normal votes, thereby enabling him to outvote the other two. It was held that: "There is no fetter which compels the company to make voting rights or restrictions of general application and—such rights or restrictions can be attached to special circumstances and to particular types of resolution": per Lord Upjohn at 1109.

[121] A similar article would scarcely be practical in most other cases.

[122] See *Re Westbourne Galleries Ltd* [1973] A.C. 360 HL, and Ch.20, below. It also seems that the court could enjoin the breach of a binding agreement between members and a director on how they should vote on any resolution to remove a director, thus, in effect, affording another method of circumventing s.168. See *Walker v Standard Chartered Bank Plc* [1992] B.C.L.C. 535 CA. Such an agreement would not be caught by s.168(1) which refers only to agreements between the director and the company.

[123] See the forthright dissenting opinion of Lord Morris of Borth-y-Gest at 1106 and D. Prentice (1969) 32 M.L.R. 693 (a note on the Court of Appeal's judgments). The development of the unfair prejudice protection further reduces the need for the decision—but it equally reduces its adverse consequences, since the exercise of the legal right to remove a director may nevertheless constitute unfairly prejudicial conduct. See para.20–7.

met. Special notice has to be given of any resolution to remove a director (and to appoint someone else instead, if that is proposed).[124] This means the proposer must give 28 days' notice to the company of the intention to propose the resolution.[125] The company must supply a copy to the director, who is entitled to be heard at the meeting.[126] Further, the director may require the company to circulate any representations which that person wishes to make.[127] The object of these restrictions is to prevent a director from being deprived of an office of profit on a snap vote and without having had a full opportunity of stating the contrary case.[128]

Director's contractual rights on termination

A more serious restraint on the members' powers of dismissal is the provision that the section shall not deprive a director of any claim for compensation or damages payable in respect of the termination.[129] This provision applies to both the termination of the directorship as such and of "any appointment terminating with that as director". Thus, compensation for termination of the executive director's service contract is included where, as is invariably the case, both directorship and service contract are terminated at the same time. In fact, the continuation of the service contract is often made conditional on the holding of the directorship, so that the service contract terminates automatically upon cessation of the directorship.

14–53

Thus, if there is a contract of service between the director and the company, as will be the case with managing and other executive directors, the probability is that the members will be able to sack the director only at the risk of imposing on the company liability to pay damages or a sum fixed by the contract as compensation. This, it may be said, is also fair, because the company has freely

14–54

---

[124] 2006 Act s.168(2). This gives rise to a potential ruse for avoiding the impact of s.168. Shortly before the meeting the directors whose removal is sought resign, having added to the board new members under their gap-filling powers (see above fn.64). The removal resolution is now unnecessary in relation to the directors who have resigned and will be ineffective in relation to their replacements (even if the resolution states as one of its objectives the removal of the replacements) because special notice will not have been given by the proposers to the company about the removal of the replacements, since the proposers will not have known who the replacements were to be at the time they served notice on the company: *Monnington v Easier Plc* [2006] 1 B.C.L.C. 283.

[125] 2006 Act s.312. The company must then give notice to the members in the notice convening the meeting or, if that is not practicable, by newspaper advertisement or other mode allowed by the articles, normally not less than 14 days before the meeting: ibid.

[126] 2006 Act s.169(1),(2). In this case a private company cannot use the written resolution procedure: a meeting has to be held.

[127] 2006 Act s.169(3). If those representations are not received in time to be circulated, the director can require them to be read out at the meeting (s.169(4)). The same rule applies if the company does not comply with its obligations under s.169(3), but the resolution is not invalidated in such a case. This would provide an easy way for the company to avoid the director's removal.

[128] But apparently the director can be deprived of this protection if the articles contain an express power to remove a director by ordinary resolution and the company acts under that power. Section 169 is expressly limited to removals "under section 168" and s.168(5)(b) provides that s.168 does not "derogate from any power to remove a director that may exist apart from this section".

[129] 2006 Act s.168(5)(a). Although those terms themselves can be subject to statutory bars: see, e.g. ss.226B–C for quoted companies.

bound itself by contract. However, once again, we encounter the risk that the director may have been present on both sides of the bargaining table when the provisions were negotiated which are now relied upon to provide compensation at the point of termination.[130] The members may therefore find that the directors have entrenched themselves by negotiating contracts of service by which the company has to pay them substantial sums if it exercises its statutory power to dismiss them by ordinary resolution—or indeed dismisses them in any other way[131]—other than for serious misconduct, although the disclosure and approval regimes noted earlier, especially for quoted companies, work against this.[132]

14–55   It must be emphasised, however, that the dismissed director can claim for damages for breach of contract only if a binding contract entitles the director either to hold that position or a related executive position for a fixed term, or to be dismissed only after prescribed or reasonable notice and that notice requirement is not observed by the company (as it rarely will be). Similarly, the dismissed director will be entitled to a contractual termination payment only if the relevant contract specifically so provides. So the important question is whether the dismissal of the director constitutes either a breach of a contract with the director (giving rise to damages) or a termination triggering specified contractual termination payments.

There are two broad classes of cases. First, if the director's contract (whether as director or as executive manager) simply incorporates the provisions of the company's articles,[133] then—like the articles themselves—the contract terms are usually regarded as inherently subject to the Act (and its statutory dismissal right) and to permissible variation if the shareholders use their powers to alter the company's underlying articles. In these circumstances if the shareholders utilise their statutory dismissal powers or change their articles to effect dismissal, then neither will count as a breach of the director's contract: they will, rather, be dismissals in accordance with the terms of the contract.[134] This approach cannot, however, be used by the company to escape past liabilities to the director: on ordinary contract principles, the shareholders' acts cannot have retrospective effect.[135]

Alternatively, and typically, the director will have a separate and independent contract with the company, whether formal or informal.[136] If this contract is for a

---

[130] See above, para.14–30.

[131] The board of directors can normally terminate a director's contract of service as an executive, and, under the usual provision in the articles, so can the general meeting by removing him as a director: see ibid.

[132] See above, paras 14–34 et seq.

[133] Recall that the articles do not operate as an enforceable contract between the director and the company: see above, paras 3–23 et seq. Instead, they define the terms of the separate contract between director and company: *Re Peruvian Guano Co, Ex p. Kemp* [1894] 3 Ch. 690, 701; *Re New British Iron Co, Ex p. Beckwith* [1898] 1 Ch. 324, 326–327; *Swabey v Port Darwin Gold Mining Co* (1889) 1 Meg. 385, 387 CA.

[134] *Swabey v Port Darwin Gold Mining Co* (1889) 1 Meg. 385 CA; *Read v Astoria Garage (Streatham) Ltd* [1952] Ch. 637 CA.

[135] *Swabey v Port Darwin Gold Mining Co* (1889) 1 Meg. 385 CA; *Bailey v Medical Defence Union* (1995) 18 A.C.S.R. 521 H Ct Australia.

[136] For the complications which are liable to occur in the latter event, see *James v Kent* [1951] 1 K.B. 551 CA; and *Pocock v ADAC Ltd* [1952] 1 All E.R. 294n.

fixed term or has a notice period, or if termination triggers a compensation payment, then such provisions will inevitably be breached or triggered if the shareholders exercise their statutory dismissal powers or exercise their power to amend the company's articles, and do so in a way which enables dismissal or prevents the director from continuing as director where that is a condition of the director's independent contract. In those circumstances, although the courts will not enjoin the shareholders from exercising their statutory or constitutional powers, the company will thereby become liable to the director either for damages for breach of contract[137] or for payment of the agreed termination payment. Depending on the terms of the director's contract, these sums can be prohibitive, so much so that dismissal can become quite impractical for the company. It is to this problem that we turn next.

Control of termination payments

This issue of prohibitive termination payments (whether paid under the contract or by way of compensation) has increasingly occupied policy-makers in recent years, at least in relation to public companies. The complaint is not only that the company's hands can be tied despite s.168 powers, but that the outcome often seems to deliver "rewards for failure" to departing directors.

14–56

A director's contract can employ a number of devices to enhance the levels of compensation payable upon termination, in particular, entering into a long fixed-term contract, perhaps one with a rolling fixed term[138]; including long notice periods for the lawful termination of the contract by the company[139]; and including express entitlements to compensation if the contract is terminated.[140] None of these provisions would operate to protect a director were the company entitled to terminate the service contract without notice on grounds of a serious breach of contract on the part of the director. However, mere lack of economic success on the part of the company is unlikely to amount to such a fundamental breach of contract: economic failure by the company does not necessarily betoken lack of effort or commitment on the part of the directors. Indeed, if

---

[137] *Southern Foundries v Shirlaw* [1940] A.C. 701 HL; *Shindler v Northern Raincoat Co Ltd* [1960] 1 W.L.R. 1038, per Diplock J. In the light of the observations in the earlier case it seems that the court will not grant an injunction to restrain the alteration of the articles.

[138] Under a rolling fixed-term contract, the fixed term is renewed from day to day, so that the full length of the term always remains to run. Under an ordinary fixed term, a director removed, for example, in the last three months of a fixed three-year term, would not receive much benefit from the fixed term; under a "three-year roller" the director will always have the full protection of the three-year term. Moreover, it is possible to structure the contract so that, although the company is bound by the fixed term, the director is permitted to terminate the contract by giving relatively short notice.

[139] In *Runciman v Walter Runciman Plc* [1992] B.C.L.C. 1084 the directors' service contracts required five years' notice for lawful termination, a provision which had been increased from three years in the face of the prospect of a takeover bid. The CGC recommends contract and notice periods of no more than one year, or at least reducing to one year even if something more is required initially to attract the director (D.1.5).

[140] This express provision may be, but need not be, a liquidated damages clause. It may give the director an entitlement which goes far beyond any compensation which would otherwise be payable to him for breach of contract. The CGC provides, however, that "the aim [when agreeing provisions which determine termination payments] should be to avoid rewarding poor performance" (D.1.4).

directors were entitled to no contractual protection on termination, they might take too cautious an approach to risky business ventures. And even where there has been clear wrongdoing by the director, the company may prefer to pay the director to go quietly, rather than insist on its contractual rights.

Company law tries to steer a course between these competing considerations by a combination of disclosure and shareholder approval requirements, both advisory and binding, in relation to agreed termination payments and other contractual terms.

Disclosure

14–57   Simple disclosure is a powerful tool. Formerly, the members might know nothing about the directors' service contracts, especially the potential consequences of any decision to remove the director. In this respect at least, their position was improved quite some time ago: each director's service contract, or a memorandum of its terms if it is an unwritten contract, must be available for their inspection at any time. This applies also to shadow directors and to service contracts with subsidiary companies.[141] The previous exemptions for service contracts with less than twelve months to run or for directors required to work wholly or mainly outside the UK have been removed.

14–58   In relation to quoted companies, as noted earlier,[142] the Act now also requires that directors produce an annual remuneration report ("DRR"), which, like the other annual reports, must be provided to the members and the Registrar.[143] The crucial features of this report are, first, that the shareholders have a binding vote on remuneration policy (s.439A), and that policy must provide details, in a prescribed and accessible form, of the company's policy on the duration of directors' contracts, on notice periods, and on termination payments.[144] Secondly, to ensure the policy and practice are aligned, the company must provide an annual implementation report, as part of the DRR, detailing all payments actually made, again broken down into accessible detail.[145]

Shareholder approval

(i) Remuneration packages—quoted companies

14–59   Failure to gain shareholder approval in advance of termination payments made to directors of quoted companies can have significant consequences. Any termination payments which are not in compliance with the company' agreed

---

[141] 2006 Act ss.228 and 229. Failure to comply constitutes a criminal offence on the part of every officer of the company who is in default. Section 228 refers to "service contracts", unlike its predecessor (s.318 of the 1985 Act) which referred to "contracts of service". It is suggested that this change makes it clear that both contracts of service and contracts for services are covered. Section 230 brings in shadow directors (on the meaning of which see para.16–8, below).

[142] Above, at para.14–44.

[143] 2006 Act ss.423(1) and 441(1).

[144] SI 2013/1981 Sch.8 Pt 4.

[145] SI 2013/1981 Sch.8 Pt 3.

remuneration policy, or have not been separately agreed by the shareholders, cannot be made (s.226C). If they are, the company can recover the payments from the recipient director; moreover, any director who authorised the payments is jointly and severally liable to indemnify the company (s.226E). On the other hand, if the payment is in compliance with the policy, but contained in an implementation report voted down by the shareholders, this will have no effect on the validity of the payment (s.439(5)).

(ii)   Terms governing the length of the contract—all companies

More generally, the legislature has sought to limit excessive termination payments by reducing the possible term for which a director can be appointed, and making sure these provisions bite whether those terms take the form of notice periods or fixed or rolling contractual terms. If such a term has the effect that the contract cannot be terminated by the company within a two-year period (referred to as the "guaranteed term"), then prior approval by a resolution of the general meeting is required.[146] In the absence of shareholder approval, the provisions establishing the guaranteed term are void and the contract can be terminated at any time by the company on reasonable notice.[147] The section applies to shadow directors and to service contracts with subsidiaries.[148]

14–60

Despite the changes made, the sections are still open to criticism on two grounds. First, by concentrating on the length of employment, s.188 seems not to catch contractual provisions which give the company the contractual right to terminate the director's employment at any time but then provide for substantial payments to be made to the director under the contract, if termination takes place. The CLR proposed that contractual covenants for severance payments "should be void to the extent that they provide for more compensation than would be available by way of compensation for breach of contract",[149] but this suggestion was not taken up.

14–61

Secondly, it is arguable that for public companies the period of two years is too long. The Greenbury Committee thought there was a strong case of reducing the period to one year.[150] As a consequence, the Listing Rules[151] now require boards to report to the shareholders annually giving "the details of any director's service contract with a notice period in excess of one year or with provisions for pre-determined compensation on termination which exceeds one year's salary

---

[146] 2006 Act s.188. Section 188(3) sets out a complex definition of the "guaranteed period" so as to prevent a company circumventing the legislative policy through a combination of fixed terms and notice periods, each shorter than two years but cumulatively longer. Section 188(4) performs the same role for guaranteed terms made up of more than one contract. Under the previous legislation the relevant period was the very long one of five years, but both the Law Commission and the CLR had recommended a reduction.

[147] 2006 Act s.189. That period of reasonable notice might be less than two years. Thus, the director pays a potential penalty for failing to secure shareholder approval, in that the contract may become subject to a notice period shorter than the two years which the contract could have contained without shareholder approval.

[148] 2006 Act ss.188(1) and 223.

[149] Final Report I, para.6.14.

[150] *Directors' Remuneration, Report of a Study Group* (Gee, 1995), para.7.13.

[151] LR 9.8.8(8).

and benefits in kind, giving the reasons for such notice period". This provision catches both notice periods and contractual severance payments and applies a one-year limit, but requires only disclosure and justification, not shareholder approval. To similar effect, the UK Corporate Governance Code, also applying to Premium Listed companies, provides: "Notice or contract periods should be set at one year or less. If it is necessary to offer longer notice or contract periods to new directors recruited from outside, such periods should reduce to one year or less after the initial period".[152] The CGC is enforceable on a "comply or explain" basis, as discussed below, and so its provisions are not mandatory, though they are generally observed.

(iii)   Termination payments

14–62   So far in our discussions, we have focused on compensation payments received by directors because their dismissal constituted a breach of contract by the company, typically because dismissal under s.168 or under the company's articles also brought to an end some other contract the director had with the company or a subsidiary, normally a service contract, and the early termination of that contract amounted to a breach. Alternatively, the contract itself may have provided for a defined termination payment.

However, it is not impossible that the remaining members of the board might choose to make a gratuitous payment to one of their number removed from office by shareholder vote, perhaps to ensure the director goes quietly, perhaps to encourage similar treatment of themselves should they suffer the same fate in the future. This, however, is a matter where the Act has required shareholder approval since 1948. What is now s.217 makes it unlawful for a company to give a director of the company (or of its holding company) any payment by way of compensation for loss of office or as consideration for or in connection with his retirement from office,[153] without particulars of the proposed payment (including its amount) being disclosed to members of the company and the proposal being approved by the members (and the members of the holding company, where appropriate). In other words, the directors cannot increase the cost of a removal without the consent of the shareholders. The section does not apply, however, to payments by way of compensation for breach of contract, to payments to which the director is contractually entitled (unless the contract was entered into in connection with the termination), or to pension payments in respect of past services, apparently whether contractually required or not.[154]

---

[152] CGC, para.D.1.5.

[153] The circumstances in which the section bites are widely defined in s.215. There are specific provisions in ss.218 and 219 dealing with compensation payments made in connection with takeover bids or transfers of the company's assets, which are discussed in para.28–28.

[154] 2006 Act s.220. The exclusion of covenanted payments, in the standard case, is in line with the previous law (*Taupo Totara Timber Co v Rowe* [1978] A.C. 537 PC; *Lander v Premier Pict Petroleum*, 1997 S.L.T. 1361) and was recommended by the Law Commission (*Company Directors: Regulating Conflicts of Interests and Formulating a Statement of Duties*, Cm. 4436 (1999), para.7.48). But, given the requirement for approval of contracts of more than two years' duration, it makes all the more peculiar the exemption from shareholder approval of covenanted termination payments equivalent to more than two years' salary.

An unauthorised payment to the director is held by the recipient on trust for the company and any director who authorised the payment is jointly and severally liable to indemnify the company for any loss suffered (for example, where the payment is not recoverable from the recipient).[155]

STRUCTURE AND COMPOSITION OF THE BOARD

14–63 When we looked at the role of the board in the first section of this chapter, we saw that, broadly, the range of business decisions to be conferred upon the board is left by the law to be determined by the company's articles of association. By contrast, in the fourth section we saw that the law plays a crucial role in setting the rules governing the removal of board members. In this fifth and final section of the chapter we look at the rules on board structure and composition. Here again the law leaves matters to be determined by the company's constitution, but this is an area in which the "corporate governance" movement of the past two to three decades has made a significant impact on listed companies, but through "soft law", in the shape of the UK Corporate Governance Code, rather than through legislation.

Legal rules on board structure

14–64 Before turning to the composition of the board, let us look at its structure. An important difference between legal systems is whether they require one-tier or two-tier boards. In Germany, for example, as we have already noted, a two-tier board is mandatory for public companies (*Aktiengesellschaften*), and so the relevant statute (*Aktiengesetz*), besides requiring both a supervisory and a managing board, stipulates the functions of each and the methods of appointment of each board. The task of running the company (in the sense of setting and executing its strategy) is entrusted to the managing board, and the supervisory board monitors the discharge by the managing board of its functions. A person may not be a member of both boards.

14–65 By contrast, in Britain, the US and the Commonwealth, the one-tier board is the norm, with managing and supervisory functions being discharged by a single body. Although this is the norm, it is not obvious that the law in Britain requires a single board. The Act does not require the directors to act as a board, and so it hardly needs to address the further question of whether the board is to be a one-tier or a two-tier board.[156] In fact, the CLR found some evidence that "the practice of delegating [from 'the board'] day to day management and major operational questions to a 'management board' is becoming increasingly common

---

[155] 2006 Act s.222(1), thus at last implementing the report of the Cohen Committee: Report of the Committee on Company Law Amendment, Cmnd. 6659 (1945), p.52. The recipient will normally be the director but the legislation covers compensation payments to persons connected with the director or at the direction of the director or a person connected with the director: s.215(3).

[156] For the same reason the Act says nothing about the division of function between the board and its committees nor about the role of the chair of the board.

in this country".[157] This infringes no provision of the statute, and, provided the articles permit such further delegation by the board and provided the board monitors effectively the functioning of the "management board", it involves no breach by the directors of their duties or risk of disqualification on grounds of unfitness.[158]

14–66 Domestic law does however formally recognise the possibility of a two-tier structure for one class of company. This is the SE (European Company) which opts to register in Britain. Under the SE Regulation of the EU, which is directly applicable in the UK, an SE may choose in its statutes (as its equivalent of the articles are termed) whether to have a one-tier board or a two-tier board consisting of a supervisory organ and a management organ.[159] Where the latter structure is adopted a German-style division of function between the two boards is applied: the management organ ("MO") "shall be responsible for managing the SE"[160]; and the supervisory organ ("SO") "shall supervise the work of the management organ", but the SO may not "itself exercise the power to manage the SE".[161] However, the statutes of the SE must list the categories of transaction (which may be extensive or limited) which require the authorisation of the SO.[162] Thus, there is some flexibility in fixing the line between supervision and management, since an extensive list of matters requiring SO authorisation would give that body a significant influence over the management of the company. Further, the SO itself (or its individual members) may require the MO to provide the information it requires for the discharge of its functions and may arrange for investigations to the same end.[163] Thus, the SO has some flexibility as to how vigorously it discharges its functions.

With one small exception, no person may be a member of both bodies.[164] The members of the MO are appointed by the SO, whose members, in the absence of employee representatives, will be appointed by the general meeting.[165] What goes for appointment must apply to removal. Consequently, the shareholders' power of removal under s.168 applies to members of the SO alone, so that the members of the MO will be removable by the shareholders only indirectly.

---

[157] Developing, para.3.139.

[158] See above at para.10–5 and below at paras 16–34 et seq.

[159] Council Regulation 2157/2001/EC art.38 and Recital 14 (see above at para.1–40).

[160] Council Regulation 2157/2001/EC art.39(1).

[161] Council Regulation 2157/2001/EC art.40(1).

[162] Council Regulation 2157/2001/EC art.48. The UK Government decided not to take up the option available under the Regulation for the SO itself to determine the list of matters requiring its authorisation.

[163] Council Regulation 2157/2001/EC art.41(3), (4). The right of individual members of the SO to information is a Member State option which the UK has exercised. See the European Public Limited-Liability Company Regulations 2005 (SI 2005/2326) reg.63 (as amended by The European Public Limited-Liability Company (Amendment) Regulations 2009 (SI 2009/2400)).

[164] Council Regulation 2157/2001/EC art.39(3). The exception is where the SO nominates one of its members to fill a vacancy on the MO, during which period that person's supervisory functions are suspended.

[165] Council Regulation 2157/2001/EC arts 39(2) and 40(2). There is a Member State option for members of the MO to be appointed directly by the shareholders, but the UK felt unable to take it up. Article 47(4) preserves appointing rights under national law of minority shareholders or other persons.

These provisions in the regulation relating to the two-tier board provide only a skeleton of the structure, however. The detail has to be fleshed out by reference to national law. Where the regulation does not deal with a matter, or deals with it only partly, then the rules of the Member State in which the SE is registered, as they apply to public limited companies, will apply to the SE. Hence the relevance of s.168 of the 2006 Act, just mentioned. This will be the case unless the Regulation requires or empowers the Member States to adopt implementing legislation specifically for the SE, in which case that implementing legislation will prevail over general public company rules as regards the matters it deals with.[166]

There are relatively few areas where specific implementing legislation is required or permitted, but one of them is in relation to the two-tier board. Where in the domestic law of a Member State "no provision is made for a two-tier board system", that Member State "may adopt the appropriate measures in relation to the SE".[167] It might be thought that the UK was quintessentially such a atate and that specific implementing measures for the two-tier board were thus required. However, the Government took the view that, since the domestic companies legislation does not require the directors to form a board in any particular way, the law permitted domestic companies to establish one-tier or two-tier boards, as they wished. The fact that UK boards were one-tier rather than two-tier in form was a result of practice, rather than legal requirement, as the CLR's evidence could be taken to suggest.

By contrast, the Government moved a little way away from this stance in relation to the duties laid on directors by statute, including now their general duties under the 2006 Act. The domestic implementing regulations do make specific provisions in relation to such duties. Their general approach is to apply the statutory duties of directors indifferently to the members of both the organs in a two-tier system, but not so as to impose on the SO a function which is managerial and so within the sole competence of the MO.[168] An example might be the production of the annual accounts, although other duties might be more difficult to classify.

It remains to be seen whether the adoption by SEs registered in the UK of two-tier board structures will create a practical "spill over" effect into domestic law. To date that seems unlikely however, since so far few SEs have been registered in the UK.

---

[166] Council Regulation 2157/2001/EC art.9(1)(c).

[167] Council Regulation 2157/2001/EC art.39(5).

[168] European Public Limited-Liability Company Regulations 2005 (SI 2005/2326) reg.78(3) and (5). Nor must the application of the statutory duties require the SO and MO to take a decision jointly: reg.78(4)—both as amended by The European Public Limited-Liability Company (Amendment) Regulations 2009 (SI 2009/2400). For the Government's views on whether domestic rules were required at all and their extent see DTI, *Implementation of the European Company Statute: A Consultative Document*, October 2003, pp.22–23 and 25; and DTI, *Implementation of the European Company Statute: Results of Consultation*, July 2004, pp.2–4.

Legal rules on board composition

Employee representatives

14–67 If the division between one-tier and two-tier board structures is an important dividing line in European jurisdictions, an even more crucial one is the requirement for employee representatives on the board. There is an inaccurate view that most continental European company laws require employee representation on the model adopted for large companies in Germany (that is, an equal division between employee and shareholder representatives), whereas that model is unique to Germany. Nevertheless, about half the Member States of the EU require minority shareholder representation on the boards of private sector companies.[169] The UK, of course, is among the half which does not have mandatory board representation for employees, i.e. does not use company law to regulate the process of contracting for labour but leaves that task to labour law and contract law. In this context, the SE is again of interest, since EU law requires SEs, even when registered in the UK, in some situations to have employee representatives at board level. This will arise when at least one of the companies forming the SE was subject to mandatory employee representation rules under its domestic laws.[170] The experience of UK-registered companies operating a system of employee representation at board level might be instructive, but again the low level of SE registrations in the UK—with or without employee representation— makes this possibility not of immediate interest.

Gender diversity—women on boards

14–68 In 2010, Lord Davies of Abersoch was commissioned to review gender diversity on boards. His report, published in February 2011,[171]presented a business case for diversity: improving performance; accessing the widest talent pool; being more responsive to the market; and achieving better corporate governance. He rejected the use of "quotas", at least for the time being, but set out recommendations

---

[169] Group of Experts, *European Systems of Worker Involvement: Final Report*, Brussels, May 1977, Annex III. The subsequent enlargement of the EU has not affected this statistic.

[170] Council Directive 2001/86/EC supplementing the Statute for a European Company with regard to the involvement of employees, implemented in the UK by the European Public Limited-Liability Company Regulations 2005 (SI 2005/2326) Pt 3 (as amended by The European Public Limited-Liability Company (Amendment) Regulations 2009 (SI 2009/2400)). The provisions of this directive are notoriously complex and include an option for the employee representatives not to take up their representation rights. For an analysis see Davies, "Workers on the Board of the European Company?" (2003) 32 I.L.J. 75. Despite the attempt to protect countries with mandatory employee representation requirements from having them undermined by the formation of an SE, it seems that some German companies have found the SE attractive because it enables them to escape some aspects of their domestic laws. Although the proportion of employees may be the same, the size of the board may be reduced for the SE, as compared with, the domestic German rules, (small boards being regarded as more efficient than large ones) and all the SE's employees will be represented at board level, not just the German ones, thus arguably diluting the employees' influence. Thus, when Allianz merged with its Italian subsidiary to form an SE its supervisory board was reduced from 20 to 12 and, of the six board members for employees, four were German, one French and one British.

[171] The "Davies Report" available at *http://www.bis.gov.uk/assets/biscore/business-law/docs/w/11-745-women-on-boards.pdf* [Accessed 27 April 2016].

designed to achieve 25 per cent female representation on boards by 2015. The effect has been positive and the target achieved,[172] with the threat of mandatory quotas no doubt providing its own incentive for action.[173] However, it is notable that most of the increase has come in non-executive board appointments, not executive ones, and in what are anecdotally described as "more junior" roles. But the pressure continues in the UK, perhaps enhanced by the EU's decision to launch its own consultation and investigation on gender imbalance as a cross-EU issue.[174] This makes rising targets increasingly likely.

Corporate governance codes, The Cadbury Report and non-executive directors

In contrast to the lack of change in the UK in the area of board representation for employees, or the slow change in gender (or other) diversity, there has been a lively debate over the past two decades about board composition, at least of listed companies. That debate has focused on the proportion and role of non-executive directors on the board, and the regulatory results have shown themselves in what is now the UK Corporate Governance Code ("CGC") rather than in legislation. Before these changes, the non-executive director held a not especially active, prestigious or powerful role, for which he (and it generally was he) was only modestly rewarded by directors' fees.[175] The executive directors were the dominant force within the company, with the CEO as the embodiment of managerial authority. All that has now changed, at least for companies subject to the CGC, although whether the changes have improved the business success of companies is still debated.[176]

14–69

The corporate governance movement in the UK can be said to have begun with the report of the Cadbury Committee in 1992.[177] As is often the case with company law reform, this committee was constituted as a result of scandal, in this case the sudden descent into insolvency of major companies which had only recently issued annual financial statements which revealed nothing of the horror to come.[178] The Cadbury Committee concluded, however, that the causes of these

14–70

---

[172] Women on FTSE 100 boards number 23.5% as at March 2015, up from 12.5% in 2010: *https://www.gov.uk/government/publications/women-on-boards-2015-fourth-annual-review* [Accessed 27 April 2016].

[173] The Equality and Human Rights Commission has issued guidance on such appointments: "Appointments to Boards and Equality Law", *http://www.equalityhumanrights.com/en/publication-download/appointments-boards-and-equality-law* [Accessed 27 April 2016].

[174] See *http://ec.europa.eu/justice/newsroom/gender-equality/news/121114_en.htm* [Accessed 27 April 2016].

[175] See para.14–30.

[176] S. Bhagat and B. Black, "The Uncertain Relationship between Board Composition and Firm Performance" (1999) 54 Business Lawyer 921. More recently, see C. Weir et al, "An Empirical Analysis of the Impact of Corporate Governance Mechanisms on the Performance of UK Firms", available at SSRN: *http://ssrn.com/abstract=286440* [Accessed 19 April 2016] or *http://dx.doi.org/10.2139/ssrn.286440* [Accessed 19 April 2016], suggesting—rather depressingly—that neither the independence of the committee membership nor the quality of the committee members had any significant effect on performance.

[177] *Report of the Committee on the Financial Aspects of Corporate Governance*, 1992.

[178] *Report of the Committee on the Financial Aspects of Corporate Governance*, Preface.

problems were not to be found in the narrow area of accounts and auditing, though it gave attention to the role of auditors, but reflected more widespread defects in the corporate governance systems of large British companies. In consequence, its proposed reforms (in the "Cadbury Code" of best practice) heralded a general reform of board composition and functioning in large UK companies, for which the scandals constituted the precipitating factor but to which they did not set a limit.

14–71   What was the corporate governance problem which Cadbury sought to address? Although it identified a number of problems, the central one might be thought to have been the domination of companies, not just by top management, but by a single over-powerful managing director or CEO. The fact that other executives may take up seats on the board gives, of course, only the illusion of constraint on the CEO in such a company, because the other directors are the latter's managerial subordinates, whilst non-executive directors may equally owe their board positions to the patronage of the CEO. Whilst not taking the view that all or even a majority of large British companies were governed in this way, the thrust of the Committee's proposals was towards putting in place a board structure which would render such dominance by a single person less likely, through the introduction of various counter-balances to the executive management of the company. From the point of view of top management, therefore, the Cadbury Code might be presented as an attack on their discretion.[179]

14–72   Indeed, in that context the subsequent review by the Hampel Committee,[180] delivered six years later, can be seen as a failed attempt by management to win back some of the ground which it had conceded to the Cadbury Committee. The Preliminary Report of the Hampel Committee[181] struck a distinctly sceptical note, asserting that "there is no hard evidence to link success to good governance", a phrase which was not repeated in the Final Report, and implicitly criticising Cadbury for giving rise to a "box ticking" approach to corporate governance. Past debate on corporate governance, it said, had focused too much on accountability and not enough on the governance contribution to business prosperity, and the Committee wished to "see the balance corrected".[182] Only in the final report could the Hampel Committee bring itself to say that it endorsed the "overwhelming majority"[183] of the recommendations of the Cadbury Committee (and of the Greenbury Committee[184] which had reported in the interim on the particular and still controversial subject of directors' remuneration). Hampel's main contribution was to propose, as indeed happened, that the recommendations

---

[179] Which, however, can be seen as a general trend in corporate law and regulation and by no means a British peculiarity: G. Hertig, "Western Europe's Corporate Governance Dilemma" in T. Baums, K.J. Hopt and N. Horn (eds), *Corporations, Capital Markets and Business in the Law* (Kluwer Law International, 2000), pp.276–278.

[180] The Hampel Committee was set up, as recommended by the Cadbury Committee, to review the operation of the Cadbury Code of Best Practice which that earlier committee had put in place. Their report is *Final Report of the Committee on Corporate Governance* (Gee, 1998).

[181] Committee on Corporate Governance, *Preliminary Report* (August 1997).

[182] This sentiment does survive to the Final Report: see *Final Report of the Committee on Corporate Governance* (Gee, 1998), para.1.1.

[183] Final Report, para.1.7.

[184] See above, fn.150.

of the Cadbury and Greenbury Committees, as refined by Hampel, should be brought together in a "Combined Code".

Following a further set of corporate failures, this time in the US and forever to be **14–73** associated with the name of the Enron company, the Government commissioned another review of the Combined Code, which was carried out by Derek Higgs. The Government's overt role in the appointment of Mr Higgs was an innovation, since the earlier bodies had been appointed by private associations, such as the Confederation of British Industry and the accounting bodies, although they were generally observed or even serviced by civil servants. The Higgs report constituted a ringing endorsement of the approach of the Cadbury committee and contained recommendations for the strengthening of the Combined Code, but along the lines already established by that Committee.[185] For example, it contained proposals, later implemented, for an increase in the proportion of non-executive directors ("NEDs") on the board from one third to one half, at least in the largest listed companies.

Developments did not stop there, but, remuneration apart (which remains under **14–74** close scrutiny, as discussed earlier), the current principles of corporate governance in the UK are in essence the product of the Cadbury Committee whose recommendations, without much violation of the truth, are often treated as a proxy for all the corporate governance reforms in the UK since the 1990s.[186] The most important requirements of the current CGC are described below, and then we consider the special mechanism by which the Code is enforced.

The requirements of the UK Corporate Governance Code

What particular practices does the UK Corporate Governance Code recommend **14–75** to listed companies as far as board structure is concerned? The principal suggestions are as follows, and they revolve around two central ideas. The primary idea is enhancement of the role of NEDs; the subsidiary one is splitting the roles of CEO and chair of the board.

---

[185] D. Higgs, *Review of the Role and Effectiveness of Non-Executive Directors* (London: The Stationery Office, January 2003). In the preface to his report Mr Higgs stated: "From the work I have done, I am clear that the fundamentals of corporate governance in the UK are sound, thanks to Sir Adrian Cadbury and those who built on his foundations". For a review of the Higgs Report (and of the contemporaneous Report by Sir Robert Smith on the role of the audit committee), see P. Davies, "Enron and Corporate Governance Reform in the UK and the European Community" in J. Armour and J. McCahery (eds), *After Enron* (Oxford: Hart Publishing, 2006).

[186] In addition to the Reports already mentioned, there are also important Reports from Turnbull (1999, updated 2005, on financial reporting, *https://www.frc.org.uk/getattachment/5e4d12e4-a94f-4186-9d6f-19e17aeb5351/Turnbull-guidance-October-2005.aspx* [Accessed 27 April 2016]); Myners (2001, on institutional investors, *http://uksif.org/wp-content/uploads/2012/12/MYNERS-P.-2001.-Institutional-Investment-in-the-United-Kingdom-A-Review.pdf* [Accessed 27 April 2016]); and Davies (2011, on women on boards, *http://www.bis.gov.uk/assets/biscore/business-law/docs/w/11-745-women-on-boards.pdf* [Accessed 27 April 2016]).

- At least one half of the board as a whole should be comprised of NEDs, all of whom should be independent.[187] As well, the board "should include an appropriate combination of executive and non-executive directors (and, in particular, independent non-executive directors) such that no individual or small group of individuals can dominate the board's decision taking".[188] As with the board as a whole, the NEDs have a role both in setting the company's strategy and supervising its implementation.[189] In the case of the non-executive directors, however, "supervising" also includes monitoring the performance of the company's executive directors.[190] The CGC provides a definition of independence, which is essentially conceived of as independence from the management. Thus, a person who has been an employee of the company within the previous five years, or has had a material business relationship with it in the previous three years, or holds cross-directorships, or represents a significant shareholder, or has been on the board for more than nine years is not categorised as independent.[191]

- The qualities and qualifications of the individuals appointed to the board are clearly crucial, and the CGC provides that there should be "a formal, rigorous and transparent procedure for the appointment of new directors to the board",[192] with the search for board candidates being conducted, and appointments made, "on merit, against objective criteria and with due regard for the benefits of diversity on the board, including gender".[193] To increase accountability and keep the board refreshed, directors of FTSE 350 companies should be subject to annual re-election, and directors of smaller companies to re-election at least every three years.[194] A measure of the perceived workload of executive directors, NEDs and chairs is evident in the CGC rule that boards "should not agree to a full time executive director taking on more than one non-executive directorship in a FTSE 100 company nor the chairmanship of such a company".[195]

- The board should have remuneration[196] and audit[197] committees on which the NEDs should be the only members, and a nomination committee on

---

[187] CGC, B.1.2. In companies below the FTSE 350 the requirement is only for two independent NEDs. Also note B.2.4 on diversity.

[188] CGC, B.1—Supporting Principle. However, there is some evidence of British boards now going in the same direction as in the US and having only one or two executive directors on them: *Financial Times*, UK edition, 31 December 2007, p.2.

[189] CGC, A.1—Supporting Principle.

[190] CGC, A.4—Supporting Principle.

[191] CGC, B.1.1.

[192] CGC, B.2—Main Principle.

[193] CGC, B.2—Supporting Principle. Gender diversity has attracted increasing concern: see the 2011 Davies Report, *Women on boards http://www.bis.gov.uk/assets/biscore/business-law/docs/w/11-745-women-on-boards.pdf* [Accessed 27 April 2016], and amended B.2.4.

[194] CGC, B.7.1.

[195] CGC, B.3.3.

[196] CGC, D.2.1. The committee may have the chair of the board as a member, provided he or she was independent upon appointment, but must otherwise consist of two or three independent NEDs.

[197] CGC, C.3.1. In smaller companies, the committee may have the chair of the board as a member, provided he or she was independent upon appointment, but must otherwise consist of at least two independent NEDs (three in larger companies).

which they should be the majority of the members.[198] These three committees clearly deal with the three most sensitive governance matters. The whole scheme will fail if the executive directors can control the appointment of the NEDs; remuneration decisions place the executive directors in a position of acute conflict of interest; and assessment by the shareholders of the performance of the management will be impossible in the absence of accurate financial data about the company but, by the same token, this is an area where the management has the greatest incentive to put an unduly optimistic interpretation on the company's position.

- The CEO and the chair of the board should not be the same person.[199] Their roles are seen as quite distinct. The chair of the board, whose role is unspecified and indeed hardly recognised in statutory company law, "is responsible for leadership of the board, ensuring its effectiveness on all aspects of its role".[200] The chairman is also responsible for "setting the board's agenda and ensuring that adequate time is available for discussion of all agenda items, in particular strategic issues. The chairman should also promote a culture of openness and debate by facilitating the effective contribution of nonexecutive directors in particular and ensuring construc- tive relations between executive and non-executive directors".[201] The chairman is responsible for ensuring that the directors receive accurate, timely and clear information.[202] The chairman should ensure effective communication with shareholders.[203]

  The CGC recognises that the chair will have such extensive contact with the executive management that his or her independence will inevitably be compromised.[204] On the other hand, the chair should be independent upon appointment.[205] From this follows one of the most contentious, and disregarded, provisions of the CGC, namely, that a retiring or recently retired CEO should not move on to become chair of the board, although exceptionally the board may so decide, subject to consulting major shareholders in advance and setting out the relevant reasons at the time of the appointment and in the next annual report.[206]

- The chairman should meet the NEDs without the executives being present (it is not stipulated how often) and once a year the NEDs should meet without the chair to appraise the latter's performance.[207]

- A senior independent director should be identified and be available as a sounding board for the chair, as an intermediary for the other directors, and as a person for shareholders to contact if they think that contact through the

---

[198] CGC, B.2.1. The chair should be either the chair of the board (unless the nomination committee is considering the chair's successor) or the senior independent NED.
[199] CGC, A.2.1.
[200] CGC, A.3—Main Principle.
[201] CGC, A.3—Supporting Principle.
[202] Also see CGC, B.5—Supporting Principle.
[203] Also see CGC, E.1—Main Principle.
[204] CGC, B.1.2.
[205] CGC, A.3.1.
[206] CGC, A.3.1.
[207] CGC, A.4.2.

CEO or chair of the board would be inappropriate.[208] All non-executive directors should be offered the opportunity to attend meetings with shareholders (and should attend them if requested by the shareholders). However, a particular obligation falls on the senior NED to "attend sufficient meetings with a range of major shareholders to listen to their views in order to help develop a balanced understanding of the issues and concerns of major shareholders".[209]

- There should be a formal statement of the matters on which the board's decision is necessary (i.e. of matters which are not simply left for management to decide and subsequently report to the board).[210]
- The NEDs should have access to appropriate outside professional advice and to internal information from the company.[211]

14–76 There are two points to be made about these provisions of the UK Corporate Governance Code. The first is that the stress on the monitoring role of the independent NEDs has the effect of reproducing within the single-tier board the distinction between management and supervision (or monitoring) that is to be found within the two-tier board system, except that in the single-tier system the NEDs are necessarily involved in the formulation of company strategy. Whether it is better to extend this functional distinction into a structural division between managing and supervisory boards depends on whether one thinks that monitoring is carried out more effectively if the executives set strategy together with the monitors or separately from them. The former provides the monitors with more information, but facilitates their capture by the executive directors.[212] In any event, one can conclude that the functions performed by one-tier and two-tier boards are not fundamentally different from one another.[213]

Secondly, although independent NEDs may no longer be the cat's-paws of the CEO, which in the past they often were, it is far from clear that the UK Corporate Governance Code provisions provide the independent NEDs with effective incentives to exercise control over strong-minded CEOs. Since executive management is unlikely easily to accept supervision by the non-executives, the non-executives may well have a battle on their hands to impose their will where there is a divergence of view. Even when explicitly trained, as Higgs recommended, why should the non-executives fight this battle rather than opt for a quiet life? Self-esteem will provide some incentive to this end, no doubt, as does the NEDs' increasingly explicit accountability to the shareholders under CGC.

But the potentially insoluble shortcomings here are, more recently, being addressed in quite a different way, by making shareholders, especially the institutional shareholders, more accountable for the exercise of their own powers

---

[208] CGC, A.4.1.

[209] CGC, E.1.1.

[210] CGC, A.1.1 cf. the similar provision relating to the role of the SO in an SE (above, para.14–66).

[211] CGC, B.5.1.

[212] See P. Davies, "Board Structure in the United Kingdom and Germany: Convergence or Continuing Divergence" (2000) 2 I.C.C.L.J. 435.

[213] What will change board methods of operation is the presence of employee representatives on them, whether on a one-tier or a two-tier board.

over the governance of their companies.[214] The explicit linking of these two powerful governance strands was promoted in the 2012 Kay Report,[215] which highlighted the serious problems of short-termism and consequential lack of trust in UK equity markets, with both executive remuneration packages and institutional investor practices coming into focus as needing reform.[216]

Enforcement of the UK Corporate Governance Code

We referred above to the UK Corporate Governance Code as "soft law". This is perhaps misleading. At the centre of the CGC there is a perfectly "hard" obligation. The Listing Rules require both UK-registered and overseas-registered companies with Premium Listing in the UK to disclose in their annual report the extent to which they have complied with the UK Corporate Governance Code in the previous 12 months and to give reasons for areas of non-compliance (if any).[217] More precisely, the company must explain how it has applied the Main and Supplementary Principles set out in the CGC (i.e. compliance at the level of principle is obligatory), and must also state whether it has complied with the lower-level specific "provisions" of the CGC and explain any areas of non-compliance. The sanctions which can be applied to both companies and directors for non-compliance with the listing rules are extensive.[218]

14–77

The "softness" of the law is a result of the lack of legal consequences if compliance with the disclosure obligation imposed by the LR reveals non-compliance with the CGC. It would be perfectly in compliance with the listing rules for the company to report that it has not complied with the CGC in any respect, provided it also gave reasons for its wholesale rejection. Any further action on the basis of the reported non-compliance is for the shareholders, as the recipients of the annual reports, not for the FCA or any other Governmental body. This has been called the principle of "comply or explain". It suggests that, even in relation to the relatively small group of Premium Listed companies, UK regulators still feel hesitant about their ability to devise governance structures which will be suitable for all the companies in the identified population. The possibility of not complying fully with the Code gives the companies in question flexibility in adapting the provisions of the UK Corporate Governance Code to their particular circumstances, whilst the need to "explain" gives the Code a somewhat greater force than a recommendation which companies are free to accept or reject. The freedom to explain rather than comply in full with the Code

14–78

---

[214] See FRC, *The UK Stewardship Code* (2012), which applies on a "comply or explain" basis (see below) to institutional investors. Also see para.15–30.

[215] *https://www.gov.uk/government/uploads/system/uploads/attachment_data/file/253454/bis-12-917-kay-review-of-equity-markets-final-report.pdf* [Accessed 27 April 2016].

[216] For the 2014 BIS Report on implementation, see *https://www.gov.uk/government/uploads/system/uploads/attachment_data/file/367070/bis-14-1157-implementation-of-the-kay-review-progress-report.pdf* [Accessed 27 April 2016]. See also para.15–30.

[217] LR 9.8.6(5) and (6), and LR 9.8.7 and 9.8.7A. UK-registered and overseas-registered companies with Standard Listing do not have to comply with the CGC, but do have to provide a statement on their corporate governance regime that meets the somewhat lower EU corporate governance standards: LR 14.3.24.

[218] See para.25–41.

has been used in particular by small listed companies.[219] "Comply or explain" clearly puts shareholders in a pivotal position in determining whether the Code's requirements will bite in practice, and much of its impact is due to the support which institutional shareholders have given to the Code.[220] In short, "softness" is not the same as self-regulation, with its risk of being merely self-interested: the compulsory disclosure regime, backed by the statutory right given to shareholders to dismiss directors, gives the CGC far greater bite.

14–79 How effective is this regime? There is evidence of some non-compliance with even the "hard" obligation of the LR; and some companies fail to explain areas of non-compliance and rather greater numbers give explanations which can hardly be considered as adequate.[221] The level of enforcement by the FCA is relatively low. Non-compliance with the CGC itself is a more slippery concept, since there is no obligation to abide by it provided non-compliance is adequately explained. But in general companies have chosen to comply; and indeed the move has often been from inadequate explanation of non-compliance to full compliance rather than to adequate explanation.[222] In this sense, the comply or explain mechanism is clearly changing corporate behaviour, although some companies do make proper use of the explanation mechanism to give good reasons why in their particular case one or more provisions of the CGC is inappropriate.[223]

14–80 The CGC is subject to both praise and criticism. For example, its application only to Premium Listed companies can be seen as too narrow. Certainly, the Cadbury Committee recommended that its Code of Practice should be observed by all large companies.[224] The restriction to listed companies seems to have arisen because the Listing Rules provided a convenient enforcement mechanism, not because this category aptly defines the companies for whom such rules are most appropriate.[225] Within this limited class, however, the regime surely succeeds in putting pressure on companies to adopt higher standards of best practice, standards which would generally be seen as to onerous to be adopted as mandatory legislative minima (the composition of audit and remunerations committees is an illustration). Moreover, these standards can be regularly and flexibly reviewed in ways not possible with statutory or regulatory rules. The best evidence of these benefits might be seen in the widespread adoption of similar regimes internationally.

---

[219] Pensions and Investment Research Consultants Ltd, *Compliance with the Combined Code* (September 1999).

[220] On the role of institutional shareholders see paras 15–25 et seq.

[221] See FRC, *Developments in Corporate Governance and Stewardship 2015* (2016, *https://www.frc. org.uk/Our-Work/Codes-Standards/Corporate-governance/UK-Corporate-Governance-Code.aspx* [Accessed 27 April 2016]). Also see S. Arcot and V. Bruno, *In Letter but not in Spirit: An Analysis of Corporate Governance in the UK* (*http://papers.ssrn.com/sol3/papers.cfm?abstract_id=819784* [Accessed 27 April 2016]). And see the enhanced demands in CGC, "Comply or Explain", para.3.

[222] See previous note.

[223] And such companies do not suffer in market terms from using such an approach and seem in fact to perform well: S. Arcot and V. Bruno, *One Size Does Not Fit All After All: Evidence from Corporate Governance* (*http://ssrn.com/abstract=887947* [Accessed 27 April 2016]).

[224] See above fn.177.

[225] Although the Code does not apply to companies with Standard Listed securities, nor to companies whose securities are traded on a public market but are not admitted to the Official List (for example, companies traded on the Alternative Investment Market).

CONCLUSION

The board of directors has long been the "black box" of British company law. In large companies, with numerous and dispersed shareholding bodies, the central management of the company's business is necessarily in the hands of the board. Yet company law has traditionally specified very little about how this body should operate. That the board is central to the operation of companies was recognised from the beginning by the development of a wide range of duties (considered in Ch.16) which apply to directors who undertake to act on behalf of the company. However, the questions of which functions should be assigned to the board and of how the board should organise itself for the effective discharge of those duties were ones that company law did not seek to answer. All that constituted the "internal management" of the company which it was for the shareholders to design.

14–81

That still remains largely the case, though the case law on the disqualification of directors (considered in Ch.10), conceived with the interests of creditors in mind, has begun to lead to the formulation of more demanding principles about the proper conduct of directors of all companies. For listed companies, however, things have changed over the past quarter of a century. Now there is not only a small-scale corporate governance industry in existence, but the central tenets of its beliefs have been given regulatory expression in the UK Corporate Governance Code which, with the support of the institutional shareholders, exerts a real, although not completely inflexible, pressure on companies to conform to a particular model of board composition and operation. A company whose business is producing outstanding profits can probably afford to ignore the CGC to large extent, but should its business performance falter, it is likely to find the pressures to conform to that model irresistible.

CHAPTER 15

SHAREHOLDER DECISION-MAKING

THE ROLE OF THE SHAREHOLDERS

The previous chapter demonstrated that most decisions about the company's **15–1**
business will be taken by the board. Nevertheless, shareholders' decision-making
still has an important, indeed crucial, role to play in the governance of companies.
Quite apart from those decisions for which the Act requires shareholder consent,[1]
the traditional model of directorial accountability to the shareholders depends
heavily upon the ability of the shareholders to review the performance of the
board (notably when the annual report and accounts are presented to them) and to
take decisions if they think that performance has not been adequate, for example,
by removing the existing directors and installing a new board.[2]

Shareholder activism depends on individual motivation, certainly, but is also **15–2**
crucially underpinned by the rights of shareholders at general meetings. Although
most intervention by substantial shareholders will take place in private, moving
into the public arena of the general meeting only if private pressure is

---

[1] See above, para.14–18.
[2] See above, para.14–48.

unsuccessful, the pressure which such shareholders can bring to bear privately depends in large part upon the prospect of their being able to get their way in the public meeting if the private pressures are unsuccessful. Without doubt, the crucial factor, if it comes to a public fight between the incumbent management and these shareholders, is the ability of an ordinary majority of the shareholders at any time to remove the directors under the provisions of s.168.[3]

15–3   Nevertheless, the shareholder meeting has had a bad press in recent years. In small companies it is argued that the meeting is an unnecessary encumbrance, because the shareholder/directors frequently meet together informally. And in large companies shareholders do not show sufficient interest in using the general meeting, often allowing it to be captured by single-issue pressure groups whose primary objective is to advance the policies they stand for rather than any interests as shareholders. The Act has been amended incrementally over recent years to address the first set of concerns. The second, and more intractable, set of problems can only be addressed with "a sharper focus on the shareholder".[4] A "more effective machinery for enabling and encouraging shareholders to exercise effective and responsible control" was one of three core policies of the CLR in the corporate governance area,[5] an approach which increasingly chimes with current government policy initiatives.[6]

15–4   Before we consider these problems, it is important to be alert to one preliminary issue, which is the question of who is entitled to vote on shareholder decisions. It should not be supposed that all shareholders, not even all ordinary shareholders, necessarily have the right to vote on shareholder resolutions or, even if they do, that they have voting rights as extensive as those attached to other shares which apparently carry the same level of risk. As we shall see,[7] the rights attached to classes of shares, including the number of votes per share, are matters for the company to determine in its articles of association or in the terms of issue of the shares. The exclusion of preference shareholders from voting rights, except in limited circumstances, is common, and the issuance of non-voting ordinary shares is not unknown, though it is fiercely opposed by institutional shareholders.[8] Thus, "shareholder democracy", which is in any event a democracy of shares rather than of shareholders, is, or may be, an imperfect one.

---

[3] See above, paras 14–48 et seq.

[4] Final Report I, para.1.56.

[5] Final Report I, para.3.4. The other two were the proposed statement of directors' duties, discussed in the following chapter, and improved disclosure and transparency provisions, discussed in a number of places in this work but especially in Ch.21.

[6] See below, para.15–22. From a governmental point of view, putting pressure on shareholders to regulate boards of directors reduces the pressure on the Government to regulate substantively in the contested area. See the example of the recent re-regulation of directors' remuneration, discussed in the previous chapter at paras 14–30 et seq.

[7] See below, Ch.23.

[8] On whom, see below. Additional voting rights may be confined to certain types of resolution, for example, the "golden share" held by the Government after some recent privatisations may operate so as to allow the Government to out-vote all other shareholders on certain specified resolutions: see Graham (1988) 9 Co. Law. 24.

Company law does not require equal voting rights for shares carrying the same risk nor equivalent rights for shares of different classes of risk.[9]

In these circumstances, there is a risk, where voting and cash-flow rights are not proportionate, that the controlling shareholder (controlling in terms of votes but not necessarily in terms of capital committed to the company) will take excessive risks with the company's business at the expense of the non-controlling shareholders (who may be the majority contributors to the company's capital) since the controller does not bear a proportionate part of the downside if the strategy is unsuccessful. Disproportionate voting structures may alternatively be used to maintain the existing directors of the company in office, because the controllers elect themselves or their nominees to the board and are reluctant to abandon their control.[10] In most cases, however, since the price of the non-controlling shares (at least where these are traded on public markets) adjusts to reflect these risks, regulatory intervention is directed at disclosure rather than prohibition.[11]

15–5

SHAREHOLDER DECISION-MAKING WITHOUT SHAREHOLDER MEETINGS

The nature of the problem

In small companies where shareholders and directors are the same people, requiring them to distinguish between the decisions they take as directors and those which they take as shareholders can seem unduly burdensome. They will tend in fact to take all decisions as directors, since the rules about board meetings are largely under their control, whereas the Act contains some mandatory rules about shareholder meetings, for example, as to the length of notice required.[12] However, this approach generates legal risks, because the rules for the two types of meeting are not the same. For example, voting is normally on the basis of "one person, one vote" on the board, but on the basis of "one share, one vote" at a shareholders meeting. If the shares are not equally divided among the directors, the outcomes in the two situations may not be the same. Normally, this does not

15–6

---

[9] 2006 Act s.284 lays down a rule of "one share, one vote" (for all shares, whether ordinary or preference), except where the vote is taken on a "show of hands" (see below, para.15–75), but allows the articles to make alternative provisions, so that the distribution of voting rights (including the creation of classes of non-voting ordinary shares) is under the control of the shareholders: s.284(4). See *Re Savoy Hotel Ltd* [1981] Ch. 351 (discussed at para.29–7) where the company had created A and B shares, ranking pari passu except in relation to voting rights, with the effect that the holders of the B shares, who owned 2.3% of the equity, could exercise 48.55% of the votes.

[10] The European Commission expressed concern with the management entrenchment qualities of disproportionate capital structures, but only introduced proposals into the Takeovers Directive on an optional basis, and its general study of the issues leans towards enhanced disclosure of voting arrangements, rather than more detailed regulation of them. For the "break-through rule" in relation to takeovers, see paras 28–22 et seq.

[11] Contrast the minority report of the Jenkins Committee in 1962 which recommended a ban on non- and restricted-voting shares: *Report of the Committee on Company Law Amendment*, 1962, Cmnd. 1749, "Note of Dissent", cf. the main report at paras 123–136. The dissentients were mainly influenced by the inconsistency between the development of a market for corporate control and the issuance of non- or restricted-voting shares.

[12] See below, para.15–60.

matter as long as all is going well, because decisions will in fact be taken unanimously. However, if relations between the entrepreneurs begin to deteriorate, as in small companies they often do,[13] clear decision-making mechanisms are required.

15–7 One straightforward way of resolving this problem would be to permit companies where shareholders and directors are the same people to operate with only a single decision-making organ, probably the board. This facility is provided by many state laws in the US, but when the CLR consulted on this proposal,[14] it did not find enough support for the idea to take it forward in Britain. Instead, the 2006 Act simply makes it easier for small companies to operate, but still with two decision-making bodies. If incorporators wish, formally, to roll the board and the shareholders' meetings into one whilst still retaining limited liability, they will have to operate as a Limited Liability Partnership.[15]

Written resolutions

15–8 By amending earlier statutory rules, the 2006 Act now provides for much simpler decision-taking within private companies. The default obligation on private companies to hold an AGM has been abolished, and resolutions of the members of a private company may now be taken either as a written resolution or by adoption at a meeting of the members.[16] Both forms of taking shareholder decisions are of equal validity and (with two limited but important exceptions, discussed below) any decision may be taken in either manner. Indeed, s.300 makes it clear that the articles may not deprive the company of its right to take statutory decisions (other than the two exceptions just noted) by written resolution, though the articles could require a meeting for decisions which are wholly within the jurisdiction of the articles. A written resolution needs to be adopted by the same percentage of support as would be needed for a resolution adopted at a meeting.[17] The necessary consequence has been a greater formalisation of the rules governing written resolutions.

15–9 This approach renders decision-taking in private companies far less cumbersome, although if a member wishes to have a meeting of members and the board is unwilling to convene one,[18] then—now that a formal AGM is not required—a meeting can only be demanded if the general provisions on the calling of

---

[13] See Ch.20, below.

[14] Developing, paras 7.95f et seq.; Completing, paras 2.35–2.36.

[15] See above, para.1–4.

[16] 2006 Act s.336, requiring an AGM, applies only to public companies and to private companies which are "traded companies" (s.336(1A)—these are defined in s.360C as companies admitted to trading on a regulated market in an EEA State by or with the consent of the company) (AGMs are discussed below at para.15–49); and s.281(1) provides for private companies to take resolutions in either way.

[17] 2006 Act s.296(4), discussed below at para.15–11.

[18] 2006 Act s.302 makes it clear that the directors may always call a general meeting of the company.

meetings by members have been observed. These provisions normally require the requisitionists to hold 5 per cent of the company's voting share capital.[19]

Where written resolutions not available

There are only two situations where the written resolution procedure is not available to private companies, and where the company must instead proceed by means of a meeting of its members. These are decisions for the removal of either a director[20] or an auditor[21] before the expiration of their period of appointment.[22] With directors, if the Act did not insist on a meeting, the director's entitlement[23] to be heard on the removal resolution at the meeting would be nugatory. An auditor does not have the same right to be heard, but only to make written representations to the meeting.[24] Here, the rationale for insistence upon a meeting seems to be to subject those shareholders who favour the removal to face-to-face questioning by the other shareholders, if they wish to put questions, presumably on the grounds that this will lead to more considered outcomes in relation to potentially significant changes of personnel in central parts of the company's corporate governance structure.

15–10

The procedure for passing written resolutions

Written resolutions require the same show of approval as would be needed to pass the resolution if it were proposed at a meeting.[25] This means either 50 per cent or 75 per cent, depending upon whether the resolution required is an ordinary or a special resolution.[26] Of course, in the case of a meeting the percentage figures refer to those who vote, whether in person or by proxy, whereas in the case of a written resolution it refers to those entitled to vote.[27] In practice, therefore, the consent of a higher percentage of the members is normally needed for the passing of a written resolution than for a resolution at a meeting where typically fewer than half the members attend either in person or by proxy. Nevertheless, the advantages of not having to call a meeting outweigh this potential disadvantage.

15–11

The Act requires a copy of the proposed written resolution to be sent at the same time (as far as is reasonably practical) to every member entitled to vote. However, if this can be done without "undue delay", the company may submit the same

15–12

---

[19] 2006 Act ss.303–306, discussed below at para.15–51. The rule for demanding that a written resolution be circulated also requires 5 per cent, or some lower threshold as specified in the articles: s.292.
[20] 2006 Act s.168. See the previous chapter at para.14–52.
[21] 2006 Act s.510. See para.22–19.
[22] 2006 Act s.288(2).
[23] 2006 Act s.169(2).
[24] 2006 Act s.511(3)–(6).
[25] 2006 Act s.296(4).
[26] See below, para.15–44.
[27] Referred to in s.292(4) as the "eligible" members, but s.289 defines the eligible members as those members who would have been entitled to vote on the date the resolution was circulated. The written resolution provisions do not alter the rules on the distribution of voting rights, discussed above at para.15–4.

copy to each member in turn (or different copies to each of a number of members in turn) or employ a combination of simultaneous and consecutive circulation.[28] It is submitted that the courts should take a rather strict view of what constitutes "undue delay". Near-simultaneous circulation is important because it prevents the proposers circulating the resolution first to its likely supporters or those with no strong view on the matter, thus securing their support before the opponents have had the opportunity to put their case to the other members. This is important, because the written resolution is passed at the point at which it secures the requisite majority of the members, whether or not all those members to whom the resolution has been sent have voted at that time, whether the period for voting has expired or whether, indeed, all the members have been sent copies of the resolution at that point.[29] If a proposed ordinary resolution is sent to a 51 per cent shareholder and he or she signifies assent to it, before any of the other shareholders have opened their emails, the resolution will be adopted at that point.

A member signifies agreement to a proposed resolution when the company receives from the member or someone acting on the member's behalf a document indicating agreement, the method of signifying agreement having been indicated when the resolution was circulated.[30] Once given, the consent cannot be revoked.[31] This is another consideration in favour of simultaneous circulation. Despite the importance of simultaneous circulation, non-compliance with the provisions of s.291 (which includes the requirements for informing the members of the method of signifying consent and the final voting date) does not affect the validity of the resolution, if it is passed, though it does constitute a criminal offence on the part of every officer in default.[32]

Written resolutions proposed by members

15–13   Resolutions may be proposed as written resolutions by directors or members.[33] Members holding at least 5 per cent (or some lower percentage if so fixed by the articles) of the total voting rights exercisable on the resolution in question may request circulation of a resolution,[34] along with a statement of up to 1,000 words

---

[28] 2006 Act s.291(3) for resolutions proposed by directors and s.293(2) for resolutions proposed by members.

[29] 2006 Act s.296(4). The period for voting is 28 days from the date of circulation or whatever other period is fixed in the company's articles: s.297. If the requisite support is not achieved by that date, the resolution lapses. The circulation date is the first date on which a copy of the resolution is sent or submitted to a member: s.290.

[30] 2006 Act s.291(2)(a). The statement accompanying the proposed resolution must also indicate the final date for voting: s.291(2)(b). Voting may be electronic: ss.296(1),(2) and 298.

[31] 2006 Act s.291(6),(7).

[32] 2006 Act s.296(3).

[33] 2006 Act s.288(3).

[34] 2006 Act s.292(4),(5). The 5 per cent figure tracks that for requiring a public company to add a resolution to the agenda of its AGM (see below, para.15–57), for which s.292 is the functional substitute, since it is not expected that private companies will typically hold AGMs. However, the original Draft Clauses had proposed that any member might require the company to initiate the written resolution procedure: *Modernising Company Law—Draft Clauses*, Cm. 5553-II, July 2002, cl.174.

in support of the resolution.[35] Once such a request has been made, the company must, within 21 days, initiate the written resolution procedure in the manner described above.[36]

This requirement is subject to three exceptions:

(i) The requisitionists must tender a sum necessary to cover the costs of the circulation, unless the company has resolved otherwise.[37] These should not be large if electronic circulation is possible.

(ii) The resolution must not be ineffective "whether by reason of inconsistency with any enactment or the company's articles or otherwise".[38] There is no point in securing a resolution for the company to do something which the company may not lawfully do, but, in the case of inconsistency with the articles, this may simply affect the level of support the resolution needs, i.e. it must be enough to alter the articles.[39] Nor need the company circulate the resolution if it is defamatory of any person or is frivolous or vexatious.[40]

(iii) The company or any other aggrieved person may apply to the court for an order that the company is not obliged to circulate the members' statement on the grounds that the members' circulation rights are being abused.[41]

Wider written resolution provisions under the articles

The 1985 Act explicitly preserved the power of companies to adopt provisions in their articles on the taking of resolutions, and art.53 of Table A 1985 contained a procedure for consenting to written resolutions unanimously without a meeting. Although the 2006 Act does not retain this explicit authorisation,[42] and although the current model sets of articles do not deal with written resolutions, it is difficult to see why the 2006 Act should be construed as taking this power away from companies which do not fall within the statutory provisions. The facility may be useful to those few public companies with small shareholding bodies. For private companies, the incentive to create a special procedure in the articles is now much less, since the 2006 statutory procedure has dropped the requirement of unanimous consent.

15–14

---

[35] 2006 Act s.292(3).

[36] 2006 Act s.293(1),(3). Non-compliance is a criminal offence on the part of every officer in default but again the validity of the resolution, if passed, is not affected by non-compliance: s.293(6),(7).

[37] 2006 Act s.294.

[38] 2006 Act s.292(2)(a).

[39] See para.3–31, above.

[40] 2006 Act s.292(2)(b),(c).

[41] 2006 Act s.295. The requisitionists may have to pay the company's costs (s.295(2)) and presumably the normal rules as to costs will apply if the application is by a person aggrieved, i.e. the requisitionists will have to pay if they lose. This is a new section, though it mirrors the provision which now appears in relation to meetings (see s.317).

[42] 2006 Act s.300 is, by contrast, concerned with restraining the (private) company's power to exclude a written resolution procedure rather than its power to have a more generous one than the statutory procedure.

Unanimous consent at common law

15–15   We touched on the common law rule on unanimous consent in the previous chapter,[43] where we saw that its main purpose is to allow shareholders to decide informally on matters within their competence. The common rule is preserved under the 2006 Act,[44] and applies to public as well as private companies, although it might be thought less necessary in relation to the latter given the revised and relaxed statutory provisions allowing for non-unanimous written resolutions. The written resolution procedure allows shareholders to adopt resolutions outside meetings; the unanimous consent rule permits wholly informal methods of giving shareholder consent, but requires that consent (being of all those entitled to vote) to be unanimous, regardless of the level of support that would have been required in a formal meeting or if the written resolution procedure been followed. The accepted explanation for this is that it would be inequitable to allow the company, or its members, to assert that they are not bound by a decision or an act which all those competent to effect have decided should be effected.[45] From this rationale follow the answers to the two issues which have most concerned the courts: what counts as informal consent and how must it be manifested; and which issues lie within the competence of the shareholders to determine in this way.

15–16   On the first of these issues, Neuberger J (as he then was) summarised the principle in the following terms in *EIC Services Ltd v Phipps*[46]:

> "The essence of the Duomatic principle, as I see it, is that [certain specified formalities, here in the company's articles] can be avoided if all members of the group [being the group entitled to determine the matter in issue], being aware of the relevant facts, either give their approval to that course, or so conduct themselves as to make it inequitable for them to deny that they have given their approval. Whether the approval is given in advance or after the event, whether it is characterised as agreement, ratification, waiver, or estoppel, and whether members of the group give their consent in different ways at different times, does not matter."

This statement is supported by earlier authorities, and has been followed subsequently. It highlights a number of important and distinct matters.

15–17   First, who must consent? Buckly J in *Re Duomatic* held that only those entitled to vote on the issue must consent, not all members regardless of that entitlement. This is especially material when, for example, the informal procedure is applied to class meetings.[47] The necessary consents can be inferred even from occasions where the shareholders wear a different hat: for example, in companies where all

---

[43] See above, para.14–15.

[44] 2006 Act s.281(4)(a): "nothing in this Part affects any enactment of rule of law as to things done otherwise than by passing a resolution". Section 281(4)(c) also preserves the estoppel-based version of the common law rules, discussed below: "nothing in this Part affects any enactment or rule of law as to cases in which a person is precluded from alleging that a resolution has not been duly passed".

[45] *Baroness Wenlock v River Dee Co* (1883) 36 Ch. D. 675n, 681-2n (Cotton LJ); *Re Duomatic Ltd* [1969] 2 Ch. 365, 373 (Buckley J); *Re New Cedos Engineering Co Ltd* [1994] 1 B.C.L.C. 797, 814 (Oliver J); *Wright v Atlas Wright (Europe) Ltd* [1999] 2 B.C.L.C. 301, 314-5 CA (Potter LJ, with whom other members of the CA agreed); *Euro Brokers Holdings Ltd v Monecor (London) Ltd* [2003] EWCA Civ 105; [2003] 1 B.C.L.C. 506 at [62] (Mummery LJ).

[46] *EIC Services Ltd v Phipps* [2004] 2 B.C.L.C. 589 at [122].

[47] *Re Torvale Group Ltd* [1999] 2 B.C.L.C. 605.

the shareholders are directors, these individuals can act as directors in a board meeting and simultaneously act as shareholders unanimously and informally approving or ratifying their own unauthorised act as directors provided, as shareholders, they are competent to do that.[48] In similar vein, individuals representing corporate shareholders (usually by virtue of being the CEO of the corporate shareholder), can give the necessary consent on behalf of their company, if competent to so act.[49] And trustees holding shares on trust can, as the registered holder, validly consent. However, here the informality of the necessary consent generates complications. If the trustee holds some of the shares personally and some as trustee, his or her consent is only taken as applying to those shares held personally unless it is expressed to apply to the other shares as well.[50] On the other hand, and in line with the justifications given for the informal consent rule, if the trustee could be compelled to vote in accordance with the wishes of the beneficial owners, then their consents are effective for the purpose of the rule.[51]

Secondly, the requirement that the consenting shareholders be aware of the relevant facts simply repeats the orthodox common law requirement that consent counts as such only when it is "fully informed". In this context, the "relevant facts" would, it seems, prima facie include any information made mandatory by statute in order for shareholders to take formal decisions on certain matters[52]: there is no reason to suppose that informal decision-making should be successful if less well informed. But it can be strongly argued that these information provisions are inserted solely for the protection of shareholders and can therefore be waived by them (although perhaps only on an informed basis or at least in a conscious fashion). Put another way, there seems no reason to suppose that the informal procedure specifically endorsed by statute would somehow be excluded in these contexts where the statute has specified information requirements, even if its application needs to be addressed thoughtfully.[53]

15–18

---

[48] *Re Express Engineering Works Ltd* [1920] 1 Ch. 466 CA. The qualification is important: for example, the shareholders cannot consent (whether formally or informally) to the directors making illegal gifts out of capital: this is now taken to be the ratio of *Re George Newman and Co* [1895] 1 Ch. 674. Also see below, paras 15–20 and 16–117 et seq.

[49] *Wright v Atlas Wright (Europe) Ltd* [1999] 2 B.C.L.C. 301 CA; *Multinational Gas Co v Multinational Gas Services* [1983] 1 Ch. 258; see also *Madoff Securities International Ltd v Raven* [2013] EWHC 3147 (Ch).

[50] *Re Tulsesense Ltd, Rolfe v Rolfe* [2010] EWHC 244 (Ch); [2010] 2 B.C.L.C. 525 at [40] (Newey J). By contrast, joint holders of shares are only entitled to one vote per share, and the assent of the "senior" holder is sufficient: *Re Gee & Co (Woolwich) Ltd* [1975] Ch. 52.

[51] *Shahar v Tsitsekkos* [2004] EWHC 2659 (Ch) at [67]. But the "control" limitation is important. More generally, the Australian case of *Jalmoon Pty Ltd (In Liquidation) v Bow* (1997) 15 A.C.L.C. 230 limits consent to the registered owner. See too *Secretary of State for Business, Innovation and Skills v Hamilton* [2015] CSOH 46 at [59], obiter, simply noting the uncertainty. If there are two or more beneficial owners, then of course all must consent: *Re Tulsesense Ltd, Rolfe v Rolfe* [2010] EWHC 244 (Ch); [2010] 2 B.C.L.C. 525 at [43] (Newey J).

[52] See, for example, ss.181(5) (directors' long-term service contracts), 696(5) and 699(6) (on repurchases of company's own shares).

[53] 2006 Act s.281(4). Also see *Wright v Atlas Wright (Europe) Ltd* [1999] 2 B.C.L.C. 301 CA, and the discussion below at para.15–20.

15–19   Finally, what is needed to signify the necessary consent? The passage already cited from Neuberger J (as he then was) in *EIC Services Ltd v Phipps*[54] illustrates the breadth of what will count as consent, as amply supported by decided cases.[55] Despite this breadth, however, the necessary consents must be objectively established,[56] and this necessarily means that they must be expressed in *some* way by each member (even if only by acquiescence[57]): the fact that the person would have consented if asked is not enough,[58] nor is a decision that is merely internal,[59] and of course express objection negates any possibility of inferring consent.[60]

In all of this, the cases which rely on something less than assent (albeit informal assent), and instead rely on the interplay of acquiescence, estoppel and laches, are perhaps the most difficult. *Re Bailey Hay & Co Ltd*[61] illustrates the problems. There, a resolution was passed by two votes in favour and three abstaining at a meeting attended by all the members of the company but of which the requisite length of notice had not been given, unbeknown to all present (it was one day short of the 14 days required). That information came to light within the next few months. The court denied a challenge to the validity of the resolution brought over three years later (and, it seems, for technical reasons as a means of defeating a counter-claim), holding that in the circumstances the shareholders should be taken as unanimously assenting to, or acquiescing, in the winding-up,[62] or, alternatively, that their delay (or "laches") in making the claim made it "practically unjust" now to upset the resolution (which had been for the appointment of a liquidator).[63] It might have been preferable to confine the finding of acquiescence to one that the non-voting shareholders could, in the circumstances, be taken to have acquiesced in the shorter period of notice. That

---

[54] *EIC Services Ltd v Phipps* [2004] 2 B.C.L.C. 589 at [122]. See above, para.15–16.

[55] See, in addition to the cases already cited, *Re Oxted Motor Co Ltd* [1921] 3 K.B. 32; *Parker & Cooper Ltd v Reading* [1926] Ch. 975; *Re Pearce Duff & Co Ltd* [1960] 1 W.L.R. 1014; *Re Duomatic Ltd* [1969] 2 Ch. 365; *Re Bailey Hay & Co Ltd* [1971] 1 W.L.R. 1357; *Re Gee & Co (Woolwich) Ltd* [1975] Ch. 52; *Cane v Jones* [1980] 1 W.L.R. 1451; *Re Moorgate Mercantile Holdings Ltd* [1980] 1 W.L.R. 227 at 242G; *Multinational Gas Co v Multinational Gas Services* [1983] 1 Ch. 258 especially at 289 CA. The unanimous consent rule is often referred to as "the *Duomatic* rule", although that case was not the first to formulate it.

[56] *Schofield v Schofield* [2011] EWCA Civ 154; [2011] 2 B.C.L.C. 319 at [32] (Etherton LJ, with whom the other members of the CA agreed).

[57] *Re Bailey Hay & Co Ltd* [1971] 1 W.L.R. 1357, 1367 (Brightman J).

[58] *Re D'Jan* [1994] 1 B.C.L.C. 561; it suffices where the only inference that can be drawn is indicative of assent and acceptance: *Hussain v Wycombe Islamic Mission and Mosque Trust Ltd* [2011] EWHC 971 (Ch) at [37] (HHJ David Cooke).

[59] *Re Tulsesense Ltd, Rolfe v Rolfe* [2010] EWHC 244 (Ch); [2010] 2 B.C.L.C. 525; see also *Bonham-Carter v Situ Ventures Ltd* [2012] B.C.C. 717 (Ch) in which the filing of relevant forms and notices was found to be insufficient to make out a *Duomatic* decision to remove the director (the decision was reversed on appeal in [2014] B.C.C. 125 but no permission to appeal had been given on this point).

[60] *Schofield v Schofield* [2011] EWCA Civ 154; [2011] 2 B.C.L.C. 319.

[61] *Re Bailey Hay & Co Ltd* [1971] 1 W.L.R. 1357. See also *Peña v Dale* [2004] 2 B.C.L.C. 508 at [120].

[62] *Re Bailey Hay & Co Ltd* [1971] 1 W.L.R. 1357 at 1366F–1367B.

[63] *Re Bailey Hay & Co Ltd* [1971] 1 W.L.R. 1357 at 1367D–E.

would have produced the same result, and was perhaps better supported by Brightman J's analysis of the facts. Nevertheless, the case is instructive in this difficult area.[64]

The second principal issue which has troubled the courts is defining which matters may be determined by the unanimous consent rule. The rule, it seems, applies whenever the shareholders are competent to act. It follows that the shareholders cannot, even by unanimous agreement, overcome prohibitions on the company's activities imposed by the general law or the Companies Act. They cannot, for example, make illegal gifts out of capital, or distribute the company's assets in ways not authorised by law, or take decisions which are not theirs to take because that right has been given to a named individual or group.[65]

15–20

Typically, then, the rule is applied when the shareholders have the power to act, but have not followed the necessary formal decision-making requirements, whether these are found in the Act or the company's articles or a shareholders' agreement.[66] The rule then appears to be that unanimous consent can operate to waive formalities required for the protection of shareholders, but not those required for the protection of other parties, notably creditors. Thus, in *Precision Dipping Ltd v Precision Dipping Marketing Ltd*[67] the requirement of auditor approval of a dividend, where the company's accounts were qualified, could not be waived by unanimous consent of the shareholders, because the provision was clearly one aimed at protecting creditors (and possibly shareholders as well). By contrast, in the *Atlas Wright* case,[68] the Court of Appeal was prepared to permit unanimous shareholder consent to override the procedural requirements set out above for the approval of a long service contract.[69] However, it may not always be easy to categorise the function of particular statutory requirements.[70] For example, it seems unlikely that the courts would permit the unanimous consent rule to operate in the two cases excepted from the written resolution procedure (removal of a director or auditor from office before the expiration of their term),

---

[64] See *Phosphate of Lime Co v Green* [1871] L.R. 7 C.P. 43, where it was held that "acquiescence" by members of a company could be established without proving actual knowledge by each individual member so long as each could have found out if he had bothered to ask; and *Ho Tung v Man On Insurance Co* [1902] A.C. 232 PC, where articles of association, which had never been adopted by a resolution but had been acted on for 19 years and amended from time to time, were held to have been accepted and adopted as valid and operative articles.

[65] *Madoff Securities International Ltd v Raven* [2013] EWHC 3147 at [288]; *Oxford Fleet Management Ltd v Brown* [2014] EWHC 3065 at [102]–[104]. In this context, see above, paras 14–11 to 14–16 (on shareholders' residual and confirmation powers).

[66] *Re Torvale Group Ltd* [1999] 2 B.C.L.C. 605; *Euro Brokers Holdings Ltd v Monecor (London) Ltd* [2003] 1 B.C.L.C. 505 at [62] CA.

[67] *Precision Dipping Ltd v Precision Dipping Marketing Ltd* [1985] B.C.L.C. 385 CA. See Ch.12, above, at para.12–5.

[68] *Wright v Atlas Wright (Europe) Ltd* [1999] 2 B.C.L.C. 301 CA.

[69] This was a strong decision because s.319(3) of the Companies Act 1985 could be read as requiring a resolution in any event in this case, so that the principle of informal unanimous consent had no operation at all. See also *Bonham-Carter v Situ Ventures Ltd* [2012] B.C.C. 717 (Ch), in which it was held obiter that informal consent of shareholders could not waive the requirements under s.169 as these were, at least in part, for the benefit of director(s) whose removal was sought.

[70] Note the contrasting approaches of Lindsay J in *Re RW Peak (King's Lynn) Ltd* [1998] 1 B.C.L.C. 183; and Park J in *BDG Roof-Bond Ltd v Douglas* [2000] 1 B.C.L.C. 401 to the construction of the rules relating to the purchase of own shares. See further *Kinlan v Crimmin* [2007] 2 B.C.L.C. 67.

since, it might be said, the purpose of these rules is to protect the director or officer by permitting him or her to make representations against the proposal.[71]

15–21   Finally, there are certain post-decision formalities which have to be complied with in relation to shareholder resolutions, most importantly the notification of certain resolutions to the Registrar and the making a record of them in the company's minute book. The obligation to notify the Registrar seems to apply to informal decisions,[72] but the requirement as to recording in the minute book seems not to.[73] Non-compliance involves a criminal sanction but the decision itself is not invalidated.

IMPROVING SHAREHOLDER PARTICIPATION

Analyses of shareholder participation

15–22   Ever since Berle and Means wrote their classic study of patterns of share ownership in large American corporations in the 1930s,[74] it has been common to think that shareholders, at least those in listed companies, are not in general interested in using the rights which the law or the company's articles confer upon them to hold the management of their company to account. This has not always been true. Although the exact historical development is still unclear,[75] there is general agreement that three distinct periods of shareholder structure in such companies can be identified. There was an initial period, beginning with the development of the large company in the nineteenth century, when the shareholdings were held mainly by the founding entrepreneurs and their families. At this time, therefore, the shareholdings were in "concentrated" form and establishing the wishes of the shareholders was relatively easy. However, as the capital needs of such companies grew, some shares were offered to the public, with the outside shareholders being, however, in the minority and with most of them holding only small stakes. By the middle of the last century, family shareholdings had declined and the small outside shareholders, collectively, made up the bulk of the shareholders. This is the second period, so brilliantly analysed by Berle and Means (see below), where the shareholdings in large companies were typically "dispersed", so that the shareholders' ability to act together in a meaningful way was doubtful.

15–23   The thesis advanced by Berle and Means was that, in large companies where shareholdings had become widely dispersed, it was not worthwhile for most

---

[71] See the discussion above, para.14–52. By contrast, the CLR recommended that the unanimous consent rule should also operate here, since it could be argued that the purpose of these provisions is solely to promote the interests of the members (enabling them to be better informed about the reasons for the proposed removal): Final Report I, para.7.22.

[72] See s.29(1)(b): "any resolution or agreement agreed to by all the members of the company" that would otherwise need to be a special resolution.

[73] 2006 Act s.356(2), referring only to "a resolution".

[74] A.A. Berle and G.C. Means, *The Modern Corporation and Private Property*, revised edn (New York: Transaction Publishers, 1968).

[75] Interesting work on the issue has been carried out by B. Cheffins. See *Corporate Ownership and Control: British Business Transformed* (Oxford: Oxford University Press, 2008).

shareholders to devote time, effort and resources to seeking to change the policies of the managements which they thought were ineffective. Any return on their relatively small investment which success might bring would be outweighed by the certain costs of seeking to achieve such change in a large company where co-ordination of shareholder action would be intensely difficult. Since these large companies were likely to be listed on a stock exchange, the alternative and cheaper responses of accepting a takeover offer or simply selling in the market were likely to prove more attractive. Shareholders in large companies were thus "rationally apathetic" towards their general meeting rights.

Whether this was ever an entirely correct picture is controversial, but in any event **15–24** it had to be modified in the third recognisably distinct historical period. Since the 1960s, there has been a partial re-concentration of shareholdings, not into the hands of entrepreneurial families, but into the hands of "institutional" shareholders, especially pension funds and insurance companies. These different patterns of shareholding have significant implications for the ability, and perhaps the willingness, of shareholders to exercise effectively the governance rights which the law confers upon them.[76] In the early 1990s, when much of the regulatory work on this issue was first conceived, institutional shareholders held about 60 per cent of the equity shares of companies listed on the London Stock Exchange. Although it would be unusual for a single institution to hold more than 5 per cent of the equities of the largest quoted companies, nevertheless the situation is one in which a small group of institutional shareholders could often bring decisive influence to bear on the management of ailing companies. Of course, they may not always wish to do so. Even institutional shareholders will not exercise their general meeting rights simply for the sake of it. If a takeover offer provides a cheaper remedy for the problem, they may be inclined to accept that, rather than take on the incumbent management of the under-performing company themselves. Nevertheless, "shareholder activism" on the part of the institutions became a bigger part of the corporate scene than it had been, say, 20 years earlier.

However, the make-up of the institutional investors and their associated attitudes towards activism have not remained the same. For reasons which do not need to be explored here, over the past two decades UK institutional shareholders have tended to reduce their exposure to UK equities, whilst foreign institutions and hedge funds have been increasing them.[77] Some of these investors may be expected to be more passive; others, certain types of hedge fund in particular, might be expected to be even more interventionist in relation to their portfolio companies, often identifying specific business decisions which they wish the board to take.[78]

---

[76] See P. Davies, "Institutional Investors in the United Kingdom" in T. Baums et al. (eds), *Institutional Investors and Corporate Governance* (1994); E. Boros, *Minority Shareholder Remedies* (Oxford, 1995), Ch.3; and G.P. Stapledon, *Institutional Shareholders and Corporate Governance* (Oxford, 1996), Ch.2.

[77] See B. Cheffins, "The Stewardship Code's Achilles' Heel" (2010) 73 M.L.R. 1004, 1017–18, indicating an increase in foreign investment from 16% to 42%, and a decrease in the holdings of UK pension funds and insurance companies from 52% to 26% between 1993 and 2008.

[78] See M. Kahan and E. Rock, "Hedge Funds in Corporate Governance and Corporate Control", ECGI Law Series 76/2006 (suggesting that some hedge funds make investments in order to become

The role of institutional investors

15–25   Given the scale of institutional investment, the role of such investor-shareholders merits attention. Both the Company Law Review ("CLR") and the Myner's Report,[79] commissioned by the Treasury, and the more recent Walker Report[80] and Kay Review,[81] all concluded that the level of institutional intervention in the affairs of their portfolio companies[82] was less than was optimal in the interests of those on whose behalf the institutions invested. This was, the CLR thought, not only a matter of concern to those investors, but also "a matter of corporate governance, impinging on the properly disciplined and competitive management of British business and industry".[83]

In order to understand the possible reasons for sub-optimal intervention and the reforms which have eventually been adopted, it is instructive to take a specific illustration. Pension funds provide a useful case study, especially as early reform proposals focused in particular upon pension funds, even though, as we shall see, they are not the only significant form of institutional investment. In simplified form,[84] a pension scheme is normally promoted by an employer, who sets up a trust into which both employer and, normally, employees pay regular contributions and out of which pensions are paid.[85] Both the pensioners and the contributing employees may be seen as beneficiaries of the trust. The trustees see to the investment of the contributions, but normally do not discharge that task themselves, but contract it out to one or more specialist fund managers. The fund managers may be freestanding institutions, but, today, they are likely to be part of larger financial groups (for example, investment banks) which offer other services in addition to fund management. The contract between the pension fund and the fund manager is likely to give the manager the right to vote the shares it purchases on behalf of the fund, although the trustees may reserve the right to take voting decisions themselves, either generally or in specific classes of case. Finally, for reasons of both efficiency and prudence, the manager is not likely itself to hold the shares it purchases on behalf of the fund, but to have them held by a separate custodian company, which may well be part of a different group of companies from that in which the fund manager sits.

---

activists rather than in order to protect an investment which has turned out not to perform as expected) and W. Bratton, "Hedge Funds and Governance Targets", ibid., 80/2007.

[79] *Institutional Investment in the United Kingdom: A Review* (London, 2001).

[80] Sir D. Walker, *A Review of Corporate Governance in UK Banks and Other Financial Industry Entities: Final Recommendations* (26 November 2009) at *http://webarchive.nationalarchives.gov.uk/ +/http://www.hm-treasury.gov.uk/d/walker_review_261109.pdf* [Accessed 27 April 2016].

[81] J. Kay, *The Kay Review of UK Equity Markets and Long-Term Decision Making* (July 2012) at *https://www.gov.uk/government/uploads/system/uploads/attachment_data/file/253454/bis-12-917-kay-review-of-equity-markets-final-report.pdf* [Accessed 30 January 2016].

[82] For example, companies in which the institution has investments.

[83] Final Report I, para.3.54.

[84] More detail can be found in Ch.5 of the Myners Report, above, fn.79.

[85] The fund may promise a certain level of benefits on retirement ("defined benefit" schemes) or only that the pensioner will be entitled to his or her share of the fund at retirement in order to purchase an annuity ("defined contribution" schemes). The distinction, though enormously important for employees in terms of the allocation of investment risk, is not significant for present purposes, though the present trend is firmly away from DB and towards DC. The proposed "activism" obligation (see below) is the same for both types of scheme.

There are three main types of argument which have been put forward to explain **15–26** the under-use by pension funds or, more often, their fund managers of the corporate governance rights which the law gives them: conflicts of interest; a desire for a quiet life; and technical difficulties of voting.

Conflicts of interest and inactivity

Conflicts of interest arise mainly where the group of which the fund manager is **15–27** part provides other financial services to corporate clients. The management of a portfolio company may be unwilling to buy, or continue to buy, these other financial services, for example in connection with public share offerings,[86] if some part of the same group is using its corporate governance rights on behalf of a pension fund to make life difficult for that management.[87] Indeed, the management of the portfolio company may actively threaten to withdraw its custom from the group if the intervention on behalf of the pension fund continues. In extreme cases, such conduct may amount to the offence of corruption, but that is likely to be very difficult to prove. After floating a number of proposals, the best the CLR could come up with was a requirement that quoted companies be required to disclose in annual reports the identity of their major suppliers of financial services. This would reveal potential conflicts of interest within financial services groups, though it would not eliminate them nor, by itself, guarantee the appropriate handling of the conflicts.[88]

Inactivity on the part of fund managers may, as we have just seen, result from conflicts of interest, but it may also result, the Myners Report thought,[89] from a lack of incentives for the fund managers to be active, for example, because the costs of intervention would depress the manager's short-term performance whilst the benefits of intervention would be reaped only in the medium term, or because the benefits of intervention would accrue to all shareholders, whether they participated in the intervention or not, including rival fund managers. A similar conclusion can be drawn from the Kay Review, where appropriate intervention was seen as compromised by market-driven short-termism, lack of trust, and the easier risk-reducing options of portfolio diversification and, if called for, "exit" rather than "voice".[90] The CLR's response to Myners' findings was a proposed requirement that managers disclose to trustees their voting record in portfolio companies on demand and a reserve power for the Secretary of State to require the publication of the voting record, so that the beneficiaries of the pension fund would be aware of it as well.[91] This proposal was controversial, to the point where the clauses were removed from the Bill in the House of Lords against the Government's wishes, but were reinstated in the Commons and are now to be

---

[86] See below, Ch.25.

[87] Even a stand-alone fund manager may suffer from conflicts of interest, for example, where it manages the pension fund of a company in which another pension fund under its management is invested.

[88] In any event, the Government was not minded to pursue this particular recommendation: Modernising, para.2.47.

[89] See above, fn.79 at paras 5.83–5.88.

[90] See above, fn.81.

[91] Final Report, I, para.6.39.

found in ss.1277–1280. In line with the CLR's recommendation, the power is one to make regulations, in relation to which the Government said that it was "willing to see how market practice evolves before choosing whether and how to exercise the power".[92] Those regulations may require institutional investors (broadly defined in s.1278) to disclose, either to the public (a particularly controversial point) or specified persons only, information about the exercise or non-exercise of voting rights by the institution or any person acting on its behalf, about the voting instructions given by the institution or person on its behalf and about the delegation of voting functions (s.1280) in relation to shares which are publicly traded and in which the institution has an interest (s.1279).

15–28 The Myners Report was bolder, proposing a substantive obligation, derived from US law, on the fund manager to monitor and attempt to influence the boards of companies where there is a reasonable expectation that such activity would enhance the value of the portfolio investments.[93] This would include, but not be limited to, the exercise of the right to vote at shareholder meetings. This would not amount to an obligation to vote the shares in portfolio companies on each and every occasion. On the one hand, voting on routine proposals might be neither here nor there in corporate governance terms; on the other, merely to vote might be an inadequate form of intervention, if, for example, a private meeting with the management might solve the problem at an earlier stage and avoid an adverse vote.

Of course, it is strongly arguable that the fiduciary duties of pension fund trustees already require them to exercise their corporate governance rights actively if they judge that this will enhance the value of the trust's assets and, therefore, to secure that a similar obligation is laid upon those to whom they contract out the exercise of their corporate governance rights. However, it may be very difficult to show that any particular piece of inaction or even a course of inaction over a period of time reduced the value of the trust's assets.

The Myners Report did not propose the embodiment of these rules in legislation, but only in voluntary Statements of Investment Principles, which the fund management industry was to observe on a "comply or explain" basis,[94] with the threat of legal regulation if voluntarism did not work. The Government, however, committed itself to legislation on the point,[95] but, for the time being, this has now been overtaken by the more general UK Stewardship Code,[96] discussed below, derived in large part from the voluntary code of practice adopted by a wide range of institutional investors (not just pension funds) in response to the Myners Report,[97] and now further strengthened in response to the Kay Review.[98]

---

[92] HL Debs, vol. 682, col. 787, 23 May 2006 (Lord Sainsbury).

[93] See above, fn.79 at para.5.89.

[94] See para.14–69.

[95] HM Treasury and Department for Work and Pensions, *Myners Review: The Government's Response*, para.11.

[96] *https://www.frc.org.uk/Our-Work/Publications/Corporate-Governance/UK-Stewardship-Code-September-2012.pdf* [Accessed 28 April 2016], as revised in September 2012.

[97] Institutional Shareholders' Committee, *The Responsibilities of Institutional Shareholders and Agents—Statement of Principles* (2002). In December 2004 the Treasury published *Myners principles*

"Fiduciary investors"

The generation of an obligation of activism in the case of pension funds takes as **15–29** its starting point, as we have seen, the fact that the trustees of pension funds owe fiduciary obligations to the beneficiaries of the fund.[99] However, outside pension fund trust structures, the relationship between investors and those who invest the money on their behalf is not usually a fiduciary one. For example, the relationship between investors and insurance companies, which are as important as pension funds in the collective investment area, is predominantly contractual. Insurance companies also play an important role in the provision of pensions, especially to those who are not part of occupational schemes, although the Myners Report made no recommendations about the activism responsibilities of insurance companies.[100]

If the value of investments will be increased by voting, or other forms of exercise of their governance rights, by institutional shareholders, it is difficult to see why this should not be required of all intermediaries, whether established as trusts or not, which acquire funds on the basis that they can manage them more effectively on behalf of investors than the investors can themselves. Indeed it was just this suggestion which the Kay Review advanced, suggesting that all intermediaries in the investment chain should be subject to fiduciary obligations in the performance of their functions.[101] However, the Law Commission, when asked to look into the possibility, came down strongly against such a rule, suggesting that it would add further confusion to an area of law which was not easily transposed to these different circumstances. Moreover, although there was a clear need for the enhanced protection of investors, the Law Commission also concluded that alternative routes, such as statutory enhancement of the provisions in FSMA s.138D to give private investors direct claims against intermediaries, were equally unworkable, especially given the potential for indeterminate liability to an indeterminate class of claimants.[102]

In short, although the objective is clear, and conceded by many to be valuable, the means of achieving it is fraught. In that climate, the task has fallen to the UK Stewardship Code, which applies—currently on a voluntary basis—to all institutional investors, whether pension funds or not, as does the reserve disclosure power contained in the 2006 Act. That regime is considered next.

---

for institutional investment decision-making: review of progress, concluding that progress had been made, that more needed to be done but that legislation was not required at that stage.

[98] See above, fn.81. Also see the Government's *Implementation of the Kay Review: Progress Report* (October 2014) at *https://www.gov.uk/government/uploads/system/uploads/attachment_data/file/367070/bis-14-1157-implementation-of-the-kay-review-progress-report.pdf* [Accessed 30 January 2016].

[99] Though the Myners Committee seems to have forgotten this for it proposed to impose its obligation on the fund managers only. The mistake was corrected by the Government: see above, fn.93, para.60.

[100] See above, fn.79, Ch.9.

[101] See above, fn.81, Recommendation 7.

[102] Law Commission, *Fiduciary Duties of Investment Intermediaries* (Law Com No.350, June 2014), especially paras 11.10–11.33, at *https://www.gov.uk/government/uploads/system/uploads/attachment_data/file/325508/41342_HC_368_LC350_accessible.pdf* [Accessed 30 January 2016].

The UK Stewardship Code

15–30   Given the UK's success with "soft law", it was perhaps inevitable that this would be the outcome here, and in 2010 the UK Stewardship Code, now revised, was promulgated by the FRC, applying, like the UK Corporate Governance Code, on a "comply or explain" basis.[103] The Code is addressed in the first instance to fund managers—that is, firms who manage assets on behalf of institutional shareholders such as pension funds, insurance companies, investment trusts and other collective investment vehicles.[104] It sets out good practice on engagement with investee companies, with the goal of helping to improve long-term returns to shareholders and the efficient exercise of governance responsibilities. The FRC expects firms subject to the Code to disclose on their websites how they have applied the Code. However, the responsibility for monitoring company performance does not rest with fund managers alone, and to that end the Code refers to "institutional investors" generally, and the FRC strongly encourages all institutional investors to report if and how they have complied with the Code. For example, pension fund trustees and other owners can comply directly, or indirectly through the mandates given to fund managers.[105]

The Code adopts a similar format to the UK Corporate Governance Code: it sets out seven Main Principles, each with supporting Guidance elaborating best practice. It indicates that institutional investors should:

1.   Publicly disclose their policy on how they will discharge their stewardship responsibilities (Principle 1) and robustly manage any conflicts of interest (Principle 2). "Stewardship activities" are widely defined to include "monitoring and engaging with companies on matters such as strategy, performance, risk, capital structure, and corporate governance, including culture and remuneration. Engagement is purposeful dialogue with companies on those matters as well as on issues that are the immediate subject of votes at general meetings" (Principle 1, Guidance).

2.   Effectively monitor their investee companies (Principle 3), including keeping abreast of the business and its general concerns, appraising their board and committee structures (especially in the light of any departures from the UK Corporate Governance Code), meeting the chairman and directors, and, where appropriate and practicable, attending general meetings of the companies in which they have a major holding and maintaining an audit trail of their formal and informal interventions.

3.   Establish clear guidelines on when and how they will escalate their stewardship activities, privately or publicly (Principle 4).

---

[103] FRC, *The UK Stewardship Code*, 2012, *https://www.frc.org.uk/Our-Work/Publications/Corporate-Governance/UK-Stewardship-Code-September-2012.pdf* [Accessed 28 April 2016]. These principles are similar to those adopted by the ISC (above, fn.97), and in Europe by the European Fund and Asset Management Association, *EFAMA Code for External Governance: Principles for the exercise of ownership rights in investee companies*, 2011, *http://www.ecgi.org/codes/code.php?code_id=336* [Accessed 28 April 2016].

[104] FSA, Conduct of Business Sourcebook COBS 2.2.3 (presumably to become the FCA rule).

[105] But for a critical assessment of the likely impact, see B. Cheffins, "The Stewardship Code's Achilles' Heel" (2010) 73 M.L.R. 1004. For its proposed broader 2012 application, see above fn.98.

4.   Be willing to act collectively with other investors where appropriate (Principle 5).

5.   Have a clear policy on voting and disclosure of voting activity, seeking generally to vote all shares held and not automatically to support the board (Principle 6).

6.   Report periodically on their stewardship and voting activities, maintaining a clear record of their activities (Principle 7).

While the ambition is clear, it is also evident from the FRC's own assessment of progress that there is still some way to go in enticing greater participation, encouraging closer adherence to best practice, and ensuring more informative reporting generally.[106] Perhaps as a result, the FRC has now adopted a policy of public assessment of Code signatories as either "Tier 1" (where reporting expectations are met), or "Tier 2" (where they are not).[107] This strategy of rewarding success (or naming and shaming failure) is designed to apply market pressure to resolve the problem.

The role of indirect investors

Under the typical arrangement for pension funds, described above, the shares in the portfolio company are held by a custodian company. That custodian company will appear on the portfolio company's share register as the holder of the shares, even though it holds them as a nominee, either for the fund manager or for the pension fund. Clearly, the custodian has no interest in voting the shares in question. Rather, the law is that, if the custodian is a bare nominee for a beneficial owner, the beneficial owner can instruct the nominee how to deal with the shares.[108] In order to bring this about, however, the custodian must confer with the fund manager and, perhaps, through the fund manager with the trustees. However, the registered holder is not placed under any obligation by company law to engage in this process, which, in any event, may not prove to be possible within the notice period for the meeting,[109] though there may be contractual arrangements in place between the member and others with an interest in the shares which require this consultation. It can be argued that this process would operate more smoothly if the company communicated directly with the beneficial owner or, going further, if the governance rights attached to the shares could be exercised by the beneficial (or "indirect") owner. **15–31**

The CLR proposed to remove any impediments which existed to the creation of contractual arrangements for giving non-members an input into the exercise of **15–32**

---

[106] See FRC, *Developments in Corporate Governance and Stewardship 2015*, at *https://www.frc.org. uk/Our-Work/Publications/Corporate-Governance/Developments-in-Corporate-Governance-and-Stewa-%281%29.pdf* [Accessed 30 January 2016].

[107] The system has a start date of July 2016: *https://www.frc.org.uk/News-and-Events/FRC-Press/ Press/2015/December/FRC-promotes-improved-reporting-by-signatories-to.aspx* [Accessed 6 February 2016].

[108] *Kirby v Wilkins* [1929] 2 Ch. 444. If the nominee votes the shares without instructions, that right must be exercised in the interests of the beneficiary.

[109] See below, para.15–61.

the governance rights attached to the shares, together with a fall-back power for the Government to require such transfers of governance rights if contractual arrangements did not continue to develop on an adequate scale.[110] The Companies Bill followed this formula but in the debates in Parliament the position of institutional investors was linked to that of many private investors who also hold shares through nominee accounts, partly as a result of the dematerialisation of shares and partly because government tax relief on private investment is often available only in relation to shares held in this way.[111] Thus, the governance rights of indirect investors became a politically much more significant matter than had been initially anticipated. The Government's fall-back proposals were defeated in the Lords.[112] The Government then consulted with those affected on alternative provisions, which contain an element of compulsion, and still have a significant fall-back element. They were introduced at a very late stage in the parliamentary process and received little debate.[113]

15–33   The reforms now contained in Pt 9 fall into two groups. As recommended by the CLR, some are purely facultative. They help companies to reassign governance rights to indirect shareholders, but do not require it. These provisions apply to all companies. The other group contains the element of compulsion, which at present relates only to shareholders' information rights in companies whose securities are traded on a regulated market, in effect the Main Market of the London Stock Exchange.[114] However, the Secretary of State has power by regulation to expand the scope of this second class of provisions so as to expand the rights provided or the types of company covered by the Act.[115]

Governance rights—voluntary transfer arrangements for all companies

15–34   Turning first to the facultative provisions applying to all companies, the view was taken in some quarters that s.126,[116] by providing that "no notice of any trust shall be entered on the register [of members] or be receivable by the registrar",[117] and a parallel provision in the articles dealing with the position of the company,[118] prevented the transfer of governance rights between the company and the holders of the beneficial interests in the shares. The CLR proposed that, if this was so, what is now s.126 be amended so as to make clear that it permits the transfer of corporate governance rights to third parties.[119] Such transfers would

---

[110] Final Report I, paras 7.1–7.4.
[111] See para.27–12.
[112] HL Debs, vol. 681, cols. 813 et seq., 9 May 2006.
[113] HC Debs, Standing Committee D, Twenty First Sitting, cols. 875 et seq., 21 July 2006.
[114] For the meaning of a "regulated market" see para.25–8.
[115] 2006 Act s.151. The regulations are subject to affirmative resolution by Parliament.
[116] The register of members is discussed below, at para.27–16.
[117] This section does not apply in Scotland.
[118] Thus art.45 of the model set of articles for public companies: "Except as required by law, no person shall be recognised by the company as holding any share upon any trust, and except as otherwise required by law or the articles, the company is not in any way to be bound by or recognise any interest in a share other than the holder's absolute ownership of it and all the rights attaching to it".
[119] Completing, paras 5.2–5.12 and Final Report I, paras 7.3–7.4.

not be compulsory, but were to be left to contractual arrangements between those holding shares on behalf of others and the persons on whose behalf the shares were held.

The drafters of the Act clearly took the view that s.126 was not an impediment to the transfer of governance rights, for it does not deal with the issue. However, s.145(1) is drafted on the basis that a company in its articles may (and always has been able to) make provision enabling a member to nominate another person to enjoy all or any of the governance rights of the member in relation to the company. That other person need not in fact be the holder of the beneficial interest in the shares, so that, for example, a custodian could nominate a fund manager as entitled to vote the shares, even though the beneficial interest is held by the pension trust. The person to whom the rights are transferred is the "nominated person".[120]

15–35

The section does not in any way require such a transfer of governance rights to be made. Its purpose rather is to ensure that the statutory provisions discussed below in relation to meetings (and, indeed, those discussed above in relation to written resolutions) work properly where contractual governance rights are held by a nominated person. In other words, where rights under the articles are transferred to a nominated person, so are the linked statutory rights. A good example is the right to vote. As we have seen above,[121] voting rights in a company are not allocated by the statute but by the company, normally through its articles. If the articles permit or require[122] those voting rights to be transferred to a nominated person and the right to vote is so transferred by a particular member, then s.145(3)(f) ensures that the statutory right to appoint a proxy to vote at the meeting on behalf of the voter[123] is also transferred to the nominated person.

15–36

Precisely which statutory rights are transferred under the section to a nominated person will depend upon which contractual rights have been transferred to the nominated person under the articles. The section potentially transfers eight statutory rights,[124] but operates only "so far as necessary to give effect to" a transfer of rights effected under the company's articles.[125] Where the right to vote is transferred, it seems that most of the listed statutory rights will also be transferred. Even so, if the company is a public company, the rights in relation to written resolutions will not be transferred and if the company is a

---

[120] An obvious, but perhaps potentially confusing, term to employ, since the nominator will often be a nominee shareholder! Any custodian of relevant shares may use the power, whether in a pension-fund context or otherwise.

[121] At para.15–4.

[122] Although the section is permissive as to the adoption of "transfer" articles by the company, there seems no reason why the articles should not be mandatory as against the member in appropriate cases.

[123] On proxies see below, para.15–67.

[124] The rights to be sent a proposed written resolution; to require circulation of a written resolution; to require directors to call a general meeting; to require notice of a general meeting; to require circulation of a statement; to appoint a proxy; to require circulation of a resolution for the AGM of a public company; to be sent the annual report and accounts. And, in addition, in relation to "traded companies" (defined in s.360C), the right to ask questions at a meeting; and the power to include matters in the business dealt with at the AGM.

[125] 2006 Act s.145(2).

private company, the right to propose a resolution at an AGM will not be transferred, since these rights are specific to private or public companies.[126]

If the linked statutory right is transferred to the nominated person, then anything the member might have done may instead be done by the nominated person and any duty owed by the company to the member is owed instead to the nominated person.[127] Thus, there is a genuine transfer of statutory powers and rights to the nominated person and away from the member, not the creation of a parallel set of provisions. However, no rights enforceable against the company by anyone other than the member are so created by the section *or* by the provisions in the articles creating the transfer system.[128] In fact, the primary sanction for many of the rights covered by the section is a criminal one, to which this provision is irrelevant, but civil rights could arise also, for example, to challenge the validity of a resolution because of an inaccuracy in the circular sent out in support of it.[129] Although the section is not absolutely crystal clear on the point, presumably its implication is that the right of the member to enforce a right against the company is not affected by the fact that the right has been transferred to a nominated person. To hold otherwise would mean a reduction in the enforceability of members' rights where there was a transfer to a nominated person.

15–37   Whether s.145 will mean much in practice will depend on the willingness of companies to adopt articles permitting or requiring the transfer of governance rights, that of nominee shareholding organisations to exercise the power of transfer (if it is permissive) and that of beneficial shareholders to put pressure on nominee shareholders to transfer rights to them and to pay for any associated costs.[130]

15–38   A further piece of apparent facilitation is to be found in s.152. This makes it clear that a member of a company holding shares on behalf of more than one person (as will typically be the case with nominees, whether they hold on behalf, ultimately,

---

[126] 2006 Act s.145(4)(b) makes it clear that the section does not affect the requirements relating to the transfer of the shares themselves.

[127] 2006 Act s.145 (2).

[128] 2006 Act s.145(4)(a). Thus, the articles may not confer enforceable rights on third parties, even if the company wishes to do so, a somewhat strange restriction. This was tested in *In re DNick Holding Plc* [2014] Ch. 196, where the claimants, being the ultimate economic owners of certain beneficial interests in the ordinary shares, applied for relief under s.98 in respect of a special resolution for re-registration as a private company. Norris J held that they were not "holders" of the shares and therefore had no standing to make an application under s.98. Moreover, s.145 could not be read as conferring rights enforceable against the company on anyone other than the registered members: the section does not mean that "if the effective exercise of the transferred right produces a result that is not to the taste of the nominated person then the nominated person can, in order to bring about his desired outcome, himself use any of the provisions of the 2006 Act available to the transferring member" at [29]. Norris J however recognised that this result would "deprive the claimants as indirect investors of the sort of protection which those who formulated the 2006 Act thought ought to be extended to minority shareholders. That is not a particularly comfortable conclusion at which to arrive: but I consider that I would have to embark upon…an 'impermissible form of judicial legislation' to reach any other conclusion" at [31].

[129] See below, para.15–65.

[130] For an excellent survey of practice as of a few years ago and proposals for reform going beyond what the CLR recommended, see R.C. Nolan, "Indirect Investors: A Greater Say in the Company?" (2003) 3 J.C.L.S. 73.

of institutional or private investors) need not exercise all the shareholders' rights (whether given under the contract of issue or provided by statute) in the same way—nor indeed need all of them be exercised on any particular occasion. Thus, the holder is enabled to give effect to the different views which the various beneficial owners may hold on the issue in question. It is doubtful whether this provision changes the previous law, although it can create its own problems.[131] What may be new, therefore, is the further provision that, if the member exercising its rights does not inform the company that not all the rights are being exercised or that some are being exercised in one way and some in another, the company is entitled to assume that all are being exercised and all in the same way.[132] Thus, this section may be more protective of the company than anything else.

An example of this form of governance contract can be found in some companies in relation to "American Depositary Receipts" ("ADRs"). A UK company acquiring a US company in a share exchange deal may not wish to issue its shares directly to the US investors, partly in order to avoid some of the complications of US securities laws and partly in order to give the US investors a security denominated in dollars. One way of achieving these consequences is the ADR, the shares being issued to a depositary institution, which in turn issues to the US investors a "depositary receipt"—one for each share—denominated in dollars, which becomes the security which is traded in the US. In some cases, the company's articles may then require the depositary institution to appoint the ADR holder as its proxy,[133] possibly just for voting purposes but possibly for all governance purposes, including the receipt of communications from the company.[134] In such a case, one sees the company using its contracting power through the articles, as facilitated by s.145, to overcome the limitations of reliance on mere conferment of information rights (which are considered below). However, there is no legal obligation upon companies to treat the holders of ADRs in this way.

15–39

Information rights—mandatory transfer options in traded companies

A member of a company whose shares are admitted to trading on a regulated market may nominate another person to enjoy those information rights, whether the company has provided in its articles for this to happen or not. This means that the rules on transfer of information rights are mandatory as against listed companies, although of course it is not mandatory for the shareholder to confer this right on someone else. Further, the rights conferred upon the other person do

15–40

---

[131] In *In re DNick Holding Plc* [2014] Ch. 196, it was noted obiter that the right of a nominee to vote both for and against particular resolutions under s.152(1) created problems, since then—for the purposes of s.98—the registered holder was "a person who has consented to or voted in favour of the resolution", and so had no standing to complain despite the partial dissenting vote [32].

[132] 2006 Act s.152(2)–(4). The provision does not specifically require the company's assumption to be a reasonable one, although the assumption only arises when the member does not inform the company otherwise, and presumably the company will need to determine this in a reasonable manner.

[133] Such provisions also prevent the depositary institution becoming a significant holder of voting rights at the company's meetings.

[134] Nolan, above, fn.130, analyses such a set of provisions in the articles of BP.

not deprive the nominating shareholder of his or her right to the same information.[135] The fact that the provisions are mandatory as against the company and increase, at least marginally, the company's costs in relation to the circulation of information was a strong argument in the Government's eyes against introducing them, and the provisions are crafted so far as possible to reduce those costs. Those costs are confined to the largest companies because the provisions, at present, apply only to companies listed on a regulated market.[136] However, there are a number of other provisions which aim to cut down the cost implications of the new rule, even for these large companies.

First, the right to nominate a recipient of information rights is restricted to those members who hold shares on behalf of another person and where the recipient is that other person.[137] Secondly, the only rights which may thus be conferred are "information rights", i.e. essentially the right to receive the communications which a company sends to its members (including its annual accounts and reports) or any class of them which includes the nominating shareholder.[138] No other governance rights may be transferred compulsorily as against the company. Thirdly, a company need not accept the conferment of only some of the shareholder's information rights.[139] The company can thus insist on an "all or nothing" conferment of information rights. Fourthly, unless the shareholder, on behalf of the nominated person, requests circulation in hard copy and provides the company with an address, the company may meet its obligation to the nominated person through website publication.[140] Fifthly, all nominations are suspended when there are more nominations in force than the nominator has shares in the company, so that the burden of sorting out the errors is moved away from the company.[141] Sixthly, the company may enquire of a nominated person once every 12 months whether it wishes to retain information rights and the nomination will cease if the company does not receive a positive response within 28 days. Seventhly, to relieve the company of the burden of staying on top of things, if the nomination is terminated or suspended for any reason,[142] the company may continue to abide by it "to such extent or for such period as it

---

[135] 2006 Act s.150(5)(a).

[136] 2006 Act s.146(1). That regulated market may be located in any Member State but the company must be one subject to the domestic companies legislation. In other words, a company registered in any jurisdiction of the UK will not escape this obligation by listing on a regulated market in, for example, France or Germany, but a company incorporated in Germany and listed on a regulated market in the UK will not be subject to the obligation.

[137] 2006 Act s.146(2). As we saw above, s.145 is not restricted in this way, though the articles are most likely to provide for transfers of rights in such a case.

[138] 2006 Act s.146(3)(a),(4). Rights to require copies of the accounts and reports or to require hard copies of documents are also included within the notion of "information rights": s.146(3)(b).

[139] 2006 Act s.146(5).

[140] 2006 Act s.147. The right to request hard copy will also give way if the company has adopted electronic communication as its way of communicating with its members generally: s.147(4) and see below, para.15–85.

[141] 2006 Act s.148(6). Section 148(7) deals with the class right variation of this problem.

[142] Besides the two situations just described, the nomination will be terminated at the request of the member or nominated person, and will cease to have effect on the death or bankruptcy of an individual or the dissolution or the making of a winding-up order of a corporate shareholder: s.148(2)–(4).

thinks fit".[143] Eighthly, the rights conferred upon the nominated person are enforceable only by the member, the rights to be treated for this purpose as if they were conferred by the company's articles.[144]

The right to enjoy information rights is thus, it may be said, rather grudgingly conferred. The main non-restrictive provision is the one which tracks s.145 and provides that any enactment or anything in the company's articles relating to communications with members has corresponding effect in relation to communications with nominated persons.[145]

The compulsory information provisions discussed above do not in any way touch on the relationship between the nominated person and the member after the information has been received. As we have seen above, the nominated person, having received notice of a meeting, for example, has power to instruct the member how to vote, if the member holds the share on a bare trust for the nominated person.[146] But there is no legal obligation upon the member, in this case or more generally, to seek the views of the nominated person before voting, in the absence of an instruction, contrary to the position in some other legal systems. Such an obligation may be created by contract, however, either between the nominated person and the member or, conceivably, between the company and the member. This is then a governance issue, as discussed earlier.

15–41

THE MECHANICS OF MEETINGS

We turn now to the various issues arising where a meeting is sought to be held, so that resolutions of the shareholders can be voted upon. This is the only method s.281 provides for the adoption of resolutions by public companies and it is open to private companies to use it instead of the written resolution method, which it may wish to do where it has a large shareholding body. These issues appear in their sharpest form where a group of shareholders wish to use the shareholders' meeting to challenge some aspect of the management of the incumbent directors. Therefore, we shall generally adopt this perspective in our analysis of the rules, though, of course, those rules may also be relevant in the more usual case where the meeting is called by the board to discuss a matter which the shareholders find relatively uncontentious.

15–42

What happens at meetings?

It is a rare shareholders' meeting which does not end up passing a resolution on some matter or another. As we saw in Ch.14, the Act requires the shareholders' consent before certain decisions can bind the company, and the articles may add to that list. By assenting to a resolution the shareholders give the consent which is necessary to make the act an act of the company. Once the shareholders have adopted an effective resolution on a particular matter, the board is empowered,

15–43

---

[143] 2006 Act s.148(8).
[144] 2006 Act s.150(2).
[145] 2006 Act s.150(3)—and even that provision is subject to qualifications in s.150(4).
[146] Above, fn.108.

and normally obliged, to take the necessary steps to put the resolution into effect. Some decisions are routinely required of shareholders, even especially important ones such as the re-appointment of directors[147] or of auditors[148] or the granting of powers to directors to issue a certain amount of shares without pre-emption rights.[149] Others occur irregularly. However, the business of general meetings does not consist entirely of the consideration of proposals for resolutions. For example, the Act requires the annual reports and accounts to be laid before the company in general meeting,[150] but does not require the meeting to consider any resolution in relation to them. The exercise is not pointless, however, because it gives the shareholders an opportunity to question the board generally on the progress of the company and to express their views on the matter. Often, this item on the agenda provides the opportunity for a wide-ranging debate which specific resolutions would not permit. Indeed, there is no reason why an item should not be placed on the agenda simply for the purposes of having a debate, without any resolution being proposed. Nevertheless, apart for the consideration of the annual reports and accounts, it is the consideration of resolutions with which the general meetings of the shareholders largely deal.

Types of resolution

15–44   For decisions required under the 2006 Act, the Act has reduced the types of resolution which the members may take to two: an ordinary resolution and a special resolution.[151] Usually the Act specifies which type is required, and the Act then governs, but where the Act is silent about the type of resolution required, then an ordinary resolution is required unless the articles specify a higher level of approval, up to and including unanimity.[152] An ordinary resolution is one passed by a simple majority of those voting.[153] A special resolution is one passed by a three-fourths majority,[154] and the notice of the meeting must specify the intention to propose the resolution as a special resolution.[155] For example, special resolutions are required before important constitutional changes can be undertaken. The higher majority required for special resolutions obviously constitutes a form of minority protection, as compared with the simple majority required for an ordinary resolution. It means, for example, that a person with more than 25 per cent of the votes, and indeed in practice often with many fewer votes, can block the adoption of a special resolution.[156]

---

[147] See above, para.14–23.
[148] See below, para.22–17.
[149] See below, para.24–10.
[150] See below, para.21–42.
[151] 2006 Act ss.282 (ordinary resolutions) and 283 (special resolutions).
[152] 2006 Act s.281(3).
[153] 2006 Act s.282.
[154] 2006 Act s.283. Confusingly, this was previously the definition of an extraordinary resolution, a special resolution being one for which a "special" notice period was required. Thus, in effect, the category of special resolution has been abolished and the extraordinary resolution re-named a special resolution.
[155] 2006 Act s.283(6). And include the text of the proposed special resolution. In the case of a written resolution the text of the resolution must state that it is proposed as a special resolution (s.283(3)).
[156] See further, Ch.19, below.

This s.282 definition of an ordinary resolution has had the (seemingly unintended[157]) effect, according to the government,[158] of making void an ordinary resolution passed at a company meeting by use of the casting vote of the chairman. This mechanism was routinely inserted in company articles to save general meeting resolutions from deadlock,[159] and has appeared in all the earlier versions of the Table A model articles, although not in the 2006 model articles. In response to adverse reaction, the government enacted a saving provision allowing those companies which had such a provision in their articles prior to 1 October 2007 to continue with it, or to revert to it if they had removed it (assuming it was ineffective).[160] This limited saving means that for all other companies the chairman's casting vote in shareholder meetings is abolished. There might be good reasons of shareholder democracy for outlawing this practice, although this instance would surely rank as a minor target. Indeed, it might be wondered whether s.282 does render this practice invalid: the section would clearly embrace as valid a resolution passed as a result of weighted voting rights given in the articles to a director in defined circumstances[161]; there seems little dividing such a case from that of the chairman's casting vote, except possibly an assumption that the chairman is a member, entitled to vote at the shareholders' meeting (an assumption which generally holds true).

As we shall see below, many votes at meetings are taken on a show of hands, and may never proceed further if no one challenges the result. The statute facilitates the continued use of such votes, though they are controversial, by providing that the majorities are then to be calculated by reference to the individuals entitled to and actually voting, rather than to the votes attached to their shares.[162] By contrast, if a poll[163] is demanded, then the requisite majority on a poll is that of the votes attached to the shares voted by members entitled to vote and actually voting either in person or by proxy, where proxy voting is allowed.[164] In the case of a meeting of a class of shareholders, where the same rules apply, this means the appropriate majority is of the votes of the class in question.[165]

15–45

For decisions other than those specified in the Act, the company's articles may make their own specific provision for the required voting entitlements and

15–46

---

[157] Since early versions of the model articles included provision for the chairman's casting vote.

[158] Please see *http://www.bis.gov.uk/policies/business-law/company-and-partnership-law/company-law/company-law-faqs/resolutions-and-meetings#8* [Accessed 31 January 2016].

[159] And still appears in the model articles in relation to directors' meetings: art.13 (private companies) and art.14 (public companies).

[160] SI 2007/3495 Sch.5 para.2(1) and (5). But note that this exemption does not apply to traded companies: SI 2007/2194 Sch.3 para.23A(4), inserted by SI 2009/1632 reg.22.

[161] See *Bushell v Faith* [1970] A.C. 1099.

[162] 2006 Act ss.282(3) and 283(4). On a show of hands, it is not known how many shares each voter represents.

[163] On a poll the votes attached to the shares are counted (see below, para.15–75) so that a single shareholder with 100 shares will outvote 99 shareholders with one vote each.

[164] 2006 Act ss.282(4) and 283(5). On proxy voting see below, para.15–67.

[165] 2006 Act s.281(1) and (2) make it clear that the same rules apply to voting at class meetings.

majorities, requiring higher, lower, weighted or even conditional (for example, conditional on the consent of a nominated person) voting requirements.[166]

Wording and notice of proposed resolutions

15–47   In order for shareholders to decide whether to attend meetings and vote, they will need to receive notice of the meeting and of "the general nature of the business to be dealt with".[167] A resolution is only validly passed if the proper notice has been given and the meeting is conducted according to the rules in the Act and the company's articles.[168] The Act adds protections. If special notice of any resolution has to be given (as is sometimes specified in the Act or the articles), then notice of "it" or "any such resolution" must be given to the company at least 28 days before the meeting.[169] Section 283(6) imposes even stricter rules for special resolutions, reflecting their more serious nature, requiring that "the resolution is not a special resolution unless the notice of the meeting included the text of the resolution and specified the intention to propose the resolution as a special resolution", and, further, that "if the notice of the meeting so specified, the resolution may only be passed as a special resolution".

All of this is clearly intended to protect those who decide not to attend the meeting, even more so than those who do attend.[170] The question then arises as to whether the meeting can vary in any way the resolution which is proposed to be passed. This, one might have supposed, would be entirely legitimate so long as the amendment was not such as to take the resolution beyond the scope of the business notified to the members in the notice of the meeting. Instead, however, the rules developed by the courts, and now reflected in both the Act and the model articles for public companies (those for private companies are silent), are far stricter in relation to special resolutions. The model articles for public companies, in art.40, allow amendments by ordinary resolution in limited circumstances: an ordinary resolution can be amended if proposed by a member and "the proposed amendment does not, in the reasonable opinion of the chairman of the meeting, materially alter the scope of the resolution" (art.40(1)(b)); while a special resolution can only be amended if the chairman so proposes and "the amendment does not go beyond what is necessary to correct a grammatical or other non-substantive error in the resolution" (art.40(2)(b)).

The potential impact of these provisions is readily illustrated by the decision of Slade J in *Re Moorgate Mercantile Holdings Ltd*,[171] from which the statutory

---

[166] For an interesting discussion on the construction of the company's bespoke article on voting entitlement and how this interacts with the corresponding Model Article regulation, see *Sugarman v CJS Investments LLP* [2014] EWCA Civ 1239 CA at [28]–[40] (Floyd LJ) and [45]–[50] (Briggs LJ).

[167] 2006 Act s.311(2), and see below, para.15–65.

[168] 2006 Act s.301.

[169] 2006 Act s.312.

[170] *Tiessen v Henderson* [1899] 1 Ch. 861, 866–7 and 870–1 (Kekewich J) recognises this as part of the purpose of notice rules.

[171] *Re Moorgate Mercantile Holdings Ltd* [1980] 1 W.L.R. 227. The case concerned the confirmation of a special resolution reducing the company's share premium account which had been "lost". The notice of the meeting proposed that the whole of it (£1,356,900.48) "be cancelled". Before the meeting was held it was realised that £327.17 resulting from a recent share issue could not be said yet to have been "lost". Accordingly, at the meeting the resolution was amended and it was resolved that

and model article rules are clearly derived. This case suggests that, in relation to special resolutions, no amendment can be made if it in any way alters the substance of the resolution as set out in the notice. Grammatical and clerical errors may be corrected, or words translated into more formal language, and, if the precise text of the resolution was not included in the notice,[172] it may be converted into a formal resolution, provided always that there is no departure whatever from the substance as stated in the notice.[173]

The learned judge thought that his decision was desirable on policy grounds,[174] as well as being demanded by the terms of the Act,[175] and that it would prevent the substantial embarrassment to the chairman of the meeting and to any persons holding "two-way" proxies on behalf of absent members,[176] that any less strict rule would cause. Slade J emphasised that his decision had no relevance to ordinary resolutions and that in relation to them the criteria for permissible amendments might well be wider.[177] This is clearly so if the precise terms of the resolution are not set out in the notice but come within a statement of "the general nature of the business to be dealt with at the meeting".[178] But even if the terms of an ordinary resolution are set out in the notice it seems that some amendments may be made at the meeting, and perhaps even that if the chairman refuses to allow a permissible amendment to be moved the resolution will be invalid.[179] It is submitted that an amendment is permissible if, but only if, the amended resolution is such that no member who had made up his mind whether or not to attend and vote and, if he had decided to do so, how he should vote, could reasonably adopt a different attitude to the amended version.[180] The criticisms of that test by Slade J[181] apply equally to an ordinary resolution but it is difficult to find any other test short of applying to ordinary resolutions that applied to special resolutions, i.e. that no amendment of substance, however trivial, may be made. And does the suggested test really face the chairman and two-way proxy-holders with the substantial embarrassments that Slade J foresaw?[182]

---

the share premium account be reduced to £327.17. Confirmation was refused on the ground that the resolution had not been validly passed. But in a later case (Unreported, but see (1991) 12 Co. Law. at 64, 65), where the facts were virtually identical, a reduction was confirmed because the "substance" (i.e. the amount of the reduction) remained unchanged.

[172] As is now in any event required by s.283(6).

[173] *Re Moorgate Mercantile Holdings Ltd* [1980] 1 W.L.R. 227 at 242C.

[174] *Re Moorgate Mercantile Holdings Ltd* [1980] 1 W.L.R. 227 at 242A–243.

[175] Which was worded in terms similar to s.312 rather than the stricter s.283(6).

[176] *Re Moorgate Mercantile Holdings Ltd* [1980] 1 W.L.R. 227 at 243F.

[177] *Re Moorgate Mercantile Holdings Ltd* [1980] 1 W.L.R. 227 at 242H; citing *Betts & Co Ltd v Macnaghten* [1910] 1 Ch. 430.

[178] 2006 Act s.311(2).

[179] *Henderson v Bank of Australasia* (1890) 45 Ch. D. 330 CA. although contrast the explicit provision in the model articles for public companies, art.40(3).

[180] This was the advice given to the chairman in the *Moorgate* case; see [1980] 1 W.L.R. at 230A.

[181] *Re Moorgate Mercantile Holdings Ltd* [1980] 1 W.L.R. 227 at 243D–G.

[182] If the articles say (as did Table A 1985, art.82) that directors' fees shall be such as "the company may by ordinary resolution determine" and the directors give notice of an ordinary resolution to increase the fees by £10,000 p.a., surely a member should be entitled to move an amendment to reduce the increase (though the directors clearly should not be permitted to move an amendment to increase it further)?

There may, nevertheless, be one type of ordinary resolution to which the stricter rule applies. This is when "special notice" of the ordinary resolution is required. Special notice is defined by s.312 as notice to be given to the company by the proposers of the resolution (not by the company to the members in general) and the length of the notice is at least 28 days before the meeting at which the resolution is to be moved. The wording of s.312(1) bears a close resemblance to that considered in *Re Moorgate Mercantile Holdings* and makes it arguable that no amendment of substance, however trivial, can be made to the resolution stated in the special notice. Hence, if, say, special notice has been given of a single resolution to remove all the directors[183] (under s.168) or both of two joint auditors (under s.510), an amendment seeking to exclude from the resolution some or one of them may be impermissible. If so, this seems a regrettable emasculation of such powers as members have (and which the relevant sections were intended to enhance) and also seems unfair to the directors or auditors whom the members may wish to retain.[184] Even where an amendment to an ordinary resolution may be proposed on the above principles, the company's articles may aim to restrict the shareholders' freedom, say, by providing that, where the text is fully set out in the notice of the meeting, the chairman has a discretion not to consider amendments of which at least 48 hours' notice in writing has not been given to the company.

Convening a meeting of the shareholders

15–48 However, in the above discussion of amendments to resolutions we are getting rather ahead of ourselves. No resolution can be debated until there is a meeting. Clearly, therefore, the shareholders' meeting is not of much value as a vehicle of shareholder control if the meeting cannot easily be convened. The law distinguishes between annual general meetings ("AGMs") and any other meeting of the shareholders.[185] The advantage of the former from our perspective is that, in principle, it must be held on a regular annual basis, whereas the Act provides procedures for the convening of other meetings but says nothing about their frequency. Even the AGM is not compulsory if the company is a private one.[186]

Annual general meetings

15–49 The law, rather oddly, whilst requiring the holding of AGMs by public companies and private companies which are traded companies, does not prescribe the business which has to be transacted at the AGM and in particular does not say

---

[183] This seems to be permissible—the singular "director" includes the plural—and s.160 relates only to voting on *appointments*, not to *removals*.

[184] Nor should proxy-holders have any doubts on how they should vote. If instructed to vote for the resolution they would vote against the amendment but, if that was passed, for the amended resolution. If instructed to vote against, they would vote for the amendment but against the resolution as amended. If given a discretion they would exercise it.

[185] The law used to distinguish between AGMs and extraordinary general meetings (EGMs) but the Act no longer uses the latter term, no doubt because in the case of a private company it is the only type of meeting that can be held.

[186] 2006 Act ss.336–340, concerning AGMs, apply only to public companies. See s.336(1).

that the annual directors' report and the accounts must be laid before the AGM[187] or that the directors due for re-election must be considered then. In fact it is normal for these matters to be taken at the AGM, and for the shareholders to have an opportunity to question the directors generally on the company's business and financial position. This customary practice has been encouraged by the UK Corporate Governance Code and its predecessors,[188] which recommends that in Premium Listed companies (i.e. those companies subjected to the requirements of the CGC) "boards should use the AGM to communicate with investors and to encourage their participation".[189]

This is now substantially strengthened by the Act: if there is enough member support,[190] s.338A allows members of traded companies to require the company to add new matters to the agenda of the AGM[191]; and at all general meetings of traded companies, the company must provide answers any question put by a member attending the meeting on any matter relating to the business being dealt with at the meeting.[192] It follows that there now seems to be no limit on the business which may be transacted at an AGM of a traded company, assuming only that it is business properly to be put before the shareholders.[193]

Following the recommendations of the CLR, the timing of the AGM is tied to the company's annual reporting cycle. The AGM must be held yearly within the six-month period (for public companies) or nine-month period (for private traded companies) following its accounting reference date,[194] which determines the beginning and end of its financial year.[195] If a company fails to comply with the requirement to hold an AGM, every officer in default is liable to a fine.[196] This puts pressure on the directors, but the power, previously contained in the

15–50

---

[187] But see s.437, which requires public companies to lay before the company, in a general meeting, copies of its reports and accounts.

[188] See above, para.14–69.

[189] Main Principle E.2. In particular the Code suggests that companies propose a resolution in relation to the report and accounts (Supporting Principle E.2.1). The Code envisages that the company's relationship with institutional investors will take the form of continuing dialogue which will extend beyond the general meeting: Main Principle E.1 and also see UK Stewardship Code, above, para.15–30.

[190] 2008 Act s.338A(3) requires the company "to include such a matter once it has received requests that it do so from—(a) members representing at least 5 per cent of the total voting rights of all the members who have a right to vote at the meeting, or (b) at least 100 members who have a right to vote at the meeting and hold shares in the company on which there has been paid up an average sum, per member, of at least £100." Section 338A(4) and (5) then set out the required format and timing (six weeks' notice, or if later, the time at which notice is given of the meeting).

[191] 2006 Act s.338A(1), and any matters may properly be added unless they are defamatory of any person or frivolous or vexatious (s.338A(2)).

[192] 2006 Act s.319A(1), with s.319A(2) relaxing the requirement slightly by providing that no such answer need be given: "(a) if to do so would—(i) interfere unduly with the preparation for the meeting, or (ii) involve the disclosure of confidential information; (b) if the answer has already been given on a website in the form of an answer to a question; or (c) if it is undesirable in the interests of the company or the good order of the meeting that the question be answered."

[193] In particular, the fact that a special resolution is required to transact a particular piece of business does not mean that that business cannot be considered at an AGM.

[194] 2006 Act s.336(1) and (1A) respectively.

[195] 2006 Act s.391. See below, para.21–8. Subsection (2) deals with the situation where the company changes, as is permitted, its accounting reference date.

[196] 2006 Act s.336(3),(4).

legislation,[197] for the Secretary of State, on the application of any member, to call or direct the calling of a meeting where the directors had failed to do so has been removed. Thus, the member has no direct and easy way of securing compliance with the AGM requirement, but must rely on the indirect impact of the criminal sanctions.

Other general meetings

15–51   As for the convening of meetings other than the AGM of a public company, such meetings are not required at any specific time. The board may convene a meeting of the members of a private or public company at any time.[198] And the Act provides that the directors must convene a meeting on the requisition of holders of not less than five per cent of the paid-up capital carrying voting rights.[199] The request must state the general nature of the business to be dealt with at the meeting. It may include the text of a resolution intended to be moved at the meeting, which facility the members will normally be well advised to take up.[200] However, the resolution must be one which may be "properly moved" at the meeting and, if it is not, it appears the directors are under no obligation to circulate it.[201]

If the directors fail to convene a meeting within 21 days of the deposit of the requisition, the meeting to be held within a further 28 days of the notice convening it, the requisitionists, or any of them representing more than half of the total voting rights of all of them, may themselves convene the meeting, and their reasonable expenses must be paid by the company and recovered from fees or remuneration payable to the defaulting directors.[202]

These provisions for requisitioning a meeting work reasonably well in private companies and also in public companies where, for example, the co-operation of only two or three institutional shareholders is required to get across the 5 per cent

---

[197] CA 1985 s.367.

[198] 2006 Act s.302.

[199] 2006 Act s.303. In the case of a company without shareholders the threshold is members holding at least one-tenth of the voting rights of the members: s.303(2)(b).

[200] 2006 Act s.303(4). This is because (a) that makes their intentions clearer and (b) if what is proposed is a special resolution, notice of it has to be given to the shareholders (see above, para.15–63). The company must then give the notice to the shareholders required for a special resolution: s.304(4).

[201] The resolution is not "properly moved" if it falls within any of the three categories of resolution which the directors may refuse to circulate as a written resolution: s.303(5) and also see above, para.15–10. For an example of the operation of this principle under the prior legislation see *Rose v McGivern* [1998] 2 B.C.L.C. 593. Here a proposed resolution "to elect a new board of not more than ten members" was held to be ineffective on the grounds that it did not provide for the removal of the existing board and there were otherwise no vacancies to which the ten could be elected (quite apart from the failure to state whether the number was in fact to be ten or some lesser number and to state who the ten were to be). The leaders of the requisition subsequently submitted 25 individual resolutions to the company, removing each of the 16 existing directors and appointing nine new ones, but the company refused to circulate the individual resolutions on the grounds they were too late.

[202] 2006 Act s.305(1),(6),(7). The effect of this is that, if more than 5 per cent requisitioned the meeting, the percentage needed to call a meeting directly is itself increased. The requisitionists may act not only where the directors fail to act in time but also where they fail to include a proposed resolution in the notice of the meeting or fail to give notice of the proposed resolution as a special resolution, if such it is: ss.304(3),(4) and 305(1)(b).

threshold.[203] However, small individual shareholders in public companies are likely to find it a matter of considerable difficulty and expense to enlist the support of a sufficient number of fellow members to be able to make a valid requisition.

The articles may make further provision for the calling of meetings, but they are unlikely to give the members an extensive right to do so, for the management would like nothing better than to be able to call meetings when it suited them, but to be under no obligation to do so when it did not. In fact, the model set of articles for public companies provides for members to convene meetings only where the number of directors falls below two and the remaining director (if any) is unwilling to appoint a further director so as to restore the board's power to act in this area[204]; and no provision for members to convene meetings is made in the model articles for private companies.

15–52

Meetings convened by the court

Finally, s.306(1) gives the court power to convene a meeting "if for any reason it is impracticable to call a meeting in any manner in which meetings of that company may be called or to conduct the meeting in manner prescribed by the articles or this Act". This power may be exercised by the court "of its own motion or on the application—(a) of any director of the company or (b) of any member who would be entitled to vote at the meeting".[205] The meeting can be "called, held and conducted in any manner the court thinks fit" and the "court may give such ancillary or consequential directions as it thinks expedient and these may include a direction that one member of the company present in person or by proxy be deemed to constitute a meeting".[206]

15–53

Most of the litigation brought under this section has revolved around responding to quorum requirements for shareholder meetings. In the absence of a required quorum, no resolution can be effectively passed. In contrast to many other jurisdictions, the quorum requirements set by the British Act are not demanding, except in relation to class[207] meetings: two members only are required for meetings of the shareholders as a whole, unless the company's constitution sets a higher figure,[208] and only one member in the case of a single-member company.[209] It is not even clear that the Act requires the quorum to be present throughout the meeting.[210] However, staying away can in principle be an effective way of preventing a meeting from being held in a private company with only two shareholders. If the board consists of the same two persons (or their

15–54

---

[203] Activist shareholders seeking to obtain changes in the board's policy have made use of it.

[204] Model articles for public companies, art.28.

[205] 2006 Act s.306(2). The section does not make the addition originally proposed of the personal representative of a deceased member of the company who would have had the right to vote at the meeting.

[206] 2006 Act s.306(2)–(4).

[207] See below, para.15–84.

[208] 2006 Act s.318(2).

[209] 2006 Act s.318(1) (in this case, the rule overrides anything to the contrary in the articles).

[210] Table A 1985 art.41 made it clear that this was required. The present model articles revert to ambiguity.

nominees) and also has a quorum requirement of two, the company may become completely deadlocked. The question the courts have had to address is whether the provisions of s.306 can be used to overcome this deadlock.

After a certain amount of litigation in recent years, the position which the courts seem to have reached as to the exercise of their discretion under the section is as follows. In principle, the section is available to break a deadlock created by quorum requirements, because, where the shareholdings are not held equally, the normal principle of majority rule is being frustrated by the quorum requirement.[211] However, it may be that the quorum requirements have been deliberately adopted in order to produce deadlock if the parties cannot agree, and in that case the section should not be used to overrule the parties' agreement. The court is likely to conclude that this is the purpose of the quorum requirement where that takes the form of a class right attached to the shares of one of the parties.[212] Other than that perhaps unusual situation, the question of whether the quorum provision was intended to create deadlock in the case of disagreement is a matter of construction of the articles or shareholders' agreement so as to provide a context for an understanding of the quorum provisions, whether contained in the articles or shareholders' agreement or applied by the Act.[213]

It might be noted that, in future, the quorum requirement will not be effective in private companies in producing deadlock where the shareholdings of the two contestants are not equal (and, of course, the quorum provision is unnecessary if they are). This is because the holder of the majority will be able to secure the passing of at least an ordinary resolution through the written resolution procedure, discussed above, without the need for a meeting. Some different protection in the articles will be required, such as a requirement for the consent of all shareholders to some or all resolutions of the company.

On the other hand, where the court takes the view that the provisions of the articles or the Act are being cynically exploited by a group of shareholders to block an effective meeting, it may exercise its s.306 powers in the broadest way. Thus, in *Re British Union for the Abolition of Vivisection*[214] a company whose articles required personal attendance in order to vote had had a general meeting badly disrupted by a minority of members, and the committee feared that other members would in future be deterred from attending. On an application by a majority of the committee the court ordered that a meeting be held to consider a

---

[211] *Re El Sombrero Ltd* [1958] Ch. 900 where the applicant shareholder held 900 of the company's 1,000 shares, the remaining 100 being held by the two directors whom the applicant wished to remove in exercise of his statutory powers under what is now s.168 and who refused to attend the meeting. The court directed that one member present in person or by proxy should constitute a quorate meeting. See also *Re Opera Photographic Ltd* [1989] 1 W.L.R. 634; *Re Sticky Fingers Restaurant Ltd* [1992] B.C.L.C. 84; and *Smith v Butler* [2012] B.C.C. 645 CA at [49]–[55] (Arden LJ).

[212] *Harman v BML Group Ltd* [1994] 1 W.L.R. 893 CA. On class rights generally see below, para.19–13.

[213] *Ross v Telford* [1998] 1 B.C.L.C. 82 CA; *Union Music Ltd v Watson* [2003] 1 B.C.L.C. 453 CA; *Re Woven Rugs Ltd* [2002] 1 B.C.L.C. 324; *Vectone Entertainment Holding Ltd v South Entertainment Ltd* [2004] 2 B.C.L.C. 224.

[214] *Re British Union for the Abolition of Vivisection* [1995] 2 B.C.L.C. 1. Contrast *Monnington v Easier Plc* [2006] 2 B.C.L.C. 283, where the judge took the view that a meeting to remove a director could be convened and conducted in accordance with the Act, but the result, as a consequence of the drafting of the removal section, would be ineffective. In that case the court had no jurisdiction to use its s.306 power to reform the Act.

resolution for the abolition of the personal attendance rule, at which meeting the personal attendance rule itself would not apply and personal attendance would be permitted only to the members of the company's committee.

What is a meeting?

Thanks to modern technology it is no longer necessary that a meeting should require all those attending to be in the same room. If more turn up than had been foreseen, a valid meeting can still take place if proper arrangements have been made to direct the overflow to other rooms with adequate audio-visual links enabling everyone to participate in the discussion to the same extent as if all had been in the same room.[215] This is now explicitly supported by the Act and model articles.[216] However, a meeting requires two-way, real time communication among all the participants. If relaxation of the real-time requirement is sought, it is necessary for the company, if a private one, to take decisions through the use of written resolutions.[217]

15–55

Getting items onto the agenda and expressing views on agenda items

Rather than going through the process of requisitioning a meeting in order to discuss a particular piece of business, the shareholders may wish simply to add an item to the agenda of a meeting which the board has called in any event. This is most likely to be attractive in relation to the AGM, which, as we have seen, a public company is obliged to hold.

15–56

Placing an item on the agenda

As we have seen, the AGM is normally convened by the board and, as part of that process, the board will be able to stipulate the items which it wishes to have discussed at the meeting. Under s.338 members representing not less than one-twentieth of the total voting rights of the members entitled to vote on the proposed resolution,[218] or 100 members holding shares on which there has been paid up an average sum per shareholder of not less than £100, may require the company to give notice of their resolutions which can then be considered at the next AGM. In a company with a large shareholding body shareholders with small shareholdings may find this second criterion easier to meet than the first, whereas a small number of institutional shareholders (perhaps even one) may be able to meet the first criterion. The second criterion for requiring a resolution to be placed on the agenda has also benefited from the steps which the Act has taken to protect the interests of "indirect" investors, i.e. those who hold their shares

15–57

---

[215] *Byng v London Life Association* [1990] Ch. 170 CA. The Company Law Review proposed that this be made clear in legislation, if there was any doubt about the principle: Final Report, para.7.7.
[216] 2006 Act s.360A; model articles for private companies, art.37, and for public companies, art.29.
[217] See above, para.15–8.
[218] Thus, the section operates on the basis of the distribution of voting rights in the company. Non-voting shares do not count, and multiple voting shares will make the 5 per cent target easier or more difficult to reach according to whether or not their holders support the requisition.

through nominees. Subject to safeguards, the 100 "members" may include those who are not members of the company but whose interest in the shares arises from the fact that a member of the company holds the shares on their behalf in the course of a business and—a very important limitation—the indirect investor has the right to instruct the member how to exercise the voting rights.[219]

However, the company is not bound to give notice of the proposed resolution unless certain conditions are met. First, the standard conditions, discussed above in relation to member's written resolutions, about the effectiveness of the resolution and so on must be met.[220] Secondly, the requisition, identifying the resolution of which notice is to be given, must be received by the company at least six weeks before the AGM or before the company gives notice to the members of the AGM.[221]

The third condition relates to the costs of circulating the resolution. In principle, those requesting the circulation must pay for it (unless the company resolves otherwise).[222] This was the previous law. However, the CLR proposed that members' resolutions received in time to be circulated with the notice of the AGM should be circulated free of charge.[223] The Act does not accept that proposal and makes only the limited concession that circulation shall be free if the request is received before the end of the financial year preceding the meeting, which may be up to six or nine months before the meeting is held.[224] The limited nature of this concession can be more fully understood when put in the context of a further reform proposal from the CLR which was rejected entirely.

15–58 One major problem with the members' resolution procedure is that it is all too likely that something in the AGM circulation from the board will trigger the wish to place a shareholders' resolution on the agenda, but, since the minimum period of notice for calling the AGM is 21 days,[225] though the company may in fact give longer notice, there may well not be time for the members to respond to the AGM documentation and get their resolution to the company within the six week limit. In addition, the company's costs of circulation would be much greater in the case where the AGM documentation has already gone out, for the proposed resolution would have to be circulated separately. The CLR proposed to address the problem, at least in part, by requiring quoted companies to put their annual reports and accounts on their website within 120 days of the end of the financial

---

[219] 2006 Act.153. The right to instruct the member as to the exercise of voting rights is most likely to arise by way of contract between the registered and beneficial owners. The safeguards are designed to verify that the non-members are indirect investors and that there is no double-counting of shares.
[220] 2006 Act ss.338(2), 338A(1) and (2). See above, para.15–13. Besides being effective, the resolution must not be defamatory or frivolous or vexatious.
[221] 2006 Act ss.338(4), 338A(4). Thus, the board cannot frustrate the requisitionists by convening a meeting on less than six weeks' notice after the receipt of the request or by giving very long notice of the AGM.
[222] 2006 Act ss.340(2), 340B(2).
[223] Completing, paras 5.33–5.35.
[224] 2006 Act ss.340(1), 340B(1), 437 and 442. However, the costs of circulation should not be large if the members' resolution can be circulated along with the general circulation for the AGM. The company is obliged to circulate the resolution with the notice if this is possible: ss.339(1).
[225] 2006 Act s.307(2). For listed companies the recommended period is rather longer (20 working days), but still not long enough to obviate the problem under discussion: CGC Provision.E.2.4. On notice periods see below, para.15–61.

year, after which there would be a "holding period" of 15 clear days, during which the company would be obliged to accept a members' resolution (having the support presently required) for circulation with the notice of the AGM and at the company's cost.[226] However, this opportunity for enhanced debate over the annual reports and accounts of large companies proved too much for management interests, who secured that this reform was not adopted.

For meetings other than AGMs there is no statutory procedure whereby members can add an item to the agenda of a meeting called by the board. However, as we have noted above, the members do have a statutory power to convene a meeting at any time (without costs to themselves) and to require circulation of a resolution to be considered at that meeting, though normally shareholders holding 5 per cent of the voting rights are needed to secure the convening of such a meeting.[227] The fact that a statutory procedure is not available for adding an item to the agenda of a meeting, other than an AGM, convened by the board probably reflects the impracticability of so doing, when the minimum notice period for convening such a meeting is only 14 days and such meetings are often held urgently.

Circulation of members' statements

However, it is not enough for the shareholders to have their resolution circulated in advance of the AGM. It will have much more effect if it is accompanied by a statement from the proposers setting out its merits. Alternatively, the shareholders may wish to circulate only a statement and not a resolution, for example, where they wish to oppose a resolution from the board rather than to propose one of their own. The directors will undoubtedly make use of their power to circulate statements in support of their resolutions. Even if the directors do not directly control many votes, they are for the moment in control of the company and they can get their say in first and use all the facilities and funds of the company in putting their views across. They will have had all the time in the world in which to prepare a polished and closely reasoned circular and with it they will have been able to dispatch stamped and addressed proxy forms in their own favour.[228] And all this, of course, at the company's expense.[229]

15–59

Until the 1948 Act, members opposing the board's resolution or proposing their resolutions had none of these advantages and, even now, only timid steps have been taken towards counteracting the immense advantage enjoyed by those in possession of the company's machinery. Such steps as have been taken are included in ss.314–316. These sections track the provisions of ss.338–340 dealing

---

[226] Final Report, paras 8.66 and 8.100–101. One can find only a pale reflection of this idea in the provisions enabling 5 per cent of the shareholders to require the company to place on its website a statement about the audit of the company's accounts or an auditor's ceasing to hold office for discussion at the company's accounts meeting (normally its AGM): ss.527–531, discussed at para.22–22.

[227] See above, para.15–51.

[228] On proxies, see below.

[229] *Peel v LNW Railway* [1907] 1 Ch. 5 CA. For an excellent description of the relative weakness of the opposition, see per Maugham J in *Re Dorman Long & Co* [1934] Ch. 635 at 657–658.

with members' requests for the circulation of resolutions and add the right, under similar conditions,[230] to have a statement of up to 1,000 words circulated to the members.

In practice, however, this provision is of limited value, except where the statement is in support of a shareholders' resolution and is dispatched with it. The expense still has to be borne by the members—unless the company otherwise resolves[231]—and no substantial saving will result from the use of the company's facilities. In other cases (for example, when the circulars are designed to oppose proposals already forwarded by the board), little extra cost will be incurred by acting independently of the company and this will have a number of advantages. It will avoid any difficulty in obtaining sufficient requisitionists and will prevent delay, which may be fatal if notices of the meeting have already been dispatched. It will also obviate the need to cut the circular to 1,000 words and will enable the opposition to accompany it with proxies in their own favour.[232] Moreover, and from a tactical point of view this is vital, the board will not obtain advance information about the opposition's case, nor be able to send out at the same time a circular of its own in reply. Moreover, in the case of large companies the institutional investors will have mechanisms for communicating with each other which are not dependent upon the company's good offices and the financial press will often report the shareholders' concerns, thus encouraging prior communication among the shareholders and attendance at the meeting.

Notice of meetings and information about the agenda

15–60   In most cases, as we have seen, shareholder meetings are convened by the board. The main protection for the shareholders in such a case lies in the information made available to them in advance of the meeting and the length of notice required. On the basis of this information and during this period, they should be able to form a view whether the matter is sufficiently important for them to vote at the meeting or to attend it, and perhaps even to form an alliance with other shareholders to oppose the board, though, as we have noted, the shareholders start off on the back foot and will not have much time to organise their opposition. Naturally, these rules apply also to meetings convened by the members, for the requisitionists may not represent a majority of the members, who, in such a case,

---

[230] Including the extension of the "100 member" right to indirect investors: s.153(1)(a). The main differences are that the request for the circulation has to be received only one week before the meeting: (s.314(4)(d)) and the company, or any person aggrieved, can make an application to the court for exemption from the obligation to circulate on grounds of abuse (s.317), as in the case of members' statements in support of written resolutions (above, para.15–13).

[231] 2006 Act s.316—subject to the limited concession where the request is received before the end of the financial year preceding the meeting. The company is likely so to resolve if the members' resolution is passed (which is unlikely) and may conceivably do so even if it is lost. In cases where it has not so resolved, there have sometimes been disputes on precisely what are properly to be regarded as "the company's expenses in giving effect" to the requisition—e.g. does it include the costs of a circular opposing the members' resolution? It ought not to.

[232] There is clearly no reason why the members' circular should not invite recipients to cancel any proxies previously given to the board but it seems that the company could refuse to despatch the members' proxy forms unless, perhaps, the words in them were counted against the 1,000 words allowed.

need to be protected against being "rail-roaded" into unwise decisions, whether the proposal emanates from the board or a minority of the members.

Length of notice

Prior to the 1948 Act, the length of notice of meetings, and how and to whom notice should be given, depended primarily on the company's articles. The only statutory regulation which could not be varied was that 21 days' notice was required for a meeting at which a special resolution was to be proposed. In other cases the Act of 1929 provided that, unless the articles otherwise directed (which they rarely did) only seven days' notice was needed. This left far too short a time for opposition to be organised.[233] Hence, it is now provided by s.307 of the 2006 Act that any provision of a company's articles shall be void insofar as it provides for the calling of a meeting by a shorter notice than 21 days' notice in the case of an annual general meeting or 14 days' notice in other cases. The company's articles may provide for longer notice but they cannot validly provide for shorter.[234] And s.307A requires traded private companies to give 21 days' notice for all meetings (not just the AGM), unless the company offers the facility of voting by electronic means, in which case the shareholders in general meeting may decide to reduce the period to 14 days for meetings other than the AGM.[235] In practice, neither of these statutory provisions has much significance for the AGMs of listed companies, since the UK Corporate Governance Code[236] suggests 20 working days' notice (in effect, 28 days' notice in statutory terms) for the AGM. However, the rules in s.307A will be significant for other meetings of listed companies.

15–61

However, if a meeting is called on shorter notice than the Act or the articles prescribe, it is deemed to be duly called if so agreed, in the case of an AGM, by all the members entitled to attend and vote.[237] In other cases a somewhat lower level of agreement will suffice.[238] This is a majority in number of those having the right to attend and vote[239] who must also hold the "requisite percentage" of the nominal value of the shares giving the right to attend and vote. That percentage is 95 per cent in the case of a public company and 90 per cent in the case of a private company (unless the article increases the percentage, which they

15–62

---

[233] Particularly as the period might be reduced still further by provisions requiring proxy forms to be lodged in advance of the meeting: see below, para.15–67.

[234] 2006 Act s.307(3). The previous requirement of 21 days' notice in the case of special resolutions has been removed. Section 360 makes it clear that in this and related contexts "days" means "clear days", i.e. excluding the day of the meeting and the day on which the notice is given.

[235] 2006 Act s.307A does not apply to meetings of shareholders called to approve defensive measures proposed by management in a takeover. See s.307(1A)(b).

[236] Supplementary Principle E.2.4. On the CGC, see above, para.14–69.

[237] 2006 Act s.337(2).

[238] 2006 Act s.307(4),(7). See also *Schofield v Schofield* [2011] 2 B.C.L.C. 319 CA, where the court held there was no agreement to a shorter notice period, and so the resolutions (dismissing the minority shareholder as director and appointing the majority shareholder in his place) were not validly passed, in circumstances where the minority shareholder had attended and voted at the meeting on the clearly maintained basis that the meeting had not been validly convened by reason of falling short of the 14-day requirement pursuant to s.307 (Etherton LJ).

[239] 2006 Act s.307(5).

may do but not beyond 95 per cent).[240] The effect of requiring, other than for AGMs where unanimity is the rule, the agreement of both a majority in number of members as well as a high percentage of the voting rights is that, where there is one or a small number of major shareholders and a number of small ones, at least some of small shareholders will need to concur in the major shareholders' view that short notice is appropriate.

Special notice

15–63   As we have seen, in certain circumstances a type of notice, unimaginatively and unhelpfully designated a "special notice", has to be given, the principal examples being when it is proposed to remove a director or to remove or not to reappoint the auditors.[241] In the light of the discussion of these examples in Chs 14[242] and 22[243] respectively, little more needs to be said here except to emphasise that special notice is a type of notice very different from that discussed hitherto in this chapter. It is not notice of a meeting given *by* the company but notice given *to* the company of the intention to move a resolution at the meeting. Under s.312, where any provision of the Act requires special notice of a resolution, the resolution is ineffective unless notice of the intention to move it has been given to the company at least 28 days before the meeting.[244] The company must then give notice (in the normal sense) of the resolution, with the notice of the meeting or, if that is not practicable,[245] either by newspaper advertisement or by any other method allowed by the articles, at least 14 days before the meeting.[246]

All this achieves in itself is to ensure that the company and its members have plenty of time to consider the resolution, but in the two principal cases where special notice is required, supplementary provisions enable protective steps to be taken by the directors or auditors concerned.

15–64   Under this heading it is also to be noted that the company's articles may require notice of certain types of resolution to be given to the company in advance of the meeting, and this requirement may limit shareholders' freedom of action at the meeting itself. For example, the articles may provide that no person shall be appointed as a director at a meeting of the company unless he or she is a director retiring by rotation, a person recommended by the board or a person of whose proposed appointment the company has been given at least 14 days' (and not

---

[240] 2006 Act s.307(5),(6). In the case of companies without share capital the percentages relate to the total voting rights of all the members at the meeting.

[241] 2006 Act ss.168 and 510. See for instance *Bonham-Carter v Situ Ventures Ltd* [2012] B.C.C. 717 (Ch).

[242] At paras 14–48 et seq.

[243] At paras 22–19 et seq.

[244] 2006 Act s.321(1). This applies whether the resolution is proposed by the board or by a member. But the notice is effective if the meeting is called for a date 28 days or less after special notice has been given, so that the board can, in effect, forgive its own tardiness: s.312(4).

[245] e.g. if notices of the meeting have already been despatched.

[246] 2006 Act s.312(2),(3). But it seems that this notice has to be given only if the resolution is to be put on the agenda and that the mover cannot compel the company to do this unless he can and does invoke s.338, above: *Pedley v Inland Waterways Ltd* [1971] 1 All E.R. 209.

more than 35 days') notice, together with the proposed appointee's consent.[247] At the general meeting of such a company it is thus not open to dissenting shareholders to put forward an alternative candidate for director on the spur of the moment, though it appears that the board could do so.

The contents of the notice of the meeting and circulars

Having previously left this matter to the articles,[248] statute now lays down some basic requirements. The notice of the meeting must give the date, time and place of the meeting; a statement of the general nature of the business to be transacted at the meeting; and any other matters required by the company's constitution.[249] The second of these three requirements is obviously the crucial one, for the member is entitled to be put in receipt of sufficient information about the business of the meeting to determine whether he or she will attend it.[250] But how specific must the notice be? If the meeting is an AGM at which all that is to be undertaken is what former Tables A described as "ordinary business",[251] all that is necessary is to list those matters. If, however, resolutions on other matters are to be proposed it is customary to set out the resolutions verbatim and to indicate that they are to be proposed as special or ordinary resolutions as the case may be. In the case of special resolutions, s.283(6) requires that the notice of the meeting contains the text of the resolution and indicates the intention to propose it as a special resolution. The notice may also indicate that the resolution shall not be passed unless passed as a special resolution. This apparently curious provision follows from the further provision that anything that may be done by ordinary resolution may also be done by special resolution.[252] In effect, this gives the proposers of the resolution an ad hoc method of raising the majority required for the passing of an ordinary resolution to that required for a special resolution.

15–65

The CLR proposed that the requirement to set out the text of the resolution should be applied to all resolutions,[253] but this suggestion was not taken up. In all cases, the directors should ensure that, if the effect of the proposed business will be to confer a personal benefit on the directors, that should be made clear either in the notice or in a circular sent with it.[254]

In practice, the notice of a meeting will be of a formal nature but, if anything other than ordinary business is to be transacted, it will be accompanied by a circular explaining the reasons for the proposals and giving the opinion of the board thereon. Indeed, it is arguable that the common law principle that members

---

[247] Such a provision was included in Table A 1985 art.76, but it no longer appears. See the difficulties caused for the requisitionists by such a provision in *Rose v McGivern* [1998] 2 B.C.L.C. 593, above, fn.201.

[248] See, for example, Table A 1985 art.38.

[249] 2006 Act s.311, with additional requirements specified in ss.311(3) and 311A in relation to traded companies where the rights and responsibilities of members at meetings must be further elaborated.

[250] Contrast *Choppington Collieries Ltd v Johnson* [1944] 1 All E.R. 762 CA; with *Batchellor & Sons v Batchellor* [1945] Ch. 169.

[251] The distinction between "ordinary" and "special" business of an AGM disappeared from Table A of 1985.

[252] 2006 Act ss.283(6)(b) and 282(5).

[253] Developing, para.4.45.

[254] On circulars and the cases applying this principle to circulars, see below.

should be put in a position to determine whether to attend the meeting requires such circulars, except where the nature of the business will be obvious to all the members from what is said in the notice of the meeting. Normally, therefore, the circular will be a reasoned case by the directors in favour of their own proposals or in opposition to proposals put forward by others. In deciding whether the nature of the business has been adequately described, the notice and circular can be read together.[255] But the circular must not misrepresent the facts; there have been many cases in which resolutions have been set aside on the ground that they were passed as a result of a "tricky" circular.[256] Misleading circulars may not only influence the vote at the meeting but also the decisions of the members whether to attend. For this reason, the fault in the circular should not be capable of cure even if the truth emerges at the meeting. For the same reason, it has been suggested that the notion of a "tricky" circular should embrace all misleading documents, whether the misinformation is the result of opportunism on the part of those putting it out or a genuine error on their part; and that the same principles should be applied to communications from shareholders to fellow members seeking their support for the requisition of a meeting of the company.[257]

If there is opposition to the board's proposals, the opposers will doubtless wish to state their case and a battle of circulars will result. It is here, however, that the superiority of the board's position becomes manifest. Even if the directors do not directly control many votes, they are for the moment in control of the company and they can get their say in first and use all the facilities and funds of the company in putting their views across. Even institutional shareholders, who may be able to stand the cost of the circulation, may find themselves on the back foot, whilst smaller shareholders may be unable to respond effectively at all. As we have seen,[258] the statutory provisions permitting 5 per cent of the members to require the company to send a statement of their views to all the members are singularly ineffective in practice.

Communicating notice of the meeting to the members

15–66   Having prescribed the basic content of the notice, the Act then goes on to specify to whom it should be given, thus giving statutory form to something previously contained in the model articles.[259] Those entitled to receive notice of the meeting are every member of the company (whether entitled to vote or not) and every director.[260] Members include those entitled to a share on the death or bankruptcy

---

[255] *Tiessen v Henderson* [1899] 1 Ch. 861 at 867; *Re Moorgate Mercantile Holdings Ltd* [1980] 1 W.L.R. 227 at 242F.
[256] *Kaye v Croydon Tramways Co* [1898] 1 Ch. 358 CA; *Tiessen v Henderson* [1899] 1 Ch. 861; *Baillie v Oriental Telephone Co* [1915] 1 Ch. 503 CA; and see *Prudential Assurance v Newman Industries Ltd (No.2)* [1981] Ch. 257; [1982] Ch. 204 CA. The circular must be construed in a commonsense way. In the case of listed companies there is a further safeguard in the requirement that non-routine circulars have to be approved in advance by the FCA: see Listing Rules 13.2 but also the exceptions set out in LR 13.8.
[257] *Rose v McGivern* [1998] 2 B.C.L.C. 593; on the former point following the Australian case of *Bain and Co Nominees Pty Ltd v Grace Bros Holdings Ltd* [1983] 1 A.C.L.C. 816.
[258] See above, para.13–56.
[259] 2006 Act s.310. For the former model provision see Table A 1985 art.38.
[260] 2006 Act s.310(1).

of a member, if the company has been notified of their entitlement.[261] However, these statutory provisions are subject to any provision in the company's articles (for example, excluding non-voting members from entitlement to receive notice). This also enables companies which need to, to deal with exceptional cases (such as that where holders of share-warrants to bearer are entitled to attend and vote).[262] The articles may also contain more prosaic matters, such as the rules identifying the address which the company will use to communicate with the members and removing the member's entitlement to be notified if the address so identified proves ineffective.[263] Accidental failure to give notice to one or more members shall not affect the validity of the meeting or resolution, and the company's articles can expand this relaxation, except for meetings or resolutions required by the members.[264]

Attending the meeting

Proxies

One of the important features of company meetings is that the members do not have to appear at the meeting in person; they may appoint another person (a proxy) to attend and vote on their behalf.[265] At common law attending and voting had to be in person,[266] but early on it became the normal practice to allow these duties to be undertaken by an agent or "proxy".[267] It should be noted that the system of proxy voting is not the same as that of postal voting. With postal voting the vote is cast directly by the member who holds the vote and he or she votes without attending a meeting. With proxy voting, the proxy votes on behalf of the member and at a meeting. In practice, there may not be much difference between the two when the proxy is given precise instructions and follows them, for then the member in effect makes up his or her mind on how the vote is to be cast in advance of the meeting. The Shareholders' Rights Directive requires Member

15–67

---

[261] 2006 Act s.310(2).

[262] The usual practice is to give notice by a newspaper advertisement. The Listing Rules require this form of communication. On bearer shares see para.24–22, below.

[263] See arts 79–80 of the model articles for public companies.

[264] 2006 Act s.313. The "accidental omission" provision, of course, would not cover the deliberate omission to give notice to a troublesome member, nor does it cover a deliberate omission based on a mistaken belief that a member is not entitled to attend the meeting: *Musselwhite v Musselwhite & Son Ltd* [1962] Ch. 964. But, if the omission is "accidental", it applies even if the meeting is called to pass a special resolution: *Re West Canadian Collieries Ltd* [1962] Ch. 370.

[265] For a discussion of the problems in this area, see Shareholder Voting Working Group, *Discussion Paper on Shareholder Proxy Voting* (July 2015) at *http://uk.practicallaw.com/9-616-7485* [Accessed 15 June 2016].

[266] *Harben v Philips* (1883) 23 Ch.D. 14 CA; and see *Woodford v Smith* [1970] 1 W.L.R. 806 at 810, per Megarry J.

[267] The word "proxy" is used indiscriminately to describe both the agent and the instrument appointing him.

States to permit companies to offer voting "by correspondence in advance of the general meeting" to their shareholders, but does not require companies to adopt this procedure.[268]

Until the 1948 Act, however, the right to vote by proxy at a meeting of a company was dependent upon express authorisation in the articles. In practice this was almost invariably given; but not infrequently it was limited in some way, generally by providing that the proxy must himself be a member. Where there was such a limitation the scales were further tilted in favour of the board, for a member wishing to appoint a proxy to oppose the board's proposals might find difficulty in locating a fellow member prepared to attend and vote on his behalf. It was also customary to provide that proxy forms must be lodged in advance of the meeting. While this is a reasonable provision, in as much as it is necessary to check their validity before they are used at the meeting, it too could be used to favour the board if the period allowed for lodging was unreasonably short. Moreover, as already pointed out, it had become the practice for the board to send out proxy forms in their own favour with the notice of the meeting and for these to be stamped and addressed at the company's expense.

For all these reasons, although proxy voting gave an appearance of stockholder democracy, this appearance was deceptive and in reality the practice helped to enhance the dictatorship of the board. In recognition of this, the Stock Exchange required that listed companies should send out "two-way" proxies, i.e. forms which enable members to direct the proxy whether to vote for or against any resolution. The FCA's listing rules currently require "three-way" proxies (i.e. for, against or abstain).[269]

15–68 The statutory provisions relating to proxies are now to be found in ss.324–331 of the Act. They show a further development in the movement of the proxy provisions from the articles to the Act. The effect is in many cases to make the proxy rules mandatory. Unless the Act expressly allows derogation from its provisions, the articles cannot reduce the statutory entitlements, though the Act gives the articles a general permission to improve them.[270] Any member is entitled to appoint another person (whether a member of the company or not) as his proxy to attend, speak and vote instead of himself at a meeting of the company.[271] In the case of a company having a share capital the member may appoint more than one proxy, provided each proxy is appointed to exercise rights attached to different shares.[272] Previously, this facility was subject to the articles of the company permitting it. It is now mandatory and is useful in the case for

---

[268] The Shareholders' Rights Directive (Directive 2007/36/EC) art.12. The Directive was implemented in the UK by the Companies (Shareholders' Rights) Regulations 2009 (SI 2009/1632). The articles may already provide for postal ballots under domestic law: see fn.297, below.

[269] LR 9.3.6. Notwithstanding recommendations that this should be a statutory requirement in all cases (e.g. by the Jenkins Committee, Cmnd. 1749, para.464) it still is not. An abstention from supporting a management proposal on the part of a larger shareholder is taken as a significant event in the case of listed companies. See also CGC Provision E.2.1.

[270] 2006 Act s.331.

[271] 2006 Act s.324(1). The restrictions under the previous law as to (a) the proxy's right to speak at meetings of public companies; (b) the proxy's right to vote on a poll; or (c) the member's right to appoint a proxy at all in a company not having a share capital, have all been swept away. The proxy may also demand a poll (s.329) and may even be elected the chair of the meeting (s.328).

[272] 2006 Act s.324(2).

fund managers or nominee custodians[273] who may hold shares on behalf of a number of different beneficial owners who may hold different views on the matters at issue.

The members must be informed of their statutory rights to attend, speak and vote by proxy (and of any more extensive rights provided under the company's articles) in the notice convening the meeting.[274] Moreover, if proxies are solicited at the company's expense the invitation must be sent to all members entitled to attend and vote.[275] Thus, the board cannot invite only those from whom it expects a favourable response. Finally, the articles may not require that proxy forms (or other documents required to validate the proxy) must be lodged more than 48 hours before a meeting or adjourned meeting.[276]

It cannot be said, however, that these provisions have done much to curtail the **15–69** tactical advantages possessed by the directors. They still strike the first blow and their solicitation of proxy votes is likely to meet with a substantial response before the opposition is able to get under way. Even if their proxies are in the "two-way" form, many members will complete and lodge them[277] after hearing but one side of the case, and only the most intelligent or obstinate are likely to withstand the impact of the, as yet, uncontradicted assertions of the directors.

It is perhaps easy to recognise that management might give biased advice, but the same concern is also voiced in relation to proxy advisers. These firms provide voting advice, especially to institutional investors, and may therefore have considerable influence on their voting behaviour. Although taking advice is often sensible, especially given the increasing complexity of the equity markets and the large number of (cross-border) holdings of shares, two shortcomings are typically noted: the advisors may have serious conflicts of interest, given that they often provide other services to issuers; and their methodologies may not be robust. Perhaps predictably, codes of best practice have been developed, with suggestions that they be adopted on a "comply or explain" basis.[278] The issue is also likely to form part of the proposed new Shareholder Rights Directive.[279]

---

[273] See above, para.15–25.

[274] 2006 Act s.325. Failure to comply does not affect the validity of the meeting or anything done at it, but does constitute a criminal offence on the part of every officer in default: s.325(2)–(4). This notice is not given to the person nominated under s.146 to receive communications from the company (see above, para.15–40). That person is told that he or she may have a right to appoint a proxy or to instruct the member how to vote, depending on the agreement between the nominated person and the member (s.149). This is not a very useful notice but it is the best that can be provided.

[275] 2006 Act s.326(1), unless a proxy form or other information is issued at the request of the member and is available to all members upon request: s.326(2). As with s.325 (previous note) non-compliance is a criminal offence. Nothing is said about the impact of non-compliance on the validity of what is done at the meeting, presumably because s.326, unlike s.325, does not concern the content of the notice of the meeting.

[276] 2006 Act s.327. Hence proxies may now validly be lodged between the original date of the meeting and any adjournment for more than 48 hours. In the case of votes taken on polls, which are sometimes delayed, the relevant time is the time the poll is demanded or, if the poll is not to be taken within 48 hours of being demanded, 24 hours before the time appointed for the taking of the poll.

[277] Encouraged by the fact that postage is prepaid. Most two-way proxies provide that if neither "for" nor "against" is deleted the proxy will be used as the proxy thinks fit (i.e. as the board wish). LR 9.3.6 requires this to be expressly stated.

[278] Following ESMA's report into the role of the proxy advisory industry, a group of six proxy advisers published a set of best practice principles for the industry in March 2014. The three main

15–70 It is, of course, true that, once opposition is aroused, members may be persuaded to cancel their proxies, for these are merely appointments of agents and the agents' authority can be withdrawn,[280] or change their instructions, since s.324A requires the proxy to vote in accordance with the member's instructions. But in practice this rarely happens.

The issue of termination of the proxy's authority is now partly addressed in s.330. The aim of the provisions is to protect things done by the proxy from being brought into question if the company[281] has not received notification of the termination of the proxy's authority before the meeting. Thus, the proxy's vote will still be valid and the proxy will still count towards the quorum and can still validly join in demanding a poll, unless the company receives notice of termination of the authority before the commencement of the meeting.[282] The company's articles may set an earlier time for the notification of the termination, but not so as to make it earlier than 48 hours before the meeting (excluding non-working days).[283] However, the section deals only with the termination of the proxy's authority by "notice of termination". It has been held that a member may attend and vote in person and the company must then accept his vote instead of the proxy's,[284] i.e. that the proxy's authority may be terminated by a personal vote. However, two points should be noted about that case. First, it was based on the construction of the particular articles of the company in question, and so does not purport to lay down a general rule. Secondly, the company was aware the shareholder had voted in person and that the votes held by the proxy were accordingly reduced—indeed the company in that case wished positively to insist on the proxy's votes having been reduced. Thus, outside the matters covered by the section, the terms of the articles and the company's knowledge seem to be the crucial determinants of the ability of the proxy to exercise his or her voting rights as against the company, despite the withdrawal of the member's authority.

---

principles, which are supplemented by additional guidance, are service quality, conflicts of interest, and communications, and they apply on a "comply or explain" basis. The group will monitor implementation of the principles and will formally review them within the next two years. ESMA is currently conducting a review of the operation of the best practice principles. See *https://www.esma. europa.eu/press-news/esma-news/esma-publishes-report-proxy-advisors%E2%80%99-best-practice-principles* [Accessed 31 January 2016].

[279] In April 2014, the European Commission published a draft Directive to revise the Shareholder Rights Directive (2007/36/EC). This includes a wide variety of different proposed measures, including a number of new provisions relating to identifying shareholdings and facilitating the exercise of shareholder rights such as shareholder voting, and enhancing the transparency of proxy advisors. Please see: *http://eur-lex.europa.eu/legal-content/EN/TXT/?qid=1398680488759&uri= COM:2014:213:FIN* [Accessed 31 January 2016]. Although mandatory rules are proposed, these seem likely to emerge in the form of "comply or explain" requirements.

[280] Unless it is an "authority coupled with an interest" (e.g. when given to a transferee prior to registration of his transfer) or is an irrevocable power of attorney under the Power of Attorney Act 1971 s.4.

[281] Or someone other than the company if the articles require or permit the notice to be given to someone else: s.330(4).

[282] 2006 Act s.330(2),(3). In the case of voting at a poll to be held more than 48 hours after it is demanded the relevant time is the time appointed for the poll (s.330(3)(b)).

[283] 2006 Act s.330(5)–(7) (noting that s.330(6)(c) has been repealed from 26 May 2015).

[284] *Cousins v International Brick Co* [1931] 2 Ch. 90 CA.

As between the member and the proxy, on ordinary agency principles a **15–71** revocation is always effective if notified to the proxy before he has voted.[285] And during the term of appointment of the proxy, s.324A (surprisingly, only since 2009) requires the proxy to vote in accordance with any instructions given by the appointing member. This would seem to overcome the problem addressed in older cases of whether there was any positive obligation on the proxy at all (or merely a negative one not to vote contrary to the principal's instructions),[286] and whether the answer depended upon whether there was a contract or a fiduciary relationship between member and proxy.[287] But failing any such statement or definite instructions from the principal, the proxy will have a discretion, and if this is exercised in good faith the proxy will not be liable, whichever way he votes or if he refrains from voting.

Corporations' representatives

Since a company or other corporation is an artificial person which must act **15–72** through agents or employees, it might be supposed that, when a member is another company, it could attend and vote at meetings only by proxy. This, however, is not so. Section 323 provides that a body corporate may, by a resolution of its directors or other governing body,[288] authorise such person or persons as it thinks fit to act as its representative at meetings of companies of which it is a member (or creditor) and that the representative may exercise the same powers as could the body corporate if it were an individual.[289] With the expansion of the powers of the proxy, on the one hand, and the removal of the previous restriction that a company could appoint only a single corporate representative, it is unclear whether the proxy or the corporate representative is the more attractive mechanism for the corporate shareholder. The representative may have the slight advantage that, unlike a proxy, he or she can simply turn up at the meeting and is not subject to any requirement for documentation to be lodged with the company in advance of the meeting, as a proxy is. This may be particularly valuable where institutional investors are in discussion with the company's management right until the last minute about the acceptability or otherwise of a resolution to be proposed at a meeting and, if those discussions break down, where it will be too late to appoint a proxy.[290]

---

[285] Unless the agency is irrevocable, see fn.280, above.

[286] This was discussed, but not decided, in *Oliver v Dalgleish* [1963] 1 W.L.R. 1274, which also left open the question of how far the company is concerned to see whether the proxy is obeying his instructions.

[287] See, e.g. *Second Consolidated Trust v Ceylon Amalgamated Estates* [1943] 2 All E.R. 567 at 570; *Re Dorman Long & Co* [1934] Ch. 635 (this case contains an admirable discussion of the general problems of proxy voting). But in both the cases the proxy-holders were present at the meeting: quaere whether (in the absence of mandatory instruction now, as per s.324A) they can be compelled to attend: see [1934] Ch. 664 at 665.

[288] e.g. its liquidator: *Hillman v Crystal Bowl Amusements Ltd* [1973] 1 W.L.R. 162.

[289] 2006 Act s.323(2). This is really a statutory example of an officer acting as an organ of the company rather than as a mere agent.

[290] 2006 Act s.323 (3) and (4) deal with the situation where more than one representative is authorised to act on behalf of the company. It has been suggested that these provisions, as revised by the Companies (Shareholders' Rights) Regulations (SI 2009/1632), now make it clear that

Voting and verification of votes

Voting as a governance issue

15–73   Company law has traditionally proceeded on the basis that voting at a general meeting is a property right for those shareholders who have voting shares. This gives rise to two problems. Shareholders may choose not to exercise their votes at all; or they may vote at the behest of a non-shareholder. Both responses are capable of undermining the legitimacy of shareholder decisions, in the first case because the result is not representative of the shareholding body as a whole and in the second because it may reflect the interests of non-shareholders.

15–74   As to the first problem, we have seen above that for "fiduciary" investors the law of trusts may impose a duty to give consideration to the question of whether voting rights should be exercised in order to promote the interests of the beneficiaries of pension trusts. Under government pressure, the institutional shareholders generally have supported the UK Stewardship Code, which embodies best practice rules on active engagement, including voting, so that for such shareholders voting is coming close to being a duty.[291] This is not a duty enshrined in the law, but a "duty" resulting from the need to ward off proposals to enshrine such a duty in the law—the typical set of factors which produces what is often referred to as "self-regulation", though that is arguably an inappropriate term. Nevertheless, these developments address to some degree the problem of non-voting. Voting levels at general meetings of large companies improved from one-half to over 60 per cent in the three years 2004 to 2007,[292] but then levelled out to just over 70 per cent by 2015.[293]

Votes on a show of hands and polls

15–75   This development has naturally led institutional shareholders to look closely at the rules on voting and to criticise rules which make their task difficult. Companies' articles normally provide for voting to be on a show of hands, unless a poll is demanded under the provisions discussed below, i.e. those present indicate their views by raising their hands. Proxies may vote on a show of hands,[294] although a proxy holding instructions both for and against a resolution

---

representatives can be assigned voting rights in respect of different parcels of shares held by the corporate shareholder in the way that is explicitly provided for in the case of a proxy. See s.324(2).

[291] See paras 15–27 et seq. Since December 2010 all UK-authorised Asset Managers are required under the FCA's Conduct of Business Rules (r.2.2.3) to produce a statement of commitment to the Stewardship Code or explain why it is not appropriate to their business model.

[292] *Review of the impediments to voting UK shares*, Report by Paul Myners to the Shareholder Voting Working Group, July 2007 (hereafter Myners 2007 Report). The issue of "empty" voting is considered at para.15–81, below.

[293] See FRC, *Developments in Corporate Governance and Stewardship 2015*, at *https://www.frc.org.uk/Our-Work/Publications/Corporate-Governance/Developments-in-Corporate-Governance-and-Stewa-%281%29.pdf* [Accessed 31 January 2016], citing figures from European Voting Results Report; ISS; September 2015.

[294] 2006 Act s.324(1). Previously this was a matter left to be regulated by the articles.

may find it very difficult to know how to act. The result on a show of hands may give a very imperfect picture of where the majority of the voting rights lie.

The alternative voting mechanism is that of the poll in which members and proxies vote the shares which they represent, though a person is not obliged to vote all the shares represented or to vote them all the same way.[295] The voting process usually involves signing slips of paper indicating how many votes are being cast in each direction and the number of abstentions. This is a more cumbersome, if more accurate, voting process, and in large meetings it may not be practical to complete it during the meeting, because of the need to check proxy forms and the votes cast, though there must be scope for increasing the speed of the voting process by use of electronic technology.[296] What is not permitted, unless the articles specifically provide for it, is voting by postal ballot.[297] The latter may be thought strange since clearly such a referendum would be a better way of obtaining the views of the members. But the fiction is preserved that the result is determined after oral discussion at a meeting, although everybody knows that in the case of public companies the result is normally determined by proxies lodged before the meeting is held.[298]

Given the potential inaccuracy of the vote on the show of hands, its retention requires some explanation, especially as it is not common in other jurisdictions and so is often misunderstood by foreign investors.[299] The main argument in its favour is its speed and simplicity, enabling the company to take uncontroversial decisions quickly, though for completely uncontroversial decisions other techniques would do equally well, such as taking decisions without a vote, if no person present demands one. Where the resolution is controversial and where the voting process therefore comes under the strongest pressure, the show of hands has two main defects. The first is that it may disguise the level of opposition to the resolution, even if the show of hands produces the same result as a poll would have done. For example, a resolution may be passed on a show of hands by 80 to 20, but if a poll had been taken it might have been revealed that 500 votes were in favour of the resolution and 400 against. It is particularly likely that the chairman of the meeting will not vote on a show of hands and yet he or she may have been appointed the person to receive the proxies solicited by the company. Such situations in particular discourage institutional shareholders from voting by proxy, because they feel their votes have no impact. In the case of companies subject to the UK Corporate Governance Code these adverse consequences are

---

[295] 2006 Act s.322. See also s.152. Thus, the chairman of the meeting, under a typical three-way proxy, will hold some votes for and some against the resolution to be voted on and some instructions to abstain, and can give effect to each set of instructions.

[296] If proxies have been gathered only by the company and have been lodged with, for example, the chairman of the meeting, calculating the vote will be easy. It is where there have been multiple proxy solicitations that the process can extend beyond the meeting.

[297] *McMillan v Le Roi Mining Co* [1906] 1 Ch. 338. The articles rarely do so provide except in the case of clubs or other associations formed as companies limited by guarantee.

[298] As was well said in an American case (*Berendt v Bethlehem Steel Corp* (1931) 154 A. 321 at 322), statements made to a meeting of proxy-holders fall "upon ears not allowed to hear and minds not permitted to judge: upon automatons whose principals are uninformed of their own injury".

[299] Nevertheless, the second sub-paragraph of art.14 of the Shareholders Rights Directive (above, fn.268) appears to permit the UK to keep it.

somewhat mitigated by the recommendation that companies should display on their websites the proxies lodged for and against a resolution where the vote was taken on a show of hands.[300]

The second, and more serious, defect in the show of hands is that it may produce a result different from that which would be revealed by a poll. This situation is addressed by the legislation through rules dealing with the question of who can demand that a poll be taken, even though a result has been achieved on a show of hands, or can demand a poll even before a decision on a show of hands has been taken.[301] The articles of companies invariably direct that a demand by the chairman shall be effective.[302] This again strengthens the position of the directors, for they run no risk of not being able to use their full voting power. Further, the Act provides that the articles must not exclude the right to demand a poll on any question, other than the election of a chairman or the adjournment of the meeting. Nor may the articles make ineffective a demand by not less than five members having a right to vote on the resolution; or by members representing not less than one-tenth of the total voting rights on the resolution; or by members holding shares having a right to vote on which a sum has been paid up equal to not less than one-tenth of the total sum paid up on all the shares conferring that right.[303] Further, a proxy may demand or join in demanding a poll.[304] This makes it difficult for the articles to hamstring a sizeable opposition by depriving them of their opportunity to exercise their full voting strength. Moreover, it is the duty of the chairman to exercise his right to demand a poll so that effect is given to the real sense of the meeting, and, if he realised that a poll might well produce a different result, it seems that he would be legally bound to direct that a poll should be taken.[305]

Verifying votes

15–76   The Company Law Review received evidence that the reliability of the results produced on a poll might not always be all it should be, because votes are "lost" somewhere in the chain between the person holding the voting power giving instructions as to how the votes are to be cast and the recording of those votes at

---

[300] CGC Provision E.2.2. For the coverage of the CGC see para.14–69, above.

[301] It is a question of construction of the relevant article whether a poll can be demanded before there has been a vote on a show of hands: *Carruth v ICI* [1937] A.C. 707 at 754–755 HL; *Holmes v Keyes* [1959] Ch. 199 CA. The model set of articles for private companies (art.44) and for public companies (art.36) provide for a poll to be demanded in advance of the meeting or at the meeting but before the show of hands decision has been taken, as well as immediately after the result has been declared of the show of hands vote.

[302] The model articles for private and for public companies, arts 44 and 36, respectively, also allow the directors to call for a poll, which facilitates the calling for a poll by the company in advance of the meeting.

[303] 2006 Act s.321. In the absence of anything in the articles any member may demand a poll (*R. v Wimbledon Local Board* (1882) 8 Q.B.D. 459 CA), and, of course, the articles may be more generous than s.321: see arts 44 and 36 of the model private and public company articles, which entitles two members, rather than the statutory five, to demand a poll.

[304] 2006 Act s.329.

[305] *Second Consolidated Trust v Ceylon Amalgamated Estates* [1943] 2 All E.R. 567. In this case the chairman held proxies (without which there would have been no quorum) which, if voted, would have defeated the resolutions passed on a show of hands.

the meeting.[306] Following this, the Act gives the same percentage of the members (including indirect members) as can place a resolution on the agenda or demand a meeting of an AGM the right to requisition an independent assessor's report (normally from the company's auditors) on a poll at a general meeting of the company (but without any cost to the requisitionists).[307] This right applies only within "quoted companies", i.e. companies incorporated in one of the jurisdictions of the UK and listed on the Main Market of the London Stock Exchange or listed on a regulated market in another Member State of the EEA or having their shares traded on the New York Stock Exchange or Nasdaq.[308] The report must give the assessor's opinion, with supporting reasons, on a number of matters, notably whether the procedures adopted in connection with the poll were adequate, whether the votes (including proxy votes) were fairly and accurately recorded and whether the validity of the members' appointment of proxies was fairly assessed.[309] The context in which the right is set strongly suggests that the assessor is required to look only at the company's practices and procedures, so that defects in the passing of voting instructions down the chain before those instructions reach the company will not be picked up.

Certainly, the rights which the assessor is given to support the discharge of the reporting function are all rights against the company and associated persons. The assessor has the right to attend the meeting of the company at which the poll is to be taken or any subsequent proceedings if the poll is not taken at the meeting itself and to be given copies of the documentation sent out by the company in connection with the meeting.[310] The assessor has a right of access to the company's records relating to the meeting and the poll and a right to require directors, officers, employees, members and agents of the company (including the operators of its share register) to provide information and explanation (unless this would involve a breach of legal professional privilege).[311] Non-compliance with the request for information or giving knowingly or recklessly misleading information in response to a request is a criminal offence.[312] The company must put on its website a copy of the report as soon as is reasonably practicable and keep the information there for two years and, at an earlier stage, must post some information about the appointment of the assessor.[313]

Non-compliance with the requirements for an assessor's report appears to have no impact on the validity of the resolution passed, though it is a criminal offence on the part of every officer in default for the company not to respond within one week of receiving a valid request by appointing an independent assessor to produce the report.[314] The request will normally be made before the meeting at

---

[306] Final Report, para.6.25. See also the Myners Report 2007 (above fn.292) pp.1–4.

[307] 2006 Act s.342. The right extends to class meetings at which it is proposed to vary the rights of any class of member: s.352. On variation of class rights see para.19–14.

[308] 2006 Act s.385. Section 354 gives the Secretary of State the power by regulations, subject to affirmative resolution in Parliament, to extend the types of company to which the assessor's report requirement applies (but also to limit them).

[309] 2006 Act s.347(1).

[310] 2006 Act s.348.

[311] 2006 Act s.349.

[312] 2006 Act s.350.

[313] 2006 Act ss.351 and 353.

[314] 2006 Act s.343.

which the poll is likely to be requested or conducted but a valid request may be made up to one week after the date on which the poll is held.[315] The appointed person must meet the statutory requirements for independence, which, however, are drawn so as not to exclude necessarily the company's auditors,[316] and the assessor must not have any other role in relation to the poll upon which a report is to be made.[317]

Establishing who is entitled to vote

15–77   One final issue which should be mentioned is the fundamental one of establishing who is entitled to vote. There are two potential problems. The first arises when the shares in a company are constantly traded. In this case, establishing who can vote can only sensibly be done by establishing some date prior to, but not too far in advance of, the meeting as the "record date". Those who are members on that date may vote, even if by the date of the meeting they have disposed of their shares, and those who have acquired shares since that date may not (except by instructing the shareholder on record how to vote). This is not an entirely satisfactory situation and in some continental European countries it is dealt with by "share-blocking", i.e. prohibiting trading between the record date and the date of the meeting. However, the disadvantages of this device, in terms of loss of liquidity, outweigh the advantages, and it has not been used in the UK and is now in any event prohibited by art.7 of the Shareholders' Rights Directive.[318] The alternative is to set the record date close to the meeting date, so as to minimise the effect of trading post the record date, but to accept that some misallocation of voting rights will inevitably occur. This is the UK approach where the record date is set at not more than 48 hours before the meeting by the Uncertificated Securities Regulations, which are determinative in the case of publicly traded companies.[319]

The second problem is one which has emerged as a practical issue only recently. Directors of public companies have powers under ss.793–797 to issue statutory disclosure notices calling for information about the persons interested in its shares. If there is non-compliance with the notice, the company can seek a court order restricting the rights attached to the relevant shares, including barring the right to vote. Given the powerful sanction, the company's right to seek to exercise the power to bar voting is subject to "proper purposes" constraints.[320]

Publicity for votes and resolutions

15–78   Whether or not an independent assessor is requested by the members, a quoted company is required to post on its website the text of any resolution voted on through a poll at a general meeting and give the details of the votes cast in favour

---

[315] 2006 Act s.342(4)(d).

[316] 2006 Act s.344. See notably s.344(2).

[317] 2006 Act s.343(3)(b).

[318] Above, fn.268.

[319] The Uncertificated Securities Regulations 2001 (SI 2001/3755) reg.41(1). See below at para.27–4.

[320] See the extended discussion of *Eclairs Group Ltd v JKX Oil & Gas Plc* [2015] UKSC 71, at paras 16–26 et seq.

of or against it.[321] This will include resolutions which are not passed. Again, failure to do so does not affect the validity of the resolution but does constitute a criminal offence on the part of every officer in default. The UK Corporate Governance Code goes a little further and suggests website publication of votes directed to be withheld and of the number of shares in respect of which valid proxy appointments were made.[322] The purpose of the latter piece of information is presumably to indicate how important or, more likely, unimportant attending the meeting actually was.

Apart from this new requirement for quoted companies, the publicity require-   **15–79**
ments for the results of meetings are of a more traditional kind. Section 355 requires every company to keep records containing the minutes of all proceedings of general meetings and copies of resolutions passed otherwise than at meetings (for example, as written resolutions or by unanimous consent), and to keep those records for 10 years.[323] Those records must be open to inspection by any member of the company (but not by the public) free of charge, who, for a prescribed fee, may require a copy of them.[324] The place of inspection is the company's registered office or some other place permitted under regulations made by the Secretary of State.[325] However, some resolutions of the company will be available publicly because they have to be supplied to the Registrar. This is true in particular of special resolutions, including such resolutions passed by unanimous consent.[326]

The minutes of the meetings and the records of the resolutions have some legal   **15–80**
significance. A record of a resolution passed other than at a meeting, if signed by a director or the company secretary, is evidence of the passing of the resolution, and the minutes of a meeting, if signed by the chair of that meeting or the following one, are evidence of the proceedings at the meeting. A record of proceedings at a meeting is deemed, unless the contrary is proved, to establish that the meeting was duly held, was conducted as recorded and all appointments made at it were valid. A record of a written resolution produces the same effect as to the requirements of the Act for passing written resolutions.[327]

"Empty" voting

The second problem identified above was that of members voting at the behest of   **15–81**
non-members. In some cases this is entirely legitimate. We have noted, for example, that a nominee shareholder must vote as instructed by the beneficial owner.[328] This is unproblematic because the effect of the rule is to reunite the

---

[321] 2006 Act s.341. This meets the requirements of art.14 of the Shareholders' Rights Directive.
[322] E.2.2.
[323] The provisions apply also to class meetings: s.359.
[324] 2006 Act s.358(3).
[325] 2006 Act ss.358(1) and 1136.
[326] 2006 Act ss.29–30.
[327] 2006 Act s.356.
[328] Above, fn.108.

voting right with the person who has the economic interest in the share.[329] The issue with "empty" voting is that the right to vote is in fact exercised by a person with no or only a limited economic interest in it, to the exclusion of the person with the greater economic interest. There are two principal ways in which voting by those with no or only a limited economic interest in the shares can come about: contracts for differences ("CfDs") and stock "lending".[330] Both are fairly sophisticated market arrangements, which do have a legitimate role, but whose impact on the allocation of voting rights has not been fully thought through.

In the first case, a person typically contracts with a counterparty for the difference in the price of a security at two points in time, and the counterparty, at least in a "long" CfD, will purchase the security in question as a hedge against its exposure under the CfD. In practice, though not as a matter of law, the holder of the CfD can often determine the way in which the counterparty exercises the votes attached to the shares acquired as a hedge. In this way a non-owner with a limited economic exposure to the share becomes in practice able to vote it. We discuss CfDs further below when dealing with takeovers, which is the one area where regulation (relating to disclosure of interests in shares) has addressed them.[331]

The second main form of "empty" voting arises out of stock "lending". This is a misnomer. With stock lending the shares are not lent by their holder to someone else but are transferred to that person on the basis that the transferee undertakes to re-transfer an equivalent number of shares (together with any dividend paid on them in the interim) upon demand to the transferor. The economic result may be near that of a loan of securities but because the legal form is an outright transfer of the shares to the other person, the right to vote is transferred to that other person as well. By the same token, because the economic effect of the transaction is that of a loan, for the transferee to exercise the voting rights leads to a disjunction between the voter and the person with the long-term economic interest in the shares (i.e. the lender). Again, there is no formal regulation of the voting rights issues arising with stock lending. The Myners Report 2007[332] reiterated its earlier recommendation that in the case of contentious votes the transferor should exercise its right to have shares re-transferred to it in order to be able to exercise the right to vote. However, it noted that, in the case of institutional shareholders, where, often, the shares were held by a custodian under a direct contract with the institution, whilst the right to vote the shares was delegated to a fund manager under a separate contract with the institution, the fund manager might be unaware whether the shares held by the custodian had

---

[329] Though perhaps less clear, other rules conferring voting rights on non-members can be justified as giving the vote to the person with the primary economic interest in the share. See, for example, the unpaid vendor of shares (*Musselwhite v CH Musselwhite & Sons Ltd* [1962] Ch. 964; but cf. *Michaels v Harley House (Marylebone) Ltd* [2000] 1 Ch. 104). Or the law may be indifferent as to the allocation by contract of the voting right as between two people each with an economic interest in the share: *Puddephatt v Leith* [1916] 1 Ch. 200 (mortgagor and mortgagee).

[330] ADRs (above, para.15–39) can also give rise to empty voting unless the depository is required to pass the governance rights onto the holder of the depository receipt.

[331] See para.28–45 and, generally, paras 26–20 et seq.

[332] Above, fn.292. The Commission has consulted on a provision to be included in a Commission Recommendation which would say that "borrowed" shares should be voted only on instructions from the "lender".

been "lent" (perhaps under an automatic stock lending programme) and so would not be in a position to ask for the re-transfer of their equivalent.[333]

Miscellaneous matters

Chairman

Every meeting needs a person to preside over it, if it is not to descend into chaos. **15–82** The Act lays down the default rule that a member may be elected at the meeting by resolution to be its chair, but states that this provision is subject to any provisions in the articles as to how that person is to be chosen.[334] The articles invariably do deal with the matter. The model articles for public companies[335] sensibly take the view that the chairman ought to be a member of the board and accordingly provide that the chairman of the board shall also be the chairman of the meeting, which is what normally happens. However, if the chairman of the board is not present with 10 minutes of the time appointed for the start of the meeting, the directors present must appoint a director or member to preside and, if there are no directors present, then those constituting the meeting do that job.

The position of chairman is an important and onerous one, for he or she will be in charge of the meeting and will be responsible for ensuring that its business is properly conducted. As chairman, he owes a duty to the meeting, not to the board of directors, even if he is a director.[336] He should see that the business of the meeting is efficiently conducted and that all shades of opinion are given a fair hearing. This may entail taking snap decisions on points of order, motions, amendments and questions, often deliberately designed to harass him, and upon the correctness of his ruling the validity of any resolution may depend.[337] He will probably require the company's legal adviser to be at his elbow, and this is one of the occasions when even the most cautious lawyer will have to give advice without an opportunity of referring to the authorities.

Adjournments

One situation in which it may be necessary to adjourn is when the meeting is **15–83** inquorate, but this is a rare situation in public companies, because the quorum requirement is so low, i.e. two persons. What may present problems is the

---

[333] This situation could also lead to the fund manager purporting to vote shares the custodian did not hold at the relevant time and to the manager's proxy instructions to the company being rejected by the company on the grounds that they related to more shares than were held.

[334] 2006 Act s.319.

[335] Model articles for public companies art.31. The model articles for private companies are in the same form (art.39).

[336] See *Second Consolidated Trust v Ceylon Amalgamated Estates* [1943] 2 All E.R. 567. Conversely, it seems a director may act as chairman of the meeting even though a resolution to be debated is critical of the board's policy: *Might SA v Redbus Interhouse Plc* [2004] 2 B.C.L.C. 449.

[337] For the sort of situation with which the chairman may have to cope if the members of a public company turn up in far larger numbers than the board has foreseen, see the case of *Byng v London Life Association Ltd* [1990] Ch. 170 CA (below) where his well-meaning efforts were in vain and the company had to convene a new meeting.

converse case where those attending the meeting are too many rather than too few, and the meeting becomes chaotic. It should be emphasised that an adjournment of a meeting is to be distinguished from an abandonment of it. In the latter case the meeting ends. If a new meeting is convened, new business, as well as any unfinished at the abandoned meeting, may be undertaken so long as proper notice is given of both. In contrast, if a meeting is adjourned, the adjourned meeting can undertake only the business of the original meeting[338] or such of it which had not been completed at that meeting. Indeed, it was thought necessary specifically to provide by what is now s.332 of the Act that where a resolution is passed at an adjourned meeting it shall "for all purposes be treated as having been passed on the date on which it was in fact passed and is not to be deemed to be passed on any earlier date".[339]

The grounds for adjournment are normally set out in the articles. Article 33 of the model set for public companies[340] provides for adjournment if those present agree, either at the chairman's suggestion or by adopting a resolution to that effect off their own motion. Basically this gives effect to the common law rule under which the chairman has no general right to adjourn a meeting if there are no circumstances preventing its effective continuance.[341] However, responding to the difficulties demonstrated in the *Byng* case,[342] the model article now further provides that the chairman may unilaterally adjourn a meeting if "it appears to the chairman of the meeting that an adjournment is necessary to protect the safety of any person attending the meeting or ensure that the business of the meeting is conducted in an orderly manner". However, this part of the model article does no more than reflect the position at common law. Helpfully, in the *Byng* case[343] this element of the common law power was held to continue to operate, even though the company's articles, reflecting the earlier model sets of articles, contained an express power to adjourn only with the consent of the meeting. But the power and duty must be exercised bona fide for the purpose of facilitating the meeting and not as a ploy to prevent or delay the taking of a decision to which the chairman objects[344]; and the chairman's exercise of the common law power must be a reasonable one.[345]

Finally, under art.33 no notice has to be given if a meeting is adjourned for less than 14 days; otherwise, seven days' clear notice must be given. Clearly if the adjournment is a temporary one and the meeting is resumed at the same place

---

[338] Model articles for public companies, art.33(6); and for private companies, art.41(6). But a meeting can be adjourned despite the fact that it was not a meeting at which any substantive resolution could be passed: see *Byng v London Life Association Ltd* [1990] Ch. 170 CA. This must be right for otherwise an inquorate meeting could not be adjourned, as all Tables A have provided that they can.

[339] Were it otherwise, the company might unavoidably contravene the obligation to deliver to the Registrar a copy of the resolution within 15 days of its passage, as required, in the case of a considerable number of resolutions, under s.380.

[340] And similarly art.41 for private companies.

[341] *National Dwellings Society v Sykes* [1897] 3 Ch. 159; *John v Rees* [1970] Ch. 345 (which concerned, not a company meeting, but one of a Divisional Labour Party); *Byng v London Life Association* [1990] Ch. 170 CA.

[342] *Byng v London Life Association* [1990] Ch. 170 CA.

[343] *Byng v London Life Association* [1990] Ch. 170 CA.

[344] If the chairman purports to adjourn for such a reason, the meeting may elect another chairman and continue.

[345] *Byng v London Life Association* [1990] Ch. 170 CA.

on the same day, this is fair enough; but otherwise it seems unfair to members who may, perhaps through no fault of their own, have found themselves unable to attend the meeting as they had intended. As a result they may not know that it has been adjourned and may be prevented from exercising their rights to attend the adjourned meeting.

Class meetings

In addition to general meetings it may be necessary to convene separate meetings **15–84** of classes of members or debenture-holders (for example, to consider variation of rights) or of creditors (for example, in connection with a reconstruction or in a winding up). Here again, the rules to be observed will depend on the company's articles construed in the light of the general law relating to meetings. However, the Act does provide that, for meetings of classes of shareholder, the statutory rules apply as they apply to general meetings, with some modifications.[346] The most important of the shareholder protections which are not applied are the members' power to require the directors to convene a meeting and the power of the court to order a meeting.[347] As we see in Ch.19, the company, if it wishes to take certain steps, may be obliged to seek the consent of a class of shareholders and convene a meeting for that purpose, but the class has no general right on its own to meet to consider issues which concern it. On the other hand, some protections are more extensive at class meetings called to vary the rights of the class members: the two people constituting the quorum must represent at least one-third of the nominal value of the class of shares in question, except at an adjourned class meeting[348]; and any one member may demand a poll.[349]

In practice, very similar arrangements are incorporated in debenture trust deeds to regulate the conduct of meetings of debenture-holders.

At class meetings all members other than those of the class ought to be excluded, but if for convenience a joint meeting is held of the company and all separate classes, followed by separate polls, the court will not interfere if no objection has been taken by anyone present.[350]

Forms of communication by the company

Much of this chapter has concerned information (about meetings, for example) **15–85** which is required to be supplied by the company to its members. In the case of AGMs of public companies that material will typically include the company's annual accounts and reports (considered in more detail in Ch.21) which are today quite bulky documents. One important issue, therefore, is the form that the communication takes. That may be by traditional hard copy, electronically or by publication on the company's website. The Act takes some tentative steps towards

---

[346] 2006 Act ss.334 and 352 (and s.335 deals with class meetings of companies without share capital).
[347] 2006 Act ss.334(2) and 335(2) and above, paras 15–48 to 15–54.
[348] 2006 Act ss.334(4) and 335(4). At an adjourned meeting one person holding shares of the class or his proxy suffices. This makes sense only if the adjournment is because there was no quorum at the original meeting.
[349] 2006 Act ss.334(6) and 335(5).
[350] *Carruth v ICI* [1937] A.C. 707 HL.

encouraging the use of the latter two forms of communication, whilst not depriving members of their traditional supply of hard copy, if they wish to have it. Thus, s.1145 provides that where a member has received a communication otherwise than in hard copy (i.e. electronically or via a website), that member is entitled to be sent, without charge, a hard copy version of the document upon request within 21 days.

More generally, before a company can validly communicate with a member[351] otherwise than in hard copy, the consent or deemed consent of that member must be obtained. Electronic communication of documents is permitted only if the member has consented to that form of communication, either generally or for a specific class of documents.[352] As to website communication, that is permitted only if there has been actual agreement by the particular member,[353] as for electronic communication, or there has been deemed agreement. Deemed agreement arises where (a) the company's articles provide for website communication or the members have resolved to permit it; and (b) the particular member has been asked by the company to agree to website communication for all or a particular class of documents and the company has not received a response within 28 days.[354] The deemed agreement may be revoked at any time by the member, but the burden is on the member to take this step.[355] To the extent that the deemed consent provisions apply to website communication only, it can be said that the Act puts more pressure on members to accept that form of communication than to accept electronic documents.

However, website communication has a number of disadvantages for the member over receiving an electronic document, which the Act aims to redress. First, unless the member constantly monitors the relevant website, he or she may not be aware of the availability of the document. Thus, the company is required to notify the member of the availability of the document, the address of the website and how to access the document.[356] This communication could be via an electronic document, if the member has consented to that form of communication. (Self-evidently, notification via the website itself will not do!) Secondly, hard copy or electronic communication gives the member their own copy of the document, whereas, unless downloaded, the member will lose access to the document when it is removed from the website. Thus, minimum rules are set for the period during which the document must be available on the website. This is 28 days from the date on which the member was notified, as above, unless a

---

[351] "Person" is the term used in Sch.5 in relation to actual consent, so that its provisions embrace not just members but also those to whom governance rights have been transferred or information rights have been given (see above, para.15–31). The deemed consent provisions (see below) apply only to "members" but that term is expanded to include the two groups mentioned in the previous sentence: Sch.5 para.10(1).

[352] 2006 Act Sch.5 para.6.

[353] 2006 Act Sch.5 para.9(a).

[354] 2006 Act Sch.5 para.10(2),(3). The request may be repeated at twelve-monthly intervals if it does not produce acceptance or deemed acceptance. Similar provisions exist for debenture-holders: para.11.

[355] 2006 Act Sch.5 para.9(b).

[356] 2006 Act Sch.5 para.13(1).

specific section of the Act sets a different period.[357] There are a number of such specific provisions relating to the passing of resolutions.[358]

Forms of communication to the company

Where the company is the communicator, it is likely to be anxious to move away from the obligation to supply hard copy. When it is the potential receiver of communications, it may not be as anxious to facilitate the members' task. With members' communications to the company, we are necessarily concerned with their freedom to use electronic communications, rather than website based communication. The general rule in the Act is that the company is not obliged to accept electronic communications from other persons unless it has actually consented to this method of communication or is deemed to have accepted it.[359] Important for our purposes is that s.333 provides, where a company gives an electronic address in a notice calling a meeting or in a document from the company inviting the appointment of proxies, it is deemed to have agreed that any document relating to the meeting or proxy solicitation may be sent to it electronically at that address. In some other cases, the Act simply imposes a mandatory obligation on the company to accept communication in electronic form, for example, with regard to communication of assent to a written resolution.[360] Of course, a difficulty with electronic communications is authentication. What is the equivalent of a signature on a hard copy? Section 1146 provides that an electronic communication is authenticated if the identity of the sender is confirmed in the manner specified by the company or, in the absence of such specification, the document contains a statement of the identity of the sender and the company has no reason to doubt the truth of the statement.

15–86

CONCLUSION

At the beginning of this chapter we pointed out that the CLR recommended reforms to improve the governance rights of shareholders, as part of its policy of making a shareholder-centred system of company law operate properly. The exercise of governance rights by shareholders may not be the only or even the most effective way of providing accountability on the part of management to shareholders—the threat of a takeover bid is probably more potent—but governance rights are certainly an important element of the accountability structure of company law. Having looked at the detail of the current law, how have the proposals of the CLR fared?

15–87

---

[357] 2006 Act Sch.5 para.14. The Act does often require a longer period, for example, quoted companies being required to maintain website availability of the annual accounts and reports until the next set is available: s.430. There are also minimum standards set for the quality of the website: para.12.

[358] For example, s.299 (written resolutions: period is from date of circulation to date resolution lapses); s.309 (general meetings: date of notification to date of conclusion of meeting, which would include any adjournment of it). The latter section is also a little more prescriptive about the detail of the notification to be given when it concerns website documents for a general meeting.

[359] 2006 Act Sch.4 para.6.

[360] 2006 Act s.296(2).

There has certainly been a great deal of tidying up and modernisation, notably the facilitation of electronic communication. Beyond that, in relation to private companies the written resolution provisions are now much simpler and likely to be more attractive, especially with the abandonment of the requirement of unanimity. For public companies, a major focus of concern was voting by the institutional shareholders, in terms of both the importance institutions attached to voting and the technical difficulties faced by indirect shareholders in casting their votes. The CLR proposed to rely mainly upon market developments and governmental suasion, rather than mandatory legal rules, to deal with both problems. Thus, there were to be fall-back powers only for the Secretary of State to require disclosure of voting by institutional shareholders[361] or to facilitate voting by indirect shareholders. As a result of pressure in Parliament, the fall-back powers designed to overcome the technical barriers to voting by indirect shareholders were given a slightly harder edge, in relation to information provision by quoted companies, but remain otherwise of a fall-back nature.[362] Meanwhile, policy-makers' understanding of the technical problems of voting has expanded with the development of the idea of "empty voting", a topic hardly touched on by the CLR, but it is not clear, even to the Shareholder Voting Working Party, consisting of those professionally involved in the area, what the correct solution should be.[363]

Finally, the CLR placed great store on the alignment of the AGM cycle with that for company reporting. Formally, that has been achieved, but the Government did not implement the further reform intended to take advantage of the alignment. This was the statutory "pause" of two weeks after circulation of the accounts and reports, during which members would be able to formulate resolutions, to be circulated by the company free of charge, to be debated at the AGM. This was undoubtedly a lost opportunity to turn the AGM into a more significant event.

---

[361] Now ss.277 et seq. See above, paras 15–25 et seq.

[362] See above, para.15–40.

[363] See the Myners Report 2007, above, fn.292. Also see Shareholder Voting Working Group, *Discussion Paper on Shareholder Proxy Voting* (July 2015) at *http://uk.practicallaw.com/9-616-7485* [Accessed 15 June 2016].

CHAPTER 16

DIRECTORS' DUTIES

INTRODUCTION

16–1   In Ch.14 we saw that it is common for the articles of large companies to confer extremely broad discretionary powers upon the boards of such companies. The arguments in favour of giving the centralised management a broad power to run the company are essentially arguments of efficiency. At the same time, the grant of a broad discretion creates a real risk that the powers will be exercised by the directors other than for the purposes for which they were conferred, and in particular will be exercised more in the interests of the senior management themselves than of anyone else. A central part of company law is thus concerned with providing a framework of rules which, on the one hand, constrains the potential abuse by directors of their powers, whilst on the other hand does not so constrain the directors that the efficiency gains from having a strong centralised management are dissipated. This is an age-old problem for company law and one that is constantly re-visited by successive generations of rule-makers, for no one approach can be shown to have struck the balance in an appropriate manner. It was a major issue in the debates leading up to the passage of the Companies Act 2006.

On the part of the rule-makers a number of distinct responses to this intractable problem can be identified. In Ch.14 we examined the extent to which rules relating to the structure and composition of the board itself and to the power of the shareholders to remove members of the board are used to constrain the exercise by the board of its powers and to produce accountability to the members of the company. In the previous chapter, we analysed the opportunities which the shareholders have to intervene directly in the management of the company by securing the passing at general meetings of resolutions binding the company or by subjecting the performance of the management to critical review. The taking of managerial decisions by the shareholders themselves is necessarily an activity of limited potential in large companies, since it flies in the face of the efficiency arguments for centralised management in the first place. Indeed, well-directed criticism of board performance may be more effective, especially if accompanied by an implicit or explicit threat of removal if performance is not improved.

In addition to rules on board structure and the governance rights of the members of the company, there is a third set of rules of great longevity in our law which are intended to operate so as to constrain the board's exercise of its powers. These are the duties which company law lays directly on the members of the board as to limits within which they should exercise their powers. These rules for directors were developed by the courts at an early stage, often on the basis of analogy with the rules applying to trustees. The substantial corpus of learning on the nature and scope of these general fiduciary or equitable duties and duties of skill and care has remained until very recently largely within the common law. Both the Law Commission and the Company Law Review ("CLR"),[1] however, recommended a "high level" statutory restatement of the common law principles. This recommendation, controversial though it was, made its way into the Companies Act 2006 Ch.2 of Pt 10 of which is headed: "General Duties of Directors".

The main aim behind the proposal for a "high level" statutory statement of directors' duties was to promote understanding of the basic principles underlying this area of law, especially among directors themselves. It was thought that this objective would be furthered if there was a relatively brief statutory statement of those principles in place of the previous situation whereby those principles had to be deduced from an elaborate body of case law. The behavioural premises upon which this view was based were never extensively investigated. And indeed the CLR and the Law Commission differed on whether the statutory statement should be comprehensive, in the sense of setting out at a high level all the duties to which directors were subject (the CLR's view) or only the principal duties, leaving the courts to develop duties which had not yet been clearly formulated in the cases (the Law Commissions' view).[2] In the end, and despite the initial behavioural premises, the Act probably comes closer to the Law Commissions' view: s.170(3) makes it clear that that only "certain" duties are set out in the statute, and so, for example, the issue of directors' duties to consider the interests of creditors is not dealt with comprehensively in Pt 10 of the 2006 Act and the

16–2

---

[1] *Company Directors: Regulating Conflicts of Interest and Formulating a Statement of Duties*, Law Com. No.261 and Scottish Law Com. No.173, Cm. 4436 (1999); CLR, Final Report, Ch.3 and Annex C. Other jurisdictions have codified directors' duties, Australia being one of them: see the major litigation in *ASIC v Healey* [2011] FCA 717 (the Centro litigation) and *ASIC v Macdonald* (2009) 256 ALR 199 (the James Hardie litigation).

[2] cf. Developing, para.3.82 and Completing, para.3.31, on the one hand, and Law Commissions, above, fn.1 at para.4.28, on the other.

courts remain free to develop this aspect of the law, even at the level of general principle.[3] But the likelihood of significant common law additions is small: the seven general duties set out in Ch.2 of Pt 10 have been long established at common law, and the courts have been able to deal with new problems by development of those general duties rather than by seeking to create new ones.

There were strong objections to codification. One, which was strongly advocated in particular by the Law Society and some of the leading commercial firms of solicitors in the City of London, was that such a reform was in danger of "freezing" the law of directors' duties and impeding its further development as circumstances changed. This contention could be refuted on two fronts. First, the statutory statement was intended to be, and in the Companies Act 2006 is, a "high level" statement, which gives the courts plenty of interpretative scope when applying the principles to the changing circumstances of commercial life. In addition, s.170(4) adds two propositions: first, the statutory general duties "shall be interpreted and applied in the same way as the common law duties or equitable principles", so that the existing case law on the common law duties will remain, in most cases, relevant to the interpretation of the statutory duties; and secondly, "regard shall be had to the corresponding common law rules and equitable principles in interpreting and applying the general principles". This second proposition is less obvious in its purpose, which seems, however, to be as follows. The law relating to directors was often developed by the courts by analogy with the rules relating to the duties of trustees to their beneficiaries and agents to their principals. Those rules continue to be embodied largely in the common law. The second proposition enables the courts, in developing the statutory duties of directors, to take into account developments in the equivalent common law duties applying to trustees and agents.[4] Thus, there was no desire on the part of the legislature to cut the law of directors' duties off from its historical roots in the duties applying to other persons acting in a fiduciary character.

A second objection to codification was that a high-level statutory statement would cause confusion or uncertainty about the relationship between the statutory statement and existing or future decisions of the courts at common law. These matters are dealt with in subss.170(3) and (4). The first subsection establishes the proposition that the general duties replace ("have effect in place of") the common law principles on which they are based. Consequently, in future, any allegation of breach of duty by the director to the company needs to be identified as a breach of one or more of the general duties set out in the statute, except insofar as the statutory statement preserves, as it does in relation to creditors' interests, the common law duties. And s.170(4) indicates, as described earlier, how the common law cases are to be used.

16–3　However, there is a difficulty underlying subss.170(3) and (4), arising from the fact that, as we shall see, the statutory statement is more than simply a restatement of the common law. In some cases it clarifies areas of uncertainty in the common law, for example, in relation to the standard of care expected of directors, whilst in other cases it adopts a different approach from that of the common law, for example, in relation to the authorisation by independent

---

[3] See above, para.9–11.

[4] HL Debs, vol.678, col.244, 6 February 2006 (Grand Committee), Lord Goldsmith.

directors of conflicts of duty. Where there is a departure in the statutory statement from the previous common law, it will obviously be inappropriate for the courts to refer to that common law in the interpretation of the statutory duties.[5] Since, however, the Act does not on its face reveal where it is confirming and where it is departing from the common law, it will be necessary to understand when the statute departs from the common law in order to determine the relevance of common law decisions to the interpretation of the statute.

The seven duties set out in Ch.2 of Pt 10 cover only the substantive content of the directors' duties. The CLR hoped to be able to recommend codification of the remedies for breaches of duty as well, but did not have enough time to produce a workable schema. The Government initially continued with this work after the CLR's final report but eventually abandoned the idea. However, the considerable work done in this direction has not been entirely lost since the work of Professor Richard Nolan, written for the CLR, has been published.[6] The failure to carry through this project is regrettable, since the remedies for breach of duty constitute an area where the law is confused and inconsistent and where practitioners as well as business people would have benefited from reform and restatement. In the result, the Act simply provides in s.178 that the civil consequences of breaches of the statutory duties are to be those which would apply at common law.

To Whom and by Whom are the Duties Owed?

To whom are the general duties owed and who can sue for their breach?

The company

Before turning to the substance of directors' duties, we need to ask who are their beneficiaries, i.e. to whom are they owed? The answer in British law is clear: the common law formulation was that the duties of the directors were owed to "the company" and that is repeated in s.170(1) in respect of the statutory duties. The importance of this point arises mainly in relation to the enforcement of those duties. First, it tells us that those duties are not owed to persons other than the company, for example, individual shareholders or employees. Secondly, it tells us that only those who are able to act as or on behalf of the company can enforce the duties. As we shall see in Ch.17, the issue of who can act on behalf of the company to enforce its rights, and in particular the question of whether an individual shareholder can do so through the so-called "derivative action", has caused considerable controversy ever since the emergence of modern company law in the nineteenth century. That is also an area where the Companies Act 2006 has introduced a major reform.

But even the seemingly straightforward notion that the company itself can enforce these duties has been subjected to some recent perturbations. The

16–4

---

[5] "The courts should continue to refer to existing case law on the corresponding common law rules and equitable principles, except where it is obviously irreconcilable with the statutory statement." (HC Debs, Standing Committee D, Thirteenth Sitting, 6 July 2006, col.536 (The Solicitor-General)).
[6] R.C. Nolan, "Enacting Civil Remedies in Company Law" (2001) 1 J.C.L.S. 245.

straightforward alignment between directors' duties being owed to the company and the company being able to sue for their breach is clearly crucial in maintaining the incentive structures underpinning directors' duties. This requires some careful thought about the rules of attribution in company law. In particular, even though a director's wrongdoing is commonly attributed to the company to make the company a wrongdoer and subject to claims brought by third parties, those same attribution rules do not necessarily apply when the company sues its directors. If they did, the company's action might be blocked on the grounds of consent or illegality. It is now recognised, in both civil[7] and criminal[8] law, that to block the company's action against the director on the grounds that the company was is some sense party to the illegality, or knew of and consented to the wrong, would be to undermine the duties owed by directors to their companies and that, except for rare cases,[9] this is not the law. Although the fact that it is not the law seems so sensible as not to merit debate, the reason why this is so is less clearly articulated than might be hoped. When, if ever, is a director's act, knowledge, or intention to be attributed to a claimant company? In *Bilta (UK) Ltd (In Liquidation) v Nazir*, Lord Neuberger put it this way[10]:

> "the question is simply an open one: whether or not it is appropriate to attribute an action by, or a state of mind of, a company director or agent to the company or the agent's principal in relation to a particular claim against the company or the principal must depend on the nature and factual context of the claim in question."

A little more guidance will undoubtedly become necessary as more cases test the boundaries, especially in the face of the contrary findings in *Safeway Stores Ltd v Twigger*.[11] A workable rule of attribution is ideally one which applies generally to individuals, not exclusively to directors, and applies whether the company is a claimant or a defendant. One suggestion is simply that no individual can benefit

---

[7] *Bilta (UK) Ltd (In Liquidation) v Nazir* [2015] UKSC 23; [2016] A.C. 1 SC at [7].

[8] *Attorney-General's Reference (No.2 of 1982)* [1984] Q.B. 624 CA; *R. v Phillipou* (1989) 89 Cr.App.R. 290 CA; *R. v Rozeik* [1996] B.C.C. 271 CA.

[9] The standout exception is *Safeway Stores Ltd v Twigger* [2010] EWCA Civ 1472 CA, which looks increasingly difficult to justify. The question the court had to answer, and one it conceded was difficult, was whether, if a company had been fixed with the improper intentions of its company officers and subjected to a regulatory sanction (under the Competition Act), could it then seek an indemnity from those same defaulting officers? The answer might seem simple: that the breach of duty by the officers had caused the company a loss, for which it could seek compensation. But this possibility was decisively rejected by the Court of Appeal. The policy underpinning the Competition Act 1998 was to impose "personal" sanctions on firms, the court held, and this liability could not then be offloaded onto individuals. To reach this end, the court relied on the illegality defence (i.e. the disqualifying principle of ex turpi causa). This decision was considered by the Supreme Court in *Bilta (UK) Ltd (In Liquidation) v Nazir* [2015] UKSC 23; [2016] A.C. 1, and although its correctness was not seriously challenged, its relevance and effect seem now very much confined to the statutory competition code (and its underlying policy): see [83] (Lord Sumption JSC) and [157]–[162] (Lords Toulson and Hodge JJSC), with whom Lord Neuberger PSC seemingly agreed though not expressing any conclusive view ([31]).

[10] *Bilta (UK) Ltd (In Liquidation) v Nazir* [2015] UKSC 23; [2016] A.C. 1 SC at [9], expressly agreeing with agree with Lord Mance's analysis at [37]–[44].

[11] *Safeway Stores Ltd v Twigger* [2010] EWCA Civ 1472 CA, and also see fn.9, above. In *Bilta (UK) Ltd (In Liquidation) v Nazir* [2015] UKSC 23; [2016] A.C. 1 SC, Lord Neuberger said, at [31], that he "would take a great deal of persuading that the Court of Appeal did not arrive at the correct conclusion in [the *Safeway*] case". However, Lords Toulson and Hodge were more critical: paras [157]–[162].

from claims which rely on *their own* acts counting as corporate acts so as to give them either a claim or a defence against the company.[12] This would explain most of the decided cases, but not all.[13]

Individual shareholders

We shall leave the derivative action until Ch.17. However, we need to touch briefly on the question of duties owed by directors directly to individual shareholders. It is clear that the statutory duties are owed only to the company, but equally clear that the Act does not purport to answer the question whether fiduciary or other duties are owed by the directors to shareholders individually. That issue is left to the common law. Traditionally, and still today, the common law has been reluctant to recognise directors' general duties as being owed to shareholders individually. This is hardly surprising. Recognition of duties owed individually would undermine the collective nature of the shareholders' association in a company. It would also undermine the rule that the duties are owed to and are enforceable by the company. If the directors owed to individual shareholders a set of duties parallel to those owed by them to the company, the restrictions on the derivative action could easily be side-stepped by means of the individual shareholder suing to enforce, not the company's rights, but his or her own rights.[14]

16–5

However, the precept that directors' duties are not owed to individual shareholders applies only to those duties which directors are subject to simply by virtue of their appointment and actions as directors. There may well be in a particular case dealings between one or more directors and one or more of the shareholders as a result of which a duty of some sort becomes owed by a director to one or more shareholders. This principle is now fully accepted in English law as a result of the decision of the Court of Appeal in *Peskin v Anderson*,[15] where Mummery LJ distinguished clearly between the fiduciary duties owed by directors to the company which arise out of the relationship between the director

---

[12] See S. Worthington, "Corporate Attribution and Agency: Back to Basics" (2017) 133 LQR (forthcoming).

[13] In particular, it does not explain *Safeway Stores Ltd v Twigger* [2010] EWCA Civ 1472 CA, already discussed; nor the case of *Stone & Rolls Ltd v Moore Stephens* [2009] UKHL 39; [2009] 1 A.C. 1391, discussed below at para.22–41, where the House of Lords concluded by a narrow majority that the illegality defence (ex turpi causa) applied to prevent a company from suing its auditors for their failure to detect fraud in circumstances where the fraud had been perpetrated by the very person who had formerly controlled the company. See however *Moulin Global Eyecare Trading (In Liquidation) v The Commissioner of Inland Revenue* [2014] HKCFA 22 Hong Kong Court of Final Appeal at [101] (Lord Walker NPJ); and *Bilta (UK) Ltd (In Liquidation) v Nazir* [2015] UKSC 23; [2016] A.C. 1 at [24]–[30] (Lord Neuberger PSC); [46]–[50] (Lord Mance JSC); [79]–[81] (Lord Sumption JSC); and [136]–[154] (Lords Toulson and Hodge JJSC). For comment on both cases, see fn.12.

[14] On similar grounds the court rejected an attempt to create a parallel set of duties owed by directors to individual shareholders via implied terms in the articles of association: *Towcester Racecourse Co Ltd v The Racecourse Association Ltd* [2003] 1 B.C.L.C. 260.

[15] *Peskin v Anderson* [2001] 1 B.C.L.C. 372 at 379. To the same end, see *Sharp v Blank* [2015] EWHC 3220 (Ch).

and the company, and fiduciary duties owed to shareholders which are dependent upon establishing "a special factual relationship between the directors and the shareholders in the particular case".

The crucial question, therefore, is what sort of dealing needs to take place between director and shareholder in order to trigger a fiduciary or other duty owed to an individual shareholder by the directors. Such a duty will certainly arise where, on the facts, the directors place themselves, as against shareholders individually, in one of the established legal relationships to which fiduciary duties are attached, such as agency. This may arise, for example, where the shareholders authorise the directors to sell their shares on their behalf to a potential takeover bidder.[16] If, in the course of such a relationship, the directors come across information which is pertinent to the shareholders' decision whether or on what terms to sell the shares, they would normally be obliged to disclose it to the shareholders on whose behalf they are acting. On the other hand, in *Percival v Wright*,[17] which is the leading authority for the proposition that the directors' duties as directors are not owed to the shareholders individually, the directors purchased shares from their members without revealing that negotiations were in progress for the sale of the company's undertaking at a favourable price. They were held not to be in breach of duty through their non-disclosure. Here, though, the shareholders approached the directors directly and sought to persuade the directors to purchase their shares themselves rather than to act as the shareholders' agents to sell the shares to third parties.

16–6   Nevertheless, there is no doubt that the directors of a company are likely to have much more information at their disposal about the company and so are likely to be at an advantage when dealing with the members. The law of agency, as we have just seen, will cover some, but not all of this ground. Can the doctrine of a "special factual relationship" be extended beyond the law of agency? Commonwealth authority established some time ago that it can. In *Coleman v Myers*[18] the New Zealand Court of Appeal found that a fiduciary duty of disclosure arose, even in the absence of agency, in the case of a small family company where there was a gross disparity of knowledge between the directors and the shareholders and where the shareholders of the company had traditionally relied on the directors for information and advice. When the directors negotiated with the shareholders for the purchase of their shares and, therefore, were clearly not acting on behalf of the shareholders, they were nevertheless held to be subject to a fiduciary duty of full disclosure of relevant facts about the company to the shareholders. The New Zealand decision was approved by the English Court of Appeal in *Peskin v Anderson*,[19] though the English decision also reveals the

---

[16] *Briess v Woolley* [1954] A.C. 333 HL; *Allen v Hyatt* (1914) 30 T.L.R. 444 PC.

[17] *Percival v Wright* [1902] 2 Ch. 421. This applies even if all the shares are owned by a holding company with which the directors have service contracts: *Bell v Lever Bros* [1932] A.C. 161 HL.

[18] *Coleman v Myers* [1977] 2 N.Z.L.R. 225 NZCA. In the Supreme Court (ibid.) Mahon J had held that *Percival v Wright* was wrongly decided but the Court of Appeal distinguished it. See also *Brunninghausen v Glavanics* (1999) 46 N.S.W.L.R. 538 CANSW.

[19] *Peskin v Anderson* [2001] 1 B.C.L.C. 372 at 397, following the decisions of Browne-Wilkinson VC in *Re Chez Nico (Restaurants) Ltd* [1991] B.C.C. 736 at 750 and, though not cited, of David Mackie QC in *Platt v Platt* [1999] 2 B.C.L.C. 745 (the Court of Appeal in that case did not deal with the point: [2001] 1 B.C.L.C. 698).

limits of the rule. In the English case, directors were not obliged to disclose to shareholders their plans for the company, even though the shareholders' decision on the sale of their shares would have been affected by the knowledge, where the directors were not parties to or otherwise involved in the sale of the shares, and the company's interests arguably required the directors' plans to be kept secret until they matured.[20]

This means that, despite the recent significant developments in English law based on a "special relationship" exception to the general proposition that directors do not owe duties directly to the shareholders, the exception is essentially one of significance for family or small companies, and does not substantially reduce, within companies with large shareholder bodies, the significance of the general proposition. The cases already noted affirm that this is true even where advice is given by directors in the course of a takeover bid. In *Re A Company*[21] Hoffmann J held that directors were not obliged to offer their shareholders advice on the bid, but, if they did so, they must do so "with a view to enabling the shareholders to sell, if they so wish, at the best price" and not, for example, in order to favour one bid, which the directors supported, over another, which they did not.[22] This identifies two strands: the directors' advice must be careful, and must also be given so as to achieve its (proper) purposes, and not the directors' own (improper) purposes.[23] Neither strand imports a "fiduciary" duty of loyalty to the shareholders.

Other stakeholders

If British company law has been reluctant to recognise general duties owed by directors to individual shareholders, it perhaps goes without saying that it has not recognised such duties owed to individual employees or creditors[24] or other groups[25] upon whom the successful functioning of the company depends. It is important to distinguish this issue (duties owed directly to stakeholder groups)

16–7

---

[20] Similarly, see *Sharp v Blank* [2015] EWHC 3220 (Ch), with Nugee J denying the directors owed a fiduciary duty to the shareholders in the context of Lloyds Banking Group's acquisition of Halifax Bank of Scotland Plc.

[21] *Re A Company* [1986] B.C.L.C. 382. The case involved an application under s.459 (see Ch.20, below), but the judge's analysis appears to have related to the common law.

[22] See also *Re Charterhouse Capital Ltd* [2014] EWHC 1410 (Ch) at [276] in particular (Asplin J), as affirmed in [2015] EWCA Civ 536 CA (in particular, [50]). In addition, takeover bids for public and listed companies will be governed by the City Code on Takeovers and Mergers (below, Ch.28), which both requires directors to give advice and attempts to ensure that that advice is given to serve the shareholders' needs. These more demanding provisions of the Code will in practice overtake those of the common law.

[23] On proper purposes requirement, see below, para.16–26.

[24] *Yukong Line Ltd v Rendsburg Investments Corporate (No.2)* [1998] 1 W.L.R. 294; and see above at para.9–11.

[25] e.g. the beneficiaries of a trust which the company, as trustee, is managing: *Bath v Standard Land Co Ltd* [1911] 1 Ch. 618; *Gregson v HAE Trustees Ltd* [2008] EWHC 1006 (Ch); [2008] 2 B.C.L.C. 542, confirming that although the beneficiary could not pursue a claim against the director directly (since the director's duty was owed to the trustee company, not to the beneficiary, although the beneficiary was in turn owed duties by the trustee company), the beneficiary would, in any event, be protected by the liquidator's ability to pursue the insolvent trustee company's claim against its defaulting director.

from the question of how far directors' duties owed to the company require the directors to take into account the interests of stakeholder groups. Explicit duties of this latter kind were recommended by the CLR and were embodied in the 2006 Act. We shall deal with them below in our analysis of the statutory duties.

By whom are the general duties owed?

De facto and shadow directors

16–8   The general statutory duties to be discussed in this chapter are clearly owed by those who have been properly appointed as directors of the company. From the early days, however, the courts have applied the common law and statutory duties also to persons who act as directors, even though they have not been formally appointed as such—normally referred as "de facto directors". There seems to be no doubt that the general statutory duties apply to de facto directors,[26] whatever the debate over whether a person is indeed a de facto director or is merely performing some lower-level management role.[27] Although there is no single test for de facto directors, the central question which the courts seek to answer is whether the individual was "part of the corporate governing structure"[28] or has "assumed the status and functions of a company director"[29] so as to attract responsibility under the Act as if he or she were a de jure director.

This factual question is often difficult to answer, but the problem is exacerbated where the issue is whether a de jure director of one company can, in the course of acting in that role, become a de facto director of another company. Does the formal role with one company protect against liability to the other company? In answering this question, the Supreme Court in *Commissioners of*

---

[26] There is some statutory support for this view in the definition of a director in s.250 as including "any person occupying the position of director, by whatever name called".

[27] The easy cases are those such as *Re Canadian Land Reclaiming and Colonizing Co* (1880) 14 Ch. D. 660 concerning a director not properly appointed because of his failure to take up shares in the company which action its articles stipulated to be a condition for appointment as director. For a more detailed discussion in a modern context of what makes a person a de facto director see *Secretary of State for Trade and Industry v Tjolle* [1998] 1 B.C.L.C. 333; and *Re Gemma Ltd v Davies, Gemma Ltd (In Liquidation)* [2008] EWHC 546 (Ch); [2008] 2 B.C.L.C. 281. This latter case, at [40], shows that the important question is whether the person is factually engaged in the central management of the company on an equal footing with the other directors and performing tasks that can only properly be discharged by directors, regardless of whether the person is held out as a director of the company (although holding out may provide important supporting evidence that the individual is acting as a director). Also see *Commissioners of HM Revenue and Customs v Holland* [2010] UKSC 51; [2010] 1 W.L.R. 2793, discussed below, declining to identify a single defining test ([26], [39], [93]) but supporting the focus on finding real influence in the central governance of the company (paras [36], [91]). See also *Elsworth Ethanol Co Ltd v Hartley* [2014] EWHC 99 (IPEC) at [54], and, as an illustration of the highly factual nature of the question, [58]–[85] (Judge Hacon); and *Smithton Ltd v Naggar* [2014] EWCA Civ 939; [2014] B.C.C. 482 at [33]–[44] (Arden LJ). See also generally *Secretary of State for Business, Innovation and Skills v Chohan* [2013] EWHC 680 (Ch) (Hildyard J); *Vivendi SA v Richards* [2013] EWHC 3006 (Newey J).

[28] *Secretary of State for Trade and Industry v Tjolle* [1998] B.C.C. 282, 290 (Jacob J).

[29] *Re Kaytech International Plc* [1999] B.C.C. 390 at 402 CA (Robert Walker LJ).

HM Revenue and Customs v Holland[30] divided 3:2 over what Lord Collins described as differences over matters of law and principle.[31] The issue was whether an individual who was the only active director of the sole corporate director[32] of the principal companies was, in those circumstances, also a de facto director of the principal companies, held to be part of the corporate governance of them and having fiduciary and other directors' duties imposed on him in relation to them. Those in the majority thought that such a finding would contradict the principle of separate legal personality, and reflect a failure to recognise the distinction between a company and its directors, where, as here (so they held), the individual had done nothing other than discharge his duties a director of the corporate director, and in circumstances where the law condones corporate directorships.[33]

This argument has its attractions. Indeed, it follows, although not explicitly, the approach adopted in determining the individual liability of company directors to third parties in contract and in tort in circumstances where the company, by virtue of the acts of its directors, is also liable to the same parties.[34] In the fiduciary arena it is suggested that the question to ask is not whether the purported director assumed fiduciary responsibilities to the company; the answer to that, at least from the director, is likely to be precisely not (and hence the corporate directorship structure). Better to ask, as in negligent misstatement cases,[35] whether, in the circumstances, and looking at what the purported director did, the company is entitled to demand that the individual be subjected to fiduciary obligations. Where the formal structure of a corporate directorship has been transparently erected, the answer is surely no, even though, absent that structure, it would perhaps equally certainly have been yes.

The practical effect in *Holland* was that the principal companies' acknowledged liability to the Inland Revenue was not met by the principals, which were insolvent, nor by the corporate director, which though liable was an undercapitalised intermediary, nor by Holland, since he was not a de facto director of the

---

[30] *Commissioners of HM Revenue and Customs v Holland* [2010] UKSC 51; [2010] 1 W.L.R. 2793 SC.

[31] *Commissioners of HM Revenue and Customs v Holland* [2010] UKSC 51; [2010] 1 W.L.R. 2793 SC at [53].

[32] This is no longer permitted: every company must now have at least one human director (s.155); and corporate directorships will be fully prohibited (subject to exceptions) as a result of new ss.156A–156C, introduced by s.87 of the Small Business, Enterprise and Employment Act 2015 (commencement expected October 2016).

[33] *Commissioners of HM Revenue and Customs v Holland* [2010] UKSC 51; [2010] 1 W.L.R. 2793 SC at [25], [28]–[29], [39]–[40], [42]–[43], [94]–[96]. Also see previous note. This follows the trend in other jurisdictions where the legislature has intervened to require that all directors be natural persons: e.g. as under the Corporations Act 2001 s.201B (Australia), the Canada Business Corporations Act 1985 s.105(1)(c), the New York Business Corporation Law s.701, and the Delaware General Corporate Law s.141(b) (see [2010] UKSC 51; [2010] 1 W.L.R. 2793 SC at [96], Lord Collins).

[34] See above, paras 7–34 and 7–37 et seq. By contrast, see [2010] UKSC 51; [2010] 1 W.L.R. 2793 SC, [117]–[118] (Lord Walker) on the approach in tort cases.

[35] Where, again, the question is often said to be simply whether the adviser "assumed" responsibility for the advice being given, although the court, taking a more objective approach, seems to search for whether the advisee is entitled to insist that the adviser did so do that.

principal companies.[36] In the circumstances it is difficult not to feel some sympathy for the views of the dissenting minority: Lords Walker and Clarke would have preferred a conclusion that, while a de facto director is not formally invested with office, if what he actually does amounts to taking all the important decisions affecting the relevant company, and seeing that they are carried out, he is acting as a director of that company.[37] Lord Walker even suggested that the majority's contrary characterisation of Holland's activities amounted to "the most arid formalism",[38] adding that if on these facts Holland could not be found to be both the de jure director of the corporate director and, at the same time, the de facto director of the principal companies, then it was difficult to imagine facts which would ever give rise to such a conclusion; the result, Lord Walker thought, would be to make it "easier for risk-averse individuals to use artificial corporate structures in order to insulate themselves against responsibility to an insolvent company's unsecured creditors".[39] This, clearly, is not the goal, although nor too is riding roughshod over legitimate corporate risk allocation structures.

16–9 As well as rules on de jure and de facto directors, some years ago the legislature created a third category of director—the "shadow director". This is a person, not formally appointed as a director, but in accordance with whose directions or instructions the directors of a company are accustomed to act.[40] A number of specific statutory duties which supplement the general duties, and are to be found in Chs 3 and 4 of Pt 10, are expressed to apply also to shadow directors. In relation to the general duties contained in Ch.2, s.170(5) initially unhelpfully provided that they apply to shadow directors "to the extent that the corresponding common law rules or equitable principles apply"; this has now been amended to provide that shadow directors will equally be subject to the general duties "where and to the extent that they are capable of so applying".[41]

This legislative change conclusively confirms the slow judicial working towards the same position. In the early case of *Ultraframe (UK) Ltd v Fielding*,[42] Lewison J had taken the view that directors' fiduciary duties did not automatically apply to shadow directors, on the grounds that a shadow director,

---

[36] Although perhaps the desired remedy might be achieved in two steps, with the principal companies suing the corporate director, liquidating it, and it (through its liquidators) then suing Holland for the liabilities his management failings had caused to it, with the proceeds of this second claim then passed down the chain to meet the corporate director's primary liability to the principal companies. The issue in *Holland* is that the wrong in the first step was wrongly paying away dividends (a strict liability claim); in the second step it would perhaps have to have been negligently advising that the payments were permissible in the circumstances, and the facts may not have readily supported such a claim (given the legal advice, etc. obtained by Holland).

[37] *Commissioners of HM Revenue and Customs v Holland* [2010] UKSC 51; [2010] 1 W.L.R. 2793 SC at [114]–[115], [129]–[134], [139], [144]–[145].

[38] *Commissioners of HM Revenue and Customs v Holland* [2010] UKSC 51; [2010] 1 W.L.R. 2793 SC at [115].

[39] *Commissioners of HM Revenue and Customs v Holland* [2010] UKSC 51; [2010] 1 W.L.R. 2793 SC at [101] and [115].

[40] 2006 Act s.251(1).

[41] See Small Business, Enterprise and Employment Act 2015 s.89(1).

[42] *Ultraframe (UK) Ltd v Fielding* [2005] EWHC 1638 (Ch) at [1279] et seq.—the case went on appeal but the CA did not consider this issue. cf. *Yukong Line Ltd v Rendsburg Investments Corp of Liberia* [1998] 1 W.L.R. 294, in which Toulson J, in a brief and unargued dictum, took the opposite view.

unlike a de facto or properly appointed director, had not undertaken to act on behalf of the company and so had not put him- or herself in a fiduciary relationship with the company. This decision showed the continuing influence of the trustee analogy in the development of directors' duties, although earlier editions of this book had suggested that the analogy was an unfortunate one, since it provided a relatively easy route for the true mover behind the company's strategy to distance him- or herself from liability for the decisions taken, by appointing a compliant board and giving it instructions at crucial points.[43] By contrast, almost a decade later the equally careful analysis of Newey J in *Vivendi SA v Richards*[44] doubted this approach and concluded that, by definition of the role,[45] a shadow director's self-appointed involvement in influencing governance decisions must at law inevitably mean that shadow directors commonly owed fiduciary duties to at least some degree.[46] This judicial and statutory change is welcome. If the purpose of the law of directors' duties is to constrain the exercise of the discretion vested in the board, it would be unfortunate if those rules did not reach all those involved in that exercise.

The early source of this definitional difficulty probably lay in the firm distinction which the courts sought to draw between a de facto and a shadow director. Although the language used to define a shadow director is of some antiquity,[47] the term "shadow director" was applied as a short-hand way of referring to the definition only in the Companies Act 1980. As we have indicated, this was done in order to make clear the scope of application of the specific duties created by that Act which applied to certain transactions entered into by directors with their companies, the modern forms of which we discuss below. The 1980 Act set the courts off on the task of defining the difference between a de facto and a shadow director. In *Re Hydrodam (Corby) Ltd*[48] Millett J took the view that in nearly all cases the two categories were mutually exclusive:

> "A *de facto* director...is one who claims to act and purports to act as a director, although not validly appointed as such. A shadow director, by contrast, does not claim or purport to act as director. On the contrary, he claims not to be a director. He lurks in the shadows, sheltering behind others who, he claims, are the only directors of the company to the exclusion of himself."

---

[43] The judge did accept that the shadow director might attract liability under the rules relating to the involvement of third parties in breaches of directors' duties (see below, para.16–134), but these provisions are relatively restrictive.

[44] *Vivendi SA v Richards* [2013] EWHC 3006; [2013] B.C.C. 771.

[45] *Sukhoruchkin v Bekestein* [2014] EWCA Civ 399 CA [39]–[41], notes the differences in approach between *Ultraframe* and *Vivendi* without preferring one or other, but also notes that any conclusions are necessarily built on the foundation of the UK statutory definition of a shadow director, and so may not be appropriate in the context of other statutory definitions (as in the instant case).

[46] See [2013] EWHC 3006 [133]–[145], especially [142]. See also *Smithton Ltd v Naggar* [2014] EWCA Civ 939 CA at [33]–[45] (Arden LJ). The Law Commissions also took the view that the shadow director was subject to the common law duties (as they then were) and certainly ought to be "where he effectively acts as a director through the people he can influence": Law Commission and Scottish Law Commission, *Company Directors: Regulating Conflicts of Interest and Formulating a Statement of Duties, A Joint Consultation Paper*, 1998, para.17.15. The CLR took a similar view: Completing, para.4.7.

[47] It seems to have been introduced by the Companies (Particulars as to Directors) Act 1917 s.3.

[48] *Re Hydrodam (Corby) Ltd* 1994] 2 B.C.L.C. 180, 183.

16–10 This view that the categories are mutually exclusive is increasingly doubted,[49] but nevertheless it remains important to draw some distinction in a statutory context because certain statutory provisions apply to both shadow directors and directors whilst others apply only to directors, in which category the courts have long included de facto directors. Nevertheless, the modern view, especially given the statutory change in terminology in s.170(5), is that the differences between the two categories of directors should not be the main focus of attention when deciding the applicability of the general statutory duties of directors. As Robert Walker LJ pointed out in *Re Kaytech International Plc*,[50] "the two concepts do have at least this much in common, that an individual who was not a *de jure* director is alleged to have exercised real influence in the corporate governance of a company".[51] In principle, the general duties should apply to all these people with "real influence". If there is a difference, it is practical, and likely to be that the general rules should be applied to shadow directors only to the extent that they have exercised control over the board: it is not inherent in the definition of a shadow director that he or she should have controlled all the activities of the board[52]; by contrast, most de facto directors assume general directorial responsibilities.

Finally, in the context of shadow directors, two statutory exceptions are provided. First, it is recognised that boards are very likely—indeed are well-advised—to act in accordance with the directions, advice or guidance of their professional advisers or of parties acting under statutory or Ministerial authority. These advisers are not thereby to be regarded as shadow directors (s.251(2)). Secondly, and perhaps more controversially, a company is not to be regarded as the shadow director of its subsidiary for the purpose of the general duties by reason only that the directors of the subsidiary are accustomed to act on the instructions of the parent (s.251(3)).[53] And, although the Act is silent on this, the parent is also unlikely to be classified as a de facto director, rather than a shadow director, if it is not involved in a direct way in the central management of the subsidiary. A parent company can thus impose a common policy on the group of companies which it controls without placing itself in breach of duty to the subsidiary (for example, because the group policy is not in the best interests of the subsidiary). Note, though, that s.251(3) does not answer the separate question

---

[49] As well as the cases which follow, see too *McKillen v Misland (Cyprus) Investments Ltd* [2012] EWHC 521, which describes de facto and shadow directors at [19]–[31], concluding at paras [32]–[34] that there is no sharp dividing line between the two classes (David Richards J); similarly, see *Smithton Ltd v Naggar* [2014] EWCA Civ 939 CA at paras [33]–[45] (Arden LJ).

[50] *Re Kaytech International Plc* [1999] 2 B.C.L.C. 351, 424 CA.

[51] Also see *Commissioners of HM Revenue and Customs v Holland* [2010] UKSC 51; [2010] 1 W.L.R. 2793 at [110] and [127]—Lords Walker and Clarke respectively, although both dissenting on the majority's finding that the defendant was not a de facto director.

[52] *Secretary of State for Trade and Industry v Deverell* [2001] Ch. 340 at [35] CA. The conclusion to be drawn from all these cases is perhaps that it is often possible to conclude that the shadow director owes all the general duties of de jure directors in relation to any decisions where he or she directed the outcome, but whether the shadow director is also subject to other duties, e.g. on pursuing corporate opportunities (see below, para.16–86), needs to be more carefully determined on a case by case basis. See also *Vivendi SA v Richards* [2013] EWHC 3006 at [133]–[145] (Newey J); and *Smithton Ltd v Naggar* [2014] EWCA Civ 939 CA at [33]–[45] (Arden LJ).

[53] A non-corporate controlling shareholder does not have the same protection.

of whether the directors of the subsidiary can agree to implement the group policy without placing themselves in breach of duty to the subsidiary, which is discussed in para.16–36, below.

Senior managers

The general statutory duties set out in Ch.2 of Pt 10 clearly do not apply to managers who are not directors of the company. However, it is important to note that, when applying the law relating to directors' duties, the courts do not distinguish between the actions of the director as director and actions as manager, where the director is an executive director of the company. Those duties will apply to both aspects of the director's activities.[54] In consequence, some actions by senior managers of the company, provided they are also directors of the company, will be subject to the controls of the general statutory duties. Although management theory may posit that it is the role of the board in large companies to set the company's strategy and to oversee its execution, rather than to execute it itself, the law of directors' duties does not make this distinction in the case of a director who has both a board position and a non-board executive function. This is consonant with the traditional provision in companies' articles that the management of the company is a matter for the board of directors.

    16–11

However, it can also be asked whether these general statutory duties (or common law fiduciary duties) apply to the senior managers of the company who are not formally appointed as directors. In *Canadian Aero Services Ltd v O'Malley* the Canadian Supreme Court approved a statement from an earlier edition of this book that directors' common law fiduciary duties (as they then were) apply to those "officials of the company who are authorised to act on its behalf and in particular to those acting in a senior management capacity".[55] That view has not been adopted expressly in any English court. Moreover, it is clear that, in principle, the employment relationship is not a fiduciary relationship, so that it would be inappropriate to apply the full range of fiduciary or directors' duties even to senior employees. However, this proposition is subject to a number of qualifications. First, a senior employee who does in fact discharge the duties of a director may be classed as a de facto director, under the principles discussed above. Secondly, the courts have held that, as a result of the specific terms of an employee's contract and of the particular duties undertaken by him or her, a common law fiduciary relationship may arise between employee and employer, even in the case of employees who are not part of senior management, though the fiduciary duty may be restricted to some part of their overall duties.[56] The view of the Canadian Supreme Court is not inconsistent with these developments, since it too was derived from an analysis of the functions of the employees in question as

---

[54] For an illustration, see *Item Software (UK) Ltd v Fassihi* [2005] 2 B.C.L.C. 91 CA, where the consequence of this approach was to subject the director to a higher standard of fiduciary duty than would have been applicable had he only been an employee, albeit a senior one.

[55] *Canadian Aero Services Ltd v O'Malley* (1973) 40 D.L.R. (3d) 371 at 381.

[56] *University of Nottingham v Fishel* [2000] I.C.R. 1462; *Shepherds Investments Ltd v Walters* [2007] I.R.L.R. 110; *Helmet Integrated Systems Ltd v Tunnard* [2007] I.R.L.R. 126 CA; *Ranson v Customer Systems Plc* [2012] EWCA Civ 841. The issues remain controversial: see the disagreement in *Generics (UK) Ltd v Yeda Research & Development Co Ltd* [2012] EWCA Civ 726 at [19]–[36] (Sir

senior management employees, though there will be scope for argument on the facts of each case about how extensive the fiduciary aspects of the employee's duties are. It goes without saying that, should a senior manager place him- or herself in an agency relationship with the company, then the normal fiduciary incidents of that relationship would arise. Thirdly, the implied and mutual duty of trust and confidence which is imported into all contracts of employment can in some cases operate in substantially the same way as certain directors' general duties.[57] This is particularly the case in relation to competitive activities on the part of an employee or the non-disclosure by senior managers of the wrongdoing of fellow employees and in some cases their own wrongdoing.[58]

16–12   The exclusion of senior managers as such from the statutory general duties of directors probably depends upon the continuation of the UK practice, as recommended in the UK Corporate Governance Code,[59] that the board should contain a substantial number of executive directors. If British practice were to move in the US direction of reducing the number of executive directors on the board, sometimes to one (the CEO), and there are indications of a move in that direction, then confining the statutory duties to members of the board might become a policy which needed to be re-considered.[60]

Finally, the above discussion has concerned the fiduciary duties of employees and directors. In relation to the statutory duty of care (see below), which equally applies only to directors, the common law duty of care required of employees

---

Robin Jacob) contrasted with [41]–[84] (Etherton LJ), with whom Ward LJ was persuaded to agree ([91]–[121]). Generally, see *Airbus Operations Ltd v Withey* [2014] EWHC 1126 QB; *Halcyon House Ltd v Baines* [2014] EWHC 2216 QB.

[57] Note, however, that the employee's duty of "mutual trust and confidence" finds its roots in contract rather than the law of fiduciary obligations, as emphasised by Lewison LJ (with whom Lloyd and Pill LJJ agreed) in *Ranson v Customer Systems Plc* [2012] EWCA Civ 841 CA, at [36]–[40]; and the distinction between the contractual duty of fidelity and the duties of a fiduciary are discussed at [41]–[43].

[58] *Shepherds Investments Ltd v Walters* [2007] I.R.L.R. 110 at [129]–[130]; *Sybron Corp v Rochem Ltd* [1984] Ch. 112 CA; *Tesco Stores Ltd v Pook* [2004] I.R.L.R. 618. On disclosure of wrongdoing, the main difference between a senior manager and a director concerns the extent to which they are obliged to disclose their own wrongdoing: see *Bell v Lever Bros* [1932] A.C. 161 HL (suggesting an employee is never under a duty to disclose his own wrongdoing); and *Item Software (UK) Ltd v Fassihi* [2005] 2 B.C.L.C. 91 CA, taking a narrower view. However, all may depend on the employee's contract: in *Ranson v Customer Systems Plc* [2012] EWCA Civ 841 CA, it was held that an employee can have an obligation to disclose his own wrongdoing, but that this can only arise out of the terms of the contract of employment, not by any analogy with the fiduciary duties owed by company directors (see [44]–[61]). The analysis may matter: *Threlfall v ECD Insight Ltd* [2012] EWHC 3543 at [111]–[126] (Lang J); *Haysport Properties Ltd v Ackerman* [2016] EWHC 393 (Ch).

[59] See para.14–69.

[60] Contrast the Australian Corporations Act 2001, which defines an "officer", in s.9, as a person "(i) who makes, or participates in making, decisions that affect the whole, or a substantial part, of the business of the entity; or (ii) who has the capacity to affect significantly the entity's financial standing", and then makes officers subject to many of the statutory duties applying to directors (see ss.179 et seq.). CA 2006 does not take this approach with directors' duties (ss.170 et seq.), although elsewhere it does make rules which apply more generally to "officers" (defined inclusively in s.1173), typically in connection with reporting requirements (see, e.g. s.113(7)). Even though corporate directors are to be abolished (see above, fn.32), it remains possible, it seems, to have "corporate officers" (see s.1122).

seems to come very close to that now required of directors (taking account of the fact that the application of the reasonable care standard will produce different results in different circumstances).[61]

Former directors

At common law the general duties of directors attach from the date when the director's appointment takes effect[62] but do not necessarily cease when the appointment ends. The second part of the common law position is explicitly confirmed by s.170(2) which provides that a person who ceases to be a director continues to be subject to two of the seven general duties, namely those relating to corporate opportunities of which he had become aware whilst still a director and the taking of a benefit from a third party in respect of acts or omissions whilst still a director. However, those two duties are to be applied by the courts to former directors "subject to any necessary adaptations", for example, to take account of the fact that the former director may no longer have up-to-date knowledge of the conduct of the company's affairs. In this way it can be said that liability is imposed in respect of actions which straddle the time before and after the director ceased to hold office.[63]

16–13

Particularly difficult issues can arise in relation to the analysis of actions by directors, whilst still directors, but after they have given notice of resignation. In such cases the director is not (yet) a former director and the issue is discussed below at para.16–94.

Directors of insolvent companies

When a company enters into an insolvency procedure (liquidation, administration or receivership), the situation under British law, unlike that in the US, is that the powers of the directors are substantially curtailed and the direction of the business passes into the hands of the insolvency practitioner appointed to act in one or other of these roles and who acts in the interests of the creditors. This is likely to have a substantial impact on what the law of directors' duties requires of the directors in practice, but does not in principle relieve the directors of their obligations to the company.[64]

16–14

---

[61] For employees see *Lister v Romford Ice and Cold Storage Co Ltd* [1957] A.C. 555 HL; and *Janata Bank v Ahmed* [1981] I.C.R. 791 CA and for the duty of care required of directors, see the following section. For a case where the defendant was sued for breach of his duty of care both as a director and as an employee, see *Simtel Communications Ltd v Rebak* [2006] 2 B.C.L.C. 571.

[62] In *Lindgren v L & P Estates Ltd* [1968] Ch. 572, the Court of Appeal rejected an argument that a "director-elect" is in a fiduciary relationship to the company.

[63] This point is discussed further below in relation to the taking of corporate opportunities, which is where it most often arises. See the approach in *Thermascan Ltd v Norman* [2011] B.C.C. 535.

[64] Directors cannot, for example, be held liable for the failure to exercise powers which they no longer have. In *Ultraframe (UK) Ltd v Fielding* [2005] EWHC 1638 at [1330] Lewison J suggested the "no conflict" rule would not apply either (though the "no profit" and basic loyalty duties would continue to bite). Also see paras 9–4 et seq. and 9–11 et seq., above.

DIRECTORS' DUTIES OF SKILL, CARE AND DILIGENCE

Historical development

16–15   We turn now to the substance of the duties which directors assume when they take up office. It is common in comparative analysis of company law systems to divide those duties into duties of loyalty and duties of care. Although the line between these two sets of duties is not absolutely clear, they broadly correspond to the two main risks which shareholders run when management of their company is delegated to the board. The board may be active, but not in the direction of promoting the shareholders' interests; or the board may be slack or incompetent. We shall adopt this division here, for it corresponds also to the two basic common law sources of the rules on directors' duties in English law: duties of loyalty based on equitable principles, developed initially by courts of equity, and duties of skill and care which now rest, with some particular twists, on the principles of the law of negligence. However, it should be noted that the general duties laid out in Ch.2 of Pt 10 are not divided in this way. The duty of care appears as the fourth of the seven duties. It is nevertheless with this duty that we begin.

The issue in this area which has long been debated is that of the appropriate standard of care to be required of directors. Historically, the common law was based upon a very low standard of care, because it was subjectively formulated. The traditional view is to be found in a stream of largely nineteenth-century cases which culminated in the decision in 1925 in *Re City Equitable Fire Insurance Co*.[65] Those cases seem to have framed the directors' duties of skill and care with non-executive rather than executive directors in mind and, moreover, on the basis of a view that the non-executive director had no serious role to play within the company but was simply a piece of window-dressing aimed at promoting the company's image.[66] The result was a conceptualisation of the duty in highly subjective terms. The proposition was famously formulated by Romer J in the *City Equitable* case that "a director need not exhibit in the performance of his duties a greater degree of skill than may reasonably be expected from a person of *his* knowledge and experience".[67] The courts were also influenced by a model of corporate decision-making which gave the shareholders effective control over the choice of directors. If the shareholders chose incompetent directors, that was their fault and the remedy lay in their hands. As we have seen,[68] that is no longer an

---

[65] *Re City Equitable Fire Insurance Co* [1925] Ch. 407, a decision of the Court of Appeal but always quoted for the judgment of Romer J at first instance, because the appeal concerned only the liability of the auditors.

[66] The most famous example of this is perhaps *Re Cardiff Savings Bank* [1892] 2 Ch. 100, where the Marquis of Bute, whose family, despite its Scottish antecedents, owned, indeed had largely rebuilt, Cardiff Castle, was appointed president of the Bank at the age of six months and attended only one meeting of the board in his whole life. He was held not liable.

[67] *Re City Equitable Fire Insurance Co* [1925] Ch. 407 at 427 (emphasis added). This test also contains *an* objective element, because the director could be held liable for failing to live up to the standard which a person of his or her skill is reasonably capable of reaching, but the strong restriction in the proposition is the subjective one, since the director can never be required to achieve a standard higher than that which he or she is personally capable of reaching.

[68] See above, Ch.15.

accurate picture of the degree of control exercised by shareholders over boards of directors in most public companies. Furthermore, the proposition formulated by Romer J was highly inappropriate for executive directors, appointed to their positions and paid large, sometimes very large, sums of money for the expertise which they assert they can bring to the business. The implicit view of the role of the non-executive director also became anachronistic after the development of the corporate governance codes in the 1990s, which allocated a major role to the non-executive directors in the monitoring of the executive directors.[69]

Even before the enactment of the Companies Act 2006 this was an area of the law of directors' duties which was beginning to change. The courts were influenced by the development of more demanding and objective statutory standards for directors whose companies were facing insolvency[70] and began to develop the common law requirements by analogy with those specific statutory provisions. The beginnings of the modern approach at common law can be found in *Dorchester Finance Co v Stebbing*,[71] but it was a pair of first instance decisions by Hoffmann J[72] in the 1990s which marked a move towards a fully objective approach. He explicitly adopted as an accurate expression of the common law the test contained in s.214(4) of the Insolvency Act in relation to wrongful trading.[73] This inchoate change in the common law was endorsed by both the Law Commissions and the CLR and now finds expression in s.174 of the 2006 Act. This section first requires that "a director of a company must exercise reasonable care, skill and diligence" and then goes on to define what is meant by reasonable care, using a formulation which tracks very closely s.214 of the Insolvency Act 1986:

"This means the care, skill and diligence that would be exercised by a reasonably diligent person with (a) the general knowledge, skill and experience that may reasonably be expected of a person carrying out the same functions carried out by the director in relation to the company, and (b) the general knowledge, skill and experience that the director has."

However, it should be noted that in one particular area the statute has exempted directors from liability for negligence. In the case of misstatements in

---

[69] See above, para.14–69.
[70] Principally the wrongful trading provisions to be found in s.214 of the Insolvency Act 1986, above, para.9–6. For a modern elucidation of this provision, see *Brooks v Armstrong* [2015] EWHC 2289 (Ch); [2015] B.C.C. 661.
[71] Decided in 1977 but fully reported only in 1989: [1989] B.C.L.C. 498.
[72] *Norman v Theodore Goddard* [1991] B.C.L.C. 1027 (where the judge was "willing to assume" that s.214 of the Insolvency Act represented the common law); and *Re D'Jan of London Ltd* [1994] 1 B.C.L.C. 561 where the director was found negligent on the basis of an objective test, though it has to be said that the director could probably have been found liable on the facts on a subjective test of diligence (he signed an insurance proposal form without reading it). See also *Cohen v Selby* [2001] 1 B.C.L.C. 176 at 183 CA; and *Brumder v Motornet Service and Repairs Ltd* [2013] 1 W.L.R. 2783 CA at [45]–[47] (Beatson LJ).
[73] See above, para.9–6.

or omissions from the directors' report and the directors' remuneration report liability arises on the part of directors to the company only on the basis of knowledge or recklessness.[74]

The statutory standard

16–16   The crucial difference between the statutory formulation and that of Romer J is that in the latter the director's subjective level of skill sets the standard required of the director, whereas under the 2006 Act the director's subjective level does so only if it improves upon the objective standard of the reasonable director. Limb (a) of the statutory formula sets a standard which all directors must meet and it is not one dependent on the particular director's capabilities; limb (b) adds a subjective standard which, however, can operate only to increase the level of care required of the director.[75] Whether the statutory provision is to be regarded as simply endorsing the current common law or, probably better, as effecting a change in the common law which was under consideration but not fully developed by the courts, this is clearly an area where a court applying s.174 should be cautious in its use of the older common law authorities as an aid to interpretation under s.170(4).

What does this all mean or not mean for directors? First, although directors, executive and non-executive, are subject to a uniform and objective duty of care, what the discharge of that duty requires in particular cases will not be uniform. As the statutory formulation itself recognises, what is required of the director will depend on the functions carried out by the director,[76] so that there will be variations, not only between executive and non-executive directors[77] but also between different types of executive director (and equally of non-executives) and between different types and sizes of company.

Secondly, the imposition of an objective duty of care does not necessarily require a directorship to be regarded as a profession. The vexed issue of what constitutes a profession does not have to be addressed; all that is required is an assessment of what is reasonably required of a person having, as the statute puts it, the knowledge, skill and experience which a person in the position of the particular director ought to have. Given the enormous range of types and sizes of companies, it would be odd if all directors were to be regarded as professional. On the other hand, as was pointed out by the Court of Appeal of New South

---

[74] 2006 Act s.463. See below, para.21–28. It should be noted that this clause exempts the director only in respect of statements in the relevant reports and not in respect of any negligent conduct to which the statements inaccurately refer.

[75] The section attributes to the director the knowledge, skill and experience of *both* the reasonable person and the particular director in question, so the latter is important only when it *adds* to the attributes of the reasonable person.

[76] One potentially significant omission from s.174 of the Companies Act in comparison with the Insolvency Act is that s.214(5) of the latter explicitly extends the meaning of "carried on" to include functions entrusted to the director as well as those actually carried out, if that should be thought necessary.

[77] Note how in the Australian case of *Daniels v Anderson* (1995) 16 A.C.S.R. 607 the Court of Appeal of NSW, applying an objective test, found that the non-executive directors were not liable for the failure to discover the foreign exchange frauds being committed by an employee, but the chief executive officer was so held.

Wales, an objective approach does require even non-executive directors, as a minimum, to "take reasonable steps to place themselves in a position to guide and monitor the management of the company".[78] The days of the wholly inactive or passive director would thus seem to be numbered—or, at least, a director who is so runs a high risk of being held negligent.

Thirdly, directors are permitted to engage in substantial delegation of management functions to non-board employees. This is an inevitable reflection of the fact that companies are organisations, sometimes very big organisations, the running of which may require a large staff. In *City Equitable* Romer J put this point in very robust terms. He said that "in respect of all duties that, having regard to the exigencies of business, and the articles of association, may properly be left to some other official, a director is, in the absence of grounds for suspicion, justified in trusting to that official to perform such duties honestly".[79] In the more recent cases of *Daniels v Anderson* and *Norman v Theodore Goddard*,[80] where objective tests were applied, at least some of the directors escaped liability as a result of the application of this proposition. However, insofar as this dictum suggests that, once an appropriate delegate has been chosen and the task delegated to that person, the director is under no further duties, it cannot stand with recent developments in the law, as the next point indicates.

Fourthly, an objective standard of care is not inconsistent with extensive delegation nor, however, does it permit the directors to escape from the second requirement of always being in a position to "guide and monitor" the management. These two things are to be reconciled by the directors ensuring that there are in place adequate internal control systems which will throw up problems in the delegated areas whilst there is still time to do something about them. As it has been put, the freedom to delegate "does not absolve a director from the duty to supervise the discharge of the delegated functions".[81] The need for adequate internal control systems was stressed by the Report of the Turnbull Committee,[82] one of the lesser known of the reports which contributed to the Combined Code, and its successor the UK Corporate Governance Code, but arguably the most important for what it has to say about directors' responsibility for sub-board

16–17

---

[78] *Daniels v Anderson* (1995) 16 A.C.S.R. 607 at 664. The language of monitoring fits in well with the views of the Cadbury and Greenbury Committees and their successors on the proper role for the board of directors.

[79] *Re City Equitable Fire Insurance Co* [1925] Ch. 407 at 429. See also *Dovey v Cory* [1901] A.C. 477 HL. But the matter must not be delegated to an obviously inappropriate employee or official, as was the case in *City Equitable* itself.

[80] See above.

[81] *Re Barings Plc (No.5)* [2000] 1 B.C.L.C. 433, 489 (per Jonathan Parker J), approved by the CA at 536. See also *Equitable Life Assurance Society v Bowley* [2004] 1 B.C.L.C. 180, 188–189. Also see *Brumder v Motornet Service and Repairs Ltd* [2013] 1 W.L.R. 2783 CA at [55] (Beatson LJ).

[82] Institute of Chartered Accountants in England and Wales, *Internal Control: Guidance for Directors on the Combined Code* (1999). The Report fleshes out the bare principles now contained in the UK Corporate Governance Code (Principle C.2) that boards should maintain sound systems of risk management and internal control, should review them annually, and should report to the shareholders that they have done so. See too the Financial Reporting Council's revised *Guidance on Risk Management, Internal Control and Related Financial and Business Reporting*, at *https://www.frc.org. uk/Our-Work/Publications/Corporate-Governance/Guidance-on-Risk-Management,-Internal-Control-and.pdf* [accessed 1 February 2016].

structures of control. Although neither the Turnbull Report nor the UK Corporate Governance Code are legislative instruments binding the courts, it is likely that, in appropriate cases, the courts' view of what an objective standard of care requires will be influenced by these provisions. Indeed, that process is already evident in the area of disqualification of directors on grounds of unfitness. Thus, in *Re Barings Plc (No.5)*[83] directors were disqualified for failing to have such internal controls in place in relation to trading activities in an overseas subsidiary, whose losses eventually caused the demise of the bank.

Fifthly, the principles relating to delegation to sub-board managers apply also to the division of functions among the directors themselves. Inevitably, executive directors will carry a greater load of management responsibility than non-executive directors and, even within the executive directors, there will be specialisation (for example, the chief financial officer will carry particular responsibility in that area). However, all directors "have a continuing duty to acquire and maintain a sufficient knowledge and understanding of the company's business to enable them properly to discharge their duties as directors" and certainly no board may permit itself to be dominated by one of their number.[84]

16–18 Further, however, it follows from the inevitable acceptance of extensive delegation, at least in large companies, that directors cannot be guarantors that everything is going well within the company. Subordinate employees may be fraudulent or negligent and the directors may not discover this in time, but this does not necessarily mean that the directors have been negligent. That conclusion will depend on the facts of the situation, including the quality of the internal controls.[85]

Sixthly, although nearly all decided English cases have arisen out of alleged failures by directors to act or to act effectively, negligence suits can equally arise where the directors have indeed acted, but their actions have delivered disastrous consequences for their company. Here too, however, since companies are in business to take risks, the fact that a business venture does not pay off and even leads the company into financial trouble does not necessarily indicate negligence, though it may encourage the shareholders to replace the directors. In the US, where an objective standard for directors' competence is well-established, the "business judgment" rule generally operates to relieve the directors of liability in

---

[83] *Re Barings Plc (No.5)* [2000] 1 B.C.L.C. 523 CA. See above, para.10–10.

[84] *Re Barings Plc (No.5)* [2000] 1 B.C.L.C. 523 CA; and *Re Westmid Packaging Services Ltd* [1998] 2 B.C.L.C. 646, 653. Also see *Weavering Capital (UK) Ltd (In Liquidation) v Peterson* [2012] EWHC 1480 (Ch), as affirmed in [2013] EWCA Civ 71 at [173]–[174] (Proudman J); and *Madoff Securities International Ltd v Raven* [2013] EWHC 3147 (Comm) in which the Court held that some directors were entitled to rely, and therefore had not failed to exercise reasonable care and skill by relying, on the expertise and experience of other members on the board. On the other hand, the failure of the directors with the appropriate experience to apply their minds to the question as to whether the transactions were in the interests of the company constituted a breach of the duty to exercise reasonable skill and care (Popplewell J).

[85] See, e.g. *Lexi Holdings Plc v Luqman* [2009] EWCA Civ 117; [2009] 2 B.C.L.C. 1 CA: the managing director of a company was found liable for stealing £59.6 million which had been lent by banks to the company. Overturning the trial judge, the Court of Appeal also held his two sisters jointly liable (with their brother) for the stolen money on the basis that the state of the company's accounts should have aroused their suspicions, given their knowledge of their brother's earlier imprisonment for deception, and they should have acted accordingly; their inactivity was a breach of duty.

such cases (i.e. cases where the directors have acted, not those where they have failed to act). The business judgment rule involves the specification of a set of procedural steps, which, if followed, will give the directors the benefit of a presumption that they were not negligent. The Law Commissions thought such a rule unnecessary in the UK;[86] and there is certainly a risk with the business judgment rule that the courts will come to regard cases where the procedural standards have not been met as presumptively negligent.[87] The Commissions thought that one could expect the courts to be alive to the probability that they are better at dealing with conflicts of interest than with the assessment of business risks and to the desirability of avoiding the luxury of substituting the courts' hindsight for the directors' foresight.[88]

Finally, as with auditors,[89] showing breach of a duty of care is one thing; showing that the loss suffered by the company was a consequence of the breach of duty may be quite another. Thus, the true explanation of the finding of no liability in *Re Denham & Co*[90] is only in part that the director was entitled to rely on others. Equally important was the judge's view that, even if the director had made the inquiries he should have made, he would probably not have discovered the fraud.

Overall, it can be said that the recent developments at common law and, now, in the Act, have brought the standard of care, skill and diligence required of directors into line with that required generally in other areas of social life by the law of negligence. However, an inevitable result of the move from a subjective to an objective test will be to give the courts a greater role in defining the functions of the board, no matter how sensitive the courts are to the need to avoid the use of hindsight. For example, the courts' decisions on the rigour with which the board has to supervise the discharge of delegated tasks will help to define the monitoring role of the board, whilst decisions about whether the audit committee of the board has sufficiently scrutinised the tasks carried out by the external auditors will help to define the relationships between audit committee, auditors and management. Twenty years ago one might have predicted that the courts would either be ineffectual in the discharge of these responsibilities (through a desire to avoid reliance on hindsight) or produce undesirable interventions. However, today, as a result of developments associated with the emergence of the UK Corporate Governance Code, discussed in Ch.14, there is a body of best practice available, on which the courts can draw, though not be bound by, at least in the case of large companies. A striking example of the creative use of such

16–19

---

[86] Law Commission and Scottish Law Commission, *Company Directors: Regulating Conflicts of Interest and Formulating a Statement of Duties*, Cm. 4436, 1999, Pt 5.

[87] cf. *Smith v Van Gorkam* (1985) 488 A. 2d 858.

[88] For a critique see C.A. Riley, "The Company Director's Duty of Care and Skill: the Case for an Onerous but Subjective Standard" (1999) 62 M.L.R. 697.

[89] See below, para.22–37.

[90] *Re Denham & Co* (1883) 25 Ch. D. 752. See also *Cohen v Selby* [2001] B.C.L.C. 176 CA, stressing the need at common law to show that the negligence caused the loss suffered by the company. The classic statement of the problem is that by Learned Hand J in *Barnes v Andrews* (1924) 298 F. 614 at 616–617.

material is to be found in the judgment of Austin J in *ASIC v Rich*[91] in which the Australian court had recourse to a wide range of "best practice" material, including corporate governance reports from the UK, in holding that the duties of the chair of the board of a listed company extended beyond responsibility for simply chairing meetings of the board.

Remedies

16–20   The standard remedy for breach of a director's duty of care is compensation for the harm caused to the company by the director's negligence. Section 178(2), specifying the remedies for breach of the general duties, may suggest that the remedy for this breach of duty (s.174) will be assessed on common law, not equitable, principles, thus laying to rest the debates in that area.[92] In any event, the better view, it is suggested, is that the remedy is not assessed differently merely because the director is a fiduciary. As Millett LJ said in *Bristol and West Building Society v Mothew*,[93] "it is inappropriate to apply the expression [breach of fiduciary duty] to the obligation of a trustee or other fiduciary to use proper skill and care in the discharge of his duties". Nor does it matter that the duty of care to which the director is subject was developed, historically, by the courts of equity before the common law developed its own more widely applicable version. This history led to the use of different terminology ("compensation" in equity; "damages" at common law), and different appropriately contextual explanations of issues of standards of care, rules on causation, remoteness and measure of damages. But even in equity the breach gave access only to compensatory remedies, and the modern tendency has been to assimilate the requirements for liability for breach of the duty of care in equity and at common law.[94]

---

[91] *ASIC v Rich* [2003] NSWSC 85. The judge referred in particular to Annex D of Mr Derek Higg's review of the role of non-executive directors: above, para.14–73.

[92] See *Henderson v Merrett Syndicates Ltd* [1995] 2 A.C. 145; *Bristol & West Building Society v Mothew* [1998] Ch. 1.

[93] *Bristol and West Building Society v Mothew* [1998] Ch. 1, CA. The case provides a good example of the difference between a compensatory and a restitutionary remedy. A building society had advanced money to a purchaser after receiving negligent information from its solicitor. The purchaser defaulted, and the building society sued the solicitor. A restitutionary claim would have required the solicitor to put the building society back in the position in was in before it made the loan (i.e. to meet the whole of the society's loss), whereas the compensatory claim required him only to compensate the society for the loss caused to it by his negligence. This might have been nil if the solicitor's negligence had not affected the building society's assessment of the ability of the purchaser to keep up the repayments on the loan.

[94] In the *Mothew* case (see previous footnote) Millett LJ referred to the distinction between equitable compensation and common law damages for breach of the duty of care as "a distinction without a difference". Now see *AIB Group (UK) Plc v Mark Redler & Co Solicitors* [2014] UKSC 58; [2015] A.C. 1503, especially at [47]–[77] (Lord Toulson JSC) and [90]–[138] (Lord Reed JSC); and *Libertarian Investment Ltd v Hall* (2013) 16 HKCFAR 681 Hong Kong Court of Final Appeal at [84]–[96] (Ribeiro PJ) and [166]–[175] (Lord Millett NPJ).

INTRODUCTION TO DIRECTORS' VARIOUS DUTIES OF GOOD FAITH AND LOYALTY

Historical background

As noted earlier, the duties of good faith and loyalty which the law requires of directors were developed by the courts by analogy with the duties of trustees. It is easy to see how, historically, this came about. Prior to the Joint Stock Companies Act 1844 most joint stock companies were unincorporated and depended for their validity on a deed of settlement vesting the property of the company in trustees. Often the directors were themselves the trustees and even when a distinction was drawn between the passive trustees and the managing board of directors, the latter would quite clearly be regarded as trustees in the eyes of a court of equity in so far as they dealt with the trust property. With directors of incorporated companies, the description "trustees" was less apposite because the assets were now held by the company, a separate legal person, rather than being vested in trustees. However, it was not unnatural that the courts should extend it to them by analogy. For one thing, the duties of the directors should obviously be the same whether the company was incorporated or not; for another, historically the courts of equity tended to apply the label "trustee" indiscriminately to anyone in a fiduciary position. Nevertheless, to describe directors as trustees is today neither strictly correct nor invariably helpful.[95] In truth, directors are agents of the company or (when acting together) one of its organs, not trustees of its property. But, as agents, the directors stand in a fiduciary relationship to their principal, the company. The duties of good faith and loyalty which this relationship imposes are in material respects identical with those imposed on trustees. Moreover, when it comes to remedies for breach of duty, the trust analogy can provide a strong remedial structure. Directors who dispose of the company's assets in breach of duty, for example, are regarded as committing a breach similar to a breach of trust, and those persons (including the directors themselves) into whose hands the assets come may find that they are under a duty to restore the value of the misapplied assets to the company.[96]

16–21

The analogy of directors as agents of the company is also less than perfect, however. As we saw in Ch.7, the authority of the directors to bind the company as its agents normally depends on their acting collectively as a board, unless authority has (or can be assumed to have) been further delegated under the company's constitution upon an individual director.[97] By contrast, their duties of loyalty are owed by each director individually. One of several directors may not

---

[95] *Re City Equitable Fire Insurance Co* [1925] Ch. 407 at 426 (Romer J).

[96] "It follows from the principle that directors who dispose of the company's property in breach of their fiduciary duties are treated as having committed a breach of trust that a person who receives that property with knowledge of the breach of duty is treated as holding it upon trust for the company. He is said to be a constructive trustee of the property", per Chadwick LJ in *JJ Harrison (Properties) Ltd v Harrison* [2002] 1 B.C.L.C. 162, 173. Also see *Madoff Securities International Ltd v Raven* [2013] EWHC 3147 (Comm) at [292] (Popplewell J); and *Fern Advisers Ltd v Burford* [2014] EWHC 762 (QB) at [18] (HH Judge Mackie QC). In this situation the trustee-like nature of the directors' duties affects also the legal position of third parties. See further below, at para.16–134.

[97] See above, para.7–17.

as such be an agent of the company with power to saddle it with responsibility for his acts, but he will invariably be a fiduciary of it, and will also owe separate but related equitable duties. To this extent, directors again resemble trustees who must normally act jointly but each of whom severally owes duties of loyalty towards the beneficiaries. Moreover, as noted earlier, when the directors act collectively as a board, the modern view is not so much that they are agents of the company but that, so long as they act within their powers, they act as the company.[98]

Given the modern statutory statement of the general duties owed by directors, these analogies and their various limitations are of less substantive importance than they once were. Nevertheless, an eye must be kept on them for two reasons: the statutory duties themselves are subject to interpretation in the light of analogous common law cases (s.170(4)); and the remedial consequences of statutory breaches remain to be determined by the appropriate corresponding common law rules (s.178).

Categories of duties

16–22 Turning now to the main elements of the directors' duties of good faith and loyalty, we divide them as below into six categories, following the scheme of the Act. The first three categories describe distinct duties, all being concerned with the manner in which directors exercise their powers, being that the directors must:

(1) act within the scope of the powers which have been conferred upon them, and for proper purposes;
(2) exercise independent judgment; and
(3) act in good faith to promote the success of the company.

The final three categories are all examples of fiduciary duties of loyalty, and in particular the rule against directors putting themselves in a position in which their personal interests (or alternatively their duties to others) conflict with their duty to the company. However, it is useful to sub-divide this "no conflict" principle further because the specific rules implementing the principle differ according to whether the conflict arises:

(4) out of a transaction with the company (self-dealing transactions);
(5) out of the director's personal exploitation of the company's property, information or opportunities; or
(6) out of the receipt from a third party of a benefit for exercising their directorial functions in a particular way.

For the purposes of statutory enactment and analysis it is inevitable that the duties are separated out in some way such as that adopted in the 2006 Act. However, s.179 specifically provides that, except where a duty is explicitly

---

[98] See above, para.14–5.

excluded by something in the statute, "more than one of the general duties may apply in any given case". This provision applies also to the duty of care. In practice, here as in other areas of the law, the facts will frequently suggest breach of more than one of the duties and, where this is so, the claimant can choose to pursue all or any of them.[99]

DUTY TO ACT WITHIN POWERS

Requiring the directors to act only within the powers that have been conferred upon them is an obvious duty for the law to impose. Indeed, this is not a duty confined to directors, or even to fiduciaries; later on we shall examine similar restrictions as they apply to shareholders.[100] As regards the directors, however, s.171 deals with two manifestations of this principle: the director must "act in accordance with the company's constitution" and must "only exercise powers for the purposes for which they are conferred". We look at each in turn.

16–23

Acting in accordance with the constitution

Constitutional limitations

As we saw in Ch.3,[101] in contrast to many other company law jurisdictions, the main source of the directors' powers is likely to be the company's articles, and the articles, therefore, are likely also to be a source of constraints on the directors' powers. The articles may confer unlimited powers on the directors, but they are likely in fact to set some parameters within which the powers are to be exercised, even if the limits are generous, as they typically will be. So, it is perhaps not surprising that s.171 contains the obligation "to act in accordance with the company's constitution". And it should be noted that the term "constitution" helpfully goes beyond the articles. It includes resolutions and agreements which are required to be notified to the Registrar and annexed to the articles, notably any special resolution of the company.[102] It also embraces any resolution or decision taken in accordance with the constitution and any decision by the members of the company or a class of members which is treated as equivalent to a decision of the company.[103] Thus, the duty includes an obligation to obey decisions properly taken by the shareholders in general meeting, for example, giving instructions to the directors without formally altering the articles.[104]

16–24

This duty was recognised in the early years of modern company law and is reflected in a number of nineteenth-century decisions, usually involving the

---

[99] Note Charities Act 2011 s.105(9): an order under this section may authorise an act even though it involves a breach of one or more of the general duties just described.

[100] See below, para.19–4.

[101] See above, para.3–13.

[102] 2006 Act ss.17, 29–30.

[103] 2006 Act s.257.

[104] As we saw at para.14–7, under the model articles the shareholders by special resolution may give directors instructions as to how they should conduct the management of the company, even in areas where the articles confer managerial powers upon the directors.

purported exercise by directors of powers which were ultra vires the company[105] or payments of dividends or directors' remuneration contrary to the provisions in the company's articles.[106] The remedies for this type of breach are considered below.[107]

Other situations?

16–25   Besides limitations on the directors' powers suggested by s.171 (i.e. limitations found in the company's constitution or in the general limitation on the exercise of powers for improper purposes), the general law may also limit what directors may do (or what companies may do, which will necessarily control the actions of the board), or limitations may be found in the Companies Act or in the common law relating to companies. Often these provisions will suggest that liability is strict, in that the motivations of the director are immaterial. As well, these provisions may set out the consequences of any failure to abide by the relevant rules, and, where this is the case, those rules will prevail. But where no remedies are specified, the law of directors' duties may provide an answer, directly or by analogy.

Improper purposes

The rule

16–26   The second proposition contained in s.171(b) is that a director must "only exercise powers for the purposes for which they are conferred". Often the improper purpose will be to feather the directors' own nests or to preserve their control of the company in their own interests, in which event it will also be a breach of one or other of the various duties, considered below, to act avoid conflicts and to act in good faith to promote the success of the company. Indeed, the particular wording of the s.172(1) statutory duty to act in good faith to promote the success of the company can be seen as assisting generally in defining proper purposes.[108] But even if no other breach is committed, directors may nevertheless be in breach of this particular duty if they have exercised their powers for a purpose outside those for which the powers were conferred upon them. The improper purposes test, like the requirement to act in accordance with

---

[105] *Re Lands Allotment Co* [1894] 1 Ch. 616 CA. On ultra vires see above at para.7–29.

[106] *Re Oxford Benefit Building and Investment Society* (1886) 35 Ch.D. 502 (an early example of a company's accounts recognising profits which had not been earned); *Leeds Estate Building and Investment Co v Shepherd* (1887) 36 Ch.D. 787. It might be said that the requirement upon the directors to repay the dividends was based on the illegality of their payment as a matter of statute or common law, but the directors were also required to repay their remuneration, the payment of which was objectionable only because it was done in breach of the company's articles. (The articles entitled the directors to remuneration only if dividends of a certain size were paid, a rule which, perhaps naturally, encouraged the directors not to be too careful about observing the restrictions on their dividend payment powers.)

[107] See below, paras 16–30 and 16–109 et seq.

[108] See paras 16–34 et seq.

the company's constitution, is an objective test.[109] Or, more precisely, the question of whether a particular purpose is proper or not is a question of law, decided objectively, while the question of which purposes actually motivated the particular director in question is, of course, subjective.[110] Notice the narrow limits to the proper purposes rule: if the directors have acted for purposes which are objectively proper, not improper, then the court will not, in addition, review the decision as also being either reasonable or unreasonable,[111] with the potential for substituting their own view as to the judgements the directors should have reached in managing the company.[112]

The leading authority in this area is the 2015 Supreme Court decision in *Eclairs Group Ltd v JKX Oil & Gas Plc*,[113] but it is helpful to begin discussion with an earlier decision. The statutory formulation of the proper purposes duty reflects the prior common law case law. That case law was reviewed by the Privy Council in *Howard Smith Ltd v Ampol Petroleum Ltd*,[114] which considered the decisions on this subject of courts throughout the Commonwealth. It concerned, as have many of the cases, the power of directors to issue new shares, but the duty is by no means so confined.[115] In this case a majority shareholder (Ampol) in a company called Millers made an offer to acquire the shares in Millers it did not already own. However, the directors of Millers preferred a takeover offer from Howard Smith, which could not succeed so long as Ampol retained a majority holding. Consequently, the directors caused the company to issue sufficient new shares to Howard Smith that Ampol was reduced to a minority position and Howard Smith could launch its offer with some hope of success, since its bid price was higher than Ampol's.

It was argued that the only proper purpose for which a share-issue power could be exercised was to raise new capital when the company needed it.[116] This was

---

[109] See *Howard Smith Ltd v Ampol Ltd* [1974] A.C. 821 at 834 PC; citing *Fraser v Whalley* (1864) 2 H.C.M. & M. 10; *Punt v Symons & Co Ltd* [1903] 2 Ch. 506; *Piercy v S Mills & Co Ltd* [1920] 1 Ch. 77; *Ngurli v McCann* (1954) 90 C.L.R. 425 Aust. HC; *Hogg v Cramphorn Ltd* [1967] Ch. 254 at 267. The "improper purpose" test, as a requirement distinct from good faith in the common law test, has been rejected, however, in British Columbia: *Teck Corp Ltd v Millar* (1973) 33 D.L.R. (3d) 288.

[110] But see *Eclairs Group Ltd v JKX Oil & Gas Plc* [2015] UKSC 71 at [15] (Lord Sumption SCJ), it seems confining himself to the latter point.

[111] Although it may of course review them as being negligent or not: s.174, above para.16–15.

[112] The best analysis of this is probably in the trusts case, *Edge v Pensions Ombudsman* [2000] Ch. 602 CA at 627E–630G; but also see *Equitable Life Assurance Society v Hyman* [2002] 1 A.C. 408 HL at [17]–[21]. And see immediately below and also paras 16–40 et seq.

[113] *Eclairs Group Ltd v JKX Oil & Gas Plc* [2015] UKSC 71. Noted, Worthington [2016] C.L.J. 202.

[114] *Howard Smith Ltd v Ampol Petroleum Ltd* [1974] A.C. 821 PC.

[115] The principle applies generally. For examples in relation to other powers, see *Stanhope's Case* (1866) L.R. 1 Ch. App. 161; and *Manisty's Case* (1873) 17 S.J. 745 (forfeiture of shares); *Galloway v Halle Concerts Society* [1915] 2 Ch. 233 (calls); *Bennett's case* (1854) 5 De G.M. & G. 284; and *Australian Metropolitan Life Association Co Ltd v Ure* (1923) 33 C.L.R. 199 Aust. HC (registration of transfers); *Hogg v Cramphorn Ltd* [1967] Ch. 254 (loans); *Lee Panavision Ltd v Lee Lighting Ltd* [1992] B.C.L.C. 22 CA (entering into a management agreement); *Equitable Life Assurance Society v Hyman* [2002] 1 A.C. 408 HL; *Criterion Properties Plc v Stratford UK Properties LLC* [2003] B.C.C. 50 CA (giving joint venture partner an option to be bought out at a favourable price); *Re HLC Environmental Projects Ltd (In Liquidation)* [2014] B.C.C. 337 (payments made when the company was in financial distress).

[116] This has often been assumed and the directors had apparently been so advised and sought, unsuccessfully, to show that this was their purpose.

rejected as too narrow.[117] There might be a range of purposes for which a company may issue new shares—a view reflected in the statutory reference to proper purposes in the plural. It might be a proper use of the power to issue shares to use that power in order to secure the financial stability of the company[118] or as part of an agreement relating to the exploitation of mineral rights owned by the company.[119] Provided the purpose of the issue was a proper one, the mere fact that the incidental (and desired) result was to deprive a shareholder of his voting majority or to defeat a takeover bid would not be sufficient to make the purpose improper. But if, as in the instant case, the purpose of the share issue was to dilute the majority voting power so as to enable an offer to proceed which the existing majority was in a position to block,[120] the exercise of the power would be improper despite the fact that the directors were acting in what they considered to be the best interests of the company, and were not motivated by a desire to obtain some personal advantage.

Which purposes are improper?

16–27   Perhaps the greatest puzzle in this area is to know by what criteria the courts judge whether a particular purpose is proper. This is generally stated to be a matter of construction of the articles of association.[121] That is all very well if the articles are prescriptive, but this is rarely the case. In *Howard Smith v Ampol*, for example, the clause giving the directors power to issue shares was drawn in the widest terms. The "purposes" limitation which the Privy Council read into the directors' powers derived not from a narrow analysis of that clause, but from placing the share issue power within the company's constitutional arrangements as a whole, as demonstrated in particular by the terms of its articles of association. In essence, to do what the directors did in that case was regarded as undermining the division of powers between shareholders and the board which the articles had created[122]; and in that context the case comes close to deciding that it is always a breach of the directors' duties to exercise their powers to promote or defeat a takeover offer, which decision should be left to the existing

---

[117] *Howard Smith Ltd v Ampol Petroleum Ltd* [1974] A.C. 821 at 835–836 PC.

[118] *Harlowe's Nominees Pty Ltd v Woodside Oil Co* (1968) 121 C.L.R. 483 Aust. HC.

[119] *Teck Corp Ltd v Miller* (1972) 33 D.L.R. (3d) 288 BC Sup.Ct.

[120] Or, conversely, to block a bid: *Winthrop Investments Ltd v Winns Ltd* [1975] 2 N.S.W.L.R. 666 NSWCA.

[121] *Re Smith and Fawcett Ltd* [1942] Ch. 304 at 306.

[122] *Howard Smith Ltd v Ampol Petroleum Ltd* [1974] A.C. 821 at 837 PC: "The constitution of a limited company normally provides for directors, with powers of management, and shareholders, with defined voting powers having to appoint the directors, and to take, in general meeting, by majority vote, decisions on matters not reserved for management. Just as it is established that directors, within their management powers, may take decisions against the wishes of majority shareholders, and indeed that the majority of shareholders cannot control them in the exercise of these powers while they remain in office so it must be unconstitutional for directors to use their fiduciary powers over the shares in the company purely for the purpose of destroying an existing majority, or creating a new majority which did not previously exist. To do so is to interfere with that element in the company's constitution which is separate from and set against their powers". This principle was applied by the Court of Appeal in *Lee Panavision Ltd v Lee Lighting Ltd* [1992] B.C.L.C. 22, where the incumbent directors entered into a long-term management agreement with a third party knowing that the shareholders were proposing to exercise their rights to appoint new directors.

body of shareholders. This is certainly the proposition upon which the City Code on Takeovers and Mergers (the Takeover Code) is based, which provisions will prevail once a bid for a listed company is imminent.[123] In *Criterion Properties Plc v Stratford UK Properties LLC*,[124] however, neither Hart J nor the Court of Appeal ruled out the possibility that in some cases it might be a proper purpose of the exercise of directors' powers for them to be used to block or discourage a takeover, but the issue was not presented in a sharp fashion in that case, since both courts were agreed that the "poison pill" adopted by the directors in that case was disproportionate to the threat faced by the company. It follows from this approach, however, that in a different type of company with a different constitution, in which, say, ownership and control were not separated, a broader view might be taken of the directors' powers under the articles.

In other words, the context is all-important. This seems to be the explanation of the expansive approach taken in *Re Smith and Fawcett Ltd*,[125] where the clause in question (regarding the admission of new members to a small company) was widely construed so as to produce the effect equivalent to the partnership rule of strict control by the board over the admission of new members.

But these illustrations indicate the difficulty, and provide little by way of real guidance when the context is novel, as it was in *Eclairs Group Ltd v JKX Oil & Gas Plc*.[126] The opposing judgments as the case made its way up to the Supreme Court are instructive. JKX suspected a hostile takeover by Eclairs, one of its shareholders, whom it alleged was seeking to destabilise it and ultimately acquire it at less than its proper value. The directors of JKX had the power[127] to request details of the parties who held interests in Eclairs' shares, and to disenfranchise Eclairs if it failed to respond adequately to the request. This the company did. It was not disputed that the power to disenfranchise had been exercised so as to disentitle these shareholders from voting at JKX's AGM, thus ensuring the passage of certain resolutions, rather than for the purpose of enforcing the company's demand for information. At first instance,[128] Mann J held this to be an improper purpose, so the purported restrictions on voting were held ineffective.

---

[123] See below, para.28–19.

[124] *Criterion Properties Plc v Stratford UK Properties LLC* [2002] 2 B.C.L.C. 151 (Hart J); [2003] 2 B.C.L.C. 129 CA. The issue was not analysed by the House of Lords, which focused on the logically prior question of the director's authority (actual or apparent) to enter into the contract on behalf of the company: [2004] 1 W.L.R. 1846. The "poison pill" arrangement entitled the joint venture partner of the potential target company (Criterion) to require Criterion to buy out its interest in the venture on terms which were very favourable to the partner and thus very damaging economically to Criterion. However, this arrangement was capable of being triggered not only by a takeover but also by any departure of the existing management of Criterion, even in circumstances, which in fact arose, which were wholly unconnected with a takeover.

[125] *Re Smith and Fawcett Ltd* [1942] Ch. 304 CA, where in a quasi-partnership company it was held that the directors, in exercising a power to refuse to register a transfer of shares, could "take account of any matter which they conceive to be in the interests of the company ... such matters, for instance, as whether by their passing a particular transfer the transferee would obtain too great a weight in the councils of the company or might even perhaps obtain control" (at 308). Similarly, see *Gaiman v National Association of Mental Health* [1971] Ch. 317. In modern law the position would now have to be considered in the light of any "legitimate expectations" enforceable under s.994. See below, Ch.20.

[126] *Eclairs Group Ltd v JKX Oil & Gas Plc* [2015] UKSC 71.

[127] Under Pt 22 of the 2006 Act (see ss.793 et seq.) and the company's articles.

[128] *Eclairs Group Ltd v JKX Oil & Gas Plc* [2013] EWHC 2631 (Ch).

The Court of Appeal allowed the appeal (Briggs LJ dissenting),[129] distinguishing previous cases of improper purposes on three overlapping grounds[130]: that here the purported "victim" was a "victim of his own choice, not a victim of any improper use of a power of the board of directors" since it was his choice how to respond to the questions properly raised[131]; that since no restrictive purposes had been expressed in the statute or the articles, none should be implied unless that was necessary to their efficacy; and, in any event, a restricted proper purpose test would essentially frustrate the purpose or utility of the provisions in question. Although the Court of Appeal did not put it so strongly, their expansive approach could essentially denude the proper purposes doctrine of any substantive role whenever a power was expressed in wide terms—as powers typically are. The Supreme Court disagreed, holding unanimously that the proper purpose doctrine had a central role to play in controlling the exercise of power by directors. But they too provided little guidance as to how these "proper purposes" should be discovered. Lord Sumption SCJ, with whom the other judges agreed, suggested that the relevant improper purposes would "usually [be] obvious from [the] context", and should be inferred from the "mischief" which might follow from exercise of the power.[132]

16–28   That is not much to go on, but, taking the cases together, perhaps two broad categories of "improper purpose" can be identified as operating quite generally, even when powers are expressed in the widest possible terms: use of a power for the purpose of "feathering the director's nest" (these are the easy cases) or for influencing the outcome of existing constitutional balances of power in the company (the harder cases) will typically be regarded as improper.[133] Note that it is not the incidental, or even inevitable, delivery of these ends which is outlawed: many perfectly proper actions by directors will deliver such results. Rather, it is this being the motivation for the exercise of the power, where that motivation has been deemed improper. But even this is not the end of the analysis; there is a further question.

When is a power exercised for improper purposes?

16–29   Directors are rarely actuated by a single purpose. This was true in the *Howard Smith* case, where the company did have a genuine need for fresh capital. If the directors are motivated by a variety of purposes, some proper and some improper, how should the courts determine whether the exercise of power is tainted? Section 171(b) indicates that a director must "only exercise powers for the purposes for which they are conferred". This suggests that *any* improper

---

[129] *Eclairs Group Ltd v JKX Oil & Gas Plc* [2014] EWCA Civ 640.

[130] As summarised by Lord Sumption SCJ at [2015] UKSC 71 at [28].

[131] *Eclairs Group Ltd v JKX Oil & Gas Plc* [2014] EWCA Civ 640 at [136].

[132] *Eclairs Group Ltd v JKX Oil & Gas Plc* [2015] UKSC 71 at [31] and [30] respectively. For earlier academic considerations, see Completing, para.3.14; and R.C. Nolan, "The Proper Purpose Doctrine and Company Directors" in B. Rider (ed.), *The Realm of Company Law* (Kluwer Law International, 1998).

[133] In the same vein, it would be improper for a director to act for the purpose of favouring his or her nominator, with the cases again suggesting, if only by inference, that a "but for" test is appropriate: see, e.g. *Kuwait Asia Bank EC v National Mutual Life Nominees Ltd* [1991] 1 A.C. 187 PC.

motivating purpose will constitute a flaw. Nevertheless, and perhaps for very pragmatic reasons, that has never been the rule applied in the corporate context except where the exercise of power is motivated by the director's dishonesty or self-interest.[134] Otherwise the courts have typically suggested that a decision will be considered flawed only if the proven improper purpose is the "primary" or dominant purpose for the decision,[135] or if the decision would not have been taken "but for" the improper purpose (even if the improper purpose was not the dominant purpose),[136] or perhaps an either/or version of these two tests[137] if it is thought that they are likely to lead to different answers on the facts. Each alternative poses enormous forensic difficulties, since all require proof of matters peculiarly within the minds of the directors and in relation to which the directors' evidence is "likely to be both artificial and defensive".[138] But in *Eclairs Group Ltd v JKX Oil & Gas Plc*, Lord Sumption SCJ (with whom Lord Hope SCJ agreed) put forward a principled preference for the "but for" test[139]:

> "The fundamental point [in selecting the right test], however, is one of principle. The statutory duty of the directors is to exercise their powers 'only' for the purposes for which they are conferred. ... If equity nevertheless allows the decision to stand in some cases, it is not because it condones a minor improper purpose where it would condemn a major one. ... The only rational basis for such a distinction is that some improprieties may not have resulted in an injustice to the interests which equity seeks to protect. Here, we are necessarily in the realm of causation. ... One has to focus on the improper purpose and ask whether the decision would have been made if the directors had not been moved by it. If the answer is that without the improper purpose(s) the decision impugned would never have been made, then it would be irrational to allow it to stand simply because the directors had other, proper considerations in mind as well, to which perhaps they attached greater importance. ... Correspondingly, if there were proper reasons for exercising the power and it would still have been exercised for those reasons even in the absence of improper ones, it is difficult to see why justice should require the decision to be set aside."

However persuasive that might seem, and whatever the practical advantages of a single simple test, the majority of the Supreme Court declined to commit themselves to this as a statement of the law, given that the issues surrounding mixed purposes had not been argued before the Supreme Court.[140] The matter thus remains unsettled. But it is hard to fault the logic that a decision should be held improper only if it would not in fact have been taken the way it was but for

---

[134] *Eclairs Group Ltd v JKX Oil & Gas Plc* [2015] UKSC 71 at [17] (Lords Sumption and Hodge SCJJ); citing *Mills v Mills* (1938) 60 C.L.R. 150 at 185–186 Aust. HC, where Dixon J indicated the difficulties.

[135] *Howard Smith Ltd v Ampol Petroleum Ltd* [1974] A.C. 821 at 832 PC (Lord Wilberforce).

[136] *Mills v Mills* (1938) 60 C.L.R. 150 at 186 Aust. HC; *Whitehouse v Carlton House Pty* (1987) 162 C.L.R. 285 at 294 Aust. HC: although this interpretation, supported in *Eclairs Group Ltd v JKX Oil & Gas Plc* [2015] UKSC 71 by Lord Sumption SCJ (with whom Lord Hope SCJ agreed) (at [21]–[22]) was doubted by Lord Mance SCJ (with whom Lord Neuberger PSC agreed) (at [53]). See also *Hirsche v Sims* [1894] A.C. 654 PC; *Hindle v John Cotton Ltd* (1919) 56 S.L.T. 625.

[137] *Eclairs Group Ltd v JKX Oil & Gas Plc* [2015] UKSC 71 at [49].

[138] *Eclairs Group Ltd v JKX Oil & Gas Plc* [2015] UKSC 71 at [20] (on the "primary" purpose test), and see too [54] (on both).

[139] *Eclairs Group Ltd v JKX Oil & Gas Plc* [2015] UKSC 71 at [21], but see generally [21]–[23].

[140] Lord Mance SCJ (with whom Lord Neuberger PSC agreed) set out his doubts at [2015] UKSC 71 at [51]–[54].

the improper consideration. If that test is not met, then—as Lord Sumption put it—no injustice has been done, and the decision should stand.

The only troubling element is the hypothetical rider aired by the court. The problem raised was this: assume the directors in fact decided the way they did only because of the presence of an improper purpose, but they might still have decided the same way had that improper purpose not been present. Should their decision then be allowed to stand? The answer, surely, is no, it should not stand. Principle suggests the court's task is simply to determine whether the decision *actually* taken by the directors should stand. It is not to hypothesise about what the directors might have done for exclusively "proper" motivating purposes. The focus of the court's intervention is not on judging the practical outcome reached, but on judging the directors' motivations in reaching it. And in any event, in practice the question would seem impossible to contemplate sensibly on most facts before the court: *JKX* and *Howard Smith* are surely illustrative of that—the directors could insist they would have taken the same decisions if acting only for proper purposes, but their targets and timing make that seem unlikely.

Despite this, in the early stages of the JKX litigation, Mann J raised this question himself, and also held that the facts supported the conclusion that the JKX directors would indeed have taken the same decision if they were acting for exclusively proper purposes, but he declined to let the company take the argument at that late stage in the litigation.[141]

Remedies

16–30   The directors necessarily breach the duty in s.171 if they act contrary to its provisions; it is irrelevant that the contravention was in the interests of the company, or that the directors were not subjectively aware of their breach of s.171.[142] In other words, directors are under a duty to acquaint themselves with the terms of the company's constitution and its limits, and to abide by them. A breach by the directors of s.171 affects the validity of any decision so made, and that in turn may affect third parties relying on the decision. In addition, if the flawed decision causes loss to the company, the company may seek compensation from its defaulting directors. The relevant remedies map the common law and equitable rules (s.178).

Starting with the validity of the flawed decision: at common law different legal consequences follow for acts done without power (or "in excess" of power, s.171(a)) and acts done within power but in abuse of it (s.171(b)). At common law, where an act or decision of the directors is beyond their constitutional capacity as set out in the company's constitution (and subject to claims of ostensible authority) (i.e. in breach of s.171(a)), it is void, i.e. of no effect. Moreover, this is also one of the situations where the trust analogy is used to strong effect. If the contravention of the constitution has involved the improper distribution of the company's assets, the directors are regarded by analogy as if in

---

[141]   *Eclairs Group Ltd v JKX Oil & Gas Plc* [2015] UKSC 71 at [42]–[43].
[142]   See the cases cited in fnn.106 and 109.

breach of trust and are liable to replace the assets, whether or not they were the recipients of them.[143] This gives the directors a strong incentive to remain within the company's constitution.[144]

Where the directors act for an improper purpose (in breach of s.171(b)), however, then at common law their act is voidable by the company (i.e. valid until set aside by the company, and incapable of being set aside if third party rights have intervened),[145] not void as in the case where the directors purport to exercise a power they do not have. Thus, bona fide third parties are safe if they act before the shareholders (or liquidator, or other) set aside the directors' decision.[146]

In both cases, however, the impact of these common law rules on third parties' interests has now been substantially softened by the statutory protections (especially s.40) for those dealing with the company in good faith.[147] In favour of such persons the powers of the directors to bind the company are treated as free of any limitation contained in the company's constitution. Helpful as this is to third parties, it does not help the directors, for s.40(5) makes it clear that liability on the part of the director to the company may be incurred under s.171, even if—perhaps especially if—the third party with whom the directors dealt on behalf of the company is able to enforce the transaction against the company.[148] In fact, to the extent that s.40 protects the position of third parties as against the company it increases in importance the company's potential remedy against the director. Companies that are now restricted in their ability to escape from transactions with third parties on the grounds that the directors have exceeded their powers may be tempted to look to the directors to recover compensation for the loss suffered as a result of entering into them.

16–31

It is also worth recalling at this point the related provisions of s.41, which apply where the third party contracting with the company is a director of the company or a person connected with the director. Then the protection afforded by

---

[143] See the cases cited in fnn.106 and 109. The most recent Supreme Court authority on quantification of this form of compensation comes from the non-company case of *AIB Group (UK) Plc v Mark Redler & Co Solicitors* [2014] UKSC 58 SC.

[144] They might escape liability, however, where, for example, the provisions of the constitution were not clear; and see also the discussion of s.1157, below, para.16–133.

[145] See the analysis of the cases in *Hunter v Senate Support Services Ltd* [2004] EWHC 1085 (Ch); [2005] 1 B.C.L.C. 175, [173]–[179]. Note the importance of the absence/excess of authority versus abuse of authority distinction in *Hogg v Cramphorn* [1967] Ch. 254—a decision to attach multiple voting rights to shares issued to the company's pension fund, in breach of the company's articles, was ineffective, whereas the issue itself, for improper purposes, was voidable only; *Guinness v Saunders* [1990] 2 A.C. 663 HL—fixing of directors' remuneration by a board committee, rather than the full board, in breach of the articles, meant that the decision was void and the recipient director had to repay the money; *Smith v Henniker-Major Co* [2003] Ch. 182 at [48]—inquorate board meeting. cf. *Hely-Hutchinson v Brayhead Ltd* [1968] 1 Q.B. 549, where the correct body acted but the director was in breach of his obligation under the articles to comply with disclosure provisions: here the decision was voidable but not void.

[146] *Bamford v Bamford* [1970] Ch. 212 CA (ratification by shareholders of decision taken for an improper purpose); and *Criterion Properties Plc v Stratford UK Properties LLC* [2004] 1 W.L.R. 1846 (on the application of the statutory protection for the benefit of third parties).

[147] See above, at para.7–9. Unless the third party is a director of the company or a person connected with the director. See s.41 and above, para.7–13.

[148] 2006 Act s.40(1).

s.40 does not apply and instead s.41 imposes liability both on directors who authorise such transactions (as s.171 does)[149] *and* on the director[150] (or connected person) who enters into the transaction with the company.[151] Both sets of directors are liable to account to the company for any gain made from the transaction and to indemnify the company for any loss which it suffered as a result of the transaction. Section 41 in its specific area of operation thus reinforces the principle underlying s.171 that directors should observe the limitations on their constitutional powers.

The jurisdiction to bring claims is worth further comment. It is clear that both duties stated in s.171 are owed to the company, as are the other statutory duties, and so may be pursued by the company directly, or by shareholders in a derivative claim. But can the defaulting directors be sued by parties other than the company? A failure on the part of the directors to observe the express limits on their powers contained in the company's constitution (i.e. s.171(a) breach) may also put *the company* in breach of the contract with the shareholders created by the articles. As we saw in Ch.3,[152] at least some breaches of the articles by the company can be complained of by a shareholder, who might, for example, obtain an injunction to restrain the company from continuing to act in breach of the articles—in effect restraining the directors from causing the company to act in breach of its articles. Equally, such acts by the directors may form the basis of a claim in unfair prejudice.

Where the breach is of the duty to act for proper purposes (i.e. s.171(b)), however, then allowing a wider class of people to complain has been more poorly defended; no case seems to have turned on standing. In some cases, minority shareholders have been allowed to sue but the question of their standing has often not been argued nor its basis explained.[153] As a matter of logic and of equitable precedent, this duty to act for proper purposes, owed by directors to the company, may also be owed (at common law only, since there is no enacted statutory equivalent) by the directors to a wider class of people, entitling this wider class to seek common law or equitable remedies from the directors for breach.[154] Alternatively, or in addition, and as described above, the directors' wrongs to the company may entitle the shareholders to pursue related or parasitic remedies,

---

[149] Liability under s.171 is preserved by s.41(1) but it would seem more attractive to proceed under s.41 where this is possible.

[150] Including a director of the company's holding company.

[151] The transaction itself is voidable by the company (s.41(2) and (4)), but not void, as it would be at common law. It will cease to be avoidable if (a) restitution of the subject-matter of the contract is not possible; (b) the company has been indemnified for the loss suffered; (c) the rights of bona fide purchasers without notice have intervened; or (d) the shareholders in general meeting have ratified the transaction.

[152] See above, para.3–18.

[153] See many of the cases cited earlier, including the leading case of *Howard Smith v Ampol* [1974] A.C. 824 PC. By contrast, in *Eclairs Group Ltd v JKX Oil & Gas plc* [2015] UKSC 71 SC, the shareholders would be expected to have jurisdiction to complain.

[154] For an attempted defence of this, see S. Worthington, "Directors' Duties, Creditors' Rights and Shareholder Intervention" (1991) 18 Melbourne University Law Review 121, 125–30. Also see *Equitable Life Assurance Society v Hyman* [2002] 1 A.C. 408 HL.

such as for breach of the contract in the articles (although note the arguments against),[155] or a claim in unfair prejudice.[156]

Finally, as noted earlier, these remedies are sometimes applied by analogy when **16–32** directors act, not contrary to the company's constitution, but contrary to some other statutory or common law rule which constrains the powers of directors to act in particular ways.[157] If the rule itself does not set out specific consequences of failure, then the law of directors' duties may provide an answer, directly or by analogy. We have already seen an example of this situation in Ch.12 where the directors, in breach of the Act, made a distribution to shareholders otherwise than out of profits. In the absence of statutory specification of the liabilities of the directors to the company in that situation, the courts have had recourse to the notion that if directors, "as quasi-trustees for the company, improperly pay away the assets to the shareholders, they are liable to replace them".[158] Another example is to be found in Ch.13,[159] where directors are regarded as having acted in breach of trust when they used the company's assets to give financial assistance for the purchase of the company's shares in breach of the statutory prohibition. In this way, directors who apply the company's assets in breach of restrictions contained in the Act are made liable to replace them. It is not thought that these liabilities, derived from the trustee-like duties imposed on directors in the handling of the company's assets, have been overtaken or displaced by the statutory duties set out in Ch.2 of Pt 10 and in s.171 in particular.

What is even more typical in this area is that different potential routes lead to the same remedial ends. An illustration is found in the decision of the Court of Appeal in *MacPherson v European Strategic Bureau Ltd.*[160] Here the directors of an insolvent company caused it to enter into a number of contracts which, the court found, amounted to an informal winding up of the company. Under the contracts, the directors as creditors were the primary beneficiaries rather than the creditors of the company as a whole, as would have been the case had the company been wound up formally under the provisions of the Act and the insolvency legislation. Chadwick LJ said that it was a breach of the duties which directors owe to the company for them to attempt such a scheme[161]:

> "It is an attempt to circumvent the protection which the 1985 Act aims to provide for those who give credit to a business carried on, with the benefit of limited liability, through the vehicle of a company incorporated under that Act."

---

[155] But for the perhaps preferable view that acting for an improper purpose is an abuse of power but not a breach of the articles see *Winthrop Investments Ltd v Winns Ltd* [1975] 2 N.S.W.L.R. 666 NSWCA. Also see *Rolled Steel Products (Holdings) Ltd v British Steel Corp* [1986] Ch. 246.

[156] *Re Sherborne Park Residents Co Ltd* (1986) 2 B.C.C. 528.

[157] See above, para.16–25.

[158] Per Sir George Jessel MR in *Flitcroft's* case (1882) 21 Ch. D. 519; quoted with approval by the Court of Appeal in *Bairstow v Queen's Moat Houses Plc* [2001] 2 B.C.L.C. 531. See above, para.12–13.

[159] At para.13–56. See also the discussion of *Re Duckwari (No.2)* [1998] 2 B.C.L.C. 315 CA, below at fn.277.

[160] *MacPherson v European Strategic Bureau Ltd* [2000] 2 B.C.L.C. 683.

[161] *MacPherson v European Strategic Bureau Ltd* [2000] 2 B.C.L.C. 683 at 701.

In consequence, the contracts were not enforceable by the directors (who were obviously aware of the facts giving rise to the breach of duty) against the company. This case can thus be seen as demonstrating a limitation on the directors' powers derived from the statutory rules on limited liability and payments to shareholders out of capital. It could also be seen as a breach of the directors' core duty of loyalty (discussed immediately below) as it applies in the vicinity of insolvency where the creditors' interests are predominant.

DUTY TO EXERCISE INDEPENDENT JUDGMENT

16–33 At common law, this issue is typically described as a duty not to fetter the exercise of discretion. In s.173, this is put in positive terms, as a duty to exercise independent judgment. At the level of principle the requirement is uncontroversial. However, there are four points relating to the practical working of this principle which need to be considered.

Taking advice and delegating authority

16–34 First, and perhaps most obviously, the principle does not prevent directors seeking and acting on advice from others. Indeed, the board might well infringe its duty to take reasonable care if it proceeded to a decision without appropriate advice from outsiders (investment bankers, lawyers, valuers). What the board cannot do is treat the advice as an instruction, although in complex technical areas the advice may leave the board with little freedom for manoeuvre, for example, where lawyers advise that the board's preferred course of action would be unlawful. The board must regard itself as taking responsibility for the decision reached, after taking appropriate advice.

Secondly, just as the duty of care does not prevent a board from delegating its functions to non-board employees (provided it has in place appropriate internal controls—see above), so the duty to exercise independent judgment does not prohibit such delegation.[162] However, it seems that s.173 was not intended to overrule the common law rule that *delegatus non potest delegare*, i.e. that a person to whom powers are delegated (as powers are to directors under the articles) cannot further delegate the exercise of those powers, *unless* the instrument of delegation itself authorises further delegation.[163] In practice, wide powers of further delegation are conferred on the directors by the articles, and it is indeed difficult to see how the board of a large company could otherwise effectively exercise its powers of management of the company. However, this rule means that the articles may effectively prevent further delegation beyond the board by simply not providing for this.

---

[162] See *Madoff Securities International Ltd v Raven* [2013] EWHC 3147 (Comm) at [191] (Popplewell J).

[163] *Cartmells'* case (1874) L.R. 9 Ch. App. 691. On the Government's intention to preserve this rule see HC Debs, Standing Committee D, Company Law Reform Bill, Fifteenth Sitting, 11 July 2006 (Afternoon), col. 600 (the Solicitor-General).

Exercise of future discretion

Thirdly, it was debated at common law whether the non-fettering rule prevented a **16–35** director from contracting with a third party as to the future exercise of his or her discretion. The answer ultimately arrived at was that this was permissible in appropriate cases. The starting point at common law, despite the paucity of reported cases on the point,[164] seems to be that directors cannot validly contract (either with one another or with third parties) as to how they shall vote at future board meetings or otherwise conduct themselves in the future.[165] This is so even though there is no improper motive or purpose and no personal advantage reaped by the directors under the agreement. This, however, does not mean that if, in the bona fide exercise of their discretion, the directors have entered into a contract on behalf of the company, they cannot in that contract validly agree to take such further action at board meetings or otherwise as is necessary to carry out that contract. As was said in a judgment of the Australian High Court[166]:

> "There are many kinds of transaction in which the proper time for the exercise of the directors' discretion is the time of the negotiation of a contract and not the time at which the contract is to be performed...If at the former time they are bona fide of opinion that it is in the best interests of the company that the transaction should be entered into and carried into effect, I can see no reason in law why they should not bind themselves to do whatever under the transaction is to be done by the board."

The principle in *Thorby v Goldberg* was applied by the English Court of Appeal in *Cabra Estates Plc v Fulham Football Club*,[167] so as to uphold an elaborate contract which the directors had entered into on behalf of the company for the redevelopment of the football ground and under which, inter alia, the club was entitled to some £11 million and the directors agreed to support any planning application the developers might make during the coming seven years. This is surely correct: if individuals may contract as to their future behaviour in these matters, it is desirable that companies should be able to do so too. The application of the "no fettering" rule would make companies unreliable contracting parties and perhaps deprive them of the opportunity to enter into long-term contracts which would be to their commercial benefit.

---

[164] But see *Clark v Workman* [1920] 1 Ir.R. 107; and an unreported decision of Morton J in the *Arderne Cinema* litigation, below, at paras 19–10 et seq.; and the Scottish decision in *Dawson International Plc v Coats Paton Plc* 1989 S.L.T. 655 (1st Div.) where it was accepted that an agreement by the directors would be subject to an implied term that it did not derogate from their duty to give advice to the shareholders which reflected the situation at the time the advice was given.

[165] Contrast the position of shareholders who may freely enter into such voting agreements: below, paras 19–25 et seq. What if the directors and the members enter into an agreement which fetters the directors' discretion? This was discussed, but not clearly settled, by the Canadian Supreme Court in *Ringuet v Bergeron* [1960] S.C.R. 672, where the majority held the voting agreement valid because, in their view, it related only to voting at general meetings. The minority held that it extended also to directors' meetings and was void, but they conceded that the position might have been different had all the members originally been parties to the agreement: see ibid., at 677. But cf. *Fulham Football Club Ltd v Cabra Estates Plc* [1994] 1 B.C.L.C. 363 at 393.

[166] *Thorby v Goldberg* (1964) 112 C.L.R. 597 Aust. HC, per Kitto J at 605–606.

[167] *Cabra Estates Plc v Fulham Football Club* [1994] 1 B.C.L.C. 363 CA; noted by Griffiths [1993] J.B.L. 576.

Section 173(2)(a) now provides that the duty to exercise independent judgment is not infringed by a director acting "in accordance with an agreement duly entered into by the company that restricts the future exercise of discretion by its directors". In the parliamentary debates this provision was described as enshrining the *Cabra Estates* decision,[168] including presumably the rider that the agreement must be one entered into by the directors in the bona fide opinion that it is in the best interests of the company to do so (i.e. "duly" entered into). Section 173(2)(b) goes on to state that no breach of the independent judgment rule arises if the director acts "in a way authorised by the company's constitution". Thus, the articles may authorise restrictions on the exercise of independent judgment, which might be a useful facility in private companies.

However, s.173(2)(a) protects the directors only from the argument that they have failed to exercise independent judgment by entering into the agreement which restricts their future freedom of action. Can the subsequent exercise of their powers as the contract demands be said to be a breach of their core duty of loyalty, if at that time they no longer believe it to be in accordance with their core duty to act in accordance with the contract? There are a number of cases in which, where shareholder consent has been required for a disposal of assets or for a takeover, the courts have been reluctant to construe agreements on the part of the directors not to co-operate with rival suitors or to recommend a rival offer to the shareholders as binding the directors, if they come to the view that the later offer is preferable from the shareholders' point of view.[169] This line of cases might be justified on the basis that shareholders are peculiarly dependent upon the advice of their directors and that they might find themselves in a poor position to take the decision which had been put in their hands, if they were given advice by the directors which did not reflect the situation as the directors saw it at the time it fell to the shareholders to take their decision. The continuing validity of the no fettering rule in this context could be reconciled with the provisions of s.173 on the basis that that section deals only with the fiduciary duties owed by the director to the company (see s.170(1)), whereas the situation just mentioned triggers the duty owed by directors to the shareholders to give them advice in the shareholders' best interest, if they choose to give them advice at all.[170]

Nominee directors

16–36 Finally, the independent judgment principle could cause difficulties for "nominee" directors, i.e. directors not elected by the shareholders generally but appointed by a particular class of security holder or creditor to protect their interests. English law solves such problems by requiring nominee directors to

---

[168] See HC Debs, Standing Committee D, Company Law Reform Bill, Fifteenth Sitting, 11 July 2006 (Afternoon), col. 600 (the Solicitor-General).

[169] *John Crowther Group Plc v Carpets International* [1990] B.C.L.C. 460; *Rackham v Peek Foods Ltd* [1990] B.C.L.C. 895; *Dawson International Plc v Coats Paton Plc*, 1989 S.L.T. 655. The correctness of these decisions was left open by the Court of Appeal in *Cabra Estates*. Even here it must be accepted that the shareholders may in consequence lose a commercial opportunity which would otherwise be open to them. See the discussion below at paras 28–36 et seq.

[170] See above, para.16–6.

ignore the interests of the nominator,[171] though it may be doubted how far this injunction is obeyed in practice. The Ghana Companies Code 1973 adopted what might be regarded as the more realistic line by permitting nominee directors to "give special, but not exclusive, consideration to the interests" of the nominator, but even this formulation would not permit the "mandating" of directors and thus the creation of a fettering problem.

DUTY TO PROMOTE THE SUCCESS OF THE COMPANY

Settling the statutory formula

The duty to promote the success of the company is the modern version of the most basic of the duties of good faith or fidelity owed by directors. It is the core duty to which directors are subject, in the sense that it applies to every exercise of judgement which the directors undertake, whether they are testing the margins of their powers under the constitution or not and whether or not there is an operative conflict of interest. Together with the non-fiduciary duty to exercise care, skill and diligence, the duty to promote the success of the company expresses the law's view on how directors should discharge their functions on a day-to-day basis. Thus, it is not surprising that its proper formulation has always been controversial, and perhaps never more so than during the deliberations of the CLR and the passage of the 2006 Act through Parliament, since this was an area of directors' duties where it was not proposed that the statute should simply repeat the common law. The common law duty was typically formulated as one which required the directors to act in good faith in what they believed to be "the best interests of the company". This, predictably, follows the equivalent formulation in relation to trustees, who are required to act bona fide in the best interests of their beneficiaries.

16–37

That historical common law formulation differs in significant ways from what is now found in s.172(1) of the Act. This section requires the director to act "in the way he considers, in good faith, would be most likely to promote the success of the company for the benefit of its members as a whole"; and then sets out a non-exhaustive list of six matters to which the directors must "have regard" when deciding on the appropriate course of action.

The common law formulation made it clear that the duty was owed to the company, so that only those who could claim to act as, or on behalf of, the company could enforce the duty. Section 170(1) repeats that. But, that aside, the common law formulation that directors must act *in the interests of* "the company" was seen by many a being close to meaningless in providing guidance to directors. Because the company is an artificial legal person, it was seen as

---

[171] *Boulting v ACTT* [1963] 2 Q.B. 606 at 626, per Lord Denning MR; *Kuwait Asia Bank EC v National Mutual Life Nominees Ltd* [1991] 1 A.C. 187 PC. The latter case shows that this principle has the advantage of not making the nominator liable for any breaches of duty to the company by the nominee director. Also see *Thompson v The Renwick Group Plc* [2014] EWCA Civ 635 CA, where the Court rejected the view that a parent assumes a duty of care to employees of its subsidiary in health and safety matters by virtue of that parent company having appointed an individual as director of its subsidiary company with responsibility for health and safety matters.

impossible to assign interests to it unless one goes further and identifies the company with the interests of one or more groups of human persons. As Nourse LJ remarked, "The interests of a company, as an artificial person, cannot be distinguished from the interests of the persons who are interested in it".[172] In practice, the common law normally identified the interests of the company with those of its shareholders, current and future if that was appropriate,[173] and thus took the further step envisaged by Nourse LJ. In addition, at common law it was seemingly permissible for the directors to take into account stakeholder interests when acting in the interests of the company. The point was made a long time ago, albeit in the context of ultra vires, by Bowen LJ, who famously said: "The law does not say that there are to be no cakes and ale, but there are to be no cakes and ale except such as are required for the benefit of the company".[174] It is in this sense that the view of the Law Society,[175] opposing any statutory reformulation as being unnecessary, can be understood; they urged instead that "the concept of the company as a legal entity separate from its members, and in whose interests the directors must act, is well understood".

16–38   If the old test of "the interests of the company" was too vague, what should a clearer statutory version require? Given the concentration of economic power in large companies, the question of which interests the directors were required to pursue when exercising their powers was of considerable interest and controversy across the political spectrum. Should the directors be required to act in the interests of the shareholders (the shareholder primacy model), or should they perhaps give equal status to all the company's various stakeholders, including not simply the shareholders but also employees, customers, suppliers, and indeed even the local community and the environment (the pluralist model)? The different interests ranged on either side added heat to the debate. The final outcome was, perhaps predictably, something between these two extremes, although undoubtedly closer to the first and so also to the old common law test. The statutory formulation clearly rejects the "pluralist" approach, at least to the extent that it might have given all stakeholders some sort of equivalent status, allowing all to have the right to enforce directors' duties. But, at the other end of the spectrum, shareholder primacy was refined: the shareholders or members are certainly to be the primary object of the directors' efforts, hence the current formulation that the director must act "in the way he considers, in good faith, would be most likely to promote the success of the company for the benefit of its members as a whole"; but the directors are also subject to an obligation (not merely a power), although clearly a subordinate obligation, to "have regard to" the interests of other stakeholders. The subordinate nature of this second duty is

---

[172] *Brady v Brady* [1988] B.C.L.C. 20 at 40 CA.

[173] *Gaiman v National Association for Mental Health* [1971] Ch. at 330: "both present and future members". Also see below, para.16–46.

[174] *Hutton v West Cork Railway* (1883) 23 Ch. D. at 673, the "cakes and ale" being in this case gratuitous benefits for the employees. For this reason directors can normally justify modest, business-related political or charitable donations on the part of their companies, though the broader public policy issues arising out of such donations are recognised in the requirement that such donations be disclosed in the directors' report and in some cases approved by the shareholders: see below, paras 16–50 and 21–23.

[175] The Law Society, *Company Law Reform White Paper*, June 2005, p.6.

made clear by the words "in doing so", i.e. in discharging the central duty. Put another way, the shareholders' position as the object of the directors' efforts is not shared with other groups of persons upon whose success the company's business may be thought to depend, for example, its employees or other stakeholders. To this extent, the rule of shareholder primacy is reiterated in the section.

The strategy of rejecting pluralism but adopting a modernised version of shareholder primacy emerged from the CLR, and was described there as a philosophy of "enlightened shareholder value (ESV)".[176] Thus, in promoting the success of the company for the benefit of its members as a whole, s.172(1) requires that the director:

"in doing so [must] have regard (amongst other matters) to—
(a)   the likely consequences of any decision in the long term,
(b)   the interests of the company's employees,
(c)   the need to foster the company's business relationships with suppliers, customers and others,
(d)   the impact of the company's operations on the community and the environment,
(e)   the desirability of the company maintaining a reputation for high standards of business conduct, and
(f)   the need to act fairly as between members of the company (s.172(1))"

The ESV approach can be said to embody the insight that the success of the company or the interests of the shareholders are not likely to be advanced if the management of the company conducts its business so that its employees are unwilling to work effectively, its suppliers and customers would rather not deal with it, it is at odds with the community in which it operates and its ethical and environmental standards are regarded as lamentable. However, it is crucial to note that the interests of the non-shareholder groups are to be given consideration by the directors only to the extent that it is desirable to do so in order to promote the success of the company for the benefit of its members as a whole. The non-shareholder interests do not have an independent value in the directors' decision-making, as they would have under a pluralist approach. For this reason, it seems wrong in principle to regard the section as requiring the directors to "balance" the interests of the members with those of the stakeholders. The members' interests are paramount, but the interests of stakeholders are to be taken into account when determining the best way of promoting the members' interests.

It may be asked whether the ESV approach amounts to a development or a **16–39** repetition of the common law. The answer is that it represents a development, but a modest one. What the Act adds to the common law is a *duty* on the part of the directors to take account of stakeholder interests when it is in the interests of the success of the company for the benefit of members to do so (but not a corresponding right in the stakeholders to enforce that duty). However, the statutory restatement may nevertheless have an impact, if only by disabusing those directors and their advisers who might have been inclined to take an unduly narrow interpretation of the duty previously held.

If the move from permission to well-described obligation is what lies at the root of the ESV approach, it becomes of great importance to know how the duty

---

[176] See Developing, Ch.3 and Completing, Ch.3.

will be enforced. As argued immediately below, s.172 imposes a mainly subjective test,[177] so, as with the predecessor common law duty, litigation is likely to be relatively uncommon and probably even less often successful. This is because it is very difficult to show that the directors have breached this duty of good faith, except in egregious cases or cases where the directors have, obligingly, left a clear record of their thought processes leading up to the challenged decision.[178]

Instead, the major role in giving some degree of practical substance to the ESV duty will lie in the extended reporting requirements to shareholders by directors, as described in Ch.21.[179] This was as envisaged by the CLR, which saw the ESV approach to directors' duties and enhanced reporting requirements as closely linked.[180]

Finally, and for the avoidance of doubt, the duty of the directors to promote the success of the company for the benefit of its members does not exempt the company from compliance with its other legal obligations, for example, health and safety or discrimination legislation, even if it could be shown that non-compliance would promote the company's overall success.

Interpreting the statutory formula

Defining the company's success

16–40   Several important points arise on the interpretation of the language contained in this section. First, it is to be noted that corporate *success* for the benefit of the members is the word used to identify the touchstone for the exercise of the directors' discretion. Success is a more general word than, for example, "value", which it might have been thought was what the shareholders are interested in. However, the more general word is clearly the appropriate one, because not all companies formed under the Act are aimed at maximising the financial interests of their members. Companies may be charitable; they may have non-profit-making objectives without being charities, as in the case of a company formed by leaseholders to hold the freehold of a block of flats; they may be companies set

---

[177] *LNOC Ltd v Watford Association Football Club Ltd* [2013] EWHC 3615 (Comm) at [64] (HH Judge Mackie QC).

[178] The classic case where the directors did all too clearly reveal their reasoning is *Dodge v Ford Motor Co* (1919) 170 N.W. 668. Henry Ford openly took the view that the shareholders had been more than amply rewarded on their investment in the company and so proposed to declare no further special dividends but only the regular dividends (of some 60 per cent per annum!) in order to reduce the price of the cars, to expand production and "to employ still more men, to spread the benefits of this industrial system to the greatest possible number, to help them build up their lives and their homes" (at 683). This was held to be "an arbitrary refusal to distribute funds that ought to have been distributed to the stockholders as dividends" (at 685).

[179] See the current regulations on narrative reporting (which apply to financial years ending on or after 30 September 2013) as set out in the Companies Act 2006 (Strategic Report and Directors' Report) Regulations 2013. These followed from a BIS consultation on narrative reporting, *The Future of Narrative Reporting—A further consultation* (2011) and *The Future of Narrative Reporting: The Government Response* (2012) *https://www.gov.uk/government/consultations/the-future-of-narrative-reporting-a-further-consultation* [Accessed 5 May 2016].

[180] Developing, para.2.22.

up within a corporate group simply to hold a particular asset rather than to exploit it, even though the overall purpose of the group is to make profits; or they may be commercially-oriented but without aiming to distribute profits, in which case the company may, but is not obliged to, be incorporated as a CIC. In all these cases, maximising the value of the company is not the primary objective of its members and perhaps not even an objective at all. Section 172(2) makes it clear that:

> "where or to the extent that the purposes of the company consist of or include purposes other than the benefit of its members, subsection (1) has effect as if the reference to promoting the success of the company for the benefit of its members were to achieving those purposes."

The underlying thrust of the section is that it is the members who are to define the purposes of the company against which the directors can give meaning to the requirement to promote its success. The definition of the purpose of the company may be set out in its constitution. This is less likely to be the case now that the company is no longer required to have an objects clause, but certainly in the case of companies with non-commercial or non-profit objectives this fact is likely to appear clearly enough from the company's articles. In other words, the position may turn out to be that the company is to be regarded as a commercial company, unless its constitution indicates otherwise, and so in the typical case the directors will define success in commercial terms.

A more important underlying question is the extent to which the section is intended to constrain directors' decisions about precisely how to pursue the success of the company. Should the company aim for expansion through a series of takeovers or by organic growth? Should the company aim for expansion at all or for exploitation of a niche position? It seems clear that the section does not intend to address this sort of issue at all. This is to be left to the directors, who in turn are accountable to the shareholders for their decisions through the company's corporate governance mechanisms rather than through the courts. To this end, the section imposes a subjective test for compliance: the director must act "in the way he considers, in good faith, would be most likely to promote the success of the company". This aspect of the statutory duty is one shared with the previous common law formulation, and that was interpreted by the courts in such a way as to leave business decisions to the directors. As Lord Greene MR put it in *Re Smith & Fawcett Ltd*, directors were required to act "bona fide in what they consider—not what a court may consider—is in the interests of the company".[181] In most cases, it is true, compliance with the rule that directors must act in good faith was tested on commonsense principles, the court asking itself whether it was proved that the directors had not done what they believed to be right, and normally accepting that they had unless satisfied that they had not behaved as honest men of business might be expected to act. However, even where the director had not acted as an honest business person might be expected to act, this is not necessarily a demonstration of breach of the duty of good faith. Thus, in one case where the directors' decision had caused substantial harm to the company it was held that this was merely a piece of evidence, perhaps a strong piece, against their contention that they had acted in good faith, rather than proof

---

[181] "and not for any collateral purpose" [this closing phrase seeing its statutory parallels in s.171(b)]: [1942] Ch. 304 at 306 CA.

absolute that they had not.[182] These decisions on the meaning of good faith in the context of the core duty of fidelity at common law seem equally applicable to the statutory duty.

Failure to have regard, or due regard, to relevant matters

16–41 The concept of ESV enshrined in the statutory duty imposes an obligation on directors to "have regard" to the list of factors set out in subs.172(1)(a)–(f). Does this give rise to a corresponding power in the courts to scrutinise the decisions of directors to establish whether they have indeed taken account of these factors, or perhaps even whether, on an objective basis, they have taken *appropriate* account of these factors? The answers to these questions seem inextricably linked to the "improper purposes" issues discussed earlier (s.171(b)); the older common law rule similarly juxtaposed the two requirements.[183]

On the first question, a proper reading of the section does suggest that a failure by directors to have regard to each item on the list of factors would constitute a breach of duty and render the directors' decision challengeable. This principle was already established at common law, although perhaps in a more limited form: although much was left to the directors' discretion (as described below) in determining what was in the interests of the company, the directors might breach that duty where they failed to direct their minds at all to the question of whether a transaction was in the interests of the company, even though a board which had considered the question might well have acted in the same way. A good illustration of the principle is afforded by *Re W&M Roith Ltd*.[184] There the controlling shareholder and director wished to make provision for his widow. On advice, he entered into a service agreement with the company whereby on his death she was to be entitled to a pension for life. On being satisfied that no thought had been given to the question whether the arrangement was for the benefit of the company and that, indeed, the sole object was to make provision for the widow, the court held that the transaction was not binding on the company.[185]

In this case it might be said that the straightforward financial success of the company was clearly compromised by the decision, since the widow was unlikely to provide the company with any corresponding corporate benefit. In such circumstances, the directors needed to be able to demonstrate that their decision was based on due consideration of the corporate benefit, and this they could not

---

[182] *Regentcrest Plc (In Liquidation) v Cohen* [2001] 2 B.C.L.C. 80. See also *Extrasure Travel Insurances Ltd v Scattergood* [2003] 1 B.C.L.C. 598 at [90]. It is to be noted that in neither the formulation of Lord Greene MR nor in s.172 is there a requirement upon the director to act "honestly" as well as "in good faith", though the word "honestly" is used in a number of court decisions in this area. However, the CLR did not believe that the adverb "honestly" added anything of importance to the requirement of good faith and its use might create uncertainty, and so it did not recommend its use either here or elsewhere in the statutory restatement: Completing, para.3.13.

[183] *Re Smith and Fawcett Ltd* [1942] Ch. 304 at 306 CA (Lord Greene MR).

[184] *Re W&M Roith Ltd* [1967] 1 W.L.R. 432.

[185] Following *Re Lee, Behrens & Co Ltd* [1932] 2 Ch. 46; but cf. *Lindgren v L&P Estates Ltd* [1968] Ch. 572 CA, where it was held that there had been no failure on the part of the directors to consider the commercial merits.

do.[186] However, had they been able to do that, the court would have been unlikely to second-guess their conclusions even if the court itself might not have reached the same decision.

But this strict approach might be thought impractical. By contrast, in **16–42** *Charterbridge Corp v Lloyds Bank*,[187] the directors of a company forming part of a corporate group had considered the benefit of the group as a whole, but without giving separate consideration to that of the company alone, when they caused the subsidiary company of which they were directors to give security for a debt owed by the parent company to a bank. It was held, perhaps surprisingly given the accepted common law formulation of the requirement on directors, that "the proper test in the absence of actual separate consideration must be whether an intelligent and honest man in the position of a director of the company concerned could have reasonably believed that the transactions were for the benefit of the company". Here the collapse of the parent company would have been "a disaster" for the subsidiary.[188] The decision perhaps suggests that although directors must act in ways *they* consider would be most likely to promote the interests (or the success) of the company, it is also true that where, objectively, on balance, their decision can be seen to do that, it will not be overturned; the directors will not be held to be in breach of their duty at common law to act in the interests of the company (or, under the statute, their duty to promote the success of the company) *merely* because they did not give explicit thought to the question, at least in the absence of proven detriment.[189]

On the other hand, and despite the *Charterbridge* decision, it must be said that the core duty of good faith does not recognise a duty "to the group" or to other companies in the group. It insists that the main focus of directors must be on the interests of their subsidiary, even if it accepts that the interests of the subsidiary are in many cases intimately related to the continuing existence of the group.[190]

---

[186] Similarly, see *Scottish Co-operative Wholesale Society Ltd v Meyer* [1959] A.C. 324 HL.

[187] *Charterbridge Corp v Lloyds Bank* [1970] Ch. 62. A similar approach has been adopted in the area of unfair prejudice. See *Nicholas v Soundcraft Electronics Ltd* [1993] 1 B.C.L.C. 360 CA.

[188] cf. *Extrasure Travel Insurances Ltd v Scattergood* [2003] 1 B.C.L.C. 598, accepting the law as stated in the *Charterbridge* case, but coming to a different conclusion on the facts because (a) the directors of the subsidiary never considered whether the survival of the parent was crucial to the subsidiary; and (b) no reasonable director would have concluded that the steps taken by the directors would lead to the survival of the parent.

[189] *Re HLC Environmental Projects Ltd (In Liquidation)* [2014] B.C.C. 337 at [92]–[93] (John Randall QC); *Green v El Tai* [2015] B.P.I.R. 24 Ch D at [110] (Registrar Jones); *Madoff Securities International Ltd v Raven* [2013] EWHC 3147 (Comm) at [194].

[190] See also *Lindgren v L & P Estates Co Ltd* [1968] Ch. 572, 595, per Harman LJ (no duty owed by director of holding company to subsidiary); and *Bell v Lever Bros Ltd* [1932] A.C. 161 at 229, per Lord Atkin (no duty owed by director of subsidiary to the parent company). The statutory qualification to the definition of a "shadow director" in s.250(3) (above, para.16–8), excluding a company in relation to its subsidiaries, supports this approach. The cases do not distinguish between wholly-owned subsidiaries and those with outside minority shareholders. Only in the latter case does the imposition of a group policy potentially have an adverse effect on the interests of the shareholders, for which the unfair prejudice provisions may now provide a remedy (see Ch.20). It should also be noted that it is apparently legitimate for the company's articles to permit or require the directors to take into account the interests of other companies in the group, because in that way it could be said that the articles have defined what is to be regarded as "success" for the company in question.

Directors in corporate groups must guard against their inevitable inclinations to promote the interests of the group as a whole (or some part of it).

16–43 These cases all concern the common law duty. Their analysis is in principle equally applicable to breaches of the statutory provisions, and indeed finding a breach of the core statutory duty of good faith on the ground that not all the required interests have been taken into account is perhaps more likely under the ESV approach because the statute is so much clearer about the precise range of matters to which directors must have regard in the discharge of their duty to promote the success of the company for the benefit of its members. To that extent, the retreat from the strict approach in *Re W & M Roith Ltd*[191] is welcome. Moreover, since the statutory list of factors is non-exhaustive, it would follow that a director would be in breach of duty in failing to take account of any matter which he or she considered relevant to the decision in question. However, in truth the statutory formulation largely makes explicit what was already implicit in the earlier common law, so it does not require boards to approach decision-making, or to document their decisions, in a totally novel fashion. Of course, to the extent that boards might previously have ignored potential adverse impacts on shareholders' interests by failing to analyse the impact of a proposed decision on non-shareholders, the section should produce a change of practice.

On the second question, of whether the directors have not simply taken account of the listed factors but have taken *appropriate* account of them, the earlier common law cases suggest that the courts will generally resist any request to second-guess the directors' judgement of how best to act in the interests of the company.[192] The only exception is perhaps when, in the court's view, no reasonable director could have considered the chosen course of action to be in the company's interests (by analogy with the public law "*Wednesbury* unreasonableness" test). Such facts as raise this concern are often seen to go to the question of whether the court believes that the director did in fact consider the relevant matter at all (and so is part of the analysis of the first question just considered), but to the extent that the court's determination is not simply evidential, but judgemental, the resulting judicial oversight of directors' management decisions has remained very restrained, and in any event is limited to overturning the impugned decision, not substituting the courts' decision (except to the extent that this is implicit in the courts' unravelling of what has been done). Indeed it is notable that the architect of the public law *Wednesbury* principle, Lord Greene MR, was also the judge who in *Re Smith & Fawcett* (quoted earlier) was concerned to stress the freedom of directors from control by the courts in the exercise of their good faith judgement, while also adding a "proper purposes" limitation analogous to the public law principle and to the statutory principle now found in s.171(b).

The most authoritative statement of this approach to judicial review is that of Lord Woolf in *Equitable Life Assurance Society v Hyman*,[193] although his

---

[191] *Re W & M Roith Ltd* [1967] 1 W.L.R. 432.
[192] See above, para.16–40; and *Edge v Pensions Ombudsman* [2000] Ch. 602 at 627E–630G CA; *Equitable Life Assurance Society v Hyman* [2002] 1 A.C. 408 at [17]–[21] HL.
[193] *Equitable Life Assurance Society v Hyman* [2000] 2 All E.R. 331 at [17]–[21] CA (per Lord Woolf). In the House of Lords ([2002] 1 A.C. 408) Lord Steyn dealt with the case as a matter of an implied term in a contract, whilst Lord Cooke, dealing with it as a matter of the exercise of a

approach was not part of the arguments of the other two judges in that case (or in the House of Lords on appeal). The complaint in this case was between groups of corporate creditors each complaining about the effect of the directors' decision; in other cases where the *Wednesbury* principle has been invoked, the disputes have typically been among members of the company about their rights and interests as shareholders rather than disagreements about the setting of the company's business strategy.[194] It might be thought, therefore, that the inclusion in subs.(1)(f) of "the need to act fairly as between the members of the company" as one of the factors of which the directors need to have regard could turn out to be significant, although the shareholders typically have more amenable avenues for complaint than reliance on a duty the directors owe to the company.

Indeed, it might be better, analytically, to see this type of objective judicial review, where relevant, as situated under s.171(b), with s.172 merely providing an explicit list of proper considerations required to be taken into account in directors' decision-making. Such an approach would effectively align s.171(b) "improper purposes" with the mandatory considerations listed in s.172, but would remind complainants of the inherent limitations in the claim being advanced. And to the extent that unfair treatment of minorities by controlling persons is the chief mischief to be dealt with, a remedy can alternatively often be provided under the unfair prejudice provisions discussed in Ch.20.

Whatever the better classification of these claims, it seems clear from the course of parliamentary debates on the Bill that the Government did not intend in its formulation of s.172 to introduce a wide-ranging judicial review of the decisions of directors. In an earlier version of what became s.172, the duty to act in good faith was set out in subs.1 and the list of ESV factors in subs.3. Later they were brought together in subs.1. As the Minister for Industry and the Regions explained in the parliamentary debates: **16–44**

> "In [the House of Lords], the clause was amended to bring together what are now its subsections and make even clearer—I hope to hon. Members and certainly to those outside who will have to use the law—our intention that, while a director must have regard to the various factors stated, that requirement is subordinate to the overriding duty to promote the success of the company."

In addition, the Minister continued, the bringing together of the two previously separate subsections involved the deletion "from the clause of a second 'must', which we considered could be perceived as creating a separate duty". Finally, and most importantly:

---

discretion for a proper purpose, did not cite the *Wednesbury* principle but confined himself to mention of the *Howard Smith v Ampol* case (see fn.109, above). See also *Hunter v Senate Support Services Ltd* [2005] 1 B.C.L.C. 175 at [165]–[232].

[194] See the previous note and the cases referred to therein. However, it should also be noted that *Re Smith & Fawcett Ltd* was itself an intra-member dispute.

"we believe it essential for the weight given to any factor to be a matter for a director's good faith judgment. Importantly, the decision is not subject to the reasonableness test that appears in other legislation.....That is in sharp contrast to, for example, decisions on public law, to which courts often apply such a test."[195]

For all these reasons, it appears that the deferential approach of the common law to directors' judgements in relation to the core duty of good faith and fidelity was intended to be applied also to its statutory reformulation.

A duty to disclose wrongdoing

16–45   In an interesting decision, in *Item Software (UK) Ltd v Fassihi*[196] the Court of Appeal held that a director was under a duty to disclose his own breaches of fiduciary duty, an obligation apparently derived from, i.e. was an aspect of, the core duty of good faith and loyalty.[197] At first sight this is a draconian duty. However, in many cases it will add little to the director's potential liability for breaches of fiduciary duty, though in some cases, as in this one, it will. The director had committed a breach of the corporate opportunity rule (discussed below) by attempting to persuade a client of the company to renew a contract with him personally rather than with the company. In the end, the client renewed the contract with neither the director nor the company. Against orthodoxy, the company sued for damages (not profits) for breach of the corporate opportunity doctrine, but failed because the trial judge had held that the client did not take the director's offer seriously. However, the court also found that, had the company known of the director's activities, it would have accepted an offer to renew from the client which it in fact rejected. Thus, the company's loss was the profit it would have made on this admittedly not favourable contract, but that loss could be recovered only if the director should have told the company of his underhand activities, a duty which the court found to exist.

The case has been thought in some quarters to create a new and free-standing "duty of disclosure" on directors, but it is submitted that this is not the case. In fact, seen as a part of the core duty of good faith and loyalty, rather than as a free-standing duty of disclosure, the decision seems unproblematic. The core duty must require a director to bring to the attention of the board threats to its business of which the director becomes aware. The twist in this case was that the duty was imposed even though the threat arose out of the director's own wrongdoing, but it would be odd if the director's wrongdoing could relieve him or her from a course

---

[195] HC Debs, Standing Committee D, Company Law Reform Bill, Fifteenth Sitting, 11 July 2006 (Afternoon), all quotations from cols 591–592. At one stage the duty of the director to take into account the listed factors was qualified by the phrase "so far as reasonably practicable" but this was deleted, perhaps because of the suggestion in the phrase of an objective test for review of the directors' decision. See also HL Debs, vol.681, cols 845–846, 9 May 2006 (Lord Goldsmith, on Report).

[196] *Item Software (UK) Ltd v Fassihi* [2005] 2 B.C.L.C. 91. Also see *GHLM Trading Ltd v Maroo* [2012] EWHC 61 (Ch); *IT Human Resources Plc v Land* [2014] EWHC 3812 (Ch).

[197] See *Stupples v Stupples & Co (High Sycombe) Ltd* [2012] EWHC 1226 (Ch) at [59] (HHJ David Cooke). Further, in *First Subsea Ltd v Balltec Ltd* [2014] EWHC 866 (Ch), Norris J emphasised (at [191]) that the duty to "self-report" is "not a discrete and free-standing duty. It is one aspect of a bundle of interrelated obligations which together constitute 'good faith' and 'loyalty'."

of action which would otherwise have to be taken.[198] The main obstacle in reaching this result was the earlier decision of the House of Lords in *Bell v Lever Bros Ltd*,[199] which had been interpreted by some as laying down a general principle that a director's own wrongdoing never had to be disclosed. The court was able to accept the result in that case by confining it to the situation where the director was negotiating compensation for the termination of his or her services with the company or an improvement in the terms of his or her employment, on the grounds that disclosure in such a case would be "contrary to the expectations of the parties".[200] However, outside the context of the director negotiating terms of service with the company, a duty to disclose others' or one's own wrongdoing can be regarded as a normal incident of the core duty of fidelity, where the director is aware that the facts of which he or she is in possession should be given to the company if it is to protect and further its own interests.

The problem of "short-termism"

The common law focus on shareholders led to a widespread but, it is submitted, erroneous view that the law required directors acting in the interests of shareholders to prioritise their short-term interests. The better view, it is suggested, is that the directors were not bound to any particular timeframe; on the contrary, they must take into account both the long- and the short-term interests of the shareholders and strike a balance between them.[201] The CLR proposed in its draft statement of directors' duties to specify an obligation on the directors to take into account "the likely consequences (short and long term) of the actions open to the director".[202] As we have seen, s.172 refers merely to "the likely consequences of any decision in the long term". If anything, the omission of the reference to short-term interests in the non-exhaustive list emphasises the importance of long-term consequences. That bias is repeated in the UK Corporate Governance Code.[203]

16–46

---

[198] See *Shepherds Investments Ltd v Walters* [2006] I.R.L.R. 110 at [132].

[199] *Bell v Lever Bros Ltd* [1932] A.C.161.

[200] *Bell v Lever Bros Ltd* [1932] A.C.161 at [57]—presumably because the parties were on opposite sides of a negotiation.

[201] See Counsel's Opinion quoted in the Report by Mr Milner Holland of an investigation under s.165(b) of the Companies Act 1948 into the affairs of the Savoy Hotel Ltd and the Berkeley Hotel Company Ltd, Board of Trade, 1954. This somewhat obscure source has long been regarded as the *locus classicus* on this point. See also *Gaiman v National Association for Mental Health* [1971] Ch. at 330: "both present and future members".

[202] CLR, Final Report I, p.345 (Principle 2, Note (1)).

[203] CGC, A.1-Main Principle. See too BIS, *A Long-Term Focus for Corporate Britain: A Call for Evidence* (2010). Responses were published, but then nothing more was done: see *https://www.gov.uk/government/consultations/a-long-term-focus-for-corporate-britain-a-call-for-evidence* [Accessed 13 February 2016].

Corporate groups

16–47   We have already considered the potential problem faced by directors within corporate groups, where their instinct may be to look to the overall success of the group, whereas their duty of good faith and loyalty is owed only to their appointing company.[204]

Employees

16–48   Among the factors to which a director of a company must have regard under s.172(1) are "the interests of the company's employees". This is as one would expect: any comprehensive list of stakeholder interests will necessarily include the employees. But the practical impact of this on employees is limited. Indeed, it was said of the predecessor provision[205] that its real impact was to dilute directors' accountability to shareholders rather than strengthen accountability to employees. This is because employees cannot use the section offensively, whilst directors can use it defensively when sued by shareholders, by arguing that a decision apparently unfavourable to the shareholders is unchallengeable because it was taken in the interests of the employees.[206] Writ large, this illustrates the argument against the pluralist approach to this core duty of good faith. So long as the duty is perceived subjectively, increasing the number of equal-status groups whose interests the directors must promote makes proof of breach difficult, almost to the point of impossibility. Correcting that defect by making the duty objective, however, paves the way for excessive judicial intervention in the taking of board-level decisions, thus inducing caution on the part of those who ought to be risk-takers. The best view is probably that any broadly-formulated pluralist provision could not by itself operate so as to alter the decision-making processes of a board unless coupled with further changes in company law, such as board-level representation for the relevant stakeholder groups.

There is, however, one particular derogation from the core duty which is made in favour of employees. This is to be found in s.247, involving the power to make gratuitous payments to employees on the cessation of the company's business, as discussed at para.7–29.

Creditors

16–49   There is one surprising omission from the statutory list of matters to which the directors must have regard, namely, the interests of the creditors, except to the extent it is embraced by subs.172(1)(c). Of course, so long as the company's business is flourishing, the creditors' position is not prejudiced by such an omission. Their contractual rights against the company plus the company's desire to preserve its reputation and thus access to future credit will act so as to protect

---

[204] See above, para.16–36.

[205] Companies Act 1985 s.309, although expressed in different terms to s.172(1)(b).

[206] cf. *Re Saul D. Harrison & Sons Plc* [1995] 1 B.C.L.C. 14 at 25 CA, where resort was had to the Companies Act 1985 s.309 to undermine the shareholder petitioning under s.459 against the board/majority shareholders of the company.

the creditors. However, once the company's fortunes begin to decline, conflict between the interests of the shareholders and the creditors may emerge in a strong form; the directors have an incentive to take excessive risks to protect their own and the shareholders' position, knowing that, if the company is in the vicinity of insolvency, the downside risk will fall wholly on the creditors, whilst the upside benefit will get the company out of trouble. We have already seen in Ch.9 how this problem is dealt with, both by statutory insolvency laws operating in the lead up to insolvency, and by common law rules operating still earlier. The CLR considered whether these statutory and common law rules should be reiterated, or even expanded, in s.172,[207] but in the end the many perceived difficulties were all avoided by the simple strategy of providing, expressly, in s.172(3), that the duty imposed under that section "has effect subject to any enactment or rule of law requiring directors, in certain circumstances, to consider or act in the interests of creditors of the company". The detail thereby comprehended is covered in Ch.9.[208]

Donations

In the abstract, a decision on the part of the directors to give the company's assets away would appear to be a *clear* example of a decision not taken in good faith to promote the success of the company for the benefit of its members. On the other hand, companies are always being approached to support various causes, worthy or less worthy, and do in fact make donations of various sorts. Company law has sought to distinguish between donations which promote the company's business (legitimate) and those which do not (illegitimate). Traditionally, that distinction was drawn by the law relating to ultra vires, but now the focus is on directors' powers: in the absence of an express provision in the articles or elsewhere conferring upon directors the authority to make donations, is there an implied power to do so in order to further the company's business?[209] And if there is such a power, has it been exercised appropriately?[210] This second question has various strands. Thus, in *Re Lee, Behrens and Co Ltd*,[211] where the company's constitution conferred an express power on the directors to make the gift in question, Eve J identified the relevant tests as follows: "(i.) Is the transaction reasonably incidental to the carrying on of the company's business? (ii.) Is it a bona fide transaction? and (iii.) Is it done for the benefit and to promote the prosperity of the company?"

In practice, the courts have tended not to examine very closely the link between the donation and the company's business when it seemed to them that

16–50

---

[207] See CLR, Final 1, para.3.17 and p.348 (Principle 9); *Modernising Company Law*, Cm. 5533-I, July 2002, paras 3.11-3.12.

[208] See paras 9–4 et seq.

[209] The courts are likely to give a positive answer to this question.

[210] Thus, in *Evans v Brunner, Mond & Co Ltd* [1921] 1 Ch. 359, where the question was whether a shareholders' resolution expressly conferring power on the directors to make a certain class of donation was ultra vires, Eve J said obiter of the authority conferred by the resolution that it "is certainly impressed with this implied obligation on those to whom it is given, that they shall exercise the discretion vested in them bona fide in the interests of the company whose agents they are".

[211] *Re Lee, Behrens and Co Ltd* [1932] 2 Ch. 46. Also see *MSL Group Holdings Ltd v Clearwell International Ltd* [2012] EWHC 3707 (QB) (Sir Raymond Jack) at [41]–[42], [45].

the donation was in the public interest, so that a substantial donation by a large chemical company to promote scientific tertiary education was upheld even though the gift might not be used to promote the study of chemistry in particular and the company had no greater claim on the graduating students than any of its rivals.[212] It seems unlikely that this approach will change in the future, in the light of pressures on companies to be "good citizens" in their communities and of the recognition that companies may secure "reputational" advantages from support-ing activities which seem remote from their businesses, for example, a bank sponsoring an opera production (presumably thus enhancing its reputation among wealthy potential customers).[213] By contrast, donations which shift assets away from shareholders in the direction of other stakeholders in the company have traditionally been treated with suspicion, but that attitude may also be undergoing a change and, in any event, it is normally possible to present such apparent gifts as part of an exchange where the company is a going concern.[214]

The upshot of the law in this area is that directors probably have some leeway to steer donations or other similar arrangements (such as sponsorship) in the direction of their favourite charities or pastimes, without serious threat of legal challenge, provided such donations are not of excessive size and provided there is some link with the company's business.

16–51　However, in one area, that of corporate political donations, such leeway is arguably constitutionally objectionable. Consequently, in that area, as we shall see, the law has required shareholder approval of donations since reforms made in 2000.[215]

OVERVIEW OF THE NO-CONFLICT RULES

16–52　As fiduciaries, directors must not place themselves in a position in which there is a conflict between their duties to the company and their personal interests or duties to others.[216] This fundamental common law principle was perhaps most famously stated by Lord Herschell in *Bray v Ford*[217]:

---

[212] *Evans v Brunner, Mond & Co Ltd* [1921] 1 Ch. 359.

[213] The donation can then be presented as a contract: a payment in exchange for exposure of the company's name before a valued target audience, in fact a form of advertising.

[214] Thus, in *Parke v Daily News Ltd* [1962] Ch. 927 the payments to the employees failed because it could not be argued that a company about to enter liquidation any longer had a (shareholder) interest in fostering good relations with its employees. The specific decision in that case was reversed, within limits, by what is now s.247, which confers a power on the company, if it would otherwise not have it, to make provisions for the benefit of employees on the cessation or transfer of its business, which power is exercisable "notwithstanding the general duty imposed by s.172 (duty to promote the success of the company)".

[215] See above, para.16–50.

[216] Overwhelmingly, the conflict is between the director's personal interest and his duty to the company of which he is director, but where the same person is director of two competing companies, he or she may then be subject to competing duties. See *Clark Boyce v Mouat* [1994] 1 A.C. 428; *Bristol and West Building Society v Mothew* [1998] Ch. 1; *Transvaal Lands Co v New Belgium (Transvaal) Land and Development Co* [1914] 2 Ch. 488.

[217] *Bray v Ford* [1896] A.C. 44 at 51–52 HL.

"It is an inflexible rule of a court of equity that a person in a fiduciary position is not, unless otherwise expressly provided,[218] entitled to make a profit; he is not allowed to put himself in a position where his interest and duty conflict. It does not appear to me that this rule is founded upon principles of morality. I regard it rather as based on the consideration that, human nature being what it is, there is a danger, in such circumstances, of the person holding a fiduciary position being swayed by interest rather than by duty, and thus prejudicing those he was bound to protect. It has, therefore, been deemed expedient to law down this positive rule."

It can be argued that this common law "no conflict" principle (often separated, as here, into no-conflict and no-profit rules) underlies all three of the remaining general duties of directors set out in the Act: the self-dealing transaction rules discussed immediately below (ss.175(3) and 177, and Pt 10, Chs 3 and 4, the latter provisions all dealing with specific and invariably substantial types of property transactions with directors); the principle that a director must not make personal use of the company's property, information or opportunities (s.175(1) and (2)); and, finally, the requirement that directors must not receive benefits from third parties in exchange for the exercise of directorial powers (s.176). In the first case (self-dealing), the conflict arises because the director is, in a very practical sense, on both sides of a transaction with the company, and so motivated perhaps by self-interest rather than by duty.[219] In the case of directorial exploitation of corporate property or opportunity, by contrast, the director uses, for his or her own ends, the company's property or opportunities, to the exclusion of the company. Finally, in the case of what the common law calls, generically, "bribes", the risk is that the director exercises his or her powers in the interests of the third party rather than the company because of the personal benefit conferred on the director by that third party.

Although, at a broad level, it is undoubtedly true that the purpose of all three duties is to discourage directors from putting their personal interests ahead of their duties to the company, it is also true that the more specific rules under each duty have now developed sufficiently separately, especially, as we shall see, in terms of the action required of the director to comply with the duty, that it is sensible to consider them separately, as the Act does.[220] **16–53**

These various "no conflict" rules are probably the most important of the directors' various duties of good faith and loyalty. As we have seen, the core good faith rule is overwhelmingly subjective and so difficult to enforce, whilst, given the width of the powers conferred upon directors by the articles, the requirement that they stay within their powers under the constitution, and use those powers for proper purposes, tends to have only a marginally constraining impact upon directors' activities.

---

[218] The rules on who needs to provide such consent differ as between the different statutory categories of conflicts, as discussed below.

[219] Or the danger of "being swayed by interest rather than driven by duty": *Breitenfeld UK Ltd v Harrison* [2015] EWHC 399 (Ch) at [68] (Norris J).

[220] On the importance of distinguishing between self-dealing transactions and personal exploitation of corporate opportunities see *Bell v Lever Bros Ltd* [1932] A.C. 161 HL, per Lord Blanesburgh; *Sinclair Investments (UK) Ltd v Versailles Trade Finance Ltd* [2011] EWCA Civ 347 CA (which has however, on the issue of proprietary remedies, been overruled by the Supreme Court in the next case); *FHR European Ventures LLP v Cedar Capital Partners LLC* [2014] UKSC 45; [2015] A.C. 250.

TRANSACTIONS WITH THE COMPANY (SELF-DEALING)

The scope of the relevant provisions

16–54   The structure of the Act is a little more complex than the above might suggest. Section 175 is the apparently general section dealing with, as the side-note says, "the duty to avoid conflicts of interest". However, self-dealing transactions are excluded from s.175 by s.175(3): "this duty does not apply to a conflict of interest arising in relation to a transaction or arrangement with the company". A number of other provisions are instead brought into play.

If we were to summarise their general effect, the general strategy adopted by the Act in managing these problematic self-dealing transactions is to put in place a fairly lenient default rule, requiring only that the self-interest of the self-dealing director be disclosed to the board in advance of the transaction being agreed to by the company (regardless of whether that agreement is then by the board or by some delegated manager). But then the Act goes on to identify particular specific categories of self-dealing transactions as being especially vulnerable to inadequate oversight by the board (either simply because of their size, or because of their commonality amongst the directors which might then risk mutual back-scratching[221]), and with these the Act requires not only disclosure to the board but also approval by the general meeting. Perhaps predictably, the protective regime is even stricter with listed companies, with particular ex ante approval rules for related party transactions, and strict ex post disclosure rules demanded by modern accounting standards. All of these various rules are examined in this section, but their significance is far more easily understood if we start with the common law rules from which these variations are derived.

As far as self-dealing transactions are concerned, by the middle of the nineteenth century it had been clearly established that the trustee-like position of directors was liable to vitiate any contract which the board entered into on behalf of the company with one of their number. This principle received its clearest expression in *Aberdeen Railway Co v Blaikie Bros*,[222] in which a contract between the company and a partnership of which one of the directors was a partner was avoided at the instance of the company, notwithstanding that its terms were perfectly fair. Lord Cranworth LC said on that occasion[223]:

> "A corporate body can only act by agents, and it is, of course, the duty of those agents so to act as best to promote the interests of the corporation whose affairs they are conducting. Such agents have duties to discharge of a fiduciary nature towards their principal. And it is a rule of universal application that no one, having such duties to discharge, shall be allowed to enter into engagements in which he has, or can have, a personal interest conflicting, or which possibly may conflict, with the interests of those whom he is bound to protect . . . .So strictly is this principle adhered to that no question is allowed to be raised as to the fairness or unfairness of a contract so entered into."

It is important to note that, provided there is a conflict of interest which is not just fanciful, a director is in breach of this duty whether or not the conflict had an

---

[221] Loans to directors and directors' service contracts are the obvious examples.
[222] *Aberdeen Railway Co v Blaikie Bros* (1854) 1 Macq. H.L. 461 HL Sc.
[223] *Aberdeen Railway Co v Blaikie Bros* (1854) 1 Macq. H.L. 461 at 471–472 HL Sc.

effect upon the terms negotiated between the parties to the transaction and whether or not the terms of the transaction could be regarded as fair in any event. It is therefore a strict liability rule. Strict though this rule is from the director's point of view, it makes the task of the courts somewhat easier. In the British jurisdiction, the courts do not scrutinise self-dealing transactions, as they do in some jurisdictions, to see if they are fair. If there is a conflict of the type covered by the self-dealing rules, there is a breach of duty on the part of the director.

Approval mechanisms

However, the lesson likely to be drawn from Lord Cranworth's statement that directors should not contract with their company was not necessarily correct or wise, even from the company's point of view. The director may in fact be the best source of a particular asset which the company wishes to acquire, and so an outright ban on self-dealing would cut against the company's interests. An obvious example is a contract between a director and the company for the provision of the full-time services of the director to the company.[224] The crucial issue underlying the rule thus became, even at common law, the identification of the procedure which the director needed to observe in order to rid him- or herself of the taint of conflicted contracting. At common law the rule was that disclosure of the conflict in advance to, and approval of the contract by, the shareholders was the appropriate procedure whereby an interested director could enter into a contract with the company. This was because the shareholders, acting as the company and thus as the beneficiaries of the directors' duty, could waive compliance with it, if they wished.

This search for the appropriate internal decision-maker to approve the self-dealing transaction is shared with the other no-conflict rules, as we shall see. Moreover, this approach had a further consequence. If the shareholders did approve the transaction, it would then be virtually impossible for the company later (via a new board, or a liquidator) to challenge it in court. In other words, shareholder approval (or "whitewash" as it is sometimes called) was a robust technique for protecting the director. Shareholder approval did not, for example, simply create a presumption of fairness which a court might overturn, as it does in some other systems. The robustness of the "whitewash" provisions is again a feature of the other no-conflict rules, as we shall see, although it is not without some limits.

Nevertheless, directors found shareholder approval an inconvenient rule and one which they regarded as in many cases tantamount to a prohibition on contracting with the company. Just as the normal restraints on trustees can be modified by express provisions in the will or deed under which they were appointed,[225] so (at common law) can the normal fiduciary duties of directors be modified by express provision in the company's articles, which of course bind all the members of the company. Directors therefore sought through provisions in the articles to substitute the more congenial requirement of mere disclosure,

16–55

---

[224] See above at para.14–30.
[225] The most common example is a "charging clause" enabling professional trustees and their firms to charge fees for acting as trustees or executors.

rather than disclosure and approval; and disclosure to the board rather than to the shareholders in general meeting. Such provisions became common-form in the articles of registered companies. Indeed, in some cases the articles gave directors permission to engage in self-dealing transactions without any form of disclosure. This practice caused the legislature to step in and require (in a provision which was introduced in 1929 and became s.317 of the 1985 Act) that directors disclose conflicts to the board, irrespective of any provisions in the articles. Thus, the board would be aware of the conflict and could decide what to do about it.

16–56   Section 177 of the 2006 Act adopts this approach and imposes a rule of disclosure to the board. Thus, the modern rule on self-dealing has become, in principle, and subject to some crucial exceptions,[226] simply a requirement of disclosure to the board. There is no duty to *avoid* such dealings (hence s.175(3)). And approval by others, whether shareholders or fellow directors, is not formally required, although presumably it could be imposed by the articles.[227]

Notice, further, that the 2006 Act deals in separate places with disclosure of interests in proposed transactions (s.177, Ch.2 of Pt 10) and disclosure in relation to existing transactions (s.182, Ch.3 of Pt 10). The former is one of the general duties imposed on directors; the latter is not. Beyond doctrinal elegance, however, the division is important in relation to the sanctions for breach of the two disclosure duties, for the categories of directors who are bound by the two duties, and to some extent for the methods of disclosure. Whether there is any merit, in remedies, in this split is questionable.

In what follows, we shall look at each of these two rules in turn, and then at the crucial exceptions noted earlier where the tougher requirement of shareholder approval is made compulsory.

Duty to declare interests in relation to proposed transactions or arrangements

16–57   A director who is "in any way, directly or indirectly" interested in a proposed transaction or arrangement with the company must declare to the other directors the "nature and extent" of that interest and do so before the company enters into the transaction or arrangement (s.177(1)). If the declaration, once made, becomes or proves to be inaccurate or incomplete, a further declaration must be made (s.177(3)).

Purpose of the disclosure requirement

16–58   The aim of s.177 is to put the other directors on notice of the conflict of interest, so that they may take the necessary steps to safeguard the company's position. What steps the other directors should take, once put on notice, is not dealt with in the section nor, indeed, in precise terms elsewhere in the Act. No doubt, they will be in breach of their duties of care and, perhaps, good faith if they take no or inadequate steps, but such a conclusion would require analysis of the other

---

[226] See below, para.16–57.
[227] See below, para.16–63.

directors' actions (or inaction) under the principles discussed above. It is not difficult to envisage a board culture in which the steps taken on the basis of the declaration are minimal, especially if all the directors from time to time make such disclosures and trust that their disclosure will be readily accepted if they readily accept disclosures by others.

It is also to be noted that the Act leaves to the company's articles the task of deciding whether, if the proposed transaction is to be entered into by the board, the interested director is entitled to vote or count towards the quorum at the meeting at which the decision is taken.[228]

Who is subject to this duty?

Since s.177, dealing with proposed transactions, is one of the general duties of directors, it applies also to shadow directors, although only "where and to the extent that [it is] capable of so applying": s.170(5).[229] By contrast, s.182, in relation to disclosure of interests in existing transactions, applies explicitly to shadow directors: s.187(1). There would seem to be no argument that s.177 is "incapable" of applying to shadow directors, all the more so in the light of the absolute rule in s.187. And the practical arguments for requiring disclosure of interests in relation to proposed transactions are even stronger than those relating to existing transactions, since in relation to the former the company has the luxury of being legally free to withdraw from negotiations if the terms seem unfavourable.[230]

16–59

The interests to be disclosed

The director must disclose interests in a "transaction or arrangement". This clearly includes contracts, which will be the paradigm example of a transaction or arrangement, but it also embraces non-contractual arrangements,[231] and it matters not whether the transaction or arrangement is entered into by the company through its board or through a subordinate manager.[232]

16–60

---

[228] The model articles for both public and private companies (arts 14 and 16 respectively) exclude the director from both, but subject to important exceptions where the director can both be counted and vote.

[229] See above, para.16–8.

[230] The argument that disclosure to the board is pointless in the case of a shadow director, because the board by definition does what the shadow director wants, needs to be qualified because (a) the definition of a shadow director requires only that the board be accustomed to do what the shadow director wants, not that it does it on every occasion (see s.251); and (b) because, if the argument is correct, it is not clear why shadow directors are required to disclose interests in relation to existing transactions.

[231] cf. *Re Duckwari (No.2)* [1998] 2 B.C.L.C. 315, 319, interpreting the word "arrangement" in what is now s.190. The predecessor to s.177 was s.317 of the 1985 Act, which made this point clear (see s.317(5)—"whether or not constituting a contract"). However, it is not thought that the omission of the words "whether or not constituting a contract" from s.177 indicates an intention to confine the section to contractual transactions or arrangements. See also *Financial Conduct Authority v Capital Alternatives Ltd* [2014] EWHC 144 (Ch) at [51].

[232] The arguments in favour of this view, given in the fifth edition of this book at p.577, in relation to Companies Act 1985 s.317 seem equally applicable to s.177. Those arguments were approved by the

Both direct and indirect interests must be disclosed. The extension of the section to "indirect" interests means that the director need not himself be the other party to the transaction. It is enough, for example, that he is a shareholder in the company which is the other party, or is a member of a contracting partnership. This is not a novel development: the common law had recognised indirect conflicts of interest during the nineteenth century.[233]

The director must disclose not only the nature but also the extent of the relevant interest.[234] It is obviously more informative to be told, not simply that X is a shareholder in the contracting party, but also whether X is a 1 per cent shareholder or holds a controlling interest.

The section includes a number of restrictive clarifications of the scope of the disclosure principle. The words of Lord Cranworth, quoted above, that the common law embraced personal interests "which possibly may conflict" with the director's duty were thought to be too broad, and in consequence s.177(6)(a) provides that a director does not have to declare an interest "if it cannot reasonably be regarded as likely to give rise to a conflict of interest".[235] This probably does no more than re-state the common law.[236]

Section 177(5) does not require the director to disclose an interest in relation to a transaction unless he or she is aware *or* ought reasonably to be aware of both the interest and the transaction. A director might be excusably unaware of an interest he or she has in a third party who is contracting with the company (for example, where the managers of a unit trust in which the director holds units have recently bought a large stake in the third party) or in the transaction (for example, where it is to be entered into at sub-board level).

Nor need the director disclose interests of which the other directors are or ought reasonably to be aware, on the grounds that such disclosure is or ought to be unnecessary (s.177(6)(b)). In particular, s.177 does not require disclosure in the case of single-member boards.[237]

---

judge in *Neptune (Vehicle Washing Equipment) Ltd v Fitzgerald* [1996] Ch. 274, whose decision was treated as authoritative by the Law Commissions, above, fn.1, at para.8.38 and was approved on consultation.

[233] See, for example, *Aberdeen Railway Co v Blaikie Bros* (1854) 1 Macq. H.L. 461 HL Sc; *Transvaal Lands Co v New Belgian Land Co* [1914] 2 Ch. 485 CA; and more recently, *Newgate Stud Co v Penfold* [2008] 1 B.C.L.C. 46, suggesting the common law rule catches transactions between the company and any person whose relationship with the director is such as to create "a real risk of conflict between duty and personal loyalties".

[234] The courts when interpreting provisions in companies' articles have long required disclosure of the extent as well as the nature of interests. See, for example, *Imperial Mercantile Credit Association v Coleman* (1873) L.R. 6 H.L. 189.

[235] A similar provision is to be found in s.175(4)(a) in relation to the statutory duty to avoid conflicts of interest.

[236] cf. *Boardman v Phipps* [1967] 2 A.C. 46 at 124 per Lord Upjohn: "In my view [the phrase] means that the reasonable man looking at the relevant facts and circumstances of the particular case would think that there was real sensible possibility of conflict".

[237] In the case where there is a single member who is also a director of the company (and may be the only director) and the company contracts with that member other than in the ordinary course of the company's business, s.231 requires that the terms of the contract are either set out in a written memorandum or recorded in the minutes of the first meeting of the directors following the making of the contract. This section aims to reduce the uncertainties which might later arise about the terms of the contract if there were to be no contemporaneous written record of it and no other person had been involved in its approval on the part of the company. This could be important, for example, if the

Also excluded is the need for a director to disclose an interest in the terms of his service contract that is being or has been considered by a meeting of the directors or the appropriate committee of the board (s.177(6)(c)). It might be thought that this last exception is covered by the previous one, and in most cases this will be so. However, where the service contract is to be decided on by a committee of the board, for example, its remuneration committee, it is conceivable that not all the other directors would be aware of the director's interest.

Methods of disclosure

Assuming the duty to disclose does bite, s.177(2) lays down three non-exhaustive methods of making the disclosure.[238] These are (i) at a meeting of the directors; (ii) by written notice to the directors (as per s.184); or (iii) by a general notice (as per s.185).

16–61

The first two options provide methods of giving notice in relation to an identified transaction. Notice given outside a meeting must be sent to each director and the notice is deemed to be part of the proceedings of the next directors' meeting and so must be included in the minutes of that meeting.[239] A general notice, by contrast, is given in the absence of any specific identified transaction, and is notice by which the director declares that he is to be regarded as interested in any transaction or arrangement which is subsequently entered into by the company with a specified company, firm or individual because of the director's interest in or connection with that other person.[240] As usual, the nature and extent of the interest has to be declared. Unlike a specific notice, however, a general notice must either be given at a meeting of the directors or, if given outside a meeting, the director must take reasonable steps to ensure that it is brought up and read out at the next meeting after it is given.[241] Thus, in relation to a general notice, the board must positively be given the opportunity to discuss the notice, though there is no obligation on the board actually to do so. The giver of a general notice is not exempted from the requirement to provide a further declaration if the first notice becomes inaccurate, as it might if the nature or extent of the director's interest in the third party altered, for example, if the

---

company subsequently went into liquidation and a liquidator had to establish the extent of the company's liabilities. The section is enforced by a summary criminal sanction but breach of it does not affect the validity of the contract (s.231(4) and (6)). However, the requirement is applied expressly to shadow directors, i.e. where the sole member is a shadow director, in which case some other person(s) will constitute the board (s.231(5)). The section implements in domestic law the requirements of art.5 of Directive 89/667 on single-member private limited-liability companies ([1989] O.J. L395/40).

[238] cf. s.177(2) ("may (but need not)"). It thus appears that an oral declaration of interest to other directors outside a directors' meeting, for example, is permissible in respect of proposed transactions.

[239] 2006 Act ss.184 and 248.

[240] 2006 Act s.185. It should not be necessary to say so, but note that it is insufficient to give general notice pursuant to ss.177(2)(b) and 185 where the transaction in question is not one which is entered into with the company (and therefore falls outside the remit of s.175(3)): *Re Coroin Ltd* [2012] EWHC 2343 (Ch) at [582]–[583] (David Richards J).

[241] 2006 Act s.185(4).

director's shareholding in the third party increased significantly. Thus, even a general notice cannot simply be given once and forgotten.

Remedies

16–62   Breach of s.177 (failure to declare interest in proposed transactions) is subject to civil sanctions, not criminal ones, but those sanctions are defined only generally. They are "the same as would apply if the corresponding common law rule or equitable principle applied".[242]

Those civil sanctions seem to be as follows. Where the self-dealing director acts in breach of the statutory disclosure rule, but subject to what is said next on special provisions in the company's articles, the transaction is voidable at the option of (i.e. not binding on, at the election of) the company, unless third party rights have intervened. On orthodox principles, avoidance (i.e. rescission) is the *only* remedy,[243] unless the director has also infringed some other rule that will deliver an alternative remedy.[244] And if rescission is no longer possible for any reason, then the court will decline to intervene. This may seem odd, especially since self-dealing transactions are illustrations of the "no conflicts" duty, for which directors are typically required to disgorge the profits they have made. But the courts in these self-dealing cases say that the director's profit is "unquantifiable", since that would involve the courts fixing a new contract price for the parties. Given all the other situations in which courts are content to make commercial assessments of value, this seems unduly reticent.

A continuing role for the articles in setting tighter constraints

16–63   We know from s.170(3) that the duties laid out in Ch.2 of Pt 10 "have effect in place" of the common law rules and equitable principles on which they are based. Consequently, in a self-dealing transaction, a director must comply with the provisions of s.177 and disclose his or her interests to the board. If the director does this, then s.180(1) provides that "the transaction or arrangement is not liable to be set aside by virtue of any common law rule or equitable principle requiring the consent or approval of the members of the company". Thus, in the standard

---

[242] 2006 Act s.178.
[243] This is especially evident in older cases dealing with promoters: *Erlanger v New Sombrero Phosphate Co* (1878) 3 App. Cas. 1218 HL; *Re Cape Breton Co* (1887) 12 App. Cas. 652 HL.
[244] And this may well be possible: for example, a misuse of the company's property (and a self-dealing transaction may fall into that category) may involve a conflict of duty and interest (for which rescission is potentially available); *and* a breach of the duty to act bona fide and for proper purposes (for which equitable compensation is recoverable, even if the director has not made a profit from the misuse (*Gwembe Valley Development Co Ltd v Koshy (No.3)* [2003] EWCA Civ 1478; [2004] 1 B.C.L.C. 131 CA)); *and* perhaps also negligence (in that the advice to the company in favour of the self-interested deal may have been poor and caused loss, for which common law damages are available). See *Costa Rica Railway Co Ltd v Forward* [1901] 1 Ch. 746; *Imperial Mercantile Credit Association v Coleman* (1873) L.R. 6 H. L.189; *JJ Harrison (Properties) Ltd v Harrison* [2001] 1 B.C.L.C. 158 Ch.D.; and [2002] 1 B.C.L.C. 183 CA; *Madoff Securities International Ltd v Raven* [2013] EWHC 3147 (Comm); *Airbus Operations Ltd v Withey* [2014] EWHC 1126 (QB).

case, compliance with s.177 disclosure rules will mean that the director is not in breach of the relevant duty of loyalty, and that the transaction is therefore binding on the company.

However, s.180(1) specifically operates without prejudice to any "provision of the company's constitution requiring such consent or approval". Thus, the company's articles may reinstate the common law principle of shareholder approval and, where this is done, a transaction entered into without such approval will not be binding on the company, subject to the protections for third parties contained in s.40 (to the limited extent that these rules may be relevant in a self-dealing transaction).[245] As we have seen already, the impact of restrictions in the articles upon the validity of the transaction will vary according to whether the restriction requires a particular organ or group within the company to take the decision on the self-dealing transaction with the director, or merely to approve it. Breach in the first case renders the transaction void; in the second, voidable only.[246] These provisions cannot, however, oust the disclosure requirements in s.177.

In short, the shareholders remain masters of the rules on self-dealing transactions but now the onus is on those who want to move away from board disclosure and require shareholder approval or some other additional control, whereas under the prior law the burden of action lay on those who wished to introduce into the articles provisions modifying the common law requirement of shareholder approval.

Duty to declare interests in relation to existing transactions or arrangements

Section 182 requires the compulsory disclosure to the board of existing self-dealing transactions, unless the interest has already been declared in relation to a proposed transaction.[247] This section catches situations such as the interests of a newly appointed director in the company's existing transactions or interests in existing contracts which an established director has just acquired, for example, because he or she has become a shareholder in one of the company's suppliers.

16–64

But why should a board wish to know about the interests of its directors in concluded transactions? What practical use can it make of the information? An example might be where the company has a power under an existing contract (for example, to terminate it unilaterally) to which knowledge of the director's interest is relevant.

---

[245] See para.7–9, above.
[246] See *Guinness Plc v Saunders* [1990] 2 A.C. 663 HL, where the wrong body under the company's articles (a committee of the board rather than the full board) acted to pay a bonus to the director so that the decision to pay the bonus was void, the committee being without power to act, and the money repayable by the director. cf. *Hely-Hutchinson v Brayhead Ltd* [1968] 1 Q.B. 549, where the correct body acted, but the director was in breach of his fiduciary obligations unless the right approvals were given: here the decision was voidable but not void.
[247] 2006 Act s.182(1).

Methods of disclosure

16–65 The details on what must be disclosed, and how, are broadly those applicable to proposed transactions (discussed immediately above), with the following amendments and exceptions. First, the disclosure must be made "as soon as is reasonably practicable".[248] Secondly, the statutory methods of giving notice discussed earlier in the non-mandatory context of s.177 are the only ones permitted in relation to existing transactions.[249] It presumably follows that a failure to make a declaration in the prescribed manner will render the declaration either a nullity or incomplete, and a further declaration will be required (s.182(3)).[250] Thirdly, a sole director is required to make a declaration only where the company is required to have more than one director but that is not the case at the time of the disclosure. That declaration must be recorded in writing and is deemed to be part of the proceedings at the next meeting of the directors after it is given.[251] Fourthly, the obligation applies explicitly to shadow directors.[252] However, not surprisingly, the method of giving notice at a meeting of the directors is not available to a shadow director nor is a general notice required to be given or brought up at a meeting of directors. Instead a general or specific notice is to be given in the case of a shadow director by notice in writing to the directors, though that will then cause the notice to be treated as part of the proceedings of the next directors' meeting and minuted accordingly.[253]

Remedies

16–66 Finally, only a criminal sanction (a fine) is provided in respect of breaches of this statutory duty to disclose.[254] This duty, being found in Ch.3, is not one of the general duties in Ch.2, and so the various common law remedies imported by virtue of s.178 do not also apply here to breaches of s.182. Nevertheless, these demands of compulsory disclosure certainly contribute, like the general duties, to aiding better corporate governance.

---

[248] 2006 Act s.182(4). The formulation in s.177(4)—before the company enters into the transaction—is clearly not available.

[249] 2006 Act s.182(2).

[250] How this requirement will be reconciled with s.182(6)(b), indicating that the duty does not apply if the other directors are already aware of the interest, or ought to be aware of the interest, is unclear.

[251] 2006 Act s.186. In the case of a proposed transaction the declaration has no point (if a further director is appointed before the transaction is completed, the s.177 obligation will arise at that point) but an interest in an existing transaction will be of continuing relevance and the declaration will be available to the new director immediately when appointed. Indeed, in most cases the sole director will have to make disclosure as soon as the proposed transaction is completed.

[252] 2006 Act.187(1).

[253] 2006 Act s.187(2)–(4).

[254] 2006 Act s.183. The disputes in relation to the remedies for breach of the predecessor provision, CA 1985 s.317 (see ninth edition of this book, p.568), have been laid to rest in the current Act.

TRANSACTIONS BETWEEN THE COMPANY AND DIRECTORS REQUIRING
SPECIAL APPROVAL OF MEMBERS

The move over the years from shareholder approval of self-dealing transactions **16–67** (as required by the common law) to mere board disclosure amounted to a significant dilution of the legal controls over this class of no-conflict cases. The move, which had been substantially achieved by the first quarter of the last century, was later shown to have weaknesses in those areas where the temptation to give way to conflicts of interest was high and scrutiny of the terms of the self-dealing transaction by the other members of board could not be relied upon to be effective. Consequently, not only did the legislature introduce what is now s.177 of the 2006 Act, but it also went further and, at various times, introduced statutory provisions which restored the common law principle of shareholder approval in certain specific classes of case. These provisions are now gathered together in Chs 4 and 4A of Pt 10 of the 2006 Act. Consequently, a complete understanding of the law relating to self-dealing transactions requires knowledge not only of s.177 and Ch.3 of Pt 10 of the 2006 Act but also of Chs 4 and 4A.

Relationship with the general duties

Where either Ch.4 or Ch.4A applies, then compliance with the general duties is **16–68** not enough to put the director in compliance with the requirements of the Act (s.180(3)). Indeed, without this rule, Chs 4 and 4A would have little point. In the interests of avoiding having to obtain multiple approvals, however, s.180(2) provides that securing shareholder approval under those Chapters will relieve the director from having to comply with ss.175 (the duty to avoid conflicts of duty and interest) and 176 (duty not to accept benefits from a third party).[255] The subsection also applies even if the situation is one which in principle falls within Chs 4 or 4A but no shareholder approval is in fact required under that Chapter, for example, because the transaction is one of small value. In such a case neither Chs 4 or 4A, nor ss.175 and 176 apply. However, since the paradigm transaction falling under Chs 4 and 4A is a transaction *with* the company, in the usual case ss.175 and 176 would not bite, even if applicable. Shareholder approval is to be given by ordinary resolution of the shareholders unless the articles of association require a higher level of approval, which might extend to unanimity (s.281(3)).[256]

However, the other general duties will apply to transactions falling within Chs 4 and 4A (s.180(2)). Thus, the duty of the directors to promote the success of the company and to act within their powers will still apply, and crucially will apply to all the directors, not just the self-dealing one. This is important because transactions within Chs 4 and 4A will typically require both board and shareholder decisions. The board in the exercise of its powers under the articles takes the decision whether to enter into the proposed transaction and the shareholders then decide whether to approve the proposal as required by

---

[255] Both duties discussed below.

[256] If approval is required under more than one of the sets of statutory provisions discussed below, the requirements of each must be met, but not so as to require separate resolutions for each: s.225.

statute.[257] Thus, it is important that directors taking the decision whether to enter into the proposed transaction should be under the core duty of loyalty and be required to act within their powers. Further, the self-dealing director will remain under the duty to disclose the nature and extent of his or her interest to the board under s.177. This may seem unnecessary because such disclosure will be part of the process of seeking shareholder approval. However, the board decision may well precede the shareholder decision by some time. In any event, the board decision will be the only one in the case of a transaction falling within Chs 4 or 4A but not requiring shareholder approval under its provisions. In either case, disclosure of the conflict to the board in advance of the board decision, as s.177 requires, is obviously desirable.

Chapter 4 of Pt 10 brings within its scope three types of transaction: (a) substantial property transactions; (b) loans and analogous transactions; and (c) two sets of decisions affecting the remuneration of directors, namely, decisions about the length of directors' service contracts and decisions about gratuitous payments to directors upon loss of office. These situations were reviewed by the Law Commission which made various proposals for reform, mainly in matters of detail.[258] A number of these provisions contain financial limits. These are capable of being altered by statutory instrument as the Secretary of State sees fit, subject to negative resolution in Parliament (s.258). Chapter 4A of Pt 10 contains special provisions dealing with the remuneration of directors of quoted companies. Its requirements were considered in Ch.14.[259] In outline, remuneration and loss of office payments are not to be made to directors of such companies unless they are consistent with an approved directors' remuneration policy, or alternatively have been specifically approved by the members (ss.226B and 226C). These additional requirements do not negate any necessary Ch.4 requirements, although approval by the members under Ch.4 will satisfy the equivalent need for Ch.4A approval (s.226F).

16–69   Unlike the position with the general duties, the statute expressly applies all the provisions of Ch.4 to shadow directors (s.223), though with the qualification that a company is not to be regarded as the shadow director of its subsidiary simply because the directors of the subsidiary are accustomed to act in accordance with its instructions or directions (s.251(3)).[260]

A further and helpful characteristic of Chs 4 and 4A, in comparison with the general duties of Ch.2, is that they stipulate not only the duties to obtain shareholder approval, but also the consequences of failure to obtain it, in terms of both the directors (and others) being in breach of duty and of the validity of the transaction in question.

---

[257] The shareholders' meeting could in principle both approve the transaction and instruct the board to enter into it, but if the transaction falls within the managerial powers of the directors, such an instruction would have to take the form of a special resolution. See above, para.14–7.

[258] Law Commissions, above, fn.1.

[259] See above, para.14–38.

[260] The statute leaves it up to the courts to decide how far the general duties apply to shadow directors, but does exclude holding companies in the circumstances set out in s.251, if the shadow director principle applies at all. See above, para.16–8.

The provisions of Ch.4 apply only to "UK registered companies".[261] These are defined as companies registered under the 2006 Act or its predecessors, but excluding overseas companies.[262] The exclusion of companies registered in other jurisdictions is not surprising. However, confining the statutory provisions to companies registered under the Companies Acts excludes also companies incorporated in the UK but in some other way than under the Companies Acts, for example, companies formed by royal charter or Act of Parliament.[263] The provisions of Ch.4A extend more broadly, to companies quoted domestically, or officially listed in an EEA State, or on the New York or Nasdaq stock exchange (s.385).

Substantial property transactions

The scope of the requirement for shareholder approval

Section 190 requires prior shareholder approval of a substantial property transaction between the company and its director. It was said of the predecessor of s.190:

16–70

> "The thinking behind that section is that if directors enter into a substantial commercial transaction with one of their number, there is a danger that their judgment may be distorted by conflicts of interest and loyalties, even in cases of no actual dishonesty … It enables members to provide a check … It does make it likely the matter will be more widely ventilated, and a more objective decision reached."[264]

Given the motivations for oversight with this type of self-dealing, it is perhaps not surprising that the definition of the transactions caught is very wide, so wide indeed that the section imposes substantial inroads on the default rule in s.177, where disclosure to the board is all that is required.

A substantial property transaction is an arrangement (note the vagueness of this term) in which the director acquires[265] from, or has acquired from him or her by, the company a substantial non-cash asset[266] of a value which exceeds either £100,000 or 10 per cent of the company's net assets (provided the latter figure

16–71

---

[261] 2006 Act ss.188(6)(a), 190(4)(b), 197(5)(a), 198(6)(a), 201(6)(a), 203(5)(a), 217(4)(a), 218(4)(a), and 219(6)(a).

[262] 2006 Act ss.1158 and 1.

[263] Above, para.1–31.

[264] *British Racing Driver's Club Ltd v Hextall Erskine & Co (A Firm)* [1996] 3 All E.R. 667 at 681–682. The case is a good illustration of the operation of both the dangers and their remedy. Technically, the transaction is not between the directors and one of their number but rather between a director and the company, but of course the decision on behalf of the company is taken by the other directors. See also *Granada Group Ltd v The Law Debenture Pension Trust Corp Plc* [2015] EWHC 1499 (Ch) in which Andrews J provides an extension discussion of the predecessor to s.190 (appeal outstanding); and *Smithton Ltd v Naggar* [2014] EWCA Civ 939; [2015] 1 W.L.R. 189 CA.

[265] Defined in s.1163 to include the creation or extinction of an estate or interest in, or right over, any property and the discharge of any person's liability other than for a liquidated sum.

[266] Also defined in s.1163 and meaning "any property or interest in property other than cash". See *Re Duckwari Plc (No.1)* [1997] 2 B.C.L.C. 713 CA; and *Ultraframe (UK) Ltd v Fielding* [2005] EWHC 1638, where the term was held to include a lease, a licence to exploit intellectual property, a supply of assets, and a sale of stock, but not a supply of services.

exceeds £5,000) (s.191).[267] The approval must be given either before the director enters into the transaction or the transaction must be conditional upon the approval being given, i.e. everything can be agreed between the parties but the transaction must not become binding on the company until the shareholders give their consent.[268] If this principle is not followed, then the director in question, the contracting party (if different) and the directors who authorised the transaction are all potentially liable to civil sanctions (as set out in s.195). However, the company itself is not subject to any liability by reason of the failure to obtain the necessary approval (s.190(3)), a necessary provision since the purpose of the rules is to protect the company's assets. Although s.190 requires prior approval of the transaction, nevertheless approval by the members of the company within a reasonable period after the transaction has been entered into will mean that the transaction can no longer be avoided by the company, but the other civil consequences of breach of s.190 will follow (s.196). Those civil consequences are dealt with below.

It will be noted that the section does not in its terms preclude the self-dealing director from voting as a member at a general meeting to approve or affirm the transaction, although the common law rules relating to the propriety of this will still apply.[269]

Approval is also required if the contracting party is a director of the company's holding company or a person connected with the director (of the company or the holding company). The extension of the section in this way is in order to pre-empt rather obvious avoidance devices. In the case of the director of a holding company (and a person connected with that director), the section requires the approval of the members of the holding company as well as of the members of the company, unless the company is a wholly-owned subsidiary of the holding company, in which case, for obvious reasons, the authorisation of the subsidiary's members is dispensed with (s.190(2) and (4)(b)).[270] The policy here appears to be that the director of the holding company may be in an institutional position to influence the actions of the subsidiary, so that the risk of unfair dealing with the subsidiary's property arises here as well. On the other hand, such a policy explains why the section is not extended to transactions between the company and a director of its subsidiary or of a sister company in the group, because those directors have no institutional position of influence over the company. If, in the particular case, such a situation of influence does exist, then it may be that the director of the subsidiary will fall within the definition of a shadow director in relation to the parent or will be regarded as a connected person in relation to a director of the parent.

---

[267] The value of the net assets is to be determined by the latest accounts or, if none have been laid, by reference to its called-up share capital: s.192(2). Non-cash transactions need to be aggregated to test for their compliance with the statutory thresholds: s.191(5).

[268] Some degree of certainty of entering into the transaction or arrangement is needed despite the fact that a conditional arrangement may otherwise fall within s.190: *Smithton Ltd v Naggar* [2014] EWCA Civ 939; [2014] B.C.C. 482 at [110] (Arden LJ, with whom Elias and Tomlinson LJJ agreed).

[269] See below paras 16–117 et seq.

[270] 2006 Act s.190(4)(a) dispenses with the requirement for shareholder approval if the company is not a UK-registered company. So, if the only British company is a wholly-owned subsidiary of a foreign company, the requirements for shareholder approval, if any, will be determined by the system of company law governing the foreign company.

The provisions on connected persons deal with a different set of avoidance devices, applicable to free-standing companies as well as companies which are members of groups, whereby the contract is diverted to a person with whom the director is connected, such as the director's spouse. However, to cover all possibilities, the resulting definition of a "connected person" is highly complex. Section 252 puts into that category members of the director's family, as widely defined in s.253. It adds companies (in fact, "bodies corporate")[271] with which the director is "connected", and s.254 defines the necessary connection as being where the director and persons connected with him or her are interested in at least 20 per cent of the equity shares of the company or control at least 20 per cent of the voting power at a general meeting. Section 252 then adds a person who is a trustee of a trust the beneficiaries (including discretionary beneficiaries) of which include the director or a person who is connected with the director under the above provisions and, finally a (business) partner of the director or of a person connected with the director. The detail need not be further examined here, but it will provide many hours of delight for those trying to avoid the provisions of Ch.4 of Pt 10 of the Act.

Exceptions

Because of the width of the connected person definition, certain transactions have to be taken out of the requirement for shareholder approval, notably certain transfers of property between group companies. Here, no director or indeed any other individual is a party to the transaction, but one of the companies might be a person connected with the director, for example, where a holding company, in which a person has a 20 per cent shareholding, enters into a substantial transaction with a subsidiary company of which that person is a director (s.192(b)). To provide a safe harbour, also excluded from s.190 are transactions between a company and a person in his character as a member of the company (even if that person is also a director of the company), thus protecting substantial distributions *in specie* to its members by the company (s.192(a)). Also excluded are transactions by a company in insolvent winding up or administration (s.193—though not transactions by a company in administrative receivership), presumably because the directors are no longer in control of the company; and certain transactions on a recognised stock exchange effected through an independent broker (s.194), presumably because the broker and the market provide the assurance that the terms of the trade are fair. Finally, s.190 does not apply to anything the director is entitled to under his or her service contract or any payment for loss of office falling under the provisions discussed below (s.190(6)).

16–72

Remedies

Section 195 provides an extensive suite of civil remedies for breach of s.190, which operate in addition to any common law remedies,[272] and which at one

16–73

---

[271] 2006 Act s.1173(1), so that bodies incorporated outside the UK are included.
[272] 2006 Act s.195(8).

stage looked likely to provide a template for the remedies to be made available for breach of the general duties.[273] The transaction or arrangement is voidable at the instance of the company unless restitution of the subject-matter of the transaction is no longer possible, third party rights have intervened, an indemnity has been paid (s.195(2)) or the arrangement has been affirmed within a reasonable time by a general meeting (s.196). It should be noted that a third party is one who "is not a party to the arrangement or transaction" entered into in contravention of s.190 (s.195(2)(c)). So, a connected person who is a party to the transaction will not count as a "third party" even if that person did not know of the connection with the director. Consequently, the connected person will not be able to prevent the transaction being avoided by the company by claiming to be a good faith third party without actual knowledge of the contravention—even though such a connected person may be relieved of liability to the company, as we see below. This statutory regime is therefore broader than its common law equivalents.

16–74   The same is true of the financial liability of those involved in the transaction. As we saw earlier, the orthodox equitable rule in relation to self-dealing transactions is that they are simply voidable.[274] Section 195(3), by contrast, contemplates liability both to account to the company for any gain which has been made by the defendant (directly or indirectly)[275] and (jointly and severally with any others liable under the section) to indemnify the company from any loss resulting from the arrangement or transaction. This has perhaps been interpreted more narrowly in some ways, and more widely in others, than might have been expected from the statutory words themselves. In the normal case, it has been held, a gain will be made by the director where the director acquires an asset from the company, and a loss suffered by the company where the company acquires an asset from the director[276]: regarded this way, the statutory provisions provide a mechanism for effecting notional rescission of the self-dealing transaction, but doing so in money rather than by re-delivery of the assets originally exchanged. This seems sensible.

So too is the notion that s.195(3) makes the remedy of accounting of profits additional to the right to avoid the transaction. Thus, any profit made by the director, but not captured by the company through avoidance of the transaction, can still be sought by the company; or the company may seek an accounting of

---

[273] See fn.6, above.

[274] Although see above, fn.244, for possible alternative claims.

[275] Thus, the duty to account is confined to the profit made by the person who is so accountable (though indirect profit is taken into account): there appears to be no duty on a director to account, for example, for a profit made solely by a connected person, though the connected person may be liable to account.

[276] *NBH Ltd v Hoare* [2006] 2 B.C.L.C. at [44]–[49]: when a director (or a connected person) sold an asset to the company at an undervalue (i.e. without loss to the company, here with that fact reinforced by the company's subsequent sale of the asset for a profit), the director was not liable for his own profits on the sale of the asset (and indeed their measurement might be difficult, and certainly could not be assumed to be the difference between the price at which the director acquired the asset, perhaps years ago, and the price for which it was later sold to the company). Also see *Re Duckwari Plc (No.2)* [1999] Ch. 253, 261 (Nourse LJ). cf. the quite different situation described in fn.277 immediately below.

profit even though the transaction cannot any longer be avoided. This is wider than the common law, but the advantages are clear.

In the case of losses, actual payment of an indemnity, by any person, removes the power to avoid the transaction. However, if the transaction has been avoided, the company could still sue for an indemnity against any losses not recovered by the reversal of the transaction. Further, and more surprisingly, the Court of Appeal has deduced from the fact that an indemnity deprives the company of its power to avoid the transaction that the indemnity, in relation to assets acquired by the company, must include losses incurred after the completion of the transaction in question, even if those losses were not caused by the absence of shareholder consent, provided the losses result from the acquisition. This means that the director is at risk of having to indemnify the company for losses caused by post-transaction adverse movements in the market.[277] Where a transaction is avoided, the company, by restoring the situation prior to the transaction, protects itself against both transaction losses and post-transaction losses, and it was held that an indemnity must go as far.

Finally, s.195(8) preserves any other remedy the company may have against the director or to avoid the transaction, for example, under the common law or any other provisions of the Act. It might be wondered what common law remedies would not be covered by the comprehensive provisions of s.195. One answer is that the remedies created by s.195 are not proprietary, because the section applies to Scotland which does not recognise proprietary remedies in this situation. However, so far as the common law applying in other parts of the UK confers a proprietary character on the company's remedies against directors,[278] s.195 preserves it.

A further notable feature of the section is the range of persons made potentially **16–75** liable. Under s.195(4)(a) and (b) liability is imposed upon the director who entered into the transaction (including the director of the holding company where the transaction is with him or her) and on the connected person if that person was the party to the transaction. This is to be expected. However, s.195(4)(c) extends liability to a director (of the company or the holding company) with whom the party to the arrangement is connected, where the transaction was with the connected person. In other words, by using a connected person to effect the transaction the director does not escape personal liability to indemnify the company against losses or to account for profits, if the director made a profit thereby—though the subsection is not confined to such instrumental cases.

---

[277] See *Re Duckwari (No.2)* [1999] Ch. 253; [1998] 2 B.C.L.C. 315 CA; and *Re Duckwari (No.3)* [1999] Ch. 268; [1999] 1 B.C.L.C. 168 CA. In these cases, the company recovered by way of indemnity the loss (with interest) suffered after the acquisition of a piece of land (at a fair price) from a director without shareholder approval when the property market subsequently collapsed, but not the higher rate of interest actually paid by the company on the funds borrowed to effect the purchase. The court in the former case based its decision that the post-acquisition loss was recoverable also on the argument that, if the statute had not made express provision for the company's remedies, the director would have been liable to restore to the company the money paid for the property (less its residual value) on the grounds that the payment amounted to receipt of corporate assets paid to the director in breach of trust on the part of the directors; and there was no suggestion in the statute that Parliament wished to give the company remedies inferior to the common law ones.
[278] See below, para.16–115.

Finally, and this is most important, s.196(4)(d) extends liability to any director of the company who authorised the arrangement, or any transaction in pursuance of it, even if neither that director nor a person connected with him entered into the arrangement. Thus, s.195 creates incentives not only for directors not to breach s.190 but also for directors to monitor compliance with the requirements of that section on the part of their fellow directors and, even more difficult, of persons connected with fellow directors. These liabilities arise whether or not the arrangement has been avoided by the company, and—perhaps oddly—they are not expressly discontinued even if the company confirms the arrangement under s.196.

16–76 This is therefore an extremely wide-ranging remedial scheme. First, the potential defendants are not just the director who was in a position of conflict of duty and interest and entered into the transaction, but also the person connected with him or her and the director so connected (where the transaction was with the connected party) and the non-self-dealing directors of the company who authorised the transaction. And secondly, the remedies range exceptionally broadly—rescission, account of profits, compensation for losses. For these reasons, two defences are provided against the liabilities created by s.195(3) and (4).

Where the arrangement is entered into by a connected person, the director with whom the connection exists is not liable if the director shows that he or she took "all reasonable steps to secure the company's compliance" with s.190 (s.195(6)). This defence does nevertheless require the director to be active, by taking "reasonable steps". For example, a director with a controlling holding in another company, which might engage in substantial property transactions with the company, would appear to be required at least to disclose to the company of which he is a director the existence of the connection and to warn of the need for shareholder approval, should a transaction be contemplated. Moreover, the director would seem required to take reasonable steps to monitor developments in both business and personal life which might give rise to "connections" of a statutory kind, so as to be able to disclose them.[279]

A further defence is provided for the connected person and an "authorising" director. They are not liable if they show that they "did not know the relevant circumstances constituting the contravention" (s.195(7)), which, given the width of the connected person definition, is not a fanciful situation. This wording does seem wide enough to cover the situation where the connected person (an estranged step-son, for example) does not know of the step-father's directorship. In this case, the connected person does not appear to be under any legal pressure to monitor the activities of the person with whom he or she is connected so as to ascertain, for example, of which companies the other person has become a director. The defence in s.195(7) is one based on simple ignorance. However, if the connected person does know of the connection, it does not appear that he or she escapes liability on the basis that there was a failure to understand that the law requires shareholder approval in such a case.

---

[279] It would not seem a legitimate reading of the section to interpret it so as to require the taking of reasonable steps only in relation to connections of which the director is actually aware, though the more remote the connection, the less the taking of reasonable steps would require.

Additional rules for listed companies

In the case of companies whose shares are Premium Listed on the London Stock Exchange, there are further requirements for shareholder approval in the Listing Rules[280] drawn up by the Financial Conduct Authority ("FCA"). Such approval is required for all "related-party" transactions, a term which includes transactions with a director or shadow director of the listed company or of another company within the same corporate group (not just of the holding company) or a person who has been such a director within the previous 12 months or an associate of such a director, or a person with significant influence.[281] On the other side of the transaction is the listed company or any of its subsidiaries. In addition, the category also includes transactions between the listed company and any person, the purpose and effect of which is to benefit a related party.[282] The requirement for shareholder approval applies to *any* related-party transaction (other than a transaction of a revenue nature in the ordinary course of business, small transactions and certain specified types of transaction),[283] so that the FCA rules have a wider range than those contained in Ch.4 of Pt 10 of the 2006 Act. The Listing Rules make every effort to ensure that the shareholders are well-advised, including requiring an independent expert's report to support the directors' statement that the transaction or arrangement is fair and reasonable as far as the security holders are concerned (LR 13.6.1(5)). Crucially, on the approval resolution the related party may not vote and the related party must also take all reasonable steps to ensure any associates do not vote either.[284] The principle of shareholder approval and disinterested voting is thus taken much further in the Listing Rules than in the Act.

16–77

Loans, quasi-loans and credit transactions

Arrangements covered

As in other areas of life—a recent example being the funding of political parties—loans constitute an easy way of avoiding the rules governing the disposition of assets. A transaction can be presented as a loan when it is in effect a gift, either because the loan is never expected to be re-paid or because the terms of the loan are non-commercial. Given their control over the company's day-to-day activities, the directors are in a good position to effect such transactions for their own benefit, thus indirectly increasing their remuneration; and history has shown that from time to time they give into the temptation to do so. Consequently, loans have long been subject to special regulation by the

16–78

---

[280] LR 11.1.
[281] LR 11.1.4.
[282] LR 11.1.5.
[283] LR 11.1.5–6. The specific exemptions are set out in LR 11 Annex 1.
[284] LR 11.1.7.

Companies Acts. In 1945 the Cohen Committee[285] recommended that the legislation move beyond requiring disclosure of the loans to directors to prohibiting them. It said: "We consider it undesirable that directors should borrow from their companies. If the director can offer good security, it is no hardship for him to borrow from other sources. If he cannot offer good security, it is undesirable that he should obtain from the company credit which he would not be able to obtain elsewhere". The 1948 Act thus introduced a prohibition on loans to directors.

Now in the 2006 Act the prohibition has been re-cast in terms of a requirement for prior shareholder approval (s.197).[286] At the same time, the criminal sanctions previously attaching to these provisions were removed so that the sanctions are now purely civil. The result is to produce a much greater degree of parallelism between the provisions on loans and those on substantial property transactions, discussed above. On the other hand, the change arguably downgrades the protection available to creditors. In owner-controlled companies making a loan to the directors can be used as a way of siphoning assets out of the company to the shareholders where the company does not have distributable profits. If the company becomes insolvent, the administrator or liquidator will not be able to sue the directors for the recovery of the loans under the 2006 Act, unless either the controllers, acting as shareholders, have forgotten to approve their decision to make the loans, taken as directors (which may happen), or the insolvency practitioner can discharge the greater burden of showing a breach of the directors' core duty of good faith or some other duty, such as the wrongful trading provisions or the common law creditor-regarding duties or can impugn the shareholder approval whitewash.[287]

16–79   As with substantial property transactions, a headache for the legislature has been the need to predict and pre-empt avoidance devices on the part of directors. With various exceptions and exemptions, the 2006 Act brings within its compass simple loans (s.197), loans to both the directors of holding companies[288] and persons connected with directors (of both the company and its holding company),[289] and also extends the rules to transactions analogous to loans. Thus, the provisions extend to what are called "quasi-loans" (s.198), to "credit transactions" (s.201) and to "related arrangements" (s.203). These provisions are hardly simple.

Sections 197 and 203 apply to any company; ss.198 and 201 only apply to a public company or a company, even if private, which is "associated with" a public company. Two companies are associated if one is subsidiary of the other or

---

[285] Report of the Committee on Company Law Amendment, Cmnd. 6659, 1945, para.94. It is interesting to note that one of the corporate governance reforms made in US federal law in the aftermath of the Enron affair was to introduce in the Sarbanes-Oxley Act 2002 a ban on loans by companies to their directors: s.402(a).

[286] This has removed a doubt arising under the old law about whether the company could seek to enforce its rights of civil recovery under the statute, on the grounds that it was seeking to rely on an illegal transaction.

[287] See above, paras 9–4 et seq. and below, paras 16–117 et seq.

[288] 2006 Act ss.197(1). See also ss.198(2) and 201(2).

[289] See ss.200 and 201(2).

both are subsidiaries of the same body corporate.[290] It does not matter which is the public and which the private company.

A loan is a well-known concept. A quasi-loan is not. Essentially, quasi-loans are **16–80** transactions, to which the company is a party, resulting in a director or a connected person obtaining some financial benefit for which the director is liable to make reimbursement to the company.[291] An example might be the company providing a credit card to the director, the company undertaking the obligation to meet the payments due to the credit card issuer and the director having an obligation to reimburse the company. This is not a loan because no funds are advanced by the company to the director, but the effect is the same as if the director took out the credit card in his or her own name and the company lent the director the money to pay the card issuer. The sections require disclosure to the shareholders of the core elements of the proposed transaction and approval from the members before the company enters into a loan or quasi-loan transaction with a director or director of the holding company or a person connected with such a director. Approval is also required if the company, instead of making the loan or quasi-loan, gives a guarantee or provides security in relation to loan or quasi-loan made by a third party. Thus, if an unconnected bank makes a loan to the director, but the company guarantees the loan, approval will be required.

Section 201 deals with credit transactions. A credit transaction is one in which goods, services or land are supplied to the director but payment for them is left outstanding, including hire-purchase, conditional sale, lease or hire agreements (s.202). Again, such a transaction is not a loan, because no funds are advanced to the director, but the economic effect is the same as if the company had made a loan to the director and the director had then used those funds to obtain the goods, land or services in question. The section applies to both credit transactions entered into by the company with the director (i.e. the company provides the goods, services or land) and transactions entered into by a third party with the director but the company gives a guarantee or security to the third person (s.201(2)).

Finally, s.203(1) requires shareholder approval for a further set of "arrangements" entered into, not by the company, but by a third party with or for the benefit of a relevant director or connected person. In order for such an arrangement to be caught it must be one which (a) would have required shareholder approval if it had been entered into by the company; and (b) the third party acquires a benefit from the company or a body corporate associated with it. Thus, the company cannot induce a third party to do without shareholder approval something which, if done by the company, requires such approval, where the third party obtains a benefit from the company for doing that thing. Section 203(1) also brings within the shareholder approval requirement situations where the company assumes responsibility under an arrangement previously entered into by a third party which, if entered into by the company, would have

---

[290] 2006 Act s.256. The reference to "body corporate" brings in companies incorporated outside the UK (s.1173(1)), so two British subsidiaries of a foreign company will be associated. If one is public and the other private, both will be caught by the quasi-loans provisions, even though the rules on quasi-loans do not apply to the holding company (see s.198(6)).
[291] 2006 Act s.199.

[535]

required the shareholders' approval. Thus, if a bank makes a loan to the director, but later the company assumes the obligation to repay the loan, the assumption of obligation by the company will require shareholder approval. By virtue of s.203 the company cannot avoid shareholder approval by doing indirectly what it cannot do directly.

Method of approval and related disclosures

16–81   Shareholder approval is by ordinary resolution, unless the articles impose a higher requirement.[292] Because of the potential complexity of the transactions covered by the provisions, it is not surprising that the Act requires full details of the proposed arrangement to be disclosed to the shareholders in writing in advance of their consideration of the approval resolution. Those details must disclose in particular the value the director will receive under the transaction and the amount of the company's liability.[293] As usual, approval is not required of the members of a wholly-owned subsidiary.[294]

Additional disclosure is required in the annual accounts issued at the end of the relevant financial year (s.413). Section 413 applies to "advances and credits" granted by the company to its directors and "guarantees of any kind" entered into by the company on behalf of its directors. The wording does not map easily onto the transactions dealt with in Ch.4 of Pt 10 of the Act and is in fact derived from the Directives on companies' accounts.[295] Given that shareholders will already have approved these arrangements, there is perhaps no need for the accounts provisions to mimic the provisions of the sections discussed above. Indeed, it is possible that nothing specific about disclosure of the above transactions in the accounts would have been required by the Act had the Directives not required otherwise.

Exceptions

16–82   Having brought a wide range of transactions within the net of those needing shareholder approval, the statute then proceeds to provide "safe harbours", i.e. to identify certain situations where the member approval requirement is not required because the transaction is thought to be legitimate or to raise only a small risk of abuse. First, the requirement does not apply to anything done by the company to put the director or connected person in funds to meet expenditure incurred for the purpose of the company or to perform properly the duties of an officer of the company or to enable the person to avoid incurring such expenditure. However, a cap of £50,000 is placed on the value of arrangements falling within the

---

[292] 2006 Act s.281(3).
[293] 2006 Act ss.197(3),(4), 198(3),(5), 200(4),(5), 201(4),(5), and 203(3),(4).
[294] 2006 Act ss.197(5)(b), 198(6)(b), 200(6)(b), and 203(5)(b).
[295] Arts 43(1) and (13) of Directives 78/660/EEC and 83/459/EEC.

exemption (s.204).[296] Thus, if the credit card mentioned above is confined to business expenditures, and has an appropriate credit limit, it will not require shareholder approval.

Secondly, shareholder approval is not required for arrangements designed to put the director of the company or holding company in a position to defend civil or criminal proceedings alleging breach of duty, to apply for relief in relation to such an action,[297] or to defend regulatory proceedings, in relation to the company or any associated company (ss.205–206). However, other than in the case of regulatory proceedings, the arrangement must be reversed (for example, the company repaid a loan) if the defence is not successful.

Thirdly, certain minor value arrangements are exempted (under £10,000 for loans and quasi-loans; under £15,000 for credit transactions) (s.207(1),(2)). Fourthly, credit transactions entered into by the company in the ordinary course of its business on no more favourable terms than it is "reasonable to expect" the company would offer to an unconnected person are exempted (s.207(3)). Fifthly, loans and quasi-loans by money-lending companies are exempted if made in the ordinary course of the company's business and no more favourable terms[298] than it is "reasonable to expect" the company would offer to an unconnected person (s.209).[299] Finally, arrangements for the benefit of associated companies[300] are permitted, even if they are connected persons, in order to facilitate intra-group transfers (s.208).

Remedies

The civil remedies provided under s.213 are similar to those under s.195 in relation to substantial property transactions, i.e. avoidance of the transaction,[301] recovery of profits made and an indemnity against loss, the latter two remedies being exercisable against the director receiving the loan, etc. those connected with that director and the directors authorising the loan.[302] The same defences are provided.

16–83

---

[296] In practice, this is likely to be a heavily used exception. Transactions have to be aggregated for the purpose of determining whether monetary thresholds have been crossed (s.209) and s.210 gives some guidance on the valuation of different types of arrangement.

[297] See below, para.16–113.

[298] However, a loan to purchase or improve a main residence for the director may be on non-commercial terms if the company has a home-loan scheme for its employees, it regularly makes such loans to its employees and the terms of the loan are the standard ones under the scheme: s.208(3),(4).

[299] 2006 Act s.208(2). This is a somewhat narrower exception than that for credit transactions because credit transactions are exempted when entered into by any company (provided this is done in the ordinary course of the company's business) whereas the loan exception applies only to money-lending companies, i.e. those whose ordinary business includes the making of such loans. So, if the ordinary course of a company's business requires it to enter into a one-off credit transaction, it may make use of s.206(3), whether or not its ordinary business includes entering into this class of transaction.

[300] See para.16–78, above.

[301] And s.214 makes the same provision as s.196 in relation to affirmation.

[302] It has been held that it is sufficient to impose liability on the director who authorised the loan (s.213(4)(d)), jointly and severally with the director who received it, that the director was aware from the annual accounts of the practice of making loans to the recipient director, even if he was unaware

Directors' service contracts and gratuitous payments to directors

16–84　A director contracting with his or her company in relation to the remuneration to be received constitutes a paradigm example of a conflict of interest, which is likely to exist in a very strong form. However, Ch.4 of Pt 10 does not in general require shareholder approval of directors' remuneration. It does so only in two specific areas. Approval is required for directors' service contracts of more than two years' duration (s.188) and of gratuitous payments for loss of office (ss.215 et seq.). These provisions are discussed elsewhere in the book, as part of our more general discussion of the control of directors' remuneration and in relation to takeovers.[303] In addition, there are the more demanding requirements of shareholder approval of the remuneration policies of all quoted companies, or, alternatively, specific approval of particular remuneration or loss of office payments.[304]

Political donations and expenditure

16–85　It may be convenient here to deal briefly with a final situation where shareholder approval of directors' acts is required, namely for political donations and expenditure. These provisions are to be found in Pt 14 of the Act, rather than Pt 10, although they can be presented as aiming to control a potential conflict of interest. That conflict is between the personal interests of the directors in promoting a particular political party and the interests of the shareholders as a body in not having corporate assets spent in ways which do not help to promote the success of the company. Of course, the provisions also have a wider constitutional significance, which is not a concern for this book, especially in the light of the long-standing regulation of the use by trade unions of their funds for political purposes.[305] What is required is not shareholder approval of a particular transaction, but shareholder approval of a company policy. The shareholder resolution approving political expenditure "must be expressed in general terms" and in fact "must not purport to authorise particular donations or expenditure".[306] If passed, the resolution has effect for four years, though the articles may impose a shorter period.[307]

　　The Act requires an authorising resolution for (a) corporate donations to political parties registered under the relevant British legislation or those which participate in elections to public office in other EU Member States, to other political organisations and to independent candidates[308]; and (b) other political

---

of the precise amounts. See *Neville v Krikorian* [2007] 1 B.C.L.C. 1 CA; followed in *Queensway Systems Ltd v Walker* [2007] 2 B.C.L.C. 577. In that case the authorising director was also held to be in breach of his general duties to the company by not seeking to recover the loans (which were repayable on demand) as soon as he knew of their existence.

[303] See para.14–30, above, and para.28–28, below.
[304] See para.14–38, above.
[305] See now the Trade Union and Labour Relations (Consolidation) Act 1992 Part I Ch.VI.
[306] 2006 Act s.367(5).
[307] 2006 Act s.368.
[308] 2006 Act s.364. A donation to the political fund of a trade union is included, but not any other type of donation to a union: s.374.

expenditure.[309] The latter is expenditure of a promotional type and other corporate activities which are "capable of being reasonably regarded as intended to affect public support for a political party or other political organisation",[310] even though there is no direct donation to a political party. A resolution is required of the shareholders (by ordinary resolution unless the articles impose a higher standard) in the case of a free-standing company; and of the shareholders of the (ultimate) holding company as well if the company is part of a group. However, in a group situation some relief is provided from the need to obtain multiple authorisations in that a resolution is not required of the company itself if it is a wholly-owned subsidiary.[311] There is one exception to this relief: even a wholly-owned subsidiary requires a resolution of its shareholders, if the parent company is not "UK registered", i.e. registered under the Act or any of its predecessors.[312] This is because a holding company which is not UK registered is not required to pass a resolution conferring approval on the political expenditure of its UK subsidiaries, so that, in such a case, the obligation on the wholly-owned subsidiary revives.[313] This may often be a rather pointless formality, but at least it will require the directors of the UK subsidiary to explain to the foreign parent the provisions of the Act on political donations.

The resolution may give authority for political expenditure generally or confine it to one or more of the following: donations to political parties and independent candidates, donations to other political organisations and political expenditure. In any event, the resolution must set a monetary limit for the expenditures during the period to which it applies.[314]

Where a free-standing company makes a political payment or incurs expenditure without the required shareholder approval, the directors of the company making the payment will be jointly and severally liable to restore to the company the expenditure (with interest) and to compensate the company for any loss or damage it has suffered in consequence, though this second head of loss might be difficult to show.[315] The liability provisions of Pt 14 also extend to shadow directors.[316] Where the company in default is a subsidiary, the directors of the ultimate UK holding company will also be liable (to the subsidiary) but only if they failed to take all reasonable steps to prevent the breach by the subsidiary.[317]

---

[309] 2006 Act s.366. There is an exemption for small donations (no more than £5,000 over any period of 12 months): s.378.

[310] 2006 Act s.365. Also included is expenditure on activity designed to influence voters' attitudes in referendums.

[311] 2006 Act s.366(3),(4). Provision is made for a single resolution to be passed in groups of companies, for example, covering donations by a holding company and any of its subsidiaries (even where those subsidiaries change during the period of the validity of the resolution): s.367(1), (2),(4),(7).

[312] 2006 Act ss.1158 and 1.

[313] 2006 Act s.366(4)(b). The 1985 Act had a series of more complex provisions attempting to deal with non-UK holding and subsidiary companies, but these have been abandoned.

[314] 2006 Act s.367(3),(6).

[315] 2006 Act s.369(1),(2),(3). If the donation is repaid by the recipient, presumably the first head of loss falls away. This was made explicit under the previous law.

[316] 2006 Act.379(1).

[317] 2006 Act s.369(3)(b),(4).

There is anecdotal evidence that the effect of these provisions of the Act (introduced in 2000) has been to persuade the directors of many companies not to make political donations from corporate funds, rather than to seek to shareholder approval to do so. Of course, wealthy business figures make large donations to political parties, but do so out of their personal wealth, which may be derived from the activities of businesses they control.

CONFLICTS OF INTEREST AND THE USE OF CORPORATE PROPERTY, INFORMATION AND OPPORTUNITY

The scope and functioning of section 175

16–86   Section 175(1) states that "a director must avoid a situation in which he has, or can have, a direct or indirect interest that conflicts, or possibly may conflict, with the interests of the company".[318] Section 175(7) makes it clear that a conflict of interests includes a conflict of duties. Subject to a restriction in relation to charitable companies,[319] s.175(3) excludes from the scope of the section one central type of situation involving conflict of interest, namely, "a conflict of interest arising in relation to a transaction or arrangement with the company". These self-dealing transactions are covered by s.177, as discussed above, rather than by s.175.[320] However, it should be noted that s.175(3) has the effect of excluding self-dealing transactions even if s.177 does not apply its normal rule of disclosure to the board of the self-dealing transaction in question, for example, decisions on directors' remuneration (s.177(6)(c)). Having excluded self-dealing transactions, s.175 applies, as is expressly stated in s.175(2), "in particular to the exploitation of any property, information or opportunity" of the company. However, this is simply an inclusive assertion: it is important to note that s.175 imposes a general obligation to avoid conflicts of interest. Any conflict situation, not excluded by s.175(3), will fall within its scope, whether or not it involves the exploitation of property, information or opportunity of the company. The example of a person acting as a director of competing companies is discussed below. Deciding whether a situation does indeed involve the necessary conflict is often

---

[318] Subject to the exception—"not reasonably regarded as likely" to give rise to a conflict—in s.175(4)(a), which parallels the provision in s.177(6)(a). See para.16–60, above.

[319] In the case of charitable companies self-dealing transactions fall within s.175, unless the articles permit the s.175 duty to be disapplied and, even then, the articles may not effect a blanket disapplication but may do so only "in relation to descriptions of transactions or arrangements specified" in the articles (s.181(2)). Thus, for charitable companies, board or shareholder authorisation will be required in many cases for directors' conflicted transactions with the company. The tougher rules for charitable companies are probably based on the premise that monitoring of the directors by the members of a charitable company is generally less effective than in the case of a non-charitable company and that the Charity Commission cannot make up the whole of the monitoring deficit.

[320] The provisions are thus described as "mutually exclusive": *Re Coroin Ltd* [2012] EWHC 2343 (Ch) at [583] (David Richards J).

the most difficult question in this area. If anything, recent developments in the case law seem to have brought an even wider range of situations within the conflicts category.[321]

As with the self-dealing transactions discussed above, the secondary aim of the rules in this area is to identify the appropriate body or bodies to handle the conflict situation on behalf of the company. As with self-dealing transactions, again, the common law rule was shareholder approval.[322] Section 175 introduces, as we shall see, the mechanism of approval by the uninvolved members of the board, as an alternative to shareholder approval. However, unlike s.177 which imposes simply an obligation of disclosure to the board for self-dealing transactions, s.175 requires the board, assuming it wishes to act, to approve the director putting him- or herself in a position of conflict of duty and interest. This difference in the roles of the board is necessary because, unlike with self-dealing transactions, situations falling within s.175 will not necessarily generate a transaction to which the company is party. An example would be where a director diverts a corporate opportunity for personal benefit. The decision for the board thus becomes not whether to enter into the transaction (the typical question in the self-dealing case), but whether to approve what would otherwise be the director's breach of duty. Nevertheless, the statute has clearly made it easier for directors to obtain approval for the exploitation of a conflict personally, by permitting the non-involved members of the board to give approval (subject to safeguards).

There are two crucial questions to be answered in the area of corporate opportunities: first, how does the law identify an opportunity as a "conflicted" one and, secondly, what processes does it specify for the company to give authority for the taking of the corporate opportunity by the director personally? The statute deals with the second issue in part but with the first issue hardly at all, where reliance is placed on the common law. We look at each of these two issues in turn.

A strict approach to conflicts of interest

The reason for depriving a director of a profit made from unauthorised exploitation of a corporate opportunity is not an objection to directors making profits as a result of or in connection with or whilst holding their office, but rather that the prospect of a personal profit may make the director careless about promoting the company's interest in taking the opportunity. If taking the opportunity personally does not involve any conflict with the interests of the company, there is no reason to deprive the director of his or her profit. It follows that some of the prior case law on corporate opportunity, which seemed to be based on a free-standing "no profit" rule, is to be regarded with caution under the

16–87

---

[321] Notably *Bhullar v Bhullar* [2003] 2 B.C.L.C. 241 CA; and *Allied Business and Financial Consultants Ltd v Shanahan* (also known as *O'Donnell v Shanahan*) [2009] EWCA Civ 751; [2009] 2 B.C.L.C. 666 CA. Also see, recently, *Sharma v Sharma* [2013] EWCA Civ 1287; [2014] B.C.C. 73 CA; and *Pennyfeathers Ltd v Pennyfeathers Property Co Ltd* [2013] EWHC 3530 (Ch).

[322] In *Queensland Mines Ltd v Hudson* [1978] 52 A.L.J.R. 379 the Privy Council appeared to accept a board decision as releasing the corporate interest in an opportunity, but in that case the only members of the company were two other companies, each represented on the board of the company in question.

new statutory provisions. However, as we shall see below, there is a high degree of overlap between a "no conflict" approach and a "no profit" approach if both are given a rigorous interpretation.

16–88   That the approach of s.175 to the "no conflict" principle is rigorous is suggested by two features of the section. First, s.175(1), echoing Lord Cranworth LC in *Aberdeen Rly Co v Blaikie Bros*,[323] includes within the principle a personal interest which "possibly may conflict" with that of the company. Secondly, s.175(2), referring to corporate opportunities, etc. says that "it is immaterial whether the company could take advantage of the property, information or opportunity". On the other hand, the primacy of the conflict approach is asserted by s.175(4)(a), which provides that the section is not infringed if "the situation cannot reasonably be regarded as likely to give rise to a conflict of interest". These parts of the section are to some degree in tension with one another. One thing is clear: it is certainly not enough for the director to escape liability under this section that he or she acted in good faith (i.e. had honestly formed the view that the company's interests were not capable of being harmed by what was done), for the question of whether an actual or potential conflict of interest has arisen is one for the court.

In identifying situations as involving a conflict, s.175 applies "in particular" to exploitation by the director of "property, information or opportunity" of the company. Misuse of corporate assets generally presents no particular problem[324]; even the most unsophisticated directors should realise that they must not use the company's property as if it was their own (although even this is frequently overlooked or ignored in a "one-man" company). It is misuse of corporate information or a corporate opportunity—in practice the two are likely to overlap—which gives rise to difficulties. The main difficulty in the law relating to the misuse of corporate information and opportunities (hereafter referred to simply as corporate opportunities) is isolating the criteria for the identification of a corporate opportunity (as opposed to one the director is free to exploit personally without seeking any authorisation from the company). To put it another way, what sorts of linkages between the opportunity and the company are needed to make the opportunity a "corporate" one, for which exploitation personally the director needs the authorisation of the company? In two relatively recent decisions, the Court of Appeal has taken a broad view of the criteria, but we need to put those decisions in the context of the prior case law.

---

[323]   *Aberdeen Rly Co v Blaikie Bros* (1854) 1 Macq. 461 HL.

[324]   Except the problem of knowing when "corporate assets" end and "corporate information" or "corporate opportunity" begin. The present law does not draw a clear distinction between them and the decisions frequently treat the latter as "belonging" to the company, i.e. as being its "property" or "asset". The modern law on remedies tends to encourage this, as precise distinction seems irrelevant for those purposes.

Identification of "corporate" opportunities

In a famous decision during the Second World War, *Regal (Hastings) Ltd v Gulliver*,[325] the House of Lords, following the law relating to trustees,[326] held directors liable to account to the company for the profit made from their personal exploitation of a corporate opportunity once it was established:

    16–89

> "(i) that what the directors did was so related to the affairs of the company that it can properly be said to have been done in the course of their management and in utilisation of their opportunities and special knowledge as directors; and (ii) that what they did resulted in a profit to themselves."[327]

Although this case is based on a "no profit" rationale which the Act now expressly rejects, it is not difficult to re-cast it in conflict terms. The facts, briefly, were as follows: company A owned a cinema and the directors decided to acquire two others with a view to selling the whole undertaking as a going concern. For this purpose they formed company B to take a lease of the other two cinemas. But the lessor insisted on a personal guarantee from the directors unless the paid-up capital of company B was at least £5,000 (which in those days was a large sum). Company A, the directors concluded, was unable to subscribe more than £2,000 and the directors, although initially willing to do so, changed their minds about giving personal guarantees. Accordingly the original plan was changed; instead of company A subscribing for all the shares in company B, company A took up 2,000 and the remaining 3,000 were taken by the directors and their friends. Three weeks later, all the shares in both companies were sold, a profit of nearly £3 being made on each of the shares in company B. The new controllers then caused company A to bring an action against the former directors to recover the profit they had made.

Issues of scope

It is not difficult to see a conflict of interest in these facts. It was the directors who decided not to give personal guarantees, thus creating the opportunity for them to participate personally in the financing of the acquisition and to share in the profits from the re-sale and depriving the company of the ability to take the whole of the profit on the sale of the subsidiary. It was the directors who, with the same result, decided not to obtain additional finance for the company to capitalise the subsidiary at the required level, even though the subsequent sale three weeks later was in contemplation when the additional cinemas were being acquired, so that it is difficult to believe that it would have been impossible for the company to obtain bridging finance for such a short period. These facts were emphasised in the judgment of Lord Russell of Killowen, even though he, like the other judges, based his reasoning on the "no profit" principle noted above.

    16–90

    Thus, it is submitted that a modern court, applying the "no conflict" principle, could come to the same result as the House of Lords in this case, especially as

---

[325] *Regal (Hastings) Ltd v Gulliver* [1942] 1 All E.R. 378; [1967] 2 A.C. 134n.
[326] Notably *Keech v Sandford* (1726) Scl. Cas. Ch. 61.
[327] per Lord Macmillan at [1967] A.C. 153.

s.175(2) provides that "it is immaterial whether the company could take advantage of the property, information or opportunity".[328] This seems at first sight a very odd provision: was it not the possibility that the company could have taken up the opportunity itself which in *Regal* provided the basis for the conflict of interest, so that the existence of that possibility can hardly be characterised as "immaterial"? However, the rule can be justified as relieving the court of having to make a judgement it was not well-placed to make, i.e. whether the company was genuinely unable to raise the finance itself. It may also be justified as a prophylactic rule. It is the duty of the director to obtain the opportunity for the company. If the director is to be relieved of this duty and made free to take the opportunity personally where there is only a low chance of the company obtaining the opportunity itself, this will give the director an incentive not to strive as hard as he or she might to promote the company's interests. Section 175(2) removes this incentive.

16–91   It will be observed, however, that the claim in *Regal* was wholly unmeritorious. Recovery by the company benefited only the purchasers, who in this way received an undeserved windfall resulting, in effect, in a reduction in the price which they had freely agreed to pay. It also appears that the directors had held a majority of the shares in company A so that there would have been no difficulty in obtaining authorisation or ratification of their action by the company in general meeting[329]; but acting, as it was conceded they had, in perfect good faith and in full belief in the legality and propriety of their actions, it had not occurred to them to go through this formality. Nor does this account exhaust the anomalies inherent in the decision. The chairman (and, apparently, the dominant member) of the board, instead of agreeing himself to subscribe for shares in company B, had merely agreed to find subscribers for £500. Shares to that value had, accordingly, been taken up by two private companies of which he was a member and director, and by a personal friend of his. It was accepted that the companies and friend had subscribed beneficially and not as his nominees and, accordingly, neither he nor they were held to be under any liability to account for the profit which they had made.[330]

The company's solicitor also escaped; though he had subscribed for shares and profited personally, he could retain his profit because he had acted with the knowledge and consent of the company exercised through the board of directors.

---

[328] More difficult to explain in this way might be the trusts case of *Boardman v Phipps* [1967] 2 A.C. 46 HL, where two of their lordships found against liability on the grounds that there was no conflict of interest on the part of the trustees, who made a profit out of confidential information obtained from the trust, which the trust itself was prohibited from acting on, whilst the majority found in favour of liability on the basis of confidential information plus profit. However, Lord Cohen (in the majority) also found that there was a conflict of interest, so that it might be argued that the majority view was that a conflict needed to be found for liability to be established. Lord Upjohn, dissenting, said that for a conflict of interest to arise there must be "a real sensible possibility of conflict" in the eyes of a reasonable person, a dictum which seems to be reflected in s.175(4)(a) of the Act.

[329] See the cogent editorial note in [1942] 1 All E.R. at 379. It was conceded that had this been done, there could have been no recovery: see further on this question, paras 16–117 et seq., below.

[330] The companies and friend had not been sued. Recovery might have been obtained from them if they had fallen within the rules relating to third parties' involvement in breaches of directors' duties. And in that case could the director be made liable for the third party's profits? See below, para.16–137.

The directors themselves could avoid liability only if a general meeting had approved,[331] but the solicitor, not being a director, could rely on the consent of the board. And this despite the fact that the board had acted throughout on his advice. Hence the two men most responsible for what had been done escaped liability, while those who had followed their lead had to pay up. What seems wrong with the application of the basic principle in this case is that recovery was not from all the right people and, more especially, was in favour of quite the wrong people.[332] Had it not been for the change of ownership it might well have been equitable to order restoration to the company, thus, in effect, causing the directors' profits to be shared among all the members. As it was, the case can be seen as one in which equitable principles were taken to inequitable conclusions.

Of the many subsequent decisions that have followed or commented on the *Regal* case, four are of particular interest: *Industrial Development Consultants v Cooley*,[333] *Canadian Aero Service v O'Malley*[334] (a decision of the Canadian Supreme Court in which the judgment was delivered by Laskin J—later the CJ), *Bhullar v Bhullar*[335] and *Allied Business and Financial Consultants Ltd v Shanahan* (also known as *O'Donnell v Shanahan*).[336]

16–92

The facts in the first two cases were very similar. In both, the companies concerned had been eager to obtain, and were in negotiation for, highly remunerative work in connection with impending projects. In both, it was unlikely that the companies would have obtained the work, but in each there was a director whose expertise the undertaker of the project was anxious to obtain. Accordingly, each of the directors concerned resigned his office and later joined the undertaker of the project, in *Cooley* directly, in *Canadian Aero Service* indirectly through a company formed for the purpose which entered into a consortium with the undertaker. In both the directors were held liable to account for the profits which they made.

In neither case is it difficult to analyse the facts through a conflict-of-interest prism, since both directors were under a duty to obtain the opportunity for the company, unlikely though it was that they would succeed, though the reasoning of the courts involved was not expressed exclusively in this way. In *Cooley*, liability was based on misuse of information,[337] the defendant, while managing director, had obtained information and knowledge that the project was to be revived and had deliberately concealed this from the company and taken steps to turn the information to his personal advantage. It was irrelevant that the approach had been made to him and that his services were being sought as an individual

---

[331] This would continue to be the case even under the Act because there appear to have been no uninvolved directors who could have given authorisation.

[332] Some American jurisdictions, in like circumstances, allow what is there known as "pro rata recovery" by those shareholders who have not profited. We, unfortunately, lack any such procedure.

[333] *Industrial Development Consultants v Cooley* [1972] 1 W.L.R. 443, per Roskill J.

[334] *Canadian Aero Service v O'Malley* [1973] 40 D.L.R. (3d) 371 Can. SC.

[335] *Bhullar v Bhullar* [2003] 2 B.C.L.C. 241 CA.

[336] *Allied Business and Financial Consultants Ltd v Shanahan* [2009] EWCA Civ 751; [2009] B.C.C. 822 CA.

[337] Roskill J presumably chose this rather than the more obvious loss of opportunity because the chance that the company could have secured the opportunity was minimal: Roskill J assessed it at not more than 10 per cent: [1972] 1 W.L.R. 443 at 454.

consultant and would be undertaken free from any association with the company.[338] "Information which came to him while he was managing director and which was of concern to the plaintiffs and relevant for the plaintiffs to know, was information which it was his duty to pass on to the plaintiffs." It might seem remarkable that the plaintiffs should receive a benefit which "it is unlikely that they would have got for themselves had the defendant complied with his duty to them" but "if the defendant is not required to account he will have made a large profit as a result of having deliberately put himself into a position in which his duty to the plaintiffs who were employing him and his personal interests conflicted".[339] This is an expression of the policy, as noted above, which now finds expression in s.175(2) of the Act. The quotation also demonstrates that the basis of the decision was not a mere misuse of information but the conflict of interest and duty to which the use gave rise.

16–93   In *Canadian Aero Service*, the decision was based firmly on misuse of a corporate opportunity, conceived of as generating a conflict of interest. On this Laskin J said[340]:

> "An examination of the case-law shows the pervasiveness of a strict ethic in this area of the law. In my opinion this ethic disqualifies a director or senior officer[341] from usurping for himself or diverting to another person or company with whom or with which he is associated a maturing business opportunity which his company is actively pursuing; he is also precluded from so acting even after his resignation where the resignation may fairly be said to be prompted or influenced by a wish to acquire for himself the opportunity sought by the company, or where it was his position with the company rather than a fresh initiative which led him to the opportunity which he later acquired."

Effect of director's resignation

16–94   Another feature of the *Cooley* and *O'Malley* cases was that the directors in question resigned, but were nevertheless held liable to account to the company for the profits subsequently made. The issue was considered by Lawrence Collins J in *CMS Dolphin Ltd v Simonet*,[342] who concluded that the answer lay in the proposition that the opportunity is treated as the property of the company, so that a director who resigns after learning about such an opportunity "is just as

---

[338] So that, "in one sense, the benefit did not arise because of the defendant's directorship: indeed, the defendant would not have got this work had he remained a director": [1972] 1 W.L.R. 443 at 451.

[339] *Industrial Development Consultants v Cooley* [1972] 1 W.L.R. 443, at 453.

[340] *Canadian Aero Service v O'Malley* (1973) 40 D.L.R. (3d) 371 at 382.

[341] See above, para.16–11 on the question of how far English fiduciary principles apply to non-board senior managers.

[342] *CMS Dolphin Ltd v Simonet* [2001] 2 B.C.L.C. 704 at 733. Alternatively, it can be said that the conflict of personal interest and duty to the company arises at the moment the opportunity emerges and that subsequent resignation does not operate retrospectively to cure the breach (indeed, it is often an expression of the director's preference for his or her personal interest). It is true that the profit arising out of the breach is made after resignation, but there is no reason why the company should not recover this if the breach occurred before resignation, just as a director who takes a decision adverse to the company in breach of the core duty of loyalty or duty of care does not reduce his or her liability to the company by resigning immediately after taking the decision. cf. *Lindsley v Woodfull* [2004] 2 B.C.L.C. 131 at [28]–[30] CA. See also *FHR European Ventures LLP v Mankarious* [2013] EWCA Civ 17; [2014] Ch. 1 at [56]–[59] CA (not affected by the appeal at [2014] UKSC 45; [2015] A.C. 250).

accountable as a trustee who retires without properly accounting for trust property". As we have seen above,[343] this approach to the issue of resignation has been confirmed in s.170(2)(a) of the Act, and without the need for dubious characterisation of the opportunity as the property of the company. It follows, of course, that if what the director has learned before his or her resignation does not fall within the category of a corporate opportunity, it is no breach of this aspect of fiduciary duties to exploit the information personally thereafter; the line can be difficult to draw.[344] This means that, beyond the boundaries of these statutory rules, or any contractual[345] or equitable restraints on the director (for example, rules on breach of confidence), he or she is otherwise free to exploit his or her enhanced knowledge, talents and skills after resignation as a director.[346]

Effect of board determinations of scope

The last two cases of the four noted earlier are in many ways the more interesting. In *Bhullar v Bhullar*,[347] in contrast to *Cooley* and *Canaero*, the defendants did not seek to divert to themselves an opportunity which their company was actively pursuing. On the contrary, the two families which had set up the company to acquire properties having fallen out, the family which constituted the claimant side of the litigation informed the family which formed the defendant side of the litigation that it did not want the company to acquire further properties. Subsequently, the defendant directors, by chance and without reliance on any information confidential to the company, discovered that a property adjacent to one of the company's properties was for sale and purchased it themselves. The claimants nevertheless succeeded in their argument that the opportunity to purchase the property should have been made available to the company, whose property would have been much more valuable if joined with the adjacent property, and that the defendants accordingly held the property on trust for the company.[348] This is a notable decision on two grounds.

16–95

First, it seems to move English law in the direction of the US "line of business test", i.e. if the opportunity falls within the company's existing business activities, not simply where the company is actively pursuing a particular opportunity, then an opportunity the director comes across is a corporate one, even if no property or

---

[343] See para.16–13, above.

[344] *Island Export Finance Ltd v Umunna* [1986] B.C.L.C. 460; *Balston Ltd v Headline Filters Ltd* [1990] F.S.R. 385; *Framlington Group Plc v Anderson* [1995] 1 B.C.L.C. 475; *Halcyon House Ltd v Baines* [2014] EWHC 2216 (QB); *First Subsea Ltd v Balltec Ltd* [2014] EWHC 886 (Ch) (appeal outstanding); *Weatherford Global Products Ltd v Hydropath Holdings Ltd* [2014] EWHC 2725 (TCC); [2015] B.L.R. 69. Also see *Imam-Sadeque v Bluebay Asset Management (Services) Ltd* [2012] EWHC 3511 (QB); [2013] I.R.L.R. 344 (in the context of a former employer-employee relationship).

[345] See, e.g. *Dranez Anstalt v Hayek* [2002] EWCA Civ 1729; [2003] 1 B.C.L.C. 278 CA, finding a restraint of trade clause too wide and therefore unenforceable.

[346] See generally *Odyssey Entertainment Ltd v Kamp* [2012] EWHC 2316 (Ch); *Halcyon House Ltd v Baines* [2014] EWHC 2216 (QB); *First Subsea Ltd v Balltec Ltd* [2014] EWHC 886 (Ch) (appeal outstanding).

[347] *Bhullar v Bhullar* [2003] 2 B.C.L.C. 241 CA. In the same vein, also see *Towers v Premier Waste Management Ltd* [2011] EWCA Civ 923; [2012] 1 B.C.L.C. 67 CA, requiring the company to be given the option to reject the opportunity.

[348] Thus, they could be obliged to convey it to the company, subject to the company's payment to them of the costs of purchase.

information of the company was deployed by the director to obtain the opportunity. There was no suggestion in *Bhullar* that the directors had used their position in the company to bring the opportunity to maturity and then diverted it for themselves, as in *Canaero*. For this reason, the decision can be seen as affecting a significant extension of the criteria for identifying a corporate opportunity. This is probably a desirable development. It recognises that, for the purpose of the conflict of interest and duty rule, the duties of a director are pervasive, not ones arising only in specific and limited circumstances.

Secondly, however, the application of the extended understanding of a corporate opportunity to the facts of the case was questionable, for the court attached no weight to the fact that, before the opportunity arose, the board decided, albeit informally, at the initiative of the claimants and for reasons which were apparent, not to acquire any more properties.[349] Nevertheless, the claimants were, in effect, able to reverse their decision once a particularly attractive opportunity arose. It is not clear why the claimants should have been permitted to act in such an opportunistic way. In *Regal*, where the claimants' behaviour was also opportunistic, as we have seen, it could be said that it was the directors who decided that the company could not afford the opportunity who were the ones who later took it themselves, and that such behaviour is necessarily suspect. In *Bhullar* it was found as a fact that the claimants, not the defendants, took the initiative to restrict the scope of company's future activities.[350]

16–96 This second point is not unrelated to the first. If the courts are, rightly it is submitted, to extend liability beyond the maturing business opportunity so as to embrace opportunities within the company's line of business, a director needs to be able to establish what the company's business actually is. Of course, this may not be simple, and it is probably right that any ambiguity ought to be resolved against the director and in favour of the company, so requiring the director to act with undeviating loyalty in furthering the company's possible wider interests.[351] On the other hand, it would seem undesirable to extend the corporate opportunity doctrine to any business opening which a director comes across and which the company could exploit, even though the company was neither already exploiting that type of opportunity nor seeking to do so.[352] To do so would come close to restoring the "no profit" rule which the section does not adopt, and indeed to do

---

[349] The issue is hardly touched upon in the reasoning of the court.

[350] It is possible that the court thought that the purchase of the adjacent property did not fall unambiguously within the decision not to purchase new properties.

[351] Companies' business models change from time to time, often quite rapidly, and the obvious place for a director to look for a current definition is in the decisions of the board setting its business strategy, but it also seems right that the company's interests might legitimately be seen as extending more widely to encompass at least those broader but related corporate endeavours that any proactive directors ought at least periodically to consider and critically review as possible new corporate endeavours. These too should be included within the compass of the directors' duties of loyalty.

[352] For example, the non-executive director of a company providing business services learns on the golf course from a friend who does not know of his directorship of an opportunity to invest in a restaurant project. Does the director need the authorisation of the company to make the investment, simply because his company is financially able to take it up? It is suggested that the answer is in the negative. For some recognition of the force of this argument see *Wilkinson v West Coast Capital* [2007] B.C.C. 717.

so without the usual limitations inherent in that common law rule.[353] This sort of rule would increase the costs of being a director (the director is at risk of losing the opportunity to the company) and in the case of non-executive directors in particular this might seem a high cost as against the potential rewards of the directorship.

In particular, an answer needs to be provided to the question posed in *Regal*: does the equitable principle involve "the proposition that, if the directors bona fide decide not to invest their company's funds in some proposed investment, a director who thereafter embarks his own money therein is accountable for any profits he may derive therefrom?"[354] The reason this question is unresolved, it is suggested, is to be found in the underdeveloped state of the law on the role of the board in the area of corporate opportunities, for the board performs two closely linked but conceptually distinct roles. It may authorise the taking by the director of an opportunity which is a corporate one, as s.175 contemplates, but, through its direction of the company's business strategy, its decisions may, or ought, to have the effect of taking some opportunities out of the category of being corporate, with the consequence that authorisation is not required, because there is no conflict of interest. As s.175(2) says, it may indeed be "immaterial" whether the company could take advantage of the opportunity, but if it is an opportunity outside the range of the company's business activities, present or in contemplation, can the situation "reasonably be regarded as likely to give rise to a conflict of interest", as s.175(4)(a) requires? It is suggested that the line of business test provides a way of reconciling these two provisions of the section, with due regard being accorded to decisions of the board in determining the company's business strategy.

This "scope of business" reasoning has, however, been dealt an unexpected and it **16–97** is suggested rather unfortunate blow in the last and most recent case on our list. In *O'Donnell v Shanahan*,[355] the deputy judge held that there had been no breach of fiduciary obligations because the impugned opportunity (which concerned a property development) arose outside the scope of the business of the principal company (which focussed upon the provision of loans, mortgages and financial advice[356]), and further there had been no use of the company's property or information in acquiring the benefit.[357] The Court of Appeal took the opposite view. The company operated as a quasi-partnership with three members, the petitioner and the two defendants (the latter also ran a property development

---

[353] That being, as stated in *Regal*, that the opportunity came to the directors "by reason and only by reason of the fact that they were directors of Regal, and in the course of their execution of that office": per Lord Russell at [1967] 2 A.C. 134, 147.

[354] per Lord Russell (quoting Greene MR) at [1967] 2 A.C. 152. cf. the answer given in *Peso Silver Mines v Cropper* (1966) 58 D.L.R. 2d 1 and the criticism of that decision by Beck in (1971) 49 Can. B.R. 80.

[355] *Allied Business and Financial Consultants Ltd v Shanahan* (also known as *O'Donnell v Shanahan*) [2008] EWHC 1973 (Ch); [2009] B.C.C. 517; overturned in [2009] EWCA Civ 751; [2009] 2 B.C.L.C. 666 CA. The case was brought as an unfair prejudice petition under CA 1985 s.459 (now CA 2006 s.994). See below, para.20–14.

[356] This was as defined in the company's constitution, although there was also the common broader power to carry on any other business considered by the directors to be advantageous.

[357] Any use of the valuation report (see below) was, if anything, in breach of the rights of the first potential buyer, not the company.

partnership on the side). Although not part of the company's usual business, the company had, in an ad hoc fashion, agreed to procure finance for and advise one particular investor who was interested in purchasing a development property. In return, the company would earn fees and a commission. Valuation reports were obtained and other work done, but the deal did not proceed. After further negotiations, the two defendants and a third party procured the opportunity for themselves, and did so on the basis that no commission would be paid to the company. The defendants did, nevertheless, pay the petitioner a sum representing her notional share of the lost commission. Later, after the falling out, the petitioner claimed that the investment in the development property was made in breach of the "no conflict" and "no profit" rules, without her consent, and that she was entitled to a share in the profits.

The Court of Appeal agreed, holding that the opportunity had arisen in the course of the directors' activities as company directors and therefore it should have been disclosed to the company which should have been given a chance to decide whether or not it wished to exploit the opportunity itself. It was immaterial that property development was not the focus of the company's activities. The "scope of business" test, described in *Aas v Benham*[358] (and heavily relied upon by the deputy judge), was held inapplicable: it was, the court held, a partnership precedent; its application was limited to partnerships where the partnership activities were clearly defined in restrictive partnership deeds; by contrast, in companies (even, it seems, quasi-partnership companies, as here) and trusts, *Aas v Benham* had no application—directors were simply fiduciaries in whatever activities they engaged. According to Rimer LJ[359]:

> "I would regard it as correct to characterise the nature of a director's fiduciary duties as being so unlimited and as akin to a 'general trusteeship'. In my judgment, the decision in *Aas v Benham* provides no assistance in determining the nature and reach of the 'no profit' rule so far as it applies to trustees and directors. In particular, in the present case, the scope of the company's business was in no manner relevantly circumscribed by its constitution: it was fully open to it to engage in property investment if the directors so chose."

And later, given this, he reached the same conclusions on the "no conflict" rule. It followed that the two directors had breached their fiduciary duties and were required to account for the profits earned on the development project (should the facts establish there were any). This would, in turn, boost the assets of the company, which would in turn increase the share price, and thus improve the return to the petitioner who was seeking to have her shares repurchased as her remedy under the unfair prejudice petition.

Moreover, the court dismissed without discussion as seemingly irrelevant the fact that the petitioner had accepted her share of the notional commission from the defaulting directors, and had at least implicitly acquiesced in the purchase of the development property by the defendants.

Finally, although it is true that unfair prejudice claims can be pursued successfully without proof of matters that would constitute legal wrongs, here the

---

[358] *Aas v Benham* [1891] 2 Ch. 244.
[359] *O'Donnell v Shanahan* [2009] EWCA Civ 751; [2009] 2 B.C.L.C. 666 at [68]–[69] CA.

entire focus of the Court of Appeal's reasoning was on the question of whether there had been a breach of the no-conflict fiduciary duties.

Where does this leave directors? It is easy to explain that it is, and ought to be, **16–98** irrelevant to the question of fiduciary breach whether the company could, or would, exploit the opportunity in question. Those questions are more relevant when the alleged breach is of the good faith duty (s.171), or even the care and skill duty (s.174). But the gist of the "no conflict" rule is to compel, so far as possible, unwavering loyalty to the corporate endeavour. Both the duty and its remedies are geared to this end. This, it is suggested, implicitly and inevitably requires the courts to pay some regard to the scope of that endeavour. Instead, the two cases just described (*Bhullar v Bhullar*[360] and *O'Donnell v Shanahan*[361]) adopt a broad approach that, taken only a little further, verges on a finding that any opportunity that is at all interesting financially will be seen as of interest to the company. This raises the risks for directors, and increases the chances of pure windfall gains to the company and its shareholders: the trend is towards there being no safe harbour other than to present every entrepreneurial idea to the board before pursuing it individually, notwithstanding the nature of the corporate business or whether there is a real, sensible prospect of a conflict. This effectively gives the company a right of first refusal on opportunities seen by the directors as worth pursuing. Within the company's scope of business, broadly interpreted, this is precisely the goal of the no-conflict rule, but outside that context the broader rule needs some justification. It raises the fiduciary "no-conflict" rule from pragmatic prophylaxis to something far more draconian.

Since all these cases were determined under the common law, it remains to be seen how far the statutory encapsulation has imposed its own pressure in s.175(4) to deny a breach if "the situation cannot reasonably be regarded as likely to give rise to a conflict of interest". However, recent authorities do not appear to deviate from these common law authorities on the tests for determining the scope of the director's duty.[362]

Competing and multiple directorships

It is common for directors to hold directorships in more than one company, **16–99** certainly where the companies are part of a group but also where they are independent of one another. In such cases an issue arises in relation to the compatibility of this practice with the no-conflict rule set out in s.175, whether conceived of as a conflict of interest and duty (s.175(1)) or a conflict of duty and duty (s.175(7)). There are two situations which need to be looked at: the first is

---

[360] *Bhullar v Bhullar* [2003] 2 B.C.L.C. 241 CA.
[361] *Allied Business and Financial Consultants Ltd v Shanahan* (also known as *O'Donnell v Shanahan*) [2008] EWHC 1973 (Ch); [2009] B.C.C. 517; overturned in [2009] EWCA Civ 751; [2009] 2 B.C.L.C. 666 CA.
[362] See *Towers v Premier Waste Management Ltd* [2011] EWCA Civ 923; [2012] B.C.C. 72 CA at [51]; *Sharma v Sharma* [2013] EWCA Civ 1287; [2014] B.C.C. 73 at [51]–[52] CA; *Richmond Pharmacology Ltd v Chester Overseas Ltd* [2014] EWHC 2692 (Ch); [2014] Bus. L.R. 1110 at [69]–[72]. Also see generally *Pennyfeathers Ltd v Pennyfeathers Property Co Ltd* [2013] EWHC 3530 (Ch); and *Invideous Ltd v Thorogood* (judgment reversed on other grounds in [2014] EWCA Civ 1511 CA).

where directorships are held in companies which are in business competition with one another, or indeed where the director in any other way enters into competition with the company; and, secondly and more commonly, where the companies are not competitors but where nevertheless their interests may conflict from time to time.

Competing with the company

16–100   One of the most obvious examples of a situation which might be expected to give rise to a conflict between two sets of a director's duties[363] is where the director carries on or is associated with a business competing with that of the company. Certainly fiduciaries without the consent of their principals are normally precluded from competing with them, and this is specifically stated in the analogous field of partnership law.[364] For a while, and strangely therefore, it was supposed that a similar rule did not apply to directors.[365] However, the one definite, if inadequately reported, decision that a director could not be restrained from acting as a director of a rival company appears to be based on the conclusion that competing directorships were not unconstitutional (i.e. not contrary to the articles or the director's contract) rather than that they were not in breach of the director's fiduciary duty.[366] It has been held that the duty of fidelity flowing from the relationship of employer and worker may preclude the worker from engaging, even in his spare time, in work for a competitor,[367] notwithstanding that the worker's duty of fidelity imposes lesser obligations than the full duty of good faith owed by a director or other fiduciary agent. It seems impossible to suggest, therefore, that a director can compete whereas a subordinate employee cannot.

---

[363] 2006 Act s.176(7) makes it clear that the section applies to a conflict of duties.

[364] Partnership Act 1890 s.30.

[365] It clearly does not apply to members, even in a private company, for members, as such, are not fiduciaries, though such conduct might give rise to a remedy under the unfair prejudice provisions. See Ch.20, below.

[366] *London & Mashonaland Exploration Co v New Mashonaland Exploration Co* [1891] W.N. 165; approved by Lord Blanesburgh in *Bell v Lever Bros* [1932] A.C. 161 at 195 HL. By contrast, the dicta in *Item Software (UK) Ltd v Fassihi* [2004] EWCA Civ 1244 at [63], per Arden LJ, suggests, it seems, that although a finding that directors could not hold multiple directorships would be a "substantive extension" of the duties of directors, there was—as in this case—no suggestion that those multiple directorships would not be subjected to the full panoply of fiduciary restrictions. See also *First Subsea Ltd v Balltec Ltd* [2014] EWHC 866 (Ch), in which the former directors were found to have breached their duties of loyalty even though the setting up of a competing business itself was not a breach (appeal outstanding).

[367] *Hivac Ltd v Park Royal Scientific Instruments Ltd* [1946] Ch.169 CA. If correct it must apply to an executive director: see *Scottish Co-op Wholesale Society Ltd v Meyer* [1959] A.C. 324 HL, per Lord Denning at 367. Also see *Allfiled UK Ltd v Eltis* [2015] EWHC 1300 (Ch) (the granting of an interim injunction restraining the use of confidential information and intellectual property in a new company pending trial, but allowing the new company to continue trading in the meantime).

In the light of the above it was not surprising that in *In Plus Group Ltd v Pyke*[368] the Court of Appeal expressed unease with the state of the law as set out above, but resisted the temptation to engage in a wholesale review of the case law in this area in the situation facing them where the defendant director had been wholly, and probably wrongfully, excluded from any influence over the operation of the claimant companies, in which he was also a substantial shareholder. The Court held that in these circumstances the claimant companies could not obtain an account of the profits made by the director as a director of a competing company which he had established. In taking this approach, the court has indicated that the logical way forward is simply to examine the rule against competition in the circumstances of each case. *The Mashonaland* case must then be seen, not as one laying down a rule that competition is in principle permitted, but as one where, as in the *Pyke* case, it was inappropriate to apply the no-competition rule.[369]

It can also be argued that s.175 has made it much easier for directors to deal with such conflicts of duty. If both companies consent to the situation, there is no breach of fiduciary duty arising simply from taking up directorships in competing companies, but so long as consent at common law required the approval of the shareholders, directors would regard the process of obtaining consent as a burdensome one. Under s.175, by contrast, the non-conflicted directors of the companies involved will normally be in a position to give their consent (subject to the different default rules for private and public companies noted below).

Two difficulties remain, however. First, the section does not contemplate, in the way that s.177 does, a general declaration of interest. The director must seek approval from the non-involved directors for taking up the position as a director of the competing company and, should the nature of that situation change—for example, should the competing company start an additional line of business in competition with the other company—a further consent would apparently be required. However, it may not always be easy to judge when a situation has arisen which requires further consent. Secondly, even if consent is given to the taking up of the directorship, the director is likely to be faced with constant difficulties in avoiding breaches of the core duty of loyalty to the companies concerned as he or she performs the duties of the directorships. The director would be required to treat both companies equally, which might reduce his or her utility to both companies.[370] It has been recognised that one who is a director of two rival   **16–101**

---

[368] *In Plus Group Ltd v Pyke* [2002] EWCA Civ 370; [2002] 2 B.C.L.C. 201 CA, especially the judgment of Sedley LJ. Also see, recently, *Halcyon House Ltd v Baines* [2014] EWHC 2216 (QB) at [220]–[227]; and *First Subsea Ltd v Balltec Ltd* [2014] EWHC 866 (Ch) at [193]–[203] (appeal outstanding).

[369] As Brooke LJ pointed out, the *Mashonaland* case was a "startling" one, but the director there had never acted as a director of the claimant company nor attended a board meeting. As for the *In Plus Group* case, Lewison J in *Ultraframe (UK) Ltd v Fielding* [2005] EWHC 1638 suggested that the "no conflict" principle applied only to the powers a director has, so that a director excluded from exercising powers, even if wrongfully, was no longer subject to the principle—and certainly not at the suit of those who excluded him.

[370] For example, if the director came across a corporate opportunity, might he not have to offer it at the same time to both companies? Consent to acting as a director of competing companies would not of course involve consent to personal exploitation of any corporate opportunity the director might come across.

concerns is walking a tight-rope and at risk if he fails to deal fairly with both.[371] However, it should be noted that the legal problem here arises not so much from the no-conflict rule as from the fact that, by becoming a director of two companies, the director owes a core duty of loyalty to each.

In practice, it is in fact rare for a director to act for competing companies, except in the very problematic case where the director forms a new company for the purpose of competing with the current company when, as he plans, he ceases to be associated with it. The tension then is to balance the freedom of individuals to exploit their talents after their association with a company ceases, and the obligations of fiduciary loyalty intended to protect the company from misuse of the company's business opportunities or trade secrets. The company cannot, of course, prevent the departing director from applying his acquired general (and non-confidential) knowledge and experience of the company's line of business and its markets for the benefit of his new employer. And, moreover, simply forming an intention to leave the company and compete with it, and indeed taking preparatory steps towards that end but without actually engaging in any competitive activity, has been held not to constitute any breach of the director's duty of loyalty, however much it may seem to be lacking in merit.[372] But actual competitive activity (such as recruiting the company's employees to work in the new business) will not only be a breach of the no-conflict rule, but the director's core duty of good faith and fidelity will require disclosure of this threat to the company's business to its board, even if it involves the director disclosing his or her own wrongdoing.[373] The rigour of the fiduciary principles is, however, somewhat abated in those cases where the resignation of the directors has been forced upon him or her and the director has not actively sought to seduce the company's customers away or to exploit an opportunity belonging to it.[374] Beyond that, the courts seem to have adopted rather pragmatic solutions based on common sense and the merits of the case. This is an area in which context is all. So in *Foster Bryant Surveying Ltd v Bryant*,[375] Rix LJ summarised the existing cases as follows:

---

[371] See, per Lord Denning in *Scottish Co-op Wholesale Society v Meyer* [1959] A.C. 324 at 366–368 HL. This concerned an application under what is now the unfair prejudice provisions (on which see Ch.20, below) but Lord Denning obviously had doubts whether the *Mashonaland* case was still good law. See also *Bristol and West Building Society v Mothew* [1998] Ch. 1, 18 (per Millett LJ); and, more recently, *Global Energy Horizons Corp v Gray* [2012] EWHC 3703 (Ch).

[372] *Balston Ltd v Headline Filters Ltd* [1990] F.S.R. 385 at 412 (Falconer J); *Halcyon House Ltd v Baines* [2014] EWHC 2216 (QB).

[373] *British Midland Tool Ltd v Midland International Tooling Ltd* [2003] 2 B.C.L.C. 523 at [77]–[92]; *CMS Dolphin Ltd v Simonet* [2001] 2 B.C.L.C. 704. On the "duty to disclose" see above, para.16–45. Also see *Allfiled UK Ltd v Eltis* [2015] EWHC 1300 (Ch); *Habro Supplies Ltd v Hampton* [2014] EWHC 1781 (Ch); *First Subsea Ltd v Balltec Ltd* [2014] EWHC 866 (Ch).

[374] *Foster Bryant Surveying Ltd v Bryant* [2007] 2 B.C.L.C. 239 CA (no breach of duty where director, forced to resign, agreed in notice period on the initiative of a major customer to work for it after the notice ran out). The case contains a full discussion of the authorities. Also see *Allfiled UK Ltd v Eltis* [2015] EWHC 1300 (Ch); *Harbo Supplies Ltd v Hampton* [2014] EWHC 1781 (Ch); and *Towers v Premier Waste Management Ltd* [2011] EWCA Civ 923 CA.

[375] *Foster Bryant Surveying Ltd v Bryant* [2007] EWCA Civ 200; [2007] 2 B.C.L.C. 239 at [76]–[77].

"At one extreme (*In Plus Group v Pyke*[376]) the defendant is director in name only. At the other extreme, the director has planned his resignation having in mind the destruction of his company or at least the exploitation of its property in the form of business opportunities in which he is currently involved (*IDC*,[377] *Canaero*,[378] *Simonet*,[379] *British Midland Tool*[380]). In the middle are more nuanced cases which go both ways: in *Shepherds Investments v Walters*[381] the combination of disloyalty, active promotion of the planned business, and exploitation of a business opportunity, all while the directors remained in office, brought liability; in *Umanna*,[382] *Balston*,[383] and *Framlington*,[384] however, where the resignations were unaccompanied by disloyalty, there was no liability." (citations added)

After resignation, however, the director will be able to compete freely subject to any contractual restraints, the law relating to trade secrets and the rules relating to conflicts which arose before resignation (see s.170(2)).

Multiple directorships

The law relating to multiple directorships of a non-competing type is basically as set out above, though obviously a directorship of another non-competing company creates a lesser conflict problem. Indeed, in the case of a non-executive director of a company (i.e. one who is not bound to devote all his time and efforts to the company) taking a non-executive directorship in another, non-competing company can be said not to raise a conflict issue at all. However, it is no doubt good practice to obtain the consent of each board to the position, and in the case of an executive director such consent would seem to be necessary.

16–102

When conflicts of interest arise at a later date, for example, where the director is on the boards of two companies which are on opposite sides of a transaction, it is common for the director simply to withdraw from a role on the board of either company. Provided the articles make provision for this solution, the Act appears to relieve the director of liability in such a case, even liability arising under the core duty of loyalty.[385] In the absence of appropriate provisions in the articles, however, the director's position is precarious. If a person is a director of two non-competing companies but one makes a takeover bid for the other, how can the director discharge the core duty of loyalty to both in such a situation? Withdrawal may ensure equal treatment but can hardly be said to amount to a discharge of the duty to promote the success of the (each) company. In that situation, resignation from one of the involved companies may be the only possible step. However, where the conflict is less pressing, the strategy of withdrawal may seem appropriate.

---

[376] *In Plus Group v Pyke* [2002] EWCA Civ 370; [2002] 2 B.C.L.C. 201 CA.

[377] *Industrial Development Consultants Ltd v Cooley* [1972] 1 W.L.R. 443.

[378] *Canadian Aero Service Ltd v O'Malley* (1973) 40 D.L.R. (3d) 371.

[379] *CMS Dolphin Ltd v Simonet* [2001] 2 B.C.L.C. 704.

[380] *British Midland Tool Ltd v Midland International Tooling Ltd* [2003] 2 B.C.L.C. 523.

[381] *Shepherds Investments v Walters* [2006] EWHC 836 (Ch).

[382] *Island Export Finance Ltd v Umunna* [1986] B.C.L.C. 460.

[383] *Balston Ltd v Headline Filters Ltd* [1990] F.S.R. 385.

[384] *Framlington Group Plc v Anderson* [1995] 1 B.C.L.C. 475.

[385] 2006 Act s.180(4)(b): general duties not infringed "where the company's articles contain provisions for dealing with conflicts of interest" and the director acts in accordance with them. Again, it will be interesting to see what types of provision are thought acceptable by the institutional shareholders in respect of listed companies.

Approval by the board

16–103   We now reach discussion of the second of the two principal issues arising under s.175. Assuming the impugned transaction does involve an unacceptable conflict, whose permission must the director obtain for personal exploitation of it? Section 175 introduces the possibility of board approval, supplementing the orthodox common law doctrine of shareholder approval which we discuss below in relation to directors' duties as a whole.[386] Previously the common law had never condoned mere board approval in these circumstances,[387] and its use by the statute in this way is a major innovation.

By virtue of s.175(4)(b), authorisation may be given by the board itself for a conflict of interest on the part of one of their number, so that no breach of duty is committed.[388] The conflicted director him- or herself is excluded in the calculation of the quorum needed for the directors' meeting at which authorisation is given, and the director's vote is disregarded in determining whether board approval has been given (s.175(6)). Any "interested" director is also similarly excluded, but when a director can be said to be interested in another director's authorisation to take a corporate opportunity is left to the courts to decide. Any other director participating in the opportunity would clearly be interested, but how far the concept of interest goes beyond that is not clear. Notably, if there is no authorisation in advance of the taking of the opportunity, subsequent ratification of the director's breach of duty by the company requires a decision of the shareholders.[389]

Nevertheless, it might be asked whether this is a wise innovation. On the one hand, a requirement of shareholder approval is a heavy one, and may deter directors from proceeding with courses of action which, if asked, shareholders would approve, thus imposing unnecessary restrictions on directors' entrepreneurial activities. On the other hand, the risk with board approval is that, although the approving directors may have no interest in the particular case, they may have an underlying interest in a culture of easy conflict approvals ("you scratch my back and I'll scratch yours"). No doubt, such conduct would be a breach of the other duties imposed on directors, discussed above, but such breaches may be difficult to detect and to prove in court.

---

[386] See below, para.16–117.

[387] See *Benson v Heathorn* (1842) 1 Y. & C.C.C. 326, per Knight-Bruce VC at 341–342; and *Imperial Mercantile Credit Association v Coleman* (1871) L.R. 6 Ch. App. 558 at 567–568 CA, per Hatherley LC. As a matter of principle, it might be asked why the board, acting properly as the company (so with the conflicted directors undoubtedly excluded from voting), could not give such informed consent: see S. Worthington, "Corporate Governance: Remedying and Ratifying Directors' Breaches" (2000) 116 L.Q.R. 638. The new statutory rule adopts precisely this approach.

[388] Nor is any transaction or arrangement with the company liable to be set aside on the grounds that the shareholders have not given their approval: s.180(1). This provision applies to conflicts of interest generally under s.175, although the present discussion relates to corporate opportunities.

[389] Section 239(2)(a), on which see below at para.16–117. It is submitted that the standard use of the word "authorise" in company law is to refer to ex ante permission, whilst ratification refers to permission given after the breach. It is clear that the CLR's proposal, on which s.175 is based, contemplated the non-involved members of the board giving permission only in advance. See Final 1, p.346, cl. 6 where the phrase adopted is "the use [of the corporate opportunity] has been proposed to and authorised by the board".

It may be for this sort of reason that the statute allows or requires the company's **16–104** constitution (notably the articles) to have some control over whether uninvolved directors can authorise conflicts of interest. In the case of private companies, the board can act as the authorising body unless something in the company's articles or other parts of its constitution restricts the board from so acting. In the case of public or charitable[390] companies, the company's constitution must positively empower the directors to act in this way, and the articles might (but need not) then regulate in further detail the scope or manner of exercise of the authorisation power. Compliance with the articles would in either case be a pre-condition for the valid exercise of the directors' powers of authorisation (s.178(5)). The more restrictive rule applied to public companies reflects the fact that their shareholding bodies tend to be more dispersed than those in private companies and their collective action problems are accordingly greater. Hence, in public companies the burden of introducing the rule of director authorisation is placed on those who want it (normally the directors themselves) rather than the burden of removing it on those who do not want it (presumably the shareholders).[391] However, the statute, surprisingly, does not adopt a proposal of the CLR that board authorisations should be reported to the shareholders in the subsequent directors' report.[392]

We shall see below that, in relation to shareholder approval, the common law developed a doctrine that certain breaches of duty are not capable of approval by the company, the case of *Cook v Deeks*[393] being a leading authority in this area. Does such a restriction apply to authorisation given by the independent members of the board? There is no mention of such a restriction in s.176 and, since independent board approval is an invention of the statute, it would seem that this limitation cannot be imported into the board's power of authorisation. Is this surprising? There are two controls over board authorisation which do not exist in relation to shareholder authorisation at common law. First, interested directors are excluded by the statute from voting on a board resolution, whereas at common law interested directors were entitled to vote as shareholders to authorise the taking of a corporate opportunity (the modern statutory rule on shareholder voting is now different[394]). The exclusion of interested directors from voting might be thought to reduce the danger of biased corporate decisions or unfair treatment of minority shareholders, although it does not eliminate it. Secondly, the non-involved voting directors, unlike shareholders, are subject to fiduciary duties when exercising their votes. The core duty of loyalty requires directors to give priority to the promotion of the success of the company when deciding

---

[390] 2006 Act s.181(2)(b).

[391] Of course, the provision may be inserted in the company's articles upon incorporation, but at least those who become its shareholders then know what they are letting themselves in for. In the case of subsequent amendments to the articles it will be interesting to see what sorts of board approval provisions institutional investors are prepared to accept in the articles of listed companies.

[392] CLR, Final Report I, para.3.25.

[393] *Cook v Deeks* [1916] 1 A.C. 554 PC.

[394] In relation to ratification, s.239(3),(4) now excludes interested directors from voting as shareholders, but it seems they are still entitled to do so on authorisations. On ratification, see para.16–118, below.

whether to authorise, for example, the taking of a corporate opportunity, though such a breach might be difficult to prove.[395]

Where the board does not have approval power (because it is explicitly removed by the articles in a private company, or not granted in a public or charitable company, or not practically possible because all the directors are conflicted), then approval will need to be obtained in accordance with any specific rules set out in the company's articles, or in accordance with the common law default rule which requires the approval of the shareholders in general meeting, as discussed below.

A conceptual issue

16–105   Section 175 is based on the existence of a conflict of duty and interest (or a conflict of duties).[396] In the area of corporate opportunity, this conflict arises because of the conflict between the interest of the director in personal exploitation of the opportunity and his or her duty to offer the opportunity to the company (or pursue it on behalf of the company). The duty to offer the opportunity to the company arises because it has been characterised as a corporate one: that is why the identification of the criteria for making the opportunity a corporate one is so central to this body of law, and why the uninhibited approach of the most recent cases seems questionable.[397]

However, one can ask, what is the nature of this duty? It is generally accepted that, if the director does not wish to exploit the opportunity personally, no breach of s.175 arises because there is then no personal interest conflicting with the director's duty to the company. In other words, a director who does nothing can never be found liable under s.175. Might the director, however, be liable for breach of some other duty, for example, the duty of care or good faith? In principle, this possibility exists. In the case of the core duty of loyalty the director would have to form the view that the promotion of the success of the company required the opportunity to be communicated to the company, and then fail to do so. The duty of care seems a more promising avenue of approach because it is based on an objective test. However, it would not necessarily be correct to infer from the existence of a duty for the purposes of the no-conflict rule a duty for the purposes of the duty of care. The courts have traditionally developed far more demanding standards of loyalty than of care and that approach may continue under the statute.[398]

---

[395]   cf. the discussion of *Regentcrest Plc v Cohen* [2001] 2 B.C.L.C. 80 in para.16–41, above.

[396]   This notwithstanding that the wording of the section itself pitches the conflict as one between the director's and the company's *interests*, not the duty of one and the interests of the other. This, it is suggested, does not evince an intention to alter the underlying premises of the common law. Rather, the director's duty is seen to be to act in the interests of the company (at common law, or, under s.171, to act to promote the success of the company—see above, paras 16–37 et seq.).

[397]   See above, para.16–89.

[398]   It is difficult to believe that the directors in *Regal*, having concluded that the company could not finance the project, would have been held liable in negligence for not putting additional money of their own into the company so that it could take up the opportunity, whereas in *Cooley* it might be said that failing to follow up for the company an opportunity of the very type the director had been hired to pursue would seem to constitute a plausible case of negligence.

Remedies

The detail of the remedies available to the company for breach by directors of **16–106** their duties to the company are dealt with later,[399] but it is useful at this stage to note their broad outline in relation to the conflicts cases, as their key characteristic differs fundamentally from the remedies so far encountered. For all breaches of directors' duties, if discovered at the planning stage, it is true that the court may be persuaded to order an injunction to prevent the plan being implemented. But, once the breach is committed, we have seen that by and large the remedy has been compensation to the company for the loss thereby caused, whether that compensation is assessed using common law or equitable rules (the former for the duty of care, it is suggested; the latter otherwise).

The only exception so far has been with the self-dealing rule, where the orthodox remedy is rescission of the contract,[400] not compensation for loss or an account of profits.[401] In these cases, as with all the "no-conflict" duties here, the aim of the remedy is to strip the defaulting director of the benefits of his or her disloyal distraction from undeviating focus on the company's interests, but the courts have typically declined to value the contract between the company and the director, and have therefore required the remedy to be solely by way of putting the parties back into their pre-contracting status.

With the conflicts of interests cases just considered, however, this difficult valuation problem does not arise. Where the conflict arises not from any self-dealing, but typically from the director's misuse of the company's property, information or opportunity, then, too, the remedy aims to strip the defaulting fiduciary of the profits of his or her disloyal activities. If the disloyal venture is not profitable, then it follows that the company does not have a remedy under this head; if it is profitable, the director must account for the profit. This seems straightforward. The point to note, however, is that the focus of these no-conflict remedies is profit-stripping; the company is not entitled, under this head, to recover losses: to recover those, the company must, and very often can on the same facts, sue its disloyal fiduciary for some other failure, be it failure to act within powers, or breach of the duty of good faith or care and skill, provided it can prove the elements of those quite different claims.[402]

---

[399] See below, para.16–109.

[400] With all the limitations inherent in that option if the company is no longer able to return the property acquired from the director. We noted earlier that the option of "pecuniary rescission", which, while requiring the court to value the assets transferred, might enable better justice to be done between the parties. This is, effectively, what the statute allows in those cases governed by statutory provisions. Indeed, where the statute has intervened, the remedies are both more varied and more extensive.

[401] Unless the facts allow reliance on the statutory remedies: see paras 16–73 and 16–83, above.

[402] For example, if the director has diverted the company's property into a loss-making conflicting opportunity, then there will be no account of profits for breach of the conflict rule (there are no profits), but the director may be compelled to restore the company's property which has been used in an unauthorised fashion, or to compensate the company for its negligent or unfaithful use.

DUTY NOT TO ACCEPT BENEFITS FROM THIRD PARTIES

The scope of section 176

16–107   Section 176 provides that a director "must not accept a benefit from a third party conferred by reason of (a) his being a director, or (b) his doing (or not doing) anything as a director".[403] A "third party" means a person other than the company, an associated body corporate or a person acting on behalf of such companies. The connection of this rule with the no-conflict principle is underlined by the provision that the duty is not infringed if the benefit "cannot reasonably be regarded as likely to give rise to a conflict of interest" (s.176(3)).[404] This being so, it may be wondered what the purpose of s.176 is, for could not the situations it deals with be handled under the general no-conflict section (s.175)? The answer, and it is an important one, is that there is no provision in s.176 for authorisation to be given by uninvolved directors for the receipt of third-party benefits. The risk of such benefits distorting the proper performance of a director's duties is so high that it is rightly thought to be proper to require authorisation from the shareholders in general meeting (even though that turns the rule into a near-ban on the receipt of third-party benefits). Although the point is not expressly dealt with in s.176, the availability at common law of shareholder authorisation is preserved by s.180(4)(a).[405] Finally, the fact that s.175 applies to a situation does not prevent s.176 being relied upon as well, i.e. the sections are cumulative rather than mutually exclusive in their operation.[406]

The common law termed such payments "bribes", although that seems a misnomer as it is enough at common law that there has been the payment of money or the conferment of another benefit upon an agent whom the payer knows is acting as an agent for a principal in circumstances where the payment has not been disclosed to the principal.[407] There is no need to show that the payer of the bribe acted with a corrupt motive; that the agent's mind was actually affected by the bribe; that the payer knew or suspected that the agent would conceal the payment from the principal; or that the principal suffered any loss or that the transaction was in some way unfair. None of these matters seem to be requirements of s.176 either. Thus, the term "third party benefits" is more appropriate than the term "bribe".

On the other hand, so far as true bribes are concerned, enormous changes have been introduced by the Bribery Act 2010, as we have seen. This Act was designed

---

[403] Benefits from associated companies are excluded as are benefits received by the director from a company which supplies his or her services to the company: s.177(2) and (3).

[404] This might be contrasted with the predominant view under the earlier common law rules that the "no profit" rule (which would catch such benefits) did not necessarily involve a conflict of duty and interest, although of course in practice it very often might: see the earlier discussion of *Regal (Hastings) Ltd v Gulliver* at para.16–89.

[405] "The general duties have effect subject to any rule of law enabling the company to give authority for anything to be done by the directors that would otherwise be a breach of duty."

[406] "Except as otherwise provided, more than one of the general duties may apply": s.179.

[407] *Industries and General Mortgage Co Ltd v Lewis* [1949] 2 All E.R. 573; *Taylor v Walker* [1958] 1 Lloyd's Rep. 490; *Logicrose Ltd v Southend United FC Ltd* [1988] 1 W.L.R. 1257. Also see, recently, *Pullan v Wilson* [2014] EWHC 126 (Ch); [2014] W.T.L.R. 669; *FHR European Ventures LLP v Cedar Capital Partners LLC* [2014] UKSC 45; [2015] A.C. 250 SC.

to bring the UK in line with international norms on anti-corruption legislation. It makes it a criminal offence to give or receive a bribe, but, most significantly, it also introduces a corporate offence of failing to prevent bribery.[408]

Remedies

At common law the remedies available in the case of third party benefits were extensive. These common law remedies, so far as they give the company remedies against the defaulting director, continue to apply by virtue of s.178, despite the change of nomenclature in s.176. Although that section imposes a duty only on the director, the common law also imposed obligations on (and provided remedies against) the third party, and these are presumably unaffected. Thus, where such a benefit has been paid to a director, the company may rescind the contract between it and the third party (provided the third party knew the recipient was a director of the company), and it matters not whether the payer is the third party or the third party's agent.[409] In addition, or instead, both the third party and the director are jointly and severally liable in damages in fraud to the company, the amount of the recovery depending upon proof of actual loss.[410] Alternatively, the company may hold both the director and the third party jointly and severally liable to pay the amount of the benefit to the company as money had and received to its use, this liability being naturally not dependent upon proof of loss. Against the director, such a personal liability to account is straightforward: the bribe is akin to a secret profit made out the director's position. Against the third party it is a rather peculiar remedy, though one which seems to be established.[411] However, the company must choose between the remedies of damages and account, the choice no doubt depending on the amount of the provable loss which the company suffered as a result of the bribe, though it need not do so until judgment.[412]

In *Attorney-General for Hong Kong v Reid*,[413] the Privy Council took the further step of recognising a proprietary remedy by way of a constructive trust in

16–108

---

[408] See above, para.7–46.

[409] *Taylor v Walker* [1958] 1 Lloyd's Rep 490; *Shipway v Broadwood* [1899] 1 Q.B. 369 CA. There is not space here to explore the complications which may arise when the payer is also the director of a company and makes unauthorised use of that company's assets to effect the bribe. See also *Airbus Operations Ltd v Withey* [2014] EWHC 1126 (QB) in relation to the position of employees.

[410] *Mahesan v Malaysia Government Officers' Co-operative Housing Society Ltd* [1979] A.C. 374 at 381 PC. The cause of action appears to lie in fraud.

[411] *Mahesan v Malaysia Government Officers' Co-operative Housing Society Ltd* [1979] A.C. 374 at 383.

[412] *Mahesan v Malaysia Government Officers' Co-operative Housing Society Ltd* [1979] A.C. 374; and *United Australia Ltd v Barclays Bank Ltd* [1941] A.C. 1 HL. Where the briber is or acts on behalf of a supplier, the damages are unlikely to be less than the amount of the bribe, but could be more.

[413] *Attorney-General for Hong Kong v Reid* [1994] 1 A.C. 324 PC; declining to follow *Metropolitan Bank v Heiron* (1880) 5 Ex. D. 319 CA; and *Lister & Co v Stubbs* (1890) 45 Ch. D. 1 CA. The decision was controversial among academic writers but was mostly followed by the courts, although see *Sinclair Investments (UK) Ltd v Versailles Trade Finance Ltd (In Administrative Receivership)* [2011] EWCA Civ 347 CA. See the judgment of Lawrence Collins J in *Daraydan International Ltd v Solland International Ltd* [2005] Ch.119; *Sinclair Investments* (ibid.); and *FHR European Ventures*

favour of the company (or other principal) against the director (or other agent) in respect of the bribe. The significance of this remedy being available, in addition to the personal remedy to account, is that the company may then make further tracing claims to any investment profits made by the defaulting director through the use of the original benefit (whilst falling back on the personal claim if the investment has been unprofitable); the company may also follow the benefit (and its traceable substitutes) into the hands of third parties who are not bona fide purchaser for value; and, importantly, all these proprietary claims will prevail over the claims of the unsecured creditors in the event of the director's (or the third party's) insolvency. After a great deal of academic and judicial debate, the Privy Council's conclusions in this case have now been confirmed by the Supreme Court in *FHR European Ventures LLP v Cedar Capital Partners LLC*,[414] as discussed in more detail below.[415]

REMEDIES FOR BREACH OF DUTY

16–109   As we have already noted, although there is a statutory statement of the general duties owed by directors, the remedies for breach of these duties is not similarly stated. Rather, s.178 simply provides that "the consequences of a breach (or threatened breach) of ss.171 to 177 are the same as would apply if the corresponding common law rule or equitable duty applied"; and that the duties contained in the sections (other than s.174) are "enforceable in the same way as any other fiduciary duty owed to a company by its directors". It should be noted that s.178 applies only to the general duties laid out in ss.171–177, not to the provisions to be found in Ch.3 of Pt 10 dealing with disclosure of interests in existing transactions (for which the statute provides only criminal sanctions)[416]; nor to the provisions contained in Chs 4 or 4A of Pt 10, requiring shareholder approval for certain transactions with directors, for which a self-contained statutory civil code of remedies is provided.[417] It should also be noted that the second proposition in s.178 is not applied to the duty to exercise reasonable care, skill and diligence, in line with the modern view that this is not a fiduciary duty. The remedy for that breach is normally confined to damages.[418]

We have sought to indicate the principal remedies available for each of the duties as we have gone along. Nevertheless, it may be useful to bring them together here, since it is important to appreciate both the areas of overlap and the areas of difference. The main remedies available are: (a) injunction or declaration; (b) damages or compensation; (c) restoration of the company's property; (d) rescission of the contract; (e) account of profits; and (f) summary dismissal.

LLP v Cedar Capital Partners LLC [2013] EWCA Civ 17 CA; affirmed [2014] UKSC 45; [2015] A.C. 250 SC for a review of both the subsequent court decisions and the academic writings. Now see para.16–115.
[414] *FHR European Ventures LLP v Cedar Capital Partners LLC* [2014] UKSC 45; [2015] A.C. 250 SC.
[415] See below, para.16–115.
[416] See above, para.16–66.
[417] See above, paras 16–67 et seq.
[418] See above, para.16–20.

(a)   Injunction or declaration

These are primarily employed where the breach is threatened but has not yet   **16–110**
occurred.[419] If action can be taken in time, this is obviously the most satisfactory
course. However, if the remedy is to be used effectively by an individual
shareholder, suing derivatively,[420] he or she will need to be well-informed about
the proposals of the board, which in all but the smallest companies will not often
be the case. An injunction may also be appropriate where the breach has already
occurred but is likely to continue, or if some of its consequences can thereby be
avoided.[421]

(b)   Damages or compensation

Damages are the appropriate remedy for breach of a common law duty of care, or   **16–111**
non-compliance with the terms of the director's contract or the company's
constitution; compensation is the analogous equitable remedy for breach of the
(originally) equitable duty of good faith (acting to promote the success of the
company) or acting for improper purposes. In practice, the common law/equity
distinction has become blurred,[422] and probably no useful purpose is served by
seeking to keep them distinct.[423] Both are inevitably personal remedies. All the
directors who participate in the breach[424] are jointly and severally liable with the
usual rights of contribution inter se.[425]

(c)   "Restoration" of property

Although the directors are not trustees of the company's property (which is held   **16–112**
by the company itself as a separate legal person), we have noted at a number of
points in this chapter that the courts sometimes treat directors as if they were such
trustees. In particular, where a director disposes of the company's property in
unauthorised ways, and in consequence the company's property comes into his or
her own hands, the director will be treated as a constructive trustee of the

---

[419] *United Pan-Europe Communications NV v Deutsche Bank AG* [2000] 2 B.C.L.C. 461 CA.

[420] See Ch.17.

[421] For example, to enjoin the delivery up of confidential documents improperly taken away by a former director: *Measures Bros v Measures* [1910] 2 Ch. 248 CA; *Cranleigh Precision Engineering Ltd v Bryant* [1965] 1 W.L.R. 1293; *Allfiled UK Ltd v Ellis* [2015] EWHC 1300 (Ch).

[422] This is especially so where the "wrong" involves a fiduciary—such as a director—failing to comply with contractual mandates. By way of illustration, see the latest authorities on quantifying equitable compensation: *Libertarian Investment Ltd v Hall* (2013) 16 HKCFAR 681 Hong Kong Court of Final Appeal at [84]–[96] (Ribeiro PJ) and [166]–[175] (Lord Millett NPJ); and *AIB Group (UK) Plc v Mark Redler & Co Solicitors* [2014] UKSC 58; [2015] A.C. 1503 SC at [47]–[77] (Lord Toulson JSC) and [90]–[138] (Lord Reed JSC).

[423] Although see the paragraph immediately following.

[424] Either actively or by subsequent acquiescence in it: *Re Lands Allotment Co* [1894] 1 Ch. 616 CA. Merely protesting will not necessarily disprove acquiescence: *Joint Stock Discount Co v Brown* (1869) L.R. 8 Eq. 381.

[425] Civil Liability (Contribution) Act 1978. The application of the principle of joint and several liability is discussed more fully below at paras 22–31 et seq. in relation to auditors.

property for the company.[426] This means that the property, or its proceeds, can be recovered by way of proprietary claim against the director, so far as traceable[427]; and that the company's claim against its defaulting director will have priority over any competing claims of the director's unsecured creditors (since the property is the company's property, not the director's). The doctrinal underpinnings of these conclusions are rarely unpicked, but they must surely rely more on analysing the claim as a profitable breach of the conflicts rules (the conflict being obvious),[428] for which proprietary disgorgement of the gains is available,[429] rather than analysing the claim as merely an unauthorised (and therefore potentially void) contract and indeed one where the identity of the counterparty is irrelevant.[430] Where these proprietary disgorgement claims are available against the defaulting directors, they can be enormously valuable to the company.

Alternatively, if the director no longer has the company's assets or their traceable proceeds, or if their use did not generate a profit, or if the company's assets were initially, and without authority, paid away to third parties rather than to the director,[431] then the company may, in the alternative, sue the director for compensation for the losses suffered by the company as a result of the director's initial unauthorised disposition of the company's property. One aspect of this is straightforward: the remedy is necessarily personal, and so the company's claim against its defaulting director will rank equally with the claims of the directors' general creditors.

But beyond that, this remedy has proved enormously controversial. It was long argued that the claim in issue was for "restoration of property" (albeit in money), and not for compensation. This had the enormous advantage, so it was said, that the claim was not dependent upon proof of loss on the part of the company, as a damages claim would be.[432] It was further suggested that it then followed that if, for example, £1 million was paid out by the director in the unauthorised purchase of X when it should have been paid out in the authorised purchase of Y,[433] then the appropriate remedy was effectively for the director to restore to the company

---

[426] *JJ Harrison (Properties) Ltd v Harrison* [2002] 1 B.C.L.C. 162 CA For an early recognition of the principle see *Re Forest of Dean Coal Co* (1878) 10 Ch. D. 450.

[427] For a recent discussion on the use of the tracing remedy, see *Relfo Ltd (In Liquidation) v Varsani* [2014] EWCA Civ 360 CA; [2015] 1 B.C.L.C. 14.

[428] Whether under s.177 (if the director has contracted with the company) or under s.175 (if not).

[429] See para.16–62 (where the self-dealing transaction is voidable); and paras 16–106 and 16–108 et seq. (on accounting for gains derived from other unauthorised conflicts).

[430] See, e.g. the void remuneration contract in *Guinness v Saunders* [1990] 2 A.C. 662 HL. Although the proprietary nature of the remedy was not in issue here (there being no insolvency risk), *Westdeutsche Landesbank Girozentrale v Islington LBC* [1996] A.C. 669 HL, is authority for it being unavailable to reverse a void contract, at least where the defendant is not a fiduciary. Although against this, see the trustee case, *Foskett v McKeown* [2001] 1 A.C. 102 HL, where the proprietary claim to stolen trust funds was considered to be "part of our law of property" (Lord Millett), not dependent on either unjust enrichment (the HL holding so explicitly) or on fiduciary disloyalty (implicitly, as the suggestion was not raised).

[431] The company may also have claims against the third parties: see below, paras 16–134 et seq.

[432] The cases typically cited are *Bishopsgate Investment Management Ltd (In Liquidation) v Maxwell (No.2)* [1994] 1 W.L.R. 261 at 265a–266a (Hoffmann LJ); *Bairstow v Queens Moat Houses Plc* [2001] 2 B.C.L.C. 531 at [49]–[54] CA (Robert Walker LJ); *Re Loquitur* [2003] S.T.C. 1394 at [135]–[137] (Etherton J); *Revenue and Customs Commissioners v Holland, In Re Paycheck Services 3 Ltd* [2010] 1 W.L.R. 2793 at [96]–[98] (Rimer LJ) and at [46], [48], [49] (Lord Hope).

[433] Or, alternatively, should have been retained by the company as part of its own assets.

the misappropriated £1 million.[434] By contrast, if the remedy were simply compensation, then the director would be required to restore to the company what effectively it *should* have had absent the breach, i.e. Y, if possible, or the monetary value of Y.[435] Moreover, this former claim to a "restoration" remedy was regarded as being available in addition to, and by way of an alternative option to, the usual compensation remedy. The effect was thus to enable a company to claim *either* £1 million (adjusted, as noted above) if the authorised investment had crashed, *or* Y (or, more accurately, it or its value, again adjusted) if the proper investment was a winner. This gave the company a "heads I win, tails you lose" remedial menu.

In fact few cases went so far, and we now seem to have reached the preferable and far more defensible position that choice between "£1 million" or "Y" is only available when the recipient of the £1 million is the defaulting director him- or herself. In these circumstances, the claim to the £1 million is better viewed as *not* for "restoration" as a self-standing option, but as a claim for disgorgement made out under one or other of the various conflicts rules. Otherwise, however, the company's claim is merely one for compensation, and—equitable or otherwise—this compensation is directed solely at reversing loss, not at some sort of free-standing "restoration" where no loss (or some far smaller loss) has been suffered.[436]

(d) Avoidance of contracts

An agreement between the director and the company that breaches the no-conflict rules may be avoided, provided that the company has done nothing to indicate an intention to ratify the agreement after finding out about the breach of duty,[437] that restitutio in integrum is possible,[438] and that the rights of bona fide third parties have not supervened.[439] It might now be doubted how strong a bar restitutio in

16–113

---

[434] Less an allowance for the value of X, being the benefit the company did receive.

[435] Again with the company giving allowance for what it had in fact received, being the value of X.

[436] See the detailed analyses in *Libertarian Investment Ltd v Hall* (2013) 16 HKCFAR 681 Hong Kong Court of Final Appeal at [84]–[96] (Ribeiro PJ) and [166]–[175] (Lord Millett NPJ); and *AIB Group (UK) Plc v Mark Redler & Co Solicitors* [2014] UKSC 58; [2015] A.C. 1503 SC at [47]–[77] (Lord Toulson JSC) and [90]–[138] (Lord Reed JSC). Also see *HLC Environmental Projects Ltd* [2013] EWHC 2876 (Ch) at [136]–[145]; *Madoff Securities International Ltd v Raven* [2013] EWHC 3147 (Comm) at [292]–[293], [296]–[306].

[437] *Lagunas Nitrate Co v Lagunas Syndicate* [1899] 2 Ch. 392 CA, a case concerning promoters' liability, but the operative principles are the same. The right to rescind will be lost if the company elects not to rescind or is too late to do so: *Re Ambrose Lake Tin Co* (1880) 11 Ch. D. 390 CA; *Re Cape Breton Co* (1885) 29 Ch. D. 795 CA (affirmed sub nom. *Cavendish Bentinck v Fenn* (1887) 12 App. Cas. 652 HL); *Ladywell Mining Co v Brookes* (1887) 35 Ch. D. 400 CA; *Gluckstein v Barnes* [1900] A.C. 240 HL; *Re Lady Forrest (Murchison) Gold Mine* [1901] 1 Ch. 582; *Burland v Earle* [1902] A.C. 83 PC; *Jacobus Marler v Marler* (1913) 85 L.J.P.C. 167n; *Hely-Hutchinson v Brayhead Ltd* [1968] 1 Q.B. 549 CA; *Salt v Stratstone Specialist Ltd t/a Stratstone Cadillac Newcastle* [2015] EWCA Civ 745 CA.

[438] *Erlanger v New Sombrero Phosphate Co* (1878) 3 App. Cas. 1218 at 1278 (Lord Blackburn); *Bentinck v Fenn* (1887) 12 App. Cas. 652, where rescission was not possible because the company had already re-sold the properties.

[439] *Transvaal Lands Co v New Belgium (Transvaal) Land & Development Co* [1914] 2 Ch. 488 CA.

integrum really is, given the wide powers the court has to order financial adjustments when directing rescission.[440]

Equally, a contract entered into by the company in breach of the directors' duties to exercise their powers for a proper purpose is in principle avoidable by the company, but again subject to the considerations noted above and the rights of good faith third parties.[441] Where, however, the directors have simply acted without power, the contract will be void, not voidable.[442]

(e) Accounting for profits: disgorgement of disloyal gains

16–114   This liability arises as a response to profitable contracts or arrangements between the director and a third party which are held to be in breach of the conflict of interest rules[443] or the duty not to accept benefits from third parties.[444] In such cases there can be no question of rescinding the contract at the instance of the company, since the company is not party to it, and an account of profits to strip the defaulting fiduciary of any benefits will be the sole remedy.

As we have seen, recovery of the profit by the company is not conditional on proof of any loss suffered by the company; the profit is recoverable not as damages or compensation but because the company is entitled to call upon the disloyal director to account to it.[445] All the profits made by the director[446] and attributable to the breach must be disgorged, but not those attributable to other sources.[447] This is sometimes ameliorated in the case of trustees, but only where

---

[440] This is certainly the case when fraud is involved and perhaps even when it is not: *Erlanger v New Sombrero Phosphate Co* (1873) 3 App. Cas.1218 HL; *Spence v Crawford* [1939] 3 All E.R. 271 HL; *Armstrong v Jackson* [1917] 2 K.B. 822; *O'Sullivan v Management Agency and Music Ltd* [1985] Q.B. 428 CA; *Salt v Stratstone Specialist Ltd t/a Stratstone Cadillac Newcastle* [2015] EWCA Civ 745 CA.

[441] *Hogg v Cramphorn* [1967] Ch. 254; *Bamford v Bamford* [1970] Ch. 212 CA; *Criterion Properties Plc v Stratford UK Properties LLC* [2004] B.C.C. 570 HL.

[442] *Guiness Plc v Saunders* [1990] 2 A.C. 663 HL. A void contract is much more threatening to the position of third parties, though in the case of third parties contracting with companies the provisions of s.40 (above, para.7–9 et seq.) may save the day.

[443] For example, in relation to the use of corporate information or opportunity discussed above, paras 16–87 et seq.

[444] See the "bribe" cases above, para.16–107, and also the secret/undisclosed commission case of *Imperial Mercantile Credit Association v Coleman* (1873) L.R. 6 H.L. 189, where the defaulting director proposed to the company a contract from the execution of which he stood to derive a secondary undisclosed profit. Also see, recently, *Airbus Operations Ltd v Withey* [2014] EWHC 1126 (QB).

[445] *Murad v Al-Saraj* [2005] EWCA Civ 959 CA.

[446] In general the director is not jointly liable for profits made by others (e.g. the company with which the director is associated, although such third parties may themselves have secondary liability, see below, para.16–134): *Regal (Hastings) Ltd v Gulliver* [1967] 2 A.C. 134; *Ultraframe (UK) Ltd v Fielding* [2005] EWHC 1638 (Ch) at [1550]–[1576], cf. *CMS Dolphin Ltd v Simonet* [2001] 2 B.C.L.C. 704. By contrast, a director may be jointly liable for the whole of the profits made by his partnership as a result of his breach: *Imperial Mercantile Credit Association v Coleman* (1873) L.R. 6 H.L. 189. Also see, more recently, *Airbus Operations Ltd v Withey* [2014] EWHC 1126 (QB) at [451]–[465]; and *Northampton Regional Livestock Centre Co Ltd v Cowling* [2015] EWCA Civ 651 CA.

[447] This can sometimes raise nice questions: *Murad v Al-Saraj* [2005] EWCA Civ 959 CA; *Warman International Ltd v Dwyer* (1995) 182 CLR 544 Aust HC (account of profits limited to first two years

their bona fides are not in question; then the courts have sometimes permitted the trustee an allowance in the accounting process to provide a reasonable remuneration (including a profit element) for the work carried out in effecting the profitable deal.[448] The fact that the director could have made the same profit without breaching his or her duty[449] or that the company, if asked, would have given its consent to the director's activities,[450] is irrelevant.

Moreover, if the disloyal gain is identifiable in the director's hands, then the **16–115** director will hold that asset on constructive trust for the company; in short, the disgorgement remedy is proprietary.[451] This conclusion has been confirmed in England only relatively recently,[452] even though it has long been the position in other common law jurisdictions.[453] In those jurisdictions, however, the courts claim to have a discretion as to whether or not to award a constructive trust on the facts before the court: they have what is described as a "remedial constructive trust", while the English courts insist that the constructive trust is "institutional" only, so that if the facts support its existence then there is not discretion in the court to deny it to a successful claimant. This latter approach seems preferable, and indeed the practice in other jurisdictions—despite their asserted flexibility—is overwhelmingly the same. The constructive trust, being proprietary, carries with it significant advantages.[454] There seems little merit in asserting that these follow from the wrong, and then denying the claimant their benefits, usually just when they are most needed.[455]

---

of operation of diverted business opportunity). Notice, too, the argument that the causal test may either *be* different, or at least have different outcomes, when applied to a third party "dishonest assistant" rather than a director/fiduciary: *Novoship (UK) Ltd v Mikhaylyuk* [2015] Q.B. 499 at [111]–[115] CA.

[448] *Phipps v Boardman* [1967] 2 A.C. 46 HL; *O'Sullivan v Management Agency and Music Ltd* [1985] Q.B. 428 CA. In *Guinness v Saunders* [1990] 2 A.C. 663 their lordships were very reluctant to entertain the possibility of an allowance for work done, but in the event the action was not decided as a breach of the conflict rules, but as a contract not properly authorised according to the terms of the articles, so the defaulting director was required to return the company's property, not account for profits made. See above, fn.246. The same hard line was taken in *Quarter Master UK Ltd v Pyke* [2004] EWHC 1815 (Ch); [2005] 1 B.C.L.C. 245 at [76]–[77].

[449] *Murad v Al-Saraj* [2005] EWCA Civ 959 at [67] CA (Arden LJ).

[450] *Regal (Hastings) Ltd v Gulliver* [1967] 2 A.C. 134 at 150 (Lord Russell); *Murad v Al-Saraj* [2005] EWCA Civ 959 at [71] CA (Arden LJ).

[451] *FHR European Ventures LLP v Cedar Capital Partners LLC* [2014] UKSC 45; [2015] A.C. 250 SC. Applying this analysis, see *FHR European Ventures LLP v Mankarious* [2016] EWHC 359 (Ch).

[452] The proprietary approach had been taken in *Attorney General of Hong Kong v Reid* [1994] 1 A.C. 324 PC, the court there declining to follow *Metropolitan Bank v Heiron* (1880) 5 Ex. D. 319 CA; and *Lister & Co v Stubbs* (1890) 45 Ch. D. 1 CA. The decision was controversial amongst academic writers but was mostly followed by the courts, although see *Sinclair Investments (UK) Ltd v Versailles Trade Finance Ltd (In Administrative Receivership)* [2011] EWCA Civ 347 CA. For a review of both the subsequent court decisions and the academic writings, see Lawrence Collins J in *Daraydan International Ltd v Solland International Ltd* [2005] Ch. 119; *Sinclair Investments* (ibid.); and *FHR European Ventures LLP v Cedar Capital Partners LLC* [2013] EWCA Civ 17 CA; affirmed [2014] UKSC 45; [2015] A.C. 250 SC.

[453] *FHR European Ventures LLP v Cedar Capital Partners LLC* [2014] UKSC 45; [2015] A.C. 250 SC at [45] (Lord Neuberger PSC). *Chan v Zacharia* (1984) 154 C.L.R. 178 Aust HC, is typically cited.

[454] These were noted earlier at para.16–112.

[455] One of the rare examples where the court's jurisdiction to do just this was both asserted and utilised is *Grimaldi v Chameleon Mining NL (No.2)* [2012] FCAFC 6, see especially [583]. But a

(f) Summary dismissal

16–116 The right which an employer has at common law to dismiss an employee who has been guilty of serious misconduct has no application to the director as such, not being an employee.[456] However, it could be an effective sanction against executive directors and other officers of the company, since it may involve loss of livelihood rather than simply of position and directors' fees. However, it tends to be used only in the clearest cases. Generally, the company prefers the director to "go quietly", which means that his or her entitlements on departure are calculated as if the contract were unimpeachable, even if there is scope for arguing that the company has the unilateral right to remove the director for breach of contract.[457]

SHAREHOLDER APPROVAL OR "WHITEWASH" OF SPECIFIC BREACHES OF DUTY

16–117 It is a normal feature of the law, including the law relating to directors, that those to whom duties are owed may release those who owe the duties from their legal obligations. Thus the company ought in principle to be able to release the directors from their general duties. But in deciding how this might be achieved in practice, a number of difficult issues emerge.

What is being decided?

16–118 The company will normally act by resolution, either of the board of directors or of the general meeting, and it is important to ask precisely what their resolution seeks to achieve. This is the first issue. Decisions to authorise or ratify a breach, where effective, have the result of putting the directors in a position where either they do not commit a breach of duty to the company or are treated as not having been in breach. Where such approval is given in advance of the breach of duty, it is normally referred to as *authorisation* and where it is given afterwards it is referred to as *ratification*.[458] Both these decisions should be distinguished from *affirmation*, where the shareholder resolution has the effect of making binding on the company a transaction which is otherwise voidable by the company because of the director's breach of duty, and from *adoption* where the transaction is one the director had no power at all to enter into, but the shareholders do,[459] and they

---

close reading of the complicated facts of that case suggest an English court might well have reached precisely the same conclusion on orthodox "institutional" constructive trust grounds.

[456] The right which the shareholders have under s.168 to remove a director at any time by ordinary resolution (see above, paras 14–48 et seq.) could be prayed in aid, and the articles sometimes provide that a director must resign if called upon by a majority of the board to do so.

[457] Hence the importance of regulating the contractual entitlements of the director when the contract is concluded. See above, para.14–56.

[458] This terminology seems to be adopted by the Act. For example, s.263, dealing with derivative actions, distinguishes between whether a breach is likely to be "(i) authorised by the company before it occurs, or (ii) ratified by the company after it occurs": s.263(2)(c) and (3)(c). See below, para.17–20.

[459] If this is to be effective, the general meeting must have the necessary authority to take the decision.

decide the company should enter into it.[460] Affirmation or adoption does not of itself constitute implicit forgiveness, and the company may (the context is important) nevertheless still enforce its remedies against the director, for example, for compensation. However, a single resolution may be intended to deliver more than one end, for example to both forgive the directors and make the transaction binding on the company, and it is a matter of interpretation whether any particular resolution does this. Finally, ratification must also be distinguished from a mere decision not to sue the director. Such a decision has no effect on the director's legal position as being in breach of duty, and unless the decision not to sue constitutes a binding contract or *waiver*, the company can always change its mind later and sue the director, subject to the statute of limitations.[461]

Ratification is inevitably given in respect of an identified wrong already committed. Authorisation, by contrast, may be given in relation to a specific breach of duty or generally, i.e. where no specific breach of duty is in contemplation or has yet occurred. The obvious mechanism to use to provide general ex ante authorisation of the release from a category of duties is an appropriate provision in the articles of association. It is also obvious that such authorisation in the articles (or elsewhere) may be regarded with more suspicion than a specific release (whether authorisation in advance or ratification after the event) because, provided that full disclosure of the relevant facts is made to the shareholders in advance of their decision,[462] they will, in the latter case, know precisely the nature of the infringement of the company's rights to which they are consenting. By contrast, a general waiver of the benefit of a nominated duty in advance is necessarily a less informed waiver, and shareholders, when voting on a change to the articles, may underestimate the chances of situations arising in the future where they would not want to give approval.[463] In other words, a provision in the articles may be less reliable an indication of shareholder preferences than specific authorisation of a particular breach. In this section we are concerned with the particular cases of what might be called "ad hoc" approval by the company, i.e. approval of a particular actual or proposed breach of duty. In the next section we discuss whether approval can be given in advance for broad categories of future breaches, where no or little detail is available concerning the particular breaches which may occur in the future.

---

[460] For an example of affirmation see ss.196 and 214 (above, paras 16–73 et seq. and para.16–83): shareholders making substantial property transactions and loan transactions binding on the company, but not relieving the directors of their breach of duty.

[461] This can be difficult. Section 239(6)(b) preserves "any power of the directors to agree not to sue, or to settle or release a claim made by them on behalf of the company" but does not tell us anything about the extent of that power. Suppose the directors in good faith enter into a contract with one of their number on behalf of the company not to sue him or her for breach of duty. Can the director obtain an injunction to stop the litigation if the shareholders in general meeting or an individual shareholder in a derivative action later institutes litigation? Since the contract gives the director nearly the whole of what is obtainable by ratification, but ratification requires shareholder approval or may not be available at all (see below), it might be thought odd policy to allow the board to enter into such a contract on behalf of the company, and yet clearly they can. The problem is discussed in H. Hirt, *The Enforcement of Directors' Duties in Britain and Germany* (2004), pp.95–96.

[462] See, for instance, *Sharma v Sharma* [2013] EWCA Civ 1287; [2014] B.C.C. 73 CA; and *Pennyfeathers Ltd v Pennyfeathers Property Co Ltd* [2013] EWHC 3530 (Ch).

[463] A fortiori if the change has already been made and the question for an investor is whether he or she should acquire shares in that company.

Authorisation and ratification are recognised in the Act. Section 180(4)(a), recognising but not seeking to amend the common law rules on authorisation, states that the directors' general duties "have effect subject to any rule of law enabling the company to give authority ... for anything to be done (or omitted) by the directors ... that would otherwise be a breach of duty".[464] And s.239 recognises the common law doctrine of ratification, but also seeks to regulate and modify it in certain important respects. This regulation is welcome by way of clarification, but one undesirable side-effect is that the rules applying to ratification are no longer in all respects the same as those applying to authorisation, so that it may matter, oddly, if the company gives its approval the day before or the day after the directors breach their duty. And it will be interesting to see if the common law on authorisation develops so as to align more with the revised statutory rules.

Who can take the decision for the company?

16–119 The next concern is which corporate organ should take the decision for the company. If the company were deciding whether or not to pursue its legal claims against third parties, or affirm voidable contracts, or waive breaches of duty committed by third parties dealing with the company, then in the ordinary course it would be the board of directors (or its delegates) who would take these decisions. But where the claims in issue are the company's claims against one or more of its directors, the common law has typically assumed that the decision will be taken by the general meeting (subject to one important qualification, noted below[465]). This appears to track the approach taken in trusts cases, where it is the beneficiaries who decide whether or not to pursue claims against wrongdoing trustees. But of course in these trusts cases the claim in issue *is* the beneficiaries' claim, whereas in the corporate scenario it is the company's. Nevertheless, there are sound and rather obvious reasons for adopting a parallel general rule, and so it has persisted.

But, whatever the advantages of such a default rule, the underlying question is simply which corporate organ should take the decision in issue, and the answer to that is not—and need not be—set in stone. The articles may make different provisions. And we have already seen that the Act itself ousts the common law default rule in certain circumstances, and hands the relevant decision to the directors. For example, advance authorisation of self-dealing transactions is determined by the board of directors (ss.177, 180(1)(b))—indeed authorisation in this context is a misnomer; mere disclosure to the board is all that is required, and the company will then go ahead with the transaction if it approves, or call it off if it does not. So too in relation to breaches of the conflict of interest rule (ss.175, 180(1)(a)), where the default rule of shareholder authorisation is again replaced by board authorisation (subject to the articles not prohibiting/permitting this for private/public companies respectively). In both these contexts, the risk profile supporting the common law default rule is considered too low to warrant the cost

---

[464] This does not necessarily mean that the doctrine of authorisation is confined to breaches of the general duties.
[465] See below, para.16–120.

and inefficiency of its use here. By contrast, there are no statutory alternatives for advance authorisation of proposed breaches of the other general duties (ss.171–174 and 176): there the common law default rules would apply.

Again, by contrast, note that there are no parallel statutory provisions for ratification decisions: if a breach is to be forgiven after the event, then the Act does not in its terms recognise a reason to relax the protections afforded by the common law default rule, which gives the decision to the general meeting. Indeed, as we will see in the next few paragraphs, the Act rather goes the other way, and stiffens the relevant restrictions.

As a result of these statutory inroads, there is no necessary alignment in the approval mechanisms for prior authorisation and for subsequent ratification, even at the level of which organ is to take the decision in question. The company's own articles might further complicate the picture. This reinforces the need identified at the outset to be clear about what the company is purporting to decide.

There is one important qualification to the preceding analysis. The underlying assumption has been that the shareholders in general meeting constitute the appropriate expression of "the company" for the purpose of approval. However, this is not always true. As we have seen,[466] when the company is in the vicinity of insolvency, the common law takes the view that the creditors are the persons with the primary economic interest in the company. One important consequence of this is that the general meeting in such a situation may no longer approve breaches of the directors' duties: that is a matter for the creditors who, however, have no means of acting until the company goes into an insolvency procedure and an insolvency practitioner is appointed to act on their behalf.[467]   **16–120**

Disenfranchising particular voters

Settling the appropriate corporate organ to take the company's decision is not the end of the analysis. Whichever organ makes the decision for the company, there is an obvious concern to see that the decision is a good one for the company. If the decision is to be taken by the board of directors, the directors' general duties, especially those in ss.171–174, go a long way to ensuring that their deliberations are appropriately focused on the corporate benefit. Even so, where the decision is one concerning authorisation or ratification of a breach of duty by one of their number, the niceties are obvious. The Act deals with these head on. In those rare cases where the authorisation decision is given to the board of directors, as it is in the s.175 conflicts cases, then conflicted directors are excluded in the calculation of the quorum, and their votes are disregarded in determining whether board   **16–121**

---

[466] Above, para.9–11.

[467] See *West Mercia Safetywear Ltd v Dodd* [1988] B.C.L.C. 250 CA; *Aveling Barford v Perion Ltd* [1989] B.C.L.C. 626; *Re DKG Contractors Ltd* [1990] B.C.C. 903; *Official Receiver v Stern* [2002] 1 B.C.L.C. 119 at 129. Also see, more recently, *Madoff Securities International Ltd v Raven* [2013] EWHC 3147 (Comm) at [272]–[288] (Popplewell J); *Goldtrail Travel Ltd (In Liquidation) v Aydin* [2014] EWHC 1587 (Ch) at [113]–[118] (Rose J).

approval has been given (s.175(6)).[468] This straightforward statutory disenfranchisement effectively eliminates the moral dilemma of "asking turkeys to vote for Christmas".[469]

The Act does not stop there. A similar approach is taken to ratification decisions, notwithstanding that these are decisions for the general meeting. Section 239(4) indicates that the ratification resolution is to be regarded as passed "only if the necessary majority is obtained disregarding the votes in favour of the resolution by the director ... and any member connected with him".[470] This may not capture every member whose motivations might be thought suspect, but it certainly goes some distance towards that.

Given these two very substantial inroads, both directed rather sensibly at disenfranchising the defaulting directors (along with certain associated parties), it is perhaps surprising that the Act did not continue in the same vein and apply the same rule to authorisation decisions taken by the general meeting. The same mischief is equally in issue in both cases. But instead these are left to the common law default rules, with the Act merely acknowledging this approach in s.180(4)(a). This reticence is seemingly repeated in the provisions of Chs 4 and 4A of Pt 10, which, as we have seen, appear to permit interested directors to vote on the resolutions required by those Chapters (subject to any stricter rules applying to listed companies). This difference in approach to authorisation and to ratification is both odd and undesirable, especially since controlling directors will generally be able to choose the timing of the necessary shareholder resolution, and thus whether it is to be a resolution of authorisation or ratification.[471]

16–122 The common law default rules on authorisation (and, prior to the Act, equally applicable to ratification) have long been a source of concern. Starting from the unexceptional position that the appropriate organ for making these decisions was the general meeting, the common law view was that it then followed that directors who were in breach of duty were entitled to cast their votes as shareholders in favour of the forgiveness of their own wrongs to the company.[472] This conclusion was seen as justified because shareholders, unlike directors, were not subject to fiduciary duties, and indeed their shares, and the rights attached to

---

[468] Any "interested" director is also similarly excluded, although when a director can be said to be so interested is left to the courts to decide.

[469] There are other illustrations of a similar approach. For example, where the board is required to decide whether the company should enter into a transaction with one of its directors (i.e. a s.177 transaction), the model articles for both public and private companies (arts 14 and 16 respectively) exclude the self-dealing director from both the quorum and vote head counts, but subject to important exceptions where the director can both be counted and vote.

[470] Section 239(4). An equivalent provision is made for written resolutions in s.239(3). Those "connected with" the director are defined by the sections discussed above in the context of substantial property transactions: see above, para.16–70, except that here a fellow director can be a connected person if he or she otherwise meets the criteria: s.239(5)(d). Also see *Goldtrail Travel Ltd (In Liquidation) v Aydin* [2014] EWHC 1587 (Ch) at [116]–[118] (Rose J).

[471] See above, para.16–118.

[472] *North-West Transportation v Beatty* (1887) 12 App. Cas. 589 PC; *Burland v Earle* [1902] A.C. 83 PC; *Goodfellow v Nelson Line* [1912] 2 Ch. 324; *Northern Counties Securities Ltd v Jackson & Steeple Ltd* [1974] 1 W.L.R. 1133. The contrary views of Vinelott J in *Prudential Assurance Co Ltd v Newman Industries Ltd (No.2)* [1981] Ch. 257, to the effect that interested shareholders may not vote on ratification resolutions, was regarded as heretical by many (see Wedderburn, (1981) 44 M.L.R. 202), but in the light of modern developments might be seen as prescient.

them, were to be regarded as their property, with all the inherent rights to use that property in their own interests. There is much to be said for the view that the law in this area should—and indeed, properly analysed, does—start from a different point. Property and fiduciary obligation do not come into it. At a most basic level, the shareholders hold, and exercise, a power on behalf of the company. All such powers come with constraints requiring that they be exercised "in good faith and for proper purposes", as it is typically put.[473] However broadly this particular approval power is conceived, it would not seem to cover use by interested members to deliver to themselves forgiveness by the company for their wrongs and relief from their need to provide the company with appropriate remedies.[474]

Voting majorities

The next issue to consider is the necessary majority for approval decisions. **16–123** Subject to what is said in the next paragraph, the common law default rule, unaffected by any of the statutory interventions noted earlier, is for company authorisation or ratification to be by an ordinary majority of either the directors or the shareholders (depending on the appropriate organ for the decision in question). The company's articles may, of course, make other provision. The Act is silent on the matter so far as authorisation is concerned, merely preserving the common law. And so far as ratification is concerned, the Act again preserves the common law, with s.239(2) stipulating that the ratification decision "must be taken by the members" and "may" be taken by ordinary majority, unless the company's articles or some common law or statutory rule requires a higher level of approval.[475]

But that is not necessarily the end of the matter. The majority, especially the majority shareholders, may approve a breach of duty by the directors and, in so doing, act unfairly towards the minority, most obviously where they themselves are the directors in question. This could be seen simply as an example of majority unfairness towards the minority which can be handled through the general mechanisms for dealing with such unfairness, and which we discuss in Pt 4. However, the issue is perhaps better dealt with—despite the precedents to the contrary—by straightforwardly addressing the core problem of the validity of the decision being taken, and to that end disenfranchising the interested directors/ shareholders, as discussed earlier.[476] Perhaps because this was not the common law approach, and yet the difficulties in this area were plain to see, an alternative tack was taken: certain breaches of directors' duties were regarded as "unratifiable". This is a difficult approach to explain or defend, and we address it briefly in the next paragraphs.

---

[473] See paras 16–117 et seq. (directors), 19–4 et seq. (shareholders), and 31–30 et seq. (bondholders).
[474] See Worthington, (2000) 116 L.Q.R. 638. Pursuing a similar line, see Completing, paras 5.85 and 5.101. The Bill preceding CA 2006, as originally introduced, also disqualified from voting those "with a personal interest, direct or indirect, in the ratification".
[475] 2006 Act s.239(7). The shareholders may also act informally by unanimous consent: s.239(6)(a).
[476] See paras 16–119 et seq.

Non-ratifiable breaches

16–124   A further question which has bedevilled the common law, and which the Act acknowledges but does not answer,[477] is whether all breaches of duty by a director are capable of being ratified. At common law it has long been held that some breaches of directors' duties are not ratifiable, but it is much less clear how wide that rule is. Moreover, it is assumed that the doctrine of the non-ratifiable breach restricts the scope of authorisation as much as it does that of ratification. Since the Act does not address either aspect of the issue, there is at least the benefit of retained equivalence, so far as non-ratifiability is concerned, between the approval rules applying before and after the breach.[478]

But which breaches are not ratifiable? The most commonly formulated proposition is that a majority of the shareholders may not by resolution expropriate to themselves company property, because the property of the company is something in which all the shareholders of the company have a (pro rata) interest. Consequently, a resolution to ratify directors' breaches of duty which would offend against this principle of equality is ineffective (unless, presumably, all the shareholders of the company agreed to the resolution and any relevant capital maintenance rules were complied with).[479] But this is a principle easier to formulate than to apply. The principle was applied in *Cook v Deeks*,[480] where the directors had diverted to themselves contracts which they should have taken up on behalf of the company. By virtue of their controlling interests they secured the passing of a resolution in general meeting ratifying what they had done. It was held that they must nevertheless be regarded as holding the benefit of the contracts on trust for the company, for "directors holding a majority of votes would not be permitted [by the law] to make a present to themselves".[481] The same may apply when the present is not to themselves but to someone else.

Where, then, is the line to be drawn between those cases where shareholder approval is ineffective, and those in which shareholder approval has been upheld? How, in particular, can one reconcile *Cook v Deeks* with the many cases in which the liability of directors has been held to disappear as a result of ratification in general meeting, notwithstanding that the voting majority has been carried by the

---

[477] 2006 Act s.239(7) says it does not "affect any rule of law as to acts that are incapable of being ratified by the company". Those rules would seem to apply equally to prior authorisation by the shareholders. Section 180(4)(a) does not require otherwise, since it preserves existing powers of authorisation only.

[478] *Franbar Holdings Ltd v Patel* [2008] EWHC 1534 (Ch); [2009] 1 B.C.L.C. 1.

[479] See *Re Halt Garage (1964) Ltd* [1982] 3 All E.R. 1016; *Aveling Barford Ltd v Perion Ltd* [1989] B.C.L.C. 626; *Rolled Steel Products (Holdings) Ltd v British Steel Corp* [1986] Ch. 246 at 296; *Madoff Securities International Ltd v Raven* [2013] EWHC 3147 (Comm) at [268]–[269]. Similarly, see s.239(6)(a).

[480] *Cook v Deeks* [1916] 1 A.C. 554 PC. See also *Menier v Hooper's Telegraph Works* (1874) L.R. 9 Ch. App. 350; cf. *Azevedo v Imcopa Importacao* [2013] EWCA Civ 364; [2015] Q.B. 1 CA at, in particular, [66] and [71].

[481] *Cook v Deeks* [1916] 1 A.C. 554 at 564. Followed by Templeman J in *Daniels v Daniels* [1978] Ch. 406, where he refused to strike out a claim alleging that the majority had sold to themselves property of the company at a gross undervalue. In that case, the majority had not actually sought to ratify their actions, but the question was whether the wrong was ratifiable so as to prevent the minority from suing in a derivative action by virtue of the rule in *Foss v Harbottle*. Today such a transaction might well be caught by s.190 of the Act (see above, para.16–70).

interested directors?[482] Why, in *Regal (Hastings) Ltd v Gulliver*,[483] did the House of Lords say that the directors would not have been liable to account for their profits had the transaction been ratified, while, in *Cook v Deeks*, the Privy Council made the directors account notwithstanding such ratification? A satisfactory answer, consistent with common sense and with the decided cases, is difficult (and perhaps impossible) to provide.[484]

Beyond the proposition that ratification is not effective where it would amount to misappropriation, or expropriation, of corporate property, it is difficult to formulate any further limitations which command general consent. But even this general consent might be misplaced. *Every* approval decision amounts to a prospective or retrospective appropriation of corporate property: in every case the company is giving up a valuable claim, typically to compensation for losses or disgorgement of gains from the director. It is not a misappropriation of corporate property for the company to do this; it is an inherent aspect of the company's legal autonomy that it can. In *Cook v Deeks*, it was surely not the nature of the corporate opportunity, or its value, or any other attribute related to the type of breach or the nature of the corporate opportunity, which denied the directors their claim to valid ratification. Had *all* the shareholders approved the ratification deal, it would have stood. What could not be tolerated was the suggestion that the three defaulting directors could *themselves* take this decision in the face of a dissenting minority holding a contrary view. If this is right, then the directors' breaches were not *un*-ratifiable; they were simply not effectively ratified by the wrongdoers themselves. The same conclusion is equally true when the company is on the brink of insolvency, or where the directors' breach consists in acting against the creditors' interests. The directors' breaches in these circumstances are not *un*-ratifiable; but they can only be ratified by the appropriate corporate organ, and, exceptionally, that is not the general meeting—even a general meeting governed by a majority of disinterested shareholders.[485] Despite the pervasiveness of the notion of un-ratifiable breaches, the relevant precedents all arguably incline more to expressing concern with the validity and appropriateness of the vote and the voting organ taking the approval decision rather than to the nature of the breach as being un-ratifiable.

If this is right, then the issue may largely disappear, since the Act has in large measure addressed the concern with interested parties voting. Section 239, by depriving the directors in breach of the right to vote, avoids the result which the Privy Council was so desirous of avoiding in *Cook v Deeks*, and does so without the need to resort to the concept of a "non-ratifiable wrong". In other words, the rule against making presents of the corporate assets seems much less strong (provided the creditors' interests are not affected) if the non-involved

---

[482] e.g. *NW Transportation Co v Beatty* (1887) 12 App. Cas. 589 PC; *Burland v Earle* [1902] A.C. 83 PC; *A Harris v Harris Ltd,* 1936 S.C. 183 (Sc.); *Baird v Baird & Co,* 1949 S.L.T. 368 (Sc.).

[483] *Regal (Hastings) Ltd v Gulliver* [1942] 1 All E.R. 378; [1967] 2 A.C. 134 HL, above, paras 16–87 et seq.

[484] It has troubled a number of writers: see, in particular, Wedderburn [1957] C.L.J. 194; [1958] C.L.J. 93; Afterman, *Company Directors and Controllers* (Sydney, 1970), pp.149 et seq.; Beck, in Ziegel (ed.), *Studies in Canadian Company Law*, Vol. II (Toronto, 1973), pp.232–238; Sealy [1967] C.L.J. 83 at 102ff.

[485] See above, para.16–120.

shareholders approve. This consideration may lead the courts in future to narrow, and maybe even eliminate,[486] the class of non-ratifiable wrongs.[487]

GENERAL PROVISIONS EXEMPTING DIRECTORS FROM LIABILITY

Statutory constraints

16–125 Although directors may secure specific authorisation or ratification of their actions from the shareholders, they are likely to regard that route to legal absolution as uncertain and unduly public. Historically, they have sought to use the articles to obtain general shareholder approval for certain categories of, or even all, breaches of duty. We have seen above that the articles were widely used in this way in respect of self-dealing transactions, and in fact the legislature in the 2006 Act accepted that outcome by re-writing the statutory duty in relation to self-dealing transactions as a duty to disclose to the board rather than as a duty to obtain the approval of the shareholders.

However, in some cases the articles went further, and included provisions exempting the directors from liability for all breaches of duty (unless fraud was involved). Parliament responded in the Companies Act 1929.[488] In the current version of that reform (s.232(1)) the principle is laid down that "any provision that purports to exempt a director[489] of a company (to any extent) from any liability that would otherwise attach to him in connection with any negligence, default, breach of duty or breach of trust in relation to the company is void".

This is a very important statutory provision. Subject to its exceptions, the section turns the directors' duties provisions into mandatory rules. Although the common law may regard those duties as existing for the benefit of the shareholders and thus to be waivable by the shareholders in the articles, the section takes a different view, perhaps reflecting doubt about the reality of the consent expressed in approvals given in advance of the event.

Conflicts of interest

16–126 Despite the general prohibition in s.232, s.232(4) then provides that "nothing in this section prevents a company's articles from making such provision as has previously been lawful for dealing with conflicts of interest". Thus it is clear that

---

[486] A wrong is only truly un-ratifiable if there is no corporate organ with the *capacity* to act. It is difficult, perhaps impossible, to conceive of circumstances where this would be the case.

[487] For further elaboration, see S. Worthington, "Corporate Governance: Remedying and Ratifying Directors' Breaches" (2000) 116 L.Q.R. 638, suggesting that the common law resolution (and so for authorisation as well as for ratification) is, as in the statute, to exclude from voting those parties who are unquestionably seen as likely to vote for improper purposes.

[488] Responding to the decision in *Re City Equitable Fire Insurance Co Ltd* [1925] Ch. 407, where a provision in the company's articles exempted the directors from liability except in cases of "wilful neglect or default".

[489] The earlier provisions applied also to any auditor or officer of the company. Since the enactment of the 2006 Act the provisions on auditors have developed in a separate direction and are discussed below at para.22–42, whilst officers have now disappeared from the section as well—and have not been replaced, it should be noted, by shadow directors.

some inroads are permitted in the articles in relation to the "no conflict" duties. This conclusion is reinforced by the provisions of s.180(4)(b) to the effect that "where the company's articles contain provisions for dealing with conflicts of interest, [the general duties] are not infringed by anything done (or omitted) by the directors, or any of them, in accordance with those provisions".[490] The test for the legality of such provisions which s.232 adopts is whether the provision had "previously been lawful for dealing with conflicts of interest"; and it seems that s.180(4)(b) must be interpreted as subject to a similar restriction.

What is the meaning of this Delphic phrase? What could the articles previously (i.e. before the 2006 Act) do in relation to conflicts of interest? In order to answer this question one needs to know the history of judicial interpretation of the predecessor of s.232, namely, s.310, later s.309A, of the 1985 Act. This was a highly debated question, arising previously mainly in relation to self-dealing transactions, because that was where the problem arose in practice. The debated question was whether articles substituting informing the board for shareholder approval were compatible with the predecessors of s.232. That particular question is no longer relevant because s.177 adopts outright the principle of disclosure to the board.[491] However, the answer given to the question under the former law may tell us how to approach under the 2006 Act an article dealing with any other conflict of interest.

The only intellectually respectable answer in that debate was given by Vinelott J in *Movitex Ltd v Bulfield*.[492] His explanation drew a distinction between (1) "the overriding principle of equity" that "if a director places himself in a position in which his duty to the company conflicts with his personal interest or duty to another, the court will set aside the transaction without enquiring whether there was any breach of duty to the company"; and (2) the director's "duty to promote the interests of [the company] and when the interests of [the company] conflicted with his own to prefer the interests of [the company]". While any proposed modification of (2) would infringe s.310 of the 1985 Act, the shareholders of the company in formulating the articles could modify the application of (1), "the overriding principle of equity", provided that in doing so they did not exempt the director from, or from the consequences of, a breach of that duty to the company.[493]

But even this is not as clear as it might be. In unravelling the issues, it seems important to recognise that "the overriding principle of equity" in (1) requires, or enables, courts to set aside self-dealing transactions whenever there is a *potential* conflict, without requiring investigation of whether the alleged conflict is real. So it might simply be this evaluative step which the articles can legitimately introduce, although if a real conflict exists they cannot go further and exempt the director from the obligation to prefer the company's interests. *Movitex* implicitly, and perhaps explicitly, takes this line. And that evaluative step could legitimately be taken by any appropriately qualified organ of the company. Again, in *Movitex*, it seemed important that the decision, allocated to the board of directors, was

16–127

---

[490] See *Bilta (UK) Ltd v Nazir* [2015] UKSC 23; [2016] A.C. 1 at [104].
[491] See above, paras 16–57 et seq.
[492] *Movitex Ltd v Bulfield* [1988] B.C.L.C. 104.
[493] *Movitex Ltd v Bulfield* [1988] B.C.L.C. 104 at 120–121d.

conditional on full disclosure and on disenfranchising the interested director from both quorum and voting numbers.[494] But to regard the board's decision as limited to this evaluative function denies reality. Indeed, the limitation seems unnecessary. We have seen that the company can prospectively authorise what *would* otherwise be a breach of the conflicts rules; there is no limitation to a mere evaluation that what is proposed would *not* constitute an actual breach. Although the common law default rule holds that this decision is for the general meeting, it must surely be open to the articles to settle an alternative but appropriately qualified organ of the company for the purposes of making this decision. This, more realistically, was what was done in *Movitex*. It is also what is now done in the current Act in ss.175 and 177. But this approach, recognising the possibility of advance authorisation, then lays bare the question at the outset: given the rigours of s.232, can ss.232(4) and 180(4)(b) legitimately permit the articles to make any inroads into the conflicts rules beyond specifying the appropriate corporate organ for any necessary evaluations, authorisations and ratifications?

Moreover, given that the duty in relation to self-dealing transactions has become, under the 2006 Act, a simple duty of disclosure, where will there be an incentive for provisions in the articles to be deployed in future which provide further inroads relating to directors' liability for conflicts of interest? The obvious areas are corporate opportunities and multiple directorships. Translated into corporate opportunity terms, however, the *Movitex* approach indicates that the articles cannot exempt the director from obtaining the company's authorisation (and note the difficulties in determining whether that is appropriately given[495]) before taking personally an opportunity the company was actually pursuing (as in *Cook v Deeks*[496] and *Industrial Development Consultants v Cooley*[497]) or probably one which the company had an interest in considering because it falls within its current line of business (as in *Bhullar v Bhullar*[498]), because in that situation there would be an actual conflict of interest. However, the articles might conceivably exempt the director from taking without authorisation an opportunity which the company (normally the board) had rejected in good faith (as in *Regal*[499]), but the better argument here is that such a decision by the board puts the opportunity outside the scope of conflicts which are caught by the equitable or statutory rule, so nothing more would need to be said in the articles, and indeed if anything were said it would be otiose.[500] Similarly, the *Movitex* case would suggest that an article permitting multiple directorships would be upheld by virtue of s.232(4) only if there is no actual conflict of duties for the director in consequence of the taking up of additional directorships. Given this, there would once again seem to be little point to such a provision.

---

[494] See above, paras 16–55 et seq., for discussion of the issues.
[495] See above, paras 16–121 et seq.
[496] *Cook v Deeks* [1916] 1 A.C. 544 PC.
[497] *Industrial Development Consultants v Cooley* [1972] 1 W.L.R. 443.
[498] *Bhullar v Bhullar* [2003] EWCA Civ 424; [2003] B.C.C. 711.
[499] *Regal (Hastings) Ltd v Gulliver* [1967] 2 A.C. 134n. Although there may be nice questions on disclosure at the board rejection stage.
[500] See above, paras 16–90 et seq.

Provisions providing directors with an indemnity

The ban, contained in s.232, on provisions exempting directors from liability **16–128** extends (subject to important exceptions) to any provision by which the company provides, directly or indirectly, an indemnity to a director or a director of an associated company in respect of these liabilities (s.232(2)). Under an indemnity arrangement the director remains in principle liable but the company picks up the financial consequences of that liability. The indemnity prohibition applies also to indemnities provided in favour of directors of associated companies, thus preventing evasion of the section in group situations, whereby all the directors have the benefit of indemnity provisions, but in no case is the indemnity provided by the company of which they are a director. The provisions referred to in the section are those "contained in a company's articles or in any contract with the company or otherwise".[501] The indemnity might be provided by means of the company promising to indemnify the director or, indirectly, by the company taking out insurance on the director's behalf, so that the indemnity is to be provided by the insurance company. As we shall see, the legislation is less strict in relation to permitted insurance than in respect of permitted direct indemnities (labelled "third party" indemnities in the Act).

Insurance

Since 1989 a company has been free (but of course not obliged) to buy insurance **16–129** against any of the liabilities mentioned in s.232 for the benefit of its directors (s.233) and it is in fact common practice to do so, at least in large companies. At first sight, this is very odd. Insurance certainly means, assuming the policy limits are large enough, that the company receives compensation for any loss it suffers as a result of the breach of duty. On the other hand, the company pays for the insurance and so, over time at least, the insurance premia will roughly equal the losses inflicted on the company by the directors, so that the company ends up paying for the directors' breaches of duty. This seems to deprive the directors' duties rules of any deterrent effect as against the directors and to mean that the insurance simply operates as a way of smoothing the losses inflicted on the company by the directors.

This argument has considerable force, but needs to be assessed subject to the following qualifications. First, the impact of s.233 depends upon the extent of the cover which the insurance market is prepared to make available at any particular time. It is unlikely that insurance is available against the consequences of a breach of duty involving fraud or wilful default, because of the moral hazard

---

[501] 2006 Act s.232(3). In *Burgoine v Waltham Forest LBC* [1997] 2 B.C.L.C. 612 it was held that the phrase "or otherwise" did not extend the section beyond indemnities, etc. given by the company (as opposed to a third party), though that is now subject to the extension of the indemnity prohibition to the directors of associated companies. Presumably, the force of these words is to ban such provisions in members' or directors' resolutions.

problem for the insurance company in providing such cover.[502] And it may be difficult to obtain cover against the liability to account for profits made as opposed to losses inflicted on the company. In any event, the policy is likely to be subject to monetary limits, so that liability remains to some extent personally with the director in the case of large claims.

Secondly, it is conceivable that insurance companies will adjust their premia according to the claims experience of the company so that a financial incentive is generated for the company to monitor the actions of its directors or refuse to insure those with a bad claims record, or insurance companies may even engage in more general monitoring of the corporate governance arrangements in the company, thus somewhat restoring the deterrent effect of the duties.[503]

Finally, it may be that qualified persons will be unwilling to take on board positions without the benefit of such insurance. This might be true particularly of non-executive directors, whose financial benefits from the company may be modest (at least in comparison with the remuneration of executive directors) and whose knowledge of and control over the company is necessarily limited. They could buy such insurance themselves, for the section does not restrict the taking out of insurance against directors' liabilities by the directors themselves.[504] However, they would no doubt expect the cost of such insurance to be reflected in their fees, and it may be cheaper and more effective for the company to provide that insurance itself.

Third party indemnities

16–130 Despite the term "third party indemnities" the indemnity under discussion here is one provided by the company in favour of the director. It is a "third party" indemnity because it relates to litigation which might be brought by a third party (i.e. someone other than the company) against the director.[505] Under an indemnity provision the company promises that the director will not be out of pocket in relation to the claim made against him or her (whether by way of a judgment against the director, a settlement of the litigation or by the incurring of legal costs), so that, to the extent of the indemnity, the cost of the director's breach of duty is borne directly by the company. As we have seen, it will be rare for breaches of the duties discussed in this chapter to lead to liability other than to the company, but this may not be the case where the liability arises under a foreign system of law, notably US law, and s.232 is not in terms confined to liabilities arising under the law of a UK jurisdiction. A director may prefer insurance to a

---

[502] The provisions to be found in such insurance contracts are analysed by C. Baxter, "Demystifying D&O Insurance" (1995) 15 O.J.L.S. 537, now a somewhat dated, but nevertheless useful, article. The insurance may extend, of course, to protection against liabilities beyond those discussed in this chapter.

[503] Evidence from the US suggests that neither form of control by insurance companies is strong, probably because the directors, who control the decision where to place the insurance, would not welcome it. See T. Baker and S. Griffin, "Predicting Governance Risk: Evidence from the Directors' and Officers' Liability Insurance Market" (2007) 74 Chicago L.R. 487; and "The Missing Monitor in Corporate Governance: The Directors' and Officers' Liability Insurer" (2007) 95 Georgetown L.J. 1795. This view is concurred in by Baxter, above, fn.502.

[504] This seems to be the implication of the *Burgoine* decision, above, fn.501.

[505] 2006 Act s.234(2).

promise of an indemnity by the company, because on insolvency the company's promise may not be worth very much, but an indemnity may be regarded by the director as better than nothing, and the company may prefer, in effect, to self-insure by promising an indemnity.

Note, however, that the company may not promise an indemnity against liability or costs incurred in an action brought by the company. This may be provided for only through the purchase of insurance by the company, as discussed above. Why is this? It may have been thought, on the one hand, that a complete indemnity would come very close to an exemption from liability, thus defeating the purpose of s.232. On the other hand, despite the failings of the insurance market, insurance requires an assessment of the extent of and the costs of the risks involved by another commercial organisation, which will exclude some risks from those it is prepared to underwrite. This provides some external control over the liabilities from which directors can be exempted, for example, where they have acted deliberately in breach of duty. Equally, the need to buy insurance will bring the cost of the protection home to the board which is arranging for it, whilst an indemnity, which carries no immediate costs for the company, might be too easy a provision to slip into the articles.

The Act prohibits provision of certain forms of indemnity (s.234(3), as elaborated in s.234(4)–(6)), in particular in relation to:

— a fine imposed on a director in criminal proceedings;
— the costs of defending criminal proceedings in which the director is convicted;
— a penalty payable to a regulatory authority;
— costs incurred in connection with an application for relief (see below) which is unsuccessful; or
— the costs of defending civil proceedings brought by the company or an associated company in which judgment is given against the director.

The last category of exclusion may seem surprising, given that liability to the company or associated company is not within the definition of a "third party indemnity" (s.234(2)) but it is to be noted that what s.234(3) deals with is not the director's liability to the company or associated company but the director's liability for costs incurred in defending civil proceedings brought by such a company, which liability may be incurred to a third party, i.e. the director's legal team. The exclusion thus completes the policy objective of preventing the indemnity from operating in respect of any aspect of a claim brought by the company or an associated company, but only if the company is successful in the claim. If no judgment is given against the director, either because the director is successful or because the case is settled, a provision requiring the company to indemnify the director against legal costs is permitted. The section achieves the same result in relation to criminal proceedings against the director: only the costs of successfully defending a criminal charge may be the subject of an indemnity provision. However, it appears that the costs of an unsuccessful defence in a regulatory procedure (for example, one brought by the Financial Conduct Authority) may be the subject of an indemnity provision (though not the cost of any penalty imposed by the FCA).

However, the real importance of the section is not revealed by what it says by way of exclusion but what it does not exclude. In the case of a civil action brought by a third party (for example, shareholders in a class action) the indemnity provision may cover both the liability of the director and the costs of defending the action, whether successfully or unsuccessfully.

16–131 An indemnity provision which meets the requirements of s.234 is termed a "qualifying indemnity provision". A qualifying indemnity provision[506] must be disclosed to the shareholders in the directors' annual report (s.236); and must be made available for inspection in the usual way by any shareholder of the company without charge, who may also require a copy of it to be provided upon payment of the prescribed fee (ss.237 and 238).

It should finally be noted that what s.234 creates is a permission for the company, not an obligation, and it is a permission to have a provision (in the company's articles or in a contract with a director, for example) which provides for an indemnity of the relevant type. The section does not deal with ad hoc decisions by boards of directors to pay an indemnity in a particular case, where there is no existing provision dealing with this matter. Such a decision is governed by the directors' duties discussed above and by the general law of the land.[507] It is also possible that a company might wish to lend the director money in advance to defend proceedings brought against him or her, whether criminal, civil or regulatory. We have already seen that a company is exempted from the normal rules on shareholder approval if it decides to make such a loan, or enter into an analogous transaction, for this purpose. However, the loan must be on terms that it is repayable if the director is unsuccessful in the proceedings.[508] A loan on different terms or for a different purpose (for example, to meet a liability in a judgment rather than to defend proceedings) would need shareholder approval.

Pension scheme indemnity

16–132 Where a company runs an occupational pension scheme (a less frequent situation these days than previously), the company may be a trustee of the trust through which the scheme is organised and the director may act on behalf of the company in its capacity as such a trustee.[509] Section 235 permits provisions indemnifying

---

[506] Whether made by the company or not, so that the directors of an associated company must report it as well; and copies must be available for inspection by the shareholders of both companies.

[507] It has been suggested in a trade union case that, whereas a once-off ex post decision to indemnify an officer against a fine was unobjectionable (if authorised by the union's rules), "continued resolutions authorising the refunding of fines might fairly be said to lead to an expectation that a union would indemnify its members against the consequences of future offences" and that would be against public policy: *Drake v Morgan* [1978] I.C.R. 56, 61.

[508] See above, para.16–82.

[509] Of course, the director may be appointed personally by the company to be a trustee of the scheme, but it may have been thought that, in such a case, any liability would not be incurred in the capacity of director but as trustee or appointee, so that any indemnity provision would not fall within s.232.

the director against any liability incurred in connection with the company's activities as trustee of the scheme, subject to the same restrictions as in s.234 in relation to criminal and regulatory proceedings. However, s.235 permits indemnity arrangements in relation to civil suits, whether brought by a third party or by the company, which indemnity may extend to both costs and liability. In other words, as far as the director's activities on behalf of the company as trustee are concerned, a complete indemnity arrangement is permissible in relation to civil liability. The same reporting and copy requirements apply in relation to a qualifying pension scheme indemnity provision as in relation to a third-party indemnity provision.

RELIEF GRANTED BY THE COURT

Whether or not the director is able to secure forgiveness from the company, the director, and any officer of the company (including auditors and liquidators), has the possibility of appealing to the court to prevent the full application to him or her of the statutory duties included in Pt 10 or indeed any analogous duties arising, for example, at common law. Under s.1157 the court has a discretion to relieve, prospectively or retrospectively, against liability for negligence, default, breach of duty or breach of trust, provided that it appears to the court that the director has acted honestly and reasonably and that, having regard to all the circumstances, he or she ought fairly to be excused. The court may relieve on such terms as it thinks fit. The requirement of reasonableness might suggest that s.1157 is not available in relation to the directors' duties of care, skill and diligence but this appears not to be the case.[510] However, the section is not available in respect of third-party (as opposed to corporate) claims against the director,[511] and, more important for present purposes, will not be applied even to corporate claims where that would be inconsistent with the purposes underlying the rule imposing the liability against which relief is sought.[512]

16–133

LIABILITY OF THIRD PARTIES

Despite the wide range of civil remedies which exist to support the substantive law of directors' duties, it is often the case that the directors are not in fact worth suing, at least if they are uninsured. They may once have had property belonging to the company but, by the time the company finds this out, may have it no longer. They may have made large profits which they should account for to the company, but may well have spent them by the time the writ arrives. Companies

16–134

---

[510] *Equitable Life Assurance Society v Bowley* [2004] 1 B.C.L.C. 180 at [45]; *Re D'Jan of London Ltd* [1994] 1 B.C.L.C. 561 at 564. For recent application, see, for instance, *Northampton Regional Livestock Centre Co Ltd v Cowling* [2014] EWHC 30 (QB) (reversed in part by the Court of Appeal) at [159]–[170]; and *Re HLC Environmental Projects Ltd* [2013] EWHC 2876 (Ch); [2014] B.C.C. 337 at [108]. And see *Re Powertrain Ltd* [2015] EWHC 3998 (Ch) (concerning liquidators).

[511] *Customs and Excise Commissioners v Hedon Alpha Ltd* [1981] 1 Q.B. 818 CA.

[512] *Re Produce Marketing Consortium Ltd* [1989] 1 W.L.R. 745 (wrongful trading liabilities excluded).

are therefore likely to want to identify some more stable third party, often a bank, which is worth powder-and-shot, either instead of or in addition to the directors.[513]

But under what conditions may the company hold a third party liable in connection with a breach of duty by the directors? This is not a matter dealt with in the Act in relation to the general duties of directors. It is left to the common law, which is rather complex, although it is an area which recent decisions of the Privy Council and House of Lords have helped to clarify. Only the briefest sketch of the relevant principles is attempted here.

16–135   It has long been recognised that there are two bases of third-party liability, one resting on receipt by the third party of company property ("knowing receipt" claims) and the other resting on complicity on the part of the third party in the director's breach of duty ("dishonest assistance" claims). The main conceptual contribution of the Privy Council in *Royal Brunei Airlines Sdn Bhd v Tan*[514] was to make it clear that the principles supporting the imposition of liability in these two situations are different from one another.

In the case of dishonest assistance claims, which the court helpfully termed "accessory" liability, the liability is a reflection of a general principle of the law of obligations. This imposes personal liability upon third parties who assist in or procure the breach of a duty or obligation owed by another, the liability of the third party being enforceable by the person who is the beneficiary of the duty whose performance has been interfered with. Provided there has been a breach of duty by the director, whether committed knowingly or not, the third party accessory will be liable to the company if the third party has acted dishonestly. After some to-ing and fro-ing, it seems, rightly, to be agreed that the test of dishonesty is objective: the accessory is dishonest if, by ordinary standards, the defendant's mental state would be characterised as dishonest, and it is irrelevant that the defendant him- or herself takes a different view.[515] The third party is often said to be obliged to account "as a constructive trustee". This label is uninformative, and indeed confusing, and should be discarded, but the cases confirm that the accessory is liable to compensate the principal (the company,

---

[513] See, for example, *Selangor United Rubber Estates v Cradock (No.3)* [1968] 1 W.L.R. 1555.

[514] *Royal Brunei Airlines Sdn Bhd v Tan* [1995] 2 A.C. 378 PC, noted by Birks, [1996] L.M.C.L.Q. 1 and Harpum, (1995) 111 L.Q.R. 545. The facts of the case did not raise an issue of directors' duties. In fact, the fiduciary duty in question was owed by the company and the principle of accessory liability was used to make the director liable to the claimant for the *company's* breach of duty. But the principle of the case is clearly of general application.

[515] *Barlow Clowes International Ltd v Eurotrust Ltd* [2005] UKPC 37; [2006] 1 W.L.R. 1476 at [15] PC (Lord Hoffmann), also excusing, at [15], as "ambiguous" the earlier majority views, including his own, in favour of subjective dishonesty in *Twinsectra Ltd v Yardley* [2002] UKHL 12; [2002] 2 A.C. 164 HL (Lord Millett dissenting vigorously), which had in turn varied the views of Lord Nicholls in *Royal Brunei Airlines Sdn Bhd v Tan* [1994] UKPC 4; [1995] 2 A.C. 378 PC, who favoured an objective test. The final position represents a return to orthodoxy, and *Starglade Properties Ltd v Nash* [2010] EWCA Civ 1314; [2011] 1 P. & C.R. D.G. 17 confirms that the *Barlow Clowes* decision represents the law in England. Also see, more recently, *Bank of Ireland v Jaffery* [2012] EWHC 1377 (Ch) (in the context of a bank's former senior executive).

here) for losses caused by the director's breach of fiduciary duty and, it seems, for any profits generated personally by the accessory from that breach.[516]

Given the dishonesty element in accessory liability, such claims are unlikely against solvent and respectable third parties.[517] The alternative is the personal claim based on "knowing receipt" of the company's property,[518] at least if the term "knowing" is given a wide enough connotation. The essence of this claim is restitutionary, being the return of the value of the company's property that was received as a result of the director's breach, and regardless of the fact that the third party may no longer have the property or its identifiable proceeds in its hands.[519] A common situation found in the cases is one where the directors have used the company's assets in breach of the statutory prohibition on the provision of financial assistance towards the purchase of its shares, and the assets in question have passed through the hands of a third party.[520]

16–136

The scope of knowing receipt liability depends heavily upon the degree of knowledge on the part of the third party which is required to trigger it, an issue which has been much discussed in the courts over recent decades. Although the issue remains unsettled, the tendency in recent decisions has been to resist imposing liability on the basis of constructive knowledge in ordinary commercial transactions, on the grounds that the doctrine of constructive knowledge presupposes an underlying system of careful and comprehensive investigation of the surrounding legal context, which is typical of property transactions but atypical of commercial transactions (including the non-property aspects of commercial property transfers).[521] This probably misconceives the notion of constructive notice, which is inherently supremely context sensitive, so that in commercial contexts the right question would be, what would a reasonable *commercial* party know in *this* context (given the usual and reasonable enquiries that such a party would—or would not—have made)?

In any event, in *Bank of Credit and Commerce International (Overseas) Ltd v Akindele*[522] the Court of Appeal struck out on a new tack. Whilst confirming that

---

[516] See *Fyffes Group Ltd v Templeman* [2000] 2 Lloyd's Rep. 643; *Ultraframe (UK) Ltd v Fielding* [2005] EWHC 1638, holding that the accessory's liability was not confined to damages but included a liability to account for profits which the accessory had made (but not profits made by the director); *Charter Plc v City Index Ltd* [2007] EWCA Civ 1382; [2008] Ch. 313; *Novoship (UK) Ltd v Mikhaylyuk* [2015] QB 499 CA; *Williams v Central Bank of Nigeria* [2014] UKSC 10; [2014] A.C. 1189. Notice in particular the argument that the causal test may either be different, or at least have different outcomes, when applied to a third party "dishonest assistant" rather than a director/fiduciary: *Novoship (UK) Ltd v Mikhaylyuk* [2015] QB 499 at [111]–[115] CA.

[517] Which is not to say that the first basis of liability is never available: see *Canada Safeway Ltd v Thompson* [1951] 3 D.L.R. 295.

[518] If the third party does still have the property or its identifiable proceeds to hand, then a proprietary constructive trust or tracing claim may be possible, subject only to the bona fide purchaser defence.

[519] *El Ajou v Dollar Land Holdings Plc* [1994] 2 All E.R. 685 at 700, per Hoffmann LJ.

[520] See above, para.13–57; and *Belmont Finance Corp v Williams Furniture Ltd (No.2)* [1980] 1 All E.R. 393 CA.

[521] See *Eagle Trust Plc v SBC Securities Ltd* [1993] 1 W.L.R. 484; *Cowan de Groot Properties Ltd v Eagle Trust Plc* [1992] 4 All E.R. 700; *Eagle Trust Plc v SBC Securities Ltd (No.2)* [1996] 1 B.C.L.C. 121.

[522] *Bank of Credit and Commerce International (Overseas) Ltd v Akindele* [2001] Ch. 437 CA. See also the use of this test in *Criterion Properties Plc v Stratford UK Properties LLC* [2003] B.C.C. 50 CA.

dishonesty is not a requirement for liability under the "knowing receipt" head, the Court abandoned the search for a single test for knowledge in this area. Instead, the question to ask was whether the recipient's state of knowledge was such as to make it unconscionable for him or her to retain the benefit of the receipt. The Court thought this would enable judges to "give common sense decisions in the commercial context", though it has to be said that the test is a very open-ended one and not likely to conduce to a common approach on the part of the courts.

16–137 Third-party liability may also arise in relation to corporate opportunities. Here, the question again arises of how far a corporate opportunity constitutes an asset of the company. We have seen above[523] that this question is relevant to the question of whether the director's taking of the opportunity can be ratified by a simple majority of the shareholders. It arises again here: does receipt by a third party either of the opportunity itself or of assets arising out of its exploitation fall within the "knowing receipt" principle? What is clear is that merely entering into a contract with the company which remains executory does not put the third party in a position in which he or she can be said to be in receipt of corporate assets.[524] Where the corporate opportunity is regarded as an asset of the company, however, it follows that the company will be able to seek to recover profits made out of exploitation of the opportunity by the third party (provided of course that the important requirement of knowledge is met), even if the defaulting director does not him- or herself make any personal profit.[525]

Whether in such a case the *director* can be held liable, with the third party, for the third party's profits is much debated. In principle this should not be possible unless the director can in some way be made personally liable for the defaults of the third party. This may be possible if the third party is a partnership of which the director is a member, but logic suggests that generally the director's own liabililty will be restricted to his or her allocated share of the profits. It will also be possible, on orthodox principles, in the narrow circumstance where the third party is a company but the company is a sham, hiding the director.[526] But where the third-party company is not a sham, it might still be disputed whether the director can be liable with the company for the company's profits on the grounds that director and company are jointly in breach of trust or whether the position is that each is liable only for the profits made personally.[527]

---

[523] Above at para.16–124.

[524] *Criterion Properties Ltd v Stratford UK Properties Ltd* [2004] 1 W.L.R. 1846 HL.

[525] As in the case of the chairman in *Regal (Hastings) Ltd v Gulliver* [1967] 2 A.C. 134n, although in that case the language of the court was not noticeably proprietary in tone.

[526] For the third-party partnership see *Imperial Mercantile Credit Association v Coleman* (1873) L.R. 6 H.L. 189; and on the sham third-party company see *Trustor AB v Smallbone (No.2)* [2001] 1 W.L.R. 1177; *Glencor ACP Ltd v Dalby* [2000] 2 B.C.L.C. 734, but note the modern analysis of these latter cases as set out in *Prest v Petrodel Resources Ltd* [2013] UKSC 34; [2013] 2 A.C. 415 SC and discussed above in paras 8–15 et seq.

[527] Contrast *CMS Dolphin Ltd v Simonet* [2001] 2 B.C.L.C. 704 at [98] et seq.; and *Ultraframe (UK) Ltd v Fielding* [2005] EWHC 1638 at [1516] et seq. See also *Novoship (UK) Ltd v Mikhaylyuk* [2015] QB 499 CA.

LIMITATION OF ACTIONS

The question of whether directors acting in breach of their fiduciary duties have **16–138** the benefit of the Limitation Acts is another area where the analogy between the director and the trustee is to the fore, the specific provisions of the Limitation Act 1980 dealing with actions by a beneficiary against a trustee being applied to actions by a company against a director.[528] The crucial question is whether there is any limitation period in such cases, for until the late nineteenth century trustees did not have the benefit of a limitation period in actions by beneficiaries.[529] Under s.21 of the 1980 Act a limitation period of six years is applied to such actions (unless some other section of the Act applies a different limitation period), but there are two exceptions where the old rule of no limitation continues to operate. These are (a) where the claim is based upon "any fraud or fraudulent breach of trust to which the trustee was a party or privy"; and (b) where the action is to recover "from the trustee trust property or the proceeds of trust property in the possession of the trustee or previously received by the trustee and converted to his use". In a standard case, therefore, of an action against a director to recover a profit made in breach of his fiduciary duties or for equitable compensation, the limitation period will be six years. Only where the claimant can go further and bring himself within either the (a) or (b) exception will the Act not apply.[530]

As to (a), it should be noted that it is a strong rule, since defendants in actions based on fraud are not generally deprived by the Limitation Act of the benefit of a limitation period. To benefit from this exception the claimant has to show not simply that the director acted in breach of duty, but that he or she intended to act either knowing that the action was contrary to the interests of the company or recklessly indifferent as to whether it was.[531]

As to (b), it means that there is no limitation period in those cases where a director has misapplied company property which has come into his or her hands and the company is seeking restoration of that property. This rule applies even though the company's property is no longer in the hands of the director.[532] As it was put some hundred years ago, the rule is intended to prevent the director from "coming off with something he ought not to have".[533]

However, in recent years the scope of both (a) and (b) has been debated in **16–139** relation to third parties who are often called "constructive trustees" by the courts under the doctrines of accessory liability and knowing receipt discussed above and in other circumstances too. The courts have drawn a distinction between two types of constructive trustee, constructive trustees properly so-called and those in respect of whom the term would better be abandoned.[534] The first case is the case of the person who, though not expressly appointed as a trustee, has assumed the

---

[528] But not to claims by third parties against a director, where the normal limitation periods apply.

[529] The position was changed by the Trustee Act 1888.

[530] *Gwembe Valley Development Co Ltd v Koshy (No.3)* [2004] 1 B.C.L.C. 131 at [111] and [118] CA.

[531] *Gwembe Valley Development Co Ltd v Koshy (No.3)* [2004] 1 B.C.L.C. 131 at [131] CA.

[532] *JJ Harrison (Properties) Ltd v Harrison* [2002] 1 B.C.L.C. 162 CA; *Re Pantone 485 Ltd* [2002] 1 B.C.L.C. 266.

[533] *Re Timmis, Nixon v Smith* [1902] 1 Ch. 176 at 186.

[534] *Paragon Finance Plc v D B Thackerar & Co* [1999] 1 All E.R. 400 CA.

duties of a trustee by a lawful transaction which was independent of and preceded the breach of trust now in issue. Such a person falls within cases (a) (if the facts fit) and (b). So a director who receives company property in breach of fiduciary duty holds that property on constructive trust, and the limitation defence is not available.

The second case is where the trust obligation arises as a direct consequence of the unlawful transaction which the claimant challenges and where the constructive trust is imposed simply to provide an effective proprietary remedy in equity.[535] Such a person does not fall within cases (a) or (b). The Supreme Court in *Williams v Central Bank of Nigeria*[536] has held, by majority, that third parties who are dishonest assistants or knowing recipients are in this fortunate position (for them), and can therefore rely on the normal limitation periods. The analysis remains controversial, however, with doctrinal and policy considerations pulling in both directions.

CONCLUSION

16–140   This is a long chapter, and its detailed rules on directors' duties are an enormously important and frequently used tool in regulating the management of companies by their directors. The most substantial reform in this area in recent times has undoubtedly been the statutory enactment of the general duties in the 2006 Act, replacing their earlier common law counterparts. This in itself was reform of a unique sort, with its careful management of the inevitable ongoing interplay between the statutory rules and their common law counterparts (see especially s.170(4)). But what can be said of the consequences? At this short distance down the track, no seismic shifts have occurred, either for good or for ill. This should come as no surprise, since what was done was largely intended to be a restatement of the past, with a few relatively minor added tweaks to improve rules and practices where problems were already well known and aired.

Section 172, imposing a general duty on directors to promote the success of the company, might be thought of as one exception to that minimal-change approach, especially as it contains an explicit recognition of stakeholder interests for the first time in British company law, which had previously referred only to members and employee interests.[537] However, those stakeholder interests are to be pursued by directors only where such action is needed to promote the success of the company for the benefit of its members. The core duty of loyalty is thus still shareholder-centred. Further, it seems clear that the prior common law permitted directors to take into account stakeholder interests where promoting the

---

[535] These are the definitions set out by Millett LJ in *Paragon Finance Plc v DB Thackerar & Co* [1999] 1 All E.R. 400 CA.

[536] *Williams v Central Bank of Nigeria* [2014] UKSC 10; [2014] A.C. 1189 SC. But note the strong dissent of Lord Mance. The issues are clearly difficult. The court's conclusions rely heavily on the judgment of Millett LJ in *Paragon Finance Plc v DB Thackerar & Co* [1999] 1 All E.R. 400 CA, although interestingly his analysis is used by both sides, and even Millett LJ, in *Paragon* at 414, had noted that "there is a case for treating a claim against a person who has assisted a trustee in committing a breach of trust as subject to the same limitation regime as the claim against the trustee".

[537] See above, paras 16–37 et seq. and for the prior statutory law see Companies Act 1985 s.309.

interests of the company (shareholders) required it.[538] Consequently, the novelty of the statutory formulation of the core duty of good faith and fidelity may be the added obligation—rather than entitlement—of directors to take stakeholder interests into account where the promotion of the success of the company requires this. This is only a marginal change in legal obligation, however, and there is as yet nothing to suggest that this revised statutory articulation of the need to take into account stakeholder interests in this way has had much impact, even when coupled with larger changes in legal rules and the social and economic context within which companies operate.[539]

The statutory rules are explicitly more constraining than the common law in their provisions on negligence (s.174), the core duty of loyalty (s.172) and the rules on ratification (s.239). The changes to the core duty of loyalty (s.172) have already been noted. So far as the duty of care is concerned, the objective standard of care introduced by s.174 is undoubtedly a strong contrast with the subjective formulation of that duty to be found in the nineteenth-century negligence cases. But common law decisions were already well-advanced in moving the law in an objective direction, and so it might be said that s.174 merely confirmed what was already emerging in the case law.[540] Equally, s.239[541] introduced important changes to the rules on who may vote on a shareholder resolution to ratify a breach of directors' duties by excluding the votes of the directors in question and those connected with them. But this trend too was evident in a trickle of cases, and clearly easily justified on policy grounds. It is undoubtedly an important reform in closely held companies, but its real impact will only be felt, even there (or especially there), if these rules also trigger a parallel change in the common law authorisation rules and their approach to disenfranchising interested voters. This, it is suggested, is a far better approach than tinkering further with the difficult notions of "un-ratifiable wrongs".[542]

Going in the other direction, and tending to relax rather than tighten the constraints on directors, perhaps the most significant statutory changes were those that allowed the independent members of the board to authorise breaches of the directors' duty not to place themselves in a position of conflict of duty and interest (or of duty and duty).[543] Although the principle of board decision-making was already established under the prior law in relation to self-dealing transactions (at least as a matter of practice, via provisions in the articles), its extension to corporate opportunities and other conflicted situations was a new step. The argument in favour of the extension is that shareholder authorisation, as the sole method of authorisation permitted by the prior law, was in practice too uncertain and too public to be a practical form of permission, so that the prior law operated in fact so as to allow directors to pursue corporate opportunities only at the risk of the company later deciding to take from the director the profit earned from the **16–141**

---

[538] *Hutton v West Cork Ry Co* (1883) 23 Ch.D. 654, per Bowen LJ: "Most businesses require liberal dealings".

[539] For example, changes within company law about narrative reporting (see paras 21–22 et seq.) or outside company law the increasing legal and political significance of environmental issues.

[540] See above, paras 16–15 et seq.

[541] Above, para.16–121.

[542] See above, paras 16–124 et seq.

[543] 2006 Act s.175 and see above, paras 16–103 et seq.

exploitation of the opportunity. The argument against the extension is that the dynamics of board relationships mean that the uninvolved members of the board may not exercise a genuinely independent judgment on whether to release the corporate interest in the opportunity, even if this is what the law requires of them. This argument may be less strong in companies listed on the main market of the London Stock Exchange and so required to comply with the provisions of the UK Corporate Governance Code as to independent non-executive directors, but that is a very small proportion of the companies incorporated under the Companies Acts. In the result, outside the area of benefits received by directors from third parties,[544] the board is now the guardian of the company's position in situations of conflict, contrary to the wisdom of the common law that only the shareholders could be relied upon for this purpose.

---

[544] See above, paras 16–107 et seq.

CHAPTER 17

THE DERIVATIVE CLAIM AND PERSONAL ACTIONS AGAINST DIRECTORS

THE NATURE OF THE PROBLEM AND THE POTENTIAL SOLUTIONS

The duties discussed in the previous chapter are not likely to play a significant **17–1** role in the governance of British companies if, for one reason or another, they are rarely enforced, either in actual litigation or in the threat of it. However, it is important not to jump from that banality to the conclusion that in every case where it is arguable that a director has infringed his or her duties to the company, the company should be contemplating litigation. The test, it is submitted, is whether "the interests of the company" require that litigation be instituted, and that question can be answered only on the facts of a particular case. It is easy to imagine many reasons why litigation would actually leave the company worse off than it was before. There may be doubts about whether a judgment in favour of the company will be obtained, either because of disputes about the law or because of difficulties of proving the events said to constitute the breach of duty. Or the defendants may not be in a position to meet the judgment even if the litigation is successful. Or the senior management time spent on the litigation might more profitably be used elsewhere or, finally, whilst winning the legal arguments and obtaining an enforceable remedy, the company may suffer collateral reputational harm which outweighs the gain from the litigation.[1] In other words, the decision whether to initiate litigation in respect of an alleged breach of directors' duty will not always be an easy one, and a negative decision is not necessarily a sign that the company is being too lax towards its directors.

On the other hand, a decision not to sue a director may indeed be heavily influenced by that director's personal interests, rather than those of the company. The conflicts of interest which we analysed in the previous chapter are not magically excluded from corporate decision-making on litigation. Thus, the need is to distinguish between litigation decisions (especially decisions not to sue) which are in the interests of the company and those which are not. Given that such decisions require a close analysis of particular cases, it is impossible to specify in advance categories of case in which litigation should always be brought and categories where it should never be. The role of the law is thus to determine the person or persons who can safely be entrusted with taking the decision whether in a particular case litigation to enforce the company's rights should be initiated or not.

The board and litigation

17–2 One possible solution to this question would be to say that the litigation decision is like any other decision the company might take and so should be left to the normal decision-making processes of the company. In most cases this approach would have the consequence of putting the litigation decision exclusively in the hands of the board. That the board will have the power under the constitutions of most companies to initiate litigation against wrongdoing directors seems clear, for it will be part of its standard management powers.[2] That the board may be unwilling always to sue the wrongdoing director even when it is in the best interests of the company to do so, however, seems equally clear. The wrongdoers may be a majority of the board or may be able to influence a majority of the board, and the same incentives which operated to cause the directors to breach their duties in the first place may cause them to utilise their board positions so as to suppress litigation against them.

Of course, this is not always the case. The board may act in an independent-minded way[3] or, perhaps more likely, the directors may have lost the influential positions on the board which they had when they committed the original wrongdoing. Thus, the previous board may have been replaced by a new set of directors as a result of a takeover[4] or, the company having become insolvent, the board has been replaced by an insolvency practitioner, acting in one

---

[1] *Taylor v National Union of Mineworkers (Derbyshire Area)* [1985] B.C.L.C. 237, 254–255 (Vinelott J).

[2] See art.3 of the model articles for both private and public companies limited by shares.

[3] cf. *John Shaw & Sons (Salford) Ltd v Shaw* [1935] 2 K.B. 113 CA, where the company's articles had allocated the litigation decision to a committee of the board from which the wrongdoers were excluded. This case shows that, where the board has the power under the articles and does decide to sue, the shareholders cannot by ordinary majority countermand its decision.

[4] See *Regal (Hastings) Ltd v Gulliver* [1942] 1 All E.R. 378 HL; above, para.16–89.

capacity or another on behalf of the creditors.[5] Indeed, the importance of litigation against wrongdoing directors (and other officers of the company) in this situation is recognised in s.212 of the Insolvency Act 1986, which gives liquidators (and others) in a winding up the benefit of a summary procedure for the enforcement of, inter alia, breaches of fiduciary duty and of the duty of care on the part of directors and to recover compensation by way of a contribution to the company's assets of such amount as the court thinks just. Under s.212 the liquidator sues in his or her own name but in substance on behalf of the company, which will be the recipient of any recovery.[6] Crucially, however, the courts regard the section as purely procedural so that it does not extend the range of the duties to which directors are subject.[7]

The shareholders collectively and litigation

Despite these examples of litigation against wrongdoing directors being initiated by those in charge of its management, it would obviously be unsound policy to leave such decisions exclusively with the board of the company. If the board decides to sue, all well and good, but it may result in less litigation than is optimal (i.e. than the interests of the company would dictate) if the board has exclusive control over the initiation of litigation in the company's name. In recognition of this argument, the common law seems to take the view that, even if the board does not wish to sue, it is open to the shareholders collectively by ordinary resolution to decide to do so.

17–3

Although sensible enough in policy terms, the reasoning by which the shareholders collectively come to have concurrent powers with the board to initiate litigation against wrongdoing directors is something of a mystery, since, as we saw in Ch.14, the allocation of a power to the board by the articles operates, in the absence of an express reservation, to remove that power from the shareholders. Consequently, in the absence of an express provision in the articles conferring upon the shareholders the power to initiate litigation, a shareholder decision to that effect would need to be passed by a special resolution, because that is the equivalent of a resolution to alter the articles. However, the common law appears to regard an ordinary resolution to initiate litigation as sufficient.

---

[5] Indeed, the replacement of the board by an insolvency practitioner was regarded under the previous law as a good reason for not allowing the individual shareholder to sue on behalf of the company. See *Ferguson v Wallbridge* [1935] 3 D.L.R. 66 PC; *Fargro Ltd v Godfroy* [1986] 1 W.L.R. 1134. In *Barrett v Duckett* [1995] 1 B.C.L.C. 243 CA the principle was even extended to deny to a shareholder who turned down the opportunity to put the company into liquidation the possibility of bringing a derivative claim: "As the company does have some money which might be used in litigating the claims, it is in my opinion manifest that it is better that the decision whether or not to use the money should be taken by an independent liquidator rather than by [the shareholder]" (at 255, per Peter Gibson LJ). These are still factors the court could take into account under s.263 (see below) but they would no longer be absolute bars to the derivative claim.

[6] Note that the court has a discretion under IA 1986 s.212 to reduce the amount that the defendant has to pay, but not to excuse liability altogether: *Revenue and Customs Commissioners v Holland* [2010] UKSC 51; [2010] 1 W.L.R. 2793 SC.

[7] *Cohen v Selby* [2001] 1 B.C.L.C. 176 at [20] CA. Nor does it allow the liquidator to escape from any limitation period to which the claim by the company would be subject: *Re Lands Allotment Co* [1894] 1 Ch. 616; *Re Eurocruit Europe Ltd* [2007] 2 B.C.L.C. 598.

This result can be rationalised on the basis that there is a rule of law, designed to promote shareholder control of the litigation decision, which overrides in this limited respect the allocation of functions by the articles. So, despite what the articles may say about the directors having general powers of management, it may be that the decision to sue may still be taken by an ordinary majority of the shareholders.[8]

However, it is still not obvious that the test of promoting the interests of the company will always be correctly applied to the litigation decision by the shareholders collectively. It is not impossible that the directors will control the general meeting through their own shareholdings, whether alone or in combination with those other shareholders whose decisions they can influence. Although the CLR proposed[9] to discount the votes of interested directors and those under their influence on decisions to sue, the Act applies that rule only to ratification decisions. If the shareholders do not purport to forgive the director's wrongdoing, but simply decide not to sue him or her (an inherently temporary commitment, unless the decision amounts to a waiver), it appears at first blush that the director in question is free to vote on that question.

Further, even in the absence of wrongdoer control of the general meeting, it is not obvious that the general meeting will come to consider the exercise of its power to initiate litigation. The wrongdoing directors, presumably, will not take steps to put the matter before the general meeting, unless they think the general meeting will support them, and so the shareholders as a whole may simply remain in ignorance of the fact that there is an issue for them to discuss. One or more shareholders may know of at least some of the relevant facts, and may seek to use their powers, discussed in Ch.15, to have the matter put on the agenda of an AGM or to have a meeting called to discuss the issue. In both cases, the support of substantial numbers of fellow shareholders will be required to force the company to take these steps and the support of half the shareholders present and voting at the meeting actually to pass a resolution in favour of litigation.

Derivative claims

17–4 In these circumstances, it is hardly surprising that provision was eventually made for giving individual shareholders standing to pursue litigation on behalf of the company against the alleged wrongdoing directors, although subject to

---

[8] See *Alexander Ward & Co Ltd v Samyang Navigation Co Ltd* [1975] 1 W.L.R. 673 at 679, per Lord Hailsham LC, quoting with approval a passage from the third edition of this book at pp.136–137. Unless this is the case, the rule in *Foss v Harbottle* (see below) made no sense, because the question that rule posed was whether the individual shareholder should be allowed to sue on behalf of the company or whether the matter should be left to a simple majority of the shareholders. On the other hand, the abolition by the 2006 Act of the rule in *Foss v Harbottle*, as far as derivative claims are concerned, reduces the force of this argument. The power of the shareholders to initiate litigation may not apply in the situation identified in the cases mentioned in fn.5, i.e. where the board has been replaced by an insolvency practitioner acting on behalf of the creditors. The not fully considered decision of Harman J in *Breckland Group Holdings Ltd v London and Suffolk Properties* [1989] B.C.L.C. 100 might seem to point in the direction of exclusive board control of the litigation, but there was in that case a shareholders' agreement in effect requiring the only two shareholders (or rather their board nominees) to support a decision to commence "material litigation".

[9] CLR, Completing, para.5.101 but contrast s.239 (above, para.16–119).

appropriate safeguards. Indeed, the principle just articulated can be said to have been accepted since 1843, when the *Foss v Harbottle* principle was formulated, because the substance of the controversy ever since has centred, not on whether such litigation should be permitted, but on the definition of the "appropriate safeguards".

On the one hand, relatively free access to the courts for individual shareholders suing on behalf of the company (or "derivatively", as the term is) will increase the levels of litigation against wrongdoing directors. If it is thought that the levels of such litigation are sub-optimal, because of the ability of the wrongdoers to influence litigation decisions at either board or shareholder level, then such an increase in litigation is likely to be welcomed. On the other hand, it is difficult to demonstrate that such litigation brought derivatively by individuals will invariably be brought in the interests of the company. It may be initiated more to promote the personal interests of the shareholder than the interests of the company (i.e. the shareholders as a whole). This is especially a risk since, as we shall see further below, in a derivative claim, recovery in the litigation goes to the company, not to the individual shareholder bringing the litigation. A person with a small shareholding thus has little financial incentive to sue on behalf of the company, because the return to that person will be, at most, a percentage of the recovery which reflects the percentage of the shares of the company that person holds.[10] So, litigation brought by such a person runs a risk of being motivated by concerns other than to increase the value of the company's business.[11] Of course, the larger the shareholder, the less this particular risk, but, by the same token, the lower the obstacles are which prevent such a shareholder from using the mechanism of the general meeting.

The English common law had always been more impressed by the risk of derivative claims being motivated by personal objectives than by the risk that confining derivative claims would lead to less litigation than the company's interests required. Accordingly, the common law, whose cumulative decisions in this area were referred to as "the rule in *Foss v Harbottle*",[12] permitted individual shareholder access to the courts on behalf of the company on only a very limited basis. The question which the rule in *Foss* set itself to answer was whether the individual shareholder should be allowed to sue derivatively or whether the litigation question would be better left to the shareholders as a whole.[13] Unfortunately, the rule was one-sided in its operation, i.e. it was effective to exclude the derivative suit if the law took the view that the decision of the shareholders as a whole should be relied upon, but it contained no mechanism whereby a meeting of such shareholders could be summoned to consider the

17–5

---

[10] Even then, the directors may choose not to pay out the recovery by way of dividend and instead to invest it in some perhaps unsuccessful venture.

[11] For an example of a derivative claim brought for what appears to be a collateral purpose, see the rather unusual case of *Konamaneni v Rolls-Royce Industrial Power (India) Ltd* [2002] 1 All E.R. 979. In the US, where derivative claims can be brought much more freely, it is sometimes argued that the drivers of the litigation are the firms of lawyers who stand to take a handsome percentage of awards obtained under contingent fee arrangements, if the derivative litigation is successful.

[12] *Foss v Harbottle* (1843) 2 Hare 461.

[13] See in particular the classic judgment of Jenkins LJ in *Edwards v Halliwell* [1950] 2 All E.R. 1064 CA.

question, and nor did it deprive interested directors of their votes.[14] Consequently, the rule did nothing to correct the deficiencies of group decision-making by the shareholders, as identified above, but simply made it difficult for the individual shareholder to sue instead.

17–6 These problems with the rule in *Foss v Harbottle* had become increasingly apparent over time and in 1997 the Law Commission advanced proposals for taking the law in a new direction by allocating the litigation decision to someone external to the company, namely, the court.[15] These proposals were largely endorsed by the CLR and are now embodied in somewhat different form in the Companies Act 2006. The Act now provides that derivative claims cannot be brought at common law but can only be brought under the statute (at least where the statute applies[16]), and so, to that extent at least, the rule in *Foss v Harbottle* need no longer be examined—to the relief of almost all those involved in company law.

Other possible solutions

17–7 Before turning to an analysis of the statutory provisions on the derivative claim, it is perhaps worth noting that the three mechanisms noted above—to have litigation decisions taken by the board, by the shareholders as a whole, or by individual shareholders—do not exhaust the possible mechanisms for handling this problem, even within the company. There are other obvious options, and to some extent the final form of the current statutory derivative action cherry-picks the better aspects of each of them.

17–8 One alternative might be to give the litigation decision to a sub-set of the members of the board, such as the uninvolved board members or its independent NEDs. As we have seen,[17] this is the approach taken in the Act to the authorisation of conflicts of interest, but not to the ratification of breaches of duty, where a shareholder decision is required. However, since the decision not to sue defaulting directors is akin to a ratification decision, it seems consistent not to use a sub-set of the board to take the litigation decision either. On the other hand, there are benefits to having director-input, especially given the powerful duties owed by directors to their companies. Recognising this, the statutory derivative framework makes it mandatory for the *court* itself to have regard to the likely approach of a disinterested director, acting in compliance with the good faith duty in s.172, to the litigation question (s.263(2)(a)). Equally, however, the ratification

---

[14] The technique endorsed in *Danish Mercantile Co Ltd v Beaumont* [1951] Ch. 680 CA, of commencing litigation in the name of the company (i.e. not derivatively) but without authority to do so and the court referring the issue to the shareholders for decision when the authority issue is raised, has not been used in practice (perhaps because the solicitors are personally liable in costs if the shareholders do not ratify the decision to sue), though it is consistent with the notion that, in the area of litigation, the shareholders have authority to decide, parallel to that of the board.

[15] Law Commission, *Shareholder Remedies*, Cm. 3769, 1997.

[16] The common law rules are still relevant for multiple derivative claims (see below, para.17–24) and claims concerning foreign registered companies (see *Abouraya v Sigmund* [2014] EWHC 277 (Ch); and *Novatrust Ltd v Kea Investments Ltd* [2014] EWHC 4061).

[17] See above, paras 16–103 and 16–117.

model, too, has its attractions, and, backing both horses, the statutory derivative claim also requires the court to consider the actual or likely views of the non-involved shareholders (i.e. those who could have voted to ratify) (ss.263(2)(b) and (c) and (3)(c) and (d)). All this is explored further below.

A further alternative would be to entrust the litigation decision to some group of shareholders, lying between the shareholders as a whole and the individual shareholder. The common law has not used this device and, although it has been used extensively in German law, the common law was perhaps right to reject it, since fixing the appropriate percentage has proved difficult. However, the strategy has been introduced into British law by the legislature in one specific context, as we will see later.[18] Where the company's claims arise in consequence of unauthorised political donations or expenditures made by the company's directors, then the right to sue in the name of the company is conferred, not on individual shareholders, but on an "authorised group" of members, defined by statute to be a minority of a particular size, but then at the same time excluding individual shareholders from suing, on the basis presumably that they might be motivated by reasons which did not relate to the company's interests.

17–9

A final and more radical approach would be to give the right to commence a derivative action to someone outside the company altogether. This is unlikely to be a sensible approach to the general run of companies, where it is difficult to identify anyone outside the company with a legitimate interest in commencing litigation on its behalf. However, some vestiges of this technique might be thought evident in the ability of a liquidator or administrator to bring all manner of claims on behalf of the company,[19] or the Secretary of State specifically to seek compensation orders against directors and other persons who are the subject of disqualification orders or undertakings where their conduct has caused loss to one or more creditors of their insolvent company.[20] Similarly, the Regulator of Community Interest Companies ("CIC") may bring proceedings (subject to a right of appeal by any director of the CIC to the court, which then has broad powers to confirm, discontinue or set terms for the litigation).[21] If the Regulator takes this step, the company must be indemnified by the Regulator against the costs and expenses of the litigation, unless, presumably, the court orders the costs should be borne by the company. This perhaps highlights a further concern with this approach in the context of viable companies.

17–10

---

[18] See below, paras 17–29 et seq.

[19] See Ch.33.

[20] See CDDA 1986 ss.15A–15C, introduced by SBEEA 2015 s.110 from 1 October 2015. The application must be made within two years of the disqualification order or undertaking (s.15A(5)). The compensation will be payable either: (i) to the Secretary of State for the benefit of a creditor or creditors specified in the order, or a class or classes of specified creditors; or (ii) as a contribution to the assets of the company (s.15B). See generally Ch.10.

[21] Companies (Audit, Investigations and Community Enterprise) Act 2004 s.44.

THE GENERAL STATUTORY DERIVATIVE CLAIM

The scope of the statutory derivative claim

The court's gatekeeper role

17–11   The novelty of the general statutory derivative claim, contained in Pt 11 of the 2006 Act, is that it places the gatekeeping decision about whether it is in the interests of the company for litigation to be commenced in any particular case in the hands of the court, i.e. an outsider to the company.[22] True, a shareholder must take the first initiative, but after the claim form has been issued, a shareholder seeking to bring a derivative claim must seek the permission of the court to take any substantive steps in the litigation (other than, in the normal case, informing the company that the claim has been issued and that the shareholder is applying to the court for permission to continue the claim).[23] It was already the case that the court had a role in the early stages of derivative claims at common law, but this was to check that the claimant had standing to sue under the rule in *Foss v Harbottle*.[24] Under the new general derivative claim the court has a broader role, namely, to exercise a constrained discretion to decide whether it is in the best interests of the company for the litigation to be brought. This new procedure has the advantages, on the one hand, that the individual shareholder can easily obtain a decision on the central question (whether it is in the interests of the company for the litigation to be brought), whilst, on the other hand, the individual shareholder's enthusiasm for derivative litigation is subject to the filter of a judge having to be convinced that this particular litigation on behalf of the company is desirable.

17–12   Whilst it is true that many of the policy issues which underlay the rule in *Foss v Harbottle* reappear under the statutory procedure,[25] they appear now not as absolute bars to a derivative claim, but as factors the court must take into account in deciding whether to allow the litigation to proceed. Thus, a claimant who is turned away by the court will receive a judgment explaining why a derivative claim in the particular case is not in the company's interests, whereas previously the court's decision said nothing about the desirability of the litigation from the company's point of view, but simply that the litigation decision was a decision for the shareholders generally rather than the individual shareholder.

---

[22] The earlier history and the purpose of the new statutory derivative claim are considered in *Iesini v Westrip Holdings Ltd* [2009] EWHC 2526 (Ch); [2011] 1 B.C.L.C. 498 at [73]–[83] (Lewison J).

[23] CPR 19.9(4), 19A(2).

[24] In *Prudential Assurance Co Ltd v Newman Industries Ltd (No.2)* [1982] Ch. 204 CA the court insisted that the question of standing to bring the derivative claim should be decided in advance of and separately from the decision on the merits of the case. This approach is embodied in CPR 19.9. Under this provision the courts recently began to take a broader look at the value to the company of the proposed derivative claim: *Portfolios of Distinction Ltd v Laird* [2004] 2 B.C.L.C. 741 at [51]–[68]; *Airey v Cordell* [2007] B.C.C. 785.

[25] See ss.263 and 268, discussed below.

The types of claims covered by the statutory regime

There are a good number of limitations to the statutory jurisdiction. The statute applies only to derivative claims or derivative proceedings, i.e. claims brought in respect of a cause of action vested in the company and seeking relief on its behalf.[26] Since the individual shareholder has no power to initiate litigation in the company's name, but the company is to be bound by and is the potential beneficiary of any judgment or order made in the derivative litigation, the Civil Procedure Rules require the company to be made a defendant in the litigation, even though it is the company's rights which are being enforced. Thus, the claim appears in the form of "Shareholder v Director and Company".[27] This can be a cause of confusion, unless it is remembered that the company is only a nominal defendant and that the real defendants are the directors.[28]

17–13

Most derivative claims can now be brought only under the Act,[29] either under the Pt 11 provisions discussed here or as a result of a court order made in unfair prejudice provisions discussed in Ch.20. The rule in *Foss v Harbottle* is thus almost entirely consigned to the dustbin. On the other hand, not all claims a shareholder might want to bring on behalf of the company may be brought under Pt 11 of the Act. The Act contemplates as derivative claims only claims "arising from an actual or proposed act or omission involving negligence, default, breach of duty or breach of trust by a director of the company".[30] Where the company has a cause of action arising in some other way (for example, a claim against a non-directorial employee), the policy seems to be that a derivative claim is not available, and the litigation decision should be taken according to the division of powers contained in the company's articles of association (i.e. normally exclusively by the board). It is only where the directors themselves are in breach of duty that the statutory derivative procedure is available, because that is when the risk of conflicted decision-making by board or shareholders generally arises. However, although the company's cause of action must arise out of breach of duty, etc. by the directors, the defendants are not necessarily limited to and may not even include the directors themselves.[31] We have seen above[32] that third parties may become liable to the company as a result of their involvement in

17–14

---

[26] 2006 Act s.260(1): derivative claims (for England and Wales and Northern Ireland). Section 265(1) provides similarly for derivative proceedings in Scotland. Because of the intimate connection between derivative claims and civil procedure, the Act contains separate provisions for Scotland (ss.265–269) and the rest of the UK (ss.260–264). However, the underlying policies are the same.

[27] CPR 19.9(3). The reason for this oddity seems to be that anyone can make another person a defendant to a claim but making a person a claimant requires that person's consent.

[28] If the shareholder has a personal claim against the directors, the statutory procedure has no application. Personal claims are dealt with below and, as we shall see, there are great complexities about remedies where both the company and the shareholder personally have claims against a director.

[29] The exceptions are those claims against directors falling outside the statutory definition of a derivate claim, in particular multiple derivative claims and claims against foreign registered companies: for the former, see below, para.17–24; for the latter, see *Abouraya v Sigmund* [2014] EWHC 277 (Ch); *Novatrust Ltd v Kea Investments Ltd* [2014] EWHC 4061 (Ch).

[30] 2006 Act ss.260(3) and 265(3).

[31] 2006 Act ss.260(3) and 265(4).

[32] See paras 16–134 et seq.

directors' breaches of duty and, in such cases, the derivative claim may be used against the third party, even if no director is sued.

17–15 Directors for the purpose of Pt 11 include former and shadow directors,[33] but this is less significant than it may seem. The Pt 11 rules do not alter the circumstances in which former or shadow directors owe duties to the company; they merely ensure that, where such duties are owed, the derivative claim can be used to enforce them. We have discussed in the previous chapter the circumstances in which the general duties of directors do in fact fall upon former or shadow directors.[34]

Shareholder claimants

17–16 A shareholder may bring a derivative claim in respect of a cause of action which arose before he or she became a member of the company.[35] On the other hand, only members of the company can bring derivative claims: a former member cannot sue even in respect of a matter which occurred when he was a shareholder.[36] This reflects the legal position of shareholders generally: the shareholder has an interest in the assets of the company as they stand during his or her membership. That interest is not confined to assets acquired during the shareholder's membership. On the other hand, once membership is relinquished, so is the interest in the company's assets, including in assets the shareholder or even the company was unaware were possessed during the period of membership (for example, the shareholder who sells the week before oil is discovered below land owned by the company just has to accept that loss).

However, there is one useful statutory extension of the notion of a "member". This term is not confined to those who have been entered on the company's register of members—which is a standard requirement for membership[37]—but is extended to those to whom shares have been transferred or transmitted by operation of law, even if not entered on the register of members.[38] The usual example of transmission is on death or bankruptcy. The extension of the meaning of membership to include mere transferees is especially useful in quasi-partnership companies where the directors normally have power under the articles to refuse to admit new members and are often prepared to use the power to keep out of the company those with whom they do not wish to work. Making the derivative claim available may enable them to challenge their exclusion or, at least, to challenge action by the controllers of the company—for example, siphoning assets out of the company to the detriment of the would-be member—designed to induce the would-be member to transfer the shares to the other members at a low price. Such action by the controllers carries the risk that the would-be member will bring a derivative action to restore the company's

---

[33] 2006 Act ss.260(5) and 265(7).
[34] See above, paras 16–8 and 16–13.
[35] 2006 Act ss.260(4) and 265(5).
[36] 2006 Act ss.260(1) and 265(1).
[37] 2006 Act s.112. For further discussion see para.27–5.
[38] 2006 Act ss.260(5)(c) and 265(7)(e).

position. A similar and even more important extension of the term "member" is to be found in the unfair prejudice provisions, discussed in Ch.20.

Deciding whether to give permission for the derivative claim

The central issue under the new statutory procedure is the nature of the discretion vested in the court to approve or not the continuance of the derivative claim. That discretion is broad but not unconstrained. The statute proceeds in three stages by requiring the claimant, first, to make out a prima facie case; then identifying three situations in which leave must be denied[39]; and then, assuming the case does not fall within any of those three situations, laying down a number of factors the court must take into account when deciding whether to give permission to proceed with the derivative claim.

The prima facie case and judicial management of proceedings

The decision whether to grant permission for the derivative claim to proceed will potentially generate a wide-ranging enquiry before the court. Although the company is a potential beneficiary of the derivative action, there is a risk that companies might find themselves subjected to overly-high levels of proposed derivative claims by shareholders who have a fanciful or even self-interested view of the likely benefits to the company from such litigation. Companies would then be distracted from more important tasks by having to explain in court why such claims should not be allowed to proceed further. In partial recognition of this issue, the statute contains a procedure whereby the court's initial consideration of the claim is on the basis of the evidence submitted by the member alone. If the court does not at this stage think the applicant has established a prima facie case for permission to be granted, the application will be refused. At this initial stage, the company is not a respondent to the application to the court for permission to continue the claim and so is not required to file evidence or be present at any hearing. Only if the application survives this initial examination will the company be invited to file evidence as to whether permission should be granted or not.[40]

Mandatory refusal of permission

Two of the situations where permission must be denied are obvious: where the actual or proposed breach of duty has been authorised or ratified in accordance with the rules set out in the previous chapter.[41] In such a case, there is no, or is no longer, any wrong by the director to the company, and, just as the company

17–17

17–18

17–19

---

[39] 2006 Act ss.263(1) and 268(1).
[40] 2006 Act ss.261(2) and 266(3). In England and Wales this procedure is fleshed out in CPR 19.9A. In some cases, the court has been inclined to merge the first two stages into one: *Mission Capital Plc v Sinclair* [2008] EWHC 1339 (Ch); *Franbar Holdings Ltd v Patel* [2008] EWHC 1534 (Ch); *Stimpson v Southern Private Landlords Association* [2009] EWHC 2072 (Ch); and *Bridge v Daley* [2015] EWHC 2121 (Ch).
[41] 2006 Act ss.263(2)(b), (c) and 268(1)(b), (c). See above, paras 16–55, 16–67 et seq., 16–103, 16–117 et seq.

cannot complain of it, neither can the shareholder suing derivatively. The important prohibition is thus the third one. The court must deny permission to continue the derivative claim where a person acting in accordance with the directors' core duty of loyalty (to promote the success of the company for the benefit of its members) "would not" seek to continue the claim.[42] Since the core duty of good faith, set out in s.172, is the modern version of the notion of acting "in the interests of the company", it is sensible to use it as the test in relation to the derivative claim, and indeed it is used both at this mandatory dismissal stage and again at the permissive stage. At this mandatory stage, the words have been interpreted as meaning *no* director would seek to pursue the claim.[43] At the permissive stage, more flexibility is both warranted and inevitable, as noted below.

Discretionary grant of permission

17–20   If the proposed litigation passes the negative test (i.e. will it fail to promote the success of the company?), one might have thought that whether it should be allowed to proceed should depend on whether it can pass that test put positively, i.e. will the litigation promote the success of the company?—or, rather, that all that is required is the positive version of the test. However, the tests which are to be applied to the proposal if it passes the negative test are more varied than that.

The statute sets out seven factors[44] which the court must take into account in deciding whether to allow the litigation to proceed once it is considered to have passed the negative test.[45] To be sure, one of those tests is "the importance that a person acting in accordance with section 172 would attach to continuing it"[46] (see below), but that is only one of the tests. The thinking behind the drafting may have been that the court should not be under pressure to allow the litigation to proceed where its financial contribution to the company was likely to be small and there were other factors pointing against the litigation,[47] though it is doubtful if the term "success" in s.172 is to be construed solely in financial terms. Alternatively, it may have been thought desirable to give the court more guidance on the factors to be considered than a single general test would provide.

17–21   The further tests, which are explicitly stated not to be exhaustive of the considerations the court should take into account,[48] are as follows:

---

[42] 2006 Act ss.263(2)(a) and 268(1)(a). On the director's core duty of good faith see above, paras 16–37 et seq.

[43] *Iesini v Westrip Holdings Ltd* [2009] EWHC 2526 (Ch); [2011] 1 B.C.L.C. 498, where the court held that the strength of the claim against the board was so weak that *no* director, acting in accordance with s.172, would seek to continue the claim.

[44] To which the Secretary of State may add by regulation: ss.263(5) and 268(4).

[45] 2006 Act ss.263(3),(4) and 268(2),(3).

[46] 2006 Act ss.263(3)(b) and 268(2)(b). *Iesini v Westrip Holdings Ltd* [2009] EWHC 2526 (Ch); [2011] 1 B.C.L.C. 498 failed this test.

[47] Although, conversely, if the potential financial gain is high, a more uncertain case might be worth pursuing: *Stainer v Lee* [2010] EWHC 1539 (Ch); [2011] 1 B.C.L.C. 537.

[48] See the words "in particular" in ss.263(3) and 268(2).

- Whether the shareholder seeking to bring the derivative claim is acting in good faith—or whether, for example, the litigation is motivated by personal interests.

- The importance that a person acting in accordance with s.172 would attach to continuing it. In that vein, it should be noted that there is one crucial difference between the court's role when it is hearing an allegation that a director has breached the core duty of loyalty and its role in the statutory derivative claim. In the former case, provided the director has properly formed a good faith view as to what promoting the success of the company requires, the court has no power to interfere. Under the statutory procedure, however, it does not appear that such deference is to be accorded at the permissive stage to the individual shareholder's decision to initiate derivative proceedings. Rather, the court will have to formulate its own view about whether the proposed litigation will fail to promote the success of the company.[49] This is difficult: as Lewison J noted in *Iesini v Westrip Holdings Ltd*,[50] it is "essentially a commercial decision, which the court is ill-equipped to take, except in a clear case."

- Whether the act or omission which constituted the breach of duty is likely to be ratified by the company (i.e. by the shareholders collectively) or—expressed as a separate test—whether in the case of a proposed breach of duty the act or omission is likely to be authorised or ratified by the company. Authorisation, as we saw in the previous chapter,[51] can sometimes be given by the non-involved members of the board. These two tests reflect a factor which was very important under the rule in *Foss v Harbottle*, but, whereas at common law the possibility of shareholder approval (normally referred to as ratifiability) of the wrong normally barred access to the derivative claim,[52] under the statutory procedure the prospect of either authorisation or ratification[53] is not a bar to the derivative claim but simply a factor weighing against giving permission. The removal of ratifiability as a bar to the derivative claim is one of the most important changes brought about by the statutory procedure. Under the common law the derivative claim was largely excluded as a mechanism for the

---

[49] See *Iesini v Westrip Holdings Ltd* [2009] EWHC 2526 (Ch); [2011] 1 B.C.L.C. 498, finding that, under s.263(3)(b), a person acting in accordance with s.172 would attach little weight to continuing the action. Also see *Re Seven Holdings* [2011] EWHC 1893; and *Kleanthous v Paphitis* [2011] EWHC 2287 (Ch).

[50] *Iesini v Westrip Holdings Ltd* [2009] EWHC 2526 (Ch); [2011] 1 B.C.L.C. 498 at [85], noting that the decision required consideration of factors which included "the size of the claim; the strength of the claim; the cost of the proceedings; the company's ability to fund the proceedings; the ability of the potential defendants to satisfy a judgment; the impact on the company if it lost the claim and had to pay not only its own costs but the defendant's as well; any disruption to the company's activities while the claim is pursued; whether the prosecution of the claim would damage the company in other ways (e.g. by losing the services of a valuable employee or alienating a key supplier or customer) and so on".

[51] Above, para.16–103.

[52] See *Edwards v Halliwell* [1950] 2 All E.R. 1064 CA.

[53] The statute specifies that this is "by the company", thus importing the mechanisms and their qualifications discussed at various stages in Ch.16, especially paras 16–117 et seq.

enforcement of ratifiable breaches of duty, and that perhaps goes some way to explaining the rise of the concept of "un-ratifiable breaches".[54]

- Whether the company (whether through a decision of the board or of the shareholders) has decided not to pursue the claim. What is at issue here is a board or shareholder resolution which, whilst not seeking to ratify the directors' breach of duty, nevertheless contains a decision not to sue the directors.[55] Such a resolution may constitute an argument against allowing the derivative claim to continue, provided the decision was not influenced by the alleged wrongdoers,[56] but it is only a factor to be taken into account. Again, this is a significant change from the common law. Under the common law regime, even a non-ratifiable wrong could not be pursued derivatively unless the alleged wrongdoers were in control of the general meeting. Under the statutory procedure, permission to continue the litigation can be granted by the court even if the alleged wrongdoers are not in control of the shareholders' meeting.[57] No doubt, however, a decision by the shareholders, uninfluenced by the wrongdoers, not to initiate litigation will count heavily against the derivative claim.

- Whether the facts give rise to a cause of action which vests in the member personally and which he or she could pursue as such rather than through a derivative claim on behalf of the company. Perhaps the most obvious claim a shareholder might bring is a petition based on unfairly prejudicial conduct by the controllers of the company, dealt with in Ch.20.[58] Apart from that, the possibilities for a personal action will be limited, since, normally, directors' duties are owed to the company, not to shareholders individually.[59] The shareholder may prefer a derivative claim because the costs of it will fall on the company (see below), but, given the courts' firm view that, outside the area of unfair prejudice, recovery cannot be obtained in a personal claim for loss to the shareholder which reflects the company's loss, the availability of the personal claim may not be a strong argument against allowing the derivative claim to proceed, even where both causes of action exist.[60]

- Finally, and by way of separate subsection, the court is required to have "particular regard" to any evidence before it of the views of the other

---

[54] On the common law's distinction between ratifiable and non-ratifiable breaches of duty, see the previous chapter at para.16–124.

[55] *Bridge v Daley* [2015] EWHC 2121 (Ch).

[56] A decision by the company not to pursue the claim should be given very little weight where the defendant directors constitute the majority of its directors: *Cullen Investments v Brown* [2015] EWHC 472 (Ch).

[57] See *Bamford v Harvey* [2012] EWHC 2858 (Ch). However, this is likely to be rare: *Cinematic Finance Ltd v Ryder* [2010] All E.R. (D) 283.

[58] See *Franbar Holdings Ltd v Patel* [2008] EWHC 1534 (Ch); [2009] 1 B.C.L.C. 1, where the shareholder's concurrent unfair prejudice claim was seen as delivering almost all the shareholder wanted, so the right to pursue the derivative claim was, to that extent, denied. Similarly, see *Kleanthous v Paphitis* [2011] EWHC 2287 (Ch); *Singh v Singh* [2014] EWHC Civ 103. The unfair prejudice alternative is important even where the shareholder does not want to be bought out.

[59] See above at para.16–5. Also see *Cullen Investments Ltd v Brown* [2015] EWHC 473 (Ch).

[60] See below, para.17–32. Also see *Cullen Investments Ltd v Brown* [2015] EWHC 473 (Ch), where the "no reflective loss" principle was one of the factors considered by the court in reaching its conclusion that no alternative remedy was available in that case.

shareholders who have no personal interest in the matter.[61] Again, this reflects an important element of the rule in *Foss v Harbottle*, which, however, appeared to say that the individual shareholder did not have standing to bring a derivative claim if a majority of the independent shareholders were against the litigation.[62] Now those views are only a factor, but are likely to be a powerful factor for or against the derivative claim where reliable evidence of those views can be provided to the court.

Varieties of derivative claim

Taking over existing claims

The discussion so far has assumed a derivative claim being brought where the company itself has failed to initiate litigation. No doubt this is the core case. However, the statute also specifically provides for a shareholder to apply to the court for permission to take over as a derivative claim litigation which the company has commenced.[63] The reasoning, perhaps, is that without this protection the directors of a company might stultify potential derivative claims by instituting litigation in the company's name but then failing to pursue it with vigour. The statute deals with this problem by allowing a shareholder to apply to take over the company's litigation in derivative form.

17–22

Of course, the company's claim must be one which falls within the scope of the derivative claim and the court must apply to the shareholder's application for permission to take over the claim the same criteria it would have applied had the litigation been commenced in derivative form.[64] In addition, the shareholder must show why he or she should be allowed to take over the company's claim. The permitted grounds are that the proceedings have been conducted by the company in a way which constitutes an abuse of the process of the court or that the company has not prosecuted the litigation diligently or that for other reasons it is "appropriate" for the shareholder to be substituted for the company.[65] However, if the company has already settled the case against the directors, there would appear to be no basis upon which the section could operate.

The statute even provides a mechanism for a shareholder to apply to the court to take over an existing derivative claim. The point seems to be to prevent the directors from stultifying litigation against themselves by securing a friendly shareholder to commence litigation in derivative form but then not prosecute the claim effectively.[66] The grounds for taking over a derivative claim are the same as for taking over a claim begun in the company's name, but of course the tests for giving permission to commence a derivative claim do not have to be applied to

17–23

---

[61] 2006 Act ss.263(4) and 268(3). Moreover, unlike the other matters to which the court must have regard, this one cannot be altered by the Secretary of State by regulation: s.263(5)(b).

[62] *Smith v Croft (No.2)* [1988] Ch. 114; cited with approval in *Franbar Holdings Ltd v Patel* [2008] EWHC 1534 (Ch); [2009] 1 B.C.L.C. 1.

[63] 2006 Act ss.262 and 267.

[64] 2006 Act ss.262(1),(3), 263(1), 267(1),(3), 268(1).

[65] 2006 Act ss.262(2) and 267(2).

[66] 2006 Act ss.264 and 269.

the claim to take over an existing derivative claim, since they will have been met at an earlier stage. It should be noted that a claim to take over an existing derivative claim can be made whether the claim was originally commenced in derivative form or was commenced by the company but later taken over derivatively; and whether the shareholder from whom the applicant wishes to take over the litigation is the originator of the litigation, took the litigation over from the company or is someone later down the chain of shareholders who have been pursuing the claim derivatively.[67]

Multiple derivative claims

17–24   The statute does not, however, cater for the possibility of "multiple derivative claims", being claims brought by a member of a corporate member of the wronged company, contrary to the suggestion of the Company Law Review.[68] A restrictive construction of the exclusive nature of the statutory scheme would mean that such actions could not be brought either under the statutory scheme (not falling within the s.260(1) definition of a derivative claim) nor at common law, but this construction has been rejected in recent cases, which have instead held that such claims can still be brought under the common law and that the court's jurisdiction in that respect has not been taken away by the statutory scheme.[69]

The subsequent conduct of the derivative claim

General issues

17–25   The statutory provisions governing the general derivative claim say nothing about the subsequent conduct of the derivative claim, except that the court is given a general power to give permission for the claim to continue "on such terms as it thinks fit".[70] It is perhaps odd that the subsequent conduct of the general derivative claim is less clearly regulated than that of the special derivative claim for unlawful political donations discussed next. In particular, there is no counterpart in the statute or Civil Procedure Rules to the duties of care and loyalty which are imposed on those bringing a derivative claim in respect of unauthorised political donations.[71] It may be that the courts could develop such provisions on the basis of the quasi-agency position in which a person bringing a general derivative claim is placed.

---

[67] 2006 Act ss.264(1) and 269(1).

[68] *Developing*, para.4.133.

[69] See *Re Fort Gilkicker Ltd* [2013] EWHC 348 (Ch); *Bhullar v Bhullar* [2015] EWHC 1943. The same argument also permits common law derivative claims concerning foreign registered companies: *Abouraya v Sigmund* [2014] EWHC 277 (Ch); *Novatrust Ltd v Kea Investments Ltd* [2014] EWHC 4061.

[70] 2006 Act ss.261(4)(a), 262(5)(a), 264(5)(a), 266(5)(a), 267(5)(a) and 269(5)(a). Contrast the provisions relating to the derivative claim arising out of unauthorised political donations or expenditure, below, at paras 17–29 et seq.

[71] See below, para.17–30.

Information rights

Those bringing general derivative claim also lack the specific information right   **17–26**
conferred by CA 2006 s.373 in favour of those seeking derivatively to recover an
unauthorised donation from the directors. It is possible that the court might deal
with this matter when setting the conditions for the conduct of the general claim.
However, another avenue may be open to secure the board's co-operation with
those responsible for the general derivative claim. By permitting the derivative
action, the court will have determined that a director acting in accordance with
the core duty of loyalty would bring the litigation and that there are no other
factors which outweigh that conclusion. In that situation it will be difficult for the
board, consistently with their duties, not to co-operate fully with the shareholder
who has charge of the derivative claim. Indeed, it may be wondered whether its
duties do not require the board to give serious consideration to bringing the claim
in the company's name, though presumably the court's permission would be
needed for the derivative claim to be superseded by a corporate one and the court
might be reluctant to so agree if the board's previous attitude towards the claim
had been one of unmitigated hostility.

Costs

The important case of *Wallersteiner v Moir (No.2)*[72] established that a   **17–27**
consequence of the derivative claim being to enforce the company's rights is that,
where permission is given, the company should normally be liable for the costs of
the claim, even, in fact especially, where the litigation is ultimately unsuccessful.
This decision is now reflected in the Civil Procedure Rules which provide that
"the court may order the company … to indemnify the claimant against any
liability for costs incurred in the permission application or in the derivative claim
or both".[73] This is a very important provision because, without it, the financial
disincentive for a shareholder to bring a derivative claim would be very strong,
no matter how relaxed the standing rules. On these rules, however, if a
shareholder can obtain permission from the court to bring a derivative claim,
there should be no financial disincentive to proceed.[74]

---

[72] *Wallersteiner v Moir (No.2)* [1975] Q.B. 373 CA.

[73] CPR 19.9. However, the court is not likely to give the claimant a blank cheque but to review the company's obligation to pay stage-by-stage as the litigation proceeds. See *McDonald v Horn* [1995] 1 All E.R. 961, 974–975 CA; *Stainer v Lee* [2010] EWHC 1539 (Ch); [2011] 1 B.C.L.C. 537 (capped at £40,000). Moreover, such an order does not give the shareholder priority over the unsecured creditors of the company (*Qayoumi v Oakhouse Property Holdings Plc* [2003] 1 B.C.L.C. 352) so that the shareholder may be unwilling to pursue a derivative claim on behalf of a doubtfully solvent company.

[74] Indeed, even greater security is given in that, in leave proceedings, the court can make a declaratory conditional order as to costs of the main litigation, requiring the company to indemnify the member at least to a certain extent: *Wishart v Castlecroft Securities Ltd* [2009] CSIH 65; [2010] B.C.C. 161. And costs might also cover the application for leave: [2010] CSIH 2. However, the court has to exercise considerable care when deciding whether to order a pre-emptive indemnity: *Bhullar v Bhullar* [2015] EWHC 1943 (Ch).

Restrictions on settlement

17–28 The Civil Procedure Rules ("CPR") also deal with one further post-permission issue. The derivative litigation is brought to enforce the company's rights for the company's benefit, but a common perversion of the procedure, known in some quarters as "greenmail", involves the shareholder being primarily interested in obtaining some private benefit from the litigation, normally as part of the terms on which the company's claim against the directors is settled. To discourage such behaviour, the CPR empower the court to order that the claim may not be "discontinued, settled or compromised without the permission of the court", thus giving the court the opportunity to scrutinise the terms of any settlement.[75]

THE STATUTORY DERIVATIVE CLAIM FOR UNAUTHORISED POLITICAL EXPENDITURE

17–29 As noted earlier, minority group shareholder action on behalf of the company has been introduced into British law by the legislature in one specific area. Under what is now Pt 14 of the Act, a company's policy to make political donations and incur political expenditure is subject to approval by the shareholders in general meeting.[76] If this requirement is contravened, every director (and shadow director) of the company at the relevant time is liable to pay to the company the amount of any donation, or expenditure and damages in respect of any loss or damage suffered by the company in consequence of the unauthorised donation or expenditure.[77] Section 370 then provides for a statutory derivative claim in order to enforce the directors' liability. However, this right to sue in the name of the company is conferred, not on individual shareholders, as in the general derivative action, but on an "authorised group" of members, meaning, in the case of a company limited by shares, the holders of not less than 5 per cent of the nominal value of the company's issued share capital or any class thereof; in the case of a company not limited by shares by not less than 5 per cent of its members; or, in either case, by not less than 50 members of the company.[78] It seems that the aim of confining the right to sue to a small group of shareholders was to provide a realistic chance of enforcement action being brought whilst at the same time excluding individual shareholders from suing, who might be motivated by reasons which did not relate to the company's interests. There is no added role for the court to act as gatekeeper giving permission to proceed.

---

[75] CPR 19.9F.

[76] See the previous chapter at para.16–85.

[77] 2006 Act s.369. In some cases, as we saw in the previous chapter at para.16–85, the liability may fall upon a director of a holding company and be a liability to the subsidiary. In such a case the derivative claim to enforce the subsidiary's rights may be brought by an authorised group of the shareholders of the holding company as well as by an authorised group of the shareholders of the subsidiary: s.370(1)(b). This will be a useful facility where the subsidiary is wholly owned by the parent.

[78] This mechanism seems to have been chosen in the original legislation of 2000 on the basis of a somewhat bizarre analogy with the group of shareholders who have the right to complain to the court about a resolution on the part of a public company to re-register as a private one: s.98. The analogy is odd because the claim arising under s.98 is not derivative.

Having conferred a statutory right of action in relation to donations upon the **17–30** approved group of members, the Act also takes some steps to facilitate the use of the power by the minority but also to ensure that the power is exercised by the group in the interests of the shareholders as a whole. In particular, the fact that the statutory derivative claim is brought on behalf and in the interests of the company is emphasised by a number of features of the legislation:

(i)   The same duties (of care and loyalty) are owed to the company by the authorised group as would be owed to the company if the claim had been brought by the directors of the company. However, action to enforce these duties against the minority cannot be taken without the leave of the court, presumably so as to protect the minority from the tactical use of counter-litigation by the alleged wrongdoing directors.[79]

(ii)   Proceedings may not be discontinued or settled by the group without the leave of the court and the court may impose terms on any leave it grants.[80] This provision reduces the risk of "gold digging" or "greenmail" claims where the purpose of the claim is to extract from the company a private benefit for the group in exchange for the settlement of the claim rather than to advance the interests of the shareholders as a whole.

(iii)   The group may apply to the court for an order that the company indemnify the group in respect of the costs of the litigation and the court may make such order as it thinks fit. The group is not entitled to be paid its costs out of the assets of the company other than by virtue of an indemnification order or as a result of a costs order made in the litigation in favour of the company.[81] These provisions both recognise the principle that the company in appropriate circumstance should pay for derivative litigation which is brought for its benefit (as is the case with the general statutory derivative claim)[82] and make it less easy for the group to pursue "gold digging" claims in the guise of generous payments by the company to the group by way of recompense for costs incurred in the litigation.

(iv)   On the other hand, there is conferred upon the group an express right to all information relating to the subject-matter of the litigation which is in the company's possession, so that the group can better decide in what way to prosecute the litigation. This right extends to information which is reasonably obtainable by the company (for example, from another group company). The court may enforce this right by order.[83]

This is quite a different model from that applying to the general derivative claim. **17–31** Section 370(5) provides that the existence of the specific procedure here does not bar access to the general statutory derivative procedure. The general procedure will normally be available because payment of an unauthorised donation or the

---

[79] 2006 Act s.371(4).
[80] 2006 Act s.371(5).
[81] 2006 Act s.372.
[82] See above, para.17–27.
[83] 2006 Act s.373. However, the right to information does not arise until proceedings have been instituted, and so the right seems not to aid the minority at the stage when it is considering whether to institute litigation.

incurring of unauthorised expenditure by the director will usually constitute a breach of the director's general duties. Whether the specific or the general statutory derivative claim will be more attractive is not clear.

SHAREHOLDERS' PERSONAL CLAIMS AGAINST DIRECTORS

17–32   The above description of the problem underlying the rule in *Foss v Harbottle* has been couched in terms of the enforcement by individual shareholders of duties owed by directors to their company. Where the duty is owed by the director to the shareholder personally, the above analysis ought to be irrelevant. If the shareholder is also the right-holder, it would seem in principle to be entirely a matter for his or her discretion whether the right is enforced. So much is indeed recognised in the statute, Pt 11 of which applies only to claims to enforce "a cause of action vested in the company".[84]

17–33   However, there are two points which call for comment. First, the range of rights owed by directors to shareholders personally is limited. We saw in the previous chapter that the general duties of directors are only rarely owed to individual shareholders rather than to the company.[85] In addition, however, the directors may owe duties to shareholders under the general law. In either case, the duties typically arise where the directors give advice to the shareholders or otherwise take action in relation to the exercise by the shareholders of the rights attached to their shares, including the sale of the shares. So although these duties, under the general law or under company law, should be freely enforceable, it is not often that shareholders have such rights to enforce.

Reflective loss

17–34   Secondly, even where the shareholder has a personal claim, the shareholder's claim may be restricted by the "no reflective loss" principle. What is required to trigger the principle is that both the company and the shareholder should have a claim against the directors arising out of the same set of facts, and part or all of the shareholder's loss can be seen as mimicking the loss caused by the directors to the company. Notice that the rule does not merely prevent potential double recovery by the shareholder: that would be unexceptional. Rather, it prevents the shareholder's *claim*, insisting that in these circumstances the shareholder's rights will be satisfied, if at all, through the company's recoveries. Perhaps predictably, there are exceptions. But we look to the general rule first. The rule applies equally to claims which the shareholder may have against the director other than in his or her capacity as a member of the company (so that the rule applies to

---

[84] 2006 Act s.260(1)(a). Section 265, applying in Scotland, is less explicit but, it is submitted, equally clear. More than one shareholder may have their rights infringed by the directors' claims, in which case the litigation may be brought in representative form by one shareholder as a representative of all shareholders who have the same interest in the matter (under CPR 19.6).

[85] Above, para.16–5. The cases below suggest that the shareholders' agreement adopts some or all of the general duties of directors and so makes them binding as between the director/shareholders parties to the agreement.

claims the shareholder brings as unsecured creditor or employee[86]). In this respect a creditor or employee who is also a shareholder is worse off than if this were not the case. The no reflective loss rule applies whether or not a derivative claim is available to enforce the company's rights and whether or not the shareholder chooses to bring a derivative claim against the director as well as a personal claim.[87]

The principle can be illustrated by the decision of the Court of Appeal in *Prudential Assurance Co Ltd v Newman Industries Ltd (No.2)*,[88] where the directors in breach of duty to the company had sold assets at an undervalue to a third party and had then obtained the shareholders' consent to the transaction by issuing a misleading circular convening a meeting of the shareholders, thus committing a wrong by way of misrepresentation against the shareholders. The Court of Appeal held that the personal claim should lead (in effect) to no recovery for the shareholder on the facts, because the only relevant loss suffered by them consisted in a diminution in the value of their shares, which was simply a reflection of the loss inflicted on the company by the sale of its assets at an undervalue, which was a wrong only to the company. The principle that a shareholder cannot recover a loss which is simply reflective of the company's loss, even though the shareholder's cause of action is independent of the company's, was confirmed by the House of Lords in *Johnson v Gore, Wood & Co*.[89]

17–35

Several rationales could be put forward for this rule limiting recovery. It might be thought to be justifiable on the grounds of preventing double recovery, i.e. to prevent the wrongdoer having to compensate both the shareholder and the company for, in effect, the same loss. However, this result could be avoided simply by preventing the company from recovering if the shareholder has recovered, and vice versa. However, the rule in fact goes further than that by always subordinating the shareholder's claim to that of the company. It applies whether or not the company has recovered from the directors. Why should this be? It might be said that it addresses the following issue: if the shareholder is allowed to recover first, he or she effectively moves assets out of the company, to the potential detriment of the creditors of the company, who can sue the company but not the shareholders. This seems a good reason for often giving the company's claim priority, but, where the company has distributable assets, the creditors cannot be said to be prejudiced by this indirect form of distribution to the shareholders. A further argument might be that the initiation of a decision to distribute is normally entrusted by the articles to the board and certainly is not

17–36

---

[86] *Gardner v Parker* [2004] 2 B.C.L.C. 554 CA.
[87] It used to be thought that it was not possible to combine a personal and a derivative claim in the same litigation, but in *Prudential Assurance Co Ltd v Newman Industries Ltd (No.2)* [1981] Ch. 257, 303–304 Vinelott J permitted it a first instance. The Court of Appeal ([1982] Ch. 204, 222–224) did not dissent from this view.
[88] *Prudential Assurance Co Ltd v Newman Industries Ltd (No.2)* [1981] Ch. 257.
[89] *Johnson v Gore, Wood & Co* [2002] 2 A.C. 1 HL. For a critique see Mitchell, (2004) 120 L.Q.R. 457. For the potential breadth of the excluded (i.e. "reflective") losses, see: *Webster v Sandersons Solicitors* [2009] EWCA Civ 830; [2009] 2 B.C.L.C. 542 CA. Also see *Waddington Ltd v Chan Chun Hoo Thomas* [2009] 2 B.C.L.C. 82 HKCA.

given to individual shareholders. The "no reflective loss" principle thus supports the principle of centralised management of the company's assets through the board.

17-37 The strength of these arguments has to be weighed against the fact that, where the principle applies, the shareholder's recovery is limited even though the company may not recover its loss from the directors, so that the shareholder's loss is not made good through the company either. Thus, the rule applies even where the company is incapable of enforcing its claim, for example, because it has been compromised or is subject to limitation or simply because the defendant has a good defence to the company's, but not to the shareholder's, claim.[90] This point led the Court of Appeal in *Giles v Rhind*[91] to refuse to apply the "no reflective loss" principle at least in the case where it was the wrongful act of the defendant himself which had put the company in a position where it could not pursue its claim. Here, by exception, if the shareholder has a separate cause of action, he or she should be able to recover damages in full, even for reflective losses.

17-38 However, the "no reflective loss" principle does not prevent the shareholder from suing to recover a loss which is separate and distinct from that suffered by the company. The distinction between reflective and separate losses is illustrated in *Heron International Ltd v Lord Grade*,[92] where, in the context of a proposed takeover, the board preferred the lower bidder to the higher bidder and, unusually, was able to take action to enforce its choice on the shareholders. The Court of Appeal distinguished between the harm inflicted on the company's assets by this decision (because it was unclear that the relevant regulator would allow the lower bidder to operate in the industry in question) and the harm suffered directly by the shareholders individually though their inability to accept a higher takeover offer for their shares (assertable in a personal claim). However, although the principle is clear, the distinction between reflective and independent losses is not always easy to draw.

CONCLUSION

17-39 Although the new statutory derivative claim is doctrinally very different from the common law it replaces, it is still not clear what its impact on the levels of derivative litigation will be. In the early days, the Law Commission was rather downbeat in its assessment. In its Consultation Paper it made the following

---

[90] *Day v Cook* [2002] 1 B.C.L.C. 1 CA; *Barings v Coopers & Lybrand (No.1)* [2002] 1 B.C.L.C. 364; *Stein v Blake* [1998] 1 All E.R. 724 CA (this last containing the probably erroneous suggestion that the rule does not apply to claims by former shareholders).

[91] *Giles v Rhind* [2003] Ch. 618 CA. The defendant's wrongful act had destroyed the company's business, so that it had no funds for litigation. This was followed in *Perry v Day* [2005] 2 B.C.L.C. 405, where the directors' wrongful act (as against both shareholder and company) consisted in accepting a settlement giving up the company's claim against the defendant directors (as vendors to the company). Contrast *Gardner v Parker* [2004] 2 B.C.L.C. 554 CA where the directors' allegedly wrongful acts as against the company had put the company into administrative receivership (not by itself enough to prevent the company commencing litigation) and where the compromise of the company's claim against the directors, although on generous terms, was not improper.

[92] *Heron International Ltd v Lord Grade* [1983] B.C.L.C. at 261–263.

remarks about the policy which underlay its proposed reforms: "a member should be able to maintain proceedings about wrongs done to the company only in exceptional circumstances" and "shareholders should not be able to involve the company in litigation without good cause ... Otherwise the company may be 'killed by kindness', or waste money and management time in dealing with unwarranted proceedings".[93] Whilst the latter remark is undoubtedly true, it is unclear whether this should lead to derivative claims being available only in exceptional circumstances, because the ability of wrongdoing directors to block decisions in favour of litigation is a matter of empirical fact which has not been extensively investigated—though the unfair prejudice cases discussed in Ch.20 below suggest it is a not uncommon feature of small companies. In its final report the Law Commission stated that "we do not accept that the proposals will make significant changes to the availability of the action. In some respects, the availability may be slightly wider, in others it may be slightly narrower. But in all cases the new procedure will be subject to tight judicial control".[94]

If the common law led to sub-optimal levels of derivative litigation, one would hope that the statutory changes would have a significant impact, even whilst the judges remain fully alive to the fact that the statute, rightly, creates no entitlement in the shareholder to bring a derivative claim. All depends on how the courts exercise their discretion. The statute does not suggest the rule in *Foss v Harbottle* should rule the courts from its grave and in due course the courts may strike out more boldly. There is some indication of this trend; as of September 2013, in the 13 reported cases where permission to continue a derivative claim was the central issue, permission was granted in just over a third of cases, suggesting that the court is not taking an unduly restrictive approach in its exercise of discretion.

---

[93] Law Commission, *Shareholders' Remedies*, Consultation Paper No.142, 1996, para.4.6.
[94] Law Commission, *Shareholder Remedies*, Cm. 3769, 1997, para.6.13.

CHAPTER 18

BREACH OF CORPORATE DUTIES: ADMINISTRATIVE REMEDIES

INTRODUCTION

A distinctive feature of British company regulation for many years has been the conferment of powers of investigation on the relevant Government Department, currently the Department of Business Innovation and Skills ("BIS").[1] Those provisions are still contained in Pt XIV of the Companies Act 1985 (rather than the 2006 Act),[2] as amended by the Companies Act 1989 and strengthened by the Companies (Audit, Investigations and Community Enterprise) Act 2004.[3] The 1985 Act, as amended, empowers the Department to launch inquisitorial raids on corporate (and even unincorporated) bodies, and BIS now has a sizeable Companies Investigation Branch ("CIB"), which in 2006 became part of the Insolvency Service Agency of the Department. The departmental powers are draconian, despite the acknowledged need to ensure that the investigatory and inspection powers comply, in both design and use, with the Human Rights Act 1998, and with the fairness standards of domestic public law, and it is perhaps the Government's desire not to spend public money on matters which should be the concern purely of the company's members or creditors which has tended to limit the scale of their use.[4]

18–1

---

[1] And in earlier guises the Department of Business Enterprise and Regulatory Reform (BERR), the Department of Trade and Industry (DTI) and the Board of Trade (BoT).

[2] Unless indicated otherwise, the references below are to the 1985 Act.

[3] Although not to the extent recommended by the Department's own review: see DTI, *Company Investigations: Powers for the Twenty-First Century* (2001).

[4] DTI, *Company Investigations: Powers for the Twenty-First Century* (2001), gives details of the costs and length of the then most recent formal s.432 inspections. For example, the inspection into Mirror Group Newspapers Ltd took nearly nine years and cost £9.5 million. However, nearly half that time was taken up with waiting for criminal trials to be completed or with dealing with challenges in the courts to the inspectors by those sought to be inspected. See fn.45, below.

[615]

Originally, appointment of outside inspectors (usually a QC and a senior accountant) was the only form of investigation power that the Secretary of State had. But an announced appointment of inspectors is likely in itself to cause damage to the company. Hence the Department was reluctant to appoint unless a strong case for doing so could be made out, and it normally made inquiries of the board of directors before doing so. Though such inquiries might cause the board to take remedial action, they might equally well provide an opportunity for evidence to be destroyed or fabricated. Hence, on the recommendation of the Jenkins Committee,[5] power to require the production of books and papers was added in 1967, a power which can be exercised with less publicity[6] and which may suffice in itself or may lead to a formal appointment of inspectors if the facts elicited show that that is needed. This power, now conferred by s.447 of the 1985 Act, is by far the one most commonly exercised.[7] It is sometimes referred to as the power of (informal or confidential) investigation, by way of contrast with the far more formal and public powers of inspection (by appointment of inspectors). It is undoubtedly the primary form of intervention, and we consider it first.

INFORMAL INVESTIGATIONS: DISCLOSURE OF DOCUMENTS AND INFORMATION

18–2 Under s.447, the Secretary of State may require or, more likely, authorise an investigator from the CIB to require a company to produce, at such time and place as are specified, such documents[8] and information as may be specified. Authorising an investigator to impose the requirement avoids the risk of the documents being destroyed or doctored; the officer will arrive without warning[9] at the company's registered office (or wherever else the documents are believed to be held).[10] The investigator may be authorised further to impose the same requirements on "any person",[11] a power to be used where, for example, the

---

[5] Cmnd. 1749 (1962), paras 213–219.

[6] The Department does not normally announce that it has mounted such an investigation and all information about it is regarded as confidential. This has its disadvantages. If a team of officials is going through the company's books and papers, this cannot be concealed from its employees and will soon become known to the Press, thus putting the company under a cloud which may never be dispersed because the ending of the inquiries will not normally be announced nor their results ever be published, notwithstanding that the conclusion may be that all is well with the company.

[7] The various powers to appoint inspectors are used only very infrequently. And the number of informal investigations has remained relatively constant at about 150 investigations per year: see *Insolvency Service Annual Report 2013–14*, at p.18; and *Insolvency Service Annual Report 2014–15*, at p.15.

[8] 1985 Act s.447(8). "Document" is defined as "information recorded in any form". The requirement to produce documents includes the power, if they are produced, to take copies of them or extracts from them: s.447(7).

[9] The investigation is an administrative act to which the full rules of natural justice do not apply: *Norwest Holst Ltd v Secretary of State* [1978] Ch. 201 at 224 CA. But "fairness" must be observed and directions to produce should be clear and not excessive: *R. v Trade Secretary Ex p. Perestrello* [1981] 1 Q.B. 19 (a case which illustrates the problems that may be met if the documents are not held in the UK). See also *R. (on the application of 1st Choice Engines Ltd) v Secretary of State for Business, Innovation and Skills* [2014] EWHC 1765.

[10] The officer may be accompanied by a policeman with a search warrant: s.448.

[11] 1985 Act s.447(3). But this is without prejudice to any lien that the possessor may have.

documents concerned are in the possession of some person other than the company. The power of an investigator to impose a requirement on "any person" in relation to the production of "information" as well as documents means that, for example, an officer or employee of the company may be required to provide an explanation of a document or, if a document is not produced by the person asked, to state to the best of his or her knowledge where it is.[12]

Failure to comply with the requirements of s.447 on the part of any person may be certified by the Secretary of State or the investigator to the court and the court may treat that person as guilty of contempt of court if, after a hearing, it concludes that the defendant did not have a reasonable excuse[13] for non-compliance with the requirement.[14] In addition, providing information known to be false in a material particular, or doing so recklessly, is a criminal offence, punishable by imprisonment or a fine.[15] Criminal sanctions are also imposed on any officer of the company who is privy to the falsification or destruction of a document relating to the company's affairs, unless the officer shows there was no intention to conceal the affairs of the company or to defeat the law.[16] In addition, fraudulently to part with, alter or make an omission in such a document is a crime.[17]

These various provisions are all aimed at extracting information from those who may be unwilling to provide it without compulsion. It may happen, however, that a person wishes to volunteer information to an investigator, but feels constrained from so doing because the information has been imparted to him or her in confidence and so disclosure might trigger an action for breach of confidence on the part of the person who provided the information to the informer. The Act now gives a limited protection against such actions. The information must be of a kind which the person making the disclosure could be required to disclose under the Act, the disclosure must be in good faith and in the reasonable belief that it is capable of assisting the Secretary of State, must be no more than is necessary for this purpose, and must not be a disclosure prohibited by or under statute or by a banker or lawyer in breach of an obligation of confidence owed in that capacity.[18]

---

[12] See *Re Attorney-General's Reference No.2 of 1998* [1999] B.C.C. 590 CA, decided on an earlier version of s.447 where this power was stated explicitly. The current version of the power is not confined to officers and employees.

[13] 1985 Act s.453C. cf. *Re An Investigation under the Insider Dealing Act* [1988] A.C. 660 HL, dealing with an analogous provision, where the court took a narrow view of reasonable excuse in the case of a journalist refusing to answer questions in order to protect his sources. This was because the information was needed for the prevention of crime, which is likely to, but need not, be the case under s.447.

[14] One effect of proceeding in this way is that the defendant is deprived of the automatic protection of legal professional privilege, which applies if, as previously, failure to comply is treated as an offence (s.1129 of the CA 2006), though the court might regard legal professional privilege as reasonable grounds for non-compliance.

[15] 1985 Act s.451. Prosecution requires the consent of the Secretary of State or DPP in England and Wales and Northern Ireland (CA 2006 s.1126(2),(3)).

[16] 1985 Act s.450(1). The same restriction on prosecution applies as under s.451: see previous note.

[17] 1985 Act s.450(2).

[18] 1985 Act s.448A.

18–3   An investigator appointed under s.447 is not confined to turning up at premises to ask questions and demand documents, running the risk that admittance will be denied. The Act provides for the investigator to be given compulsory powers of entry and search.[19] These come in escalating tiers. A Justice of the Peace, if satisfied on information given on oath by the Secretary of State or by a person appointed or authorised to exercise powers under Pt XIV, that there are on any premises documents, production of which has been required under that Part and which have not been produced, may issue a search warrant.[20] Under that provision a search warrant cannot be issued unless there has first been a requirement to produce the documents sought. The company, thus forewarned, could destroy the documents before the search took place, even if such action might be a crime.[21]

Hence, the 1989 Act added a further provision under which a warrant may be issued if a J.P. is satisfied: (a) that there are reasonable grounds for believing that an indictable offence has been committed and that there are on the premises documents relating to whether the offence has been committed; (b) that the applicant has power under Pt XIV to require the production of the documents; and (c) that there are reasonable grounds for believing that if production was required it would not be forthcoming but the documents would be removed, hidden, tampered with or destroyed.[22] Though narrowly circumscribed by the need to satisfy a J.P. of conditions (a)–(c), this enables the search for the documents to be undertaken by the police rather than by the (possibly self-interested) officers of the company.

Although the search warrant power introduced in 1989 undoubtedly increased the investigators' powers, in many cases it is not available, particularly given conditions (a) and (c) above. Where it is not, the investigator might still be left standing on the doorstep. Consequently, in the 2004 Act a right of entry to premises was introduced which was not dependent on a warrant issued by a J.P., nor subject to onerous conditions. Whenever authorised by the Secretary of State to do so, and provided the investigator[23] thinks it will materially help in the exercise of his or her functions, the investigator may require entry to premises believed to be used wholly or partly for the purpose of the company's business and may remain there for such time as is necessary to discharge those functions.[24] The power of entry extends to accompanying persons whom the investigator

---

[19] These powers apply also to inspectors, discussed below: s.448(1). Note also that there is a power under CA 2006 s.1132 whereby (on application of the DPP, the Secretary of State or the police) a High Court judge, if satisfied that there is reasonable cause to believe that any person, while an officer of a company, has committed an offence in its management and that evidence of the commission is to be found in any books or papers of, or under the control of, the company, may make an order authorising any named person to inspect the books and papers or require an officer of the company to produce them: see *Re A Company* [1980] Ch. 138 CA (reversed by the House of Lords sub nom. *Re Racal Communications Ltd* [1981] A.C. 374, because, under the express provisions of subs.(5), there can be no appeal from the judge and it was held that this included cases where he had erred on a point of law—and, having discovered that other judges had taken a different view, had volunteered leave to appeal!).

[20] 1985 Act s.448(1).

[21] See fn.6 above.

[22] 1985 Act s.448(2).

[23] Or inspector (see below).

[24] 1985 Act.453A(1)–(3).

thinks appropriate.[25] The section does not give the investigator powers of search but it does potentially give him or her access to relevant persons from whom the production of documents or information can be demanded. Intentional obstruction of the exercise of this power of entry is an offence, punishable with imprisonment or a fine,[26] and non-compliance with a requirement imposed under the section may be certified to the court to be dealt with as a contempt of court.[27] The power is subject to some procedural safeguards, notably a requirement that the investigator and accompanying persons identify themselves,[28] and the investigator must give a written statement as soon as practicable after entry to the occupiers of the premises about the investigator's powers and the rights and obligations of the persons on the premises.[29]

The powers discussed above are cumulatively very considerable, but it is worth remembering that over three-quarters of the investigations initiated are prompted by allegations of fraudulent trading,[30] so that attempts to side-step the investigation are likely. Despite the width of the power to appoint investigators, this fact also illustrates the reluctance of the Department to use it unless wrongdoing and a strong public interest in taking action are present.

18–4

Part XIV also contains further provisions common to both departmental investigations and to inspections, but these are left until after a description of the latter. What should be emphasised, however, is that an investigation by the Department's officials under s.447 is very far from being merely a preliminary step towards the appointment of inspectors if the documentary evidence thus discovered justifies that. On the contrary, in most cases it will be the only investigation undertaken and will lead either to a decision that no further action is needed or that some non-inspection follow-up action should be taken.[31] The time taken to decide may vary from a few days to several months and, while the investigation continues, the officials will probe deeply and in a way which from the viewpoint of the company is just as traumatic as a formal inspection.

---

[25] 1985 Act s.453A(4).

[26] 1985 Act s.453A(5),(5A).

[27] 1985 Act s.453C(1); and see para.18–2, above.

[28] 1985 Act s.453B(3).

[29] 1985 Act s.453B(4)–(10); and the Companies Act 1985 (Power to Enter and Remain on Premises: Procedural) Regulations 2005 (SI 2005/684), which, together, go into considerably more detail than is indicated in the text.

[30] The two other main grounds for appointing an investigator after fraudulent trading are the involvement of a disqualified person or an undischarged bankrupt in the management of the company and using the company to promote an unlawful pyramid selling scheme.

[31] See para.18–13, below.

FORMAL INVESTIGATIONS BY INSPECTORS

When inspectors can be appointed

18–5   Sections 431 and 432 set out circumstances in which the Secretary of State is empowered to appoint one or more competent inspectors[32] to investigate the affairs[33] of a company and to report the result of their investigations to him; and one situation where the Secretary of State is obliged to do so. This last is where the court by order declares that the affairs of the company ought to be so investigated.[34] The courts rarely make use of this power. As to those situations in which the Secretary of State has a discretion, s.431 deals with cases where the company, formally, takes the initiative to suggest the appointment (almost never used) and s.432 with cases where the Secretary of State acts of his or her own motion (as it turns out, rather rarely used).

Under s.431, the Secretary of State may appoint on the application of: (a) in the case of a company with a share capital, not less than 200 members or members holding not less than one-tenth of the issued shares; (b) in the case of a company not having a share capital, not less than one-fifth of the persons on the company's register of members; or (c) in any case, the company itself.[35] However, appointments under this section hardly ever occur.[36] This is due not only to the fact that, before appointing under the section, the Secretary of State may require applicants to give security to an amount not exceeding £5,000 for payment of the costs of the investigation,[37] but also because the application has to be supported by evidence that the applicants have good reason for the application.[38] If they have, the Secretary of State will normally have power to appoint of his own motion under s.432(2), below, and it is far better for those who have good reasons to draw them quietly to the attention of the Department, requesting that there should be an appointment under that section. Proceeding thus avoids the danger, inherent in s.431, that the malefactors in the company will tamper with the evidence once they learn of possible action under that section and thus frustrate effective intervention by the Department, whether by the appointment of inspectors or the appointment of an investigator under s.447 (see above).

---

[32] As already mentioned, the usual appointees are a QC and a chartered accountant but less expensive mortals may be appointed in the rarer case when the Department appoints in relation to a private company.

[33] i.e. its business, including its control over its subsidiaries, whether that is being managed by the board of directors or an administrator, administrative receiver or a liquidator in a voluntary liquidation: *R. v Board of Trade Ex p. St Martin Preserving Co* [1965] 1 Q.B. 603.

[34] 1985 Act s.432(1). This seems to make the Secretary of State's refusal to appoint reviewable by the court if an application is made to it by anyone with locus standi, and to enable a court, in proceedings before it (e.g. on an unfair prejudice petition), to make an order declaring that the company's affairs ought to be investigated by inspectors. A copy of the inspectors' report will be sent to the court: s.437(2).

[35] 1985 Act s.431(2)(c).

[36] It is believed that there have been no appointments since 1990.

[37] 1985 Act s.431(4). The £5,000 can be altered by statutory instrument. In the 1948 Act it was only £100 which, even then, would not have kept a competent QC and chartered accountant happy for the time that most inspections take.

[38] 1985 Act s.431(3).

Section 432(2) empowers the Secretary of State to appoint inspectors[39] if it appears that there are circumstances suggesting one (or more) of four grounds, the first two of which are:

"(a)   that the company's affairs are being conducted or have been conducted with intent to defraud creditors or the creditors of any other person or otherwise for a fraudulent or unlawful purpose or in a manner which is unfairly prejudicial to some part of its members;[40] or

(b)   that any actual or proposed act or omission of the company (including an act or omission on its behalf) is or would be so prejudicial, or that the company was formed for any fraudulent or unlawful purpose."

These, it will be observed, in part adopt the wording of s.994 on unfair prejudice petitions,[41] but in addition they enable the Secretary of State to appoint where the company has been operated with intent to defraud creditors or was formed or conducted for a fraudulent or unlawful purpose.

In addition an appointment may be made on the ground:

"(c)   that persons concerned with the company's formation or the management of its affairs have in connection therewith been guilty of fraud, misfeasance or other misconduct towards it or towards its member; or

(d)   that the company's members have not been given all the information with respect to its affairs which they might reasonably expect."[42]

Given the availability of the more attractive, cheaper and speedier option of investigations (considered earlier), appointments of formal inspectors under s.432(2) have become far less common, except in major cases where there are circumstances suggesting malpractice (such as companies formed or used in unlawful, dishonest, fraudulent or improper ways) and a strong public interest in having an inspection. Had the reforms proposed in 2001 been implemented, this would have become the sole basis for the s.432(2) discretion.[43]

18–6

Conduct of inspections

Extent of the inspectors' powers

The Act itself contains a number of sections on the conduct of inspections. Under s.433, if inspectors appointed to investigate the affairs of a company think it also

18–7

---

[39]   Even if the company is in the course of being voluntarily wound up: s.432(3).

[40]   "Member" includes a person to whom shares have been transmitted by operation of law: s.432(4).

[41]   See Ch.20. Although s.432(2)(a) refers only to "some part of the members", rather than using the CA 2006 s.994 wording of "members generally or some part of the members", this is unlikely to have the absurd result that, strictly speaking, the Secretary of State should not appoint inspectors if it is thought that *all* the members are unfairly prejudiced. This is especially so since the precise grounds for action do not have to be stated (see *Norwest Holst v Trade Secretary* [1978] Ch. 201 CA).

[42]   This wording implies that members may "reasonably expect" more information than that to which the Act entitles them. But it seems that s.432(2) does not entitle the Secretary of State to appoint merely because the directors or officers of the company appear to have breached their duties of care, skill or diligence: see *SBA Properties Ltd v Cradock* [1967] 1 W.L.R. 716 (which, however, was concerned with an action by the Secretary of State under what is now s.438, below).

[43]   DTI, *Company Investigations: Powers for the Twenty-First Century* (2001), para.97.

necessary for the purposes of their investigation to investigate the affairs of another body corporate in the same group, they may do so and report the results of that so far as it is relevant to the affairs of the company.[44] Under s.434 inspectors have powers similar to those of investigators under s.447 (above) entitling them to require the production of documents and information. They may also require any past or present officer or agent of the company to attend before them and otherwise to give all assistance that he is "reasonably" able to give.[45] In addition, they may examine any person on oath.[46] If any person fails to comply with their requirements or refuses to answer any question put by the inspectors for the purposes of the investigation, the inspectors may certify that fact in writing to the court which will thereupon inquire into the case and, subject to the important defence of reasonableness, may punish the offender in like manner as if he had been guilty of contempt of court.[47]

Control of the inspectors' powers

18–8   This topic can be looked at from two points of view: control over the inspectors by the Secretary of State and control over the inspectors in the interests of third parties. The former control was considerably strengthened by Pt 32 of the Companies Act 2006, inserting new provisions in the 1985 Act, although to some extent they reflect what was probably already administrative practice. In any event, the inspectors are now under a statutory obligation to comply with any direction given to them by the Secretary of State as to the subject-matter of the investigation, the steps to be taken in the investigation, and whether to report or not report on a particular matter or in a particular way.[48] The Secretary of State may also terminate an investigation.[49]

Perhaps anticipating that exercise of these powers may lead to dissatisfaction among inspectors, they are given an express statutory right to resign, and the Secretary of State a corresponding power to revoke an appointment as inspector.[50] However, former inspectors are under an obligation to produce to the Secretary of State or a replacement inspector the documents and information

---

[44] Most major corporate scandals involve the use of a network of holding and subsidiary companies, the extent of which may only become apparent during the course of the investigation: s.433 avoids the need for a formal extension of the inspectors' appointment each time they unearth another member of the group. The extended power applies to bodies corporate (i.e. not just Companies Act companies) but does not extend to unincorporated bodies, which, however, may be subjected to investigation on the grounds that associated unincorporated bodies are part of the affairs of the corporate body with which they are associated.

[45] 1985 Act s.434(1) and (2). On the use of the "reasonableness" defence to protect a director against oppressive use by the inspectors of their powers, see *Re Mirror Group Newspapers Plc* [1999] 1 B.C.L.C. 690. Agents include auditors, bankers and solicitor (s.434(4)).

[46] 1985 Act s.434(3).

[47] 1985 Act s.436.

[48] 1985 Act s.446A.

[49] 1985 Act s.446B(1)—though in the case of inspectors appointed as a result of a court order, only if matters have come to light suggesting the commission of a criminal offence and those matters have been referred to the appropriate prosecuting authority: s.446B(2).

[50] 1985 Act s.446C—and the Secretary of State can fill any vacancy: s.446D.

obtained or generated in the course of the inspection.[51] These provisions make it very clear that the inspector is a creature of the Department.

As to control in the interests of the investigated, a number of matters have been established by practice and case law. The process of inspection is undoubtedly an inquisitorial one. However, as noted, since the aim of the inspection is to establish facts rather than to determine legal rights, in domestic law the process has been characterised as administrative rather than judicial, so that the inspectors are obliged to act fairly but are not subject to the full requirements of natural justice. The European Court of Human Rights has adopted a similar stance in relation to the applicability of art.6 of the European Convention (right to a fair trial) to inspections.[52] Consequently, it would seem that the use of compulsion in investigations and inspections to secure information from those investigated, including compulsion to answer questions put by inspectors, is not in principle unlawful, as a matter of either domestic or European Convention law. However, as we shall see below, European Convention law has had a significant impact on what can be done subsequently, for example by the prosecuting authorities, with compelled testimony obtained by inspectors, and the Act was amended by the Criminal Justice and Police Act 2001 to take account of the jurisprudence of the European Court of Human Rights.

Although the full rules of "natural justice" do not apply, the inspectors must act fairly. This involves letting witnesses know of criticisms made against them (assuming that the inspectors envisage relying on, or referring to, those criticisms in their report) and giving them adequate opportunity of answering. But the inspectors are not bound to show them a draft of the parts of their report referring to them, so long as they have had a fair opportunity of answering any criticisms of their conduct. Inspectors are free to draw conclusions from the evidence about the conduct of individuals, but should do so only with restraint.[53]

Inspectors sit in private (and probably do not have the power to sit in public),[54] but allow witnesses to be accompanied by their lawyers—although the latter's role is limited, since the questioning is undertaken by the inspectors and neither the witness nor his lawyers can cross-examine other witnesses. Although the range of persons whom the inspectors may question is very wide, the Act provides that such persons cannot be compelled to disclose or produce any information or document in breach of legal professional privilege, except that lawyers must disclose the names and addresses of their clients.[55] A banker's duty of confidentiality is protected more narrowly.[56] In particular, it may be overridden by the Secretary of State.[57]

18–9

---

[51] 1985 Act s.446E. The inspector is under a duty to comply but no sanction is specified— presumably *in extremis* the Department could obtain a court order.

[52] *Fayed v United Kingdom* (1994) 18 E.H.R.R. 393.

[53] *Re Pergamon Press Ltd* [1971] Ch. 388 CA; *Maxwell v DTI* [1974] Q.B. 523 CA; *R. (on the application of Clegg) v Secretary of State* [2003] B.C.C. 128 CA.

[54] *Hearts of Oak Assurance Co Ltd v Attorney-General* [1932] A.C. 392 HL.

[55] 1985 Act s.452(1),(5). This applies to Departmental investigations as well as to inspections: s.452(2).

[56] 1985 Act s.452(1A),(1B).

[57] 1985 Act s.452(1A)(c). The bankers' protection in relation to s.447 investigations is differently worded. It can be overridden by the Secretary of State only when it is thought necessary for the

Reports

18–10   The inspectors may, and if so directed by the Secretary of State shall, make interim reports, and (subject to what is said below) on the conclusion of the investigation must make a final report.[58] If so directed by the Secretary of State, they must also inform the Minister of matters coming to their knowledge during their investigation.[59] The Secretary of State may, if thought fit, forward a copy of any report to the company's registered office and, on request and payment of a prescribed fee, to any member of the company or other body corporate which is the subject of the report, any person whose conduct is referred to in the report, the auditors, the applicants for the investigation[60] and any other person whose financial interests appear to be affected by matters dealt with in the report.[61] And the Secretary of State may (and generally will, though not until after any criminal proceedings have been concluded[62]) cause the report to be printed and published.[63]

There is one exception to this, however. Under s.432(2A), inspectors may be appointed under s.432(2) on terms that any report they make is not for publication, in which case s.437 does not apply. Since, under that section, a report does not have to be published unless the Secretary of State thinks fit, it might be thought that subs.(2A) was unnecessary. But it has two advantages: it protects the Secretary of State from pressure to publish even though advised that that might prejudice possible criminal prosecutions; and, since it is an ex ante rule, it makes it clear to the proposed appointees that they will not be able to bask in publicity resulting from their efforts.[64]

POWER OF INVESTIGATION OF COMPANY OWNERSHIP

18–11   The above provisions relate to the appointment of inspectors or investigators to examine the affairs of the company in general (even if in particular cases they may be given a more limited remit). There is, however, one situation in which the Secretary of State's powers to appoint inspectors or investigators are limited by the statute to a particular topic. This is the power of investigation into company

---

purpose of investigating the affairs of the person carrying on the banking business, or the customer is a person upon whom a s.447 requirement has been imposed: s.452(4).

[58] 1985 Act s.437(1).

[59] 1985 Act s.437(1A).

[60] This is not relevant to inspections under s.432(2) when the Secretary of State appoints of his or her own motion.

[61] 1985 Act s.437(3).

[62] For an unsuccessful attempt to force the Secretary of State to publish while criminal proceedings were still being considered: see *R. v Secretary of State Ex p. Lonrho* [1989] 1 W.L.R. 525 HL.

[63] 1985 Act s.437(3)(c). Thus making the reports available for purchase from HMSO by any member of the public so long as the reports remain in print. They often make fascinating reading for anyone interested in "the unacceptable face of capitalism".

[64] It may also tend to make the officers of the company more co-operative.

ownership.[65] This may be a controversial issue and the facts may not be clear, because, although the name of the shareholder has to be entered on the company's share register, that shareholder may be a nominee rather than the beneficial owner of the share. The circumstances in which large beneficial shareholders are required to disclose their positions or in which a company may require a person to reveal the extent of a beneficial holding in the company are discussed in Chs 2,[66] 26[67] and 28.[68] The Secretary of State's investigatory powers are essentially supplementary to these provisions.

In the first instance, if the Secretary of State is persuaded that there may be good reasons for intervening, he or she will probably institute preliminary investigations under the powers conferred by s.444. Under this provision, the Secretary of State can require any person whom he or she has reasonable cause to believe to has, or is able to obtain, information as to the present and past interests in a company's shares or debentures to disclose this information.

If this fails to produce a satisfactory answer the Secretary of State may then appoint inspectors under s.442.[69] The Secretary of State may do so at will and must do so if application is made by members sufficient to instigate an appointment of inspectors under the general powers.[70] A fully-fledged investigation may afford the best chance of getting at the truth, but it is expensive and time-consuming.[71] Hence, the amendments to the section made by the 1989 Act provide that the Secretary of State shall not be obliged to appoint inspectors if satisfied that the members' application is vexatious and, if an appointment is made, may exclude any matter if satisfied that it is unreasonable for it to be investigated[72]; and the applicants may be required to give security for costs as in a general investigation initiated by the members.[73]

The inspectors' powers in this area are supported by the sanctions mentioned above[74] but what makes the foregoing sections more effective than they would otherwise be is that, if there is difficulty in finding out the relevant facts on an investigation under ss.442 or 444, the Secretary of State may by order direct that the securities concerned shall, until further notice, be subject to restrictions on their transfer and the exercise of rights attached to them. These restrictions are discussed further in Ch.28.[75]

---

[65] There was also a power of investigation into share dealings (s.446), but this was repealed by the Companies Act 2006 from October 2007, but the Financial Conduct Authority has a like investigatory power and is now regarded as the more appropriate body to exercise this type of power. See para.30–48.

[66] At para.2–42.

[67] At para.26–17.

[68] At para.28–51.

[69] This section is directed not merely to determining share and debenture ownership but "the true persons who are or have been primarily interested in the success or failure (real or apparent) of the company or able to control or materially to influence its policy": s.442(1).

[70] 1985 Act s.442(3) and see above, para.18–2, though under s.442(3) the appointment is mandatory.

[71] It is believed that no appointments have been made since 1992.

[72] 1985 Act s.442(3A).

[73] See above, para.18–5.

[74] 1985 Act s.443.

[75] At para.28–53.

LIABILITY FOR COSTS OF INVESTIGATIONS

18–12   Under s.439, the expenses of any investigation under Pt XIV of the Act[76] are to be defrayed in the first instance by the Department, but may be recoverable from persons specified in that section. These expenses include such reasonable sums as the Secretary of State may determine in respect of general staff costs and overheads. The persons from whom costs are recoverable include: anyone successfully prosecuted as a result of the investigation; the applicants for the investigation where inspectors were appointed under s.431, to the extent that the Secretary of State directs[77]; any body corporate dealt with in an inspectors' report when the inspectors were not appointed on the Secretary of State's own motion, unless the body corporate was the applicant, or except so far as the Secretary of State otherwise directs.[78] Thus, in the case of investigations under s.447, the only persons at risk of costs are those subsequently prosecuted and, even where inspectors are appointed, the same is true if the Secretary of State takes the initiative to appoint the inspectors.

FOLLOW-UP TO INVESTIGATIONS

18–13   Following an investigation, whether by inspectors or otherwise, the Secretary of State has a number of powers. Apart from the obvious one of causing prosecutions to be mounted against those whose crimes have come to light, which prosecutions may be mounted by the Department itself or by others such as the Serious Fraud Office, the Secretary of State may petition under s.8 of the Company Directors Disqualification Act 1986 for the disqualification of a director or shadow director on grounds of unfitness.[79] The Secretary of State may also petition the court for an appropriate order if unfair prejudice to all or some of the company's members has been revealed.[80] Alternatively, or in addition, he or she may petition for the winding-up of the company under s.124A of the Insolvency Act 1986. Under that section, if it appears to the Secretary of State as a result of any report or information obtained under Pt XIV of the Companies Act that it is expedient in the public interest that a company should be wound up, he or she may present a petition for it to be wound up if the court thinks it just and equitable. In 2014–15, 102 companies were wound up on the Secretary of State's petition, and 58 disqualification orders obtained as a result of investigations.[81]

---

[76] Which in the case of inspections are likely to be heavy; the Atlantic Computers investigation cost £6.5 million and the Consolidated Goldfields one nearly £4 million: DTI, *Company Investigations: Powers for the Twenty-First Century* (2001), Annex A. And the total costs to the companies and their officers were probably as great or greater.

[77] Or the equivalent provisions relating to ownership investigations: s.439(5).

[78] 1985 Act s.439(4). Inspectors appointed otherwise than on the Secretary of State's own motion may, and shall if so directed, include in their report a recommendation about costs: s.439(6). Note also the provisions regarding rights to indemnity or contribution (s.439(8) and (9)).

[79] See para.10–5.

[80] See para.20–1.

[81] *Insolvency Service Annual Report 2014–5*, at pp.14 and 15. The winding-up application cannot be made on the basis of information supplied under the voluntary method (see para.18–2, above): Insolvency Act s.124A(1)(a).

What the Secretary of State can no longer do is initiate proceedings in the name and on behalf of the body corporate, indemnifying it against any costs or expenses incurred by it in connection with the proceedings. This power was removed by the 2006 Act,[82] perhaps on the basis that remedies for the benefit of the company should be a matter for its members.[83] By contrast, taking companies off the register and disqualifying unfit persons from future involvement in the management of companies may well be steps which no member has an interest in taking.

Since the majority of investigations and inspections are driven by allegations of potentially serious wrongdoing on the part of those involved in companies, it is hardly surprising that the Department does not simply receive the information produced by the investigation machinery, but makes use of the possibilities just described to take remedial steps of one sort or another. That this is contemplated by the Act is revealed by s.449, which contains a long list of exceptions to the starting proposition that information obtained under the s.447 investigation powers is confidential to the Department and cannot be disseminated more widely without the consent of the company.[84] These so-called "gateways" permit the information to be provided to those who are best placed to take the consequential action.

However, this possibility of subsequent action brings into sharp focus the rules **18–14** which permit investigators and inspectors to secure information compulsorily. Although the domestic courts had held to the contrary (before the enactment of the Human Rights Act 1998), the European Court of Human Rights, in litigation arising out of the *Guinness* affair, concluded that evidence given to inspectors under threat of compulsion cannot normally be used in subsequent criminal proceedings against those investigated, on the grounds that this would infringe their privilege against self-incrimination.[85] The Act now provides that compelled testimony (but not documents produced under compulsion) may not be used in either primary evidence or cross-examination in a subsequent criminal trial of the person providing the testimony, unless the defendant him- or herself brought the compelled testimony in, or unless the offence in question is giving false evidence to the investigator or certain offences under the general perjury legislation.[86]

However, this restriction does not apply to subsequent use of the testimony in proceedings for disqualification under s.8 of the Company Directors Disqualification Act. Indeed, s.441 specifically provides that an inspectors' report can be

---

[82] 1985 Act s.438 was repealed by s.1176 of the CA 2006 as from April 2007.

[83] For the same reason the Department seems to make little or no use of its power to bring unfair prejudice petitions.

[84] The gateways are set out in Schs 15C and 15D of the Act. The same provisions apply to information provided voluntarily: see para.18–2, above.

[85] *Saunders v United Kingdom* [1998] 1 B.C.L.C. 362 ECtHR; *IJL v United Kingdom* (2001) 33 E.H.R.R. 11 ECtHR. For a sceptical assessment, see P. Davies, "Self-incrimination, Fair Trials and the Pursuit of Corporate and Financial Wrongdoing" in B. Markesinis (ed.), *The Impact of the Human Rights Bill on English Law* (Oxford: OUP, 1998). The House of Lords refused to quash the convictions of those involved despite the breach of the Convention: *R. v Saunders, Times Law Reports*, 15 November 2002.

[86] 1985 Act s.447A. Nor do the amendments specifically exclude evidence to which the prosecuting authorities were drawn as a result of the compelled testimony, where the answers themselves are not used in the criminal trial.

evidence as to the opinion of the inspectors in such an application, and the courts have come to the same conclusion in respect of a report by investigators under s.447.[87] Both the domestic courts and the ECHR seem to be in agreement that disqualification applications are not criminal proceedings.[88] However, disqualification applications, if not criminal proceedings, clearly are proceedings falling within art.6 of the European Convention, because they determine the legal rights of the person to be disqualified. Unlike the investigation process itself, which lies outside art.6,[89] disqualification proceedings will have to comply with Convention standards appropriate for civil proceedings. These standards do not specifically include a privilege against self-incrimination, but they do involve general standards of fairness. Especially since disqualification has a penal element, the presumption of innocence might be relevant.[90] Presumably, the same considerations will apply where it is proposed to use compelled testimony in purely civil litigation[91]: there will be no ban in principle, but the court conducting the civil trial will need to have regard to general fairness issues. One such issue, already identified by the English courts in the context of the Insolvency Act powers of compulsory examination, is the undesirability of allowing statutory powers to give one party a litigation advantage over another in purely civil litigation, which it would not have were the company not insolvent.[92]

CONCLUSION

18–15   Since the scheme of administrative remedies under the Act is dominated by the power of investigation, and this power is predominantly used in cases of suspected fraudulent trading or breach of the disqualification provisions, it is far from clear that these remedies constitute an important element in the British system of corporate governance, if that is defined as the accountability of the senior management to the shareholders as a whole. These provisions might be better seen as seen as supporting the provisions analysed in Part Two of this book, dealing with the abuse of limited liability. It would seem that the Department leaves allegations of breaches of the duties discussed in Ch.16 to be pursued by companies or shareholders themselves, perhaps now through the reformed derivative action procedure,[93] unless either there is a strong public interest in favour of intervention by the Department or the misconduct of the directors has been egregious. Nevertheless, administrative remedies are an important part of

---

[87] *Re Rex Williams Leisure Plc* [1994] Ch. 350 CA.

[88] *R. v Secretary of State for Trade and Industry Ex p. McCormick* [1998] B.C.C. 379 CA; *DC v United Kingdom* [2000] B.C.C. 710 ECHR.

[89] *Fayed v United Kingdom* (1994) 18 E.H.R.R. 393.

[90] *Albert and Le Compte v Belgium* (1983) 5 E.H.R.R. 533 ECHR. The Court of Appeal remains of the view that general fairness does not in principle require the exclusion of compelled testimony: *Re Westminster Property Management Ltd* [2000] 2 B.C.L.C. 396 CA.

[91] Where the inspectors' report is also admissible: s.441.

[92] *Cloverbay Ltd v BCCI SA* [1991] Ch. 90 CA.

[93] See Ch.17.

corporate law, and shareholders may benefit from them indirectly, as where inspectors' reports reveal matters which lead to the reform of company law.[94]

---

[94] Substantial elements in Pt X of the Act (see Ch.16) are the response to abuses revealed in inspectors' reports.

PART 4

CORPORATE GOVERNANCE—MAJORITY AND MINORITY SHAREHOLDERS

An important determinant of behaviour in a company is the structure of its shareholding along the continuum between highly dispersed and atomised shareholdings to one person holding all the shares. Where there are many shareholders, each with only a very small shareholding, the risk to the shareholders is that the management will be the true controllers of the company and they may not give the shareholders' interests proper consideration. We looked at the legal mechanisms which may address those issues in Part Three. On the other hand, where there is a controlling shareholder—or a small group of shareholders who can exercise control—the management will certainly be accountable to the controlling shareholders, but the latter may act opportunistically towards the non-controlling shareholders. (Where there is only one shareholder, then neither problem exists.) Some consequences of majority control do not merit legal intervention. For example, in most cases the non-controlling shareholders will have to accept that the controlling shareholders will set the company's business policy. In return, the minority may benefit from being able to "free-ride" on the majority's efforts to ensure that its chosen policy is effectively implemented by the management of the company.

However, the majority shareholders may also use their power to divert to themselves a greater part of the company's earnings than their contribution to the company's share capital justifies. Such "private benefits of control" are probably impossible to eradicate without interventionist rules whose costs would probably outweigh the rewards—and, in any event, some benefits constitute legitimate returns for the majority's monitoring efforts. Nevertheless, if the law is to encourage investors to place their money in companies controlled by a small group of shareholders, then it must deal with the more outrageous examples of majority opportunism. Apart from the unfairness of majority exploitation of the minority, there is a strong efficiency argument in favour of minority protection. If the holders of minority stakes of ordinary shares in companies are not so protected, they will protect themselves, probably by being prepared to buy such shares only at a lower price, thus in effect buying insurance against the majority's unfair treatment of them. This will raise the company's cost of capital, so that the cost of the unfair treatment is ultimately transferred back to the controllers of the company. On this argument, it is as much in the interests of the majority as it is of the minority shareholders that effective legal limits should be placed on the freedom of the majority to act opportunistically towards the minority.

Unfair treatment of the minority by the majority most obviously occurs through decisions taken by shareholders in general meeting. Thus the general meeting is one focus of the rules designed to protect the minority, and these rules are examined in the next chapter. However, the majority of shareholders has the power to replace the members of the board at any time and for any reason (see Ch.14), so the majority's influence may equally be articulated through decisions of the board. In fact, given the division of powers between the board and the general meeting, generally favouring the former in all but small companies, majority shareholder influence over the company is very likely to involve some element of board decision-making. Sometimes the rules on directors' duties will catch action by directors aimed at diverting corporate assets to themselves, for example, the rules on self-dealing.[1] However, effective control of the majority clearly requires rules which operate on the "controllers" of the company, whether they act through the board or through shareholder decision-making. In recent times the legislature has tried to provide such a remedy in the shape of the "unfair prejudice" provisions. We shall examine these rules in Ch.20.

---

[1] Above, paras 16–54 et seq.

CHAPTER 19

CONTROLLING MEMBERS' VOTING

INTRODUCTION

In any company law system a number of techniques are in principle available to **19–1**
control the unfair exercise of voting power by the majority of shareholders. We
have encountered several such techniques already, and it is useful to draw them
together briefly, before going on to discuss in more detail some techniques not
previously dealt with.

Perhaps most obviously, the law could identify specific decisions which the
majority is simply not permitted to take. There are one or two examples of this
approach in the Act and at common law. For example, s.25[1] provides that a
member is not bound by an alteration of the articles after the date upon which he
or she became a member if its effect is to require the member to take more shares
in the company or in any other way increases the member's liability to contribute
to the company's share capital or otherwise pay money to the company. In other
words, the size of a shareholder's investment in the company is a matter for
individual, not collective, decision. Another is the admittedly controversial
common law rule may be that certain majority shareholders cannot ratify
wrongdoing by a director which involves the appropriation by the director of
corporate property.[2] However, it is impossible for the legislature or the judges to

---

[1] See above, para.3–31.
[2] See above, para.16–124.

identify in advance very many substantive decisions which should be prohibited on the grounds that they will always be unfair to the minority. Normally, fairness and unfairness are fact-specific assessments and therefore not appropriate for ex ante decision-making on the part of the rule-maker.

An obvious response of the rule-maker in this situation is to move from substance to procedure, and in fact the legislature does make much greater use of rules which determine *how* the shareholders are to decide than it does of rules which determine *what* they shall decide. Chapter 14[3] provides a list of decisions which the Act requires to be taken by the shareholders. Often those decisions must also be taken by a three-quarters majority of those voting (a "supermajority") rather than a simple majority (an "ordinary majority"). The statutory categorisation of decisions as requiring ordinary or supermajority voting is not entirely consistent in policy terms, but decisions affecting the rights of the shareholders under the constitution generally require a supermajority. Of course, a three-quarters majority requirement does not obviate all cases of unfair prejudice of the minority, but it reduces the incidence of such problems because, under a supermajority requirement, only a quarter of the votes is needed to block the resolution.

19–2 An approach lying in between the substantive and the procedural is to leave the shareholders largely free to take what substantive decision they will, but to control those elements of the decision which are most likely to cause prejudice to the minority. This policy is often effected through an equal treatment or sharing rule. Thus, when a company repurchases its shares and does so through market purchases,[4] the Listing Rules insist on equality of treatment of the shareholders, either by controlling the price at which the repurchase is made or by requiring the repurchase to be made by way of a tender offer to all shareholders.[5] This does something to prevent insiders from taking undue advantage of the repurchase exercise or the repurchase having an effect on the balance of power within the company to the benefit of the majority. In the same vein, the common law requires dividends to be paid equally to shareholders according to their shareholdings. The common law took as its test for equality the nominal value of the shares, though the articles normally adjust this so as to use the amount paid up on the shares where the nominal value differs from the amount paid up.[6] This makes it difficult for the majority to use the mechanism of dividend distribution to allocate a disproportionate share of the company's earnings to themselves.[7]

Three further minority protection techniques are worth mentioning at this stage. The new statutory derivative action procedure makes it more difficult for a controlling shareholder/director to block access to the courts by the minority to

---

[3] See above, at para.14–18.

[4] See above, at para.13–19.

[5] Listing Rules 12.4.1–2.

[6] *Birch v Cropper* (1889) 14 App. Cas. 525 HL; cf. art.71 of Model Articles for Public Companies. The Model Articles for Private Companies Limited by Shares needs no equivalent since art.21 requires all shares (other than those initially subscribed) to be fully paid as to nominal value and any premium.

[7] This provides a possible rationale for the exemption of dividends from the rules on financial assistance, especially as creditors are also protected by the rule that dividends are payable only out of profits. See above at para.13–45.

enforce the company's rights against the controller acting as director.[8] The derivative action allows the minority to side-step the majority's control of the board or shareholder decision-making and to seek court (rather than corporate) approval to initiate litigation. Of course, the derivative action is not available if the shareholders have ratified the wrongdoing. However, the statute now prevents interested directors from voting on a shareholder resolution to ratify the wrongdoing.[9] Thus, two techniques are used. One is the essentially procedural one of structuring the vote at shareholder level by excluding the votes of those interested in the decision. The other is novel, i.e. shifting the litigation decision to an outside authority free of majority influence.

Excluding the controllers, when interested, from voting on the decision in question is a technique taken further by the Listing Rules of the Financial Conduct Authority and applying to companies listed on the Main Market of the London Stock Exchange. More importantly, those Rules impose a requirement for shareholder approval of transactions with significant shareholders which is not to be found in general company law. Under the rules for "related party" transactions, the Listing Rules exclude the related party from voting on the decision in question and require that party to take all reasonable efforts to ensure that associates do not vote either. Crucially, the term "related party" is widely defined so as to include a person who can control 10 per cent or more of the voting rights in the company or who can exercise substantial control over the company. "Associate" is widely defined, rather in the manner of a "connected person" in s.252 of the Act. Finally, a "related party transaction" is widely defined so as to include not only transactions between the company and the related party but also transactions in which the company and related party together finance a transaction or project and any other similar transaction which benefits the related party.[10]

The final technique to be mentioned is that of giving the minority the right to exit the company at a fair price if certain decisions with which they disagree are taken by the majority. Such exit rights are usually referred to as "appraisal" rights. Crucially, they are not simply rights to exit the company, which in a listed company the shareholder hardly needs, but rights to leave at a fair price. Although in some company law systems this is a rather well-developed minority protection remedy,[11] the British legislation uses it only very sparingly. This is perhaps because, whether the right is to be bought out by the company or by the majority shareholder, the effect is to place a potentially substantial financial hurdle in the way of the decision which triggers the appraisal right. Nevertheless, an appraisal right can be found in ss.110 and 111 of the IA 1986 (reflecting provisions introduced in the nineteenth century) which deal with the reorganisation of companies in liquidation.[12] More important, it is also to be found in both

19–3

---

[8] See above, Ch.17.

[9] See above, para.16–121.

[10] See Listing Rules 11.1 et seq. The closest the general law comes to requiring shareholders' approval of transactions with significant shareholders is where that shareholder falls within the category of "shadow director" and thus is subject to the statutory rules on self-dealing contained in Ch.4 of Pt 10 (above, paras 16–54 et seq.).

[11] For example, the US (see R. Clark, *Corporate Law* (Little Brown, 1986) pp.444 et seq.

[12] See below, para.29–24.

the Companies Act and the Takeover Code where it provides an exit right at a fair price where there has been an acquisition or transfer of a controlling block of shares in the company. In this second situation, the exit right is not tied to the taking of a business decision but rather to a shift in the composition of the shareholder body, though the basis of the exit right is, in part, that the shift in the identity of the controller of the company may well have an adverse impact upon the minority shareholders.[13]

In this chapter, however, we shall look at two further minority protection techniques. The first consists of giving power to the court to review the decision of the majority on the grounds that it is in some sense unfair to the minority. In specific instances we have seen that the Act gives such a right of appeal to the minority. The question now is whether the common law gives such a general right. The second is treating the shareholders whose interests are at risk from the decision as a separate group whose consent is needed for the decision to go ahead, whether or not under the company's constitution the separate consent of that group would be required. The first of these two techniques obviates the difficulty of having to predict in advance which decisions are acceptable and which not, for the decision is subject to ex post scrutiny on a case-by-case basis by the courts. The second technique is an extension of the policy of excluding interested parties from voting on a decision. Sometimes this negative technique is enough by itself. In other cases, however, the law may need to go further and specify those who are entitled to vote as well as those who are not, rather than leaving the determination of those entitled to vote to the rules contained in the company's articles.

REVIEW OF SHAREHOLDERS' DECISIONS

The starting point

19–4   Scattered throughout the reports are statements that members must exercise their votes "bona fide for the benefit of the company as a whole",[14] a statement which, read casually, might suggest that shareholders are subject at common law to precisely the same basic principle as directors. This would be highly misleading, however, and the decisions do not support any such parallel. Indeed, to the contrary, it has also been repeatedly laid down that votes are proprietary rights, like other incidents of shares, which the holder may exercise in his or her own

---

[13] See paras 28–41 and 28–75. The statute recognises the exit right only if the new controller holds 90% of the voting rights after a takeover bid; the Code gives an exit opportunity at the 30% level, no matter how the 30% has been acquired and so goes much further than the statute.

[14] The original source of this oft-repeated (but potentially misleading) expression seems to be Lindley MR in *Allen v Gold Reefs of West Africa* [1900] 1 Ch. 671–2, and merits full citation: "The power thus conferred on companies to alter their articles is limited only by the provisions contained in the statute and the conditions contained in the company's memorandum of association. Wide, however, as the language of [the Act] is, the power conferred by it must, like all other powers, be exercised subject to those general principles of law and equity which are applicable to all powers conferred on majorities enabling them to bind minorities. It must be exercised, not only in the manner required by law, but also bona fide for the benefit of the company as a whole, and it must not be exceeded. These conditions are always implied, and are seldom, if ever, expressed".

selfish interests even if these are opposed to those of the company.[15] A shareholder may even enter into a contract to vote or not vote in a particular way, and that contract may be enforced by injunction.[16] Moreover, as we have seen, directors themselves, even though personally interested, can vote in their capacity as shareholders at that general meeting,[17] unless the Act or the Listing Rules specifically deprive them of the right to vote.[18] And this is so also as regards the transactions which, under Chs 4 and 4A of Pt 10 of the Act, require the prior approval of the company in general meeting.

Thus, it is wrong to see the voting powers of shareholders as being of a fiduciary character. Unlike directors' powers, shareholders' voting rights are not conferred upon them in order that they shall be exercised in the way which prefers the interests of others over the interests of the voting shareholder where the two are in conflict (as the fiduciary rule requires), and this is so whether those others are seen to be "the company" or the minority shareholders or, indeed, any other group.

However, to deny the fiduciary character of shareholders' voting rights and to assert their proprietary nature is not to say that the exercise of shareholders' voting powers is, or should be, unconstrained by the law. The controlling shareholders may not be required to exercise their powers in the best interests of the non-controlling shareholders, but this does not mean they may trample over the interests of the latter with impunity. There are many situations in the modern law, and not just within company law, where the exercise of property rights or personal powers is subject to some sort of review by the courts. The issue which arises, therefore, is not the one of principle, but whether it has proved possible for the courts or the legislature to develop a set of criteria for the effective review of majority shareholders' decisions. As we shall see below, this task was addressed by the courts at an early stage in the development of British company law, but the results of that exercise have not been spectacularly successful. The courts have hovered uncomfortably between an unwillingness to determine how businesses should be run and an equally deeply felt unease that simple majoritarianism would leave the minority exposed to opportunistic treatment by the majority.

The principle which the courts have found so difficult to develop and apply to **19–5** shareholder decisions was articulated as early as 1900 by the Court of Appeal in *Allen v Gold Reefs of West Africa Ltd*[19] in the context of a vote to alter the company's articles. The Court of Appeal held that because the power to alter the

---

[15] *North-West Transportation Co v Beatty* (1887) 12 App. Cas. 589 PC; *Burland v Earle* [1902] A.C. 83 PC; *Goodfellow v Nelson Line* [1912] 2 Ch. 324.

[16] *Greenwell v Porter* [1902] 1 Ch. 530; *Puddephatt v Leith* [1916] 1 Ch. 200—in which a mandatory injunction was granted. Contrast the rules on directors' fettering their discretion: above, para.16–35.

[17] *NW Transportation Co v Beatty* (1887) 12 App. Cas. 589 PC; *Burland v Earle* [1902] A.C. 83 at 93 PC; *Harris v A Harris Ltd* (1936) S.C. 183 (Sc); *Baird v Baird & Co*, 1949 S.L.T. 368 (Sc). And see the remarkable case of *Northern Counties Securities Ltd v Jackson & Steeple Ltd* [1974] 1 W.L.R. 1133 where it was held that, although to comply with an undertaking given by the company to the court the directors were bound to recommend the shareholders to vote for a resolution, they, as shareholders, could vote against it, if so minded.

[18] See, for example, s.239 excluding the interested director from voting on a resolution to ratify his or her wrongdoing (above, para.16–119) or the Listing Rules provisions on related-party transactions, discussed above.

[19] *Allen v Gold Reefs of West Africa Ltd* [1900] 1 Ch. 656 CA. See fn.14, above, for the full quotation.

articles was a power which enabled the majority to bind the minority, it must therefore be exercised "not only in the manner required by law, but also bona fide for the benefit of the company as a whole, and it must not be exceeded. These conditions are always implied, and are seldom, if ever, expressed". This explanation might be thought to embrace the ideas of absence of power, good faith, and abuse of power. Despite that, for much of the early development in this area, the focus was almost exclusively on "bona fide for the benefit of the company as a whole", and the difficult task of deciding what this required.

In examining the case law, it is useful to divide the cases into those where the shareholders' decision clearly concerns and affects the company's rights and those where it does not, but merely affects the members' rights as between themselves; and, with the latter, subdividing those cases into alteration of the articles involving an expropriation of the member's shares, and those not having that effect, although all these distinctions are becoming less marked in light of recent cases.

Resolutions where the company's interests are centre stage

19–6   We have already seen the tension in reviewing voting decisions brought to the fore in Ch.16. The company, like any legal person, can forgive directors for the wrongs they do to the company. This inevitably comes at a financial cost to the company, since it gives up an otherwise valuable claim. Nevertheless, the decision, typically taken by the general meeting on behalf of the company, can be taken for perfectly proper reasons. But we rightly doubt that the reasons are "perfectly proper" when the decision is carried by the votes of the wrongdoing directors themselves. This is true even if the range of "perfectly proper" reasons is very much at large; there is something unpalatable about forgiveness driven by the wrongdoers themselves. In this context we have seen the common law's struggle between holding certain decisions "un-ratifiable" (i.e. the general meeting simply does not have the power to act) and, alternatively, disenfranchising the interested shareholder directors (i.e. focusing on the propriety of their decision-making).[20] We have also seen the modern statutory preference for the latter approach.[21] The same approaches are evident in other contexts: denying shareholders the right to dispose of corporate assets when the company is

---

[20] *Prudential Assurance Co Ltd v Newman Industries Ltd (No.2)* [1981] Ch. 257; *Smith v Croft (No.3)* [1987] B.C.L.C. 365, neither adopted with great vigour in subsequent cases, although clearly influential.

[21] See paras 16–121 et seq.

insolvent has parallels with "un-ratifiable" decisions[22]; occasionally disenfranchising shareholders thought to be inevitably conflicted is an example of the latter approach.[23]

Resolutions more generally

However intuitively compelling these approaches, they are rarely defended on the basis of principle. That makes it difficult to settle on the appropriate approach in the more difficult, and more common, cases. These are the cases where the general meeting has the undoubted power to take decision, but their objective is not straightforwardly to advance the interests of the company (although sometimes it can be framed that way), but merely to determine relative rights as between the shareholders. In this context, it is inevitable that the majority's preferences will be favoured, even in circumstances where there can be no rational complaint that the decision was somehow inappropriate or improper: consider decisions to sack directors, or change the articles. When are these decisions reviewable? It is clear that they are reviewable, but, as one judge put it with some understatement, the current British law is "somewhat untidy".[24]

19–7

Resolutions to expropriate members' shares

In expropriation (or compulsory transfer) cases, the arguments for judicial intervention might seem to be at their strongest, but the law falls far short of prohibiting changes in the articles aimed at introducing such clauses. On the contrary, it is clear that compulsory transfer articles may be introduced into the company's articles, and the debate is about the level of judicial scrutiny to which such amendments will be subject. The relevant authorities start with *Brown v British Abrasive Wheel Co*,[25] a decision at first instance in which a public company was in urgent need of further capital which shareholders, holding 98 per cent of the shares, were willing to put up but only if they could buy out the 2 per cent minority. Having failed to persuade the minority to sell, they proposed a special resolution adding to the articles a provision to the effect that any shareholder was bound to transfer his shares upon a request in writing of the holders of 90 per cent of the shares. Although such a provision could have been

19–8

---

[22] See *West Mercia Safetywear Ltd v Dodd* [1988] B.C.L.C. 250 CA; *Aveling Barford v Perion Ltd* [1989] B.C.L.C. 626; *Re DKG Contractors Ltd* [1990] B.C.C. 903; *Official Receiver v Stern* [2002] 1 B.C.L.C. 119 at 129. Also see, more recently, *Madoff Securities International Ltd v Raven* [2013] EWHC 3147 (Comm) at [272]–[288] (Popplewell J); *Goldtrail Travel Ltd (In Liquidation) v Aydin* [2014] EWHC 1587 (Ch) at [113]–[118] (Rose J).

[23] *Bamford v Bamford* [1970] Ch. 212 CA. The directors had issued shares for improper purposes. In a ratification by shareholders of this decision, it was conceded that the holders of the newly issued shares could not vote.

[24] *Constable v Executive Connections Ltd* [2005] 2 B.C.L.C. 638, the judge refusing to dispose of an expropriation claim summarily.

[25] *Brown v British Abrasive Wheel Co* [1919] 1 Ch. 290. For a stimulating analysis of these cases see Hannigan, "Altering the Articles for Compulsory Transfer" [2007] J.B.L. 471.

validly inserted in the original articles,[26] and although the good faith of the majority was not challenged, it was held that the addition of a general provision enabling the majority to expropriate the minority could not be for the benefit of the company as a whole but was solely for the benefit of the majority. Hence an injunction was granted restraining the company from passing the resolution.

This decision, however, was almost immediately "distinguished" by the Court of Appeal in *Sidebottom v Kershaw, Leese & Co Ltd*.[27] There, a director-controlled private company had a minority shareholder who had an interest in a competing business. Objecting to this, the company passed a special resolution adding to the articles a provision empowering the directors to require any shareholder who competed with the company to sell his shares at a fair value to nominees of the directors. This was upheld on the basis that it was obviously beneficial to the company. In contrast, shortly thereafter in *Dafen Tinplate Co v Llanelly Steel Co*,[28] it was held at first instance that a resolution inserting a new article empowering the majority to buy out any shareholder as they thought proper, was invalid as being self-evidently wider than could be necessary in the interests of the company.

So far, all these decisions suggest that adding to the articles a provision enabling the shares of a member to be compulsorily transferred will be upheld only if passed bona fide in the interests of the company, with that judged not just by the members but also reviewable by the court, on a basis which in some ill-defined way goes beyond the general meeting merely showing good faith and rationality. However, in *Shuttleworth v Cox Bros Ltd*,[29] a case concerning not the expropriation of shares but the removal of an unpopular life director, the Court of Appeal, in upholding the validity of a resolution inserting in the articles a provision that any director should vacate office if called upon to do so by the board, held that it was for the members, and not the court, to determine whether the resolution is for the benefit of the company and that the court will intervene only if satisfied that the members have acted in bad faith.[30] If the same applies to expropriation of shares, it is difficult to understand why what is now s.979 of the Act was needed. That section[31] enables a takeover bidder who has acquired 90 per cent or more of the target company's shares to acquire compulsorily the remainder. There would have been no need for that section if a bidder, having acquired a controlling interest, could then cause the target company to insert in its articles a similar power. That might suggest that mere bona fides, directed to the

---

[26] *Phillips v Manufacturers Securities Ltd* (1917) 116 L.T. 209; in *Borland's Trustees v Steel Bros* [1901] 1 Ch. 279 an even wider article was inserted with the agreement of all the members. Presumably too a compulsory transfer article could be introduced by majority vote which would affect only shares acquired in the future.

[27] *Sidebottom v Kershaw, Leese & Co Ltd* [1920] 1 Ch. 154 CA.

[28] *Dafen Tinplate Co v Llanelly Steel Co* [1920] 2 Ch. 124.

[29] *Shuttleworth v Cox Bros Ltd* [1927] 2 K.B. 9 CA.

[30] The court conceded that if the resolution was such that no reasonable man could consider it for the benefit of the company as a whole that might be a ground for finding bad faith, [1927] 2 K.B. 9 at 18, 19, 23, 26 and 27. This exception was affirmed in *Re Charterhouse Capital* [2015] EWCA Civ 536. Another, it is submitted, would be if the majority was trying to acquire the shares of the minority at an obvious undervalue.

[31] Dealt with in Ch.28 at paras 28–68 et seq., below.

benefit of the company, does not quite capture the approach being applied by the court. And yet going further has proved controversial.

An issue akin to the *Brown* facts was considered by the High Court of Australia in **19–9** *Gambotto v WCP Ltd*,[32] where it was proposed to alter the articles to allow a 90 per cent shareholder to acquire the shares of minority shareholders at an objectively fair price (the majority holder in fact holding 99.7 per cent of the shares). The motivation for the change was to convert the company into a wholly owned subsidiary, which would bring enormous tax advantages for the company. Nevertheless, the court refused to allow the change, holding explicitly that the majority's decision could only be upheld if it were taken in good faith *and* for proper purposes. In the court's view, the general meeting's power to expropriate shares could legitimately be used to save the company from "significant detriment or harm" (as in *Sidebottom v Kershaw, Leese and Co Ltd*) but not to advance the commercial interests of the majority (as in this case, where the tax advantages to the company would indirectly, but greatly, benefit its controlling shareholders). "English authority", presumably *Shuttleworth v Cox Bros Ltd*, was disapproved on the grounds that "it does not attach sufficient weight to the proprietary nature of a share".[33] On one view, there is something of this same approach implicit in *Brown*, in Astbury J's judgment, where he too could be seen as denying the majority the right to use their power to expropriate the minority to their own corresponding advantage.[34] And yet English courts have on occasion explicitly distanced themselves from the objective "proper purposes" approach in *Gambotto*, even in the context of expropriation decisions.[35]

However, the recent decision of *Re Charterhouse Capital Ltd*[36] perhaps puts suggestions of continuing adherence to a more relaxed British test in doubt. The Court of Appeal approved an amendment of the articles to permit expropriation of shares, and affirmed the broadly subjective test in *Shuttleworth*, but, in setting out the full detail of the appropriate test, the court consistently referred to the test as embracing not only bona fides but also the intended proper purpose of the power,[37] here being a tidying-up exercise designed to implement the agreed terms of a shareholder agreement which was expressed to take priority over the articles.

---

[32] *Gambotto v WCP Ltd* (1995) 182 C.L.R. 432.

[33] *Gambotto v WCP Ltd* (1995) 182 C.L.R. 432 at 444.

[34] *Brown v British Abrasive Wheel Co* [1919] 1 Ch. 290, 296, per Astbury J: "The defendants contend that it is for the benefit of the company as a whole because in default of further capital the company might have to go into liquidation. The plaintiff is willing to risk that. The proposed alteration is not directly concerned with the provision of further capital, nor does it insure that it will be provided. It is merely for the benefit of the majority. If passed, the majority may acquire all the shares and provide further capital. That would be for the benefit of the company as then constituted. But the proposed alteration is not for the present benefit of this company". It may be that the decision can be put on the basis, as found by the judge, that the majority did not think about the benefit to the company's business at all, but only their own benefit, for example, because financing was available on equivalent terms from those who did not require complete control.

[35] See *Citco Banking Corp NV v Pusser's Ltd* [2007] UKPC 13; [2007] 2 B.C.L.C. 483 PC.

[36] *Re Charterhouse Capital Ltd* [2015] EWCA Civ 536, especially at [90], [92], [96]–[108] (Etherton C for the court).

[37] *Re Charterhouse Capital Ltd* [2015] EWCA Civ 536, see especially [90].

In such circumstances it would seem difficult for any minority shareholder to argue that the amendment was either irrational or for improper purposes, or in bad faith.

Other resolutions

19–10   If it is not clear what English law requires in cases of compulsory transfer of shares, where the arguments can typically be framed in terms of corporate benefit even if there are also substantial benefits to the majority, then how much more difficult is the issue likely to be where that claim cannot be made, and it is simply a battle of wills between the majority and minority as to how their relations should be regulated by the articles? In these circumstances, many cases appear to adopt the view that the *only* test can be good faith, as in *Shuttleworth*, since the courts can have no objective standard of their own to judge whether a decision is for the benefit of the company (other than shareholder irrationality, perhaps, and even that requires some conception of "the interests of the company"). In the difficult case of *Greenhalgh v Arderne Cinemas Ltd*,[38] where the proposed amendment was to remove a pre-emption clause so as to facilitate a sale of control to a third party, Sir Raymond Evershed MR tried to preserve the application of the traditional test by saying that in such cases "the company as a whole" did not mean the company as a corporate entity but "the corporators as a general body", and that it was necessary to ask whether the amendment was, in the honest opinion of those who voted in favour, for the benefit of a hypothetical member. Since the case was before the court precisely because of a division of opinion on the issue, this test is hardly illuminating. As was pointed out by the High Court of Australia in its famous inter-war decision, *Peter's American Delicacy Co Ltd v Heath*,[39] it is "inappropriate, if not meaningless" to ask whether the shareholders had considered the amendment to be in the interests of the company as a whole. Some other test of validity is required.

On what that might be, little progress has been made over the intervening 75 years. Thus, in *Citco Banking Corp NV v Pusser's Ltd*[40] the Privy Council upheld a change in the articles which entrenched the existing controller of the company (who before the change controlled 28 per cent of the company's shares) by permitting the conversion of his existing shares (carrying one vote per share) into a new class of share carrying 50 votes per share. This was said by those who supported the alteration to be a bona fide decision in the interests of the company because it enabled the company to raise further finance for expansion, the financiers requiring that the existing controller remain in charge. The genuineness

---

[38] *Greenhalgh v Arderne Cinemas Ltd* [1951] Ch. 286 CA; and [1950] 2 All E.R. 1120 where the judgment of Evershed MR is reported more fully.

[39] *Peter's American Delicacy Co Ltd v Heath* (1939) 61 C.L.R. 457, 512 (Dixon J). Here the amendment provided that shareholders should thenceforth receive dividends rateably according to the amounts paid up on their shares rather than, as previously, according to the number of shares (fully or partly paid) which they held. A fortiori the test is not useful if the group in question is made up of a number of distinct sub-groups: *Redwood Master Fund Ltd v TD Bank Europe Ltd* [2006] 1 B.C.L.C. 149, not an expropriation case and involving a "class" of creditors rather than of shareholders, but applying the same principles.

[40] *Citco Banking Corp NV v Pusser's Ltd* [2007] UKPC 13; [2007] 2 B.C.L.C. 483 PC.

of this belief on the part of the majority was not challenged by the other party to the litigation and the court found that a reasonable shareholder could have held this view about the proposed alteration. Applying the *Shuttleworth* test and reiterating that the burden of proof is on those who challenge the resolution, the court found the test of bona fide in the interests of the company to have been met.

This may all seem unexceptional, yet working through the potential ramifications must give some cause for concern. At face value, it appears to suggest that a majority could use its power to deliver differential benefits to itself to the exclusion of the minority (here, conversion of a tranche of A shares carrying one vote per share to a tranche of B shares carrying 50 votes per share). If that can be done, would it not be equally permissible to reclassify the majority's tranche of ordinary shares to give differential dividend rights, or rights to capital on winding up? Even if it is thought that does not offend the rules on amending a company's articles—which is doubted—it must surely fail the statutory requirements for protection of shareholders' class rights and pre-emptive rights. The minority would effectively be reduced to advancing s.994 complaints of unfair prejudice. The remedies there are typically that the minority is bought out, and thus excluded completely from further participation in the company. Looking back to the problem, notice that what is intuitively objectionable is not that the minority is overpowered; that is inevitable with majority rule. It is that the majority can use its power for the purpose of delivering differential benefits *to itself* to the exclusion of the minority. Lord Hoffmann, in *Citco*, would not disenfranchise the interested shareholder (here one Tobias), especially as there was no attack on his bona fides, but he did note that, even without his votes, the resolution would still have been carried by 78 per cent of the shareholders. In these circumstances, there seems little cause for complaint by the losing minority. But absent these circumstances, and despite the prevailing analysis in the cases, surely there is a justifiable concern?[41]

The future

But perhaps, finally, the future is looking a little more certain. All the cases so far illustrate a set of common concerns in this area. Of itself, this suggests a common approach is warranted: there is little point in different tests for different sub-categories of shareholder decision-making, although of course, whatever the test, the particular power and the context for its exercise will be a material consideration.[42] In determining the appropriate tests for judicial review, there seem to be three broad ways forward in this area. The first is to demand little of shareholders in their decision-making other than rationality and bona fides. Many

19–11

---

[41] Note the different approach in *Rights & Issues Investment Trust Ltd v Stylo Shoes Ltd* [1965] Ch. 250, cited in *Citco*, although not followed in its detail. In *Stylo*, along with a substantial increase in the issued ordinary share capital, the articles were amended to double the number of votes attached to special management shares so as to maintain the control of the existing management. In upholding the shareholders' resolution, Pennycuick J noted, at 255–256, that the rules on class rights needed to be followed, and that here the resolution was effective because the management shares had not voted, and yet nevertheless 92 per cent of the ordinary shareholders, being those with no personal interests to gain in the matter, had voted in favour.

[42] See also Completing, para.5.98.

cases are illustrative,[43] but so too their problems. The second is to adopt a safe mid-way point, permitting an objective element in the test applied by the court, and keeping that test focused on "the interests of the company", but not going so far as to allow the court to substitute its own commercial view of what might have been best in the circumstances. *Brown v British Abrasive Wheel Co*,[44] discussed earlier, might be illustrative.[45] Whatever the merits, such an approach seems difficult to justify in principle and impossible to administer with certainty. The third, and certainly the most interventionist approach, is to embrace the twin tests of subjective bona fides and objective proper purposes, as in *Gambotto*. Despite the criticisms visited on that case, this does increasingly appear to be the modern approach, both with shareholder decision-making and more generally.[46] It has a respectable pedigree: it is evident in the explicit language of the much-cited *Allen v Gold Reefs of West Africa Ltd*,[47] as well as in the more controversial *Gambotto*, and is also evident in all the most recent considered English decisions.[48] Moreover, although it was not the language used, it might be seen as a better explanation of some of the earlier English cases.[49]

Its starting point is the perfectly general one that no grant of power is absolute, at least when its exercise binds dissenting parties. The minimum constraints are that the power must be exercised rationally, in good faith, and for the purposes for which the power is granted. It is this last feature which typically provides the potential tripwire in authorisation and ratification decisions, in expropriation decisions, and in governance decisions such as *Citco*. But in different contexts the concerns (or "purposes") are different; for example, the relevant "proper purposes" might give free rein to shareholders in their appointment and dismissal of directors.[50] This variability might not make the relevant distinctions much easier to solve when presented in terms of improper purposes (or fraud on the power), rather than in terms of "bona fide in the interests of the company", but at least the principles being pursued are clearer.

---

[43] There is some indirect support for this approach in English law in *Citco Banking Corp NV v Pusser's Ltd* [2007] UKPC 13; [2007] 2 B.C.L.C. 483 at [20] PC, where a subjective approach was endorsed even in what came close to an expropriation case.

[44] *Brown v British Abrasive Wheel Co* [1919] 1 Ch. 290.

[45] And was criticised on precisely that basis in *Shuttleworth* and (perhaps) *Citco*.

[46] Any number of cases might be cited. The rule does not depend on the identity of the power-holder, and in particular does not depend on the power-holder being a fiduciary. See as illustrative *Eclairs Group Ltd v JKX Oil & Gas Plc* [2015] UKSC 71 SC (directors); *Assénagon Asset Management SA v Irish Bank Resolution Corp Ltd (formerly Anglo Irish Bank Corp Ltd)* [2012] EWHC 2090 (Ch) (creditors); *Burry & Knight Ltd v Knight* [2014] EWCA Civ 604 (shareholders).

[47] *Allen v Gold Reefs of West Africa* [1900] 1 Ch. 671.

[48] See especially the earlier discussion of *Re Charterhouse Capital Ltd* [2015] EWCA Civ 536. See also fn.46, above.

[49] In particular, the test applied by the courts is not to look at the controlling director-shareholder's *actual* bona fides, nor even to assert that *no* reasonable director-shareholder could have thought the decision to be bona fide in the interests of the company (i.e. either an irrationality test, or an indication that he court was simply not persuaded that bona fides were proven). Rather, it is, it seems, to apply a more objective test, and to assume an improper motivation, or a use of the power for improper ends.

[50] Although even here there are some constraints: the potential pay-back for appointment of a board of directors intended to serve as the appointer's puppet is classification of the appointer as a shadow director.

As evidence of this trend, Sir Terence Etherton C in *Re Charterhouse Capital,* indicated, obiter, that he preferred the formulation in *Peters' American Delicacy Co Ltd v Heath,*[51] that in the case of an amendment in which the company as an entity has no interest, the test should be whether the amendment amounts to oppression of the minority or is otherwise unjust or is outside the scope of the power. This is the sort of test which also applies more broadly, to decision-making by other power-holders.[52]

Voting at class meetings

The rules discussed above apply not only to decisions by the shareholders at large but also to votes at meetings of classes of shareholders. These rules and their use are described in the next section, but we might immediately note that here, too, the cases adopt the same approach to decision-making as described immediately above. Sometimes this is very clearly so. *Re Holders Investment Trust*[53] concerned a capital reduction scheme requiring the confirmation of the court. Megarry J approached the matter on the basis that he had to be satisfied, first, that the resolution of the preference shareholders had been validly passed bona fide in the interest of that class; and then that, in the court's view, the scheme was fair to all classes.[54] The application failed at the first step. By analogy with the cases considered earlier, the law required members voting in class meetings to use their votes for the purpose of—or in the interests of—the class. Here, confirmation was refused because the resolution of the class meeting of the preference shareholders had been passed as a result of votes of trustees who held a large block of the preference shares but a still larger block of ordinary shares. In casting their votes, the trustees had deliberately voted in the way best designed to favour the ordinary shareholders, since that was what would best serve the interests of their beneficiaries (as of course their trustee obligations required). The court held that use of their power in this way was not permitted. We might now say it was contrary to the protective purposes underpinning the required class meetings.

CLASS RIGHTS

We have already noted that the principle discussed in the previous section applies to class meetings as well as to general meetings of the shareholders. Now we need to turn to the question of when separate meetings of classes of shareholders are required and how the class in question is defined. The separate consent of shareholders particularly affected by a proposed resolution may be required by statute or by the company's own constitution. For example, as we shall see, the

19–12

19–13

---

[51] *Peters' American Delicacy Co Ltd v Heath* (1939) 61 C.L.R. 457, 512 (Dixon J).

[52] See paras 16–26 et seq. (directors); and *Redwood Master Fund Ltd v TD Bank Europe Ltd* [2006] 1 B.C.L.C. 149; and *Assénagon Asset Management SA v Irish Bank Resolution Corp Ltd* [2012] EWHC 2090 (Ch) (bondholders).

[53] *Re Holders Investment Trust* [1971] 1 W.L.R. 583.

[54] See below, para.29–11.

principle of separate consent is well-established in relation to proposed alterations of the articles where these alterations affect the "rights" of a class of members.

The procedure for varying class rights

19–14   Where a proposed alteration of the articles involves "the variation of the rights attached to a class of shares", the Act supplements the general supermajority provisions of s.21 with additional protective mechanisms for members of the affected class. The technique deployed in ss.630 and 631 is to require the separate consent of the class, usually by way of a 75 per cent majority, to any proposal to alter the articles in such a way as would vary the class rights. Without this important protective technique, the class might be swamped by the votes of other classes of shareholders. Indeed, the class in question might not otherwise have any say in the matter at all, if, for example, it was a class of non-voting shareholders. Preference shares are often non-voting, at least if their dividends are being paid on time, and classes of non-voting ordinary shares are not unknown. The alteration of their rights would otherwise be a matter entirely for the voting shareholders. The Act thus provides the class in question with a veto over the proposed change, even if the company's constitution gave the class members no right to vote on the issue. Of course, the alteration must also be approved in the normal way under s.21 (approval by a three-quarters majority of those shareholders entitled to vote under the company's articles), but that is not normally a problem in the cases considered in this section.

The statutory provisions on variation in the 2006 Act are considerably simpler than their predecessors. Section 630 in effect lays down a single default rule,[55] with equivalent provision being made in s.631 for companies without shares. Variation of the rights attached to a class of shares requires the consent of three-quarters of the votes cast at a separate meeting of that class or a written resolution having the support of holders of three-quarters of the nominal value of the class (excluding treasury shares) (s.630(4)). That default rule may be displaced by explicit provisions in the company's articles, which may set a higher or a lower standard. This is very straightforward and is enough to deal with most cases which will arise.

The complexity of the section, such as it is, derives from its attempt to answer the question of what rules should govern any attempt to amend the procedure in the articles for the variation of class rights, if the articles contain such a procedure. If the variation procedure in the articles could be freely amended in the same way as any other article of the company, the protection intended to be afforded by the articles to the class could easily be undermined. The section begins by stating that any amendment to the variation procedure contained in the articles itself attracts the provisions protecting class rights (s.630(5)).[56] Without

---

[55] The Model Articles for private and public companies contain no variation of rights procedure, so, in effect, the statute is the default model.

[56] Both in relation to variation of rights and amendments to variation procedures, variation includes abrogation: s.630(6). Class rights and variation procedures contained in the memorandums of existing companies are treated as being contained in the articles: s.28.

this provision, a variation procedure in the articles requiring a higher level of consent could be reduced to, or even below, the level of the statutory default by simply following the requirements of s.21 for general alterations to the articles (for example, no class meeting). This is now not possible as a result of s.630(5), unless, presumably, the articles themselves expressly provide a less demanding way of amending the variation procedure than the default rule in the statute.

In the same vein, the subsection also treats as a variation of class rights the introduction of a variation procedure into the articles, for that might set a lower standard than the statutory default rule previously applicable. Finally, the section is without prejudice "to any other restrictions on the variation of rights".[57] This appears to mean that a company could use the entrenchment mechanism of s.22[58] to set an even higher requirement for amendments to the variation procedure contained in the articles than that otherwise required by s.630. For example, the articles could provide that amendments to the variation procedure require the consent of all the members of the class.

So far, we have observed that the statutory provisions on class rights use two protective techniques, at least on a default basis: a separate meeting of the class (the main protection) and the supermajority protection of a three-quarters majority to obtain an effective decision of the class meeting. However, s.633 also makes use of a third technique analysed in the first part of this chapter, namely, court review of the majority's decision.[59] This acknowledges the fact that, even within a class meeting, it is possible for the majority of the class to act opportunistically towards the minority of the class. Section 633 may be particularly useful where the articles adopt a variation procedure considerably less demanding than the default statutory one. As we have seen,[60] those voting at class meetings are subject to the general common law requirements as to proper decision-making, but s.633 (with equivalent provisions in s.634 for companies limited by guarantee) goes further. It affords a dissenting minority of not less than 15 per cent of the issued shares of a class,[61] whose rights have been varied in manner permitted by s.630, a right to apply to the court to have the variation cancelled. Application must be made within 21 days after the consent was given or the resolution passed, but can be made by such one or more of the dissenting shareholders as they appoint in writing. Once such an application is made, the variation has no effect unless and until it is confirmed by the court. If, after hearing the applicant "and any other persons who apply to be heard and appear to the court to be interested",[62] the court is satisfied that the variation would

19–15

---

[57] 2006 Act s.630(3).
[58] Discussed below at para.19–23.
[59] This court review applies to all variation procedures, whether specified in the Act or in the company's articles: s.633(1).
[60] See above, para.19–12.
[61] Provided that they have not consented to or voted in favour of the resolution—an unfortunately worded restriction which effectively rules out nominees who have not exercised all their votes in one way.
[62] This clearly includes representatives of other classes affected and of the company.

"unfairly prejudice"[63] the shareholders of the class represented by the applicant, it may disallow the variation but otherwise must confirm it.[64] It is expressly provided that "the decision of the court is final",[65] which presumably means that it cannot be taken to appeal.[66]

The dearth of reported cases on s.633, and earlier versions of it, suggests that applications under it are made rarely if at all. Nevertheless, it probably serves a useful purpose in specifically drawing the attention of boards of directors to the need to ensure that variations of class rights treat classes fairly. But, should they ignore that warning, they are more likely to face an application under the unfair prejudice rules in Pt 30 rather than under s.633.

The sections analysed above provide a procedure whereby the company can vary class rights. Sometimes, a variation of class rights is effected by an order of the court. Section 632 makes it clear that the courts' powers under Pt 26 of the Act (dealing with arrangements and reconstructions (see Ch.29)) and Pt 30 (unfair prejudice—see the following chapter) and, less importantly, s.98 (cancellation of resolution of public company to re-register as private) are not affected by ss.630 and 631.

What constitutes a "variation"

19–16 Although the Act deals at some length with the procedure for varying class rights, it says very little, if anything, about what a variation of class rights is or, indeed, what a class right is. Both these matters are defined principally by the common law. As a matter of logic, however, the statutory or constitutional procedure is only relevant once it is clear that there is to be a variation of a class right. We will look first at "variation" and then at "class right".

Prior to the enactment of statutory provisions in this area, it was commonly assumed that rules specified in the articles required class consent only of the class whose rights were being altered in a manner adverse to that class. But the statutory provisions on "variation" (even if coupled with the statement that it includes "abrogation") cannot reasonably be construed as meaning only "*adverse variation*", and, to avoid any subsequent attack on the validity of the resolution, the formal consent of the benefited class should be obtained, even though it might appear a foregone conclusion.

---

[63] This is the same expression as that used in Pt 30 (see Ch.20, below), which would seem to provide a better alternative remedy not demanding 15 per cent support and strict time limits and with a wider range of orders that the court can make.

[64] 2006 Act s.633(5). The company must within 15 days after the making of an order forward a copy to the Registrar: s.635.

[65] 2006 Act s.633(5).

[66] This was certainly the intention of the Greene Committee on whose recommendation the section was based: Cmnd. 2657, para.23. But the need for speedy finality seems no greater than on an application under the general unfair prejudice provisions where there is no such provision and cases can be taken to the House of Lords. But if the application under s.633 is struck out on the ground that the time-limit was not complied with, that can be taken to appeal and was in *Re Suburban Stores Ltd* [1943] Ch. 156 CA. See also *Re Sound City (Films) Ltd* [1947] Ch. 169 which seems to be the only officially reported case on the predecessors to s.633. Cases in which it might have been invoked (e.g. *Rights & Issues Investment Trust v Stylo Shoes Ltd* [1965] Ch. 250) have been taken instead under the unfair prejudice sections or earlier versions of those sections.

However, the real problem lies where a class is adversely affected by what is proposed, but the courts, by placing a narrow technical construction on what constitutes a variation of rights, have declined to hold that the proposal falls within the class rights provisions of either the statute or the articles. Thus a subdivision[67] or increase[68] of one class of shares has been held not to vary the rights of another class notwithstanding that the result was to alter profoundly the voting equilibrium of the classes. Similarly, where preference shares were non-participating as regards dividend but participating as regards capital on a winding-up or reduction of capital, a capitalisation of undistributed profits in the form of a bonus issue to the ordinary shareholders was not a variation of the preference shareholders' rights notwithstanding that the effect was to deny them their future participation in those profits on winding up or reduction.[69] In the contrary situation, where the shares were participating as regards dividends but not in relation to return of capital on a winding-up, a reduction of capital by repayment of irredeemable preference shares in accordance with their rights on a winding-up (i.e. at their nominal value) was not regarded as a variation or abrogation of their rights, even though the shareholders were deprived of valuable dividend rights.[70] Even if the dividend rights of the preference shareholders were fixed, those rights might be valuable, if interest rates had fallen after the issuance of the preference shares. The obvious unfairness of this led to a contractual solution: the practice of providing, on issues by public companies of preference shares which are non-participating in a winding-up, that on redemption or any return of capital the amount repaid should be tied to the average quoted market price of the shares in the months before (the market price reflecting the value of the dividend rights rather than the nominal value of the shares). This, so-called "Spens formula", named after its inventor, affords reasonable protection in the case of listed companies but preference shareholders in unquoted companies still remain at risk.

Finally, an issue of further shares ranking pari passu with the existing shares of a class was not regarded as a variation of rights.[71] And, where there were preference and ordinary shares, an issue of preferred ordinary shares ranking

---

[67] *Greenhalgh v Arderne Cinemas* [1946] 1 All E.R. 512 CA, where the result of the subdivision was to deprive the holder of one class of his power to block a special resolution.

[68] *White v Bristol Aeroplane Co* [1953] Ch. 65 CA; *Re John Smith's Tadcaster Brewery Co* [1953] Ch. 308 CA.

[69] *Dimbula Valley (Ceylon) Tea Co v Laurie* [1961] Ch. 353. On the meaning of "participation" in this context see para.23–7 and on bonus shares see para.11–18. And see the startling decision in *Re Mackenzie & Co Ltd* [1916] 2 Ch. 450 which implies that a rateable reduction of the nominal values of preference and ordinary capital (which participated pari passu on a winding up) did not modify the rights of the preference shareholders notwithstanding that the effect was to reduce the amount payable to them by way of preference dividend while making no difference at all to the ordinary shareholders.

[70] *Scottish Insurance Corp v Wilson & Clyde Coal Co* [1949] A.C. 462 HL; *Prudential Assurance Co v Chatterly Whitfield Collieries* [1949] A.C. 512 HL; *Re Saltdean Estate Co Ltd* [1968] 1 W.L.R. 1844; *House of Fraser v AGCE Investments Ltd* [1987] A.C. 387 HL (Sc.); *Re Hunting Plc* [2005] 2 B.C.L.C. 211. But contrast *Re Old Silkstone Collieries Ltd* [1954] Ch. 169 CA, where confirmation of the repayment was refused because it would have deprived the preference shareholders of a contingent right to apply for an adjustment of capital under the coal nationalisation legislation.

[71] See the cases cited above, but contrast *Re Schweppes Ltd* [1914] 1 Ch. 322 CA, which, however, concerned s.45 of the 1908 Act, which forbade "interference" with the "preference or special privileges" of a class.

ahead of the ordinary but behind the preference was not a variation of the rights of either existing class.[72] The principle applied in all the above cases was that the formal rights of the complaining shareholders had not been varied, even if the change had adversely affected the value of those rights.

19–17   However, just as it is possible for the articles to require a variation procedure which is more demanding than the statutory default procedure in terms, for example, of the level of approval required, so it is possible for the articles to require a wider range of variations to be subject to the procedure than the statute requires. Thus, in the wake of the decisions on reduction of capital referred to in the previous paragraph, it became common to introduce special provisions into a company's articles to protect preference shareholders. In *Re Northern Engineering Industries Plc*[73] a clause in the articles deeming a reduction of capital to be a variation of rights was upheld and enforced when the company proposed to cancel its preference shares. But very clear wording will have to be used if such a provision is to be construed as affording any greater safeguards. In *White v Bristol Aeroplane Co*[74] and *Re John Smith's Tadcaster Brewery Co*,[75] the relevant clauses referred to class rights being "affected, modified, dealt with or abrogated". At first instance Danckwerts J[76] held that bonus issue to the ordinary shareholders could not be made without the consent of the preference shareholders because, although their rights would not be abrogated or varied, they would be "affected" since their votes would be worth less in view of the increased voting power of the ordinary shareholders. But the Court of Appeal reversed his decision. They said that the rights of the preference shareholders would not be affected; the rights themselves—to one vote per share in certain circumstances—remained precisely as before. All that would occur was that their holders' enjoyment of those rights would be affected. If that eventuality was to be guarded against, more explicit wording would have to be used, making it clear that the clause was intended to protect economic interests as well as rights.

It seems, therefore, that if s.630 is effectively to prevent class rights from being "affected as a matter of business",[77] it is necessary to find a formula for a variation of rights clause which will expressly operate in relation to an alteration which affects the enjoyment of their rights (as opposed to the rights themselves). In the absence of such a clause in the model articles, however, such rights are likely to be granted by companies only if it is thought that the securities on offer would not otherwise be acceptable to potential purchasers or, at least, not acceptable at the price the company wishes to issue them at.

---

[72] *Hodge v James Howell & Co* [1958] C.L.Y. 446 CA; *The Times*, 13 December 1958.
[73] *Re Northern Engineering Industries Plc* [1994] 2 B.C.L.C. 704 CA.
[74] *White v Bristol Aeroplane Co* [1953] Ch. 65 CA.
[75] *Re John Smith's Tadcaster Brewery Co* [1953] Ch. 308 CA.
[76] Only his judgment in the latter case is fully reported: see [1952] 2 All E.R. 751.
[77] The words are those of Greene MR in *Greenhalgh v Arderne Cinemas* [1946] 1 All E.R. 512 at 518.

The definition of class rights

Before it is possible to decide whether a class right has been varied, it is necessary to know what a class right is. This is a matter upon which there is a surprising degree of doubt. Section 629 tells us that shares are to be regarded as of one class if the rights attached to them "are in all respects uniform", so that merely attaching different names to groups of shares does not turn them into different classes of share if the rights attached to them are the same.[78] This definition of a class of shares applies to the Act generally, not just in relation to the variation of class rights.

19–18

Beyond that, the statute gives no help. It does not even state expressly, as s.127(1) of the 1985 Act did, that class rights can arise only if there is more than one class of share. It seems likely that no change was intended on this point, since, where there is only one class of share, s.21 (alteration of the articles) and s.630 (variation of class rights) would overlap to an unacceptable extent, if s.630 applied in this case as well. However, assuming two or more classes of share, what then counts as a class right? The choices range from only the rights attached to any one of the classes which are unique to it (i.e. not held in common with any of the other classes of share) to all the rights attached to any of the classes. An intermediate position adds to the first group the core rights of shareholders (relating to voting, dividends and return of capital on a winding-up) whether or not those rights are unique to the class in that particular case. There is little authority on the choice to be made, although in *Cumbrian Newspapers Group Ltd v Cumberland and Westmoreland Newspaper and Printing Co Ltd*[79] Scott J seemed to favour the first and narrowest view. The second view might be thought to protect more adequately the expectations of shareholders. On the first and narrowest view a shareholder seeking protection of dividend, voting and return of capital rights which were not unique to the class would have to ensure that there was a variation of rights clause in the articles and that that clause defined class rights in an appropriately broad way. This seems undesirable. The right to class consent at least for the variation of core rights would be what companies and, for example, preference shareholders would expect and the law should give effect to that expectation.

Whilst this basic issue about the definition of a class right continues unresolved, a more sophisticated aspect of the same question has been considered judicially and has received a surprisingly liberal response. The question is whether there are class rights where nominally the shares are of the same class but special rights are

19–19

---

[78] This definition does not solve all the problematic cases. Suppose the only difference between the classes is a difference in par values (thought by the Court of Appeal in *Greenhalgh v Arderne Cinemas Ltd* [1946] 1 All E.R. 512 CA, to be enough to create separate classes); or suppose the par values are the same but some shares are fully paid-up and others only partly. The statute provides that its definition is satisfied even if the rights to dividends of shares in the 12 months after allotment are different from those of other shares with otherwise similar rights—as they might be if additional shares were issued part-way through a financial year.

[79] *Cumbrian Newspapers Group Ltd v Cumberland and Westmoreland Newspaper and Printing Co Ltd* [1987] Ch. 1 at 15. Earlier editions of this book have argued for the second view. For a full discussion see E. Ferran and L.C. Ho, *Principles of Corporate Finance Law*, 2nd edn (Oxford: OUP, 2014), Ch.6.

conferred on one or more members without attaching those rights to any particular shares held by that member or members. This was the question facing Scott J in the *Cumbrian Newspapers* case.[80] Two companies, publishing rival provincial weekly newspapers in an area where it had become apparent that only one was viable, entered into an arrangement designed to ensure that one of the companies (Company A) would publish that one newspaper but that it would issue 10 per cent of its ordinary share capital[81] to the other company (Company B). Company B was anxious to ensure that the paper should remain locally owned and controlled, and to this end the articles of Company A were amended in such a way as to confer on Company B pre-emptive rights in the event of any new issue of shares by Company A or on a disposal by other shareholders of their shares in Company A. These rights were not attached to any particular shares but conferred on Company B by name. Further, another new article provided that: "If and so long as [company B] shall be the holder of not less than one-tenth in nominal value of the issued ordinary share capital of" Company A, Company B "shall be entitled from time to time to nominate one person to be a director of" Company A. Company A's articles contained a variation of rights clause. Eighteen years later, Company A's directors proposed to convene a general meeting to pass a special resolution deleting the relevant articles. Company B thereupon applied to the court for a declaration that Company B's rights were class rights that could not be abrogated without its consent.

Scott J pointed out that special rights contained in articles could be divided into three categories.[82] First, there are rights annexed to particular shares. The classic example of this is where particular shares carry particular rights not enjoyed by others, e.g. in relation to "dividends and rights to participate in surplus assets on a winding up".[83] These clearly were "rights attached to [a] class of shares" within the meaning of what is now s.630. He also held that this category would include cases where rights were attached to particular shares issued to a named individual but expressed to determine upon transfer by that individual of his shares.

The second category was where the articles purported to confer rights on individuals not in their capacity as members or shareholders.[84] Rights of this sort would not be class rights, for they would not be attached to any class of shares.[85] But Company B's rights did not fall within this class; the articles in question were

---

[80] *Cumbrian Newspapers Group Ltd v Cumberland and Westmoreland Newspaper and Printing Co Ltd* [1987] Ch. 1 at 15.

[81] It also had preference shares but nothing turned on that. Clearly an attempt to vary their class rights would have been subject to the equivalent of s.630.

[82] *Cumbrian Newspapers Group Ltd v Cumberland and Westmoreland Newspaper and Printing Co Ltd* [1987] Ch. 1 at 15A–18A.

[83] *Cumbrian Newspapers Group Ltd v Cumberland and Westmoreland Newspaper and Printing Co Ltd* [1987] Ch. 1 at 15.

[84] He instanced *Eley v Positive Life Assurance Co* (1875) 1 Ex.D. 20, on which see paras 3–16 and 3–23, above. It seems clear that in such a case the individual will have no enforceable rights in the absence of an express contract with the company additional to the articles.

[85] *Cumbrian Newspapers Group Ltd v Cumberland and Westmoreland Newspaper and Printing Co Ltd* [1987] Ch. 1 at 16A–E.

"inextricably connected with the issue to the plaintiff[86] and the acceptance by the plaintiff of the ordinary shares in the defendant".[87]

This left the third category: "rights that, although not attached to any particular shares were nonetheless conferred upon the beneficiary in the capacity of member or shareholder of the company".[88] In his view, rights conferred on Company B fell into this category.[89] But did they come within the words in the then equivalent of s.630(1) as "rights attached to any class of shares"? After an analysis of the various legislative provisions and of the anomalies which would result if they did not,[90] he concluded that the legislative intent must have been to deal comprehensively with the variation or abrogation of shareholders' class rights and that he should therefore construe what is now s.630 as applying to categories one and three. He accordingly granted the declaration sought.[91]

This decision of Scott J might have been easier to reach under the 2006 Act. In effect, the learned judge treated the expressions "the rights of a class of members" and the "rights...attached to a class of shares" as synonymous. The 2006 Act, by contrast, deals explicitly with variations of the former type in s.631, and the latter in s.630. In short, Scott J may have anticipated by a few decades the position now provided for by statute.

19–20

Other cases

There are some statutory procedures for taking corporate decisions which explicitly require the separate consent of each class of shares, for example, Pt 26 dealing with schemes of arrangement, but there the definition of a "class" of shares is interpreted functionally rather than literally, in contrast with the variation of rights cases.[92]

19–21

---

[86] i.e. Company B.

[87] *Cumbrian Newspapers Group Ltd v Cumberland and Westmoreland Newspaper and Printing Co Ltd* [1987] Ch. 1 at 16G.

[88] *Cumbrian Newspapers Group Ltd v Cumberland and Westmoreland Newspaper and Printing Co Ltd* [1987] Ch. 1 at 16A–17A.

[89] *Cumbrian Newspapers Group Ltd v Cumberland and Westmoreland Newspaper and Printing Co Ltd* [1987] Ch. 1 at 17. He instanced as other examples, *Bushell v Faith* [1970] A.C. 1099 (above, para.14–51); and *Rayfield v Hands* [1960] Ch. 1 (above, para.3–24).

[90] *Cumbrian Newspapers Group Ltd v Cumberland and Westmoreland Newspaper and Printing Co Ltd* [1987] Ch. 1 at 18A–22B.

[91] *Cumbrian Newspapers Group Ltd v Cumberland and Westmoreland Newspaper and Printing Co Ltd* [1987] Ch. 1 at 22F–G. But he refrained from granting an injunction on the ground that this would "prevent the company from discharging its statutory duties in respect of the convening of meetings" (instancing s.368—though there had not in fact been any requisition by its members under this section). The result was therefore that Company A could hold the meeting if it wished but, if the resolution was passed, it would nevertheless be ineffective in the light of the declaration unless Company B consented.

[92] See below, Ch.29.

19–22 It is wrong to think that protection for minority shareholders is to be found only in mandatory provisions of company law. Provided the minority shareholder has sufficient bargaining power, for example at the point a much-needed investment is made in the company, that shareholder may be able to negotiate for protections over and above those to be found in company law. These contractual protections may then be reflected in the company's constitution or in an agreement existing separately from and outside the constitution.

Indeed, across the board there is a considerable incentive for shareholders themselves to provide, in advance of a dispute arising, for a substantive or procedural rule which will govern the case. Individuals reading the previous pages would be justified in feeling somewhat gloomy about the extent to which minority shareholder interests are truly protected by the rules there analysed, and so might well feel that such contractual protections would be essential. Where class rights are not involved, the scope of the objective controls upon the voting decisions of the majority is still very unclear. Even where class rights are involved, the protection afforded still has its weaknesses, notably the limited view taken by the courts of what constitutes the variation of a class right. Indeed, the statutory class-rights procedure encourages self-help because it sets out only default rules and limited ones at that.[93]

As an added advantage, the techniques described below may be used quite generally to exert control in the interests of minority shareholders in any corporate decision, regardless of whether that decision needs to be taken by the shareholders or may be taken by the board of the company. As such, the following discussion constitutes a bridge to the statutory unfair prejudice provisions discussed in the following chapter.

Provisions in the constitution

19–23 The articles provide an obvious place in which to locate any agreements reached for the protection of minority shareholders, because the articles bind the company and its members as they exist from time to time (s.33) so that future members are bound by the provisions of the articles protecting the minority without further ado.

Protective provisions in the articles will be an effective way of safeguarding minorities only if they can be enforced. Often the minority shareholder will want to assert that a decision taken in breach of the protective provisions is not binding on the company and that an injunction should be granted to enjoin the company and its directors from acting on the invalid resolution. In principle, such an action should be available since, as we saw in Ch.3, the articles are enforceable as a contract, although the discussion in Ch.3 also set out several important and probably unexpected limits to the general principle.[94]

---

[93] See above, para.19–16.
[94] See especially para.3–27 on "mere internal irregularities".

The weakness with protective provisions in the articles, however, is that they are alterable by special resolution of those entitled to vote on shareholder resolutions (s.21). This may provide a way to defeat the expectations of non-voting shareholders or even those of minority voting shareholders, because a previous protection may simply be removed from the articles, at least provided no class rights have been created.

The Act itself suggests one possible solution to the risk of future amendment, namely, use of the entrenchment powers contained in s.22. Under this section a provision in the articles can be declared to be alterable only through a more restrictive procedure than that required for a special resolution under s.21. The entrenchment provision may go so far as to require unanimity for a particular change, although it cannot render the provision unalterable if all the members agree to the change (s.22(3)). Thus, s.22 provides a mechanism whereby a provision protective of the minority can be included in the company's articles and that protective provision can be declared to be alterable only in the desired way, most obviously only if those it is intended to protect agree to the change. However, the entrenchment provision may have a powerful and adverse effect on those it does not benefit and so s.22(2) provides that entrenchment provisions may be included only in the company's articles on formation or, subsequently, with the consent of all the members of the company. Entrenchment is, thus, essentially a small company facility.

Consequently, it may be more attractive to provide the required minority protection in a company already in existence by creating a new class of shares carrying the relevant protection, issuing those shares to the shareholder to be protected, and then including a broad variation of rights clause in the articles, so that, for example, the consent of the protected shareholder becomes necessary for the alteration of the protection. Alternatively, the shareholder may be given in effect control over the taking of any resolutions by the shareholders through provisions which in principle are alterable but in practice cannot be. An example would be a rule that the quorum for a meeting of the shareholders cannot be constituted unless the minority shareholder is present, either in person or by proxy. Thus, the shareholder would be given a veto over decisions of the shareholders, exercisable by refusing to participate in the meeting.[95] This provision would be ineffective where the shareholders decide by written resolution, but in that case it might be possible to provide a solution by requiring the particular shareholder's consent for a written resolution or through weighted voting rights.[96]

19–24

Shareholder agreements

Alternatively, the parties may prefer to proceed by way of an agreement existing outside and separate from the articles. This has the advantage of privacy because such an agreement, unlike the company's constitution, does not have to be filed at

19–25

---

[95] As we have seen at para.15–53, the courts have been unwilling to undermine such arrangements through use of their powers under s.306 of the Act.

[96] See *Bushell v Faith* (above, para.14–51).

Companies House. However, an issue immediately arises as to whether the company can effectively be made party to such an agreement, as it would be if the agreement were embodied in the company's articles. Here, there are two apparently conflicting principles: first, that a company, like any other person, cannot with impunity break its contracts and, secondly, that a company cannot contract out of its statutory power under s.21 to alter its articles by special resolution.

The second proposition was favoured by the House of Lords in *Russell v Northern Bank Development Corp Ltd*.[97] It was clear to their lordships that "a provision in a company's articles which restricts its statutory power to alter those articles is invalid"[98] and they applied that principle to the agreement before them, existing outside the articles among the shareholders and to which the company purported to be a party. That agreement provided that no further share capital should be created or issued in the company without the written consent of all the parties to the agreement. Consequently, it would seem that the company cannot validly contract independently of the articles not to alter those articles.[99] However, that proposition is heavily qualified by two further propositions which may render the initial proposition ineffective in practice, at least for those who are well advised.

Prior contracts

19–26   The first qualification is that the principle of invalidity, laid down in *Russell*, does not apply where the company has entered into a previous contract on such terms that for the company to act upon its subsequently altered article would involve it in a breach of the prior contract. In this situation the term of the earlier contract, which would be breached if the company acted upon the altered article, is not invalid. The *Russell* principle is not relevant here because the term in the earlier contract is not broken when the company alters its articles, but only when it acts upon the altered article. Although the case law has tended to focus on directors' service contracts, its implication for shareholder agreements is that a company would be a party to them and agree not to act in a particular way in the future, provided it did not agree to refrain from amending its articles. Thus, in *Southern Foundries (1926) Ltd v Shirlaw*[100] the company altered its articles so as to introduce a new method of removing directors from office and then used the new method to dismiss the managing director in breach of his 10-year service contract. The managing director successfully obtained damages for wrongful dismissal. The provision as to the term of the service agreement was thus clearly held by the House of Lords to be valid. Lord Porter said: "A company cannot be precluded from altering its articles thereby giving itself power to act upon the provisions of the altered articles—but so to act may nevertheless be a breach of

---

[97] *Russell v Northern Bank Development Corp Ltd* [1992] 1 W.L.R. 588 HL. See Sealy, [1992] C.L.J. 437; Davenport, (1993) 109 L.Q.R. 553; Riley, (1993) 44 N.I.L.Q. 34; Ferran, [1994] C.L.J. 343.

[98] *Russell v Northern Bank Development Corp Ltd* [1992] 1 W.L.R. 588 at 593.

[99] In this case what was proposed was an increase in the company's authorised capital laid down in the memorandum. Whether the quoted principle applies to all powers conferred on the company by the statute is unclear.

[100] *Southern Foundries (1926) Ltd v Shirlaw* [1940] A.C. 701 HL.

contract if it is contrary to a stipulation in a contract validly made before the alteration".[101] In this case the contract protected a manager but the principle is equally applicable to a contract protecting a shareholder.

The unresolved issue in relation to this first qualification is whether a claimant seeking to enforce his or her contractual rights against the company is confined to the remedy of damages or whether and, if so, how far, injunctive relief is available to enforce the earlier contract. In *Baily v British Equitable Insurance Co*,[102] the Court of Appeal granted a declaration that to act on the altered article would be a breach of the plaintiff's contractual rights. More surprisingly, in *British Murac Syndicate Ltd v Alperton Rubber Co Ltd*[103] Sargant J went so far as to grant an injunction to restrain an alteration of the articles which would have contravened the plaintiff's contractual rights. Although Sargant J's decision is generally regarded as based upon a misunderstanding of the previous authorities, some sympathy with this approach was expressed by Scott J in the *Cumbria Newspapers* case,[104] where he said that he could "see no reason why [the company] should not, in a suitable case, be injuncted from initiating the calling of a general meeting with a view to the alteration of the articles". To the extent that injunctive relief is made available in this way not simply to restrain acting upon the altered article but to restrain the operation of the machinery for effecting the alteration itself, the notion that the company cannot validly make a direct contract not to alter its articles becomes hollow. Such an extension of injunctive relief would also contradict the dictum of Lord Porter in *Shirlaw*[105]: "Nor can an injunction be granted to prevent the adoption of the new articles". However, injunctive relief merely to prevent the company acting upon the new articles would not fall foul of this principle.

19–27

Binding only the shareholders

The second qualification is that an agreement among the shareholders alone as to how they will exercise the voting rights attached to their shares is not caught by the principle that a company cannot contract out of its statutory powers to alter its articles. This rule was applied to save the agreement in *Russell*, the House of Lords benignly severing the company from the agreement in question. Lord Jauncy said that "shareholders may lawfully agree inter se to exercise their voting rights in a manner which, if it were dictated by the articles, and were thereby binding on the company, would be unlawful".[106] The claimant was granted a declaration as to the validity of the agreement, and it seems that their lordships would have been happy to grant an injunction had the claimant objected

19–28

---

[101] *Southern Foundries (1926) Ltd v Shirlaw* [1940] A.C. 701 at 740–741.

[102] *Baily v British Equitable Insurance Co* [1904] 1 Ch. 373 CA.

[103] *British Murac Syndicate Ltd v Alperton Rubber Co Ltd* [1915] 2 Ch. 186. The case concerned the right of the plaintiff, under both the articles and a separate contract, to appoint two directors to the board so long as he held 5,000 shares in the company. Today, after the *Cumbria Newspaper* decision (see para.19–18, above) the claimant might be protected as the holder of a class right.

[104] *Cumbrian Newspapers Group Ltd v Cumberland and Westmoreland Newspaper and Printing Co Ltd* [1987] Ch. 1 at 24.

[105] *Southern Foundries (1926) Ltd v Shirlaw* [1940] A.C. 701 HL.

[106] *Russell v Northern Bank Development Corp Ltd* [1992] 1 W.L.R. 588 at 593.

substantively to the course of action proposed by the company, as against wishing to establish the principle that his consent to the change was required.[107] This conclusion flows from the more general proposition that the vote attached to a share is a property right which the shareholder is prima facie entitled to exercise and deal with as he or she thinks fit.[108] Since the company can act only through its members to alter the articles, an agreement binding all the members is as effective as one to which the company is party as well.

However, in one respect a members' agreement is less secure than one which binds the company as well. On a subsequent transfer of a shareholding covered by the agreement the new shareholder will not be bound without his or her express adherence to the agreement among the other shareholders.[109] Nevertheless, the shareholders' agreement does play an important role in establishing the requirement for minority shareholder consent to important changes in the company's financial or constitutional arrangements in situations such as management buy-outs, venture capital investments and joint ventures.[110]

Finally, a device analogous to the voting agreement should be noted. Closely associated with, but more sophisticated than, the voting agreement is the voting trust, not uncommon in the US but less common in the UK. Under this, in effect, voting rights are separated from the financial interest in the shares, the former being held and exercisable by trustees while the latter remains with the shareholders. Voting policy then becomes a matter for the trustees, who may use their powers to protect minority shareholders, though the voting trust may be driven by other considerations, such as a desire to make a takeover bid more difficult and thus protect the incumbent management.[111]

CONCLUSION

19–29 The mandatory protections for minority shareholders identified in this chapter are rather patchy. They apply only to voting at general meetings and not to majority control exercised via the board and, even then, only to certain types of shareholder decision. In the case of the requirements for shareholder voting, the

---

[107] *Russell v Northern Bank Development Corp Ltd* [1992] 1 W.L.R. 588 at 595.

[108] On the enforcement of shareholder agreement see *Greenwell v Porter* [1902] 1 Ch. 530; and *Puddephatt v Leith* [1916] 1 Ch. 200, where a mandatory injunction was granted to compel a shareholder to vote in accordance with his agreement. Some shareholder agreements may make their adherents "concert parties", thus triggering provisions which impose obligations on a member of the shareholder group because of the size of the group interest. See paras 26–19, 28–44 and 28–54, below.

[109] cf. *Greenhalgh v Mallard* [1943] 2 All E.R. 234 CA. Of course, the selling shareholder may be contractually bound to secure the adherence of the acquiring shareholder, but even so it is difficult to make the arrangement completely water-tight by purely contractual means, especially at the remedial level.

[110] See, for example, *Growth Management Ltd v Mutafchiev* [2007] 1 B.C.L.C. 645; and, generally, K. Reece Thomas and C. Ryan, *The Law and Practice of Shareholders' Agreements*, 4th edn (London: LexisNexis, 2014). If the power which it is sought to control is one which is exercisable by the board of directors, it may in addition be necessary to alter the articles so as to shift the power in question to the general meeting or to provide for its exercise by the board only with the consent of the general meeting or to provide that the shareholders shall take all appropriate action to prevent the company taking the steps to which a shareholder, exercising its rights under the agreement, objects.

[111] An offeror, where a trust is in operation, may acquire the majority of the shares but still not be able to dismiss the incumbent management. Such trusts are common in the Netherlands. See Ch.28, below.

protection provided manages to be, at once, both limited and uncertain in scope. It is perhaps not surprising that shareholders have resorted to private means, and that the legislature has attempted make more far-reaching protections available. The development and current status of these alternative means are considered in the next chapter.

CHAPTER 20

UNFAIR PREJUDICE

INTRODUCTION

The statutory unfair prejudice provisions are surprisingly wide-ranging, espe-   **20–1**
cially viewed against the patchy protections considered in the previous chapter.
Section 994(1),[1] the first of the six sections which constitute Pt 30 of the Act,
provides that any member may petition the court for relief on the ground:

> "(a) that the company's affairs are being or have been conducted in a manner which is unfairly
> prejudicial to the interests of members generally or some part of its members (including at
> least himself), or (b) that an actual or proposed act or omission of the company (including any
> act or omission on its behalf) is or would be so prejudicial."

This provision repeats rather than reforms the provisions previously found in
s.459 of the Companies Act 1985, so the older cases remain relevant.

Controlling shareholders are not in terms excluded from using the section,
although normally any prejudice they are subject to will be remediable through
the use of the ordinary powers they possess by virtue of their controlling position,
and so the conduct of the minority cannot be said in such a case to be *unfairly*

---

[1] The procedure for petitions is governed mainly by the Companies (Unfair Prejudice Applications)
Proceedings Rules 2009 (SI 2009/2469), but also by the Civil Procedure Rules and the practice of the
High Court, where not inconsistent with the 2009 Rules. Section 994(1A), somewhat bizarrely,
specifically states that the removal of an auditor in certain circumstances falls within (a). The reasons
for this provision are dealt with at para.22–18. Such claims should generally be heard in public open
court: *Global Torch Ltd v Apex Global Management Ltd* [2013] EWCA Civ 819 CA.

prejudicial to the controllers.[2] The section thus operates primarily as a mechanism for minority protection—or, at least, for the protection of non-controlling shareholders, for petitions are often brought where there is an equal division of shares in the company.

By referring to the conduct of the company's affairs, the section is clearly wide enough to catch the activities of controllers of companies, whether they conduct the business of the company through the exercise of their powers as directors or as shareholders or both. The section can even apply to the conduct of corporate groups. Although the conduct of a shareholder, even a majority shareholder, of its own affairs is excluded from the section, nevertheless, where a parent company has assumed detailed control over the affairs of its subsidiary and treats the financial affairs of the two companies as those of a single enterprise, actions taken by the parent in its own interest may be regarded as acts done in the conduct of the affairs of the subsidiary; and in some cases conduct of the subsidiary's business may amount to conduct of the business of the parent.[3] The "outside" shareholders in the subsidiary may thus use the section to protect themselves against exploitation by the majority-shareholding parent company.

20–2   The right to petition for relief under s.994 is conferred upon the members of the company,[4] but s.994(2) extends this right to non-members to whom shares have been transferred[5] or transmitted by operation of law.[6] As in the case of the derivative action, where a similar extension applies, this provision is useful in small companies where the directors of the company may exercise the power they have under the articles to refuse to register as a member a person to whom shares have been transferred, especially as s.771 now requires directors to give reasons for their refusal. If not within this extension, however, a non-member will not be able to petition under the section.[7] For example, if the registered shareholder is a nominee, the person with the beneficial interest in the shares cannot petition; the

---

[2] *Re Legal Costs Negotiators Ltd* [1999] 2 B.C.L.C. 171 CA; cf. *Parkinson v Eurofinance Group Ltd* [2001] 1 B.C.L.C. 720—majority shareholder, removed from the board, not able to use his shareholding to obtain redress in respect of a sale of the company's assets by the directors to a company controlled wholly by them, and so able to use the unfair prejudice provisions.

[3] On conduct of the parent as conduct of the subsidiary see *Nicholas v Soundcraft Electronics Ltd* [1993] B.C.L.C. 360 CA; expanding upon the approach taken in *Scottish Co-operative Wholesale Society Ltd v Meyer* [1959] A.C. 324 HL, by not confining the principle to companies engaged in the same type of business. See also *Re Dominion International Group (No.2)* [1996] 1 B.C.L.C. 634. On conduct of the subsidiary as conduct of the parent see *Rackind v Gross* [2005] 1 W.L.R. 3505.

[4] And, accordingly, members can agree to waive or vary those rights, or, as in *Fulham Football Club (1987) Ltd v Richards* [2011] EWCA Civ 855; [2012] Ch. 333, have disputes determined by arbitration instead.

[5] An agreement to transfer is not enough; a proper instrument of transfer must have been executed and delivered to the transferee: *Re a Company (No.003160 of 1986)* [1986] B.C.L.C. 391; *Re Quickdome Ltd* [1988] B.C.L.C. 370. However, the fact that the directors have refused to register the transfer does not deny the transferee standing: *Re McCarthy Surfacing Ltd* [2006] EWHC 832 (Ch).

[6] See *Re a Company (No.007828 of 1985)* [1986] 2 B.C.C. 98,951 at 98,954 (Harman J): "In my view, transmission by operation of law means some act in the law by which the legal estate passes even though there be some further act (such as registration) to be done; and in my view the mere allegation that there arises a constructive trust cannot possibly amount to a transmission by operation of law".

[7] Exceptionally, in *Re I Fit Global Ltd* [2013] EWHC 2090 (Ch), the court held that a person whose name was not entered in the company's register as required under s.112 was a shareholder and could

nominee will, however, be a legitimate petitioner and the interests the nominee may seek to protect include those of the beneficiary.[8]

Section 995 permits the Secretary of State to petition if, as a result of an investigation carried out into a company,[9] he concludes that the affairs of the company have been carried on in a way that is unfairly prejudicial to the members (or some part of them).

Finally, when an administration order is in force, s.994 is supplemented by para.74 of Sch.B1 to the Insolvency Act 1986, permitting any creditor or member to apply to the court on the grounds that the administrator has acted in a way which has unfairly harmed the interests of the applicant (or proposes to do so) or on the grounds that the administrator is not performing his or her functions as quickly or as efficiently as is reasonably practical.[10]

When this section was first introduced in its modern form in 1980, it posed a considerable challenge to the traditionally non-interventionist attitudes of judges in relation to the internal affairs of companies.[11] The extent to which the modern judges have thrown off that traditional attitude emerges very clearly in this chapter. The statutory remedy is capable of ranging very widely over the conduct of corporate affairs; it can address control of both shareholders' voting powers, examined in the immediately preceding chapter, and directors' powers, examined in Ch.14, as well as more subtle forms of unfairly prejudicial management.

20–3

SCOPE OF THE PROVISIONS

Since the right to petition is drafted in deliberately wide terms, the first problem for the courts has been to define its scope. It is suggested that three main questions have arisen, all requiring the court to decide whether to give the section (or, more accurately, its predecessors) a wide or narrow operation.

20–4

---

bring a petition. This was because during the trading of the company, there had been wholly inadequate formal corporate documentation and records.

[8] *Atlasview Ltd v Brightview Ltd* [2004] 2 B.C.L.C. 191. Also, the conduct of which a petitioner may complain embraces conduct occurring before the petitioner became a member, even if that conduct is not continuing (though it must prejudice the petitioner), so that the beneficial holder will be able to petition if the shares are transferred to him by the nominee: *Lloyd v Casey* [2002] 1 B.C.L.C. 454.

[9] See Ch.18, above. A petition under s.995 may be instead of, or in addition to, a petition by the Secretary of State to have the company wound up under s.124A of the Insolvency Act (see para.18–13, above), but it is notable that the Companies Act power does not require the Secretary of State to be of the opinion that the public interest would be furthered by the bringing of an unfair prejudice petition. The Secretary of State's power of petition also applies to any company capable of being wound up under the Insolvency Act (including in some cases companies not incorporated in the UK), whilst the general right to petition under s.994 applies only to companies incorporated under the Companies Acts and statutory water companies: s.994(3) and (4).

[10] The Insolvency Act provision is not considered in any detail in this chapter. For administration in general, see para.32–43. An unfair prejudice challenge may also be made to proposals adopted by way of a company voluntary arrangement (see s.6 of the Insolvency Act 1986) but the court's powers here are confined to setting aside the proposals adopted at the creditors' meeting and ordering meetings to consider revised proposals.

[11] See the lament of the Lord President (Cooper) in *Scottish Insurance Corp v Wilsons & Clyde Coal Co*, 1948 S.C. 376.

First, should the reference to conduct which is unfairly prejudicial to "the interests of members" be interpreted as referring only to their interests "*as* members", as with the jurisprudence on the statutory contract in the articles?[12] Decisions under very early predecessors to s.994 transposed this restriction with full effect,[13] but modern courts now take a more flexible view. The point is an important one, since one very common form of minority oppression is the expulsion of the minority shareholder from a position on the board. Under a narrow interpretation, this could not give rise to a remedy, since it amounts to oppression qua director, not qua member.[14] Now, however, although the qua member restriction remains as part of the unfair prejudice provisions, it is much more flexibly interpreted, and its practical significance is therefore much reduced. It is now accepted that the interests of a member, at least in a small company, may be affected by his or her expulsion from the board, whether because it was expected that the return on investment would take the form of directors' fees or because a board position, even in a non-executive role, may be necessary to monitor and protect the member's investment.[15] This approach is now settled, and not considered further.

Secondly, should the sections be seen simply as aimed at providing a more effective way of remedying harms which, independently of the unfair prejudice provisions, are in any case unlawful, or should the remit be wider? This may be termed the "independent illegality" issue. Once the modern statutory wording had been adopted, the courts opted quite early on for the wider approach,[16] holding that the provisions are not concerned simply with greater access and better remedies but, in addition, are designed to render unlawful some types of conduct which, apart from the sections, are not in any way unlawful. In many ways this constitutes one of their most important judicial contributions to the development of these provisions, although the move creates its own problems. Deprived of the familiar landmarks of established illegalities, what criteria should the courts deploy in determining whether conduct is unfairly prejudicial, i.e. unlawful in s.994 terms? This is the second main issue which has faced the courts and it is the one which has absorbed the greatest amount of judicial thought and effort. It is considered in more detail below. In the courts' handling of this issue we see most

---

[12] See above, paras 3–23 et seq.

[13] *Re A Company* [1983] Ch. 178, decided under s.210 of the 1948 Act. Section 210 referred to "oppression" rather than "unfair prejudice", and was generally interpreted very narrowly, hence the statutory amendments delivering the form we now have, first in s.459 of the 1985 Act, and now s.994 of the 2006 Act.

[14] *Re Lundie Bros* [1965] 1 W.L.R. 1051; *Ebrahimi v Westbourne Galleries Ltd* [1973] A.C. 360 HL.

[15] *Re A Company* [1986] B.C.L.C. 376; *Re Haden Bill Electrical Ltd* [1995] 2 B.C.L.C. 280.

[16] Under s.210 of the 1948 Act, the House of Lords had defined "oppression" as conduct which was "burdensome, harsh *and wrongful*" (emphasis added): *Scottish Co-operative Wholesale Society Ltd v Meyer* [1959] A.C. 324. This was the point which gave rise to the notion that the oppression section was aimed only at providing better remedies for existing wrongs. The Jenkins Committee recommended that the restriction, if it existed, should be removed (Report of the Company Law Committee, Cmnd. 1749 (1962), paras 203–206), and the courts, from an early stage, interpreted the substitution of the words "unfairly prejudicial" for "oppressive" as intended to achieve that result: see Hoffmann J in *Re A Company (No.8699 of 1985)* [1986] B.C.L.C. 382 at 387. The courts had already arrived at this position some years previously in the case of petitions to wind up the company. See *Ebrahimi v Westbourne Galleries Ltd* [1973] A.C. 360 HL; below, para.20–21.

clearly what amounts to a partial revolution in judicial attitudes to becoming involved in the internal affairs of companies.

Finally, whether or not the courts had extended the range of unfairly prejudicial conduct beyond conduct which is independently unlawful, there remains an important issue of the relationship between the unfair prejudice remedy and the derivative action. When a wrong *has* been committed against the company, may a shareholder leap over the restrictions on bringing a derivative action, formerly contained in the rule in *Foss v Harbottle* and now set out in the statute,[17] by presenting a petition founded upon unfair prejudice and obtaining in this way a remedy for the company? Or is the petitioner under s.994 confined to the recovery of personal losses? In other words, are the unfair prejudice petition and the derivative action aimed at redressing different wrongs and, if so, how does one distinguish between them? This is the third issue which we shall consider in more detail after taking a closer look at the second.

20–5

INDEPENDENT ILLEGALITY AND LEGITIMATE EXPECTATIONS OR EQUITABLE CONSIDERATIONS

In modern law, giving courts the power by statute to control the exercise of discretion by persons or institutions on grounds of "unfairness" is hardly novel.[18] Yet such open-ended legislation, which in effect involves a sharing of the legislative function between Parliament and the courts, always presents the courts with the challenge of how to develop on a case-by-case basis criteria by which the imprecise concept of "fairness" can be given operational content. As we remarked above, the challenge was particularly acute for the courts in relation to the unfair prejudice remedy, for the tradition of the courts was not to interfere in the internal affairs of companies.

20–6

The important steps taken by the courts can be characterised by saying that the courts recognised that s.994 protects expectations and not just rights. Borrowing from public law, it is sometimes said that the section protects the "legitimate expectations" of the petitioner, though more recently the courts have preferred the private law phrase "equitable considerations".[19] Whatever the language used, the difficult issue is to distinguish those expectations of the petitioner which are to be classified as "legitimate", and so deserving of legal recognition and protection, from those expectations which the petitioner may harbour as a matter of fact but which the courts will not protect. Put in more modern terms, the task is to distinguish those equitable considerations which merit a judicial response from those which do not. It is suggested that the decisions of the courts to date have succeeded in identifying one clear class of legitimate expectation or equitable consideration, and have hinted at a range of other situations where s.994 may be

---

[17] Analysed in Ch.17, above.

[18] See, for example, the law relating to unfair dismissal of employees by employers, introduced in 1971 and now contained in the Employment Rights Act 1996.

[19] "Legitimate expectations" was the phrase endorsed by the Court of Appeal in *Re Saul D Harrison & Sons Plc* [1995] 1 B.C.L.C. 14 at 19, per Hoffmann LJ; but in *O'Neill v Phillips* [1999] 1 W.L.R. 1092; [1999] 2 B.C.L.C. 1 HL, the same judge led the House of Lords to adopt the phrase "equitable considerations" for fear that the former phrase carried connotations which were too wide.

prayed in aid, but without developing any of them in a comprehensive way. We begin with the clearly established category.

Informal arrangements among the members

20–7 This category of legitimate expectation or equitable consideration has been described as follows: it "arises out of a fundamental understanding between the shareholders which formed the basis of their association but was not put into contractual form".[20] What this principle recognises is that the totality of the agreement or arrangements among the members of the company may not be captured in the articles of association. This may be so for a number of reasons, but predominantly, it is suggested, because of a desire to avoid transaction costs when establishing a company or when admitting a new person to membership of the company. It will be cheaper to adopt some standard, or only slightly modified, form of articles rather than to bargain out in detail and then incorporate into the articles a customised set of rules dealing with every aspect of the company's present and likely future method of operation, the future being in any case inherently unpredictable. This is especially likely to be the case for small "quasi-partnership" companies where the incorporators[21] know each other well and may have worked out a successful method of operation when trading in unincorporated form whose translation into a formal document they would see as a needless expense. However, it would seem that the correct analysis is that a company is a quasi-partnership because of the particular understandings among its members, not that the understandings exist because the company is a quasi-partnership.

When things eventually go wrong—and small companies emulate marriages in the frequency and bitterness of their breakdown—the precise provisions of the articles may seem almost irrelevant to the petitioner's sense of grievance. The unwritten understandings upon which the members of the company operate will come to the fore. Adding to the complications, these understandings will also include assumptions that, where powers are exercised, they are exercised within the law—for example, powers conferred upon the board will be exercised in accordance with the fiduciary duties of directors—with the result that breaches of fiduciary and other duties may be tied into the shareholders' arrangements as well.[22]

---

[20] *Re Saul D Harrison & Sons Plc* [1995] 1 B.C.L.C. 14 at 19.

[21] Though the legitimate expectation often arises when the company is formed, it may arise at a later date, for example, when the petitioner becomes a member: *Tay Bok Choon v Tahanson Sdn Bhd* [1987] 1 W.L.R. 413 PC; *Strahan v Wilcock* [2006] 2 B.C.L.C. 555 CA. Equally, a legitimate expectation based on informal agreement among all the members is most often recognised in a quasi-partnership company, but may arise in any small company, whether the company is to be operated as an incorporated partnership or not: *Re Elgindata Ltd* [1991] B.C.L.C. 959.

[22] *Re Saul D Harrison* [1995] 1 B.C.L.C. 14 at 18. This aspect of unfair prejudice is, of course, not peculiar to small companies but applies across the full range of companies. Hence, it is suggested, the importance of the question, discussed above at para.20–14, whether s.994 provides corporate or only personal relief to the petitioner.

The range of expectations which may be protected in this way is open-ended, although the most common is undoubtedly the petitioner's expectation that he or she would be involved in the management of the company through having a seat on the board.[23]

It is important to grasp, however, that this category of legitimate expectation depends crucially upon the factual demonstration that an informal agreement or arrangement, generating the expectation relied upon, did exist outside the articles and supplementing them. The "starting point"[24] of the court's analysis will be the articles of association and "something more" will be required to move the court from the view that "it can safely be said that the basis of association is adequately and exhaustively laid down in the articles".[25] If that factual demonstration cannot be made, the petitioner's case will fail,[26] For example, in *Re Coroin Ltd*,[27] David Richards J refused to recognise legitimate expectations where the founding members of the company were a group of highly sophisticated and experienced investors with little by way of prior relationship, investing in a project worth many hundreds of millions of pounds, and governed by lengthy and complex formal documentation. As he put it, "I find it hard to imagine a case where it would be more inappropriate to overlay on those arrangements equitable considerations of the sort discussed by Lord Wilberforce[[28]] and Lord Hoffmann[[29]]". It follows from this that this category of protected expectations is almost wholly confined to companies with small, even very small, numbers of members, probably with relatively unsophisticated governance arrangements. Beyond such companies it becomes increasingly difficult to demonstrate, first, that there was any relevant informal arrangement; and, secondly, that all the members of the company were parties to it.[30]

This approach on the part of the courts was confirmed, indeed re-emphasised, in the first decision of the House of Lords on what is now s.994, *O'Neill v Phillips*.[31] The leading judgment was given by Lord Hoffmann, whose own rise through the judicial hierarchy has roughly coincided with that of the unfair prejudice case law and who has had a particular influence upon its development. Their lordships' endorsement of the dominant approach in the lower courts was

20–8

---

[23] So that s.994 may qualify not only the formal articles, but also the statutory powers of the majority under s.168. In this respect the s.994 decisions reinforce the decision of the House of Lords in *Bushell v Faith*, above, para.14–51.

[24] *Re Saul D Harrison* [1995] 1 B.C.L.C. 14 at 18.

[25] *Ebrahimi v Westbourne Galleries Ltd* [1973] A.C. 360 at 379 HL.

[26] See *Re Saul D Harrison* [1995] 1 B.C.L.C. 14 itself; but also *Re Posgate and Denby (Agencies) Ltd* [1987] B.C.L.C. 8; *Re A Company* [1987] B.C.L.C. 562; *Re A Company* (1988) 4 B.C.L.C. 80; *Re Ringtower Holdings Plc* (1989) 5 B.C.C. 82; *Currie v Cowdenbeath Football Club Ltd* [1992] B.C.L.C. 1029; *Re JE Cade & Sons Ltd* [1992] B.C.L.C. 213; *Murray's Judicial Factor v Thomas Murray & Sons (Ice Merchants) Ltd* [1993] B.C.L.C. 1437 at 1455; *Khoshkhou v Cooper* [2014] EWHC 1087.

[27] *Re Coroin Ltd* [2012] EWHC 2343 (Ch) at [636] (the point not disturbed on appeal, [2013] EWCA Civ 781; [2013] 2 B.C.L.C. 583).

[28] In *Ebrahimi v Westbourne Galleries Ltd* [1973] A.C. 360 HL.

[29] In *O'Neill v Phillips* [1999] 1 W.L.R. 1092; [1999] 2 B.C.L.C. 1 HL.

[30] *Re Blue Arrow Plc* [1987] B.C.L.C. 585; *Re Tottenham Hotspur Plc* [1994] 1 B.C.L.C. 655; *Re Astec (BSR) Plc* [1998] 2 B.C.L.C. 556.

[31] *O'Neill v Phillips* [1999] 1 W.L.R. 1092; [1999] 2 B.C.L.C. 1 HL.

accompanied, however, by a shift in terminology from the public law language of "legitimate expectations" to the more traditional private law phraseology of constraining the exercise of legal rights by reference to "equitable considerations".

Although on its face not obviously more restrictive than "legitimate expectations", the purpose of the phrase "equitable considerations" was to anchor more firmly the courts' assessment of what might constitute unfair conduct in the face of the formal and informal bargain struck by the shareholders of the company. Their lordships feared that lower courts might treat the legitimate expectations test as a licence to "do whatever the individual judge happens to think fair"[32] in the light of the petitioner's expectations. Instead, the correct approach was to ask whether there were equitable considerations which required the exercise of the majority's undoubted powers under company law or the company's constitution to be constrained in any way by reference to the bargain which the members of the company had struck, a bargain which, in its totality, might be located in informal, non-legally enforceable understandings between the members as well as in the company's formal constitution.[33] This more "contractual" approach to the assessment of unfairness under s.994 might admit not only of an approach based on analogy with breach of contract but also with other doctrines for the discharge of contracts, for example, frustration, where the majority used its legal powers to keep the association on foot in circumstances in which the original agreement between the parties had become fundamentally changed.[34]

Their lordships thought that legal certainty would be promoted by the expulsion from this area of "some wholly indefinite notion of fairness"[35] and the costs of litigation would be reduced by discouraging lengthy and expensive hearings which ranged over the full history of the company and the relationships among its members. They rejected the view of the Law Commission[36] that the contractual definition of unfair prejudice would unduly limit the scope of the section, but seemingly more on the grounds that some limitation was a price worth paying for legal certainty than on the grounds that all deserving cases would in fact fall within the section on the contractual approach.[37] The CLR endorsed the policy balance struck by the House of Lords,[38] and the 2006 Act thus seeks to repeat rather than to reform the unfair prejudice provisions previously contained in the 1985 Act.

---

[32] *O'Neill v Phillips* [1999] 2 B.C.L.C. 1 at 7e HL.

[33] *O'Neill v Phillips* [1999] 2 B.C.L.C. 1 at 10–11 HL. In *Re Guidezone Ltd* [2000] 2 B.C.L.C. 321 at 356 Jonathan Parker J took the equitable analogy a stage further by requiring that non-contractual understandings be relied upon by the minority before they could form the basis of an unfair prejudice petition.

[34] *O'Neill v Phillips* [1999] 2 B.C.L.C. 1 at 11b–d HL.

[35] *O'Neill v Phillips* [1999] 2 B.C.L.C. 1 at 9a HL.

[36] *Shareholders' Remedies*, Cm. 3769 (1997), para.4.11. An example might be mismanagement of the company not amounting to a breach of directors' duties (see *Re Elgindata* [1991] B.C.L.C. 959; but cf. *Re Macro (Ipswich) Ltd* [1994] 2 B.C.L.C. 354); but with the rise in the standard of care required of directors (above, para.16–16) it may be that this is a declining problem, because such cases will fall within the category of "indirect" wrongs (below, para.20–14).

[37] *O'Neill v Phillips* [1999] 2 B.C.L.C. 1 at 8g–h HL.

[38] Final Report I, para.7.41; Completing, paras 5.77–5.79.

In *O'Neill* itself, the not-uncommon situation arose in which the founding **20–9** entrepreneur, who had built up the business, increasingly handed over control to a trusted employee (the petitioner), allowing him to acquire a quarter of the shares in the company. Later the petitioner became managing director of the company, receiving half its profits, and there were talks about his acquiring one-half of the share capital. However, an economic downturn occurred and the company began to falter; the founder removed the petitioner from his managing directorship, taking back the reins himself, and paid the petitioner only a salary and the dividends due on his 25 per cent shareholding. This treatment of the petitioner, who resigned, was held not to be unfairly prejudicial because there was no agreement between the parties, even at an informal level, that the petitioner should be entitled to receive half the profits, except for so long as he acted as managing director, or that he should be entitled to increase his shareholding to one-half.

The result is that the strict legal rights of the majority, deriving from the articles of association or the Companies Act, may be subject to "equitable considerations"[39] which channel and restrict the discretion which the majority would otherwise have, where it can be shown that the members came together on the basis that those legal rights should not be entirely freely exercisable. It is suggested that putting the proposition in this way enables us to explain both the vigour with which the courts have developed this aspect of unfair prejudice and the limited conceptual nature of the development. As we have already said, the difficulty for the courts, when they abandon illegality as the touchstone of unfairness, is that the choice of criteria for judging whether s.994 has been breached seems to be at large. The "informal arrangement" category of unfair prejudice provides a partial answer to this problem. The courts can claim to be, and indeed are, using as the criteria for judging unfairness the standards laid down, albeit informally, by the members themselves, and the judges can thus avoid the more challenging task of developing their own criteria. These considerations explain, it is suggested, the emphasis in the *Ebrahimi* case[40] that the equitable considerations do not flow simply from the nature of the company as a quasi-partnership but require "something more" in the shape of proof of the existence of an informal agreement concerning, say, the participation by the minority in the management of the company. As we have seen, this requirement has been fully absorbed into the unfair prejudice case law. The company's formal constitution is the "starting point" for judicial analysis because "keeping promises and honouring agreements is probably the most important element of commercial fairness".[41] Informal qualifications and supplements to the written constitution must be proved to have been agreed. And even when they are proved, the "extended" agreement sets the boundaries of the courts' intervention. Thus, in *Re JE Cade and Son Ltd*,[42] Warner J denied the proposition that:

---

[39] *Ebrahimi*'s case [1973] A.C. 360 HL.
[40] *Ebrahimi*'s case [1973] A.C. 360 at 379. This was a winding-up case, but, as we shall see below at para.20–21, similar considerations apply there too and the winding-up case-law has strongly influenced the development of this category of unfair prejudice.
[41] *Re Saul D Harrison* [1995] 1 B.C.L.C. 14 at 18.
[42] *Re JE Cade and Son Ltd* [1992] B.C.L.C. 213.

"where such equitable considerations arise from agreements or understandings between the shareholders dehors the constitution of the company, the court is free to superimpose on the rights, expectations and obligations springing from those agreements or understandings further rights and obligations arising from its own concept of fairness. There can in my judgment be no such third tier of rights and obligations."

The balance between dividends and directors' remuneration

20–10   Where the petitioner has never been, or has ceased to be, a director of the company, a frequent cause of dispute is the payment of excessive remuneration to the directors of the company and the failure to declare dividends payable to all the shareholders. However, absent any special agreements (whether formal or informal), minority shareholders have no legitimate expectation that dividends will be paid just because they are shareholders, even shareholders in a quasi-partnership company.[43] On the other hand, there may be particular circumstances in which the payment of no or only derisory dividends (or the failure to consider properly whether or not dividends should be declared[44]) will amount to unfair prejudice, for example, where there was an arrangement that all the profits of the company would be taken out of the company in one way or another; that the fiscally efficient way of doing this had been to pay large remuneration to the directors; and that the fact that the petitioner was not a director deprived the petitioner of any share of the profits.[45] The court has also refused to strike out a petition alleging that the non-payment of dividends produced a disparity between the petitioner and the respondents as far as their participation in the profits of the company was concerned, because the respondents obtained their return through the payment of directors' remuneration and other benefits provided by the company to the directors, whilst the petitioners were excluded from any substantial return.[46]

As far as the payment of directors' remuneration to the controllers is concerned, which is often the other side of the coin of the non-payment of dividends, it is perhaps obvious that it may be a ground for a successful petition if the directors have fixed their remuneration in disregard of the provisions of the articles governing that matter.[47] Where the controllers have executive positions within the company and the petitioner does not, it may well be fair that the returns which the controllers receive via directors' salaries and perks exceed those of the petitioner, obtained via dividends. However, where the proper procedures for fixing the directors' remuneration have not been followed, the courts, perhaps surprisingly, have not shrunk from embarking on the exercise of determining whether the directors' remuneration package is excessive in order to establish whether the petitioner has suffered from unfair prejudice. The appropriate level of remuneration for the directors is to be determined by

---

[43] *Irvine v Irvine (No.1)* [2007] 1 B.C.L.C. 349, 421.

[44] *Re McCarthy Surfacing* [2008] EWHC 2279 (Ch); [2009] B.C.L.C. 622; *Re J&S Insurance & Financial Consultants Ltd* [2014] EWHC 2206 (Ch).

[45] *Irvine v Irvine (No.1)* [2007] 1 B.C.L.C. 349, 421; *Re McCarthy Surfacing* [2008] EWHC 2279 (Ch); [2009] B.C.L.C. 622; *Sikorski v Sikorski* [2012] EWHC 1613 (Ch).

[46] *Re Sam Weller & Sons Ltd* [1990] B.C.L.C. 80.

[47] *Irvine v Irvine (No.1)* [2007] 1 B.C.L.C. 349; *Re Ravenhart Services (Holdings) Ltd* [2004] 2 B.C.L.C. 375.

reference to "objective commercial criteria" in order to see whether the remuneration was "within the bracket that executives carrying that sort of responsibility and discharging the sort of duties [the respondent] was would expect to receive".[48]

As described in the previous section, any consideration of breaches of the articles or general law in the context of unfair prejudice petitions must inevitably be modified in the light of the parties' own private agreements, both formal and informal. It seems that there are no special rules about unfair prejudice applicable in this situation, but rather that the principles discussed above should be applied.

Any charge of unwarranted intervention by the courts in the internal affairs of companies can be easily rebutted, because it is the members' own standards which the courts are purporting to enforce.[49] On the other hand, because, at least in small companies, the articles systematically fail to capture the full agreement between the members, the development of this case law has brought company law into much greater touch with corporate reality and, as the amount of litigation shows, has addressed a previously unmet legal need.

20–11

Other categories of unfair prejudice

Although the case law is dominated by the informal arrangement category of unfair prejudice, the wording of the section in no way permits the courts to confine its scope to such cases. However, beyond informal arrangements and the linked argument that the controllers have committed breaches of their fiduciary duties, the issue of how to set the bounds of the courts' intervention arises in an acute way. Probably for this reason alone, no further, clearly defined categories of unfair prejudice can be found in the case law, though one can find a number of cases where allegations of unfair prejudice have been accepted outside the categories mentioned above. An examination of these cases is of particular importance in assessing the significance of s.994 outside the small company field.

20–12

A feature of some of them is reasoning by analogy from established standards, that is, using the unfair prejudice provisions to extend established rules into related areas where the provisions do not formally apply. Thus, in *Re A Company*[50] the court used the provisions of the City Code on Takeovers and Mergers as a guide to what s.994 requires the directors of a target company to do by way of communication with their shareholders, even though the target was a private company and so outside the formal scope of the Code.[51] In *McGuinness v*

---

[48] *Irvine v Irvine (No.1)* [2007] 1 B.C.L.C. 349, 420. Guidance can be taken from guidelines on the remuneration of directors in listed companies: *Re Tobian Properties* [2012] EWCA Civ 998 at [36].

[49] This is not to deny that the degree of proof which the court requires of the informal arrangement may vary according to whether the alleged arrangement is usual or unusual in the type of company in question.

[50] *Re A Company* [1986] B.C.L.C. 382. See also *Re St Piran Ltd* [1981] 1 W.L.R. 1300; but cf. *Re Astec (BSR) Plc* [1998] 2 B.C.L.C. 556 at 579. Also see *Re Phoenix Contracts (Leicester) Ltd* [2010] EWHC 2375 (Ch).

[51] See below, para.28–15. The Code was used only as a guide. In particular, the judge borrowed from the Code the proposition that any advice given by the directors should be given in the interests of the shareholders, but he did not borrow the further proposition that the directors were obliged to give the shareholders their view on the bid.

Bremner Plc[52] the judge found a useful analogy in art.37 of the then current version of Table A, even though the company in question had not adopted that version, when deciding whether delay on the part of the directors in convening a meeting requisitioned by the petitioners was unfairly prejudicial. Again, such reasoning by analogy plays a useful role in defending the courts against the charge of unwarranted or inexpert interference.

However, an appropriate analogy will not be available in all cases. Then the court may have to face the task of developing its own criteria of fairness. For example, the company may have adopted a policy of paying only low dividends, although financially able to do better and even though the controllers have been able to obtain an income from the company by way of directors' fees. Is that unfairly prejudicial to the interests of the non-director shareholders, even in the absence of any informal understanding as to the level of dividend pay-outs or as to the participation of the petitioner in the management of the company as a director (thus entitling him to directors' fees)? The courts have shown themselves willing to entertain such claims under s.994, but have not yet had to adjudicate on their merits in cases where there is otherwise no breach of general duties or private arrangements.[53] The issue could be approached on the basis that the court undertakes the task of working out the appropriate distribution policy for the company (or for companies of that type), which seems unlikely, or by asking the question whether the policy in question unfairly discriminated between the insiders with their directorships and the outsiders who were only shareholders.[54]

PREJUDICE AND UNFAIRNESS

20–13   In a number of cases the courts have stressed that the section itself requires prejudice to the minority which is unfair, and not just prejudice per se. Sometimes what was done to the petitioner was unfair, but it caused him or her no prejudice,

---

[52] *McGuinness v Bremner Plc* [1988] B.C.L.C. 673. See also *Bermuda Cablevision Ltd v Colica Trust Co Ltd* [1998] A.C. 198 PC (analogy with the criminal law, though the directors were acting, presumably, in breach of fiduciary duty). However, the courts have not in general been prepared to use the unfair prejudice petition as a way of curing defects in the statutory protections conferred upon minorities: see *CAS (Nominees) Ltd v Nottingham Forest FC Plc* [2002] 1 B.C.L.C. 613 (avoidance of minority power to block share issue—see below, para.24–4); and *Rock Nominees Ltd v RCO (Holdings) Plc* [2004] 1 B.C.L.C. 439 CA (avoidance of minority's power to reject a "squeeze out" after a takeover—see below, para.28–69).

[53] *Re Sam Weller Ltd* [1990] Ch. 682, where the judge refused to strike out the claim. The case was largely concerned with the now irrelevant issue of whether the dividend policy affected all the shareholders equally: cf. *Re A Company Ex p. Glossop* [1988] 1 W.L.R. 1068. Where the decisions on policy are in breach of the general law, see para.20–10, above, and *Re McCarthy Surfacing Ltd* [2008] EWHC 2279 (Ch); [2009] B.C.L.C. 622.

[54] *Re A Company (No.004415 of 1996)* [1997] 1 B.C.L.C. 479.

for example, because no loss was inflicted: in these cases s.994 is not open.[55] Usually, however, prejudice, typically of a financial sort, is obvious in these cases.[56]

More commonly, it is the unfairness requirement which debated. In many cases "unfairness" is simply another way of putting the point that only legitimate expectations are protected by the section, not every factual expectation which the petitioner may entertain. Thus, a shareholder who needs the money may be prejudiced by the failure of the company to adopt a scheme for the return of capital to its shareholders, but it does not follow that there was anything unfair in the company's decision to retain the capital in the business, in the absence of a formal or informal understanding that the company's capital would be returned at a certain point in its life.[57]

In other and more interesting cases the petitioner appears to have a prima facie case for the protection of s.994, but the petitioner's own conduct means that he or she is not granted relief. There is no requirement that the petitioner come to the court with clean hands, but the petitioner's conduct might mean that the harm suffered was not unfair or that the relief granted should be restricted. Thus, in *Grace v Biagioli*[58] the petitioner had been removed from his directorship, contrary to the agreement between himself and the three other persons involved when the company was set up, which would normally be a clear example of unfair prejudice. However, the petitioner had put himself in a position of conflict by seeking to purchase a competing company, which act was held by the Court of Appeal to justify his removal in breach of the agreement, so that the prejudice to the petitioner could not be said to be unfair to him. Again, the petitioners may have consented to, and even benefited from, the company being run in a way which would normally be regarded as unfairly prejudicial to their interests[59]; or they might have shown no interest in pursuing their legitimate interest in being involved in the company.[60]

The test of whether the prejudice was unfair is an objective one, but this means no more than that unfair prejudice may be established even if the controllers did not intend to harm the petitioners.[61] The question is whether the harm which the petitioner has suffered is something he or she is entitled to be protected from. It

---

[55] *Guinness Peat Group Plc v British Land Co Plc* [1999] 2 B.C.L.C. 243 CA—exclusion of petitioner from an interest in a company where the shareholder's equity was negative. However, the case was mainly concerned with the inappropriateness of making such a determination at the strike-out stage of litigation where the experts on each side were in sharp disagreement as to the applicable valuation methodology.

[56] Some guidance on the broad meaning of "prejudice", and its possible financial and non-financial aspects, is usefully discussed in the judgment of David Richards J in *Re Coroin Ltd* [2012] EWHC 2343 (Ch) at [630]–[631] (affirmed on appeal, [2013] EWCA Civ 781).

[57] *Re A Company* [1983] Ch. 178; as explained in *Re A Company* [1986] B.C.L.C. 382 at 387; *Re Guidezone Ltd* [2002] 2 B.C.L.C. 321; *Re J&S Insurance & Financial Consultants* [2014] EWHC 2206 (Ch).

[58] *Grace v Biagioli* [2006] 2 B.C.L.C. 70 CA; following *Re London School of Electronics* [1986] Ch. 211. Also see *Re Home & Office Fire Extinguishers Ltd* [2012] EWHC 917.

[59] *Jesner v Jarrad Properties Ltd* [1993] B.C.L.C. 1032 Inner House; but note the qualifications in *Re J&S Insurance & Financial Consultants* [2014] EWHC 2206 (Ch).

[60] *Re RA Noble & Sons (Clothing) Ltd* [1983] B.C.L.C. 273.

[61] *Bovey Hotel Ventures Ltd, Re* unreported, but this view is set out and approved in [1983] B.C.L.C. 290; *Re Saul D. Harrison & Sons Plc* [1995] 1 B.C.L.C. 14 at 17.

has been suggested that a fall in the value of the petitioners' shares is a touchstone of unfairness, but this seems to be incorrect. The exclusion of petitioners from the management of the company in breach of their legitimate expectation of involvement would not necessarily have any impact upon the value of the company's shares, whilst, on the other hand, those shares might fall in value as a result of a managerial misjudgement which was in no way unfair to the petitioners.

UNFAIR PREJUDICE AND THE DERIVATIVE ACTION

20–14   It may seem odd at first sight that a right of petition vested in the individual member might potentially be used to secure the redress of wrongs done to the company, especially those committed by its directors. Directors' duties are owed, normally, to the company, not to individual shareholders. However, the unfair prejudice provisions are drafted so as to protect the *interests* of the members and not just their rights,[62] and it cannot be denied that a wrong done to the company may affect the interests of its members. Before the introduction by the 1989 Companies Act of the words "of its members generally" into s.459 of the 1985 Act, there was an argument that a wrong done to the company, which affected all the members equally, fell outside the section,[63] but that argument is no longer available.

The Jenkins Committee, whose report recommended the introduction of the unfair prejudice remedy, envisaged that it would have a role in relation to wrongs done to the company:

> "In addition to these direct wrongs[64] to the minority, there is the type of case in which a wrong is done to the company itself and the control vested in the majority is wrongfully used to prevent action being taken against the wrongdoer. In such a case the minority is indirectly wronged."[65]

However, there is an ambiguity here: did the Committee mean simply that, where a wrong done to the company has also inflicted harm on the shareholder, the member should be able to use s.994 to obtain redress for that personal harm? If so, that seems uncontroversial: there are a number of reported cases under the current legislation in which petitions have been entertained by the courts where the wrongdoers' conduct consisted wholly or partly of wrongs done to the company.[66] The courts have even gone so far as to refuse to accept that the actual

---

[62] A point to which the courts have attached some importance. See above, para.20–6.

[63] The argument was accepted by Vinelott J in *Re Carrington Viyella Plc* (1983) 1 B.C.C. 98, 951, though the exact scope of the point was never finally settled.

[64] "Direct wrongs", i.e. where the harm is inflicted directly on the minority and not via a diminution in the value of their stake in the company.

[65] Report of the Company Law Committee, Cmnd. 1749 (1962), para.206.

[66] *Re Stewarts (Brixton) Ltd* [1985] B.C.L.C. 4; *Re London School of Electronics* [1986] Ch. 211; *Re Cumana Ltd* [1986] B.C.L.C. 430 (all involving various forms of diversion of the company's business to rival companies in which the majority were interested, i.e. situations of the type found in *Cook v Deeks* [1916] 1 A.C. 553 PC, above, at para.16–124); *Re A Company Ex p. Glossop* [1988] 1 W.L.R. 1068; and *McCarthy Surfacing Ltd* [2009] B.C.L.C. 622 (both involving exercise of directors' powers for an improper purpose); *Re Saul D. Harrison & Sons Plc* [1995] 1 B.C.L.C. 14 (failure of directors

availability of a derivative action constitutes a bar to an unfair prejudice petition.[67] As Hoffmann LJ (as he then was) has said: "Enabling the court in an appropriate case to outflank the rule in *Foss v Harbottle* was one of the purposes of the section".[68]

Alternatively, the Committee may have meant that the court could award relief to the *company* in a s.994 petition to redress the harm done to it. This approach raises a difficulty in the light of the reforms to the derivative action made by the 2006 Act and discussed in Ch.17. Thus, the question is, what sort of "outflanking" of the derivative action rules is envisaged? Whereas it may just possibly have been legitimate to view the unfair prejudice remedy as designed to overcome the excessively strict limitations on the derivative action imposed by the common law, it will hardly conduce to a coherent reading of the statute to allow the unfair prejudice provisions to be interpreted so as routinely to side-step the reformed statutory regime governing the derivative action.

The problem is not material if the "outflanking" is merely that s.994 provides another route to a court-ordered derivative claim seeking a remedy for wrongs done to the company. This is expressly acknowledged in the Act.[69] In addition, the court, in the exercise of its remedial discretion under s.996, may have regard to the range of factors listed in Pt 11 of the Act as applying to the standard statutory derivative action. These recognise it is not always in the company's interests to enforce its legal rights, even when enforcement is likely to be successful. And in any event, it will not normally be attractive for a shareholder to bring a petition to obtain authority to commence a second piece of litigation as opposed to seeking permission directly under Pt 11 to commence derivative litigation.

But even in this regard, notice that the pre-requisites for success on each route are different. An attempt to address this difficult problem by distinguishing between corporate and personal loss was made by Millett J in *Re Charnley Davies Ltd (No.2)*,[70] which involved a petition under the Insolvency Act claiming that the administrator had breached his duty of care to the company by selling its business at an undervalue and ought to pay compensation to the company. Whilst holding that on the facts there had been no breach of duty, he nevertheless went on to consider in dicta the relationship between a petition based on unfair prejudice and the derivative action. The learned judge thought that an allegation that the controllers as directors had breached their duties to the company was not sufficient to found a petition. What needed to be shown was that there was also conduct on the part of the controllers which was unfairly prejudicial to the

20–15

---

to act bona fide in the interests of the company). In not all these cases was the allegation in question made out on the facts. Indeed, so long as the "independent illegality" theory held sway, proving breaches of directors' duties was a way of bringing the controllers' conduct within the unfair prejudice provisions.

[67] *Re A Company (No.5287 of 1985)* [1986] 1 W.L.R. 281; *Re Stewarts (Brixton) Ltd* [1985] B.C.L.C. 4; *Lowe v Fahey* [1996] 1 B.C.L.C. 262.

[68] *Re Saul D Harrison & Sons Plc* [1995] 1 B.C.L.C. 14 at 18.

[69] Note that Pt 11 of the Act makes it clear that derivative actions can be brought only under its provisions or "in pursuance of an order of the court in proceedings under section 994": s.260(2). The provision for Scotland is in s.265(6)(b).

[70] *Re Charnley Davies Ltd (No.2)* [1990] B.C.L.C. 760.

minority. If the shareholder wished to complain simply of the breach of duty by the directors, this could not be done by petition. The shareholder must sue instead on behalf of the company and subject to the standing restrictions of the derivative action. In the petition the gist of the action is not the wrong done to the company but the disregard by the controllers of the interests of the minority.

This suggests that the answers to the difficult questions of which complaint the petitioner is seeking to make and of whether the petition is the appropriate vehicle turn very largely on the nature of the remedy sought. In *Re Charnley Davies* the petition sought compensation for the company, for which, it was said, an unfair prejudice petition was inappropriate, whereas a claim that the controllers purchase the petitioners' shares at an appropriate price would have indicated that the gist of the complaint was unfair prejudice to the minority.[71] In short, the suggestion was that, whilst an unfair prejudice petition might arise out of breaches of duty owed by directors to the company, unfair prejudice to the petitioner was the ground for any relief granted; and the relief that might be claimed in a petition was confined to personal remedies and might not include corporate relief. This approach might be thought to fit in well with the view of the Jenkins Committee[72] that the harm to the shareholders in such cases is "indirect" and that the wrong to them consists, not in the wrong done to the company, but in the controllers' use of their position to prevent action being taken to redress the wrong done to the company. The remedy in the petition should thus address the indirect wrong to the shareholder, not the direct wrong to the company. Admittedly this might be done very straightforwardly by ordering pursuit of a derivative claim, but the analysis delivering this conclusion does rather suggest that the claimant has selected the wrong starting point, and should have commenced the claim under Pt 11. And this in turn seems to contradict the explicit inclusion in s.996(2)(c) of the remedial option of a derivative claim.

Whatever the answer to the previous question, it deals with process more than substance. On substance, the crucial questions in this area are two: first, in a s.994 petition, can the court order a remedy in favour of the company rather than the petitioner? And, secondly, if it does not do that, can it order a remedy in favour of the petitioner which might be characterised as representing an impermissible claim to recover reflective losses?[73]

20–16 Given the breadth of the courts' discretion as set out in s.996, the answer to the first question is surely yes. Despite initial caution, there have been a number of cases at appeal court level in which corporate remedies have been granted in an unfair prejudice petition. In *Anderson v Hogg*[74] the Inner House of the Court of Session (Lord Prosser dissenting) awarded relief to the company, where the unfair prejudice was based on an unlawful payment by the respondent director of remuneration to himself. Without detailed consideration of the point, the director was ordered to return the money to the company. More important, perhaps, the court came close to rejecting Millett J's proposition in *Re Charnley Davies* that

---

[71] This is, of course, a remedy very commonly sought by s.994 petitioners (see below, para.20–19).
[72] See above.
[73] See *Atlasview Ltd v Brightview Ltd* [2004] 2 B.C.L.C. 191, para.20–20, below, and the discussion of reflective loss at paras 17–34, above.
[74] *Anderson v Hogg*, 2002 S.L.T. 354, Inner House.

proof of illegality on the part of the director as against the company is not by itself enough to demonstrate unfair prejudice to the petitioning shareholder. Since that case involved in essence a two-person company which was in course of solvent liquidation, the distinction between illegality to the company and unfairness to the shareholder was in that instance very fine. *Clark v Cutland*[75] was a somewhat similar case involving a petition about a two-person company where the controlling director had made large and unauthorised payments to himself, this time by way of contributions to his pension fund. Although the decision was principally about other matters, the Court of Appeal did order the unauthorised payments to be restored to the company and indeed was prepared to contemplate that, as in a derivative action,[76] the costs of the litigation should be borne by the company. However, this decision may not be as dramatic as it seems, since the litigation began as separate derivative and unfair prejudice cases, which were later consolidated into the unfair prejudice application.[77] Thus, at an early stage in the derivative action the then applicable standing rules were presumably satisfied, so that granting corporate relief in the unfair prejudice petition would not be objectionable on the ground identified above.

In the corporate opportunity case, *Bhullar v Bhullar*,[78] which we considered in Ch.16 and which again concerned a two-person—or, at least, a two-family company—the litigation was always in the form of an unfair prejudice petition and, indeed, the petitioners sought the traditional personal relief in such a petition, namely, the compulsory purchase of their shares at a fair price by the respondents. However, the initial petition also sought permission to bring a derivative action in the company's name. The trial judge refused the compulsory purchase order but ordered direct corporate relief by declaring the property in question to be held on trust for the company. The Court of Appeal did not demur from this way of proceeding. It may be that in this case the court took the view that the facts upon which a derivative suit would be based and the petitioner's standing to sue derivatively had been clearly established in the petition and that it would be simply a waste of time and money to have a further action commenced by writ, and so corporate relief was granted immediately. However, it is notable that the Court of Appeal did not think it necessary to address this issue.

The most extensive discussion of the principles at issue in this area is to be found a decision of only persuasive authority, *Kung v Kou*, a decision of the Court of Final Appeal of Hong Kong.[79] Although petition in the case was ill-conceived and there were some differences of emphasis in the judgments of

---

[75] *Clark v Cutland* [2004] 1 W.L.R. 783 CA (considered by Payne, (2004) 67 M.L.R. 500 and [2005] C.L.J. 647).

[76] See above at para.17–13.

[77] *Clark v Cutland* [2004] 1 W.L.R. 783 at [2] CA.

[78] *Bhullar v Bhullar* [2004] 2 B.C.L.C. 241. The early stages of the litigation are recounted at [3]–[4]. See above at paras 16–95 et seq.

[79] *Kung v Kou* (2004) 7 HKCFAR 579. The decision was mentioned by the Privy Council in the case of *Gamlestaden Fastigheter AB v Baltic Partners Ltd* [2007] B.C.C. 272 PC, where the judgment of the PC, delivered by Lord Scott of Foscote, makes no reference to the restrictive conditions set out in the Hong Kong decision and seems to treat it as a general permission to award damages to the company. Even stranger, the company being hopelessly insolvent, the benefit to the petitioner from any payment by the directors to the company would be obtained only as lender to the company, whose loans would achieve a higher percentage recovery.

Bokhary PJ and Lord Scott of Foscote NPJ, the issue of whether an unfair prejudice petition could be used to avoid the standing rules of *Foss v Harbottle* was addressed head-on and answered in the negative. This answer did not mean that allegations of breaches of duty by directors are irrelevant in unfair prejudice proceedings, for example, as a basis for making out a claim for relief to be granted to the member. Nor did it mean that the court can never at the end of an unfair prejudice petition hearing grant a remedy in the company's favour. However, in order to do that the court would have to hear both the company's claim and the member's claim together. This would be appropriate only in "rare and exceptional" circumstances (per Bokhary PJ) or where at the pleading stage of the petition it was clear that "the director's liability at law to the company can conveniently be dealt with in the hearing of the petition" (per Lord Scott of Foscote). Otherwise, the petitioner should seek an order in the petition to bring a derivative action on behalf of the company or, under the new Act, make such an application directly to the court rather than through the unfair prejudice petition.

20–17 It is submitted that the decision in *Kung v Kou* is based on the correct principles and that the unfair prejudice petition is normally confined to relief in respect of harm personal to the minority shareholder.

As to the second question, and whether personal remedies in favour of the petitioner are subject to the "no reflective loss" principle, the answer is less clear. The most common remedy in s.994 cases is an order for the compulsory purchase of the petitioner's shares. The purchase price may indeed contain an element which would otherwise constitute reflective loss, but that is by way of delivering a clean break to the petitioner in circumstances where it is the proven unfairly prejudicial conduct which has reduced the value of the petitioner's shares. The cases are considered below.[80]

REDUCING LITIGATION COSTS

20–18 A major issue which has emerged under the unfair prejudice jurisdiction is the length and, therefore, the cost of trials of these petitions. Although the decision of the House of Lords in *O'Neill v Phillips*[81] has done something to reduce the scope of the issues to be explored, the court may still find itself trawling through a great deal of the history of the relations between petitioner and respondent, to establish, first, the existence of any informal understandings and, secondly, whether they have subsequently been breached. All this will typically occur in relation to small companies, whose net value may not be large. Both the Law Commission and the CLR investigated a number of ways of reducing the costs of unfair prejudice litigation, but all were ultimately rejected as ineffective, either by the Commission or the Review,[82] except for a suggestion that an arbitration

---

[80] See below, para.20–19, and the discussion of reflective loss, above, at paras 17–34 et seq.

[81] *O'Neill v Phillips* [1999] 1 W.L.R. 1092 HL.

[82] These were (a) a new unfair prejudice remedy for those excluded from the management of small companies (rejected by the Law Commission, *Shareholders' Remedies*, Cm. 3769 (1997), at para.3.25, as likely to lead to "duplication and complication of shareholder proceedings"; (b) a presumption of unfairness in certain cases of exclusion from management (recommended by the Commission but rejected by the CLR after the proposal received little support from consultees: Developing,

scheme be developed as an alternative to litigation before the High Court,[83] plus reliance on the newly introduced general system of case management in the civil courts for those cases not going down the arbitral route.

However, the courts themselves have developed a technique for encouraging an agreed solution to unfair prejudice claims. Where it is clear, as it will normally be, that the relationship between the petitioner and the remainder of the members cannot be reconstituted by the court and that the only effective remedy available to the minority is to have their shares purchased at a fair price, then if a suitable ad hoc offer is made to the petitioner for the purchase of the shares or there is a suitable mechanism to this effect in the company's articles, but the petitioner decides to proceed with the petition, rather than to accept the offer or use the mechanism, that will be seen to be an abuse of the process of the court and the petition will be struck out. In *O'Neill v Phillips*[84] Lord Hoffmann was as keen to endorse and encourage this procedure as he was to set out the basis of the unfair prejudice claim itself. His lordship thought that a petitioner could not be said to have been *unfairly* prejudiced by the respondent's conduct if:

(a)   the offer was to buy the shares at a fair price, which normally would be without a discount for their minority status (see below);

(b)   there was a mechanism for determination of the price by a competent expert in the absence of agreement;

(c)   to encourage agreement the expert should not give reasons for the valuation;

(d)   both sides should have equal access to information about the company and equal freedom to make submissions to the expert; and

(e)   the respondent should be given a reasonable time at the beginning of the proceedings to make the offer and should not be liable for the petitioner's legal costs incurred during that period.

Cases where an offer from the respondent has not blocked a petition have usually involved offers which did not give the petitioner all he or she would get if successful at trial[85] or have involved valuation by a non-independent expert.[86] The offer which the court has to evaluate may be an ad hoc one or may result from the application of provisions in the company's articles laying down a mechanism to be used where a shareholder wishes to dispose of his or her holding. Although the courts once took a different view, it does not now appear

---

para.4.104); (c) the development of a model exit article (recommended by the Law Commission, above, Pt V, but rejected by the CLR, Developing, para.4.103, on the grounds that it was not likely to be used by the well-advised and would be a trap for the ill-advised).

[83]   Final Report I, para.2.27 (this proposal was not confined to unfair prejudice petitions).

[84]   See above, fn.81 at pp.16–17. This approach was applied to the winding-up remedy (below, para.20–21) in *CVC/Opportunity Equity Partners Ltd v Demarco Almeida* [2002] B.C.C. 684 PC.

[85]   *North Holdings Ltd v Southern Tropics Ltd* [1999] 2 B.C.L.C. 624 CA; *Harbourne Road Nominees Ltd v Kafvaski* [2011] EWHC 2214 (Ch).

[86]   *Re Benfield Greig Group Plc* [2002] 1 B.C.L.C. 65 CA, where, in fact, the non-independence of the expert constituted the alleged unfair prejudice.

that an offer arising out of the mechanism contained in the articles is to be treated differently from an ad hoc offer, in terms of its effect in excluding an unfair prejudice provision.[87]

REMEDIES

20–19   Section 996 gives the court a wide remedial discretion to "make such order as it thinks fit for giving relief in respect of the matters complained of". In addition to this general grant, five specific powers are given to the court by s.996(2), of which undoubtedly the most commonly used is an order that the petitioners' shares be purchased by the controllers or the company.[88] The reason for the popularity of this remedy, with both petitioners and courts, is readily explained. Unfair prejudice jurisprudence is most firmly established in relation to quasi-partnership companies. When business and, often, personal relations between quasi-partners have broken down and are incapable of reconstitution by a court, the only effective remedy is the minority's exit. A share purchase order gives the petitioner an opportunity to exit from the company with the fair value of his or her investment, a result which is usually impossible in the absence of a court order, since often no potential purchasers of the shares are available or, even if they were, the purchase price a third party would be willing to pay would reflect, rather than remedy, the harm inflicted on the seller by the unfairly prejudicial conduct.[89]

The crucial question in this buy-out process is how the court is to assess the fairness of the price to be paid for the shares. Two important issues have emerged in the valuation process. The first is whether the petitioner's shareholding should be valued pro rata to the total value of the company or whether its value should be discounted on the basis that it is ex hypothesi a minority holding and so does not carry with it control of the company. In this context the notion of a "quasi-partnership" company has become important. Although many unfair

---

[87] On the original approach see *Re A Company Ex p. Kremer* [1989] B.C.L.C. 365; and on the later developments *Virdi v Abbey Leisure Ltd* [1990] B.C.L.C. 342; *Re A Company Ex p. Holden* [1991] B.C.L.C. 597; *Re A Company* [1996] 2 B.C.L.C. 192.

[88] 2006 Act s.996(2)(e). In the latter case the company's share capital must be reduced. The statutory power is widely enough drawn to include an order that the minority purchase the majority's shares, which has occasionally been ordered: *Re Brenfield Squash Racquets Club Ltd* [1996] 2 B.C.L.C. 184. The other specific powers are the authorisation of proceedings to be brought in the company's name (s.996(2)(c) and above, para.20–14); requiring the company to do or refrain from doing an act (s.996(2)(b)); requiring the company not to make alterations to its articles of association without the leave of the court (s.996(2)(d)); and regulating the conduct of the company's affairs in the future (s.996(2)(a)). Whatever remedy is contemplated, the court must choose what is appropriate at the time it is granted: *Re A Company* [1992] B.C.C. 542. Indeed, the court is not limited to ordering the remedy requested by the petitioner: *Hawkes v Cuddy (No.2)* [2009] EWCA Civ 291; [2009] 2 B.C.L.C. 427 (although in this case, and as is specified now in the Companies (Unfair Prejudice Applications) Proceedings Rules (SI 2009/2469), the petitioner specifically requested particular remedies or "that such other order may be made as the court thinks fit"). Sections 757 and 758 give the court a further specific power in the case where the unfair prejudice consists of a public offer of shares by a private company: see para.24–2.

[89] See *Grace v Biagioli* [2006] 2 B.C.L.C. 70 CA, for a good example of the court's preference for a "clean break" via a share purchase as against a compensation order, which might have remedied the specific harm suffered by the petitioner but would have left him exposed in the future.

prejudice proceedings concern such companies, the statutory provisions are not confined to them. However, in relation to whether a minority shareholding should be discounted, the courts have developed a presumption that it should not in a quasi-partnership company, whereas no such presumption applies for other categories of company.

In *Re Bird Precision Bellows Ltd*[90] it was established that the principle was pro rata valuation where the company could be characterised as a quasi-partnership. This is because, in a true partnership, upon dissolution of the partnership the court orders a sale of the partnership business as a going concern and divides the proceeds among the partners according to their interests in the former partnership.[91] However, the normal principle in company law of discounting a minority shareholding applies if the company is not a partnership carried on in corporate form or if the petitioner had bought the shareholding at a price which reflected its minority status or it had devolved upon him or her by operation of law.[92] The concept of a quasi-partnership involves more than simply the company having a small number of members. The members must have set up their association on the basis of mutual trust and confidence, expect to be involved in the management of the company (though the existence of clearly defined "sleeping partners" would not defeat this requirement), and there must be some degree of lock-in of the members to the company,[93] although these are cumulative preconditions and the presence of one or more of these factors may suffice.[94]

The second question is whether the valuation should be on the basis that the company will continue as a going concern, or on a liquidation or break-up basis, which would normally yield a lower value for the company. The going concern basis will normally be appropriate, but this will depend to some degree on the facts of the case, as will the precise method to be adopted for valuing the going concern.[95]

20–20

A further issue concerns timing. The value put on shares, whether on a pro rata or a discounted basis, will often depend crucially on when the value of the company is assessed. The courts have given themselves the widest discretion to

---

[90] *Re Bird Precision Bellows Ltd* [1984] Ch. 419, per Nourse J, approved on appeal [1986] Ch. 658.

[91] *CVC/Opportunity Equity Partners Ltd v Demarco Almeida* [2002] 2 B.C.L.C. 108 at [41]–[42]; *Strahan v Wilcock* [2006] 2 B.C.L.C. 555. The court might instead work out what the former partner's interest would be worth upon the hypothesis of a sale, without actually holding one.

[92] *Irvine v Irvine (No.2)* [2007] 1 B.C.L.C. 445; *Re Elgindata Ltd* [1991] B.C.L.C. 959 at 1007. See also *Re DR Chemicals* (1989) 5 B.C.C. 37.

[93] These criteria are taken from *Ebrahimi v Westbourne Galleries Ltd* [1973] A.C. 360, 371 (a winding-up case considered further below, para.20–21) and applied by the Court of Appeal to unfair prejudice valuations in *Strahan v Wilcock* [2006] 2 B.C.L.C. 555. What was initially a quasi-partnership may have ceased to be one by the time the facts supporting the petition take place, thus changing the basis of valuation: *Re McCarthy Surfacing Ltd* [2008] EWHC 2279 (Ch); [2009] B.C.L.C. 622.

[94] *Khoshkhou v Cooper* [2014] EWHC 1087 (Ch) at [25], where a company with no restriction on the transfer of shares was nevertheless held to be a quasi-partnership company since it was closely dependent on the personal relationship between the original members.

[95] *CVC/Opportunity Equity Partners Ltd v Demarco Almeida* [2002] 2 B.C.L.C. 108; *Parkinson v Eurofinance Group Ltd* [2001] 1 B.C.L.C. 720; *Guinness Peat Group Plc v British Land Co Plc* [1999] 2 B.C.L.C. 243 CA; *Re Planet Organic Ltd* [2000] 1 B.C.L.C. 366. See also *Re Annacott Holdings Ltd* [2013] EWCA Civ 119 CA, where it was held that there is no rule that a going-concern valuation can only be adopted for quasi-partnerships.

choose the most appropriate date. The competing dates are usually a date close to when the shares are to be purchased or the date when the petition was presented. In *Profinance Trust SA v Gladstone*,[96] the Court of Appeal thought that the former had become the presumptive valuation date, but that there were many circumstances when an earlier date might be chosen, for example, where the unfairly prejudicial conduct had deprived the company of its business, where the company had reconstructed its business or even that there had been a general fall in the market since the presentation of the petition. In *Re KR Hardy Estates Ltd*,[97] however, the court held that on the particular facts of that case, the date of the order was the most appropriate date since it had the advantage of certainty and seemed to be the most fair.

Although a buy-out of the minority is the most common remedy, it is not always the most appropriate one, and s.996 gives the courts a wide range of other possible remedies. These include compensation, to which it is not yet clear whether the "no reflective loss" principle applies.[98]

WINDING UP ON THE JUST AND EQUITABLE GROUND

20–21   Legal protection for minority shareholders is now dominated by the unfair prejudice remedy, but, despite its remedial flexibility, the court cannot thereby order the winding-up of the company in question. The Law Commission recommended that this power should be added to the range of remedies available to the court for the redress of unfair prejudice,[99] but the CLR rejected this on the ground that it was open to abuse for the reasons discussed below.[100] There is, instead, a separate procedure by which a minority shareholder may seek to have the company wound up. A company may be wound up compulsorily by the court on a petition presented to it by a contributory[101] if the court is of the opinion that

---

[96] *Profinance Trust SA v Gladstone* [2002] 1 B.C.L.C. 141 CA, where the earlier authorities are reviewed. Also see *Re McCarthy Surfacing Ltd* [2008] EWHC 2279 (Ch); [2009] B.C.L.C. 622, for a valuation taking into account the depreciation due to the wrongs complained of.

[97] *Re KR Hardy Estates Ltd* [2014] EWHC 4001 (Ch) at [89]–[93].

[98] *Atlasview Ltd v Brightview Ltd* [2004] 2 B.C.L.C. 191. This case, rightly it seems, suggests that proper quantification of remedies would be alert to double recovery. If so, the principle underpinning the rules on reflective loss would be upheld. This principle is discussed above at para.17–34.

[99] *Shareholders' Remedies*, Cm. 3769 (1997), paras 4.24–4.49.

[100] Developing, para.4.105.

[101] 2006 Act s.124(1). Petitions may also be brought by creditors, directors or the company itself, though such applications are rare. The Secretary of State may petition under s.124A in the public interest on the basis of information received as a result of an investigation into the company's affairs. See above, para.18–13. However, public interest grounds for a winding-up are not available other than to the Secretary of State: *Re Millennium Advanced Technology Ltd* [2004] 2 B.C.L.C. 77. The term "contributory" includes even a fully paid-up shareholder provided he or she has a tangible interest in the winding-up, which is usually demonstrated by showing that the company has a surplus of assets over liabilities, though that will not be required if the petitioner's complaint is that the controllers failed to provide the financial information from which that assessment could be made: see *Re Rica Gold Washing Co* (1879) 11 Ch. D. 36; *Re Bellador Silk Ltd* [1965] 1 All E.R. 667; *Re Othery Construction Ltd* [1966] 1 W.L.R. 69; *Re Expanded Plugs Ltd* [1966] 1 W.L.R. 514; *Re Chesterfield Catering Ltd* [1977] Ch. 373 at 380; *Re Land and Property Trust Co Plc* [1991] B.C.C. 446 at 448; *Re Newman & Howard Ltd* [1962] Ch. 257; *Re Wessex Computer Stationers Ltd* [1992] B.C.L.C. 366; *Re A Company* [1995] B.C.C. 705. The Jenkins Committee recommended (para.503(h)) that any member

it is "just and equitable" to do so. This provision, now contained in s.122(1)(g) of the Insolvency Act 1986, has a long pedigree in the law relating to companies, and the power can be traced back to the Joint Stock Companies Winding-up Act 1848. The provision was influenced by (then uncodified) partnership law and was originally used mainly in cases where the company was deadlocked. In the course of the twentieth century it has been moulded by the courts into a means of subjecting small private companies to equitable principles derived from partnership law when they were in reality incorporated partnerships. The apotheosis of this use of the section, the decision of the House of Lords in *Ebrahimi v Westbourne Galleries Ltd*,[102] was also highly influential in the courts' development of their powers under the predecessors of s.994.

Despite its remarkable substantive development, the winding up provision always suffered from a weakness at the remedial level: if the company was prospering, presenting a "just and equitable" petition was tantamount to killing the goose that might lay the golden egg (although the threat of liquidation might induce the parties to negotiate an alternative solution to their dispute). So long as the oppression remedy was hobbled by the restrictive wording and interpretation associated with s.210 of the Companies Act 1948, the winding-up petition was better than nothing. But, with the introduction of the unfair prejudice remedy, one might argue that the role of the winding-up remedy should now be restricted.

A winding-up petition triggers s.127 of the Insolvency Act 1986, which requires the court's consent for any disposition of the company's property after the petition is presented. This ability to paralyse, or at least disrupt, the normal running of the company's business adds to the negotiating strength of the petitioner, but is hardly legitimate if an unfair prejudice petition could give him or her all that is warranted. Consequently, a Practice Direction[103] seeks to discourage the routine joining of winding-up petitions to unfair prejudice claims, unless a winding-up remedy is what is genuinely sought. The force behind the Practice Direction is provided by s.125(2) of the Insolvency Act 1986, to the effect that the court need not grant a winding-up order if it is of the opinion that some alternative remedy is available to the petitioners and that they have acted unreasonably in not pursuing it.[104] It would seem an appropriate use of this power for the courts to insist that, where a more flexible s.996 remedy is available, the petitioner should be confined to it. That would be a natural consequence of the fact that the statutory alternative to a winding-up order has finally come of age.

---

should be entitled to petition, presumably on the grounds that this remedy was aimed primarily at protecting minorities rather than at winding up companies.

[102] *Ebrahimi v Westbourne Galleries Ltd* [1973] A.C. 360 HL.

[103] CPR Practice Direction, Applications under the Companies Act and Other Legislation Relating to Companies, para.9(1). See *Re A Company (No.004415 of 1996)* [1997] 1 B.C.L.C. 479 where the judge struck out the alternative petition for winding up on the just and equitable ground on the basis that there was no reasonable prospect that the trial judge would order a winding up as against a share purchase under what is now s.996.

[104] The alternative remedy need not be a legal one. For example, it may be an offer to purchase the petitioner's shares on the same basis as the court would order on an unfair prejudice petition: *Virdi v Abbey Leisure Ltd* [1990] B.C.L.C. 342. See also *Maresca v Brookfield Development & Construction Ltd* [2013] EWHC 3151 (Ch), where the alternative remedy was for the shareholder to demand repayment of her interest from the company.

20–22 On the other hand, there are situations where a winding up order is the only option. This observation is sometimes taken as proof that the grounds of unfairness upon which a company can be wound up under s.122(1)(g) of the 1986 Act are wider than those which will found an unfair prejudice remedy under s.994 of the 2006 Act. Certainly the grounds do not overlap completely, but this in itself does not determine which has greater width. The cases, it is suggested, roundly accord that accolade to the unfair prejudice petitions. But the important point here is that there are reported cases in which the court has denied a petition based on unfair prejudice, because the conduct of the petitioner did not merit it, but has granted a winding-up order on the grounds that mutual confidence among the quasi-partners had broken down,[105] or that the substratum had failed.[106] In other words, in these cases the mere fact of breakdown or deadlock is sufficient to ground a winding-up order, whereas an unfair prejudice petition is seen as requiring some assessment of the comparative blame-worthiness of petitioners and controllers. This simply reinforces the legislative sense in providing two distinct options, expressed in different terms and designed to deliver remedies in different circumstances.[107]

CONCLUSION

20–23 Part 30 of the Act does not provide, and on no conceivable interpretation could provide, a unilateral exit right for minority shareholders, i.e. a right for minority shareholders at any time to withdraw their capital from the company. Indeed, it might be thought that such a right would be inconsistent with the nature of shareholding in companies. The shareholder is locked into the investment in the company unless he or she is able to find someone else to purchase the shares and thus stand in the shareholder's shoes in relation to the company.[108] Compulsory purchase appears under Pt 30, not as a right for the minority, but as a remedy—and not even a remedy the minority can insist upon, though it is the most common—in respect of unfair prejudice committed by the company's controllers. Thus in *Re Phoenix Office Supplies Ltd*[109] the Court of Appeal refused a shareholder's petition to have his shares acquired at a non-discounted value, even though he had been removed from his directorship by the other two incorporators in breach of their common understanding. The reason for the decision was that the conduct of the others had been a response to the petitioner's unilateral decision to sever his relations with the company, which could be seen as a prior and more fundamental breach of the original understandings among the

---

[105] *Re RA Noble & Sons (Clothing) Ltd* [1983] B.C.L.C. 273; and *Jesner v Jarrad Properties Ltd* [1993] B.C.L.C. 1032 Inner House; *Loch v John Blackwood Ltd* [1924] A.C. 783 PC; and *Re Brand & Harding Ltd* [2014] EWHC 247 (Ch). See also *Re Full Cup International Trading Ltd* [1995] B.C.C. 682, where the judge found himself in the presumably unusual position of being unable to fashion an appropriate remedy under s.996 but of being prepared to wind up the company.

[106] *Re Kitson & Co Ltd* [1946] 1 All E.R. 435 CA.

[107] *Hawkes v Cuddy (No.2)* [2009] EWCA Civ 291; [2009] 2 B.C.L.C. 427 CA; overruling on this point, *Re Guidezone Ltd* [2000] 2 B.C.L.C. 321 at 357.

[108] Of course, if the company and the shareholder wish expressly to bargain for "redeemable" shares, they are free to do so (above, para.13–2).

[109] *Re Phoenix Office Supplies Ltd* [2003] 1 B.C.L.C. 76 CA.

three people involved. Of course, members may bargain for rights of unilateral exit to be incorporated in the articles of particular companies[110]; but they are rare, since a general right for minority shareholders to withdraw their capital when they will would seem likely wholly to undermine the financing function of shares.

Finally, there is some evidence that the unfair prejudice remedy, whatever its imperfections, has successfully "crowded out" alternative techniques of controlling the exercise of majority power through board decisions. Thus, the Law Commissions' draft statement of directors' statutory duties[111] included a requirement that directors act fairly as between shareholders, a duty reflected at least at first instance in the current case law.[112] The CLR's initial draft statement contained the same duty,[113] but fairness between shareholders was later reduced to one of the factors to be taken into account by the directors when discharging their duty to promote the success of the company for the benefit of its members.[114] The explanation given for this development was a desire to "make it clear that fairness is a factor in achieving success for the members as a whole, rather than an independent requirement which could override commercial success".[115] It is difficult to believe that this argument would have been accepted in the absence of Pt 30 as an overriding instrument of minority protection.

---

[110] See above, para.19–23.
[111] *Company Directors: Regulating Conflicts of Interest and Formulating a Statement of Duties*, Cm. 4436 (1999), Appendix A.
[112] See especially *Mutual Life Insurance Co of New York v Rank Organisation Ltd* [1985] B.C.L.C. 11.
[113] Developing, para.3.40.
[114] Final Report I, Annex C, Sch.2. On the nature of the general duty see para.16–37, above.
[115] Final Report I, Annex C, Explanatory Notes, para.18.

PART 5

ACCOUNTS AND AUDIT

It has been accepted since the early days of modern company law that mandatory publicity about the company's affairs was an important regulatory tool. For shareholders in large companies with dispersed shareholdings it operates to reduce the risk of management incompetence or self-seeking. The non-director shareholders of a company will have a difficult task to judge the effectiveness of the management of the company if they do not have access to relevant data about the company's financial performance. For creditors it operates to reduce the risks of dealing with an entity to whose assets alone the creditors can normally look for re-payment. In fact, mandatory disclosure has long been seen as something which could legitimately be asked for in exchange for the freedom to trade with limited liability,[1] though there has been controversy throughout the history of company law about how extensive the disclosure rules should be. Today, therefore, there is a major difference between the disclosure rules applicable to ordinary partnerships (without limited liability) and those applicable to companies, with limited liability partnerships being rightly placed in the company category for these purposes, because they benefit from limited liability.[2] Given this range of interests in disclosure of information by companies, it is not surprising that successive company scandals have provoked demands for ever more far-reaching mandatory disclosure of information, and such demands have often been successful.

As far as the companies legislation is concerned, the main instrument for delivering mandatory disclosure has been the annual accounts and reports—which the directors are required to produce, have verified by the company's auditors (in most cases), lay before the members in general meeting (or otherwise distribute to them in the case of private companies) and register in a public registry. This development over the years has produced an elaborate body of rules. The desire of the Company Law Review to use mandatory disclosure to promote an "enlightened shareholder value" approach to company law has led to reforms which require disclosure of information which is not directly financial,

---

[1] An unlimited liability company is not normally required to make its accounts available to the public: see para.21–36, below.
[2] See G. Morse et al., *Palmer's Limited Liability Partnership Law*, 2nd edn (London: Sweet & Maxwell, 2012), Ch.3.

but concerns the quality of the company's relationships with those who are capable of making a major contribution to the success of the business or about the impact of the company's operations upon the community in which it operates. Further, at EU level the impact of various corporate scandals in the early years of this century only served to make those rules even more elaborate, especially in relation to the verification of the accounts through the process of audit. The recent financial crisis has ensured that these concern remains at the centre of public policy discussions. Accounts and audit are the subject of the two chapters in this Part.

However, mandatory disclosure can be seen as an instrument, not only of corporate law (for the benefit of shareholders, creditors and other stakeholders) but of financial services or securities law (for the benefit of investors and the efficient functioning of the capital markets). Consequently, we shall return to the issue of mandatory disclosure in Pt 6, where we analyse the additional disclosure requirements which apply to companies whose securities are traded on a public securities market.

CHAPTER 21

ANNUAL ACCOUNTS AND REPORTS

INTRODUCTION

Scope and rationale of the annual reporting requirement

On the basis that "forewarned is forearmed" the fundamental principle underlying   **21–1**
the Companies Acts has always been that of disclosure. If the public and the
members were enabled to find out all relevant information about the company,
this, thought the founding fathers of our company law, would be a sure shield.
The shield may not have proved quite so strong as they had expected and in more
recent times it has been supported by offensive weapons. However, disclosure
still remains the basic safeguard on which the Companies Acts pin their faith, and
every succeeding Act since 1862 has added to the extent of the publicity required,
although, not unreasonably, what is required varies according to the type of

company concerned. Not only may disclosure by itself promote efficient conduct of the company's business, because the company's controllers (whether directors or large shareholders) may fear the reputational losses associated with the revelation of incompetence or self-dealing, but the more interventionist legal strategies, going beyond disclosure, depend upon those who hold the legal rights being well-informed about the company's position. For example, those in a position to enforce the company's rights against directors for breach of duty[1] or to bring claims of unfair prejudice[2] or shareholders holding rights to remove directors,[3] if rational persons, will not turn their minds to the exercise of those rights unless they think there are grounds for so doing. Finally, self-help, such as taking contractual protection or altering the pricing of credit, depends upon good knowledge of risks embedded in the company's operations. Thus, disclosure is the bed-rock of company law.

This chapter is focused on what has always been the central disclosure mechanism of the British companies legislation, namely, the obligation laid on the directors to produce annual accounts (referred to in EU law as annual financial statements) relating to the financial position of the company and to accompany those accounts with a report on the company's activities, including their own stewardship of the company. Those accounts and reports are then typically considered by the shareholders at an annual general meeting of the company, though, as we have seen, only public companies are now required to hold an AGM.[4] Over the years, what is required of large companies by way of accounts and reports has expanded. By contrast, the recent tendency has been to reduce the reporting requirements of small companies.

The production of the annual accounts has generated an industry of professionals to help the company meet its statutory obligations. Notably, the accounting profession has played a major role in developing the standards which determine how the raw financial data is to be analysed and presented in the accounts, the law having rightly shied away from doing more than setting the broad parameters for this task.[5] That profession then re-appears in the guise of auditors to verify that the accounts do meet those standards and the applicable legal rules and, in particular, present a "true and fair view" of the company's financial position.[6]

This is an area where the harmonisation programme of the EU has had a significant impact. This is hardly surprising since the utility of accounts is enhanced if they are comparable across companies and increasingly investors (shareholders and creditors) and others are interested in the financial position of non-domestic companies. The first EU rules related to the presentation of accounts,[7] and were extended later to the use of accounting standards[8] and to the

---

[1] See Chs 16 and 17, above.
[2] See Ch.20, above.
[3] See Ch.14, above.
[4] See para.15–8.
[5] See below, para.21–14.
[6] See Ch.22.
[7] Notably the Fourth Council Directive on the Annual Accounts of Certain Types of Companies, Directive 78/660/EEC ([1978] O.J. L222/110), as amended (hereafter "Fourth Directive") and the

provision of non-financial information.[9] In 2013 the core provisions were modernised and consolidated into Directive 2013/34/EU.[10] References to the "Directive" in this chapter are to the 2013 Directive as amended[11] (unless the context indicates otherwise). Since the leading EU instrument in this area is a Directive (rather than a Regulation), it needs to be transposed into domestic law. This is done partly by amendments to the Companies Act 2006 and, to a significant extent, by secondary legislation. Both the Act and the secondary legislation were recently amended by the Companies, Partnerships and Groups (Accounts and Reports) Regulations 2015/980, in order to implement the 2013 Directive.

The classification of companies for the purposes of annual reporting

As we have hinted, the accounting rules have developed a classification of companies which is more sophisticated than the core division deployed in the Act between public and private companies. That distinction turns on whether the company is permitted to offer its shares to the public or not.[12] The accounting classification turns mainly on the economic size of the company. However, the public/private distinction still plays a role because public companies are excluded from the two smallest categories of company (micro and small) for (most) accounts purposes.[13] Since the ramifications of the classification run throughout the substantive rules on accounts, it is important to set it out at the beginning. The criteria upon which the classification is based are set out principally in the Directive and the Member States have only limited freedom to amend them.

There are five categories of company for accounts purposes: micro, small,[14] medium-sized, large and "public interest entities" ("PIE"). The criteria for identifying the first four categories are quantitative indicators of the economic size of the company and are designed to be capable of application in a fairly mechanistic way. The PIE category is a cross-cutting category but, for the general run of companies in the UK, it will form a sub-set of the large company category. The criteria used refer to the company's "balance sheet total", a perhaps not entirely clear phrase which refers to amount of the company's assets (without

21–2

Seventh Council Directive on Consolidated Accounts, Directive 83/349/EEC ([1983] OJ L193/1), as amended (hereafter "Seventh Directive")—both repealed by the 2013 Directive.

[8] Regulation (EC) No.1606/2002 on the Application of International Accounting Standards ([2002] O.J. L243/1) (hereafter "IAS Regulation").

[9] Directive 2003/51/EC ([2003] O.J. L178/16) (hereafter the "accounts modernisation directive"), which amended the Fourth and Seventh Directives.

[10] Directive 2013/34/EU [2013] O.J. L182/19.

[11] As it was by Directive 2014/95/EU ([2014] O.J. L330/1) on the disclosure of non-financial information.

[12] See para.1–8.

[13] 2006 Act ss.384(1)(a) and 384B(1)(a).

[14] Small Business Enterprise and Employment Act 2015 ss.33 and 34 envisage the use of the micro and small business definitions in subordinate legislation to relieve these categories of regulatory duties beyond the accounting area. If and when such regulations are made, the domestic definitions might shift from the Act to these regulations, but the controlling definitions would still be in the Directive.

subtracting liabilities)[15]; its net turnover[16]; and the number of persons employed by it on average over the year.[17] In order to classified as micro, small or medium-size the company has to meet two of the three applicable criteria; the "large" category is a residual one into which companies otherwise fall; and the PIE classification turns on a different approach.

Micro companies

21–3   Micro companies are private companies[18] for which the balance sheet maximum is £316,000; the maximum net turnover £632,000 and the maximum number of employees is 10.[19] However, a micro company will not have access to the reporting relaxations if it is a member of a corporate group,[20] presumably because those relaxations might undermine the group accounts. In short, the micro exemptions are available to stand alone companies only, which reinforces their focus on very small businesses.

Companies on the borderline of the criteria might find themselves drifting in and out of qualification as micro companies. This problem is addressed, as it is with the other categories, by requiring that companies meet the criteria for two years in order to qualify as micro and equally by providing that micro status will not be lost unless the criteria are not met for two consecutive years.[21] As is to be expected, the micro company benefits from the least demanding reporting regime. The category was the result of an EU level initiative in 2012.[22] It operates by giving Member States the option to remove from micro companies requirements that would otherwise apply to them under the regime for small companies. The UK chose to take up most of the options made available in the Directive.[23] Of course, the directors of micro companies may choose to report more fully.

---

[15] 2006 Act s.306(5) of the Act: "The balance sheet total means the aggregate of the amounts shown as assets in the company's balance sheet", implementing art.3(11) of the Directive.

[16] "'net turnover' means the amounts derived from the sale of products and the provision of services after deducting sales rebates and value added tax and other taxes directly linked to turnover" (Directive art.2; Act s.474(1)). The Directive (art.3(12)) allows Member States to add other items of income to the net turnover but the UK has chosen not to do so.

[17] Employed means only those employed under a contract of service (s.306(6)).

[18] Other than charities and financial companies which are excluded from the micro regime: s.384B.

[19] 2006 Act s.384A. The slightly odd amounts result from the translation into pounds of the more rounded figures set out in art.3 of the Directive, i.e. €350,000 and €700,000 respectively. The Member State not using the euro can adjust the figure upwards or downwards by 5 per cent when translating into their own currencies. The UK government chose to increase the number resulting from a strict application of the exchange rate, i.e. so as to increase the number of companies covered.

[20] 2006 Act s.384B(2). On group accounts see below para.21–9.

[21] 2006 Act s.384A(3). By way of qualification to this, in its first year of operation the company's status is determined by whether it meets the criteria at the end of that year (s.384A(2)), so that a small start-up does not have to wait for a second year to benefit.

[22] Directive 2012/6/EU [2012] O.J. L81/3, whose provisions are now incorporated into the 2013 Directive.

[23] BIS, *Simpler Financial Reporting For Micro-Entities: The UK's Proposal To Implement The "Micros Directive": Government Response*, September 2013 (BIS/13/1124).

Small companies

The criteria for small companies are also set out in the Directive, but, unlike with   **21–4**
micro companies, Member States may increase the monetary criteria by up to 50
per cent. The UK chose to take advantage of this flexibility (i.e. to include more
companies in the small category). The resulting numbers are: £5.1 million for
balance sheet; £10.2 million for turnover; and 50 employees (this last being a
number fixed in the Directive).[24] A company which qualifies as small can
normally benefit from the "small companies regime" for the accounts and reports,
which is less stringent than that for larger companies. Moreover, having qualified
in a particular year, the company retains its status as "small" unless it fails to
meet the criteria for two successive years.[25] Some 3 million of the approximately
3.5 million companies in the UK fall within either the "small" or "micro"
categories, so that in numerical terms the relaxations for small companies are
very important and the full accounting regime is of concern only to the numerical
minority of companies.[26]

A company which meets the numerical criteria nevertheless cannot count as a
small company if it is a public company or carries on insurance, banking or fund
management activities or is a member of a group which contains an "ineligible"
member.[27] The thought here appears to be that such companies (or groups of
which they are members) are engaged in sufficiently sensitive activities that full
disclosure is required, especially for the benefit of the relevant regulators, and, in
the case of public companies, the fact that they are free to offer their shares to the
public suggests that a full financial record should be available.

Medium-sized companies

Somewhat misleadingly placed some 80 sections away from the provisions on   **21–5**
small companies is to be found, in the "supplementary provisions" to Pt 15, the
definition of a medium-sized company. The criteria here are: balance sheet total
of not more than £18 million, turnover not more than £36 million and not more
than 250 employees.[28] There are similarly-motivated, but not identical,
exclusions from this category as we saw in the small category, amongst which,
crucially, are public companies.[29] In some ways, however, placing these
definitions in the "supplementary provisions" of the Part dealing with accounts is
appropriate, for medium-sized companies and groups benefit from rather fewer
relaxations from the full accounts requirements, as compared with small
companies. The CLR recommended the removal of this category on the grounds
that it was neither much used nor valued, but this suggestion was not taken up.[30]

---

[24] 2006 Act s.382.
[25] 2006 Act s.382(2).
[26] BIS, *UK implementation of the EU Accounting Directive: Chapters 1-9: Impact Assessment*, 2014
(BIS/14/1055).
[27] 2006 Act s.384(1). The definition of ineligibility for groups includes a somewhat wider range of
financial companies (s.384(2)).
[28] 2006 Act s.465(3).
[29] 2006 Act s.467(1).
[30] *Developing*, para.8.35.

Large companies and public interest entities

21–6 Large companies are simply those which not meet the quantitative criteria needed to fall within the medium-sized category.[31] Public interest entities are companies whose securities are admitted to trading on a regulated market in the EU,[32] which the Act terms a "traded company".[33] In addition, the category includes any bank or insurance company (whether so traded or not), plus any other category of company added to the list for its jurisdiction by a Member State (the UK has not done so). PIEs are already subject to special audit treatment, as we shall see in the next chapter. As for core accounting, the principal requirement is that PIEs should always report as large companies even if otherwise qualified as medium-sized.[34] It is seriously open to doubt whether in the UK any PIE would qualify as medium-sized even without this express exclusion. The PIE category is, in fact, of most interest in the context of non-financial reporting, as we shall see below.

There is a further dimension to financial reporting by companies traded on public markets. Those who introduced the annual reporting obligation in the nineteenth century probably saw it as informing two groups of people: the shareholders of the company, so that they could assess whether the company's management was doing an acceptable job; and the creditors of the company, whose claims are confined to the company's assets (except in the rare case of an unlimited company). However, the modern view includes a further group as having an interest in this matter. At least with companies whose securities are traded on a public market, disclosure of information about the company is crucial for the accurate pricing of the companies' securities and hence for the efficient operation of the securities market. This is true both of equity securities (shares) and debt securities (bonds) which are traded on public markets.

So strong is the markets' demand for information that it is not satisfied by the annual reporting obligations discussed in this chapter. As we shall see in Ch.26, publicly traded companies are now subject to extensive disclosure requirements which operate throughout the company's financial year. Such rules include more frequent periodic reporting than the annual requirements of the Companies Act, as well as significant requirements for the episodic or ad hoc reporting of particular events. Even in relation to the annual reports, which remain a very significant reporting occasion, it is the point at which the company makes a preliminary announcement to the market of its financial results for the previous year (the "prelims")[35] which moves the market. Such announcements—and the

---

[31] Directive art.3.

[32] Directive 2013/34/EU art.2. For the meaning of a "regulated" market see para.25–8. In the UK the principal such market is the Main Market of the London Stock Exchange, but a company will be a PIE if it is traded on such a market anywhere in the EU.

[33] 2006 Act s.474(1).

[34] This is achieved by excluding "traded companies" from medium-sized status (s.467(2)(a)). Since public companies may not be small or micro companies (above, para.21–2) and private companies may not offer their securities to the public, explicit exclusion from only medium-sized status is necessary.

[35] Such a preliminary statement used to be obligatory for listed companies, but ceased to be so in January 2007, in the light of the implementation of the Transparency Directive, though companies continue to make such announcements and the Listing Rules regulate the form they must take, if made. See LR 9.7A.1 and Ch.26, below.

later full accounts and reports, though they are somewhat stale news by then—are pored over by analysts, whose task it is to generate advice for investors.

THE ANNUAL ACCOUNTS

Accounting records

The statutory provisions relating to the annual accounts begin by imposing on the company a continuing obligation to maintain accounting records.[36] This is logical enough, because, although these records are not open to inspection by members or the public, unless they are kept it will be impossible for the company to produce verifiable annual accounts. Hence, s.386 provides that every company—no matter how categorised for other accounting purposes—shall keep records sufficient to show and explain the company's transactions, to disclose with reasonable accuracy at any time its financial position and to enable its directors to ensure that any balance sheet and profit and loss account will comply with the relevant accounting standards.[37]

21–7

A company which has a subsidiary undertaking to which these requirements do not apply[38] must take all reasonable steps to secure that the subsidiary keeps such records as will enable the directors of the parent company to ensure that any accounts required of the parent company comply with the relevant requirements.[39]

Failure to comply with the section renders every officer of the company (but not the company itself) who is in default guilty of an offence[40] unless he shows that he acted honestly and that, in the circumstances in which the company's business was carried on, the default was excusable.[41] More effective in practice is probably the duty laid on the auditor to check whether adequate accounting records have been kept and to reveal failure to do so in the auditor's report.[42]

Section 388 provides that accounting records are at all times to be open for inspection by officers of the company.[43] If any such records are kept outside the UK,[44] there must be sent to the UK (and be available for inspection there by the officers) records which will disclose with reasonable accuracy the position of the business in question at intervals of not more than six months and which will enable the directors to ensure that the company's balance sheet and profit and loss

---

[36] 2006 Act ss.386–389.

[37] 2006 Act s.386(3) adds certain specific requirements the records must meet, but, except for unsophisticated businesses, the general standards are likely to be more important.

[38] e.g. because it is a foreign subsidiary or a partnership.

[39] 2006 Act s.386(5).

[40] Punishable by fine or imprisonment or both: s.387(3).

[41] 2006 Act s.387(2).

[42] 2006 Act s.498(2). Failure to keep adequate accounting records could also form the basis of a disqualification of a director under the general heading of unfitness (*Re Galeforce Pleating Co Ltd* [1999] 2 B.C.L.C. 705).

[43] For this reason, accountants may not exercise a lien for unpaid fees over such documents: *DTC (CNC) Ltd v Gary Sargeant & Co* [1996] 1 B.C.L.C. 529. Of course, other persons may also have the right of access to the records, for example, the company's auditors: s.499.

[44] e.g. because the company has a branch outside Great Britain.

account comply with the statutory requirements.[45] All required records must be preserved for three years if it is a private company or for six years if it is a public one.[46]

The financial year

21–8   The first step in the production of the annual accounts is to fix the company's financial year. Sections 390–392 prescribe how this is to be done. Despite its name the financial year is not a calendar year nor, necessarily, a period of 12 months. What period it is depends on its "accounting reference period" ("ARP"), which in turn depends on its "accounting reference date" ("ARD"), which is the date in each calendar year on which the company's ARP ends. For companies incorporated after 1 April 1996, the company's ARD will be the anniversary of the last day of the month in which it was incorporated.[47] However, the company may choose a new ARD for the current and future ARPs and even for its immediately preceding one.[48] This it may well want to do for a variety of reasons; for instance, if the company has been taken over and wishes to bring its ARD into line with that of its new parent.[49] The new ARD may operate either to shorten or to lengthen the ARP within which the change is made,[50] but in the latter case the company may not normally extend the ARP to more than 18 months[51] and may not normally engage in the process of extending the ARP more than once every five years.[52] These are necessary safeguards against obvious abuses, for constantly changing ARPs make comparisons across the years difficult. The company's financial year then corresponds to its ARP, as fixed according to the above rules, except that the directors have a discretion to make the financial year end at any point up to seven days before or seven days after the end of the ARP.[53]

---

[45] 2006 Act s.388(2),(3). The six-monthly requirement seems remarkably lax in the light of both modern management practice and modern electronic technology.

[46] 2006 Act s.388(4). An officer of the company is liable to imprisonment or a fine or both if he fails to take all reasonable steps to secure compliance with the preservation requirement or intentionally causes any default: s.389(4). If there has been villainy, destroying all record of it is all too likely.

[47] 2006 Act s.391(4). For companies in Northern Ireland the relevant date is 22 August 1997. For methods of determining the ARD for earlier incorporations see s.391(2),(3).

[48] 2006 Act s.292. This section applies no matter when the company was incorporated.

[49] Indeed, in this particular situation, in order to promote the production of group accounts, the directors of the parent company are under a presumptive duty to ensure that the financial years of subsidiaries coincide with that of the parent: s.390(5).

[50] 2006 Act s.392(2).

[51] 2006 Act s.392(5), unless an administration order is in force in relation to the company, presumably because the administrator, who is responsible to the court, can be trusted in a way the directors cannot.

[52] 2006 Act s.392(3), unless an administration order is in force (see previous note) or the step is taken to make the ARD coincide with that of an EEA undertaking which is the company's parent or subsidiary company, or the Secretary of State permits it.

[53] 2006 Act s.390(2),(3).

Individual accounts and group accounts

Subject to a very limited exception[54] s.394 imposes on the directors of every **21-9** company the duty to prepare for each financial year a set of accounts of the company (its "individual accounts"). This duty applies even to the directors of small and micro companies, though the requirements as to what the accounts have to contain in those cases are less onerous. Section 399 imposes a duty on directors of a company which is a parent company additionally to prepare a consolidated balance sheet and profit and loss account ("group accounts"). Those group accounts must deal with the state of affairs of the parent company and its "subsidiary undertakings"—taken together.[55]

However, the obligation to produce group accounts is qualified by one very significant exception: it does not apply to parents of groups subject to the small companies regime. Many businesses, even quite small ones, operate as groups. However, that exemption could undermine the requirement for group accounts, for example, where those in control of the business ensured that the operations of the group were carried on and its employees were employed principally in companies below the parent which itself was a small company. Consequently, in order to benefit from the small company group exemption, the test is not whether the parent is small, but whether the group as a whole meets the relevant criteria.[56] The size tests for a small group are the same as for a stand-alone company except that intra-group transactions may be eliminated when calculating turnover and balance sheet totals; alternatively, the parent company may choose instead to benefit from higher levels (by one fifth) without eliminating intra-group transactions.[57] However, the legislature recently expanded the group accounts exemption in one significant way, by extending it to small public companies. Provided the size criteria are met, it does not matter that the parent or the subsidiaries are public companies, provided none of them is a traded company.[58]

There is no special exemption for micro companies in relation to group accounts. Indeed, if a micro company is part of a group, the micro relaxations are not available for its individual accounts.[59] However, since, by definition, a micro company will also be a small company, it will be able to benefit from the small company regime when producing its individual accounts as a member of a group and will benefit from the small company exemption from the requirement to produce group accounts if it is the parent company.

---

[54] The exception for dormant subsidiaries is discussed in para.21-10.

[55] 2006 Act s.404(1).

[56] 2006 Act s.383(1).

[57] 2006 Act s.383(4)–(7). The choice is available separately in relation to each of the turnover and balance sheet tests: s.383(6).

[58] 2006 Act ss.399(2A) and 384(2)(a). For the meaning of a "traded company" see para.21-6, above. The other accounting advantages of being a "small" company continue to be unavailable to "small" public companies.

[59] 2006 Act s.384B(2).

There is a similar approach to the definition of a medium-sized group to that used for a small group—except, of course, that a medium-sized group is not exempted from the obligation to produce group accounts, but it may report less fully.[60]

Parent and subsidiary undertakings

21–10   The obligation to produce group accounts does not relieve the directors of the parent company from the obligation to produce individual accounts for the parent[61] nor, subject to one exception, the directors of the other companies in the group from that obligation in relation to their company.[62] The individual and group accounts of companies within a group should be produced, in principle, using the same financial reporting framework.[63] The exception relates to subsidiaries which have been dormant throughout the relevant financial year (unless the subsidiary is a traded company—a rare situation). They are not required to produce individual accounts, subject to certain conditions, in particular that all the members of the subsidiary agree (easy enough if the subsidiary is wholly owned), that the parent is incorporated in the EEA and that the parent guarantees the liabilities of the subsidiary as they existed at the end of the year in relation to which the exemption applied (and all this is disclosed).[64] The principle that the production of group accounts should not normally remove the obligation to render individual accounts is as it should be. Creditors, in particular, may well have claims only against particular companies in the group, unless they have contracted for guarantees from other group members, and so the group picture alone might be misleading. By contrast, the shareholders of the parent have an economic interest in the performance of the group as a whole, since subsidiary profits may eventually come to them as dividends from the parent company, and so are interested primarily in the group accounts.[65]

---

[60] 2006 Act s.466.

[61] 2006 Act s.399(2)—"as well as producing individual accounts". Section 408 permits certain relaxations for the individual accounts of a company which produces group accounts, notably that the company's individual profit and loss account need not be circulated to the shareholders or filed with the Registrar, if notes to the group accounts show the profit and loss of the company for the financial year.

[62] 2006 Act s.394—"the directors of every company".

[63] 2006 Act s.407. However, this section does not apply if the parent uses IAS for both the consolidated and its individual accounts. For the meaning of "financial reporting framework" see para.21–13.

[64] 2006 Act ss.394A–C. Even so, the usual financial companies cannot take advantage of the exemption nor may a dormant subsidiary which at any time in the relevant financial year has been a traded company (see para.21–6, above). All this may seem rather elaborate for exempting a company from producing individual accounts when, by definition (see s.1169), it has engaged in no significant accounting transactions during the financial year. At times the authorities have considered a wider policy of exempting subsidiaries generally from producing individual accounts in exchange for a parent company guarantee. However, the policy has always failed on the basis that it would reduce the amount of information available about the activities of potentially economically important subsidiaries.

[65] Nevertheless, it is crucial to remember that dividends are paid on the basis of only individual accounts alone. If the profits of a subsidiary are paid directly to the shareholders of the parent, all sorts of legal problems arise. See Ch.12, fn.24.

The obligation to produce group accounts gives rise to the need to define a subsidiary undertaking. The situation may be clear when Company A holds all the voting shares in Company B, but suppose it holds only 30 per cent of them. What is then the position? The answer is provided by ss.1161 and 1162 and Sch.7. The term "undertaking" is used rather than "company" because consolidation of the accounts is required even if the subsidiary business does not take the form of a company or some other body corporate, but is a partnership or other unincorporated body.[66] Thus, although group accounts are required by the Act to be compiled only by entities which are companies,[67] the shareholders and creditors of and investors in those companies are to be provided with financial information relating to all the businesses the parent controls, no matter what legal form they may take.

But what is control? The Act, building on art.22 of the Directive, sets out five situations where control will be found to exist. Briefly summarised, these situations are where the parent company:

(a)   holds a majority of voting rights in the undertaking[68];

(b)   is a member of the other undertaking and has the right to appoint or remove a majority of its board of directors[69];

(c)   by virtue of provisions in the constitution of the other undertaking or in a written "control contract", permitted by that constitution, has a right, recognised by the law under which that undertaking is established, to exercise a "dominant influence" over that undertaking (by giving directions to the directors of the undertaking on its operating and financial policies which those directors are obliged to comply with whether or not the directions are for the benefit of the undertaking)[70];

(d)   has the power to exercise or actually exercises dominant influence or control over the undertaking or the parent and alleged subsidiary are actually managed on a unified basis[71];

(e)   is a member of another undertaking and alone controls, pursuant to an agreement with other members, a majority of the voting rights in that undertaking[72];

---

[66] 2006 Act s.1161(1).

[67] 2006 Act s.399(2).

[68] 2006 Act s.1162(2)(a).

[69] 2006 Act s.1162(2)(b). Membership includes "indirect" membership, i.e. where a subsidiary of the parent is a member of the undertaking in question: s.1162(3).

[70] 2006 Act s.1162(2)(c) and Sch.7 para.4. This situation of "contractual subordination" is probably never found in the UK, though it is provided for in Germany, where, however, it is rarely found in practice. See paras 9–21 et seq. There would be great difficulties with the legality of such a contract under the law of the UK.

[71] 2006 Act s.1162(4). This is a reference to actual domination and the qualifications needed to establish contractual domination do not apply here: Sch.7 para.4(3).

[72] This brings in shareholder agreements which are an established way of exercising control over companies in some continental European jurisdictions, but note that the effect of the agreement must be to give the alleged parent sole control.

and sub-subsidiaries are to be treated as subsidiaries of the ultimate parent also.[73]

Despite the complexities of this definition, which arise partly out of the need to address control structures across the EU, it is clear that the most important case in the UK is (a). Thus, the answer to our question is that a holding of 30 per cent by Company A in Company B will not, by itself, make Company B its subsidiary. However, companies are not permitted to remain entirely silent about their significant relationships with companies other than subsidiaries. Companies have to disclose in their individual or group accounts certain information about companies, not being subsidiaries, in which they have nevertheless a significant holding.[74] However, such affiliated companies do not have to be consolidated into the group accounts.

Parent companies which are part of a larger group

21–11 A parent/subsidiary relationship will exist even where the parent (the "intermediate parent") is itself the subsidiary of another company. In groups of companies this situation often exists. There may be a chain of companies in which all but the bottom company meet the statutory definition for being a parent of the company (or companies) below them in the chain. The resulting proliferation of group accounts of varying scope is not likely to be helpful. Consequently, there are exemptions which apply in such cases. The terms of the exemption vary according to the level of the parent's shareholding in the intermediate parent, since the "outside" shareholders in the intermediate parent have an economic interest in that company's subsidiaries and so may wish to have intermediate group accounts.

Subject to certain further conditions, an intermediate parent which is a wholly-owned subsidiary of another company is relieved of the obligation to produce group accounts.[75] Where the parent of the intermediate parent holds 90 per cent or more of the subsidiary's shares, the exemption needs the approval of (presumably a majority of) the remaining shareholders of the intermediate parent.[76] Where the parent of the intermediate parent holds more than 50 per cent of the allotted shares[77] (but less than 90 per cent), exemption is the default rule. However, if the holders of at least 5 per cent of the total allotted shares in the

---

[73] 2006 Act s.1162(5). For this reason it is important that the section refers to parent undertakings, since the immediate parent of the indirect subsidiary might not itself be a company.

[74] See, for example, paras 4–6 of Sch.4 to the Large and Medium-Sized Companies and Groups (Accounts and Reports) Regulations 2008 (SI 2008/410, as amended) requiring a company's individual accounts to give certain information about companies in which the reporting company has a "significant holding"—defined as 20 per cent or more of any class of shares in the other company. Similar rules apply to group accounts (para.20–22) with more detail being required in the cases where the "significant holding" makes the other company an "associated" undertaking or a joint venture with the reporting company (paras 18–19).

[75] 2006 Act ss.400(1)(a) and 401(1)(a).

[76] 2006 Act ss.400(1)(b) and 401(1)(b).

[77] It does not matter whether the allotted shares carry voting rights or not, but unless the "parent" undertaking controls 50 per cent of the voting rights, it will not be under an obligation to produce consolidated accounts in any event. See below. In effect, the requirement to hold 50 per cent of the allotted share capital means that the parent company, which passes the 50 per cent figure by holding weighted voting rights in the subsidiary, will have access to the exemption only if the parent also holds non-voting shares in sufficient quantities.

intermediate parent serve a notice, within six months of the end of the financial year in question, requiring the production of group accounts by their company, then those group accounts must be produced.[78] The higher level of protection where the "outside" shareholders constitute 10 per cent or less of the shareholders is perhaps explicable by reference to the fact that the governance rights of such shareholders are very limited. For example, they are unable to block a special resolution. None of the above exemptions is available, however, if the intermediate parent is a traded company.[79] This is particularly important in relation to the default exemption. For such companies, there will necessarily be a significant block of the company's shares which are not held by that company's parent but are in the hands of public investors. Their interests dictate that the traded company should produce accounts which cover its position together with the position of the undertakings it controls, for that is the economic entity in which the public have invested.[80]

Even where the exemption is available in principle, certain other conditions have to be met. First, the intermediate parent must actually be included in the accounts of a larger group; those accounts must be drawn up in accordance with the standards contained in the Directive or equivalent standards, and must be audited.[81] Secondly, the individual accounts of the intermediate parent must disclose that it is exempt from the obligation to produce group accounts and give prescribed information in order to identify the parent undertaking that draws up the group accounts.[82] Thirdly, the intermediate parent must deliver the group accounts to the Registrar, translated into English, if necessary.[83]

Companies excluded from consolidation

Even if a company is in principle subject to the obligation to produce group accounts, nevertheless some subsidiary companies may be omitted from the consolidation. Subsidiaries may be omitted if (a) their inclusion is not material for giving a true and fair view of the group (for example, if they are inactive companies); (b) "severe long-term restrictions" substantially hinder the exercise of the parent's rights over the assets or management of the company (a situation most likely to arise from restrictions in foreign legal systems); (c) the necessary information cannot be obtained "without disproportionate expense or undue delay"; and (d) the parent's interest is held exclusively with a view to resale.[84] If

21–12

[78] 2006 Act ss.400(1)(c) and 401(1)(c).

[79] See para.21–6, above.

[80] Of course, those investors may also be strongly interested in the traded company's relations with its parent, for fear that the parent may seek to take a disproportionate share of the company's earnings. But that is a different issue.

[81] 2006 Act ss.400(2)(a)–(b), 401(2)(a)–(c). The requirement for audit is stated expressly in relation only to non-EEA parent companies, but in the case of EEA companies this requirement follows from the provisions of the Audit Directive (see Ch.22, below).

[82] 2006 Act ss.400(2)(c)–(d), 401(2)(d)–(e).This is not necessarily its immediate holding company, since that company, by operation of the same rules, might be exempt from the need to produce consolidated accounts. Thus, where there is a chain of three wholly-owned subsidiaries, only the top company will normally have to produce consolidated accounts.

[83] 2006 Act ss.400(2)(e)–(f), 401(2)(f)–(g).

[84] 2006 Act s.405.

all the subsidiaries fall within one or other of these categories, no group accounts need be produced—no doubt a rare situation.[85]

Form and content of annual accounts

Possible approaches

21–13 Broadly, there are two model approaches for the legislature to take to the rules governing the financial analysis of the transactions the company has engaged in during the year and the presentation of the results of that analysis in the company's individual or group accounts. It could lay down one or more very general principles and leave it to the accounting profession to develop more specific rules (usually referred to as "accounting standards"), to which, however, legal force might or might not be attached; or the legislature could try to set out a detailed set of rules itself. The British tradition is closer to the former model. However, the continental European tradition, which is closer to the second model, had an impact on British law in the 1980s, because that tradition influenced the Fourth and Seventh Directives on companies' accounts,[86] though not to the extent by any means of a complete shift to the latter approach. However, in a later development, the EU moved towards giving standard setters a bigger role in the setting of the detailed rules, through the adoption of International Accounting Standards ("IAS"), though with the rider that standard-setting should no longer be purely a matter for the professions and the public interest should be represented in the standard-setting exercise.

The result is that the current rules are a mixture of legislative provision and accounting standards, to which different degrees of legal recognition are accorded. Moreover, there are two sets of rules, with different mixtures. Here lies the significance of the term "accounting framework". A company which is under an obligation to produce individual accounts is free to do so either by reference to the rules contained in the Companies Act and regulations made thereunder or by reference to IAS.[87] These accounts are called, helpfully if unimaginatively, "Companies Act individual accounts" and "IAS individual accounts" respectively. The same choice is available to companies under an obligation to produce group accounts, except that companies which in domestic terminology are traded companies[88] must use IAS for their group accounts, as required by EU law.[89] Thus, there are also "Companies Act group accounts" and "IAS group accounts".

---

[85] 2006 Act s.402.

[86] See fn.7, above.

[87] 2006 Act s.395. A company which is a charity must provide Companies Act individual and group accounts: ss.395(2) and 403(3).

[88] See para.21–6. By virtue of s.407 (above, fn.63) there is some pressure to use IAS for the individual accounts of group companies as well.

[89] IAS Regulation art.4. Since the Regulation is directly applicable in the Member States, the provisions of art.4 are not reproduced in the Act, though s.403(1) refers to the EU obligation. In fact, IAS accounts are mandatory on a wider basis than the Regulation suggests because the London Stock Exchange requires EEA-incorporated companies traded on the Alternative Investment Market to use them as well: LSE, *Aim Rules for Companies*, 2014, r.19.

The IAS Regulation permits Member States to permit or require domestic companies to use IAS more widely.[90] The UK adopted the permissive approach but made it widely available, for even small companies may use IAS.[91] Having switched to IAS, a company may change back to Companies Act accounts provided it has not changed to Companies Act accounts during the five-year period leading up to the most recent year of IAS accounts. This rule is clearly aimed at preventing chopping and changing, which would reduce the comparability of the accounts. If the company wishes to change back to Companies Act accounts within that period, it must show that "there is a relevant change of circumstance".[92] Similar rules apply on a reconversion to IAS.[93]

We will now look at Companies Act accounts and IAS accounts in turn, but first it is necessary to look at a two provisions which applies to both Companies Act and IAS accounts.

True and fair view

The traditional British approach to the accounts has long focused around the general principle that the accounts must "give a true and fair view of the assets, liabilities, financial position and profit or loss"[94] of the individual company or the companies included in the consolidation in the case of group accounts. For many years this was virtually all the companies legislation said about the content of the accounts. It remains an overriding principle, no matter which accounting framework is used for the presentation of the accounts. The directors must not approve accounts unless they provide a true and fair view.[95] The overriding nature of the requirement is reflected in art.4 of the Directive.

If compliance with the Act or provisions made under it would not be sufficient to give a true and fair view, the necessary additional information must be given in the accounts or notes to them.[96] Further, if in "exceptional" or "special" circumstances compliance with the statutory provisions would put the accounts in breach of the "true and fair" requirement, the directors must depart from the statute or subordinate legislation to the extent necessary to give a true and fair view.[97] What this qualification seems not to permit, though standard-setters have sometimes taken a different view, is the issuance of a standard which gives a general dispensation to companies to depart from a provision in or made under

21-14

---

[90] IAS Regulation art.5.

[91] 2006 Act s.403.

[92] 2006 Act ss.395(3)–(4B) and 403(4)–(5B). The changes identified in the Act, and they are apparently exclusive, are becoming a subsidiary of a company which does not prepare IAS accounts and the company or its parent ceasing to have securities traded on a regulated market: ss.395(4) and 403(5). Until 2012 the company always had to show a relevant change of circumstance in order to revert to Company Act accounts.

[93] 2006 Act ss.395(5) and 403(6).

[94] 2006 Act s.393(1).

[95] 2006 Act s.393(1). The strength of UK commitment to this principle is demonstrated by the modifications to it which were thought necessary when micro companies were relieved of compliance with many standards. See para.21–17.

[96] 2013 Directive art.4(3) and, for Companies Act accounts, ss.396(4) and 404(4) (for individual and group accounts respectively).

[97] 2013 Directive art.4(4) and ss.396(5) and 404(5).

the Act, on the grounds that a true and fair view requires this. These provisions of the Directive and of the Act contemplate only ad hoc departures from the statutory requirements in the case of particular companies in particular circumstances.

The prohibition on signing accounts which do not give a true and fair view applies equally to IAS accounts as to Companies Act accounts. However, with IAS accounts, domestic law says nothing about what must or may be done to produce that view if the applicable standards by themselves do not achieve it.[98] Nevertheless, the position is probably the same, since the provisions of the Directive apply to all accounts, no matter what accounting framework is employed. IAS 1 requires that the accounts "present fairly" the company's or group's financial position, which presumably may be equated with a "true and fair view".[99] The application of IAS (or rather International Financial Reporting Standards ("IFRS"), as they have now become) is presumed to lead to fair presentation, but IAS 1 recognises that further disclosure may be necessary to achieve this result. Departure from IFRS in order to achieve fair presentation is recognised as permissible but only "in extremely rare circumstances".

Going concern evaluation

21–15 Much less obvious in the domestic legislation than the true and fair requirement, but often as important, is the requirement that directors form a view, when they draw up the accounts, whether the company is a going concern. Article 6 of the Directive lays down as one of its "general financial reporting principles" that "the undertaking shall be presumed to be carrying on its business as a going concern", so that, if the company is in danger of ceasing to be a going concern, this fact must disclosed and appropriate valuations made. This principle is important because the numbers in the accounts are likely to look very different where a company may have to sell assets off on a break-up basis. Both the national and international accounting standards (discussed below) require that the directors make this assessment when preparing financial statements.[100] In addition, the Listing Rules require the directors of a company with a premium listing on the Main Market[101] of the London Stock Exchange to insert in its annual financial report a statement that the company is a going concern, together with any assumptions underlying that statement and any qualifications to it.[102] In the recent financial crisis, and especially when liquidity was in short supply, the issue came to the fore. The Financial Reporting Council (see below) established a

---

[98] 2006 Act s.393(1) applies but not ss.396 and 405.

[99] If this is not the case, then there is a flat contradiction between the requirements of s.393 and art.4 of the Directive, on the one hand, and the obligations of companies under the IAS accounting framework. Furthermore, the Commission is to endorse an IAS for use in the EU only if it considers it will result in a true and fair view (Regulation, Recital 9). The FRC strongly argues that "true and fair" remains fully applicable to IAS accounts: FRC, *True and Fair*, June 2014.

[100] See International Accounting Standard 1 and Financial Reporting Standard 18.

[101] For the definition of these terms see para.25–6 and 25–9.

[102] LR 9.8.6(3).

committee to examine the lessons to be drawn from how this matter was handled in the crisis and later issued revised guidance.[103]

Companies Act accounts

At the core of Companies Act accounts are a traditional balance sheet and a profit and loss statement.[104] The balance sheet provides a statement of the company's assets and liabilities, as at a particular point in time, i.e. the last day of the financial year. If, as is to be hoped, the former are greater than the latter, the difference between the figures is sometimes referred to as the shareholders' equity. It is the theoretical amount which the shareholders would receive if the company's business were then sold as a going concern.[105] If the assets are less than the liabilities, the shareholders have no equity in the company and the people with the strongest interest in its economic performance are its creditors.[106] The profit and loss account indicates the company's performance over the financial year: has it generated more value than it has consumed? Profit is different from cash flow. A profitable company may have a negative cash flow over a particular period, for example, where it has used a previously large cash balance to buy a new (and profitable) business. Although the new business may have generated cash during the financial year in which it was bought, it is highly unlikely that this cash income will come anywhere near the amount expended to acquire the business. Conversely, a company which has been unprofitable over the year but has managed to dispose of a large fixed asset during that year may end the year with more cash than at the beginning of it.

What does the Act say about the format of these two accounts? With the enactment of the Fourth and Seventh Directives, UK law also adopted the Continental practice of dealing with matters of form and content to some extent in the legislation itself, and so the domestic legal provisions dealing with the accounts were expanded. Those provisions are now in the Large and Medium-Sized Companies and Groups (Accounts and Reports) Regulations 2008,[107] and the Small Companies and Groups (Accounts and Reports) Regulations 2008,[108] both as subsequently amended. This account of the Regulations is necessarily brief and we shall omit entirely the special provisions applying to banking and insurance companies.

Following the Directive, Pt 1 of Sch.1 to both sets of Regulations[109] provides two alternative formats in which the balance sheet may be presented and four possible formats for the profit and loss account. However, the directors cannot shift from the formats adopted in the previous year "unless in their opinion there

21–16

---

[103] FRC, *Guidance on Risk Management, Internal Control and Related Financial and Business Reporting*, September 2014.

[104] 2006 Act s.396. See the similar s.404(1) for group accounts.

[105] Theoretical because what the shareholders will actually receive is what a buyer of the business is willing to pay for it.

[106] We saw at para.9–6 that this situation may induce directors responsive to shareholder interests to embark on projects with a low chance of a high return and high chance of making a loss.

[107] SI 2008/409 (hereafter the "Large Accounts Regulations"). They were previously in Schedules to the 1985 Act.

[108] SI 2008/410 (hereafter the "Small Accounts Regulations").

[109] Schedule 6 makes some additional provisions in relation to group accounts.

are special reasons for a change".[110] The formats concern simply the questions of how the accounting information is grouped and the order in which the information, so grouped, is presented to the reader. More important, therefore, are the provisions of the Schedule which go into issues relating to the proper accounting treatment of transactions carried out by the company or contain rules about the valuation of assets and liabilities. These are contained in Pt 2 of the Schedule under the heading "Accounting Principles and Rules". This is where the "going concern" principle of the Directive is transposed into domestic law. However, these rules are (strong) default rules, for the directors may depart from them if there are "special reasons" for so doing, provided the nature of the departure, the reasons for it and its effect are stated.[111] Furthermore, the Schedule explicitly provides a choice to the directors as to the fundamental accounting approach which will be adopted. No longer is a historical cost approach mandatory (under which, for example, assets are carried in the books at their original acquisition price, less depreciation, even though their current market price is much higher) but rather various forms of "marking to market" are permitted.[112]

Finally, it is clear that the "Accounting Principles and Rules" contained in the Schedule are not sufficient to produce a set of accounts for any particular company, except perhaps one of the simplest character. More detailed accounting standards need to be deployed, which are not to be found in the Regulations implementing the Directives but in standards developed by the standard-setters, to which we now turn.

Accounting standards

21–17　In the UK the professional accountancy bodies had begun as early as 1942[113] to issue accounting standards. At that time and for a long while thereafter they provided the only authoritative guidance on what the "true and fair" requirement meant in particular situations. Those standards covered ever more topics and became ever more sophisticated over time; and, as we have seen, their centrality to the accounts-producing exercise was not ended by the transposition in the UK of the Fourth and Seventh Directives. Two important developments have accompanied the expansion of the role of accounting standards. These two developments are probably not unconnected with one another, their common feature being a recognition of the quasi-public role played by accounting standards. First, accounting standards have achieved legal backing; secondly, the professional bodies have lost their previously complete control over the standard-setting process.

---

[110] Regulations Sch.1 para.2.

[111] Regulations Sch.1 para.10.

[112] See Sch.1 Pt 2 ss.C and D. The introduction of "fair value accounting" into the Fourth and Seventh Directives was effected by Directive 2003/53/EC ([2003] O.J. L178) as a direct result of the adoption by the EU of the IAS for companies on regulated markets, where this approach was required. See now art.8 of the 2013 Directive. In this way, IAS have expanded as well the scope of action of purely domestic standard-setters.

[113] In that year the Institute of Chartered Accountants in England and Wales began to issue Recommendations on Accounting Principles.

Although the 1942 standards were termed "Recommendations", it became accepted in the accounting profession that compliance with the legal obligation to present a "true and fair" view of the company's financial position required in principle adherence to accounting standards – even if on rare occasions that legal obligation had the contrary effect of requiring directors to override the requirements of a particular standard.[114] A good example of this reasoning in action was provided on the occasion of the introduction of a set of extensive reporting relaxations for micro companies (see below). The Directive provides that where advantage is taken of these relaxations, the micro company's annual financial statements "shall be regarded as giving the true and fair view required by Article 4(3)[115] [which refers to the provision of additional information to give a true and fair view]". This was argued to rule out the application of accounting standards to the relevant items in the micro company's accounts, because these typically would require additional information. But, if accounting standards could not be applied, directors and auditors would be in danger of not meeting the "true and fair" obligation. Consequently, the Act's formulation of the directors' true and fair obligation was amended specifically to require directors of micro companies to ignore accounting standards when making that judgement if those standards would require the provision of further information.[116]

This process described in the previous paragraph was supported by the courts' acceptance of the professional standards as the best evidence of the standard of care required by the law of negligence in relation to accountants performing their professional duties, especially when acting as auditors, though the courts are not bound by the professionally developed standards.[117] In the case of large companies the resulting position was recognised legislatively in a provision added in 1989. This provides that "it must be stated whether the accounts have been prepared in accordance with applicable accounting standards and particulars of any material departure from those standards and the reasons for it must be given".[118] This in effect puts accounting standards on a "comply or explain" basis, and it was probably the first example of the use of this technique in company law.[119]

The second development—the injection of a public element into the standard-setting bodies—occurred when the Companies Act 1989 conferred on the Secretary of State the power to determine which body or bodies have authority to issue accounting standards which have statutory recognition.[120]

---

[114] See para.21–14, above.

[115] Ibid. The implementing domestic provision is s.396(2A).

[116] 2006 Act s.393(1A).

[117] *Lloyd Cheyham & Co v Littlejohn & Co* [1987] B.C.L.C. 303; but cf. *Bolitho v City and Hackney Health Authority* [1998] A.C. 232 HL (court not bound by professional standards where "in a rare case" it is convinced they are not reasonable or responsible).

[118] Large Accounts Regulations Sch.1 para.45. Medium-sized companies are exempt from this obligation (see reg.4(2A)) and the Small Accounts Regulations 2008 do not contain a impose a similar rule.

[119] For its use in relation to the Corporate Governance Code, which was developed only in the 1990s, see above at para.14–69.

[120] Now s.464 of the 2006 Act. The current arrangements are set out in the Statutory Auditors (Amendment of Companies Act 2006 and Delegation of Functions etc) Order 2012/1741. Previously, the delegation was directly to an Accounting Standards Board which was a subsidiary of the FRC.

Under the current arrangements the Secretary of State has delegated this power to the Financial Reporting Council Ltd ("FRC"). The FRC is a private company (limited by guarantee), but the Chair and Deputy Chair of the FRC are appointed by the Secretary of State; the remaining directors, executive and non-executive, are appointed and removed by the board itself. Those who have practised in the accounting profession within the previous five years are excluded, so that the board appears to be weighted towards the users of accountants' services. Some of the work of the FRC in the accounting standards area is delegated to a Codes and Standards Committee. The FRC is funded in its accounting, audit and corporate governance activities by the accountancy profession and the preparers of financial statements, though the "preparers' levy" paid by public traded and large private (i.e. non publicly traded) companies.[121] Overall, the public authorities, despite no longer making any significant contribution to the funding of the FRC, can be said to have considerable potential control over its activities. On the other hand, the governmental bodies do not interfere in the day-to-day running of the FRC. Thus, the current structure can be said to combine the technical competence and flexibility of setting rules through expert bodies exercising delegated powers with the safeguarding of the public interest through ultimate public control.

IAS accounts

21–18   If the Directive represents the use by the EU of (partial) legislative specification of the form of the accounts, the IAS Regulation[122] represents the EU's adoption of the alternative strategy of reliance on the standard-setters. Companies subject to the IAS, whether mandatorily or by their own choice, are to prepare their accounts in conformity with international accounting standards as laid down by the International Accounting Standards Board and as adopted by the Commission.[123] True it is that such companies remain subject to the Directive, but the predecessors of the current Directive, the Fourth and Seventh Directives, were amended so as to ensure that they permitted companies to adopt the IAS approach. A good example is the fact that IAS 1 does not require the production of a profit and loss account but rather of income and cash flow statements, which necessitated an adjustment of the Fourth Directive.[124] At domestic level, since the IAS Regulation applies directly in the UK, the national provisions dealing with the form and content of the accounts are applied only to companies producing Companies Act accounts.[125] For IAS accounts, these matters are dealt with in the international standards themselves.

---

[121] See FRC, *Plan and Budget and Levies 2015/16*, March 2015. Section 17 of the Companies (Audit, Investigation and Community Enterprise) Act 2004 gives the Secretary of State the power to make the levy binding, but currently the levy is paid on a "voluntary" basis.

[122] Above, fn.8.

[123] IAS Regulation art.2.

[124] Thus, in the current Directive art.13(2) permits the use of a "statement of performance", as required by IAS, rather than a profit and loss account, whilst art.8(6) permits derogations from the Directive's fair value rules in order to facilitate compliance with IAS.

[125] Both Large (regs 3 and 9) and Small (regs 3 and 8) Accounts Regulations exempt companies from the operation of their Schs 1 (individual accounts) and 6 (group accounts) if they use IAS. Of course, a small company need not produce group accounts at all (see para.21–9) but may choose to do so.

The effect of the IAS Regulation is to give the standards produced by the IASB (now called International Financial Reporting Standards ("IFRS")) an even more explicit legal position than domestic standards. The appropriate IAS and IFRS must be followed under the terms of the IAS Regulation.[126] Not surprisingly, and in line with the domestic developments, the more prominent role afforded to the international standards was accompanied by the loss of purely professional control over the setting of those standards. The IASB became an independent body in 2001, having been founded in 1973 by the professional accountancy bodies of nine leading countries. However, close ties with a particular government, on the model of the FRC, were hardly feasible for the IASB, which adopted a different path away from professional control. In brief, its members are appointed by the trustees of a foundation,[127] which trustees are a self-perpetuating body (i.e. they appoint their own successors). However, this arrangement was subject to criticism, notably from the European Commission, and was modified by the addition of a Monitoring Board consisting of representatives of the public authorities (mainly regulators, including the European Commission).[128]

The IASB is not a European but an international organisation, as its name suggests. Given its wider scope, the obligation of companies within the IAS Regulation to apply IAS and IFRS, and the reluctance of the European Commission to lose all control over this important area, it is perhaps not surprising that there is a filter in place between the adoption of a standard by the IASB and its becoming mandatory for European companies subject to the IAS Regulation. The filter is that the standard produced by the IASB must have been adopted by the Commission of the European Union, which is advised by a technical committee (European Financial Reporting Advisory Group ("EFRAG")) and a committee consisting of representatives from the Member States (Accounting Regulatory Committee ("ARC")) before it endorses an international standard.[129] The nature of the filtration process is perhaps less clear. Adoption is not permitted if the IASB standard is contrary to the "true and fair view" principle,[130] but if the "fair presentation" principle of IAS 1 is the same as a true and fair view,[131] then that judgment will have been made already by the IASB. Nor may the Commission adopt an IASB standard if it fails to "meet the criteria of understandability, relevance, reliability and comparability" required of such standards. However, it is highly unlikely that the IASB would adopt a standard which it considered infringed this principle either. In effect, the filter operates as an opportunity for the same issues to be debated again at EU level as were considered internationally in the adoption of the initial IAS or IFRS. Such a re-hashing of the arguments occurred in relation to the IAS standard on the market valuation of financial instruments. After a long debate IAS 39 was

21–19

---

[126] Companies using IAS shall produce their accounts "in conformity with the international accounting standards": Regulation arts 4 and 5.

[127] Currently termed the IFRS Foundation.

[128] The role of the Monitoring Board is described at: *http://www.iasplus.com/en/resources/ifrsf/governance/monitoring-board* [Accessed 27 April 2016].

[129] IAS Regulation arts 3 and 6.

[130] IAS Regulation art.3(2).

[131] See para.21–14, above.

adopted but with two significant carve outs.[132] The other IAS and IFRS have been adopted straightforwardly, though not always on time.[133] It is clear that extensive use of the blocking power by the Commission would be likely to lead to a collapse of the IASB venture.

It may be wondered why the EU threw its weight behind the IAS and the IASB rather than keeping closer control over accounting standards itself. It seems to have recognised that producing accounting standards for the largest companies is necessarily a global rather than a regional activity.[134] Globalisation has led multinational companies to acquire not only cross-border business activities, but also cross-border groups of investors. Both investors, seeking to compare companies from different jurisdictions, and companies, seeking to raise money in more than one country, have generated a demand for international uniformity in accounting standards, so that accounts do not have to be constantly restated according to different countries' "generally accepted accounting principles" ("GAAP"). The only other contender for a global role is the US national standards (US GAAP). The IASB provides a platform from which convergence may be pursued with the US standards rather than a simple adoption of them.[135]

Applying the requirements to different sizes of company

21–20   We have seen that the form and content of the accounts result from a complex interaction of rules set out in legislation (which itself may be national or EU legislation and primary or secondary legislation) and accounting standards (which may be national or international). This is a far cry from the days when there was only national legislation, when that legislation confined itself to the requirement of a true and fair view, and the rest was national accounting standards. It does not help that the balance between legislation and standards varies somewhat according to whether national or international standards are used by the company. There is one further cross-cutting set of divisions which we need to notice. This is the varying intensity of the rules and standards across companies of different sizes. We need to consider this point only briefly, since this is not a textbook on accounting. The rules we consider here relate to the different requirements for the production of accounts. As we shall see later, differences in economic size are also relevant a number of other accounting matters: what goes into the notes to the accounts and into narrative reporting or the level of publicity to be given to those accounts once produced (through their filing in a public registry). The full force of the rules and standards applies only to large companies and groups and PIEs which are required to report as large

---

[132] Commission Regulation (EC) No.2086/2004. The IASB later amended IAS 39 and one of the carve outs was dropped (Commission Regulation (EC) No.1864/2005), the hedge fund carve out remaining. The economic crisis has continued to keep this issue at the forefront of regulators' attention.

[133] The current state of play on endorsement is given by EFRAG, *The EU endorsement status report*, April 2012.

[134] Among the countries, outside the EU, which allow or require their companies to use IFRS are Australia, India, Japan and South Korea.

[135] The FRC also has a policy of producing convergence with IAS, so that in the end there may be relatively little difference between Companies Act and IAS accounts, though the IASB would be in the lead.

companies, even though they are only medium-sized.[136] Medium-sized companies and groups benefit from a modest set of derogations from the requirements for large companies. In particular, the UK has not taken up the permission in art.23 of the Directive to exempt the parent of medium-sized groups from the obligation to draw up group accounts.

For small companies the derogations are more substantial. As we have seen above, a small company is not required to produce group accounts, though it may choose to do so. Further, the Directive (art.14) permits Member States to allow small companies to produce only "abridged" profit and loss accounts and balance sheets. This means that some items normally required to be shown separately may be combined in a single heading. So, the accounts are less granular, but equally cheaper to produce and less helpful to competitors. Until recently, domestic law has permitted small companies to *publish* abbreviated accounts.[137] Drawing up abridged accounts raises additional issues because the accounts are then less useful for shareholders as well as outsiders (shareholders receive the accounts as drawn up and are not reliant on the published ones). The UK decided to take up the option to permit abridged accounts to be drawn up only where all of the members of the company consent to this course of action.[138] This is designed to allow the company to cut costs when all the shareholders are insiders but to allow outside shareholders to protect themselves by withholding consent. Finally, the accounting standards applying to small companies have been simplified, both by the FRC and the IASB.[139]

The largest set of derogations is reserved for the smallest companies, i.e. micro companies. The permissible derogations from the accounts preparation requirements are set out in art.36 of the Directive, and the UK has taken advantage of nearly all of them[140] for free-standing micro entities.[141] Accounting standards are further simplified for micro entities.[142]

Notes to the accounts

Although the British tradition has been for the legislature not to specify the form and content of the accounts, but to leave that to standard-setters, the legislature

21–21

---

[136] See above, para.21–6

[137] See below, para.21–36.

[138] Small Accounts Regulations Sch.1 Pt 1 para.1A.

[139] The FRC's had previously operated a separate Financial Reporting Standard for Smaller Entities ("FRSSE"). The Directive required a change of approach but not of principle. See FRC, *Accounting Standards for Small Enterprises: Consultation Document*, September 2014 and *Consultation Overview*, February 2015. For the IASB, see *IFRS for SMEs* ("International Financial Reporting Standards for Small and Medium-sized Enterprises").

[140] See BIS, *Simpler Financial Reporting For Micro-Entities: The UK's Proposal To Implement The "Micros Directive": Government Response*, September 2013. The exception was the decision not to take up the option to relieve micro companies from the obligation to use accrual accounting. Cash accounting was thought to be potentially misleading: for example, pre-payments received in year 1 would show up without off-setting costs where the supply of the good or service was not due until year 2 (when the costs would show up without the associated income). The Directive itself prohibits micro companies benefitting from the derogations from using fair value accounting: art.36(3).

[141] 2006 Act s.394B(2)(b); see para.21–3, above.

[142] For the FRC see *Draft FRS 105 The Financial Reporting Standard applicable to the Micro-entities Regime*, discussed in the documents cited in fn.139, above.

has long seen the accounts as a useful place to require the disclosure of specific pieces of information. These are not required to be part of the accounts proper but are to be given in "notes" to the accounts.[143] The notes requirements apply whether the company has produced Companies Act or IAS accounts.[144] The information required to be disclosed is often designed to make the information contained in the accounts complete.[145] We have seen above the example of the requirement to give information in the notes about non-subsidiary companies in which the reporting company has a significant holding.[146] Another example is the requirement for companies (other than small ones) to disclose 'off balance-sheet' transactions, without knowledge of which the balance sheet may be entirely misleading.[147]

Most of what is required by way of notes in arts 16–18 of the Directive falls into the "completeness" category. However, in this context there is again room for debate about whether the notes requirements should apply uniformly across all sizes of company. The Directive requires compliance with the art.16 list by all companies, except that Member States may choose to exempt micro companies from nearly all of them, as the UK did.[148] Small companies are in principle exempted from the more advanced disclosures required by art.17. However, Member States may choose to apply five of the more advanced disclosures to small companies, but may not impose notes requirements on small companies beyond this level.[149] The UK decided to apply all five additional disclosures to small companies, on the grounds that they were not burdensome and were needed to understand properly the financial position of the company, e.g. material post-balance sheet events.[150] Finally, art.18 (disclosure of turnover by reference to different geographical markets) applies only to large companies and PIEs.[151]

However, the information provided in the notes may reinforce the shareholders' governance rights as well as supplying potentially useful financial information. We have seen that the issue of transactions between companies and those who are in a position to influence the terms of those transactions or their associates is a central regulatory problem in relation to both directors and controlling shareholders. Transactions between directors and their companies are

---

[143] Unless it is a micro company, the company may, but is not required to, put them in a separate document annexed to the accounts: s.472.

[144] The Directive makes no derogation for IAS accounts, but in that case the notes requirements may be found in the international standards themselves rather than in domestic law transposing the Directive.

[145] Much of the information required to be disclosed in notes under Pt 3 of Sch.1 to the Large and Small Accounts Regulations 2008 is of this character.

[146] Above, fn.74. This part of the Regulations is made under ss.409 and 410 of the Act and extends to information about subsidiaries as well as about affiliates.

[147] 2006 Act s.410A, introduced in 2008, in the wake of the Enron collapse in the US which was in part brought about by the acquisition of liabilities by Special Purpose Vehicles ("SPVs") connected with Enron but not counting as its subsidiaries.

[148] The option is provided by art.36(1)(b). It is implemented in the UK in the Small Regulations reg.5A. The matters still required to be disclosed in the notes to micro companies' accounts relate to contingent liabilities and capital commitments: Sch.3 para.57.

[149] 2013 Directive art.16(2) and (3).

[150] BIS, *UK Implementation of the EU Accounting Directive*, August 2014 (BIS/14/1025).

[151] For smaller companies such disclosure might give competitors valuable information which could be used to undermine the company's business.

subject to special rules about disclosure to the board or even shareholder approval,[152] whilst similar transactions by controlling shareholders, though in general less well policed by British company law, may give rise to claims of unfair prejudice.[153] Article 17(1)(r) requires disclosure of information about material related party transactions not concluded under normal market conditions, and this is one of the provisions of art.17 which the UK has applied to small companies.[154] Shareholders reading the notes are thus in a better position to decide whether to seek to invoke their remedies in this area.

NARRATIVE REPORTING

The company's financial statements, naturally, are dominated by numbers. But the annual circulation by the directors to the shareholders includes some predominantly non-numerical documents. This is now conventionally referred to as "narrative reporting". Until about a quarter of a century ago, the only statutorily required narrative report was the directors' report, the content of which was determined largely by the directors themselves. Since then, the mandatory content of narrative reporting has expanded enormously and, as part of that process, further reports have been added to the directors' report. Just as important, the notion of the audience to whom the narrative reports are addressed has expanded. Originally, directors thought of their report as addressed to shareholders and, perhaps, potential investors in the company. Today, it is common to say that the narrative reports are addressed to all "stakeholders" in the company—though the term "stakeholder" is usually undefined and the action which stakeholders might take in response to the information provided left unspecified.[155]

In consequence, the disclosures required are sometimes only indirectly linked to the financial interests of the shareholders.[156] Indeed, in some cases narrative reporting may be intended to induce changes in corporate behaviour which the shareholders might not wish to induce, if left to themselves. Thus, the recent addition of "extractive industry" reporting requires the directors of large companies and PIEs active in those industries to produce an annual report which discloses payments made to foreign governments. The purpose of this

21–22

---

[152] Above, paras 16–54 et seq.

[153] Above, Ch.20.

[154] Small Companies Regulations Sch.1 para.66; Large Companies Regulations Sch.1 para.72. The requirements are applied more stringently to large than medium or small companies. These provisions apply formally only to companies preparing Companies Act accounts, but those preparing IAS accounts are under a similar obligation because of the provisions in IAS 24 (Related Party Disclosures). The two are further tied together by the adoption in paras 66 and 72 of the same definition of "related party" as in the IAS—though unhelpfully it does not reproduce it. IAS 24.9 defines a related party widely so as to include controlling shareholders as well as directors.

[155] A typical statement (in this case from BIS, *The Future of Narrative Reporting: Consultation*, September 2011 (BIS/11/945)) is: "Narrative reporting provides an important link between companies and their investors and wider stakeholders. It is a key element in the framework that allows investors to hold companies to account, both in terms of achieving sustainable long term returns and on the impact of the business to society and the environment." So, reporting is presented as addressed to stakeholders as well as investors, but only investors are mentioned in relation to accountability.

[156] See below, para.21–24.

requirement is so that "we can provide citizens [of foreign countries] with the detailed information they need to hold their governments to account".[157] The implication is that such payments are often bribes to local politicians or senior officials. The shareholders' interests are not placed centre-stage in this case, but rather those of the foreign citizens. Indeed, if because of corruption or lack of democratic process in those countries, no such accountability occurs, the reporting companies will find themselves at a competitive disadvantage as against companies from jurisdictions which do not impose (or effectively enforce) this reporting requirement. If, on the other hand, the foreign citizens are successful, the benefits will accrue mainly to them rather than the company's shareholders.[158] Perhaps for this reason, the Directive and the domestic regulations, whilst requiring the payment report to be made public (through filing at Companies House), do not require it to be laid before the shareholders.[159] Narrative disclosure can thus be used to bolster policies whose drivers are located outside company law, as conventionally conceived.

In this section we consider the various items that contribute to narrative reporting, with the exception of the directors' remuneration report, important though that is. This has been dealt with in Ch.14[160] and need not be further considered here.

Directors' report

21–23   The directors' report ("DR"), to accompany both the individual and group accounts, has long been a statutory requirement in the UK. However there is no longer a requirement for micro companies to produce a directors' report[161] and small companies benefit from a lower disclosure regime.[162]

The statute requires the report to contain some fairly straightforward information, for example, a list of those who were directors of the company at any time during the year.[163] It must also state the amount the directors recommend to be paid by way of dividend to the shareholders.[164] However, this latter requirement does not apply to companies entitled to the "small company exemption". Presumably, this is because in small companies public disclosure of dividend recommendations may reveal the income of easily identifiable individuals, for example, where the directors are the only shareholders. This exemption is available not only to small companies falling within the small

---

[157] BIS, *UK Implementation of the EU Accounting Directive, Chapter 10: Consultation*, March 2014, p.4 (BIS/14/622).

[158] On the assumption that bribes do not increase the overall costs of the company but rather are recovered by a lower formal contractual payment to the foreign government. There may be some marginal gains to the company from operating in countries which have less corruption.

[159] See the Reports on Payments to Government Regulations 2014/3209, implementing Ch.10 of the Directive.

[160] At paras 14–44 et seq.

[161] 2006 Act s.415(1A).

[162] 2006 Act s.415A and contrast Sch.5 to the Small Companies Regulations with Sch.7 to the Large Companies Regulations.

[163] 2006 Act s.416(1).

[164] 2006 Act s.416(3).

companies regime for the accounts but also to small companies which would so fall but for the fact that they are members of a group of companies which contains an ineligible member.[165] Thus, the relaxations for small companies in relation to the DR go somewhat wider than in relation to the accounts. More generally, the DR must state any important events which have affected the company since the end of the financial year and indicate the likely future development of its business.[166]

None of the above is very demanding. However, when one turns from the Act to Sch.7 of the Large Companies Regulations, one finds a number of disclosure requirements which are not closely related to the financial interests of the shareholders.[167] Thus Pt 3 requires information to be given about the employment, training and promotion of disabled persons.[168] Part 4 requires information about "employee involvement", i.e. the extent to which employees are systematically given information, consulted, and encouraged to join employee share schemes. Part 7 requires traded companies[169] to disclose their greenhouse gas emissions. These provisions seek to co-opt large companies to support (usually laudable) non-corporate policies which the government is pursuing.

Even the requirement in Pt 1 for separate disclosure of the amounts of political donations is not generally necessary to form a view on the financial position of large companies in view of the minimal amounts needed to trigger this requirement and the modest amounts normally donated. However, this disclosure clearly facilitates the operation of the controls over political donations laid down in Pt 14 of the Act.[170] One can say the same of the buy-back disclosures required in Pt 2, which reinforce the rules in Pt 18 of the Act. One might even take the same view of Pt 6 of the Schedule, implementing for traded companies art.10 of the Takeover Directive on the disclosure of a company's control structures.[171] Such disclosures facilitate takeover bids.

The strategic report

Rationale and history

Section 414A requires all companies, other than those benefiting from the small companies regime,[172] to produce an annual strategic report ("SR"). The requirement for a SR reflects the perception that shareholders and investors need more than financial data to understand fully the prospects of the company. They need also to be able to gauge the quality of the company's relationships with

21–24

---

[165] 2006 Act s.415A. For the meaning of "ineligible" companies see above, para.21–4.

[166] Large Companies Regulations Sch.7 para.7.

[167] This information may be laid out in the strategic report (below) instead.

[168] This disclosure and disclosure of political donations are required also of small companies: Small Companies Regulations Sch.5.

[169] See para.21–6, above.

[170] See para.17–29, above. Until recently the amount of charitable donations had to be stated as well.

[171] See para.28–25, below.

[172] The requirements are relaxed for medium-sized companies, but not excluded entirely. A small company excluded from the small company regime because a member of an ineligible group may also take advantage of this exemption: s.414B.

those upon whose contributions or cooperation the success of the company depends (sometimes called "stakeholders"). For stakeholders, as well, this information may be useful, even if company law itself gives them no particular platform from which to take action on the basis of the information.[173] As the CLR put it, "companies are increasingly reliant on qualitative and intangible assets such as the skills and knowledge of their employees, their business relationships and their reputation. Information about future plans, opportunities, risks and strategies is just as important as the historical review of performance which forms the basis of reporting at present".[174]

The second argument for a broader review of the company by the directors was the need to provide a check on the discharge by directors of their "inclusive" duty[175] to promote the success of the company for the benefit of its members but on the basis of taking into account the company's need to foster its relationships with stakeholders, its impact upon communities affected and environmental and reputational concerns. This duty is specifically referred to in s.414C(1). Thus, there was a close link between the shareholder-centred statement of directors' duties recommended by the CLR and the desire to provide some mechanism whereby its "enlightened" elements meant something significant in practice and were not just self-serving.

Despite broad agreement on these principles, producing a steady-state set of rules to implement them proved surprisingly controversial. There have been three iterations of the rules, which have come close to going around in a circle. The first set of rules was recommended by the CLR under the name of an Operating and Financial Review. At first, all seemed to be going well with the OFR proposal. In fact, it was introduced by regulation in 2005 under powers contained in the Companies Act 1985 in advance of the enactment of the 2006 Act,[176] after extensive consultation among those affected.[177] Whilst the companies affected were preparing their first OFRs, the then Chancellor of the Exchequer, in a speech to the Confederation of British Industry,[178] and apparently after exiguous consultation with the Department of Trade and Industry (the then name of the governmental department responsible for company law),[179] announced the repeal[180] of the OFR on the grounds it was "a gold-plated regulatory requirement"—but without showing any appreciation of its place in the wider scheme of reforms proposed by the CLR. The DTI, re-stating its commitment to

---

[173] Trade unions might use the information in collective bargaining with the company or they and other stakeholders might use it in making representations to government or taking other sorts of political action.

[174] Final Report I, para.3.33.

[175] See above at paras 16–37 et seq.

[176] Companies Act 1985 (Operating and Financial Review and Directors' Report etc.) Regulations 2005 (SI 2005/1011).

[177] DTI, *The Operating and Financial Review and Directors' Report: A Consultative Document*, May 2004 (URN 04/1003).

[178] Speech by the Rt. Hon. Gordon Brown MP, Chancellor of the Exchequer, at the CBI Annual Conference in London, 28 November 2005.

[179] Somewhat more is known about the internal workings of government on this issue than might be expected as a result of documents produced in judicial review proceedings brought by Friends of the Earth over the abolition decision. See *Financial Times*, UK Edition, 8 March 2006.

[180] Effected by the Companies Act 1985 (Operating and Financial Review) (Repeal) Regulations 2005 (SI 2005/3442).

"strategic forward-looking narrative reporting", then undertook consultation on how far this commitment could be implemented within what it called a Business Review requirement without imposing on companies "unnecessary burdens". However, the coalition agreement of the government which took office in 2010 included a commitment to "reinstate" the OFR. The implementation of that commitment gave us the current strategic review. In the meantime, the EU legislature became more involved in the area. The "management report" (in effect a DR) required by arts 19 and 29 of the Directive (for individual and group accounts respectively) contains some non-financial requirements and in 2014 those requirements were strengthened by an amending Directive, adding arts 19a and 29a to the 2013 Directive.[181]

Contents of the Strategic Review

Section 414C states that the purpose of the SR is to "inform members of the company" and to help them assess whether the directors have performed their duty under s.172 of the Act to promote the success of the company for the benefit of its members.[182] Although placing the emphasis on the members ties in well with the shareholder-centred focus of s.172, the CLR proposed that the OFR should not be so narrowly targeted.[183] Section 414C(2) requires the directors to produce a SR containing a fair review of the company's business and a description of the principal risks and uncertainties facing it—or them in the case of group accounts.[184] The review required is "a balanced and comprehensive" analysis of the development and performance of the company's business during the financial year and of its position at the end of the year.[185] To the extent that it is necessary for an understanding of the business the review must make use of "key performance indicators", both financial and non-financial.[186] This is an attempt to inject some quantitative analysis into what might otherwise be a set of generalities. These parts of the section simply track art.19(1) the Directive, whose requirements are indeed rather general.

21–25

For quoted companies[187] the SR must deal with further matters, largely as a matter of domestic law. At the most general level, the company is required to describe its strategy and its business model.[188] Then the SR must address "to the extent necessary for an understanding" of the company's business[189]—with KPIs

---

[181] Directive 2014/95/EU [2014] O.J. L330/1.
[182] Above at para.16–37.
[183] Completing, para.3.33. Thus, non-shareholders would have been included among the addresses of the OFR.
[184] 2006 Act s.414C(13).
[185] 2006 Act s.414C(3).
[186] 2006 Act s.414C(4)(5), unless the company qualifies as medium-sized, or would do were it not for the fact that it is a member of an ineligible group, in which case it need not use KPIs in relation to non-financial matters: ss.414C(6) and 467(4).
[187] 2006 Act s.385. This definition includes not only companies included on the "official list" in an EU state (see para.25–9) but also those UK-incorporated companies traded on the New York Stock Exchange or Nasdaq. Nevertheless, this is a narrower set than proposed by the CLR which wished to apply the OFR requirement to most public and some large private companies as well.
[188] 2006 Act s.414C(8)(a)(b).
[189] 2006 Act s.414C(7).

where necessary—certain specific issues. The phrase in quotes does not give the directors a discretion whether to deal with a matter: it simply recognises that not all the additional matters will be relevant to the businesses of all companies, though few will not have to comment, for example, on the employees. The list of additional matters potentially to be commented on is:

(a) "the main trends and factors" likely to affect the future of the company's business;
(b) the impact of the company's business on the environment;
(c) the employees;
(d) social, community and human rights issues.[190]

Finally, whether or not this is necessary to an understanding of the company's business, the SR must disclose the number of persons of each sex who were (i) directors; (ii) senior managers; and (iii) employees of the company. This is an example of disclosure being used to promote the government's diversity policies, this time at senior levels in companies. The amending Directive of 2014, operative from January 2017, requires some expansion of the additional information to be provided by public interest entities employing on average 500 employees over the financial year, but it will not bring any novel departures from the existing categories of additional disclosure. At the time of writing the government is consulting on the potentially significant move of confining all the additional elements of SR reporting to companies with this number of employees.[191]

None of these provisions requires disclosure of impending developments or matters in the course of negotiation if, in the directors' opinion, disclosure would be seriously prejudicial to the interests of the company.[192] Matters of strategic significance which are required by regulation to be included in the DR may be included instead, at the directors' choice, in the SR, a move likely to make discussion of strategic issues more coherent.[193]

Verification of narrative reports

21–26   There is a risk that narrative reporting requirements will produce only self-serving and vacuous descriptions rather than analytical material which is of genuine use to those who read the report. There are two traditional ways of dealing with this issue in relation to financial statements: audit and accounting

---

[190] The BR required information about supply chains and out-sourcing arrangements (s.417(5)(c)). This was highly controversial because it was introduced only at a very late stage in Parliament, though it had been part of the OFR. It has not made its way into the SR.

[191] BIS, *The Non-Financial Reporting Directive*, BIS/16/35, February 2016. Since companies traded on a regulated market fall within the definitions of both "quoted company" and "public interest entity", the main impact of the change would be to remove the higher level reporting requirement from quoted companies with fewer than 500 employees. The consultation document also floats the proposal to allow some of the non-financial reporting to be released on a more relaxed time-table than that for the annual accounts.

[192] 2006 Act s.414C(14).

[193] 2006 Act s.414C(11).

standards. The risk with applying audit to the DR and SR is that it will take away from the desirability of those reports constituting the directors' view of the business rather than that of its auditors. Consequently, the Act formerly restricted the audit requirement for the DR and SR to certification that the reports were consistent with the accounts (which are required to be audited). Under the current version of the Act[194] the auditor must state in addition whether he has identified material misstatements in the SR or DR (and describe their nature) in the light of the knowledge of the company acquired in the course of the audit.

The auditor must also state whether the SR and DR have been prepared in accordance with "applicable legal requirements". This phrase obviously covers statutory provisions but it also raises the question whether there are professional standards for these reports just as there are for the financial statements. The OFR Regulations in fact contained the familiar requirement from the accounts provisions that the Review must state whether it had been prepared in accordance with the relevant reporting standard and give reasons for any departure[195]; and a "reporting standard" was defined, as with an accounting standard, as a "statement of standard reporting practice" relating to OFRs and issued by a body authorised by the Secretary of State, i.e. (then) the Accounting Standards Board.[196] The ASB duly produced its reporting standard (RS 1) in May 2005. However, the Business Review provisions contained no statutory underpinning for reporting standards and so the ASB turned RS 1 into Reporting Statement of best practice, changing its language so as to reflect its new voluntary status, and that situation has continued with the SR.[197]

Liability for misstatements in narrative reports

An alternative approach to verification is to impose liability ex post for misstatements in narrative reports. There are two areas of potential negligence liability to be considered. First, there is liability on the part of the directors to the company under what is now s.174 of the Act. Secondly, there is liability on the part of the directors or the company (and conceivably others) to third parties, including investors in the market, under the general law on misstatements, whether negligent or fraudulent. However, the extension of narrative reporting prompted reforms, now to be found in s.463, whose aim is not to strengthen the ex post liability regime but to circumscribe it. The case for providing a "safe harbour" in relation to directors' forward-looking statements is that no one can predict the future with certainty and if directors were to be exposed to litigation, or the threat of it, whenever their forward-looking statements turned out to be untrue, they would be very cautious in the statements they made This caution might undermine the value of narrative reporting to its users.[198]

21–27

---

[194] 2006 Act s.496. This tracks art.35 of the Directive. The expanded audit requirement is more in line with what the CLR proposed: Final Report I, para.8.63.

[195] OFR Regulations reg.8.

[196] OFR Regulations reg.11.

[197] FRC, *Guidance on the Strategic Report*, June 2014. The question of developing reporting standards for the DR seems never to have been actively pursued.

[198] CLR, Final Report I, para.8.38.

Section 463, in fact, goes well beyond forward-looking statements, apparently on the grounds that it would be difficult to distinguish them from other types of statement. The section applies to the entire content of the three narrative reports: DR, SR and the directors' remuneration report.[199] The effect of s.463 is to exclude directors' liability in negligence to the company entirely. The director is so liable in respect of untrue or misleading statements in the reports or omissions from them only if the director has been fraudulent.[200] Fraud is defined in the way it is in the common law of deceit: the maker of the statement must know it is untrue or misleading or be reckless as to whether this is the case.[201] Thus, a genuine belief in the truth of the statement, no matter how unreasonable, will save the director from liability.

21–28   If the directors' liability to the company is preserved in the case of fraud, their liability to other persons is excluded entirely, even in the case of fraud.[202] Moreover, the liability which is excluded is the liability of "any person", not just of the directors, provided it is not a liability to the company. Thus, investors (including existing shareholders) cannot impose liability on the company in respect of unsuccessful investment decisions which are based on inaccurate information in the narrative reports. It is in fact very unclear whether, even without the section, liability in negligence towards investors on the part of the company or the directors would exist under the general law. The issue has been tested at the highest levels only in respect of auditors, where, as we shall see, the starting point of the courts is one of non-liability.[203] The exclusion of liability towards third parties in the case of fraud in narrative reports is more questionable, since the common law does impose liability in principle for fraud and it is unclear why fraud should be condoned. In fact, however, the exclusion of liability to third parties is qualified by the provisions of s.90A of and Sch.10A to FSMA 2000, applying to companies with securities traded on a regulated market, which imposes liability in fraud on the company in relation to certain statements made to the market (which might include the narrative reports).[204]

Section 463 excludes the third-party liability of "any person", but it is not clear who might be liable beyond the directors and the company in respect of errors in the narrative reports. A number of professionals may be consulted and have a hand in the compilation of the reports but they are not normally identified in those reports as responsible for particular parts of it and thus as having particular statements attributed to them, since the reports are the reports of the directors. However, if this did occur, s.463 would protect these persons (other

---

[199] 2006 Act s.463(1). The inclusion of the remuneration report is particularly bizarre, since it requires statements of policies but very little in the way of forward-looking statements. See paras 14–44 et seq.

[200] 2006 Act s.463(2),(3). The liability excluded is only the liability to compensate the company, though it will be rare for any other liability to be in issue.

[201] Recklessness means making the statement not caring whether it is true or untrue, accurate or misleading: *Derry v Peek* (1889) L.R. 14 App. Cas. 337 HL. In the case of omissions there must be "a dishonest concealment of a material fact".

[202] 2006 Act s.463(4),(5). The liability here excluded is not confined to liability to compensate but embraces any civil remedy, including self-help remedies.

[203] See para.22–44.

[204] See below at para.26–25.

than in respect of their liability to the company). The auditors are required to report on the narrative reports to some extent, as we have seen, but the auditor's report is a separate document and so would not be covered by s.463.

APPROVAL OF THE ACCOUNTS AND REPORTS BY THE DIRECTORS

That the narrative reports are the reports of the directors is clear.[205] The accounts as well are the product of the directors: the directors must draw them up,[206] although in this case, because of the role played by the auditors in verifying the accounts and, in practice, in drawing them up, they are often misconceived as the auditors' accounts. With the collapse of the Enron Company and other companies renewed emphasis was placed on the directors' responsibility for the accounts. At EU level the Fourth and Seventh Directives were amended so as to impose on directors a "collective duty" to ensure that the annual financial statements and management report are drawn up in accordance with the Directive or the IAS Regulation.[207] The Government took the view that this requirement was met by the existing domestic provision that the annual accounts and narrative reports must be approved by the directors and signed on behalf of the board by a director or the secretary.[208] If the directors approve accounts or reports that do not comply with the Act, every director who knows that they do not comply or is reckless as to whether or not they comply and who fails to take reasonable steps to secure compliance or to prevent the accounts being approved is guilty of an offence.[209]

21–29

The Member States are also required to ensure that their "laws, regulations and administrative provisions on liability" to the company apply to the directors who breach their collective duty.[210] This provision does not require the Member States to have any particular liability regime in place. In the case of the UK this requirement is met presumably through the general law on directors' duties and, in the case of the narrative reports, by the preservation of the directors' liability in fraud to the company.[211]

THE AUDITOR'S REPORT

The final document that has to accompany the annual accounts is the auditor's report thereon—assuming the company is one which is required to have its accounts audited or has chosen to do so. This has to be addressed to the company's members[212] and to state whether in the auditors' opinion on a number

21–30

---

[205] See ss.414A, 415 and 420: directors' duties to prepare narrative reports.

[206] 2006 Act ss.394 and 399.

[207] Now art.33 of the Directive.

[208] 2006 Act ss.414(1), 414D(1) and 419(1). Section 419A imposes the same duty in relation to the corporate governance report, if it is a separate document, but lays down no specific penalties for non-compliance.

[209] 2006 Act s.414(4),(5), 414D(2)(3) and 419(3)(4). This re-states the previous law somewhat more simply by dropping the requirement that the director be a party to the approval and presuming the existing directors to be parties.

[210] 2013 Directive art.33(2).

[211] See above, para.21–27.

[212] 2006 Act s.495(1).

of matters, notably whether the annual accounts have been properly prepared in accordance with the Act or the IAS Regulation, as appropriate and whether they give a true and fair view of the company's financial position.[213] The rights and duties of the auditor in the preparation of the audit report are considered more fully in the following chapter. The auditors' report must state the names of the auditors and be signed by them.[214] However, those names need not appear on the published copies of the report or on the copy filed with the Registrar (see below) if the company has resolved that the names should not be stated on basis that there are reasonable grounds for thinking that publication would create a serious risk of violence to or intimidation of the auditor or any other person, and has provided that information instead to the Secretary of State.[215]

REVISION OF DEFECTIVE ACCOUNTS AND REPORTS

21–31   Despite the requirements for director and auditor approval, noted above, it is not inconceivable that accounts and reports will be produced by the company which are later discovered to be incorrect. Until the passing of the Companies Act 1989 there were no statutory provisions for revising incorrect accounts and reports. However, it has never been doubted that, if directors discover such defects, they can, and should, correct them. Section 454 makes it clear that the directors may revise the accounts and narrative reports on a voluntary basis. Where the accounts have not yet been sent to the Registrar or the members (see below), the directors have a pretty free hand as to revisions, but if either of those events has occurred, as is likely, the corrections must be confined to what is necessary to bring the accounts and reports into line with the requirements of the Act or the IAS Regulation.[216] Regulations made under the section provide that the revised accounts or reports become, as nearly as possible, the reports and accounts of the company for the relevant financial year, to which the other provisions of the Act apply. For example, they will be subject to audit.[217]

More significant are the statutory powers to compel revision of defective accounts. The Secretary of State has power to apply to the court for a declaration that the accounts or the DR or SR (but not, it seems, the remuneration report) do not comply with the Act or the IAS Regulation and for an order that they be brought into line, with consequential directions.[218] The court may order the costs of the application and of the production of the revised accounts to be borne by the directors in place at the time of the approval of the accounts or report, unless a director can show that he or she took all reasonable steps to prevent approval, though the court also has power to exclude from liability a director who did not

---

[213] See para.22–3 for more detail.

[214] 2006 Act s.503.

[215] 2006 Act s.506. The reasons for this measure or secrecy in relation to the auditors are the same as those which led to the suppression of public information about directors' residential addresses: see above at para.14–23.

[216] 2006 Act s.454(2).

[217] Companies (Revision of Defective Accounts and Reports) Regulations 2008/373 (as amended).

[218] 2006 Act s.456(1)–(3).

know and ought not to have known of the defects.[219] Notice of the application and of its result must be given to the Registrar.[220]

However, in practice this is not an activity the Secretary of State undertakes. There is power under s.457 for authorisation to make applications to the court to be conferred upon persons appearing to the Secretary of State "to have an interest in, and to have satisfactory procedures directed to securing, compliance by companies" with the Act and the IAS Regulation and "to have satisfactory procedures for receiving and investigating complaints" about annual accounts and the DR and SR and otherwise to be "fit and proper". Such authorisation is now conferred on the Conduct Committee of the Financial Reporting Council ("FRC").[221] In practice, the task of dealing with defective reports is discharged by the Conduct Committee, rather than by the Department, except in relation to small companies.[222] The Committee has statutory authority to require the production of documents, information and explanations if it thinks there is a question-mark over the compliance of a company's accounts or reports with the Act or IAS Regulation.[223] It must keep the information received confidential, except for disclosure to a list of approved recipients (relevant Government Departments and Regulators).[224]

The FRRP, predecessor of the Conduct Committee, was criticised for being reactive, i.e. acting only on complaints or media revelations that a particular set of accounts was defective rather than checking or investigating of its own motion. Partly because of EU pressure to produce equivalent mechanisms in the Member States for the enforcement of international accounting standards, the FRRP agreed in 2002 to adopt a proactive review policy,[225] though it did not have to resort to a court order to secure the necessary changes, a threat of an application being enough. In 2014/15 the Conduct Committee reviewed the reports of some 252 companies, sent letters raising queries to 76, and in nine cases there was a restatement of the numbers in the accounts or a significant change in disclosure policy.[226]

21–32

With regard to companies with securities traded on a regulated market, the obligation to secure compliance with the periodic reporting requirements of such companies (which include but extend beyond the annual reports and accounts)[227] is allocated by EU law to the Financial Conduct Authority ("FCA"), but the

---

[219] 2006 Act s.456(5)–(6).

[220] 2006 Act s.456(2)–(7).

[221] Supervision of Accounts and Reports (Prescribed Body) and Companies (Defective Accounts and Directors' Reports)(Authorised Person) Order 2012/1439 reg.4. Previously, the task was delegated to the Financial Reporting Review Panel.

[222] Where Companies House takes the lead: CLR, Completing, para.12.48.

[223] 2006 Act s.459.

[224] 2006 Act ss.460–462.

[225] DTI, *Final Report of the Co-ordinating Group on Audit and Accounting Issues*, URN 03/567, paras 4.11 et seq. Such a policy, including the identification of "priority sectors" for review, has been developed and since 2006 the FRRP included the directors' report, and so the business review, in its activities.

[226] FRC *Corporate Reporting Review 2014*, pp.7–9. The restatement occurs in the following year's accounts.

[227] These requirements are discussed in Ch.26, below.

relevant Directive permits the FCA to delegate the tasks conferred upon it.[228] Accordingly, the Conduct Committee has been authorised[229] by the Secretary of State to keep under review not only the accounts and reports required by the Act but also those required under the provisions of the Transparency Directive to be produced by companies whose securities are traded on regulated markets. In this case, there is an obvious need for close liaison with the FCA.[230] The Conduct Committee is under a duty to report its findings to the FCA in appropriate cases and the FCA may expand the Conduct Committee's remit.[231]

FILING ACCOUNTS AND REPORTS WITH THE REGISTRAR

21-33 The statutory requirement to produce accounts and reports would be of little use if there were no provisions for the information so generated to reach the hands of those who might make use of it. This is done in two ways under the Act: circulation to the members (discussed below) and delivery of the accounts to the Registrar.[232] By delivery to the Registrar, the accounts and reports become public documents.

Speed of filing

21-34 A source of complaint in the past has been the length of the gap between the end of the financial year and the date laid down for filing the accounts and reports with the Registrar. The CLR thought that modern technology permitted speedier filing than had been required in the past and recommended that the period be reduced from seven to six months for public companies and ten to seven for private companies.[233] Section 442 implements the former reform but only marginally reduces the private company period (to nine months), which is a pity.[234] For public companies whose securities are traded on a regulated market[235] the period for publication of the annual accounts and reports is four months from the end of the financial year,[236] though the core elements in the accounts may have been made available earlier through a preliminary public announcement of the results.

---

[228] Directive 2004/109/EC art.24 (the Transparency Directive).

[229] See fn.221, made in part under s.14 of the Companies (Audit, Investigations and Community Enterprise) Act 2004. The tests laid down in s.14 of the 2004 Act are similar to those contained in s.457 of the 2006 Act.

[230] The FRRP concluded a "memorandum of understanding" with the FSA in 2005 about their joint working, which is available on the FRRP website. Indeed, there was some debate at the time as to whether these powers should not be retained by the FCA.

[231] 2006 Act s.14(2),(7). The Conduct Committee's power to apply for a court order appears to be limited to annual accounts and reports only (s.456(1)), so that it would fall to the FCA to take action in respect of the semi-annual reports required of companies on regulated markets.

[232] 2004 Act s.441.

[233] CLR, Final Report I, paras 4.49–4.32 and 8.80 et seq.

[234] 2006 Act s.442 deals with some exceptional cases as well.

[235] See para.25–8, essentially those traded on the Main Market of the London Stock Exchange.

[236] See FCA, Disclosure and Transparency Rule 4.1.3, implementing art.4 of the Transparency Directive 2004/109/EC. See Ch.26, below.

A linked source of complaint has been non-compliance with the filing time-limits, though the UK's record in this area is superior to that of some Member States of the EU. The formal sanctions are criminal liabilities on the directors and civil penalties on the company. If the filing requirements are not complied with on time, any person who was a director immediately before the end of the time allowed is liable to a fine and, for continued contravention, to a daily default fine, unless the director can prove that he took all reasonable steps for securing that the accounts were delivered in time.[237] Furthermore, if the directors fail to make good the default within 14 days after the service of a notice requiring compliance, the court, on the application of the Registrar or any member or creditor of the company, may make an order directing the directors or any of them to make good the default within such time as may be specified and may order them to pay the costs of and incidental to the application.[238]

To these criminal sanctions against directors, the Act adds civil penalties against the company.[239] The amount of the penalty, recoverable by the Registrar, varies according to whether the company is private or public and to the length of time that the default continues; the minimum being £150 for a private company and £750 for a public company when the default is for not more than one month, and the maximum £1,500 for a private and £7,500 for a public company when the default exceeds six months.[240] There are obvious attractions in affording the Registrar an additional weapon in the form of a penalty recoverable by civil suit to which there is no defence once it is shown that accounts have not been delivered on time. Presumably, the thought is that civil sanctions on the company will put pressure on shareholders to intervene and secure compliance on the part of the directors, but it is not clear how effective this mechanism is. It may be that the shareholders simply lose dividends as well as suffer from a failure on the part of the directors to perform a duty intended to protect them.[241] In 2014/15 the compliance rate was nearly 99 per cent across the UK but nevertheless some 2,100 convictions for failure to file accounts were obtained and late filing penalty worth over £81 million were issued (mainly in relation to private companies), but it is not clear how much was collected.[242]

---

[237] 2006 Act s.451. But, to spike the guns of barrack-room lawyers, it is expressly stated that it is not a defence to prove that the documents required were not in fact prepared in accordance with the Act!

[238] 2006 Act s.452. If they fail to do so, they will be in contempt of court and liable to imprisonment. The subsection does not say who may serve such a notice so presumably anyone can: but in practice it is likely to be the Registrar who does so—though the subsection makes it pretty clear that a member or creditor could.

[239] 2006 Act s.453 and the Companies (Late Filing Penalties) and Limited Liability Partnerships (Filing Periods and Late Filing Penalties) Regulations 2008/497.

[240] The Scheme withstood judicial review in R. (Pow Trust) v Registrar of Companies [2003] 2 B.C.L.C. 295.

[241] The company could, presumably, sue the directors to recover its loss resulting from their default. But unless the company goes into liquidation, administration or receivership this is unlikely to happen.

[242] Companies House, Statistical Tables on Companies Registration Activities 2014/15, Tables A7, A8 and D2. Curiously, late filing does not appear to be prosecuted in Scotland.

Modifications of the full filing requirements

21–35   Filing with the Registrar is such a sensitive issue precisely because the information in the accounts and reports thus becomes publicly available. The Act itself makes some concessions to the fear of publicity in the case of small, medium-sized and unlimited companies, by way of derogations from the full filing regime. The full regime requires filing of the annual accounts, the directors' report, the strategic report and (in the case of a quoted company) the directors' remuneration report and conceivably a corporate governance statement, and the auditor's report on those accounts and reports (assuming the company is subject to audit).[243] If the company has been required to produce group accounts, then the full regime applies to both the group and individual accounts.[244] The balance sheet must contain the name of the person who signed it on behalf of the board.[245] As we have noted along the way, some categories of company are not required to produce the full range of these accounts and reports, especially small and micro companies. Naturally, they are not required to file a document they are not required to produce. The issue here is whether directors are required to give publicity to, i.e. file or file in full, a document they are required to produce for their shareholders.

21–36   Unlimited companies are in principle exempt from filing any accounts and reports, provided the unlimited company is not part of a group containing limited companies and is not a banking or insurance company.[246] This is a good example of the link between limited liability and public financial disclosure, i.e. the latter is dispensed with if the former is not present.[247] Of course, the unlimited liability company still has to produce and circulate accounts to the members, who have perhaps an even bigger interest in the proper running of the company if their liability is unlimited.

Small companies (and thus also micro companies) subject to the small company regime are required to produce only individual accounts and, in addition, they may choose to file only a balance sheet and not the profit and loss account and directors' report though they may make more publicly available, if they wish.[248] Until recently, there was a further relaxation for small companies in that the filed copy of the balance sheet (and the filed copy of the profit and loss account, if one was filed at all) were permitted to be less detailed than the accounts made available to the members, at least where the company produces Companies Act accounts. These were the so-called "abbreviated" accounts.[249]

---

[243] 2006 Act ss.446 and 447.

[244] 2006 Act s.471.

[245] See above, para.21–30.

[246] 2006 Act s.448. There are certain other disqualifications set out in the section.

[247] The same distinction can be found between partnerships (accounts need not be made public) and limited liability partnerships (public disclosure required).

[248] 2006 Act s.444(1). On the exemption from group accounts see para.21–9. Small companies excluded from the small companies regime because a member of an ineligible group may choose not to file a directors' report, but must file a profit and loss account: s.444A.

[249] 2006 Act s.444(3)—as originally enacted.

However, in 2015 changes were made which withdrew this facility.[250] The CLR would have required small companies to file both balance sheet and profit and loss account as prepared for the members. It took the view that the filed accounts of small companies were "not meaningful".[251] The general conclusion that little insight into the financial position of a company subject to the small company regime will normally be obtained from consulting its filed accounts probably remains true, given that the option not to file a profit and loss account is still available.

Other information available from the Registrar

The annual accounts and reports are probably the most important documents filed with the Registrar[252] and thus made public, because they give reasonably current (though by no means completely up-to-date) information about the company's financial position.[253] However, the accounts and reports do not constitute the whole of the information about the company which is publicly available from the Registrar, as we see at various points in this work. The next most important document thus made available is probably the company's constitution, mainly its articles of association.[254] After that is the list of the company's directors, which must be updated as changes occur.[255] Amongst the other information available through the Registrar are the list of those with significant economic interests in the company,[256] the address of its registered office,[257] the amount of its issued share capital[258] and details of charges on its property.[259]

21–37

---

[250] Companies, Partnerships and Groups (Accounts and Reports) Regulations 2015/980 reg.8. This step was less radical than it might seem at first sight, since a small company may prepare (and therefore publish) abbreviated accounts if all shareholders agree (see para.21–20) and, even if they do not, the disclosure requirements of the Small Regulations are much less demanding than those of the Large Regulations. These regulations also removed the facility for medium-sized companies to file an abbreviated profit and loss account (previously in s.445(3)(4)).

[251] CLR, Developing, paras 8.32–8.34. Although using the term "abbreviated accounts", the CLR appears to include in it the option not to file a profit and loss account at all. The CLR would have dealt with small company sensitivities through the simplified format rules for the accounts prepared for the members.

[252] Actually, there are three Registrars—one for each of the UK jurisdictions—though their functions are similar: s.1060.

[253] Hence with companies whose securities are traded on a regulated market the obligation on the company (a) to produce reports more often than annually and (b) to report material changes as they occur. See Ch.26, below.

[254] See para.3–13.

[255] See para.14–23. Also to be disclosed is the identity of the company's secretary, if there is one: s.276.

[256] See para.2–42.

[257] See ss.9(5)(a) and 86–87. This is important because it is there that legal process can be served on it.

[258] See para.11–11. The returns of allotments will show to whom the shares were initially issued but not who now owns them.

[259] See Ch.32. This is likely to be more up-to-date than the filed accounts and so a better indicator of creditworthiness.

"Any person" has the right to inspect the register maintained by the Registrar, subject to certain limited limitations imposed in the interests of privacy.[260] There is also a right to obtain a copy of material on the register, subject to a fee,[261] and a copy duly certified by the Registrar is evidence in legal proceedings of equal validity to the original.[262] The applicant has the choice in relation to the most central items of information to make the request for inspection or copy electronically or in hard copy, and to receive the information in either way.[263]

Confirmation statement

21–38   This document used to be called the "annual return" until the current term was substituted by the Small Business, Enterprise and Employment Act 2015. As the former name suggested, the confirmation statement is produced each year by the company. It is delivered to the Registrar by the company,[264] but, unlike the accounts and reports considered above, it is not a document sent to the members. The Registrar is the principal addressee of the annual return[265] (though, of course, any member may access it under the provisions discussed in the previous paragraph). Nevertheless it is convenient to consider it here. Moreover, it is a document required to be submitted by every company, whatever its obligations as to accounts and reports.

The 2015 Act reduced the significance of the previous annual return, which was already a rather historical document. The annual return collated much information that should have been, and probably had been, delivered to the Registrar when the relevant transactions occurred, so that an enquirer might find it unnecessary to search back beyond the latest annual return on the file. Since the annual return was often reduplicative of information already provided, the advantage to the company of the confirmation statement is that it simply requires the company to confirm to the Registrar that the information which the company is under a duty to supply to the Registrar has already been provided or is being provided along with the confirmation statement. In the first case, the statement will be a bare confirmation statement. Since we have noted at the appropriate points in the book when information must be supplied by the company to the Registrar, such as the statement of capital or the statement of persons with significant control, we need not rehearse those matters again here. With the 2015 reform, the confirmation statement ceases to be a significant piece of disclosure by the company and its main function is to jog the corporate memory about its filing obligations. Despite the criminal sanctions[266] for non-compliance with the

---

[260] See ss.1085 and 1087, the latter excluding access, for example, to directors' residential addresses (see para.14–23).

[261] 2006 Act s.1086.

[262] 2006 Act s.1091(3).

[263] 2006 Act ss.1089 and 1090. The information in relation to which this right exists is set out in s.1078, which implements art.3 of the First Company Law Directive (68/151/EEC) as amended by Directive 2003/58/EC art.1.

[264] 2006 Act s.853A. The return date is normally the anniversary of the company's incorporation.

[265] Hence the provisions about the confirmation statement are set out in a separate Part of the Act (Pt 24).

[266] 2006 Act s.853L: offence by company, every director, shadow director and secretary, and every other officer who is in default. Compliance with the annual return requirement was about one

obligation to provide a confirmation statement and provision by the Registrar of electronic means for submitting it, companies are not always prompt in complying with this obligation. In fact, failure to file the annual return (or, in future, the confirmation statement) often alerts the Registrar to more fundamental issues with the company and may lead to the taking of steps which culminate in the company's removal from the register.

Other forms of publicity for the accounts and reports

Although filing with the Registrar is the only form of publicity for the annual accounts and reports mandated for all companies by the Act, in fact large companies often, and other companies sometimes, make their annual statements available more generally; and quoted companies are now required to provide website publication.[267] Where a company chooses to make its annual statements available in a way which is calculated to invite members of the public generally, or a class of them, to read it, then the Act requires the name of the person who signed the balance sheet or the narrative reports on behalf of the company to be stated.[268] If a company publishes its accounts in this way, they must be accompanied by the auditor's report (if there is one) and a company preparing group accounts cannot publish only its individual accounts.[269] In short, a non-quoted company is not required to publish its annual accounts other than via the Registrar, but if it does so, it must do so in full.

21–39

The accounts described above are known as the company's "statutory accounts". A company is not prohibited from publishing other accounts dealing with the relevant financial year, thought this is in fact rare. If the company does so, it must include with them a statement that these accounts are not the statutory accounts and disclose whether the statutory accounts have been filed and whether the auditors have reported on them and, if so, whether the auditors' report was qualified. Nor may an auditors' report on the statutory accounts be published with the non-statutory accounts.[270] If the company is listed on a regulated market in the EU, it will be required by the Transparency Directive[271] to produce a set of (less elaborate) accounts and a management report six months into the financial year, as well as annual ones, though such accounts do not fall into the category of "non-statutory accounts" because they do not cover an entire financial year.

---

percentage point less than for the accounts filing requirement. Some 1,200 directors were convicted of this offence in 2014/15 in England and Wales: above fn.242, Tables A7 and D2.

[267] 2006 Act s.430 and para.21–40.
[268] 2006 Act ss.433 and 436.
[269] 2006 Act s.434.
[270] 2006 Act s.435.
[271] See Ch.26, below. This aspect of the Directive is implemented in the UK by Disclosure and Transparency Rule 4.2, made by the Financial Conduct Authority.

CONSIDERATION OF THE ACCOUNTS AND REPORTS BY THE MEMBERS

Circulation to the members

21–40   Since the accounts and reports are communications from the directors to the members, it is not surprising that the Act requires their circulation to the members.[272] However, not only the members but also the company's debenture-holders (i.e. its long-term lenders holding the company's debt securities)[273] must receive copies, since their chances of being repaid depend upon the financial health of the company. Thirdly, so must anyone who is entitled to receive notice of general meetings of the company be sent the accounts and reports, a category which includes the directors themselves (hardly a necessary requirement) and anyone else entitled to notice under the particular company's articles.[274] This obligation arises only if the company has a current address for the person in question.[275] Finally, those nominated to enjoy information rights will receive copies of the accounts and reports.[276] Just to make sure, the Act also provides that shareholders and debenture-holders can at any time demand copies of the most recent annual accounts and reports and the company must comply with the request within seven days.[277]

Circulation of the Strategic Report only

21–41   There are two linked problems with the circulation requirements. First, the full accounts and reports may be grist to the mills of the analysts, but lots of individual shareholders find the full set more daunting than useful. Secondly, the circulation requirement is an expensive one for the company to meet.[278] Both these concerns are addressed by the provisions which allow companies to circulate something less than the full accounts and reports. Initially, that something less was a "summary financial statement", but with the introduction of the strategic report,[279] that document became the substitute.

This facility was previously available only to companies whose securities were traded on certain public markets, but now it is in principle open to all companies.[280] Moreover, the burden is on the recipient to ask to continue to receive the full accounts and report. If, after being sent an appropriate notice from the company, the recipient does not respond with a contrary statement within 28

---

[272] 2006 Act s.423(1). The content of the "annual accounts and reports" is specified in s.471(2) separately for unquoted and quoted companies.

[273] See Ch.31, below.

[274] 2006 Act s.307. In the case of companies without share capital only this third category need be circulated: s.423(4).

[275] 2006 Act s.423(2),(3).

[276] 2006 Act s.146. See para.15–40.

[277] 2006 Act ss.431 (unquoted companies) and 432 (quoted companies). This right is also extended to those nominated to enjoy information rights: s.146(3)(b).

[278] It is reported that in 2006 postmen in the UK were restricted as to the number of sets of the annual accounts and reports of HSBC bank they were permitted to carry at any one time, because of the weight of the document.

[279] Above, para.21–24.

[280] 2006 Act s.426.

days, he or she will be deemed to have opted for the summary, though that "choice" can be reversed at any time.[281] The provisions are, however, default rules, in the sense that the company in its constitution or the instrument creating the debentures may deprive itself of this facility. The right to make use of the summary is also dependent on the company observing the relevant provisions of the Act relating to the audit, filing and approval of the full accounts and reports.[282] The SR must be accompanied by a warning that it is only part of the annual accounts and reports; informing the reader how to obtain full copies; stating whether any of the required auditor certifications was qualified; and containing one (clearly important) figure from outside the strategic report, i.e. the "single total remuneration" figure from the directors' remuneration report in the case of quoted companies.[283]

An alternative, or additional, way, of addressing circulation costs is to encourage members to receive communications (whether full accounts and reports or only the SR) from the company in electronic form or via the company's website. This has been discussed in Ch.15.[284] A quoted company is in any event required to put its current annual accounts and reports on its website and to maintain it there throughout the following financial year.[285]

Laying the accounts and reports before the members

Circulating the accounts and reports to the members and others allows them to consider them on an individual basis, but such consideration is not likely to lead to significant action in the case of companies with larger bodies of shareholders, unless there is some facility for collective consideration of the accounts and reports. As far as private companies are concerned, there is no longer any statutory requirement for such collective consideration, no matter how large a shareholding body that company may have. A private company is required by the statute to circulate its annual accounts and reports at the time it delivers them to the Registrar,[286] and any further action is a matter for the shareholders or the company's articles. The shareholders might seek to convene a meeting[287] or the articles might require annual consideration of the accounts and reports at a meeting, which the directors would be obliged to convene.

21–42

---

[281] 2006 Act s.426(2)(3) and Companies (Receipt of Accounts and Reports) Regulations 2013/1973. The consultation may take place as part of the circulation of the annual accounts and reports (and relate to future years) or be a free-standing consultation. Requesting to continue with the full set must be made easy, depending simply on ticking a box on a form, postage on which has been pre-paid by the company, at least if the recipient has an address in the EEA. Those who enjoy information rights are within this procedure as well: s.426(5).

[282] Receipt Regulations reg.5.

[283] 2006 Act s.426A. On the "single total remuneration" figure see para.14–45.

[284] At para.15–85.

[285] 2006 Act s.430.

[286] 2006 Act s.424(2). For delivery to the Registrar, see above, para.21–33. Of course, the company cannot evade this obligation simply by not filing the accounts and report with the Registrar: s.424(2)(a).

[287] See para.15–48.

As far as public companies are concerned, the traditional obligation "to lay the accounts and reports before a general meeting" still applies.[288] This formulation implies that the shareholders are not required to consider a resolution to approve the accounts and reports (as is the case in many countries), but they must be afforded an opportunity to discuss them. Indeed, this item on the agenda is normally used to allow a wide-ranging discussion of the company's business.[289] The meeting at which the accounts and reports are considered is termed the "accounts meeting"[290] and it is in fact normally the company's annual general meeting. The accounts and reports must be circulated at least 21 days before the accounts meeting and the accounts meeting itself must be held not later than the end of the period for the filing of the accounts and reports with the Registrar, i.e. six months after the end of the financial year in the case of a public company. As we noted in Ch.15,[291] the Government backed away from the CLR's proposal that, after circulation, there should be a pause of two weeks, during which shareholders could formulate, if they wished, resolutions on the accounts and reports to be considered at the meeting.

CONCLUSION

21–43 Part 15 of the Act, dealing with the annual accounts and reports, constitutes a substantial part of the Companies Act 2006, long though that Act is. Part 15 contains nearly 100 sections, and this is an indication of the central role played by annual reporting in the structure of the companies legislation. Excessive though the detail of the Act, subordinate legislation and accounting standards is to anyone not an accountant, an understanding of the central principles of the annual reporting process is central to understanding the philosophy of company law.

The developments in this part of company law reflect very well a broader trend in the subject towards greater refinement of the applicable rules according to the economic importance of different types of company. This classification proceeds broadly by reference to direct indicators of economic size (turnover, balance sheet total and number of employees) or by reference to the divorce between ownership and control (i.e. whether the shares are publicly traded) though this indicator is also correlated with economic size. For the largest publicly traded companies,[292] not only is financial reporting increasingly demanding, as International Financial Reporting Standards expand their scope, but so are the demands of narrative reporting. This expansion of reporting requirements is driven substantially by investor demand but also in part by a governmental desire to encourage investors (and in some cases pressure-groups) to engage with the management of their investee companies, even beyond what they might themselves do, if left to their own devices. At the other end of the

---

[288] 2006 Act ss.437–438.

[289] See para.15–43.

[290] 2006 Act s.437(3).

[291] At para.15–58.

[292] A particular feature of the rules applying to these companies is the differences in the range of publicly traded companies caught by different rules. In descending order of breadth, sometimes the rules apply on to companies traded on "regulated" markets, sometimes to "quoted" companies and sometimes to companies on "prescribed" markets.

scale, micro companies have obtained a further relaxation of the relaxed rules which apply to small companies. In between, medium-sized companies benefit from some relaxations whilst large, but not publicly traded, companies are subject to broadly the same reporting regime as publicly traded companies, but have to cover less in their strategic report.

CHAPTER 22

AUDITS AND AUDITORS

INTRODUCTION

22–1 The statutory accounts and reports discussed in the previous chapter are the responsibility of the directors. However, all modern company law systems have long accepted the principle that the reliability of the accounts and reports will be increased if there is in place a system of independent third-party verification of them. The temptation to present the accounts in a light which is unduly favourable to the management is one likely to afflict all boards of directors at one time or another—and the temptation is likely to be at its strongest when the financial condition of the company is at its weakest and shareholders, creditors and investors are most in need of access to the truth. To provide such third-party verification is the traditional role of the audit.

Sources of audit law

22–2 We saw in the last chapter that the global nature of modern large businesses creates a strong pressure for global accounting standards (though a single set of such standards is still some way off) and for regulation of accounts within the EU to be something which takes place to a significant extent at EU level. Equally this is the case with auditing, as an essential complement to accounts. Global auditing standards are being developed, as we shall see below, and auditing is a matter which has been regulated to an increasing degree at EU level. The process began with Directive 84/253 on auditors' qualifications, but in the wake of various corporate scandals at the beginning of the century (in the US as much as in Europe) that Directive was replaced by one which regulated in addition the process of auditing. Directive 2006/43/EC was in turn amended after the financial crisis in 2013 by Directive 2013/34/EU and, again, by Directive 2014/56/EU.[1] However, in 2014 an additional crucial step was taken. In respect of the largest companies, i.e. companies whose securities are traded on regulated markets, termed "public interest entities" ("PIEs"),[2] an extended supplementary set of rules was introduced. As important, that supplementary set of rules was laid down in a Regulation,[3] whose provisions are, therefore, directly applicable in the UK (though domestic rules are needed to exercise any choices which the Regulation specifically gives to Member States). Domestic rules are still needed to transpose the amended Directive and to deal with matters not dealt with by either the Regulation or the Directive.[4] Domestic rules on auditing are contained in the

---

[1] In this chapter references to the "Directive" are to the 2006 Directive as amended; where it is necessary to mention the other directives, they are referred to as the "2013 Directive" and the "2014 Directive" respectively.

[2] Regulation art.1, cross-referring to art.1(2)(f) of the Directive. The PIE definition embraces in addition banks and insurance companies, whether their securities are traded on a regulated market or not, but the special rules for financial institutions are ignored in this chapter. For the definition of regulated markets see para.25–8. In the UK one can think of the term as referring to the Main Market of the London Stock Exchange.

[3] Regulation (EU) No.537/2014. Some rules specific to PIEs had been included in the 2006 Directive. References in this chapter to the "Regulation" are to the 2014 Regulation.

[4] The 2014 Directive was transposed by the Statutory Auditors and Third Country Auditors Regulations 2016, which made changes to the Companies Act 2006 (hereafter "Statutory Auditors

Companies Act 2006, as amended, and the Statutory Auditors Regulations but also in rules ("standards") made by the Financial Reporting Council or by the relevant professional bodies.[5] The structure of the domestic institutional arrangement was changed (and simplified) in the light of the requirements of the Regulation and, to a lesser extent, the Directives, so that the 2014 EU level reforms were significant for structural as well as substantive reasons.

The duties of the auditor

To summarise briefly the role of the auditor, the core element of it is the production of a report to the members of the company which gives the auditor's opinion on a number of issues. The core opinion is whether:

22–3

(a)   the annual accounts give a true and fair view of the financial position of the company (or the group in the case of group accounts)[6]; have been properly prepared in accordance with the relevant financial reporting framework[7]; and have been prepared in accordance with the requirements of the Act or the IAS Regulation[8];

(b)   the directors' report is consistent with the accounts, has been prepared in accordance with the applicable legal requirements and whether any material misstatements have been identified[9] (the same or similar duties arise in relation to the strategic report and the separate corporate governance statement, if the company has produce either)[10]; and

(c)   the auditable part of the directors' remuneration report (DRR) has been properly prepared in accordance with the Act.[11]

The auditor's report must be either "qualified" or "unqualified".[12] An unqualified report is one where the auditor is able to give the opinions mentioned above; a qualified report (which is a serious thing for the company and its members) is one

---

Regulations"). In addition, the domestic Regulations embedded the EU Regulation in domestic law and exercised the choices given to the UK under the Regulation. At the time of writing only a draft of this statutory instrument was available.

[5]   See para.22–11, below.

[6]   For the distinction between individual and group accounts see para.21–9.

[7]   On the meaning of this term see para.21–16.

[8]   2006 Act s.495(3). On the role of the IAS Regulation see para.21–18. For micro-company accounts the requirement about accounting standards is qualified by s 495(3A) for the reasons explained in para.21–20.

[9]   2006 Act s.496. On the directors' report see para.21–23.

[10]   2006 Act ss.496 and 497A. On the strategic report see para.21–24, and on the corporate governance statement Disclosure and Transparency Rules 7.2, made by the FCA. In the case of the latter the auditor must report whether the DTR of the FCA have been complied with. The mandatory report on this statement indicates, among other things, the increased importance attached to internal control and risk management, as does the requirement on the auditors to state whether a separate corporate governance statement has been prepared if the directors have not chosen to include in their report (s.498A).

[11]   2006 Act s.487. The auditable part of the DRR is that set out in Pt 3 of Sch.8 to the Large and Medium-sized Companies and Groups (Accounts and Reports) Regulations 2008/410 (see reg.11(3)). On the directors' remuneration report see para.14–44.

[12]   2006 Act s.495(4).

where one or more of the opinions mentioned above cannot be given.[13] The auditor's report to the members must contain opinions on matters (a)–(c) above. In addition:

(d)   In relation to PIEs the Regulation requires discussion in the report of the risks of fraud or misstatement in the company's accounts.[14] This falls short of requiring an opinion on whether there has been fraud or misstatement, but the report must "explain to what extent the statutory audit was considered capable of detecting irregularities, including fraud".

Under domestic law and according to the circumstances, the auditor's report may also have to deal with further items. The most important potential matters that may need discussion are:

(e)   those "which cast significant doubt about the company's ability to continue as a going concern".[15]

In addition, certain matters may need to be mentioned arising out of the auditor's duty, in preparing the report, to carry out investigations so as to be able to form a view as to whether:

(f)   adequate accounting records have been kept by the company;
(g)   the company's individual accounts are in agreement with the accounting records; and
(h)   the auditable part of the DRR is in agreement with the accounting records.[16]

If all is well in relation to the above three issues, the auditor need say nothing in the report. If it is not, the auditor must state this fact.

(i)   in addition, if the auditor has failed to obtain all the information and explanations which he or she believes to be necessary for the purposes of the audit, that fact must be stated in the report.[17]

Finally, there are two specific provisions relating to the small company accounts and the DRR:

---

[13] The auditor may refer to matters to which attention needs to be drawn without necessarily qualifying the report: s.495(4)(b).
[14] Regulation art.10.
[15] 2006 Act s.495(4)(c). This is a new requirement in the Act (as from 2016) but auditing standards previously required such discussion.
[16] 2006 Act s.498(1),(2).
[17] 2006 Act s.498(3).

(j)   Where the directors have taken advantage of the relaxations for small companies when preparing the company's accounts or the directors' report, the auditor must state in the report his opinion that they were not entitled to do so, if he forms such an opinion.[18]

(k)   If the auditor finds that the statutory provisions on the disclosure of directors' remuneration have not been complied with, there is a duty upon the auditor, so far as he or she is reasonably able, to provide the particulars which should have been given in the directors' report or the DRR.[19] Apart from this, however, the auditor is not under an obligation the revise the accounts and reports so as to bring them into line with the applicable requirements: that is the task of their authors, the directors.

In the not uncommon case where more than one person is appointed auditor, it must be disclosed whether they all agree on the matters contained in the report and the reasons for any disagreement must be given.

Undoubtedly, the most important and time-consuming of the auditor's tasks is that listed at (a) above, because it amounts to a general endorsement of the accuracy of the accounts, though (d) is likely to add considerably to the auditor's burdens (and the company's costs) in the case of a PIE. In some cases, the auditor may also be required to report facts uncovered to third parties, especially regulators, though this development has been controversial, as we shall see.[20]

Overarching issues

There are three main issues of principle about audits and auditors. First, is the benefit of the audit greater than its costs for all companies? If not, is there a case for exempting some classes of company from the requirement[21] to have an audit? Secondly, once an audit is required, the temptation on management to present the accounts in an unduly favourable light can be given effect only if they can persuade the auditors to accept such an unduly favourable presentation. What steps, then, can and should be taken to ensure the independence of the auditors from the management of the company? Thirdly, even if the auditor is independent, what steps should be taken to ensure that a good job will be done, in particular what role should be played by civil liability in damages on the part of the auditor towards those who relied on the reports? We shall look at these issues in the remainder of this chapter.

22–4

The auditor today, at least in large firms, is not an individual practitioner but a member of a firm, often of international scale, and the audit is carried out by a team of auditors under the leadership of one or more partners in the firm. Where necessary, the text below will refer to these realities. Otherwise, the word "auditor" is used, but to cover both firms and sole practitioners, individuals and teams of auditors.

---

[18] 2006 Act s.498(5). On the small business definition see para.21–4.

[19] 2006 Act s.498(4).

[20] Below, para.22–21.

[21] The basic principle of a mandatory audit of the statutory accounts is laid down in s.475.

AUDIT EXEMPTION

Small companies

22–5   Over a little more than a decade a very substantial set of audit exemptions has been introduced, to the point where some 88 per cent of non-dormant companies are exempt from audit of their annual accounts (both individual and group).[22] Of course, one must not exaggerate the economic significance of the companies so exempt, because the exemption is applied to small companies. Nevertheless, the definition of what counts as "small" for this purpose has been progressively enlarged over this relatively short period of time. This was a significant change of policy on the part of Government, for previously it had been committed to a universal audit requirement.[23] What triggered the reversal seems to have been the additional costs generated by the implementation in the Companies Act 1989 of Directive 84/253 on auditors' qualifications,[24] which was alleged to have a disproportionate impact on the audit costs of very small firms. Once begun, the exemption process seems to have acquired a life of its own. Despite the opposition from some users of accounts, notably the HM Revenue and Customs and some banks, the deregulatory pressure was successful.

An indication of the spread of the small company exemption from audit can be gained from looking at how the upper turnover figure for exemption has increased over the years. In 1994, this was set at £90,000[25]; it was raised to £300,000 in 1997[26]; and in 2000 to £1 million.[27] The CLR recommended a further increase, namely, to the level of the requirement for being a small company for accounts purposes, and that at the same time the UK's definition of a "small" company should be revised upwards to the level permitted by EU law.[28] This raised the turnover figure to £4.8 million. With a further raising of the EU limit, we reach the current number of £10.2 million.[29] Thus, there has been a move from a very cautious approach to audit exemption, where the domestic rules remained well within the upper limit set by EU law, to one of taking full advantage of the exemption permitted at EU level.[30] In consequence, over a short period a very substantial process of removal of third party assurance in relation to the accounts of small companies has taken place.[31]

---

[22] BIS, *Consultation on Audit Exemptions and Change of Accounting Framework*, October 2011 (URN 11/1193), para.32.

[23] DTI, *Accounting and Audit Requirements for Small Firms: A Consultative Document* (1985) and *Consultative Document on Amending the Fourth Company Law Directive on Annual Accounts* (1989). The Fourth Directive, however, permitted Member States to exempt small companies from the audit.

[24] Repealed and replaced by Directive 2006/43/EC as from June 2006.

[25] Companies Act 1985 (Audit Exemption Regulations) 1994 (SI 1994/1935).

[26] Companies Act 1985 (Audit Exemption) (Amendment) Regulations 1997 (SI 1997/936).

[27] Companies Act 1985 (Audit Exemption) (Amendment) Regulations 2000 (SI 2000/1430).

[28] Final Report I, paras 4.29–4.31 and 4.43–4.45.

[29] See para.21–4.

[30] Exemption from audit for small companies is permitted by art.34 of the 2013 Directive.

[31] However, all but the smallest charitable companies remain subject to audit under the Charities Act 2011. The reason for these more stringent requirements for charities appears to be that the persons with the strongest financial interest in whether a charitable company uses its money properly are its donors, but they are not typically members of the company and so do not have access to the control

After a period in which access for small companies to the audit exemption was **22–6**
somewhat more restricted than access to the small company accounting regime,
the government decided in 2012 to adopt the simple rule that companies which
are small for accounts purposes are also entitled to the audit exemption.[32] Even if
the company meets this condition, it may be excluded from the audit exemption,
on grounds which parallel the loss of small company status for accounts
purposes.[33] In particular, the company must not be a public company.[34] In
addition, if the company is a member of a group, it will qualify for the exemption
only if the group qualifies as small and is not an ineligible group.[35]

Further, even if a company is exempt from audit on the ground of its size (or
the ground of dormancy, discussed below) members representing at least 10 per
cent of the nominal value of the company's issued share capital (or any class of
it)[36] may demand an audit for a particular financial year, provided the notice is
given after the financial year commences and within one year of its end.[37] Thus,
notice must be given on a year-by-year basis and the members cannot make a
demand relating to future financial years (when they might not meet the size
threshold).

Where the exemption applies and is used, the directors must confirm in a
statement attached to the balance sheet that the company was entitled to the
exemption, that no effective notice has been delivered requiring an audit and that
the directors acknowledge their responsibilities for ensuring that the company
keeps accounting records and for preparing accounts which give a true and fair
view of the state of the company's affairs.[38]

However, none of this means that small companies will not have their
accounts audited in fact. If a company sees value in providing such assurance to
members, creditors or investors, it may choose to have an audit. More likely,
banks or other large creditors may insist on an audit as part of the process of
considering whether to make a loan to the company. Where the company which
chooses to have an audit is a "micro" company, however, the audit will not cause
the company to reveal more information where it has chosen to stick to the
minimum standards for such companies.[39]

rights over the management of the company which members have. Thus, there is a stronger case for
third-party verification than in the case of the accounts on non-charitable small companies. No doubt
for this reason as well one sees in the charities legislation full use made of the technique of requiring
auditors or reporting accountants to make reports to the regulator, the Charities Commission.

[32] 2006 Act s.477(1) and see para.21–4.
[33] 2006 Act ss.478–479.
[34] 2006 Act ss.478(a),(b). Also excluded are companies in the financial services sector.
[35] 2006 Act s.479(1). The concept of an "ineligible group" we have analysed at para.21–10.
[36] Or 10 per cent in number of the members if there is no share capital.
[37] 2006 Act s.476.
[38] 2006 Act s.475(2)–(4). This provision applies to the exemption on grounds of dormancy as well.
[39] 2006 Act s.495(3A). On the accounting standards for micro companies see para.21–20.

Subsidiaries

22–7   Subsidiary companies, of any size, are exempt from the audit requirement, under reforms introduced in 2012, subject to certain conditions.[40] The central requirement is that the parent company guarantees all the liabilities of the subsidiary as they stand at the end of the financial year, until they are satisfied, and that the guarantee is enforceable against the parent.[41] Apart from extensive publicity requirements, this exemption is confined in various ways. It is available only where the parent is incorporated in the EEA; it is not available to subsidiaries whose securities are traded on a regulated market—a rare, but not unknown, situation in the UK; all the members of the company must agree to forego the audit; and the subsidiary's accounts must be included in the consolidated accounts of the parent.[42] It is thus most easily available to wholly-owned subsidiaries of EEA parents. The underlying policy argument is that the audit of the subsidiary's accounts in such case adds little by way of value to the audit of the consolidated accounts—though, equally, given the requirement for audit at group level, the savings from omitting the subsidiary audit are probably not enormous.

Dormant companies

22–8   A further and less controversial type of company which is exempt from audit is the so-called "dormant" company.[43] A company is dormant during a period when there is "no significant accounting transaction" in relation to it, an accounting transaction being one which needs to be recorded in the company's accounting records.[44] Where the company has been dormant since its formation, no other conditions need be met before the exemption is granted.[45] The most obvious and common example of such a company is a "shelf company"[46] while it remains on the shelf (though there may be legitimate reasons for incorporating a company which is intended to remain dormant indefinitely). If the company becomes dormant after a period of activity, then its audit exemption is more circumscribed. It depends on the company not being a parent company required to produce group accounts and its being entitled to produce its individual accounts under the small companies regime[47] or being entitled to do so but for the fact that it is a public company or a member of an ineligible group.[48] In practice, the most important extension which the dormant company exemption makes to that already provided for small companies is that it extends to small public companies.[49]

---

[40] 2006 Act s.479A.
[41] 2006 Act s.479C(3).
[42] 2006 Act ss.479A(1)(2) and 479B(a).
[43] 2006 Act s.480(1).
[44] 2006 Act s.1169.
[45] 2006 Act s.480(1)(a).
[46] See above, para.4–9.
[47] See above, para.21–4.
[48] 2006 Act s.480(2).
[49] The dormant company exemption is not available to companies whose securities are traded on a public market, but it is rare for such a company to be dormant (s.481(za)).

Non-profit public sector companies

This exemption does not need detailed consideration because the companies   **22–9**
entitled to it, although incorporated under the Companies Acts, are part of the
public sector and are subject to public sector audit.[50] A company is non-profit
making if it is so for the purpose of art.54 of the Treaty on the Functioning of the
European Union—though that article in fact contains no definition of "non-profit
making". Such companies are excluded from audit because they are outside the
scope of art.50(1) TFEU, under which the audit Directives were made.

AUDITOR INDEPENDENCE AND COMPETENCE

Although the issue of small company exemption from audit has been important   **22–10**
over the past two decades, the most important policy issue relating to auditors
concerns their independence. This was an issue brought to the fore by the
collapse of the Enron Company and others in the US in the early years of this
century, which collapses were thought to reveal weaknesses in the provisions on
auditor independence.[51] At least in the eyes of the EU, the same issue arose out of
the experience of the financial crisis 2007–9.[52] The essence of the independence
issue is that the auditor is appointed and remunerated by the company whose
accounts and reports are to be audited. Although companies are required to have
their accounts audited (unless exempted), they are not required to employ any
particular auditor or to pay that auditor any particular level of remuneration.
There thus develops the possibility that auditors will compete for mandates on the
basis that they will engage in only a cursory scrutiny of the company's accounts
or that they will act in this way in return for excessive remuneration (which might
be disguised as remuneration for the provision of non-audit services to the
company). The traditional response to this argument is that in the long- or even
the medium-term such a business model is self-destructive. The auditor will
obtain a reputation for laxness, which will, perversely, destroy its business.
Whilst the company's management may want a lax audit, it is crucial that those
who rely on the audit believe that the appropriate checks have been carried out. A
lax audit by an auditor known to be lax is no good, even for evasive management,
because the management will not obtain the benefit it desires from the audit
opinion. Whilst the reputation argument may have much force, recent experience
suggests that it does not operate at all times and in all circumstances so as to
guarantee an appropriate level of audit scrutiny. Individuals within the audit firm
may have perverse short-term incentives which outweigh the firm's longer term
incentive to do a good job or the investors may move away from attaching much
importance to the audited accounts in periods of market exuberance.

Consequently, there is a case for regulation to reinforce the market incentives
supporting auditor independence. Much the same arguments can be made in
relation to auditor competence. An audit firm has reputational reasons for

---

[50] 2006 Act s.482(1).

[51] See J. Coffee Jr, *Gatekeepers* (Oxford: OUP, 2006), especially Ch.5.

[52] European Commission, "Proposal for a Regulation . . . on specific requirements regarding statutory
audit of public interest entities", COM(2011) 779 final, 30 November 2011, p.2.

providing a good service in general but in particular cases there may be incentives on individuals to operate inefficiently. Nor should the independence and competence issues be viewed as completely separate: a non-independent auditor displays dependence on management precisely by carrying out an inadequate audit. However, the fact the market cannot guarantee independence and competence does not mean that regulation can (some aspects of the problem might be insoluble) nor that all types of regulation are equally appropriate.

There are eight strategies which have been deployed by the law to address these problems.

(1) Laying down specific rules disqualifying persons from acting as auditor of a particular company on grounds of conflict of interest.

(2) Constraining the provision of non-audit services to audit clients.

(3) Requiring the mandatory rotation of auditors.

(4) On the basis that the board is the body within the company which has the greatest interest in a lax audit, increasing the role of the shareholders in relation to audit decisions.

(5) On the basis that, within the board, it is the executive directors who have the greatest interest in a lax audit and that shareholders have serious collective action problems, increasing the role of the non-executive directors in relation to auditor decisions, notably via an audit committee consisting wholly of independent non-executive directors.

(6) Attacking the problem not from the side of the company but from the side of the auditor by subjecting auditors to greater regulatory control and more effective disciplinary mechanisms.

(7) Increasing the powers of the auditors as against the company.

(8) Imposing civil liability on auditors to those who rely on the audited accounts and reports where the auditors have been negligent and imposing criminal liability for false statements in audit reports.

Each has been deployed with greater vigour in recent years, except civil liability, where indeed the tendency has been to restrict liability.

Regulatory structure

22–11   Before we do so, however, a short word is necessary about the structure of the regulation. The Directive requires Member States to appoint a "competent authority" with the function of approving auditors and putting in place a system of "public oversight" of the work of those auditors who have been approved.[53] In the UK that competent authority is the Financial Reporting Council.[54] Whilst the competent authority has ultimate responsibility for the tasks assigned to it, the Directive permits delegation of its tasks to other bodies "authorised by law" to carry out the delegated tasks—though in the case of PIEs the Regulation forbids the delegation of many tasks beyond the FRC.[55] This delegation is subject to the

---

[53] Directive art.32.
[54] On the FRC see para.21–17.
[55] Directive art.32(4b) and Regulation art.24(1).

condition that the competent authority may reclaim the delegated power on a case-by-case basis. Under the Statutory Auditors Regulations, the FRC must itself oversee the creation of the standards which auditors are required to meet and the manner of their application in practice, but "must consider whether and how" other aspects of the public oversight function (for example, quality assurance and discipline) can be delegated to "recognised supervisory bodies" ("RSBs").[56] The RSBs are, in brief, the professional accounting bodies which meet the standards set in the Act for recognition.[57] An elaborate system of regulation of auditors and auditing is thus envisaged. Some matters are determined in the Act or the Statutory Auditors Regulations (or in the EU Regulation in the case of PIEs), some in standards developed by the FRC and some matters by the RSBs. However, the division of powers between the FRC and the RSBs is not a novel feature of EU Regulation. It was in place before the recent elaboration of the EU requirements and, in fact, the impact of those requirements has been somewhat to simplify the domestic relationships. However, it is still the case that the obligation to comply with the FRC's standards flows from the requirements that a statutory auditor be a member of a RSB[58] and that the RSB's rules require compliance with standards laid down by the FRC.[59]

DIRECT REGULATION OF AUDITOR INDEPENDENCE

Non-independent persons

A person may not act as an auditor if he is an officer or employee of the company to be audited or a partner or employee of such an officer or employee or, in the case of the appointment of a partnership, if any member of the partnership is ineligible on these grounds.[60] Nor may a person act if any of these grounds apply in relation to any associated undertaking[61] of the company. An auditor who comes within these provisions must immediately resign and give notice to the company of the reason for the resignation.[62] Failure to do so is a criminal offence. Further, the appointment or continuation in office of an auditor who is not independent within the statutory section triggers a power in the Secretary of State to require the company to appoint a proper person to conduct a second audit or to

22–12

---

[56] Statutory Auditors Regulations reg.3(1)(2)
[57] 2006 Act s.1217 and Sch.10 Pt 1.
[58] 2006 Act s.1212(1)(a).
[59] 2006 Act Sch.10 para.9.
[60] 2006 Act s.1214(1)–(3). Section 1214(5) expressly states that, for this purpose, an auditor is not to be regarded as an "officer or employee". This hardly needs saying, for if he were, he would become ineligible immediately upon appointment! The definition of "officer" in the Act ("officer—includes a director, manager or secretary or, where the affairs of the company are managed by its members, a member": s.1261(1)) might seem in any event to exclude auditors. Nevertheless, they have been held to be "officers" in a number of corporate contexts: *Mutual Reinsurance Co Ltd v Peat Marwick Mitchell & Co* [1997] 1 B.C.L.C. 1 CA; *Re London & General Bank (No.1)* [1895] 2 Ch. 166 CA; *Re Kingston Cotton Mills (No.1)* [1896] 1 Ch. 6 CA.
[61] 2006 Act s.1214(6); i.e. a parent or subsidiary undertaking of the company or a subsidiary undertaking of any parent undertaking of the company.
[62] 2006 Act s.1215(1).

review the first audit, and the company may recover the costs of the additional audit work from the first auditor, provided that person knew he or she was not independent.[63]

Clearly, however, an employer-employee relationship with the company being audited is far from being the only type of relationship which might impair the independence of the auditor, e.g. a debtor-creditor relationship or a substantial shareholding[64] in the company might do so. The prohibition is clearly not a sufficient compliance with the requirements of art.22 of the Directive which imposes a general requirement upon Member States to ensure the independence of auditors and to exclude a person from acting as auditor if there is *any* relationship between the auditor and audited company "from which an objective, reasonable and informed third party would conclude that the statutory auditor's independence is compromised". To meet this requirement, the Statutory Auditors Regulations[65] require the FRC to make standards aimed at ensuring auditor independence on appointment and during the audit. This mandate is discharged by the FRC through its ethical standards.[66]

Non-audit remuneration of auditors

22–13   Apart from remuneration for the audit itself, the most common conflicted relationship which an auditor may have with the audit client arises from the fact that the auditor is normally a member of a firm of accountants which is capable of providing a wide range of services—well beyond audit or even accountancy services—to clients. These non-audit revenues from audit clients of accountancy firms have increased substantially in recent years.[67] Disclosure of the amount of these payments is provided for under regulations requiring companies to disclose on a disaggregated basis in notes to the accounts the non-audit remuneration received by their auditors. The Regulations[68] divide the auditor's potential sources of remuneration into eight categories (including remuneration from the audit itself), require separate disclosure of remuneration earned from the company (and its subsidiaries) and from associated pension schemes,[69] and require disclosure of amounts paid to the auditor's "associates" as well as to the

---

[63] 2006 Act ss.1248–1249. The provisions also apply—and in practice are probably more important—where the auditor is ineligible to be appointed (for example, because not qualified) rather than prohibited from acting on grounds of lack of independence: s.1248(3). The sections appear not to apply to lack of independence solely under the FRC's standards discussed below.

[64] Though the shareholding might make the auditor a more diligent watchdog over the members' interests—but members are not the only people whose interests he should protect.

[65] Statutory Auditors Regulations Sch.1 paras 3–6.

[66] FRC, *Ethical Standard*, 2016, §2, which devotes some twenty pages to the topic.

[67] See D. Kershaw, "Waiting for Enron: The Unstable Equilibrium of Auditor Independence Regulation" (2006) 33 Journal of Law and Society 388, 394. This is a valuable article on the whole issue of auditor independence.

[68] The Companies (Disclosure of Auditor Remuneration and Liability Limitation Agreements) Regulations 2008/489 (as amended by SI 2011/2198) reg.5(3) and Sch.2A, made under s.494 of the Act.

[69] Remuneration and Liability Regulations reg.5(4).

auditor.[70] The disclosure obligation imposed on small or medium-sized[71] companies extends only to the audit fee.

However, regulation of this issue extends beyond disclosure. For PIEs a long list of non-audit services is simply prohibited from the beginning of the period subject to audit to the completion of the audit. These are non-audit services where the risk of conflict of interest is thought to be high. They may not be provided by the auditor or any member of its network[72] or to a PIE or any member of its group, if incorporated in the EU.[73] Even permitted non-audit services are subject to controls. Their provision must be approved by the company's audit committee (see below).[74] In addition, the amount that is permitted to be paid for the non-audit services is capped at 70 per cent of the average audit fees paid over the previous three years.[75]

For non-PIEs the Directive applies its general principle that auditors must assess and handle appropriately threats to their independence, into which category non-audit remuneration falls. In the UK this requirement is implemented via ethical standards made by the FRC. However, these standards go beyond the essentially procedural requirements of the Directive and make the provision of certain high-risk non-audit services inconsistent with an audit engagement.[76] This approach on the part of the FRC, which was in place before the most recent EU reforms, essentially follows, but makes binding, the recommendations contained in Commission Recommendation 2002/590/EC on statutory auditors' independence in the EU.[77]

Auditors becoming non-independent

It may be that, although the auditor may have no other relationship with the company, over a period of time the auditor relationship itself becomes a threat to independence. The auditor may build up personal relationships with the management of the audited company which make him or her reluctant to challenge the management's picture of events. The watchdog may have become a lap dog. This argument is accepted at EU level in relation to PIEs. The "key audit partners" are required to rotate every seven years and not to take up appointment again for three years.[78] The notion of a "key audit partner" is one derived from

22–14

---

[70] Remuneration and Liability Regulations reg.5(1)(b)(ii) and Sch.1.

[71] Remuneration and Liability Regulations reg.4. For the definition of medium-sized, see para.21–5, above.

[72] The major accounting firms are organised as more or less closely linked partnerships operating under a single brand.

[73] Regulation art.5. Examples are tax advice and services involving taking management decisions. If the group member is incorporated outside the EU, the requirement is that the auditor assess the level of conflict and be able to justify the continued provision of the non-audit services—but some of the services prohibited within the EU are regarded as incapable of justification (art.5(5)).

[74] Regulation art.5(4).

[75] Regulation art.4(2). This constraint applies only if the auditor has supplied both types of service over a period of three consecutive years.

[76] FRC, *Ethical Standards*, §5.

[77] Commission Recommendation 2002/590/EC on statutory auditors' independence in the EU [2002] O.J. L191/22.

[78] Regulation art.17(7).

the Directive and it means the auditor designated by the audit firm as primarily responsible for carrying out the audit (normally referred to in the UK as the "engagement auditor") but also the auditor who signs the report, if different.[79] In fact, the FRC's rules take up the option to make the rotation rules more demanding and impose a five-year rotation and a five-year gap.[80] In addition, the Regulation requires the phased rotation of all the senior personnel in the audit team.

Rotation of the key audit partner has been required since 2006 Directive,[81] but the Regulation introduces in addition a requirement for the rotation of the audit firm of a PIE. The argument against mandatory rotation of firms is that it means the loss of the expertise of the whole of the existing audit team, which occurrence would be likely to reduce the quality of the audits immediately following a change of firm (unless, of course, the audit team simply changed firms, thus defeating the object of the exercise). In its 2011 proposals for an Audit Regulation the Commission put forward, nevertheless, a rule requiring for PIEs rotation of the audit firm every six years (or a little longer in some cases).[82] As enacted, the firm rotation proposal survived but with considerably longer intervals. The provisions are complex, reflecting their heavy negotiation in the EU's legislative process. In principle, rotation of the firm is required every ten years, but Member States may opt for a 20-year rule, as the UK has done, provided a public re-tendering process is carried out after ten years.[83]

Firm rotation can be looked at as a competition issues as well as an independence issue. Since a mere four firms dominate the global accounting market, choice for large companies is necessarily limited. In an attempt to address this issue, the Competition and Markets Authority made an order in 2014 requiring mandatory re-tendering of audit engagements at least every ten years for the largest 350 companies on the Main Market of the London Stock Exchange.[84] The aim was to give second-tier audit firms an opportunity to break into the market for the provision of audit services to this class of company and to make it worthwhile for those firms to gear up to provide the audit services. The Regulation now goes further than the order in that it requires a change of auditor after 20 years, not just a re-tendering process, and matches the order's requirement of re-tendering within the first ten years.

---

[79] Regulation art.2(16), apparently translated in the Act as "senior statutory auditor": s.504.
[80] FRC, *Ethical Standards*, para.3.10.
[81] 2006 Act Sch.10 para.10c(1) reflects the original Directive requirements but note para.10(1A) requiring compliance with the stricter rules of the FRC, taking up an option under the Regulation.
[82] Above fn.52, para.3.3.3. In 2012 the FRC amended the CGC to recommend that FTSE 350 companies put their audit business out to competitive tender at least every 10 years. In the light of the EU Regulation this recommendation has been removed from the 2016 CGC.
[83] Regulation art.17. The tendering process is governed by art.16. This Member State choice is implemented in the UK by s.491(1A)(1B). Although not absolutely clear from the Regulation, the UK rules allow a re-tendering process to occur after less than ten years and for the incumbent auditors, if successful, to remain for ten years after that process.
[84] The Statutory Audit Services for Large Companies Market Investigation (Mandatory Use of Competitive Tender Processes and Audit Committee Responsibilities) Order 2014.

Both independence and competition goals might be hindered if there were contractual restrictions in place on the choice of auditor. The Regulation renders such clauses "null and void";[85] the Statutory Auditors Regulations treats them as of "no effect".[86]

Auditors becoming prospectively non-independent

An auditor may have no current relationship with the company which creates a **22–15** conflict of interest (nor may he or she have a long association with the company as auditor) but there may be an understanding, falling short of a contract, that the auditor will resign in due course and take up a role in the management of the company. Since accountancy skills are much prized in some areas of management, movement from professional practice to management is quite common. Article 22a of the Directive, however, imposes a two-year "cooling off" period between ceasing to be the statutory auditor or key audit partner and the taking up of a "key" management position in a PIE and a one-year period in any other case. The same periods are applied if the new post is as a non-executive director of the client company or a member of its audit committee (without being either a key manager or a non-executive director—a rare situation). This rule too is implemented via ethical standards in the UK.[87]

THE ROLE OF SHAREHOLDERS AND THE AUDIT AUTHORITIES

The traditional regulatory strategy deployed by the domestic legislation to **22–16** reinforce auditor independence has been to enhance the role of the shareholders. In many ways this is an obvious strategy. The accounts and reports are statements from the directors to the members and so putting control over those who verify those statements in the hands of the recipients rather than the originators of the statements appears to be an appropriate strategy. The auditor's relationship with the shareholders is underlined by the provision which gives him or her a right to be sent all notices and other communications relating to general meetings, to attend them and to be heard on any part of the business which affects or concerns the auditor.[88] In the case of a private company which takes its decision by written resolution, the right transmogrifies into a simple right to receive the communications relating to the written resolution, but there is no general right to make representations to the shareholders before they decide.[89] This is a pretty ineffective provision—though it needs to be recognised that many private companies will be exempt from audit on grounds of being "small". However, the shareholders have limited opportunities to exercise control, since they meet infrequently, and in addition may face co-ordination problems in large companies

---

[85] Regulation art.16(6).
[86] Statutory Auditors Regulations reg.12.
[87] Statutory Auditors Regulations Sch.1 para.7; FRC, *Ethical Standards*, paras 2.47 et seq.
[88] 2006 Act s.502(2).
[89] 2006 Act s.502(1).

over the exercise of the powers which are conferred on them. Perhaps for this reason, the auditor's information obligations to the shareholders are often extended to the audit authorities.

Appointment and remuneration of auditors

22–17   The normal rule is that the appointment of the auditors must be done at each accounts meeting, normally the annual general meeting,[90] and the appointment is from the conclusion of that meeting until the conclusion of the next such meeting.[91] There are only exceptional circumstances in which the directors may appoint auditors.[92] However, the proposal to appoint the auditors, to re-appoint them or to appoint others in their place comes normally from the board (though it need not) and the meeting, almost invariably, will agree with the board's proposal. This is an example of a situation where the shareholders' co-ordination problems make it difficult, though not impossible, for them to generate a proposal of their own. They might do so if they had reason to believe that the auditor was in the board's pocket, but they rarely have grounds for so thinking, in which case accepting the board's proposal seems the rational course of action. In the case of PIEs the audit committee (see below) is required to put forward recommendations to the shareholders.[93] This both recognises shareholders' potential co-ordination problems and attempts to shift the de facto nomination role out of the hands of the executive directors of the company.

Where the auditors are appointed by the members in general meeting, their remuneration shall be fixed by the company in general meeting or in such manner as the general meeting shall determine.[94] This, too, is intended to emphasise that the auditors are the members' watchdogs rather than the directors' lapdogs. But in practice it serves little purpose since the members normally adopt a resolution proposed by the directors to the effect that the remuneration shall be agreed by the directors—as the provision permits them to do. Even if the shareholders actually fixed the auditor's remuneration, rather than fixing the method for fixing it, they would invariably act on a recommendation from the board. A more effective protection, perhaps, is that the amount of the remuneration, which includes expenses and benefits in kind (the monetary value of which has to be estimated) has to be shown in a note to the annual accounts, thus enabling the members to criticise the directors if the amount seems to be out of line.[95]

For private companies shareholder meetings are not required to be held, but, assuming the company is subject to audit, the principle of shareholder appointment and determination of remuneration still applies, except that the

---

[90] See para.21–42.
[91] 2006 Act ss.489(4) and 491(1)(b).
[92] 2006 Act s.489(3)—to fill a casual vacancy, after a period in which the company has not been required to have an audit, before its first accounts meeting.
[93] Regulation art.16.
[94] 2006 Act s.492(1).
[95] 2006 Act s.493 and the Companies (Disclosure of Auditor Remuneration and Liability Limitation Agreements) Regulations 2008/489 regs 4 and 5 (hereafter the "Remuneration and Liability Regulations"). Generally, they criticise only if the amount seems abnormally high; they should perhaps be more alarmed if it is abnormally low.

shareholders may act by written resolution and the rules are re-drafted so as to apply with reference to, not the accounts meeting, which will probably not be held, but the period of 28 days beginning with the day on which the accounts and reports were circulated to the members or, if later, the last day for circulating them.[96] Suppose, however, that no resolution with regard to the auditors is circulated to the shareholders, a not inconceivable situation in a private company. The Act provides that, unless the auditor was appointed by the directors under their exceptional powers,[97] failure to re-appoint or to appoint someone else at the end of the year will mean the auditors in place are deemed to be re-appointed.[98] This process of deemed re-appointment in private companies, which may otherwise continue indefinitely, can be excluded by the company's articles.[99] More important in practice, the auditor in post may be required to undergo re-election as a result of a resolution adopted by the members[100] or a notice received from members holding at least five per cent of the voting rights entitled to be cast on a resolution that the auditor should not be re-appointed.[101] The last of these is the least demanding method of preventing deemed re-appointment.

Removal and resignation of auditors

Requirement for shareholder resolution

As in the case of directors,[102] a company may by ordinary resolution passed at a meeting at any time remove an auditor from office.[103] However, the auditor, unlike a director, may not be removed prior to the expiration of the term of office other than by resolution of the shareholders.[104] In this way the auditor is given some protection against management pressure. If management wish to remove the auditor prematurely, they must do so by means of a proposal to the shareholders. If management goes down that route, further provisions of the Act come into play designed to permit or even require the auditor to put the contrary case to the shareholders. Hence, not only has special notice (28 days)[105] to be given to the company of a resolution to remove an auditor, but notice of the proposed resolution has to be given to the auditor.[106] The auditor is entitled to make written representations which, if received in time, have to be sent to the members with the notice of the meeting, and which, if not received in time, have

22–18

---

[96] 2006 Act ss.485, 487. We ignore the special rules which apply to private companies which are PIEs because this categories embraces only financial institutions (and probably very few of them). See fn.2, above.

[97] 2006 Act s.485(3).

[98] 2006 Act s.487.

[99] 2006 Act s.487(2)(b).

[100] 2006 Act s.487(2)(d).

[101] 2006 Act ss.487(2)(c) and 488.

[102] See para.14–49.

[103] 2006 Act s.510. A meeting is required, as for the removal of a director, even in the case of a private company: s.288(2).

[104] 2006 Act s.510(4). The articles often provide for directors to be removed by resolution of the board.

[105] 2006 Act s.511.

[106] 2006 Act s.511(2).

to be read out at the meeting.[107] If the resolution is passed, the auditor still retains the right to attend the general meeting at which the term of office would otherwise have expired or at which the vacancy created by the removal is to be filled.[108] Nor does removal deprive the auditor of any right to compensation or damages, arising, for example, under the contract between auditor and company, in respect of the termination of the appointment as auditor or any appointment terminating with that as auditor.[109]

A feature of the above rules is that, whilst protecting the auditor to some degree against management pressure, they give the shareholders a free hand over the removal of the auditor. If, for example, the shareholders of their own motion wish to remove an auditor they regard as too friendly with management, they are free to do so, provided the special notice and auditor statement provisions are complied with. However, art.38 of the Audit Directive requires Member States to ensure that auditors may be removed only on "proper grounds". It provides that "divergence of opinion on accounting treatments or audit procedures shall not be proper grounds for dismissal". The aim is clearly to give the auditor further protection against management pressure where the auditor has fallen out with the management, but the provision appears to be general and makes it less easy for the shareholders to act where they think the auditor has become too cosy with the management.

In countries with controlling shareholders as the predominant form of shareholding even in large companies (common in continental Europe), it may have been thought unrealistic to regard the directors and the (majority of the) shareholders as two separate groups. However, it is not unrealistic in dispersed shareholding jurisdictions such as the UK, and the Government was clearly reluctant to implement the Directive in the obvious way, i.e. by building a "proper grounds" qualification into the shareholders' removal power in s.510.[110] Instead the Government opted to amend s.994 dealing with unfair prejudice.[111] Removal of an auditor on ground of divergence of opinion or any other improper ground is deemed to be conduct unfairly prejudicial to the interests of some part of the members.[112] This approach has the merit of addressing the policy issue probably underlying the Directive, i.e. unfair treatment of minority shareholders. However, it is difficult to see that it transposes the Directive's formal requirement that the auditor "may be dismissed" only on proper grounds. The dismissal, even if challengeable under the unfair prejudice provisions by a shareholder, still seems to be effective as far as the auditor is concerned nor, whether the dismissal is effective or not, does the new provision give the auditor any rights as against the company. Further, there is no requirement that the court exercise its remedial

---

[107] 2006 Act s.511(3)–(5). The auditor should ensure that it is received in time since otherwise members may return proxy forms before they see his representations. But see subs.(6) regarding restraint by the court if the section is being abused "to secure needless publicity for defamatory matter". The auditor also has a general right to attend and speak at shareholder meetings. See para.22–24, below.

[108] 2006 Act ss.513 and 502(2).

[109] 2006 Act s.510(3).

[110] DTI, *Implementation of Directive 2006/43/EU: A Consultation Document*, March 2007, at paras 3.34 et seq.

[111] See Ch.20.

[112] 2006 Act s.994(1A).

powers under s.996 to secure the reinstatement of the auditor. Whether this way of proceeding meets the Directive's requirements must be open to doubt.

In the case of PIEs the Directive[113] requires that 5 per cent of the shareholders or the competent authority should be able to bring proceedings before a court for the dismissal of the auditor on proper grounds. Unlike the provision just discussed, this expands the powers of (minority) shareholders though in a rather cumbersome way.

A breakdown in relations between auditor and management is more likely to reveal itself in the resignation of the auditor rather than an attempt by the management to persuade the shareholders to remove the auditor. Few auditors will want to retain office if relations with the management of the company have become seriously strained. At first glance the Act makes resignation an easy matter: the auditor resigns by sending a notice to that effect to the company.[114] In this case what is needed are provisions which make it difficult for the auditor to "go quietly", i.e. to resign office without ensuring that any matters which have caused concern will be ventilated. The Act contains two sets of notice provisions designed to achieve this objective, requiring notice to be given to the company, on the one hand, and the regulatory authorities on the other. The information may put these bodies on the alert about possible mismanagement of the company. However, the Act also imposes notification requirements in the case of dismissal. We therefore discuss the notification requirements together in the following sub-section.

Notifications

An auditor of a PIE who leaves office at any time and for any reason must send the company a statement of reasons for this occurrence.[115] In the case of a non-PIE such a statement may be required. It will not be required where the departure from office occurs in circumstance which the legislature has determined in advance raise no concerns.[116] Nor will it be required of an auditor who leaves office at the end of an accounts meeting,[117] i.e. the rule here is aimed a departures during a financial year. For both PIEs and non-PIEs the statement must include reference to matters connected with the departure from office which the auditor thinks should be brought to the attention of the company's members or creditors.[118] This is the "section 519 statement".

Having produced the statement, an auditor resigning from a PIE can seek to replicate the situation in relation to a dismissal by requiring the directors to

22–19

---

[113] Directive art.38—an example of a PIE provision being contained in the Directive. This is implemented in the UK by 2006 Act s.511A.

[114] 2006 Act s.516(1).

[115] 2006 Act s.519(1). The statement must be virtually contemporaneous with the departure.

[116] These circumstance are set out in s.519A(3).

[117] 2006 Act s.519(2A)—or its equivalent in the case of a private company.

[118] 2006 Act s.519(3A). In the case of a dismissal this obligation to the company may be overtaken in practice by the auditor's entitlement (discussed above) to circulate representations to the meeting at which the dismissal is to be considered (an opportunity which arises before the dismissal whilst the statement of circumstances is to be made only after dismissal). A statement by a non-PIE auditor must state that there are no matters to be drawn to the attention of shareholders and creditors, if this is the case.

convene a meeting of the shareholders to consider it,[119] though if "going quietly" was the motivation behind the resignation, the auditor is pretty unlikely to take this step.[120] Whether or not the resigning auditor triggers this right, the company must send circulate any s.519 statement received from a departing auditor to those entitled to receive copies of the company's accounts.[121] This too is unlikely to generate action on the part of dispersed shareholders, unless the statement reveals egregious conduct.

Of greater significance is the obligation to inform a regulator of the s.519 statement. The auditor must send the statement to the Registrar,[122] so that it gets onto the company's public file at Companies House, and to the appropriate audit authority,[123] both obligations being sanctioned by criminal sanctions. The appropriate audit authority for a PIE is the FRC and for a non-PIE a RSB. Where the s.519 statement is made by an auditor who is ceasing office other than at the end of an accounts meeting (or its private company equivalent), the company must forward to the appropriate audit authority a statement of its reasons for the occurrence of this event, though the company may simply say that it agrees with the reasons given by the departing auditor. Thus the regulator is informed of both sides of the dispute, if there is one, and is perhaps more likely to take action than dispersed shareholders, at least where the dispute reveals a public interest element. Overall, the management cannot remove an auditor prematurely, whether by dismissal or forced resignation, without facing a serious risk of a row at the general meeting (and, in the case of a listed company, adverse press publicity) and with the auditing and accounting authorities.

Failure to re-appoint an auditor

22–20   Finally, a management which has fallen out with its auditors may simply wait until the end of the term of office and replace them. As we have seen, in the case of a public company this is an annual opportunity, since the term of office of the auditor runs, normally, from one accounts meeting to the next, and in the case of a private company the deemed re-appointment mechanism can be brought to an end by appointing substitute auditors during the annual period for appointing them.[124] Moreover, since a change of auditors, for good reasons, is not an uncommon event and is now encouraged by the authorities, failure to re-appoint

---

[119] 2006 Act s.518—or, without requisitioning a special meeting, the auditor might require the statement to be read out at the next regular accounts meeting: s.518(3).

[120] The section might be used by a resigning auditor who does not want to go quietly, but wishes to avoid the ignominy of being sacked.

[121] 2006 Act s.520—unless the statement says that there are no matters to be drawn to the attention of members or creditors. The company may alternatively apply to the court to be relieved of the circulation obligation if the auditor is using the provision to secure publicity for defamatory matter. The company must then send to members or debenture-holders a statement setting out the effect of the order. There is a risk that a company will use the appeal procedure simply to delay circulation of the auditor's statement, discontinuing the application just before it is due to be heard. Such action places the company at risk of having to pay the auditor's costs on an indemnity basis: *Jarvis Plc v Pricewaterhouse Coopers* [2000] 2 B.C.L.C. 368.

[122] 2006 Act s.521.

[123] 2006 Act s.522.

[124] Above, para.22–18.

may not be suspicious. Alternatively, auditors who have fallen out with the management may simply not seek re-appointment. However, the Act does take steps to flush out information about failures to re-appoint which are questionable. First, a resolution to appoint someone other than the existing auditors must be a resolution of which special notice (at least 28 days)[125] has been given to the company, and the company must make use of the advance notice to inform the outgoing auditor and the proposed replacement of the resolution.[126] The outgoing auditor then has the right to have representations circulated in advance of the meeting or read out at the meeting, similar to the rights arising on a resolution to dismiss.[127] If, in the case of a private company, the decision is to be taken by written resolution, the right is to have the representations circulated to the members of the company.[128]

More important, because obligatory, the rules applying to PIEs concerning the auditor's duty to deposit a statement of circumstances with the company apply to the outgoing auditor.[129] Following on from that, the auditor must supply a copy of the statement to the Registrar and the FRC[130] and the company must circulate the statement to those entitled to receive the accounts,[131] but the company is not required to supply a statement of its reasons to the FRC.[132]

Whistle blowing

The auditor's relationship with the authorities is strengthened, possibility to the detriment of the quality of its relationship with the company, by whistle-blowing provisions, meaning a duty laid on the auditor to report certain categories of facts discovered in the course of the audit to the relevant authorities. In the case of PIEs the Regulation not surprisingly requires auditors to report suspected fraud or other irregularities to the company, but if the company does not investigate the suspicions, the auditor must report them to the relevant authorities.[133] This is supplemented by an obligation to report directly to the authorities evidence discovered in the course of the audit about "material" breaches of the law or regulation or which throws doubt on the continuous functioning of the PIE or which lead the auditor to form the intention not to issue an opinion on the financial statements or to issue a qualified opinion.[134] In the latter two cases the

22–21

---

[125] 2006 Act s.312.

[126] 2006 Act s.515(2),(3). The provisions of the section apply also where the period for re-appointment has passed without an appointment being made and the company later decides to appoint someone other than the outgoing auditors. Otherwise the section's requirements could be easily avoided.

[127] 2006 Act s.515(4)–(7).

[128] 2006 Act s.514.

[129] 2006 Act s.519(1), which applies where an auditor "ceases for any reason to hold office".

[130] 2006 Act ss.521(1) and 522(1).

[131] 2006 Act s.520(1). All this is somewhat pointless if the auditor is ceasing to hold office as the result of a re-tendering exercise.

[132] 2006 Act s.523(1) applies only where the auditor is ceasing to hold office other than at the end of an accounts meeting (or its private company equivalent).

[133] Regulation art.7.

[134] Regulation art.12. These provisions are reflected in International Standard on Auditing (UK and Ireland) 210, issued by the FRC.

auditor is not necessarily reporting any wrongdoing to the authorities, but is giving them advanced notice of something which will necessarily become public in due course. Disclosure under the above provisions does not make the auditor liable under any contractual or legal restriction on the disclosure of information.[135] The relevant authority in the UK will often be the FRC but might be different body in some cases, such as the Serious Fraud Office.

Although general whistle-blowing provisions of this kind were previously not part of UK law, UK auditing standards have for some time required auditors to consider whether the public interest requires such action,[136] and on the basis of this professional guidance it has been held that the auditor's legal duties to the company could embrace, as a last resort, a duty to inform relevant third parties of suspected wrongdoing.[137]

Shareholders and the audit report

22–22   The focus on the shareholder role in relation to the appointment and removal of auditors rather obscures the fact that the audit report is a report to the shareholders, to which they might be expected to react. Until recently, the Act provided no specific channels for these reactions. It was assumed that the shareholders would use their general governance powers (for example, to remove directors) or impose market pressure on the company by selling their shares. We have seen above[138] that the Government did not take up the CLR's general proposal for a "pause" between the delivery of the annual accounts and reports to the members and the holding of the annual general meeting, during which period shareholders would have an opportunity, at no cost to themselves, to require the company to circulate resolutions for consideration at the AGM in relation to those documents. However, a weak form of that proposal is to be found in ss.527–531 of the Act. Shareholders of a quoted company[139] may require the company to post on its website a shareholder statement about the audit of the company's accounts or about the circumstances in which an auditor has ceased to hold office, for consideration at the company's accounts meeting (normally its AGM). The tests for defining the members entitled to require website publication are the same as those for requiring circulation of a resolution to be considered at an AGM,[140] that is, members representing at least 5 per cent of the total voting rights of those entitled to vote at the accounts meeting or 100 voting members holding shares

---

[135] Regulation art.12(3).

[136] See International Standards on Auditing (UK and Ireland) No.110, *Fraud and Error*; and No.250A, *Consideration of Laws and Regulations in an Audit of Financial Statements*, both 2009. In the financial services area extensive reporting obligations are imposed on auditors in favour of the regulator: FSMA 2000 Pt XXII.

[137] *Sasea Finance Ltd v KPMG* [2000] 1 All E.R. 676 CA, where the court refused to strike out a claim for loss suffered by the company where the auditors discovered fraud on the part of those in control of the company and failed to report it to the relevant authorities.

[138] Ch.15 at para.15–58.

[139] One listed in the UK or any other EEA state or on the New York Stock Exchange or Nasdaq: ss.531 and 385.

[140] Above, para.15–56.

upon which an average of at least £100 has been paid up.[141] The company is required to post the statement on its website within three working days of its receipt and to keep it there until after the accounts meeting,[142] unless the company persuades a court that the shareholders are abusing their rights.[143] A copy of it must be sent to the auditor at the same time as it is posted.[144] The company may not charge the shareholders for the costs of website publication, which will normally be negligible.[145] Finally, when it gives notice of the accounts meeting, the company must draw attention to the existence of this facility and that it is without cost to the members, which may encourage them to take it up.

THE ROLE OF THE AUDIT COMMITTEE OF THE BOARD

Introduction

The argument in favour of conferring a greater role on directors in relation to the audit is that the board is able to give more continuous attention to the audit than are the shareholders, whose contribution is naturally episodic, normally at the annual general meeting when the auditors' report is considered and the auditors appointed or re-appointed. The conflict of interest which the board may have on audit matters can be dealt with, it is argued, by entrusting this supervisory role not to the board as a whole but to an appropriate committee of the board. Audit committees are now common among UK companies traded on public securities markets. This is partly because successive versions of the UK Corporate Governance Code ("CGC") have recommended, on a comply or explain basis, that companies with a premium listing[146] on the Main Market of the London Stock Exchange establish such committees of the board, along with remuneration and appointment committees.[147] However, in relation to public interest entities there is now a mandatory requirement for audit committees contained in the Directive. The provisions of the Directive in relation to audit committees are transposed into domestic law via rules made by the Financial Conduct Authority ("FCA"), notably its Disclosure and Transparency Rule ("DTR") 7.[148] Present practice is thus an amalgam of these two streams of rules, though their coverage is not exactly the same. Premium listing is a voluntary choice on the part of the listed company, whereas the definition of 'public interest entities' embraces all companies with securities traded on a regulated market.

22–23

---

[141] 2006 Act s.527(2),(3). This is one of the sections where those to whom governance rights have been transferred may act: s.153(1)(d) and above, para.15–34.

[142] 2006 Act s.528(4). Failure to do so is a criminal offence on the part of every officer in default.

[143] 2006 Act s.527(5),(6).

[144] 2006 Act s.529(3).

[145] 2006 Act s.529(2).

[146] See para.25–6.

[147] See para.14–75.

[148] The core obligation to "comply or explain" in relation to the CGC is also embodied in FCA rules (Listing Rule 9.8.6(5)(6)). Since PIEs are essentially listed companies, use of FCA rules is a convenient way of focusing on the correct sub-set of companies as far as their governance structure is concerned.

Composition of the audit committee

22–24   Article 39 the Directive is headed "audit committee" and art.39(1) appears to require most PIEs[149] to establish an audit committee, so that this is no longer a "comply or explain" obligation for companies with securities listed on the Main Market of the London Stock Exchange. In fact, art.39(4) allows Member States to dispense with the audit committee if there is some other body within the company performing equivalent functions. Consequently, DTR 7.1.1 is drafted in terms of requiring a listed company to have a "body" which discharges the functions assigned to the audit committee by the Directive. However, since the UK Corporate Governance Code (C.3.1) recommends the establishment of an audit committee of the board, we assume in this account that the "body" will take the form of such a committee.[150] It is possible, however, that in small companies the task could be discharged by the board as whole, since the drafting of DTR 7 permits this and the company could explain its non-compliance under the CGC.[151] Under the Directive the committee is to be composed of non-executive members of the board or of appointees of the shareholders, of whom the majority (including the chair) are to be independent of the company. The UK CGC does not envisage members of the audit committee being directly appointed by the shareholders but rather that the members should all be members of the board. Shareholder appointments directly to board committees is not part of UK practice and it is unlikely that the Directive will encourage the adoption of this approach.[152] However, the CGC recommends that all members of the audit committee be independent, and this is likely to continue to be UK practice. Both sets of rules agree that at least one member of the committee "shall have competence in accounting and/or auditing" (Directive) or "recent and relevant financial experience" (CGC).

Functions of the audit committee

22–25   The Regulation indicates the importance it attaches to the audit committee by conferring on it a list of functions which, together, make the audit committee the central focus for dealings between the auditor and the PIE:

(a)   The appointment of the auditor is a process run by the audit committee.[153] That committee makes a recommendation for the appointment of the auditor and, except for the renewal of an existing engagement, that recommendation must contain at least two choices, with a reasoned

---

[149] There are some exceptions in art.39(3), of which the most important for our purposes is a subsidiary where the requirements of the Directive are met at group level.

[150] Under art.39(1) it could be a "stand-alone" committee, but we ignore this possibility as unrecognised in UK practice.

[151] Because of the flexibility inherent in the "body" requirement the UK has not taken up the specific Member States option (art.39(2)) to assign to the board as a whole the audit committee's functions in small and medium-sized companies and companies with small market capitalisation.

[152] Shareholder appointment to the audit committee fits more naturally with systems where the audit committee is a stand-alone committee.

[153] Regulation art.16.

statement of the committee's preference among them. The choices must have resulted from an open and transparent tendering process organised by the committee.[154] Although the detail of the procedure are left up to the committee to determine, the selection is required to be made according to publicised selection criteria and to be capable of justification according to those criteria. The aim appears to be to avoid "sweet heart" deals between auditor and the company. Although the committee's recommendations go to the full board and the full board makes the final recommendations to the shareholders, it is likely that the board will simply follow what the committee recommends. If the full board makes a different proposal, it must justify its departure from the committee's proposals and, in any event, the board's list may not include an auditor who has not participated in the selection process.[155]

(b) Whilst the appointed auditor reports to the members of the company,[156] the audit committee must receive at the same time or earlier a more detailed report which delves into some sensitive matters.[157] These include the methodology underlying the audit, the quantitative criteria used to determine materiality,[158] the valuation methods used in the financial statements and the judgements underlying the auditor's 'going concern' conclusions. The report to the audit committee must also give details of any significant deficiencies in the financial statements and of any areas of non-compliance (actual or suspected) with the applicable legal rules or the articles of association, explain the grounds on which companies were included in or excluded from the consolidated accounts, report any significant difficulties arising during the conduct of the audit and, finally, describe the extent of the auditor's interaction with the management of the company. It is clear that this list adds considerably to the auditor's standard reporting duties but also that the audit committee will require a significant level of expertise to understand and evaluate the report it receives.

(c) The approval of the audit committee is required for the provision to the PIE of permitted non-audit services.[159]

(d) Where the audit fee received from the PIE exceeds 15 per cent of the auditor's total fee income over a period of three years, the audit committee must decide whether the audit engagement should continue (in any case it may not continue for more than two years) and whether the audit report should be subject to review by another statutory auditor.[160] The danger here is perceived to be that the auditor has become too dependent on a single

---

[154] Except in the case of PIEs which are small or medium-sized or have a market capitalisation of less than €100 million. "Small or medium-sized" has a special meaning here which is not the same as for the accounts directives (see para.21–4) but is a more expansive set of criteria derived from the prospectus directive, involving meeting two of the following three criteria: an average number of employees during the financial year of fewer than 250, a total balance sheet not exceeding €43 million and an annual net turnover not exceeding €50 million (art.16(4)).

[155] Regulation art.16(5).

[156] See paras 22–4 and 22–5.

[157] Regulation art.11.

[158] Many accounting rules require the disclosure of only "material" items.

[159] Regulation art.5(4). See para.22–13, above.

[160] Regulation art.4(3).

client and so is less likely to be rigorous in its scrutiny. Given the adverse consequences for the auditor of exceeding the 15 per cent threshold over the three year period, it is likely that auditors will not allow this situation to arise. Ironically, the risk of exceeding the threshold is greater for small auditors trying to break into the PIE market than it is for the established "big four" global auditing networks.

(e)   In addition to the Directive's general independence requirements for auditors,[161] the Regulation requires a PIE auditor annually to confirm its independence in writing to the audit committee and to discuss with the committee any threats to its independence and potential safeguards.[162]

(f)   Finally, audit committees are themselves subject to periodic review of their effectiveness by the FRC.[163]

In addition to these specific duties the Directive adds a group of more general duties to the list of the audit committee's tasks. These are to monitor the financial reporting process, the company's internal quality assurance and risk management systems and the conduct of the statutory audit and to report to the board as a whole on the outcomes of the statutory audit.[164] The inclusion of internal risk management review is a significant addition to the committee's tasks, since it gives the committee a very important internal governance role.

Despite this formidable list of tasks, it is doubtful whether the Regulation and the Directive substantially upgrade what has been expected from audit committees in the UK for some years. The UK CGC covers a lot of the same ground.[165] In addition the Code recommends that a separate section of the annual report to the shareholders should explain how the audit committee has discharged its obligations during the year and that the chair of the audit committee should be available at the AGM to answer shareholders' questions.[166] In 2002, as a result of the efforts of a committee chaired by Sir Robert Smith, extensive extra-Code guidance for audit committees was produced, which, whilst having no formal status, even on a "comply or explain" basis, strongly indicates the enhanced importance of the audit committee.[167] The FRC has also produced guidance on risk management which stresses the potential role of the audit committee.[168] Nevertheless, the embodiment of these requirements in hard law may lead to greater regulatory, and potentially litigation, focus on these matters.

---

[161] See para.21–12, above.

[162] Regulation art.6(3).

[163] Regulation art.27(1)(c), though this provision is placed in an article dealing predominantly with the operation of the market for audit services.

[164] Directive art.39(6).

[165] UK CGD, C.3.2-7.

[166] C.3.8 and E.2.3.

[167] For the present version of that guidance see FRC, *Guidance on Audit Committees*, 2012, likely to be revised soon in the light of the Directive and Regulation.

[168] FRC, *Guidance on Risk Management, Internal Control and Related Financial and Business Reporting*, 2014.

AUDITOR COMPETENCE

So far in this chapter we have focused on the issue of auditor independence. But competence is important as well. Shareholders, investors and creditors may suffer if the auditor, whilst not beholden to management, just does not do a good job and produces accounts which are not reliable. Moreover, as noted, one sign of lack of independence may be a lax audit which does not meet professional standards, so that tackling competence is an indirect way of tackling lack of independence. Rules aimed at increasing competence may be aimed at controlling those permitted to carry out audits, at controlling how audits are carried out or at sanctioning those who have carried out incompetent audits. The sanctions may be criminal, administrative or civil. Competence may also by enhanced by extending the auditor's powers.

22–26

Qualifications

An early concern of the EU law on auditors was to require that they be appropriately trained and qualified and continue to be so.[169] We do not need to go into the details in this book. It is enough to note that the rules of the recognised supervisory bodies (i.e. normally the professional institutes)[170] must provide for appointment as statutory auditor to be confined to those who hold appropriate qualifications (or in the case of appointment of a firm that each individual responsible on behalf of the firm is so qualified and that the firm is controlled by such persons).[171] Schedule 11 then lays out in some detail the terms on which bodies may award professional qualifications. The discharge by the RSBs of this function is overseen by the FRC.[172] Since a person who acts as an auditor without the appropriate qualifications is ineligible to do so,[173] the POB has the power to require a second audit in such cases and the ineligible auditor may be liable for its costs.[174] An auditor may also be appropriately qualified by virtue of a qualification granted in another EEA State and of having passed an aptitude test and spent an adaptation period in the UK.[175] The FRC also has power to recognise qualifications obtained outside the EEA where it is thought that they are equivalent and where the country in question would provide reciprocal treatment of persons qualified in the UK.[176] The names of statutory auditors must be entered into a public register, which must include an indication of the other Member States (if any) in which the auditor is registered. It must also contain the names of third country auditors who sign the audit reports of third country companies whose securities are traded on a regulated market in the EU.[177]

22–27

---

169 Directive, Ch.2.
170 See above, para.22–11.
171 2006 Act Sch.10 para.6.
172 Statutory Auditors Regulations reg.3(1)(f)–(j).
173 2006 Act s.1212(1)(b).
174 See above, para.22–12.
175 2006 Act Sch.10 para.6.
176 2006 Act s.1221.
177 2006 Act ss.1239–1247 and the Statutory Auditors Regulations Pt 4.

Auditing standards

22–28 Auditing standards play a similar role in relation to the function of auditing as accounting standards play in relation to drawing up the accounts. An auditor is necessarily concerned with both sets of standards: the auditor must establish that the accounts have been drawn up properly (including in accordance with the relevant accounting standards) and he or she must carry out the job of checking the financial statements in a proper manner (in accordance with auditing standards). In the case of a negligence claim against the auditor, compliance with both accounting and auditing standards is likely to be a matter to which the courts attach great weight.[178] As with accounting standards, auditing standards are becoming internationalised. Article 26 of the Directive requires Member States to secure compliance on the part of statutory auditors (in all cases, not just the audits of PIEs) with international standards issued by the International Auditing and Assurance Standards Board ("IAASB"), based in New York, once these have been adopted by the Commission. In default of adoption of international standards, Member States apply national standards though only "to the extent necessary to add to the credibility and quality of financial statements". However, the process of adoption of auditing standards for the EU lags behind that of adopting accounting standards, and, at the time of writing, none has been adopted. In the UK, this delay is of little consequence since the approach of the FRC to auditing standards has been to adopt those laid down by the IAASB, but with additional explanatory material.

Quality assurance, investigation and discipline

22–29 A central function of the FRC is to oversee the monitoring of audit quality in general and to carry out investigations into particular cases of suspected inadequate audit and to secure (subject to appeal) disciplinary sanctions.[179] This has been so since the substantial domestic reform of auditor regulation initiated by the Companies (Audit, Investigation and Community Enterprise) Act 2004, which effectively did away with professional self-regulation in these areas. In respect of PIEs the Regulation requires these functions to be carried out by the FRC itself.[180] In other cases, the task may be delegated by the FRC to or shared with the RSBs. Quality assurance means the periodic inspection of audits carried out in particular companies accompanied by possible recommendations for improvement—a process now familiar in many walks of life. Both the Directive[181] and the Regulation[182] require quality assurance arrangements to be put in place but the latter, applying to PIEs, is more prescriptive about the nature of the process, requires quality assurance reviews more frequently (every three years rather than every six) and makes the "recommendations" of the inspectors binding. In order to facilitate this work of the FRC the Regulation requires an

---

[178] For accounting standards see, above, at para.21–16.
[179] Statutory Auditors Regulations reg.3(1)(l)(m).
[180] Regulation art.24(1).
[181] Regulation art.29.
[182] Regulation art.26.

"annual transparency report"[183] by the auditor to the authority, setting out information such as the PIEs for whom it acts, the firm's governance and remuneration structure and its practices designed to ensure independence.

In the case of suspected inadequate audits the Directive contains a series of provisions requiring effective investigation powers and a range of potential sanctions to be available, and lays down criteria for determining the severity of the sanction in particular cases.[184] The Regulation adds information and access rights in the case of PIEs.[185] The disciplinary sanctions range from private censure, through public censure to a prohibition on acting as an auditor and imposing a financial penalty.[186] In important cases the disciplinary proceedings are commenced in the UK by the FRC, which initiates proceedings before Disciplinary Tribunal, established by but independent of the FRC. The Tribunal is chaired by an experienced lawyer, and appeal lies to an Appeal Tribunal.

Empowering auditors

Even if the statutory and professional rules produce loyal and competent auditors, auditors may fail to detect impropriety in the company if they are not given the co-operation of those who work for it. If an auditor does not receive the co-operation needed to assess the company's accounts, that fact can be reflected in the ultimate report to the shareholders,[187] but it is obviously more desirable that the auditor should be able obtain the necessary information. The issue of the auditor's powers as against the audited company and its management is one to which the legislature has given increasing attention in recent years.

22–30

Auditors have a right of access at all times to the company's books, accounts and vouchers.[188] They are entitled to require such information and explanations as they think necessary for the performance of their duties. Those under the obligation to provide the information and explanations now go beyond the company's officers and embrace (present or past): employees of the company; persons holding or accountable for the company's accounts (for example, where the company has outsourced this function); subsidiary companies incorporated in the UK; and persons falling within the above categories in relation to the subsidiary and the subsidiary's auditor (if different).[189] More problematic, though of great importance, is the position of subsidiaries incorporated outside the UK and the relevant persons connected with them. Here the problem of comity of legal systems is dealt with by putting an obligation on the parent, if required by its auditors to do so, to take such steps as are reasonably open to it to obtain such

---

[183] Regulation art.13.
[184] Regulation arts 30–30b. The investigation provisions are transposed into domestic law by Sch.2 to the Statutory Auditors Regulations.
[185] Regulation art.23(3).
[186] Regulation art.30a, reflected in the Statutory Auditors Regulations reg.5.
[187] As the Act requires: s.498(3).
[188] 2006 Act s.499(1).
[189] 2006 Act s.499(2). Statements so made may not be used in subsequent criminal proceedings against the maker (except in respect of offences connected with the making of the statement) and the requirement is subject to an exception for legal professional privilege: s.499(3),(4).

information and explanations from the subsidiary and the relevant persons.[190] A failure to respond "without delay" to a request for information is a criminal offence, unless compliance was not reasonably practicable. Also criminal is knowingly or recklessly making to the auditors a statement which conveys or purports to convey any information or explanation which is misleading, false or deceptive in any material particular.[191]

The above rights for the auditor depend upon the auditor knowing which questions to ask. Since the auditor is by profession an investigator, it is reasonable to suppose that he or she will often be in a position to ask the right questions. However, the CLR[192] thought there was a good argument for requiring directors to "volunteer" information rather than leaving the auditor to find everything out. This reform was implemented via an addition to the matters required to be disclosed in the directors' report.[193] That report must contain a statement on the part of each director to the effect that (a) so far as the director is aware, there is no information needed by the auditor of which the auditor is unaware; and (b) the director has taken all steps he ought to have taken to make him- or herself aware of such information and to establish that the auditor is aware of it.[194] This may require the director to reveal his or her wrongdoing or that of fellow directors to the auditor.[195] The full extent of what is required of the director is to be assessed by reference to the director's objective duty of care,[196] but the Act specifically recognises that making enquiries of fellow directors and the auditor might be enough to discharge the duty (i.e. that the director can rely on satisfactory answers from such sources to appropriate questions).[197] A director is criminally liable if the statement is false but only if the director knew of the falsity or was reckless as to whether the statement was true or false and if he or she failed to take reasonable steps to prevent the (inaccurate) directors' report from being approved.[198] However, as we shall see below, failure to comply with this provision may also limit the auditor's civil liability towards the company by virtue of the doctrine of contributory negligence.

---

[190] 2006 Act s.500.

[191] 2006 Act s.501. However, for the foreign subsidiary or those connected with it to make an inaccurate statement is not a criminal offence (s.501(1) applies only to s.499), probably an unavoidable loop-hole, since otherwise British law would be criminalising conduct committed abroad.

[192] CLR, Final Report I, paras 8.119–8.122.

[193] See para.21–22.

[194] 2006 Act s.418(2). Wilfully suppressing relevant information may be a ground for disqualification—potentially lengthy—of a director. See *Re TransTec Plc (No.2)* [2007] 2 B.C.L.C. 495; and Ch.10.

[195] A result which, as we have seen, the director's core duty of loyalty may also produce: above, para.16–78.

[196] See para.16–24.

[197] 2006 Act s.418(4).

[198] 2006 Act s.418(5),(6). For the process of approving the directors' report, see para.21–30.

LIABILITY FOR NEGLIGENT AUDIT

The nature of the issue

Imposing civil liability on an auditor towards the company in the case of a negligent audit is an obvious way of encouraging diligence on the part of auditors. It is also a liability which arises naturally out of the law of tort, once negligence liability was extended to misstatements. If an auditor produces an audit report which is misleading and the inaccuracy can be traced to a lack of care, skill or diligence on the part of the auditor, then those to whom the auditor owed a duty to take care will be in a position to sue the auditor for damages, if they can show that the inaccurate report caused them loss. In the case of a single auditor, the liability will lie with that person; in the more common case of a firm being appointed auditor, then the individuals who were negligent will be liable but so also will the firm, either because the negligence of the individuals is regarded as the negligence of the firm or because the firm is vicariously liable for the negligence of the individuals. Nevertheless, as we shall see below, the question of how wide that liability should be (both in terms of the range of potential claimants and the quantum of liability) raises difficult policy issues.

22–31

The rules for determining the underlying liability of the auditor rests, even after the 2006 Act, with the common law,[199] though statute has played a role in fashioning the way that common law liability applies to auditors. It is important to distinguish among the potential claimants against the auditor between the audit client and everyone else. That the audit client in principle has a claim against the negligent auditor is well-established, that claim being based either on the contract between the auditor and the company or on the tort of negligence.[200] In relation to claims by persons other than the audit client, however, the question of how widely the duty of care in tort is owed has been, as we shall see, fiercely debated in the courts and the upshot of the litigation is a rather restricted duty of care. Of course, the matter might be decided by contract even in relation to non-clients, but there is less likely to be an explicit contract between the auditor and the non-client upon which the claimant can rely. However, as we shall see, the thrust of the court decisions on the tortious liability of auditors is that liability exists in relation to non-clients only where a relationship akin to a contract has arisen.

The formulation of the duty of care owed by auditors to non-client claimants is but one example of a generally cautious attitude on the part of legislators towards auditors' civil liability. One might have thought that increasing the civil liability

---

[199] In the case of the appointment of a firm as auditor, the senior statutory auditor must sign the report (s.503(3)), but s.504(3) provides that the person identified as the senior statutory auditor is not thereby subject to any civil liability to which he or she would not otherwise be subject. Nor would it seem that members of the audit team who would otherwise be liable are protected from liability by the signature of the senior statutory auditor.

[200] It makes little difference which way the claim is put, since the implied term in the contract to provide audit services will be, as in tort, only a duty to take reasonable care. In particular, the defence of contributory negligence is available whichever way the claim is put: *Forsikringsaktieselskapet Vesta v Butcher* [1989] A.C. 852 at 858–868 CA. Of course, the parties could by contract seek to increase the level of the duty (for example, to a warranty that the audit report was accurate), but their freedom to lower the duty is subject to the statutory provisions discussed below.

of the auditor would be an effective way of providing incentives to auditors to be both independent and competent. However, unlike all the legal strategies discussed above, which in one way or another have seen some expansion in recent years, judicial decisions and legislative rules have ensured that there has been no such expansion in relation to civil liability; in fact, the tendency in recent years has been to rein in civil liability.

22–32   As regards liability to non-clients, there is a particular problem that liability arises out of the fact that the accounts and reports and the auditor's report thereon are placed in the public domain.[201] It is therefore possible that a very large number of people will rely on them in order to carry out a wide range of transactions. Unrestricted liability on the part of auditors to third parties who rely on the accounts thus raises the prospect, as it was once famously described, of "liability in an indeterminate amount for an indeterminate time to an indeterminate class".[202] We discuss this problem further below in relation to the decision of the House of Lords in *Caparo Industries Plc v Dickman*,[203] but, at its worst, the liability rules might cause the audit market to unravel through the withdrawal of financially sound auditors.

22–33   Even in relation to actions by audit clients, there are difficult issues about the proper scope of the liability rules. Thus, the general tort doctrine of joint and several liability may significantly increase the tort exposure of auditors. Under this doctrine, if two or more tortfeasors are liable in respect of the same loss, the injured party may recover from any one of them for the whole of the loss, leaving the defendant to seek contributions from the other tortfeasors. In the classic case, where the misstatements in the company's accounts result from the fraud or negligence of someone within the company and the failure of the auditors to discover the wrongdoing, the claimant[204] may recover the whole of the loss from the auditor, leaving the auditor to bear the risk that the original wrongdoers (usually directors or employees of the company) are judgment proof. Thus, claimants are encouraged to sue the defendants with "deep pockets" for the recovery of the whole of their loss, even though the auditor may be only the minor party at fault. Again, there is a risk the audit market will unravel in these circumstances.

The above problems are only partially addressed (and may even be exacerbated) by the professional indemnity insurance (or equivalent arrangements) which audit firms are obliged to carry.[205] That insurance may be very expensive and so increase the cost of audits and it may not be available for the full extent of the claim, so that the liability risk is only partially collectivised through the insurance mechanism. More problematically, the presence of insurance may actually encourage litigation against auditors, since claimants will know that auditors are worth suing and auditors will have an incentive to settle

---

[201]   See para.21–33.

[202]   *Ultramares Corp v Touche* (1931) 174 N.E. 441 at 441, per Cardozo CJ.

[203]   *Caparo Industries Plc v Dickman* [1990] 2 A.C. 605 HL.

[204]   In the case of actions by the company, this position is significantly qualified by the defence of contributory negligence (see para.22–39), but the point provides a potential rationale for restricting auditor liability to third parties.

[205]   2006 Act Sch.10 para.17.

quietly rather than fight the issue in court provided they keep the liability within the insurance limits. There has been some movement in the common law world towards the substitution of "proportionate" liability for joint and several liability for auditors (i.e. the auditor is liable only for the share of the loss which is fairly attributable to the auditor's negligence).[206] However, in the UK, despite pressure from the accounting profession, there has been resistance to such a move on the grounds that it simply shifts the risk of insolvency from the auditor to the wholly innocent claimant.[207] Nevertheless, a British solution has emerged in the 2006 reforms permitting a "liability limitation agreement" between auditor and audit client, as discussed below. A restriction of liability to the auditor's proportionate share of the loss is a permissible type of agreement. This reform, of course, does not address third party claims against auditors.

Providing audit services through bodies with limited liability

Where the auditor is an audit firm taking the form of a traditional partnership, further issues are raised. The assets of the firm as a whole become available to satisfy the claimant in the case of loss caused by a partner (or employee) acting in the ordinary course of the business of the firm.[208] In addition, given the absence of limited liability in the traditional partnership, the personal assets of both the negligent partner and fellow partners may be called on to meet the claim.[209] The prospect of personal liability (uncovered by insurance) might induce such defensive action on the part of auditors that utility of the audit is reduced, because, for example, auditors began to give qualified audit opinions based on trivial grounds. Something has been done to address the issue of personal liability. Audit services may now be provided to a company by an accounting firm which is not a partnership. The Act provides that both individuals and firms are eligible to be appointed as auditors[210] and then defines a "firm" as "any entity, whether or not a legal person, that is not an individual".[211] Thus, the old idea that it was the hallmark of a professional that he or she provided services on the basis of personal liability for their quality has gone. Some accounting firms have set up their auditing arms as limited companies, but, by and large, the company form of internal organisation is not attractive to professional partnerships. The accounting firms therefore pressed for, and ultimately obtained in 2000, a new corporate vehicle, the limited liability partnership,[212] which has the internal structure of a partnership but benefits from limited liability in its external dealings. The origins

22–34

---

[206] See, for example, R. Austin and I. Ramsay, *Ford's Principles of Corporations Law*, 12th edn (Australia, 2005) pp.609–610.

[207] DTI, *Feasibility Investigation of Joint and Several Liability by the Common Law Team of the Law Commission*, (1996); CLR, Final Report I, para.8.138. As to situations where the claimant is not wholly innocent, see below, para.22–39.

[208] Partnership Act 1890 s.10.

[209] Partnership Act 1890 s.12. Joint and several liability operates again, this time among the partners.

[210] 2006 Act s.1212(1).

[211] 2006 Act s.1173(1).

[212] See above, para.1–4.

of this new vehicle are demonstrated by the fact that, when originally proposed, it was to be confined to professional businesses, but in the end it was made generally available.[213]

Conducting the audit through a vehicle with limited liability certainly protects the personal assets of the non-negligent partners. Whether the personal assets of the negligent partner are so protected depends on whether the negligent misstatement in the audit report is analysed as having been made by the member, for whose tort the corporate body is vicariously liable (personal assets of the negligent member not protected), or whether the negligent misstatement is analysed as having been made by the corporate body through the auditor, in which case the personal assets of the negligent member are not at risk. The decision of the House of Lords in *Williams v Natural Life Health Foods*[214] suggests the latter analysis (personal assets not at risk) but it is unclear whether the *Williams* rationale extends to statements by professionals.[215]

22-35   Even if *Williams* does apply, the benefits of corporate personality and limited liability are restricted to the personal assets of the members: the business of the corporate body itself could still be destroyed by a large claim which exceeded the insurance cover and pushed the body into insolvency. This is, indeed, the public policy crux. If there were many competing firms of auditors, the occasional insolvency of one of them might not matter in public policy terms. However, there are now only four international networks of firms capable of carrying out the audits of the largest multinational firms, and the collapse of Arthur Andersen in the aftermath of the Enron scandal in the US is a reminder of how quickly such international firms can disintegrate.[216] The disappearance of another such firm would further reduce competition in the market for the audit of multinational companies from its already low level. However, this fear should not push legislators into hasty acceptance of arguments for the reduction of auditors' liability without rigorous scrutiny of the likely impact. For example, it was argued that a cap on auditors' liability would increase competition in the audit market, especially for large firm audits, on the grounds that a cap would encourage medium-sized audit firms to move up into the "big league". However, an analysis by the Office of Fair Trading concluded that such a result was not a likely impact of the reform.[217] A more robust approach might be to seek to open up the audit market, especially the market for the audit of the largest companies, to a wider range of firms. As we have seen above, rules relating to mandatory re-tendering of audit contracts were driven as much by competition concerns as by concerns for auditor independence.[218]

---

[213] For the origins of the LLP see G. Morse et al. (eds), *Palmer's Limited Liability Partnership Law*, 2nd edn (London: Sweet & Maxwell, 2012), Ch.1.

[214] *Williams v Natural Life Health Foods* [1998] 1 W.L.R. 830; above, para.7–32.

[215] *Merrett v Babb* [2001] Q.B. 1171 CA; *Phelps v Hillingdon LBC* [2001] 2 A.C. 619 HL. For discussion see Whittaker, [2002] J.B.L. 601.

[216] Arthur Andersen did not collapse because of a large liability claim but because of loss of reputation resulting from its being charged with and convicted of criminal offences (even though these convictions were overturned on appeal).

[217] OFT, *An Assessment of the Implications for Competition of a Cap on Auditors' Liability*, OFT 741, July 2004.

[218] See para.22–14.

We now turn to the ways in which the current liability rules reflect the above concerns, looking separately at claims by the audit client and by others.

CLAIMS BY THE AUDIT CLIENT

Establishing liability

As we have already noted, the audit client's cause of action in negligence is easily established in principle. Thus, the litigation is likely to focus on the question of whether the auditor has in fact been negligent and, if so, whether and how much loss has been caused to the claimant. As far as the standard of care is concerned, it is clear in law, though often not accepted in the commercial world, that the auditor is not a guarantor of the accuracy of the directors' accounts and reports. Indeed, in an old case the auditor was given a broad discretion to rely on information provided by management, so long as no suspicious circumstances had arisen which should have put the auditor on inquiry.[219] However, the modern law is different. As Lord Denning once put it, the auditor, in order to perform his task properly, "must come to it with an inquiring mind—not suspicious of dishonesty, I agree—but suspecting that someone may have made a mistake somewhere and that a check must be made to ensure that there has been none".[220] Auditor scepticism is now firmly established in audit regulation. The Directive requires Member States to ensure that the auditor "maintains professional scepticism throughout the audit".[221] As to what "scepticism" will require, the existence of accounting and auditing standards helps the courts to concretise the duty of care in any particular situation, even though they are not formally binding on the courts.[222] A court which relies on these standards can be sure that it is not imposing unexpected standards of care on auditors and that there has been some 'public interest' input into the formulation of the standards.

As to the quantum of liability, the auditor's failure to detect error in the company's financial statements deprives the directors (or shareholders) of knowledge which could have afforded them an opportunity to take remedial action or to prevent the company from proceeding with some action on a false basis (for example, by declaring a dividend or making representations and warranties in a contract for the sale of the company's business). That remedial action might take a number of forms, ranging from preventing a continuance of

22–36

---

[219] *Re Kingston Cotton Mill (No.2)* [1896] 2 Ch. 279 CA, where the auditors relied on certificates as to levels of stock which were provided by the managing director who for years had grossly overstated the true position. cf. *Re Thomas Gerrard & Son Ltd* [1967] 2 All E.R. 525, where the discovery of altered invoices, it was held, should have caused the auditors to carry out their own check on the stock.

[220] *Formento (Sterling Area) Ltd v Selsdon Fountain Pen Co Ltd* [1958] 1 W.L.R. 45 HL; and see also the remarks of Pennycuick J in *Re Thomas Gerrard* (cited in previous note).

[221] Directive art.21. Transposition in the UK is via standards made by the FRC: Statutory Auditors Regulations reg.2. Scepticism means "an attitude that includes a questioning mind, being alert to conditions which may indicate possible misstatement due to error or fraud and a critical assessment of audit evidence". Standards issued by the FRC already recognised the importance of professional scepticism before this change, made in 2014, to the Directive.

[222] *Lloyd Cheyham & Co Ltd v Littlejohn & Co* [1987] B.C.L.C. 303.

mismanagement or fraud to deciding to sell a company whose business model a proper audit would have shown to be under serious threat from changing economic circumstances. However, the auditor is not liable on a simple "but for" test for the company's failure through ignorance to take such action. For liability to arise, the action which the company might have taken or avoided must be one that was within the scope of the auditor's duty of care. This principle will embrace liability in respect of decisions that companies normally take on the basis of the accounts, such as declaring dividends or paying bonuses, whether to staff or policy-holders.[223] Thus, the auditor's liability will embrace losses caused to the company where the directors would have acted differently in these areas if they had known the full facts, even if the decision actually taken was perfectly lawful. Beyond such decisions, the auditor's duty of care will depend in large part on the scope of the audit engagement. The auditor's liability may extend to wider classes of decision, including strategic corporate decisions, if it is clear that the audit engagement contemplated that the company needed the audit information to make such decisions.[224]

22–37   In many cases, for example where the remedial action was the possible sale of the company's undertaking, what the company will have lost is really the chance to take a particular step, i.e. to find a purchaser at an acceptable price—who might or might not have been forthcoming. The pecuniary value to be placed on that lost opportunity depends upon the degree of likelihood that action would have been taken and that it would have led to the outcome the company alleges would have been reached. The court will have to assess the value of that chance, awarding the chance no value if it thinks it purely speculative.[225] Even where there was a course of action the directors could have taken which was wholly within their own control, liability will depend on its being shown that the step would have been taken. Often this will be difficult to do, especially in the case of fraud or mismanagement, when those involved included the directors. Then, it would seem, to establish any loss the claimant would have to show on the balance of probabilities that, had the auditors' report been properly qualified, action would have been taken by the shareholders which would have led to the removal of the directors. To recover any substantial damages, the claimant would have to establish, further, a probability that the ill-consequences of the former directors' negligent or fraudulent reign would have been effectively remedied by the steps which would have been taken. The difficulties of establishing all this are obvious.

---

[223] *Leeds Estate, Building and Investment Co v Shepherd* (1887) 36 Ch.D. 787; *Barings Plc (In Liquidation) v Coopers & Lybrand (No.1)* [2002] 2 B.C.L.C. 364; *Equitable Life Assurance Society v Ernst & Young* [2003] 2 B.C.L.C. 603 CA; cf. *MAN Nutzfahrzeuge AG v Freightliner Ltd* [2007] B.C.C. 986 CA.

[224] *Equitable Life Assurance Society v Ernst & Young* [2003] 2 B.C.L.C. 603 CA; *Sayers v Clarke-Walker* [2002] 2 B.C.L.C. 16.

[225] *Equitable Life Assurance Society v Ernst & Young* [2003] 2 B.C.L.C. 603 CA.

Limiting liability

Even if the claimant can establish liability and substantial loss, there are two types of argument available to the auditors to reduce their liability for the whole of that loss, one based on general defences (full or partial) to tortious liability and the other on contract.

22–38

General defences

The most obviously available defence is contributory negligence, whereby a claimant, who suffers loss as a result partly of his or her own fault and partly of the defendant's fault, will have the damages payable by the latter reduced by such amount as the court thinks just and equitable, having regard to the claimant's share of the responsibility for the damage.[226] Thus, where harm has been inflicted on the company through fraud committed by its employees which the directors failed to discover because they had inadequate internal controls in place and which the auditors failed to discover because they did not realise the internal controls were inadequate, the failures of the directors are the failures of the company which the auditors can pray in aid to reduce the damages payable. The disclosure statement now required of directors in the directors' report is likely to increase the incidence of this defence being run by the auditors.[227]

22–39

In fact, a somewhat similar result seems to have been obtained before this reform through the use by auditors of "representation letters", which auditors require companies to sign before the auditors will certify the accounts. In these letters the company typically promises "to the best of its knowledge and belief" that certain important matters concerning the company's financial situation are in a particular state.[228] If such a representation letter is signed negligently on behalf of the company, the auditors will have the partial defence of contributory negligence if subsequently sued by the company and it can be shown that the auditors would not have certified the accounts, or not certified them without further investigation, had they known the true facts. If the representation letter is signed fraudulently, the auditors have a complete defence, because any damages due from the auditors to the company can be wholly set off in the claim the auditors have against the company for deceit committed by the company against the auditors.[229]

In the above cases the situation is one where the both the auditors and the directors or senior management of the company failed to discover the fraud or negligence of a subordinate employee and where both are at fault in failing to do so. Reducing the company's recovery seems acceptable in this context for otherwise the existence of auditor liability would provide an incentive for companies not to manage their internal risk systems effectively. What is much

---

[226] Law Reform (Contributory Negligence) Act 1945 s.1(1).

[227] Above, para.22–30. Although misleading disclosure is not a civil wrong under the Act, it can still constitute "fault" on the part of the company for the purposes of the contributory negligence rule.

[228] The representations may include, for example, that "there have no irregularities involving management or employees who have a significant role in the system of internal control".

[229] *Barings Plc (In Liquidation) v Coopers & Lybrand (No.2)* [2002] 2 B.C.L.C. 410, where an example of a representation letter can be found.

less clear is whether the auditors should be permitted to build a defence of contributory negligence directly on the actions of the subordinate employee, i.e. in a situation where the only failure to discover the fraud or negligence is that of the auditors. The argument against allowing contributory negligence on this basis is that it reduces the incentive of the auditors to discover wrongdoing within the company—sometimes put as the argument that contributory negligence should not be based on conduct within the company which was "the very thing" (or one of those things) the auditors were under a duty to discover.

22–40 In *Barings Plc (In Liquidation) v Coopers & Lybrand*[230] the judge took account of both management failings and the undiscovered fraud of the employee (which was attributed to the company) in assessing the level of the company's contributory negligence. Applying this approach the judge assessed the company's contributory negligence at a high level, varying over the time of the fraud, beginning at a 50 per cent contribution and ending at 95 per cent. However, the judge did recognise some force in "the very thing" argument,[231] for it appears that he would otherwise have attributed the employee's fraud to the company so as to allow the auditors to avoid all liability. We need thus to consider again the rules on attribution, which we looked at in Ch.7, but here in a different context. In Ch.7 we considered attribution in the context of litigation by third parties against the company; here we consider litigation by the company against third parties. It is not obvious that the attribution rules should be the same, at least where the third party is the auditor, precisely because of the protective function of the auditors as against the company, which a broad set of rules on attribution might undermine.

22–41 The issue arose in an extreme form in *Stone & Rolls Ltd v Moore Stephens*[232] where the defendant auditors sought to raise the defence of illegality as a complete defence to liability. In this case a person who was the sole beneficial shareholder and controlling shadow director of a company established it for the purpose of committing large-scale fraud on banks. The company, in liquidation, sought compensation through its liquidator (acting in the economic interests of the creditors) for the allegedly negligent failure the defendant auditor to discover the fraud. The defendant sought to strike out the claim on the basis of an illegality defence usually referred to by its Latin name: ex turpi causa non oritur actio (roughly translated as "disgraceful conduct does not give rise to a cause of action"). This is a rule of public policy that the court will not allow its processes to be used by a claimant to benefit from its own illegal conduct. In this case, the majority by three to two allowed the defence, because of the controller's fraud, though on rather different grounds. As the Supreme Court itself said in a later

---

[230] *Barings Plc (In Liquidation) v Coopers & Lybrand* [2003] EWHC 1319 (Ch); [2003] Lloyd's Rep. I.R. 566 (the trial of the action whose interlocutory proceedings are cited in the previous note).
[231] Basing himself on *Reeves v Commissioner of Police of the Metropolis* [2000] 1 A.C. 360 HL.
[232] *Stone & Rolls Ltd v Moore Stephens* [2009] A.C. 1391 HL.

case, *Jetivia SA v Bilta (UK) Ltd*,[233] "it is very hard to derive much in the way of reliable principle from the decision" in the earlier case.

In the later case, however, all the judges seemed to agree on one proposition, namely, that the ex turpi defence is available only if there are no "innocent" (i.e. uninvolved in the fraud) shareholders or directors in the company. The decision thus affects only a limited number of claims by companies against their auditors. There was disagreement, however, on whether the defence was always available in the absence of innocent shareholders (and, perhaps, directors).[234] This was the most significant dividing line among the judges in *Stone & Rolls* itself. Since the company was in liquidation at the time of the litigation, the persons with an economic interest in the success of the claim were its creditors (i.e. the defrauded banks), who were "innocent". If the presence of innocent shareholders would have been enough to prevent use of the ex turpi defence by the auditors, presumably on the grounds that a public policy defence should not be deployed to deprive non-involved persons of the value of their interest in the company, it can be argued that the presence of innocent creditors of a company in liquidation should have the same negative impact on the availability of the defence. This argument does not involve acceptance of the proposition that auditors' duties are owed to the company's creditors (an argument which, as we see in the next section, the courts have accepted only in limited situations). The duty here is still one owed by the auditors to the company; the litigation is brought by the body which has the management of the company—the liquidator in this case; and the basis of the auditor's liability remains restoration of the company's assets to the level they would have enjoyed had the auditors not been negligent. The point rather is that, so long as the company is a going concern, the residual economic interest in the company's assets lies with the shareholders, so that excluding liability where all the shareholders are involved in the fraud is understandable. However, once the company is in the vicinity of insolvency, the residual economic interest shifts to the creditors, as the law now clearly recognises.[235] If the interests of non-involved shareholders trump the ex turpi defence when the company is a going concern, it would be consonant with recent developments in company law that the interests of non-involved creditors should be taken into account in the same way.[236]

---

[233] *Jetivia SA v Bilta (UK) Ltd* [2015] 1 B.C.L.C. 443 at [46], per Lord Neuberger, a case involving attribution in a third context, i.e. where the company sues a director. "We conclude that *Stone & Rolls* should be regarded as a case which has no majority ratio decidendi" (per Lords Toulson and Hodge at [154]).

[234] Lords Mance and, less strongly, Neuberger thought the point was still open; Lords Sumption, Toulson and Hodge thought the defence was always available in this situation.

[235] See para.9–11.

[236] This was essentially the reasoning of Lord Mance in *Stone & Rolls*, except that he attached significance to the fact that the company was insolvent at the time of the negligent audit. It might be that a better test is the presence of innocent creditors or shareholders at the time of the litigation. It would be odd if the presence of an innocent shareholder at the time of the negligence should facilitate an action by the company against the auditors even though that shareholder had left the company by the time of the litigation; and equally odd if the defence were available despite the fact that the fraudsters had sold out to a new set of shareholders by the time of the litigation.

Limitation by contract

22–42   It was formerly impossible for auditors to limit their liability to the company by means of a contract with it or by provision in the company's articles, or to obtain an enforceable promise of an indemnity from the company in respect of such liability,[237] but one of the main changes in the 2006 Act was to permit such contracts, subject to safeguards.[238] The indemnity prohibition did and does not apply if it relates to an agreement or provision to indemnify the auditor against a liability incurred in defending proceedings, criminal or civil, in which the auditor is successful or in making a successful application for relief under s.1157 of the Act.[239] This is a limited qualification to the prohibition which does no more than track the provisions relating to directors.[240]

The innovation is the permission for the auditor and company to contract to limit the amount of a liability the auditor owes to the company arising out of a breach of duty in the conduct of the audit. The section is widely enough drafted to permit the parties to introduce proportionate liability by agreement. This reform was recommended by the CLR but it is subject to reasonably strict safeguards. The principal ones are as follows:

(a)   The agreement is effective to limit the auditor's liability only to the amount that is fair and reasonable in the circumstances, having regard, amongst other things, to the auditor's responsibilities under the Act and the professional standards expected of the auditor.[241] If the agreement goes further than is permitted by this provision, then it operates so as to limit liability to the permitted level, i.e. the agreement does not fail altogether.[242] The agreement is exempted from the control provisions of the Unfair Contract Terms Act 1977,[243] which applies a reasonableness standard to similar limitations of negligence liability in many contracts. In short, the auditor limitation clause is subject to ex post court control by reference to a broad standard, as under UCTA, but the significance of the exclusion from UCTA 1977 is that a clause which fails the test under the 2006 Act still operates, but at a lower level of substantive protection.

---

[237] This is still the starting point of the Act: s.532.

[238] Limitation of liability is also promoted at EU level: see Commission Recommendation concerning the limitation of the civil liability of statutory auditors and audit firms ([2008] O.J. L162/39). However, in the US the Securities Exchange Commission opposes agreements on limitation, whilst accepting mandatory limits on auditors' liability, thus making the 2006 Act provisions unusable by UK-incorporated companies which are cross-listed in the US (*Financial Times*, 10 May 2009). The SEC fear apparently is that the need to negotiate a limitation undermines the independence of auditors (rather than giving clients the opportunity to obtain improvements in audit quality). This is somewhat ironic in view of the fact that the liability of auditors is limited by statute to proportionate liability in the US.

[239] Essentially, the auditor may rely on a promise by the company to pay the costs of a successful defence.

[240] See para.16–130.

[241] 2006 Act s.537(1). In determining what is fair and reasonable the court must ignore matters occurring after the loss or damage has been incurred (an attempt to restrain hindsight) and the possibility of recovering compensation from other persons.

[242] 2006 Act s.537(2).

[243] 2006 Act s.534(3).

(b)   The agreement may relate to only a single financial year, i.e. a new agreement is needed for each set of annual reports and accounts.[244]

(c)   The agreement must be approved by the members, though in the case of a private company the members, before the company enters into the agreement, may pass a resolution waiving the need for approval.[245]

To provide a check that these requirements have been met, a note to the companies accounts must set out the principal terms of the liability limitation agreement and the date on which it was approved by the members (or approval was waived).[246]

The FRC produced guidance on the operation of these provisions,[247] which contemplates three main types of agreement: proportionate liability, a "fair and reasonable" test and a cap on liability, which could be expressed in a number of ways, but most obviously as a multiple of the audit fee. However, institutional shareholders have indicated that they will normally vote in favour only of proportionate liability agreements and, in particular, will be opposed to caps on liability.[248] Further, they will expect an improvement in audit quality in exchange for the agreement, in particular, less defensive auditing.

Criminal liability

The 2006 Act reform, permitting auditor liability limitation agreements, was accompanied by an increase of criminal liability for an auditor who knowingly or recklessly makes a statement in the audit report which is misleading, false or deceptive.[249] In other words, the deterrent effect of unlimited liability in damages for negligence was to some extent replaced by a narrower criminal liability for intentional or reckless misstatements.[250] The liability applies to the statement that the accounts give a true and fair view[251] and to statements in the audit report about the compliance of the company's accounts with its accounting records, about whether the necessary information and explanations were forthcoming from management and others, and about whether the company was entitled to prepare accounts under the small companies regime.[252] Curiously, however, the liability applies only to that part of the auditor's report which deals strictly with the accounts. Thus, it does not apply to the auditor's report on the directors' or strategic report, the separate corporate governance statement or the auditable part

22–43

---

[244] 2006 Act s.535(1).

[245] 2006 Act s.536. Approval may be given before or after the company enters into the agreement; in the former case only the "principal terms" of the agreement need to be approved. In the case of public companies approval is likely to be sought at the AGM which also functions as the "accounts meeting" for the previous year.

[246] The Companies (Disclosure of Auditor Remuneration and Liability Limitation Agreements) Regulations 2008 (SI 2008/489) reg.8.

[247] FRC, *Guidance on Auditor Liability Limitation Agreements*, June 2008.

[248] Institutional Shareholders' Committee, *Statement on Auditor Liability Limitation Agreements*, June 2008.

[249] 2006 Act s.507.

[250] HL Debs, Grand Committee, Eighth Day, col. 407, 14 March 2006 (Lord Sainsbury of Turville).

[251] And associated matters set out in s.495.

[252] 2006 Act s.507(1)–(3).

of the directors' remuneration report. In this respect, the criminal liability of auditors is narrower than that of directors, which extends to knowing or reckless authorisation of publication of non-compliant directors' reports as well as of accounts.[253] There was much pressure in Parliament from the auditing profession to remove the liability for recklessness, but the Government stoutly resisted it.[254]

CLAIMS BY THIRD PARTIES

The duty of care in principle

22–44   The issues discussed above relating to breach of duty and loss arise in relation to third-party claims (i.e. claims by anyone other than the audit client) as well, but the prior and most controversial issue has been to define the circumstances in which a duty of care will be owed at all by the auditors to third parties. Here the courts have applied in the auditing context the general common law rules governing the duty of care in relation to economic loss caused by negligent misstatement. Until less than 50 years ago, this was not a live issue, because until the decision in *Hedley Byrne & Co Ltd v Heller & Partners Ltd*[255] the law of negligence did not recognise a general duty to take care to avoid misstatements causing economic loss. Liability in damages could, and still can, be based on the tort of deceit, as had been recognised in the nineteenth century, but that liability is subject to two major restrictions. First, liability arises only if the maker of the statement knows that it is false or makes it not caring whether it is true of false, so that an honest, even if unreasonable, belief in the truth of the statement protects its maker from liability in deceit (or fraud).[256] Secondly, the maker of the statement must intend the claimant (or a class of persons of whom the claimant is one) to rely on the statement.[257] The effect of the first limitation is to restrict the circumstances in which liability in deceit will arise and the effect of the second is to restrict the range of potential claimants if it does arise. The impact of the decision in *Hedley Byrne* was to side-step both these limitations, which are not part of the tort of negligence. However, it was not at all clear from *Hedley Byrne* (which was not a case concerning the audit) when the new duty of care to avoid misstatements[258] causing economic loss would be imposed on auditors.

22–45   The answer to these questions, at least in broad outline, was provided by what is undoubtedly the leading case on the application of these rules to auditors, the

---

[253] See ss.414(4) (accounts), 414D(2) (strategic report), 419(3) (directors' report), 422(2) (directors' remuneration report).

[254] 2006 Act ss.508–509 provide for the Secretary of State or, in Scotland, the Lord Advocate to give guidance to the regulatory and prosecuting authorities about how misconduct should be handled which appears to fall both within the criminal prohibition and the regulatory provisions discussed above.

[255] *Hedley Byrne & Co Ltd v Heller & Partners Ltd* [1964] A.C. 465 HL.

[256] *Derry v Peek* (1889) 14 App. Cas. 337 HL. The terms "deceit" and "fraud" (in the civil sense) seem to be used interchangeably.

[257] *Bradford Equitable BS v Borders* [1941] 2 All E.R. 205 HL.

[258] The auditors' public statement is contained in their report (above, para.22–3) but in that they opine about the accuracy of the accounts and reports generally, so that their failure to pick up inaccuracies in those documents is inevitably in issue.

decision of the House of Lords in *Caparo Industries Plc v Dickman*,[259] and was provided in a way which gave greater comfort to auditors than to investors. The facts of the case are worth recounting briefly. Like many of the cases decided around this period, the factual background of *Caparo* involved the purchase of a company whose economic prospects were discovered after the purchase to be less promising than the purchaser had thought beforehand. The purchaser then looked around for someone to sue in respect of what was alleged to be the misleading information about the company which had been made available. In *Caparo* the purchase was of a target company listed on the London Stock Exchange by another such company through a takeover offer preceded by share purchases in the market. The target company had issued a profit-warning in March 1984, which caused its share price to halve. In May 1984 the directors of the target made a preliminary announcement of its annual results for the year to March 1984, which confirmed that profits were well short of expectations. This caused a further, though less dramatic, fall in the share price. In June the annual accounts were issued to the shareholders. Shortly before the June date, Caparo, which had previously owned no shares in the target, began acquiring shares in tranches until it reached a shareholding of 29.9 per cent, at which point (after the accounts had been circulated) it made a general offer for the remaining shares, as the Takeover Code required it to do if it was to acquire any more of the target's shares.[260] Caparo asserted that the 1984 accounts, although gloomy, in fact overvalued the company and that the auditors had been negligent in not detecting the irregularities or fraud which had led to the overstatements in the accounts and in certifying the accounts as representing a true and fair view of the company's financial position.

The House of Lords' examination of the statutory framework for company accounts and audits led them to the following conclusions. The statutory provisions establish a relationship between those responsible for the accounts (the directors) or for the audit report (the auditors), on the one hand, and some other class or classes of persons, on the other, and this relationship imposes a duty of care owed by the directors or auditors to those persons. Among these "persons" is the company itself, to which, apart altogether from the statutory provisions, the directors are in a fiduciary relationship and the auditors in a contractual relationship by virtue of their employment by the company as its auditors. However, the statutory provisions do not establish such a relationship with everybody who has a right to be furnished with copies of the accounts or report or, a fortiori, with everybody who has a right to inspect or obtain copies of them from the Registrar of companies (i.e. the world at large).[261] If a relationship other than with the company is to be established so as to give rise to a duty of care, it can be only with the members of the company (and perhaps debenture-holders) and, even in their case, the scope of the resulting duty of care extends only to the protection of what may be described as the members' corporate governance

---

[259] *Caparo Industries Plc v Dickman* [1990] 2 A.C. 605 HL. The litigation concerned the preliminary issue whether on the facts pleaded a claim against the auditors could succeed. What the facts of the case actually were was never decided.

[260] See below at para.28–41.

[261] On the circulation and filing of the company's annual reports and accounts, see paras 21–33 et seq.

powers to safeguard their interests in the company. Not within the scope of the duty are shareholders' decisions to buy further shares in the company even if it is a perusal of the annual accounts and reports that led them to do so.[262]

22–46   To establish a duty of care to members which is greater in scope than this, or to establish any duty of care to other persons, there must be an additional "special" relationship with the person who suffered loss as a result of relying on the accounts or report. To succeed in establishing that additional relationship, the claimant must show that the auditors (or directors) contemplated that the accounts and report:

> "would be communicated to the plaintiff either as an individual or as a member of an identifiable class, specifically in connection with a particular transaction or transactions of a particular kind (e.g. in a prospectus inviting investment)[263] and that the plaintiff would be very likely to rely on it for the purpose of deciding whether or not to enter upon that transaction or upon a transaction of that kind."[264]

Caparo thus represented a firm rejection by the House of Lords of the proposition that negligent auditors were liable to those who it was reasonable to foresee would rely on the audited accounts and who suffered loss as a result of such reliance.[265] Instead, the House confined the common law duty of care more narrowly. For the reasons given below this policy has much to commend it. However, deducing it from the statutory framework set by the Companies Act for company accounts and their audit is not straightforward.[266] Their lordships' analysis of that framework gives very little weight to the purposes Parliament

---

[262] This was the specific point that had to be determined in *Caparo*. The Court of Appeal had held unanimously that auditors owed no duty of care to members of the public who, in reliance on the accounts and reports, bought shares (in the absence of a special relationship—see below) but, by a majority, that they did owe such a duty to existing shareholders who, in such reliance, bought more shares. The House of Lords thought the distinction between liability for investment decisions made by shareholders and investment decisions made by non-shareholders unsustainable.

[263] As pointed out below at para.25–32 the statute law on prospectus liability has gone beyond the common law which will normally be irrelevant. But it remains highly relevant where the statute does not apply. See *Al-Nakib Investments Ltd v Longcroft* [1990] 1 W.L.R. 1390; and the comment thereon at para.25–37, below.

[264] Per Lord Bridge at 621E–F. This was clearly the unanimous view, adopting the dissenting judgment of Denning LJ in *Candler v Crane Christmas & Co* [1951] 2 K.B. 164 CA; and affirming the decision of Millett J in *Al Saudi Banque v Clark Pixley* [1990] Ch. 313; but rejecting the wider views expressed in *JEB Fasteners Ltd v Marks Bloom & Co* [1981] 3 All E.R. 289; and in *Twomax Ltd v Dickson, McFarlane & Robinson*, 1982 S.C. 113; and by the majority of the New Zealand Court of Appeal in *Scott Group Ltd v McFarlane* [1978] N.Z.L.R. 553.

[265] The case concerned only the purchase of shares and the court left open the question of whether sales of shares (for example, where the accounts negligently undervalued the company) were within the scope of the duty, on the grounds that only shareholders could sell shares so that sales were necessarily a shareholder activity. However, the judges showed little enthusiasm for this argument; and a thorough-going governance analysis would seem to exclude sales as well as purchases on the grounds that both are investment, not governance, decisions.

[266] For a similar refusal to use the common law to supplement the statutory framework but within an analysis of the statutory purposes which seems more faithful to the legislative intent (in this case the New Zealand Securities Act 1978) see *Deloitte Haskins & Sells v National Mutual Life Nominees* [1993] A.C. 774 PC.

might have had in mind when steadily requiring ever greater levels of public disclosure of financial reports rather than just their circulation to members and other current investors in the company.

Assumption of responsibility

Not surprisingly, the case law after *Caparo* has concentrated on seeking to determine the basis or bases upon which it will be possible for claimants to establish a "special relationship" or, as it is now often called in the light of subsequent general developments in the law of negligence, an "assumption of responsibility" on the part of the auditors towards the claimant. Third parties naturally seek to point to facts from which liability could be inferred; auditors to include statements in their report which disclaim any liability to third parties. A crucial initial issue is that the special relationship does not require that the auditor should consciously have assumed responsibility. The test is an objective one and the question for the court is whether, in all the circumstances, it is appropriate for the auditors to be treated as having assumed responsibility.[267]

22–47

In *Barclays Bank Ltd v Grant Thornton UK LLP*[268] the judge held that a disclaimer in an audit report of liability to third parties was effective to negative[269] liability on the part of the auditor towards a sophisticated third party. The disclaimer was clear[270] and its inclusion in a short audit report was enough to bring it to the attention of the sophisticated third party. The main issue was whether the disclaimer satisfied the "reasonableness" requirement of s.2 of the Unfair Contract Terms Act 1977, from which a disclaimer, unlike a limitation of liability agreement,[271] is not exempted. The judge thought that the bank's argument that the clause was unreasonable had no real hope of success and so struck out the claim. Not only was Barclays in general terms a sophisticated third party, but it was aware of the practice of auditors' disclaiming liability to third parties. Indeed, in other aspects of the same transaction the bank had expressly contracted with the auditors to accept liability, which the auditors had agreed to do, subject to a cap on their liability. The bank was in effect seeking to be better off for not having contracted (because liability would be uncapped) than it was in the situations where it had expressly contracted with the auditors to accept liability.

22–48

---

[267] *Electra Private Equity Partners v KPMG Peat Marwick* [2001] 1 B.C.L.C. 589 CA; *Caparo Industries Plc v Dickman* [1990] 2 A.C. 605 at 638 HL, per Lord Oliver.

[268] *Barclays Bank Ltd v Grant Thornton UK LLP* [2015] 2 B.C.L.C. 537.

[269] Because the clause operated to negative liability (rather than being an exemption clause) it was not subject to the convention that it should be construed narrowly.

[270] "To the fullest extent permitted by law, we do not accept or assume responsibility to anyone other than the company and the company's directors ... for our audit work, for this report, or for the opinion we have formed." Although given in the context of an audit of the company's accounts for non-statutory purposes, the clause was a variation of the formula recommended by Institute of Chartered Accountants in England & Wales for statutory audit reports (with the substitution of "members" for "directors").

[271] See para.22–42. In particular, if the disclaimer is caught by s.2 it fails entirely.

22–49   A number of different situations have been considered by the courts where no disclaimer has been present, though one may imagine that express disclaimers are becoming routine. First, within groups of companies, the courts have accepted that it is arguable that the auditors of a subsidiary company owe a duty of care to the parent company, since the production of individual accounts is an integral part of the process of producing both the parent's accounts and consolidated accounts.[272] However, the losses for which the auditors are potentially liable in such a case will be restricted by the uses to which it can be contemplated the accounts will be put by the parent. Thus, in the standard case the subsidiary's auditors should contemplate that the parent will use the consolidated or parent's accounts for the purposes to which parent companies normally put them (payment of dividends to shareholders of the parent or bonuses to senior staff), but this will not necessarily lead to the auditors being liable for other types of loss, in this case loss flowing from the parent's decision to continue to fund the subsidiary.[273] It is less obvious that, on the above argument, the auditors of the parent will owe a duty of care to subsidiary companies of which they are not the auditors, but the Court of Appeal refused to strike out such claim where, because of the way the group was run in practice, the auditors of the various group companies co-operated to a high degree.[274]

A second established area of tortious duty to "third" parties involves the directors of the company by which the auditors have been engaged. Although the Act presents the compilation of the accounts by the directors and their audit as consecutive and separate events, in practice the two overlap, with the directors finalising the accounts at the same time as the audit is in progress on the basis of draft accounts. On this basis, it has been held to be arguable that the auditors are under a duty to alert the directors immediately if the auditors form the view that the directors' approach to the accounts is misconceived in some respect. The directors are not obliged to accept the auditors' views but are entitled to be informed before they commit themselves, with the risk that their approach may lead to the accounts being qualified by the auditors.[275]

22–50   However, the most obvious strategy suggested by the *Caparo* decision for investors in or lenders to the company (or, sometimes, its regulator), who do in fact propose to rely on the company's accounts, is to seek to make the auditors aware of their intentions in advance of the transaction and to secure from the auditors an ad hoc assumption of responsibility for the accounts in relation to the contemplated transaction. Where such an approach is made explicitly and openly and the auditors accept responsibility, there is little to be said against holding the auditors liable for negligent audit. The auditors have the opportunity not to accept

---

[272] *Barings Plc (In Administration) v Coopers & Lybrand* [1997] 1 B.C.L.C. 427 CA.

[273] *Barings Plc (In Liquidation) v Coopers & Lybrand (No.1)* [2002] 2 B.C.L.C. 364; *MAN Nutzfahrzeuge AG v Freightliner Ltd* [2008] 2 B.C.L.C. 22 at [56].

[274] *Bank of Credit & Commerce International (Overseas) Ltd v Price Waterhouse* [1998] B.C.C. 617 CA, where, as is often the case in groups, the group's activities were arranged and carried on along lines which cut across the separate companies in the group and their respective auditors.

[275] *Coulthard v Neville Russell* [1988] 1 B.C.L.C. 143 CA. The claimant directors, who were subsequently disqualified, sought compensation from the auditors for the losses caused by the disqualification. The court refused to strike out the claim. If the loss as a result of the failure to inform the directors is suffered by the company, then no issue of liability to a third party arises.

wider responsibility or to do so on explicit terms, which may limit their liability and involve compensation being paid to them for assuming the additional risk. The question is whether the auditors can or should be made liable on the basis of anything less than a near-explicit bargain with the lender or investor. It has been held that it is not enough to attract liability to the third party that the auditor repeated its conclusions to that person. The crucial question is whether the terms of the request from the third party can be said to have made it clear to an auditor in the defendant's position the purpose for which the repetition was required and the fact that the auditor's skill and judgment were being relied upon.[276] Although this approach falls short of an explicit bargain, it does require that the auditor be made aware of the nature of its commitment before liability in tort is imposed for the benefit of the third party.

Although the *Caparo* decision was controversial amongst those interested in the **22–51** general theory of the law of tort (because of its rejection of the foreseeability test in the area of negligent misstatements) and although the court's reliance on the statutory structure for the accounts seems overblown, the line drawn in that case has been followed by other top-level courts in the common law world, notably Australia and Canada.[277] Its effect, in the core case where no duty arises, is to insulate the audit transaction (and thus the fee charged by auditors to companies for carrying it out) from having to bear the investigation costs of other transactions which third parties may wish to carry out (whether by way of loan or equity purchase) with the company. Since the auditors are in a very poor position to estimate the risks associated with those other transactions, about which they will have little, if any, information, exclusion of liability is probably necessary for the maintenance of the market in audit services. The burden thrown on third parties by this approach is, by contrast, relatively slight. If the state of the company's finances is important to their transaction, as it often will be, they can either pay someone else to replicate the due diligence which the auditors have carried out or, more likely, seek through the special circumstances exception to persuade the auditors to accept responsibility for their report in the context of the third party's transaction. This gives the auditors the opportunity to assess the risks of the particular transaction and to respond appropriately.[278] In principle, there seems to be no reason why the audit should subsidise investigation activities necessary for transactions between third parties and the company in the absence of near-express agreement by the auditors to accept the potential liability.[279]

---

[276] *Andrew v Kounnis Freeman* [1999] 2 B.C.L.C. 641 CA (where the tests were held to have been satisfied); *James McNaughton Papers Group Ltd v Hicks Anderson & Co* [1991] 2 Q.B. 113 CA (where they were not); *Galoo Ltd v Bright, Grahame Murray* [1994] 1 W.L.R. 1360 CA (claims partly struck out and partly allowed to proceed). For the application of this approach to circulars issued in the course of takeover bids, see para.28–64.

[277] *Essanda Finance Corp Ltd v Peat Marwick Hungerford* (1997) 188 C.L.R. 241 High Court of Australia; and *Hercules Management Ltd v Ernst & Young* (1997) 146 D.L.R. (4th) 577 Supreme Court of Canada.

[278] This analysis depends, of course, on the courts not expanding the special circumstances exception so as to swallow up the *Caparo* rule. Contrast the sophisticated approach in *Peach Publishing Ltd v Slater & Co* [1998] B.C.C. 139 CA with the rather easy way in which assumption of responsibility was found in *ADT Ltd v BDO Binder Hamlyn* [1996] B.C.C. 808.

[279] If those costs were imposed on auditors, it is likely companies would end up paying them (by way of higher audit fees), so that, for example, the company would be subsidising the due diligence efforts

Other issues

22–52 Even if duty is established, the claimant will still have to satisfy the other ingredients for tortious liability which have been discussed above in relation to claims by the audit client. Thus in *JEB Fasteners Ltd v Marks Bloom & Co*,[280] which would today be regarded as a "special circumstances" case, Woolf J held that, although all the conditions necessary for success other than causation had been established, the claimant failed on that since it would have entered into the transaction (a takeover) even if the accounts on which it had relied had presented a wholly true and fair view of the company's financial position, its main object having been to secure the managerial skills of two executive directors.[281]

CONCLUSION

22–53 The audit has been subject to two very different legislative policy influences in recent years: on the one hand, a desire to relieve small companies of the need to have one and, on the other, a desire to make the audit of large, especially listed, companies a more effective check on the financial probity and corporate governance standards of management. The former is easy to effect as a matter of legal technique, though conclusive cost/benefit analysis of the audit of small companies is not available to demonstrate where the line should be drawn and the audit should remain mandatory. The latter policy drive has had a positive consequence so that the status of company auditors has, in the course of the past century, been transformed from that of somewhat toothless strays given temporary house-room once a year, to that of trained rottweilers, entitled to sniff around at any time and, if need be, to bite the hands that feed them. However, even rottweilers may learn that biting the hand that feeds you is not a policy conducive to happiness for the biter. Through a combination of domestic and EU initiatives a substantial structure has been put in place aimed at addressing issues of independence and competence, using a wide range of legal techniques, some more firmly located in company law than others. In the course of this process EU law has come to play an increasingly central role.

---

of a potential acquirer. In some cases, the company might want to do so (see for an example para.13–49) but that can again be done through express contract.

[280] *JEB Fasteners Ltd v Marks Bloom & Co* [1981] 3 All E.R. 289; affirmed on other grounds [1983] 1 All E.R. 583 CA.

[281] Who, in fact, resigned!

PART 6

EQUITY FINANCE

In the course of the book we have referred frequently to the rights of shareholders but less often to the function which they perform in the company. In Part Four, for example, we discussed the accountability of management to the shareholders, but did not investigate in any detail what the shareholders contribute in return for that ultimate control over the company. In very small companies, the purpose of issuing shares may indeed be simply to give the shareholders control over the company. In a two-person quasi-partnership, for example, the founders of the company may take one low-value share each, and no other shares may be issued by the company. The issue of shares in such a case operates to give the partners complete control over the running of the company, for, in all likelihood, they will use their voting rights as shareholders to appoint themselves as directors of the company. Financing for the company will come from elsewhere, probably in the form of a bank loan secured on the partners' personal assets.

However, in larger companies the purpose of share issues is not simply, or even primarily, to allocate control over the company but also to raise finance for it, and it is on that function of the share issue that we concentrate in this part. As we have seen,[1] ordinary shares constitute a particularly flexible form of finance for companies, because, so long as the company is a going concern, the shareholders are entitled to no particular level of return by way of dividend and cannot withdraw the contribution made in exchange for their shares without the company's consent, given either at the time of issue of the shares (e.g. where the shares are issued as redeemable at the option of the shareholder) or later (e.g. where the company offers to re-purchase some of its shares). During periods of economic strain the company can hang on to the finance provided by the shareholders but reduce or eliminate its dividends, whilst the shareholders hope that things will turn around eventually and they will be well rewarded for their patience. Even where the company is wound up and the shareholders obtain rights to repayment of their investment, they stand at the end of the queue after the creditors and so may find that their rights are in fact worthless.[2] The

---

[1] Chs 12 and 13.
[2] IA 1986 ss.107 and 143. See generally Ch.33.

economic exposure of the ordinary shareholders goes a long way to explain the traditional practice of allocating control rights over the management to those shareholders.

However, not all shares are "ordinary" or "equity" shares, though it is rare for a company not to issue some shares of this type. The economic and control rights of shareholders are a matter largely of contract between company and investor, rather than of statutory stipulation, so that a company may issue several classes of share, with differing rights attached to them. As we have already seen,[3] this can create risks of oppression of one class of shareholder by another, to combat which the statute has developed special protective mechanisms. More important for this Part, the rights conferred upon "preference" shares may make it difficult to distinguish in practice between share-based finance of companies and debt-based finance, considered in the final Part of this book. A preference shareholder may have a right under the terms of issue of the share to a particular level of dividend each year (assuming the company has profits to cover the dividend entitlement). This makes the preference shareholder look in some ways like a lender, entitled to interests on a loan (though that interest is payable whether or not the company has profits to cover it). However, a lender to a company does not become a member of it and thereby obtain control rights over it. Nevertheless, since the terms of a loan contract can be structured so as to give the lenders considerable control over what the management of the company does, whilst preference shareholders may have limited voting rights, the line between debt and equity is sometimes difficult to identify. Even the feature that a loan is normally repayable after a fixed period may be replicated by making the preference shares redeemable, and even if the preference share is, at least on the surface, a permanent contribution to the company's capital, the preference shareholders can usually be squeezed out if the company (ie the management and the ordinary shareholders) so wishes.[4]

Since the ordinary shareholder's contribution to the company is normally "locked in" until the point of winding up, an investor is likely to look more favourably shares which can easily be sold to another investor if the holder of them wishes to exit from the shareholding. Thus, large companies, contemplating a public offer of shares, are likely to ensure that the public offer is accompanied by an introduction of the shares to trading on a public securities market. This will restore liquidity to investors by enabling them to dispose of the shares to another investor at any time through the "stock exchange" (if not necessarily at an attractive price). This has generated a demand for rules regulating public offerings of shares. In addition, it has generated a strong interest in the proper regulation of secondary trading on public markets (i.e. trading among investors, not with the company), especially continuing disclosure requirements. This regulatory impulse extends to the "market for corporate control", whereby control of a company passes into new hands through the acquisition by a bidder of a majority of the shares traded on a public exchange. Finally, the price at which the shares trade in the secondary market may reveal important information about the company's prospects, which may not only influence investors' decisions, but also

---

[3] See above, paras 19–13 et seq.
[4] On the ability to the company to squeeze out unwanted preference capital see para.19–16.

the exercise of governance rights by shareholders or directors. At the same time, with the goal of creating a single market, much of the regulatory initiative has passed from domestic bodies to the EU. In fact, the EU has had a much bigger impact on the laws governing the public share markets than it has had on general company law. As a result of both domestic and European initiatives there has been a not insignificant revolution in the structure and content of the relevant rules, to which the financial crisis of 2007 onwards has given further impetus. By contrast, shareholders in non-publicly traded companies must rely for protection on the mechanisms discussed in Chs 19 and 20.

CHAPTER 23

THE NATURE AND CLASSIFICATION OF SHARES

LEGAL NATURE OF SHARES

What is the juridical nature of a share? At the present day this is a question more   **23–1**
easily asked than answered. In the old deed of settlement company, which was
merely an enlarged partnership with the partnership property vested in trustees, it
was clear that the members' "shares" entitled them to an equitable interest in the
assets of the company. It is true that the exact nature of this equitable interest was
not crystal clear, for the members could not, while the firm was a going concern,
lay claim to any particular asset or prevent the directors from disposing of it.
Even with the modern partnership, no very satisfactory solution to this problem
has been found, and the most one can say is that the partners have an equitable
interest, often described as a lien, which floats over the partnership assets
throughout the duration of the firm, although it crystallises only on dissolution.
Still, there is admittedly some sort of proprietary nexus (however vague and
ill-defined) between the partnership assets and the partners.

At one time it was thought that the same applied to an incorporated company,
except that the company itself held its assets as trustee for its members.[1] But this
idea has long since been rejected. Shareholders have ceased to be regarded as
having equitable interests in the company's assets; "shareholders are not, in the
eyes of the law, part owners of the undertaking".[2] As a result, the word "share"
has become something of a misnomer, for shareholders no longer share any
property in common; at the most they share certain rights in respect of dividends,
return of capital on a winding up, voting, and the like.

Today it is generally stated that a share is a chose in action.[3] This, however, is
not helpful, for "chose in action" is a notoriously vague term used to describe a

---

[1] *Child v Hudson's Bay Co* (1723) 2 P. Wms. 207. As in the case of partnerships it was clear long
before the express statutory provisions to this effect (see now s.541) that shares were personalty and
not realty even if the company owned freehold land.

[2] per Evershed LJ in *Short v Treasury Commissioners* [1948] 1 K.B. 122 CA. See also the discussion
of "asset partitioning" in para.8–3, above.

[3] See, per Greene MR in [1942] Ch. 241; and *Colonial Bank v Whinney* (1886) 11 App. Cas. 426 HL.

mass of interests which have little or nothing in common except that they confer no right to possession of a physical thing, and which range from purely personal rights under a contract to patents, copyrights and trade marks.

It is tempting to equate shares with rights under a contract, for as we have seen[4] the articles of association constitute a contract of some sort between the company and its members and it is this document which directly or indirectly defines the rights conferred by the shares. But a share is something more than a mere contractual right in personam. This is suggested by the rules relating to infant shareholders (minors), who are liable for calls on the shares unless they repudiate the allotment during infancy or on attaining majority,[5] and who cannot recover any money which they have paid unless the shares have been completely valueless.[6] As Parke B said[7]:

"They have been treated, therefore, as persons in a different situation from mere contractors for then they would have been exempt, but in truth they are purchasers who have acquired an interest not in a mere chattel, but in a subject of a permanent nature."[8]

23–2   The definition of a share which is, perhaps, the most widely quoted is that of Farwell J in *Borland's Trustee v Steel*[9]:

"A share is the interest of a shareholder in the company measured by a sum of money, for the purpose of liability in the first place, and of interest in the second, but also consisting of a series of mutual covenants entered into by all the shareholders *inter se* in accordance with [s.33]. The contract contained in the articles of association is one of the original incidents of the share. A share is not a sum of money . . .but is an interest measured by a sum of money and made up of various rights contained in the contract, including the right to a sum of money of a more or less amount."

It will be observed that this definition, though it lays considerable stress on the contractual nature of the shareholder's rights, also emphasises the fact that the holder has an interest *in* the company. The theory seems to be that the contract constituted by the articles of association defines the nature of the rights, which, however, are not purely personal rights but instead confer some sort of proprietary interest in the company though not in its property. The company itself is treated not merely as a person, the subject of rights and duties, but also as a res, the object of rights and duties.[10] It is the fact that the shareholder has rights in the

---

[4] See above, at paras 3–18 et seq.

[5] *Cork & Brandon Railway v Cazenove* (1847) 10 Q.B. 935; *N.W. Railway v M'Michael* (1851) 5 Exch. 114. If they repudiate during infancy it is not clear whether they can be made liable to pay calls due prior thereto: the majority in *Cazenove*'s case thought they could, but Parke B in the later case (at 125) stated the contrary.

[6] *Steinberg v Scala (Leeds) Ltd* [1923] 2 Ch. 452 CA.

[7] *N.W. Railway v M'Michael* (1851) 5 Exch. at 123.

[8] Later he suggested that the shareholder had "a vested interest of a permanent character in all the profits arising from the land and other effects of the company" (at 125). This can hardly be supported in view of later cases.

[9] *Borland's Trustee v Steel* [1901] 1 Ch. 279 at 288. Approved by the Court of Appeal in *Re Paulin* [1935] 1 K.B. 26, and by the House of Lords ibid., sub nom. *IRC v Crossman* [1937] A.C. 26. See also the other definitions canvassed in that case.

[10] "A whole system has been built up on the unconscious assumption that organisations, which from one point of view are considered individuals, from another are storehouses of tangible property": T. Arnold, *The Folklore of Capitalism* (New Haven, Conn., 1959), p.353. The proprietary analysis of the

company as well as against it, which, in legal theory, distinguishes the member from the debenture- or bond-holder whose rights are also defined by contract (this time the debenture itself and not the articles) but are rights against the company and, if the debenture or bond is secured, in its property, but never in the company itself.

Farwell J's definition mentions that the interest of a shareholder is measured by a sum of money. Reference has already been made to this[11] and it has been emphasised that the requirement of a nominal monetary value is an arbitrary and illogical one which has been rejected in certain other common law jurisdictions. The nominal value is meaningless and may be misleading, except insofar as it determines the minimum liability. Even as a measure of liability, it is of less importance now that shares are almost invariably issued on terms that they are to be fully paid-up on or shortly after allotment and are frequently issued at a price exceeding their nominal value. But reference to liability is valuable in that it emphasises that shareholders *qua* members may be under obligations to the company as well as having rights against it.

This analysis may seem academic and barren, and to some extent it is, for a closer examination of the rights conferred by shares and bonds or debentures will show the impossibility of preserving any hard and fast distinction between them which bears any relation to practical reality. Nevertheless, the matter is not entirely theoretical, for in a number of cases the courts have been faced with the need to analyse the juridical nature of a shareholder's interest in order to determine the principles on which it should be valued. The most interesting of these cases is *Short v Treasury Commissioners*[12] where the whole of the shares of Short Bros were being acquired by the Treasury under a Defence Regulation which provided for payment of their value "as between a willing buyer and a willing seller".[13] They were valued on the basis of the quoted share price, but the shareholders argued that, since all the shares were being acquired, stock exchange prices were not a true criterion and that either the whole undertaking should be valued and the price thus determined apportioned among the shareholders, or the value should be the price which one buyer would give for the whole block, which price should then be similarly apportioned. The courts upheld the method adopted and rejected both the alternatives suggested, the first because the shareholders were not "part owners of the undertaking" and the second because the regulation implied that each holding was to be separately valued. It is the rejection of the first argument which supports the view that the shareholder has no proprietary interest in the company's assets.[14]

One thing at least is clear: shares are recognised in law, as well as in fact, as objects of property which are bought, sold, mortgaged and bequeathed. They are

23–3

share (even if it does not extend to the company's assets) sometimes makes courts resistant to compulsory acquisition of shares, even at a fair price. See *Gambotto v WCP Ltd* (1995) 127 A.L.R. 417 High Ct, Australia, above para.19–9.

[11] See above, para.11–3.

[12] *Short v Treasury Commissioners* [1948] 1 K.B. 116 CA; affirmed [1948] A.C. 534 HL.

[13] This popular formula is much criticised by economists who argue with some force that the willingness of the buyer and seller depends on the price and not vice versa.

[14] The rejection of the second argument illustrates the expropriatory nature of the legislation. Had the willing buyer been characterised as a buyer of control, there is no doubt that a premium to the market

indeed the typical items of property of the modern commercial era and particularly suited to its demands because of their exceptional liquidity. To deny that they are "owned" would be as unreal as to deny, on the basis of feudal theory, that land is owned—far more unreal because the owner's freedom to do what he likes with his shares in public companies is likely to be considerably less fettered. Nor, today, is the bundle of rights making up the share regarded as equitable only. On the contrary, as Ch.27 will show, legal ownership of shares is recognised and distinguished from equitable ownership in much the same way as a legal estate in land is distinguished from equitable interests therein. Nor must this emphasis on the proprietary and financial aspects of a shareholder's rights obscure the important fact that shares cause their holder to become a member of an association, with rights, at least in relation to ordinary shares, to take part in its deliberations by attending and voting at its general meetings.

THE PRESUMPTION OF EQUALITY BETWEEN SHAREHOLDERS

23–4   A company limited by shares must necessarily issue some shares, and the initial presumption of the law is that all shares issued by the company confer the same rights and impose the same liabilities. As in a partnership[15] equality prevails in the absence of agreement to the contrary. Normally the shareholders' rights will fall under three heads: (i) dividends; (ii) return of capital and participation in surplus assets on a winding up (or authorised reduction of capital); and (iii) attendance at meetings and voting. Unless there is some indication to the contrary, all the shares will confer the like rights to all three. So far as voting is concerned this is a comparatively recent development, for, on the analogy of the partnership rule, it was felt in the early days that members' voting rights should be divorced from their purely financial interests in respect of dividend and capital, so that the equality in voting should be between members rather than between shares. A stage intermediate between these two ideas was reflected in the Companies Clauses Act 1845[16] which provided that, in the absence of contrary provision in the special statute, every shareholder had one vote for every share up to ten, one for every additional five up to a hundred and one for every ten thereafter, thus weighting the voting in favour of the smaller holders. However, attempts to reduce the proportion of voting rights as the size of holdings increased were doomed to failure since the requirement could be easily evaded by splitting holdings and vesting them in nominees. Whilst "voting caps" may still be inserted into the articles, it is today more usual to create separate classes of shares if voting rights are to vary, so that the different number of votes can be attached to the shares themselves and not to the holder. Even today, however, the older idea still prevails on a vote by a show of hands, when the common law rule is that each member entitled to vote has one vote irrespective of the number of shares held; a rule which, although it can be altered by the constitution, is

---

price would have been payable, even though no individual seller had control, because some sharing of the benefits of control would have been necessary to induce the shareholders to sell. See Ch.28, below.

[15] Partnership Act 1890 s.24(1).
[16] Companies Clauses Act 1845 s.75.

normally maintained, because it provides a speedy, if somewhat inaccurate, way of establishing the views of the meeting.[17]

There is in fact a strong argument in favour of applying the equality rule to the voting rights attached to shares which otherwise have the same rights and duties, because a shareholder's influence in the company is then linked to the size of his or her investment in it. Governance rights are then coterminous with the financial risk to which each holder is exposed. In 1962 the Jenkins Committee on Company Law considered the adoption of a rule which would have prohibited non- or restricted-voting ordinary shares. The majority rejected the proposition as an interference with freedom of contract, but three members of the committee, including the original author of this book, dissented.[18] More recently, the EU tried, but failed, to build support for the principle of "one share one vote".[19] So, the equality rule is not mandatory and companies are free to issue shares with no, restricted or, even, weighted voting rights. It is relatively rare for listed companies to do so because institutional shareholders have traditionally been reluctant to buy shares whose votes do not reflect the financial risk. The solution to the problem in the UK is thus a market driven rather than a regulatory one.

There is a similar presumption of equality in relation to shareholders' liabilities **23–5** but it too can be altered by provisions in the articles. In the case of a company limited by shares, normally the only liability imposed on a shareholder as such will be to pay up the nominal value of the shares and any premium insofar as payment has not already been made by a previous holder. This, however, does not mean that all the shares, even if of the same nominal value and of the same class, will necessarily be issued at the same price, or that, even if they are, all shareholders will necessarily be treated alike as regards calls for the unpaid part. Section 581 provides that a company, if so authorised by its articles, may: (a) make different arrangements between shareholders on an issue of shares as to the amounts or times of payments of calls; (b) accept from any member the whole or part of the amount remaining unpaid although it has not been called up; or (c) pay a dividend in proportion to the amount paid up on each share where a larger amount is paid up on some shares than on others.[20] Subject to that, however, calls must be made pari passu.[21]

CLASSES OF SHARES

As will have become apparent, the prima facie equality of shares can be modified **23–6** by dividing the share capital into different classes with different rights as to dividends, capital or voting or with different nominal values. Even this way of proceeding was once open to doubt. For many years it was thought that, in the

---

[17] As we have seen above (para.15–75), the rule has been criticised, and it is tolerated only because it is easy for a shareholder who thinks the result would be different on a poll to trigger the poll process.
[18] Report of the Company Law Committee, Cmnd 1749, paras 123–140 and pp.207–210.
[19] See Commission of the European Communities, *Impact Assessment on the Proportionality between Capital and Control in Listed Companies*, SEC(2007) 1705, 12 December 2007.
[20] Table A 1985 appeared to authorise (a) only (see art.17) probably rightly in view of the complications which (b) and (c) would cause a public company.
[21] *Galloway v Halle Concerts Society* [1915] 2 Ch. 233.

absence of express provision in the original constitution, the continued equality of all shares was a fundamental condition which could not be abrogated by an alteration of the articles so as to allow the issue of shares preferential to those already issued.[22] This idea was, however, finally destroyed in *Andrews v Gas Meter Co*[23] where a company, whose original constitution provided for only one class of shares, was permitted to alter it so as to issue a second class of shares with rights which ranked to some extent ahead of the existing shares.

Today, the number of possible classes is limited only by the total number of shares issued by the company, since the number of available combinations of the incidents attached to shares is infinite. On the whole, however, it is not the present fashion for publicly traded companies to complicate their capital structures by having a large number of share classes. But, both in the case of public and private companies, there may well be two or three different classes and sometimes more. The division of shares into classes and the rights attached to each class will normally be set out in the company's articles but, in contrast with the Companies Acts of some other common law countries, that is not compulsory.[24] However, steps have been taken to ensure that the classes and their rights can be ascertained from the company's public documents. For this purpose the "return of allotments" (i.e. the information which the company has to provide to the Registrar of companies within one month of the allotment of shares)[25] is used. This must give the "prescribed particulars" of the rights attached to the shares in relation to each class of shares.[26] If the company assigns a class a name or other designation or changes an existing one, that too must be notified.[27] The same applies if and when there is any variation of the class rights.[28]

Preference shares

23–7 Where the differences between the classes relates to financial entitlement, i.e. to dividends and return of capital, the likelihood is that the classes will be given distinguishing names, though these may be no more informative than "preference" and "ordinary" (perhaps, in the case of the former, preceded by "first" or "second" where there are two classes of preference shares). The preference normally is that the preference shareholder receives a fixed dividend and/or a return of capital before (in preference to) any payment to the ordinary shareholders. If a potential investor should assume that "preference" means that he should prefer them to the ordinary shares he would be sorely in need of

---

[22] *Hutton v Scarborough Cliff Hotel Co* (1865) 2 Dr. & Sim. 521.

[23] *Andrews v Gas Meter Co* [1897] 1 Ch. 361 CA.

[24] This is now true even in relation to redeemable shares, provided the articles or a resolution of the company authorises the directors to determine the terms of redemption: s.685. See para.13–10. Shareholders' rights are sometimes set out on the back of the share certificate (where such is issued) but a misstatement of the rights on the certificate will not override the statement in the articles or in the offer document: *Re Hunting Plc* [2005] 2 B.C.L.C. 211.

[25] On allotment see the following chapter at para.24–18.

[26] 2006 Act ss.555(4)(c) and 556(3), applying to limited and unlimited companies respectively, and the Companies (Shares and Share Capital) Order 2009/388.

[27] 2006 Act s.636.

[28] 2006 Act s.637. The question of how class rights may be varied is discussed in Ch.19, above.

professional advice. The advice received would probably not be couched in terms of relative merits and de-merits of preference and ordinary shares but of security and levels of risk. And if the client's needs suggested the former, the investor would probably be advised to invest not in shares but in bonds or debentures. For preference shares may often be virtually indistinguishable from bonds except that they afford less assurance of getting one's money back or a return on it until one does. On the other hand, if in addition to being "preferential" the shares are also "participating" (i.e. have a right, beyond the preference, to share in the profits of the company after the ordinary shareholders have received a specified return), they may be regarded rightly as a form of equity shares with preferential rights over the ordinary shares (and in consequence should be, and often are, designated "preferred ordinary"). The Act defines the company's equity share capital as all its issued share capital except that part which "neither as respects dividends nor as respects capital, carries any right to participate beyond a specified amount in a distribution".[29] Participating preference shares will thus normally fall within the definition of equity capital, even if the right to participation is confined to surplus assets when the company is wound up, whilst the shareholders' dividend right is limited to a fixed (and perhaps not very generous) amount.

The truth of the matter is that an enormous variety of different rights, relating to dividends, return of capital, voting, conversion into ordinary shares,[30] redemption and other matters, may be attached to classes of shares, all of which are conventionally described as "preference" shares. What these rights are in any particular case and whether any particular issue of preference shares is located more at the debenture end or the ordinary share end of the spectrum will depend on the construction of the articles or other instrument creating them. Unfortunately, in the past the drafting of these documents has often been deplorably lax.[31] Hence the courts had to evolve various "canons of construction" of the documents which, even more unfortunately, have themselves fluctuated from time to time, with the courts overruling earlier decisions and defeating the legitimate expectations of investors who purchased preference shares in reliance on the construction adopted earlier.[32] In former editions of this book the story of these vacillations was traced in some detail,[33] starting with the virtually irreconcilable decisions of the House of Lords[34] and the Court of Appeal[35] relating to the winding-up of the Bridgewater Navigation Company in

---

[29] Thus, a limitation on either dividends or a return of capital on a winding up will take the share out of the ordinary class.

[30] The apparently simple matter of converting preference shares into ordinary shares can become one of considerable complexity, at least where the nominal value and number of the ordinary shares into which the preference shares are to be converted differ from those of the preference shares to be converted, so that there is a danger that the transaction will involve an unauthorised return of capital, on the one hand, or the issue of shares at a discount, on the other. For a clear explanation of the ways of avoiding this result, see (1995) VI *Practical Law for Companies* (No.10) at p.43.

[31] Even to the extent of simply providing that the share capital is divided into so many X per cent Preference Shares and so many Ordinary Shares and issuing them without further clarification.

[32] The classic illustration is the overruling, by the House of Lords in *Scottish Insurance v Wilsons & Clyde Coal Co* [1949] A.C. 462, of the Court of Appeal decision in *Re William Metcalfe Ltd* [1933] Ch. 142.

[33] 4th edn (1979), pp.414–421.

[34] *Birch v Cropper* (1889) 14 App. Cas. 525 HL.

[35] *Re Bridgewater Navigation Co* [1891] 2 Ch. 317 CA.

1889–1891. Since, at long last, a reasonably clear finale now appears to have been reached, there is no longer a justification for that indulgence. It suffices to summarise what the present canons of construction appear to be.

Canons of construction

23–8

1. Prima facie all shares rank equally. If, therefore, some are to have priority over others there must be provisions to this effect in the terms of issue.

2. If, however, the shares are expressly divided into separate classes (thus necessarily contradicting the presumed equality) it is a question of construction in each case what the rights of each class are.[36]

3. If nothing is expressly said about the rights of one class in respect of (a) dividends, (b) return of capital, or (c) attendance at meetings or voting, then, prima facie, that class has the same rights in that respect as the residuary ordinary shares. Hence, a preference as to dividend will not imply a preference as to return of capital (or vice versa).[37] Nor will an exclusion of participation in dividends beyond a fixed preferential rate necessarily imply an exclusion of participation in capital (or vice versa) although it will apparently be some indication of it.[38]

4. Where shares are entitled to participate in surplus capital on a winding-up, prima facie they participate in all surplus assets and not merely in that part which does not represent undistributed profits that might have been distributed as dividend to another class.[39]

5. If, however, any rights in respect of any of these matters are expressly stated, that statement is presumed to be exhaustive so far as that matter is concerned. Hence if shares are given a preferential dividend they are presumed to be non-participating as regards further dividends,[40] and if they are given a preferential right to a return of capital they are presumed to be non-participating in surplus assets.[41] The same clearly applies to attendance and voting[42]; if shareholders are given a vote in certain circumstances (e.g.

---

[36] *Scottish Insurance v Wilsons & Clyde Coal Co* [1949] A.C. 462; *Re Isle of Thanet Electric Co* [1950] Ch. 161 CA.

[37] *Re London India Rubber Co* (1868) L.R. 5 Eq. 519; *Re Accrington Corp Steam Tramways* [1909] 2 Ch. 40.

[38] This is implied in the speeches in *Scottish Insurance v Wilsons & Clyde Coal Co* [1949] A.C. 462; and in *Dimbula Valley (Ceylon) Tea Co Ltd v Laurie* [1961] Ch. 353.

[39] *Dimbula Valley (Ceylon) Tea Co Ltd v Laurie* [1961] Ch. 353; *Re Saltdean Estate Co Ltd* [1968] 1 W.L.R. 1844. These cases "distinguished" *Re Bridgewater Navigation Co* [1891] 2 Ch. 317 CA (on the basis that the contrary decision of the Court of Appeal depended on the peculiar wording of the company articles) but it is thought that *Bridgewater* can now be ignored; in *Wilsons & Clyde Coal Co* Lord Simonds pointed out the absurdity of supposing that "parties intended a bargain which would involve an investigation of an artificial and elaborate character into the nature and origin of surplus assets": [1949] A.C. at 482.

[40] *Will v United Lankat Plantations Co* [1914] A.C. 11 HL.

[41] *Scottish Insurance v Wilsons & Clyde Coal Co* [1949] A.C. 462; *Re Isle of Thanet Electric Co* [1950] Ch. 161 CA.

[42] Quaere whether attendance at meetings and voting should not really be treated as two separate rights. It seems, however, that express exclusion of a right to vote will take away the right to be summoned to (or presumably to attend) meetings: *Re MacKenzie & Co Ltd* [1916] 2 Ch. 450. If, under this canon shareholders have votes but the articles do not say how many, the effect of s.284 appears to

if their dividends are in arrears), it is implied that they have no vote in other circumstances. It is in fact common to displace the preference shareholders' presumed equality in relation to voting by expressly restricting their voting rights to situations in which their dividends have not been paid for a period of time, on the basis that only in such cases will the preference shareholders need to assert their voice in the management of the company.[43]

6.   The onus of rebutting the presumption in 5 is not lightly discharged and the fact that shares are expressly made participating as regards either dividends or capital is no indication that they are participating as regards the other—indeed it has been taken as evidence to the contrary.[44]

7.   If a preferential dividend is provided for, it is presumed to be cumulative (in the sense that, if passed in one year, it must nevertheless be paid in a later one before any subordinate class receives a dividend).[45] This presumption can be rebutted by any words indicating that the preferential dividend for a year is to be payable only out of the profits of that year.[46]

8.   It is presumed that even preferential dividends are payable only if declared.[47] Hence arrears even of cumulative dividends are prima facie not payable in a winding-up unless previously declared.[48] But this presumption may be rebutted by the slightest indication to the contrary.[49] It may thus be advantageous to specify that the dividend is automatically payable on certain dates (assuming profits are available) rather than upon a resolution of the directors or shareholders. When the arrears are payable, the presumption is that they are to be paid in the winding up provided there are surplus assets available, whether or not these represent accumulated profits

---

be that they have one vote per share or, if their shares have been converted to stock (on which see para.23–11, below) per each £10 of stock and that if the company has no share capital each member has one vote.

[43] See, for example, *Re Bradford Investment Ltd* [1991] B.C.L.C. 224.

[44] *Re National Telephone Co* [1914] 1 Ch. 755; *Re Isle of Thanet Electric Co* [1950] Ch. 161 CA; and *Re Saltdean Estate Co Ltd* [1968] 1 W.L.R. 1844. This produces strange results. If, as the House of Lords suggested in the *Scottish Insurance* case, the fact that shares are non-participating as regards dividends is some indication that they are intended to be non-participating as regards capital (on the ground that the surplus profits have been appropriated to the ordinary shareholders), where the surplus profits belong to both classes while the company is a going concern, both should participate in a winding-up in order to preserve the status quo.

[45] *Webb v Earle* (1875) L.R. 20 Eq. 556.

[46] *Staples v Eastman Photographic Materials Co* [1896] 2 Ch. 303 CA.

[47] *Burland v Earle* [1902] A.C. 83 PC; *Re Buenos Ayres Gt Southern Railway* [1947] Ch. 384; *Godfrey Phillips Ltd v Investment Trust Ltd* [1953] 1 W.L.R. 41. *Semble*, therefore, non-cumulative shares lose their preferential dividend for the year in which liquidation commences: *Re Foster & Son* [1942] 1 All E.R. 314; *Re Catalina's Warehouses* [1947] 1 All E.R. 51. But, if the terms clearly so provide, a prescribed preferential dividend may be payable so long as there are adequate distributable profits in accordance with Ch.12, above: *Evling v Israel & Oppenheimer* [1918] 1 Ch. 101.

[48] *Re Crichton's Oil Co* [1902] 2 Ch. 86; *Re Roberts & Cooper* [1929] 2 Ch. 383; *Re Wood, Skinner & Co Ltd* [1944] Ch. 323.

[49] *Re Walter Symons Ltd* [1934] Ch. 308; *Re F de Jong & Co Ltd* [1946] Ch. 211 CA; *Re E.W. Savory Ltd* [1951] 2 All E.R. 1036; *Re Wharfedale Brewery Co* [1952] Ch. 913.

which might have been distributed by way of dividend,[50] but that they are payable only to the date of the commencement of the winding-up.[51]

The effect of applying these canons of construction has been, as Evershed MR pointed out,[52] that over the past 100 years:

"the view of the courts may have undergone some change in regard to the relative rights of preference and ordinary shareholders and to the disadvantage of the preference shareholders whose position has . . .become somewhat more approximated to [that] of debenture holders."

Unless preference shareholders are expressly granted participating rights they are unlikely to be entitled to share in any way in the "equity" or to have voting rights except in narrowly prescribed circumstances. Yet they enjoy none of the advantages of debenture-holders; they receive a return on their money only if profits are earned[53] (and not necessarily even then), they rank after creditors on a winding-up and they have less effective remedies against the company. Suspended midway between true creditors and true members they may get the worst of both worlds, unless the instrument creating the preference shares is carefully drafted.

Ordinary shares

23–9   Ordinary shares (as the name implies) constitute the residuary class in which is vested everything after the special rights of preference classes, if any, have been satisfied. They confer a right to the "equity" in the company and, insofar as members can be said to own the company, the ordinary shareholders are its proprietors. It is they who bear the lion's share of the risk and they who in good years take the lion's share of the profits (after the directors and managers have been remunerated). If, as is often the case, the company's shares are all of one class, then these are necessarily ordinary shares, and if a company has a share capital it must perforce have at least one ordinary share whether or not it also has preference shares. It is this class alone which is unmistakably distinguished from debentures both in law and fact.

But as we have seen, the ordinary shares may shade off imperceptibly into preference, for, when the latter confer a substantial right of participation in income or capital, or a fortiori both, it is largely a matter of taste whether they are designated "preference" or "preferred ordinary" shares. Moreover, distinctions may be drawn among ordinary shares, ranking equally as regards financial participation, by dividing them nevertheless into separate classes with different voting rights. In this event they will probably be distinguished as "A" "B" "C" (etc.) ordinary shares. Some public companies have issued non-voting A ordinary

---

[50] *Re New Chinese Antimony Co Ltd* [1916] 2 Ch. 115; *Re Springbok Agricultural Estates Ltd* [1920] 1 Ch. 563; *Re Wharfedale Brewery Co* [1952] Ch. 913; not following *Re W.J. Hall & Co Ltd* [1909] 1 Ch. 521.

[51] *Re E.W. Savory Ltd* [1951] 2 All E.R. 1036.

[52] *Re Isle of Thanet Electric Co* [1950] Ch. 161 at 175.

[53] This necessarily follows from the principle laid down in s.830(1) that "a company shall not make a distribution except out of profit available for the purpose". See above, para.12–2.

shares. Alternatively, both classes of ordinary share may have voting rights but the votes of a share of one class may be a high multiple of the votes attached to a share of another. In either case, control may be retained by a small proportion of the equity leading to a further rift between ownership and control.[54]

Special classes

Although in most cases the shares of a company will fall into one or other of the primary classes of preference or ordinary, it is, of course, possible for the company to create shares for particular purposes and containing terms which cut across the normal classifications. An example of this is afforded by employees' shares. Frequent references have already been made to "employee share schemes". Under the present definition of such schemes,[55] the beneficiaries of them may include not only present employees of the company concerned, but also employees, or former employees, of it or any company in the same group, and the spouses, civil partners, children or stepchildren under the age of 18, of any such employees. When employees' share schemes first came to be introduced, the normal practice was to create a special class of shares with restricted rights regarding, in particular, votes and transferability; only in relation to share option schemes, designed as incentives to top management, were ordinary voting equity shares on offer. Now, however, that is usual in all cases[56] in order that employees' share schemes may enjoy the special tax concessions conferred on "approved" schemes. Hence, today such schemes will rarely lead to the creation of a special class of share; it is only in relation to their allotment, financing, and provision for re-purchase by the company or the trustees of the scheme that there will be special arrangements which the Act facilitates by exclusions from the normal restrictions on purchase of own shares and on the provision of finance by a company for the acquisition of its shares.[57]

23–10

Conversion of shares into stock

Shares may no longer be converted into stock.[58] This is a change made by the 2006 Act, though one of minor, almost undetectable, significance, since companies had abandoned the practice for the reason that, today, stock has no advantage over shares. In the case of shares the size of a person's holding in the company is measured by the number of shares held, whereas with stock the person's holding is measured by the total par value of the stock held, the stock not being divided into separate units. From the stockholder's point of view this makes it easier to transfer very small proportions of the holding, whereas a

23–11

---

[54] See para.23–4.

[55] 2006 Act s.1166.

[56] But it would be rare indeed for this to have led to employees controlling a large public company—as has occurred in the USA.

[57] See paras 13–5 and 13–50. And note also the special treatment in relation to pre-emptive rights: below, para.24–7.

[58] 2006 Act s.540(2). See also the prohibition in s.617 on a company altering its share capital, except as permitted by that section, which permissions no longer include conversion into stock.

shareholder can never transfer less than one share. However, this is a small advantage since companies tend to take steps to keep the market value of the shares to a manageable size (for example, through bonus issues[59] if the market value becomes large). From the company's point of view there were until the 1948 Act some administrative savings associated with stock.[60] The 2006 Act still permits stock to be re-converted to shares by ordinary resolution of the shareholders, but this is now an irreversible decision.[61] Thus, the phrase "stock exchange" becomes even more of a misnomer than it was previously. However, turning debentures into debenture stock does retain some advantages and may still be done.[62]

---

[59] See para.11–59.

[60] This was the requirement that, throughout its life, each share had to have a distinctive number, thus creating some bureaucratic work for the company, whilst stock did not. However, this is no longer required of shares which are fully paid up and rank pari passu (s.543).

[61] 2006 Act s.620.

[62] See para.31–12.

CHAPTER 24

SHARE ISSUES: GENERAL RULES

In the previous chapter we examined how the company attaches rights to shares. **24–1** We now need to look at the process by which a company issues shares to those who wish to invest in it. The crucial regulatory divide is between offers to the public to acquire the company's shares and offers which are non-public. The regulatory regime is much more elaborate in the former case. In addition, since a public offer is often combined with the provision of a trading facility for the shares on a stock exchange or other trading platform (though it need not be), the rules governing that process become of crucial importance as well. Where there is no public offer, the relevant rules are still to be found mainly in the Companies Act and the common law of companies, rather than in the Financial Services and Markets Act 2000 and in rules made by the FCA. In this chapter we deal with the rules that apply to offers of securities, whether the offer is a public one or not. The additional requirements applying only to public offers are treated in the following chapter. However, some of the rules discussed in this chapter, for example, the pre-emption rules, have their greatest impact when the offer is a public one. The domestic law considered in this chapter has been substantially influenced by the Second Company Law Directive of the Community,[1] but, in contrast with its provisions on legal capital, its rules on share issuance have generally been welcomed by shareholders as strengthening their position, though, often, not as strongly as they would wish.

---

[1] Directive 77/91/EEC ([1997] O.J. L26/1), subsequently amended and re-stated as Directive 2012/30/EU ([2012] O.J. L315/74). The references in this chapter are to the re-stated Directive.

PUBLIC AND NON-PUBLIC OFFERS

24–2   A public company has a choice whether to make a public offer of its shares. It is not obliged to do so and if it refrains from making a public offer, it will escape the regulation analysed in the following chapter, although it will find that its fund-raising possibilities are much constrained. Hence arises an ambiguity in the meaning of the term "public company". By those concerned with capital markets the term is used to refer to companies which have indeed made a public offering of their securities and introduced those shares to trading on a public market. However, under the Companies Act a public company is simply one that may lawfully make a public offering of its securities, whether it has actually done so or not. In this book, the term "public company" means one that is public in the Companies Act sense of the term, whilst one which has actually made a public offer of its securities is referred to as a "publicly traded"[2] company or one which has "gone public". Under the Companies Act the contrast between a "public" and a "private" company is that a private company is prohibited from offering securities[3] to the public, either directly or through an offer for sale via an intermediary.[4] Thus, a private company may make only a non-public offer of its shares, and, indeed, this is the defining characteristic of a private company; but a public company (under the Companies Act) may or may not have made a public offer.

If a private company does make a public offer, the validity of any agreement to sell or allot securities or of any sale or allotment is not affected by breach of the prohibition, thus protecting innocent third parties who wish to enforce their rights under the contract of issuance of the shares,[5] and the criminal sanctions which previously underlay the prohibition have been removed. Nevertheless, the court has a wide range of powers to deal with the consequences of a breach or potential breach, on application of any member or creditor of the company or the Secretary of State or on its own motion in an unfair prejudice application. The court may enjoin the proposed issue[6]; require the company to re-register as a public company (the statute's preferred ex post remedy)[7]; and, if it decides against re-registration, it may wind the company up or make a remedial order.[8] The purpose of the remedial order is to put the person in whose favour it is made (who may be a subsequent holder of the share) in the position they would have been in had the breach of the prohibition not occurred.[9] The court has a wide discretion as to the contents of the remedial order, including the power to order the company

---

[2] Even this term is not fully precise, since a company may make public offer of its shares without securing their admission to a trading facility.

[3] 2006 Act s.755. The prohibition applies to both shares and debentures: s.755(5). Nor may a private company secure admission of existing securities to the official list without making a public offer: FSMA 2000 s.74 and the Financial Services and Markets Act 2000 (Official Listing of Securities) Regulations 2001 (SI 2001/2956) reg.3. On the "official list" see the following chapter at para.25–9.

[4] See para.25–12 for a discussion of direct and indirect share offerings.

[5] 2006 Act ss.755(1) and 760.

[6] 2006 Act s.757.

[7] 2006 Act s.758(2)—but not if it is "impracticable or undesirable" to do so.

[8] s2006 Act s.758(3). The remedial order may be make whether or not the company is ordered to be wound up.

[9] s2006 Act s.759(1).

and any others "knowingly concerned" in contravention of the prohibition to offer to purchase the securities at a price determined by the court.[10] For a private company to contemplate breaching the prohibition is, thus, a highly risky business, both for it and its officers and advisers. On the other hand, the requirements for becoming a public company are not onerous and the company can even leave conversion until after the issue has succeeded, provided conversion is part of the terms of issue.[11]

The definition of what is a public offer for the purpose of the Act is in s.756. This section makes it clear that "public" includes a section of the public ("however selected").[12] On the other hand, the definition excludes an offer which "can properly be regarded, in all the circumstances, as not being calculated to result, directly or indirectly, in the shares or debentures becoming available for subscription or purchase by persons other than those receiving the offer or invitation".[13] Also excluded are offers which are of "domestic concern" to the company, into which category fall, presumptively, offers to the company's existing members or employees, their families, debenture-holders of the company or a trustee for any of the above.[14]

24–3

The main issue with this definition is that it does not correspond exactly to the definition of a "public offer" used for the purposes of determining the applicability of the additional regulation discussed in the next chapter. In particular, it does not replicate the definition of a public offer in the Prospectus Directive,[15] which determines whether a prospectus is required (and regulates its contents, if it is). On the one hand, some offers regarded as private under the Act might be public under the Directive. This is because the "offerees only" exemption of the Act appears to set no limit on the number of people who receive the offer nor to impose any qualification as to their experience or qualifications as investors, whilst the central exemptions in the Directive are based on one or other of these limitations.[16] In other words, a private company might make what is a public offer for the purposes of the Directive without contravening the prohibition in the Act. In such a case, of course, the private company will have to comply with the requirements of the Directive, as transposed into domestic law, and so no real conflict arises, provided those concerned realise that private companies may fall within the prospectus rules in some cases.

On the other hand, a private company may be prevented by the Act from making an offer in respect of which, if it were a public company, it would not need to produce a prospectus, because the offer would fall within one of the exemptions contained in the Directive. The Company Law Review, whilst

---

[10] 2006 Act s.759(3) and (5). Those involved could include advisers, such as investment banks. Where the company is ordered to re-purchase, the court may reduce its capital.

[11] 2006 Act s.755(3)(b)(4). On the requirements of converting to a public company see para.4–40.

[12] 2006 Act s.756(2).

[13] 2006 Act s.756(3)(a). If the securities do in fact end up in public hands within six months of their initial allotment or before the company has received the whole of the consideration for the shares, the company is presumed to have allotted them with a view to their being offered to the public: s.755(3).

[14] 2006 Act s.756(3)(b)–(6). Such offers may be renounceable in favour of other persons, provided such persons also fall within the "domestic" category.

[15] Discussed at paras 25–18 et seq.

[16] See para.25–19.

recommending that some alignment of the definition of "public offer" in the Act with that in the Directive, did not think that the lack of fit was in principle objectionable, because different policies were being pursued by the two sets of rules. There might be good reasons for preventing a private company from making a public offer, even if such an offer would not attract the requirement for a prospectus under EU law. The CLR's view was that some of these exemptions from the prospectus requirement were "wholly inappropriate" for a private company, because they might allow the private company to reach "very large economic scale". This should be permitted only if the company were prepared to undertake the burdens of a public company.[17] Of course, most share issues by private companies come nowhere near being classified as public for the purposes of either the Act or the Directive.

DIRECTORS' AUTHORITY TO ALLOT SHARES

24–4   Issuance of shares by a company involves essentially three steps. First, the company must decide to make an offer of shares, public or non-public, and set the terms of the offer. Secondly, some person or persons must agree with the company to take the shares (at which point the shares are said to have been "allotted"). Thirdly, in implementation of that contract, those persons must take the shares and be made members of the company, thus completing the process of issuance. We shall look at each stage in turn.

The first question is whether the decision to allot shares[18] is one for the board alone or whether the shareholders' concurrence is required. We have seen that the company's decision to allot shares ranking along with or even ahead of the company's existing shares does not normally amount to a variation of the rights of the existing shareholders, so that their consent will not be required under the variation of class-rights procedure,[19] even though the practical value of those rights may well be affected by such an issue. Even if the new shares are to rank behind the existing shares, the shareholders may still have doubts about the directors' plans for the use of the finance which will be raised. Thus, it is a matter of some importance whether the Act requires the shareholders' consent to a share issue or whether the matter is left entirely to the company's articles of association. If the Act does not intervene, the situation is likely to be that the board has power to issue shares as part of its general management powers, and the articles may or may not give the shareholders a role in the decision-making process. Thus, the question becomes whether the Act should make shareholder consent mandatory or leave this issue to be determined by the company's articles.

The Second Company Law Directive[20] contains the principle that consent of the shareholders is required. The Directive applies only to public companies,

---

[17] Completing, paras 2.77–2.82; Final Report I, paras 4.57–4.58. Examples of exemptions under the Directive which might be thought inappropriate for private companies were offers to professional investors, as part of takeovers, and of large denomination shares.

[18] The rules discussed in this section, unlike those relating to public offers, do not apply to debt securities which have no equity element.

[19] See para.19–16.

[20] Directive art.29. Even then, only the consent of shareholders with voting rights under the company's articles.

although the Government, when transposing it into domestic law in 1980, chose to apply the principle to private companies as well, albeit in a more flexible way. However, the CLR proposed[21] to remove the requirement of shareholder authorisation for the issuance of shares by private companies, except where the company already had or the directors' proposal would create more than one class of shares. This would be a default rule, for private companies' articles might restore the requirement of shareholder approval. This reform was implemented in the 2006 Act.[22] The requirement for shareholder consent was thought to be an unnecessary formality in private companies, with their greater overlap of directors and members. However, such overlap would not necessarily obtain, and there would be the risk of greater opportunism, if the company had, or was about to create, more than one class of share.

Except in relation to the private company with only one class of share, however, shareholder consent, in one form or another, is still required for the allotment of shares. Not to obtain it is a criminal offence on the part of the directors knowingly involved,[23] although such failure does not affect the validity of the allotment.[24] The requirement is applied not only to the allotment of shares but also to the grant of rights to subscribe for or to convert a security into shares in the company in the future, for example, a convertible bond.[25] Otherwise, the requirement of shareholder consent could be avoided easily, for example, by issuing a debt security convertible at a later stage into shares. In this case, the requirement for shareholder approval is imposed at the stage of issuance but is not repeated at the conversion stage.[26] However, if, unusually, a convertible bond is convertible into existing, rather than new, shares of the company, then shareholder consent would not be needed at the allotment stage either.[27]

    Shareholder authorisation may take the form of the directors putting before the shareholders a proposal for the issuance of a particular amount of shares to fund a specific project, with full details of how the finance raised will be used. This is authorisation for "a particular use of the power".[28] However, authorisation can be given generally, either in the articles or by (ordinary) resolution, for (renewable)

24–5

---

[21] Developing, paras 7.28–7.33.

[22] 2006 Act s.550.

[23] 2006 Act s.549(3)–(4).

[24] 2006 Act s.549(6).

[25] 2006 Act s.549(1). This may help to explain in part why the "shareholder rights plan" or "poison pill" against takeovers is uncommon in the UK, for the effectiveness of the plan depends heavily upon the directors being able to issue warrants to subscribe for shares without shareholder approval.

[26] 2006 Act s.549(3).

[27] When the section talks about rights to "convert any security into shares in the company" it means newly created shares, not shares already in existence.

[28] 2006 Act s.551(2). The section does not in terms require details of the use to which the funds will be put to be given to the shareholders. However, if the directors are also seeking authority in relation to a specific allotment to remove pre-emption rights, they are obliged to put forward a justification: see s.571(6) and fn.62, below. Moreover, the general rules on resolutions at meetings of shareholders may require it. See para.15–47. The resolution need only be an ordinary resolution, even if it amends the company's articles (s.551(8)), but the resolutions must be notified to the Registrar (s.551(9)). Authorisation can be given in the articles, but this is unlikely in the case of "particular" authorisation.

periods of up to five years.[29] With general authorisation, where no specific use of the power may be under contemplation at the time, information about how the funds raised will be used will necessarily be very general and will be phrased so as to give management maximum freedom of action. However, the authority, whether general or particular, must state the maximum number of securities which can be allotted under it and the date at which the authority will expire.[30] Moreover, the authorisation may be made conditional,[31] and it may be revoked or varied at any time by resolution of the company, even if the original authority was contained in the articles.[32] Institutional shareholders do attach importance to the general requirement for shareholder authorisation of share issues by the board. Guidance from the Association of British Insurers indicates that its members will not vote in favour of resolutions giving authority above a certain size. That size used to be one third of the company's existing issued share capital. In 2008 the limit was increased, under the pressures discussed in the next section, to two thirds, provided that the second third could be issued only on a pre-emptive basis and the authorisation for the second third was renewed yearly.[33]

PRE-EMPTIVE RIGHTS

Policy issues

24–6 Whether or not collective shareholder consent is required for allotment of shares, there is a further issue whether the existing shareholders individually should have a "right of first refusal" over the new shares or, in company law terms, whether the shares should be issued on a pre-emptive basis. The basic principle underlying the pre-emption rules is that a shareholder should be able to protect his or her proportion of the total equity by having the opportunity to subscribe, in proportion to the existing holding, for any new issue for cash of equity capital or securities having an equity element.[34] There are two main reasons why a shareholder might wish to exercise this right and thus to prevent the "dilution" of his or her holding of equity shares. First, if new voting shares are issued and a shareholder does not acquire that amount of the new issue which is proportionate

---

[29] 2006 Act s.551(2), (3), (4). Renewals of authority are to be given by resolution, even if the original authority was contained in the articles: s.551(4)(a). As s.551(7) makes clear, the time limit relates to the directors' authorisation of the share offer, not to the allotment of the shares (which might occur after the time limit had expired). A time limit is required even for particular exercises of the power.
[30] 2006 Act s.551(3). In relation to allotments of rights to subscribe or to convert, what has to be stated is the maximum number of shares that can be allotted pursuant to the rights: s.551(6).
[31] 2006 Act s.551(2).
[32] 2006 Act s.551(4)(b). This will be a case of an ordinary resolution amending the articles. See fn.28, above.
[33] See now Investment Association, *Share Capital Management Guidelines*, 2014, 1.1 (available at *https://www.ivis.co.uk/media/11164/Rebranded-Share-Capital-Management-Guidelines-3-June-2015-.pdf* [Accessed 26 January 2016].
[34] This principle is also to be found in the Second Directive (art.33) but has again been applied in the UK to private as well as public companies. Pre-emption in relation to new shares issued by the company should be sharply distinguished from pre-emption on the transfer of shares by a shareholder, common in private companies, but entirely a matter for private contracting through the articles. See para.27–7.

to the existing holding, that person's influence in the company may be reduced because he or she now has control over a smaller percentage of the votes. In listed companies this is likely to be of concern only to large, often institutional, shareholders, but in small companies the issuance of new shares may well have a significant impact upon the balance of power within the company, and perhaps be motived by a desire to bring this change about. Here, pre-emptive rights operate as a potential limit on the freedom of the directors to affect a shift in the balance of control in the company by issuing new equity shares carrying voting rights to new investors.[35]

Secondly, large issues of new shares by a publicly traded company are likely to be priced at a discount to the existing market price, in order to encourage their sale. Once the new shares are allocated, all the shares of the relevant class, new and old, will inevitably trade on the market at the same price. This new price will be somewhere between the issue price of the new shares and the previous market price of the existing shares, depending upon the size of the discount and the size of the new issue. In the absence of protective regulation, if an existing shareholder does not acquire the relevant proportion of the new shares, the loss of market value of the existing holding will be uncompensated. The new shareholders, in effect, will have been let into the company too cheaply, and the existing shareholders will have paid the price for that decision.[36]

The protection against voting dilution afforded by a bare pre-emptive right is only partial. The shareholder must also be in a position financially to take up the shares on offer.[37] A financially constrained existing shareholder is thus not protected against voting dilution by pre-emption. The same might seem to be true of financial dilution. However, here the addition of a further feature to the basic pre-emption model can help. If the shareholder is able to sell his or her pre-emptive rights in the market, that will provide compensation for the loss suffered. The rights will have a value equal to the difference between the issue price of the new shares and the (higher) price at which the whole class will trade after the issue, which will compensate the shareholder for loss caused by the difference between the pre-issue value of that person's holding and the (lower) value it will have after the new issue.[38] However, for the rights to be marketable they must be transferable to third parties. There is an established way of providing this facility. The company issues a "renounceable" letter of allotment, which gives the shareholder the option to subscribe for the new shares or to

---

[35] See also para.16–26 on the collateral purposes doctrine which has a similar effect but operates only when the directors' predominant purpose is an improper one, and Ch.20 on the unfair prejudice remedy.

[36] See the distinction drawn between the loss suffered by the company and that by the shareholders when shares are issued for an inadequate consideration in *Pilmer v Duke Group Ltd* [2001] 2 B.C.L.C. 773 Aus. HC.

[37] In the case of small companies, the shareholder may be able to challenge the decision to issue new shares under the unfair prejudice procedure. See *Re A Company* [1986] B.C.L.C. 362; and *Re Sam Weller Ltd* [1990] Ch. 682.

[38] For a worked example of this analysis see Bank of England, *Guidance on Share Issuing*, 1999, Technical Annex, showing that the total value of the rights will always match the loss of value on the holding, no matter the size of the discount or the proportion of the existing shares to be issued on a discounted basis. At the time of the trading of the rights the actual post-issue price is unknown but a "theoretical ex rights price" can be easily calculated.

transfer the right to subscribe to a third party, the overall process being known as a "rights issue".[39] Provided the shareholder transfers the right to acquire the new shares before the time for exercising it expires (i.e. "renounces" it) the third party will pay the company for the new shares, having paid the shareholder for the acquisition of the right to subscribe.[40]

The scope of the statutory right

24–7   The Act creates a pre-emptive right in favour of existing shareholders, but it does not require companies to add the additional feature of a rights issue.[41] The company may simply make what is usually termed an "open" offer to its existing shareholders: the shareholder either takes the shares at the price asked or passes up the offer altogether. It is, however, common practice in listed companies for pre-emptive offers to be made on a renounceable basis.[42] We will first examine the shareholder's legal entitlements and then see how institutional pressure has moved practice beyond the statute in many cases.

The ambit of the statutory pre-emptive provisions extends only to issues for cash of "equity securities". These are defined as ordinary shares (and rights to subscribe for or convert securities into ordinary shares); and an ordinary share is any share other than one where the holder's right to participate in a distribution (whether by way of dividend or return of capital) is limited by reference to a fixed amount.[43] It does not matter whether the existing shares carry votes or not, and in fact it can be argued that pre-emptive rights are particularly important for the holders of non-voting shares, who will obtain no protection from the rules on shareholder authorisation discussed in the previous section. Certain types of share issue are excluded from the pre-emption rules, even if they arguably involve the issue of equity shares for cash: bonus shares (where the pre-emption problem does not arise)[44] or shares to be held under an employees' share scheme.[45] Nor do the rules apply to shares taken by subscribers on the formation of a company.[46]

---

[39] See para.25–14.

[40] A third course of action is for the shareholder to sell part of the rights and to exercise the other part, so as to maintain the value of his or her shareholding in the company (but not the proportion of the shares held), rather than simply to receive compensation for that drop in value by selling all the rights. This action is called, obscurely, "tail-swallowing". The "discount" referred to in this discussion is, of course, a discount to the prevailing market price of the shares, not to their par value, which is not permitted (see para.11–4, above).

[41] It recognises, of course, that a rights issue is a permissible way of providing the pre-emptive right. See the reference to renouncement of rights to allotment in s.561(2).

[42] For further discussion see E. Ferran, "Legal Capital Rules and Modern Securities Markets" in K.J. Hopt and E. Wymeersch (eds), *Capital Markets and Company Law* (Oxford: OUP, 2003).

[43] 2006 Act s.560(1). There is no upper limit to this amount (and it would be impracticable to set one) with the result that it is possible to fix a dividend limitation so high that the holders would in fact be entitled to the whole or the lion's share of profits without affording existing shareholders pre-emptive rights.

[44] 2006 Act s.564. See para.11–20. Since issuance of a bonus share involves the capitalisation of the company's reserves, no payment by shareholders is involved and the shares must be allotted pro-rata to those entitled to the reserve, were it distributed, or, in the case of an undistributable reserve, whose contributions constituted the reserve (as in the case of the share premium account).

[45] 2006 Act s.566. Even if those scheme members may be entitled to renounce or assign their rights so that, if they do, the shares when allotted will not be "held in pursuance of the scheme". Employees'

Moreover, pre-emptive rights will be triggered only if the proposed issue is exclusively for cash.[47] For example, if a company wishing to acquire a business proposed to allot ordinary shares as consideration to the vendor, it would be impracticable to make a pre-emptive offer to the existing shareholders on the same terms. Nevertheless, the restriction of the statutory pre-emptive provisions to cash issues, even if compelled by necessity, does make a severe hole in the principle of protecting shareholders against dilution, especially dilution of their voting position. In relation to financial dilution some alternative protection is provided by Ch.6 of Pt 17 of the Act, requiring an independent valuation report in the case of share issues by public companies for a non-cash consideration,[48] but, even so, that section does not confer individual rights upon shareholders in the way that the pre-emption rules do.

Futhermore, the exclusion of share issues which are wholly or partly other than for cash gives rise to possibilities of manipulation so as to avoid the pre-emption rules. For example, if any part of the consideration, even a minor part, is not cash, then it appears that the pre-emption rules are excluded. This may be of particular interest to private companies. In other cases it may well be possible to restructure the transaction so that the cash is provided otherwise than to the issuer in exchange for its shares. Thus, where Company A wishes to acquire part of the business of Company B, the latter wishing to receive cash, Company A might issue new shares to raise the necessary money, if it does not have sufficient available cash, thus attracting the pre-emption provisions in relation to its shareholders. Instead, however, Company A might issue its shares to Company B, in exchange for the latter's assets and thus without attracting the pre-emption provisions, Company A having previously arranged for an investment bank to offer to buy the shares from Company B at a fixed price and to place them with interested investors. Such a "vendor placing" gives Company B the cash it wanted, whilst relieving Company A of the need to abide by the pre-emption rules.[49]

24–8

Assuming none of the above limitations apply, the pre-emption obligation requires the company not to allot equity securities to any person unless it has first offered, on the same or more favourable terms, to each person who holds shares covered by the right a proportion of those equity securities which is as nearly as

24–9

---

share schemes would be unworkable if every time a further allotment was to be made pursuant to them all equity shareholders had to be offered pre-emptive rights. If, however, equity shares have been allotted under the scheme, the employee holders should have the same rights to protect their proportion of equity as any other shareholder.

[46] 2006 Act s.577. Indeed, it is difficult to see how the rules could be so applied.

[47] 2006 Act s.565.

[48] See above, para.11–16. But the chapter does not apply to private companies or to share issues even by public companies in connection with takeover offers or mergers, where there is in fact a considerable risk of financial dilution. Listed company shareholders are better protected, for the rule restricting discounts to 10 per cent (see para.24–13) applies also to a "vendor consideration placing".

[49] It is difficult to regard this scheme with great disapprobation, since, if Company B had been prepared to take the shares of Company A in exchange for its assets, and then immediately sold them, no question of pre-emption would have arisen. A legitimate concern of the existing shareholders in such a case arises if the shares are placed with their new holders at a discount to the market price. For listed companies, the Listing Rules restrict the discount to 10 per cent, unless the shareholders have approved something larger: LR 9.5.10.

practicable equal to the shareholder's existing proportion in nominal value of the existing shares.[50] Only if the period for the existing shareholders to accept the offer has expired (now at least 14 days)[51] without the offer being accepted (or if it was positively rejected within this period) may an offer be made to outsiders. If the pre-emptive offer is not accepted in full, shares not taken up may be allotted to anyone; accepting existing shareholders do not have further pre-emptive rights in respect of those unaccepted shares.

Waiver

24–10   The shareholders collectively can forego their statutory pre-emption rights: they can be excluded or disapplied. Exclusion means the statutory provisions do not operate at all; disapplication may mean that but it also embraces the situation where the statutory provisions apply "with such modifications as the directors may determine"[52] or such modifications as are specified in the disapplication resolution.[53] Not surprisingly, both exclusion and disapplication are easier for private than for public companies. A private company may exclude the obligation to offer pre-emptive rights (or a provision relating to the method of offering, most likely the time during which the offer must be open) through a provision in its articles—either generally or in relation to allotments of a particular description.[54] As for disapplication, if the private company has only one class of shares, so that the directors do not need shareholder authority to issue new shares, its articles or a special resolution of the shareholders may remove the pre-emptive obligation or give the directors power to modify the statutory scheme.[55]

In relation to public companies exclusion is available only where the articles provide a pre-emptive alternative to the statutory scheme. This provision is designed to deal with situations where the company has more than one class of ordinary share.[56] The statutory pre-emptive obligation[57] is drafted in such a way as not to differentiate among different classes of ordinary shares, so that an offer of ordinary shares of one class would have to be made pre-emptively to all classes of ordinary shareholder. Section 568 permits a company to substitute an alternative pre-emption scheme in its articles which operates on a class basis. Non-compliance with the procedure in the articles carries the same consequences as non-compliance with the statutory procedure.[58]

As for disapplication, the provisions applicable to public companies (and private companies with more than one class of share) are built onto the rules on

---

[50]   2006 Act s.561. Treasury shares are excluded from the calculations required by this section: s.561(4). The details of how communication is to be made with the shareholders are set out in s.562.

[51]   2006 Act s.562(5). Nor can the offer be withdrawn, once made: s.562(4).

[52]   2006 Act ss.569(1), 570(1).

[53]   2006 Act s.571(1).

[54]   2006 Act s.567. A provision in the memorandum or articles which is inconsistent with ss.561 or 562 has effect as an exclusion of that subsection: s.567(3).

[55]   2006 Act s.569. On shareholder authority to issue in private companies see para.24–4, above.

[56]   2006 Act s.568. The problem does not arise if the other classes of share are not ordinary but preference shares, because they will not benefit from a pre-emption right.

[57]   2006 Act s.561.

[58]   2006 Act ss.568(4),(5), on which see below.

directors' authority to issue shares, discussed above. Where such authorisation is needed and has been given "generally",[59] the articles or a special resolution may disapply the pre-emption rights entirely or give the directors a discretion to apply them with such modifications as they may determine.[60] The disapplication lasts only so long as the general authority and, if the authority is renewed, the disapplication will need renewal as well. In other words, the disapplication can be for a maximum period of five years.

Alternatively, where authorisation is required, and it has been given either generally or specifically, a special resolution may disapply the statutory provisions in relation to a particular issuance of shares or determine that they shall apply only with such modifications as are specified in the resolution.[61] Again, the disapplication lasts only so long as the authorisation to which it relates, though this is a less important provision in relation to specified allotments. Unusually for British company law, a special resolution in relation to a specified allotment may not be proposed unless it has been recommended by the directors, and there is circulated a written statement by the directors of their reasons for making the recommendation, the amount to be paid to the company in respect of the proposed issue, and the directors' justification of that amount.[62] A person, director or otherwise, who knowingly or recklessly authorises or permits the inclusion in the statement of information which is misleading, false or deceptive commits a criminal offence.[63]

It is relatively common for public companies to make use of the disapplication provisions, even where the directors have every intention of respecting the principle of pre-emption, because greater flexibility can be built into the arrangements. A common desire is to exclude from the offer shareholders in foreign jurisdictions whose securities laws are regarded as excessively burdensome in relation to the number of the company's investors located there.[64] Even if the statutory rules have been disapplied, however, a publicly traded company is likely to be subject to the Listing Rules,[65] but these specifically permit pre-emptive offers to exclude holders whom the company considers "necessary or expedient to exclude from the offer on account of the laws or regulatory requirements of" another country.[66] Finally, there may be disapplication in relation to treasury shares, whether held by a public or a private company.[67] The

24–11

---

[59] See para.24–5, above, for the meaning of "general" authorisation.

[60] 2006 Act s.570.

[61] 2006 Act ss.571.

[62] 2006 Act ss.571(5)–(7). These provisions track art.33.4 of the Directive, but the common law would produce a similar disclosure requirement.

[63] 2006 Act s.572.

[64] *A Report to the Chancellor of the Exchequer by the Rights Issue Review Group*, November 2008, 6.5.

[65] See para.24–13.

[66] LR 9.3.12. This is primarily designed to deal with the situation where a company has shareholders resident in the USA. Under the Federal securities legislation it may have to register with the SEC if it extends the offer to such shareholders. Hence the present practice is to exclude such shareholders and to preclude those to whom the offer is made from renouncing in favour of a US resident. This practice was upheld in *Mutual Life Insurance of N.Y. v Rank Organisation* [1985] B.C.L.C. 11, but a fairer arrangement would surely be for the rights of the American shareholders to be sold for their benefit?

[67] On which see para.13–26, above.

directors do not require shareholder consent to sell treasury shares (since they are already in issue) but such sales are caught in principle by the statutory pre-emption right.[68] However, the directors may be given power to allot free of that right, either generally (by the articles or by special resolution) or in relation to a specified allotment (by special resolution).[69] One of the arguments for permitting treasury shares was that it gave companies freedom to raise relatively small amounts of capital quickly, which a pre-emption right would hinder, so that it seems correct policy to facilitate the disapplication of the pre-emption right to treasury shares.[70]

Sanctions

24–12 A civil (but not a criminal) sanction is provided by the Act. When there has been a contravention of the pre-emption right (either by not providing it all or by not providing it in the way required by the Act), the company and every officer of it who knowingly authorised or permitted the contravention are jointly and severally liable to compensate any person to whom an offer should have been made for any loss, damage, costs or expenses.[71] Where under the provisions discussed immediately above, the statutory provisions are applied in a modified way, these sanctions will equally apply to a contravention of the modified provisions.[72] The Act does not invalidate an allotment of shares made in breach of the pre-emptive provisions, no doubt in order to protect the legitimate interests of third parties. However, in *Re Thundercrest Ltd*[73] the judge was prepared to rectify the register[74] as against the directors of a small company, with only three shareholders, where the directors responsible for the breach of the pre-emptive provisions had allotted the shares in dispute to themselves.

Listed companies

24–13 Institutional shareholders (pension funds and insurance companies in particular) have traditionally held a very significant proportion of the shares of publicly traded companies.[75] For a long time they have placed a high value on pre-emptive rights. Consequently, market practice, influenced by the institutional shareholders, goes beyond the statutory rights embodied in the Act. Indeed, pre-emptive rights were a feature of market practice in London before the statutory pre-emption right was introduced into legislation in 1980. There are two channels

---

[68] 2006 Act s.560(2)(b).

[69] 2006 Act s.573.

[70] However, existing shareholders in listed companies are protected against dilution by the imposition of a limit of 10 per cent to any discount applied on the sale of the treasury shares: LR 9.5.10.

[71] 2006 Act s.562. Proceedings must be commenced within two years of the filing of the relevant return of allotments or, where rights to subscribe or convert are granted, within two years from the grant: s.563(3). As noted, the same applies to contraventions of the substitute right in the company's articles relating to classes of ordinary shares: s.568(4),(5).

[72] 2006 Act ss.569(2), 570(2), 571(2), 573(3),(5).

[73] *Re Thundercrest Ltd* [1995] 1 B.C.L.C. 117.

[74] See para.27–19.

[75] See para.15–25.

through which the institutional shareholders have been able to advance their views. First, they have been able to influence effectively the rules made by the FCA relating to the listing[76] of companies and the rules made by the London Stock Exchange relating to the admission of securities to trading (though the former are the more important source of rules). Secondly, they have taken collective action to draw up rules to govern what action they will or will not support as shareholders in the pre-emption area. We will look first at the Listing Rules.

The most important Listing Rule in this area is probably the one which limits the discount at which a company may issue shares, other than by way of a rights issue, to 10 per cent of the prevailing market price, unless the shareholders approve a higher discount.[77] This means that, if the company sticks to the bare pre-emptive entitlement set out in the statute, those shareholders who cannot afford to take up their rights face only a limited financial loss, as a result of the cap on the discount. To put the matter from the company's point of view, if the success of the pre-emption offer is thought to require a greater discount than 10 per cent, the directors will need the shareholders' consent to proceed with the issue other than as a rights issue.[78] The rule is thus an important restraint on the directors' powers to proceed with an open offer and pushes them instead in the direction of a rights issue, where the shareholders' financial interests are protected.

Pre-emption guidelines

The overall picture which emerges of the above analysis is that existing shareholders' right to pre-emption, which the Act creates, and to pre-emption on a rights basis, which the Listing Rules indirectly create, may be removed by collective decision of the shareholders. So the impact in practice of both the statute and the Listing Rules turns on shareholders' willingness (or otherwise) to forego their rights. Since institutional shareholders are strongly opposed to dilution of their positions, they have sought to agree guidelines determining the circumstances in which consent to disapplication will be given. Originally, the institutions acted alone in drawing up the guidelines but, given their importance for the financing of companies and the operation of the capital markets, an element of public interest has been injected by conducting the discussions under the auspices of, first, the Bank of England, then the London Stock Exchange and, now, the Financial Reporting Council.[79] Institutionally, this development has resulted in the creation a Pre-emption Group,[80] which issues the guidelines which determine institutional shareholders' attitudes to disapplication resolutions,

24–14

---

[76] On listing see para.25–9.

[77] LR 9.5.10. This rule applies only to companies with a premium listing, on which see para.25–6.

[78] Since the requirement is that "the terms of the offer or placing at that discount have been specifically approved by the issuer's shareholders", the shareholder approval cannot be given in practice in advance of the decision to issue.

[79] On which see para.21–17.

[80] *http://www.pre-emptiongroup.org.uk* [Accessed 26 January 2016]. The first guidelines were adopted in 1987. The Principles are supported by the National Association of Pension Funds and the Investment Association.

whether under the statute or the Listing Rules. The guidelines have no legal status but they articulate a strongly held and practically significant attitude on the part of the institutions about the value of pre-emptive rights. This policy of the institutional investors has turned pre-emption on a rights basis into an example of a "strong" default rule whose alteration creates a significant hurdle for the management of the company. Thus, the statutory provisions and the Listing Rules have much more bite because of the difficulty of securing shareholder consent to their disapplication other than in accordance with the guidelines. On the other hand, if there were no default rules in the statute and Listing Rules, the institutional shareholders would face the more demanding task of securing an amendment to a company's articles of association, introducing a pre-emption right.[81]

The guidelines, currently in the form of a Statement of Principles,[82] distinguish between general and specific disapplication resolutions. The institutional investors will vote in favour of general disapplication resolutions where the authority is limited to no more 5 per cent of the ordinary share capital of the company in any one year (plus a further 5 per cent for an acquisition or capital investment which is identified at the time the resolution is put forward). When acting under the general disapplication resolutions, the company should raise no more than 7.5 per cent in any rolling period of three years (excluding the capital investment addition), without consulting with its shareholders. Authority should not be sought for more than 15 months or until the next AGM, whichever is the sooner.[83] In consequence, disapplication resolutions have become a common feature of the AGM agenda.

Controversy has raged over the rules relating to specific, non-routine (often large-scale) disapplication resolutions, where the institutions need to be persuaded to vote in favour of the disapplication resolution and so need to be presented with the business case for proceeding on a non-rights basis. It used to be thought in some corporate circles that institutions would normally vote against specific disapplication resolutions, but after criticism from a government review,[84] the rules were re-drafted to make it clear this was not the case. What is abundantly clear from the Principles, however, is that, where the institutional shareholders hold sway, the company will have no chance of securing a general, large-scale disapplication of the pre-emption requirement. The Principles envisage specific resolutions being supported only in the context of a specific project, where the need for non-pre-emptive finance can be demonstrated and justified.[85]

---

[81] Hence the reported opposition of the institutional investors to the removal of the pre-emption requirement from the Second Directive: *Financial Times*, UK edn, 22 October 2007, p.18 and ibid. 23 October 2007, p.23. Of course, the removal of the right from the Second Directive would not prevent the UK from maintaining the statutory default.

[82] The latest version dates from 2015 and is available on website identified in fn.80. The Principles are said to apply formally only to companies listed on the Premium Listing segment of the Main Market of the London Stock Exchange, but standard listing companies and those on the Alternative Investment Market are "encouraged" to apply them.

[83] Principles, Pts 2A and 2B.

[84] DTI, *Pre-Emption Rights: Final Report*, February 2005 (URN 05/679). It was in this re-drafting process that the "Guidelines" became "Principles", perhaps to emphasis this point.

[85] Principles, Pt 3.

Criticism and further market developments

The pre-emptive right, and the rights issue in particular, have always been **24–15** unpopular amongst management, just as it has been popular amongst shareholders. Two main criticisms are advanced. First, that it reduces the pool of investors to whom a company may turn for additional equity finance and so it pushes up the cost of equity finance. Secondly, a rights issue takes longer to carry out than either an open offer or a placing (i.e. raising finance from a small number of investors without making a public offer) and so exposes the company to market risk during the offer period. The arguments in principle for and against the rights issue were examined in the Myners Review of 2005.[86] Paul Myners came out in favour of rights issues. He was particularly impressed by the corporate governance argument in favour of pre-emption. This is that this doctrine makes it difficult for a management, which has failed its existing shareholders, to obtain finance from a new group of investors, letting them into the company cheaply (and at the expense of the existing investors) as part of an implicit bargain to back the existing management against the complaints of the first group of investors. By contrast, pre-emption makes management seeking further equity finance sensitive to the views of the existing investors from whom it must be raised.

In 2008, the first full year of the financial crisis, the issue came to fore again as a number of banks had to raise large sums of fresh capital. All succeeded in doing so, but often only after great difficulties. The Rights Issue Review Group[87] was appointed to see if the principle of rights issues could be maintained whilst mitigating the associated fund-raising difficulties. The main issue was perceived to be one of timing. If the length of the rights issue process could be reduced, the issuer's exposure to market risk (possibly even to market manipulation)[88] would also be reduced, an important development in turbulent markets.[89]

An obvious first step, already implemented, was to reduce the period for **24–16** shareholders to decide whether to take up their rights from 21 to 14 days, the minimum specified in the Second Directive.[90] However, the main timing problem was seen to flow from the need to both secure shareholders' consent and to provide the (now) 14-day period for shareholders to decide whether to take up their rights, and the inability to have those two activities running concurrently. It may not be clear why shareholder consent should be needed if what is proposed is a rights issue. There are three possible answers. First, the directors may not have in place a large enough authority to issue shares (in any way) without shareholder consent, though the changes recently made to the Investment Association Guidance[91] make that now less likely. Second, the directors may wish to make a non-statutory pre-emption offer and so need shareholder consent to disapply the

---

[86] See fn.84.
[87] Above, fn.64.
[88] On which see para.30–39.
[89] The discussion below focuses on speeding up the formal offer process.
[90] 2006 Act s.562(5). The change was made in 2009. Similar changes were made to LR 9.5.6 to cater for non-statutory rights issues and to the *AIM Rules for Companies* (notes to rr.24 and 25).
[91] Above para.24–5.

statutory pre-emption provisions.[92] Thirdly, the Pre-emption Group's Principles suggest, though not clearly, that institutional shareholders expect shareholder approval for deeply discounted rights issues (above 5 per cent), even though the statute does not specify any cap on the level of discount nor does the Listing Rules cap apply if a rights issue is proposed.

Assuming shareholder approval is required, the difficulty about making the offer to the shareholders before that approval is obtained is that trading in the rights (so-called "trading in nil paid form") necessarily begins as soon as the offer is made (since the trading must be completed within 14 days). If, however, shareholder approval for the issue is not ultimately obtained, unscrambling the trading may prove very difficult. Consequently, practice is to obtain approval before making the offer. An open offer does not suffer from this difficulty and so the offer can be launched and shareholder approval sought at the same time, the offer being conditional upon shareholder approval being obtained. However, the open offer gives no protection against dilution to the shareholder who cannot take up the offer. Consequently, market practice has developed recently the "compensatory open offer", under which any shares not take up by the shareholder are sold by the company (or its underwriters) into the market and any premium obtained over the offer price is paid to the shareholder who did not take up the offer.[93] In effect, the burden of trading the rights to the new shares passes from the shareholder under a rights issue to the company under the compensatory open offer, but the economic impact on the shareholder should be very similar.[94] This may be a burden the company is happy to accept in order to speed up the fund raising process.[95]

THE TERMS OF ISSUE

24–17 As noted in the previous chapter,[96] the rights attached to the shares to be issued are likely to be set out in the company's articles. What will not be set out there is the price or other consideration to be asked in exchange for the shares. Here the directors have a free hand, subject to the rules on capital raising discussed in Ch.11.[97] As far as private companies are concerned, these rules are not demanding, consisting mainly of the rules on commissions and requiring shares not to be issued at a discount to their nominal value (not to be confused with a discount to the market price, against which the pre-emption right, as we have just

---

[92] See para.24–11.

[93] See above para.24–6 as to why the market price can be expected to be higher than offer price. LR 9.5.4 already imposed this rule in favour of offerees in a rights issue who did not take up the offer, so that those unfamiliar with the rights issue procedure were not disadvantaged.

[94] However, a shareholder cannot engage in tail swallowing (above fn.40) under the compensatory open offer.

[95] Because of these market developments the FSA recommended against some of the more radical suggestions from the RIRG which would allow offer and approval periods to run simultaneously. See FSA, *Report to HM Treasury on the implementation of the recommendations of the Rights Issue Review Group*, April 2010.

[96] See above, para.23–6.

[97] See above, paras 11–13 et seq.

seen, aims to provide protection). With regard to public companies, the rules, implementing the Second Directive, are more constraining, though they have recently been relaxed somewhat.

ALLOTMENT

The process by which the company finds someone who is willing to become a shareholder of the company is not something about which the law says very much if there is no offer to the public of the company's shares[98]—although, as we shall see in the next chapter, this is in fact now a very heavily regulated area, if there is a public offer. What the Act does assume is that the process of becoming a shareholder is a two-step one, involving first a contract of allotment and then registration of the member. As Lord Templeman said in 1995:

24–18

> "The Act of 1985 preserves the distinction in English law between an enforceable contract for the issue of shares (which contract is constituted by an allotment) and the issue of shares which is completed by registration. Allotment confers a right to be registered. Registration confers [legal] title."[99]

This is consistent with the 2006 Act which defines the point at which shares are allotted as the time when a person acquires the unconditional right to be included in the register of members, but does not require actual entry in the register.[100]

Renounceable allotments

In the case of a private company the processes of agreement and registration will be achieved with little formality and without the issue of allotment letters. If someone wants to become a shareholder and the company wants him to, he will be entered on the register and issued with a share certificate without more ado. However, the advantage of constituting the agreement to become a member in a formal letter of allotment is that it facilitates the process described above in relation to rights issues[101] of "renouncing" the entitlement to be registered as a member in favour of someone else, though the technique is not confined to rights issues. Printed on the back of the letter there will be forms enabling, for a short specified period, the allottee to renounce the right to be registered as a member and the person to whom they are ultimately renounced to confirm that he or she accepts the renunciation and agrees to be entered on the register. Normally the original allottee will not insert the name of the person to whom they are to be renounced and the effect is then to produce something similar to a short-term

24–19

---

[98] The general common law rules on fraud, misrepresentation and negligence will provide some protection to investors: see paras 25–31 et seq., below.

[99] *National Westminster Bank Plc v IRC* [1995] 1 A.C. 111 at 126 HL. From this, Lord Templeman reasoned that shares were not "issued" (the Companies Act does not define the term) for the purposes of a taxing statute until the applicants for the shares were registered as members of the company.

[100] 2006 Act s.558.

[101] See above, para.24–7. Of course, a private company may not want to grant this facility, which might be inconsistent with its articles (see para.27–7, below). The statutory scheme of pre-emption rights does not *require* renouncing to be made available.

share-warrant to bearer.[102] It is not a negotiable instrument but once the renunciation is signed by the original allottee, the rights can be assigned by manual delivery of the allotment letter without a formal transfer. Before the stated period ends, however, it will be necessary for the name of the ultimate holder to be inserted, a signature obtained, and the allotment letter lodged with the company or its registrars.

Failure of the offer

24–20 Implementing art.32 of the Second Directive, the Act lays down a default rule for public companies that no allotment of shares shall be made pursuant to an offer to subscribe[103] for shares (whether the offer is to the public or not) unless the shares on offer are taken up in full.[104] This rule is designed to prevent an investor ending up holding shares in a company which is less fully capitalised than was expected when the offer was accepted. If a full take-up of the shares is not achieved within 40 days of making the offer, the money[105] received from the offerees becomes repayable in full, though without interest,[106] and must actually be repaid within a further eight days. The sanction for this latter requirement is that the directors then become jointly and severally liable to repay the money, with interest.[107] If the company actually proceeds with an allotment in breach of the Act then the allotment is voidable by the offeree within one month of the allotment (even if the company is in course of winding up),[108] and any director who knowingly contravenes or permits the contravention of the prohibition on allotment becomes liable to compensate the allottee and the company for any loss, damages, costs or expenses.[109] Despite these fearsome sanctions, the rule is not enormously important in practice, for two reasons. First, if the offer in terms says that the allotment will proceed, even if not fully subscribed, or will proceed if conditions falling short of full subscription are met, the prohibition on allotment does not apply.[110] So, the rule is really one which requires only that the investors be told what risk they run in relation to the take-up of the offer. Secondly, in relation to offers to the public, failure to achieve a full take-up of the offer is a serious matter, not only for the investors, but also for the issuer, so that companies will

---

[102] See below, para.24–22.

[103] The section thus does not apply to offers for sale of shares (see para.25–12) and does not need to because the issue has been in effect underwritten.

[104] 2006 Act s.578(1). In fact, however, the rule has a much longer pedigree: CA 1948 s.47.

[105] The rule applies, mutatis mutandis, where the consideration for the offer is wholly or partly otherwise than in cash: s.578(4),(5).

[106] 2006 Act s.578(2).

[107] 2006 Act s.578(3). A director can escape liability if it can be shown that the failure was not due to misconduct or negligence on the director's part. If the company promises to keep the monies advanced by a subscriber in a separate bank account and does so, it seems that the monies will be held on trust by the company in favour of the investors: *Re Nanwa Gold Mines Ltd* [1955] 1 W.L.R. 1080.

[108] 2006 Act s.579(1),(2). This means the assets contributed by the allottee are taken out of the insolvent company's estate, but only if the allotee acts within the one-month period.

[109] 2006 Act s.579(3), subject to a two-year limitation period: s.579(4).

[110] 2006 Act s.578(1)(b)—or if the offer is stated to be subject only to certain conditions (such as a 75 per cent acceptance) and those conditions are met.

arrange for the offer to be "underwritten" in some way (i.e. normally an investment bank agrees to take up the shares which are not bought by the public).[111]

Once the shares have been allotted, the company must make a return of allotment to the Registrar of companies, as discussed in the previous chapter.[112]

REGISTRATION

As Lord Templeman indicated, allotment does not make a person a member of the company. Entry in the register of members is also needed to give the allottee legal title to the shares. Section 112(2) says explicitly that a person "who agrees to become a member of the company and whose name is entered on the register of members is a member of the company".[113] The Act now requires registration "as soon as practicable" and in any event within two months of the date of allotment.[114] Even when registered, the shareholder will find difficulty in selling the shares, if they are to be held in certificated form, until a share certificate is received from the company. If the shares are to be held in uncertificated form,[115] then by definition no share certificate will be issued. Instead, the company, by computer instruction, will inform the operator of the electronic transfer system of the identity of those to whom the shares have been allotted and of the number of shares issued to each person.[116] The lapse of time between allotment and registration in the share register by informing the operator of the electronic transfer system of what the company has done should be very much shorter than the gap between allotment and the issue of share certificates, where the Act gives the company up to two months to complete the process.[117]

24–21

Bearer shares

A major exception in principle, though much less so in practice, to the requirement of entry on the register in order to become a member of the company was created by share-warrants to bearer. Section 779 provided that a company, if so authorised by its articles, could issue with respect to any fully paid shares a warrant stating that the bearer of the warrant is entitled to the shares specified in it. If similarly authorised, it could provide, by coupons attached to the warrant or

24–22

---

[111] See para.25–11.

[112] At para.23–6.

[113] On which, see *Re Nuneaton Football Club* [1989] B.C.L.C. 454 CA, holding that "agreement" requires only assent to become a member. The subscribers to the memorandum of association (above, para.4–5) are the first members of the company and should be entered on its register of members, but in their case it appears that they become members, whether this is done or not: *Evans' Case* (1867) L.R. 2 Ch. App. 247; *Baytrust Holdings Ltd v IRC* [1971] 1 W.L.R. 1333 at 1355–1356.

[114] 2006 Act s.554. Failure to register is a criminal offence on the part of the company and every officer in default.

[115] See Ch.27.

[116] Uncertificated Securities Regulations 2001 (SI 2001/3755) reg.34.

[117] 2006 Act s.769.

otherwise, for the payment of future dividends.[118] Title to the shares specified then passes by manual delivery of the warrant,[119] which is a negotiable instrument.[120] On their issue, the company removed from its register of members the name of the former registered holder and merely states the fact and date of the issue of the warrant and the number of shares to which it relates.[121] The bearer of the warrant from time to time was unquestionably a shareholder but to what extent, if at all, he was a member of the company depended on a provision to that effect in the articles.[122] Hence shareholding and membership are not necessarily coterminous if share warrants are issued. However, again subject to the articles, the bearer of the warrant was entitled, on surrendering it for cancellation, to have his name and shareholding re-entered on the register.[123] In practice this exception was unimportant because bearer securities have never been popular with British investors or British companies and are rarely issued and hardly ever in respect of shares, as opposed to bearer bonds (i.e. debt securities which are sometimes issued to attract continental investors who have a traditional liking for securities in bearer form). It is fortunate that bearer shares were such a rarity for, if they became common, it would play havoc with many provisions of the Act. In the end, amendments made by the Small Business, Enterprise and Employment Act 2015 prohibited companies from issuing share warrants in the future and made provision for the mandatory conversion of existing warrants back into shares, precisely because they were thought likely to undermine that Act's enhanced provisions on disclosure of share ownership.[124]

CONCLUSION

24–23   Where a company makes a non-public offer of shares, a situation which will necessarily include most share offers by private companies, the rules discussed above are all that the company will need to concern itself with. Where, however, a public offer of shares is to be made, the extensive regulation considered in the next chapter will come into play. Even then, the relevant regulation is additional to the rules considered in this chapter and, though it may supplement, does not replace them. In fact, rules discussed in this chapter, for example those relating to pre-emptive rights, can be very important in public offers, but the point is that such rules are not confined to public offers but apply to share issues of a non-public type as well. Protection of the position of existing shareholders through pre-emption is as important in a private as in a public company, indeed

---

[118] 2006 Act s.779(3). Share-warrants to bearer must be distinguished from what is perhaps the more common type of warrant, which gives the holder the right to subscribe for shares in the company at a specific price on a particular date or within a particular period. Such warrants are a form of long-term call option over the company's shares. They may be traded, but their transfer simply gives the transferee the option and does not make him or her a member until the option is exercised.

[119] 2006 Act s.779(2).

[120] *Webb, Hale & Co v Alexandria Water Co* (1905) 21 T.L.R. 572.

[121] 2006 Act s.122(1).

[122] 2006 Act s.122(3).

[123] 2006 Act s.122(4)—now repealed.

[124] 2006 Act s.779(4), as added; 2015 Act s.84 and Sch.4. The prohibition operated from May 2015; the period for mandatory reconversion ended a year later.

arguably more so in the absence of a market upon which the shares of a disgruntled shareholder can be disposed of.

PUBLIC OFFERS OF SHARES

INTRODUCTION

This chapter is concerned with a subject that takes us into the area of securities **25–1** regulation or capital markets law. Nevertheless, it is not a subject which books on company law can ignore; how public companies go about raising their capital from the investing public and the legal regulations that have to be complied with when they do are central to the operations of large companies. An elaborate discussion of this specialised branch of legal practice is inappropriate in a book of this sort but an outline is essential. The rules considered in this chapter generally apply to "securities", i.e. both to shares and debt instruments (for example, bonds). The focus of this chapter will be on share issues but we will notice the major divergences when debt securities are issued, as and when is relevant. Debt securities are the lesser subject in this chapter, because they are less often offered to the public even by companies which issue shares to the public and because bonds are less frequently traded on public markets (as opposed to "over the counter"). Nevertheless, to an extent, this chapter crosses the divide between Pts 6 and 7 of the book.

Public offers and introductions to public markets

25–2   There are two distinct, though usually combined, operations which may take place when a large company seeks to raise finance from the investing public. In the first place, it needs to make its case to those people who may be interested in investing in it by purchasing its securities. As we shall see below, the company may choose among a number of different ways of putting itself before investors. The most heavily regulated of these methods is the public offer of securities, simply because the company addresses its publicity to a wide range of persons who may include the ill-informed and the gullible as well as the experienced and well-informed. When a company makes a public offer of its shares for the first time, that is usually termed an "initial public offering" ("IPO"), and this is often a major event in the life of the company. But it may well make further public offerings at a later stage ("secondary" offers). The document (the "prospectus") through which public offers are made is regulated heavily by the law. From this perspective, the law relating to prospectuses can be viewed as a branch of consumer protection legislation, but concerning a product which is very difficult to evaluate. The value of shares depends heavily upon the future performance of the company and cannot be ascertained, as with a motor car, for example, by visual inspection and a test drive.

It will normally be the case that a company seeking to raise substantial funds from investors will also secure that the securities to be issued will be admitted to trading on a public securities market, such as one of the markets operated by the London Stock Exchange. The reason the company will normally take this extra step is that the willingness of investors to buy its securities will be increased if there is a liquid market upon which those securities can be traded after they have been issued. As we have seen, a shareholder is normally "locked into" the company after the shares have been purchased, in the sense that the investor, short of winding up, cannot require the company to buy back the shares, even at the later prevailing market price, except in the case of some types of redeemable share. Equally, bonds are not normally redeemable at the request of the investor until after some specified period has elapsed and perhaps not before they reach their maturity date. Therefore, a person who wishes to withdraw from an investment will normally be constrained to find another investor willing to purchase the securities. A liquid securities market will facilitate this operation, to the benefit of both investors and the company, which is likely to be able to sell its securities at a higher price if they have access to the liquidity afforded by a public market.

However, the mere admission of securities to trading on an public market also involves putting those securities before the investing public, even if there is no concomitant public offer, since it is now open to the public to acquire the company's securities, this time not directly from the company but from those who already hold them. Hence, there is a strong argument for having the same information disclosure upon admission of securities to a public market as when the company offers its securities directly to the public. The argument is even stronger if, as is usual, both events occur at the same time. However, there is no legal requirement that this should be so. A company may offer its securities to the public without securing their admission to public market (for example, where it does not expect or want the securities to be traded to any significant degree and so is content to rely on sellers seeking out potential purchasers privately). Or the driving force[1] behind the admission of the securities to the market may be an existing large shareholder (for example, the Government in a de-nationalisation issue) which wishes to liquidate or reduce its holding, but the company does not intend at that time to raise additional finance.

Our main concern in this chapter is with the financing of the company and the public offer of securities as a form of corporate finance. Consequently, the core transaction which we examine is one in which the company both makes a public offer of its shares and, at the same time, secures the admission of the shares to trading on a public market.

Regulatory goals

We have referred above to the law relating to public offers as consumer law and that is a very strong strand in the thinking of those responsible for the rules in this area. However, it would be wrong to see the regulation as nothing but a form of consumer protection. In fact, scholarship today stresses the function of regulation in this area as a way of promoting "allocative efficiency", that is, of promoting investment on the basis of an accurate understanding of the risk and reward profile of particular projects which the issuance of the shares will finance. This objective furthers the interests not only of investors but of companies and of the economy generally, for effective regulation promotes the allocation of scarce investment resources to the projects with the highest returns. But what sort of regulation will best facilitate the accurate assessment of different projects?

25–3

It is conventional in this branch of law to make a distinction between "merit" regulation and disclosure of information. Under the former approach, a regulator permits an offer to be made to the public only if the securities on offer or the company issuing them ("the issuer") pass certain quality tests, whereas the latter simply puts information in the hands of investors and leaves it up to them to make up their own minds about investing. Although the early regulation of public offers (at state level in the US) adopted the merit regulation approach,[2] the disclosure approach has been the predominant one in all jurisdictions since its adoption by federal US law in the great reforms of 1933 and 1934.[3] However, disclosure has never driven out all elements of merit regulation. Although what is required varies from market to market, disclosure is never all that is required. As a Canadian committee once remarked, with heavy irony, "it would be improbable that a securities commission in a disclosure regime would approve a prospectus that said, truthfully, that the promoters of the company intended to abscond with the proceeds of the public offering, or that the company's business enterprise had

---

[1] Securities cannot be admitted to the official list (see below) without the consent of the issuer (FSMA 2000 s.75(2)), but the impetus for the listing may come from the shareholder.
[2] Often referred to as "blue sky laws" because the securities on offer were backed, it was said, only by the blue sky. The first significant State law in the US seems to have been that of Kansas in 1911.
[3] The Securities Act 1933 and the Securities Exchange Act 1934.

no hope of success".[4] Thus, elements of merit regulation, referred to in the UK as "eligibility requirements", survive in even the most disclosure-oriented regime.

The triumph of disclosure as the predominant regulatory philosophy in this area is probably a reflection of the decision the investor has to make. Prospective subscribers to the ordinary shares to be issued by a company normally obtain no legal entitlement to a return on their investment and so they are essentially making a judgment about the company's business prospects in the future and the appropriate price to pay in the light of those prospects. If the company makes good profits, the ordinary shareholders will benefit; if it makes heavy losses, those will fall first on the same people. The prospective purchaser of shares has to take a view about how the industry in which the company is active will evolve and about the qualities of the company's management.[5] Nobody can be sure about the future. Using merit regulation to exclude certain public offers risks excluding a company whose track record is not good but which has a perfectly decent story to tell about its future. Further, heavy merit regulation may carry the implication that those offers that are permitted to proceed benefit from some sort of public guarantee of the company's future success, something the public authorities are unlikely to wish to provide. Merit regulation thus tends to play a limited role. Even disclosure of information does not make the investor's task easy, because the one piece of hard information the investor requires—what will be the issuer's financial results in the future?—is by definition not available. However, information about the company's present and recent activities, its proposals for the future and the terms of the securities on offer can help to guide the investment decision, even if it cannot take all risk out of the process. Indeed, if all risk could be eliminated, there would be no need for equity finance in the first place.

25–4   A further question about the disclosure regime, which has been hotly debated, is whether production of the requisite level of information requires mandatory disclosure rules. It can be argued that, a prospectus being a selling document, those companies with good stories to tell would make full disclosure of information and use private "bonding" mechanisms (such as certification by independent third parties) to convince investors of the truth of what they say. Companies with less good stories would follow suit, for fear that investors would deduce from inadequate disclosure that the prospects for the company were dire. Only companies with truly dire prospects would make inadequate disclosure and investors would draw the correct conclusions from such inadequate prospectuses. Whether this theory works in practice seems never to have been tested satisfactorily, but even if self-interest would generate extensive disclosure, mandatory disclosure rules have certain advantages over leaving it to the issuers to decide for themselves the extent of the disclosure. First, the state sanctions available for breaches of the mandatory rules (criminal, civil and regulatory sanctions) may be more credible to investors than the private bonding

---

[4] Toronto Stock Exchange, *Toward Improved Disclosure*, Interim Report of the Committee on Corporate Disclosure, 1995, para.3.9.

[5] For debt issues the investor's concern is whether the debt will be re-paid on time and in full. Because debt has priority over equity in an insolvency and because debt has no exposure to the up-side of a company's performance, less disclosure is generally required for bond issues in comparison with share issues. See para.25–17.

mechanisms companies themselves could produce. Secondly, mandatory rules may produce more uniformity in disclosure than disclosure decisions taken by issuers on an individual basis (thus helping investors to compare different public offerings). Thirdly, mandatory rules may overcome forces acting against full disclosure even when, from one point of view, disclosure is in the company's interest. An example is the disclosure of information which, whilst it would make the company attractive to investors, would also help the company's competitors.[6]

In any event, the detail required by the disclosure rules applicable on public offerings is now staggering. Since, as we have noted, the information available is only indirectly relevant to the future-oriented decision the investor has to make, there comes a point where the marginal gain from more information may outweigh the costs of providing it. This issue has been debated especially in relation to small and medium-sized entities ("SMEs") since the financial crisis. SMEs traditionally relied on bank funding, which became difficult to obtain post the crisis. Many advocated greater use by SMEs of the financial markets to raise capital. However, the largely fixed costs of capital raising from the public markets absorb a relatively high proportion of the funds raised in the case of small offerings. So, the question of a relaxed disclosure regime for SMEs moved centre stage, as we discuss below.

Turning to the admission of securities to trading on public markets, a regulatory goal has been to ensure that those who control the operation of public markets exercise their admission and expulsion powers fairly. This might be thought necessary to protect the interests of both issuers which wish to make public offerings and investors who have bought the securities on the basis that they would continue to be publicly traded. In practice, this has turned out to be a less important regulatory objective, since competition among public markets for offerings has itself constrained any impulse to act unfairly.

Listing

The meanings of a public offer and admission to trading on an exchange are easy enough to grasp. Somewhat less obvious is the concept of "listing". This is partly because of the varying ways in which the term is used. Sometimes it is used to refer to any security which is traded on a public market (i.e. it is on the "list" of securities traded on that market), in which case it adds nothing to what we have already said. In this book, however, we use the term in a narrower sense: a listed security is one which has been admitted to the "official list". The first point to note is that inclusion in the official list is not a pre-requisite for admission to trading on all public markets. For example, it is possible to make a public offer of "unlisted" securities and to secure the admission of those securities to trading on the Alternative Investment Market ("AIM") of the London Stock Exchange ("LSE"). On the other hand, the Main Market of the LSE is a market for listed securities only. So, the question arises as to why a company should wish its securities to be included in the official list. The answer to that is that admission to the official list constitutes a quality mark, which companies may be anxious to

25–5

---

[6] J. Coffee Jr, "Market Failure and the Economic Case for a Mandatory Disclosure System" (1984) 70 Virginia L.R. 717.

have in order to encourage investors to acquire their securities.[7] For this reason, admission to the official list is an important element in the public offer and admission to trading process.

Inherent in the concept of an official list is the idea that somebody controls admission to it in order to ensure that the standards for admission are met. That task used to be discharged by the LSE itself, but, with the demutualisation of the LSE, the Exchange no longer wished to carry out this regulatory function, which was transferred,[8] in consequence, to what is now the Financial Conduct Authority ("FCA"),[9] established under the Financial Services and Markets Act 2000,[10] as amended. Section 74 of FSMA requires the FCA to maintain the "official list" and to include securities in it only in accordance with the provisions of the Act and it gives the FCA the power to make listing rules ("LR") for the purpose of governing admission to the official list and the subsequent conduct of listed companies.[11] However, as is generally true in the area of public offers of securities, much of the controlling legislation is now made at EU level. Under art.5 of the Consolidated Admissions Requirements Directive[12] (or "CARD") Member States are required to "ensure [that] securities may not be admitted to official listing" on a stock exchange operating in their territory "unless the conditions laid down by this Directive are satisfied" and it is from this Directive that certain "merit" or "eligibility" requirements flow, as we shall see below. Article 105 requires that Member States appoint a "competent authority" for the purposes of the Directive, and in the UK that authority is the FCA, acting as the UK Listing Authority ("UKLA").

Premium and standard listing

25–6   However, it would be wrong to think that the FCA's Listing Rules exist only for the purpose of implementing the CARD Directive in the UK. The Listing Rules are of some antiquity and deal with many matters falling outside the scope of CARD or any other EU Directive or add to the requirements of those Directives.[13] For example, the LR contain corporate governance rules and rules on related-party transactions which, as we have seen, add significantly to the Companies Act requirements.[14] These additional requirements substantially contribute to the "quality mark" impact of admission to the official list. On the other hand, the additional requirements add to the regulatory burdens on a company and may discourage it from listing in London—as opposed to New York or Hong Kong. Consequently, in 2010 the FCA's predecessor introduced two classes of listing. Companies may choose between "standard" and "premium"

---

[7] Indeed, some investment institutions may be permitted only to acquire listed securities or may be restricted in the proportion of unlisted securities they may hold in their portfolio.

[8] By the Official Listing of Securities (Change of Competent Authority) Regulations 2000 (SI 2000/968). In other European countries the exchange typically still acts as the competent authority.

[9] Previously the Financial Services Authority.

[10] This is the primary piece of domestic legislation considered in this chapter.

[11] FSMA s.73A.

[12] Directive 2001/34/EC ([2001] O.J. L184).

[13] CARD art.8 makes it clear it is a "minimum harmonisation" Directive, to whose requirements the Member States may add.

[14] Above, paras 14–77, 16–77 and 19–6.

listing for equity shares, standard listing requiring compliance only with the minimum EU standards and not with the additional domestic rules.[15] Those additional rules concern predominantly corporate governance requirements to be observed after listing, but to a lesser extent they relate to the process of listing itself. Companies may choose a premium share listing for reputational reasons or under investor pressure.

Types of public market

Most people, if asked, would probably say that there is one stock market in the UK and that is the LSE. However, this is not the case. The LSE itself runs two separate markets for shares, namely the "Main Market" and the "Alternative Investment Market" ("AIM")[16] for well-established and less well-established companies respectively; and two separate markets for bonds (the Gilt-edged and Fixed-Interest Market ("GEFIM") and the Professional Securities Market ("PSM")).[17] However, the LSE has no monopoly on the operation of public markets in securities, even in the UK, and there exist a number of smaller share markets, of which the best known are probably those operated by ICAP Securities & Derivatives Exchange ("ISDX"), which operates partly in competition with those run by the LSE and partly to provide a market for companies needing to raise smaller sums of money than is usual on AIM. However, there is no legal reason why a British registered company should not have its securities traded on a public market in another country. A number of large British companies have primary listings in London and secondary listings elsewhere, usually in continental Europe or the US, and some non-British companies equally have secondary listings in London. More interestingly, a small number of British companies have their primary listings outside the UK and a somewhat larger number of foreign companies have their primary listings in London. Indeed, there has been a certain international competition in recent years among the exchanges to secure such listings, notably from Chinese and Russian companies. Bonds issued by UK-incorporated companies are often listed in Luxembourg.

25–7

Regulated markets and multi-lateral trading facilities

Carrying on the business of operating a stock market is, not surprisingly, one of the activities regulated under the FSMA. Those who operate the exchange must either be persons authorised to carry on financial business in the UK or the investment exchange must be a "recognised" investment exchange ("RIE").[18] Applications for recognition can be made under Pt XVIII of FSMA to the FCA,

25–8

---

[15] LR 1.5. This choice, which had previously been available only to foreign-incorporated issuers, was made available to domestic issuers in 2010. The choice may be changed subsequently, but subject to supermajority shareholder approval in the case of transfer from premium to standard listing (LR 5.4A). Bonds will always be listed on the standard basis.

[16] AIM replaced the previous and more usefully entitled Unlisted Securities Market (USM) in 1995.

[17] There are also a number of other markets or segments of markets run by the LSE which, however, need not concern us here.

[18] Otherwise they will fall foul of the "general prohibition" in s.19 of FSMA 2000 on carrying on regulated financial activities in the UK.

which is the primary regulator in the area covered by this chapter. The requirements[19] which have to be met relate to both the initial setting up of the exchange and its continued operation. Thus, any public market in securities operating in the UK will be subject to the regulation of the FCA.

The purpose of the above regulation of investment exchanges is to ensure the security of their operation. Thus, the recognition requirements deal with matters such as the suitability of the persons running the exchange and the level of financial resources available to them. As with the minimum requirements for listing, the underlying rules for exchange regulation are set out in EU law, in this case the Directive on Markets in Financial Instruments ("MIFID").[20] This Directive distinguishes a regulatory point of view between "regulated" markets and "multilateral trading facilities" ("MTF"). The Community requirements for a regulated market are now set out in Title III of MIFID. Article 44 states that "Member States shall reserve authorisation as a regulated market to those systems which comply with the provisions of this Title". The Title then sets out a number of requirements for acquiring the status of a regulated market, many of which cover the same ground as is to be found in the domestic rules governing the award of recognised investment exchange status.

It might therefore be thought that all RIEs would seek to have all the markets they run characterised as regulated markets.[21] However, there is no obligation on an RIE to apply for regulated status for all or any of its markets and not having regulated status does not prevent that market from continuing to operate in the UK, provided it continues to meet the domestic law requirements. In the language of MIFID a market which is not a regulated market is a MTF.[22] On the other hand, a market which does not obtain regulated status under MIFID loses the benefits and the burdens placed by EU law on regulated markets, those benefits and burdens being found across the EU law governing securities. For RIEs, therefore, the question is whether the benefits EU law attaches to a regulated market outweigh the burdens. The LSE decided not to seek regulated status for AIM,[23] but the Main Market of the LSE is a regulated market. For bonds, GEFIM is a regulated market and PSM is not.[24]

Listing and regulated markets

25–9 Although official listing is a concept which refers to the quality of the securities and the issuer, whilst regulated markets are markets of a particular quality, there is a close link between them, at least in the case of shares. The Listing Rules

---

[19] Set out in more detail in the Financial Services and Markets Act 2000 (Recognition Requirements for Investment Exchanges and Clearing Houses) Regulations 2001 (SI 2001/995).

[20] 2014/65/EU ([2014] O.J. L173/349). This is "MIFID II" replacing "MIFID I" (Directive 2004/39/EC) as from January 2017.

[21] Especially as the requirements for recognition were upgraded in response to Title III of MIFID: see subs.(4A) to (4E) inserted into FSMA 2000 s.286 by SI 2006/2975.

[22] See MIFID, Title II. Where trading takes place outside both a regulated market and a MTF, it is generally called "over the counter" trading (OTC).

[23] This decision was taken in 2004 under the then applicable Directive concerning regulated markets, i.e. Directive 93/22/EEC, the investment services Directive, which was repealed by MIFID.

[24] MIFID also identifies "organised trading facilities" ("OTF"), but since these are not venues for share trading, we shall ignore them: MIFID art.4(23).

provide that "equity shares must be admitted to trading on a regulated market for listed securities operated by a RIE".[25] Thus, the listing process is not complete unless the shares have been admitted to trading on a regulated market. On the other side, it is only companies whose shares are in the official list which will be admitted by the LSE to its Main Market.[26] Thus, listed shares must be traded on a regulated market and the Main Market of the LSE will admit only listed securities. The FCA (or the competent authority in some other EEA State in the case of companies incorporated there) controls inclusion in the official list and the LSE controls admission of the securities to trading on the Main Market.[27] The company has to satisfy both sets of requirements in order to give its securities the status of being on the official list and its shareholders the facility to trade in those securities.

By contrast, listed debt securities must be admitted to trading on a market for listed securities operated by a RIE, but that market need not be a regulated market. On the LSE, GEFIM is a regulated market and the PSM is exchange-regulated, but nevertheless trades listed debt securities.

The regulatory structure

The document containing the information which must be put before potential investors in a public offering is termed a prospectus. Domestic statutory law regulating prospectuses has a long history: the Directors' Liability Act 1890,[28] imposing liability for negligent misstatements in prospectuses, was an advanced piece of legislation for its time and significantly influenced the US Securities Act 1933. However, over the past 30 years EU law has gradually occupied the legislative space in relation to public offers, admission of securities to public markets and listing, as part of a broader strategy to create a single European financial market[29]—though remedies for breaches of the rules still remain substantially in the hands of the Member States. The result of EU occupation of the field, together with the additional rules adopted at national level, has been a multi-layered regulatory structure, where six distinct layers can be identified: primary community law; secondary community law; primary domestic legislation; secondary domestic legislation; FCA rules; and rules generated by stock exchanges.

25–10

---

[25] LR 2.2.3.

[26] LSE, *Admission and Disclosure Standards*, June 2013, para.1.1 note.

[27] Just to complicate things further, the fact that a listed security has been admitted to a regulated market does not mean that trading has to take place on that market. It was reported that less than 50 per cent of the trading in FTSE 100 companies (all listed) had taken place in certain weeks in the middle of 2011 on the Main Market of the LSE, the main competitors being the MTFs (above, para.25–8) or private markets organised by large investment banks ("dark pools") (*Financial Times*, 19 September 2011, p.20 (UK edn)).

[28] The modern version of that law can be found in FSMA 2000 s.90.

[29] For an excellent general analysis of this process see E. Ferran, *Building an EU Securities Market* (Cambridge: CUP, 2004).

The modern EU legislative instruments aimed at regulating this area were proposed in the Financial Services Action Plan ("FSAP"),[30] adopted in 1999 for the period up to 2005 and substantially achieved in that period. We shall look at some of the FSAP instruments in this and the following chapter. As far as disclosure of information in prospectuses is concerned the central piece of EU law is currently Directive 2003/71/EC on prospectuses (the "Prospectus Directive" or "PD") as amended in 2010,[31] whilst admission to listing is regulated by CARD.[32]

As far as the PD is concerned, it has two features which need to be noted. First, it is what is inelegantly referred to as a "maximum harmonisation" Directive. This means that it sets out not only standards below which the Member States may not fall but also standards above which they may not rise. Since it is also a very detailed Directive, especially when taken with the subordinate EU legislation—see below—the Member States have rather little discretion over its implementation in domestic law and it functions more like a Regulation than a Directive.[33] The reason for this approach was the EU's desire to produce a prospectus which, without changes other than translation, could be used simultaneously in more than one Member State in a cross-border offer. We shall look at this "EU passport" concept in more detail below.[34]

The second notable feature of the PD results from an adaptation of the EU legislative process introduced for FSAP instruments and known as the "Lamfalussy process", after the name of the chairman of the committee which put forward this proposal. An important part of this process is that the European Commission obtained the power to make what we would call subordinate legislation (through *Commission* Directives or Regulations), without going through the full EU legislative process but after consulting the Member States,[35] where the parent Directive provides for such "second-tier" legislation. In fact, in the case of disclosure of information in public offers the detailed information required is to be found in Commission Regulation (EC) No.809/2004,[36] as amended, a document of some 100 pages and being, as a Regulation, directly applicable[37] in the Member States and so not requiring transposition by them. The purpose of this shift of legislative power to the Commission was said to be to enable the details of the FSAP legislation to be adapted more quickly to changing

---

[30] COM(1999) 232, 11 May 1999. It was succeeded by a less ambitious White Paper on Financial Services Policy 2005–2010, which is also less relevant to the concerns of this book than its predecessor.

[31] Directive 2003/71/EC on prospectuses [2003] O.J. L345/64, as amended by Directive 2010/73/EU ([2010] O.J. L327/1).

[32] Above, fn.12. This Directive consolidated Directives going back to 1979, when the EU first became interested in regulating the admission of securities to public markets. Substantial parts of the 2001 Directive have now been themselves replaced by Directives adopted under the FSAP.

[33] The PD is thus some distance from the description of a Directive in art.288 TFEU as an instrument "which is binding as to the result to be achieved but shall leave to the national authorities the choice of form and methods".

[34] See para.25–44.

[35] This consultation takes place through the European Securities and Markets Authority ("ESMA"). In fact, directives today make a distinction between "delegated acts", where ESMA only gives advice to the Commission, and "technical standards", where ESMA draws up draft rules.

[36] Commission Regulation (EC) No.809/2004 [2004] O.J. L215/3.

[37] Article 288 TFEU.

market practices than would be the case if the full EU legislative process had to be used. Law-making by the Commission thus constitutes the second layer of rules in this area, after the adoption of the parent legal instrument by the EU legislature.

However, the PD, the parent EU instrument in our area, and Commission instruments taking the form of a Directive do require transposition into national law. This gives rise to the third level of law-making, i.e. by the British legislature (which itself may take the form of primary or secondary legislation). The most obvious expression of the domestic law-making process is FSMA 2000, as subsequently amended, especially its Pt VI. FSMA 2000 contains three broad types of rules: those simply transposing the EU law, those both transposing and adding to the EU requirements (where EU law permits this) and those dealing with matters not subject to EU regulation. However, from the outset of domestic financial services regulation, the policy of embodying all the relevant rules in a statute or even in statutory instruments was rejected in favour of conferring broad rule-making and enforcement powers on a regulator, now the FCA. This is a statutory body[38] but funded by market participants and designed to be more attuned to the needs of the markets than would be a governmental department. It has a very wide remit in the financial services area but for the purposes of this chapter we concentrate on its role in public offerings. Rules made by the FCA or its predecessor thus constitute the fifth level of rule-making. For the purposes of this chapter particularly important are its Prospectus Rules ("PR"), though on some matters its Listing Rules ("LR") are relevant as well.

The sixth layer of regulation is that done by the exchanges themselves, as a matter of private contract with the issuers which seek to have their securities traded on a securities market.

It is likely that the balance within the above structure will change in the future. In November 2015 the European Commission proposed to replace the PD with a Prospectus Regulation, as well as making some changes to the substantive rules, which we note as appropriate below.[39] This proposal was part of a more general scheme to create a "capital markets union" within the EU. To the extent that this proposal is successful, EU rules would become relatively more important and domestic rules relatively less so, since a Regulation does not need transposition into domestic law.

Types of public offer

The EU and domestic rules discussed in this chapter are concerned with public offers of transferable securities. The whole of this body of regulation can be avoided by offering non-transferable securities to the public.[40] However, the

25–11

---

[38] Established under FSMA 2000, as amended by the Financial Services Act 2012 Pt IA.

[39] COM(2015) 583 final.

[40] As Caxton*fx* did in September 2011 when it offered to the public non-transferable debt securities with a four-year maturity, but paying a high interest rate. The main regulation in such a case lies in FSMA s.21, which requires the offer document to be approved by a person authorised by the FCA. The authorised person will need to be concerned with the adequacy of the disclosures contained in the invitation document.

illiquidity embodied in non-transferable securities is likely to make them unattractive to investors. Assuming an issue of transferable securities, the company's choices appear to be as follows. On an initial public offering of shares, a company's choice of method will be severely restricted. If the issue is large it will have to proceed by way of an offer for sale or subscription coupled with admission to listing (or admission to AIM), whilst smaller amounts may be raised via a placing plus an introduction to a public market. (A placing is an offer to a selected group of investors and so is not a general offer.) In the case of bonds, even large amounts are normally raised by means of a placing, because bonds are traditionally bought by institutional, not retail, investors. In the case of shares, a third way of proceeding may be available. Where the company's shares have somehow become sufficiently widely held (which is unlikely without a public offer but conceivable) it may be possible to raise the new money needed by a rights or open offer to its existing shareholders, but this course of action is normally available only on subsequent offers, not on an IPO. We shall look briefly at each type of offer.

Offers for sale or subscription

25–12 A full-blown public offer will prove to be an expensive and time-consuming operation. The company's finance director (and probably other executives) and representatives of the advising investment bank and their respective solicitors will for weeks or months devote most of their time to working as a planning team. At a later stage the services of a specialist share registrar will generally be needed to handle applications and the preparation and dispatch of allotment letters. The offer will have to be made through a lengthy prospectus which will have to be published. To ensure that the issue is fully subscribed, arrangements will have to be made for it to be underwritten. Today this is normally achieved by the sponsoring investment bank agreeing to subscribe for the whole issue and for it, rather than the company, to make the offer. Thus, large public offers are normally in the form of offers for sale not offers for subscription, the investment bank having already subscribed for all the shares on offer.[41] In major offerings, such as the privatisation issues,[42] a syndicate of investment banks may be employed. The banks will endeavour to persuade other financial institutions to sub-underwrite. Ultimately the cost of all this, including the commissions payable to underwriters and sub-underwriters,[43] will have to be borne by the company.

The most ticklish decision that will have to be made is the price at which the securities should be issued and, for obvious reasons, this is normally left to the

---

[41] In an offer for subscription the underwriters simply take up the shares for which the public have not subscribed. Even if there is no underwriting, large offers are often distributed to the public by financial intermediaries, perhaps over a period of weeks. Even in an offer for sale the prospectus is normally drawn up by the issuer and then relied on by the intermediaries, but some difficult issues have to be resolved to bring this result about. See ESMA, Consultation Paper 2011/444, Pt 3 and art. 5 of the Commission's 2015 reform proposals (above, fn.39).

[42] Most of the UK privatisation offers were not primary distributions (i.e. offers of securities by the company) but secondary distributions (i.e. offers by a large or sole shareholder of its shares to the public). This chapter is concerned mainly with the raising of capital by a public offer by the company.

[43] On which see para.11–14, above.

last possible moment. If it proves to have been set too low, so that the issue is heavily over-subscribed, the company will be unhappy, while, if it is set too high so that much of the issue is left with the underwriters, it is they who will be unhappy since their commission rates will have assumed that they will end up with a handsome profit and not be left with securities that, initially, they cannot sell except at a loss. Nor, probably, will the company be best pleased since it is generally believed that an under-subscribed issue will reduce the company's prospects of raising further capital in the future. The nightmare of all concerned is that there will be an unforeseen stock market collapse between the date of publication of the prospectus and the opening of the subscription list.[44] The sweet dream is that the issue will be modestly over-subscribed and that trading will open at a small premium.

If the issue is over-subscribed it will obviously be impossible for all applications to be accepted[45] in full. The issuer decides how to deal with this situation and the prospectus will need to say how it intends to do so. Normally this will be by accepting in full offers for small numbers of shares and scaling down large applications, balloting sometimes being resorted to. The company will probably wish to achieve a balance between private and institutional investors. To succeed in that aim multiple applications by the same person will probably be expressly prohibited.[46] An abuse which also needs to be guarded against is that "stags" will apply but seek to withdraw and stop their cheques if it seems likely that dealings will not open at a worthwhile premium to the offer price. However, offer documents will require applications to be accompanied by cheques for the full amount of the securities applied for, the cheques being cleared immediately on receipt and any refund sent later. This means that an applicant may not only fail to get all or any of the shares he hoped for but may, for a period, lose the interest that he was earning on his money.[47]

The offer price is normally stated as a fixed and pre-determined amount per share. It can however, be determined under a formula stated in the offer, though this is uncommon except in offers addressed to professional investors. Alternatively applicants can be invited to tender on the basis that the shares will be allocated to the highest bidders. This, however, is rarely used in relation to issues of company securities.

Placings

Obviously, the expense of an offer for sale plus introduction to listing is prohibitive unless a very large sum of money is to be raised. For lesser amounts the placing may be more attractive (and may be used for large amounts in the

25–13

---

[44] Which came true in the case of one of the privatisation issues in the "Crash of 1987". Yet thousands of small investors continued to put in applications notwithstanding that the media were warning them that trading would open at a massive discount.

[45] The so-called "offer" by the issuer is normally not an offer (as understood in the law of contract) which on acceptance becomes binding on the offeror. It may be in the case of a rights issue (see below) but on an offer for sale or subscription it is an invitation to investors to make an offer which the company may or may not accept.

[46] Breaches are difficult but not impossible to detect where applications are made in different names.

[47] This causes bona fide applicants who are unsuccessful understandable resentment.

case of bonds). Under this method the investment bank or other adviser to the issuer obtains firm commitments, mainly from its institutional investor clients (instead of advertising an offer to the general public), coupling this with an introduction to trading. The absence of the need for newspaper advertisements, "road-shows" and the like makes this a much less expensive procedure. On the other hand, it prevents the general public from acquiring shares at the issue price. Another way of proceeding is the "intermediaries offer", whereby financial intermediaries take up the offer for the purpose of allocating the securities to their own clients. This way of proceeding should be only marginally more expensive than a straightforward placing, but has the advantage that it is more likely to result in a wide spread of shareholders and a more active and competitive subsequent market. Although these are not "public" offers as far as the financial community is concerned, unless carefully controlled they may end up being public offers under the prospectus rules (as we see below).

Rights offers

25–14 Once a company has made an initial public offering of shares it will have additional methods whereby it can raise further capital and, even if it proceeds by an offer for sale, this will be less expensive if the securities issued are of the same class as those already admitted to listing or to the AIM. More often, however, it will make what is called a "rights issue" and, if it is an offering of equity shares for cash, it will generally have to do this, or make an open offer, unless the company in general meeting otherwise agrees. This is because of the pre-emptive provisions discussed in the previous chapter.[48] In one sense a rights issue is considerably less expensive than an offer for sale: circulating the shareholders is cheap in comparison with publishing a lengthy prospectus in national newspapers and mounting a sales pitch to attract the public. But in another sense it may be dearer: if the issue price is deeply discounted the company will have to issue far more shares (on which it will be expected to pay dividends) in order to raise the same amount of money as on an offer. In any event, as we shall see, a rights issue will normally be a public offer for the purposes of the prospectus rules.

Other methods of issue, which can be used in appropriate circumstances, include exchanges or conversions of one class of securities into another, issues resulting from the exercise of options or warrants, and issues under employee share-ownership schemes—though these will not necessarily raise new money for the company. Nor, of course, will capitalisation issues, dealt with in Ch.13, above. We do not discuss them further in this chapter.

---

[48] Discussed at paras 24–6 et seq., above.

ADMISSION TO LISTING AND TO TRADING ON A PUBLIC MARKET

Eligibility criteria for the official list

We have already noted that admission to trading on a public market is a normally **25–15** a concomitant feature of a public offer. Although it might seem logical to look at the rules on disclosure of information in relation to offers before looking at the rules governing admission to trading, there are good reasons for the opposite approach. First, the admission rules are generally less elaborate. Secondly, the admission rules contain merit requirements, i.e. rules permitting securities resulting from only certain types of public offer to be publicly traded. The admission requirements therefore feed back into decisions about the types of public offers than can considered and the public markets available for the resulting securities to be traded.

The principal source of admissibility requirements are the Listing Rules made by the FCA, partly transposing into domestic law the EU rules from CARD on admission to the official list and partly adding to those minimum requirements. Chapter II of Title III of CARD lays down certain conditions for the admissibility of shares to the official list, and Ch.III lays down a lesser set of requirements for debt securities.[49] Since securities admitted to the official list must also be admitted to trading on a regulated market,[50] the rules on admission to the official list in effect control admission to trading as well. However, the operators of any market may lay down conditions for the admission of securities to trading on that market, though competition considerations constrain operators from going very far in controlling admissions. We look first at the rules on admission to the official list.

The admissibility conditions may be divided into those related to the issuer and those related to the securities on offer. In relation to both equity and debt securities one of two major policy concerns of CARD and the LR is to ensure that there should be a liquid market in the securities in question after listing, so that subsequent trading in the securities is not unacceptably volatile.[51] The following requirements promote this goal.

(i)   The expected market value of the securities to be admitted must be at least £700,000 for shares and £200,000 for debt securities.[52]

(ii)   All the securities of the class in question must be admitted to listing.[53]

---

[49] The merit requirements are less for debt securities presumably because the security itself will normally give the investor greater contractual protections than in the case of an equity security.
[50] See para.25–9.
[51] Where there is only a thin market in a security, the prices at which those securities can be traded may be volatile.
[52] CARD arts 43 and 58; LR 2.2.7. This rule does not apply if the shares on offer are of a class already listed; and, in any event, the FCA may grant a derogation if satisfied that nevertheless there will be "an adequate market for the securities concerned".
[53] CARD arts 49, 56, 62; LR 2.2.9. The LR do not avail themselves of the exemption in art.49(2) for the non-admission to listing for "blocks serving to maintain control of the company".

(iii)   The securities must be freely transferable.[54] Without this requirement the development of a market in the securities would clearly be inhibited.

(iv)   In the case of shares a "sufficient number" of the class of shares in question must be distributed to the public (as opposed to being held in non-trading blocks by insiders), which is translated as a rule of thumb into 25 per cent of the shares for which admission is sought.[55]

The other main driver of the CARD rules is that the issuer should have a certain quality. These requirements apply to the issue of shares only.

(v)   The company must produce audited accounts for a period of three years, ending not earlier than six months before the application for admission.[56]

(vi)   Going beyond CARD, for premium listing the company must show that "at least 75% of the applicant's business is supported by a historic revenue earning record" for the three years in question and that it will be carrying on an independent business as its main activity.[57] The aim of these requirements is not that the applicant show that it has been profitable over the three years (though it may not find takers for its shares if it has not been) but that its current business has a three-year track record and is not contingent on some other person's consent.[58] As a result of opportunistic behaviour on the part of controllers of certain listed companies, the LR were modified in 2015 so as to require controlling shareholders (30 per cent of more of the voting rights) to enter into a written and legally binding agreement with the company, designed to safeguard its independence, especially in relation to related-party transactions and the election of independent directors, in the absence of which the LR's standard related-party transactions are applied to the issuer with particular rigour.[59]

(vii)   Again going beyond CARD and for premium listing, the applicant must show, subject to exceptions, that it will have sufficient working capital to meet its requirements for the 12 months after listing.[60] This is some protection against the company suffering a "cash crunch" in the short-term after listing. Of course, where the admission is coupled with a public offer, the working capital is likely to be raised in that offer. The purpose of this requirement is that the applicant shows it has made a realistic forecast of what needs in the near term.

---

[54] CARD arts 46, 54, 60; LR 2.2.4. The FCA may make arrangements to accommodate the transfer of partly paid shares. In exceptional cases where it is convinced the market in the shares will not be disturbed the FCA may list shares whose transfer needs the consent of the issuer (rare in listed companies but found in some denationalised companies in order to subject control transfers to scrutiny).

[55] CARD art.48; LR 6.1.19, 14.2.2. The rule applies on an EU-wide basis.

[56] CARD art.44; Commission Regulation (EC) No.809/2004 Annex 1, 20.1; LR 6.1.3 (premium listing only). For premium listing the accounts must normally have an unqualified audit certificate (not a requirement of CARD).

[57] LR 6.1.3B, 6.1.4.

[58] The FCA may dispense with the requirements of LR 6.1.3 and 6.1.4 where it thinks this desirable in the interests of investors and that investors have the necessary information to arrive at an informed judgment: CARD art.44 and LR 6.1.13.

[59] LR 6.1.2A, 6.1.4B & D, 11.1.1A & C. The related party transactions are discussed in para.16–77.

[60] LR 6.1.16. This is a more effective protection for investors than the minimum capital rule for public companies. See para.11–9.

In addition to these specific requirements in relation to the company and its securities, there is a general power in art.11 of CARD for Member States to reject an application for listing "if, in their opinion, the issuer's situation is such that admission would be detrimental to investors' interests". This is transposed into domestic law by FSMA 2000 s.75(5), which gives the power of rejection to the FCA as the competent authority. It is unclear in what circumstances this power might be used, though no doubt it is a useful back-stop to deal with the unexpected.

Exchange admission standards

Since admission to listing requires admission to a market for listed securities, the   **25–16**
admission standards of the exchange are also relevant to the listing process. Taking the admission standards of the LSE for its Main Market as an example, these largely track the eligibility requirements of the LR but add to them in some ways. Thus, the shares sought to be traded "must be capable of being traded in a fair, orderly and efficient manner" and the Exchange may refuse an application for listing if the applicant's situation is such that admission "may be detrimental to the orderly operation of the Exchange's markets or to the integrity of such markets".[61]

In the case of unlisted securities, the eligibility rules of the exchange to which admission is sought are naturally central, since the LR have no application. For the AIM, run by the LSE, the exchange in fact lays down no general eligibility requirements for admission other than the appointment of a "nominated adviser".[62] This is because the responsibility for assessing the suitability of the applicant for AIM is placed by the Exchange on the adviser (usually referred to as the "nomad").[63] However, eligibility requirements are laid down in certain specific cases. For example, r.7 of the *AIM Rules for Companies* stipulates:

> "Where an applicant's or quoted applicant's main activity is a business which has not been independent and earning revenue for at least two years, it must ensure that all related parties and applicable employees as at the date of admission agree not to dispose of any interest in its securities for one year from the admission of its securities."

This rule obviously reflects in a muted way the independence requirements of the LR. The Exchange has also reserved to itself the power to subject any applicant for admission to a special condition.[64]

---

[61] LSE, *Admission and Disclosure Standards*, April 2013, 1.4 and 1.5.
[62] LSE, *AIM Rules for Companies*, May 2014, r.1.
[63] LSE, *AIM Rules for Nominated Advisers*, 2014, especially Sch.3.
[64] Above, fn.61, r.9.

THE PROSPECTUS

25–17   The core mechanism by which the law achieves its disclosure objectives is the prospectus. The relevant EU rules are in the PD, a maximum harmonisation Directive,[65] and in subordinate EU law made by the Commission. They are transposed, as necessary, into domestic law by amendments to FSMA, statutory instruments and through rules made by the FCA—the Prospectus Rules ("PR"). There are two triggers for the requirement to produce a prospectus: a public offer and the admission of shares to trading on a regulated market.[66] Where, as is usual, shares are both offered to the public and at the same time admitted to trading on a regulated market, both triggers will be pulled, but either will do. We have also noted that AIM is not a regulated market and so simple admission to trading on AIM will not trigger the prospectus requirement. However, the PD rules will be triggered if the admission is accompanied by a public offer. To escape the PD the issuer must both avoid admission to trading on a regulated market and make an offer which falls outside the definition of a public offer, as certain types of placing, for example, will.

Even in this case the issuer must normally meet some disclosure requirements. For example, the LSE's own rules for AIM have disclosure obligations built into them. Those rules require an applicant for admission to AIM to produce a publicly available "admission document". This document is a slimmed down version of what is required under the PD: in fact the information required for the admission document is defined by express reference to the annexes of Commission Regulation which contain the detailed requirements for disclosure under EU law.[67]

The same two-trigger mechanism applies in relation to bonds. Thus, if the bonds are admitted to the PSM (an MTF or exchange regulated market), rather than the GEFIM (a regulated market), and there is no public offer, then no prospectus is required. However, there is a twist here. The PSM, although exchange-regulated, is a market for listed securities only, and the process of listing entails disclosure obligations under CARD for the applicant.[68] The disclosure is effected not through a prospectus but through listing particulars.[69] However, the detail of what is required for particulars, laid down in the LR,[70] is in general less demanding than that required for a prospectus. FSMA makes it clear that listing particulars are the more junior instrument, for the FCA has no power to require listing particulars in any situation where a prospectus is required.[71] Consequently, where shares are admitted to the official list as part of a public offer, it is the prospectus rules which count, not those governing listing. The same is true if bonds are to be admitted to the official list as part of a public offer. However, because bonds are often offered in a placing which does not

---

[65] See above, para.25–10.
[66] PD art.3; FSMA s.85(1),(2). The meaning of a regulated market is discussed above at para.25–6.
[67] Above, fn.62, r.3, Sch.2 and Glossary.
[68] This is by way of contrast with AIM, to which non-listed securities are admitted, which explains why the LSE has to stipulate its own disclosure requirements for AIM.
[69] CARD art.20; FSMA s.80(1).
[70] Notably LR4.2.
[71] FSMA s.79(3A).

constitute a public offer and then admitted to trading on the PSM (an exchange-regulated market), the disclosure obligations attached to listing are more important for bonds than shares. In this chapter, however, the core of our analysis will be the prospectus, because our focus is on capital raising through share issues.[72]

The public offer trigger

Producing an acceptable definition of a public offer has long proved a difficult exercise. The predecessor of the current PD[73] did not even attempt the exercise, noting rather disarmingly in its preamble that "so far, it has proved impossible to furnish a common definition of the term 'public offer' and all its constituent parts". It was lauded as one of the achievements of the current PD that it does contain such a definition. That definition is as follows:

25–18

> "'offer of securities to the public' means a communication to persons in any form and by any means, presenting sufficient information on the terms of the offer and the securities to be offered, so as to enable an investor to decide to purchase or subscribe to these securities."

This, it will be observed, is not a great example of the drafter's art, for it is hardly helpful to define the trigger for a disclosure obligation in terms of the information which is in fact disclosed. Thus, as before, one has to proceed by taking an essentially broad and imprecise concept ("communication to persons in any form and by any means") and then seeking to give meaning to it by examining the specific provisions in the Directive which state when something is not a public offer, even though on the general approach it might otherwise be.

Of central importance, therefore, are the reasons for excluding some types of offer from the category of a "public" offer. Producing and verifying the information required for a prospectus is a costly and time-consuming business. There is therefore a strong argument for not requiring a prospectus if its recipients do not need the information it contains. This could be for a number of reasons. Even if the information would be of benefit to the recipients, the costs of providing it may outweigh the benefits of having it provided. This is likely to be true of small offers. The provisions of the PD can be seen to reflect these concerns.

Exemptions from the prospectus requirement on a public offer

The policies underlying the various exemptions from the requirement to produce a prospectus can be roughly categorised as follows.

25–19

---

[72] In any event, the admission of bonds to listing and to trading on a public market is a somewhat artificial exercise, driven by the fact that many institutions are unable to purchase non-listed securities. Much of the trading in bonds is done between institutions over the counter. So, this is an example of listing and admission being driven by a regulatory requirement rather than a need for liquidity.

[73] Directive 89/228/EEC.

First there are exemptions which seek to identify the investors who can look after themselves and so do not need the mandatory prospectus information:

(i) Offers addressed to "qualified investors" only.[74] These are defined so as to include legal entities authorised to operate in the financial markets (for example, fund managers or investment banks); governmental bodies at both national and international level; institutional investors and, large companies.[75] Member States are also given the power to include in the category of qualified investors individuals who satisfy two of the following criteria and who ask to be considered as qualified investors. The criteria are: having carried out at least ten transactions of significant size per quarter over the previous four quarters; having a securities portfolio of at least half a million euros; working or having worked for a year in the financial sector in a position requiring knowledge of securities investment.[76] Member States may also apply the exemption to SMEs which asked to be so considered, the criteria then applying to those taking financial decisions on behalf of the SME. A register of these last two categories of qualified investor has to be kept by the competent authority. The UK has taken up both these options.[77] The British legislation makes an important clarification that included in the category of qualified investor is the offeree who is not qualified but whose agent is, provided the agent has authority to accept the offer without reference to the client.[78] To avoid a rather obvious way around the prospectus requirements, it is provided that, if there is a subsequent resale of the securities by a qualified investor, the question of whether that resale counts as a public offer is to be tested afresh.[79]

(ii) Offers of securities where each investor is to pay at least €100,000 in response to the offer.[80] The idea is that such a large consideration will deter all but investors who can look after themselves.

(iii) Offers of securities in denominations of at least €100,000—another way of expressing the same point.[81]

---

[74] PD art.3(2)(a); FSMA s.86(1)(a). Even though no prospectus is required, information given to some qualified investors must be given to them all: PD art.15(5). Bond issues are often directed only at financial institutions which fall within this category. Offers to the public of debt securities are relatively rare, though not unknown.

[75] This is a default classification; such investors may ask to be treated as non-professional investors. This exemption was originally stated in arts 2(1)(e) and 2(2) of the PD but now that directive operates by reference to the (slightly wider) definition of "professional investors" in the Markets in Financial Instruments Directive (2004/39/EC), Annex II Part 1. This is to be replaced from January 2017 by MIFID II (2014/65/EU) but with only minor changes in relation to the definition of a professional investor.

[76] ibid.

[77] FSMA ss.86(7) and 87R and PR 5.4.

[78] FSMA s.86(2).

[79] PD art.3(2).

[80] PD art.3(2)(c); FSMA s.86(1)(c). The original figure of 50,000 was increased to 100,000 by Directive 2010/73/EU as from July 2012.

[81] PD art.3(2)(d); FSMA s.86(d). But the Commission's 2015 proposals (above, fn.39) seek to remove this exemption on the grounds it has had a distorting effect on the size of issued securities (especially debt securities) which has reduced market liquidity.

A second category of those who, it can be said, do not need the prospectus information, are those who will receive the relevant information through some other mechanism. The PD identifies[82] on this basis the target's shareholders in a share-exchange takeover bid[83] and the shareholders of companies involved in a merger.[84] Controversy has surrounding the question whether rights issues[85] should fall into this category. In principle an offer to existing shareholders is a public offer, but it is argued that the continuing disclosure obligations of listed companies, discussed in the following chapter, make a prospectus unnecessary in this case. Initially, the PD made no concessions to this argument but in 2010 the full prospectus requirement was reduced to a "proportionate level"[86] (fixed in secondary EU legislation). However, there is continued debate about what that proportionate level should be.[87]

The third category where a prospectus is not regarded as useful is where those who receive the offer do so other than as part of a fund-raising exercise by the company. The PD identifies[88] on this basis those receiving new shares in substitution for their existing shares, if there is no increase in the issued share capital; bonus shares and script dividends[89]; and shares issued under employee or directors' share schemes.

The fourth and most contentious case is where the prospectus information is admittedly useful to potential recipients but the cost of providing it is thought to be out of proportion to the benefits flowing from it. The Directive as a whole does not apply where the total amount to be raised in the offer is no more than 5 million over a period of 12 months.[90] Somewhat oddly, there is then a separate exemption from the definition of a public offer for "an offer of securities with a total consideration of less than EUR 100,000" over a period of 12 months.[91] The policy seems to be to leave the Member States free to impose or not their domestic prospectus rules on offers below the 5 million limit, but to prohibit them from so doing in the case of offers below 100,000.[92] A further important example of this policy is the exclusion from the prospectus requirement of offers addressed to fewer than 150 persons (natural or legal) per EEA State, and any qualified investor offerees do not count against this number.[93]

A contentious issue has been how far SME offerings fall within the category of "useful but too expensive" information. Initially, no concession was made to

---

[82] PD art.4(1)(b),(c); FSMA s.85(5)(b); PR 1.2.2.
[83] See below at para.28–61. Where, as is common, the offer is in cash, the issue does not arise, because the target's shareholders are not acquiring any securities.
[84] See below at para.29–7. The provision introduced in 2010 ensuring that only a single prospectus is required for "retail cascades" falls within this category as well: PD art.3(2).
[85] See para.24–6.
[86] PD art.7(2)(g).
[87] For the Commission's latest contribution see above fn.39, p.16.
[88] PD art.4(1)(a),(d),(e); FSMA s.85(5)(b); PR 1.2.2.
[89] See para.11–20.
[90] PD art.1(2)(h); FSMA s.85(5)(a) Sch.11A para.9. In the UK this figure was raised to its present level from 2.5 million in July 2011.
[91] PD art.3(2)(e); FSMA s.86(1)(e),(4).
[92] This interpretation is confirmed in the Commission's 2015 reform proposals (above, fn.39) which propose to increase the relevant amounts to €500,000 and €10 million respectively.
[93] PD art.3(2)(b); FSMA s.86(1)(b). Section 86(3) treats as an offer to a single person as an offer made to the trustees of a trust, the members of a partnership as such and two or more persons jointly.

SMEs but in 2010 the size of the issuer was made a criterion for determining the extent of the required disclosure.[94] This is a difficult issue: provision of what investors regard as inadequate information might reduce their willingness to subscribe for the securities of such issuers, even if the reform cuts down the costs of making public offers, so that SMEs overall could be worse off. The Commission's reform proposals of 2015[95] propose to solve the problem by offering substantial relaxations to SMEs but only where the securities are not to be listed on a regulated market. Those using MTFs are thought to better understand the risks they run.

Probably the most practically significant of these exemptions, to date, are those for offers to qualified investors and to small numbers of investors. An offer made by a company to institutional investors and brokers operating discretionary portfolios for clients, followed by admission to trading on AIM, can escape the statutory prospectus requirements, though not the Exchange's own disclosure rules.

The admission to trading trigger

25–20   The second trigger for the prospectus is a request for admission of securities to a regulated market.[96] Thus, if shares are to be introduced onto the Main Market of the LSE, even though there is no offer to the public by the company, a prospectus will normally be required. However, there are exemptions from the second trigger as well. Consequently, if an issuer can bring itself within both the public offer and the admission to trading exemptions, it may avoid the need for a prospectus even though it appears to have pulled both triggers. Some of the admission exemptions[97] repeat those available in relation to public offers, mainly those noted in categories two and three above. Thus, the takeovers and mergers exceptions to the public offer trigger appear again in relation to the admission trigger. Otherwise, in the case of share-exchange takeover, a prospectus would often have to be produced because the securities offered in the bid are to be admitted to trading on a regulated market.

25–21   On the other hand, the first category of exemptions for public offers (qualified investors) is missing in the case of admission to trading, presumably because, once the securities are admitted, they are in fact freely available to everyone. The fourth category (burdens outweigh benefits) is present in the case of admission but formulated in a rather different way. Again a limitation on the number of offerees will not work effectively once there is trading on a public market. Instead, the exemption applies to the admission of shares representing less than 10 per cent of the number of shares of the same class already admitted to trading on that regulated market (measured over a 12-month period).[98] The policy argument is that, if the class of share is already traded on the market, there will be

---

[94] PD art.7(2)(e), implemented by Commission Delegated Regulation (EU) No.486/2012.
[95] Above, fn.39, p.16.
[96] PD art.3(3); FSMA s.85(2).
[97] PD art.4(2); PR 1.2.3.
[98] PD art.4(2)(a); PR1.2.3(1). The 2015 reform proposals (above, fn.39, p.7) are to raise the percentage to "at least 20%".

a lot of information about them and the issuer in the market[99] and a relatively small offering of additional shares will not mark a dramatic change of direction for the company. Combined with the qualified investor exception for public offers, the 10 per cent rule enables companies to raise relatively small amounts of new capital via a carefully structured placing, even if the shares in question are admitted to trading on a regulated market.[100]

In order to encourage a single financial market in the EU, securities already admitted to trading on one regulated market to be admitted to trading on another without the production of a prospectus.[101] This facility is subject to conditions, notably that securities of the same class shall have been traded on the other market for at least 18 months[102] and that the ongoing obligations for trading on that other market have been complied with.

The form and content of prospectuses

Subject to the exemptions discussed above, a prospectus must be made available before an offer is made to the public or a request is made for admission of securities to trading on a regulated market.[103] The prospectus is a disclosure document and the overriding rule to which it is subject is that it "shall contain all information which is necessary to enable investors to make an informed assessment of the assets and liabilities, financial position, profit and losses, and prospects of the issuer and of any guarantor, and of the rights attaching to [the] securities".[104] However, the PD does not content itself with this important general rule: far from it. This is an area where the Commission is given law-making powers in relation to the format and content of the prospectus and in pursuance of this power has produced a Regulation,[105] containing more than 40 articles (more than the PD itself) and, remarkably, some 19 annexes. The Regulation is directly applicable in Member States (and so does not need transposition).[106] The purpose of the "sweeping up" rule in the Directive is thus to require those drawing up a prospectus, after they have complied with the detailed rules in the Regulation, to ask themselves, as a final check, whether overall it gives the investors all the information they require. In some cases the competent authorities may—or

25–22

---

[99] As we have noted above, this argument has now been extended to justify reducing the level of disclosure on pre-emption issues.

[100] The LSE does not normally require an admission document for a further issue of shares of any size on AIM (above, fn.61 at r.26) and so in the case of an AIM company only the exceptions to the public offer trigger are relevant in the standard case.

[101] PD art.4(2)(h); PR 1.2.3(8).

[102] Reflecting the EU's traditional fear that otherwise there would be a regulatory "race to the bottom" with a companies securing admittance to the laxest market and then immediately moving to the market of choice. Given that the PD is a maximum harmonisation Directive, this may be thought an over-blown worry.

[103] PD art.3; FSMA s.85(1),(2).

[104] PD art.5(1); FSMA s.87A(2). Although this sounds like a strict liability provision, the rules governing civil liability for omissions and misstatements (see below paras 25–33 et seq.) are negligence based (albeit with the burden of proof reversed).

[105] Commission Regulation (EC) No.809/2004, as amended.

[106] In a number of places the PR (made under powers conferred by FSMA s.84) repeat rules from the Commission Regulation but do not seek to transpose it into domestic law.

must—add to the minimum disclosure requirements if this is necessary to meet the standard of "all information necessary".[107]

In a work of this nature the Commission Regulation does not need to be analysed in detail. Despite its formidable size it is not quite as fearsome as it seems. First, it contains rules which to some extent were previously to be found in Directives[108] and so it is not as big a regulatory extension as it seems. Indeed, one of the purposes of giving the Commission law-making powers in this area was to remove a lot of the detail from EU Directive to Commission subordinate law, which could more easily be adjusted to changing needs. Secondly, the annexes contain "building blocks" to be used in the construction of the prospectus, but only some, often a small number, of those building blocks will be relevant to any one prospectus.[109]

Despite these disclosure requirements, there is likely to be one crucial piece of information which it may not be possible to insert into it, namely, the price of the security. For the reasons given above,[110] those involved will want to leave this to the last possible moment, in order to be able to react to late changes in the market. Connected with the price uncertainty, it may not be possible to say how many securities will be on offer. Omission of these matters is permissible provided either the prospectus contains the criteria by which these matters will be determined or anyone who has accepted the offer before the final price and amount of securities on offer have been published is allowed to withdraw their acceptance during the following two working days.[111]

Summary

25–23   Overall, a prospectus is likely to be a forbiddingly long and detailed document, a tendency to which the civil liability rules, discussed below, only contribute. It is doubtful whether many retail investors read it in full or at all before deciding whether to invest. Professional investors and analysts may pore over it, but most retail investors will not find it a user-friendly document, despite the requirement that the information in it "shall be presented in an easily analysable and comprehensible form".[112] It is therefore sensible that a summary is required to be part of the prospectus, conveying "the essential elements of the securities concerned" but with a warning that it should be read only as an introduction to

---

[107] Commission Regulation arts 3 and 4a.

[108] Most recently in Directive 2001/34/EC Annex 1 (now repealed).

[109] Commission Regulation art.3. For example, the Regulation distinguishes between offers of equity and debt securities and has special provisions for asset-backed securities, depository receipts, derivative securities, closed-end collective investment schemes and public authority offerors, some or all of which will be irrelevant in many cases.

[110] At para.25–12.

[111] PD art.8; FSMA s.87Q. In practice, companies will structure matters so that acceptances are received only after the final price has been announced. However, they will probably have given an indicative price range to investors whilst drumming up support for the offer. Somewhat similar reasoning underlies the notion of a "base prospectus" which, however, is confined to the issuance of debt securities on "a continuous and repeated manner": art.5(4).

[112] PD art.5(1); FSMA s.87A(3). This is not to say that the prospectus may not influence retail investors' decisions indirectly, for example, through the comments of financial journalists or financial advisers who, one hopes, have read it.

the prospectus.[113] The significance of the summary was underlined in the 2010 revisions which require the summary to be drawn up in a common form and to contain "key information" (both to be determined by subordinate EU legislation)[114] and impose civil liability for the omission of key information.[115]

Supplementary prospectus

It is also not a rare event that information becomes available after the prospectus has been published which requires the published information to be qualified. Article 16 of the PD requires "every significant new factor, material mistake or inaccuracy" relating to the information contained in the prospectus which "arises or is noted" after its approval and before the closing of the offer to be the subject of a supplementary prospectus, if the new information is capable of affecting the investors' evaluation of the offer. In the case of an offer to the public investors have a right of withdrawal during the two working days after the supplementary prospectus is published. The transposing British legislation puts any person responsible for the prospectus who knows of the change under a duty to notify it to the company or the applicant for admission, if different.[116] It is unclear whether duty to produce a supplement arises if the issuer is unaware of the event and it cannot be said that it should have been.[117]

25–24

Registration statement and securities note

The traditional British prospectus has been a single document containing all the relevant information. Under the Directive it may consist of two documents (the summary is in addition) and incorporate some information by reference. Where there are two documents, the prospectus will consist of a "registration statement" and a "securities note".[118] The registration statement, containing information about the issuer, can be filed with the relevant authority and, if approved, be valid for 12 months. This is sometimes termed "shelf registration". The securities note can then be produced later and contain the information about the securities on offer plus updated information, if any is needed, about the issuer. When the

25–25

---

[113] PD art.5(2); FSMA s.87A(5),(6). The Directive does not require the production of a summary in the case of "heavy weight" debt securities (denominations of €100,000 or above) except in cross-border offerings where Member States may require a summary in their official language if the prospectus is not in that language. The argument, presumably, is that these securities are likely to be bought only by professional investors who can be expected to read the whole prospectus. Although offers of such securities do not count as public offers (see above, para.25–19), a prospectus is required if they are to be admitted to trading on a regulated market.

[114] Nevertheless, the Commission's 2015 proposals (above, fn.39) are based on the proposition that the summary provision have not been a success and a further, and more elaborate attempt, is to be made to standardise them, using an approach which is to be applied across all packaged retail investment and insurance products (the so-called "PRIIPS" products).

[115] PD arts 5(2) and 6(2); FSMA s.90(12). On civil liability generally see below.

[116] FSMA s.87G.

[117] The phrase "is noted" might suggest knowledge is required but "arises" does not. Section 81 creates a similar obligation to produce supplementary listing particulars, but s.81(3) makes it clear that knowledge of the new event is required to trigger the obligation.

[118] PD art.5(3).

securities note and the summary are produced they can be put together with the registration statement to form a valid prospectus (which will in turn be valid for 12 months).[119] The purpose of this facility is to cut down the time needed between the decision to raise capital and the making of the public offer by obtaining approval in advance for part of the required information.[120]

Incorporation of information by reference was not previously permitted in the UK, on the grounds that it makes the information less accessible to the reader of the prospectus. Article 11 of the PD now requires Member States to allow certain information to be incorporated in this way (other than in the summary) and art.28 of the Commission Regulation spells out which information may be incorporated by reference. The list is reasonably long, though most of it ought to be available electronically, for example, the company's audit reports and financial statements and earlier approved prospectuses.

Verifying the prospectuses

25–26   As we shall see below, the law provides ex post remedies for those who suffer loss as a result of omissions or inaccuracies in a prospectus or supplementary prospectus. However, it is obviously more desirable if the law or regulation can provide ex ante mechanisms designed to ensure that the information as provided is complete and accurate before it is published. A number of such mechanisms are to be found in the PD or domestic rules.

Reputational intermediaries

25–27   A first mechanism, long relied on in the UK, not regulated by the PD but evidently not regarded as prohibited by it, is the use of a "sponsor" as a reputational intermediary. The sponsor guides the applicant for admission to trading through the applicable rules and certifies that there has been compliance. Certification of compliance with the requirements by the intermediary may be more reliable than that by the company alone because of the intermediary's greater experience in the field and because the intermediary's business model depends on its certifications being accurate, for otherwise future issuers will not have an incentive to use that intermediary, as opposed to one of its competitors and the intermediary may be removed from the list of sponsors. Use of an intermediary in this way involves in effect a partial delegation by the FCA or the Exchange of its supervisory powers to an adviser to the company, who is of course paid for by the company.

---

[119] PD arts 12 and 9(3); PR 2.2–6.

[120] This two-part arrangement is particularly convenient for "programme" sales, i.e. where similar securities are offered in relatively small batches on a relatively frequent basis. Short- and medium-term debt instruments ("commercial paper" and "notes") are often offered in this way. The Commission's 2015 proposals aim to increase the speed advantages of the registration statement, renaming it the "universal registration document".

A company applying for a premium listing of its equity securities on the Main Market of the LSE must appoint a sponsor[121] whose role is defined in general as being to "(1) provide assurance to the FCA when required that the responsibilities of the listed company or applicant under the listing rules have been met"; (2) to provide the FCA with any requested explanation or confirmation to the same end; and (3) guide the listed company or applicant in "understanding and meeting its responsibilities" under the FCA's rules.[122] The sponsor thus owes duties to both its client (to use reasonable care in guiding it through the application process) and to the FCA when providing assurance to the regulatory body that those requirements have been met. It is the sponsor (normally an investment bank) which submits the application for listing to the FCA and accompanies it with a "sponsor's declaration" that it has fulfilled its duties and provides information to the FCA about the outcome of the offer.[123] In the case of an application for listing of equity securities where the production of a prospectus is required, the sponsor must not submit such an application "unless it has come to a reasonable opinion, after having made due and careful enquiry" that the applicant has satisfied all the requirements of the Listing and Prospectus Rules.[124]

Secondly, certain specific items of information in the prospectus may be subject to third-party verification. We have already noted the requirement on applicants for admission to the official list to produce three years' of accounts which have been audited.[125] However, backward-looking information is less useful to—or at least less likely to impress itself upon—investors than future-regarding statements, which directly address their concerns about how well is the company likely to do in the future. On the other hand, a requirement to state the company's prospects gives the directors a golden opportunity to present the company in a rosy light for the future, without the check which historical data provides on their descriptions of the past. Accordingly, the Commission Regulation is keen to expose to public light and professional scrutiny the assumptions upon which statements about the future are based. This is especially true of profit forecasts, which are likely to be especially influential with unsophisticated investors. The assumptions underlying profit forecasts contained in prospectuses must be stated and a distinction made between assumptions directors can influence and those outside their control. The assumptions must be specific and precise and readily understandable by investors. The company's

---

[121] LR 8.2.1, made under FSMA s.88. Since the sponsor is a purely domestic requirement, the relevant rules are found in the LR rather than the PR. The "nominated adviser" (or "nomad") plays a similar role in relation to the admission document (see above, para.25–17) required for admission to AIM. A sponsor is also required on certain other occasions, for example, when the company issues a "Class 1" circular (see para.14–20), but a listed company is not required to have a sponsor at all times, unlike a company admitted to AIM where a condition for continued admission of the company is that it always has a nomad: LSE, *AIM Rules for Companies* 2014, r.1. The nomad has similar responsibilities to the sponsor at admission stage and must give the Exchange the same assurance: *AIM Rules for Nominated Advisers*, 2014, Sch.2.

[122] LR 8.3.1.

[123] LR 8.4.3. Given the importance of sponsors, provisions have to be made for their independence, qualifications and supervision. See, for example, LR 8.6 and 8.7, but those matters do not need to be considered further in this book.

[124] LR 8.4.2 and 8.4.8. And has procedures in place to facilitate compliance with the Transparency and Disclosure Rules discussed in the following chapter.

[125] Above, para.25–15.

auditors or reporting accountants must confirm that the forecast has been properly compiled on the basis stated in the forecast; that the accounting presentation used in the forecast is compatible with the issuer's general accounting policies; and that the forecast is compatible with the company's historical accounts.[126]

Vetting by the FCA

25–28 Before publication, the prospectus must be vetted by the FCA.[127] Submission of a draft prospectus, and indeed various other documents, to the FCA must occur at least 10 business days prior to the intended publication date.[128] The purpose of the vetting is to put the FCA in a position to assure itself that the information is complete before it is published.[129] Inevitably, given the time and resources available, the FCA can concern itself only to a limited extent with the accuracy of the information put forward by the company, for example, it should spot glaring inaccuracies appearing on the face of the document. Nor can the FCA guarantee even completeness, except to the extent of seeing that something is said on all the matters upon which the Commission Regulation requires information and that, once again, the information is not obviously inadequate. Nevertheless, the obligation to obtain the prior approval of the FCA is, no doubt, a valuable discipline upon the issuer and its professional advisers, especially the sponsor. It should also be noted in this regard that the FCA and its officers are protected from liability in damages for acts and omissions in the discharge of the functions conferred upon them, unless bad faith is shown or there has been a breach of the Human Rights Act 1998 s.6 (unlawful for a public authority to act in a way incompatible with a convention right), so that it will be rare for the FCA to be worth suing if the prospectus turns out to be incomplete or inaccurate.[130] A refusal of approval on the part of the FCA must be accompanied by reasons and the applicant may appeal to the Tribunal (see below) against the decision.[131] The regulator is more likely simply to require that information be corrected or provided and to refuse approval only if that is not forthcoming.[132]

Authorisation to omit material

25–29 A particularly important part of the approval role of the FCA is the power given it by, to authorise omissions from the prospectus of information which would normally be required to be included.[133] Given the range of information which the Commission Regulation requires to be included, it is likely that the applicant will

---

[126] Commission Regulation (EC) No.809/2004, Annex 1, para.13.
[127] PD art.13; FSMA s.87A.
[128] FSMA s.87C: 20 days if the issuer has no securities traded on a regulated market and has never previously made a public offer. This follows from the fact that s.87C determines the periods within which the FCA must make its decision. The submitted information must include the documents which the prospectus incorporates by reference: PR 3.1.1.
[129] PD art.13(4).
[130] PD art.13(6); FSMA Sch.1ZA para.25.
[131] FSMA s.87D.
[132] FSMA s.87J, following art.21(3)(a)–(c) of the PD.
[133] PD art.8(2); FSMA s.87B.

regard some disclosure to be commercially harmful, because, for example, it will aid competitors. Apart from omission of information "in the public interest" on a certificate from the Treasury,[134] however, the grounds for omission are limited, in the sense that the interests of investors are given predominant weight in the balance over the interests of the issuer and its current shareholders. Omissions may be authorised only if (a) the disclosure would be "seriously detrimental" to the issuer *and* the omission would be unlikely to mislead the public over matters "essential" for an informed assessment of the offer; or (b) if the information is only of minor importance for the offer and unlikely to influence an informed assessment of the offer.[135] One might summarise the policy underlying these rules as being that, where the information is important to investors, they should be provided with it, despite the harm to the company.

Publication of prospectuses and other material

All the effort involved in drawing up a prospectus and having it approved by the FCA is, of course, simply a prelude to its publication when the securities are offered to the public. The issuer is given a choice of methods of publication to the public (except that some form of electronic publication is mandatory): insertion in a widely circulating newspaper; in hard copy available free of charge to the public from the issuer, its financial advisers or the regulated market in question; in electronic form on the website of the issuer, financial adviser or regulated market. Where publication is in electronic form, any member of the public is entitled to a hard copy upon request.[136]

25–30

Despite the requirement that the prospectus include a summary, designed to be more easily accessible to unsophisticated investors, it is likely that an issuer will want to publish documentation in addition to the prospectus, designed to generate interest in the offer. Such "advertisements", as the PD terms them, run the risk of subverting all the careful regulation of the prospectus, if unsophisticated investors read only the advertisements and those documents are carelessly constructed. Consequently, any advertisement[137] must be clearly recognisable as such; must state that a prospectus is or will be available and how it may be obtained; must not contain inaccurate or misleading information; and the information in it must be consistent with the prospectus.[138] However, unlike previously,[139] advertisements do not need to be submitted to the FCA in advance or to be approved by it. On the other hand, s.85 makes it unlawful to offer

---

[134] FSMA s.87B(1)(a),(2).

[135] FSMA s.87B(1)(b),(c). The same two exemptions are found for AIM admissions documents: *AIM Rules for Companies*, r.4. A similar exemption power also exists in relation to listing particulars (s.82).

[136] PD art.14; PR 3.2.4–5. There is further detail in arts 29, 30 and 33 of the Commission Regulation.

[137] Widely defined in art.34 of the Commission Regulation.

[138] PD art.15; PR 3.3.2–3. The FCA's guidance is that the advertisement should state that it is not a prospectus and contain the warning that investors should not subscribe for securities without reading the prospectus.

[139] FSMA s.98, requiring prior approval, was repealed in 2005 when the PD was transposed in the UK. The wide definition of "advertisement" makes such a requirement impractical.

securities to the public before publication of the prospectus required by FSMA, so any "warm-up" material will have to stop short of actually offering the securities to the public.[140]

SANCTIONS

25–31 The rules examined above aim to put at the disposal of investors a considerable amount of information about companies and their securities when the latter are offered to the public. Although there may be adverse market consequences for companies which issue misleading prospectuses (their future fundraising efforts are likely to be greeted with scepticism), nevertheless an effective prospectus regime is likely to require legal sanctions as well. There are three categories of sanctions in principle available for breach of the disclosure regime: criminal, civil and administrative or regulatory. However, the criminal and regulatory sanctions are today effectively in the hands of the FCA and so can be looked at together. We start with an analysis of the civil sanctions.

Compensation under the Act

25–32 Before turning to the statutory provisions which create a compensation remedy for those who have suffered loss as a result of misstatements in or omissions from prospectuses, we should note that the Act provides a civil remedy also for a person who has suffered loss as a result of a breach of the prohibition on offering shares to the public before a prospectus is published. The contravention is treated as a breach of statutory duty.[141] As for misstatements and omissions in the prospectus, art.6 of the PD requires Member States to apply "their laws, regulations and administrative provisions on civil liability" to those responsible for the information contained in the prospectus, but it does not seek to stipulate what that liability regime shall be. Consequently, despite the maximum harmonisation characteristic of the PD, the impact in practice of the rules may vary from Member State to Member State, because of differences in their enforcement regimes. The same point can be made in relation to enforcement by the "competent authority": art.21(3) of the PD stipulates the powers each regulator must have but not the sanctions available to enforce them.

In relation to compensation the UK has long had a strong regime in place, basing liability on negligence and, indeed, reversing the burden of proof on this matter. That regime dates back to the Directors' Liability Act 1890, passed in reaction to the decision of the House of Lords in *Derry v Peek*[142] which, by insisting upon at least recklessness, exposed the inadequacy of the common law

---

[140] FSMA s.102B. This is not necessarily straightforward, since the Commission does not accept that merely refraining from inviting offers removes the advertisement from the category of prospectus. The 2015 reform proposals (above fn.39) give the Commission power to issue delegated legislation in this area.

[141] FSMA s.85(4). There is no equivalent in relation to listing particulars.

[142] *Derry v Peek* (1889) 14 App. Cas.337 HL. At this time, of course, liability in the tort of negligence for purely economic loss caused by misstatements was not accepted either (and that remained in effect

tort of deceit as a remedy for investors who suffered loss as a result of misleading prospectuses. The modern version of liability under the 1890 Act is now located in s.90 of FSMA.

(a)   Liability to compensate

Subject to the exemptions in (b), below, those responsible for the prospectus (or supplementary prospectus)[143] are liable under s.90 to pay compensation to any person who has acquired any of the securities to which it relates and suffered loss as a result of any untrue or misleading statement in it or of the omission of any matter required to be included under the Act.[144] This is a considerable improvement on the former provisions, contained most recently in the Companies Act 1985, which applied only in favour of those who subscribed for shares and therefore excluded from protection those who bought on the market when dealings commenced. Now anyone who has acquired[145] the securities whether for cash or otherwise and whether directly from the company or by purchase on the market and who can show that he or she suffered loss as a result of the misstatement or omission will have a prima facie case for compensation.[146]

25–33

This may seem at first sight an unreasonable extension of liability from the company's point of view, but in fact the prospectus is normally intended to influence not only applications to the company for shares but also the initial dealings in them in the market (the "after market"), since the company has an interest in the securities not trading at below the offer price after issue.[147] In addition, whereas the former version applied only to misleading "statements", the new provisions specifically include omissions. Furthermore, the provisions do not require the claimant to show that he or she relied on the misstatement in order to establish a cause of action: it is enough that the error affected the market price, even if the claimant never read the prospectus. This is sometimes referred to as the "fraud on the market" theory of liability.[148] Obviously, however, a causal connection between the misstatement or omission and the loss will have to be proven. So, for example, market purchasers who buy after such a lapse of time that the prospectus would no longer have a significant influence on the price of the securities will not be able to satisfy this causal test. Finally, the statute does

---

the case until the House of Lords' decision in *Hedley Byrne & Co Ltd v Heller & Partners Ltd* [1964] A.C. 465), so that the tort of negligence could not be used to circumvent the restrictions on liability under the tort of deceit.

[143] The rules discussed in this section also apply to misstatements and omissions in listing particulars. Indeed, the section is drafted in terms of listing particulars and only s.90(11) makes it clear that it covers prospectuses.

[144] FSMA s.90(1). Where the rules require information regarding a particular matter or a statement that there is no such matter, an omission to provide either is to be treated as a statement that there is no such matter: s.90(3).

[145] "Acquire" includes contracting to acquire the securities or an interest in them: s.90(7).

[146] To be assessed presumably on the tort measure, i.e. to restore the claimant to his or her former position: *Clark v Urquart* [1930] A.C. 28 HL, i.e. normally the difference between the price paid and the value of the securities received.

[147] For the difficulties the common law has had with this point, see below, para.25–38.

[148] This is the securities litigation term deployed in the US. It is not really apt in this context: "negligence on the market" would be more accurate if less resonant.

not require the maker of the statement to have "assumed responsibility" towards the claimant, a requirement that limits the operation of the common law of negligent misstatement.[149]

On the other hand, as far as public offers are concerned, the statutory provisions under discussion apply only to misstatements in prospectuses. This will now include the summary, which is part of the prospectus, but here liability is restricted to situations where the summary is misleading when read together with the rest of the prospectus or where liability is based on the omission of key information.[150] However, the section does not apply to advertisements issued in connection with a public offer but separately from the prospectus. Nor, it seems, does the section apply to the Admission Document required for an AIM admission (assuming no public offer triggering the requirement for a prospectus, even for admission to AIM). In such cases compensation might be available at common law or under the Misrepresentation Act but, as the origins of the current legislation suggest, investors in that situation will in all likelihood benefit from a lower level of protection than if they could invoke the civil liability provisions of FSMA.[151]

(b) Defences

25–34 Schedule 10 provides persons responsible for the misstatement or omissions with what the headings in the schedule describe as "exemptions", but which are really defences that may be available if a claim for compensation is made. The purpose of Sch.10 is to implement the policy of imposing liability on the basis of negligence but with a reversed burden of proof. The overall effect[152] of these defences is that defendants escape liability under s.90, if, but only if, they can satisfy the court (a) that they reasonably believed that there were no misstatements or omissions and had done all that could reasonably be expected to ensure that there were not any, and that, if any came to their knowledge, they were corrected in time; or (b) that the claimant acquired the securities with knowledge of the falsity of the statement or of the matter omitted. Defence (a) disproves negligence and defence (b) disproves a causal link between the defendant's conduct and the claimant's loss. Where the statement in question is made by an expert and is stated to be included with the expert's consent, the rules are that a non-expert escapes liability on the basis of a reasonable belief that the expert was competent and had consented to the inclusion of the statement. The expert will be subject to the same test for liability as any other responsible person, but what is "reasonable" is likely to be assessed at a higher standard.

---

[149] See above, para.22–44 in relation to auditors, and below, para.25–38.

[150] PD art.6(2); FSMA s.90(12). On key information see para.25–23.

[151] The common law rules are discussed briefly below. It is not entirely unarguable that s.90 applies to an AIM admission document, which is a cut-down version of the PD prospectus. The function of the two types of document is the same. The section does not in terms say that it applies only to prospectuses required by the PD. Nor is it clear that a "prospectus" (not defined for the purposes of s.90) is confined to the documentation accompanying a public offer of shares. Nevertheless, s.90 is probably understood by most people to be limited in the way stated in the text.

[152] This sentence merely summarises the very complex drafting of Sch.10.

(c)   Persons responsible

The sensitive question of who are "persons responsible" and thus liable to pay the compensation is now dealt with by the PR.[153] In the case of an offer of equity shares, they are[154]:

25–35

(a)   the issuer—a further improvement on earlier versions which did not afford a remedy against the company itself;

(b)   directors of the issuer, unless the prospectus was published without the director's knowledge or consent;

(c)   each person who has authorised himself to be named, and is named in the prospectus, as having agreed to become a director, whether immediately or at a future time;

(d)   each person who accepts, and is stated as accepting, responsibility for, or for any part of, the prospectus, but only in relation to the part to which the acceptance relates[155];

(e)   each other person who has authorised the contents of the prospectus or any part of it, but again only in relation to the part authorised; and

(f)   the offeror of the securities or the company seeking admission and its directors where it is not the issuer.[156]

In the case of offers of other types of security,[157] directors of the issuer or offeror are excluded, unless they fall within one of the other categories (stated as accepting responsibility for the prospectus, for example), whilst the guarantor (if there is one, as there might be for offers of debt securities) is made liable for information relating to the guarantee. However, nothing in the rules is to be construed as making a person responsible by reason only of his giving advice in a professional capacity.[158]

A crucial problem facing misled investors is to identify all the "persons responsible" so as to be in a position to decide whether any of them is worth powder-and-shot. The PD requires those responsible to be identified in the prospectus and it must also contain a declaration by them that, to the best of their knowledge, the prospectus is not misleading. Somewhat stealthily, the Commission Regulation requires the declaration to state that it is made after "having taken all reasonable care to ensure that such is the case".[159] In some Member States this by itself might be used to ground liability, but in the UK s.90 of FSMA would seem to be a more secure basis for liability.

---

[153] PR 5.5. In the case of listing particulars the persons responsible are set out in FSMA 2000 (Official Listing of Securities) Regulations 2001 (SI 2001/2956) reg.6.

[154] PR 5.5.3.

[155] For example, the reporting accountant and any other "experts".

[156] This takes account expressly of secondary offers (above, fn.42), but the offeror will not be liable if it is making the offer in association with the issuer and the issuer has taken the lead in drawing up the prospectus.

[157] PR 5.5.4.

[158] PR 5.5.9. This clearly does not exclude the main functions of sponsor required by the Listing Rules.

[159] PD art.6; Commission Regulation, Annex I para.1.

Civil remedies available elsewhere

25–36   The liability created by s.90 is not exclusive. Section 90(6) says that the section "does not affect any liability which any person may incur apart from this section", but s.90(8) limits the disclosure obligations of promoters and other fiduciaries to those required under the statutory regime.[160]

As explained above, the damages remedy available under the Act is superior to that available under the general law. However, there may be cases where the legislation does not apply. The most obvious examples are non-prospectus material issued in connection with public offers or, where there is no public offer, an Admission Document issued in connection with an application for admission to AIM, which Document does require, as we have seen,[161] significant disclosure by applicants, even if less than under the PD. Alternatively, the claimant may want a remedy other than damages, such as rescission. Thus, a brief examination of the law relating to misrepresentation as it applies to issue documents is in order, but only a sketch of the relevant principles will be provided.

(a)   Damages

25–37   The common law provides civil remedies for misrepresentations which have caused loss to those who have relied upon them. A misrepresentation is understood at common law as being a misstatement of fact rather than an expression of opinion or a promise or forecast. There must be a positive misstatement rather than an omission to state a material fact. However, this requirement is heavily qualified by a further rule that an omission which causes a document as a whole to give a misleading impression or falsifies a statement made in it is actionable.[162]

Historically, the common law has provided a damages remedy only for fraudulent misstatements through the tort of deceit. This requires the maker of the statement to know that it is false or at least to be reckless as to its truth. An honest, even if wholly unreasonable, belief in the truth of the statement will not amount to deceit. As we have seen, it was the decision of the House of Lords to this effect in *Derry v Peek*[163] which led to the introduction of the predecessor of the statutory provisions relating to misstatements in prospectuses which we discussed above. In addition, the tort of deceit requires reliance by the recipient on the statement and, further, that the maker of the statement should have intended the recipient to rely on it. These are formidable hurdles to liability.

Since then, however, there have been two significant developments. Section 2(1) of the Misrepresentation Act 1967 introduced a general statutory remedy for negligent misstatement, which also reverses the burden of proof. The 1967 Act was in effect a generalisation of the principle contained in the statutory provisions

---

[160] No person, by reason of being a promoter or otherwise, is to incur any liability for failing to disclose in a prospectus information which would not have had to be disclosed by a person responsible for the prospectus or which a person responsible would have been entitled to omit by virtue of the Act.

[161] Above, para.25–17.

[162] *R. v Kylsant* [1932] 1 K.B. 442 CCA.

[163] *Derry v Peek* (1889) 14 App. Cas. 337.

relating to prospectus liability, and will therefore be of use where the misstatement was not contained in a prospectus but in some other document issued in connection with the offer. However, the generalisation in s.2(1) extends only to misstatements made by a party to the subsequent contract[164] and the section gives a cause of action only to the other party to it, so that it would seem impossible to use it to sue directors or other experts or advisers who are involved in public offers of shares by the company.

The company itself may be sued, certainly in an offer for subscription or a rights issue or an open offer and perhaps even on an offer for sale, since a new contractual relation between a purchaser and the company comes into existence when the purchaser is registered as the holder of the securities. Where the subsection applies, it makes the misrepresentor liable as if fraudulent. This had led the Court of Appeal to conclude that the measure of damages under s.2(1) is a tortious, rather than a contractual, one, but that the rules of remoteness are those applicable to actions in deceit, so that the person misled can recover for all losses flowing from the misstatement.[165]

Because of these limitations on the new statutory cause of action, it can be said that the more significant development in recent times has been the acceptance of liability for negligent misstatement at common law following the decision of the House of Lords in *Hedley Byrne & Co Ltd v Heller & Partners Ltd*.[166] This is a general principle of liability, not confined within the precise words of a statutory formulation, and so capable of being used against directors and advisers as well as the company itself in the case of negligent misstatements in prospectuses and other documents associated with public offers. Nevertheless, the burden of proof is not reversed under the common law rule, so that the FSMA provision will be more attractive where it is available; and in the case of individual defendants it will be necessary to show that they accepted personal responsibility for the statements made.[167]

25–38

There is also uncertainty, which emerged in the nineteenth century fraud cases, about the range of possible claimants, in particular whether there is a firm rule that only subscribers may sue[168] or whether this is only a presumption, perhaps

---

[164] Or his agent, but even then not so as to make the agent liable but only the principal: *The Skopas* [1983] 1 W.L.R. 857—though presumably the agent's state of mind is relevant in establishing the reasonableness of the belief in the truth of what was said. In the case of statements in the prospectus, even by experts, it seems that the company will be prima facie liable for them and that it carries a heavy burden to disassociate itself from them. See *Mair v Rio Grande Rubber Estates Ltd* [1913] A.C. 853 HL; *Re Pacaya Rubber Co* [1914] 1 Ch. 542 CA.

[165] *Royscot Trust v Rogerson* [1991] 2 Q.B. 297 CA. However, in *Smith New Court Securities Ltd v Scrimgeour Vickers (Asset Management) Ltd* [1997] A.C. 254, a case of deceit, where the consequences of adopting the fraud measure were particularly onerous for the defendant, the House of Lords refused to commit themselves to acceptance of the proposition laid down in the *Royscot Trust* case.

[166] *Hedley Byrne & Co Ltd v Heller & Partners Ltd* [1964] A.C. 465.

[167] This last requirement is discussed further in para.28–64.

[168] As suggested by *Peek v Gurney* (1873) L.R. 6 H.L. 377 HL.

not a very strong one, capable of being rebutted on the facts.[169] The issue continues to trouble modern judges. In *Al-Nakib Investments Ltd v Longcroft*[170] it was held that allegedly misleading statements in a prospectus issued in connection with a rights issue could form the basis of a claim by a shareholder who took up his rights in reliance upon the prospectus but not when the (same) shareholder purchased further shares on the market. By contrast, in *Possfund Custodian Trustees Ltd v Diamond*[171] the judge refused to strike out a claim that an additional and intended purpose of a prospectus issued in connection with a placing of securities was to inform and encourage purchasers in the aftermarket, so that such purchaser could sue in respect of misstatements. Drawing a distinction between subscribers and market purchasers in the immediate period after dealings commence is, in commercial terms, highly artificial. Companies have an interest not only in the issue being fully subscribed but also in a healthy aftermarket developing so that subscribers can easily dispose of their shares, if they so wish.[172] The statutory provisions on liability for misstatements recognise the force of this argument.[173] Perhaps the way forward in the common law would be for the courts to take a more inclusive view of the issuer's purposes.

(b) Rescission

25–39   The common law has traditionally permitted rescission (i.e. reversal) of contracts entered into as a result of a misrepresentation, whether that misrepresentation be fraudulent, negligent or wholly innocent (so that no damages remedy is available). This remedy is a potentially useful supplement to the right to claim damages, even when an extensive damages remedy is provided through the special statutory provisions relating to prospectuses. In many cases, all the investor may wish or need to do is to return the securities and recover his or her money. However, there are two significant limitations on its use. First, s.2(2) of the Misrepresentation Act 1967 gives the court a discretion in appropriate cases to substitute damages for the rescission, a provision included largely for the benefit of misrepresentors.[174] This subsection might be invoked, for example,

---

[169] As suggested by *Andrews v Mockford* [1892] 2 Q.B. 372 CA, where the jury were held to be entitled to conclude that the false prospectus was only one of a series of false statements made by the defendants, whose purpose was not simply to induce subscriptions but also to encourage purchases in the market when dealings began.

[170] *Al-Nakib Investments Ltd v Longcroft* [1990] 1 W.L.R. 1390.

[171] *Possfund Custodian Trustees Ltd v Diamond* [1996] 1 W.L.R. 1351. At the time the relevant provisions of the companies legislation conferred a statutory entitlement to compensation only upon subscribers.

[172] "The issue of a prospectus establishes a basis for valuation of the securities and underpins the development of a market in them, irrespective of the precise circumstances of the initial offer": DTI, *Listing Particulars and Public Offer Prospectuses: Consultative Document* (July 1990), para.10.

[173] Above, para.25–33.

[174] However, in *Thomas Witter Ltd v TBP Industries Ltd* [1996] 2 All E.R. 573 there is a dictum of Jacob J to the effect that the court's power to award damages under s.2(2) is not limited to situations where the misrepresentee still has the right to rescind, thus opening up the possibility of damages under the statute for non-negligent misstatements, a development which would benefit misrepresentees. This dictum was not followed in *Government of Zanzibar v British Aerospace (Lancaster House) Ltd* [2000] 1 W.L.R. 2333.

where the court thought that the rescission was motivated by subsequent adverse movements in the stock market as a whole rather than the impact of the misrepresentation as such.

Secondly, and more important, the right to rescind expires in practice much more quickly than the right to damages, which is subject only to a long limitation period. By contrast, the right to rescind is quickly "barred". If, after the truth has been discovered, an investor accepts dividends, attends and votes at meetings or sells or attempts to sell the securities, the contract will be taken to have been affirmed,[175] and even mere delay may defeat the right to rescind. The reason for this strictness is that the company may well have secured loans from third parties who have acted on the basis of the capital apparently raised by the company, which appearance the rescission of the shareholder's contract would undermine. A rescission claim is also defeated by the liquidation of the company (at which point the creditors' rights crystallise), or even perhaps by its becoming insolvent but before winding up commences,[176] so that the shareholder must have issued a writ or actually had his name removed from the register before that event occurs.[177] Finally, inability to make restitutio in integrum will bar rescission, though in the case of shares that principle would seem to be relevant mainly where the shareholder has disposed of the securities before discovering that a misrepresentation has been made.[178]

(c) Breach of contract

Finally, in the general law of contract it not uncommonly occurs that the courts **25–40** treat a misrepresentation as having been incorporated in the subsequent contract concluded between the parties. The advantage of establishing this would be that the misrepresentee would have a claim to damages to be assessed on the contractual basis, rather than on a tortious basis as is the position with claims based on the statutory prospectus provisions, the Misrepresentation Act or, of course, the *Hedley Byrne* principle. In particular, the shareholder might be able to claim for the loss of the expected profit on the shares. However, a difficulty facing such claims against the company is that the processes of allotment of shares and entry in the register entail a complete novation, i.e. the substitution of a new contract with the company upon registration for the old contract based on

---

[175] *Sharpley v Louth and East Coast Railway Co* (1876) 2 Ch. D. 663; *Scholey v Central Railway of Venezuela* (1869) L.R. 9 Eq. 266n; *Crawley's Case* (1869) L.R. 4 Ch. App. 322.

[176] *Tennent v The City of Glasgow Bank* (1879) 4 App. Cas. 615.

[177] *Oakes v Turquand* (1867) L.R. 2 H.L. 325; *Re Scottish Petroleum Co* (1882) 23 Ch. D. 413. Whether this would apply in the case of rescission as against a transferor (rather than the company) is less clear, but the liquidator's consent would be needed for the re-transfer: Insolvency Act 1986 s.88.

[178] Even in this context one should note the dictum of Lord Browne-Wilkinson in *Smith New Court Securities Ltd v Scrimgeour Vickers (Asset Management) Ltd* [1996] 4 All E.R. 769 at 774: "if the current law in fact provides that there is no right to rescind the contract for the sale of quoted shares once the specific shares purchased have been sold, the law will need to be carefully looked at hereafter. Since in such a case other, identical shares can be purchased on the market, the defrauded purchaser can offer substantial *restitutio in integrum* which is normally sufficient". However, this comment was made in the context of a purchase from a shareholder, not a subscription to shares issued by the company.

the prospectus.[179] It has to be said, too, that prospectuses normally stop short of making explicit promises about future value or performance, so that the basis for finding a promise to be enforced may not be available.

Criminal and regulatory sanctions

25–41 Criminal sanctions play a rather limited role in the area of public offers, but it is to be noted that the central obligation in this area—not to make a public offer of securities or to request admission of securities to a regulated market unless an approved prospectus has been made publicly available—is supported not only by civil but also by criminal sanctions.[180] The principal non-civil sanctions, however, are regulatory ones in the hands of the FCA, which also has power to invoke the criminal law just mentioned.[181] The FCA's sanctions vary considerably according to whether or not the breach of the rules is discovered before or after the public offer or introduction has been completed.

Ex ante controls

25–42 The FCA has two veto powers relevant to the public offering process. It must refuse admission to listing where the applicant does not meet the eligibility requirements and may or must do so in certain other cases.[182] The decision must be taken by the Authority normally within six months of the application and failure to do so may be treated by the applicant as a refusal to admit. If the FCA proposes not to accept an application for listing, it must give the applicant a "warning notice", giving the applicant a reasonable period within which to make representations, and if the proposal is confirmed, the matter may be referred to the Upper Tribunal.[183] Secondly, the FCA must not approve a prospectus if it does not contain the required information or other breaches of the applicable rules are detected, thus preventing the public offer or admission to a regulated market from proceeding.[184] These are both potentially significant enforcement powers, though, as suggested above, it is probably easier for the FCA to

---

[179] The possibilities and problems arising out of breach of contract claims against the company are illustrated by *Re Addlestone Linoleum Co* (1887) 37 Ch. D. 191 CA, which, however, must now be read in the light of the abolition of the rule that a shareholder cannot recover damages against the company unless the allotment of shares is also rescinded. See CA 2006 s.655.

[180] FSMA s.85(3): on indictment the maximum penalty is a prison term of not more than two years or a fine or both.

[181] FSMA s.401.

[182] FSMA s.75(4). See para.25–15, above. Other cases include issues of securities by private companies (s.75(3) and FSMA 2000 (Official Listing of Securities) Regulations 2001/2956 reg.3) and securities already listed in another EEA state where the issuer is in breach of those listing rules (s.75(6)).

[183] The warning notice procedure is laid down in s.387 of FSMA 2000 and fleshed out in the following provisions of Pt XXVI of the Act. In 2010 the Upper Tribunal replaced the Financial Services and Markets Tribunal, which had previously discharged this function. Appeal lies on a point of law to the Court of Appeal or Court of Session.

[184] FSMA s.87A.

determine whether the eligibility criteria for listing have been met than to make a comprehensive determination at the vetting stage whether the prospectus contains any misrepresentations or omission.

Admission to listing is a binary decision. If the securities are admitted to listing, but should not have been because, for example, they did not meet the eligibility requirements, it appears that the admission is effective. However, the Authority may discontinue listing "if it is satisfied that there are special circumstances which preclude normal regular dealings in them",[185] but it may need to proceed carefully if the securities subsequently have been offered to the public and admitted to trading, since investors will find themselves holding an illiquid security as a result of the cancellation.[186] By contrast, approval of a prospectus is a step in a process of making a public offer and it may be possible to halt the process, even after the prospectus has been approved, if breaches of the rules are later discovered. Thus, even after approval, the FCA has power to suspend the offer for a period of up to 10 days, if it has reasonable grounds for suspecting that a provision of Pt VI of FSMA (the relevant Part for most of the sections considered in this chapter) or of the PR or any other provision required by the PD has been infringed. If it finds that such a provision has been infringed or even if it concludes that such infringement is likely, it may require the offer to be withdrawn or the market operator to prohibit trading in the securities.[187] The suspension or prohibition decision of the FCA may take effect immediately, without the issuer or other involved person having the opportunity to make representations, for such action may be urgent. However, in these cases, or where the FCA refuses to approve the prospectus, the FCA must issue a notice, stating the reasons for the action and giving the applicant or other person involved the possibility of making representations (which may cause the FCA to vary or revoke its decision).[188] The notice must also notify the person of the right to refer the FCA's decision to the Tribunal.

Where admission to trading is refused under the LSE's own rules,[189] an appeal process is also provided. There is now a fairly elaborate system for appeals against both disciplinary and non-disciplinary decisions of the Exchange. This tracks the FCA arrangements but with an Appeal Committee, established by the

---

[185] FSMA s.77(1). A more common use of this power is where the "free float" has fallen below 25 per cent (above, para.25–15) and is not likely to return to that level in the near future. See further, LR 5.2.2.

[186] The issuer may refer the cancellation to the Upper Tribunal (s.77(5)), but the shareholder has no right of appeal, nor even to be consulted by the Authority before the decision is taken, even though his or her financial position is crucially affected. In *R. v International Stock Exchange Ex p. Else (1982) Ltd* [1993] Q.B. 534 CA it was held that the EU Directives did not require that access to the courts be granted to the shareholders. The Court was influenced by the argument that to decide otherwise would enormously slow down decision-taking by the competent authority.

[187] FSMA ss.87K and 87L. In the case of admission to trading, there is no withdrawal power where the FCA concludes only that it is likely a requirement will be infringed. This is presumably because of the adverse impact of ending trading on those who have invested in the company's securities, whereas if an offer is withdrawn, the securities on offer are simply not taken up. These provisions follow those of art.21(3)(d)–(h) of the PD.

[188] FSMA ss.87D and O. The "person" (other than the offeror) could be, for example, the operator of the market.

[189] See para.25–16.

Exchange, acting as the final appeal body instead of the Upper Tribunal.[190] Further, judicial review of the Exchange's exercise of its powers is a possibility and the elaboration of the Exchange's disciplinary and appeals procedures in recent years constitutes an obvious response to that legal risk.[191]

Ex post sanctions

25–43   The sanctions discussed in the previous paragraph can be applied effectively only to breaches of the rules which the FCA picks up in advance of completion of listing, the public offer or admission to trading. The FCA will obviously be reluctant to use its powers to prohibit trading once admission has been secured, and cannot do anything about a public offer which has been carried through to the point of the allotment of securities. Furthermore, it can be said that the regulatory sanctions considered so far impose costs on the issuer (i.e. its shareholders) rather than on the officers of the company who may be those responsible for the non-compliance. It is therefore of some significance that the FCA has the power to impose monetary penalties where there has been a breach of Pt VI of FSMA or the prospectus or listing rules.[192] The FCA may impose a penalty of such amount as it considers appropriate on the corporate bodies involved. Significantly, this penalty-imposing power extends to any person who was a director of the company where the director was "knowingly concerned" in the contravention.[193] The FCA may engage in public censure in lieu of imposing a penalty.[194] In the case of suspected breaches of Pt VI of FSMA or of the PR or LR the FCA also has formal investigatory powers which may help it to uncover the truth.[195]

This penalty-imposing power is naturally surrounded by some safeguards. The FCA is required to develop outside the context of a particular case a policy about the circumstances in which it will exercise its powers and the amount of the penalty it will impose.[196] A proposal to impose a penalty must be communicated to the person in question by means of a "warning notice", giving at least 28 days for representations to be made, and a decision to impose a penalty may be appealed to the Tribunal.[197]

---

[190] LSE, *AIM Disciplinary and Appeals Handbook*, 2014.

[191] cf. *R. (on the application of Yukos Oil Co) v Financial Services Authority and London Stock Exchange* [2006] EWHC 2044.

[192] FSMA s.91(1) and (1A). Section 91(1) includes breaches of the listing rules other than at the public offer stage, as we shall see in the next chapter. Section 91(1A) implements art.25 of the PD. It will be recalled that an FCA penalty is one of the matters against which a company may not agree in advance to indemnify the director: above, Ch.16 at para.16–130.

[193] FSMA s.91(2). Since 2012 sponsors are also subject to FCA disciplinary powers: s.88A.

[194] FSMA s.91(3).

[195] FSMA s.97 and Pt XI. The investigatory powers are not confined to authorised persons, as they normally are under Pt XI.

[196] FSMA s.93.

[197] FSMA s.92 and s.387 on warning notices.

CROSS-BORDER OFFERS AND ADMISSIONS

We have noted above that the EU's strong drive to remove obstacles to **25–44** cross-border offers and admissions to regulated markets led to the maximum harmonisation character of the PD. The notion is that an issuer should be able to use the same documentation (subject in some cases to translation requirements) when it makes offers or seeks admission to trading in more than one Member State. Since there is not currently a single EU regulator, an immediate question which arises is where regulatory responsibility should be allocated in cross-border offers. The basic choice in the PD is to allocate responsibility to the state in which the company is incorporated (has its registered office) in the case of companies incorporated within the EU (the "home state"). The competent authorities of "host states", i.e. states in which an offer to the public is made or admission to trading is sought, "shall not undertake any approval or administrative procedures relating to prospectuses".[198]

This choice, which applies even if there is to be no public offer or admission in the home state, is controversial. It potentially puts regulatory responsibility in the hands of inexperienced regulators in countries with undeveloped markets and prohibits the authority in the jurisdiction where the offer or trading will occur from taking action, even though the latter has the stronger incentive to discharge its regulatory functions effectively. If the host state regulator finds that breaches of the relevant rules have occurred or are taking place, it is obliged to refer the matter to the home state authorities, and, only if this is ineffective, may the host state regulator act, informing the Commission at the same time.[199] Equally, if the host state authority forms the view that a supplementary prospectus is needed, it is the home state authority which must require it and the host state authority is permitted simply to draw the home state authority's attention to the need.[200] Consequently, FSMA is drafted so that the obligation to seek FCA approval of a prospectus is applied only to issuers whose home state is the UK,[201] and most of the PR apply only to offers and admissions involving issuers whose home state is the UK.[202] It follows as well that the regulatory sanctions for breach of the PR apply only to issuers incorporated in the UK, but the domestic statutory and common law compensation regimes may apply (subject to the relevant conflicts of law rules).

There are two exceptions to the rule of home state regulation. First, a home state has to be attributed to companies incorporated outside the EEA, and this is the state in which securities are first offered to the public or where the first admission to trading on a regulated market is made, at the issuer's choice.[203] For non-EEA issuers, therefore, the home state is what would be the host state for an EEA issuer. However, third-country issuers may also benefit from a further

---

[198] PD arts 17(1) and 2(1)(m)(n). There are procedures to be followed by the home State to certify to the FCA its approval of the prospectus: PD art.18; FSMA s.87H.

[199] PD art.23.

[200] PD art.17(2).

[201] FSMA s.87A(1)(a).

[202] PR 1.1.1. However, the FCA does have the task of applying the eligibility requirements (above, para.25–15) to all applicants, for CARD does not insist on home state regulation.

[203] PD art.2(1)(m)(iii).

relaxation. The chosen EU regulator may permit the third-country issuer to draw up a prospectus under the third country's laws if the information is equivalent to that required by the PD and the third country rules meet international standards.[204] No doubt this is done in the expectation that EEA issuers will be treated similarly, so that international offerings will be promoted. Secondly, even for EU-incorporated issuers, issuers of debt securities denominated in amounts of at least €1,000 may choose as regulator the state of incorporation, the state of offer or the state of admission to trading.[205]

The second contentious issue with cross-border offerings is that of language. If a translation is required in all the official languages of the states in which the offering is to take place and where the securities are to be admitted to trading and in the language of the state of incorporation, then the additional costs of the cross-border offer are likely to be substantial. On the other hand, the Member States can hardly be expected to agree a single language in which alone prospectuses need be circulated. The result, however, is a complex set of rules. The language issue is solved in the following way in art.19. Where the offer or admission takes place in the home state only, then the competent authority of the home state determines the appropriate language. Where the offer or admission takes place in one or more Member States *not including the home state*, then the offeror or person seeking admission has a choice between a language acceptable to each the competent authorities in those Member States or "a language customary in the sphere of international finance" (though the competent authorities of the host states can require the summary to be translated into its official language). How far this Delphic phrase goes to embrace languages other than English is anyone's guess—and, indeed, that was probably the primary virtue of the phrase in the EU legislator's mind. Of course, the issuer will need home state approval of the prospectus, even if it is not issuing there, and for that purpose it may choose either a language acceptable to the home state authority or a customary language. Thus, where the offer is not made in the home state, the incentive created by these rules is clearly for the offeror, etc. to use "a language customary in the sphere of international finance", since that language can be used for both home and host state purposes (unless home and host states share a language which does not fall within the "customary" category).

Where the offer or admission to listing is to take place in two or more Member States, *including* the home state, then the prospectus must be produced in a language acceptable to the home state competent authority and, in addition, in either a language acceptable to each host state or a language customary in the sphere of international finance. Here, therefore, the burden of translation costs turns on the home state's willingness to accept a "customary" language.

However, in the case of admission to trading of heavy-weight debt securities (i.e. those denominated in amounts of €100,000 or more), the offeror, etc. always has the choice of using a customary language only, even where admission will

---

[204] PD art.20; PR 4.2. See Commission Regulation (EC) No.1569/2007. An issuer using IFRS will always be in the clear since this is the EU requirement.

[205] PD art.2(1)(m)(ii). This rule applies to non-EU incorporated issuers as well, who, however, cannot choose the State of incorporation because they are not within the EU. The advantage for them of being within (ii) rather than (iii) appears to be that the choice arises each time a relevant issue of debt securities is made, under (iii) the choice is otherwise a once-and-for-all one.

occur in the home state, or it may instead choose a language acceptable to both home and host state competent authorities.

DE-LISTING

This chapter has focused on the processes by which the securities of a company become publicly held and traded on a public market. Whilst a completed public offering cannot easily be reversed,[206] admission to trading is a reversible process. Companies may seek voluntarily to retire from a market upon which their securities are traded, notably after a successful takeover bid (discussed in Ch.28), as a result of which the majority of its shares are held by the bidder. If the securities of the company are all held by one person as a result of the bid, this is a straightforward exercise. If, however, there are some outside shareholders, they may oppose the proposal to de-list because it will reduce the liquidity of the securities even further. Indeed, the proposal to de-list may be part of an attempt by the controllers of the company to squeeze out the minority in a situation where the statutory squeeze-out provisions (also discussed in Ch.28) would not operate. The requirement previously was that companies simply inform their shareholders of the decision to de-list, but the LR now require requests from companies with a premium listing for the cancellation of a primary listing of equity shares to be approved by a three-quarters majority at a meeting of the class of shareholders in question and, where there is a controlling shareholder, a majority of the non-controlling shares, after the circulation to them of a statement, approved by the FCA, of the reasons for this step.[207] This is a significant increase in minority shareholder protection and should increase the willingness of investors to take minority stakes in companies that are controlled by a single investor or are likely to become so.

25–45

---

[206] See the constraints on companies' acquisition of their own shares discussed in Ch.13.

[207] LR 5.2.5. For the meaning of a controlling shareholder see text attached to fn.59, above. There are certain exceptions to the requirement for shareholder approval, for example, where the shares are already traded on a regulated market in another EEA State (though this may be a significant event for shareholders); if the company is in severe financial difficulties; or the securities in question are debt securities; or the controller has reached a 75 per cent holding as a result of a takeover bid in which the offer document made clear the offeror's intention to de-list.

CHAPTER 26

CONTINUING OBLIGATIONS AND DISCLOSURE OF INFORMATION TO THE MARKET

INTRODUCTION

Even after a company has been admitted to a public market, in accordance with **26–1**
the rules discussed in the previous chapter, the law imposes "continuing
obligations" in relation to disclosure *by* publicly traded companies. These
obligations are discussed in the first half of this chapter. In addition, however, the
law requires those associated with the company, as directors or major
shareholders, to make certain disclosures *to* the company and, through the
company, to the market. We turn to them in the second half.

The continuing obligations laid on the company largely reflect the disclosure **26–2**
philosophy which dominates the rules on public offerings and admission to
trading,[1] but that theory is applied now to the post-admission period so as to
inform trading among investors in the securities of the company. Investor
protection and allocative efficiency are most obviously advanced by continuing
disclosure when a traded company returns to the market to raise further capital,
especially in cases where it may do so without issuing a new prospectus.[2] More
generally, investors' willingness to purchase securities in publicly traded
companies (whether on a public offering or from existing shareholders) is likely
to be enhanced if they think that market prices reflect the true state of the

---

[1] See para.25–3.
[2] See para.25–21.

company's business.[3] In addition, the prompt disclosure of significant information by the company will reduce the opportunities for insiders to trade in the securities before the market is aware of new developments. Further, disclosure rules may benefit shareholders, whether or not they contemplate trading in the company's securities. The market price of the stock may indicate to shareholders (or independent directors acting on their behalf) whether all is well with the company's business and whether the exercise of their governance rights would be appropriate—though it would be unwise for shareholders to react to short-term movements in share prices. Continuing disclosure by the company thus has both market and corporate governance implications, which we will explore in this chapter.[4]

Insider trading may also be discouraged by requiring those closely associated with the company's central management (notably its directors) to make disclosures *to* the company and to the market about their trading in the company's securities, since directors are structurally well placed to acquire inside information. Finally, within the shareholder body disclosure of beneficial ownership of shares may also reveal who is really in a position to influence decisions in shareholder meetings and so to determine the future course of the company (for example, through the selection of directors). So, the rules about disclosure to the company and the market have market "cleanliness" and corporate governance objectives as well as the rules on disclosure by the company.

As with the disclosure rules operating at the time of admission to the market, the structure of domestic law is now heavily influence by EU law, notably the Transparency Directive ("TD")[5] and the Market Abuse Regulation ("MAR").[6] The TD has generated the same multi-layered rule-making structure which we identified in relation to the Prospectus Directive.[7] At the bottom of the structure, but very important in practice, are the Transparency Rules ("TR") made by the FCA. Under the TD the domestic rules are somewhat more important than under the PD because, unlike the PD, the TD is not a maximum harmonisation instrument. In principle Member States can add to its provisions, which the UK, because of its long history of regulating continuing obligations, has often done. Market abuse was previously dealt with at EU level through directives, generating the same multi-layered structure. However, in the post-crisis reforms

---

[3] The "semi-strong" version of the efficient capital market hypothesis states that all publicly available information about the company is immediately incorporated into market prices. The ongoing mandatory disclosure rules are a crucial mechanism whereby corporate information becomes public. See R. Gilson and R. Kraakman, "The Mechanisms of Market Efficiency" (1984) 70 Virginia L.R. 549, and see later by the same authors on the same topic: (2003) 28 Journal of Corporation Law 215 and (2014) 100 Virginia L.R. 313.

[4] But we shall not deal in any detail with companies incorporated in other EEA States or outside the EU whose securities are traded on a London market or with UK-incorporated companies whose sole or primary listing is outside the UK.

[5] Directive 2004/109/EC ([2004] O.J. L390/38), as amended, notably by Directive 2013/50/EU ([2013] O.J. L294/13). The necessary changes to the FSMA 2000 were made by the Transparency Regulations 2015/1755.

[6] Regulation (EU) No.596/2014 ([2014] O.J. L173/1), in effect in part from July 2016 and in part from January 2017. The non-disclosure aspects of this Regulation are discussed in Ch.30.

[7] See para.25–10.

the EU moved to a Market Abuse Regulation[8] which, as a regulation, does not require transposition into domestic law but operates directly as part of UK law. However, it too provides largely minimum standards to which domestic law may add.

PERIODIC REPORTING OBLIGATIONS

We saw in Ch.21 that all companies must report on an annual basis to their shareholders and that such reporting is now extensive, especially for "quoted" companies.[9] However, for a long time companies with securities[10] traded on public markets have been subject to more frequent reporting requirements, for the market's appetite is not satisfied by yearly reporting. Such companies may be required to report half-yearly and even quarterly. In the case of regulated markets[11] these obligations currently stem from the TD.

26–3

Article 4 of the TD requires the publication of audited annual accounts and reports. By and large, the requirements of this article are met by the rules contained in the Companies Act 2006 and considered in Chs 21 and 22.[12] However, the Directive's requirement for speedier publication of accounts than the 2006 Act requires (four, rather than six, months from the end of the financial year) is implemented domestically in the DTR.[13] Further, TD art.4 requires a more explicit "responsibility statement" than is to be found in the case of accounts approved by the directors and signed by a director on behalf of the board under the Act.[14] The TD requires the names of all those responsible within the issuer for the accounts and reports to be stated and the responsibility statement must certify that, to the best of their knowledge, the accounts have been prepared in accordance with the relevant standards and give a true and fair view of the company's financial position, and the management report includes a fair review of the company's business.[15]

More significant is the TD's requirement for half-yearly reports, to which there is no Companies Act equivalent, to be published within two months of the end of the half year. The half-yearly reports are required to be less detailed than

---

[8] One impact of this change is that the FCA loses its power to make Disclosure Rules (though it may provide guidance) so that "DTR" will come to stand for "Disclosure Guidance and Transparency Rules" rather than, as previously, "Disclosure and Transparency Rules".

[9] "Quoted companies" are those officially listed in any EEA State or admitted to trading on the New York Stock Exchange or Nasdaq: CA 2006 s.385.

[10] The provisions discussed in this section normally apply whether the traded securities are equity or debt instruments.

[11] For the meaning of a "regulated market" see para.25–8. In the case of shares, the term can be equated in the UK, with some degree of inaccuracy, with the Main Market of the LSE. The Alternative Investment Market ("AIM") is not a regulated market, but the LSE's own rules for that market require half-yearly statements (but not quarterly reports): LSE, *AIM Rules for Companies*, 2014 r.18.

[12] The CA contains some rules specific to quoted companies, for example, the requirement for website publication: s.430.

[13] DTR 4.1.3. Some statutory material is repeated in the DTR in order to make it applicable to companies not incorporated in the UK but which have their securities traded on a regulated market in the UK.

[14] See para.21–29.

[15] DTR 4.1.12.

the annual ones and are not required to be audited (though if they are audited or reviewed, the audit report or review must be published).[16] The accounts required to be produced are a condensed set of financial statements, the directors' report is an "interim review" and the responsibility statement is adjusted accordingly.[17]

26–4 The issue of quarterly reporting has been contentious. Some argue that it adds to the efficiency of securities markets; others than it encourages management to focus on the short-term. The original TD required, not a set of quarterly accounts but only a quarterly "interim management statement", giving an explanation of material events and transactions which had taken place and their impact on the issuer and a general description of the company's financial position and performance.[18] However, in the 2013 amendments the short-termism argument won out and the quarterly reporting requirement was removed.[19]

As we have noted in Ch.21, the power to review the accounts and reports of companies for compliance with the relevant requirements is one which has been delegated by the Government to the Financial Reporting Council; and that body's powers extend to all the periodic reports required to be produced by listed companies, whether annual or otherwise.[20]

EPISODIC OR AD HOC REPORTING REQUIREMENTS

26–5 In addition to the requirement to make reports every six months, publicly quoted companies are required to report events as they occur. There are two main arguments behind this requirement. First, it can be seen as a way of keeping shareholders and investors up-to-date about developments in the business of the company or about other factors which affect its business. The information should be disclosed because it is relevant to investors and shareholders. The second argument, reflected in the fact that at EU level this disclosure obligation is located in MAR rather the TD, is that the information should be disclosed publicly in order that it shall no longer be known only to a small group of persons who may be tempted to trade on the basis of the information to their profit precisely because it is not known to the market in general. On this rationale disclosure is a way of reducing opportunities of "insider trading", i.e. trading in securities on the basis of price-sensitive information which is not generally available. On both arguments, the purpose of the rules is to have the information disclosed to the market, but, in the first argument because market participants and shareholders need the information to inform action they might take and, on the second argument, because disclosure is the way of depriving the information of its "inside" character.

---

[16] TD art.5(4). The FRC has produced guidance on the review of interim statements.

[17] TD art.5(2). Some detail about what is required in the half-yearly accounts and reports is set out in Commission Directive 2007/14/EC ([2007] O.J. L69/27) art.3. The transposing domestic legislation is in DTR 4.2.

[18] Original art. 6.

[19] The UK might have chosen to retain the requirement as a domestic rule but in fact opted not to do so.

[20] See para.21–32.

The current version of these disclosure requirements is to be found in art.17 of MAR, applying to companies whose securities are traded on a multi-lateral trading facility as well as on a regulated market.[21] The emphasis in MAR is on disclosure by the company of inside information "as soon as possible". The essence of inside information is that it is information which is not known to the market but, if it were known, would have a significant effect on the price of the company's securities.[22] This is discussed further in Ch.30.

In the design of any rules relating to the disclosure of events "as soon as possible", there are two problems which have to be faced. One is to define the point at which the event has crystallised and so triggers the disclosure obligation. If impending developments or matters under negotiation are disclosed too soon, their completion may be jeopardised and the market possibly be given information whose value is difficult to assess because it relates to inchoate matters. The injunction to act "as soon as possible" gives the issuer some leeway, for example, where it receives unexpected information whose ambit is not clear and which it needs to clarify. Beyond that, MAR permits issuers "on their own responsibility" (i.e. they cannot require the national regulatory authority to give advance clearance of non-disclosure, though the regulator must be informed of the decision not to disclose)[23] to delay disclosure to protect their "legitimate interests", but subject to the riders that the non-disclosure must not be likely to mislead the public and that the company can ensure the confidentiality of the information on the part of those to whom it will have to be disclosed.[24] This permission is particularly important since art.7(2) states that, in principle, "an intermediate step in a protracted process shall be deemed to be inside information if, by itself, it satisfies the criteria of inside information as referred to in this Article".[25]

MAR provides for the European Securities Markets Authority ("ESMA") to produce guidelines on the tricky issues of what constitutes a legitimate interest and action likely to mislead, though some examples of legitimate interest are given in Recital 50 to the Regulation. The indicative list of such legitimate interests produced in the draft guidance from ESMA[26] focuses on the negotiation

---

[21] MAR art.2. The domestic provisions on insider trading, however, have always applied to public, not just regulated, markets. For the meaning of MTF and regulated market see para.25–8.

[22] MAR art.7.

[23] In addition to the fact of delay art.17(4) states that the national competent authority must require the notification to be accompanied by an explanation of how the conditions set out in the text are met or require the issuer to provide the explanation upon request of the regulator. The UK seems likely to take the second option: FCA, *Policy proposals and Handbook changes related to the implementation of the Market Abuse Regulation*, November 2015, 2.8. The definition of the relevant competent authority is likely to give somewhat greater role to the authority of the state in which the securities are traded than under the PD (see para.25–44). Unless the issuer has securities traded in the state of registration, the competent authority will be (one of the) the states where trading occurs even if that is different from the state of registration: ESMA, *Technical advice on possible delegated acts concerning the Market Abuse Regulation: Final Report*, 2015, §4.

[24] MAR art.17(4). Where confidentiality has been breached, the withheld information must be disclosed as soon as possible, including in some cases of market rumours relating to the information: 17(7).

[25] Following the prior CJEU decision in Case C-19/11 *Geltl v Daimler AG*, decision of 28 June 2012.

[26] ESMA, *Draft guidelines on the Market Abuse Regulation*, Consultation Paper, January 2016. This follows the guidance issued under the pre-MAR law.

or implementation of transactions which are likely to be prejudiced if they are revealed, for example, negotiations for a major contract or negotiations to sell a major holding in the company. However, even where the issuer has a legitimate interest in non-disclosure, it may refrain from disclosing only if non-disclosure is not likely to be misleading to the market. Here the indicative list suggests non-disclosure will be misleading if (i) the information is inconsistent with some prior public statement by the issuer to the market; (ii) casts doubt on the issuer's prospects of meeting its financial objectives where these have been the subject of prior public guidance from the company; or (iii) the information goes against the market's current expectations where these have been set by signals from the issuer. As is to be expected, investors' interests appear to receive more weight than issuers' concerns.[27]

26–7 The second problem is that public disclosure of adverse developments may make it more difficult for the issuer to handle them. In principle, this situation is also handled under the above rules, but in one case the balance is re-weighted in favour of the issuer. Where the issuer is a financial institution and disclosure of the information would threaten the financial viability of the issuer *and* of the financial system, disclosure can be delayed, subject to the confidentiality test and a public interest test and the consent of the competent financial regulator.[28] The reason for downgrading investors' interests in this case is that instability in the financial system is likely to be more costly to society as a whole than the costs to investors of non-disclosure. This provision reflects experience in the financial crisis where, at least in the UK, the regulators interpreted the prior EU law strictly so as to require immediate disclosure of the existence of banks' liquidity problems whilst permitting non-disclosure only of the state of the negotiations to solve them—arguably the worst of both worlds.[29]

26–8 Where information is required to be disclosed the Regulation requires that to be done in a way which "enables fast access and complete, correct and timely assessment of the information by the public".[30] It also requires it to be displayed on the company's website for an appropriate period, but this is not in fact a very good way of disclosing information simultaneously to all market participants. In practice, Dissemination will occur in the UK via a "Primary Information Provider" ("PIP"), i.e. one approved by the FCA, which carries news about all companies in the market and so does not favour those who happened to be logged onto a particular company's website at the time the information was posted. Further, information required to be disclosed under art.17 of MAR constitutes

---

[27] The third category is the most controversial since inside information, if it is to move the market, will necessarily alter the market's expectations, so much depends on what is understood by "signals from the issuer".

[28] MAR art.17(5)(6).

[29] The strongest case in point was the run on the Northern Rock Building Society in 2007, when it appeared that the immediate cause of the run was the required disclosure by Northern Rock that it had approached the Bank of England for liquidity support, after it was no longer able to fund itself in the inter-bank market, even though, logically, the provision of the Bank support increased the Rock's stability. See HM Treasury, *Financial Stability and Depositor Protection*, Cm 7308, January 2008, paras 3.41 and 3.43. Article 17(5) does not in terms appear limited to liquidity problems, though that is the only example of a threat to financial stability which it gives.

[30] MAR art.17(1).

"regulated information" which, by virtue of art.21 of TD, is subject to additional requirements, notably that it be disseminated to the public simultaneously, as nearly as possible, in all EEA Member States.[31]

Somewhat bureaucratically, art.18 of MAR[32] requires issuers to draw up and keep updated, lists of those working for them (whether as employees or self-employed persons) who have access to inside information; and to send the lists to the relevant national regulator, if so requested. Each list must be kept for five years. Those acting on behalf of the issuer (for example, an investment bank or law firm) must also draw up such a list.[33] The list must give the reason why a particular person is on the list. All those on the list must be acknowledge in writing their duties under the insider dealing rules and of their awareness of the sanctions for breaking them.

DISCLOSURE OF DIRECTORS' INTERESTS

In the previous sections we have examined the disclosure obligations imposed on publicly traded companies. We now turn to the obligations imposed on those associated with the company as either directors or major shareholders.

26–9

Since shortly after the Second World War the Companies Acts required directors to disclose to their companies their interests in the securities of the companies of which they are directors, an obligation which was later extended so as to impose upon the director the duty to disclose the interests of spouses, civil partners and children. In the case of a company with securities listed on a recognised investment exchange[34] the company was then under an obligation to notify the exchange, which was permitted to publish the information to the market. Following the implementation of the Market Abuse Directive[35] in the UK, these disclosure obligations were transferred wholly to rules made by the FCA[36] and confined to companies whose securities were admitted to trading on a regulated market (or where an application for admission has been made). With the adoption of MAR[37] to replace the Directive the controlling obligation is now to be found in art.19 of that instrument and, as we have noted, MAR applies to multi-lateral trading facilities as well as to regulated markets.[38] However, the substantive provisions of the Regulation are not enormously different from the prior combination of EU and domestic law.

---

[31] DTR 6.3.4. "Regulated information" is any information required to be disclosed under art.6 of MAD, the TD, the LR or the DTR (FSA Handbook, Glossary). There must also be a central storage system for regulated information: TD art.21; FSMA s.89W.

[32] SMEs whose securities are traded on a SME growth market need draw up a list only if requested by the regulator to do so (art.18(6)).

[33] ESMA, *Final Report: Draft technical standards on the Market Abuse Regulation*, 2015, §8 and Annex XIII.

[34] For the meaning of this term see para.25–5.

[35] Directive 2003/6/EC ([2003] O.J. L96/16).

[36] Or rather the FSA, as it then was.

[37] At the time of writing the Commission and domestic rules required to fully implement the Regulation exist only in draft form.

[38] Above, para.26–5. So, it will apply to companies traded on AIM, which, however, already imposed a disclosure obligation in respect of directors' dealings: *Aim Rules for Companies*, 2014, r.17 and Sch.5.

29–10   The principal, though not the exclusive, rationale behind this disclosure requirement is to combat insider trading. Although directors are not the only people under a temptation to engage in insider dealing, they are particularly at risk because their relationship with the company will routinely generate inside information, i.e. information which, at least for a short while, is known to them but not outside the company. The original provisions requiring disclosure of directors' securities dealings were introduced following a recommendation from the Cohen Committee (1945), which identified the insider dealing rationale for requiring the disclosure:

> "The best safeguard against improper transactions by directors and against unfounded suspicions of such transactions is to ensure that disclosure is made of all their transactions in the shares or debentures of their companies."[39]

Insider dealing is now a prohibited activity,[40] but the disclosure provisions still operate to supplement the operation of the prohibition, by making detection of improper transactions easier. However, these disclosure rules should not be regarded as aimed solely at insider trading. As the Law Commissions put it:

> "the interests which a director has in his company and his acquisitions and disposals of such interests convey information about the financial incentives that a director has to improve his company's performance and accordingly these provisions form part of the system put in place…to enable shareholders to monitor the directors' stewardship of the company".[41]

So, there are two rationales for director disclosure, insider dealing and corporate governance.

Who has to disclose?

26–11   The disclosure obligation is imposed on any "person discharging managerial responsibilities" ("PDMR") and those "closely associated" with them. PDMRs are defined so as to go somewhat wider than just directors so as to include senior (but non-directorial) executives who (i) have regular access to inside information relating to the issuer; and (ii) have power to make managerial decisions affecting the future development and business prospects of the issuer.[42] This is a welcome recognition of the importance of senior executives, though condition (ii) will bring only a small number of non-directorial executives within the definition. In this respect the current law goes beyond the scope of the former companies legislation. On the other hand, the prior law applied the disclosure obligation to shadow directors,[43] who would not seem to fall within the definition of a PDMR, since they will not typically be executives of the company. For example, a large shareholder will not fall within this definition, though its transactions may be

---

[39] Board of Trade, *Report of the Committee on Company Law Amendment*, Cmd. 6659, June 1945, para.87.
[40] See Ch.30, below.
[41] Law Commission and Scottish Law Commission, *Company Directors: Regulating Conflicts of Interest and Formulating a Statement of Duties: A Joint Consultation Paper* (1998), para.5.2.
[42] MAR art.3(1)(25).
[43] Companies Act 1985 s.324(6). However, a de facto director is probably within the definition.

caught by the less demanding rules on "vote holder" disclosure, discussed below. "Closely associated" persons are, in relation to natural persons, spouses and partners, dependent children and any relative who has shared the same household for at least twelve months at date of the transaction. A complex definition of connected artificial persons adds any legal person, trust or partnership, which is managed by a PDMR or a connected natural person and which is directly or indirectly controlled by the PDMR or connected person or which is set up for that person's benefit.[44] The notification obligation is imposed on the person who engages in a relevant transaction (see below); a director who does not transact is not obliged to disclose the information relating to connected person's transactions. However, the PDMR must inform connected persons of their obligations under the Regulation, which means the PDMR must identify them, but the connected person's disclosure obligation is not expressly conditioned upon such notification. Equally, the issuer must notify the PDMRs of their obligations, which again involves identifying them, a useful exercise in relation to non-board PDMRs in particular.[45]

What has to be disclosed, to whom and when?

MAR requires those subject to it to disclose "transactions on their own account relating to the shares or debt instruments" of the issuer. Transactions "relating to" securities clearly embraces much more than their purchase of sale. In addition, transactions relating to "derivatives or other financial instruments linked to" those securities are covered—an important extension. Nevertheless, this is narrower in one respect than the former domestic rules. Those required disclosure of interests in the securities of other companies in the same corporate group by a person who was a director of any one group company.[46]

26–12

The Commission is required[47] to produce "delegated acts" specifying what constitutes a transaction on own account, although art.19(7) already includes pledging or lending of securities and the execution of transactions by a third party where that third party acts on behalf of the PDMR or connected person. ESMA's advice[48] devotes a lot of attention to the situation where the director or connected person buys or sells units or otherwise invests in a fund which itself has invested in securities of the issuer. In principle, such transactions should be disclosed, unless information about the fund's investments is not available to the PDMR. Assuming access to this information, transactions are to be disclosed where the issuer's securities constitute at least 20 per cent of the value of the fund. This means that most retail fund investments are excluded, because such funds are not normally allowed such a high degree of investment concentration. Moreover, the test is applied at the point of investment or disinvestment by the PDMR. If the

---

[44] MAR art.3(1)(26); or, the definition Delphically adds, "the economic interests of which are substantially equivalent to those of such a person".

[45] Regulation art.19(5).

[46] Companies Act 1985 s.324(1). A director of a parent company may well be able to influence what a subsidiary does, even though s/he is not an executive of the subsidiary. However, unless the subsidiary's shares are publicly traded, the point is not important.

[47] Regulation art.19(14).

[48] Above fn.23, 5.2.

test is not met on acquisition, for example, the PDMR will not have to disclose if the fund manager later buys securities which take the fund over the threshold, unless the situation is an unusual one where the PDMR can influence the managers' investment decisions.

In addition to funds, the ESMA advice suggests the disclosure obligation should apply, amongst others, to contracts for differences (equity swaps),[49] options under directors' remuneration schemes, gifts and donations and share borrowing. The transactional scope of the disclosure obligation is in fact very wide, though Member States are free to add to it. However, the Regulation contains one limitation not previously present in UK law. If the value of the transactions in a calendar year does not exceed €5,000, then no disclosure is required and, once that threshold is reached, only transactions above it are disclosable.[50]

26–13   The Regulation[51] requires information about the transaction to be disclosed to the company (issuer) and, normally, to the competent authority of the issuer's state of registration (in the UK the FCA).[52] The information to be given to the issuer includes "the price and volume of the transaction" (so that the director cannot simply say that he or she has bought some shares in the company).[53] Given the complexity of the connected persons definition the information is wisely required to specify "the reason for the notification", which both requires the notifying person to work out how the definition applies to them and enables the company to check the reasoning. The financial instrument and the nature of the transaction must also be described. The transaction must be notified to the FCA and the issuer not later than three business days after the day of the transaction, and the issuer must release the information to the market (throughout the EU) within the same time-scale (unless national law transfers that obligation to the competent authority).[54] The information disclosed by directors and others under the above mechanism, is regulated information under art.21 of TD and so Member States must ensure it is held in a central database.[55]

DISCLOSURE OF MAJOR VOTING SHAREHOLDINGS

Rationale and history

26–14   This is a further area where British law has long required disclosure but where EU legislation (via the TD) has now become dominant, leading to a transfer of a substantial part of the disclosure requirements from the Companies Acts to FSMA. There is an initial puzzle about why these provisions are necessary at all. It is rare for companies in the UK to issue "bearer" shares, and the Small

---

[49] See para.26–23.
[50] Regulation art.19(8). National competent authorities may raise the threshold to €20,000, but the FCA does not propose to do so: FCA, above fn.23, 2.16.
[51] Regulation art.19(1).
[52] Regulation art.19(2), assuming the company is registered in the EEA.
[53] Regulation art.19(6)(g).
[54] Regulation art.19(2)(3).
[55] Above para.26–8.

Business, Enterprise and Employment Act 2015 now prohibits their issuance,[56] so that shares are issued instead in the name of a person (natural or corporate) and are referred to as "registered" shares. The names of the holders of such shares, as we have seen,[57] must be entered in a register, which is kept by the company, and reported to Companies House in the confirmation statement, so that the names of the shareholders are public knowledge. It may be wondered why further provision is required. However, the requirement that the shareholder's name be registered in the company's share register does not mean that the name of the beneficial owner needs to be registered. The use of nominee names has long been popular among big investors and now the dematerialisation of shares[58] has put some pressure upon even small investors to use nominees. Thus, inspection of the share register will not necessarily, perhaps not even typically, reveal who has the beneficial interest in the share.[59] Finally, the list of shareholders in the confirmation statement may not be up-to-date.

Granted this, it is still necessary to say why holders of large shareholdings should be required to reveal their interests publicly. In part, but only in small part, these provisions aim to deter insider dealing, as with those discussed in the previous section. However, the main purpose of these provisions is better put as follows:

> "A company, its members and the public at large should be entitled to be informed promptly of the acquisition of a significant holding in its voting shares in order that existing members and those dealing with the company may protect their interests and that the conduct of the affairs of the company is not prejudiced by uncertainty over those who may be in a position to influence or control the company."[60]

This statement explains the concentration in the successive legal regimes on disclosure of holdings of voting shares, because it is disclosure of actual or potential control of the company that is aimed at, rather than interests in its securities in general.

However, the statement might also be thought to run together two rationales for the disclosure provisions. One is protection of the management of the company and its members, by making them aware of who is building up a stake in the company. Disclosure here operates as an early-warning device about potential takeover bids in particular. But the statement refers also to the protection of "the public". Public disclosure may be said to be promoting the conceptually separate goal of "market transparency". The argument here is that disclosure of the identity of those with important share stakes in the company is (or could be) an important element in the market's assessment of the value of the company. Obviously, a single set of disclosure rules might aim to promote both policies.

---

[56] See para.24–22.
[57] See above, at paras 21–37 et seq.
[58] See Ch.27, below.
[59] We have discussed in Ch.15, above, the problems which this causes in relation to shareholders' governance rights.
[60] Department of Trade, *Disclosure of Interests in Shares* (1980), p.2.

26–15   The current law in fact contains two different types of disclosure rule. One requires the disclosure of shareholdings once a certain size threshold has been crossed. This is an obligation generated automatically by the law once the appropriate threshold has been reached. The second, still contained in the Companies Act, is triggered by the company asking any person to reveal the extent of their interest in the company's voting shares. This latter set of disclosure rules we discuss not in this chapter but in Ch.28 dealing with takeovers, because their main impact is in that context.

The principle of automatic disclosure of major shareholdings was introduced as a result, again, of the recommendations of the Cohen Committee[61] in 1945 that the beneficial ownership of shares be publicly disclosed. Over time, the starting threshold has been lowered, the speed of the required disclosure increased and the range of interests to be disclosed made more sophisticated. EU law also showed an interest in this topic at an early stage.[62] The current EU principles are laid down in the TD.[63] The main impact of the TD in the UK was, once again, to spark off a fundamental review of the purposes of these disclosure rules. In particular, the emphasis in the Directive upon disclosure as an instrument to improve the functioning of the securities markets[64] led the DTI to propose[65] that the "market transparency" rationale be given pre-eminence over the others. This policy was implemented by the removal of the automatic disclosure requirements from the companies legislation whilst at the same time the Companies Act 2006 Act amended FSMA so as to permit the area to be regulated by FCA rules, thus giving rise to the current regulatory structure.[66] The result, as with directors' disclosures, was an overall narrowing of the range of companies covered by the regime. At this point the domestic rules still went beyond the minimum EU requirements in a number of ways, but that gap has been substantially narrowed by the TD amendments of 2013.[67]

---

[61] Report of the Committee on Company Law Amendment, Cmd. 6659 (1945), pp.39–45. It is to be noted that the domestic legislation has still not been lowered to the one per cent threshold recommended by that Committee.

[62] Its first Directive on disclosure of major shareholdings was Directive 88/627/EEC, [1988] O.J. L348/62 (17 December 1988), later consolidated into Directive 2001/34/EC, arts 89–97.

[63] Chapter III, as amended. The fact that the major shareholding rules are in the TD and not MAR perhaps shows that insider trading is the lesser rationale for the required disclosure.

[64] See especially the preamble to the TD.

[65] DTI, *Proposals for Reform of Part VI of the Companies Act 1985* (April 1995). The CLR touched only lightly on this topic, largely endorsing the 1995 proposals: Completing, para.7.32.

[66] Companies Act 2006 s.1266, introducing new FSMA 2000 s.89A–G.

[67] By Directive 2013/50/EU. This directive required relatively little in the way of substantive amendment to the UK rules. See Treasury and FCA, *Implementation of the Transparency Directive Amending Directive (2013/50/EU) and other Disclosure Rule and Transparency Rule Changes*, March 2015.

The scope of the disclosure obligation

Which companies are subject to the regime?

The 1985 Act regime applied to all public companies (in the company law sense of that term—Plcs).[68] The Directive applies only to companies (issuers) whose securities are admitted to trading on a regulated market.[69] The domestic regime implementing the Directive applies to all companies with securities traded on a prescribed market, which includes any market operated by a Recognised Investment Exchange, on the grounds that transparency of shareholding is as important on exchange-regulated as on regulated markets.[70] Thus, both the Main Market of the LSE and AIM are covered by the current domestic disclosure obligation, but not Plcs which are not publicly traded.

26–16

When does the disclosure obligation arise?

The rules are concerned with disclosure of the percentage of voting rights held in a company, as certain thresholds are passed, rather than just holdings of shares. For that reason DTR 5 is entitled "Vote Holder Notification". Holdings of non-voting shares do not have to be disclosed, because they do not contribute to the ability to exercise control over the company. Nor do holdings of shares which are entitled to vote only in particular circumstances have to be disclosed, for example, non-voting preference shares whose shareholders can nevertheless vote when class rights are being varied under the statutory procedure[71] or which are entitled to vote if their preference dividend has not been paid, provided, of course, that the event has not occurred which gives the class of shares general voting rights.[72] By contrast, those exercising managerial responsibilities do have to disclose holdings in non-voting shares under the rules discussed in the previous section, because opportunities to engage in insider dealing can easily arise in relation to such shares, and holdings of non-voting equity shares may provide economic incentives for directors to act in particular ways, despite the absence of a vote.

26–17

The disclosure thresholds are three percent of the total voting rights in the company and every 1 per cent increase thereafter. Decreases must also be notified on the same scale.[73] These disclosure triggers are more demanding than those in the TD,[74] but reflect the prior domestic law. Almost as important as the definition of the threshold is the question of how soon after the threshold has been crossed

---

[68] Companies Act 1985 s.198.

[69] TD art.2(1)(d).

[70] FSMA 2000 s.89A(1),(3)(a); DTR 5.1.1(3); Glossary, *Issuer* (2B); Financial Services and Markets Act 2000 (Prescribed Markets and Qualifying Investments) Order 2001 (SI 2001/996) art.4. For the distinction between "regulated" and "prescribed" markets see para.25–8.

[71] See para.19–25.

[72] DTR 5.1.1(3).

[73] DTR 5.1.2.

[74] TD art.9(1), which has triggers only at 5, 10, 15, 20, 25, 30, 50 and 75 per cent. Only these triggers are used by the British law in relation to non-UK incorporated companies on a regulated market for which the UK is nevertheless the Home State.

does the notification obligation have to be discharged. A notification obligation which did not have to be discharged until, for example, a month after the threshold had been crossed would be of very little use to the company, its shareholders or the market in general. In fact, the current regime, following the 1985 Act, imposes a "two-day" rule, i.e. disclosure as soon as possible but in any event by the end of the second trading day following the day on which the obligation to disclose arose.[75]

26–18 In the simple case, the event giving rise to the obligation to disclose will be the purchase or sale of the voting shares of the issuer by an investor who is then obliged to make the notification. However, if the disclosure rule did not extend beyond this, it would be inadequate. For example, Company A, holding 2 per cent of the voting shares of Company X, acquires control of Company B, which also holds two per cent of the shares. Neither company had a notifiable interest in Company X beforehand, but after the acquisition Company A will have a notifiable interest. The notification obligation in relation to X's shares is thus triggered by the acquisition of B's shares by A, not the acquisition of X's shares by A or B, which could have occurred much earlier. Much more complex cases are possible to imagine, which is why, no doubt, the obligation to disclose is imposed on a person who "learns of the acquisition or disposal or the possibility of exercising voting rights" or "having regard to the circumstances, should have learned of it", rather than the date on which the acquisition, disposal or possibility actually occurred or arose.[76]

The obligation to disclose might even arise as a result of events with which the person upon whom it falls is wholly unconnected. For example, a company engages in a share buy-back programme in relation a class of voting shares. The shareholder does not participate in the buy-back, but as a result of other shareholders' decisions the shareholder finds that his or her holding now exceeds one of the notification thresholds. The opposite development could occur if the company issued new voting shares other than to the existing shareholders. The scheme of the FCA rules on this point is that the company is required at the end of the month in which there has been an increase or decrease in the number of its voting shares to give details of the resulting voting structure; and that is the event which causes the disclosure obligation to arise.[77]

Indirect holdings of voting rights

26–19 In order to bring in situations other than the simple acquisition or disposal the Directive contains two provisions extending its scope. First, art.10 brings in certain holdings of shares of the issuer where the holding is indirect. Among them are[78]:

---

[75] DTR 5.8.3. This applies to UK incorporated companies only; for non-UK companies the rule is the Directive minimum "four-day" rule (i.e. the end of the fourth trading day following—art.12(2)).
[76] DTR 5.8.3, following art.12(2) of the TD.
[77] DTR 5.8.3, 5.1.2(2), 5.6, following TD arts 12(2), 9(2) and 15.
[78] Article 10 of the TD is "copied out" in DTR 5.2.1.

(i)   Voting rights held by an undertaking controlled by a person are to be treated as voting rights of that person.[79] The FCA rules suggest the use of the definition of parent and subsidiary in the 2006 Companies Act to identify a controlled undertaking, with the extension that the controller can include a natural person and not be confined to a controlling company.[80] The controlled undertaking would also have to notify its holding, if one of the triggering events applied.

(ii)   Voting rights attached to shares held by a nominee on behalf of another will constitute an indirect holding of voting rights by that other person.[81] The nominee will be a direct holder of the voting rights unless, as will often be the case, the nominee may exercise those rights only on the instructions of the beneficial owner.[82]

(iii)   Voting rights attached to shares deposited with someone are to be treated as voting rights of the depositee, if the depositee has the right to exercise the votes at its discretion in the absence of instructions from the shareholder.[83] In the same way, a person engaged in investment management is to be treated as the holder of voting rights if it can effectively determine the manner in which voting rights attached to shares under its control are exercised, in the absence of specific instructions from the shareholders.[84] One or other of provisions (ii) and (iii) is likely to be applicable in the common situation in the UK where an institutional shareholder has outsourced the management of its investment portfolio to a fund manager, though the shares themselves may be vested in a custodian.[85] The fund manager will be an indirect holder of voting shares, assuming, as will usually be the case, the relevant discretion. The custodian will not have to disclose if, as is usual, it can vote only upon instruction (see (ii) above).

A further issue arises where, as is common, the investment management company is part of a larger financial conglomerate. The rules on controlled undertakings ((i) above) would suggest the parent of the group must aggregate the fund-management subsidiary's indirect holdings with its own. However, art.12(5) of the TD provides an exemption from this further aggregation, subject to certain conditions, notably that the fund management subsidiary exercises its voting rights independently of the parent.[86] This seems correct in principle, since the fund manager will be required to exercise the voting rights attached to the shares it controls in the interests of the beneficial owner (the institutional shareholder) and not those of its parent.

(iv)   Where there is an agreement between two or more people under which they are obliged to implement "a lasting common policy" towards a company

---

[79] TD art.10(e). See the example given above.
[80] FSA, *Handbook, Glossary*; FSMA 2000 s.420.
[81] TD art.10(g).
[82] DTR 5.1.3(3).
[83] TD art.10(f).
[84] TD art.10(h).
[85] See above at para.15–31.
[86] These provisos are fleshed out in Commission Directive 2007/14/EC art.10. Both art.12 of TD and art.10 of the implementing Directive are transposed in DTR 5.4.

through a concerted exercise of voting rights, then each of the parties to the agreement will have the voting rights of the other parties attributed to it.[87] Such "concert parties" are a common feature of the long-term governance of companies in some continental European jurisdictions. Although they are less popular in the UK, they do arise, for example in connection with takeover bids, where the Takeover Panel has developed its own sophisticated and more far-reaching definition of "acting in concert".[88]

(v) A person will be regarded as an indirect holder of voting rights if he or she has concluded an agreement with the shareholder for the temporary transfer of voting rights.[89] A linked question concerns disclosure obligations in relation to stock lending,[90] which does not fall conceptually within this category (because the shares are transferred as well as votes), but which serves a similar function. The borrower will be treated as acquiring voting rights if such are attached to the stock borrowed. However, will the lender of the stock be regarded as disposing of voting rights, thus potentially triggering a disclosure obligation? When implementing the original TD the FSA was anxious to continue the prior rules which relieved the lender of the duty to notify on the grounds that its right to call for the re-delivery of the stock was an acquisition of voting rights and that acquisition could be netted off against the loss of voting rights arising out of the stock-lending agreement, thus producing no overall change in its position. However, the ESMA indicative list of financial instrument under the amended art.13 of the TD (discussed below) made it clear that "the right to recall lent shares" was a notifiable event which must be disclosed.[91]

Financial Instruments

26–20 The second extension, contained in the revised art.13, relates to interests in the voting shares of the issuer acquired via holdings of other types of financial instrument which are linked to the issuer's securities. The operation of some of these linked instruments is easy to grasp because they generate rights to acquire or dispose of the issuer's voting rights. Thus an option to buy from or sell the issuer's voting shares to a third party must be disclosed at the time the option is acquired, even though it has not been exercised (and my never be).[92] However, whilst financial instruments generating "an unconditional right to acquire a share

---

[87] Directive art.10(a). The requirement for a "lasting common policy" means that this disclosure rule will not apply to temporary coalitions of shareholders designed to bring about specific changes in the running of the company.

[88] See para.28–44. "Acting in concert" is defined in the Code so as to include "understandings" as well as agreements and the Code contains an extensive list of "presumed" cases of acting in concert (see *The Takeover Code*, C1). On the other hand, the Code only applies where the common policy towards the company is to obtain or consolidate control of it.

[89] Directive art.10(b).

[90] See above at para.15–81.

[91] See ESMA, *Indicative list of financial instruments that are subject to notification requirements according to Article 13(1b) of the revised Transparency Directive*, December 2015. The ESMA list is produced under the provisions of art.13(1)(b).

[92] However, options to subscribe to new shares to be issued by the company appear to be excluded from art.13(1), though actual acquisition would need to be notified (subject to the thresholds).

carrying voting rights" have been within the scope of the TD from the beginning,[93] more recent debate has focussed on instruments which do not give a right to acquire or dispose of the issuer's voting shares but rather which, in the words of ESMA, "exposes the holder to the benefits of an upward movement and/or the damages of a downward movement of the price of these shares (i.e., the value of the financial instrument is positively correlated with the underlying equity instrument)".[94] In this case, the holder of the financial instrument does not have the right to acquire (dispose of) ownership of the underlying voting shares, but does have the economic exposure of an owner.

The classic example of such a financial instrument are "contracts for differences" ("CfDs"). In these contracts, as more fully explained in Ch.28,[95] the subject-matter of the contract is the difference in the price of a security at two points in time, rather than the actual security itself. As such, it would seem to give rise to no disclosable issue at all, since the holder of the CfD does not acquire a share and, in particular, its voting rights but only an economic interest in it. However, in relation to "long"[96] CfDs the counterparty to the contract (usually an investment bank) will often hedge its position under the contract by buying the underlying security. In some cases this will enable the other person entering into the CfD contract to influence the way the votes attached to those shares are exercised by the bank or to acquire the shares from the bank when the CfD is settled. If that person has a contractual right to either of these things under the CfD, then there is no doubt that there is a potentially disclosable interest, assuming the CfD relates to voting shares. The debate concerned the much more common situation where no such contractual right exists, but in practice the CfD holder can either acquire the shares or influence the exercise of voting rights.

The UK decided to include CfDs before this step was taken by the EU in the amending Directive of 2013. Consulting on the issue the FSA, noting that today some 30 per cent of equity trades are by way of CfDs, usually in order to increase leverage or to avoid stamp duty, concluded that investment banks normally require the CfDs to be "closed out" with cash (rather than the delivery of the underlying shares) and are resistant to CfD holders seeking to influence voting rights attached to the shares bought as a hedge. Nevertheless:

26–21

"There are some instances of CfDs being used in ways which the intention of the current regulatory regime is designed to catch . . .Specifically, we conclude that CfDs are sometimes being used, firstly, to seek to influence votes and other corporate governance matters on an undisclosed basis and, secondly, to build up stakes in companies, again without disclosure. We have therefore decided that we should take action now to address these failures."[97]

---

[93] Commission Directive 2007/14/EC art.11(1), containing "second level" implementing rules.

[94] ESMA, *Consultation Paper on Draft Regulatory Technical Standards on major shareholdings and indicative list of financial instruments subject to notification requirements under the revised Transparency Directive*, 2014, para.178.

[95] At para.28–45.

[96] If the investment bank has to pay the CfD holder any increase in the value of the share, the holder can be said to have a "long" position and the bank can protect itself by buying the underlying share; if the bank has to pay the holder the decrease in the value of the share, the holder can be said to have a "short" position, but purchasing the underlying share does not protect the bank in that case. It must hedge its exposure in some other way.

[97] FSA, *Disclosure of Contracts for Difference*, CP 07/20, November 2007, para.1.24.

After some havering about how to implement this policy, the FSA changed the rules so as the require disclosure of all "long" positions under CfDs.[98] The amended TD followed suit. Article 13(1) includes not only financial instruments giving an entitlement to acquire or dispose of ownership of voting shares ("point (a) instruments") but also "financial instruments which are not included in point (a) but which are referenced to shares referred to in that point and with economic effect similar to that of the financial instruments referred to in that point, whether or not they confer a right to a physical settlement". ESMA had no difficulty in concluding that this included CfDs.[99] The contrary argument is that, since most CfDs are settled for cash and the bank's voting behaviour is usually not influenced by the CfD holder, requiring disclosure of all CfDs potentially gives the market a great deal of useless information. However, no one has been able to find a reliable method of distinguishing between those CfDs which will and those which will not be used to build up a stake in the issuer.

Exemptions

26–22   Given the range of notifiable interests, some exemptions needed to be provided, in the interests of both disclosers and recipients of disclosures. We have already noted the one relating to custodians.[100] Another is the acquisition of shares for the purposes of clearing and settlement, i.e. of completing a bargain to buy and sell shares.[101] Probably the most significant is that relating to "market makers", i.e. those who hold shares (usually in a particular range of companies) on their own account in order to be able to offer continuous trading opportunities to those who want to buy or sell those shares.[102] Market makers enhance the liquidity of public securities markets but they do not provide this service for altruistic reasons but in the hope of making a profit overall out of the difference between the prices at which they acquire and dispose of the securities. If they were obliged to disclose the details of their purchases and sales, their ability to make this profit and so their willingness to offer their services as market makers would be reduced. Even this exemption is limited: it does not apply when the market maker's holding in a particular company reaches 10 per cent and it is conditional upon the market maker not intervening in the management of the company or exerting any influence over the company to acquire its shares. There is a similar exemption for financial instruments held in the trading books of banks and related institutions,

---

[98] DTR 5.3.3(2). For its earlier preference see previous note at paras 1.28 and 5.32–5.34.

[99] ESMA, *Final Report on draft Regulatory Technical Standards on major shareholdings and an indicative list of financial instruments subject to notification requirements under the revised Transparency Directive*, 2014, Part IV. This involved minor changes to ss.89A, 89C and 89F of FSMA. The interests falling within art.13 must be aggregated with those falling within arts 9 and 10 for the purpose of calculating thresholds (art.13a).

[100] See para.26–19, above.

[101] Directive art.9(4); DTR 5.1.3(1). On clearing and settlement see para.27–2. This is a limited exemption since it applies only to acquisitions made for the sole purpose of settlement and is limited to acquisitions made during the three trading days following the striking of the bargain to which it relates.

[102] Directive art.9(5); DTR 5.1.3(3) and 5.1.4.

but in this case the disclosure obligation bites at the 5 per cent level.[103] The amendments of 2013 added an exemption for acquisitions during the price stabilisation process after a new issue.[104]

The disclosure process

Assuming a disclosure obligation has arisen, the person upon whom it falls must act within the time limits discussed above and give the required information. In the case of a direct acquisition or disposal of voting shares the required information is straightforward: simply the "resulting situation in terms of voting rights", i.e. the percentage of shares now held and the date upon which the threshold was crossed. Unlike in the case of disclosure by directors there is no obligation to disclose information about the terms upon which the shares were acquired or disposed of. In the case of indirect holdings of shares, some further information is required. For holdings via controlled companies the chain of control must be identified, partly, no doubt, to encourage disclosers to give their mind to this issue. The identity of the shareholder must be given (even if that shareholder has no notification obligation, for example a custodian voting only under instructions) and that of the person entitled to exercise the voting rights, if not the shareholder.[105] For voting rights exercisable through financial instruments, some basic information about those instruments must also be given, notably, the name of the underlying issuer and details about the exercise period (if any) and the date of maturity or expiry of the instrument.[106]

This information must be given to the company. However, the purposes of the disclosure rules can be met only if the information given to the issuer is publicised further. The DTR require issuers on a regulated market to make public the information received as soon as possible and, in any event, by the end of the following trading day, as is the rule for directors' notifications. In the case of issuers whose securities are traded on a prescribed (but not a regulated) market the maximum period for the further disclosure is the end of the third trading day following.[107] There must be a single national storage point for the information and, in due course, the national registers will be linked up via an EU portal.[108]

Overall, it can be said that the rather simple objective of achieving disclosure of vote-holdings at and above the three per cent level has generated a fearsomely complex set of rules.

26–23

---

[103] Directive art.9(6) (as amended); DTR 5.1.3(4). This exemption will normally permit the bank party to the CfD (see above, para.26–22) which buys the underlying shares as a hedge not to disclose its holding of the shares. The FCA had previously included a free-standing "client-serving intermediary" exception, not subject to a cap, but art.13(2) makes no mention of it and so it was deleted in the post-amendment UK reforms.

[104] Directive art.9(6a); DTR 5.1.3(7). On stabilisation see para.30–45, below.

[105] DTR 5.8.1.

[106] DTR 5.8.2. For some types of CfDs calculating the number of shares the counterparty would buy for hedging purposes may not be straightforward and may involve an excursion into option pricing. See art.13(1a) and Commission Regulation (EU) 2015/761 art.5.

[107] DTR 5.8.12 (the period for prescribed markets is that required by the TD art.12(6)).

[108] Directive arts 21, 21a, 22.

SANCTIONS

26–24 Although EU law is the controlling law in relation to the continuing obligations discussed in this chapter, enforcement action is still a matter for national authorities and litigants. The link between the substantive obligations and national enforcement is made through provisions in the TD and MAR which require certain sanctions to be made available in national law, though those provisions do not purport to determine when the sanctions should be deployed. Broadly, sanctions may be private or public. Private remedies are sought by persons who have suffered loss as a result of the breaches of the disclosure obligations (and so are usually aimed at compensation). Public sanctions are initiated by the public authorities, notably national regulators (the FCA in the case of the UK), normally seeking to punish infringers.[109] Those sanctions may be administrative or criminal.

Compensation for misleading statements to the market

26–25 The most obvious basis for a private claim for compensation is where an issuer is required to make a disclosure to the market but fails to disclose, delays disclosure in circumstances where it is not legitimate to do so or makes a misleading disclosure. Assuming full disclosure would have moved the price of the security, those who bought or sold shares[110] during the period before the emergence of the truth might have a claim for the difference between the actual price and the price the securities would have had if the disclosure obligations had been complied with.[111] The EU instruments actually say rather little about private actions for compensation. The TD states, but only in relation to its periodic reporting requirements, that Member States "shall ensure that their laws, regulations and administrative provisions on liability apply to the issuers, [the administrative, management or supervisory bodies of the issuer] or the persons responsible within the issuers".[112] The reference to the "laws" of the Member States means that they must enable private litigants to sue on the basis of their domestic civil liability rules, but does not require any alteration to the domestic liability regime. Moreover, the TD gives the Member States a choice in relation to the defendants against whom the liability may be asserted. Furthermore, this provision on civil liability in the TD does not apply to the disclosure of major shareholdings under that Directive. Nor is there any equivalent to it in MAR, i.e. in relation to episodic disclosures and disclosure of interests by directors and others. Member States are thus have considerable freedom in fashioning civil liability rules.

---

[109] There is, however, some overlap. See para.26–28, below.

[110] Whether buyers or sellers would sue would depend on the direction of the price movement had the information been disclosed.

[111] There are also issues of causation here. If I buy at an artificially high price (because the issuer has concealed adverse information) but sell before the truth emerges, I have suffered no loss. If I sell at an artificially low price (because the issuer has concealed positive information), it can be argued that I have suffered a loss only if the price was the main motivation for my sale (rather than some personal financial emergency).

[112] TD art.7.

After extensive policy debate, the UK introduced an explicit liability regime (in Sch.10A to the FSMA) but for issuers only and only for intentional or reckless statements. The statutory liability applies to information notified or communicated to the market by issuers through a PIP[113] or other recognised communication service.[114] It thus embraces communications to the market by issuers of information communicated to them by PDMR or major vote-holders and to the market-moving episodic disclosures required by MAR as well as to the issuer disclosures required by the TD. However, the issuer is unlikely to attract liability if it accurately passes on the information communicated to it, unless it is aware of the inaccuracy of the information it received. The main focus of the debate was in relation to communications where the issuer is both the generator and communicator of the information, i.e. in relation to periodic and episodic disclosures by the issuer.

It is a controversial issue whether compensation should be available to investors in relation to misleading periodic or episodic statements put out by companies. Until 2006, FSMA 2000 made no specific provision for compensation to be available directly to investors as a result of misleading statements or non-disclosure to the market—in contrast to the extensive statutory liabilities created in the case of misstatements in prospectuses.[115] It was possible to bring an action in the common law of deceit, but the requirements for that head of tortious liability are particularly demanding, notably the requirements for knowledge of the falsity of the statement or recklessness as to its truth on the part of the maker of the statement, for reliance on the statement by the claimant and that the defendant should have intended the claimant to rely on the statement. An action in common law negligence for purely economic loss reduces the first and third requirements, but brings with it an additional high hurdle for liability, namely, that the defendant should have assumed responsibility to the claimant for taking care in relation to the truth of the statement.[116] Thus, actions for compensation by investors who had taken investment decisions on the basis of false statements to the market were extremely rare.[117]

By and large, government was content with this situation, and it moved to legislate only in the light of art.7 of the TD, which was thought capable of undermining the "assumption of responsibility" requirement in the domestic law of negligence. After enacting a stop-gap measure in 2006, a more considered solution was put in place as from October 2010.[118] The purpose of the new regime was slightly to relax the requirements for liability in fraud (for fear that the domestic remedies would not otherwise meet the EU requirement for "effectiveness"), whilst confirming the virtual absence of a role for negligence

26–26

---

[113] Above para.26–6 and FSMA s.89P.

[114] 2006 Act Sch.10A para.2.

[115] See paras 25–32 et seq.; and, at least at first instance, the courts refused to find a breach of statutory duty on the basis of FSMA's disclosure rules: *Hall v Cable and Wireless Plc* [2010] 1 B.C.L.C. 95.

[116] *Caparo Industries Plc v Dickman* [1990] 2 A.C. 605. See para.22–36.

[117] The pre-2006 position is described in HM Treasury, *Davies Review of Issuer Liability: Discussion Paper*, March 2007.

[118] 2006 Act s.90A and Sch.10A.

liability in this area.[119] The new statutory scheme applies to statements made on multi-lateral trading facilities as well as regulated markets and covers statements required by MAR as well as the TD.[120] The aim was to put in place a comprehensive statutory regime for misstatements to the market.

As far as liability on the part of the company for knowing or reckless misstatements is concerned, it is enough under the statutory scheme that the claimant's reliance on the statement was reasonable.[121] It does not matter whether the company intended to induce reliance. Furthermore, the scheme imposes liability for dishonest delay in making a required announcement, even though at common law failure to speak would not normally trigger liability.[122] The other requirements for the common law of deceit are, however, maintained under the statutory scheme.[123] In principle, the issuer is liable for misleading statements to the market only under the special statutory regime, whilst any other person (e.g. a PDMR who was responsible within the company for the statement) is relieved of all responsibility, except to the company.[124] However, certain other liabilities are preserved.[125] Liability for negligent misstatement is maintained provided there has been an assumption of responsibility on the part of the issuer or PDMR for the truth of the statement (thus preserving the common law of tort). Liability will also arise where the issuer (or, much less likely, the PDMR) has contractually promised the truth of its statement to the claimant, where the requirements of liability under the Misrepresentation Act 2007[126] are satisfied, or where the statement falls within the prospectus liability provisions and in certain other limited cases.[127] In short, the idea is the issuer and a PDMR should not be liable in negligence to an investor unless they have promised, formally or informally, to that investor to take care in making statements.

26–27 The principal argument for excluding liability on the part of the issuer for misstatements to the market is that shifting the loss from claimant to issuer (i.e. its shareholders) has very little social utility. A generous liability rule in effect shifts the loss from a sub-set of the shareholders to the shareholders as a whole, i.e. from the investors who bought shares on the basis of a false statement to the market and were still holding the shares when the truth emerged to the shareholders as a whole.[128] A regular investor in the market is as likely, over the long term, to find itself a shareholder in the company who did not buy shares in

---

[119] See HM Treasury, *Davies Review of Issuer Liability, Final Report* (June 2007).

[120] 2006 Act Sch.10A paras 1 and 2.

[121] 2006 Act Sch.10A para.3(4)(b).

[122] Unless the failure to speak rendered a previous statement misleading. The statutory provision is in para.5. It was a controversial decision to impose liability for delay, but, since liability is confined to dishonest delay, defined narrowly (para.6), it is unlikely to be widespread.

[123] For the purpose of the issuer's liability the attribution rule (see para.7–2) used is whether "a person discharging managerial responsibilities" within the company knew of the falsehood, was reckless as to its truth or was dishonest as to the concealment (paras 3(2) and 8(5)).

[124] 2006 Act Sch.10A para.7(1)(2).

[125] 2006 Act Sch.10A para.7(3).

[126] See para.25–37.

[127] 2006 Act Sch.10A paras 7(1) and (3).

[128] If the investor disposes of the shares before the truth emerges, then of course no loss is suffered by that investor. See *Hall v Cable and Wireless Plc* [2010] 1 B.C.L.C. 95 at [43]–[46]. This argument assumes the typical situation, i.e. that the company's statement was falsely optimistic.

the company whilst the misstatement was operative in the market as among those who did. That investor would rationally favour a rule which leaves the loss where it lies rather than transfers it, at considerable transaction costs (the costs of litigation), from one group of shareholders to the shareholders as a whole. This argument might be thought to apply as much to liability in fraud as to liability in negligence, and yet the statutory scheme shifts the loss in the case of fraud. One response might be that the TD does not permit Member States to remove liability completely; a more principled response might be that fraud has a corrosive effect on markets and the deterrent impact of imposing liability for fraud is useful addition to the law's armoury against fraud.

A striking feature of the new statutory scheme is that, whilst it makes the company liable in fraud to investors, it removes liability to third parties entirely, including for fraud, from PDMR who were involved in making the false statement or were responsible for the dishonest delay.[129] At first sight this seems odd, for the argument against transferring loss does not apply if the loss is transferred from investors to PDMR, rather from investors to shareholders as a whole. Why not make the PDMR liable for both fraudulent and negligent misstatements to the market so as to encourage them to provide accurate statements on behalf of the company? There are two arguments against negligence liability to investors on the part of PDMR in respect of misstatements to the market. First, liability might encourage the PDMR to be excessively cautious in what they say to the market and thus deprive investors of useful information.[130] Secondly, given the prevalence of insurance bought by companies to protect their directors against negligence claims,[131] liability for PDMR would again shift the loss to the shareholders as a whole, through the cost of the insurance premiums payable over the years. There is probably a stronger case for maintaining individual liability to investors in the case of fraud. The statutory scheme does impose that liability, but it lies only to the company.[132] Deterrence of misleading statements is thus to be achieved, not under the statutory compensation scheme, but, if at all, as a result of penalties imposed by the FCA, as discussed below.

Compensation via FCA action

An alternative route to compensation for investors is via FCA action on their behalf. FSMA 2000 appears to provide such a mechanism. Under ss.382 and 383 the FCA has the power to apply to the court for an order, in cases of market abuse or contravention of its rules,[133] where profits have accrued to the person in

26–28

---

[129] 2006 Act Sch.10A para.7(2). Of course, individuals will be liable if they have assumed responsibility to the claimant for the truth of their statement or contractually bound themselves in that respect.

[130] See the similar argument developed in para.21–27.

[131] See para.16–129.

[132] For these arguments in greater detail see P. Davies, "Liability for Misstatements to the Market: Some Reflections" (2009) 9 J.C.L.S. 295; and for comment Ferran, ibid., 315.

[133] FSMA 2000 s.382 applies to breaches of the FCA's rules or a "qualifying EU provision" (s.382(9)(a)) and s.383 to market abuse. The powers conferred are similar as far as the company's liability for non-disclosure is concerned.

breach, or loss or other adverse consequences were suffered by other persons.[134] The order may be sought against the issuer itself or individuals, including directors of the company.[135] The court may order the person in breach to pay to the FCA such amount as it thinks just, having regard to the profits made or loss suffered. That amount is to be paid out by the FCA to such persons as the court may direct who fall within the categories of those who have suffered loss or are the persons to whom the profit is "attributable".[136] This provision is potentially important. It constitutes a form of class action for investors, with the costs paid by the FCA. However, the FCA's Enforcement Guide suggests that it will not use its powers to seek restitution whenever they are available but only when it regards their use as more effective than alternative courses of action, open to the FCA or to the potential beneficiaries of FCA action. In particular, "instances in which the [FCA] might consider using its powers to obtain restitution for *market counterparties* are likely to be very limited."[137]

Were the FCA to use its restitution powers in this area, the court would be faced with two difficult questions: how much should be paid and to whom should it go? Depriving the issuer of the profit made may be uncontroversial, but losses may have been suffered on a wide scale in the market which go far beyond the profit made. For example, where a company makes an inaccurate statement to the market which moves the market price upwards, but the price later falls when the truth emerges, losses may well have been suffered by all those who bought shares in the market after the statement and still held them at its correction. Making the company or individuals provide compensation for all those losses might be disproportionate to the wrong involved. As to who should share in the restitution, here the difficulties are the other way around. Those who have suffered loss should presumably share in the pay-out, but where there are no losses but only profits made, to whom are those profits "attributable"? If all those who traded in the market at the relevant time, whether with the defendant or not, share in the profits, then the share of any individual beneficiary will be limited, thus reducing the FCA's incentives to make use of the procedure in the first place.

The above powers to seek restitution extend to the situation where the defendant has committed the criminal offence of making an intentionally or recklessly misleading statement considered below.[138] If such conduct leads to an actual conviction, a further avenue to compensation may be opened up, namely compensation orders made under the general criminal law provisions.[139]

---

[134] FSMA 2000 s.384 empowers the FSA to make a restitution order under its own authority, but only in relation to persons authorised by it to carry on financial business, a category into which neither issuer nor director is likely to fall.

[135] In respect of directors, liability for breach of the FCA's rules is imposed on a person "knowingly concerned" in the company's contravention (s.382(1)), whereas for market abuse the liability is on the basis that a person "has required or encouraged" another person [the company] to engage in behaviour which, if engaged in by the person would amount to market abuse (s.383(1)(b)).

[136] FSMA 2000 ss.382(3),(8), 383(5),(10).

[137] FCA, *Enforcement Guide* (EG) 11.2.

[138] See below, para.26–32.

[139] See *R. v Rigby and Bailey* [2006] 1 W.L.R. 3067 (though the FSA's attempted use of general confiscation powers was unsuccessful). Some £200,000 was paid to Morley Fund Management and £120,000 to Standard Life.

The Act also gives the FCA power to seek injunctions from the courts in respect of apprehended or repeated violation of its requirements.[140]

Administrative penalties for breaches

The TD and the MAR are more prescriptive in relation to administrative sanctions for breaches of their provisions, though not to an extent which adds significantly to the sanctions already developed domestically. The original TD required competent national authorities to have certain essentially investigative powers,[141] but the amending Directive added requirements as to sanctions. These relate to all breaches of the TD, not just the periodic disclosure requirements, and by all persons, not just issuers, but the required penalties are of an administrative nature.[142] The general principle underlying the extended sanctioning powers is now expressed as follows:

26–29

> "Member States shall lay down rules on administrative measures and sanctions applicable to breaches of the national provisions adopted in transposition of this Directive and shall take all measures necessary to ensure that they are implemented. Those administrative measures and sanctions shall be effective, proportionate and dissuasive."[143]

MAR follows a similar approach. "Member States shall, in accordance with national law, provide for competent authorities to have the power to take [sic] appropriate administrative sanctions and other administrative measures",[144] though it goes into considerable detail about the required minimum. It should be noticed that, even though MAR is a Regulation, this part of it requires transposition by the Member States because it is addressed to them.

The rules and procedures governing the imposition of penalties and the FCA's investigatory powers[145] have been described in the previous chapter in relation to breaches of LR and PR.[146] The FCA's powers are further discussed in Ch.30 on market abuse. In this chapter we note only those provisions which are particularly relevant to misstatements to the market.

26–30

First, where the issuer or a PDMR has contravened the FCA's transparency and disclosure rules, they are liable to the imposition of penalties[147] or to public censure by the FCA.[148] Moreover, even where the breach is the issuer's alone,

---

[140] FSMA 2000 ss.380 and 381.

[141] TD art.24.

[142] New TD arts 28–28b.

[143] TD art.28(1), but there is a list of more specific requirements for the core obligations under the TD (arts 28a and 28b).

[144] TD art.30(1).

[145] Under s.97.

[146] See above, para.25–43.

[147] Both the TD (art.28(1)(c)) and MAR (art.30(2)(i)(j)) lay down substantial maximum penalties, whose purpose seems to be, not to protect infringers, but to ensure that competent authorities have sufficiently deterring penalty powers available to them.

[148] FSMA 2000 s.91(1ZA),(1B),(3). The implementation of MAR will require the Disclosure Rules to be replaced with Disclosure Guidance (above fn.8) but it assumed that the FCA's penalty-imposing powers will be amended so as to refer to breaches of MAR. However, this has not been done at the time of writing.

directors may be penalised where they were knowingly concerned in the contravention by the issuer.[149] Thus, directors and PDMR are more exposed to liability under the administrative regime than they are under the rules on compensation.[150]

Secondly, the standard for liability is lower for breaches of the FCA rules than under the "intention or recklessness" standard for compensation under Sch.10A. Breach of the rules might involve the company not disclosing on time or disclosing on time but inaccurately or incompletely (or, of course, both). Whereas complete non-disclosure seems to be subject to strict liability under the FCA's rules, in relation to inaccurate or partial disclosure the standard is one of negligence:

> "An issuer must take all reasonable care to ensure that any information it notifies to [the market] is not misleading, false or deceptive and does not omit anything likely to affect the import of the information."[151]

The FCA makes relatively light use of its penalty-imposing powers.[152] However, it has used them to pick up egregious cases of misleading statements to the market[153] or of failure to disclose market-moving information.[154]

26–31   Thirdly, in relation to breaches of the major vote-holding disclosure obligation, the 2013 amendments to the TD introduced an additional sanction not previously available to the FCA. This is the sanction of suspension of the voting rights attached to the shares whose beneficial ownership has not been revealed.[155] As we shall see in Ch.28, a similar, in fact somewhat broader, power exists under domestic law in relation to non-disclosure under the company-triggered provisions there discussed. In relation to major vote-holding disclosure, the FCA now has power to apply to the court (High Court or Court of Session) for a suspension of voting rights, which the court may impose in the case of a "serious" breach of the disclosure provisions.[156]

---

[149] FSMA s.91(2A)(2B).

[150] The civil penalty liability is expressly preserved in Sch.10A para.10(3)(b).

[151] DTR 1.3.4 and 1A.3.2. Again with the change from disclosure rules to disclosure guidance, the latter obligation will need to be reformulated. See FCA above fn.[44], 4.100.

[152] See HM Treasury, *Davies Review of Issuer Liability: Discussion Paper*, March 2007, Table 1: nine cases over four years, including the cases on breach of s.397, discussed below. The FCA increased its enforcement activity after the financial crisis and adopted a much stronger approach to the size of penalties (see FCA, *Decision Procedures and Penalties Manual*, Pt 6).

[153] For example, FSA, *Cattles Ltd*, Final Notice, March 2012 (and its directors) for misleading statements in the annual report, penalties imposed on directors but not on the company because of its parlous financial state.

[154] For example, FSA, *Entertainment Rights Plc*, January 2009, delay of 78 days, fine of £224,000 on the company; FSA, *Photo-Me International Plc*, Final Notice, June 2010, delay of 44 days, fine of £500,000.

[155] TD art.28b(2). This is most likely to happen where an intermediary states that it is holding the shares on behalf of another person but refuses to reveal the identity of that other person, possibly because the laws of the jurisdiction in which the intermediary is situated prohibit disclosure without the consent of the other person.

[156] FSMA s.89NA. The criteria for assessing seriousness are set out in subs.(4).

Fourthly, the TD applies only to companies with securities admitted to trading on a regulated market, for example, the Main Market of the LSE.[157] The same was true of the Market Abuse Directive, repealed by MAR. However, the AIM rules impose similar disclosure obligations in relation to market-moving information (episodic disclosures) and a negligence standard of care in relation to the disclosure, but enforcement of that obligation is a matter for the LSE, as the market operator, rather than the FCA.[158] The implementation of MAR will change this: the disclosure rules of MAR will apply directly to AIM-listed companies, thus displacing the AIM rules, and enforcement will move to the FCA.

Fifthly, we have discussed MAR in this chapter because it contains specific disclosure rules, notably in relation to market-moving information. However, quite apart from the specific disclosure requirements, supplying misleading information to the market may constitute conduct which amounts to breach of the substantive market abuse provisions of MAR (discussed more fully in Ch.30). The definition of market abuse includes "disseminating information...which gives, or is likely to give, false or misleading signals as to the...price of a financial instrument".[159] This reflects the prior substantive law on market abuse, which, in contrast to the disclosure requirements, the UK had applied to AIM as well as to regulated markets.[160] Thus, AIM securities were covered by the substantive market abuse rules, but not by the MAD disclosure rules. A striking example of the operation of the substantive market abuse provisions can be seen in the fine of £17 million imposed by the then FSA on Shell in August 2004 in relation to misstatements made to the market over a number of years about the extent of its oil and gas reserves.[161]

Criminal sanctions

In extreme cases non-disclosure or inaccurate disclosure might also constitute the offence now contained in s.89 of the Financial Services Act 2012. Breaches may be prosecuted by the FCA.[162] This offence can be traced back to s.12 of the Prevention of Fraud (Investments) Act 1939 and consists of making a statement knowing it to be false or misleading or reckless whether it is so, or dishonestly concealing material facts. The statement or concealment must be for the purpose, among others, of inducing someone[163] (or reckless whether it may induce

26–32

---

[157] DTR 1.1.1.

[158] *AIM Rules for Companies*, February 2014, rr.10, 11 and 42; and *AIM Rules for Nominated Advisers*, February 2014, r.17.

[159] MAR art.12(1)(c).

[160] FSMA 2000 s.118(1); Financial Services and Markets Act 2000 (Prescribed Markets and Qualifying Investments) Order 2001 (SI 2001/996) reg.4.

[161] In the *Shell* case (FSA, Final Notice, 24 August 2004, *The "Shell" Transport and Trading Company Plc and The Royal Dutch Petroleum Company NV*) that company was fined for misleading disclosures to the market on the basis that its actions constituted market abuse, the DTR not being in force at the relevant time. Clearly Shell is a listed company but the analysis would seem equally applicable to an AIM company.

[162] FSMA s.401 (except in Scotland).

[163] The person thus persuaded to act need not be the same person as the one to whom the statement is made: s.89(2).

someone) to deal in securities (whether as principal or agent).[164] The section is a useful weapon in the prosecutor's armoury since only recklessness (not intent) needs to be established.[165] However, the misleading disclosure must be made for the required purpose: the fact that a recipient of the statement makes an investment decision on the basis of a statement which its maker knows to be false would not be enough to secure a conviction. Conviction on indictment may lead to a sentence of imprisonment of up to seven years.[166] All the ingredients for criminal liability were found in *R. v Bailey and Rigby*,[167] where the chief executive and chief financial officers of a company were convicted of issuing a misleading trading statement[168] which caused its share price to rise and investors to purchase its shares when the contracts on which the trading statement had been based had not been concluded and in fact never were. The basis of the conviction was recklessness, both as to the truth of the statement and as to whether investors would rely on it. When the truth emerged the share price fell to one-fifth and then one-tenth of its pre-correction level.

CONCLUSION

26–33   There is more than one way in which the efficient functioning of the market is promoted by the requirements discussed in this chapter. The reduction of insider trading opportunities is promoted by rules requiring price-sensitive information about the company to be made public or revealing directors' trading in the shares of their companies. However, continuous disclosure of information about companies also helps the accuracy of the price-formation process in securities markets, whilst information about directors' holdings helps shareholders assess the financial incentives to which the management is subject—and perhaps reveals information about the company's prospects. Thus, both market efficiency and corporate governance objectives are promoted by the disclosure requirements. The vote-holder disclosure rules address a different need of investors: to know who is in a position to control the company or, perhaps more importantly, who may be building up a stake in the company as a prelude to effecting a change in the current control position. As so often in company law, the substance of the legal requirement may be the modest one of disclosure, but the underlying objectives, which the disclosure requirements are aimed to promote—it is unclear how effectively—are fundamental.

---

[164] FSA 2012 s.89(2) and the Financial Services Act 2012 (Misleading Statements and Impressions) Order 2013/637 art.2.

[165] Where the statement is true, but designed to create a false or misleading impression, it may fall within s.90 of FSA 2012. This section is discussed in Ch.30.

[166] FSA 2012 s.92.

[167] *R. v Bailey and Rigby* [2006] 2 Cr. App. R.(S.) 36. Although custodial sentences were upheld, the CA reduced them from three-and-a-half years to 18 months and from two-and-a-half years to nine months. The case was decided on an earlier version of the prohibition.

[168] A statement updating the market on the company's trading performance.

CHAPTER 27

TRANSFERS OF SHARES

Once shares have been issued by the company, it is only infrequently that the **27–1** company will buy them back. Moreover, this cannot happen without the company's consent, either at the time the shares were issued (as with shares which are issued as redeemable at the option of the shareholder)[1] or at the time of re-acquisition (as in the case of shares redeemable at the option of the company or a re-purchase of shares).[2] In any event, the re-acquisition cannot occur unless the rules on capital maintenance, imposed for the benefit of creditors, are observed.[3] Although companies occasionally use surplus cash to re-purchase shares rather than to pay a dividend, a shareholder who wishes to realise his or her investment in the company will normally have to find, or wait for, another investor who will purchase the shares and take the shareholder's place in the company. This is precisely the reason why a company which secures the admission of its shares to a public market is likely to find it easier to persuade investors to buy the shares in the first place.

Although the above principle is true of all types of company, there is a major difference between companies with large and fluctuating bodies of shareholders whose shares are traded on a public exchange ("listed" companies) and companies with small bodies of shareholders whose composition is expected to be stable and where the allocation of shares is as much about the allocation of control in the company as it is about its financing ("non-listed" companies). In

---

[1] See above, para.13–9.
[2] See above, para.13–9.
[3] See above, para.13–11.

the former case, the law or the rules of the exchange will require the shares to be freely tradable as far as the issuer is concerned,[4] so that except in a few cases the transfer of the shares will be simply a matter between the existing shareholder and the potential investor. Free transferability tends to be taken for granted in listed companies, but it does become controversial when what is proposed is the wholesale transfer of the shares to a single person, in the shape of a takeover bidder, because in that situation, even in an open company, the transfer of the shares has clear implications for the control of the company. We shall examine takeovers in the following chapter.

In non-listed companies, by contrast, even the transfer of shares by a single shareholder may have implications for the control of the company and often also for its management, since a shareholding in such a company may be perceived as giving rise to a formal or informal entitlement to membership of the board of directors and participation in the management of the company.[5] In those companies, therefore, it is common for the articles of association to contain some restrictions on the transferability of the shares, perhaps by making transfers subject to the permission of the board or requiring the shares to be offered initially to the other shareholders before they can be sold outside the existing shareholder body. The latter obligation is normally referred to as giving the other shareholders pre-emption rights, but these are pre-emption rights arising on transfer and are to be distinguished from pre-emption rights arising on issuance, which are discussed in Ch.24. The latter bind the company; the former the selling shareholder.

27–2 Share transfers involve a two-step process. In the first step the buyer and the seller conclude a sales contract where they agree on the price which the shares are sold for and on other terms of the transaction. Bankers sometimes refer to this first step as "trading". In the second step the transfer is carried out. At the end of the second step the buyer becomes the owner of the shares that formed part of the sales transaction. This second step is sometimes referred to as "settlement". Settlement is a process which in itself consists of two or more stages depending on whether certificated or uncertificated shares are sold.

When shares in private companies and non-listed public companies are sold the buyer and the seller frequently know each other's identity and are often personally involved in negotiating the terms of the transaction. Sales transactions are completed by way of delivery of certain transfer documents from the seller to the buyer and by way of registering the buyer's name on the shareholder register.

When listed shares are sold, the transaction is frequently more standardised. In most cases, the seller does not go out to find a buyer him- or herself, but enlists the services of a broker who sells the shares for him or her. The broker does this either through the electronic trading system operated by a stock exchange or by making a contract with another financial services provider directly. In both cases buyer and seller rarely know each other's identity. After the contract has been

---

[4] Listing Rules r.2.2.4 as of April 2016.

[5] In the case of an informal entitlement, it may be protected by the unfair prejudice remedy: above, Ch.20.

concluded, the buyer's name is also entered on the shareholder register, but this settlement process is carried out electronically through a settlement system known as CREST.

In this chapter we will focus on the second step of the transfer process, the completion of the sales transaction. We shall examine the difference between certificated and uncertificated shares, transfers of certificated and transfers of uncertificated shares as well as the rules governing the shareholder register and transmission of shares by operation of law. We shall first address the difference between uncertificated and certificated shares.

CERTIFICATED AND UNCERTIFICATED SHARES

In the UK, shares are predominantly issued in registered form. Companies issuing registered shares keep a register of the names of their shareholders. Until 1996 all registered shares were issued in what is now called the "certificated form". This means that, in addition to having his or her name noted on the shareholder register, every shareholder receives a paper certificate evidencing his or her shareholding. When shares are transferred the seller completes and signs a transfer form and delivers this together with the share certificate to the buyer. The buyer then lodges the certificate with the company to have his or her name entered on its shareholder register.

This paper-based transfer process still applies to non-listed shares. These are shares in private companies and shares in public companies which are not listed on the London Stock Exchange ("LSE").

Until 1996 listed shares were also transferred by means of paper documents. The LSE operated a transfer system entitled TALISMAN. Under the TALISMAN regime, the LSE received transfer forms and share certificates from buyers and ensured that the sellers' names would be registered on the shareholder register. There was a gap of two to three weeks between trading and settlement. If shares were sold in the meantime, TALISMAN would keep track of that transaction and arrange for the name of the ultimate buyer to be registered.

In the years leading up to the introduction of CREST in 1996, the UK privatised a large number of previously state-owned enterprises. The number of listed shares and with that the number of share transactions increased significantly. When share prices fell sharply on 19 October 1987, trading volumes soared and substantial delays in settlement occurred. Delays in settlement pose a significant risk to a share market. The longer the delay between trading and settlement the greater the risk that parties suffer loss by transactions not completing successfully. In many cases, the law will provide remedies if the transaction comes to a halt part way through, but the enforcement of those rights will be expensive and in some cases, for example, in the insolvency of an involved party, the rights may not have any value.

27–3

In the discussion following the 1987 market crash, it became apparent that the paper-based transfer process was unable to cope with large volumes of share transactions. It was decided that paper transfers should be phased out for listed shares and that a new electronic share transfer system should be introduced. This process of replacing paper with electronic shares transfers is referred to as

27–4

dematerialisation. Listed shares were dematerialised in the UK in 1996 when the CREST system went live. Since then, all UK shares listed on the LSE must be compatible with electronic settlement.[6] CREST operates on the basis of ss.784–790 of the 2006 Act and of the Uncertificated Securities Regulations 2001 (USR 2001).[7] These Regulations have termed electronic shares as uncertificated shares and paper shares as certificated shares.[8]

The introduction of uncertificated shares requires the consent of a number of parties. CRESTCo, as the operator of the electronic system, must agree to admit the securities of the company in question to the system, though it clearly has a strong commercial incentive to do so, if the shares are heavily traded. Moreover, since an operator of an electronic system of share holding and transfer requires the approval of the Treasury and that approval requires the operator's rules not to distort competition,[9] it will not be in a position to set rules which discriminate improperly among companies.

In addition, the company itself must agree to permit its securities to be held in uncertificated form. Shares or individual classes of shares are in principle admissible to the electronic system only where the holding of shares in uncertificated form and their transfer electronically is permitted by the company's constitution.[10] The standard constitution requires the company to issue shareholders with a certificate of their holding.[11] To facilitate the change-over to uncertificated shares, USR 2001 reg.16 permits such provisions in the articles to be disapplied by resolution of the directors, rather than by the normal route for altering the articles by resolution of the shareholders,[12] provided the shareholders are given prior or subsequent notice of the directors' resolution. The Regulations then provide that the shareholders by ordinary resolution may vote to overturn the directors' resolution, but, unless they do so, the articles will be modified pro tanto without the shareholders' positive approval. Thus, the Regulations encourage uncertificated shares by putting the burden of objection on the shareholders.

For the time being shareholders can opt to have uncertificated shares converted into certificated shares. If a shareholders exercises this option conversion is recorded on the central CREST register, the company is notified, updates the register and issues the shareholders with a share certificate.[13] On July 2014 the EU adopted a Regulation requiring all securities that are transferable on a regulated market to be issued in book entry form.[14] The Regulation will come

---

[6] Listing Rules rr.6.1.23–6.1.24.

[7] USR 2001 (SI 2001/3755).

[8] Certificated and uncertificated shares do not constitute separate classes of shares (*Re Randall ad Quilter Investment Holdings Plc* [2013] EWHC 4357 (Ch)).

[9] USR 2001 Sch.1.

[10] USR 2001 reg.15.

[11] The Companies (Model Articles) Regulations 2008 Sch.1 reg.24 and Sch.3 reg.46.

[12] See above, para.3–31.

[13] USR 2001 reg.28.

[14] Regulation (EU) No.909/2014 of the European Parliament and of the Council on improving securities settlement in the European Union and on central securities depositaries (CSDs) (CSDR) ([2014] O.J. L257/1) art.3(1).

into force on 1 January 2023 by which point the UK will have to abolish the option to convert shares into certificated form for those shares who are transferable on regulated markets.[15]

Having briefly looked at the characteristics of certificated and uncertificated shares in this section, we shall examine transfers of certificated shares in the following section. After that transfers of uncertificated shares will be addressed.

TRANSFERS OF CERTIFICATED SHARES

Legal ownership

To transfer certificated shares, the seller needs to complete a transfer form and deliver that form together with the share certificate to the buyer. The transfer form needs to comply either with the requirements contained in the company's constitution or with the simplified requirements put in place by the Stock Transfer Act.[16]

This, however, is not enough to make the transferee a member of the company. Neither the agreement to transfer nor the delivery of the signed transfer form and share certificate will pass legal title to the transferee (though it may pass an equitable interest in the shares to the transferee).[17] The normal rule is that a person becomes a member of a company and the legal owner of the shares when they have agreed to this and their name has been entered into the company's register of members. The company enters the transferee's name on the register of members in place of the transferor's name.[18] It is precisely this requirement which gives a closed company the opportunity to control the process of transfer of shares to new holders.

It also follows from this analysis that a share certificate is not a negotiable instrument. Legal title does not pass by mere delivery of the certificate to the transferee but upon registration of the transferee by the company. In fact, even registration is not conclusive of the transferee's legal title. Section 127 provides that the register of members is only "prima facie evidence" of matters directed or authorised to be inserted in it and s.768 correspondingly says that a share certificate issued by the company (for example, to the transferee) is "prima facie evidence" of the transferee's title to the shares.[19] Where there is a conflict

27–5

---

[15] CSDR art.76(2).

[16] Stock Transfer Act s.770(1).

[17] See below, para.27–8.

[18] And, it seems, what then occurs is a novation (i.e. the relationship between the company and the transferor is ended and is replaced by a new relationship between the company and the transferee) rather than an assignment of the transferor's rights to the transferee (*Ashby v Blackwell* (1765) 2 Eden 299 at 302–303; 28 E.R. 913 at 914; *Simm v Anglo-American Telegraph Co* (1879) 5 Q.B.D. 188 at 204; E. Micheler, "Legal Title and the Transfer of Shares in a Paperless World—Farewell Quasi-Negotiability" [2002] J.B.L 358). If this is the rule, it is favourable to transferees, for in general on assignment the assignee is in no better position than was the assignor.

[19] Or in Scotland "sufficient evidence unless the contrary is shown". It is not thought that the reference in s.768 to a certificate "under the common seal of the company" requires the use of the common seal, if it instead uses an official seal which is a facsimile of its common seal (see s.50) or has the certificate signed by two directors or one director and the secretary (see s.44). Section 768 (2) makes the position clear for Scotland.

between the register and the certificate, the former is stronger prima facie evidence than the latter but neither is decisive. Ownership of the shares depends on who is entitled to be registered. Suppose, say, that A, who is registered and is entitled to be registered, loses his certificate, obtains a duplicate from the company[20] and transfers to B who is registered by the company. Subsequently A finds the original certificate and, either because he has forgotten about the sale to B or because he is a rogue, then purports to sell the shares to C. The company will rightly refuse to register C whose only remedy will be against A (who may by this time be a man-of-straw).

More importantly, suppose D loses the certificate to E, a rogue, who forges D's signature and secures entry on the register in place of D. D will nevertheless be entitled to have the register rectified[21] so as to restore D's name, because D is still the holder of the legal title to the shares and so is entitled to be entered on the register. This appears to be so, even if D's conduct has been such as to provide the opportunity for E to commit the fraud, for example because D had deposited the certificate with E.[22] Furthermore, D will be entitled to insist on rectification if, as is all too likely, E has made a further transfer of the shares to a wholly innocent third party, F, who is registered before D learns of the fraud. D may still rectify the register against F. This system of rules provides a high level of protection of D's legal rights, but is hardly conducive to the free circulation of shares.

Estoppel

27–6   However, the position of people such as F is ameliorated by the doctrine of estoppel by share certificate, which may give F a right to an indemnity against the company, if D insists on rectification of the register. In other words, the risk of fraud (or other unauthorised transfer) falls on the company, which is perhaps defensible on the grounds that it is the company which benefits from legal rules which encourage the free circulation of shares.[23] The doctrine of estoppel by share certificate produces what has been termed "quasi-negotiability".[24]

A share certificate contains two statements on which the company knows that reliance may be placed. The first is the extent to which the shares to which it relates are paid up. The second is that the person named in it was registered as the

---

[20] Companies do this readily enough so long as the registered holder makes a statutory declaration regarding the loss and supplies the company with a bank indemnity against any liability it may incur.
[21] On rectification, see below, para.27–19.
[22] *Welch v Bank of England* [1955] Ch. 508; *Simm v Anglo-American Telegraph Co* (1879) 5 Q.B.D. 188.
[23] The company may in turn be entitled to an indemnity from the person who asked it to register the transfer which led to the issuance by the company of the misleading certificate. An indemnity against the fraudster is likely to be worthless, but the entitlement embraces also the broker who acted on behalf of the fraudster, who may well be worth suing. See *Royal Bank of Scotland Plc v Sandstone Properties Plc* [1998] 2 B.C.L.C. 429, where the earlier cases are reviewed. Presumably, the rationale for the company's entitlement is that the broker is in a better position to detect unauthorised transfers than is the company. No liability arises, however, if the broker who instructed the issuer to amend the register did so in reliance on genuine but inaccurate share certificates issued by the issuer or its registrar (*Cadbury Schweppes Plc v Halifax Share Dealing Ltd* [2007] 1 B.C.L.C 497).
[24] E. Micheler, "Farewell to Quasi-negotiability? Legal Title and Transfer of Shares in a Paperless World" [2002] J.B.L. 358.

holder of the stated number of shares. The company may be estopped from denying either statement if someone in reliance upon it has changed his position to his detriment. This may afford a transferee who, in reliance on the transferor's share certificate, has bought what he believed, wrongly, to be fully paid shares a defence if the company makes a call upon him.[25] The company will also be estopped if the transferee has relied on a false statement in his transferor's certificate that the transferor was the registered holder of the shares on the date stated in the certificate.[26] Thus, F, the transferee from the rogue, will be entitled to an indemnity from the company if the company rectifies the register in favour of D, the legal owner, because F will have relied upon the certificate issued by the company to the rogue.

However, this argument will rarely[27] benefit an original recipient of the incorrect certificate because receipt of the certificate normally marks the conclusion of the transaction and is not something which was relied on in deciding to enter into it. In the example above, E, the rogue, is the original recipient of the incorrect certificate and we need have no regrets about the weakness of E's legal position. However, suppose E, instead of transferring the shares fraudulently into his own name and then disposing of them to F, in fact, as is all too likely, short-circuited this procedure by transferring them directly to F, and the company then issued a new certificate to F. F could not claim to have relied on the new certificate when entering into the transaction which pre-dated its issue. F did rely on the certificate issued to D but E's fraud did not turn on a denial of D's ownership of the shares but rather upon E pretending to be D. In this situation, only a transferee from F would be able to rely on the doctrine of estoppel by share certificate. Perhaps this result may be justified on the basis that D is in a better position to detect E's fraud than is the company.

Restrictions on transferability

The directors of non-listed companies are frequently empowered by the articles to refuse to register transfers or there will be provisions affording the other members or the company[28] rights of pre-emption, first refusal or even compulsory

27–7

---

[25] *Burkinshaw v Nicholls* (1878) 3 App. Cas. 1004 HL; *Bloomenthal v Ford* [1897] A.C. 156 HL. If the reason why the shares were not fully paid up is a contravention of the provisions regarding payment in ss.553 et seq. of the Act (see Ch.11, above, at para.11–14) a bona fide purchaser and those securing title from him will be exempted from liability to pay calls by virtue of s.588(2) and s.605(3) and will not have to rely on estoppel.

[26] *Cadbury Schweppes Plc v Halifax Share Dealing Ltd* [2007] 1 B.C.L.C 497; *Dixon v Kennaway & Co* [1900] 1 Ch. 833; *Re Bahia and San Francisco Railway Co* (1868) L.R. 3 Q.B. 584. This, in contrast with resisting a call, may seem to be committing the heresy of using estoppel as a sword rather than a shield. The justification is that a purchaser who has bought from the registered owner has a prima facie right to be registered in his place and that the company is estopped from denying that the transferor was the registered owner.

[27] But in exceptional circumstances it may do so: *Balkis Consolidated Co v Tomlinson* [1893] A.C. 396 HL; *Alipour v UOC Corp* [2002] 2 B.C.L.C. 770 (where the holder was even held entitled to be registered as a member, since no innocent party was thereby prejudiced).

[28] Acquisition by the company itself will, of course, be lawful only if it is able to comply with the conditions enabling a company to buy its own shares: see above, at para.13–7. Less usually, the provision may impose an obligation on other members to buy.

acquisition. This does not apply to listed shares because the Listing Rules require there to be no restrictions of the transfer of shares.[29]

Provisions restricting share transfers require the most careful drafting if they are to achieve their purpose; and have not always received it, thereby facing the courts with difficult questions of interpretation. The following propositions can, it is thought, be extracted from the voluminous case law:

(a) The extent of the restriction is solely a matter of construction of the company's constitution. But, since shareholders have a prima facie right to transfer to whomsoever they please, this right is not to be cut down by uncertain language or doubtful implications.[30] If, therefore, it is not clear whether a restriction applies to any transfer or only to a transfer to, say, a non-member,[31] or to any type of disposition or only to a sale[32] the narrower construction will be adopted.

(b) However, this does not help the courts much when faced with a common provision in the articles that a shareholder "desirous" or "intending" or "proposing" to transfer his or her shares to another must give notice to the company to trigger pre-emption procedures. On the one hand, the provision would be unworkable if the courts had held that as soon as a shareholder formed the relevant intention, the provision in the articles was triggered, especially as the shareholder is normally permitted to withdraw the notice, if he or she does not wish to sell to the person who comes forward to buy the shares. There must be something in addition to the required intention. On the other hand, a shareholder who enters into an agreement with an outsider to sell the shares to that person or to give that person an option to buy them will fall within the provision in the articles, even if the outsider has not completed the agreement (and so has only an equitable interest in the shares) or has not taken up the option to purchase.[33] Drafters have spent much ingenuity on producing agreements which do not fall within the second category and have been rewarded. The courts have held that agreements do not trigger the notice provision if they transfer only the beneficial interest in the shares and entitle the transferee to be registered as the legal owner of the shares only once the pre-emption right has been removed from the articles.[34] The execution of a transfer form and its

---

[29] Except for any restrictions imposed for failure to comply with a notice under CA 2006 s.793 (notice by company requiring information about interests in its shares): Listing Rules r.2.2.4.

[30] per Greene MR in *Re Smith & Fawcett Ltd* [1942] Ch. 304 at 306 CA. See also *Re New Cedos Engineering Co Ltd* [1994] 1 B.C.L.C. 797 (a case decided in 1975); *Stothers v William Steward (Holdings) Ltd* [1994] 2 B.C.L.C. 266.

[31] *Greenhalgh v Mallard* [1943] 2 All E.R. 234 CA; *Roberts v Letter "T" Estates Ltd* [1961] A.C. 795 PC; see also *Rose v Lynx Express Ltd* [2004] 1 B.C.L.C. 455.

[32] *Moodie v Shepherd (Bookbinders) Ltd* [1949] 2 All E.R. 1044 HL.

[33] *Lyle & Scott Ltd v Scott's Trustees* [1959] A.C. 763 HL; distinguished in *Re Coroin Ltd McKillen v Misland (Cyprus) Investment Ltd* [2013] EWCA Civ 781; [2013] 2 B.C.L.C. 583.

[34] *Re Sedgefield Steeplechase Co (1927) Ltd, Scotto v Petch* [2000] All E.R. (D) 2442 CA (Lord Hoffmann sat as an additional judge of the Chancery Division, where the previous cases are reviewed); *Theakston v London Trust Plc* [1984] B.C.L.C. 390; see also *Safeguard Industrial Investments Ltd v National and Westminster Bank Ltd* [1980] 3 All E.R. 849.

deposit with the company's auditor, however, can amount to a transfer which triggers pre-emption rights contained in the company's constitution.[35]

(c) Where the regulations confer a discretion on directors with regard to the acceptance of transfers, this discretion, like all the directors' powers, is a fiduciary one[36] to be exercised bona fide in what they consider—not what the court considers—to be in the interest of the company, and not for any collateral purpose. But the court will presume that they have acted bona fide, and the onus of proof of the contrary is on those alleging it and is not easily discharged.[37]

(d) Prior to the Companies Act 2006 it was possible for the articles of association to stipulate that the directors shall not be bound to state their reasons for not registering a transfer.[38] The Companies Act 2006 now states in s.771 that the company must provide the transferee with such further information about the reasons for the refusal as the transferee may reasonable request. This, however, does not include minutes of the meetings of directors. The CLR hopes that this will make it possible to apply the fiduciary tests and s.994 on unfair prejudice in a transparent way to such refusals.[39]

(e) If, on the true construction of the articles, the directors are entitled to reject only on certain prescribed grounds and it is proven that they have rejected on others, the court will intervene.[40] If the directors state their reasons (as they are now obliged to do) the court will investigate them to the extent of seeing whether they have acted on the right principles and would overrule their decision if they have acted on considerations which should not have weighed with them, but not merely because the court would have come to a different conclusion.[41] If the regulations are so framed as to give the directors an unfettered discretion the court will interfere with it only on proof of bad faith.[42]

---

[35] *Hurst v Crampton Bros (Coopers) Ltd* [2003] 1 B.C.L.C. 304; *Re Claygreen* [2006] 1 B.C.L.C. 715.

[36] For the application of the fiduciary principle to the transfer of shares in the context of takeover bids, see paras 28–26 to 28–36, below.

[37] In *Re Smith & Fawcett Ltd* [1942] Ch. 304 CA, the directors refused to register but agreed that they would register a transfer of part of the shareholding if the transferor agreed to sell the balance to one of the directors at a stated price. It was held that this was insufficient evidence of bad faith but it might today be "unfairly prejudicial" under s.994; see Ch.20. See also *Village Cay Marina Ltd v Acland* [1998] 2 B.C.L.C. 327 PC.

[38] *Berry & Stewart v Tottenham Hotspur Football Co* [1935] Ch. 718; see also *Sutherland v British Dominions Corp* [1926] Ch. 746.

[39] Final Report I, paras 7.42–7.45.

[40] *Re Bede Steam Shipping Co* [1917] 1 Ch. 123; see also *Village Cay Marina Ltd v Acland (Barclays Bank Plc third party)* [1998] 2 B.C.L.C 327 PC; and *Sutherland v British Dominions Corp* [1926] Ch. 746.

[41] *Re Bede Steam Shipping Co* [1917] 1 Ch. 123; *Re Smith & Fawcett Ltd* [1942] Ch. 304 CA. Indeed, if there are rights of pre-emption at a fair price to be determined by the auditors the court can investigate the adequacy of this price only if the auditors give a "speaking valuation" stating their reasons: *Dean v Prince* [1954] Ch. 409 CA; *Burgess v Purchase & Sons Ltd* [1983] Ch. 216.

[42] *Re Smith & Fawcett Ltd* [1942] Ch. 304 CA; *Charles Forte Investments Ltd v Amanda* [1964] Ch. 240; *Village Cay Marina Ltd v Acland (Barclays Bank Plc third party)* [1998] 2 B.C.L.C 327 PC.

(f)   If, as is normal, the regulations merely give the directors power to refuse to register, as opposed to making their passing of transfers a condition precedent to registration,[43] the transferee is entitled to be registered unless the directors resolve as a board to reject. Hence in *Moodie v Shepherd (Bookbinders) Ltd*[44] where the two directors disagreed and neither had a casting vote, the House of Lords held that registration must proceed. The directors have a reasonable time in which to come to a decision,[45] but since s.771(1) imposes an obligation on them to give to the transferee notice of rejection within two months of the lodging of the transfer, the maximum reasonable period is two months.[46]

The positions of transferor and transferee prior to registration

27–8   It may be of importance to determine the precise legal position of the transferor and transferee pending registration of the transfer which, if there are restrictions on transferability, may never occur. As we have seen, only if and when the transfer is registered will the transferor cease to be a member and shareholder and the transferee will become a member and shareholder. However, notwithstanding that registration has not occurred, the beneficial interest in the shares may have passed from the transferor to the transferee. In the case of a sale of certificated shares the transaction will normally go through three stages: (1) an agreement (which, particularly if a block of shares conferring de facto or de jure control is being sold, may be a complicated one); (2) delivery of the signed transfer form and the certificate by the seller and payment of the price by the buyer and; (3) registration of the buyer's name on the shareholder register.

Notwithstanding that the transfer is not lodged for registration or registration is refused, the beneficial interest in the shares will, it seems, pass from the seller to the buyer at the latest at stage (2) and, indeed will do so at stage (1) if the agreement is one which the courts would order to be specifically enforced.[47] The seller then becomes a trustee for the buyer and must account to him for any dividends he receives and vote in accordance with his instructions (or appoint

---

[43] It is common to state that transfers have to be passed by the directors but under normal articles that is not so (the Companies (Model Articles) Regulation 2008 Sch.1 reg.26) and in the light of s.771 it is doubtful if the articles could make the directors' approval a condition precedent.

[44] *Moodie v Shepherd (Bookbinders) Ltd* [1949] 2 All E.R. 1044 HLSc.

[45] *Shepherd*'s case (1866) L.R. 2 Ch. App. 16.

[46] *Re Swaledale Cleaners Ltd* [1968] 1 W.L.R. 1710 CA; *Tett v Phoenix Property and Investment Co Ltd* [1986] B.C.L.C. 149; *Re Inverdeck Ltd* [1998] 2 B.C.L.C. 242. And normally it seems that they will not be treated as acting unreasonably if they take the full two months: *Re Zinotty Properties Ltd* [1984] 1 W.L.R. 1249 at 1260.

[47] The fact that the agreement is subject to fulfilment of a condition beyond the control of the parties will not prevent it from being specifically enforceable, notwithstanding that the condition has not been fulfilled, if the party for whose benefit the condition was inserted is prepared to waive it. In *Wood Preservation Ltd v Prior* [1969] 1 W.L.R. 1077 CA, where the condition was for the benefit of the buyer, the court was prepared to hold that the seller ceased to be "the beneficial owner" on the date of the contract notwithstanding that the buyer did not become the beneficial owner until he later waived the condition. In the interim, beneficial ownership was, apparently, in limbo! See also *Michaels v Harley House (Marylebone)* [1997] 2 B.C.L.C. 166; *Philip Morris Products Inc v Rothmans International Enterprises Ltd* [2001] All E.R. (D) 48 (Jul); *Re Kilnoore Ltd (In Liquidation) Unidare Plc v Cohen* [2006] 1 Ch. 489.

him as his proxy).[48] This, however, begs several questions. The first arises because at stage (2) delivery of the documents may not necessarily be matched by payment of the full price; the agreement may have provided for payment by instalments[49] and the seller will then retain a lien on the shares as an unpaid seller. This will not prevent an equitable interest passing to the buyer but the court will not grant specific performance unless the seller's lien can be fully protected,[50] and until paid in full he is entitled to vote the shares as he thinks will best protect his interest.[51] Instead of being a bare trustee his position is analogous to that of a trustee of a settlement of which he is one of the beneficiaries.

The second begged question is whether the foregoing can apply when the articles provide for rights of pre-emption or first refusal when a shareholder wishes to dispose of his shares. In such a case the transferor (perhaps with the full knowledge of the transferee[52]) has breached the deemed contract under s.33 between him and the company and his fellow shareholders. There are observations of the House of Lords in *Hunter v Hunter*[53] to the effect that accordingly the transfer is wholly void, even as between the transferor and transferee.

However, in later cases[54] courts have refused to follow this and, it must surely be right (at any rate if the price has been paid) that the buyer obtains such rights as the transferor had. This will not benefit the buyer if all the shares are taken up when the transferor is compelled to make a pre-emptive offer, but it does not follow that all of them will be taken up and, if not, the transferee has a better claim to those shares not taken up than has the transferor.

When the transaction is not a sale but a gift, there need be no agreement. Even if there is, it will not be legally enforceable under English law because there will be no valuable consideration and because, under the so-called rule in *Milroy v Lord*,[55] "there is no equity to perfect an imperfect gift". One might have supposed, therefore, that if the donor has chosen to make the gift by handing to the donee a signed transfer and the share certificate, rather than by a formal declaration of trust in favour of the donee, the gift would not be effective unless

27–9

---

[48] *Hardoon v Belilios* [1901] A.C. 118 PC; distinguished in *Wise v Perpetual Trustee Co* [1903] A.C. 139 PC.

[49] The normal practice then is to provide that the transfer and share certificate shall be held by a stakeholder and not lodged for registration until released to the buyer on payment of the final instalment.

[50] *Langen & Wind Ltd v Bell* [1972] Ch. 685; *Prince v Strange* [1977] 3 All E.R. 371.

[51] *Musselwhite v Musselwhite & Son Ltd* [1962] Ch. 964; *JRRT (Investments) Ltd v Haycraft* [1993] B.C.L.C. 401; *Michaels v Harley House (Marylebone)* [1997] 2 B.C.L.C. 166; *Stablewood v Virdi* [2010] EWCA Civ 865; [2010] All E.R. (D) 204.

[52] As in *Lyle & Scott Ltd v Scott's Trustees* [1959] A.C. 763 HLSc.

[53] *Hunter v Hunter* [1936] A.C. 222 HL.

[54] *Hawks v McArthur* [1951] 1 All E.R. 22; *Tett v Phoenix Property Co* [1986] B.C.L.C. 149, where the Court of Appeal was not required to rule on this point because the appellants did not argue that the decision on it at first instance was wrong. *Re Walls Properties Ltd v PJ Walls Holdings Ltd* [2008] 1 I.R. 732; *Cottrell v King* [2004] 2 B.C.L.C. 413; but see *Re Claygreen Ltd; Romer-Ormiston v Claygreen Ltd* [2006] 1 B.C.L.C. 715.

[55] *Milroy v Lord* (1862) 4 De G.F. & J. 264.

and until the transfer was registered. In modern cases,[56] however, it has been held that so long as the donor has done all he needs to do, or there has been detrimental reliance by the donee, the beneficial interest passes from him to the donee.[57]

Priorities between competing transferees

27–10   Questions may also arise in determining the priority of purported transfers of the same shares to different people. In answering these questions the courts[58] have relied on two traditional principles of English property law: i.e. (1) that as between two competing holders of equitable interests, if their equities are equal the first in time prevails; and (2) that a bona fide purchaser for value of a legal interest takes free of earlier equitable interests of which he has no notice at the time of purchase.

In applying these principles to competing share transfers, a transferee prior to registration is treated as having an equitable interest only but registration converts his interest into a legal one.[59] Hence if a registered shareholder, A, first executes a transfer to a purchaser, B, and later to another, C, while both remain unregistered B will have priority over C. If, however, C succeeds in obtaining registration before B, he will have priority over B so long as he had no notice, at the time of purchase, of the transfer to B. If C did have notice, although he has been registered, his prima facie title will not prevail over that of B, who will be entitled to have the register rectified (assuming that there are no grounds on which the company could refuse to register B) and in the meantime C's legal interest will be subject to the equitable interest of B.[60] If both transfers were gifts, the position would presumably be different; the gift to B[61] would leave A without any beneficial interest that he could give to C and, not being a "purchaser", C could not obtain priority by registration; his legal interest, on his becoming the registered holder, would be subject to the prior equity of B.

It should perhaps be pointed out once again that even registration affords only prima facie evidence of title. If the registered transferor, A, was not entitled to the

---

[56] *Re Rose* [1949] Ch. 78; *Re Rose* [1952] Ch. 499 CA; *Pennington v Waine* [2002] 2 B.C.L.C. 448 CA; *Kaye v Zeital* [2010] 2 B.C.L.C. 1; *Curtis v Pulbrook* [2011] 1 B.C.L.C. 638.

[57] Thus, until the transfer is registered, placing the donee in the same position as if the donor had instead made a declaration of trust.

[58] The leading cases are *Shropshire Union Railway v R.* (1875) L.R. 7 H.L. 496; *Société Générale v Walker* (1885) 11 App. Cas. 20 HL; *Colonial Bank v Cady* (1890) 15 App. Cas. 267 HL. For more recent decisions, see *Hawks v McArthur* [1951] 1 All E.R. 22; *Champagne Perrier-Jouet v Finch & Co* [1982] 1 W.L.R. 1359; *Macmillan Inc v Bishopsgate Investment Trust Plc (No.3)* [1995] 3 All E.R. 747.

[59] Notwithstanding a suggestion by Lord Selbourne (in *Société Générale v Walker* (1885) 11 App. Cas. 20 HL) that "a present absolute right to have the transfer registered" might suffice, it seems that nothing less than actual registration will do. In *Ireland v Hart* [1902] 1 Ch. 521 the transfer had been lodged for registration and the directors had no power to refuse but it was held that the legal interest had not passed.

[60] *France v Clark* (1884) 26 Ch.D. 257 CA; *Earl of Sheffield v London Joint Stock Bank* (1888) 13 App. Cas. 332 HL; *Rainford v James Keith & Blackman* [1905] 2 Ch. 147 CA.

[61] So long as it has been "perfected"—as interpreted in the cases following *Re Rose* [1949] Ch. 78; and *Re Rose* [1952] Ch. 499 CA.

shares, what will pass when he transfers to B or C is not, strictly speaking, either a legal or equitable interest but only his imperfect title to it, which will not prevail against the true owner. If, for example, the transfer to A was a forgery the true owner will be entitled to be restored to the register.[62] Hence a transferee can never be certain of obtaining an absolute title in the case of an off-market transaction. But his risk is slight so long as he promptly obtains registration of the transfer. And this he can do unless there are restrictions on the transferability of the shares or unless there are good reasons for failing to apply for registration.

The principal example for the latter occurs when the shareholder wants to borrow on the security of his shares. This can be done by a legal mortgage, under which the shareholder transfers the shares to the lender (who registers the transfer) subject to an agreement to retransfer them when the loan is repaid. Generally, however, this suits neither party; the lender normally has no wish to become a member and shareholder of the company and the borrower does not want to cease to be one. Hence a more usual arrangement is one whereby the shareholder deposits with the lender his share certificate and, often, a signed blank transfer, this usually being accompanied by a written memorandum setting out the terms of the loan. The result is to confer an equitable charge which the lender can enforce by selling the shares if he needs to realise his security. Custody of the share certificate is regarded as the essential protection of the lender.[63] In the case of shares, dealt with through CREST,[64] its rules provided for uncertificated shares to be held in "escrow" balances, which provision appears to give the bank an equivalent security.[65]

The company's lien

As we have seen,[66] a public company is not permitted to have a charge or lien on its shares except (a) when the shares are not fully paid and the charge or lien is for the amount payable on the shares; or (b) the ordinary business of the company includes the lending of money or consists of the provision of hire-purchase finance and the charge arises in the course of a transaction in the ordinary course of its business.[67] Neither exception is of much importance in the present context.

Hence it is only in respect of private companies that problems are still likely to arise when their articles provide, as they frequently do, that "the company shall

27–11

---

[62] The transferee will have no remedy against the company based on estoppel by share certificate: it made no false statement: see para.27–6, above. The Forged Transfers Acts 1891 and 1892 enabled companies to adopt fee-financed arrangements for compensating innocent victims of forged transfers but this is purely voluntary and seems to have been virtually a dead-letter since its inception.

[63] Banks usually grant their clients overdrafts on the security of an equitable charge by a deposit of share certificates without requiring signed blank transfers.

[64] Shares not listed or dealt with on the AIM are rarely accepted as security for loans because of their illiquidity and, usually, restrictions on their transferability. Banks will instead want a charge on the undertaking and assets of the company itself plus, probably, personal guarantees of the members or directors.

[65] See Evans, (1996) 11 J.I.B.F.L. 259; see also in relation to the Financial Collateral Directive and its implementation in the UK: Ho, [2011] J.I.B.L.R. 151; and *Cukurova Financial International Ltd v Alfa Telecom Turkey Ltd* [2009] 3 All E. R. 849 PC; *Mills v Sportsdirect.com* [2010] 2 B.C.L.C. 143.

[66] See para.13–2, above.

[67] 2006 Act s.670; for listed companies see also Listing Rules r.2.2.4.

have a first and paramount lien on shares, whether or not fully-paid, registered in the name of a person indebted or under any liability to the company". Since the decision of the House of Lords in *Bradford Banking Co v Briggs, Son and Co*[68] it appears to be accepted that the effect of such a provision is that:

(a) once a shareholder has incurred a debt or liability to the company, it has an equitable charge on the shares of that shareholder to secure payment which ranks in priority to later equitable interests and, it seems, to earlier ones of which the company had no notice when its lien became effective; and

(b) in determining whether the company had notice,[69] s.126 has no application; if the company knows of the earlier equitable interest (because, for example, a transfer of the shares has been lodged for registration even if that is refused) it cannot improve its own position to the detriment of the holder of that known equitable interest.

An interesting modern illustration is afforded by *Champagne Perrier-Jouet v Finch & Co.*[70] There the company's articles provided for a lien in the above terms. One of its shareholders[71] had been allowed to run up substantial debts to the company resulting from trading between him and the company and it had been agreed that he could repay by instalments. Another creditor of the shareholder subsequently obtained judgment against him and a charging order on the shares by way of equitable execution. It was held that the company's lien had become effective when the debts to it were incurred (even though they were not then due for repayment) and as this occurred before the company had notice of the charging order,[72] the company's lien had priority.[73]

As this case shows, an equitable charge on shares in a private company with articles conferring a lien on the company is likely to be an even more undesirable form of security than shares in private companies always are. It may, however, be the only security obtainable, for an attempt to obtain a legal charge will almost certainly be frustrated by the refusal of the directors to register the transfer. If, *faute de mieux*, it has to be accepted, notice should immediately be given to the company, making it clear that this is a notice which it cannot disregard in relation to any lien it may claim, and an attempt should be made to obtain information about the amount, if any, then owed to the company.

---

[68] *Bradford Banking Co v Briggs, Son and Co* (1886) 12 App.Cas.29, HL.

[69] It is not altogether clear why notice should be relevant. Since the company's lien is merely an equitable interest, its priority over another equitable interest should depend on the respective dates of their creation. But the decisions seem to assume that the company's lien will have priority over an equitable interest if the company has not received notice of the latter.

[70] *Champagne Perrier-Jouet v Finch & Co* [1982] 1 W.L.R. 1359.

[71] He had also been a director and it was argued that the debt he incurred to the company was a loan unlawful under what is now s.197 so that the company could not have a valid lien. It was held that it was not a loan; it would, however, today be "a quasi-loan" as defined in s.198 and as such unlawful if the company was a "relevant company" (e.g. a subsidiary of a public company) as defined in s.198.

[72] It also ante-dated the charging order but the court seems to have regarded the date of notice as decisive: see at s.1367B–E.

[73] It was also held that if the company enforced its lien by selling the shares it would have to comply with provisions in the articles conferring pre-emptive rights on the other members of the company.

TRANSFERS OF UNCERTIFICATED SHARES

We have seen in the previous section that certificated shares are transferred by **27–12** way of delivery of certain transfer documents to the company. The company being so notified of a transfer then registers the transferee's name on the shareholder register. When uncertificated shares are sold, the register is updated through electronic instructions.

For a transfer of uncertificated shares to be possible, both the seller and the buyer need to have access to the CREST system. There are three ways in which investors can access CREST. They can either hold an account with CREST themselves and acquire the hard- and software necessary to establish a safe connection with CREST. The cost involved in doing this makes this option unappealing to small scale private investors. An investor can also have his or her account with CREST operated by a broker who accesses the system or his or her behalf. This option is referred to as personal membership in the CREST documentation. With both options, the account is operated in the name of the investor who holds legal title to the shares. The third option for an investor is not to hold an account with CREST but to instruct a broker to act as a nominee on his or her behalf. In that case, the investor's name does not appear on the company's register. The nominee rather than the investor has an account with CREST and holds legal title to the shares. This form of holding shares has recently come under scrutiny (BIS Research Paper 261, *Exploring the Intermediated Shareholding Model*, January 2016).

When uncertificated shares are transferred, both the selling and the buying account holder need to instruct the system to carry out the transfer. When shares are sold through the Stock Exchange's electronic trading system, the sales information is transferred into the CREST system automatically and the selling and the buying account holder have an opportunity to verify the data before the transfer is effected.

Upon receiving transfer instructions, CREST verifies them, matches them and carries them out on the day specified by the parties. On that day CREST transfers the shares from the seller to the buyer and causes the purchase price to be paid over to the seller. The buyer becomes the legal owner of the shares when they are credited to his or her account. This is because, since 2001, CREST not only operates an electronic transfer system, but also keeps the shareholder register for all UK uncertificated shares.[74] Having updated the register, CREST needs to immediately inform the issuing company which keeps a record of all transfers relating to uncertificated shares.

In order to preserve the integrity of the shareholder register, the USR 2001 **27–13** stipulates that the Operator must not amend the shareholder register, except on completion of a trade in uncertificated units, unless ordered to do so by a court[75]

---

[74] USR 2001 reg.27(1) obliges the Operator upon settlement of the transfer to amend the operator register (unless the shares thereafter are to be held in certificated form). The Operator must also, immediately after making the change, notify the company: reg.27(7).

[75] USR 2001 reg.27(5)—for example, upon rectification of the register. Or unless it receives an issuer instruction to the effect that the shares have been converted into uncertificated form or there has been a compulsory acquisition of shares after a takeover (see para.28–69): reg.27(1).

or unless shares have been transferred by operation of law.[76] Equally, there are only limited circumstances in which the Operator may or must refuse to alter the operator register if it has received appropriate instructions from system members. Of course, the Regulations recognise that, in rare cases, events outside the system may impinge on the Operator's freedom of action in relation to the Operator register, just as they do on the issuer register kept by the company (for the uncertificated shares) or the share register, also kept by the company, for companies which have not entered the electronic transfer system. Thus, unless it is impracticable to stop it, CREST must not make a change in the Operator register which it actually knows is prohibited by an order of a court or by or under an enactment or involves a transfer to a deceased person.[77] There are further cases where CREST may refuse to make a change, for example, where the transfer is not to a legal or natural person or is to a minor.[78] Section 771(1)[79] applies in cases where CREST refuses to register a transfer,[80] but a two-month limit for notifying transferees of a failure to register hardly seems an appropriate one for an electronic system.

Title to uncertificated shares and the protection of transferees

27–14   The CREST system has reduced the time that lapses between trade and settlement. It has also caused transfers of uncertificated shares to be carried out almost simultaneously with payment of the purchase price. This has significantly reduced the transactional risk investors in shares are exposed to. The risk involved in shares transaction has, however, not been eliminated completely. In particular, the Regulations do not introduce a rule to the effect that entry on the Operator register confers title to the shares on the person registered. On the contrary, reg.24(1) provides, in the same way as the Act,[81] that "a register of members" is simply prima facie evidence of the matters directed or authorised to be stated in it, and "register of members" is defined to include both the issuer and Operator register of members.[82] In principle, therefore, a legal owner of shares may seek rectification of the Operator register if CREST removes his or her name from it without cause, and a court order restoring the legal owner to the register would be, as we have seen, something to which the Operator is obliged to respond.[83] In fact, it is doubtful whether the statutory provision under which the Regulations were made is wide enough to effect a general change in the rules as to the status of the register.

This is not to say, however, that the protection of transferees is provided in the same way or to the same extent under the Regulations in relation to uncertificated

---

[76] USR 2001 reg.27(6). On transfer by operation of law, see below, para.27–21.
[77] USR 2001 reg.27(2) and (3).
[78] USR 2001 reg.27(4).
[79] See above at para.27–7.
[80] USR 2001 reg.27(8) and (9).
[81] 2006 Act s.127; below, para.27–16. Naturally, s.768 (certificate to be evidence of title) has no application to uncertificated shares, though the section seems still to apply to certificated shares of participating companies.
[82] USR 2001 reg.3(1).
[83] USR 2001 reg.27(5).

shares as it is in relation to certificated shares. As we have seen, that protection in relation to the latter class of shares depends heavily upon the doctrine of estoppel by share certificate. Since, by definition, there is no share certificate in relation to uncertificated shares, the immediate position seems to be that the third party cannot be protected by this doctrine. Is this in principle a problem for the transferee of shares? The answer is that, if the matter were not dealt with in the Regulations, it would be. There are obvious risks that either an unauthorised person obtains access to the system or a person with authorised access uses the system in an unauthorised way, in both cases sending an instruction to transfer shares not belonging to him or her to an innocent third party. Can the former holder of the shares secure the restoration of his or her name to the Operator register to the detriment of the third party?

One technique for protecting the third party might be to transfer the doctrine of estoppel by share certificate to the entry on the register, but it is no accident that, in relation to certificated shares, the doctrine is based on the certificate, not on the register entry, even though both are available. This is because it is rare for a transferee to rely on the register entry before committing him- or herself to the transaction. This is true of both the Operator register and the issuer register, and so estoppel does not seem an effective protective device as against either the company or CREST.

In fact, the Regulations take an entirely different approach to the protection of transferees. If the unauthorised instruction in the situations above is sent in accordance with the rules of the Operator, the recipient of the instruction is entitled, subject to very few exceptions, to act on it and the person by whom or on whose behalf it was purportedly sent may not deny that it was sent with proper authority and contained accurate information.[84] Unlike at common law, where even careless conduct does not prevent the legal owner from asserting his or her title to the shares,[85] even a legal owner who was in no way to blame for the fraud may find that title to the shares has been lost. The transferor may have a remedy in such a case against the system participant whose equipment was used to send the unauthorised instructions.[86] There may also be a liability of the Operator in such a case, but only if the instruction was not sent from a system computer or the system computer it purported to be sent from. Thus, purely unauthorised activity by a broker's employee is not caught.[87] In any event, the liability is capped at £50,000 in respect of each instruction[88] and falls away entirely if the Operator identifies the person responsible, even if the transferor is not able to recover any compensation from that person.[89]

Thus, it seems right to conclude that transferees are somewhat better protected under the Regulations than under the common law doctrine of estoppel, since

27–15

---

[84] USR 2001 reg.35.

[85] See above, para.27–5.

[86] The Regulations do not create such a liability but do preserve it if it exists under the general law (USR reg.35(7)), for example, as between the transferor and his or her broker.

[87] See the definition of "forged dematerialised instruction" in USR reg.36(1). In effect, the Operator is liable for security defects in its system but not for unauthorised use of the system.

[88] USR reg.36(6).

[89] USR reg.36(4), unless the Operator has been guilty of fraud, wilful neglect or negligence (USR reg.36(9)).

even first transferees from the rogue are protected. However, that protection is provided at the expense of the transferor, rather than of the company, as at common law, and it is certainly arguable that company liability is the better principle because of the benefit companies obtain from effective markets.[90]

Because the transfer of legal ownership is so closely linked to payment, the rules on beneficial ownership have less practical relevance in relation to transfers of uncertificated shares.[91] When uncertificated securities are used as collateral, however, equity continues to play an important role. Moreover, the Financial Collerateral Directive,[92] which aims at reducing the formalities required to create a security interest over securities, has had significant impact on English law.[93]

THE REGISTER

27–16   We have already seen that companies issuing registered shares must keep a register containing the names of their members.[94] We shall now examine the rules governing the shareholder register more closely. The register of companies which issue only certificated shares is subject to the 2006 Act. Companies which issue only uncertificated shares or both certificated and uncertificated shares are subject to the Uncertificated Securities Regulation 2001 (USR 2001).[95]

Under both regimes, the register contains the name and address of each member and the date on which each person was registered as a member and the date on which any person ceased to be a member.[96] It also states the number and class[97] of shares held by each member and the amount paid up on each share.[98] In

---

[90] E. Micheler, fn.18, above.

[91] Equitable ownership arises, however, when uncertificated securities are transferred to a person who opts to have them converted in to certificated securities (USR 2001 reg.31(2)).

[92] Directive 2002/47/EC of the European Parliament and of the Council of 6 June 2002 on financial collateral arrangements [2002] O.J. L168/43 implemented in the UK by the Financial Collateral Arrangements Regulation (No.2) 2003 SI 2003/3226.

[93] Ho, [2011] J.I.B.L.R. 151; *Mills v Sportsdirect.com* [2010] EWHC 1072 (Ch); [2010] 2 B.C.L.C. 143; see also *Cukurova Financial International Ltd v Alfa Telecom Turkey Ltd* [2009] 3 All E.R. 849 PC.

[94] 2006 Act s.113; The Small Business, Enterprise and Employment Act 2015 (2015 c. 26) s.94 and Sch.5 amend the Companies Act 2006 to give private companies the option of keeping the register of members on the register kept by the registrar instead of keeping it on their own register. This will come into force at a date to be appointed (SBEE Act 2015 s.164(1)). Companies House's website contains information suggesting that this will be in June 2016 (*https://www.gov.uk/government/news/the-small-business-enterprise-and-employment-bill-is-coming* [Accessed 26 May 2016].

[95] The USR 2001 (SI 2001/3755) was introduced to bring forward the point in time at which an investor acquires legal title to uncertificated shares from the moment at which the company amends the shareholder register to the moment at which the Operator of the uncertificated transfer system credits the shares to the buyer's securities account (HM Treasury, *Modernising Securities Settlement*, 2001; Bank of England, *Securities Settlement Priorities Review*, September 1998 and March 1998). This was done by entrusting the Operator of the uncertificated transfer system with the maintenance of the shareholder register for uncertificated shares.

[96] 2006 Act s.113; USR 2001 Sch.4 paras 2(1), (2) and 4(1).

[97] In the case of a company without a share capital but with different classes of membership the register has to state the class to which each member belongs (s.113(3); USR 2001 Sch.4 para.2(2)). This fills the lacuna revealed in *Re Performing Right Society Ltd* [1978] 1 W.L.R. 1197.

[98] 2006 Act s.113(3); USR 2001 Sch.4 paras 2(2), (3), 4(1) and 5(1). In the case of the amount paid up, this appears only on the issuer's record.

the case of a private company there must also be noted on the register the fact and the date of the company becoming, or ceasing to be a single member company.[99]

The register of members of both certificated and uncertificated shares constitutes prima facie evidence of any matters which are by the respective regulatory regime directed or authorised to be inserted in it.[100]

In order to become a member or shareholder of a company an investor has to have his or her name entered on that shareholder register. A buyer normally acquires legal title to shares at the point in time at which his or her name is entered on the shareholder register.[101] This rule applies irrespective of whether shares are held in the certificated or in the uncertificated form.

Certificated and uncertificated shares differ in terms of who maintains the shareholder register. The register for certificated shares is maintained by the company itself or by a registrar on behalf of the company. The register for uncertificated shares is maintained by the Operator of the uncertificated transfer system, CREST. The register of companies which issue certificated shares and uncertificated shares consists of two parts. Entries relating to certificated shares are maintained by the company. They are referred to as the "issuer register of members". Entries relating to uncertificated shares are maintained by the Operator of the uncertificated transfer system, and are referred to as "Operator register of members". The company maintains a "record" relating to uncertificated shares. This record does not constitute a shareholder register. It must be regularly reconciled with the Operator register of members.[102] In relation to uncertificated shares, the Operator register prevails over the record kept by the company.[103] The record does not provide for prima facie evidence. It enables the company to inform those inspecting the register about entries that have been made on the register maintained by CREST.

27–17

The issuer register may be kept at the company's registered office or at a place specified in regulations under s.1136.[104] If kept otherwise than at the company's registered office, notice must be given to Companies House (and thus to the public) of the place where it is kept and of any change of that place.[105]

---

[99] s2006 Act s.123(2); USR 2001 Sch.4 para.3. It is rather unlikely that a company issuing uncertificated shares would fall into the state of having only one member, but it might do if it became part of a group of companies.

[100] 2006 Act s.127; USR 2001 reg.24(1).

[101] 2006 Act s.112; *J Sainsbury Plc v O'Connor (Inspector of Taxes)* [1991] 1 W.L.R. 963 at 977 CA; *Re Rose* [1952] Ch. 499 at 518–519 CA; *Kaye v Zeital* [2010] 2 B.C.L.C. 1 at [40].

[102] USR 2001 reg.23 and Sch.4 para.5(2).

[103] USR 2001 reg.24(2).

[104] Companies (Company Records) Regulations 2008 (SI 2008/3006).

[105] 2006 Act s.114(2); USR 2001 Sch.4 para.6(3) and (4). The place must be in England or Wales if the company is registered in England and Wales or in Scotland if it is registered in Scotland. But if the company carries on business in one of the countries specified in s.129(2) it may cause keep an "overseas branch register" in that country (s.129(2)). This, in effect, is a register of shareholders resident in that country, a duplicate of which will also be maintained with the principal register (s.132). This provision is not affected by the Uncertificated Securities Regulations (USR 2001 Sch.4 paras 2(7) and 4(4)).

If a company has more than 50 members then, unless the register is kept in such a form as to constitute an index of names of members, such an index must be kept at the same place as the register.[106]

27–18 The shareholder register and the index are available for public inspection. Any member of the company may inspect the register free of charge.[107] Any other person may inspect the register on payment of such fee as may be prescribed.[108] In the case of uncertificated shares, the inspection right is granted against the record held by the company rather than against the Operator register itself.[109] This exposes the searcher to the risk that the company's record will not accurately reflect the Operator register. Provided the company regularly reconciles its record with the Operator register, except insofar as matters outside its control prevent such reconciliation, the company is not liable for discrepancies between the record and the register.[110]

The right to inspect the register is a legitimate help to a takeover bidder and makes it possible for members to communicate with each other. It also has, in the past, been abused by traders who advertised their wares by unsolicited mail or telephone calls and who were able to obtain more cheaply than in any other way a list of potential victims by buying a copy of the shareholder register of, say, British Telecom or British Gas. With a view to putting an end to this illegitimate use of the shareholder register, the 2006 Act revised the right to inspect the register. The right to inspect the register may now be denied by the Court if it is satisfied that the request was not sought for a proper purpose.[111]

Under s.358 of the 1985 Act a company had the power to close the shareholder register for any time or times not exceeding in total 30 days in any year. The provision enabled companies to draw up a list of those who are entitled to attend the annual general meeting or to receive dividends. The 2006 Act does not contain a power to that effect.

Under the USR 2001, companies participating in CREST are entitled to specify a time not more than 48 hours before a general meeting by which a person must have been entered on the register in order to have the right to attend and vote at the meeting and may similarly choose a day not more than 21 days before notices of a meeting are sent out for the purposes of determining who is entitled to receive the notice.[112] This way of proceeding enables transfers to continue in the period before the meeting (thus reducing the risk to transferees) without landing the company in the position of having to deal with a constantly changing body of shareholders.

---

[106] 2006 Act s.115.

[107] 2006 Act s.116.

[108] 2006 Act s.116.

[109] USR 2001 Sch.4 para.9.

[110] USR 2001 Sch.4 para.5(3).

[111] 2006 Act s.117; For examples of this see: *Burry & Knight Ltd v Knight* [2014] EWCA Civ 604; [2014] 1 W.L.R. 4046 where it was held that the communication with fellow shareholders about the manner in which company shares are proposed to be valued was a proper purpose, but the communication to fellow shareholders of unsubstantiated allegations about directors' remuneration was not. See also *Burberry Group Plc v Fox-Davies* [2015] EWHC 222 (Ch) where an application of a tracing agent attempting to find "lost" shareholders was refused because the real motive was to extract a fee from these shareholders and that was not a proper purpose.

[112] USR 2001 reg.40.

Rectification

The register is "prima facie evidence of any matters which are by this Act **27–19** directed or authorised to be inserted in it".[113] It is not, however, conclusive evidence for, as we have seen, membership is dependent both on agreement to become a member and entry in the register, and it may be that other requirements in the company's articles have to be met. If they are not, it seems that the registered person does not become a member.[114] In any event, if the entry does not truly reflect the agreement or other requirements, the register ought to be rectified. Hence s.125 provides a summary remedy whereby:

> "(a)   the name of any person is without sufficient cause entered in or omitted from a company's register of members, or
>
> (b)   default is made or unnecessary delay takes place in entering on the register the fact of any person having ceased to be a member, the person aggrieved or any member of the company, or the company may apply to the court for rectification of the register."[115]

This wording is defective because it ignores the fact that the register is not just a register of members but also a register of shareholdings and that a likely error is in the amount of a member's shareholding. However, common sense has prevailed and in *Re Transatlantic Life Assurance*[116] Slade J felt able to hold that "the wording is wide enough in its terms to empower the court to order the deletion of some only of a registered shareholder's shares".[117] It must follow that it is similarly empowered to order an addition to the registered holding.

On an application the court may decide any question relating to the title of any person who is a party to the application whether the question arises between members or alleged members,[118] or between members or alleged members on the one hand and the company on the other hand,[119] and may decide "any question necessary or expedient to be decided for rectification...".[120] A rectification may

---

[113] 2006 Act s.127; USR 2001 reg.24. In case of conflict between the issuer and Operator registers, the latter prevails (USR 2001 reg.24(2)). The rule applies to the Operator register provided the transfer has occurred in accordance with the Regulations.

[114] *POW Services Ltd v Clare* [1995] 2 B.C.L.C. 435; *Domoney v Godinho* [2004] 2 B.C.L.C. 15. The issue of restrictions in the articles is not one which arises in relation to listed companies or companies whose shares are held in uncertificated form, since the Listing Rules and the rules of CREST require such shares to be freely transferable.

[115] 2006 Act s.125(1). This power operates equally in relation to shares held in uncertificated form (USR 2001 reg.25(2)(b)).

[116] *Re Transatlantic Life Assurance* [1980] 1 W.L.R. 79. The case arose because the allotment of some shares was void because Exchange Control permission had not been obtained as at that time was necessary. See also *Re Cleveland Trust Plc* [1991] B.C.L.C. 424.

[117] *Re Transatlantic Life Assurance* [1980] 1 W.L.R. 79 at 84F–G.

[118] e.g. when A and B are disputing which of them should be the registered holder.

[119] e.g. when there is a dispute between the company and A or B on whether either should be.

[120] 2006 Act s.125(3). Despite this wide wording, it has been held the summary procedure of CA 1985 s.359 should not be used where there was an unresolved and substantial dispute as to the entitlemet to shares (*Nilon Ltd v Royal Westminster Investment SA* [2015] UKPC 2 rejecting the view expressed by the Court of Appeal in *Re Hoicrest Ltd* [2000] 1 B.C.L.C. 194 CA).

also be carried out with retrospective effect.[121] Moreover, the court may order payment by the company of "damages sustained by any party aggrieved".[122]

27–20 There is some uncertainty as to the extent to which the company can rectify the register without an application to the court. But in practice here again commonsense prevails. Sections 113, 115 and 122 envisage, and indeed demand, alterations without which the register could not be kept up-to-date and fulfil its purpose, and although there is no express provision for alterations of members' addresses that takes place all the time. Indeed it would be quite absurd if companies could not correct any mistake if all interested parties agree.

The USR 2001 also contemplate that a company may rectify the issuer register other than by order of a court, but, in order to preserve the integrity of the electronic transfer system, require the company in such a case to have the consent of the Operator of the system if the change would involve rectification of the Operator register. Equally, the Operator may rectify the Operator register, but must inform the issuer and the system-members concerned immediately when the change is made.[123]

It must be emphasised, however, that although the register provides prima facie evidence of who its members are and what their shareholdings are, it provides no evidence at all, either to the company or anyone else, of who the beneficial owners of the shares are.[124]

TRANSMISSION OF SHARES BY OPERATION OF LAW

27–21 The Act[125] recognises that shares may be transmitted by operation of law and that, when this occurs, the prohibition on registering unless a proper instrument of transfer has been delivered does not apply.[126] The principal examples of this are when a registered shareholder dies or becomes bankrupt. As regards the death of a shareholder, the Act further provides that a transfer by the deceased's personal representative, even if he is not a member of the company, is as valid as if he had been.[127] The company is bound to accept probate or letters of administration granted in any part of the UK as sufficient evidence of the personal representative's entitlement.[128] However, he or she does not become a

---

[121] *R I Fit Global Ltd* [2013] EWHC 2090 (Ch); [2014] 2 B.C.L.C. 116.

[122] 2006 Act s.125(2). "Compensation" would be a better word than "damages" and "party aggrieved" is an expression which courts have constantly criticised, but apparently without convincing Parliamentary Counsel responsible for drafting Government Bills.

[123] USR 2001 reg.25.

[124] For the rules dealing with the disclosure of beneficial interests, see paras 26–14 to 26–22, above.

[125] And see the Companies (Model Articles) Regulations 2008 Sch.1 reg.27.

[126] 2006 Act s.773; for uncertificated shares see USR reg.27(6).

[127] 2006 Act s.773.

[128] 2006 Act s.774. If it does so without such production of the grant it may become liable for any tax payable as a result of the transmission (*NY Breweries Co v Attorney-General* [1899] A.C. 62 HL) but in the case of small estates, companies may be prepared to dispense with production of a grant if the Revenue confirms that nothing is payable. If the deceased was one of a number of jointly registered members, the company, on production of a death certificate, will have to recognise that he has ceased to be a member and shareholder and that the others remain such. But the whole beneficial interest in the shares will not pass to them unless they and the deceased were beneficial owners entitled jointly rather than in common.

member unless he or she elects to apply to be registered and is registered as a member. In the meantime, the effect is that he has the "same rights as the holder had".[129]

> "But transmittees do not have the right to attend or vote at a general meeting, or agree to a proposed written resolution, in respect of shares to which they are entitled by reason of the holder's death or bankruptcy or otherwise unless they become the holders of those shares."[130]

If the shares are those of a listed company, this anomalous position can be ended rapidly because, unless the shares are not fully paid, there will not be any restrictions on transferability and the personal representative will either obtain registration of him- or herself or execute a transfer to a purchaser or to the beneficiaries. In relation to a private company, however, it may continue indefinitely and prove detrimental to the personal representative, the deceased's estate and, sometimes, the company. The personal representative may suffer because it may not be possible for him fully to wind up the estate and to obtain a discharge from his fiduciary responsibilities. The estate may suffer because it may be impossible for the personal representative to sell the shares at their true value, especially if any attempt to dispose of them would trigger rights of pre-emption or first refusal.[131] The company may suffer because, as we have seen,[132] unless such rights have been most carefully drafted, they will not come into operation so long as no action regarding registration is taken by the personal representative. In order to assist personal representatives, the statute has extended the remedies afforded to members so that they can be invoked by personal representatives of members.[133] It is also now obligatory for the company to give reasons explaining the refusal to register a transferee.[134]

The position on bankruptcy of an individual shareholder[135] is broadly similar. His rights to the shares automatically vest in the trustee in bankruptcy as part of his estate.[136] But, as in the case of a personal representative, until he elects to become registered and is so registered, he will not become a member of the company entitled to attend meetings and to vote. In contrast, however, with the position on the death of a member, the bankrupt will remain a member and be entitled to attend and vote—though he will have to do so in accordance with the directions of the trustee. As in the case of personal representatives, the company's articles will probably provide that any restrictions on transferability apply on any

---

[129] The Companies (Model Articles) Regulations 2008 Sch.1 reg.27(2).

[130] The Companies (Model Articles) Regulations 2008 Sch.1 reg.27(3).

[131] If there are any restrictions on transfers all the articles relating to restriction on transfers apply both to a notice that the personal representative wishes to be registered and to a transfer from him (The Companies (Model Articles) Regulations 2008 Sch.1 reg.28(3)).

[132] See above, para.27–7.

[133] See, in particular, s.994(2) which makes it possible for personal representatives to invoke the "unfairly prejudicial" remedy which might well be effective if it could be shown that the directors were exercising their powers to refuse transfers in order to enable themselves or the company to acquire the shares of deceased members at an unfair price: see Ch.20, above.

[134] 2006 Act s.771.

[135] On winding up of a corporate shareholder there is no transmission of the company's property; it remains vested in the company but most of the directors' powers to manage it pass to the liquidator.

[136] Insolvency Act 1986 ss.283(1) and 306. But not if the shareholder held his shares as a trustee for another person: ibid., s.283(3)(a).

application to be registered and to any transfer by him or her[137] and these restrictions may handicap the trustee in obtaining the best price on a sale of the shares, particularly if the articles confer pre-emption rights.[138] If a personal representative or trustee in bankruptcy elects to be registered, and is, he becomes personally liable for any amounts unpaid on the shares and not merely representationally liable to the extent of the estate. Trustees in bankruptcy, but not personal representatives, may disclaim onerous property,[139] which the shares might be if they were partly paid or subject to an effective company lien.

---

[137] The Companies (Model Articles) Regulations 2008 Sch.1 reg.28.

[138] In *Borland's Trustee v Steel Bros* [1901] 1 Ch. 279, a provision in the articles that in the event of a shareholder's bankruptcy (or death) his shares should be offered to a named person at a particular price was held to be effective and not obnoxious to the bankruptcy laws; for this see most recently *Belmont Park Investment Pty Ltd v BNY Corporate Trustee Services and Lehman Brothers Special Financing Inc* [2012] 1 All E.R. 505 SC.

[139] Insolvency Act 1986 s.315. Disclaimer puts an end to the interest of the bankrupt and his estate and discharges the trustee from any liability: ibid., s.315(3).

CHAPTER 28

TAKEOVERS

INTRODUCTION

A takeover bid consists of an offer from A (an acquirer—usually another **28–1**
company) made generally to the shareholders of T Co (the "target" company) to
acquire their shares for a consideration which may be cash or securities of the
offeror or a mixture of both. The legal mechanism at the heart of the bid is thus a
contractual transfer of shares, but the rules on transfers of shares, discussed in the
previous chapter, although relevant, do not capture the significance of the
takeover bid. A takeover offer has the aim not simply of a transfer of shares but a
shift in the control of the T Co—or at least a consolidation of control. Previously,
T Co may have been under the control of its board (for example, where its
shareholdings were widely dispersed) or of one or a few shareholders with a
controlling block of shares. After a successful bid (i.e. one where all or most of
the T Co's shareholders accept A's offer) T Co will be controlled by A. Depending
upon who previously had control of the company, that change of control will
therefore be a matter of some moment to the board of T Co (who will have lost

control) or the minority shareholders[1] of T Co (who will be faced with a new controller, unless they themselves have accepted a cash offer). The change of control may also affect other stakeholders in the company (for example, employees) because bidders do not normally expend large resources to obtain control of companies simply to run them in the same way as previously. The change of control of T Co may thus have wide ramifications for those who have interests in the businesses run by T Co.

This little description reveals the two main issues which takeover regulation has to address. First, should it seek to prevent the management of the target company from taking any steps to discourage a potential bidder from putting an offer to its shareholders or from discouraging those shareholders from accepting it? In other words, is the takeover bid to be analysed as a transaction purely between bidder and target company shareholders or as one in the outcome of which the management of the target company also has a legitimate self-interest which it may take steps to defend? As we shall see, the rules in the UK have traditionally been based on the former view (no frustration of the bid by the target management). This rule is expressed in a strong form once a bid is imminent, and somewhat less strongly and more diffusely in relation to defensive action taken by target management in advance of any specific offer. This policy gives the acquirer or offeror a free run at the target shareholders and prevents the board from using its management powers so as to frustrate the bid. It is a policy which can be justified on the grounds that it supports the principle of free transferability of the shares of listed companies and, more importantly, on the grounds that it is a significant element in the British system for disciplining management and reducing the agency costs of dispersed shareholders. A board, it is argued, which is at risk of an unwelcome takeover bid will be sure to promote the interests of its shareholders, in order to decrease the chances of a bid being made (because the share price will be high) and increase the chances that those shareholders will reject an offer if one is made (because they think they will be at least as well off with the current management). In this way, the accountability of the board to the shareholders is promoted by the threat of takeovers, especially "hostile" ones, i.e. offers not recommended by the target board to its shareholders but rather made over the heads of the incumbent management to the shareholders.[2]

The second major issue for takeover regulation concerns the steps to be taken to protect non-controlling shareholders if a bid is launched. Obviously, the transfer of shares could be left, like any other commercial transaction, to be regulated by the ordinary law of contract. In the case of controlling shareholders, who are well-placed to take care of themselves, this is probably sensible policy. However, in the typical case in the UK, where the shareholdings in the target are dispersed, the shareholders may lack information needed to evaluate the offer which has been made to them (especially information about the likely benefits of

---

[1] Where T Co was previously controlled by one or more large shareholders, they too will have lost control to A, but that is the result of a voluntary transaction between them and A. In so far as issues arise on this aspect of the takeover they can probably be resolved by the law of contract.

[2] This is a crucial and highly controversial proposition. For a balanced assessment see J. Coffee Jr, "Regulating the Market for Corporate Control" (1984) 84 *Columbia Law Review* 1145. See also P. Davies, K.J. Hopt and G. Ringe "Control Transactions" in R. Kraakman et al. (eds), *The Anatomy of Corporate Law*, 3rd edn (Oxford: OUP, 2016).

the takeover to the acquirer). Moreover, if left to its own devices, the offeror may be able to put pressure in various ways on the shareholders of the target company to accept the bid, often by proposing to treat some groups of target shareholders more favourably than others. To counter these risks we shall see that takeover regulation puts considerable emphasis on two policies: disclosure of information (by both bidder and target) to the shareholders of the target, and equality of treatment of the target shareholders. Equality means that some shareholders of the target cannot be offered a better deal than is available generally. As we shall see below,[3] this second policy is taken even to the point of requiring a bid to be launched where an offeror company has acquired in the market or by private treaty a sufficient shareholding in the target to give it control. The "mandatory bid" permits non-controlling shareholders to exit the company at a fair price upon a change of control, even though the bidder would prefer not to acquire any further shares.

Thus, the two central tenets of the British regulation of takeovers are that the shareholders alone decide on the fate of the offer and equality of treatment of shareholders. The regulation is both orthodox and rigorous in putting the target shareholders centre stage, and in this respect it differs from takeover regulation in both the US and some, though not all, continental European countries (for example, Germany). However, these are not the only objectives of takeover regulation. A takeover offer is disruptive of the normal running of the target company's business and it is therefore politic that this period of disruption should be minimised by the setting of a firm timetable for the bid. Thus, a bidder which has indicated it might make a bid is required to do so or to withdraw within a relatively short period ("put up or shut up"); the offer, if made, remains open only for fixed period; and a bidder whose offer fails is not permitted immediately to come back with another bid. Thus, the bid is a relatively quick and self-contained event and is not capable of infinite repetition.

    We shall look at these and other aspects of the substantive rules for the regulation of takeover bids below, but we begin by examining the rather special machinery which exists in the UK for the creation and application of those rules.

28–2

---

[3] Below, para.28–41.

THE TAKEOVER CODE AND PANEL

28–3   Since the takeover does not require a corporate decision on the part of the target company,[4] there is no obvious act of the target upon which company law can fasten for the purposes of regulating the transaction.[5] For this reason, most European countries treat takeover regulation as part of their securities laws, i.e. they rightly take the transfer of the shares as the central act. The UK follows this pattern, but it developed takeover regulation long before statutory regulation of the securities markets was established, and so the regulation of takeovers took initially a quasi self-regulatory approach. In the 1950s and 1960s, bidders took full advantage of the absence of regulation.[6] Alarmed by what was happening,[7] a City working party published in 1959 a modest set of "Queensberry Rules" entitled *Notes on Amalgamation of British Businesses*, which was followed in 1968 by a more elaborate *City Code on Takeovers and Mergers* and the establishment of a Panel on Takeovers and Mergers to administer and enforce it. It is this Code, in its various editions, which has since constituted the main body of rules relating to takeovers, with the Companies Act and the Financial Services and Markets Act, and rules and regulations made thereunder, performing an accessory role. However, the element of self-regulation in this arrangement could easily be overestimated. Although the Panel had no statutory authority, its success as a regulator depended largely on the recognition on the part of those routinely involved in advising on takeovers (mainly investment banks and large law firms) that to flout its authority would probably induce Parliament to replace the Code and Panel with something they liked even less.

---

[4] Sometimes the approval of the *offeror* company's shareholders is required under the Listing Rules if the proposed transaction is a very large one: above, at para.14–20. However, the relationship between acquirer and its shareholders is not dealt with by takeover regulation in the UK, though it has sometimes been suggested that it should be. Rather, that relationship is left to the general rules concerning shareholder approval of transactions, notably the "significant transactions" requirements of the Listing Rules. Other than the Listing Rules, general company law, notably the rules on directors' duties, is rather weak: it would be a bold court which concluded that an offeror board's decision to launch a takeover offer constituted a breach of duty. See A. Kouloridas, *The Law and Economics of Takeovers: An Acquirer's Perspective* (Oxford: Hart, 2008).

[5] As we shall see below, where the takeover is effected by means of a scheme of arrangement (Ch.29), a corporate decision of the target, which company law can regulate, is required, but the scheme is in practice available only where acquirer and target board are in agreement on the desirability of the takeover, so that at least the first main issue in takeover regulation (see para.28–1) will not be present.

[6] A. Johnston, *The City Take-over Code* (Oxford: OUP, 1980), Chs 1–4.

[7] Which, in some cases, was horrendous, with rival bidders badgering each of the target's shareholders by night and day telephone calls offering him a special price because, so it was falsely alleged, only his holding was needed to bring that bidder's acceptances to over 50 per cent. In one case the result was that the bidder who eventually succeeded paid prices ranging from £2 to £15 per share.

The Panel and its methods of operation

The status and composition of the Panel

In any event, discussion of the self-regulatory status of the Panel is now rather beside the point. The regulation of takeovers is a further area where EU Law has come to be a significant source of the relevant rules. After a very long gestation period the EU eventually adopted Directive 2004/25/EC on takeover bids (hereafter the "takeover directive").[8] One of the requirements of the Directive is that Member States should "designate the authority or authorities competent to supervise bids" (art.4(1)), so that the UK was required to place the takeover rules on some sort of a statutory footing. In fact, the proposed change in the legal status of the Panel was the basis for the UK Government's initial opposition to the Directive, despite the fact that the Directive's substantive content was heavily influenced by the City Code.[9] During the EU legislative process changes were made in the draft Directive so as to allay, as far as possible, the Government's fears that the Panel's flexible way of working would be undermined by the statutory basis required by the Directive. The Government's goal when implementing the Directive was to produce a situation in which the Panel could carry on in practice much as before, even though now with its powers derived from statute. Article 4 of the Directive makes it clear, which might otherwise be in doubt, that the designated authorities may be "private bodies recognised by national law".[10] Thus, s.942 of the Companies Act 2006 simply confers certain statutory powers upon the Panel but does not seek to regulate the constitution of the Panel, in contrast to the way in which, for example, the constitution of the FCA is regulated by FSMA 2000. The composition of the Panel is to be found, not in legislation, but in the Code itself.[11] It consists of a Chairman and up to three Deputy Chairmen appointed by the Panel itself, up to a further 20 members appointed by the Panel, and individuals appointed by representative bodies of

28–4

---

[8] For an excellent early analysis of the impact of the Directive on the UK see J. Rickford, "The Emerging European Takeover Law from a British Perspective" [2004] E.B.L.R. 1379.

[9] Reflecting the fact that a very high proportion of the EU's total of takeover bids (especially "hostile" ones) takes place in the UK.

[10] The competent authority may be, of course, a public body of a more traditional kind. The Government did toy, probably not very seriously, with the idea of giving takeover regulation to the FCA, or alternatively keeping the Panel on a non-statutory basis but treating breaches of the Code as breaches of the FCA's rules, but rejected both ideas. See DTI, *Company Law Implementation of the European Directive on Takeover Bids: A Consultation Document* (January 2005, URN 05/11) paras 2.7 and 2.17—hereafter "DTI Consultation Document". That idea does demonstrate, however, that the Government was not obliged to give these functions to the Panel nor is it obliged to leave them there, should the Panel act in a way the Government finds unacceptable.

[11] See *The Takeover Code*, 11th edn, 2013, *Introduction*, A8 (hereafter the "Code"). This perhaps illustrates better than anything the self-created nature of the Panel, since it is circular for the Code, which is the responsibility of the Panel, to determine the composition of the body which creates the Code. Under earlier editions of the Code the chair and two deputies of the Panel were appointed by the Governor of the Bank of England, which reflects the historical reality of how the self-regulatory process was initiated, but he no longer has a formal role in the Panel's composition. Sections 957–959 also maintain the Panel's present funding arrangements. It is not supported out of taxation, but by fees for its services and a levy on share transactions, but of course a statutory body could be funded in a similar manner, as the FCA is.

those involved in takeovers, such as the Association of British Insurers, the National Association of Pension Funds, the Association of Investment Companies and other investor groups, the British Bankers' Association, the Institute of Chartered Accountants and the Confederation of British Industry. The Panel appointees come from similar backgrounds as those of the representative appointees, though they include a former general secretary of a large trade union.

Internal appeals

28–5 However, the Panel's and the Government's central concern, when implementing the Directive, was not with the formal status of the Panel but with preserving in the statutory framework its way of working, in particular its freedom to give flexible and speedy binding rulings in the course of the bid, which could not be easily challenged in litigation before the ordinary courts. A particular concern was to discourage "tactical litigation", i.e. litigation designed to disrupt the bid timetable or to delay the operation of a decision of the Panel which is against the interests of a particular party, but at the same time providing a method of appeal for those with a genuine grievance. Before the implementation of the Directive, this result was achieved through a system of speedy appeal within the Panel itself, coupled with the courts' adoption of a limited and after-the-event approach to judicial review of the Panel's decisions. Article 4(6) of the Directive does its best to preserve the viability of this system by providing that:

> "this Directive shall not affect the power of the Member States to designate judicial or other authorities responsible for dealing with disputes and for deciding on irregularities committed in the course of bids or the power of Member States to regulate whether and under which circumstances parties to a bid are entitled to bring administrative or judicial proceedings. In particular, this Directive shall not affect the power which courts may have in a Member State to decline to hear legal proceedings and to decide whether or not such proceedings affect the outcome of a bid."

Thus fortified, the relevant government department decided to maintain the Panel appeal system rather than seek to devise a new system.[12] The Panel Executive (i.e. its full-time employees, some of whom are seconded from investment banks, law firms, accountancy firms and similar bodies) gives rulings on the Code in the course of a bid, either on its own initiative or at the request of one or more parties to the bid.[13] Rulings of the Executive may be referred to the Panel's Hearing Committee (or the Executive may refer a matter to the Hearing Committee itself), and disciplinary proceedings for breach of the Code or a ruling may be initiated before the Hearing Committee by the Executive. The Executive may require any appeal to the Hearing Committee to be lodged within a specific

---

[12] DTI Consultation Document, paras 2.35–36. The system is set out in the Code, *Introduction*, §§6–8.

[13] Delegation by the Panel of functions to officers or members of staff is specifically provided for by s.942(3)(b). In practice, the Panel's efficiency depends upon the parties or their advisers bringing issues to the Panel at an early stage and disclosing full information. The obligation to do so is laid down in the *Introduction* to the Code, paras 6(b) and 9(a). See Panel Statement 2015/15, *Asia Resource Minerals plc (Formerly Bumi plc)*.

period, possibly a period as short as a few hours. The Hearing Committee normally sits in private and operates informally, but does issue public statements of its rulings.

A party to the hearing before the Hearing Committee may appeal to the Takeover Appeal Board, normally within two business days of receipt in writing of the ruling of the Hearing Committee. The Board was formerly known as the "Appeal Committee" and the change of name indicates that the Board is now an organisation independent of the Panel.[14] This is a rather wider right of appeal than existed previously when many appeals required leave of the Appeal Board. The Appeal Board is an independent body, whose chairman and deputy chairman, appointed by the Master of the Rolls, will usually have held high judicial office[15] and whose other members (normally four) are experienced in takeovers. The Appeal Board operates in a similar way to the Hearing Committee, including the publication of its decision. It may confirm, vary, set aside or replace the ruling of the Hearing Committee. This was, broadly, the system in operation before the Act came into force and s.951 requires that system to be maintained. The section requires, as was the previous practice, that a Panel member who is or has been a member of its Code Committee (responsible for drawing up the Code) may not be a member of the Hearing Committee or Appeal Board. The separation of the Code Committee from the committees involved in administering the Code and the organisational separation of the Appeal Board were responses to the Human Rights Act 1998.[16]

Judicial review

The second limb of the pre-Directive system for dealing with tactical litigation **28–6** consisted of restraint by the courts in exercising their powers of judicial review. Article 4(6) (above) of the Directive permits the British courts to maintain their restraint, but, of course, does not require it. The Act does not seek explicitly to regulate the process of judicial review of the Panel by the courts, probably wisely, and so the matter is left to the domestic courts themselves. It was perhaps surprising that the pre-Directive Panel, as a body which, as it was put in *R. v Panel on Take-overs and Mergers, Ex p. Datafin Ltd*,[17] performed its functions "without visible means of legal support", was made subject to judicial review at all. However, that was the step taken in the *Datafin* case on the grounds that the Panel, although then a private body, was performing a public function. Its susceptibility to judicial review is now beyond doubt. Having taken that decision of principle, the then Master of the Rolls set out his "expectations" as to how judicial review of the Panel would operate, emphasising its limitations.

---

[14] With its own website: *http://www.thetakeoverappealboard.org.uk/* [Accessed 26 April 2016]. For an instructive example of its operating methods see Takeover Appeal Board, *Principle Investment Capital Trust Plc*, decision 2010/1.

[15] Currently Lord Collins of Mapesbury as chairman and Sir John Mummery as deputy chairman.

[16] The Takeover Panel, *Report on the Year Ended March 31, 2001*, pp.8–9.

[17] *R. v Panel on Take-overs and Mergers, Ex p. Datafin Ltd* [1987] Q.B. 815 CA. See Cane, "Self Regulation and Judicial Review" [1987] C.J.Q. 324. See also *R. v Takeover Panel, Ex p. Guinness Plc* [1990] 1 Q.B. 146 CA.

First, it was expected that the Panel would require obedience to its rulings and the parties would abide by them, even if one of them had signalled it was intending to seek judicial review. Secondly, the grounds for review would be limited: an argument that the Panel had propounded rules which were ultra vires was "a somewhat unlikely eventuality"; the Panel in its interpretation of its rules must be given "considerable latitude"; attacks on the Panel's dispensing powers would be successful only in "wholly exceptional circumstances"; and the Panel's exercise of its disciplinary powers would not be open to attack "in the absence of any credible allegation of lack of bona fides". Thirdly, and most importantly, the expectation was that the courts would only intervene after the bid was concluded ("the relationship between the panel and the court [would] be historic rather than contemporaneous"), perhaps to relieve individuals of disciplinary sanctions, perhaps to deliver a declaratory judgment to guide the Panel in the future. Thus, a party involved in a bid (most obviously the board of the target company) was given little incentive to seek judicial review during the offer in order to secure a tactical advantage (most obviously delay, during which the target's defences could be better organised), but the Panel was not given an entirely free hand in interpreting the Code or its own jurisdiction.

It seems likely that this attitude of deference on the part of the courts to the Panel (and especially the Takeover Appeal Board) will continue, despite the statutory framework within which the Panel is now placed. The statute does one or two things to encourage the courts in that direction. The Panel is given power to "do anything that it considers necessary or expedient for the purpose of, or in connection with, its functions", thus protecting the Panel's vires in its new statutory guise; it is given a wide rule-making power; it is explicitly given a dispensing power; and it is explicitly given the power to make rulings and give directions.[18] Overall, the Government's policy seems to have been to fit the requirements of the Directive to the existing practice of the Panel, rather than vice versa.[19]

Nevertheless, the fact of putting the Panel on a statutory footing potentially opens up avenues of civil litigation not previously available. The Act seeks to block off these paths to the courts. This seems to be permitted by the further sentence in art.4(6) of the Directive that "this Directive shall not affect the power of the Member States to determine the legal position concerning the liability of supervisory authorities or concerning litigation between the parties to a bid". Consequently, no action for breach of statutory duty lies in respect of contravention of a requirement imposed by or under the Panel's rules or a requirement imposed by the Panel to produce information or documents.[20] Contravention of a rule-based requirement does not render the transaction in which it occurs void or unenforceable or affect the validity "of any other thing" (unless the rules so provide).[21] However, civil litigation between the parties is not

---

[18] See ss.942(2), 943, 944(1) and 945.

[19] "It is intended that the implementing legislation should neither undermine nor be inconsistent with the principles established in the Datafin case." (DTI Consultation Document, para.2.38.)

[20] 2006 Act s.956(1). The definitions of "rule-based requirement" and "disclosure requirement" are given in s.955(4), the latter referring to the Panel's disclosure powers in s.947, which are discussed below.

[21] 2006 Act s.956(2).

entirely excluded by these provisions. A claim based on fraudulent or negligent misstatement, for example, arising out of the documentation put out by bidder or target, is not excluded, but, as we shall see below, such claims were in any event possible before the Directive, though they were, and are, constrained by the general law of misstatement.

Finally, the Panel itself is not liable in damages in connection with the discharge of its functions, unless it was acting in bad faith or there is a claim against it for breach of s.6(1) of the Human Rights Act 1998 (which in the circumstances laid down in s.8 of that Act could lead a court to award damages for breach by a public authority of the rights guaranteed by the European Convention on Human Rights).[22] This protection extends to members, officers and employees of the Panel and any person authorised by the Panel to act under its information disclosure powers. Thus, the risk of tactical litigation is minimised, but cannot be entirely eliminated (see below).

Powers of the Panel

This and the following section deal with the areas where there has been the biggest formal change in the Panel's position as a result of its being put on a statutory basis. At least the basic elements of the Panel's powers and the sanctions to support them had to be set out in, or provided for by, the legislation, since art.4(5) of the Directive requires that "supervisory authorities shall be vested with all the powers necessary for the purpose of carrying out their duties, including that of ensuring that the parties to a bid comply with the rules made or introduced pursuant to this Directive". Again, however, the aim of the legislation was to reflect, rather than substantially to alter, the Panel's existing methods of working. The main powers of the Panel are as follows.

28–7

First, the Panel is given both an obligation and a power to make rules to govern the conduct of bids.[23] Thus, the legislation does not purport to discharge that rule-making function itself but requires or empowers the Panel to do so. The Panel is required to make rules in those areas where the Directive requires Member States to introduce rules, thus ensuring that the UK is not in breach of its obligations under the Directive, but the Panel is empowered to make rules more generally, a power which is very widely formulated.[24] In consequence, the whole of the Panel's regulatory activity is placed on a statutory basis. It would have been possible to confine the statutory structure to the bids and topics covered by the Directive, leaving the remainder of the Panel's activities to continue on a

---

[22] 2006 Act s.961. The provisions of the Convention most likely to affect that Panel are those of a procedural nature, for example, art.6 relating to the fair trials in civil disputes. The liability of the Panel under the Human Rights Act 1998 is not new.

[23] 2006 Act s.943. It is not absolutely clear that art.4 of the Directive contemplates that the supervisory authority shall make the rules, but the Directive does not explicitly forbid it, which one would have expected it to do if its authors had wanted to bring about such a major change in British practice, which was very much to the forefront in the formulation of art.4.

[24] 2006 Act s.943(2),(3). Section 944(1) permits the Panel to make rules in a flexible form.

non-statutory basis, but that was thought likely to cause confusion.[25] The Panel is permitted to arrange for its rule-making power (and, indeed, any of its functions) to be discharged by a committee of the Panel, so that there can be a further stage of delegation before the power to make rules is actually exercised.[26] This reflects the fact that, since the enactment of the Human Rights Act 1998, responsibility for the rules has been assigned to a Code Committee of the Panel and that membership of the Hearing Committee (see above) and of the Code Committee does not overlap. Thus, the "legislative" and "judicial" functions of the Panel have been separated.

Secondly, the Panel "may give rulings on the interpretation, application or effect of rules", in the way described in above, such rulings having binding effect.[27] This is the Panel's "judicial" function. Giving the Panel's rulings binding effect is, of course, new, and the sanctions available to support this provision are discussed below. Further, art.4(5) of the Directive permits Member States to give supervisory authorities powers to waive national rules, either to "take account of circumstances determined at national level" or "in other specific circumstances, in which case a reasoned decision must be required", provided in either case that the derogation does not contravene the general principles laid down in art.3(1) of the Directive (see below). Section 944(1)(b) takes up the former option by authorising the Panel to make rules which are "subject to exceptions or exemptions" in the rules themselves. Section 944(1)(d) takes up this latter option by authorising the Panel "to dispense with or modify the application of rules in particular cases and by reference to any circumstances", subject to the requirement to give reasons. This reflects the Panel's traditional practice to use its dispensing power where a rule "would operate unduly harshly or in an unnecessarily restrictive or burdensome, or otherwise inappropriate, manner".[28]

The rules may, and do, also confer upon the Panel the power to give directions to secure compliance with the rules. In practice, this is a very important power for the Panel. Having identified a breach of the rules, its focus in practice is on requiring remedial action which will enable the bid to continue in the normal way.[29] This is the great virtue of having a regulator which can give rulings during the course of a bid, as contrasted with a body which comes to the matter only after the bid has succeeded or failed and so no longer has the possibility of getting the transaction back on track.

28–8   Thirdly, the Panel may require a person by notice in writing to produce to it specified documents or to provide specified information, where such disclosure is "reasonably required in connection with the exercise by the Panel of its functions".[30] This again is a new legal power for the Panel, which in the past has

---

[25] DTI Consultation Document para.2.10. The Directive applies only to bids for companies whose shares are traded on a regulated market, whilst the Code applied more broadly (see below), and even in relation to regulated markets the Code covers a number of topics not touched on by the Directive.

[26] 2006 Act s.942(3)(a).

[27] 2006 Act s.945, but binding effect only "to the extent and in the circumstances specified in the rules".

[28] City Code, *Introduction*, 2(c).

[29] 2006 Act s.946 and City Code, *Introduction*, 10.

[30] 2006 Act s.947(1)–(3). This section can also be seen as implementing art.6(5) of the Directive. The Code itself requires those dealing with it to disclose any known and relevant information (Code,

been able to survive without it. There is the usual protection for legal professional privilege (or confidentiality of communications in Scotland).[31] There is also the usual requirement that the Panel keep confidential information disclosed to it (whether under the compulsory disclosure power or not) which relates to the private affairs of an individual or to any particular business. A person who breaches this requirement is guilty of a criminal offence unless that person had no reason to suspect that the information had been provided to the Panel in connection with its functions or that the person took all reasonable steps and exercised all due diligence to avoid disclosure in breach of the statute. However, this confidentiality provision is subject to the usual long list of permitted "gateways" for disclosure of the information to other official bodies, and to disclosure by the Panel itself for the purpose of facilitating the carrying out of any of its functions (so that some such information may be found in the public rulings of the Hearing Committee or Takeover Appeal Board).[32]

Sanctions

Thus, the Act confers upon the Panel three core powers: to make rules for takeover bids, to interpret those rules and to require the disclosure of information. None of these functions is new for the Panel: all were previously carried on, though without legislative support. Having put those powers in place, the statute was required by the Directive to go on and provide sanctions for non-compliance with them on the part of bid participants. As a self-regulatory body and, in particular, as a body with not even a contractual relationship with those involved in takeovers, whether as participants or advisers, the Panel's formal sanctions were previously extremely limited. The Panel itself could administer only a private reprimand or public censure if there was non-compliance with the Code. For more pressing measures it was dependent on the action of other regulatory authorities, such as the Department of Trade and Industry, the FCA or the Stock Exchange. However, these bodies, even if willing to act, might not have appropriate sanctions at their disposal.[33] In the early days of the Panel such problems threatened the Panel's credibility and even its future, but gradually the Panel gained acceptance for its rulings, partly because of a realisation among

28–9

Introduction, 9(a)) and the Panel expects this to be the power it normally relies on rather than the statutory one. Those firms subject to the jurisdiction of the FCA are required under its rules to provide information and documents to the Panel and to provide such other assistance which the Panel requests in the performance of its functions and the firm is reasonably able to provide: see MAR 4.3.5 and below, fn.41. This disclosure obligation is also subject to an exemption relating to legal professional privilege: see s.413 of FSMA.

[31] 2006 Act s.947(10).

[32] 2006 Act ss.948 and 949 and Sch.2. In the parliamentary debates it was controversial that the Panel has no responsibility for the further disclosure of the information by a body which receives it through one of the gateways, though it is difficult to see how in practice the Panel could have exercised such supervision.

[33] In one notorious case, concerning St Piran Ltd, such action by the Exchange proved singularly ineffective, despite belated undertakings by the guilty party to behave in future. See the Annual Reports of the Panel for 1981 and 1984. See also *Re St Piran Ltd* [1981] 1 W.L.R. 1300 CA, where intervention by the Secretary of State was saved from futility only because a shareholder in the company was prepared to bring a petition for the winding-up of the company on the just and equitable ground.

advisers in particular that an ineffective Panel was likely to lead to the transfer of its functions to a statutory regulator.[34] Further, the Panel's relationship with the FSA in particular was placed on a more explicit footing when FSMA was enacted in 2000.[35]

Perhaps the strongest expression of the new policy of giving the Panel statutory sanctions is to be found in s.955 which confers upon the Panel a power to apply to the court (High Court or Court of Session) where a person has contravened or is likely to contravene a requirement imposed by or under a Code rule or has failed to comply with a disclosure requirement under the statutory provisions just discussed. The court may then make such order as it thinks fit to secure compliance with the requirement, which order will be backed by the sanctions for contempt of court. The Panel, no doubt, expects not to have to make use of this new power, just as it has operated effectively in the past without it.

One important question which arises is whether this section will provide an avenue whereby a party can obtain judicial scrutiny of the Panel's or Appeal Board's rulings during the course of the bid. Of course, the decision to apply to the court for an enforcement order is in the hands of the Panel, so that a party cannot trigger the procedure.[36] However, if the Panel does so apply, the question will be whether the courts in this new context will maintain the after-the-event approach which has been adopted for judicial review and simply enforce the Panel's ruling without scrutinising its legality or without scrutinising it rigorously. This may be a more difficult line for the court to take where the court's order is backed by the sanctions for contempt of court than when the Panel's rulings lacked extensive formal sanctions. Further, if the question is raised whether the Panel's ruling is compatible with the Directive, the court would have to consider making a preliminary reference to the Court of Justice of the European Union (with all the delay that implies).

28–10   The statute places at the disposal of the Panel two other important sanctions, relating to compensation and discipline, but they both require adoption by Panel rules in order to be brought into force. Section 954 provides that the rules may confer power on the Panel to order a person to pay such compensation as it thinks just and reasonable if that person is in breach of a rule "the effect of which is to require the payment of money". This power thus falls short of a general remit to require compensation for breaches of the rules, but it covers the situations where in the past the Panel has required monetary payments.[37] The Code now applies this section to those rules which determine the price at which an offer has to be made or the form of the consideration (for example, where cash or a cash alternative is required).[38]

---

[34] Thus, in *R. v Takeover Panel, Ex p. Guinness Plc* [1990] 1 Q.B. 146 CA, the bidder agreed to pay £85 million to the shareholders of the target company in order to comply with a ruling of the Panel.
[35] See in particular ss.138 and 143 of FSMA 2000. The current provisions are discussed further below.
[36] 2006 Act s.955(2) makes it clear that only the Panel can so apply and not, for example, the party to the bid which stands to benefit from the Panel's ruling.
[37] See fn.17, above, where the company had been in breach of a Code rule requiring the bidder to increase the price offered to the target shareholders because shares had been purchased in the market at that higher price. For the current version of that requirement, see below at para.28–39.
[38] Code, *Introduction*, 10(c).

As to discipline, there is a general provision in s.952 that the rules may give the Panel the power to impose sanctions on a person who has acted in breach of the rules or of a direction given by the Panel to secure compliance with the rules (see above). This is the section on which the Panel now bases its disciplinary powers, which are exercised, except in case of agreement with the offender, by the Hearings Committee (with appeal to the Takeover Appeal Board). The Code sets out the Panel's disciplinary powers and they are the established ones of private or public censure, reporting the offender's conduct to another body for that body to take action against the offender if thought appropriate, and triggering the "cold shouldering" of the offender.[39] It is clear that s.952 permits the rules to adopt a wider range of penalties, notably financial penalties of the type available to the FCA. However, where the Panel adopts a sanction of a kind not previously provided for by the Code, it must produce, again following the FCA model, a policy statement with respect to the imposition of that sanction and, in the case of a financial penalty, the amount of the penalty.[40] So far, the Panel has not ventured into this territory.

The "cold shoulder" and criminal sanctions

Where the Panel reports conduct to a third party, it is up to that regulator (domestic or overseas) or a professional body to decide whether it is appropriate to take further action. The most likely recipient of such a report from the Panel is the FCA. The FCA might conclude that a person who has broken the Takeover Code is also in breach of its obligations under the FCA's rules and impose sanctions upon that person. The persons most obviously within the FCA's scope are those who need its authorisation to carry on their professional activities within the financial services sector. This will cover the principal advisers to bidders and target companies (notably investment banks) but not bidder and target companies themselves or their directors. To deal with this lacuna, a system of FCA-required "cold shouldering" was introduced in FSMA 2000 and is carried forward under the new arrangements. Cold shouldering involves advisers within the scope of the FCA's powers being required not to deal with those who are likely not to observe the Code. In this situation, there is no suggestion that the adviser is in breach of the Code. Indeed, the "cold shoulder" operates generally and covers all those who might act for persons likely not to observe the Code, whether they have acted for that person in the past or not. In this way, the range of the FCA's sanctions is extended to companies and their directors: if they act, or are likely to act, in breach of the Code, they may find that they are denied the facilities of the City of London in relation to takeover bids. The FCA's rules, as contained in its Code of Market Conduct ("MAR"), require firms not to act in connection with transactions to which the Takeover Code applies if they have reasonable grounds to believe that the person in question is not likely to act in

28–11

---

[39] Code, *Introduction*, 11(b). The Panel may also withdraw or qualify any special status or exemption it has granted the offender, for example, as an "exempt principal trader".

[40] 2006 Act s.952(2)–(8). For a discussion of the FCA's penalty powers, see above at para.25–41.

accordance with the Takeover Code.[41] The Hearing Committee has the power, as a disciplinary sanction under the Code, to make a public statement that a person is, in its view, not likely to comply with the Code. In such a case the FCA "expects" that the above rule will require the firm not to act for the person in question.

28–12   Apart from the sanctions which the Act places in the hands of the Panel, the legislation creates a criminal offence in addition to the one we have already discussed in relation to the disclosure of confidential information. This concerns non-compliance with the Code's rules on bid documentation. As we shall see below, much of the Code is concerned with specifying the information a bidder or target must provide, and failure to comply with these rules will clearly fall within the powers and sanctions of the Panel, discussed above. It is also the case that there might be civil litigation between those involved in the bid in the case of misstatements in the bid documentation. Despite this, the Government was convinced that the Directive's (standard) requirement that the sanctions provided for breaches of the transposing national rules should be "effective, proportionate and dissuasive" (art.17) necessitated an additional criminal sanction to be provided in domestic law. The Government feared that inadequacies in the bid documentation might emerge only after the bid had been completed (and when the Panel might be reluctant to involve itself again) so that the Panel's sanctions could not be relied upon, whilst the possibilities of civil litigation were uncertain. Consequently, s.953 creates a narrow criminal offence. It applies only to offers for companies whose voting securities are quoted on a regulated market (which is the scope of the Directive) and it imposes liability on a person only if he knew the offer documentation did not comply with the Code's requirements (or was reckless as to that) and failed to take all reasonable steps to secure compliance. In the case of a response document, the liability falls on any director or officer of the target company; in the case of an offer, which need not be made by a company, on the person making the bid and, in the case of a bid by "a body of persons", any director, officer or member of the body who caused the document to be published. Typically, this will be the directors and officers of the bidder company.[42]

Overall, the policy of the Act in relation to the Panel and the Code can be said to have been that of "replicating, to the greatest extent possible, the Panel's current jurisdiction, practices and procedures within a statutory framework".[43]

---

[41] The FCA rules discussed in this paragraph are set out in MAR 4.3. These rules were made by the FSA under what is now FSMA 2000 s.137A. The range of prohibited services in connection with a bid is widely defined (MAR 4.3.3–4), though it does not extend to the giving of legal advice. S.143, dealing with formal endorsement of the City Code by the FSA, was repealed in the light of the statutory sanctions given to the Panel.

[42] 2006 Act s.953(2),(4). In the parliamentary debates the Solicitor-General gave an assurance that the provision was not intended to reach investment banks when they make offers as agents of bidders—though it must be said that it would be a pretty poor investment bank which knew of the defect in the documentation and did not take reasonable steps to correct it. See HC Debs, Standing Committee D, Nineteenth Sitting, 18 July 2006, cols 804–806.

[43] DTI Consultation Document para.2.18. See also Panel on Takeovers and Mergers, *Implementation of the Takeover Directive, Consultation Paper*, PCP 2005/5, November 2005, (hereafter "Panel Consultation Document") para.2.4: "Overall, the Panel remains confident that while its status and the

THE SCOPE OF THE CITY CODE

The scope of application of the City Code (i.e. the types of companies and types **28–13** of transactions to which it applies) is wider than that of the Directive. The latter applies to public offers to the holders of securities in the target company, where those securities are traded on a regulated market in the EEA and where the objective of the offer is to secure control of the target company.[44] For present purposes it is enough to equate a "regulated market" in the UK with the Main Market of the London Stock Exchange. The Code is not confined to companies whose securities are traded on a regulated market (and thus covers companies whose securities are traded on AIM) and it takes in certain transactions which are analogous to public offers. The expanded scope of the Code (or, alternatively put, the narrow scope of the Directive) would raise no particular problems in the light of the decision (discussed above) to put the whole of the Panel's operations on a statutory footing, were it not for the fact that the two take a different approach to the regulation of takeovers which have a cross-border element. The approach of the Directive, as laid down in art.4, is to divide jurisdiction in such cases among the relevant regulators. By contrast, the Panel's approach, as a national body, is either to accept jurisdiction over all aspects of the offer or not to accept it at all. Consequently, it is necessary to identify not only the offers to which the Code applies (anything outside this set is not regulated at all by the Code) but also the narrower set of offers to which the Directive applies, at least in cross-border takeovers, in order to establish the precise jurisdiction of the Panel (is it all or only some aspects of the bid process?).[45]

Transactions in scope

Let us turn first to the range of transactions covered. The crucial point here is that **28–14** the Directive applies only to the core method of implementing a takeover, namely a public offer by the bidder to the holders of the securities of the target, which "follows or has as its objective" the acquisition of control of the offeree company (art.2.1(a)). This is, at bottom, a contractual mechanism. The Code traditionally has applied more widely, i.e. beyond takeover offers, though obviously it includes them. It is, in fact, not uncommon for non-hostile takeovers to be implemented in the UK via a scheme of arrangement, to which the Code in principle applies.[46] The scheme of arrangement, which is not confined to control-shift transactions, is

---

status of the Code will be different under the new statutory regime, there will be little material substantive change either to its procedures or to the Rules of the Code".

[44] Directive, arts 1(1) and 2(1)(a). On the definition of a "regulated market" see above at para.25–7.
[45] We have also noted above that the criminal sanctions for inaccuracies in the bid documentation apply only to offers within the scope of the Directive. See para.28–12.
[46] The Code's provisions, discussed in this and the following paragraph, are set out in its *Introduction*, 3(b). Although a control shift by means of a scheme of arrangement has long fallen within the Panel's jurisdiction, only in 2008 was the Code amended to indicate more fully how it applies to schemes (because of the "significant increase in recent years in the use of schemes of arrangement in order to implement transactions which are regulated by the Code"). See Panel Consultation Paper, PCP 2007/1, *Schemes of Arrangement*, and App.7 to the current Code. For a more detailed analysis see J. Payne, *Schemes of Arrangement* (2014), Ch.3.

discussed in Ch.29, but the essence of the scheme, when used as a substitute for a takeover offer, is that the company, through a decision of its shareholders in general meeting, adopts a proposal the end result of which is the same as that achieved by the contractual offer (the shares in the target company end up with the bidder and the shareholders receive a consideration in exchange). The scheme has certain advantages in the case of a non-hostile offer (notably that all the shareholders are bound once the scheme is adopted and approved by the court), so that the squeeze-out mechanism referred to later in this chapter does not have to be used. However, technically the offer is implemented not through each individual shareholder's decision to accept a contractual offer made for the transfer of their shares but by the shareholders collectively, acting as the company, voting to adopt a scheme of arrangement. In this case, a mechanism of corporate law is used to effect the takeover. For this reason, a takeover effected by a scheme of arrangement appears not to fall within the Directive's definition of a takeover,[47] so that a scheme is outside the scope of the Directive, even if it involves companies whose securities are traded on a regulated market. For this reason, the jurisdiction splitting provisions of the Directive will not apply to a takeover effected by a scheme of arrangement which has a cross-border element, which may itself be regarded as an advantage by the parties involved.

The Code also applies to offers by a parent company to acquire outside shares in its subsidiary. It is unclear whether this transaction is within the Directive because it is not clear how closely the Directive requires the public offer to "follow" the acquisition of control. The Code applies as well to other mechanisms which have "as their objective or potential effect (directly or indirectly) obtaining or consolidating control". This covers a wide range of possible methods, not involving a general offer to acquire securities, such as the issue of new shares and share capital reorganisations, which, if structured appropriately, could shift control of the company into new hands. Although not much invoked in practice, the inclusion of these analogous control-shift mechanisms removes any temptation for the parties to seek to avoid the Code's provisions by adopting one or other of them.

Companies in scope

Full jurisdiction to the Panel

28–15   The range of companies within scope of the Directive or the Code is defined by focusing on the status of the target company. Let us look first at the cases where the Panel will be the sole regulator, i.e. where the target is what might be called a

---

[47] A takeover bid is defined in art.2(1)(a) as "a public offer (other than by the offeree company itself) made to the holders of the securities of a company to acquire all or some of those securities, whether mandatory or voluntary, which follows or has as its objective the acquisition of control of the offeree company in accordance with national law".

purely UK company. The Code divides such companies into two categories.[48] The first category consists of those companies incorporated in the UK (i.e. they have their registered offices in the UK) and having any of their securities admitted to trading on a regulated market or multilateral trading facility (such as AIM) in the UK.[49] The second category consists of companies registered in the UK, which do not have their securities traded on a public market in the UK but do have their place of central management and control within the UK. Whereas the first category is necessarily confined to companies which are public in the Companies Act sense of the term, the second category is capable of embracing private companies. However, private companies are brought within the Code only where in the previous decade their securities have been traded in a public or semi-public way or a prospectus has been issued in relation to them. In quantitative terms, the second category is subject to takeover offers, but their inclusion at least means the Code's provisions cannot be evaded by first de-listing the target company from a public market.

Thus, the Panel's sole jurisdiction extends far beyond companies traded on regulated markets. Before the adoption of the Directive, the Code applied only to companies "resident" in the UK, i.e. both incorporated in the UK and having their central management in the UK. That requirement for jurisdiction was ruled out by the Directive in the case of UK companies traded on regulated markets and the Code has now abandoned it in respect of companies traded on multilateral trading facilities. To this extent, the Directive expanded the jurisdiction of the Panel compared to the pre-Directive position. However, the residence requirement has been retained in relation to the second category of companies.[50]

Divided jurisdiction

In the above cases Panel has jurisdiction over all aspects of the bid. In the cases now to be examined the Panel's jurisdiction will be shared with another regulator, because there is some "cross-border" element in the target. This division results from the approach adopted by art.4 of the Directive. Because division of competence is a Directive concept, it applies only to bids for target companies whose securities are traded on a regulated market. The issue arises where the two factors the Directive uses to identify its scope (incorporation in the EU; trading on a regulated market in the EU) are satisfied in different jurisdictions, for example, a target incorporated in one Member State but having its securities traded on a regulated market in another Member State. The Directive could have

28–16

---

[48] *Introduction*, 3(a)(i) and (ii). The starred note makes it clear that "company" for the purposes of the Code includes UK unregistered companies, to which, in addition, the statutory provisions of Chs 2 and 3 of Pt 28 are applied by regulation. See para.1–16. The term also embraces European companies which are incorporated in the UK.

[49] References to the UK include the Channel Islands and the Isle of Man. This is necessary to meet the EU obligations of the UK, but we do not further refer to this extension.

[50] For a good example of the significance of the residence requirement see *Xstrata Plc*, Panel Statement 2002/7: company incorporated in the UK and to be listed on the Main Market of the LSE not within the jurisdiction of the Panel under the pre-Directive rules because the place of its central management was Switzerland. The Panel's insistence on the central place of management being in the UK seems to have been linked to the question of whether that management would be amenable to its authority.

allocated jurisdiction wholly to the State of incorporation, as is done with the Prospectus Directive,[51] but this is hardly feasible with takeover regulation, which involves much more than information disclosure and is in parts intimately related to the operation of the market on which the target's securities trade. Alternatively, jurisdiction could have been allocated wholly to the State where the target's securities trade. In fact, art.4 of the Directive appears initially to proceed in this way by identifying the competent authority to supervise the bid as the one in the Member State where the company's securities are admitted to trading on a regulated market (even if the company is incorporated elsewhere). If the securities are admitted to trading on a regulated market in more than one Member State, the competent authority is the State where the securities were first admitted. If the securities are admitted to markets in more than one Member State (other than the State of incorporation) simultaneously, the company makes the choice of competent authority from among the various Member States, but must do so in advance, that is, the choice must be made on the first day of trading, and the choice seems subsequently to be unalterable.[52]

However, art.4(2)(e) then proceeds to say, not simply that the takeover rules of the Member State of incorporation shall be the operative ones for certain matters, but also that in respect of those matters the competent authority shall be that of the State of incorporation. In this way, the Directive does end up with a divided jurisdiction. In particular, what the Directive refers to as "company law" matters are allocated to the competent authority of the State of incorporation. These include the definition of the threshold at which a mandatory bid shall be launched and any derogations from the obligation to launch such a bid, the rules governing frustrating action by the directors of the target company and the provision of information to employees. By contrast, the competent authority of the Member State where the securities are traded will deal with the rules relating to the price to be offered, bid procedure, disclosure and the contents of the offer document.

For the Panel this means that (a) where a company is incorporated in the UK but traded on a regulated market in another EEA Member State, the Panel will deal with the "company law" aspects of the bid, including the rules on information to be provided to employees. (b) Where the company is incorporated in an EEA Member State (other than the UK) but traded only on a regulated market in the UK, the Panel will deal with the "bid procedure" aspects of the offer. (c) Where the company is incorporated as in (b) but traded on regulated markets in more than one Member State of the EEA, including the UK but excluding its state of incorporation, the Panel will be the competent authority to deal with the "bid procedure" aspects of the offer, provided the UK is the state of first admission or has been chosen by the target in the case of multiple first admissions.[53]

---

[51] See para.25–44.

[52] Directive art.4(2)(b) and (c). If the simultaneous listing had occurred before the Directive came into force, the relevant competent authorities must agree within four weeks of that date which of them is to be the competent authority for that company or, in default of agreement, the company chooses on the first day of trading after that four-week period.

[53] If, on the date for transposition of the Directive (20 May 2006) there were already multiple first admissions, either the regulators have to agree who has jurisdiction or the target chooses.

The division of applicable rules and competent authorities is very important, both **28–17** because the Directive itself gives the Member States significant choices about how they implement the Directive's provisions and because Member States are free to add to those provisions in many cases. For example, as we have noted,[54] the UK has a strong "no frustration" rule, which a company incorporated in the UK will be subject to even if its shares are listed and its shareholders mainly located in a jurisdiction where this rule is not applied; whereas a company incorporated in a Member State which does not impose the "no frustration" rule will not become subject to it by listing its securities on a regulated market in the UK.

Finally, it should be noted that, for the Directive to apply the target company must be both incorporated in a Member State of the EEA and have some of its securities traded on a regulated market in the EEA.[55] However, the Code, as we have seen, does apply to target companies incorporated and having their central management and control in the UK, no matter where, or indeed whether, their securities are publicly traded. Thus, a bid for a company incorporated outside the EEA will escape British regulation even if its securities are listed on a public market in the UK; whilst a bid for one which is incorporated in and has its central management in the UK will be regulated by the Panel, even if its securities are traded on a public market outside the EEA or, even, on a non-regulated market within the EEA (but outside the UK). For this reason, no doubt, s.950 requires the Panel to co-operate not only with foreign national authorities designated for the purposes of the Directive but also with any foreign regulator that appears to exercise functions similar to those of the Panel.

THE STRUCTURE OF THE CODE

The Code consists, in its eleventh edition of 2013 (as amended), and always has **28–18** consisted, of a small number of General Principles and a larger number of Rules. Currently, there are six General Principles ("GPs") and 38 rules. Before the amendments made in 2006 to accommodate the Directive, there were 10 General Principles and the same number of rules as currently. The current six GPs are simply a copy out of the general principles laid down in art.3 of the Directive. The decision simply to substitute the Directive's GPs for those previously in place seems to have been driven in part by the consideration that the Panel's derogation powers must be exercised in such a way as not to contravene the Directive's GPs. It was thought that the cleanest way of implementing this requirement was to simply adopt the Directive's list of GPs.[56] The original notion behind the GPs was that they constituted high-level standards, compliance with which was required even though no specific rule of the Code had been broken.

---

[54] At para.28–1.

[55] Directive art.1(1).

[56] Panel Consultation Document para.2.1. On the Panel's derogation and waiver powers, see above at para.28–7. Of course, the Directive restricts the Panel's derogation powers only by reference to its GPs and not by reference to any additional GPs which a Member State chooses to adopt, but copying out the Directive's GPs at least removes a source of possible confusion about which of the domestic GPs simply implement the Directive's GPs and which add something beyond the Directive's requirements.

This was thought to be a desirable regulatory technique because, as it was put in the seventh edition of the Code, "it is impracticable to devise rules in sufficient detail to cover all the circumstances which can arise in offers".[57] However, the reduction in the number of GPs in the current Code has somewhat reduced the force of this regulatory argument, not simply because the current GPs cover less ground than those previously in place and because, where they cover the same ground, the Directive's GPs are in general more weakly expressed, but also because the Rules have been amended to take account of the loss of coverage at GP level.[58] This movement of material between GPs and Rules casts some doubt on the significance of the distinction between those two types of norm.

In any event, it is also the case that, over successive editions of the Code, the Rules had become more detailed and elaborate, so that the gap-filling rationale given for the GPs had become less convincing. The Rules acquired sub-rules and both acquired "notes", some of which are prescriptive and not just explanatory. It is perhaps not surprising that the view just quoted about the role of GPs is not repeated in the current version of the Code. The best view is probably now that the GPs are there because the Directive requires them to be and that they serve to highlight some, but not all, of the fundamental principles underlying the Code. It seems likely in the future that the Rules will continue to grow in importance in comparison with the GPs. Both Rules and GPs are interpreted by the Panel purposively,[59] so that no penalty in terms of rigidity of interpretation is paid by dealing with a matter in the Rules. Further, if the content of the GPs is effectively controlled by the Directive, the responses to domestic pressures for change or elaboration of takeover regulation will have to be revealed in changes to the Rules. Such changes in the Rules can be readily made through the Code Committee of the Panel, whose task it is to keep the Code under review and to propose changes, after public consultation,[60] whereas, on the Panel's current approach, changes to the GPs would require legislation at EU level.

The current General Principles are as follows:

1. All holders of securities in the offeree company of the same class must be afforded equivalent treatment. Where a person acquires control of a company, the other holders of securities must be protected. These are the two limbs of GP 1 and they constitute a partial expression of a more elaborate notion of equality which underlies the Code and which is discussed below.

2. Holders of securities in the offeree company must have sufficient time and information to enable them to reach a properly informed decision on the bid. When advising the shareholders, the board of the offeree company must give its views on the effects of the implementation of the bid on employment, conditions of employment and the location of the company's place of business. The first part of GP 2 is clearly central to any takeover regulation; the second part, specifically requiring the provision of

---

[57] City Code, 7th edn, 2002, B1.
[58] Panel Consultation Document para.2.1.
[59] City Code, *Introduction*, 2(b).
[60] City Code, *Introduction*, 4(b).

employee-related information, constitutes a relatively minor protection of the interests of the employees. They or their representatives are given no formal role in the takeover decision, but the provision of the required information may enable them to apply pressure outside the formal requirements of the Code. Although the second part of the GP is conditional upon the board of the offeree company giving advice to the shareholders of the target company, in fact, as we shall see, the Code requires such advice to be given.

3. "The board of an offeree company must act in the interests of the company as a whole and must not deny the holders of securities the opportunity to decide on the merits of the bid." The phrase "the company as a whole" is, as ever, ambiguous as to whether it means only the shareholders as a whole or includes stakeholder interests.[61] The answer to that question may not be very significant since the second part of the principle puts the decision on the bid in the hands of the shareholders, to whom the "company as a whole" duty does not apply. As already noted, the allocation of the decision on the bid as between target board and target shareholders is a crucial question for takeover regulation. The City Code has always allocated that decision to the shareholders, though, somewhat oddly, the Directive permits Member States to opt out of art.9 of the Directive, which gives effect to GP 3 (see below).

4. False markets should not be created, whether in the securities of the offeror, offeree or any other company concerned in the bid.

5. An offeror may announce a bid only if has ensured that it can meet in full any cash consideration payable and after taking "all reasonable steps" to secure the implementation of any other type of consideration. Thus, offers may be opportunistic in some ways (for example, a bid for a target which is suffering from a temporary set-back) but not in terms of financing.

6. The offeree company should not be hindered in the conduct of its affairs by the bid for longer than is reasonable. This is a GP not expressed in the Code before the transposition of the Directive, though the policy underlying it was certainly implemented in the Code, and so it was rather odd that it was not there. The point is that a bid is likely to cause the senior management of the target to divert their attention wholly to the bid from the moment it is imminent to the point where it succeeds or fails, so that there is a strong argument that this distraction from the other aspects of company's activities should be subject to limits.

THE ALLOCATION OF THE ACCEPTANCE DECISION

As already indicated at the beginning of this chapter, a, perhaps the, crucial question for takeover regulation is whether the decision on the bid should be that of the shareholders alone or one to which both shareholders and the target board must consent. Allocating the decision to the shareholders alone facilitates the creation of a market in the control of companies, which acts as a powerful

28–19

---

[61] See para.16–65.

incentive for the managements of companies, at all times and not just when a bid is imminent, to act in the interests of the shareholders. Bidders are able to make "hostile" takeover offers, i.e. offers which the board of the target opposes but which it is not able to prevent being put to the shareholders. The market in corporate control is probably a much more powerful mechanism for the promotion of the interests of shareholders than all the corporate governance techniques discussed in Part Three of this book, including the law of directors' duties. On the other hand, some have argued that the threat of a takeover makes management too responsive to shareholder needs, in particular by inducing management to take a short-term view of the company's success, which may be detrimental to the longer term development of its business and thus to the long-term interests of the shareholders themselves. Those taking this latter view would wish to permit management to have some say in whether the bid is successful and would not allocate the decision wholly to the shareholders. Those concerned about the impact of takeovers on non-shareholder groups, notably employees, tend to support this managerialist stance, as being the best protection they can secure in the absence of a stakeholder input into the acceptance decision.[62]

Since the standard takeover transaction is necessarily one between the bidder and the shareholders of the target company (there is no corporate decision), how can the board of the target company, which is not a party to the transaction, have a say on whether the bid is to succeed? The answer is that the board has many possibilities to exercise its general powers of management so as to discourage an offeror from making or continuing with a bid. Thus, the question is whether, in the particular context of a takeover bid, the board should be permitted to use its normal management powers, for example by issuing new shares to a friendly investor or by disposing of assets the bidder is anxious to acquire. This is usually referred to as the issue of whether takeover regulation should adopt a "no frustration" rule, i.e. whether the board of a target is to be prohibited from taking action which constrains the freedom of the shareholders as a whole to decide to accept an offer, even though such action would normally be within the scope of the board's powers of management. This issue needs to be addressed at two different points of time: when a bid is imminent and when no bid is in prospect. The reason for this distinction is that the imposition of a strict no frustration rule is feasible once a bid is imminent, because it will operate only so long as the bid is current. The imposition of a strict "no frustration" rule where no bid is imminent (i.e. at all times) would limit the board's powers of management in a way which is undesirable even from the shareholders' point of view (because it reduce the benefits shareholders obtain from centralised management), whilst the risk of self-serving decisions by management is less severe when a bid is not imminent. Thus, even those in favour of the "no frustration" principle would not necessarily want the same rules to apply both pre- and post-bid. In the UK this distinction in point of time is reinforced by a division in terms of regulatory responsibility, for the Takeover Code applies only once a bid is imminent.

---

[62] For an analysis of the competing views see R. Kraakman et al. (eds), *The Anatomy of Corporate Law*, 3rd edn (Oxford: OUP, 2016), Ch.8.

Post-bid defensive measures

The Code has always adopted a strong "no frustration" rule, thus helping to make **28–20** the UK a very active takeover market. The principle used be expressed in GP 7, which said that after a bona fide offer had been communicated to the board of the target or the board had reason to believe that such an offer was imminent, no action might be taken by the board without the approval of the shareholders in general meeting which could result in the offer being frustrated or to shareholders being denied an opportunity to decide on its merits.[63] This language no longer appears in the GPs, though there is a paler version of it in the current GP 3. In a strong example of the GP to Rule transfer brought about by the Directive, however, this exact formulation can be found in r.21.1(a) of the current Code. This rule makes it difficult for the existing controllers to erect any of the defences against being ousted from control by an unwelcome takeover unless they have succeeded in doing so in advance of a threatened takeover. Even then, the pre-bid defence must be one that does not require board action post-bid, for the post-bid action will be caught by r.21.[64] It is a particularly strict rule. Unlike the common law relating to improper purposes,[65] r.21 requires shareholder approval for any action proposed by the directors of the target company which could have the result of preventing the shareholders of the target company from deciding on the merits of the bid. Whether the directors of the target had this purpose in mind or whether it was their predominant purpose in proposing the action in question is beside the point under the rule. The rule looks to consequences, not to purposes. Equally important, the rule requires shareholder approval to be given for the specific defensive measure proposed by the target board and thus to be given in the context of the bid; it cannot be given in general and in advance of the bid.

Rule 21.1(b), together with r.37.3, spells out some common specific situations where the approval of the shareholders will be required, for example, in relation to share issues; acquisition or, more likely, disposals of target company assets of a "material amount"[66]; entering into contracts other than in the ordinary course of business (which may include the declaration and payment of interim dividends); and the redemption or purchase of shares.[67] But r.21.1(a) covers any frustrating action, whether specifically mentioned in the rules or not, and it has been held by the Panel to cover even the initiation of litigation on behalf of the target once an

---

[63] This prohibition, however, seems to be restricted to internal corporate action of the sort specified in r.21 and it is not regarded as breached by lobbying the competition authorities seeking to persuade them to take action to prohibit the bid or subject it to conditions unacceptable to the offeror.

[64] Thus, a power conferred by shareholders pre-bid upon the board to issue shares or warrants post-bid would not escape r.21, because that rule would catch the post-bid decision by the board to make the issue.

[65] See paras 16–26 et seq., above.

[66] On which see Note 2 to r.21.1.

[67] Of course, the management of the target company may, and often do, promise as part of their defence to the bid to carry out one or more of these actions after their shareholders have rejected the offer.

offer is imminent.[68] The overall effect of the rule is to reduce the defensive tactics available to the management of the target company to three general categories: convincing the shareholders that their future is better assured with the incumbent management than with the bidder; persuading the competition authorities, at national or EU level, that the bid ought to be referred on public interest grounds; and encouraging another bidder to come forward as a "white knight" and make an alternative offer to the shareholders. In all three situations the directors of the target are thrown back on their powers of persuasion: in all three cases the final decision on the success of these defensive moves rests with others. However, the board of the target company is not required as a general rule to co-operate with the bidder and to smooth its path. Rule 21 is framed by way of stipulations about what the board must not do, not about how it should act positively. Thus, the board may find itself in a stronger negotiating position than r.21 might suggest if either (a) a recommendation in favour of the offer from the target board is, for one reason or another, important to the bidder; or (b) the bidder needs the target board's cooperation to launch the bid. We discuss such situations below under "bid procedure".

The requirement for shareholder approval for frustrating action is reflected in art.9 of the Directive, but this is one of the articles out of which Member States are permitted to opt by choosing not to apply the "no frustration" rule to companies within their jurisdiction. Not surprisingly, the UK chose not to opt out, since art.9 reflects the established policy of the Code. However, there is a further issue about opt outs from the no-frustration rule. Although not completely clear on the point, art.12(3) can be interpreted so as to permit Member States to permit companies to opt out of the no-frustration rule of art.9 in limited circumstances, namely, when faced with a bid from a company to which art.9 does not apply (for example, because the bidder is from a Member State which has opted out of art.9). This is the so-called "reciprocity" principle, i.e. a target should be subject to the ban on frustrating action only where the bidder is subject to it. However, the UK chose not to adopt this more limited form of company-level opting-out either, on the grounds that it was not part of the existing Code structure and that the benefits to the UK of an open market for corporate control obtained even if the bidder is not an available target.[69]

In short, r.21 is a mandatory rule out of which companies may not opt, either generally or on a reciprocity basis. It is arguable that a strictly mandatory "no frustration" rule does not fit well with policies to encourage shareholder engagement, as discussed in paras 15–30 et seq. There may be a case for permitting the shareholders of the company, by an appropriate majority, to opt out

---

[68] See Panel Statement 1989/7, *Consolidated Gold Fields* and Panel Statement 1989/20, *BAT Industries*, which explore the complications which arise when the litigation is initiated in a foreign jurisdiction by a partially owned subsidiary or when the "litigation" takes the form of enthusiastic participation in regulatory hearings.

[69] DTI Consultation Document para.3.12. The most prominent country which does not apply the board neutrality rule in takeovers is Germany, though even there defensive measures need (a) the approval of the shareholders which can be given in general and for periods of up to eighteen months and need not be given in the face of the bid, as the Code demands; or (b) the approval of the supervisory board. See W. Underhill and A. Austmann, "Defensive Tactics" in J. Payne (ed.), *Takeovers in English and German Law* (Oxford: Hart Publishing, 2002), pp.95–98.

of the "no frustration" rule for a period of time. This would enable the management of a company to embark on the implementation of a strategy which might not benefit the share price in the short-term, secure in the knowledge that they would be free from the risk of an opportunistic takeover offer, at least where the shareholders also conferred upon the board the power to put in place an effective takeover defence.

Defensive measures in advance of the bid

This is an area where the Code does not operate. Rule 21 applies only once the "board has reason to believe that a bona fide offer might be imminent". Before that point regulation is left to general company law,[70] which, however, has not developed a single rule to deal with pre-bid defensive tactics. Rather, a number of rules may be relevant, depending upon the precise action the directors of a potential target company wish to take. The most general of these company law rules is s.171 of the Companies Act requiring the directors to exercise their powers for a proper purpose or to obtain shareholder approval of action not proposed for a proper purpose. As we have noted in relation to pre-bid defences, however, because that section focuses on the directors' purpose, rather than on the effects of their acts, and indeed on their predominant purpose, where there is more than one, the section is a weaker control than r.21. Provided there is a commercial justification which the directors can plausibly put forward as the predominant purpose of their action, it will be difficult for a shareholder to challenge it on the grounds that an effect of the decision will be to make the company less attractive to a bidder or less easy to acquire. In the absence of a current bid, there is also less incentive for a shareholder to seek to challenge the directors' action through a derivative action. An example of a board decision, having the effect of making the company less easy to take over but having also a plausible commercial justification, might be the creation of a joint venture with another company, to which each commits part of its existing assets, on terms that a change of control in either partner permits the other partner to buy the first partner out.[71] Alternatively, the board of a company might seek to make it less attractive to a bidder by gearing up its balance sheet (i.e. altering the ratio of debt to equity in the company's financial structure) and distributing the immediate gains of that exercise to the shareholders, on the basis that the opportunity of carrying out this exercise is what makes the company attractive to a private equity bidder. It is not surprising that s.171 is less stringent than r.21. Rule 21 is very restrictive of managerial initiative, because of its requirement for shareholder consent. This is a policy which may be sustainable for the short period after a bid has been launched and before its fate is decided, but applied to

28–21

---

[70] These rules apply to post-bid defensive tactics as well, but there their impact is normally hidden beneath that of r.21 of the Code. They might be important, even post-bid, in the exceptional case where the Code did not apply to the target company, for example, where it was a private company or a public company whose securities were not publicly traded in the UK and whose central management was outside the UK. See para.28–15, above.

[71] For an example of the legal pitfalls which can be created if the drafters of the joint venture agreement are overly ambitious see *Criterion Properties Plc v Stratford UK Properties LLC* [2004] 1 W.L.R. 1846 HL.

corporate decision-making across the board it would subvert the delegation in the articles of managerial powers to the board whenever a decision might have the effect of making the company a less attractive bid target.[72]

Other rules can be pointed to which require shareholder consent in specific circumstances for pre-bid defences. Thus, s.551 requires shareholder authorisation for decisions by the directors of public companies to issue shares or to grant rights to subscribe for or convert any security into shares.[73] This section, together with the improper purposes doctrine, makes it much more difficult for a British company to adopt a US-style "poison pill" or "shareholder rights plan". In the US the efficacy of that device depends crucially on the board being able to adopt the plan without the consent of the shareholders and upon the courts not regarding the adoption of such a plan as a breach of fiduciary duty on the part of the directors. Section 551 lays down the principle of shareholder consent for the conferment of such rights, and a poison pill might well be regarded by British courts as falling foul of the proper purposes doctrine, since the pill has no commercial rationale except in the context of the bid and its role then is simply to make it very unattractive for a bidder to put an offer to the shareholders of which the target board does not approve.[74] However, s.551 is again a less rigorous provision than r.21 of the Code, because it allows shareholders to approve the issuance of shares by directors up to five years in advance, though institutional shareholders are in fact reluctant to give a blank cheque to the directors for such a long period. Asking shareholders to approve share issues in advance, for which permission there may well be good commercial reasons, does not focus shareholders' attention as sharply on the potential costs to them as where approval is required, as under r.21, in the course of a bid, when the shareholders know the terms of the offer they will be rejecting if they adopt the defensive measures.[75]

However, it should be noted that pre-bid and post-bid defensive measures do not fall into fully separate categories. For example, a pre-bid defensive tactic (obtaining authority to issue shares to defeat a bidder) which requires action by the directors post-bid (actually to issuing the shares) will be caught by r.21 at the point of exercise of the share-issue power. Thus, r.21 has some chilling effect on pre-bid defensive measures despite its post-bid operation.

The break-through rule

28–22   The drafters of the Takeover Directive, however, were concerned with a different form of pre-bid defensive measure. This was the creation by companies of capital structures in which the voting rights attached to equity shares are not proportionate to the economic interests held by the equity shareholders, or where

---

[72] On the division of powers between shareholders and the board see para.14–1.

[73] See para.24–4.

[74] The shareholder rights plan, which comes in many varieties, in its core version gives shareholders other than the bidder the right to subscribe for shares in the target company at a very attractive price. Given the discrimination between the bidder and non-bidder shareholders a rights plan would also cause difficulties for the target board under s.172(1)(f).

[75] Pre-emption rights, which might also stand in the way of rights plans, suffer from the same weakness of disapplication in advance. See s.570 and, above, at para.24–6.

there were restrictions on the transferability of the shares. Both arrangements make future bids less likely to succeed, in the former case because the voting shares may be concentrated in the hands of those, for example members of the founding family, who oppose a change of control in principle; and in the latter because it may simply not be possible for shareholders to accept the bidder's offer. A disjunction between voting and economic rights can be achieved in a number of different ways, of which the most obvious are the creation of a class of non-voting equity shares or a class of shares with multiple voting rights. Let us assume that in each case there is also a class of equity shareholder having one vote per share, but with rights and obligations otherwise the same as those of the other class of equity shareholder. In the case of non-voting shares, the class with one vote per share will control the company, even though they have contributed only a part of the company's equity share capital. In the case of multiple vote shares, this class will have a disproportionate influence over (perhaps even control) the company, even though the holders of the shares with multiple votes have not contributed a proportion of the company's equity capital that is equivalent to their votes. In either case, by ensuring that the voting or multiple voting shares are in "friendly" hands, no bid will succeed, even if a majority of the equity shareholders (by capital contributed) would wish it to.

In the discussions on the drafts of the Takeover Directive the concern was with deviations from the proportionality principle in the specific context of takeovers. The "Winter group",[76] to whom the issue was referred by the EU, wished, putting the matter broadly, to assert the mandatory operation of a "one share, one vote" rule in two bid situations. These were: (a) any vote by shareholders called to approve or not post-bid defensive measures; (b) at a general meeting called after the bidder has acquired a specified proportion of the company's equity for the purpose of installing its own nominees as directors of the target or changing the target's articles of association. This so-called "breakthrough" rule would also apply to restrictions on the transferability of shares, whether to be found in the company's articles or in contracts with or among shareholders. The aim of the break-through rule was to render nugatory the defensive qualities of the capital structures or of the transfer restrictions once a bid emerged. This was a controversial proposal, which was ultimately implemented in art.11 of the Directive only in an optional form.

There is no doubt that the issue identified in art.11 of the Takeover Directive is an important one. To take an extreme example, r.21 of the Code, requiring shareholder approval of post-bid defensive measures, would be of little value if the company's articles allocated the voting rights on such a question entirely to the board of the target company. However, this theoretical problem has never loomed large in British policy-making. As we have seen in Ch.23 there is nothing in British law that prohibits or regulates such capital structures. Nevertheless, they are uncommon, mainly because of the opposition of institutional shareholders to acquiring non- or limited-voting equity shares. This is not to say that such capital structures do not exist in British companies, but that, broadly, where they continue, institutional shareholders have been convinced that there is

28–23

---

[76] *Report of the High Level Group of Company Law Experts on Issues Related to Takeover Bids*, Brussels, 10 January 2002, Ch.1, especially pp.28–36.

a good reason for that situation. In other words, the solution to the problem in the UK has traditionally been market-led rather than to be found in the law, and British law, in consequence, has not regulated disproportionate voting arrangements, either generally or in the context of a takeover bid, for example, through a break-through rule. In those Member States which make extensive use of disproportionate capital structures or restrictions on transfer, there was strong opposition to an EU rule which would set them aside, even in the limited, if important, context of a takeover bid. The result was that art.11 of the Directive, like art.9, was made optional for the Member States at the final point in the EU's legislative process.

The British Government decided to opt out of art.11 (not to apply it to UK companies), contrary to its decision in relation to art.9. However, in policy terms the reasoning was consistent, i.e. the choices made in relation to both articles reflected the prior position in UK law.[77] One might think, therefore, that the break-through rule needs no further attention in this book. Unfortunately, art.12, which provides for the opt-out, also stipulates that where a Member State has opted out, it must permit opting back in on a company-by-company basis.[78] In short, a company may override the decision of the Member State to opt out of art.11, so far as that particular company is concerned. Article 12 further provides that Member States may permit companies, which have opted back in, to opt out again on the reciprocity principle, i.e. when faced with a bid from a company that is not subject to art.11. Here, as with art.9, the British Government decided not to permit opting out at company level on the basis of the reciprocity principle, though, as we shall see, the decision on the part of a company to opt into the break-through rule is reversible under certain conditions. Thus, the choice for a company incorporated in the UK and having its securities traded on a regulated market is, during any single period of time, to be wholly within or wholly outside the break-through rule. This choice, which the Directive requires to be provided, is given not in the Code, but in the Companies Act (in Ch.2 of Pt 28), since it involves the amendment of vested rights, and the choice is made available only to companies falling within the Directive's scope, i.e. companies with voting shares admitted to trading on a regulated market.

28–24   The eighth edition of this book dealt with the break-through rule in some detail.[79] However, it appears that no UK company has chosen to opt into the break-through rule and so a shorter treatment is justified in this edition. A number of reasons could be put forward for this lack of take up of the break-through rule by individual companies. First, the incentives to do so are not strong. As already indicated, disproportionate voting rights are not a major issue in the UK. A company which has them has presumably managed to convince its shareholders (at least when it raised new capital) that it is useful to retain them. If the

---

[77] DTI Consultation Document para.3.9. In opting out of the breakthrough rule the UK followed the "vast majority" of the Member States: see Commission of the European Communities, *Report on the implementation of the Directive on Takeover Bids*, SEC (2007) 268, February 2007, para.2.1.4 (hereafter "Commission Report").

[78] Directive art.12(2). This provision applies to opt-outs from both arts 9 and 11, though only the latter is relevant in the UK, because the UK did not opt out of art.9. Article 12(3) provides for the reciprocity exception.

[79] At paras 28–19 to 28–26.

shareholders cease to be convinced, they are likely to press the board to remove them entirely and not just in the context of a takeover. A company which has proportionate voting rights and an absence of restrictions on the transfer of shares might still wish to opt into the break-through rule in order to prevent a target in another Member State from taking defensive measures against it on the reciprocity basis. However, since most Member States have opted out of the break-through rule and apparently no companies in those states have opted back in, this incentive is very weak.[80]

Secondly, the break-through rule deals with restrictions in both the articles and restrictions in private contracts. As far as restrictions in the articles are concerned, the Act deals with them by simply making their removal a pre-condition for a company to opt into the break-through rule.[81] However, this puts those shareholders likely to lose from the removal of restrictions in the articles in a strong position to prevent the necessary changes. If the necessary changes to the articles involve an amendment of the rights of any class of shareholder (for example, reducing the votes attached to their shares to one from some higher number), the separate consent of that class by supermajority resolution will be required—and may not be obtainable.[82] If the necessary changes to the articles cannot be obtained, the company will not be in a position to opt into the rule.

Thirdly, while the removal of restrictions on voting rights or on the transfer of shares which are contained in contracts (either contracts with the company or contracts wholly among the shareholders) is not a pre-condition for opting into the rule, nevertheless compensation is required to be paid when those contractual rights are infringed by the company's adherence to the break-through rule. For the purposes of compensation, therefore, the contractual provisions are not in fact broken through. The significance of the break-through rule is thus that it excludes the possibility of a contracting party seeking an injunction to prevent the transfer of shares or the argument that a shareholder decision is void because not taken in accordance with the agreed arrangements for voting. Section 968(6) deals with compensation by providing a right to compensation for loss (of such amount as the court thinks just and equitable) from those persons who, but for the statutory break-through, would be liable to the claimant in contract for breach of contract or in tort for inducing breach of contract. The "just and equitable" formula for the assessment of the compensation renders the extent of the liability uncertain and will thus act as a disincentive to opting in. In practice, the compensation may be offered by the bidder, but the bidder is not formally liable to pay compensation unless it is a party to the contract or has committed the tort of inducing breach of contract.

---

[80] The extent to which such defensive measures on the part of the target are permitted and the extent to which opting back into art.11 by the UK company would be effective against such defensive measures depends upon some difficult issues in the interpretation of the singularly ill-drafted art.12(3) of the Directive. First, it is not clear whether reciprocity is permitted to companies to which either arts 9 or 11 applies on a mandatory basis. The strict wording of the Directive suggests not, but this seems an odd result and the Commission seems to take a different view. See Commission Report para.2.1.3. Secondly, it is not clear on what precise basis the equivalence of the positions of the bidder and target companies is to be assessed, so as to exclude retaliatory measures. See Rickford, above, fn.8 at pp.1406–1408.

[81] 2006 Act s.996(3).

[82] For the variation of class rights procedure, see para.19–13.

However, the Act does provide one incentive for opting in. This is that it is not an irreversible decision. Subject to a minimum period of one year, a company which, by special resolution of its shareholders, has opted into the break-through rule may opt out of it, again by special resolution—and presumably opt back in again and out again as many times as it wishes.[83]

Disclosure of control structures

28–25 Given the optional nature of the break-through rule, it may well be in practice that art.10 of the Directive turns out to be more important than art.11. The purpose of this article, as Recital 18 of the Directive recounts, is to make "defensive structures and mechanisms" more transparent. Consequently, companies within the scope of the Directive (i.e. with securities admitted to trading on a regulated market) are required to give information on them as part of their annual report and the board must give an "explanatory report" on them, though it is rather unclear what sort of explanation is called for and how far it should include elements of justification. In the UK the mechanism used for this disclosure is the directors' report.[84] The domestic rules, following the Directive, require a wide range of information to be given, though some of it will either not be relevant to British companies or is already required to be disclosed. The main items to be covered are:

(a)   the structure of the company's capital, notably the rights and obligations of each class of share, whether all those classes of capital are traded on a regulated market or not;

(b)   restrictions on the transfer of securities (i.e. both shares and debentures);

(c)   the identity of persons with significant direct or indirect holdings of securities in the company and the size and nature of that holding, so far as known to the company[85];

(d)   similar information about a person with "special rights" with regard to the control of the company;

(e)   how control rights are exercised under employee share schemes, where the rights are not exercisable by the employees directly;

(f)   restrictions on voting rights, notably voting caps (restricting the percentage of total votes a shareholder has, no matter that the shareholding exceeds that percentage) or arrangements for splitting the financial and control rights of securities and placing them in different hands, where the company cooperates in making these arrangements;

---

[83] 2006 Act ss.966–7.

[84] The Large and Medium-sized Companies and Groups (Accounts and Reports) Regulations 2008 (SI 2008/410) Sch.7 Pt 6. The information might conceivably be set out in the strategic report instead: s.414C(11).

[85] In the case of "vote-holding" such disclosure by the vote-holder to the company and then by the company is required by the Transparency Directive (see para.26–14), but this disclosure obligation goes wider to embrace not just voting shares, though it is not accompanied by any obligation of disclosure on the security-holder.

(g)   agreements between holders of securities, if known to the company, which contain restrictions on transfer or the exercise of voting rights[86];

(h)   powers of the board to issue or buy back shares in the company[87];

(i)   significant agreements to which the company is party which will operate differently if there is a change of control (such as loans containing repayment covenants upon a change of control—sometimes referred to as "poisoned debt"), but subject to the exception that disclosure is not required if that would be "seriously prejudicial" to the company;

(j)   agreements between the company and its directors or employees for compensation payments to be made upon a change of control.[88]

TARGET MANAGEMENT PROMOTION OF AN OFFER

In the previous section we have proceeded on the assumption that the target board's conflict of interest in relation to a bid leads them to seek to maintain the independence of the target company and thus of their positions within it, and hence the "no frustration" rule. This does indeed constitute the most obvious expression of the target board's conflict of interest, but it is not the only one. The board might perceive its future interests as being best served by the company coming under a new controller, especially, for example, where the bidder is a private equity group which wishes to retain the existing senior management of the target and give them a much larger financial stake in the company than they had when it was in public ownership and traded on a stock market.[89] It is thus incorrect to think that the conflict of interest of the target board will always take the form of resisting the bid, to the detriment of the interests of the shareholders. The board may promote the bid—or, if there are competing bids, one of the bids—to the shareholders, again possibly to their detriment. The Code and the general law use a number of different techniques for addressing the problem of conflicted promotion of a bid by target management.

28–26

Disclosure and independent advice

One technique is to inject an element of independence into the advice which the board is required to give to the shareholders on any offer made to the shareholders by a bidder. Under r.3.1 the board is required to obtain competent

28–27

---

[86] Shareholder pacts are particularly important in some continental European countries in giving groups of investors holding a substantial, but nevertheless minority, stake in the company complete control of it. See *Financial Times*, 28 March 2007, UK edition, p.15 (discussing Italy).

[87] These are likely to be the subject of annual shareholder resolutions in any event: see paras 13–19 and 24–10 et seq.

[88] Which in the UK will often be required as part of the directors' remuneration report: see para.14–43.

[89] It does not necessarily follow that a private equity group will want to keep the existing management of the target in place. Conversely, a public bidder may be happy to keep the existing management, where it is buying the target for synergy reasons rather than because it thinks the target badly run.

independent advice[90] on any offer and the substance of that advice must be made known to the shareholders.[91] Independent advice is regarded as of particular importance on a management buyout or an offer by controlling shareholders.[92] However, r.25 requires the board to circulate its own opinion on the offer to the shareholders (that is, they cannot simply hide behind the independent advice). If there is a divergence of views within the board or between the board and the independent adviser, this must be disclosed and the arguments for and against acceptance given.[93]

Where directors have a conflict of interest, they should not normally join with the other members of the board in expressing a view on the offer. In the case of a management buy-out, the director will normally be regarded as having a conflict of interest if he or she is to have a continuing role in either offeror or offeree company.[94] Thus, where the whole of the executive director team of the target is to be taken on by the bidder, the conduct of the target company's response falls on the non-executive directors and if, as happened in a one case, the non-executives are conflicted because they are involved with the bidder as well, the chair of the board may become largely responsible for the target board's response to the bid. Some help is provided to the independent directors by r.20.3, which requires the offeror to provide to the independent directors, on request, all the information which the offeror has furnished to the potential external providers of finance in relation to the buy-out. This does something to equalise the information available to the independent directors and the executive directors who are part of the bidding team. Overall, the distinction between executive and independent non-executive directors, which has become formalised in the Corporate Governance Code, is used by the Takeover Code to handle the most pressing examples of conflict of interest which might lead the board to promote a bid, though at the cost of the non-executive directors suddenly finding themselves more heavily involved in the affairs of the company than they probably contemplated when taking on that role.

Looking at these matters from the bidder's point of view, r.24.6 requires the bidder to disclose in its offer document "any agreement, arrangement or understanding" between it (or any person acting in concert with it) and any of the target's directors or recent directors which are connected with or dependent on the offer, giving full particulars of them. This would clearly include the details of any proposed arrangement concerning employment of the directors of the target in either the target or the offeror after the bid. Rule 16 requires Panel consent for special deals offered by the bidder to some shareholders where that deal is not

---

[90] Normally from an investment bank not disqualified under r.3.3. A similar obligation applies to the board of the offeror when the offer is made in a "reverse takeover" (i.e. one in which the offeror may need to increase its issued voting equity share capital by more than 100 per cent: see fn.2 to r.3.2) or when the directors are faced with a conflict of interests: r.3.2.

[91] In its 2010 review of the Code following the politically controversial takeover of Cadbury Plc by Kraft, the Panel considered the suggestion that independent advice should be required to be given to the shareholders directly, but this was not thought to add significantly to the existing r.3 requirements. See Code Committee of the Takeover Panel, *Review of Certain Aspects of the Regulation of Takeover Bids*, 2010/22, paras 6.10–6.12.

[92] Note 1 to r.3.1.

[93] Note 2 to r.25.2.

[94] Notes 4 and 5 to r.25.2.

being extended to all shareholders. This rule creates a potential problem for management buy-outs, where, as will be usual, the target management holds shares in the target company but is also part of the bidding entity and is being offered the special deal that it will continue to be involved in the running of the target if the bid is successful or if only the management shareholders in the target company are being offered shares in the acquirer (the other shareholders being offered cash). In practice, the Panel will give its consent so as to facilitate management buy-outs where the management of the target can be regarded as a joint bidder with the other bodies which are financing the bid. For this reason "joint offerors may make arrangements between themselves regarding the future membership, control and management of the business being acquired".[95]

Compensation for loss of office

A much cruder form of conflict of interest which gives rise to managerial promotion of a bid arises out of the compensation which a director may expect to receive if the bid is successful and he or she is removed from office. The anticipation of a large windfall may shape the directors' response to the bid, consciously or unconsciously. Moreover, a part of the consideration which the bidder is willing to pay for the target may be diverted to the directors in such a case. In those jurisdictions which allocate to the target board a major role in the determination of the fate of an offer, such monetary incentives to accept the bid may well be viewed with favour, as aligning shareholder and directors' interests. However, in the UK, where the decision on the fate of the bid is allocated primarily to the shareholders, such financial incentives for target directors have been viewed as distorting the direction of the consideration the bidder is willing to pay and the incentives of the target management to advise the target shareholders dispassionately.

28–28

The Act has long contained provisions which require shareholder approval for payments in respect of loss of office.[96] These clearly catch "gratuitous" payments for loss of office (i.e. payments to which the director has not contractual entitlement) where the risks of distortion are significant. In the past, contractual entitlements to loss of office compensation were excluded from the member approval requirement, but the Act has now taken modest steps to include some of these within the principle as well.

Gratuitous payments

The provisions on gratuitous transfers apply to takeovers of both public and private companies. Where the loss of office accompanies a takeover bid, two features of the shareholder approval requirement show that the offeree shareholders are the persons the Act aims to protect. First, approval is required from the holders of the shares to which the offer relates ("relevant" shareholders), and the bidder and associates are excluded from voting in respect of any shares

28–29

---

[95] Panel Statement 2003/25, *Canary Wharf Ltd*, para.12.
[96] Now set out in Pt 4 of Pt 10 of the Act.

they hold.[97] Obtaining such consent may be problematic indeed in the case of payments made under an arrangement entered into after the transfer of the shares to the bidder and in such cases the requirement for shareholder consent may operate in practice as a prohibition on such payments.[98] Even in the course of the bid the bidder and target management may regard holding a meeting to obtain shareholder approval as a very unwelcome distraction, although it is possible for the approval to be sought by way of a written resolution where the target company is a private company. Information about the proposed payment, notably its amount, must be made available to the shareholders in advance of the vote.[99] Secondly, if approval is not obtained but a payment is nevertheless made, it is treated as held on trust by the recipient for those who have sold their shares as a result of the offer and the expenses of making the distribution to those entitled to it are to be borne by the recipient.[100] Here, therefore, the legislation has avoided the absurdity illustrated in *Regal (Hastings) Ltd v Gulliver*,[101] by providing restitution to those truly damnified, rather than to the company when, in effect, that would result in an undeserved reduction of the price that the successful offeror has paid.

28–30 These provisions apply also to payments made in connection with a takeover bid for the shares of a subsidiary of the paying company. This extension might be important where there are outside minority shareholders in the subsidiary.[102] "Takeover bid" is not defined for the purpose of this section, and so it is unclear whether the section embraces a takeover effected by means of a scheme of arrangement. The requirements ought to apply, since the risks are the same, and they are easier to comply with in a takeover by way of a scheme since a shareholder meeting is an essential part of the scheme procedure. However, "payment for loss of office" is defined. Among other things, s.215(1) includes payments for loss of any other office or employment held in conjunction with the directorship which involves the management of the company or its subsidiaries. This is a very important provision, since compensation payments are often made to executive directors in connection with the loss of their management positions in the company, rather than in connection with the loss of the directorship itself. For this reason, it is also sensible to bring shadow directors within the scope of s.219. Although loss of the status of shadow director itself is not within the

---

[97] 2006 Act s.219(1)(2)(4). Non-bidder holders of shares of the class may vote, even if their shares are not subject to the offer—a rare situation given the Code's equality rules.

[98] The Act does not require shareholder approval before the transfer of shares to the bidder under the offer but only before the payment is made. However, failure to achieve a quorum at two successive meetings triggers the rule that the payment is deemed to have been approved: s.219(5).

[99] 2006 Act s.219(3). The director is no longer under a statutory obligation, as was the case with the 1985 Act, to take all reasonable steps to secure that details of the proposed payment are included in the offer document, though r.24.5 (above) of the Code requires the offeror to include such information.

[100] 2006 Act s.222(3).

[101] See para.16–91, above.

[102] 2006 Act s.219(6) makes it clear that approval is not required where compensation is paid in relation to the takeover of a wholly-owned subsidiary. The requirement for shareholder approval also applies only to payments by UK-registered companies.

section, compensation payments for the loss of other offices or employment within the company held by the shadow director will be caught.[103]

Although the payer is typically the target company after the takeover has succeeded, the requirement for shareholder approval applies to payments for loss of office made by "any person".[104] This will clearly include payments by a parent company (i.e. the successful bidder) or a subsidiary of the target. Payments to a director include payments to a person connected with a director and payments to any person at the direction or on behalf of the director or connected person.[105] Payments are rebuttably presumed to be payments for loss of office if made in pursuance of an arrangement (not necessarily a contract) made within the period extending from one year before to two years after the transfer of the shares and either bidder or target is privy to the arrangement.[106] So, the provisions cannot be avoided simply by waiting for the transaction to be concluded. If the price paid to the director for his or her shares is in excess of that available to other shareholders or if, in connection with the transfer of the shares, any valuable consideration is given to the director by any person, the excess is irrebuttably treated as a payment for loss of office.[107] Finally, compensation is treated as including benefits otherwise than in cash, though cash is in fact the typical form of compensation provided.[108] On the other hand, there is a de minimis exception for payments by the company or its subsidiaries where the amount or value of the payment does not exceed £200, a very small amount.[109]

28-31

Contractual compensation

Although r.25.5 of the Code requires disclosure in the target's first circular to the shareholders of particulars of the directors' service contracts and of any earlier contract which has been replaced in the six months preceding the circulation, it contains no shareholder approval requirement for contractual payments. Nor does the Act, as a matter of general principle, but there are two situations where it does require shareholder approval.

28-32

First, the contract might explicitly say that upon a takeover the director is entitled to the payment of a sum of money by the company. These are sometimes

---

[103] 2006 Act s.223. This might seem to mean that a company could escape the statutory controls by paying a shadow director compensation for loss of the shadow directorship. However, since the shadow directorship is not a formal position, payment for loss of it is likely to be a breach of duty on the part of the non-shadow directors and recoverable from the shadow director who has received it, knowing of the facts which make its payment improper.

[104] 2006 Act s.219(1).

[105] 2006 Act s.215(3). The definition of a connected person is given in s.252 and discussed above at para.16–71.

[106] 2006 Act s.219(7). The date of the transfer of the shares is presumably the date upon which the bid became unconditional as to acceptances.

[107] 2006 Act s.216.

[108] 2006 Act s.215(2).

[109] 2006 Act s.221. The Secretary of State has power to raise the figure: s.258.

referred to as "covenanted payments".[110] Whilst payments "in discharge of an existing legal obligation"[111] are in principle excluded from the approval requirements of Ch.4 of Pt 10, this is so only if the obligation "was not entered into for the purpose of, in connection with or in consequence of" the takeover".[112] Thus, covenanted payments entered into in the face of a bid (even, in appropriate circumstances, before the bid is formally announced) will need shareholder approval under the provisions discussed above. The Act accurately assesses the risks to the offeree shareholders in this case to be substantially the same as with a gratuitous payment.

Secondly, payments to directors by way of damages for breach of an existing legal obligation or by way of settlement of a claim arising in connection with the termination of a director's office or employment were and remain excluded from the provisions discussed above. Thus, payments to directors, especially executive directors, representing compensation for dismissal without the proper notice due to them under their service contract or settlements of claims for such payments fall outside the provisions of Ch.4.[113] This is a significant exemption, since large sums may be payable to an executive director by way of breach of a fixed-term or long-notice service contract, even if it contains no "covenanted payments". In addition, payments "by way of pension in respect of past services" are exempted from the need for shareholder approval,[114] apparently even if they are gratuitous. Directors towards the end of their careers may positively welcome compensation payments which take the form of a pension.

However, under the provisions of Ch.4A, introduced in 2013[115] and applying only to "quoted companies",[116] payments for loss of office must either be "consistent with" the company's remuneration policy, as approved by the shareholders,[117] or receive specific shareholder approval.[118] Thus, if the director's contractual notice period or contractual term exceeds that stated in the remuneration policy, payment of damages for breach will need shareholder approval, at least in relation to the "excess" period, as will the payment of a pension beyond what the policy contemplates. The new rule applies in principle to all payments for loss of office, but it is made clear that, if the payment falls within Ch.4, Ch.4A does not apply.[119] So the relevance of Ch.4A is for payments

---

[110] *Taupo Totara Timber Co v Rowe* [1978] A.C. 537 PC; *Lander v Premier Pict Petroleum*, 1997 S.L.T. 1361. In the former case the director's service contract provided that, if the company were taken over, he could within 12 months resign from the company and become entitled to a lump-sum payment of five times his annual salary.

[111] 2006 Act s.220(1)(a).

[112] 2006 Act s.220(3).

[113] 2006 Act s.220(1)(b), (c). Such payments must be made "in good faith" and so the parties to the transaction run a legal risk if they use a damages claim to inflate the compensation payable to the director beyond his or her contractual or statutory entitlements.

[114] 2006 Act s.220(1)(d). Again the payment must be made "in good faith", which may constrain egregious use of this provision. For an unsuccessful attempt to use s.320 of the 1985 Act (now s.190 of the 2006 Act, see para.16–70) to impose a requirement for shareholder approval in relation to pensions, see *Granada Group Ltd v Law Debenture Pension Trust Corp Plc* [2015] 2 B.C.L.C. 604.

[115] By the Enterprise and Regulatory Reform Act 2013.

[116] i.e. companies with equity quoted on a top-tier public market: s.385.

[117] See para.14–44.

[118] 2006 Act s.226C.

[119] 2006 Act s.226F.

excluded from Ch.4. The detailed provisions of Ch.4A largely track those of Ch.4. In particular, the recipient of an inconsistent and unauthorised payment holds it on trust for those who sold their shares into the offer.[120]

Competing bids

One post-bid defensive measure which the Code does permit is the search by the target board for an alternative bidder. Such action is not held to breach the non-frustration rule, because the decision on the bids still rests with the shareholders of the target company, whose choices have in fact been widened by the presence of the so-called "white knight". The Directive makes it clear that "seeking alternative bids" is not caught by the prohibition on post-bid defensive action.[121] However, conflicts of interest on the part of the target board may arise here also, either because the board wishes to discourage a competitor because its interests will be better served by the initial bidder or, vice versa, where the target board seeks a competitor because it does not favour the initial bidder. Of course, in either case the board's decisions may be driven by a desire to promote the interests of the shareholders of the target, rather than the directors' interests, and so the Code and other rules need to focus on this problem with some degree of sophistication. Another troublesome question is whether it is, in fact, in the interests of the shareholders to encourage competing bids. In the context of a particular offer, that is clearly so, since the competitor drives up the price and may even trigger an auction. However, the initial bidder often loses out in the auction, thus throwing away the costs it has incurred in identifying a target and mounting a bid. Knowing of this risk, companies may be less willing to bid initially than if they could be sure that there would be no competitor, thus reducing the incidence of bids, arguably to the detriment of shareholders. It is thus conceivable that the encouragement of competing bids would mean fewer bids overall. In this situation, devising an appropriate policy for competing bids is not easy.

28–33

A duty to auction or a duty to be even-handed?

A conceivable policy would be to require the target board to seek out any available competing offers. In bid situations there will often be pressure from shareholders on the board of the target to do this. However, the Code itself contains no such obligation, only a permission for the target board to take this step. In the case law on fiduciary duties the question has sometimes arisen, but the upshot of that limited case law seems to amount to no more than the proposition that, if a competing bid does in fact emerge, the directors may not obstruct the shareholders from accepting the bid the latter prefer, but the directors are not obliged to further that offer by, for example, assenting their own shares to it. In *Heron International Ltd v Lord Grade*[122] there were two competing bids for a company whose directors held over 50 per cent of the shares and where,

28–34

---

[120] 2006 Act s.226E(4).
[121] Directive art.9(2).
[122] *Heron International Ltd v Lord Grade* [1983] B.C.L.C. 244 CA.

unusually for a public company, the consent of the directors was required for the transfer of shares. The directors had given irrevocable undertakings to accept what turned out to be the lower bid and stood by those undertakings, so that the higher bidder was defeated. The Court of Appeal declared that:

> "Where directors have decided that it is in the best interests of a company that the company should be taken over and there are two or more bidders the only duty of the directors, who have powers such as those in [the company's articles], is to obtain the best price. The directors should not commit themselves to transfer their own voting shares to a bidder unless they are satisfied that he is offering the best price reasonably available."[123]

This dictum clearly suggests that the directors' freedom to assent their own shares to the bidder favoured by them is restricted by their duty as directors to the other shareholders. In *Re A Company*,[124] where a similar issue arose in the context of unfair prejudice petition but involving this time a small private company, Hoffmann J, however, refused to accept "the proposition that the board must inevitably be under a positive duty to recommend and take all steps within their power to facilitate whichever is the highest offer", especially where that alleged duty restricted the directors' freedom of action in relation to their own shares. Their duty went no further than requiring them not to exercise their powers under the articles so as to prevent those other shareholders, who wished to do so, from accepting the higher offer, and requiring them, if they gave advice to the shareholders, to do so in the interests of those shareholders and not in order to further the bid preferred by the directors. The view of Hoffmann J seems more in accord with generally accepted principles of fiduciary law and with the Code which, as we have seen above, requires the directors to give advice to the shareholders in order to promote the interests of the latter, but stops short of requiring directors to take decisions in relation to their shares other than in their own interests.

More generally in relation to the exercise of directorial discretion, the Code can be said to adopt the policy of requiring the directors to be even-handed as between competing bids: they are not required to seek out alternative offers but, if such emerge, the choice between them should be one for the shareholders. This can be seen as an application or, perhaps, extension of the "no frustration" principle in the context of competing bids. The central provision here is r.20.2 which requires the target board to provide information to an offeror or potential offeror which it has made available to another offeror or potential offeror "even if that other offeror is less welcome". This is an important provision, because, as we shall see below, the target board is not normally under an obligation to provide information to a potential bidder to help it decide whether to make an offer or on what terms. However, if the board decides to do so for one offeror or potential offeror, it cannot refuse this facility to a competitor. This principle is applied not only to the information itself but also to the terms on which it is made available (for example, confidentiality requirements). However, the rule does not permit the competitor to ask simply for all the information given to the initial offeror: the competitor has to specify the questions to which it wants answers, and the target

---

[123] *Heron International Ltd v Lord Grade* [1983] B.C.L.C. 244 at 265.
[124] *Re A Company* [1986] B.C.L.C. 382.

company must answer them if it has done so for the other bidder.[125] There is an obvious difficulty in applying this rule in relation to a management buy-out, because the existing management element of the bidder will have comprehensive knowledge of the target company. Note 3 to r.20.2 confines the disclosure obligation in such a case to the information provided to the external providers of finance for the buy-out bid.

Quite apart from regulation of the conduct of the target board towards competing bidders, the question can be asked whether the design of the takeover Code facilitates the emergence of competitors. In many ways it does, though mainly as a side-wind from the implementation of policies designed to further other goals. Thus, as we shall see below, the timetable for the offer (the gap between the initial approach and the formal offer, the need for the formal offer to be open for a minimum period of time) does create a space in which competing bidders have the opportunity to put together an alternative offer. The offeror may seek to dilute this risk by buying shares in the target on the market in advance of the public announcement of the approach or offer. The insider dealing legislation is so drafted as not to catch a bidder who buys shares in the market knowing that it intends to make a bid at a higher price in the near future.[126] Nevertheless, market purchases on any scale are likely to drive up the price of the potential target's shares very rapidly as they become disclosable under the major shareholdings rules. Alternatively, the bidder may deal privately with the larger shareholders in the target (if there are any) and seek their agreement, in advance of the bid, to accept an offer if one is made (i.e. to give what are known as "irrevocable commitments"). However, those who give such commitments normally in fact reserve the right to withdraw the acceptance if a competitor emerges. More simply, the bidder might simply seek to buy the shares of any large shareholders in advance of the bid, but their willingness to sell might be forthcoming only in situations where they think the company is unlikely to attract rival bids.[127] Moreover, as we shall see below, pre-bid purchases may restrict the freedom of the bidder to determine the level of its offer. Overall, the Code does expose a bidder to a significant risk that a rival bid will emerge.[128]

28–35

---

[125] Note 1 to r.20.2.

[126] See paras 30–28 and 30–38.

[127] Code r.5 forbids pre-bid purchases (at least once a bid is in contemplation) which would take the bidder over the 30 per cent threshold, which triggers a mandatory bid (see below), or over the 50 per cent threshold, giving de jure control of the company, except purchases from a single shareholder (and in certain other cases). The purpose of r.5 is to ensure that "the board of the company has a sufficient opportunity to make the company's shareholders aware of all relevant matters before control of the company passes". See Panel Consultation Paper 2005/5, para.6.1. (However, the rules on Substantial Acquisitions of Shares, which previously formed an addendum to the Code and prevented, or at least slowed down, market raids, were repealed in 2006.)

[128] However, the Code does not encourage competing bids, as some systems do, by automatically releasing those who have accepted the offer if a competing bidder emerges, but only if the offer has not become unconditional as to acceptances within 21 days of the first closing date of the initial offer (r.34). For this reason, experienced investors do not accept an offer until the final moment, so as to be able freely to consider competing offers, whilst those who find the terms of the offer attractive may simply sell their shares in the market. On the other hand, once a competing bidder emerges, the bid

Binding the target board by contract

28–36   Given the risks just alluded to, the initial bidder may well seek, by contract, to enlist the directors of the target on its side in dealing with any future competitor. There are two main contractual techniques which have been used to this end, though obviously they are potentially available only where the target board approves of the proposed bid. First, the initial bidder may wish to secure from the directors of the target company a legally binding undertaking to recommend the bid to the shareholders of the target in any event and not to seek, encourage or co-operate with any "white knight". Such an agreement with the directors is not necessarily against the interests of the target's shareholders, for the initial bidder may not be willing to make a bid at all for the target unless such undertakings are forthcoming. The courts, however, have been unwilling to give full effect to such agreements, especially the commitment always to recommend the initial offer, even if a better one emerges. They have subjected the contractual undertaking to recommend the bid to an implied limitation, which in fact deprives the undertaking of most of its utility to the offeror, that the directors should be free to recommend the competing bid if they form the view that it would be in the best interests of the shareholders that the bid be accepted.[129] There is in fact a lot to be said for this approach, for to hold otherwise would be to undermine both the basic allocation of decision-making power on the fate of the bid to the shareholders and General Principle 2 of the Code that the shareholders must be given the information necessary to enable them to reach a properly informed decision on the bid.

Given the uncertainties surrounding agreements which seek to control the target board's actions towards competing bidders, it is not surprising that alternative contractual arrangements were developed. A common form of agreement was the "break fee" or "inducement fee", i.e. an agreement between the target company (through its directors) and the initial bidder that, if the bidder's offer is not accepted for one of a number of reasons, which might include the shareholders' acceptance of an alternative offer, the target company becomes liable to pay a sum of money to the disappointed bidder. In this way, the initial bidder seeks to protect itself against the financial costs of its failed bid. However, the effect of a large break fee may be to discourage a competing bidder, since it effectively reduces the value of the target in the hands of the competitor, but not in the hands of the bidder which has negotiated the break fee.

The break fee was always regarded with some suspicion by the Code, which imposed a cap on the level of the fee (or similar inducement) at 1 per cent of the offer price. However, in the course of the Panel's 2010 review of the Code it was

---

timetable is re-set for both offerors according to that appropriate for the competitor (see fn.4 to r.31.6) so that the offer period is extended to give target company shareholders adequate time to consider both offers.

[129] *Dawson International Plc v Coats Paton Plc* [1991] B.C.C. 278; *Rackham v Peek Foods Ltd* [1990] B.C.L.C. 895; *John Crowther Group Ltd v Carpets International Plc* [1990] B.C.L.C. 460. See also the decision of the Inner House in the interlocutory proceedings in the *Dawson* case: (1989) 5 B.C.C. 405. This is sometimes called the "fiduciary out" though it is to some degree unclear in these cases whether the result was arrived at as a matter of interpretation of the contract in question or of the application of a mandatory rule of the law of directors' duties.

concluded that break fees and other "deal protection measures", including "no cooperation" agreements, should be prohibited, except in very limited cases. The Code Committee was sceptical about the benefits to target shareholders of inducement fees and other deal protection devices, which it regarded as often imposed by the acquirer for its benefit.[130] Rule 21.2 now prohibits in most situations "offer-related arrangements",[131] a term which includes but goes beyond inducement fees and embraces commitments by the offeree board not to cooperate with competing bidders.[132] However, the potentially adverse impact upon shareholder choice of prohibiting inducement fess is recognised in two situations. Subject to the 1 per cent cap and disclosure, the target company may agree an inducement fee with a competing offeror where an initial, but not recommended, bid has been launched (so that a competitor can be encouraged). Further, where the board of the target had initiated a formal sale of the company before any firm offer for the target was announced, and sought bidders in that context, it will normally be permitted to agree an inducement fee (and perhaps other arrangements) with a bidder who participated in that process in order to encourage it to make a formal bid.[133] Here, the formal sale process operates as the assurance that all serious offers have been flushed out.

EQUALITY OF TREATMENT OF TARGET SHAREHOLDERS

Since the UK Code places the decision on the offer firmly in the hands of the target shareholders, it follows that there is a strong regulatory interest in protecting the target shareholders from being manipulated by the offeror into accepting an offer they think is sub-optimal. The possibility of manipulation arises, on the one hand, from the bidder's freedom under the law of contract to formulate the offer as it wishes (in the absence of regulation) and, on the other, from the dispersed nature of the shareholders in a typical UK target company, so that coordination amongst them is too costly to be effective. Although "the Code is not concerned with the financial or commercial advantages or disadvantages of a takeover",[134] it does contain a wide range of rules designed to preserve the integrity of the target shareholders' decision-making and these rules do shape the substantive content of the offer. The most obvious (but not the only) technique the bidder might deploy to manipulate the target shareholders' decision-making is unequal treatment of the offerees. For example, a bidder might make an attractive

28–37

---

[130] Above fn.91 at para.5.15.
[131] Code r.21.2(b) contains a list of agreements which are permitted because they do not infringe substantially the principle of shareholder choice. This new approach also renders less important, but does not remove, the difficult question of whether a break fee constitutes financial assistance under the statute (para.13–44): *Paros Plc v Wordlink Group Plc* [2012] EWHC 394 (Comm).
[132] The Code Committee review (above fn.91 at para.5.16) makes it clear that the intention was to include undertakings "to refrain from taking any action which might facilitate a competing transaction" as well as commitments to positive action in relation to the initial bid. The prohibition on agreements to take positive action might be thought to impede the implementation of agreed takeovers by way of schemes because the scheme arrangements are in the hands of the offeree (see para.29–5) and offeror will want the target to commit to propose the scheme. However, the necessary obligation is now laid on the offeree by the Code itself: App.7.3(f).
[133] Notes 1 and 2 to r.21.2.
[134] Code, *Introduction*, 2(a).

offer for target shares, but only for a certain percentage of them, with the offer being open only for a short-time. Once this offer is satisfied, the bidder might make a lower offer to the remaining shareholders or no offer at all. Although the shareholders collectively might be better off if they all refused the offer and forced the acquirer to bid for all the target shares on the same terms, any individual shareholder will maximise his returns by accepting the partial offer. Or the inequality strategy may be implemented the other way around. The acquirer makes a low-level bid for all the shares. Having picked up the unsophisticated shareholders in this way, it makes a higher offer to those who hold out. From the beginning the Code has addressed these "divide and rule" issues though the requirement for equal treatment of target shareholders, a notion which has now been developed to a considerable degree of sophistication. Reflecting the Directive, GP 1 of the Code stipulates that "all holders of the securities of an offeree company of the same class must be afforded equivalent treatment" but the Rules in fact go beyond this. The equality principle, in all its manifestations, is another demonstration that, whilst the Code facilitates takeovers, it does not make the maximisation of the number of bids its goal, for otherwise it would permit differential offers. However, this policy is not without its costs. Some of the bids which are discouraged by the equality rules would come from financially constrained bidders who nevertheless would run the company more efficiently than the current controllers.

Partial bids

28–38   Perhaps the most obvious way of implementing the equality principle is to prohibit partial bids, i.e. offer for only some of the outstanding shares in the target. Through a partial bid the offeror acquires sufficient shares to obtain control of the company, but not all the shares are acquired. If the offer is made on a "first come, first served" basis, offerees may rush to accept it, either because it is pitched at an attractive level or, even though it is not, offerees wish to exit the company because of doubts about how well the acquirer will run it in the future. As we shall see in para.28–58 a floor is put under the partial bid strategy by the requirement that the bidder must end up with at least 50 per cent of the voting rights in the target; otherwise the bid will be ineffective. However, the Code goes much further: by r.36 the Panel's consent is needed for partial offers. Consent will normally be given if the offer could not result in the offeror being interested in shares carrying 30 per cent or more of the voting rights of the target company, since at this level the acquirer is not regarded as having control.[135] If the partial offer could result in the offeror holding more than 30 per cent but less than 100 per cent, consent will not normally be granted if the offeror or its concert party has acquired, selectively or in significant numbers, interests in shares in the target company during the previous 12 months or if any shares were acquired after the partial offer was reasonably in contemplation.[136] Nor, without consent, may any

---

[135] Code r.36.1. In fact, where the other shares are very dispersed, less than 30 per cent could in fact give control. However, the Code is constructed on the basis of equating a 30 per cent holding with control. See the discussion of the mandatory bid below.
[136] Code r.36.2.

member of the concert party purchase any further interests in shares within 12 months after a successful partial bid.[137] Both rules promote equality of treatment, since the sellers outside the offer may have been able to dispose of the entirety of their shareholdings and at a better price.

If the Panel does give its consent to a partial offer, some restrictive conditions apply to it. First, all the accepting shareholders must be able to dispose of the same proportion of their holdings.[138] Secondly, the offer must state the precise number of shares bid for and the offer must not be declared unconditional unless acceptances are received for not less than that number.[139] Thus, the offeror does not have freedom to relax the acceptance condition, which is normally possible in a full offer. More interestingly, where the partial offer could result in the offeror being interested in more than 50 per cent of the votes, shareholders are asked to vote on two questions. The first is, as ever, whether to accept the offer for their shares; and the second is whether they approve of the offer, irrespective of their decision to sell their shares. Given the "same proportion" rule, the existing shareholders will remain members of the target company, at least as to part of their shareholdings, even if the bid is successful. They may well regard this as unsatisfactory: hence the requirement that shareholders should have a double opportunity to vote. Shareholders may vote to accept the offer in relation to the relevant proportion of their shares, thus enabling them to benefit from the disposal of part of their holding if the bid does go through, whilst voting not to approve the bid. The partial bid will be successful only if the acquirer obtains at least 50 per cent approval for the bid as well the number of shares bid for. Finally, to induce shareholders to exercise both voting opportunities, an offer which could result in the offeror holding shares carrying over 50 per cent of the votes must contain a prominent warning that, if the offer succeeds, the offeror will be free, subject to the twelve-month post bid prohibition, to acquire further shares without incurring an obligation to make a mandatory offer.[140]

These Rules of the Code display an obvious antipathy to partial offers, even though formal equality of treatment is maintained by the requirement that all shareholders who accept the offer must have the same proportion of their holdings acquired by the bidder. In consequence, partial bids are infrequent, though not unknown.

Level and type of consideration

In pursuit of the equality principle the Code contains rules which determine the minimum level of consideration which is required to be offered for the shares, even when the offer is made to all target shareholders. The purpose of these equality rules is to prevent the offeror from distorting the decision of the target's shareholders by offering an attractive price to some shareholders to gain control whilst offering an inadequate price to the remainder, who then have the choice of accepting the low offer or being locked into the company under a new controller.

28–39

---

[137] Code r.36.3.
[138] Code r.36.7.
[139] Code r.36.4.
[140] Code r.36.6.

The first and most obvious expression of the equality principle is to be found in the requirement that, if the offer is revised upwards after an initial offer at a lower price, the original acceptors are entitled to the higher consideration.[141] This rule probably does more to protect inexperienced shareholders (who accept early) than to prevent opportunistic behaviour on the part of offeror companies.[142] The function of the rule giving an entitlement to offer increases is supported by r.16.1, whereby, except with the consent of the Panel, the offeror may not make any special arrangements, either during an offer or when one is reasonably in contemplation, whereby favourable conditions are offered to some shareholders which are not extended to all of them.[143]

A more significant expression of the equality principle is between those who accept the offer and those who sell their shares to the offeror outside the offer, either before the offer is made or during the offer period. Again, r.6 of the Code seeks to prevent private and favourable deals being done with a few shareholders. An offeror (or person acting in concert) which purchases shares of a relevant class in the three months before the offer period[144] or during that period[145] must make or raise the level of the offer for that class to that paid outside it, if it is higher.[146] However, r.6 distinguishes between purchases made before the offer period begins and those made after a firm intention to make an offer has been announced. In relation to purchases made beforehand, it is clear that the rule does not necessarily require that the offer be in cash even if the prior acquisitions have been for cash. To that extent, r.6 permits inequality: the offer later made may be on a share-exchange basis but the securities offered by the bidder must have the value equal to the highest consideration paid outside the offer. However, if the post-announcement acquisitions at above the offer price are for cash, the offer will have to be (or become) a cash offer or be accompanied by a cash alternative.[147]

28–40   However, even in respect of acquisitions made before the offer period, the subsequent offer will have to be in cash (or accompanied by an alternative cash offer, probably provided by the offeror's investment bank rather than the offeror itself), if the conditions of r.11.1 are met. Where the offeror and persons acting in concert acquire "for cash" shares of a class in the target company, which carry at least 10 per cent of the voting rights of the class, in the 12 months prior to the offer, the subsequent offer must be in cash or be accompanied by a cash

---

[141] Code r.32.3.

[142] The pressures in favour of thoughtless acceptance are further mitigated by the procedural rules requiring the initial offer to be open for acceptance for at least 21 days (r.31.1) and revised offers to be open for at least 14 days (r.32.1).

[143] Note 1 makes it clear that this bans the not-unknown practice of buying a shareholding coupled with an undertaking to make good to the seller any difference between the sale price and the higher price of any successful subsequent bid. It also covers (Note 3) cases where a shareholder of the target company is to be remunerated for the part he has played in promoting the offer ("a finder's fee").

[144] Code r.6.1 or even earlier if the Panel thinks this is necessary to give effect to General Principle 1: r.6.1(c).

[145] Code r.6.2.

[146] Before an announcement is made of a firm intention to make an offer the Panel has a discretion to relax the rule, though it will do so only rarely, but not thereafter. Compare rr.6.1 and 6.2.

[147] Note 3 to r.6. For this reason some systems prohibit post-offer purchases outside the bid if the offer is on a share-exchange basis.

alternative at the highest level of the prices paid outside the offer.[148] In this rule "cash" has an extended meaning in its application to acquisitions "for cash", though it bears its ordinary meaning in relation to the requirement that the offer be "in cash". In relation to acquisitions the phrase includes acquisitions by the offeror company in exchange for securities, unless the exiting shareholder is not free to dispose of the securities until the offerees in the general bid receive their consideration (or the offer lapses).[149] The thinking is that, since securities are saleable, they are the equivalent of cash. The overall effect of r.11.1 is that the offer must be in cash or accompanied by a cash alternative because the sellers prior to the bid have received cash (or its equivalent). The rule is triggered only at the 10 per cent level and so it can be argued that r.11.1 is not a full implementation of the equality principle. Beneath the 10 per cent threshold, r.6.1 applies, not normally requiring a cash offer and applying only in the three-month period before the bid. The contrary argument is that a stronger rule would discourage bids because bidders would either have to forgo pre-bid acquisitions or always launch cash bids where they had made previous acquisitions for cash. Building up a pre-bid stake is a way of obtaining some degree of protection against a competing offer, either because the stake will deter a competitor or because, if the initial bidder fails, it can recoup some of its costs by selling its stake at a profit to the successful bidder.

Rule 11.1 does not deal with the converse case, i.e. where the prior acquisitions were in exchange for securities but the bid is in cash and the target shareholders claim they should be offered the securities provided in the prior acquisitions. This is a rarer situation than the one where the general offerees claim cash, because cash is in general more attractive than securities, but there might be exceptional circumstances where the securities were attractive but not readily available on the market. In the light of this, a new rule was introduced in 2002, similar, but not identical, to r.11.1, but requiring securities to be offered in the general bid. Under r.11.2, if, during the three months prior to the commencement of the offer and during the offer period, the offeror has acquired shares of a class in the target which carry 10 per cent of the voting rights of the class in exchange for securities, then the general bid must offer the same number[150] of securities to the target shareholders. However, this will not displace the obligation to offer cash or a cash alternative under r.11.1, if the securities accepted outside the bid have triggered r.11.1.[151] Rule 11.2 is less far-reaching than the combined effect of rr.6.2 and 11.1 because it is triggered only by the 10 per cent threshold (even if the securities have been offered during the bid) and because it reaches back only to the three months before the bid.

---

[148] The Panel has a discretion to apply the cash rule even if fewer than 10 per cent of the voting rights have been acquired (see r.11.1(c)), something Note 4 to r.11.1 suggests it might do, and at a considerably lower level than 10 per cent, if the vendors were directors of the target.

[149] See Note 5 to r.11.1.

[150] Which may not now have the same value as when offered prior to the offer: see Note 1 to r.11.2.

[151] Or under the mandatory bid rule, see below.

Mandatory offers

28–41   The strongest expression of the equality rule, however, is to be found in the mandatory bid rule. Here, a bidder is obliged to make an offer in a situation where it has obtained without a general offer what the Code regards as effective control of the company and might not therefore wish to make a general offer to the shareholders of a company it already controls. However, because the sellers to the new controller were able to exit the company upon a change of control, the Code requires the remaining shareholders to be given the same opportunity. A mandatory bid rule is now required of Member States by art.5 of the Takeover Directive. This led to some minor changes to the Code rules, though in general the mandatory bid rule contained in the Code is tougher than that required by the Directive.

Under r.9.1 a mandatory bid is required when:

(a)   Any person acquires an interest in shares which (with any shares held or acquired by any persons acting in concert) carry 30 per cent or more of the voting rights of a company.

(b)   Any person who, with persons acting in concert, already holds not less than 30 per cent but not more than 50 per cent of the voting rights and who, alone or with persons acting in concert, acquires an interest in additional shares.

In those cases, unless the Panel otherwise consents, such a person must extend offers, on the basis set out in subsequent provisions of r.9, to the holders of any class of equity share capital, whether voting or non-voting, and also to the holders of any other class of transferable securities carrying voting rights. Offers for the different classes of equity share capital must be comparable and the Panel should be consulted in advance.

The effect of this Rule is that, once acquirers have secured "control" (circumstance (a)) or acquisitions have been made to consolidate control[152] (circumstance (b)), a general offer must be made, thus giving all equity shareholders an opportunity of quitting the company and sharing in the price paid for the control or its consolidation. However, the force of the requirement lies not in the obligation to make an offer by itself, but in the supplementary rules which determine the level and nature of the offer which has to be made. After all, an

---

[152] In the case of consolidation, the holder will necessarily have been able to cross the 30 per cent threshold without triggering the mandatory bid, notably where it falls into one of the exceptions discussed below. The Code used to allow consolidation of control at the rate of 1 per cent a year without imposing a mandatory bid requirement. However, this facility was removed, seemingly in response to the decision in *Re Astec (BSR) Plc* [1998] 2 B.C.L.C. 556, in which the court took a narrow view of the application of the unfair prejudice remedy in relation to future actions of a shareholder which had obtained "creeping control" of a company under this facility. In this case the target company was non-resident in the UK, and so not subject to the Code when it acquired 45 per cent of the target, but it then entered into an agreement with the other investors under which it made itself subject to the Code. Today, the company's initial purchase would be subject to the Code since the company was incorporated in the UK and its shares were traded on the Main Market of the LSE, and the fact that its headquarters were in Hong Kong would not put it outside the Code. See above, para.28–15.

obligation to make an offer which none of the offerees would find attractive would be a futile gesture on the part of the rule-maker. Crucial here are the requirements that a mandatory offer must be a cash offer, or with a cash alternative, and be pitched at the highest price paid by the offeror or a member of his concert party within the 12 months prior to the commencement of the offer.[153] As we have seem, in a voluntary offer this level of consideration is required only if shares carrying 10 per cent or more of the voting rights of that class were purchased in the previous 12 months. An acquirer cannot escape the cash requirement for a mandatory bid by waiting a year before acquiring the shares which carry it over the 30 per cent threshold. In addition, a mandatory bid must not contain any conditions other than that it is dependent on acceptances being such as to result in the bidder holding 50 per cent of the voting rights;[154] on a voluntary offer, there may well be further conditions.[155]

Furthermore, where directors of the target company (or their close relatives and family trusts) sell shares to a purchaser as a result of which the purchaser is required by r.9 to make a mandatory offer, the directors must ensure that, as a condition of the sale, the purchaser undertakes to fulfil its obligations under the rule and, except with the consent of the Panel, the directors must not resign from the board until the closing date of the offer or the date when it becomes wholly unconditional, whichever is the later. Further, whether the directors have been involved on the sell side of the acquisition or not, a nominee of the new controller may not be appointed to the board of the target company nor may it exercise the votes attached to any shares it holds in the target company until the formal offer document has been posted.[156]

The mandatory bid requirement of the Code is one of its outstanding features, even if relatively few mandatory bids are made. Being aware of the rule, acquirers normally sit just below the 30 per cent threshold and then make a voluntary bid when they want to go further. This is because, as we have just seen, the acquirer has more flexibility with the formulation of a voluntary bid, so that it is normally desirable to avoid triggering a mandatory one. Even so, a bid made in these circumstances is not truly "voluntary": the acquirer might really have wanted to go to 40 per cent and then rest satisfied that it had enough votes to control the company, but that option is not open to it. The effect of the mandatory bid rule is, usually, to require a person who wishes to obtain control of a company to do so by offering to acquire all or most of the equity share capital of the company. This discourages acquirers who aim to extract benefits from the

28–42

---

[153] Code r.9.5. Unless the Panel agrees to an adjusted price in a particular case: see Note 3 to r.9.5 for the factors the Panel will take into account in considering whether to grant a dispensation from the highest price rule. For a strong example of the application of the "highest price" rule, even in the face of a serious market decline triggered by the terrorist bombings in New York, see Panel Statement 2001/15 (WPP Group Plc).

[154] Code r.9.3. But, when the mandatory offer comes within the provisions for a possible reference to the competition authorities, it must be a condition of the offer that it will lapse if that occurs. But, in contrast with voluntary offers (r.12), it *must* be revived if the merger is allowed and, if it is prohibited, the Panel may require the offeror to reduce its holdings to below 30 per cent: r.9.4, Note 1.

[155] e.g. on a share for share offer that it is conditional on the passing of a resolution by members of the offeror to increase its issued capital.

[156] Code rr.9.6 and 9.7.

company personally ("private benefits of control") rather than increase the value of the company for the benefit of all shareholders. The personal benefit strategy clearly has little attraction for someone who in any event owns all or most of the company. On the other hand, it discourages acquisitions by those who would increase the value of the company for the benefit of all shareholders but who are wealth constrained and so cannot raise the finance needed to bid for all the outstanding shares. Non-controlling shareholders might be better off if the latter sort of partial bid were allowed to proceed.[157]

Exemptions and relaxations

28–43   Given the major financial consequences for an acquirer of triggering a mandatory bid, one can expect acquirers to take great pains to avoid it. In some cases this may discourage activities which are viewed as entirely legitimate. In this situation, a great deal of attention comes to be focused on the Panel's discretion to exempt acquirers, wholly or partly, from the mandatory bid obligation, which the notes to r.9 indicate it is prepared to do in certain circumstances, sometimes on its own decision and sometimes only if a majority of the shareholders of the potential target company agree, though these notes do not constrain the Panel's discretion to grant exemptions in other cases. For example, if a shareholder envisages that a particular financial operation, such as a share issue via a placing,[158] will take it over the 30 per cent limit, it may escape the obligation to bid if it adopts in advance firm arrangements to off-load the shares to non-connected parties within a very short period after their acquisition.[159] Otherwise, the company's capital raising abilities might be reduced. Again, a redemption or repurchase by a company of its shares may take a shareholder over the 30 per cent mark without the shareholder having taken any action at all. This situation is given a rule of its own (r.37), in which the Panel states that it will normally[160] waive the bid obligation, provided the Panel is consulted in advance and the independent shareholders of the target agree and the stringent "whitewash" procedure (set out in App.1 to the Code) is followed. Finally, a Note on Dispensations from r.9, appended to the Rules, lists six situations where a mandatory bid is not normally required, either because the policy behind the rule has not in truth been infringed or because it is subordinated to other policies regarded as of greater value to the company and its shareholders than the equality policy. Into the first category fall (a) inadvertent mistakes, provided the holding is brought below the threshold within a limited period; and (b) situations where, in addition to the person who would otherwise be required to launch a mandatory

---

[157] For discussion of the mandatory bid see fn.62, above, Ch.8.3.5.

[158] See para.25–13.

[159] Note 7 to r.9.1. Notes 8 to 15 deal with a number of other cases where dispensation may be granted, for example, indirect acquisitions of controlling interests, convertible securities, further acquisitions after a reduction of the holding below 30 per cent; share lending arrangements.

[160] But not if the person seeking the waiver bought shares in the target company after the point at which it had reason to believe that a redemption or repurchase would take place: Note 2 to r.37.1.

bid, another single person holds 50 per cent of the voting rights (so that the acquisition of the 30 per cent or more does not in fact confer control on the acquirer).[161]

Into the second category fall situations where the 30 per cent threshold is breached as a result of (c) a rescue operation of a company in a serious financial position, even if the independent shareholders of the target have not approved the acquisitions, since insolvency is a more serious threat to shareholder wellbeing than a new controller; (d) where a lender enforces its rights and acquires shares given as security (for otherwise the value of shares as collateral would be undermined); (e) where a holding of more than 30 per cent of the voting rights results from an enfranchisement of previously non-voting shares (showing that enfranchisement is to be encouraged); and (f) where a company issues new shares either for cash or in exchange for an acquisition, provided a majority of the independent shareholders agree to removal of the bid obligation, through what is known as the "whitewash" procedure.[162] This last covers a variety of situations, including that where an offeror company makes a share exchange offer as a result of which a large shareholder in the target, who is perhaps already a significant shareholder in the offeror, ends up with more than 30 per cent of the combined entity.[163] Thus, the mandatory bid rule, although strictly formulated in r.9, is applied with some flexibility by the Panel.

Acting in concert

Although the definition of "acting in concert" is relevant to the percentage tests used in all the rules which implement the equality principle, the consequences of the mandatory bid rule focus particular attention on the concept in this context. Indeed, in its introduction to the notes on r.9.1 the Code states that "the majority of questions which arise in the context of r.9 relate to persons acting in concert", and the notes then provide five pages of guidance on the concept in the context of r.9, in addition to what is said in the "Definitions" section of the Code about the concept in general. When a group of persons act in concert to acquire control of a company, r.9.2 and the note thereto impose the obligation to make a general offer on the person whose acquisition takes the group's holding over the relevant threshold, but also extend the obligation to each of the "principal members" of the group, if the triggering acquirer is not such a member. It appears that the offer need not be made to the other members of the concert party, but only to the outside shareholders.

The "Definitions" section lays down the following general principle:

28–44

---

[161] Dispensation Notes 4 and 5. Note 5 also waives the bid where the holders of 50 per cent of the voting rights indicate they would not accept the bid, no matter by how many people those rights are held.

[162] Dispensation Notes 3, 2, 6 and 1 respectively. In the case of (d) the security must not have been taken at a time when the lender had reason to believe that enforcement was likely, and of (e) the shares must not have been purchased at a time when the purchaser had reason to believe that enfranchisement was likely. The "whitewash" procedure is set out in App.1 of the Code, which involves tight Panel control over the procedure.

[163] In the case of entities of equal size, this could occur if a person held 15 per cent of the voting rights of both offeror and target companies.

"Persons acting in concert comprise persons who, pursuant to an agreement or understanding (whether formal or informal) co-operate to obtain or consolidate control of a company or to frustrate the successful outcome of an offer for a company."

The "Definitions" section then goes on to provide that six categories of persons are presumed to be acting in concert unless the contrary is proved.[164] In the context of r.9, a troublesome question has been the relationship between shareholder activism, which the Government encourages,[165] and acting in concert and the mandatory bid obligation. Shareholders are likely to be deterred from coming together to influence the board if they fear that they will be required by the Code to make a general offer for the company's shares. In principle r.9 does apply to shareholders who obtain control of a company by pooling their existing shares. However, there is one limitation on the pooling rule. Note 1 makes it clear that shareholders are not caught by the mandatory bid obligation at the moment they come together in order to obtain control of a company, even if at that point their prior and independently acquired shareholdings together exceed the 30 per cent threshold. What will trigger the mandatory bid is their subsequent acquisition of further interests in shares. However, it may discourage institutional shareholders from coming together to exercise their rights as shareholders if the price of so doing is their inability to acquire further shares in the company. Since successful activism will increase the share price, an important method for the activists to gain some reward for their activism is to invest in the company in advance of their intervention but after they have decided to intervene. If they are prohibited from making such acquisitions, a greater part of the benefits of intervention will simply go to the non-intervening shareholders who free ride on the activists' actions.

The relationship between shareholder activism and the mandatory bid rule has received explicit attention from the Code Committee[166] and the results of its deliberations are now reflected in Note 2 to r.9.1. The Panel's prior position was that shareholders who come together to seek control of a company's board are presumed to be acting in concert in respect of their subsequent actions. (If the intervention contemplated falls short of seeking control of the company's board, for example, voting against the Directors' Remuneration Report, then the issue of conflict with r.9 does not arise.) The Panel was clearly under some pressure not to place obstacles in the way of an important government policy and the new Note means that "the Panel will be less likely than it has been in the past to rule that activist shareholders are acting in concert".[167] Although not altering its fundamental approach in this area, the Panel through the new Note makes the

---

[164] This definition reflects art.2(1)(d) of the Directive. The presumed categories of acting in concert are: (i) a company with any others in the group and associated companies (widely defined, so as to make a company an associated company if another company controls 20 per cent of its equity share capital); (ii) a company with any of its directors and their close relatives and related trusts; (iii) a company with any of its pension funds or the pension funds of other group or associated companies; (iv) a fund manager with any of its discretionary managed clients; (v) a connected adviser with its client; (vi) the directors of the target company.

[165] See above, paras 15–25 et seq.

[166] *Shareholder Activism and Acting in Concert*, Consultation Paper 10, issued by the Code Committee of the Panel (2002).

[167] *Shareholder Activism and Acting in Concert*, para.1.6.

crucial clarification that, even where the shareholder coalition seeks to change the whole of a company's board, their efforts will not be classified as "board control seeking" if there is no "relationship" between the activist shareholders and the proposed directors. Thus, voting a new management team into place, or even finding it as well, will not trigger a finding of acting in concert if the new directors' relationship with the activists does not go beyond the normal board/shareholder relationship. Even if such a relationship does exist, the acting in concert rule may not be triggered, depending on the circumstances.

Interests in shares

A second notable feature of the percentage tests to be found in the equality rules **28–45** of the Code is that they apply, not just to the acquisition of shares, but to the acquisition of "interests in shares". A definition of "interests in shares" was introduced as part of a major reform of the Code in 2005. The "Definitions" section of the Code sets out a list of situations which will be regarded as involving the acquisition of an interest in a share. Some of them are quite obvious, such as the acquisition of the right to control the exercise of voting rights attached to shares, without actually owning them, as where a shareholder agrees, as is permissible, to vote in the way the other party to a contract directs.[168] However, the main impetus for the 2005 changes was to deal with the issue of derivatives, and, in particular, with the form of derivative known as a "contract for differences" (CfD), the only form of derivative which will be discussed here. The essence of the problem of the CfD is that it is a contract which, on its face, gives the holder of it only an economic interest in the movement of the market price of the security over a period of time and not an entitlement to exercise any of the rights attached to the share. On this basis, a CfD is irrelevant to control of a company. In practice, however, the holder of a CfD is often able to control the exercise of voting rights attached to the shares in question and sometimes even to acquire them at the end of the contract. In brief, the holder of a "long" CfD contracts to receive from the counterparty any upward difference between the market prices of the security at two points in time (or the contract may be based on a starting "reference" price, which is something other than the then current market price). The counterparty, usually an investment bank or securities house, will normally hedge its position, but is not obliged to do so, by acquiring a corresponding number of underlying securities at around the "start" price of the CfD. It is this action on the part of the counterparty, usually found but not legally required, that generates the problem for control rights. The counterparty holds the shares only for hedging, and will normally be prepared to exercise its voting rights as the holder of the CfD requires (if only to obtain repeat CfD business from the holder) and at the end of the contract may well be happy to close out its position by transferring the shares to the holder of the CfD, if the holder so requires.[169]

---

[168] *Puddephat v Leith* [1916] 1 Ch. 200.

[169] Panel Consultation Papers 2005/1–3, *Dealings in Derivatives and Options*, set out the nature of the problem (see in particular PCP 2005/1, section A) and the Panel's proposals for reform of the Code. The CfD may work in the opposite way (i.e. the holder obtains the downward difference in the

Thus, a person seeking to exercise control over a company, but being aware of the restrictions in the Code, could have sought to circumvent its restrictions by exercising some or all of its control rights via CfDs. The changes made prevent that step. The definition of "interests in securities" now provides, generally, that "a person who has long economic exposure, whether absolute or conditional, to changes in the price of securities will be treated as interested in those securities", and, in particular, that a person will be regarded as having an interest in securities if "he is party to any derivative: (a) whose value is determined by reference to their price; and (b) which results, or may result, in his having a long position in them". It should be noted that the Panel's rules contain no "safe harbour" for a person who does have a purely economic interests in shares arising out of CfDs, for example, where the counterparty has not bought the shares in question as a hedge. A person might trigger the mandatory bid rule purely on the basis of such interests, and would be reliant on the consent of the Panel to escape the consequences of that rule.

Conclusion

28–46 The mandatory bid rule is a very strong expression of the Code's principle that all shareholders in the target company must be treated equally upon a change of control. Without it, those to whom the offeror makes approaches when building the controlling block might be under pressure to sell for fear that no comparable later general offer will be forthcoming. From a more corporate law point of view the mandatory bid rule might be seen as a form of minority shareholder protection. The prospects of minority equity shareholders in a company depend crucially upon how the controllers of the company exercise their powers and the provisions of company law proper, even after the enactment of the new "unfair prejudice" provisions of the Companies Act (discussed in Ch.20), could be seen as incapable of providing comprehensive protection of minority shareholders against unfair treatment. Consequently, when there is a change of control of a company, it could be said that all the shareholders should be given an opportunity to leave the company and to do so on the same terms as have been obtained by those who have sold the shares which constitute the new controlling block.[170]

It should be noted that there are two aspects of the policy underlying r.9. The first is the opportunity for all shareholders to exit the company upon a change of control by selling their shares to the new controller, and the second is the opportunity to do so on the most favourable terms that have been obtained by those who sold to the holder of the 30 per cent block. Of these two aspects it is

---

market prices) but then the counterparty will protect itself by selling "short", which does not create the control problems noted in the text. Why should anyone enter into such a contract? Essentially, it allows the derivative holder to speculate in relation to the price of the underlying shares without having to spend the money to acquire them. The fee paid to the investment bank for entering into the contract is a form of recompense to the bank for making the acquisition instead of the derivative holder (a sort of interest payment).

[170] Of course, 30 per cent is only a rough approximation of the point at which a change of de facto control of a company occurs. In the early versions of the Code the figure was set at 40 per cent, but it was reduced to 30 per cent in 1974. However, a precise percentage makes the Rule easier to operate than would a case-by-case examination of whether a particular shareholder had acquired sufficient shares in a particular company to enable it to control that company.

the second which is the more controversial. In particular, the latter aspect of the Rule makes it impossible for the holder of an existing controlling block of shares to obtain any premium for control upon the sale of the shares. Since the purchaser of the block will know that the Code requires it to offer the same price to all shareholders, the purchaser is forced to divide the consideration for the company's securities rateably among all the shareholders. In the UK, where shareholdings in listed companies are widely dispersed, this is probably not an important issue, but in countries where family shareholdings in even listed companies are of significant size, the Rule might operate as a disincentive to transfers of control.

To whom must an offer be made?

A final form of equality is as between voting and non-voting shares in all types of bid. Where the target company has more than one class of equity share capital, r.14 requires a "comparable" offer[171] to be made for each class, including non-voting classes, if the acquirer decides to offer for at least one of the classes. Thus, an offeror company may not bid only for equity shares carrying voting rights but must bid for all classes of equity share. This reflects the policy that a change of control in a company is a significant event for equity shareholders (whose returns depend on the discretion and success of the controllers) and so all such shareholders should be given the opportunity to exit the company on fair terms when a change of control is in prospect.[172] The rule is a protection of non-voting shareholders rather than aimed at controlling coercive offers. Separate offers must be made for each class of equity share. The offer for the non-voting equity must not be made conditional upon any particular level of acceptances by that class, unless the offer for the voting shares is conditional upon that same level of acceptances by the non-voting equity shareholders. In other words, the non-voting equity shareholders may not be left locked into the target if the offeror company obtains control through acceptance from the voting shareholders. Either there will be no acceptance condition for the non-voting shares or, if there is and it is not met, the offer for the voting shares will lapse as well. However, the offeror can protect itself against ending up with a majority of the non-voting equity but too little of the voting equity by inserting identical conditions, relating to the voting equity, into both (or all) offers.

28–47

In a voluntary bid, classes of non-equity shares need not be the subject of an offer, even if they carry voting rights.[173] Of course, an offeror company may wish to make an offer for non-equity shares carrying voting rights, but an offer is not required, presumably on the theory that the non-equity shareholders are normally protected by their contractual entitlements.[174] However, r.15 requires that, on an

---

[171] Notes to r.14 make it clear that comparable is not the same as identical and that normally the difference between the offers should reflect the differences in market prices over the previous six months. "Equity share capital" seems to be as defined in CA 2006 s.548. See para.23–7.

[172] See in relation to mandatory bids, para.28–46, above.

[173] The implication from Note 3 to r.14.1 is that equity share capital is defined in the same was as in the Companies Act 2006 s.548, so that preference shares are not included.

[174] See para.23–7, above.

offer for voting equity share capital, an appropriate offer or proposal must be made to holders of securities convertible into equity shares (who clearly are potentially affected by the change of control).

Wait and see

28–48   It is possible to create pressure on shareholders to accept an offer, even though the same offer is made to all the shareholders. From the point of view of an offeror, there are only two possible outcomes: the offer is accepted by the majority of the shareholders or it is not. From the point of view of an individual shareholder, considering whether to accept an offer and unable to predict the actions of fellow shareholders, there are three possible outcomes. First, the bid may not be accepted by the majority, in which case it does not matter how the individual votes. Secondly, it may by accepted by the majority and the individual is among the accepting majority. Thirdly, the bid is accepted by the majority and the individual is among the non-accepting minority. Where the bid is not particularly attractive in the eyes of the individual but that shareholder has misgivings about how the bidder will run the company if it obtains control, the individual's preferences may be ranked in the same order as the outcomes just listed. But since that shareholder has only one decision (accept/not accept) he or she cannot rank those preferences fully. In order to avoid the worst outcome (three), he or she may vote for the second outcome, even though the first outcome is the preferred one. If many shareholders considering the offer have the same set of preferences and reason in the same way, the offer may be accepted, even though their first choice is rejection.

There is in fact a simple procedural solution to this problem, which the Code adopts. As we see in para.28–75, the Code requires the bidder to keep the offer open for a further 14 days after it has achieved the level of acceptances the bidder requires and this fact has been publicly announced. During that period those who had previously not accepted the bid can change their minds. Since the offeree shareholders now have two decisions, they can rank the three preferences fully. When the offer is first made, it is not accepted (decision 1); if and when it becomes clear the majority are in favour of the bid, the offer is accepted (decision 2). Decision 1 gives effect to the first preference; when it becomes clear that the first preference is not available, decision 2 gives effect to the second preference.

THE PROCEDURE FOR MAKING A BID

28–49   Having dealt with the two central features of the Code, the allocation of decision-making on the bid to the shareholders of the target company and equal treatment of target shareholders, we now turn briefly to the procedure for making the offer. Much of this is concerned with putting the shareholders of the target in a position in which they can effectively take the decision which has been allocated to them, but other policy goals are also evident, such as that the company should not be subject to a bid or bid speculation for an excessive period of time or that false markets in the securities involved should not be created.

However, since the Code applies only once a potential acquirer has decided it wishes, or might wish, to put an offer to the shareholders of the target company, there is a prior period which may be important for the success of the bid but where the relevant rules are not to be found in the Code. We divide the bid process into three periods: before an approach is made by the bidder to the target board; before a firm offer is made to the target shareholder; and after a firm offer has been made to the target shareholders.

Before the approach to the target board

The main issues here relates to the acquisition of shares in the potential target company. A potential acquirer, although not yet committed to making a bid, may want to increase the chances of the bid ultimately succeeding by building up as large a stake in the company as possible before hand. As we have seen, the mandatory bid rule puts a cap of 30 per cent on this strategy, but, in fact, long before that stage is reached, the potential bidder's stake in the company will have become public knowledge in the market and the share price will have responded appropriately. A more important question, therefore, may be how far the potential bidder can go in acquiring shares in the company without knowledge of the acquisitions seeping into the market. Such shares may be particularly valuable to the potential bidder, not only because they are acquired cheaply but also because, if the bidder is defeated in the event by a "white knight" competitor, the defeated bidder can assent these shares in the competitor's bid and make a profit, which may help to off-set some of the costs of its failed bid.[175] So, the central question is one of disclosure of acquisitions of shares. Conversely, the board of a potential target company will want to keep a close eye on its share register, both in order to see if a potential bidder is building up a stake in the company and to see if shareholders are appearing who are likely to be susceptible to an offer, if one is made (for example, certain types of hedge fund). Most of these events are likely to take place before the Takeover Code applies and so the relevant rules are to be found in the Companies Act and other legislation.

28–50

An initial apparent advantage for the board and disadvantage for the acquirer is that the names of those who are on its register of shareholders are known both to the company and the public.[176] However, the registered shareholder is often not the beneficial owner of the share,[177] and so the appearance of a new name on the register does not necessarily reveal much useful information, whilst large shareholdings can be split up across a number of registered nominee holders. Information about beneficial holders of shares is obtainable under two sets of provisions. First, beneficial holdings at the 3 per cent level and above are required to be disclosed under the vote-holding disclosure rules discussed in

---

[175] On the disincentives of potential bidders to bid because of the wasted costs point, see para.28–33 above. As we have seen, the insider dealing rules are formulated so as to allow defeated bidders to profit in this way. See para.28–35. However, the shares the bidder "acquires" through acceptance of its offer cannot be used in this way, because, if the initial bidder does not obtain the level of acceptances it seeks, its offer will lapse and so the assenting shareholders, rather than the initial bidder, will be able to accept the competing bid.

[176] See para.27–16.

[177] As we have seen in para.15–31, above.

Ch.26.[178] It is not intended to repeat that discussion here but its importance should be noted. In effect, a cap of 3 per cent is set on the shares an acquirer can obtain cheaply in order to offset the costs of a failed bid, so that there must be doubts about the financial adequacy of this method of combating the disincentive effect of permitting competing bids.

Company-triggered disclosures

28–51   The second set of disclosure provisions contain no threshold requirements, and so are potentially more extensive than the general vote-holder disclosure rules, but they do not operate automatically but must be triggered by the company on each particular occasion it requires information and in relation to each potential holder. These rules are in Pt 22 of the Companies Act 2006. They enable the directors of a public company to serve a notice upon persons suspected of being interested in its voting shares seeking information about that interest and permitting the company to apply to the court for restrictions on the voting and transfer of the shares if that information is not forthcoming. The statutory provisions are often supplemented by provisions in the company's articles which expand the board's powers, for example, by permitting the directors to impose the restrictions without application to the court and to impose them in a wider range of situations.[179]

Section 793 provides that a public company (whether its shares are traded on a public market or not) may serve notice on a person whom it knows to be, or has reasonable cause to believe to be, or to have been at any time during the three years immediately preceding the date of the notice, interested in voting shares of the company. The notice may require that person to confirm that fact and, if so, (a) to give particulars of his own past or present interest; (b) where the interest is a present interest and any other interest subsists or subsisted during the three-year period at a time when his own interest did, to give particulars known to him of that other interest; or (c) where his interest is a past interest, to give particulars of the identity of the person to whom that interest was transferred.[180] In cases (a) and (b) the particulars to be given include the identity of persons interested and whether they were members of a concert party or there were any other

---

[178] See paras 26–16 et seq.

[179] Where the directors impose the restrictions, their freedom of action is limited by the "proper purpose" doctrine applying generally to the exercise by directors of their powers under the articles (see para.16–26). In particular, the purpose of the power to impose restrictions is to further the purpose underlying the statutory provisions (revelation of beneficial interests in shares). Failure to disclose does not give the directors a general power to impose restrictions, for example, for the purpose of defeating a resolution to remove the directors: *Eclairs Group Ltd v JKX Oil & Gas Plc* [2015] UKSC 71.

[180] 2006 Act s.793(2) and (6).

arrangements regarding the exercise of any rights conferred by the shares.[181] The notice must require a response to be given in writing within such reasonable time as may be specified in the notice.[182]

The initial notice will normally be sent to the person named on the shareholder register and, if he is the sole beneficial owner of the shares, he will normally say so (at any rate once the likely consequences of refusing to respond are explained to him). But in other cases the notice may merely be the beginning of a long and often abortive paper-chase. If the recipient of the notice is a nominee it may well decline to say more than that, claiming that a duty of confidentiality forbids disclosure or, if the nominee is, say, a foreign bank, that the foreign law makes it unlawful to disclose the name of the person on whose behalf the nominee holds the shares. In principle, this is a breach of the duty under s.793 (since the nominee is bound to give details of the "other interests" known to it, i.e. that of the person upon whose behalf the nominee holds the shares). Alternatively, the nominee may disclose the nominator's identity, but the latter, if resident abroad, may refuse to provide any further information. Ultimately, as a result of the possibility of the freezing and disenfranchisement of the shares (see below), the true ownership may be disclosed—but not always.[183] Such information regarding interests in the shares as may be elicited as a result of the notice (or a succession of notices as the company follows the trail) must be entered on a public register, with the information being entered against the name of the present holder of the shares.[184] The rules applying to this register, including court control of public access for a non-proper purpose, are the same as those applying to the company's register of members, and most companies will use the share register for this purpose as well.[185]

The Act recognises that members of the company may have a legitimate interest in securing that the company exercises its powers under s.793, even if the board does not want it to (perhaps because the directors or some of them may fear that it may bring to light breaches by them of their obligations to notify their dealings under the rules discussed in Ch.26). Hence, under s.803, members holding not less than one-tenth of the paid-up voting capital—a very high threshold in the case of a publicly traded company—may serve a requisition stating that the requisitionists require the company to exercise its powers under s.793, specifying the manner in which those powers are to be exercised[186] and giving reasonable grounds for requiring the powers to be exercised in the manner specified.[187] It is

28–52

---

[181] 2006 Act s.793(5). In the light of the complications of the statutory provisions defining "interests" and "concert party agreements" (see below) a lengthy explanation accompanying the notice may be needed if the recipient (particularly if a foreigner) is to understand precisely what is being asked.

[182] If the time allowed is unreasonably short, the notice will be invalid: *Re Lonrho Plc (No.2)* [1989] B.C.L.C. 309.

[183] In some cases the information sought has never been obtained and the shares have remained frozen.

[184] 2006 Act s.808. Assuming there is a present holder and assuming the holder's identity is known. If not, the information must be entered against the name of the holder of the interest. The entry must state the fact that, and the date when, the requirement was imposed.

[185] 2006 Act ss.808–819. For discussion of the share register, see paras 27–16 et seq.

[186] In particular, of course, in respect of which persons they require notices to be served.

[187] 2006 Act s.803(2) and (3).

then the company's duty to comply.[188] If it does not, every officer of the company who is in default is liable to a fine.[189] On the conclusion of a shareholder-initiated investigation, the company, under s.805, has to prepare a report of the information received which has to be made available at the company's registered office within a reasonable time[190] after the conclusion of the investigation.[191] If it is not concluded within three months beginning on the day after the deposit of the requisition, an interim report on the information already obtained has to be prepared in respect of that and each succeeding three months.[192] Any report has to be made available for inspection by any person at a place notified to the registrar, unless the company chooses to make it available at its registered office[193] and the requisitionists must be informed within three days of the report becoming available.[194]

Sanctions

28–53 A person who fails to comply with a s.793 notice, whether initiated by board or shareholders, or, in purported compliance with the notice, knowingly or recklessly makes a false or misleading statement commits an offence, which can be sanctioned by imprisonment, unless the defendant shows the requirement was frivolous or vexatious.[195] What, however, makes the foregoing sections more effective than they would otherwise be is that, if a notice is served on a person who is or was interested in shares of the company and that person fails to give any information required by the notice, the company may apply to the court for an order directing that the shares in question be subject to restrictions.[196] However, it should be noted that the information a company may require under the notice is, perhaps not surprisingly, limited by what the person asked knows. If the company obtains no useful information, because the person asked does not have it, there is no breach of s.793 and restrictions cannot be imposed on the shares.[197]

The restrictions are that:

(a) any transfer of the shares is void;

---

[188] 2006 Act s.804.

[189] 2006 Act s.804(2).

[190] Not exceeding 15 days: s.805(1).

[191] 2006 Act s.805(1). On the meaning of "concluded", see s.805(7).

[192] 2006 Act s.805(2).

[193] 2006 Act ss.805(5) and 807. Not to give notice to the registrar is an offence on the part of the company and any officer in default, as is a failure to make the report available for inspection: ss.806 and 807. There is no "proper purpose" control over public access to the report.

[194] 2006 Act s.805(6) and it must remain available for inspection at the registered office for at least six years: s.805(4).

[195] 2006 Act s.795. After consulting the Governor of the Bank of England, the Secretary of State may exempt persons from compliance with a s.793 notice where for "special reasons" an undertaking is substituted for the obligation to comply with the section: s.796.

[196] 2006 Act s.794.

[197] It appears to be open to companies—and some have taken this step—to make provisions in their articles entitling the board to impose restrictions in a wider range of circumstances, including where information is not forthcoming following a request, even if the person asked does not have the information.

(b)   no voting rights are exercisable in respect of them;
(c)   no further shares may be issued in right of them or in pursuance of an offer made to their holder; and
(d)   except in a liquidation, no payment by the company, whether as a return of capital or a dividend, may be made in respect of them.[198]

Thus, although the company may never track down the ultimate beneficial owner of the shares, it can take them out of consideration with regard to a takeover bid through the restrictions imposed by the court or under the articles. Nevertheless, the restrictions constitute a draconian penalty,[199] which may be detrimental to wholly innocent parties, for example bona fide purchasers of, or lenders on the security of, the shares. Although the court has a discretion whether to make the order imposing the restrictions, an order should normally be made if that knowledge has not been obtained, since "the clear purpose [of Pt 22 of the Act] is to give public companies, and ultimately the public at large, a prima facie unqualified right to know who are the real owners of its voting shares". If an order is made, it has to impose all four restrictions without any qualifications designed to protect innocent parties.[200] However, an application can be made to the court by the company or any aggrieved person for the restrictions to be relaxed on the grounds that they "unfairly affect" the rights of third parties, and the court is given a broad power to do so.[201] The court also has the power to remove the restrictions altogether,[202] but this normally can be done only if the court is "satisfied that the relevant facts about the shares have been disclosed to the company and no unfair advantage has accrued to any person as a result of the earlier failure to make that disclosure".[203] To this there are two exceptions. If the shares are to be transferred for valuable consideration and the court approves the transfer,[204] an order can be made that the shares should cease to be subject to the restrictions.[205] Further, the court, on application by the company, may order the shares to be sold,[206] subject to the court's approval as to the terms of the sale,[207] and might then also direct that the shares should cease to be subject to the restrictions.[208]

---

[198] 2006 Act s.797(1).
[199] Made the more so since any attempt to evade the restrictions may lead to a heavy fine: s.798.
[200] *Re Lonrho Plc (No.2)* [1990] Ch. 695.
[201] 2006 Act s.799.
[202] 2006 Act s.800: on the application by the company or any person aggrieved.
[203] 2006 Act s.800(3)(a).
[204] 2006 Act s.800(3)(b).
[205] But the court has a discretion whether to allow the transfer and whether or not also to remove the restrictions; in particular it may continue restrictions (c) and (d) either in whole or in part so far as they relate to rights acquired or offered prior to the transfer: see s.800(4).
[206] 2006 Act s.801. The only transaction that can be *ordered* is a sale. The word is used in conscious contradistinction to "transferred for valuable consideration" in s.800(3), which would include a share exchange takeover offer: cf. *Re Westminster Group Plc* [1985] 1 W.L.R. 676 CA.
[207] 2006 Act s.801(1). The court may then make further orders relating to the conduct of the sale: s.800(3). The proceeds of sale have to be paid into court for the benefit of the persons who are beneficially interested in the shares who may apply for the payment out of their proportionate entitlement: s.802.
[208] Though it appears that it does not have to remove them.

Interests in shares and acting in concert

28–54   As is usual in the disclosure area, what has to be disclosed is not just ownership of shares but "interests in shares". However, the legislation does not use the Code's definition of "interests in shares" but has its own, set out in ss.820 to 823. It is widely formulated so as to include an interest in shares "of any kind whatsoever", but it is not so wide as to include interests in shares of a purely economic character, such as CfDs.[209] Part 22 also contains a "concert party" provision, again not that of the Code, but set out in ss.824 and 825, under which the interests of one concert party can be attributed to all members. The agreement must relate to the acquisition of interests in shares and indeed the agreement is not caught by the section until an interest in securities is in fact acquired by one of the parties to it in pursuance of the agreement.[210] Thus, the section does not apply to a simple voting agreement between existing shareholders. Further, the agreement must include provisions imposing restrictions on dealings in the interests so acquired[211]: an agreement to acquire shares which the acquirer is then free immediately to dispose of is not caught by the section. The "agreement" need not be an enforceable contract, but the section does not apply to an agreement which is not legally binding "unless it involves mutuality in the undertakings, expectations or understandings of the parties to it".[212] Each member of the concert party is taken for the purposes of the disclosure notice to be interested in all shares in which any member of the concert party has an interest, whether or not those interests were acquired in pursuance of the agreement.[213] Any notification which a party makes with respect to his interest must state that he is a party to a concert party agreement, must include the names and (so far as known to him) the addresses of the other parties and must state whether or not any of the shares to which the notification relates are shares in which he is interested by virtue of the concert party provision and, if so, how many of them.[214]

Before a formal offer is made to the target shareholders

28–55   Once a bid is imminent, the Takeover Code rules become the dominant source of obligation, though the rules discussed in the previous section continue to operate. Rule 1(a) of the Code prohibits an offeror from simply putting its offer directly to the shareholders of the target: it must "notify a firm intention to make an offer in the first instance to the board of the offeree company or its advisers". This is to

---

[209] 2006 Act s.820(1). For a discussion of CfDs, see para.28–45, above.

[210] 2006 Act s.824(2)(b). Though, see below, once an agreement is triggered by an acquisition, the notification requirements extend beyond interests acquired in pursuance of it.

[211] 2006 Act s.824(2)(a).

[212] 2006 Act s.824(5)(6). Of course, the presence of mutuality will normally make the agreement legally binding, but the subsection deals with the doctrine of intention to create legal relations, which the parties might use to declare an agreement not binding at law. The subsection also excludes an underwriting or sub-underwriting agreement provided that that "is confined to that purpose and any matters incidental to it".

[213] 2006 Act s.825(1)–(3).

[214] 2006 Act s.825(4).

enable the board of the target to form a view on the merits of the offer and to advise the shareholders accordingly. As we have seen above, the Code requires the board to give such advice to the shareholders and, indeed, to obtain independent advice on the bid and make it known to the shareholders. Rule 1 facilitates this process: without it, the board of the target might be left scrambling around trying to fulfil its duties under r.3.

Apart from this, there are two different timing problems relating to the public disclosure of the bid proposal with which the Code has to deal. The bidder may delay disclosure, perhaps in order to continue acquiring shares in the target company. Alternatively, the bidder may be eager to put the possibility of a bid into the public domain. As r.1(b) recognises, what the board of the target often first receives is not so much the details of a firm offer proposed to be made to the shareholders as "an approach with a view to an offer being made". There are a number of good reasons why this should be. First, the offeror may wish to obtain the target board's recommendation of the offer and so wishes to indicate that there is some flexibility in the terms of its offer and that it is prepared to negotiate with the board for its support. Secondly, the offeror may genuinely be in doubt about the value of the target and may wish to secure access to the target's books in order to be able to formulate a precise offer to be put to the shareholders. Especially in the case of highly leveraged bids, it is crucial for the offeror not to find any unpleasant surprises after it has obtained control which would jeopardise its ability to pay the interest on or repay the often very large loans it has taken out to finance the bid. Offers by private equity bidders, accordingly, are rarely hostile. This puts the target board in a negotiating position, because there is nothing in the Code or the general law which requires the board to give the potential bidder such access. Thirdly, the bidder may make an informal approach, but also let it be known publicly that such an approach has been made, in order to induce the larger shareholders to put pressure on their board to co-operate with the bid, notably by granting access to the company's books. This third situation caused the Panel some concern in its 2010 review, on the grounds that it created a "virtual bid" period of uncertain duration, i.e. one in which the company is effectively "in play" but no firm offer for the company has been announced. We begin with discussion of this problem.

Put up or shut up

Where a public but non-firm approach, which puts the company "in play", has been made, senior management of the potential target will concentrate on little else until the acquirer walks away or a firm offer is made and is either accepted or rejected. However, no firm intention to make an offer having yet been announced, the time limit contained in the Code for posting the offer to the target shareholders is not triggered. On the other hand, the announcement of a possible offer triggers the Code's definition of the "offer period", at which point the ban on defensive action by the target board without shareholder approval is

28–56

triggered.[215] So, the target board is stymied, but the acquirer used to be under no obligation to push on with its offer. To meet this concern, the Code for some time contained a "put up or shut up" (PUSU) provision, enabling the potential target to request the Panel to set a time limit within which the bidder had either to make an announcement of a firm intention to make an offer or to state that it did not intend to make a bid, and in the latter case the bidder (and a person acting in concert) would not normally be able to bid until six months had passed. Such applications to the Panel by potential targets were not infrequent, but in its 2010 review the Code Committee concluded that boards were often reluctant to make such applications, presumably for fear of shareholder ire, even though the company's management was "destabilised" by the possible offer announcement. Consequently, it recommended shifting the burden of action under the PUSU rule.[216] Except with the consent of the Panel, a possible offeror, who must be named in the possible offer announcement, must make a further announcement one way or the other within four weeks of the possible bid announcement, with the consequence noted above if the further announcement is that it will not proceed with an offer.[217] However, the Panel will normally extend the deadline for the further announcement if the target board requests this. This amendment clearly promotes the policy underlying GP 6 that "an offeree company must not be hindered in the conduct of its affairs for longer than is reasonable by a bid for its securities".

Faced with the PUSU requirement, a potential bidder might move on to make an announcement of a firm intention to make an offer, but hedge that offer about with conditions, so that it can react appropriately to any negative information about the target which subsequently emerges. Where a bidder seeks to make an actual offer subject to conditions, its freedom to do so is severely constrained by the provisions of r.13, but originally that rule did not apply to announcements of a firm intention to make an offer, where, in consequence, the bidder had a freer hand. However, in 2004 the Panel decided to apply the provisions of r.13 (discussed below) to "firm intention" statements as well.[218] This Rule promotes certainty, for both the shareholders and the board of the target company. Thus, the "PUSU" rule forces the potential bidder to clarify its intentions since r.13 now constrains the bidder's freedom to avoid PUSU by employing a heavily conditional firm intention statement.

Once a "firm intention" announcement is made, whether because of the operation of the PUSU rule or not, the offeror becomes obliged in the normal case to proceed with its bid and to post the formal offer document to the shareholders

---

[215] The "Definitions" section of the Code makes it clear that the offer period is triggered by an announcement of a possible offer (not necessarily a firm one) and the possible offeror can make that announcement itself or easily put the offeree company in a position where it is required to make an announcement under rr.2.2 and 2.3.

[216] Above fn.91, paras 3.1 and 5.7.

[217] Code rr.2.6 and 2.8. The deadline is set much later if a competing offeror announces a firm bid for the company before the deadline expires. And the rule will not normally apply to participants in a formal sale process which the company is conducting, presumably because any destabilising effect has been precipitated by the company's management itself.

[218] PCP 2004/4, *Conditions and Pre-Conditions*, especially s.7. The "pre-conditions" to an offer are the conditions attached in the "firm intention" statement. See now r.2.7.

within 28 days of the announcement.[219] Moreover, at the firm announcement stage a good deal of information about the forthcoming bid must be provided.

Initial announcements

The bidder strategy discussed above depends on an announcement of a possible offer being made at an early stage. However, there are incentives for potential bidders to delay announcements in some situations. A possible bid creates tempting opportunities for insider trading on the part of those privy to the bid preparations, not only those within the bidder itself but those involved as financial or legal advisers. We have seen that the acquisition of shares in the target by or on behalf of the bidder itself does not normally amount to insider trading, but acquisitions by or on behalf of other persons would.[220] Insider dealing also constitutes market abuse under the Market Abuse Regulation, in respect of which the FCA can impose civil penalties, including, in this case, on corporate bodies involved. In spite of the frequent and unexplained rises in the share prices of target companies in the period before takeover announcements are made, the FCA has not had great success in identifying the culprits.[221]

The Code approaches this problem by, first, insisting on the "vital importance of absolute secrecy before an announcement of a bid" (r.2.1) and, secondly, and probably more effectively, by requiring a public announcement if that secrecy is not or is not likely to be maintainable, for example, where the target is subject to "rumour and speculation" or where the bidder is taking its discussions about a possible bid beyond "a very restricted number of people" (r.2.2). Once an approach has been made to the board of the offeree company, the primary responsibility for making an announcement rests with that board, but what is announced will depend upon how far matters have progressed when an announcement has to be made. As we have seen, it may be no more than a statement that an offer may possibly be forthcoming (but with no guarantee that it will). Rule 13 about conditions does not apply to announcements which are not firm.[222]

28–57

---

[219] Code rr.2.7 and 30.1.

[220] Above, para.28–35. Even those acting on behalf of the bidder may find themselves caught by the insider trading prohibition, if as a result of being granted access to the target's books, they obtain, as is likely, price-sensitive but non-public information. This is because the exemption in Sch.1 to the CJA 1993 is confined to "market information" which is information about the acquisition or disposal of securities. Thus, to take an extreme example, if the bidder's due diligence reveals the company has just made a potentially very lucrative discovery, the fact that the bidder is now prepared to pay more for the target's shares is market information, but the fact of the discovery would appear not to be.

[221] FSA, *Market Watch*, No.21, July 2007.

[222] Code rr.2.3 and 2.4 and n.1 to r.2.4, though the Panel must be consulted in advance if it is proposed to include conditions and there are some requirements in the note designed to make the potential bidder's intentions clear. The Panel (above, fn.218) took the view that, since a "possible bid" announcement was not binding on the bidder in any event, more information was preferable to less.

The formal offer

Conditions

28–58 Once a company posts its formal offer documents to the shareholders of the target, the bid is open to acceptance by the shareholders to whom it is addressed. One aim of the Code in this situation is that the shareholders should have a clear proposition to accept or reject. As we have noted already, r.13 of the Code imposes restrictions on the conditions which the bidder can attach to its offer. An offer must not be subject to conditions which depend solely on subjective judgments by the directors of the offeror or the fulfilment of which is in their hands. Otherwise, offerors would be free to decide at any time to withdraw an offer, whereas one purpose of the Code is to ensure that only serious offers are put forward for consideration. The note to r.13.4 makes it clear that this means that normally the bidder cannot make its offer subject to satisfactory financing being available for the offer: the bidder must not make an offer, or even announce a firm intention to make an offer, if the financing is not already in place.[223] This implements GP 5. The main exception to this principle arises where the bidder intends to raise the cash for the bid through a new issue of shares and its shareholders' approval is required for the share issue, either by the Act or under the rules applicable to the market on which the shares are traded. In this case, the offer must be made conditional on the necessary consent and the condition is not waivable by the bidder.[224] Even if the inclusion of the condition does not fall foul of the above restriction, the condition must not actually be invoked by the bidder unless the circumstances which have arisen are of "material significance" to the offeror in the context of the bid.[225]

However, some conditions are common in offers, and are even required by the Code. The offeror is required by r.10 to make its offer for voting securities conditional on acceptances of a sufficient level to give it, together with securities already held, 50 per cent of the voting rights in the offeree company. Thus, the bidder must either end up with legal control of the target company or the bid must lapse and the bidder acquires none of the shares which have been assented to the offer. This is regarded by the Panel as a very important provision, as the extensive notes to r.10 make clear, dealing with the operation of the Rule in a variety of circumstances likely to arise in practice. As r.9.3 makes clear, it also applies to

---

[223] In the case of pre-conditions the Code shows a little more flexibility, notably where a regulatory condition must be satisfied for the bid to proceed and that is likely to take a long time, and it would thus not be "reasonable" for the potential offeror to have to maintain, and pay for, committed financing throughout this period.

[224] In fact, this concession may enable the company to escape having to proceed with the bid. The shareholders (including the directors in their capacity as shareholders) will not be obliged to approve the share issue (especially if they think conditions have changed since the offer was first announced): *Northern Counties Securities Ltd v Jackson & Steeple Ltd* [1974] 1 W.L.R. 1133. And it is not even clear that the Code can require the directors to recommend approval to the shareholders if the directors think it would be a breach of their core fiduciary duty to do so: see above, para.28–36. (In the *Jackson & Steeple* case the contrary was held, but on the basis that the directors had already given an undertaking to the court to recommend positively.) Perhaps for this reason, the Code attempts to prevent this situation arising in the case of a mandatory bid: r.9.3(b).

[225] Code r.13.5 and see the WPP case, above, fn.153.

mandatory bids. The offeror may choose to, and often does, make a voluntary offer conditional upon a higher level of acceptances, though it will normally also reserve to itself the right to waive the higher condition during the bid. The offer may be conditional upon the offeror achieving 75 per cent of the voting rights, so as to be able to pass a special resolution; or even on achieving 90 per cent of the shares bid for (so as to be able to avail itself of the statutory squeeze-out procedure discussed below). Hence, an important stage in the progress of a bid is when it becomes or is declared "unconditional as to acceptances".

Rule 12 requires a condition to be inserted in the offer to deal with the fact that a competition authority consent may be needed for the offer to be consummated. The condition is to the effect that the bid will lapse if there is a reference to the competition authorities before the offer becomes unconditional as to acceptances. Except for a mandatory bid, where reinstatement is mandatory, the offeror has a choice whether to reinstate its bid, if the competition authorities ultimately clear it.[226]

Timetable

We have already seen that r.30.1 imposes a 28-day-limit for the posting of the offer document after a firm intention to bid has been announced. That is a maximum limit in order not to leave the target board and shareholders in a state of uncertainty. Once the offer is posted, the Code is still concerned with the overall length of the process and r.31.6 stipulates that the offer may not remain open for acceptances once the 60th day after the offer was posted has passed. There are some exceptions, in particular that the "60th day" is set by reference to the competing bidder's timetable if there is a competing offer or can be adjusted where the board of the target company agrees to a longer period.

28–59

However, within the offer period, the Code is also concerned with setting minimum time periods, in order that the shareholders have an opportunity to properly consider the offer and are not pushed into a "snap" decision on it. An offer must initially be open for acceptance for at least 21 days, as required by r.31.1. This date is referred to as the "first closing date" of the offer. If this is later extended, as it normally may be, a new date must be specified, but there is no obligation to extend an offer (rr.31.2 and 31.3). Moreover, if it is stated that the offer will not be extended, only in exceptional cases will the Panel allow it to be so. This is laid down in r.31.5, not merely because the offeror should not break its promises but in order to prevent shareholders being pressurised into accepting before the current closing date by false statements that they will lose all chance of availing themselves of the offer unless they accept before that date.

In some cases the offer may be revised (i.e. improved), sometimes more than once. This is particularly likely to occur if there is a contested takeover. In such circumstances each rival bidder, having already incurred considerable expense, is likely to go on raising its bid and trying to get its new one recommended by the board of the target. Even if it loses the battle, the defeated bidder will at least be

---

[226] Normally a lapsed bid cannot be revived within 12 months: see r.35 below. However, the bidder must decide whether to re-offer within 21 days of the clearance: note on r.35.1 and 35.2. The new offer need not be on the same terms as the lapsed one. For the mandatory bid, see note on r.9.4.

able to recover part of the expenses out of the profit it will make by accepting the winner's bid in respect of its own holdings.[227] Moreover, even if there is no contest, an offeror may be forced to increase its bid if proves unattractive to the target shareholders or if the bidder or its associates or members of its concert party acquire shares outside the offer at above the price of its offer, as we have seen above. If an offer is revised, it must be kept open for at least 14 days after the revised offer document is posted (r.32.1). All shareholders who have accepted the original offer are entitled to the revised consideration (r.32.3) and new conditions must not be introduced except to the extent necessary to implement an increased or improved offer and with the prior consent of the Panel (r.32.4). "No increase" statements are treated by r.32.2 in essentially the same way, and for the same reasons, as "no extension" statements, i.e. the bidder is allowed to go back on them only in "wholly exceptional" circumstances, unless the bidder has specifically reserved its freedom in the "no increase" statement to increase the offer in the circumstances which have arisen.

28–60   In general, as r.33.1 makes clear, the foregoing rules apply equally to alternative offers in which the target's shareholders are given the option to choose between different types of consideration (e.g. shares or cash). In other words, the shareholders retain their options so long as the offer remains open. But where the value of a cash alternative provided by a third party is more than half the maximum value of the primary share option, the offeror is not obliged to keep that offer open, or to extend it, if not less than 14 days' written notice to shareholders is given reserving the right to close it on a stated date.[228] This "shutting off" of the cash alternative provided by a third party is permitted because underwriters will be reluctant to agree to remain at risk for an indeterminate period. However, the bidder's freedom to "shut off" a cash alternative does detract from the offeree's freedom to wait and see what the other shareholders do before accepting the offer. It is significant that it is not permitted in mandatory bids, where a cash offer or a cash alternative is required, and there is no danger of bidders responding to the lack of a "shut off" opportunity by simply not arranging for a cash alternative to be available.

The combination of the maximum period for the formal offer (normally 60 days) and the minimum period for revised offers to remain open (14 days) means that an offer cannot normally be revised after the 46th day. However, where there are competing bidders still in the field at this point, the Panel has come to the conclusion that this freezing of the offers on the 46th day is an unacceptably inflexible rule. It will therefore conduct an auction, with revisions being announced into the final period, according to a procedure determined ad hoc for the particular bid (r.32.5).

---

[227] By contrast, the successful bidder may suffer from the "winner's curse" of having overpaid for the target.
[228] Code r.33.2. But such a notice must not be given if a competing offer has been announced until the competitive situation ends. For the exclusion of mandatory offers see fn.2 to r.33.2.

Bid documentation

The offer will, of course, be a longer and more detailed document than the **28–61** announcement of the firm intention to make a bid. After a general statement in r.23 that shareholders must be given sufficient information and advice to enable them to reach a properly informed decision as to the merits or demerits of an offer and early enough to decide in good time, r.24 (divided into 16 sub-rules) states what financial and other information the offer document must contain and r.25 (divided into nine sub-rules) what information must be contained in circulars giving advice from the target company's board. The information required is extensive but need not be considered in detail here, beyond saying that it is very much what one would expect in the light of the nature of the documents. It is worth noting that the documentation issued by a bidder on a share-exchange offer need no longer comply with the FCA's rules, since it does not constitute a prospectus.[229]

Employees' interests

Following the adoption of the Directive, the interests of employees received **28–62** slightly more explicit consideration in the Code than before, mainly at the level of information provision, and these provisions were further strengthened in the 2010 review. Rule 24.2 requires the bidder to state in its offer document "its intentions with regard to the future business of the offeree company and explain the commercial justification for the offer" as well as its intentions with regard to continued employment of the employees and management of the offeree company, material changes in working conditions, strategic plans for the offeree company and their likely impact on employment, and the redeployment of the fixed assets of the company. It must also state its intentions on these matters in relation to the business of the offeror company. So, much more is required to be stated about intentions vis-à-vis employees than previously. Rule 25.2 requires the board of the target, when giving its opinion on the offer, to include its views, and the reasons for those views, on the implications of the bid for the employees and its views on the offeror's strategic plans. These documents, and any revised offer and a target board opinion thereon, must be made available to the representatives of the employees or, in their absence, to the employees themselves[230]; and the offeree board must attach the opinion of the employee representatives to its response circular or publish it on its website.[231] None of this gives the employees any formal say in the bid decision, though it may give them information upon which to organise political or social pressure in relation to the offer. For a more formal input to the bid decision, the employees or their representatives must look elsewhere. Thus, where a statutory information and

---

[229] PR 1.2.2(2) and 1.2.3(3).
[230] Code rr.23.2. The same obligation is imposed in relation to bid announcements: r.2.12.
[231] Code r.25.9. Rule 32.6 makes the same provision in relation to the offeree's circular on any revised offer.

consultation arrangement is in place, both bidder and target may need to consult employee representatives on the employment consequences of the bid or of defensive measures.[232]

In the takeover of Cadbury by Kraft in 2009 the bidder unwisely committed itself not to close a factory in the UK which the target management had decided to shut down. Having obtained control, the bidder discovered there were very good reasons for the previous management's decision and reneged on its commitment. This caused a political storm, as a result of which r.19 was amended to deal with "post offer" statements and undertakings, i.e. statements made during an offer about how a party (typically the bidder) intends to act after the end of the offer period. The amendments apply generally to post-offer statements and undertakings, but these will often be given in relation to employment matters in order to defuse employee or public opposition to the bid. The amendments first require the party to be clear whether it is making a statement of intention (r.19.8) or giving an undertaking (r.19.7) about its post-offer conduct. The requirements on intention statements are less demanding than those on undertakings. For intention statements the statement must accurately reflect the party's intentions at the time it is made and be made on reasonable grounds. For 12 months after the offer has closed (or such other period given in the statement), a party intending to depart from its statement must consult the Panel and, having done so, it must publicly announce its change of heart and explain the reasons for it. The intention statement rules recognise that intentions may genuinely change but they impose a form of "comply or explain" rule, first in relation to the Panel and then in relation to the market and public opinion, in an attempt to control opportunistic changes of mind.

The rules on undertakings are, not surprisingly, more robust. The Panel must be consulted in advance of the undertaking being given and the undertaking must be precisely formulated. In particular, qualifications or conditions attached to the undertaking must be capable of objective assessment (ie not be dependent on the subjective judgement of those giving the undertaking). Even if these conditions are met, a person seeking to invoke a condition or qualification post-bid must obtain the Panel's consent. The giver of the undertaking must report periodically to the Panel on progress, or lack of it, towards its implementation, which reports the Panel may publish. If the Panel has doubts about the quality of these reports, it may appoint an independent supervisor to monitor compliance and to report to the Panel. The regulation of intention statements and undertakings was not an easy issue for the Panel, because it required regulation of post-offer behaviour. Once the offer period is over the Panel's role has traditionally been limited, as discussed below, essentially confined to enforcing its rules on when a failed bidder may bid again. It is notable that in extending its regulatory reach the Panel

---

[232] Information and Consultation of Employees Regulations 2004 (SI 2004/3426) reg.20. The FCA's rules indicate that it will not be market abuse for a company involved in a bid to disclose information to an employee representative in fulfilment of an obligation imposed by the Regulations, provided the information is subject to a confidentiality requirement: MAR 1.4.5(2)(e). Equally, disclosure of inside information to an employee representative will not be a criminal offence on the part of a manager under s.52 of CJA 1993 if the disclosure is "in the proper performance of the functions of his employment", though it might be for the representative to trade on the information or to further disclose it. See C-384/02 *Criminal Proceedings against Gröngaard* [2006] I.R.L.R. 214 ECJ.

did not put in the forefront the use of its new legal powers,[233] but relied instead on the domestic remedies of Panel consultation and approval and disclosure.

Curiously, however, the strongest mechanism for the protection of employee interests may found in the pensions legislation. Where a highly leveraged bid for a target company is successful, the level of risk in the target company increases, including the risk that the company will default on its obligations under an occupational pension scheme. In that situation, the Pensions Regulator has a, still somewhat ill-defined, power to require the bidder to make extraordinary payments into the fund, which the bidder may either do, and so give the pensioners greater financial protection, or refuse to do and decide not to make an offer. The potential power of the Regulator puts the pension scheme trustees in a position to negotiate with the bidder as to the terms upon which they will regard it proper not to seek the Regulator's intervention.[234]

Profit forecasts and valuations

In the case of an agreed recommended takeover with no rival bidders, no more may need stating than the Code requires. But, in the case of a hostile bid or where there are two or more rival bids, each of the companies involved will probably want to make optimistic profit forecasts about itself[235] and to rubbish those of the others. All profit forecasts are unreliable and those made in a takeover battle more unreliable than usual. Hence, r.28 (with eight sub-rules) lays down stringent conditions about them. In particular, the forecast "must be compiled with due care and consideration by the directors whose sole responsibility it is" but "the financial advisers must satisfy themselves" that it has been so compiled.[236] The assumptions on which the forecast is based must be stated both in the document and in any press release.[237] Except for a bidder's forecast in a pure cash offer, the forecast must be reported on by the auditors or consultant accountants (and sometimes by an independent valuer[238]) and the report sent to the shareholders[239] and, if any subsequent document is sent out, the continued accuracy of the forecast must be confirmed.[240] All this is wholly admirable but the evidence does not suggest that it has made such forecasts significantly more reliable.

28–63

---

[233] See para.28–9, above.

[234] Pensions Act 2004 ss.43–51 ("financial support directions"). The point is that the pension deficit revealed in the accounts may no longer be an accurate indication of the amount of money needed to secure the pension obligations, if the bidder's risk profile changes significantly. A better test might be the amount an insurance company would require to transfer to itself the company's pension obligations. In the case of the takeover of Boots by a private equity bidder in 2007 the trustees negotiated additional payments of £418 million over 10 years into the pension fund: *Financial Times fm*, 25 June 2007, p.6. In the earlier case of WH Smith it appears that a potential bidder decided not to make a bid because of the target's pension fund deficit.

[235] The offeror will not need to do so on a pure cash offer for all the shares; but the target will.

[236] Code r.28.1.

[237] Code r.28.2 (and see the Notes thereto).

[238] Code r.28.3.

[239] Code r.28.4.

[240] Code r.28.5.

Somewhat similar requirements apply when a valuation of assets is given in connection with an offer.[241] These valuations tend to vary according to whether it is in the interests of the company which engages the "independent" valuer that the value should be high or low; but at least the valuer of real property is likely to have more objective evidence in the form of prices recently paid for comparable properties. Rule 19.1 lays down a general principle that all documents, advertisements and statements made during the course of an offer "must be presented with the highest standards of care and accuracy and the information given must be adequately and fairly presented". Note 9 makes it clear that statements about the expected financial benefits of a takeover to the bidder (often referred to as "synergies"), which fall short of constituting profit forecasts, are nevertheless regulated in a similar manner, with assumptions stated and reports from financial advisers.

Liability for misstatements

28–64 Although there has not been space here to discuss the details, it is clear that the Code attaches the highest importance to the provision to shareholders of complete and accurate information about the bid and any defence to it. Without such guarantees, the Code's purpose of placing the decision on the commercial acceptability of the offer in the hands of the shareholders of the target company might seem unrealistic, as might the Panel's own refusal to make any assessment of the commercial merits of the bid.[242]

Suppose, however, an inaccuracy is present in the information put out by the bidder or target companies and a person later wishes to claim compensation for the loss said to have been suffered thereby. The Panel now has the power to award compensation but this is not one of the areas in which it has sought to implement the power, nor will compensation under FSMA normally be available.[243] However, this is an area in which the Code intersects with the general law, in the sense that there may well be legal remedies available to shareholders who have suffered loss as a result of inaccurate or incomplete information provided in the course of a takeover bid.[244] Applying generally, that is, to both bidder and target documentation, is the common law liability for negligent misstatement, which, even after the decision of the House of Lords in *Caparo Industries Plc v Dickman*,[245] would seem capable of imposing liability upon the issuers of documentation in the course of takeover bids towards the shareholders of the target company, to whom it is clearly addressed, where such shareholders act in reliance upon the information to either reject or accept the

---

[241] Code r.29.

[242] Code, *Introduction*, 2(a).

[243] On the Panel's powers to award compensation, see above, para.28–9.

[244] In addition to the liabilities discussed in the text, the bidder might also be liable in damages under s.2(1) of the Misrepresentation Act 1967 (unless it could disprove negligence) or to have its contract with the accepting shareholders rescinded in equity, though in both cases this could apply only between the bidder and the target company shareholders and where the shareholders had accepted the bidder's offer.

[245] *Caparo Industries Plc v Dickman* [1990] 2 A.C. 605. See paras 22–36 et seq., above.

offer made.[246] Indeed, in the post-*Caparo* case of *Morgan Crucible & Co v Hill Samuel & Co*[247] the Court of Appeal refused to strike out a claim by the bidding company against the directors of the target that inaccurate statements made by the target company in the course of a bid had been intended to cause the bidder to raise its bid, which it had done to its detriment.

Dealings in shares

General Principle 4 states that "false markets must not be created in the securities" of the offeror or offeree company. The Code has always sought, however, to permit dealings in the securities of companies involved in a bid to continue during the bid period. Apart from the insider dealing laws, already discussed, the main restrictions are these. Once the "offer period" starts (triggered by the first public announcement about the bid, even if it is only about a possible offer) and has not ended (with the first closing date or, if later, the offer becoming or being declared unconditional as to acceptances),[248] the offeror and persons acting in concert with it must not sell any securities in the target company without the consent of the Panel.[249] Moreover, during that period requirements for disclosure of dealings, additional to and stricter than that required by the Act, come into operation.[250]

28–65

---

[246] Proving that the negligent misstatement caused the plaintiff the loss in question may be, of course, a very difficult matter. See *JEB Fasteners Ltd v Marks Bloom & Co* [1981] 3 All E.R. 289 (above, para.22–52).

[247] *Morgan Crucible & Co v Hill Samuel & Co* [1991] Ch. 295 CA. However, this decision has to be read in the light of subsequent developments on assumption of responsibility. See *Partco Group Ltd v Wragg* [2002] 2 B.C.L.C. 323 CA, where a successful bidder sued the directors of the target on the basis of statements made to the bidder in the course of due diligence carried out by the bidder prior to making a recommended offer. The CA refused to strike out the claim but were clearly sceptical as to whether it would ultimately succeed, because the directors could be said to have assumed responsibility for the accuracy of the statements only on behalf of the target (now owned by the bidder) and not personally. See also above, at para.22–44. See further the refusal to strike out in a claim by the bidder against the target's auditors on special facts in *Galoo Ltd v Bright Grahame Murray* [1994] 1 W.L.R. 1360 CA.

[248] See Code, "Definitions".

[249] Code r.4.2. Such action is likely to cause great confusion in the market. If the Panel does consent, it will require 24 hours' notice to be given to the market and will require the sale to be at above the offer price. Not abiding by the Code's provisions on sales might well be a criminal offence under Pt 7 of the Financial Services Act 2012, if the object was to rig the market by causing a fall in the quoted price of the target's shares, thus making the offer more attractive; or under the insider dealing legislation if information available to the offeror suggested that its offer would not succeed and it wanted to "make a profit or avoid a loss" by selling before the quoted market price fell back when the offer lapsed. See Ch.30, below.

[250] In brief, "Opening Disclosures" must be made by any person at the 1 per cent level (instead of 3 per cent) and full disclosure by the parties to the bid or their "associates" (as defined in "Definitions") and "Dealing Disclosures" must be made daily by those parties. Dealings in derivatives must also be disclosed. See rr.8.1–8.3 and notes. However, in the case of cash offers, dealings in the shares of the offeror do not have to be disclosed.

Solicitation

28–66   There is an obvious temptation for both bidder and target to engage in high-pressure salesmanship in the case of a hostile or, especially, a contested takeover. There are firms specialising in the art of persuading reluctant shareholders. It is increasingly common for the services of such firms to be recruited by the parties or their financial advisers. Rule 19 of the Code is designed to curb the excesses which may result (and sometimes have done). The sub-rules of particular interest include r.19.4 which prohibits the publication of an advertisement connected with an offer unless it falls within one of nine categories, and, with two exceptions,[251] it is cleared with the Panel in advance. The Panel does not attempt to verify the accuracy of statements,[252] but if it subsequently appears that any statement was inaccurate the Panel may, at least, require an immediate correction.[253] This pre-vetting, however superficial, is a powerful disincentive to window-dressing and to "argument or invective".[254] The rule applies not only to press advertisements (which must not include acceptance or other forms[255]) but also to advertisements in any of the ever-expanding media available[256] and in each case the advertisement must "clearly and prominently" identify the party on whose behalf it is being published.[257]

The Rule, however, covers only advertising material of which there will be a record. The greater danger arises from unrecorded oral communications, which cannot be vetted in advance or scrutinised afterwards. However, an attempt is made to control these. Rule 19.5 provides that, without the consent of the Panel, campaigns in which shareholders are contacted by telephone may be conducted only by "staff of the financial advisers who are fully conversant with the requirements of, and their responsibilities under, the Code", and it adds that only previously published information which remains accurate and not misleading may be used, and that "shareholders must not be put under pressure and must be encouraged to consult their financial advisers". However, in recognition, no doubt, that the parties will have selected their financial advisers on the basis of their financial expertise and reputation rather than their ability to woo, the Panel may consent to the use of other people, subject to the Panel's approval of an appropriate script which must not be departed from, even if those rung up ask questions which cannot be answered without doing so, and to the operation being supervised by the financial adviser.[258]

---

[251] A product advertisement, not bearing on the offer (which is not really an exception), and advertisements in relation to schemes of arrangement (when the relevant regulator is the court): see Ch.29, below.

[252] Time constraints do not permit this to be done; the Panel requires only 24 hours to consider the proof of the advertisement which must have been approved by the company's financial adviser: r.19.4, Note 1.

[253] Code r.19.4, Note 2.

[254] Specifically excluded from exceptions (iii) and (iv) to r.19.4.

[255] Code r.19.4, Note 5.

[256] Code r.19.4, Note 4.

[257] Code r.19.4, Note 3.

[258] Code r.19.5, Note 1. It is difficult to see how the financial adviser can supervise effectively unless it insists upon all calls made being recorded; but the rules and notes do not require or suggest that.

The telephone campaign rules focus on solicitations in favour of or against a bid **28–67** which is on the table. But campaigning may begin before this. Rule 4.3 provides that any person proposing to contact a private individual or small corporate shareholder with a view to seeking an irrevocable commitment consult the Panel in advance. An irrevocable commitment is an undertaking to accept the offer, if one is made, though they often contain qualifications which release the promisor if a rival bid emerges at a higher price. A Note to r.4.3 states that the Panel will need to be satisfied that the proposed arrangements will provide adequate information as to the nature of the commitment sought and a realistic opportunity to consider whether or not it should be given and with time to take independent advice. It adds that the financial adviser will be responsible "for ensuring compliance with all relevant legislation and other regulatory requirements".[259] Furthermore, Note 3 to r.19.5 stipulates that the Panel must be consulted before a telephone campaign is conducted with a view to gathering irrevocable commitments in connection with an offer. Short of a total ban on cold-calling this seems to regulate it in this context as satisfactorily as is reasonably possible—assuming that financial advisers can be relied on to observe the Rules.

Rule 19.6 says that parties, if interviewed on radio or television, should seek to ensure that the interview, when broadcast, is not interspersed with comments or observations made by others. It also provides that joint interviews or public confrontations between representatives of the contesting parties should be avoided.

The more serious problem, arising from meetings with shareholders or those who are likely to advise them, is dealt with in r.20.1 which provides that "information about companies involved in an offer must be made equally available to all offeree company shareholders as nearly as possible at the same time and in the same manner".[260] Despite this, meetings with institutional shareholders, individually or through their professional bodies, are likely to be held, as, often, are meetings with financial journalists and investment analysts and advisers. Note 3 to the Rule permits this, "provided that no material new information is forthcoming and no significant new opinions are expressed". If that really is strictly observed, one wonders why anybody bothers to attend such meetings.[261] But many do, and when a representative of the financial adviser or corporate broker of the party convening the meeting is present (as must be the case unless the Panel otherwise consents), the representative generally seems able to confirm in writing to the Panel (as the Note requires) that this Rule was observed. If such confirmation is not given, a circular to shareholders (and, in the later stages, a newspaper advertisement also) must be published giving the new information or opinions supported by a directors' responsibility statement.

---

[259] This warning ought to frighten the financial adviser!

[260] This does not preclude the issue of circulars to their own investment clients by brokers or advisers provided that the circulars are approved by the Panel.

[261] The risk of new information being given out on a partial basis in such cases materialised in the Kvaerner bid for AMEC, where a financial public relations company employed by the target made statements in closed meetings about the target's future profits which had not been contained in the defence document: Panel statement 1995/9. The PR company was censured by the Panel and dismissed by the target.

The post-offer period

Bidding again

28–68   If the first offer fails, the Code's policy is that the target should be given some respite before the acquirer makes a second offer. Rule 35.1 provides that, except with the consent of the Panel, when an offer[262] has not become wholly unconditional within the bid timetable or has been withdrawn or has lapsed, neither the offeror nor any person who has acted or now is acting in concert with it, may, within the next 12 months: (a) make or announce another offer for the target company; (b) acquire any shares of the target company which would require a mandatory bid on the part of the acquirer; (c) be a member of a concert party which acquires 30 per cent or more of the voting rights in the offeree company[263]; (d) make any statement which raises the possibility that an offer might be made for the offeree company; (e) take any preliminary steps in connection with an offer (to be made after the end of the 12 months) which might become known outside the immediate circle of the company's top management and its advisers. Similar restrictions apply following a partial offer, if one is permitted. Interestingly, the restrictions apply to a partial bid for between 30 and 50 per cent of the target, even if that bid is successful. In other words, having had one bite at the cherry, the bidder cannot come back for a second within 12 months: if the bidder wants to obtain a legally controlling interest through a partial bid, it must try for this the first time around.[264] Furthermore, if a person or concert party following a takeover offer holds 50 per cent or more of the voting rights it must not, within six months of the closure of the offer, make a second offer, or acquire any shares from the shareholders on better terms than those under the previous offer.[265] This is another expression of the equality principle. Overall, these provisions prevent the offeror from continuously harassing the target and, while the maximum waiting period is only 12 months, that may be long enough to enable the target's board to strengthen its defences against further hostile bids by the offeror.

The bidder's right to squeeze out the minority

28–69   Here we deal with the post-bid consequences of a successful offer. These are regulated by the Act rather than the Code, since they involve the compulsory acquisition of shares. It is virtually unknown for even a well-supported offer to achieve 100 per cent acceptance. As we have seen above, although a bidder is normally required to offer for all the equity shares, it may declare the offer "unconditional as to acceptances" at a less than full acceptance, provided it ends up with at least 50 per cent of the voting rights. However, where it is important to

---

[262] Or even if no offer has been made but a firm announcement of an intention to bid has been made. A bidder is not normally free simply to withdraw a bid, but may do in some limited circumstances.

[263] As we have seen above (para.28–42), the obligation to bid might not fall to the particular member of the concert party who is the former bidder.

[264] Code r.35.2.

[265] Code r.35.3.

the bidder to obtain complete control of the target (for example, where it wishes to conduct its business in a way which will not necessarily be in the interests of the minority shareholders of the target), it will seek to get to a position where it can squeeze out any dissenting (or simply non-responsive) minority shareholders. This may be particularly true of private equity bidders, which will want to use the target's assets to secure the loans made to the bidder to finance the bid. Moreover, the existence of the squeeze-out removes to some degree the incentive for target shareholders not to accept an offer from a bidder who they think will run the target well, so that a target shareholder will be better off not accepting the bid (provided the majority do so).

Since 1929, the Companies Act has contained a provision enabling the bidder to squeeze out a minority after a successful bid. Article 15 of the Takeover Directive now requires Member States to provide a squeeze-out right, and the Directive's provisions led to some amendments in the 2006 Act to the previous legislation, though the report of the Company Law Review was a more significant source of reforms.[266] Despite the number of statutory provisions devoted to the squeeze-out, its practical importance is less extensive as it constitutes only one way of ejecting an unwanted minority. One attraction of the scheme of arrangement mechanism (discussed in the following chapter) for effecting a takeover is that, once the scheme has been approved by a resolution of the shareholders and approved by the court, dissenting minorities (or those who simply do not accept the offer as a result of inertia) will be bound to transfer their shares, though a scheme is not attractive in a competitive situation.[267] Moreover, the majority required for a scheme is 75 per cent of those voting on the resolution, rather than 90 per cent of those to whom the offer is addressed required (see below) for a post-bid squeeze-out. Not only is a higher percentage required for the squeeze-out, but under that mechanism apathy always counts against the bidder. A de-listing of the company from the public equity markets will also act as a strong incentive for the minority to throw in the towel. Again, this step requires only a 75 per cent vote in favour and, indeed, no vote at all if the intention to de-list has been stated in the offer document and the offeror reaches the 75 per cent figure as a result of the offer.[268]

The current rules on squeeze-outs are set out in Ch.3 of Pt 28 of the Act. The **28–70** basic principle is quite straightforward, though its implementation gives rise to some complicated provisions. Assuming a single class of shares has been bid for, the offeror is entitled to acquire compulsorily the shares of the non-acceptors if

---

[266] Final Report I, pp.282–300. However, that report rejected the argument that a squeeze-out right should be extended so as to operate whether the 90 per cent holding results from a takeover or not, largely on the grounds that valuation in such a case would be difficult. Nevertheless, the functional arguments for the squeeze-out from the 90 per cent holder's point of view are just as strong in such a case. The European Commission included such a proposal in its draft Directive amending the Second Directive (see COM(2004) final, 21 September 2004, proposed new art.39a) but it was later dropped.

[267] See para.29–3.

[268] See para.25–46. This is a situation where non-acceptors are likely to change their minds once the acceptance level is known. See para.28–60, above. In companies with a small number of shareholders there are sometimes contractual provisions (in the articles or a shareholder agreement) requiring the minority to accept on the same terms an offer which the majority have accepted ("drag along" provisions). See *Re Charterhouse Capital Ltd* [2015] B.C.C. 574 CA.

the offer has been accepted by at least 90 per cent in value of the shares "to which the offer relates" and, if the shares are voting shares, those shares represent at least 90 per cent of the voting rights carried by those shares.[269] Note that the 90 per cent figure relates to the shares bid for, not to the total number of shares of the class, some of which may be held by the offeror before the bid is launched. These shares are to be excluded from both the numerator and the denominator when working out whether the appropriate fraction of the shares has been acquired as a result of the bid.[270] Where there is more than one class of shares bid for, the 90 per cent test is applied to each class separately, so that a bidder could end up in a position to squeeze out the minority of one class but not that of another.[271]

In contrast to the Code, Ch.3 applies to takeovers of any type of company within the meaning of the Act whether it is public or private.[272] The offeror need not be a company though in practice it will usually be a body corporate[273] (or in some cases two or more such bodies).[274] The definition of "takeover offer" is one to acquire (a) all[275] the shares of the company (or all the shares of a class) which on the date of the offer the offeror does not already hold[276]; and (b) to do so on the same terms for all the shares (or all the shares of a particular class).[277]

28–71 All the apparently simple terms used above are capable of raising questions of interpretation, most, though not all, of which are expressly addressed now in the legislation. What, for example, is an "offer"? In *Re Chez Nico (Restaurants) Ltd*,[278] Browne-Wilkinson VC held that this definition had to be construed strictly, since the provisions enabled a bidder who had acquired 90 per cent of the shares to expropriate the remaining shares, and that accordingly they operated only if the bidder had made an "offer" in the contractual sense of the word. In the instant case two directors of the company who were its major shareholders had circulated the other shareholders inviting them to offer to sell their shares to them and indicating the price that those directors would be prepared to pay if they accepted the offers. As a result, the directors succeeded in acquiring over 90 per cent and then sought to acquire the remainder. On an application by one of the remaining shareholders, the court declared that the directors were not entitled to

---

[269] 2006 Act s.979(2). If, as is usual, the voting rights are on a one vote per share basis, the two requirements amount to the same thing.

[270] See further below.

[271] 2006 Act s.979(4). In the case of a company with voting shares or debentures admitted to trading on a regulated market, debentures carrying voting rights are treated as shares of the company: s.990. This provision is necessary because art.15 of the Directive refers to "securities" (not just to shares), though art.2(1)(e) makes it clear that the Directive includes only securities carrying voting rights. Voting debentures are uncommon in the UK.

[272] 2006 Act s.974(1); and see *Fiske Nominees Ltd v Dwyka Diamond Ltd* [2002] 2 B.C.L.C. 123.

[273] But it could be an unincorporated body, e.g. the trustees of a pension fund.

[274] See s.987 on joint offers, which deals with the problem identified in *Blue Metal Industries v Dilley* [1970] A.C. 827 PC, that the legislation at the time of that case was not well-adapted to deal with joint offers.

[275] Hence it does not apply to "partial offers": but, where the Code applies, the Panel would not be likely to allow a partial offer which might lead to the acquisition of 90 per cent.

[276] "Shares" here means shares allotted at the date of the offer and excludes treasury shares (s.974(4)) but see below for the handling of these shares.

[277] 2006 Act s.974(2) and (3). "Shares" here means shares allotted at the date of the offer but the offer may include shares to be allotted before a specified date: s.428(2).

[278] *Re Chez Nico (Restaurants) Ltd* [1992] B.C.L.C. 192.

do so, since they had not made any "offer" but instead had invited the shareholders offer to them. While this produced the right result in the instant case,[279] the importation into company law of the subtle distinctions drawn by the law of contract seems regrettable; in company law many transactions are described as "offers" or "offerings" when strictly they are invitations to make offers.[280] Moreover, the decision has adverse consequences for a minority shareholder who, instead of wanting to remain a shareholder in the taken-over company, wishes to exercise his rights to be bought out (see below); the effect of the decision is that he will not be entitled to do so if the bidder has proceeded as the directors did in this case.

The requirement that the offer be on the same terms is relaxed in two minor respects by s.976. If the difference simply reflects differences in the dividend entitlements (for example, because later allotted shares carry a lower dividend entitlement in that particular financial year as contrasted with shares allotted earlier), the offer is nevertheless on the same terms. This is deemed to be the case also where an offer is made of "substantially equivalent" consideration to those outside the UK whose law either prohibits or subjects to unduly onerous conditions the consideration offered to the main body of the shareholders.[281]

A similar problem to this second one arises with the requirement that the offer be made to all the shareholders (of the relevant class) where the target has a few shareholders resident in countries with elaborate securities laws and where the inclusion within the offer of such shareholders is likely to trigger the need to comply with those laws. An established technique for dealing with this situation is to make the offer capable of acceptance by the foreign shareholders but to take elaborate steps to ensure that the formal offer documentation is not addressed to them. When challenged in court, this practice was upheld with some unease by the Court of Appeal on the specific facts of the case.[282] Section 978 now gives specific statutory cover to this technique, where the offer was not communicated in order to avoid contravention of local law. In order to deal with the difficulty that the foreign resident might never know of the offer until it receives the compulsory acquisition notice from the offeror, the offer is normally placed on a website and the website address given in the *Gazette*.[283] Section 978(2) also saves from failure under the squeeze-out provisions an offer which is communicated but whose acceptance is made impossible or difficult as a result of local law.

---

[279] Since the directors had failed to make proper disclosure to the other shareholders.

[280] Browne-Wilkinson VC emphasised that his decision was only on the meaning of "takeover offer" for the purposes of the squeeze-out and sell-out provisions and that he had no doubt that what had occurred would be a takeover offer for the purposes of many statutory or non-statutory provisions. This is certainly true of the non-statutory Code. Indeed, the Panel had treated the *Chez Nico* takeover as subject to the Code (the company had been a Plc at the time of the circularisation and remained subject to the Code after its conversion to a private company since, while a public company, it had made a public offering) but the only penalty that the Panel had imposed was to criticise the two directors for their ignorance of, and failure to observe, the Code: see p.200.

[281] For example, local securities laws might make a share-exchange offer in a particular jurisdiction "unduly onerous". The requirement for "equivalent consideration" is a better solution than that adopted by the directors in *Mutual Life Insurance Co of New York v The Rank Organisation Ltd* [1985] B.C.L.C. 11, in order to avoid US securities laws, which was simply to exclude the US shareholders from any pre-emption entitlements in a public offering.

[282] *Re Joseph Holt Plc* [2001] 2 B.C.L.C. 604 CA.

[283] Final Report I, paras 13.24 and 13.43–13.45.

Finally, s.978(3) makes it clear the courts should not deduce from the section that, in all other cases, a failure to communicate the offer to each holder or an offer which it is impossible or more difficult for some shareholders to accept fails to be a "takeover offer" within the meaning of the Act: the courts will decide on a case-by-case basis.

28–72 Further, there is the question of which are the shares "already held by the offeror" at the date of the offer.[284] In general, the larger the stake held by the offeror before the bid, the more difficult it is for it to achieve the 90 per cent, since the smaller becomes the proportion of the class as a whole which is needed to stop it reaching the threshold.[285] In consequence, it becomes important to know how one determines whether a share is acquired before or after the offer is made. Section 975(2) states that shares conditionally acquired before the offer do not count towards the 90 per cent except where the promise by the existing holder is to accept the offer when and if it is made ("irrevocable undertakings") and the undertaking is given for no significant consideration beyond, if this is the case, a promise to make the offer.[286]

Finally, the bidder's ability to reach the 90 per cent threshold will be enhanced if it can count shares acquired after the date of the offer but outside the bid. The effect of the Act is that such shares count towards the 90 per cent but only if the price paid does not at that time exceed the value of the consideration specified in the offer or the offer is subsequently revised so that it no longer does so.[287] As we have seen, where the Code applies, inequality of consideration is unlikely to arise.

There are also potentially tricky issues about shares which are allotted after the bid is made (for example, as a result of a conversion of another security into shares of the class in question) and about treasury shares, which may be held in treasury throughout the bid or become or cease to be treasury shares during the bid period. The statute handles this point by giving the bidder a choice whether it includes in the shares to which the offer relates after-allotted shares or treasury shares of different categories.[288] If it decides to include them in the offer, a cut-off

---

[284] 2006 Act s.974(2).

[285] This is not compensated for by the fact that the number of shares which the bidder has to acquire to reach 90 per cent acceptances is also reduced. Thus, if there are 200 allotted shares and the bidder holds none of them at the outset, it takes a holding of 21 shares to block the squeeze-out, but if the bidder holds 100 at the outset, 11 objectors are enough to block it, i.e. the blocking percentage falls from just over 10 per cent of the class to just over five per cent of the total shares in issue. This would not matter if the bidder could rely on having acquired shares pre-bid rateably from acceptors and non-acceptors, but, in the nature of things, the non-acceptors are likely to be underrepresented among those who have sold out voluntarily to the bidder.

[286] The reason for insisting on no significant consideration is to maintain the rule that the offer must be on the same terms to all the shareholders. In general, shares conditionally acquired ahead of the bid do count as shares already held: s.975(1).

[287] 2006 Act ss.977, 979(8)–(10). This rule is also applied to acquisitions by associates.

[288] 2006 Act s.974(4)–(7). A decision to exclude all or any such shares from the offer does not cause it to fail to meet the requirement that the offer be for all the shares or all the shares of a class: s.974(4), which excludes such shares from the universal obligation. Convertible securities, so long as they remain unconverted into shares, are treated as shares of the company but as a class of shares separate from the class into which they can be converted: s.989. Rule 15 of the Code normally requires the bidder to bid for convertible shares. For the problems caused by convertible shares before the introduction of these statutory reforms see *Re Simo Securities Trust* [1971] 1 W.L.R. 1455. Rule 4.5

date must be specified in the offer beyond which such shares will not be regarded as being within the offer. If any of those categories of shares are included within the offer, then the 90 per cent threshold is calculated by taking into the account the shares allotted or which have ceased to be treasury shares on the date on which the bidder triggers the compulsory acquisition procedure (s.979(5)). Subsequently allotted shares or shares subsequently ceasing to be treasury shares do not affect that determination, once made, though if the offeror gives a subsequent notice (for example, because the first is defective in some way) the 90 per cent figure will have to be calculated on that second date. If the offeror chooses not to make an offer for after-allotted or treasury shares, then, naturally, the compulsory transfer provisions will not apply to them.

Challenging the squeeze-out

Given the demanding nature of the 90 per cent threshold, the above detailed provisions may well be of practical importance in particular cases in establishing whether the threshold has been exceeded. Assuming it has, the successful bidder triggers the compulsory acquisition process by giving notice to the non-accepting shareholders, with a copy to the target company, accompanied by a statutory declaration of its entitlement to serve the notice.[289] That notice must normally be given within three months of the last day on which the offer could be accepted.[290] The effect of the notice is, under s.981(2), that the offeror becomes entitled and bound to acquire the shares on the final terms of the offer. If the offer gave shareholders alternative choices of consideration (e.g. shares or a cash alternative), the notice must offer a similar choice and state that the shareholder may, within six weeks from the date of the notice, indicate the choice by a written communication to the offeror and must also state which consideration will apply in default of a choice. This applies whether or not any time limit or other conditions relating to choice contained in the offer itself can still be complied with and even if the consideration was to have been provided by a third party who is no longer bound or able to provide it.[291] The remainder of ss.981 and 982 prescribes in detail the procedures that have to be adopted to ensure that the

28–73

---

prohibits an offeree company from accepting an offer in respect of shares still held in treasury until after the offer is unconditional as to acceptances. On treasury shares, see above at para.13–27.

[289] 2006 Act ss.979(2), 980. This requirement is buttressed by criminal sanctions for failing to send a notice to the company or for intentionally or negligently making a false statement in the declaration. Section 986(9),(10) provide a limited exemption from the 90 per cent threshold: if the failure to reach it is due entirely to the non-response of untraceable shareholders, the court may permit the bidder to serve a compulsory acquisition notice, provided it is satisfied (a) the consideration is fair and reasonable and (b) it is just and equitable to do so (taking into account in particular the number of untraceable shareholders).

[290] Where the offer is not governed by the Code, so that there is no fixed closing date for the offer, the period is six months from the date of the offer.

[291] 2006 Act s.981(4),(5). Normally the alternative which was to have been provided by a third party will have been cash, in which case the bidder now has to supply it. If the consideration which cannot now be provided, whether by bidder or third party, was a non-cash one, a requirement for equivalent cash applies. This adopts and codifies the effect of the decision of Brightman J in *Re Carlton Holdings Ltd* [1971] 1 W.L.R. 918.

shares which the offeror is bound to acquire are transferred to it and that the consideration that it is bound to pay reaches the shareholders concerned.[292]

The dissenting shareholder does not have to take the notice lying down. He or she can appeal to the court under s.986(1) for an order either (a) that the offeror shall not be entitled to acquire the shares; or (b) that the terms of the acquisition shall be amended "as the court thinks fit".[293] The shareholder must act within six weeks of the date on which the acquisition notice was given by the bidder, but the application has the effect of suspending the bidder's rights until the appeal is disposed of. Section 986(4) provides that, where the petitioner seeks relief of type (b), the court may not increase the level of consideration to be provided by the bidder beyond that available in the offer, unless "the holder of the shares shows that the offer value would be unfair" (but it cannot in any event require a consideration of lower value). Thus, the burden of showing unfairness is on the challenger.

28–74 What are the petitioner's chances of success? They will be excellent if the petitioner can show that the statutory requirements for a "takeover offer" have not been met or that the 90 per cent threshold has not been reached, under the provisions discussed above, because then the court will have no jurisdiction to make an order for the compulsory acquisition of the shares.[294] However, it should not be thought that the merits are always on the side of the non-accepting minority. They may simply be interested in exploiting to the full the position of power which the bidder's desire for complete control has given them. If the court cannot order a compulsory acquisition because the statutory requirements have not been met, the bidder may think of other devices to achieve the same result.

In *Rock Nominees Ltd v RCO (Holdings) Plc*[295] the bidder, faced with highly opportunistic conduct on the part of a shareholder which narrowly blocked achievement of the 90 per cent threshold, caused the newly acquired subsidiary to sell its business to another company in the same group (at a fair price) and then put the seller into voluntary liquidation, for which only a special resolution is required, distributing the price received on the sale to the shareholders (including the minority) and thus achieving the same result as a compulsory acquisition. The Court of Appeal refused to hold that this was unfairly prejudicial conduct on the part of the majority.[296]

---

[292] The main problem that has had to be solved is that many of the non-acceptors of the offer will probably be untraceable. The solution adopted causes the offeror little trouble (see ss.982(4) et seq.), but the target company, now a subsidiary of the offeror, may have to maintain trust accounts for 12 years or earlier winding-up and then pay into court.

[293] It seems that the offeror cannot deprive the court of its jurisdiction to amend the terms of the squeeze-out by accepting the petitioner's right not to be squeezed out, at least where the petitioner has not indicated he or she seeks only the right not to be compulsorily acquired: *Re Greythorn* [2002] 1 B.C.L.C. 437. In this case the petitioner had reasons for thinking that the closely-held target company had been taken over at a gross undervalue, and the bidder evidently preferred to allow the petitioner to remain in the company than to have that issue examined in court.

[294] Formally, this will not help a petitioners who want a higher price, but they may be able to negotiate one if the bidder cannot squeeze them out at the offer price.

[295] *Rock Nominees Ltd v RCO (Holdings) Plc* [2004] 1 B.C.L.C. 439 CA.

[296] This way of proceeding was undoubtedly more expensive for the bidder than a compulsory acquisition. On unfair prejudice, see Ch.20, above, and on voluntary winding up, para.33–9, below.

Where the court has jurisdiction, the petitioner will have a more uphill struggle. Section 986(4) (above) indicates the nature of the difficulty: if 90 per cent of the shareholders have accepted the offer, that is normally strong evidence that it is a fair one. Indeed, that subsection, introduced as a result of the Directive, appears to put a very high burden on the petitioner seeking to amend the bid terms: the petitioner must show, not simply that the offer value is unreliable, but that it was too low and, by implication, what the right price should be.[297] Consequently, the petitioner may have a better chance of success if he or she simply seeks an order that there should be no compulsory acquisition, for there the requirement to show that the offer value is unfair does not apply. Even in relation to simple denial of the compulsory purchase request, however, the British courts have traditionally relied on the high level of acceptances achieved to conclude that they should exercise their discretion in favour of the compulsory acquisition.[298] However, in more recent times the courts have been prepared to refuse compulsory acquisition where, unusually, the acceptances are an unreliable indicator of fairness, without requiring the petitioner to establish what the correct level of consideration should have been. Two such indicators of unreliability have emerged in particular in the cases. If the acceptors of the offer are not independent of the bidder or if the acceptors were not given adequate information upon which to take their decision, the court will not necessarily draw the conclusion that a 90 per cent acceptance indicates a fair offer.[299] In practice, this means the petitioner's chances of success are much greater if the bid was not governed by the Code than if it was.

The sell-out right of non-accepting shareholders

The squeeze-out provisions introduced in 1929 were not originally accompanied by a right on the part of the non-accepting minority to have their shares bought by the bidder. This right was added only in 1948. Although formally reciprocal, in fact the two rights perform very different functions. The sell-out right permits the shareholder, who does not wish to accept the bid, but who, if the majority do accept, would rather leave the company as well, to give effect to that set of preferences. He or she can refuse to accept the offer, but then change his or her mind, once the results of the other shareholders' decisions have become clear. However, as we have noted, the Code already provides a more effective mechanism for giving the shareholder that facility. Rule 31.4[300] requires the offeror to keep the offer open for a further 14 days after it has become unconditional as to acceptances. Since the Code rule is not dependent upon the 90 per cent threshold and it operates without a court order, it is a much more

28–75

---

[297] For the courts' traditional reluctance to fix a price (as opposed to simply ratifying or not the bid price) see *Re Grierson, Oldham & Adams Ltd* [1967] 1 W.L.R. 385.

[298] *Re Hoare & Co Ltd* (1933) 150 L.T. 374; *Re Press Caps Ltd* [1940] Ch. 434.

[299] *Re Bugle Press Ltd* [1961] Ch. 270 CA; *Re Chez Nico (Restaurants) Ltd* [1992] B.C.L.C. 192; *Re Lifecare International Plc* [1990] B.C.L.C. 222; *Fiske Nominees Ltd v Dwyka Diamond Ltd* [2002] 2 B.C.L.C. 123.

[300] Subject to the shut-off of cash alternatives: see above, para.28–60.

attractive mechanism for those who are quick enough to use it. This perhaps explains why there has been little litigation on the sell-out right provided by the statute.

The sell-out right, like the squeeze-out right, depends upon there having been a takeover offer which relates to all the shares in the company, as those terms are defined for a squeeze-out.[301] However, the 90 per cent threshold is calculated in relation to a different set of shares. The question is whether the shares acquired through the offer *together with* other shares which the offeror (or an associate of the offeror) held before the offer or acquired during the offer but outside it constitute 90 per cent of the shares in the company (and, where relevant, 90 per cent of the votes). If there is more than one class of share, this rule is applied class by class.[302] In other words, unlike in the squeeze-out, the question is not whether there has been a 90 per cent level of acceptance of the offer, but rather whether the bid has left the offeror holding 90 per cent of the shares. This seems the correct test: the mischief which is sought to be remedied is the minority position into which the bid has put the applicant shareholder and the precise degree of enthusiasm displayed by the other shareholders for the offer is of secondary importance.[303] It is probably rather easier for the sell-out threshold to be attained than the squeeze-out threshold, because, in a sell-out, a lower level of acceptances might be compensated for by a higher level of pre-bid holdings on the part of the bidder or its associates.

28–76   The offeror must give each of the non-accepting shareholders notice of their entitlement to be bought out within one month of the end of the offer period. The shareholder wishing to take up this right must give notice to the offeror, either within three months of the end of the offer period or, if later, as it usually will be, of the notice given by the offeror.[304] Provisions apply as to the consideration to be provided which are equivalent to those for a squeeze-out.[305] It is in this case, rather than in relation to a squeeze-out, that the need to provide a choice of all the original alternatives (including a cash underwritten alternative) is so unpopular with offerors and their advisers. And it is, perhaps, rather remarkable and not altogether easy to reconcile with the provisions of the Code. As we have seen, under the Code an offer has to remain open for at least 14 days after it becomes unconditional as to acceptances. However, an offeror is not obliged to keep most types of cash underwritten alternatives open if it has given notice to shareholders that it reserves the right to close them on a stated date being not less than 14 days after the date on which the written notice is given.[306] The effect of the Act is

---

[301] 2006 Act s.983(1).

[302] 2006 Act s.983(2)–(4),(8). "Associate" is broadly defined in s.988. If conditionally acquired shares are not in fact ultimately acquired and that would mean the threshold would not be met if they were excluded, there is a standstill procedure which may result in the shareholder losing the right to be bought out: s.983(6),(7).

[303] As with the squeeze-out right, however, this is not a general right for a minority to be bought out: if the final step in the process whereby the majority acquires 90 per cent of the shares is not a takeover bid, the right to be bought out does not arise in the UK, unlike in some other jurisdictions.

[304] 2006 Act s.984(1)–(4). The offeror's obligation is supported by criminal sanctions on the bidder and any officer in default: s.984(5)–(7).

[305] 2006 Act s.985.

[306] Above, para.28–59.

virtually to keep the offer open for considerably longer than is required under the Code in all cases where the offer has achieved 90 per cent success. And clearly the parties cannot contract out of the statutory provisions. Nor can the Panel or the Code waive them. The CLR endorsed this position.[307]

However, it is sometimes argued that what is now s.985 does not apply if the cash alternative is described in the offeror's offer document as a separate offer by the underwriting investment bank. In the light of the section that argument seems unsustainable. The fact is that, as the section and the Code clearly recognise, the offeror's "offer" may and probably will contain a number of separate offers and that some of those offers may be made by third parties. All fall within the phrase "the terms of the offer". The only way, it is submitted, in which offerors and their investment banks might be able to achieve their aim is by making no mention at all of a cash underwritten alternative hoping that an independent investment bank, not acting on behalf of, or paid for its services by, the offeror will come forward and make an offer on its own account to the target's shareholders to buy the shares of the offeror received on the takeover. That is a somewhat unlikely scenario.

Under s.986(3), when a shareholder exercises his sell-out rights by notice to the offeror, an application to court may be made either by the shareholder or the offeror and the court may order that the terms on which the offeror shall acquire the shares shall be such as the court thinks fit. The parties may be in disagreement about whether there is an obligation on the offeror to acquire the shares at all or they may be in disagreement about the terms. The same provisions about raising or lowering the consideration in relation to the bid value apply as in a squeeze-out, since art.16 of the Directive requires Member States to provide a sell-out right; and the shareholder will be in the same difficulty when arguing that the sell-out should be at a higher level than was provided for in the bid.

Conclusion

UK takeover regulation is committed to the principle that the decision on the **28–77** offer should lie in the hands of the shareholders rather than the management of the target company (assuming no competition concerns). Especially important in this regard are the restrictions imposed by the Code on the defensive steps which are open to the management of the target company and its insistence that the shareholders of the target should not be denied the opportunity to decide on the merits of the bid. In other countries, it is easier for the incumbent management to take steps to defend itself against unwelcome bids, though not necessarily to the point of preventing them entirely. The argument in favour of the regime adopted by the Code is that it provides a cheap and effective method of keeping management on their toes and protects shareholders from management slackness or self-dealing—or, in any event, provides a method for the shareholders to exit the company on acceptable terms if such managerial misbehaviour produces a takeover bid. Further, this rule makes it less easy for target management to resist offers driven by the potential benefits of combining the businesses of offeror and

---

[307] Final Report I, para.13.61.

target companies, where target management are nevertheless likely to lose their jobs in the process. The potential disadvantages of this stance are that it deprives the board of the target of full-scale role in either negotiating on behalf of the shareholders or protecting them from coercive bids. The latter concern is addressed by other provisions of the Takeover Code regulating the format in which offers may be put, in particular, the requirements for equal treatment and the Panel's reluctance to sanction partial bids. The board's negotiating role is not entirely removed by the "no frustration" rule but the board cannot in the end insist that its valuation of the company is correct and the shareholders' mistaken, if the target shareholders take a different view.

The Code's orientation seems to reflect the dominance of the institutional shareholders in the UK which naturally favour a set of rules which maximise their gains from bids but which also reduce their managerial agency costs. Thus, the institutions have also set their faces against the adoption in pre-bid situations, where the Code does not apply, of defensive devices by the management of potential takeover targets. However, it is perhaps easy to overestimate the beneficial effect upon management performance of the threat of the takeover bid, which is not to say that the takeover bid has no role to play in the British system of corporate governance. The core decision to side-line target management in the decision on the takeover offer also makes it difficult to build any protection for non-shareholders, notably employees, into the Takeover Code—though in this respect the Code simply imitates the general orientation of British company law.[308]

---

[308] For a general review of these issues see P. Davies, "Control Shifts via Contracting with Shareholders" in G. Ringe and J. Gordon (eds), *The Oxford Handbook of Corporate Law and Governance* (Oxford: OUP, 2017 (forthcoming publication)).

CHAPTER 29

ARRANGEMENTS, RECONSTRUCTIONS AND MERGERS

THE FUNCTION OF SCHEMES OF ARRANGEMENT

Part 26 of the Act applies "where a compromise or arrangement is proposed   **29–1**
between a company and its creditors or any class of them or its members or any
class of them" (s.895). Proposals made under this Part are normally referred to as
"schemes of arrangement". Schemes are frequently used to effect "game-
changing" transactions as a company's business strategy develops, especially in
the case of public and publicly-traded companies. They are very important in
practice. Yet, someone who comes to the statute without any knowledge of how
schemes can be used finds the language of the statute uninformative. This is
mainly because the scheme provisions are very widely drawn and can be used to
carry through a number of different types of transaction which, in other
jurisdictions, are often made the subject of separate statutory procedures. It is
therefore useful to begin by identifying the principal types of activity for which
schemes are or could be used.

Mergers

In most countries' companies legislation there is to be found a section headed   **29–2**
"Mergers" which will contain language somewhat along the following lines:

> "Any two or more corporations existing under the laws of this State may merge into a single
> corporation, which may be any one of the constituent corporations, or may consolidate into a

new corporation formed by the consolidation, pursuant to an agreement of merger or consolidation, as the case may be, complying and approved in accordance with this section."[1]

The assets of the merging companies will end up in the "resulting company" (which may be a new company formed for the purpose of the merger or one of the merging companies). As to the shareholders of the merging companies, traditionally they too end up as shareholders of the resulting company, each of the previously separate bodies of shareholders holding, more or less, the proportion of shares in the resulting company which reflects the respective valuations of the companies which came together to form that company. In liberal jurisdictions, such as the UK, cash may be permitted as merger consideration. In that case, some or all of the shareholders of a merging company exit the company rather than transfer to the combined enterprise. If, in addition, one merging company is already wholly owned by the controlling shareholder of the second merging company and only cash is offered to the non-controlling shareholders of the second company, then the merger constitutes a method of squeezing out the minority shareholders in the second company.

Although it is perhaps not obvious that s.895 contemplates the use of a scheme of arrangement to effect a merger, later sections make it clear that this is the case. Section 900 deals specifically with compromises or arrangements under s.895 "proposed for the purpose of or in connection with a scheme for the amalgamation of two or more companies" and involving the transfer of the undertaking or property of one company involved in the scheme to another.[2] Section 900 gives the court the power to make ancillary orders so as to transfer the undertaking from transferor to transferee company (without the parties having make arrangement to do this themselves by contract) and to dissolve the transferor company without winding it up.[3] Equally, the scheme can be used for a "de-merger" or division of a company, whereby part of its undertaking is transferred to another company, again either one formed for the purpose of the de-merger or an existing company.[4] In certain merger and de-merger cases, the transaction will have to comply in addition with the provisions of Pt 27 of the Act, which implements in the UK the Third and Sixth Company Law Directives of the EU.[5]

In addition to the scheme of arrangement under the Companies Act, it is possible to effect a merger under provisions of the Insolvency Act 1986. Sections 110 and 111 of that Act are precisely targeted at the transfer of a company's undertaking to another company, in exchange for shares "or other like interests"

---

[1] Delaware General Corporation Law s.251.

[2] 2006 Act s.900(1). The section also applies to the "reconstruction" of a company by way of the transfer of its undertaking or property to another company.

[3] 2006 Act s.900(2)(a),(d).

[4] That a de-merger is a valid scheme is clear, but the courts' powers under s.900 apply only to de-mergers which count as "reconstructions". From this the courts have reasoned that a reconstruction requires that the shareholding structure of the transferee company must substantially reflect that of the transferor company (but liabilities may be left with the transferor): *Re South African Supply and Cold Storage Co* [1904] 2 Ch. 268, 281–282; *Re MyTravel Group Plc* [2005] 2 B.C.L.C. 123 (Mann J).

[5] See para.29–12, below.

in the transferee company, which are distributed to the transferor's shareholders. However, the transferor must be in voluntary winding up to take advantage of this procedure.[6]

Takeovers

As we shall see,[7] it is in fact relatively uncommon for the scheme to be used to effect a merger. More often, what is produced is the scheme equivalent of a takeover, as discussed in the previous chapter. A simple example is the "transfer scheme" whereby the shares in the target not already held by the bidder are transferred to it in exchange for a consideration in cash or shares, provided by the bidder.[8] A scheme can be used in this way to replicate all of the outcomes of a successful takeover bid.[9] The resulting position is, formally, different from a merger. The target company ends up as a subsidiary of the bidder (i.e. the separate legal personality of the two companies is maintained), though a single legal entity may be produced ultimately through a squeeze out merger of the parent and its new subsidiary. As we have seen above, effecting an agreed takeover through a scheme is an increasingly popular move, so that the Takeover Panel, which has always applied its rules to takeovers through schemes (where its rules are not displaced by statutory rules specific to schemes), has now set out on a systematic basis how its rules apply to schemes.[10]

An advantage of the scheme is that it becomes binding on all the shareholders in question if approved by three-quarters of the shares (and a majority in number of them),[11] whereas, as we have seen,[12] a takeover offer becomes binding on all shareholders only if accepted by 90 per cent of the shares offered for (which allows the company compulsorily to acquire the shares of the non-accepting shareholders). For this reason, it was argued that, if the scheme procedure was

29–3

---

[6] See para.29–24, below.

[7] See para.29–12, below.

[8] This way of proceeding under what is now Pt 26 was sanctioned a century ago: *Re Guardian Assurance Co Ltd* [1917] 1 Ch. 431, despite the fact that the element of "arrangement" between the target company and its shareholders is vanishingly small, consisting of no more than the company facilitating the transfer of their shares to the bidder. See also *Re Jelf Group Plc* [2016] B.C.C. 289.

[9] Popular in the past, because it avoided the payment of stamp duty on the transfer of the shares from target shareholders to the "bidder", was the "reduction" scheme, under which the shareholders of the target agreed to the cancellation of their shares in the target company; the reserve so created in the target was used by the target to pay up new shares which were issued to the offeror; and the shareholders of the target received in exchange for their cancelled shares cash or shares in the offeror company. The company's role in a reduction scheme is thus more significant. However, the Treasury removed the stamp duty advantage in 2015 by prohibiting the first step (cancellation of the shares) when this is part of scheme to allow the bidder to obtain all the shares in the target company. However, the reduction scheme is still available for the equivalent of share exchange bid. See the Companies Act 2006 (Amendment of Part 17) Regulations 2015/472, inserting new s.641(2A) and (2B).

[10] Above, at para.28–14. On the complications which can arise when competing bids are put through the scheme mechanism see *Re Allied Domecq Plc* [2000] 1 B.C.L.C. 134; and *Re Expro International Group Plc* [2010] 2 B.C.L.C. 514. For this reason acquirers proceeding by way of a scheme often reserve the right to revert to a contractual offer if a competing bidder emerges.

[11] 2006 Act s.899(1).

[12] See above at paras 28–69 et seq.

used where a takeover offer could be made, the court should insist on 90 per cent approval of the scheme by the shareholders. However, the argument was rejected on the grounds that in the scheme procedure the shareholders have the protection of the requirement of prior court approval of the scheme, an element not present in the contractual takeover offer.[13] A crucial step in this reasoning is that the court must form its own judgment on the merits of the scheme when it comes to consider its approval and not grant approval simply because the appropriate proportion of the members have approved it. Whether this is in fact the case we shall consider below.

In the case of a hostile offer, the disadvantages of the scheme normally outweigh its advantages as against the takeover offer. The main disadvantage is that the shareholders are not bound until they have voted in favour of the scheme or, even, until the court has sanctioned it, and the necessary delays involved in calling a shareholder meeting give rival bidders the time to organise a competing bid. By contrast, in a takeover offer the bidder can start soliciting "irrevocable commitments"[14] even before the formal offer is made, and those who accept the offer, whether before or after it is formally launched, are not released from their acceptances simply because a rival offer has appeared.[15] It is also easier to make use of the scheme procedure if the cooperation of the target board is forthcoming, though that cooperation is not a formal condition for a successful scheme, whereas one of the advantages of the contractual offer is that the legal transaction is solely between acquirer and target shareholder. Therefore, a scheme is likely to prove attractive only where the takeover is agreed with the board of the target and is not likely to precipitate a rival offer and the offeror is keen to achieve complete ownership of the target.

Other cases

29–4   Although a merger (potentially) and a take-over (actually) constitute important uses of the scheme of arrangement, the width of the statutory language means that many other uses are possible. The scheme may be particularly convenient where UK company law does not appear to offer a customised procedure for carrying out the transaction in question. Besides the merger, another example is use of the scheme to shift the jurisdiction of incorporation of the company or of the parent of a corporate group—usually termed "redomiciling" the company. As we have noted,[16] British company law does not provide a simple mechanism for transferring jurisdictions, not even between the jurisdictions which constitute the UK. Forming a new company in the preferred jurisdiction which acquires the assets of the existing company at a market price is likely to prove expensive in tax terms. However, a transfer scheme whereby the court uses its powers to transfer the assets of the existing company makes this transaction fiscally

---

[13] *Re National Bank* [1966] 1 W.L.R. 819; *Re BTR Plc* [2000] 1 B.C.L.C. 740 CA.
[14] See above, at para.28–67.
[15] See para.28–35 at fn.128—though those accepting may contract for this right.
[16] See para.6–18.

feasible.[17] It should be noted that the scheme provisions do not require that the transferee company be incorporated in the same jurisdiction as the transferor or in a UK jurisdiction at all.

Overall, whether the scheme involves just a single company or more than one company, the courts have construed "arrangement" as a word of very wide import and as not to be read down by its association with the word "compromise" in the section, so that an arrangement involving members need not, and usually does not, involve an element of compromise.[18] The term covers almost every type of legal transaction, and, as the takeover example shows, in substance the transaction may be between the shareholders and a third party, though a scheme will only be available if the company is formally a party to the transaction. Only the case of unvarnished expropriation of the shareholders has so far been excluded by the courts from the scope of the term.[19]

Creditors' schemes

The arrangement may not be with the company's members at all but with its creditors. In fact, when the scheme provisions were introduced by the Joint Stock Companies Arrangement Act 1870, they applied only to arrangements with creditors (and indeed only to arrangements proposed by companies in the course of being wound up). The members were added in 1900 but not until the Companies (Consolidation) Act 1908 was the winding-up requirement dropped and the forerunner of the modern provisions emerged. In practice, a very common use of the provisions today is to secure compromises with creditors of a company in financial trouble—and perhaps at the same time with its shareholders.[20] In some cases the getting in and distribution of the company's assets can be effected more quickly and expeditiously through a scheme than a winding-up, in which case the scheme will operate alongside the winding-up, but in effect be determinative of most of the substantive issues; or the company may be able to reconstruct itself as a viable going concern under a scheme without entering formal insolvency.[21] We do not consider creditors' interests in schemes in any detail in this book, since they are better located in works on insolvency. It is

29–5

---

[17] In this case the problems mentioned in fn.4, relating to the use of courts' ancillary powers, are unlikely to arise.

[18] Re National Bank Ltd [1966] 1 W.L.R. 819 at 829; Re Calgary and Edmonton Land Co [1975] 1 W.L.R. 355 at 363; Re Savoy Hotel Ltd [1981] Ch. 351 at 359D–F; Re T&N Ltd (No.3) [2007] 1 B.C.L.C. 563 at [46]–[50].

[19] Re NFU Development Trust Ltd [1972] 1 W.L.R. 1548: held that the court had no jurisdiction to sanction a scheme whereby all the members were required to relinquish their financial rights without any quid pro quo. However, the decision in Re MyTravel Group Plc [2005] 2 B.C.L.C. 123, makes it less easy for companies to use the scheme to effect a debt-for-equity swap. The lack of congruence between the transferor and transferee companies' shareholding structures was brought about in that case by the fact that, under the scheme, the existing shareholders were to be heavily diluted and most of the shares in the transferee were to be held by the former creditors of the transferor. However, the scheme did in fact proceed in that case but without the exercise of the court's ancillary powers (see the decision of the CA in that case). It is unclear why the ancillary powers are not made available for all schemes which get through the statutory procedure.

[20] See the debt-for-equity swap discussed in the previous note.

[21] For a modern example see Re T&N Ltd (No.3) [2007] 1 B.C.L.C. 563.

worth noting, however, that where the company is in financial difficulty the English courts have been willing to accept jurisdiction over schemes proposed by companies which are not incorporated in the UK and even have no assets here, for example, where the creditors' rights are governed by English law. However, such reasoning would have no application to solvent companies where the scheme concerns wholly or primarily the members' rights.[22] Even in members' cases, creditors' interests may possibly be affected and, if so, their consent will be needed.

THE MECHANICS OF THE SCHEME OF ARRANGEMENT

29–6   Given the significance of the scheme for the company's future development, it is not surprising that the scheme procedure is designed with the aim of ensuring that the shareholders of the company or companies involved in the scheme are content with it. Special resolution approval of the scheme is required, to be given separately by each class of affected shareholders. But since even a supermajority approval requirement may not protect minority shareholders, court approval of the scheme is also required—though the effectiveness of this piece of minority protection depends on the rigour of the court's scrutiny of the scheme. Thus, there are three main steps in a scheme of arrangement:

(a)   A compromise or arrangement must be proposed between the company and its members.[23]

(b)   Meetings of the members must be held to seek approval of the scheme by the appropriate majorities. These meetings are convened by the court on application to it.[24]

(c)   The scheme is sanctioned by the court.[25]

Proposing a scheme

29–7   This first stage, which is often overlooked, is important because, in practice, it is difficult to use the scheme procedure unless the scheme is approved by the board, which then proposes it on behalf of the company. Formally, it would seem that the general meeting could propose a scheme on behalf of the company,[26] but the shareholders' co-ordination problems make this course of action often difficult. The point is illustrated by the decision in *Re Savoy Hotel Ltd*,[27] which is instructive in a number of ways. The company, which had survived a hostile

---

[22] *Re Drax Holdings Ltd* [2004] 1 B.C.L.C. 10, where Lawrence Collins J (as he then was) said obiter at [29]: "It is almost impossible to envisage circumstances in which the English court could properly exercise jurisdiction in relation to a scheme of arrangement between a foreign company and its members, which would essentially be a matter for the courts of the place of incorporation".

[23] 2006 Act s.895(1).

[24] 2006 Act ss.896–899(1).

[25] 2006 Act s.896.

[26] The possibility of shareholder proposal was recognised in *Re Savoy Hotel Ltd* [1981] Ch. 351.

[27] See previous note.

takeover bid in the early 1950s,[28] introduced a dual-class share structure, consisting, at the time of the litigation, of some 28 million A shares and some 1.3 million B shares, with identical financial entitlements, but with the B shares having (in effect) 20 times the number of votes attached to the A shares. The board held directly or indirectly some two-thirds of the B shares. Such a degree of voting leverage may have been thought to have rendered the company impregnable to a takeover. However, this distribution of voting rights did mean that the A shareholders held just over half the votes in the company. This did not create the risk of an ordinary takeover offer succeeding, because it was reasonable to assume that enough holders of the A shares would oppose a bid to prevent the bidder obtaining 50 per cent of the total votes, as required by the Takeover Code,[29] given that the B shareholders would be solidly against an offer.

Instead, the bidder (THF) sought to put forward a scheme for the transfer to it of the A and B shares in exchange for cash, the scheme providing that if one class of shareholders did not approve of it (the B shareholders), the scheme could proceed in favour of the other class alone (the A shareholders). It was reasonable to suppose that three-quarters in value and a majority in number of the A class shareholders[30] might approve the scheme. The dissentient A class shareholders would then be bound by it (subject to court sanction) and the bidder would end up with just over half the voting shares in the company, even if the scheme were rejected by the B class shareholders. THF, which held a few A class shares, applied to the court as a member[31] under step (b) above for an order for separate meetings of the A and B shareholders to be held to consider the scheme. Nourse J held that he had power to order such meetings but declined to do so, on the grounds that they would be futile. This was because the scheme had not been proposed by the company but by a shareholder (THF). Thus, step (a) was not satisfied and so the court would not have jurisdiction to sanction it at stage (c).[32]

Convening and conducting meetings

When the proposed scheme has been formulated, the first step is an application (normally ex parte) to the court by or on behalf of the company (or companies) to which the compromise or arrangement relates for the court to order meetings of the members or classes of members to be summoned.[33] This the court will generally do and will give directions about the length of notice, the method of

29–8

---

[28] See para.15–4 at fn.9.

[29] See para.28–58.

[30] The required level of approval of a scheme. See below.

[31] 2006 Act s.896(2) contemplates applications under step (b) by a creditor or member as well as by the company or its liquidator or administrator.

[32] THF would not be able to get around this problem by seeking to convene a general meeting to propose the scheme, because at a general meeting both A and B shareholders would vote together and the reasons given in the text why a bid would fail would apply also to a shareholder resolution to adopt a scheme.

[33] 2006 Act s.896(1). Sensibly, the courts will recognise that a meeting can occur even if the company has only one shareholder, for otherwise schemes would be less freely available within groups (*Re RMCA Reinsurance Ltd* [1994] B.C.C. 378), but no meeting can be said to have occurred when in a multi-member class only one member in fact attends: *Re Altitude Scaffolding Ltd* [2006] B.C.C. 904.

giving it and the forms of proxy. In the case of shareholders—unlike with creditors where the question has generated endless difficulty—this is a relatively easy task, since the practice of splitting shares into different classes in the articles is a general feature of company law. However, the fact that the members in question have the same rights as against the company does not necessarily mean that they are part of the same class for scheme purposes, because the scheme may propose to treat different groups of those members differently Equally, the fact that shareholders are in different classes under the articles does not necessarily mean they should not be put together for the purposes of voting on the scheme.

The general test for determining whether the members should meet as a whole or in one or more separate classes is whether the rights of those concerned "are not so dissimilar as to make it impossible for them to consult together with a view to their common interest".[34] However, it is easier to state this test than to apply it. In general, it can be said that, the greater the number of classes, the greater the chances the scheme will fail to obtain the consent of one or more of those classes.[35] Further, the tests for determining classes should be reasonably simple and applicable by the company without extensive investigation into the position of particular members. For this reason, the courts have used the rights of shareholders (as against the company and under the scheme) as the touchstone for determining the class issue, rather than their interests. Interests, it is said, can be taken into account by the court at the third stage when it decides whether to sanction the scheme. However, the courts cannot take a radically different approach at the third stage without affecting the way classes are defined at the second stage. Thus, in *Re BTR Plc*,[36] a case of a takeover being effected through a scheme, the judge sanctioned the scheme which had been approved in a single meeting of the target's shareholders and rejected the argument that those shareholders of the target company who already held shares in the bidder should have been put in a separate class. The judge distinguished the earlier case of *Re Hellenic and General Trust*,[37] where the judge had refused sanction because the ordinary shares already held by a subsidiary of the bidder in the target had been voted in favour of the scheme at a meeting of the ordinary shareholders. The explanation of *Re Hellenic* was that the subsidiary's shares had been excluded because the scheme did not concern them: in effect, they were already held by the bidder.

29–9   The issue of how classes should be composed for scheme purposes was rendered particularly acute by the former practice of the courts of leaving the decision about class meetings at stage (b) almost wholly to the company (i.e. of simply accepting what the company proposed) and taking a view whether that decision was correct only at stage (c), by which time it was too late to do anything about it and the court could only refuse to sanction the scheme on the grounds it had no jurisdiction to do so, since the proper meetings had not been held!

---

[34] *Sovereign Life Assurance Co v Dodd* [1892] 2 Q.B. 573 at 583, per Bowen LJ.

[35] *Re Equitable Life Assurance Society* [2002] 2 B.C.L.C. 510.

[36] *Re BTR Plc* [1999] 2 B.C.L.C. 675. The decision and reasoning were upheld on appeal: [2000] 1 B.C.L.C. 740 CA. See also *Re Industrial Equity (Pacific) Ltd* [1991] 2 H.K.L.R. 614.

[37] *Re Hellenic and General Trust* [1976] 1 W.L.R. 123. On the view of this case adopted in *BTR* it was not fatal to the scheme that the subsidiary's shares were voted at the class meeting, but they were to be discounted at the third stage when deciding whether to approve the scheme.

This approach was roundly criticised by Chadwick LJ in *Re Hawk Insurance Co Ltd*[38] and, as far as creditors are concerned, where identifying the correct classes is often particularly difficult, a Practice Direction was subsequently issued designed to produce substantive consideration of the classes issue at stage (b). Although a creditor may still challenge the way the meetings were convened at stage (c), the court "will expect them to show good reason why they did not raise a creditor issue at an earlier stage".[39] The CLR proposed that the court should have the general discretion to determine the appropriate classes at stage (b), when asked to do so by the company, and that, if it exercised its discretion at this stage, it should be bound by it when it came to consider sanctioning the scheme after member or creditor approval (stage (c)).[40] It further proposed that the court should have a discretion to sanction the scheme even if the appropriate class meetings had not been held, provided the court was satisfied that the incorrect composition of the meetings had not had any substantive effect on the outcome, i.e. it would no longer be a matter going to the jurisdiction of the court.[41] However, these proposed reforms were not taken up in the Act and so the procedure in relation to classes of members remains somewhat obscure. It seems likely that the courts will adapt the creditor procedure so that members who think the company's class proposals are inappropriate should object at stage (b) and not wait until (c).

Section 897 requires any notice sent out summoning the meetings to be accompanied by a statement explaining the effect of the compromise or arrangement and in particular stating any material interests of the directors (whether in their capacity of directors or otherwise) and the effect on those interests of the scheme in so far as that differs from the effect on the interests of others.[42] Where the scheme affects the rights of debenture-holders, the statement must give the like statement regarding the interests of any trustees for the debenture-holders.[43] If the notice is given by advertisement,[44] the advertisement must include the foregoing statements or a notification of where and how copies

29–10

---

[38] *Re Hawk Insurance Co Ltd* [2001] 2 B.C.L.C. 480. He thought it particularly unfortunate that the court should feel obliged to raise the issue of its own motion at stage (c), even though no member or creditor sought to argue that class meetings should have been held.

[39] Practice Direction [2002] 1 W.L.R. 1345. For an account of modern practice, see *Re T&N Ltd (No.3)* [2007] 1 B.C.L.C. 563 at [18]–[20].

[40] The court does already decide at stage (b) issues relating to the jurisdiction of the court to sanction a scheme at stage (c), though not issues going to the fairness of the scheme: *Re Savoy Hotel* [1981] Ch. 351; *Re Telewest Communications Plc (No.1)* [2005] 1 B.C.L.C. 752 at [14]–[15]; *Re My Travel Group Plc* [2005] 2 B.C.L.C. 123.

[41] Final Report I, paras 13.6–13.7. This would not otherwise affect the tasks to be performed by the court at the sanctioning stage, on which see below.

[42] 2006 Act s.897(1),(2).

[43] 2006 Act s.897(3). If the interests of the directors or the trustees change before the meetings are held, the court will not sanction the scheme unless satisfied that no reasonable shareholder or debenture-holder would have altered his decision on how to vote if the changed position had been disclosed: *Re Jessel Trust Ltd* [1985] B.C.L.C. 119; *Re Minster Assets* [1985] B.C.L.C. 200.

[44] Which will be the only way of notifying holders of bearer bonds. It may also be necessary to advertise in this way to creditors.

of the circular can be obtained, and on making application a member or creditor is entitled to be furnished with a copy free of charge.[45] The level of approval required at the meeting is a majority in number,[46] representing three-fourths in value,[47] of its creditors or members present and voting in person or by proxy.[48] The question of whether the approval of both creditors and members or of a particular class of member or creditor is required in any case is to be answered by determining with whom the company proposes to effect a compromise or arrangement. If members or creditors or any class of them are not included within the scheme, their consent is not required, but the company runs the risk that the implementation of the scheme may later be held to infringe the rights of those left out of it.[49]

The sanction of the court

29–11   The application for the court's approval is made by petition of the applicants and may be opposed by members and creditors who object to the scheme. In the oft-quoted words of Maugham J,[50] the duties of the court are twofold:

> "The first is to see that the resolutions are passed by the statutory majority in value and number...at a meeting or meetings duly convened and held. The other duty is in the nature of a discretionary power...[W]hat I have to see is whether the proposal is such that an intelligent and honest man, a member of the class concerned and acting in respect of his interest, might reasonably approve."

The first of these duties involves not only ensuring that the meeting was given the information the statute requires and that the requisite majority was obtained, but also that the class was fairly represented at the meeting. Thus, the sanction of the court can be refused if the meeting was unrepresentative of the class as a whole or if those whose votes were necessary to secure the required level of approval did so in order to promote some special interest which they did not share with the ordinary members of the class.[51] This seems to involve something akin

---

[45] 2006 Act s.897(1)(b),(4). A default in complying with any requirement of the section renders the company and every officer, liquidator, administrator, or trustee for debenture-holders liable to a fine unless he shows that the default was due to the refusal of another director or trustee for debenture-holders to supply the necessary particulars of his interest: s.897(5)–(8). In that case the criminal offence is committed by that director or trustee: s.898.

[46] The CLR recommended the removal of the number requirement, which does indeed appear anomalous in the context of the Companies Act approach to shareholder approval: Final Report I, para.13.10. However, the "number" requirement does constitute an additional element of minority protection where 75 per cent of the shares are concentrated in one or a few persons.

[47] In relation to creditors further difficulties may arise in valuing their claims and thus determining whether the majority does represent three-fourths in value. This is a problem met whenever this formula is employed in respect of creditors—as it is throughout the Insolvency Act.

[48] 2006 Act s.899(1).

[49] Re MyTravel Group Plc [2005] 2 B.C.L.C. 123 CA; Re Bluebrook Ltd [2010] 1 B.C.L.C. 338.

[50] In Re Dorman Long & Co [1934] Ch. 635, 655 and 657. See also Re National Bank Ltd [1966] 1 W.L.R. 819, 829.

[51] Re BTR Plc [2000] 1 B.C.L.C. 740 at 747. For an extreme case, see Re PCCW Ltd [2009] 3 HKC 292 Hong Kong Court of Final Appeal.

to the "bona fides" test applied to majority decisions to change the articles.[52] The second part of the test is relatively weak, since it is a rationality rather than a reasonableness test. The court should not differ from the majority view "unless something is brought to the attention of the Court to show that there has been some material oversight or miscarriage".[53]

The scheme becomes binding on the company and all members (or all members of the class concerned) and, if the company is in liquidation, on the liquidator, once it is sanctioned by the court and a copy of the court's order is delivered to the Registrar (so that knowledge of the scheme is publicly available).[54] Indeed, the binding effect of schemes on minorities is one of its attractions over a takeover bid.[55] In addition, implementation of an approved scheme will not lead to liability for any unlawful act contained in the scheme, for example, unlawful financial assistance for the purchase of shares.[56]

Additional requirements for mergers and divisions of public companies

Under British practice, amalgamations of domestic companies are rarely carried out by means of transfers of undertakings (as opposed to shares) using a scheme of arrangement. For this, there are said to be two reasons. First, there are limitations on what s.900 can achieve. It was held in *Nokes v Doncaster Amalgamated Collieries*[57] that the section does not operate to transfer contracts of employment and that principle has been applied to any rights which as a matter of general law are not transferable. Even if the contract is in principle transferable, the counterparty may have negotiated a right to terminate the contract or to insist on different terms of business if the transferor is replaced by the transferee as the contracting party. Any court order under s.900 (transferring property) will not override these third-party rights and so transferor and transferee will have to negotiate an acceptable set of arrangements with the third party. However, it should be noted that contractual restrictions can easily be drafted so as to apply where control of the company changes without there being any transfer of assets (as in a takeover, whether effected by a scheme or not), so

29–12

---

[52] Above, at para.19–7. At this point the first and second parts of the test began to overlap.

[53] per Lindley LJ in *Re English, Scottish, and Australian Chartered Bank* [1893] 3 Ch. 385. See also *Re Alabama, New Orleans, Texas and Pacific Junction Railway Co* [1891] 1 Ch. 213, per Fry LJ; *Re Telewest Communications Plc (No.2)* [2005] 1 B.C.L.C. 772; *Re Apcoa Parking Holdings GmbH* [2014] EWHC 3849 (Ch). These were all creditors' cases but the same principle applies to members' schemes.

[54] 2006 Act s.899.

[55] The courts have rejected arguments that a scheme which satisfies the requirements of the Act might nevertheless amount to deprivation of possessions contrary to art.1 of the First Protocol of the European Convention on Human Rights: *Re Equitable Life Assurance Society* [2002] 2 B.C.L.C. 510; *Re Waste Recycling Group Plc* [2004] 1 B.C.L.C. 352.

[56] *British and Commonwealth Holdings Plc v Barclays Bank Plc* [1996] 1 W.L.R. 1 CA; *Re Uniq Ltd* [2012] 1 B.C.L.C. 783—though it is unlikely that the judges will give wholesale exemptions from the financial assistance rules just because the assistance is embodied in a scheme.

[57] *Nokes v Doncaster Amalgamated Collieries* [1940] A.C. 1014 HL; *Re TSB Nuclear Energy Investment UK Ltd* [2014] B.C.C. 531—though the Transfer of Undertakings (Protection of Employment) Regulations 2006/246 largely solve the employment issue.

that in this respect a merger may put the company in no worse a position. Whether or not the third party has negotiated contractual protection, s.900(2)(e) gives the court power to require protection for any creditor (or, indeed, member) who dissents from the transfer. This issue will not arise in the case of a takeover, since the court is not involved in approving it.

A second part of the explanation may be that a merger effected by a scheme is very likely to trigger Pt 27 of the Act, which imposes extra requirements and costs on the implementation of schemes for reconstruction[58] or amalgamation involving a public company, in order to meet the requirements of the Third Company Law Directive on mergers of public companies.[59] Part 27 does not apply where a scheme is used to effect a takeover, because bidder and target remain separate companies after the scheme has been effected. There are three major additional requirements,[60] of which the most important is the third, which deploys the protective device, not otherwise found in the domestic rules on schemes of arrangement, of an independent expert's report. However, although no formal independent expert's report may be required of the bidder in the case of a proposed takeover by means of a scheme, the Takeover Code lays down extensive rules on the provision of information to the "target" shareholders, including an independent expert's opinion on the fairness of the offer and the Code's rules will apply to takeovers by way of a scheme.[61] Thus, Pt 27 may not add much in substance to the bidder's costs. Perhaps the truth is that tax rules make amalgamations through schemes unattractive or that British practitioners have become so familiar with the takeover that alternative means of amalgamation are not seriously explored. In any event, the scheme-based domestic merger seems to be rare.

29–13   The additional requirements of Pt 27 are:

1.   Normally, a draft scheme has to be drawn up by the boards of all[62] the companies concerned and publicised via the *Gazette* or, more likely, the company's website. All this must be done at least one month before the meetings are held.[63]

---

[58] See fn.4, above.

[59] Directive 78/855/EEC (now Directive 2011/35/EU ([2011] O.J. L110/1)). The requirements of this Directive were somewhat reduced by two subsequent amending directives: Directives 2007/63/EC and 2009/109/EC, both of which have been implemented in the UK. Directive 82/891/EEC (the "Sixth" Directive) deals with the division of public limited companies.

[60] The details differ somewhat according to the "Case" (see below) within which the scheme falls, the main differences being between those within Case 1 or 2 (mergers) and Case 3 (divisions).

[61] See para.28–14.

[62] This includes the transferee company, whose consent is not required under a scheme governed purely by Pt 26, unless the rights of the shareholders or creditors of the transferee are proposed to be changed. However, it is enough that the members of the transferee are given the option to call a meeting (on the basis of a five per cent threshold: ss.918 and 932) so that the burden of action falls on the shareholders rather than the company in such a case. Of course, if the transferee is a UK listed company, the large transaction provisions of the Listing Rules might require it to obtain shareholder approval. See para.14–20.

[63] 2006 Act ss.905–6A, 920–921A.

2.   What has to be stated in the board's circulars is considerably amplified as compared with the rules for a standard scheme, but perhaps not as compared with the Takeover Code rules.[64]

3.   In addition, generally[65] separate written reports on the scheme have to be provided to the members of each company by an independent expert appointed by that company or, if the court approves, a single joint report to all companies by an independent expert appointed by all of them.[66]

However, the Directive, although widely framed, does not apply to all forms of merger, and Pt 27 goes no wider. Hence, there is some considerable scope for framing a merger scheme which avoids the additional requirements. In particular, Pt 27 applies only where the consideration for the transfer is or includes shares in the transferee, so that a merger for a purely cash consideration is excluded.[67] Secondly, in the case of a merger "by absorption" (see below), where the transferee company already holds all, or in some cases 90 per cent, of the securities carrying voting rights in the transferor, the requirements mentioned above are substantially reduced.[68] This facilitates mergers within corporate groups and, in particular, a merger of parent and new subsidiary following a successful takeover bid. Thirdly, Pt 27 does not apply if the transferor company is being wound up,[69] rather than being dissolved without winding-up after the merger. Thus, the requirements of Pt 27 can be avoided by incurring the expense of putting the transferor into liquidation—probably not an attractive course of action.

Finally, the merger must fall within one of two "Cases" specified in the Directive. The two "Cases" are: **29–14**

1.   Where the undertaking, property and liabilities of the public company are to be transferred to another public company, other than one formed for the purpose of, or in connection with, the scheme ("merger by absorption").[70]

2.   Where the undertakings, property and liabilities of each of two or more public companies, including the one in respect of which the arrangement is proposed, are to be transferred to a new company, whether or not a public company, formed for the purpose of, or in connection with, the scheme ("merger by formation of new company").[71] Thus, a transfer to a new

---

[64] 2006 Act ss.908, 910, 923, 925.

[65] As a result of amendments to the Directives introduced by Directive 2007/63/EC the requirement for an independent report can be dispensed with if all the shareholders agree. See s.918A.

[66] 2006 Act ss.909, 924 and 935–937. The matters to be dealt with in the report are specified in some detail. In some respects it resembles the report required (also as a result of an EU Directive) when a public company makes an issue of shares paid-up otherwise than in cash: see paras 11–16 et seq., above.

[67] 2006 Act s.902(1)(c).

[68] 2006 Act ss.915 and 915A. In these cases, as well, the requirement for a meeting of members is relaxed: ss.916–917 and 931.

[69] 2006 Act s.902(3).

[70] 2006 Act ss.904(1)(a) and 902(2)(b).

[71] 2006 Act ss.904(1)(b) and 902(2)(a).

company, public or private, by a single public company escapes from both 1 and 2, and equally a reconstruction of a single company can be carried out purely under Pt 26.[72]

3. There is a third Case, which applies to divisions. Where, under the scheme, the undertaking, property and liabilities of the public company are to be divided among, or transferred to, two or more companies each of which is either a public company or a company formed for the purposes of, or in connection with, the scheme ("division by acquisition" or "division by formation of new company").[73]

29–15 Despite the discouraging history of the use of schemes to effect true mergers, the CLR consulted on the issue of whether there should be introduced into the Act a statutory merger procedure, as in many other jurisdictions.[74] For the CLR the crucial element of a statutory merger procedure was that the merger should not require approval by the court, though in appropriate cases those adversely affected by the proposal should have a right of appeal to the court. Its goal of providing a "court free" merger procedure was thus in line with what it recommended in the case of reductions of capital.[75] However, it also took the view that, where the Third Directive applied, it would be impractical to implement a proposal except under the supervision of the court.[76] The result of the restrictions in effect imposed by the Directives was that the statutory merger procedure seemed to the CLR to be feasible only in two cases. The first was the merger of wholly-owned subsidiaries of a parent company. The CLR thought this a useful reform, and it was supported on consultation, because "many groups of companies include subsidiaries which are kept alive for no good reason other than to avoid the expense and problems associated with getting rid of them".[77] The second and somewhat more general area for the operation of a statutory merger procedure was where a company formed a new wholly-owned subsidiary, into which the assets and liabilities of an existing company were transferred, the transferor being dissolved. On consultation a majority thought the new procedure should be made available in this situation as well.[78] However, neither of these proposals was taken up in the Act.

CROSS-BORDER MERGERS

29–16 Despite the limited utilisation of the scheme of arrangement to produce true mergers between domestic companies, the merger procedure has begun to be used by UK companies involved in cross-border mergers since the adoption by the EU

---

[72] See the scheme proposed in *Re MyTravel Group Plc* [2005] 2 B.C.L.C. 123.
[73] 2006 Act ss.919 and 902(2). The Sixth Directive applies to divisions. See fn.59, above.
[74] Completing, paras 11.40–11.53.
[75] See paras 13–39 et seq.
[76] Completing, para.11.46.
[77] Completing, para.11.50. A potential use for the SE (above, para.1–40) is to achieve a similar result within multinational groups.
[78] Final Report I, paras 13.14–13.15.

of the Cross-Border Mergers Directive.[79] The objective is often to simplify the structure of a multi-national corporate group, The Directive is implemented in the UK by the Companies (Cross-Border Merger) Regulations 2007.[80] Thus, for cross-border mergers UK law does now have a customised merger procedure, i.e. one not tied to the scheme of arrangement. Given their EU origin, the Directive and Regulations reflect the approach of the Third Directive, but subject to the important extension that they cover mergers involving private as well as public companies. They provide a mechanism to effect both mergers by absorption and mergers by formation of a new company. Within the absorption category a distinction is made between standard absorptions and absorption of a wholly-owned subsidiary.[81]

Even before the adoption of the Directive, the CJEU had held that the blanket exclusion of a company incorporated in another EU state from the domestic merger procedure of a Member State was an infringement of a company's freedom of establishment under the Treaty.[82] However, an effective cross-border merger procedure requires the coordination of the laws of different Member States, which is difficult to achieve via decisions of the CJEU, but which EU legislation is uniquely well-placed to bring about. The Regulations apply only to mergers involving both a UK and a non-UK company incorporated in the EEA, so that purely domestic mergers are excluded.[83] Equally, the Regulations are not available for cross-border mergers involving a non-EEA company.[84]

Subject to the always thorny issue of employee representation on the board of the resulting company (see below), the scheme of the Directive and the Regulations is simple and relatively elegant. Each company in the cross-border merger is subject to its national merger procedure, on the basis of a common merger plan, drawn up by the directors.[85] That merger plan must be accompanied by a report from the directors, setting out, amongst other things, the rationale for the merger and its likely impact on members, creditors and employees.[86] As under the Third Directive, a report by an independent expert is normally also required.[87] An expert is one who is eligible to be appointed as a statutory auditor and is

29–17

---

[79] Directive 2005/56/EC on cross-border mergers of limited liability companies ([2005] O.J. L310/10).

[80] SI 2007/2974, as amended, a self-standing set of regulations made under the European Communities Act 1972 and constituting a major piece of corporate law which is not located in the 2006 Act at all.

[81] SI 2007/2974 reg.2.

[82] TFEU art.49. See Case C-411/03 *SEVIC* [2005] E.C.R. I-10805, concerning German merger procedure.

[83] SI 2007/2974 reg.2. In the case of merger by formation of a new company the diversity requirement is applied to the transferor companies (reg.2(4)(a)).

[84] See art.1 of the Directive.

[85] SI 2007/2974 reg.7. It thus appears that the merger cannot proceed unless the directors of all the companies involved approve the idea.

[86] SI 2007/2974 reg.8.

[87] SI 2007/2974 reg.9. An expert's report is not required where the merger is between a wholly-owned subsidiary and its parent and where the transferee holds 90 per cent of the securities of the transferor carrying voting rights and an exit right on fair terms is afforded to the minority: regs 9 and 9A.

independent if he meets the statutory tests for independence as an auditor.[88] This report is concerned principally with the exchange ratio proposed as between the shares in the transferor company (or companies) and in the transferee company involved in the merger.[89] The consideration for the merger will often be shares in the transferee company but the UK regulations take up the option to make cash available as consideration without restriction.[90] In the case of merger by absorption of a wholly owned subsidiary, the Regulations anticipate that no consideration at all will be provided[91] (since consideration has no function in this situation). In the other types of merger it has been held that, within a wholly-owned group structure, the members of the transferor company can waive their right to shares in the transferee, so that here, as well, consideration is dispensed with.[92]

29–18 Publicity is to be given to these documents in various ways, for the benefit of members, creditors and employees, but normally in practice by their publication on the company's website.[93] Publicity is a necessary part of the process whereby consent is sought from these groups for the merger proposal. As far as members are concerned, in principle consent is required from each of the UK companies involved in the merger. The approval level, as under a scheme, is 75 per cent in value and a majority in number of each class of members.[94] Again, as under a scheme, the court has power to order meetings of the members or classes of them, and the same issues are likely to arise in relation to the definition of classes as under schemes.[95] Creditor approval does not appear to be mandatory, but any creditor of a UK merging company may apply to the court to summon a meeting of creditors or classes of creditors, and the transferor company itself will normally do so, if the rights of creditors are affected (for example, because their claims will lie in future against a foreign company).[96] The level of creditor approval required at a meeting is again 75 per cent in value and a majority in number.[97] Employee consultation is considered below.

29–19 After the relevant procedure has been followed (including the employee aspects—below), the UK court performs one of two roles, depending on whether the transferee company is a UK company or not. If it is not, the UK transferor

---

[88] Reg.9(7)–(8), invoking ss.1212 and 1214 of the Act, on which see para.22–12.

[89] The transferor company or companies will have their assets and liabilities transferred if the merger goes through and the transferee company is the company which will receive those assets and may be an existing company or one formed for the purposes of the merger.

[90] SI 2007/2974 reg.2.

[91] SI 2007/2974 reg.2(3).

[92] *Re Olympus UK Ltd* [2014] EWHC 1350 (Ch)—an interesting example of the interpretation of the English version of the Directive so as to maximize its harmonising effect, despite an ill-advised use of words in that version.

[93] SI 2007/2974 regs 10, 12–12A.

[94] SI 2007/2974 reg.13. Transferor member approval is not required in the case of merger by absorption of a wholly owned subsidiary and, where the transferee company is an existing company, approval of its members is required only if the holders of 5 per cent or more of the voting rights call a meeting to consider the merger.

[95] SI 2007/2974 reg.11, and see para.29–8, above.

[96] SI 2007/2974 reg.11. The transferor company may pay off or secure the creditors' claims in advance of the merger.

[97] SI 2007/2974 reg.13.

company or companies may apply to the court for a certificate (a "pre-merger certificate") that the UK procedure has been followed.[98] The UK company may use that certificate before the competent authority in the jurisdiction where the transferee company is incorporated in order to complete the merger in that jurisdiction. If the transferee company is a UK company, the UK court may order the completion of the cross-border merger on the basis of the pre-merger certificates provided by the UK court and by the competent authority of the jurisdictions in which the non-UK merging companies are incorporated.[99] The core function of the court at this stage is to ensure that the merging companies have all approved the same draft merger terms and that the employee participation arrangements have been determined, where this is necessary. However, it has been said that the court also has a more general power to review the merger substantively to see whether it will adversely affect any member, creditor or employee in a material way and whether there is any other good reason not to approve it.[100] Upon approval and notification to the registrar of companies, all the assets and liabilities of the transferor companies go across to the transferee company,[101] the members of the transferor companies receiving securities become members of the transferee company and the merging companies cease to exist.[102]

Employee participation

The Directive and domestic Regulations become complicated over the issue of whether the transferee company is required to have in place a system of worker participation in relation to its board. Participation includes not only the right to elect or appoint members of the board but also rights to recommend or oppose board members.[103] No more than a sketch of the provisions can be offered here, but in general the rules follow those for the SE (European Company).[104] However, there is one very important difference from the scheme contained in the SE Regulations: the default system of representation which applies in the absence of agreement between company and employee representatives may be capped by

29-20

---

[98] SI 2007/2974 reg.6. The court's role here is presumably similar to that under a scheme.

[99] SI 2007/2974 reg.16. The court may order completion even where the merger agreement is conditional, provided the court has a high degree of confidence that the conditions will be met, that the conditions are aimed at facilitating the merger which the shareholders approved and that they do not amount to giving a party other than the court a discretion whether the merger goes ahead: *Re International Game Technology Plc* [2015] 2 B.C.L.C. 45; *Nielsen Holdings Plc* [2015] EWHC 2966 (Ch); *Re Livanona Plc and Sorin SpA* [2015] B.C.C. 914. This reflects practice under domestic schemes (*Lombard Medical Technologies Plc* [2015] 1 B.C.L.C. 656).

[100] *Re Diamond Resorts (Europe) Ltd* [2013] B.C.C. 275. The judge also held that the rigor of that enquiry would also depend on the extent of the investigations undertaken by the competent authority (which may not be a court) in the other EEA jurisdictions involved.

[101] Including the rights and obligations of the merging companies under contracts of employment: reg.17(1). It seems likely that reg.17 will be interpreted as transferring all contractual rights and liabilities, no matter whether they are transferable under general law. See fn.57, above.

[102] SI 2007/2974 reg.17, widely construed in *Re Lanber Properties LLP and Lanber II GmbH* [2014] EWHC 4713.

[103] SI 2007/2974 reg.3(1).

[104] See para.14–67.

the transferee company at one third of the seats for the employees, even if a more extensive system applied to one of the constituent companies.[105] There is no such cap in the SE rules and so there may be some incentive for cross-border mergers to take place via the Directive rather than under the SE Regulation.

29–21 The following additional points can be made about the employee participation rules, looking at the matter from the point of view of a UK-incorporated transferee company:

(1) The general rule (though it has significant exceptions) is that the transferee is subject to the participation rules applying in its State of registration.[106] On this basis a resulting company registered in the UK would not be subject to participation rules.

(2) However, participation is the default rule even in UK transferee companies in three situations,[107] of which the most important is probably that where any merging company in the six months prior to the publication of the draft terms of the merger had an average number of employees exceeding 500 and operated a system of employee participation. The default rule covers any merging company (not just a UK one) and any system of employee participation, whether based on board level representation or some other form of influence over the composition of the board. In this way, a UK transferee company may exceptionally become subject to mandatory employee participation rules.

(3) Where participation rules apply to the UK transferee, the merging companies (unanimously) may choose unilaterally to apply to the transferee company the "standard rules" (set out in the Regulations) on participation, i.e. without any negotiation with the employee representatives and without the loss of time such negotiation entails.[108] In that case, the employees of the transferee company obtain participation rights in relation to that number of board members which is equal to the highest proportion to be found in any of the merging companies in which participation rights existed. Thus, the strongest system applying in any of the merging companies will apply to the transferee company, where "strength" is measured by the number of board seats subject to employee influence, not the form of that influence. The right to oppose the appointment of three members trumps the right to elect two.

(4) Alternatively, the merging companies may choose to negotiate with representatives of the employees of the merging companies with the aim of agreeing on some alternative to the standard rules. This involves the creation of a "Special Negotiating Body" ("SNB") of employee representatives to negotiate on behalf of the employees of all the merging

---

[105] SI 2007/2974 reg.39. This follows art.16(4)(c) of the Directive, which permits, but does not require, Member States to adopt a cap and confines that cap to one-tier boards.

[106] Directive art.16(1) and reg.22.

[107] Directive art.16(2) and reg.22.

[108] Directive art.16(3)(h), (4)(a) and regs 36 and 38. However, the one third cap can be imposed only if there have been negotiations with the employee representatives. Completion of the employee participation arrangements is a condition for the registration of the resulting company: reg.39.

companies.[109] The parties have six months (extendable by agreement once to 12 months) to reach a participation agreement, which agreement will then determine the participation arrangements in the company.[110] That agreement may increase or reduce the participation rights of the employees.[111] The SNB can even decide not to negotiate participation arrangements, in which case the employees of the transferee company are subject to the rules on participation of the Member State in which that company is incorporated.[112] In the case of a UK transferee this would mean no mandatory participation rights.

(5)   If the parties either do not reach agreement within the specified period or agree that the standard rules shall apply, then the resulting company will be subject to those rules.[113] In this case, however, the transferee company may impose the cap mentioned above.

(6)   The employee participation system applied by the Directive to the first transferee company must be applied to a subsequent domestic merger by that company for a period of three years, so that the second transferee company cannot escape the participation rules imposed on the first transferee company.[114] However, after three years it would appear to be open to the first transferee company, in a jurisdiction which does not require employee participation, to merge with a domestic company under the domestic merger procedure and thus escape from the Directive's participation requirements.

Further uses of cross-border mergers

In addition to the simplification of the structure of cross-border groups, the Regulations could be used to effect an amalgamation between two or more separately owned companies, in place of a cross-border takeover bid. For the reasons given in relation to schemes of arrangement,[115] the cross-border merger is unlikely to replace the cross-border hostile bid, especially as the directors of the merging companies are even more strongly entrenched in the case of cross-border merger than a scheme.[116] However, the cross-border merger could perform a role in relation to agreed takeovers, where a competing offer is unlikely to emerge,

29–22

---

[109] Regulations Ch.2 of Pt 4.

[110] SI 2007/2974 regs 28 and 29.

[111] But if at least one-quarter of the employees of the merging companies had participation rights, any decision by the SNB on an agreement which reduces participation rights below the highest proportion previously operating requires a two-thirds majority of the members of the SNB: reg.30.

[112] SI 2007/2974 reg.31. This requires not only a two-thirds vote of the SNB, but also that those voting in favour should represent two-thirds of the employees of the merging companies.

[113] SI 2007/2974 reg.36. However, failure to agree will trigger the standard rules where fewer than one-third of the employees of merging companies were subject to participation only where the SNB has positively opted (by a majority of its members) for them. Thus, a majority of representatives, perhaps from countries not having a participation system, could block its imposition on the resulting company, perhaps in exchange for some different type of concession from the companies.

[114] SI 2007/2974 reg.40.

[115] Above, para.29–3.

[116] Above, fn.85. *Re International Game Technology Plc* [2015] 2 B.C.L.C. 45 concerned a genuine cross-border merger, not just an intra-group restructuring.

especially where the bidder is from a culture less committed to the takeover form of amalgamation. On the other hand, the takeover avoids the creation of novel employee participation rights: the bidder and target remain subject to whatever, if anything, their national laws provide in this regard.[117]

29–23 A rather different potential use of the cross-border merger is to change a company's jurisdiction of incorporation. The cross-border merger Directive and Regulations appear to give the merging companies a free choice as to the Member State jurisdiction in which the transferee company is incorporated. If a jurisdiction is desired which is not one in which any of the merging companies is currently incorporated, then a new transferee company can be incorporated in the desired jurisdiction and the existing companies merged into it. However, if the desired jurisdiction is a "real seat" state, then the Directive appears to permit the authorities of that state not to register the resulting entity, if the company's "central administration" is not also in that state.[118] This is a significant obstacle to a merger based solely on choice of law considerations.

Finally, it is worth noting that it is possible to produce a cross-border merger through a "dual-listed structure". In this arrangement the companies remain formally independent (i.e. they do not merge) nor does the one become a subsidiary of the other, as in a takeover. Instead, by contract, including provisions in their respective constitutions, the companies produce a unified management (i.e. the same people sitting on the boards of directors of the two companies or, normally, top companies of the two groups of companies which are coming together). The shareholder bodies remain separate but each body is given voting rights in the meetings of the other, so as to produce a single decision from the two votes; and the profits of the two companies are equalised. Such structures are complex to create (and to understand) but may have advantages over a merger, for example, where national susceptibilities are involved. There are not many such companies but a number of well-known multinational companies take this form (Unilever, BHP Billiton, Reed Elsevier) and others did so for a substantial period of time before moving to a more conventional single company (or group) structure (Shell, ABB).

---

[117] This is in fact highly unsatisfactory in one respect. Where a German company, subject to co-determination, takes over a British company, the British workers will have no right to participate in board level representation arrangements of the German parent, even though the strategy of both companies is probably determined at that level, unless, as sometimes happens, voluntary arrangements are made to accommodate the interests of the non-German workers.

[118] Directive art.4(1)(b). For discussion of this issue, and a number of other pertinent observations on the Directive, see J. Rickford, "The Proposed Tenth Company Law Directive on Cross Border Mergers and its Impact in the UK" [2005] E.B.L.R. 1393.

REORGANISATION UNDER SECTIONS 110 AND 111 OF THE INSOLVENCY ACT 1986

Under this type of reorganisation the company concerned resolves first to go into voluntary liquidation[119] and secondly to authorise by a special resolution the liquidator to transfer the whole or any part of the company's business or property to another company[120] or a limited liability partnership ("LLP") in consideration of shares or like interests in that company (or membership in the LLP) for distribution among the members of the liquidating company. This procedure affords a relatively simple method of reconstructing a single company or of effecting a merger of its undertaking into that of another. It is often used as a tax-efficient way of effecting a demerger or division of a business.

29–24

Use of this method has the advantage, over a scheme, that confirmation by the court is not required,[121] and the advantage over a takeover that all the shareholders of the company are bound by the decision. But what it can achieve is somewhat limited. Creditors of the transferor will be entitled to prove in its liquidation and the liquidator must ensure that their proved claims are met and cannot rely upon an indemnity given by the acquiring company.[122] A high level of member agreement on the use of the sections is also desirable. This is because s.111 provides that, in the case of a members' voluntary winding-up, any member of the company who did not vote in favour of the special resolution may, within seven days of its passing, serve a notice on the liquidator requiring the liquidator either to refrain from carrying the resolution into effect or to purchase the member's shares at a price to be determined either by agreement or by arbitration.[123] It is normally essential if advantage is to be taken of stamp duty concessions that the membership of the old company and the new should be very largely the same. If a number of the members elect to be bought out, there is a grave risk that the reorganisation will have to be abandoned as prohibitively expensive.

The CLR found the Insolvency Act procedure to be a popular method for reconstructing private or family-controlled companies or groups and also for

29–25

---

[119] Under former versions of these provisions it had to be a *members'* voluntary liquidation, i.e. one in which the directors have made a "declaration of solvency" declaring that all the company's debts will be paid in full within 12 months. It can now be employed also in a creditors' voluntary liquidation so long as it is sanctioned by the court or the liquidation committee (Insolvency Act s.110(3)) but that sanction is unlikely to be given unless all creditors are paid in full.

[120] Whether or not the latter is a company within the meaning of the Companies Act (Insolvency Act s.110(1)) so that it could be a company registered in another jurisdiction.

[121] Though the court's sanction may be needed if the company is to be wound up in a creditors' winding-up.

[122] *Pulsford v Devenish* [1903] 2 Ch. 625. But the sale of the undertaking will be binding on the creditors who will not be able to follow the assets transferred to the transferee company: *Re City & County Investment Co* (1879) 13 Ch. D. 475 CA.

[123] This is an example, rare under UK law (but more widely used in some other common law jurisdictions) of protecting dissenting members by granting them "appraisal rights". The courts will not permit the company to deprive members of their appraisal rights under the section by purporting to act under powers in its articles to sell its undertaking in exchange for securities of another company to be distributed *in specie*: *Bisgood v Henderson's Transvaal Estates* [1908] 1 Ch. 743 CA.

reconstructing investment trust companies.[124] It therefore recommended its retention with, however, the modernisation of the arbitration procedure which operates when a member exercises the appraisal right and a valuation of the member's interest cannot be agreed. The procedure under the current law is antiquated, invoking as it does the arbitration provisions of the Companies Clauses Consolidation Act 1845 or its Scottish equivalent,[125] doubtfully in compliance with the Human Rights Act and unclear about the basis upon which the member's interest should be valued. The CLR proposed that the valuation should be based on the dissentient's proportionate share of the consideration offered by the transferee for the transferor's business.[126] However, these provisions being in the Insolvency Act 1986, they were not touched by the Companies Act 2006.

CONCLUSION

29–26   We remarked at the beginning of this chapter that the Companies Act does not contain a statutory merger procedure of the type typically found in other jurisdictions. Whilst this statement is true, somewhat oddly a true merger procedure is now provided for cross-border mergers within the EU as a result of the Cross-Border Merger Directive and implementing Regulations. For purely domestic mergers, however, the scheme of arrangement is available for this purpose, but that procedure is available also to achieve a number of other objectives which have nothing to do with mergers of two or more companies. Indeed, since the scheme procedure, although available, is rarely used to achieve a true merger, it would be odd to use the term statutory merger procedure to refer to the scheme of arrangement. Just to confuse things further, the alternative to the merger—the takeover bid—can be, and increasingly is, affected by means of a scheme. The scheme of arrangement is thus an immensely flexible instrument. However, because it is as much an instrument of insolvency law as of corporate law and because it elides what is regarded in other jurisdictions as the fundamental difference between a takeover bid and a merger, the scheme of arrangement has a rather uncertain image. There can be almost as many types of schemes of arrangement as there are inventive corporate and insolvency lawyers, which indicates both the significance of the scheme procedure and the impossibility of identifying such a thing as a typical scheme of arrangement.

---

[124] Completing, para.11.13.
[125] Clauses Consolidation Act 1845 s.111(4).
[126] Final Report I, para.13.13.

CHAPTER 30

MARKET ABUSE

INTRODUCTION

With these topics we reach the margins of company law. Market abuse can occur   **30–1**
in all markets and the relevant rules apply equally widely. We are concerned in
this book, however, only with abuse in the markets for company securities (shares
and bonds) and their derivatives. Our analysis will accordingly be so confined.

Market abuse is conventionally regarded, at least within the EU, as covering
two rather different activities: insider dealing and market manipulation. Insider
dealing (or trading)[1] occurs when a person in possession of price-sensitive
information about a company buys or sells securities in that company and so
obtains better terms in the transaction than would have been the case had the
counterparty been aware of the information in question. In that way, the insider
can either make a profit or avoid a loss, depending on whether the information,
once public, will drive the price of the security up or down.[2] The issue is at the
margins of company law because the insider dealer does not have to be an insider

---

[1] The Criminal Justice Act 1993 Pt V and the Market Abuse Regulation (Regulation (EU)
No.596/2014) (MAR) use the word "dealing".
[2] Clearly, the insider buys in the former case and sells in the latter.

of the company, for example a director, though he or she very often is. A governmental official may know that the agency for which he or she works is about to issue an adverse report on a particular company which will affect the price of its shares and then trade in the company's shares before the report is published.

Market manipulation involves conduct which moves the price of the securities to a position which is different from that which the market would have set in the absence of the conduct. Penalising such behaviour thus involves drawing a distinction between legitimate and illegitimate behaviour within markets. If a company announces a bid for another company at a price above the prevailing market price for the shares, that announcement will move the price in an upward direction, but such behaviour is not only regarded as legitimate, it may also be required by takeover rules (as we saw in Ch.28). On the other hand, if I move the market price by making statements which I know to be false, that will be regarded as illegitimate behaviour. In a very early example of market manipulation, from the beginning of the nineteenth century, the fraudsters pretended to be soldiers returning from France with news of the defeat of Napoleon (before this event actually came to pass some time later). The false rumours which they spread caused the price of British government bonds to rise, thus enabling the accused to dispose of their holdings of those bonds at a profit.[3] However, as we shall see below, distinguishing legitimate from illegitimate behaviour in more marginal cases is not easy.

In the case of manipulation it is clear that market participants may suffer loss as a result of the behaviour. They will have acquired or disposed of shares on the basis of an artificial price and may suffer loss when the truth emerges.[4] Equally, the allocative efficiency of the market may suffer. Investors use market prices to determine how to target their resources and so manipulated prices may produce a misallocation of those resources. In the case of insider dealing the harm to the market and its participants is less clear. The insider dealing may not move the share price very much, if at all, and, in so far is it does, it moves the price towards, not away from, its "true" value (i.e. towards the value it will have when the full information is eventually publicly disclosed). Since insider dealing can be avoided by not trading and in public markets many of the other market participants would have traded, whether or not the insider traded, the harm to them is difficult to identify.[5] It is easier to see the harm if there are rules, as is now the case, requiring inside information to be disclosed.[6] If the information had been in the market, the prices would have been different and this can be used as a starting point for calculating loss.[7] On this basis, the harm-causing event is not

---

[3] *R. v De Berenger* (1814) 3 M. & S. 68. This was long before there was specific legislation on market manipulation but the defendants were convicted of the common law offence of fraud. The case was also an example of manipulation in the government bond, rather than the corporate securities, market.

[4] Of course, those who buy and sell before the truth emerges may suffer no loss but may actually benefit from the manipulation, so the loss is normally suffered by those holding the securities at the moment of truth.

[5] The analysis might be different in face-to-face transactions but in fact the market abuse rules apply only to securities which are publicly traded.

[6] See para.26–5, above.

[7] The loss is in fact crystallised only when the truth emerges. See fn.4.

the insider dealing as such but the non-disclosure of the inside information, but non-disclosure is an inherent part of the insider dealer's strategy.[8]

In insider dealing rules a crucial task is distinguishing between information which the insider cannot use privately and information which can be used privately. This is not an easy task. It cannot be said, though it often is, that the aim of the insider dealing rules is to put all market participants in possession of the same information, because then there would be no incentive for analysts (and others) to seek out information about companies which is not known to the market in general. Analysts fulfil an important function in keeping the market information-ally efficient because they provide information to the market after, or often as, they trade on the information for their profit.[9] If they had to disclose the information before trading, their incentive to acquire it in the first place would disappear. As with market manipulation, it can be argued that the key objective is to distinguish legitimate from illegitimate means of acquiring information which is not generally known to the market. Only information acquired by illegitimate means should count as "inside" information. So, for example, an analyst who carefully pieces together public but not easily accessible information to arrive at new facts about the company should not be classified as a holder of inside information. On the other hand, a director, who routinely acquires information about the company before the market does because of his or her position in the company, has no socially valuable claim to be allowed to trade on the basis of that information.

30–2

The above arguments provide reasons why securities market authorities would wish to control market abuse. But they do not tie the regulation very closely to the objectives of corporate law. It is possible to make this connection by focusing on the interests of the company (the issuer) in having effective regulation in place. If insider dealing is rife in the market, the non-insider will know that the market prices will systematically fail to reflect all the available information about the company and will do so in a way which is unfavourable to the outsiders. In the absence of regulation, this will be an inherent risk of holding shares in companies and outsiders will build this risk into their investment decisions, by lowering the price they are prepared to pay for companies' shares. This in turn will increase companies' cost of capital because they will be able to issues shares on less favourable terms than if investors could be assured that there was no or little insider trading in the market. Thus, companies have an interest in effective insider dealing legislation or regulation.[10]

30–3

---

[8] So, the distinction between trading and non-disclosure may seem trivial. However, without the disclosure rule, the insider could plausibly say that s/he could have complied with the insider trading provisions by simply not dealing.

[9] The very act of trading will reveal some information to the market about the analysts' position.

[10] See H. Schmidt, "Insider Dealing and Economic Theory" in K.J. Hopt and E. Wymeersch (eds), *European Insider Dealing* (Butterworths, 1991).

The same general argument can be made in relation to market manipulation.[11] If extensive, such behaviour may systematically produce prices which are unfavourable to outsiders, thus again causing them to re-assess the riskiness of corporate securities as a class.

30–4 The law on market abuse has developed rapidly over the past 40 years. The first sanctions against insider dealing were criminal and were introduced by the Companies Act 1980. Those sanctions are now in Pt V of the Criminal Justice Act 1993. Market manipulation was criminalised (beyond the common law) a little later in the Financial Services Act 1986. The present provisions are in Pt 7 of the Financial Services Act 2012. The Financial Services and Markets Act 2000 added administrative sanctions against market abuse (of both types) and widened the definitions of the behaviour which was open to sanction. Enforcement of both the administrative penalties and the criminal law lies in the hands of the Financial Conduct Authority ("FCA"), previously the Financial Services Authority ("FSA").

Market manipulation is an area where EU law has played an important role. Initially, the EU operated via Directives which required transposition into domestic law by the domestic legislator. After the financial crisis, in the name of greater uniformity, the EU adopted a Market Abuse Regulation ("MAR"),[12] most of whose provisions do not require transposition.[13] However, in the case of the UK, the EU rules tended to lag behind the reforms made at domestic level, so that their impact on the rules applicable to the UK markets was also limited. Even the extensions contained in the new Regulation relate primarily to markets other than the markets in corporate securities. Consequently, for the matters considered in this chapter, the impact of the Regulation has been more on the structure of the law and less on its substantive content. Its impact on the structure or sources of the law is profound. EU rules, in the shape of the Regulation and "secondary legislation" made by the Commission under the Regulation, become the important first-line sources of law in relation to market abuse in securities markets and domestic sources, whereas rules made by Parliament or the FCA, become less important than in the past.

This is the position in relation to administrative sanctions against market abuse. In relation to criminal law, the position is different. There is a new Market Abuse Directive on criminal sanctions,[14] but this is a Directive out of which the UK may opt and it has chosen to do so. In the criminal law, therefore, the domestic rules remain in the front line.

We analyse first the rules on insider dealing and then those on market manipulation.

---

[11] For an example see *R. v De Berenger* (1814) 3 M. & S. 68. For the specific statutory definition of market abuse in the current legislation, see para.30–29, below.

[12] Above fn.1. MAR is in force, for the most part, as from July 2016, but at the time of writing not all the Commission's delegated legislation was in place.

[13] The area of enforcement and sanctions is the most important one where Member State transformation is required, because there the Regulation is formulated as a direction to the Member States to introduce specified powers.

[14] Directive 2014/57/EU. But the Government has committed itself to the principle that the UK criminal sanctions should be at least as tough as those in the Directive. See Treasury, Bank of England, FCA, *Fair and Effective Markets Review: Final Report*, June 2015, 6.3.1.

APPROACHES TO REGULATING INSIDER DEALING

Disclosure

A number of approaches to the regulation of insider dealing are to be found in the **30–5** current law. Mandatory disclosure has long been used, but disclosure may be used to control insider dealing in a number of different ways. For example, as we saw in Ch.26, directors, as potential insider dealers, may be required to disclose dealings in their company's securities on the theory that, if they know that their dealings will be public knowledge, they will be less likely to trade on the basis of inside information.[15] Indeed, this is the oldest anti-insider dealing technique, having been introduced upon the recommendation of the Cohen Committee of 1945.[16]

Alternatively, or in addition, the disclosure rules may aim at those who have the inside information and require them to disclose it, whether or not they are likely to trade on the basis of it. The point here is that putting the information into the public domain reduces the opportunities of others to engage in insider dealing. This, too, we have discussed above in the shape of the obligation laid upon issuers to disclose inside information promptly to the market.[17] Even the obligation to disclose the beneficial ownership of shares at the 3 per cent level and above[18] may constitute a disclosure obligation of this type, for it shows who is accumulating a stake in a company, perhaps preparatory to a bid.[19]

Prohibiting trading

At the other end of the spectrum, the law could ban trading by potential insiders, **30–6** irrespective of whether they are in possession of inside information or not. This is a blunt instrument, since it deprives those without inside information of trading opportunities. However, this approach is used in a targeted way in relation to particular "high risk" groups. The clearest example of this strategy was the requirement of the *Model Code* that directors, subject to exceptions, should not deal in securities of the company within a period of two months preceding the preliminary announcement of the company's annual results and similar limitations were imposed in relation to the announcement of the half-yearly and quarterly[20] reports. In addition, clearance to deal at any time had to be obtained in advance from the chairman of the board, the CEO or the company secretary, as appropriate.[21] Compliance with the Code was not required by legislation but was

---

[15] See above, paras 26–9 et seq.

[16] *Report of the Company Law Committee*, Cmnd. 6659 (1945), paras 86–87.

[17] See above, paras 26–5 et seq.

[18] See above, paras 26–14 et seq.

[19] Though note that for the prospective bidder itself to buy shares on the basis of its knowledge that it is going to launch a bid is not regarded as insider trading (see below, para.30–28), but it would be for a person in the know to do so for his or her own account.

[20] Which are, of course, no longer mandatory. See para.26–4.

[21] Nor might the company or any other company in the group trade in its securities at a time when the director was prohibited from trading, unless this was done in the ordinary course of securities dealing or at the behest of a third party: LR 9.2.7.

one of the continuing obligations imposed upon companies with a premium listing by the Listing Rules.[22] Such companies were required to ensure that those discharging managerial responsibilities complied with the Code or such stronger requirements as the company might impose. Thus, the Code was not directly binding on directors but was a model which premium listed companies were required to adopt with such refinements as were thought desirable. In practice it was normally adopted virtually verbatim. The company was required to take "all proper and reasonable" steps to secure compliance with the Code by those discharging managerial responsibilities within it.[23]

The notion of a prohibition on trading during a closed period preceding the company's required regular reports was taken up in MAR, though with a lesser closed period of 30 days.[24] The prohibition now applies to all companies traded on the Main Market, whether with a premium listing or not, and companies traded on AIM. MAR covers "persons discharging managerial responsibilities" as well as directors (but not "closely associated" persons[25]); extends to trading on the account of a third party as well as to own account trading; and brings in trading in derivatives and other financial instruments as well as directly in the company's securities. As under the Model Code, the issuer may allow trading in this period in "exceptional circumstances, such as severe financial difficulty", as further elaborated in Commission delegated acts.[26] Since the MAR provisions overlap with the Model Code, the FCA proposes to remove it from the Listing Rules.[27] However, this leaves two areas where the Model Code applied more widely than MAR. First, it applied to preliminary announcements of annual results, which are not required, and so fall outside MAR, but are market practice in the UK and are in effect the market moving event rather than the later full publication. Secondly, MAR has no equivalent to the clearance rules which applied whenever a director proposes to deal (not just during the closed period). On the second issue the FCA proposed to provide guidance for issuers in place of the present obligation to have clearance rules.[28] Its policy on the first issue is unclear: it may take the view that the provisions of MAR cannot be added to.[29]

---

[22] LR 9.2.8. The code itself was appended to Ch.9. On listing and premium listing see para.25–6.

[23] LR 9.2.8. On the meaning of those "discharging managerial responsibilities", which term includes both directors and senior executives, see para.26–11.

[24] MAR art.19(11).

[25] See para.26–11 for the meaning of these two terms.

[26] MAR art.19(12)(13). Certain limited routine trading is permitted, for example, in relation to employee share schemes. ESMA's advice is that a narrow view be taken of "exceptional circumstances", embracing only situations which are "extremely urgent, unforeseen and compelling and where their cause is external to the person discharging managerial responsibilities who has no control over them" (ESMA, *Final Report: ESMA's technical advice on possible delegated acts concerning the Market Abuse Regulation*, 2015, 5.4).

[27] FCA, *Policy proposals and Handbook changes related to the implementation of the Market Abuse Regulation (2014/596/EU)*, November 2015, paras 4.130 et seq.

[28] FCA, *Policy proposals and Handbook changes related to the implementation of the Market Abuse Regulation (2014/596/EU)*, November 2015, paras 4.130 et seq.

[29] Of course, the insider trading prohibition itself will apply during the run-up to the preliminary announcement, but that is hardly an adequate response if one thinks the blanket ban on trading is a valuable technique during pre-result periods.

Relying on the general law

A third approach is to not to legislate specifically for insider dealing but to rely   **30–7**
instead on established doctrines of the common law to deal with it. Company law
offers its fiduciary duties for this purpose, and more general doctrines of the
common law may also have a role. For one reason or another, however, these
doctrines fail to capture the problem of insider dealing comprehensively. Yet they
need to be borne in mind because they offer civil remedies under the control of
private parties, whereas, as we shall see, the specific insider dealing rules rely
wholly on criminal or regulatory sanctions which are, in effect, under the control
of the FCA.

Directors' fiduciary duties

As pointed out in Ch.16,[30] if directors make use of information acquired as   **30–8**
director for their personal advantage they may breach their fiduciary duties to the
company and be liable to account to it for any profits they have made. A great
advantage of the civil suit brought by the company for breach of fiduciary duty is
that it does not have to show that it has suffered loss as a result of the insider
dealing, simply that the insider fiduciaries have made a profit in breach of the
rules on conflicts of interest.[31] In practice, however, it is unlikely that the
company will call them to account unless and until there is a change of control. If
only one director has committed the breach, the others may cause the company to
take action against him but most public companies are likely to avoid damaging
publicity by persuading the errant director to resign "for personal reasons" and to
go quietly.

It is also possible that, for example, in relation to a takeover of a small
company,[32] the directors may place themselves in the position of acting as agents
negotiating on behalf of the individual shareholders and thereby, despite *Percival
v Wright*,[33] owe fiduciary duties to the shareholders. If so, they would breach
those duties if they persuaded any shareholder to sell at a price which they knew
(and the shareholders did not) was materially lower than their likely value on the
basis of full disclosure of the information the directors hold about the company. It
is, however, highly unlikely that the directors of a listed company would create
such a relationship. If they did engage in insider dealing, it would be by dealing
impersonally on a stock exchange so that no fiduciary relationship was created.

Hence, the general equitable principle is, on its own, rarely an effective
deterrent. Moreover, the law relating to directors' fiduciary duties is simply
incapable of applying to the full range of insiders and, except in the rare case
where the decision in *Percival v Wright* can be overcome, it has the demerit of

---

[30] See paras 16–86 et seq., above.
[31] The leading case is the decision of the New York Court of Appeals in *Diamond v Oreamuno* (1969)
248 N.E. 2d 910. The precise situation has not yet arisen in an English court.
[32] For an early example of the directors constituting themselves agents in this way, see *Allen v Hyatt*
(1914) 30 T.L.R. 444 PC. Or the court may find a fiduciary relationship in a small company even in
the absence of agency: see para.16–6, above.
[33] *Percival v Wright* [1902] 2 Ch. 421: see para.16–5, above.

concentrating on the relationship between the director and the company rather than on the relationship between the director and other traders in the market.

Breach of confidence

30–9 Somewhat similar criticisms can be made of the second source of equitable obligation which is relevant here, namely that imposed by the receipt of information from another person where the recipient knows or ought to have known that the information was imparted in confidence. However, the range of persons potentially covered by this obligation is much wider that those covered by the fiduciary duties applying to directors of companies. It will extend to the professional advisers of companies who, say, are involved in preparing a takeover bid which the company is contemplating, and to the employees of such advisers, since no contractual link between the confider and the confidant is necessary to support this fiduciary obligation. Indeed, the obligation extends to anyone who receives information knowing that they are receiving it in breach of a duty of confidentiality imposed upon the person communicating the information.[34]

If the duty attaches, the holder of the information may not use it (for example, by trading in securities) or disclose it (for example, to another person so that that person may trade)[35] without the permission of the confider. Breach of the duty gives rise to a liability to account for the profits made, potentially the most useful civil sanction in the case of insider dealing on securities markets. The confidant may have to pay damages to the confider but it is far from clear that the confider actually suffers any loss if the confidant uses the information for the purposes of insider dealing and does not, in so doing, communicate the information to other persons. However, the cause of action again lies in the hands of the person to whom the fiduciary obligation is owed (i.e. the confider), not in the hands of the person with whom the confidant has dealt in the securities transaction or other participants in the market at the time. This might not matter if in fact the duty of confidence was routinely used to deprive insiders of their profits,[36] but, although much inside information must also be received in confidence and although the law in this area has achieved much greater prominence in recent years than it had previously, there are no reported cases of its use against insider dealers. This may be because the difficulties of detection and proof, which abound in this area, operate so as to deprive confiders of the incentive to use their private law rights to secure the transfer of insider dealing profits from the insiders to themselves.

Misrepresentation

30–10 When in 1989 the Government was considering its response to the EU's first Directive on insider dealing, it decided to continue its policy of not providing civil sanctions under the insider dealing legislation partly on the grounds that

---

[34] For both these propositions see *Schering Chemicals Ltd v Falkman Ltd* [1982] Q.B. 1 CA.

[35] And by virtue of the *Schering Chemicals* case (see previous note) the recipient of the information (the "tippee") would also be in breach of duty by using or disclosing the information if aware that it had been communicated in breach of the duty of confidence imposed on the tipper.

[36] That is, one might be more concerned with depriving the insiders of their profits than with working out who precisely are the best persons to receive them.

these worked satisfactorily only in face-to-face transactions and that the general law already provided remedies in that situation.[37] Apart from the insider's liability to the company, discussed above, the Government referred to liability for fraudulent misrepresentation. Misrepresentation-based liability, however, whether for fraudulent, negligent or innocent misrepresentation, faces a formidable obstacle in relation to insider trading. This is the need to demonstrate either that a false statement has been made or that there was a duty to disclose the inside information to the other party to the transaction. As to the former, the insider can avoid liability by not making any statements to the other party relating to the area of knowledge in which he holds the inside information. Liability might arise if the other party to the transaction has the good luck or the right instinct to extract a false statement from the insider by probing questions, but liability on this basis is unlikely to be widespread.

As to non-disclosure, the current legislation does not adopt the technique contained in some earlier proposals for insider dealing legislation: requiring insiders in face-to-face transactions to disclose the information before dealing.[38] Consequently, the potential plaintiff has to fall back on the common law, which imposes a duty of disclosure in only limited circumstances. The most relevant situation would be where the insider was in a fiduciary or other special relationship with the other party, but, as we have seen above, even as between directors and shareholders, the current law recognises such a relationship only exceptionally, whilst many insiders and their counterparties are simply not in the relationship of director and shareholder at all.[39] There is also little evidence at present of a willingness on the part of the courts to expand the categories of fiduciary or other special relationships in this area[40] or to bring securities contracts within the category of contracts uberrimae fidei.

Prohibiting insider dealing

The above analysis leaves only the approach of prohibiting dealing by those who actually possess inside information. This can be said to constitute the core of the current law. However, the prohibition can take two forms. The first involves the criminalisation of insider dealing and certain associated acts. The original criminal legislation was contained in Pt V of the Companies Act 1980 and was later consolidated in the Company Securities (Insider Dealing) Act 1985. As a result of the adoption by the European Community of the Insider Dealing Directive in 1989,[41] some amendment of the British law became necessary, and the Department of Trade and Industry also took the opportunity to simplify the

30–11

---

[37] DTI, *The Law on Insider Dealing: A Consultative Document* (1989), paras 2.11–2.12.

[38] Companies Bill, Session 1978/79, H.C. Bill 2, cl.59. As we saw in Ch.26 those with management responsibilities in companies traded on regulated markets are obliged to disclose inside information, but this requirement is likely to pick up a few face-to-face transactions.

[39] For example, where the director is selling shares in the company to a person who is not presently a shareholder or where the insider is not a corporate fiduciary at all.

[40] See *Chase Manhattan Equities v Goodman* [1991] B.C.L.C. 897, where the judge passed up the opportunity to use the FCA's *Model Code* as the basis of an extended duty of disclosure.

[41] Directive 89/592/EEC [1989] O.J. L334/30. This Directive was replaced by Directive 2003/6/EC (the Market Abuse Directive) in 2003, but the Government took the view that the criminal law

1985 Act in some respects. However, Pt V of the Criminal Justice Act 1993, the current law, is still recognisably in the mould established by the 1980 Act, though it contains some interesting new features and has abandoned some old obfuscations.[42] Experience showed, however, that it was difficult to secure convictions for this offence, partly because of difficulties of detection but partly also because of the standards of evidence and proof required in criminal trials. The legislature responded in the market abuse provisions of the FSMA 2000, which allow the FCA to impose administrative penalties upon those who engage in this activity, which is defined so as to include insider dealing. Thus, the second main form of the prohibition on trading is the deployment of regulatory sanctions against insider dealing, which is the area where EU law has been most influential.

THE CRIMINAL JUSTICE ACT 1993 PART V

30–12 Section 52(1) of the 1993 Act defines the central offence which it creates in the following terms: "An individual who has information as an insider is guilty of insider dealing if, in the circumstances mentioned in subs. (3), he deals in securities that are price-affected securities in relation to the information". This definition, however, conceals as much as it reveals, for it is much elaborated and qualified in the remaining sections of the Part. It is proposed in the following sections to try to elucidate the central elements of the offences created and of the defences available.

Regulating markets

30–13 Pursuing the reference to s.52(3), contained in the above definition, reveals at once that the Act does not aim to control all dealings in shares where one of the parties has price-sensitive, non-public information in his or her possession. On the contrary, it is only when the dealing takes place "on a regulated market" and in certain analogous situations does the Act bite. If, say, the transaction occurs face-to-face between private persons, then the situation is outside the control of this particular legislation. The Act leaves regulated markets to be identified by statutory instrument and that instrument includes any market established under the rules of the London Stock Exchange (thus including AIM).[43]

However, the legislation has always applied to certain "off-market" deals and these are now defined as those where the person dealing "relies on a professional intermediary or is himself acting as a professional intermediary".[44] Section 59 makes it clear that the profession in question must be that of acquiring or

---

provisions of domestic law did not require amendment as a result, though the 2006 Directive had a substantial impact on the administrative sanction regime. The 2006 Directive was repealed by MAR.
[42] For an analysis of the changes see Davies, (1991) 11 O.J.L.S. 92.
[43] Insider Dealing (Securities and Regulated Markets) Order (SI 1994/187) art.10, as amended. Confusingly, the term "regulated market" in the 1993 Act does not have the meaning attached to the term in the EU instruments: see para.25–8. In particular, trading on AIM does fall within the CJA (AIM being a market established under the rules of the LSE), even though AIM is not a regulated market for EU law purposes but a multi-lateral trading facility.
[44] 1993 Act s.52(3).

disposing of securities (for example, as a market maker[45]) or acting as an intermediary between persons who wish to deal (for example, as a broker[46]), and that a person does not fall within the definition if the activities of this type are merely incidental to some other activity or are merely occasional.

Despite this extension, which was in any event required by the 1989 Directive,[47] **30–14** the main thrust of the legislation is the regulation of dealings on formalised markets, and the extension was designed to prevent the evasion of such regulation, which might occur if trading were driven off formalised markets into less efficient, informal arrangements. The concentration of the prohibition on formal markets also makes it much easier to justify the restriction of the sanctions for breaches of the Act to the criminal law. In addition to the other difficulties which surround the creation of a coherent civil remedy in this area, the fact that the trading has occurred on a public exchange means that the identity of the counterparty to the transaction with the insider is a matter of chance. In any liquid stock many thousands of persons may be trading in the market at the same time as the insider. To give a civil remedy to the person who happened to end up with the insider's shares and not to the others who dealt in the market at the same time in the security in question would be arbitrary, whilst to give a civil remedy to all relevant market participants might well be oppressive of the insider.[48] By confining the sanction to the criminal law, Parliament avoided the need to address these difficulties. Moreover, if the main argument against insider trading is that it undermines public confidence in the securities markets, the criminal law is capable of expressing the community's view of that public interest, provided it can be effectively enforced.[49]

Finally, in this section on the definition of markets a few words should be said about the international dimension of insider dealing. It is now extremely easy, technically, for a person in one country to deal in the shares of a company which are listed or otherwise open to trading in another country; or for a person to deal in shares of a company quoted on an exchange in his or her own country via instructions placed with a foreign intermediary. For the domestic legislator not to deal with this situation runs the risk that the domestic legislation will be circumvented wholesale. To apply the domestic sanctions irrespective of the foreign element, on the other hand, is to run the risk of creating criminal law with an unacceptable extra-territorial reach. The latter risk is enlarged by the 1989 Directive's requirement that the Member States must prohibit insider dealing in transferable securities "admitted to a market of a Member State"[50] and not just those admitted to its own markets. In line with this requirement, the 1994 Order

---

[45] A firm which has undertaken to make a continuous two-way market in certain securities, so that, in relation to those securities, it will always be possible to buy from or sell to the market maker, though, of course, at a price established by the market maker.

[46] Following the "Big Bang" on the Stock Exchange in 1986 it is no longer required that market makers and brokers be entirely distinct functions, though equally it is not required that brokers make a continuous two-way market in any particular securities. Some broking firms act as market makers as well; others are only intermediaries.

[47] 1989 Directive art.2(3).

[48] In some cases it might not even be possible to identify the counterparty.

[49] See further below, para.30–30.

[50] 1989 Directive art.5.

extends the application of the Act to securities which are officially listed in or are admitted to dealing under the rules of any investment exchange established within any of the states of the European Economic Area.[51]

This clearly should not mean, however, that a French citizen dealing on the basis of inside information on the Paris *Bourse* or even on the Milan Exchange in the shares of a British company (or a company of any other nationality) is guilty of an offence under UK law. Consequently, s.62(1)[52] of the Act lays down the requirement of a territorial connection with the UK before a criminal offence can be said to have been committed in the UK. This requires the dealer or the professional intermediary to have been within the UK at the time any act was done which forms part of the offence or the dealing to have taken place on a regulated market situated in the UK.[53] Consequently, our French citizen will commit a criminal offence in the UK only if the deal is transacted on a regulated market located in the UK,[54] unless the trader or the professional intermediary through whom the deal is transacted is in the UK at the time of the dealing.[55] This approach does not eliminate all potential of the insider dealing legislation for extra-territorial effect, but it does limit it to situations where there is some substantial connection between the offence and the UK.

Regulating individuals

30–15 A striking feature of the 1993 Act is that it regulates insider dealing only by individuals. The Act does not use the more usual term "person" to express the scope of its prohibition, so that bodies corporate are not liable to prosecution under the Act. Corporate bodies were excluded, not because it was thought undesirable to make them criminally liable but because of the difficulties it was thought would be faced by investment banks when one department of the bank had unpublished price-sensitive information about the securities of a client company and the dealing department had successfully been kept in ignorance of that information by a "Chinese Wall"[56] or otherwise. If someone in the dealing

---

[51] Above fn.43, arts 4 and 9 and Schedule.

[52] 1993 Act s.62(2) provides that in the case of the offences of encouraging dealing or disclosing inside information (see para.30–25, below) either the encourager or discloser must be in the UK when he did the relevant act or the recipient of the encouragement or information must be.

[53] See above, para.30–10.

[54] If French law adopts the same territorial rules as the UK, the citizen would also commit a criminal offence under French law if he gave the instructions to deal from France. His liability in the UK would not depend, of course, upon the nationality of the company in whose shares on a UK regulated market the trading occurred.

[55] If the French citizen is in the UK at the relevant time, he will commit a criminal offence in the UK even if the trading occurs on a regulated market outside the UK but within the EEA. However, if the market is outside the EEA (say, New York or Tokyo) and involves no professional intermediary who is within the UK it would seem that the offence of dealing is not committed in the UK even if the instruction to deal is given by a person in the UK. This is because the dealing will not have taken place on a regulated market within s.52(3) and the 1994 Order and will not have involved a professional intermediary who is within the scope of s.62. However, the offence of encouraging dealing may have been committed, the encourager being in the UK even if the person encouraged is not. See fn.52, above.

[56] An arrangement designed to prevent information in one part of a firm from being available to individuals working elsewhere in the firm.

department entered into a trade, it was thought to be arguable that the bank as a single corporate body would have committed an offence, had the Act applied to corporate bodies, the act of one employee and the knowledge of the other being attributed to the bank. However, it should be noted that these arguments were not regarded as decisive by those who drafted the various versions of the administrative sanction regime. Their policy was to bring insider dealing, even by corporate bodies, within the scope of the regulatory prohibitions but then to deal expressly with the problem of attributed knowledge.[57]

In any event, it should be noted that an individual can be liable under the Act even if the dealing in question is done by a company. Companies can act only through human agents, and, as we shall see below,[58] the Act's prohibition on dealing extends to procuring or encouraging dealing in securities. Thus, if the individuals who move the company to deal do so on the basis of unpublished price-sensitive information, they may well have committed the criminal offence of procuring or encouraging the company to deal, even if the company itself commits no offence in dealing. These extensions embrace encouraging and procuring "persons" to deal—though, of course, the encourager or procurer must be an individual.

Inside information

The definition of inside information is a core feature of the Act and has always   **30–16**
been controversial. The general principle stated in the preamble to the 1989 Directive was: investor confidence in security markets depends inter alia on "the assurance afforded to investors that they are placed on an equal footing and that they will be protected against the improper use of inside information". However, it is much easier to state this general principle than to cast it into precise legal restrictions. As we have noted, placing investors "on an equal footing" cannot mean that all those who deal on a market should have the same information.[59] The aim of the legislation is not to eliminate all informational advantages, but to proscribe those advantages whose use would be improper, often because their acquisition is not the result of skill or effort but of the mere fact of holding a particular position. This general issue will be seen to recur in relation to all four of the limbs of the statutory definition of "inside information".

Section 56 defines inside information as information which:

(a)   relates to particular securities or to a particular issuer of securities and not to securities generally or to issues of securities generally;
(b)   is specific or precise;
(c)   has not been made public;
(d)   if it were made public would be likely to have a significant effect on the price of any securities.

---

[57] See para.30–38, below.
[58] See below, para.30–25. Otherwise a person could avoid the prohibition on insider dealing simply by setting up a company to do the trading.
[59] Above, para.30–2.

Particular securities or issuers

30–17   The first limb of the definition is the subject of a crucial clarification in s.60(4) that information shall be treated as relating to an issuer of securities "not only where it is about the company but also where it may affect the company's business prospects". This makes it clear that the definition of inside information includes information coming from outside the company, for example, that the Government intends to liberalise the industry in which the company previously had a monopoly, as well as information coming from within the company, for example, that the company is about to declare a substantially increased or decreased dividend or has won or lost a significant contract. This casts the net very wide, but it is difficult to see that any narrower formulation would have been appropriate.

Whatever the source of the information, it must relate to particular securities or a particular issuer[60] or particular issuers of securities and not to securities or issuers generally. So information relating to a particular company or sector of the economy is covered, but not information which applies in an undifferentiated way to the economy in general. This is not an entirely easy distinction; nor is its policy rationale self-evident. It would seem to mean that knowledge that the Government is, unexpectedly, to increase or decrease interest rates would fall within the definition in relation to bank shares (because interest rates are central to the bank's business of borrowing and lending money) but not in relation to the shares in all companies (where the implication of the rate rise is simply a less rapid future growth of the economy).

Specific or precise

30–18   The second limb of the definition restricts the scope of inside information further: the information must also be specific or precise.[61] The 1989 Directive required simply that the information be "precise",[62] but this was thought by Parliament to be possibly too restrictive, so the alternative of "specific" was added. The example was given of knowledge that a takeover bid was going to be made for a company, which would be specific information, but might not be regarded as precise if there was no knowledge of the price to be offered or the exact date on which the announcement of the bid would be made.[63] However, the crucial effect of this restriction is that it apparently relieves directors and senior managers of the company and analysts who have made a special study of the company from falling foul of the legislation simply because they have generalised informational advantages over other investors. Having a better sense of how well or badly the company is likely to respond to a particular publicly known development does not amount to the possession of precise or specific information.

---

[60] The Act uses the term "issuer" rather than "company" because the Act applies not only to securities issued by companies but also to government securities or even, though this is unlikely, securities issued by an individual: s.60(2).

[61] 1993 Act s.56(1)(b).

[62] 1989 Directive art.1.

[63] HC Debs, Session 1992–93, Standing Committee B, col. 174 (10 June 1993). It seems that, on this argument, precise information will always be specific.

Made public

The tension between the policy of encouraging communication between **30–19**
companies and the investment community and of stimulating analysts and other
professionals to play an appropriate role in that process, on the one hand, and that
of preventing selective disclosure of significant information to the detriment of
investors who are not close to the market, on the other, is further revealed in s.58
of the Act, which deals with the issue of when information can be said to have
been "made public". The Government initially proposed to leave the problem to
be solved by the courts on a case-by-case basis, but came under pressure in
Parliament to deal with the issue expressly. The pressure probably reflected the
accurate perception that, with the broadening of the definition of "insider",[64]
more weight would fall on the definition of "inside information" and especially
this limb of the definition. Section 58 is not, however, a comprehensive attempt
to deal with the issue. It stipulates four situations where the information shall be
regarded as having been made public and five situations where the court may so
regard it; otherwise, the court is free to arrive at its own judgment.[65]

The most helpful statement in s.58 from the point of view of analysts is that
"information is public if it is derived from information which has been made
public".[66] It is clear that this provision was intended to protect analysts who
derive insights into a company's prospects which are not shared by the market
generally (so that the analyst is able to out-guess competitors) where those
insights are derived from the intensive and intelligent study of information which
has been made public. An analyst in this position can deal on the basis of the
insights so derived without first disclosing to the market the process of reasoning
which has led to the conclusions, even where the disclosure of the reasoning
would have a significant impact on the price of the securities dealt in. This seems
to be the case even where the analyst intends to and does publish the
recommendations after the dealing, i.e. there is what is called "front running" of
the research.[67]

The utility of this subsection to the analyst and others is enhanced by the other **30–20**
provisions of s.58(2). Section 58(2)(c) comes close to providing an overarching
test for whether information is "made public" by stating that this is so if the
information "can readily be acquired" by those likely to deal in the relevant
securities. In other words, the public here is not the public in general but the
dealing public in relation to the securities concerned (which is obviously
sensible) and, more controversially, the issue is not whether the information is

---

[64] See para.30–22, below.
[65] In the permissive cases the situation is, presumably, that the facts described in the subsections do
not prevent the court from holding the information to have been made public, but whether the court in
a particular prosecution will so hold will depend on the circumstances of the case as a whole.
[66] 1993 Act s.58(2)(d).
[67] Query whether front-running a recommendation, not based upon any research but where its
publication will have an impact on the price of the securities because of the reputation of the
recommender, would be protected by s.58(2)(d). cf. *US v Carpenter* (1986) 791 F. 2d 1024. The trader
might have a defence under para.2(1) of Sch.1 to the Act, but that would depend upon his having
acted "reasonably": see para.30–28, below. Such conduct might in extreme cases even be a breach of
Pt 7 of the FSA 2012. See para.30–29, below.

known to that public but whether it is readily available to them. This is a more relaxed test than that applied under the previous legislation, which required knowledge of the information on the part of the public.[68] The former test in effect required those close to the market to wait until the information had been assimilated by the investment community before trading. Now it appears that trading is permitted as soon as the information can be readily acquired by investors, even though it has not in fact been acquired. In other words, a person who has advance knowledge of the information can react as soon as it can be "readily acquired" and reap a benefit in the period before the information is in fact fully absorbed by the market. This consequence of s.58(2)(c) is strengthened by the express provisions that publication in accordance with the rules of a regulated market or publication in records which by statute are available for public inspection mean that the information has been made public.[69]

However, the extent of the move away from actual public knowledge in the current legislation should not be exaggerated. The test laid down in s.58(2)(c) is not that information is public if it is available to the relevant segment of investors but whether it "can readily be acquired" by them. That information could be acquired by investors, if they took certain steps, is surely not enough in every case to meet the test of ready availability. One can foresee much dispute over what in addition is required to make information readily available. Section 58(3) helps with this issue to the extent of stating that certain features of the information do not necessarily prevent it from being brought within the category of information which "can be readily acquired". Thus, information is not to be excluded solely because it is published outside the UK, is communicated only on payment of a fee, can be acquired only by observation or the exercise of diligence or expertise, or is communicated only to a section of the public. However, in the context of particular cases, information falling within these categories may be excluded from the scope of "public information", for instance because the information is supplied for a (high) fee or is supplied to a very restricted number of persons. To this extent, the legislation has necessarily ended up adopting the Government's initial standpoint that much would have to depend upon case-by-case evaluation by the courts in the context of particular prosecutions.

Impact on price

30–21   The final limb of the definition is the requirement that the information should be likely to have "a significant effect" on the price of the securities, if it were made public.[70] The law has chosen not to pursue those who will reap only trivial advantages from trading on inside information. At first sight, the test would seem to present the court (or jury) with an impossibly hypothetical test to apply. In fact, in most cases, by the time any prosecution is brought, the information in question will have become public,[71] and so the question will probably be answered by

---

[68] Company Securities (Insider Dealing) Act 1985 s.10(b).

[69] 1993 Act s.58(2)(a) and (b) respectively. The former would cover publication on a Regulatory News Service and the latter documents field at Companies House or the Patents Registry.

[70] 1993 Act s.56(1)(d).

[71] Insiders have little incentive to trade on the basis of inside information which will never become public or will do so only far into the future.

looking at what impact the information did in fact have on the market when it was published. However, it would seem permissible for an insider to argue in an appropriate case that the likely effect of the information being made public at the time of the trading was not significant, even if its actual disclosure had a bigger effect, because the surrounding circumstances had changed in the meantime.

Insiders

We have already noted[72] the important restriction in the legislation that insiders must be individuals. Beyond that, it might be thought that nothing more needs to be said other than that an insider is a person in possession of inside information. In other words, the definitional burden should fall on deciding what is inside information and the definition of insider should follow as a secondary consequence of this primary definition. The Government's consultative document on the proposed legislation[73] rejected this approach as likely to cause "damaging uncertainty in the markets, as individuals attempted to identify whether or not they were covered". This is not convincing. Either the definition of inside information is adequate or it ought to be reformed. If it is adequate, so that it can be applied effectively to those who are insiders under the Act, then it is not clear why it cannot be applied to all individuals, whether they meet the separate criteria for being insiders or not. If the definition of inside information is not adequate, it is not proper to apply it even to those who clearly are insiders under the legislation and it should be changed. In fact, the proposal that insiders should be defined as those in possession of inside information would to some extent reduce uncertainty, because the only question which would have to be asked is whether the individual was in possession of inside information and the additional question of whether the individual met the separate criteria for being classed as an insider would be irrelevant.

30–22

However, the Government stuck to its guns whilst simplifying the criteria which had been used in the earlier legislation and, following the Directive, expanding the category of insiders quite considerably.[74] By virtue of s.57(2)(a) two categories of insider are defined. The first are those who obtain inside information "through being" a director, employee or shareholder of an issuer of securities.[75] Although it is not entirely clear, it seems that the "through being" test is simply a "but for" test. If a junior employee happens to see inside information in the non-public part of the employer's premises, he or she would be within the category of insider, even if the duties of the employment do not involve acquisition of that information. On the other hand, coming across such information in a social context would not make the junior employee an insider, even though the information related to the worker's employer. In other words,

---

[72] See above, para.30–15.

[73] DTI, *The Law on Insider Dealing* (1989), para.2.24.

[74] In particular, the requirement of "being connected with the company" was removed. See the Company Securities (Insider Dealing) Act s.9.

[75] The relationship does not have to exist with the issuer of the securities which are dealt in. So a director of Company A who is privy to his or her company's plans to launch a bid for Company B is an insider in relation to the securities of Company B (as well as those of A).

there must be a causal link between the employment and the acquisition of the information, but not in the sense that the information must be acquired in the course of the employee's employment (though the latter remains a possible interpretation of the subsection). It may be thought that shareholders, who were excluded from the definition of insider in the previous legislation, are unlikely to obtain access to inside information "though being" shareholders, but this is in fact a likely situation in relation to large institutional shareholders, which may, either as a general practice or in specific circumstances, keep in close touch with at least the largest companies in their portfolios.

The second category of insider identified by s.57(2)(a) is the individual with inside information "through having access to the information by virtue of his employment, office or profession", whether or not the employment, etc. relationship is with an issuer. Thus, an insider in this second category maybe, or be employed by, a professional adviser to the company[76]; an investment analyst, who has no business link with an issuer; a civil servant or an employee of a regulatory body; or a journalist or other employee of a newspaper or printing company.[77] Again, the question arises about the exact meaning of the phrase "by virtue of": is it again a simple "but for" test or does it mean "in the course of" (perhaps a slightly stronger suggestion in this second situation)? Even if the latter interpretation is ultimately adopted, this second category would be wide enough to embrace partners and employees of an investment bank or solicitors' firm retained to advise an issuer on a particular matter, employees of regulatory bodies who are concerned with the issuer's affairs, journalists researching an issuer for a story and even employees of a printing firm involved in the production of documents for a planned but unannounced takeover bid.[78] If the broader "but for" test is adopted, then employees of these organisations, not employed on the tasks mentioned, but who serendipitously come across the information in the workplace, would be covered too.[79]

Recipients from insiders

30–23 In practice, the need to define the exact scope of the second category of insider is reduced by the third category, created by s.57(2)(b). In the US persons in this third category are distinguished from primary insiders by the use of the graphic expression "tippee",[80] but the British legislation lumps them in with primary

---

[76] In the course of their professional duties such individuals may well obtain inside information in relation to a company other than the instructing company. Thus, employees of an investment bank preparing a takeover bid would become insiders in relation to both the proposed bidder (i.e. the bank's client) and in relation to the target company.

[77] Of course, the journalist's employer may be a listed company, in which case he would seem to fall within the first category as well.

[78] cf. *US v Chiarella* (1980) 445 U.S. 222.

[79] An even more restrictive test would be in the course of an employment which is likely to provide access to inside information. Such a test would exclude the famous, if unlikely, example of the cleaner who finds inside information in a waste-paper basket. However, there seems to be no warrant in the Act or the Directive for such a restrictive test, which would come close to reinstating the clearly discarded test of s.9(b) of the 1985 Act.

[80] The guru of securities regulation, Professor Louis Loss of Harvard Law School, first used this expression and the Oxford English Dictionary has credited him with this fact.

insiders. This third category consists of those who have inside information "the direct or indirect source of" which is a person falling within either of the first two categories. Thus, subject to the point about mens rea made in the next paragraph, the employee of an investment bank who overhears a colleague talking about a takeover bid on which the latter is engaged would be in all probability an insider in the third category if he or she does not fall within the second category. This example also makes it clear that the more striking American terminology might be somewhat misleading. It does not matter whether the primary insider has consciously communicated the information to the secondary insider (i.e. "tipped the latter off"). Provided the latter has acquired the information from an inside source, even indirectly, he or she will fall within the scope of the Act; indeed, as in the example, the "tipper" may be entirely unaware that inside information has been communicated to anyone else.[81] Furthermore, a certain type of tipping will not in fact make the tippee liable for dealing. If the insider within the first two categories encourages another person to deal without communicating to that other person any inside information, the latter can deal without being exposed to liability under the Act—though the tipper would be liable for encouraging the dealing.[82]

Mental element

Finally, the requirement of having information "as an insider" in s.57 was used by the drafters to put a crucial limitation on the scope of the offence created by the Act. This is the required mental element, a not surprising precondition for criminal liability, but nevertheless one which has made enforcement of the legislation often difficult.[83] The requirement in this regard is a two-fold one: the accused must be proved to have known that the information in question was inside information and that the information came from "an inside source", i.e. accused knew the information was obtained in one of the three ways discussed above. The requirement of knowledge is likely to be difficult to meet, especially in the case of recipients of information from insiders via a chain of communications. Proving that a "sub-tippee" or even a "sub-sub-tippee" knew that the ultimate source of the information was a primary insider could be fraught with problems.

30–24

Prohibited acts

What is an individual with inside information and who is an insider and meets the required mental element prohibited from doing? There are four prohibitions and, before describing them, it should be pointed out that it is not necessary that the

30–25

---

[81] Moreover, since it is enough that the individual in the third category "has" the information from a source falling within the first or second categories, it does not matter either whether the "tippee" has solicited the information. Inadvertent acquisition of inside information is covered. This was a point of controversy under the previous legislation until cleared up by the House of Lords, in favour of liability. See *Attorney-General's Reference (No.1 of 1988)* [1989] A.C. 971.

[82] See para.30–25, below.

[83] See para.30–30, below.

accused should be an insider at the time he or she does the prohibited act. Once inside information has been acquired by an insider, the prohibitions apply even though the accused resigns the directorship or employment through which he obtained the information.[84] On the other hand, if by the time of the dealing the information enters the public domain, the prohibitions of the Act will cease to apply. It should also be noted that the prohibitions apply not only to the company's securities but also to futures contracts[85] and contracts for differences,[86] where the reference security is a security issued by the company.[87]

First, and most obviously, there must be no *dealing* in the relevant securities.[88] The relevant securities are those which are "price-affected", i.e. those upon the price of which the inside information would be likely to have a significant effect, if made public.[89] Dealing is defined as acquiring or disposing of securities.[90] Thus, a person who refrains from dealing or cancels a deal on the basis of inside information is not covered by the legislation.[91] In principle, it is difficult to defend this exclusion since the loss of public confidence in the market will be as strong as in a case of dealing, if news of the non-dealing emerges. The exclusion was presumably a pragmatic decision based on the severe evidential problems which would face the prosecution in such a case. The dealing prohibition is broken quite simply by dealing; the Act does not require the prosecution to go further and prove that the dealing was motivated by the inside information, though the accused may be able to put forward the defence that he would have done what he did even if he had not had the information.[92] The Act covers dealing as an agent (not only as a principal) even if the profit from the dealing is thereby made by someone else, for one can never be sure that the profit made by the third party will not filter back to the trader in some form or other. And it covers agreeing to acquire or dispose of securities as well as their actual acquisition or disposal, and entering into or ending a contract which creates the security[93] as well as contracting to acquire or dispose of a pre-existing security.

---

[84] This is the significance of prohibiting acts by a person who has information "as an insider", which s.57 makes clear refers to the situation at the time of the acquisition of the information, rather than the simpler formulation of prohibiting acts *by* an insider, which might well refer to the accused's status at the time of the prohibited acts.

[85] A contract of the sale or purchase of securities at a future date.

[86] A contract not involving an agreement to transfer an interest in the underlying securities but simply to pay the difference between the price of the securities on a particular date and their price on a future date. For discussion of the problems which CfDs have created in relation to disclosure obligations, see above at para.26–20 and at para.28–45.

[87] Certain types of security are omitted, perhaps most notably the purchase or sale of units in unit trusts, though shares in companies which operate investment trusts are within the scope of the Act. Presumably, the former were excluded on the pragmatic grounds that it was unlikely that a person would have inside information which would significantly affect the price of the units, which normally reflect widely diversified underlying investments, though query whether this is always the case with more focused unit trusts. See para.26–12. In any event, the Treasury has power to amend the list of securities contained in Sch.2 (see s.54(2)).

[88] 1993 Act s.52(1).

[89] See s.56(2) and para.30–21, above.

[90] 1993 Act s.55.

[91] Ditto an individual who discovers good news and decides not to dispose of its shares.

[92] See below, para.30–27.

[93] As is the case with derivatives.

Secondly, the insider is prohibited from *procuring*, directly or indirectly, the acquisition or disposal of securities by any other person. Technically, this result is achieved by bringing procuring within the definition of dealing.[94] Procurement will have taken place if the acquisition is done by the insider's agent or nominee or a person acting at his or her direction, but this does not exhaust the range of situations in which procurement can be found.[95] Since the person procured to deal may well not be in possession of any inside information and the procurer has not in fact dealt, without this extension of the statutory meaning of "dealing" there would be a gap in the law.

Thirdly, there is a prohibition on the individual *encouraging* another person to deal in price-affected securities, knowing or having reasonable cause to believe that dealing would take place on a regulated market or through a professional intermediary.[96] Again, it does not matter, for the purposes of the liability of the person who does the encouraging, that the person encouraged commits no offence, because, say, no inside information is imparted by the accused. Indeed, it does not matter for these purposes that no dealing at all in the end takes place, though the accused must at least have reasonable cause to believe that it would. The existence of this offence is likely to discourage over-enthusiastic presentations by company representatives to meetings of large shareholders or analysts.

Finally, the individual must not *disclose* the information "otherwise than in the proper performance of the functions of his employment, office or profession to another person".[97] Unlike in the previous two cases, the communication of inside information is a necessary ingredient of this offence, but no response on the part of the person to whom the information is communicated need occur nor be expected by the accused. However, in effect, this element is built into the liability, for the accused has a defence that "he did not at the time expect any person, because of the disclosure, to deal in securities" on a regulated market or through a professional intermediary.[98] So, even if it occurs outside the proper performance of duties, disclosure which is not expected to lead to dealing will not result in liability, but the burden of proving the absence of the expectation falls on the accused. This prohibition helps to put the issuer in the position of being the sole source of the disclosure of internally generated inside information to the market.[99]

---

[94] 1993 Act s.55(1)(b).
[95] 1993 Act s.55(4) and (5).
[96] 1993 Act s.52(2)(a).
[97] 1993 Act s.52(2)(b).
[98] 1993 Act s.53(3)(a).
[99] See paras 26–5 et seq.

Defences

30–26   The Act provides a wide range of defences,[100] which fall within two broad categories. First, there are two general defences which carry further the task of defining the mischief at which the Act is aimed.[101] Secondly, there are the special defences, set out mainly but not entirely, in Sch.1 to the Act, which frankly accept that in certain circumstances the policy of prohibiting insider trading should be overborne by the values underlying the exempted practices. These special defences, which were foreshadowed in the recitals to the 1989 Directive, will be dealt with only briefly here.[102]

General defences

30–27   The more important of the general defences is that the accused "would have done what he did even if he had not had the information".[103] This defence benefits liquidators, receivers, trustees, trustees in bankruptcy and personal representatives who may find themselves in the course of their offices advised to trade when in fact themselves in possession of inside information.[104] Thus, a trustee, who is advised by an investment adviser to deal for the trust in a security in relation to which the trustee has inside information, will be able to do so, relying on this defence. But the defence applies more generally than that and would embrace, for example, an insider who dealt when he did in order to meet a pressing financial need or legal obligation. However, the accused will carry the burden of showing that his or her decision to deal at that particular time in that particular security was not influenced by the possibility of exploiting the inside information which was held.

The other general defence is that the accused did not expect the dealing to result in a profit attributable to the inside information.[105] Although the defence is general in the sense that it is not confined to particular business or financial transactions, the range of situations falling within it is probably quite narrow. The

---

[100] We have already dealt, in the previous paragraph, with one of the defences relevant to the disclosure offence.

[101] Though s.53 makes it clear that the burden of proof falls on the accused, thus obviating a possible ambiguity which was found by some in the previous legislation. See *R. v Cross* [1991] B.C.L.C. 125.

[102] Sch.1 may be amended by the Treasury by order (s.53(5)), presumably so that it may be kept current with developments in financing techniques.

[103] 1993 Act s.53(1)(c) and (2)(c). This defence does not apply to the disclosure offence, though it is an essential ingredient of that offence that the disclosure should not have occurred in the proper performance of the accused's functions.

[104] Previously they were covered by more targeted provisions: 1985 Act ss.3(1)(b) and 7.

[105] 1993 Act s.53(1)(a). The same defence is provided, mutatis mutandis, in relation to the other offences by s.53(2)(a) and (3)(b). Making a profit is defined so as to include avoiding a loss: s.53(6). This is considerably narrower than the defence in the 1985 Act s.3(1)(a), which applied when the individual traded "otherwise than with a view to the making of a profit".

Government's attempts in the parliamentary debates to produce examples of situations for which this defence was needed and which were at all realistic were not entirely convincing.[106]

Special defences

The Act provides six special defences, two in the body of the Act and four in Sch.1. One of those provided in the body of the Act appears to be a general defence and is to the effect that dealing is not unlawful if the individual "believed on reasonable grounds that the information had been disclosed widely enough to ensure that none of those taking part in the dealing would be prejudiced by not having the information".[107] In fact, however, this defence is aimed particularly at underwriting arrangements,[108] where those involved in the underwriting may trade amongst themselves on the basis of shared knowledge about the underwriting proposal but that information is not known to the market generally. The other defence provided in the body of the Act[109] concerns things done "on behalf of a public sector body in pursuit of monetary policies or policies with respect to exchange rates or the management of public debt or foreign exchange reserves". So reasons of state, relating to financial policy, trump market integrity.[110]

30–28

The four special defences provided in the Schedule do not extend to the disclosure of inside information. Where these defences apply, those concerned may trade or encourage others to do so but may not enlarge the pool of persons privy to the inside information. In all four cases, what are judged to be valuable market activities would be impossible without the relaxation of the insider dealing prohibition. Thus, market makers[111] may often be in possession of inside information but would not be able to discharge their undertaking to maintain a continuous two-way market in particular securities if they were always subject to the Act. So para.1 of Sch.1 exempts acts done by a market maker in good faith in the course of the market-making business. More controversially, para.5 does the same thing in relation to price stabilisation of new issues.[112]

The final two special defences relate to trading whilst in possession of "market information", which is, in essence, information about transactions in securities being contemplated or no longer contemplated or having or not having taken place. First, an individual may act in connection with the acquisition or disposal of securities and with a view to facilitating their acquisition or disposal where the information held is market information arising directly out of the individual's

---

[106] HC Debs, Session 1992–93, Standing Committee B (10 June 1993). A suggestion was where the insider sold at a price which took into account the impact the (bad) information would have on the market when released.

[107] 1993 Act s.53(1)(b),(2)(b) provide a similar defence in relation to the encouraging offence.

[108] On underwriting, see para.25–12, above.

[109] 1993 Act s.63, applying to all offences under the Act. Technically, s.63 does not provide a defence but rather describes a situation where the Act "does not apply".

[110] As art.2(4) of the Directive permits.

[111] See above, fn.45.

[112] This is discussed further below at para.30–45.

involvement in the acquisition or disposal.[113] An example is where the employees of an investment bank advising a bidder on a proposed takeover procure the acquisition of the target's shares on behalf of the bidder but before the bid is publicly announced, in order to give the bidder a good platform from which to launch the bid. This defence would not permit the employees to purchase shares for their own account, because they would not then be acting to facilitate the proposed transaction out of which the inside information arose. Even so, permitting a bidder to act in this way is somewhat controversial for those who procure the purchase of the shares know that a bid at a price in excess of the current market price is about to be launched and those who sell out to the bidder just before the public announcement may feel that they have been badly treated.[114] Another situation covered by the provision is that of a fund manager who decides to take a large stake in a particular company. The manager can go into the market on behalf of the funds under management and acquire the stake at the best prices possible, without announcing in advance the intention to build up a large stake, which would immediately drive up the price of the chosen company's shares.

Under the second and more general "market information" defence the individual may act if "it was reasonable for an individual in his position to have acted as he did" despite having the market information.[115] This is so broadly phrased that it would seem wide enough to cover the situations discussed in the previous paragraph. The more specific provisions were included as well presumably in order to give comfort to those who would otherwise have had to rely on the general reasonableness provision and who might have wondered whether the courts would interpret it in their favour.

CRIMINAL PROHIBITIONS ON MARKET MANIPULATION

30–29   The criminal prohibitions on market manipulation are now to be found in Pt 7 of the Financial Services Act 2012. Section 89 creates an offence in relation to misleading statements made in order to induce trading in securities. It can clearly be used to catch egregious cases of market manipulation[116] and has been discussed in Ch.26.[117] The second offence is more interesting and was introduced by s.47(2) of the Financial Services Act 1986 (now repealed). As reformulated by s.90 of the 2012 Act, this criminalises an act or course of conduct[118] which

---

[113] See para.3.

[114] Nevertheless, the Code on Takeovers and Mergers adopts the same approach as the Act. See r.4.1. However the potential bidder would have to comply with the statutory provisions on the disclosure of shareholdings. See paras 26–17 et seq.; and P. Davies, "The Takeover Bidder Exemption and the Policy of Disclosure" in K.J. Hopt and E. Wymeersch (eds), *European Insider Dealing* (London, 1991). Even so, the bid facilitation argument ought not to be employed to justify the purchase of derivatives where the aim of the purchase is simply to give the bidder a cash benefit rather than to take a step towards the acquisition of voting control.

[115] See para.2(1). Some guidance on what is reasonable is given in para.2(2).

[116] As in *R. v De Berenger* (1814) 3 M. & S. 68.

[117] See para.26–32, above.

[118] 2012 Act s.90(1). The act or course of conduct must occur in the UK or the misleading impression must be created in the UK: s.90(10).

creates a false or misleading impression as to the market in or price or value of any investment (as widely defined), if done for one or other (or both) of two purposes. The first is where the defendant intends by creating the impression to induce a person to acquire or dispose of investments or to refrain from doing so or to exercise or not to exercise rights attached to investments.[119] It is to be noted that the offence is complete whether or not the accused knew that, or was reckless whether, the impression created was misleading: all that has to be shown is that he acted for the purpose of creating an impression which was in fact misleading. However, a defence is provided where the accused can show that he reasonably believed that the impression was not misleading.[120] In effect, negligence as to the misleading nature of the impression is made a crime and the burden of disproving negligence is placed upon the maker of the impression.

The second purpose does depend upon the creator of the impression knowing that it is false or misleading or being reckless as to whether this is the case. If the defendant intends through the impression to make a gain for himself or another or cause loss (or the risk of loss) to another, that person commits an offence, as will also be the case where the defendant is aware that these consequences are likely to result.[121] Thus, if in the *De Berenger* case,[122] the fraudsters had acted somewhat more subtly and refrained from openly stating that Napoleon had been killed but had allowed that impression to arise (for example, through their joyous behaviour as if by soldiers released from a successful army), they would be caught by this version of the second offence.

Some basic forms of manipulative behaviour are offences at common law,[123] but the statute extends and makes clearer the reach of the criminal law in this area. This offence is rarely prosecuted,[124] but the following examples of contraventions can be given. The promoters of a company fund the underwriters of a share issue to buy shares in the market when dealings begin in order to give the impression that there is a greater market interest in the shares than is in fact the case[125]; or the directors of a company, believing the market price of its shares not to reflect the net tangible asset value of the company, persuade its brokers to buy shares in the market at some four times the previous market price, in order to move the market price closer to what the directors believe to be the "true" value of the shares.[126]

---

[119] 2012 Act s.90(2).

[120] 2012 Act s.90(9)(a).

[121] 2012 Act s.90(3)(4).

[122] *R. v De Berenger* (1814) 3 M. & S. 68 (see para.30–1, above).

[123] *Scott v Brown Doering & Co* [1892] 2 Q.B. 724.

[124] Though there has been recent interest in relation to the manipulation of interest-rate or foreign exchange benchmarks, topics outside the scope of this chapter.

[125] As in *Scott v Brown Doering & Co* [1892] 2 Q.B. 724. There is a defence in s.90(9)(b) for such behaviour carried out in accordance with the price stabilisation rules. See para.30–45.

[126] *North v Marra Developments* (1981) C.L.R. 42 HCA. Both this and the case mentioned in the previous note were civil actions in which the criminal nature of the activity was used to defeat a contractual claim on grounds of the illegality of the contract.

REGULATORY CONTROL OF MARKET ABUSE

Background

30–30 So far, we have looked at the criminal prohibitions on insider dealing and market manipulation. We now turn to the practically more important form of control of market abuse, namely, that administered by regulators, which do not require resort to the criminal law and the criminal courts. In fact, with the enactment of the FSMA 2000, the main thrust of the legal rules controlling market abuse, in which term is to be included both insider dealing and market manipulation, shifted from the criminal law to administrative sanctions which have been placed in the hands of the FCA. At this point, the main source of the rules was Pt VIII of FSMA which was used later to transpose the first EU Directive on market abuse,[127] but in significant ways went beyond that Directive. From the beginning the regulatory sanctions were applied to companies as well as to individuals. Moreover, they applied to all those whose actions had an effect on the market, whether they were persons authorised to carry on financial activities or not. They thus applied as much to industrial companies and their directors, for example, as to investment banks and their directors and employees. These statements are true also of the MAR, now the central legal instrument on administrative control.

Part of the reason for the emphasis on administrative penalties from 2000 onwards was that successful deployment of the criminal law on a wide scale against insider dealing and market manipulation proved difficult. Only after the financial crisis of 2007/8 did the FSA/FCA put substantial resources into the enforcement of the relevant criminal laws. Even so, between 2009 and mid-2015 there were only 27 successful prosecutions for insider dealing (about four a year), of which 23 resulted in custodial sentences (in no case for more than four years).[128] The move towards a regime based on administrative penalties was driven by the desire to address two of the obstacles raised by the criminal offences, namely the need to show intention, at least in relation to insider dealing,[129] and the high evidential requirements of the criminal law. Even so, in the 12 years to March 2015 the FSA/FCA issued only 85 "Final Notices" in relation to market abuse, i.e. about seven a year.[130]

However, the proposals which were eventually embodied in the FSMA 2000 proved highly controversial during the parliamentary debates on the Bill, those opposing it claiming that it would infringe rights conferred by art.6 of the European Convention on Human Rights (right to a fair trial).[131] The central claim of the opponents was that the penalty regime proposed by the Government,

---

[127] Directive 2003/6/EC on insider dealing and market manipulation (market abuse) [2003] O.J. L96/16.

[128] Treasury, Bank of England, FCE, above fn.14, Chart 11. In general those convicted were not sophisticated criminals.

[129] As we have seen, in relation to misleading impressions, mens rea is required only in an attenuated form under what is now the Financial Services Act 2012.

[130] Above, fn.128, p.85.

[131] See Joint Committee on Financial Services and Markets, First Report, *Draft Financial Services and Markets Bill*, Vol. I, Session 1998/99, HL 50-I/HC 328-I, pp.61–67 and Annexes C and D; Second Report, HL 66/HC 465, pp.5–10 and Minutes of Evidence, pp.1–27.

although clearly not part of the domestic criminal law, would be classified as criminal by the European Court of Human Rights, whose classification criteria are independent of those used domestically. Without ever conceding the correctness of this claim, the Government nevertheless did make substantial amendments to its proposals in order to promote the fairness of the new regime, the regime being subject in any event to a general fairness test under the European Convention, even if regarded as civil rather than criminal in nature. These amendments involved in particular the elaboration by the then FSA of a Code on Market Abuse in order to give guidance on the scope of the prohibitions, and the creation of rights of appeal to an independent tribunal (now the Upper Tribunal) to be granted to persons penalised by the FCA.[132]

In the aftermath of the financial crisis, the debate turned on its head. Now, it was argued that the market abuse provisions were inadequate. This was an argument advanced at EU level as well as at domestic level. It led to the replacement of the EU Directive by a Regulation on market abuse (MAR). MAR both expanded the scope of the substantive EU laws on market abuse, but also removed the need for domestic transposition of those laws, thus bringing about a major change in the structure of the domestic law. In fact, with regard to the securities markets aspects of market abuse, which are the focus of this chapter, the structural changes were probably more important than the substantive ones. In particular, MAR led to the removal of the FCA's power to make a Code in this area.[133]

Insider dealing

The definition of insider dealing in MAR is somewhat more simply phrased than under the CJA.

30–31

> "For the purposes of this Regulation, insider dealing arises where a person possesses inside information and uses that information by acquiring or disposing of, for its own account or for the account of a third party, directly or indirectly, financial instruments to which that information relates."[134]

As to inside information, as far as trading in corporate securities is concerned, this is:

> "information of a precise nature, which has not been made public, relating, directly or indirectly, to one or more issuers or to one or more financial instruments, and which, if it were made public, would be likely to have a significant effect on the prices of those financial instruments or on the price of related derivative financial instruments"[135]

---

[132] The Financial Services and Markets Tribunal, the predecessor to the Upper Tribunal, tended to view the penalty proceedings as being criminal in nature for the purposes of the Convention. However, the standard of proof required by the Convention is not necessarily that of "beyond reasonable doubt". The standard will depend, as is the case with the civil burden in domestic law, on the seriousness of the allegation which has to be proved. See *Davidson & Tatham v FSA*, FSM Case No. 31; *Parker v FSA* [2006] UKFSM FSM037; *Mohammed v FSA* [2005] UKFSM FSM012.

[133] FCA, above fn.27, para.3.15.

[134] MAR art.8(1).

[135] MAR art.7(1).

Since these definitions, not surprisingly, are substantially similar to those to be found in the CJA, it is proposed only to highlight the main features of the regulatory prohibition.

Dealing

30–32   First, the crucial difference between the MAR approach to insider dealing and that of the CJA is that there is no requirement for a mental element, i.e. no equivalent to the requirement in s.57(1) of the CJA that the person know the information is inside information and know that he or she has it through being an insider.[136] This was the case also under FSMA. Article 14 of MAR simply says that "a person shall not engage in insider dealing" and the definition of insider dealing (above) contains no requirement as to a mental element. The lack of mental element was further emphasised by the CJEU when it held that a person who "possesses" inside information and trades is presumed to "use" it, i.e. to trade on the basis of the information—though that presumption is rebuttable.[137]

30–33   Secondly and new in the UK, art.14 prohibits attempts to engage in insider dealing, so that even if no dealing occurs, there is exposure to penalties if the person attempted to deal (for example, placed an order with a broker which, for some reason, the broker failed to implement).

30–34   Thirdly, again new in the UK, MAR catches a limited number of decisions not to trade or to trade differently, i.e. where the person cancels or amends an order for trading already given after receiving the inside information. A simple addition to a trading order would seem to be caught in any event by the prohibition on trading but an alteration of the price at which a person is prepared to trade might not be and is picked up by the provision on amending an existing order. However, a person who is contemplating an order but has not placed one before receiving the inside information is still outside the prohibition.

30–35   Fourthly, the definition of insider dealing in art.8(1), unlike the CJA,[138] appears not to contain a requirements that the possessor of the inside information be, in addition, an insider. However, art.8(4) says that the prohibition applies only to those who acquire the information "as a result of" being a director or shareholder of the company, having access to the information "through the exercise of an employment, profession or duties" or through criminal activities. So, art.8(4), like the CJA, in fact builds in a requirement of being an insider into its prohibition—though the extension of the insider concept to criminals is novel. In addition to the above categories, art.8(4) imposes liability on any person "who possesses inside information under circumstances…where that person knows or ought to know that it is inside information". In this final case, a mental element is

---

[136] See above, para.30–24. However, knowledge or negligence might to relevant to the size of the penalty imposed: art.31.

[137] Case C-45/08 *Spector Photo Group NV v CBFA* [2010] 2 B.C.L.C. 200. Rebuttable presumably involves showing that the insider would have traded whether he had the inside information or not. A specific defence of this sort is provided in art.9(3)—trading carried out under an obligation which had come into effect before the inside information was acquired.

[138] Above, para.30–22.

required to bring the person within the category of insider: either knowledge or negligence as to the inside quality of the information. Subject to that mental element, however, a person with inside information is an insider, and how that person acquired the information is relevant only to the assessment of the holder's mental state.

Fifthly, like the CJA, the prohibition extends beyond dealing. It extends to the situation where the person with inside information "recommends" or "induces" another person to trade (or cancel or amend an order), irrespective of whether the inside information was communicated to the person who trades or, in the case of a recommendation, irrespective of whether trading occurs.[139] If the third party actually responds by trading, etc. that person will also be liable provided that he knows or ought to know that the recommendation or inducement is based on inside information.[140] Mere disclosure of inside information, unaccompanied by any recommendation or inducement, is also prohibited, unless this occurs "in the normal exercise of an employment, a profession or duties".[141] The onward transmission by its recipient of a recommendation or inducement also falls within this prohibition where the recipient knows or ought to know that the recommendation or inducement was based on inside information.[142] This prohibition does not seem confined to the first recipient of the recommendation or inducement.

30–36

Inside information

Sixthly, the definition of inside information is slightly broader than its CJA equivalent in that the information does not have to relate to particular securities or particular issuers of securities, so that information which has an impact on the securities markets generally could be inside information for the purposes of MAR. As with the prior domestic law (under FSMA), the likely impact of the information on the market is tested by reference to what "a reasonable investor" would regard as relevant information.[143] The CJEU has held that the "market impact" test can be satisfied even if the direction of the impact (upwards or downwards) cannot be predicted at the time of trading.[144] Whilst this seems odd at first sight, in situations of market volatility a particular piece of information might predictably move the market without the direction of the movement being clear in advance. A person holding the information could then profit from it by acquiring appropriate financial instruments one of which will pay off in either

30–37

---

[139] MAR art.8(2).

[140] MAR art.8(3). MAR inelegantly talks about the third party 'using' the recommendation or inducement.

[141] MAR art.10(1). The CJEU has indicated that this exception is to be construed narrowly: Case C-384/02 *Criminal Proceedings against Grongaard* [2005] E.C.R. I-9939.

[142] MAR art.10(3). Unless the transmitter knows the information underlying the recommendation or inducement, that person would not otherwise fall within the prohibition because not in possession of inside information.

[143] MAR art.7(4).

[144] Case C-628/13 *Lafonta v Autorité des marchés financiers* [2015] Lloyd's Rep FC 113. This was in fact a disclosure case, but its rationale seems equally applicable to trading. The Upper Tribunal had taken a different view: *Hannam v Financial Conduct Authority* [2014] UKUT 0233 (TCC).

event, for example, both call and put options over the issuer's securities, only one of which would be exercised depending on the direction of the market impact.[145]

The headline definition of inside information requires that it be "precise" but, unlike the CJA,[146] does not say that it is enough that it is specific, even if not precise. However, art.7(2) says that information about events or circumstances "shall be deemed to be of a precise nature…where it is specific enough to enable a conclusion to be drawn as to the possible effect of that set of circumstances or event on the prices of the financial instruments". This does not in terms say that specific but not precise information may always be inside information, but comes close to it.

As with disclosure of information,[147] knowing when information about a developing situation becomes inside information raises difficult issues. The CJEU held under the prior EU law that the information might cross that threshold before the situation was fully developed and MAR reflects that view.[148] Article 7(2) states that "an intermediate step in a protracted process shall be deemed to be inside information if, by itself, it satisfies the criteria of inside information as referred to in this Article". More generally, art.7(2) treats information as inside information where it relates to circumstances or events which "which may reasonably be expected" to occur as well as circumstances which already exist or have occurred. That same CJEU decision equated a reasonable expectation with a realistic prospect, not a high probability, of occurrence.

MAR does not contain one extension beyond inside information which was part of the prior domestic regime. This covered "information which is not generally available" (RINGA) and not just to "inside information",[149] provided a "regular user of the market" would regard the information as relevant to the transaction in question. The effect was to extend the prohibition to information which would not meet the definition of inside information, because it was not specific or precise, but which market users would regard as an illegitimate basis for trading. Domestically, this was a controversial extension, which was kept going from year-to-year until the end of 2014, when it was allowed to expire under the latest version of its "sunset" provision.[150] The Commission proposed a more rigid version of RINGA in its initial proposals for MAR, but in the end the uncertainties thought to be generated by the concept led to its exclusion from MAR.[151]

---

[145] In this respect it is important to note that the definition of insider trading quoted above embraces "financial instruments" and not just the securities issued by the company.

[146] Above, para.30–18.

[147] Above, para.26–6.

[148] Case C-19/11 *Geltl v Daimler AG*, decision of 28 June 2012, also a disclosure case.

[149] FSMA s.118(4).

[150] FSMA s.118(9).

[151] The FCA's Code of Market Conduct gave the following example of RINGA: "An employee of B Plc is aware of contractual negotiations between B Plc and a customer. Transactions with that customer have generated over 10 per cent of B Plc's turnover in each of the last five financial years. The employee knows that the customer has threatened to take its business elsewhere, and that the negotiations, while ongoing, are not proceeding well. The employee, whilst being under no obligation to do so, sells his shares in B Plc based on his assessment that it is reasonably likely that the customer will take his business elsewhere". Query whether this situation would fall within art.7(2) of MAR (above).

Persons covered and exemptions

Seventhly, like the prior FCA rules but unlike the CJA, MAR imposes liability on **30–38**
the company as well as on natural persons, but makes it clear that corporate
liability does not remove the liability of the persons who traded on behalf of the
company.[152] The problem of over-extensive attribution is addressed by removing
liability from the company if it has effectively instituted a "Chinese wall"
between those within the company who traded and those who held the inside
information.[153]

Eighthly, inevitably a range of exemptions from the prohibition is provided in
order to deal with situations where the otherwise prohibited activity is thought to
have a higher value than reducing the incidence of insider trading. Besides the
usual exemptions from liability for market makers and brokers acting in the
normal course of their business, MAR pay a lot of attention to insider trading in
the course of takeovers and mergers. Article 9(5) provides that a person's
knowledge that it has decided to acquire or dispose of securities, where that fact
is not known to the market, does not "of itself" constitute the use of inside
information when that person implements its decision. This provision applies
generally (for example, to fund managers who have decided to take a major
position in a company) but would appear to permit a bidder to build up a stake in
the potential target before announcing a bid, at least to the point where the rules
on disclosure of major shareholding are triggered.[154] Article 9(4) applies
specifically to inside information obtained "in the conduct of" a merger or public
takeover. A person holding such information is not "deemed" from the mere fact
of its possession to have used it when proceeding with the merger or takeover,
provided the inside information has ceased to be such by the time the
shareholders accept the takeover offer or approve the merger. The purpose of this
provision, which is expressly said not to apply to "stake-building", might be to
deal with the situation where a bidder or potential merger partner obtains
information in private discussions with the target company before making an
offer or putting forward a merger proposal. The offer or proposal, when made,
might constitute a recommendation or inducement to acquire shares (in the
bidder) or dispose of shares (in the target), even though that offer or proposal,
when initially announced as required by MAR itself, might not be accompanied
by all relevant information.

An exemption from the obligation not to disclose inside information is
provided, subject to extensive safeguards, in relation to "market soundings", i.e.
discussion with selected market participants about a possible course of action in
order to establish the market's likely reaction to it. The most common situation is
where those acting on behalf of an issuer wish to establish whether the market
would absorb a public offering of shares within a price range the issuer would
find acceptable. However, market soundings also embrace talks by a potential
bidder with large shareholders in the target in order to establish the likelihood of

---

[152] MAR art.8(5). "National law" is left to determine how these natural persons are identified. In the
UK the rules of agency and employment will presumably be used, in a form of "reverse" vicarious
liability.
[153] MAR art.9(1).
[154] See para.26–14.

their accepting an offer, if one were made.[155] The information in question here is clearly likely to constitute inside information of the utmost salience. Indeed, unusual trading in advance of a bid announcement is a common feature of securities markets. MAR seeks to address this risk by requiring the discloser to assess whether it will be disclosing inside information during the market soundings (and to keep a written record of its assessment and of the inside information disclosed, if any). If so, the consent of potential recipients of the information to receive it must be obtained (a process sometimes called "[Chinese] wall crossing") and the implications for the recipients of being put in possession of inside information must be explained. The recipients must themselves assess whether they are in possession of inside information.[156] Finally, the Commission is to adopt regulatory technical standards and ESMA guidelines for market soundings.[157]

Market manipulation

Transactions and orders to trade

30–39   Market manipulation is defined very broadly in art.12 of MAR, as it was under the previous regime. Many of its manifestations have little relevance to the public markets in securities, with which we are primarily concerned. We concentrate on the forms of manipulation which are relevant to such markets. The first two aspects of the definition both arise out of effecting transactions or orders to trade (for example, in securities). The first covers trades which give or are likely to give a false impression as to the market supply or demand or price of a financial instrument or secure the price of the financial instrument at an abnormal or artificial level.[158] As we have seen above, such behaviour constitutes a criminal offence if done for the purpose of inducing investment decisions,[159] but MAR applies on the basis simply of engaging in the proscribed behaviour (subject to the defences discussed below).[160] Indeed, as with insider dealing, attempting to engage in the behaviour is also prohibited. The second covers transactions or orders which employ some form of deception.[161] Annex 1 to MAR gives a non-exhaustive list of the matters national regulators should take into account when applying these two aspects of the prohibition.

The market itself has developed graphic terms to refer to some of the forms of behaviour falling within these prohibitions. Examples are "wash trades" (where a person trades with himself or two persons acting together trade between themselves, but so that there is no real transfer of beneficial ownership or market risk) and "painting the tape" (entering into a series of transactions that are

---

[155] MAR art.9(1)(2).
[156] MAR art.9(5)(7).
[157] ESMA, *Final Report: Draft technical standards on the Market Abuse Regulation*, 2015, §4 and Annex VIII; ESMA, *Consultation Paper: Draft guidelines on the Market Abuse Regulation*, 2016.
[158] MAR art.12(1)(a).
[159] FSA 2012 s.90. Above, para.30–29.
[160] MAR art.15.
[161] MAR art.12(1)(b).

publicly reported for the purpose of suggesting a level of activity or price movement which do not genuinely exist) fall within the first type of behaviour.[162]

Dissemination of information

Given the reliance of markets on information, it is not surprising that a common form of market manipulation consists of supplying misleadingly good or bad information to the market. Colourful examples are "pump and dump" (taking a long position in an investment, disseminating misleading positive information about it, and then selling out) and its opposite, "trash and cash" (taking a short position in a security and disseminating misleading negative information before closing out the short position) fall within this type of market manipulation.[163] The third aspect of prohibited manipulation thus consists of disseminating information which gives or is likely to give a false or misleading impression as to the demand for, supply of or the price of a financial instrument where the disseminator knew or ought to have known that the information was false or misleading.[164] In this case, a negligence standard is built into the definition of the prohibited conduct.[165] In effect, a person who makes a negligent misstatement to the market about a financial instrument is exposed to the FCA's penalties, but without it being a requirement for liability that the maker of the statement should have intended or expected that any particular person or class of person should rely on it, still less that any such reliance should have occurred.[166] As we have seen,[167] there is liability under s.91 of FSMA to the FCA's penalties on the part of an issuer (and its directors) which negligently make a misleading disclosure required by the Transparency Rules. However, liability under the market abuse provisions (which was invoked in the *Shell* case)[168] is a useful supplement because MAR, unlike the TD, is not confined to regulated markets.[169]

30–40

Misleading behaviour and market distortion

The final forms of market manipulation identified in MAR target various forms of behaviour which may mislead the market but which are not central to the manipulation of securities markets. An example is securing a dominant position in the market for a financial instrument ("cornering" it) so as to establish unfair

30–41

---

[162] See FCA, Code of Market Conduct, 1.6.2.

[163] FCA, Code of Market Conduct, 1.7.2.

[164] MAR art.12(1)(c). See also art.12(2)(d) dealing with statements (not required to be false or misleading) about a financial instrument where the maker of the statement already has a position in the instrument but has not disclosed it.

[165] Though the defences discussed below are still available.

[166] The breadth of the prohibition was thought to put financial journalists at particular risk and so art.21 provides that the liability of journalists is to be assessed on a basis which takes into account the codes of conduct governing that profession, provided the journalist derives no direct or indirect benefit from the dissemination of the information and did not intend to mislead the market.

[167] See Ch.26 at para.26–29, above.

[168] See above, Ch.26 at para.26–31.

[169] MAR art.2(1) applies the Regulation to MTFs as well as regulated markets and to derivatives referencing securities so traded.

trading conditions.[170] This can happen in securities markets but is difficult and expensive in a deep and liquid market. More common perhaps is trying to influence the opening or closing prices of certain financial instruments, in order to influence the settlement terms of derivatives linked to those prices[171] or placing artificial orders which make it difficult for market participants to identify genuine orders or for the market to establish the price of the financial instrument.[172]

Accepted market practices

30–42   The principal difficulty with prohibitions on market manipulation is that any effective definition is likely also to catch some behaviour which market participants regard as legitimate. MAR recognises this by exempting from the prohibition on manipulation acts which are done "for legitimate reasons, and conform with [sic] an accepted market practice".[173] A further issue here is that accepted market practices ("AMP") are specific to particular markets and so need to be defined at that level. This created a particular problem for the drafters of MAR, whose objective is uniformity of regulation across the EU. One can see their reluctance to delegate an important regulatory power, not just to Member States, but to the regulators of particular markets. Having accepted therefore the principle that AMP are to be established by the relevant market regulators,[174] MAR constrains the decisions of those regulators to a considerable extent. Seven criteria are laid out which competent authorities have to take into account when establishing an AMP and those criteria are supplemented by regulatory technical standards adopted by the Commission.[175]

None of the criteria is surprising but setting them creates a framework of EU law within which competent authorities must operate. That framework is enforced through the requirement that a competent authority, before establishing an AMP, must notify ESMA, giving its analysis justifying the establishment of an AMP under the criteria.[176] ESMA then carries out its own analysis at the EU level to determine whether the AMP would "threaten the market confidence in the Union's financial market," publishing that opinion on its website.[177] The competent national authority is not bound to accept ESMA's view but must publish on its website within 24 hours of establishing the AMP what is in effect a rebuttal of ESMA's analysis.[178] This very public "comply or explain" procedure is clearly designed to give ESMA a major oversight role in the establishment of an AMP: a national competent authority which wants a quiet life will clearly

---

[170] MAR art.12(2)(a).

[171] MAR art.12(2)(b).

[172] MAR art.12(2)(c). There is considerable debate about the extent to which high frequency or algorithmic trading can or bring about such distortions.

[173] MAR art.13.

[174] MAR art13(2).

[175] MAR art.13(2) and ESMA, above fn.157, §5 and Annex X.

[176] MAR art.13(3).

[177] MAR art.13(4).

[178] MAR art.13(5).

consult informally with ESMA before it provides its initial analysis in order to maximise the chances of that analysis being acceptable to ESMA.

However, this is not an end to ESMA's role. Other competent authorities (from other Member States) are co-opted into the scrutiny process. Another competent authority may complain that the AMP has been established in breach of the criteria laid out in MAR. In that case ESMA is to assist the competent authorities to reach an agreement, but, if this does not occur, ESMA may give a decision which is binding on the competent authorities involved in the dispute.[179] Enforcement of the decision may lead ESMA to give instructions directly to market participants. Although this procedure is dependent on complaint by the competent authority of another Member State, no doubt there are ways and means of informally encouraging such complaints.

Safe harbours

MAR provides safe harbours, for two types of activity, in relation to both the insider trading and market manipulation manifestations of the prohibition on market abuse. These activities are share buy-backs and stabilisation occurring in the period after a public offer of securities. In both cases, the exemptions are tightly drawn and must comply with regulatory technical standards drawn up by ESMA and adopted by the Commission.[180] Both exemptions were contained in the prior law and were there subject to Commission second-level rules. The UK has chosen to extend the protection to the criminal provisions[181] on misleading statements.

30–43

Share buy-backs

The creditor and shareholder protection aspects of share buy-backs have been considered in Ch.13.[182] It is by no means impossible for a company to effect a buy-back programme for its shares without falling foul of the market abuse prohibition, especially as issuers in any event must disclose inside information to the market "as soon as possible"[183] and so should not be holding it when effecting the buy-back. However, it seems to have been thought that buy-backs were an important corporate tool, so that companies should be given a "safe harbour" for their implementation.

30–44

The conditions laid down for access to the safe are not particularly novel in the UK, where the Listing Rules have contained similar provisions for permissible buy-backs some time.[184] Putting together the provisions of MAR and the likely content of the technical standards, the following main points emerge:

---

[179] MAR art.13(6). ESMA's procedure for giving a binding decision is set out more fully in art.19 of Regulation (EU) No.1095/2010, which establishes ESMA. ESMA's power to give binding decisions in inter-Member State disputes is not confined to this instance, but it must be specifically provided for in the relevant EU instrument dealing with the subject in question.

[180] MAR art.5; ESMA, above fn.157, §3 and Annex 7.

[181] FSA 2012 ss.89(3),90(9).

[182] At paras 13–11 et seq.

[183] See para.26–6.

[184] See, for example, FSA, *The Listing Rules*, May 2000 edition, Ch.15.

(a)   The purpose of the buy-back programme must be to reduce the company's capital or to meet its obligations under a debt instrument convertible into equity or an employee share scheme. This appears to mean that the shares bought back will be required to be either cancelled or re-issued for the permitted purposes (rather than held in treasury subject to the board's discretion). And the safe harbour applies only to behaviour directly related to the purpose of the buy-back programme.

(b)   Apart from meeting the requirements for shareholder approval and so on,[185] details of the buy-back programme must be disclosed to the market in advance of any purchases and the issuer must report purchases actually made to the competent authority within seven working days, giving amounts acquired and prices. Thus, the acquisitions cannot occur clandestinely and the market will know what may happen and what has happened.

(c)   The acquisitions must not be at a price higher than the prevailing market price (even if the authorisation from the shareholders permits a higher price) and, normally, not more than one quarter of the average daily volume of the shares may be bought in any one day. This rule reduces the impact of the acquisitions on the trading price of the share.

(d)   The issuer may not sell its own shares (presumably those held in treasury) during the programme, thus removing an incentive to pay an above-market price. Nor may it effect acquisitions under its programme at a time when it is making use of the permission not to disclose otherwise disclosable inside information. Finally, it may not make purchases under the programme during a "closed period".[186] However, the issuer can avoid all three restrictions by either adopting a programme under which the amounts and times of the acquisitions are set out in the public disclosure required above (a "time-scheduled" programme) or by outsourcing the programme to an investment bank which makes the trading decisions independently of the issuer.

Price stabilisation

30–45   Share or price stabilisation is, as its name suggests, a somewhat more questionable procedure from the point of view of market abuse than share repurchases, since the very purpose of the behaviour is to set the market price of the security at a different level from that which would otherwise prevail. However, it is permitted in connection with new shares issues, for reasons which have been put as follows:

> "Because new securities are usually issued at irregular intervals, they may result in a temporary oversupply of those securities leading to an artificially low market price during and immediately after issue. Such short-term price fluctuations may be to the detriment of both

---

[185] See above, para.13–15.
[186] See above, para.30–6.

issuers and investors. Price stabilising activity involves the lead managers of a new issue of securities supporting the price of those securities for a limited period, thereby reducing the risk of price falls."[187]

Putting together the provisions of MAR and the technical regulatory standards of the Commission developed under the prior EU law, the main conditions to be met for the price stabilisation safe harbour are likely to be, briefly, as follows:

30–46

(a)　The stabilisation may be carried out only within a limited period of time, for example, in the case of shares, within 30 calendar days of the date on which shares offered in an initial offer commence trading.[188]

(b)　The market must be informed before the shares are offered to the public that stabilisation may be undertaken (but that there is no guarantee that it will or that it will be at any particular level) and of the period during which it may be undertaken and who will be undertaking it.[189] Stabilisation activity must be reported to the FCA within seven working days of its taking place, and within one week of the end of the stabilisation period the market must be informed of what stabilisation activity occurred, including the dates and prices.[190]

(c)　The price at which the stabilisation activity took place must not be above the offer price.[191]

ENFORCEMENT AND SANCTIONS

Although the substantive rules on market abuse are set at EU level, enforcement and sanctions are in the hands of national competent authorities. However, this does not mean that MAR ignores these topics. Rather, it proceeds by requiring Member States to confer on their national authorities at least the investigatory and sanctioning powers specified in Chs 4 and 5 of MAR and by imposing obligations to cooperate on those authorities. Although the range of powers and sanctions contained in these chapters is wide, by and large they are not new powers for the FCA. The current investigation and penalty powers of the FCA in relation to market abuse are set out in Pts VIII and XI of FSMA but will need some amendment to deal with the provisions of MAR.

30–47

Investigation into market abuse

MAR requires competent authorities to have 13 powers so that they may police and enforce the prohibition on market abuse effectively.[192] Among the more notable ones, are access to data in any form, the right to summon persons and

30–48

---

[187] FSA, *The Price Stabilising Rules*, CP 40, January 2000.
[188] Commission Regulation (EC) No.2273/2003 issued under the former Market Abuse Directive art.8.
[189] This matter is currently covered in the Commission Regulation (EC) No.809/2004, Annex III para.6.5, implementing the Prospectus Directive.
[190] Commission Regulation implementing the Market Abuse Directive art.9.
[191] Commission Regulation implementing the Market Abuse Directive art.10.
[192] MAR art.23(2).

demand answers to questions, to carry out on-site inspections (other than residences), to enter premises and seize documents (subject to judicial control if the Member State requires it), to require recordings of telephone conversations and copies of emails from financial institutions, to require traffic data from telecom operators (if national law permits this) and, crossing the border into remedies, to impose various interlocutory remedies and to require the correction of misstatements to the market. Information obtained must be subject to confidentiality requirements and be governed by national data protection laws.[193]

In order to maximise the chances of national regulators learning of potential infringements of MAR, Member States are required to ensure that "whistle-blowing" procedures exist, both for the provision of information to the competent authority and for the provision of information to the employer concerned, where the employer is engaged in providing regulated financial services.[194] However, there is no obligation on the whistle-blower to report first to the employer before approaching the competent authority. In relation to reporting to the competent authority the Commission Implementing Directive[195] provides that there should be a dedicated function within the authority to receive the reports, that its operation should be explained on the authority's website and that, in all normal circumstances, the identity of the reporting person should not be revealed and that that person should be protected against discriminatory acts of the employer, if the identity does become known. MAR permits the provision of financial inducements to make reports, provided the informer is not under an existing legal or contractual duty to report and that the report leads to the imposition of a penalty or sanction.[196]

30–49 Since market manipulation is often a cross-border activity, MAR requires national competent authorities to cooperate both with ESMA (mainly in the communication of information)[197] and with other national authorities and ESMA for the purposes of investigation, supervision and enforcement.[198] The latter form of cooperation is likely to involve the provision of information but may go much further. For example, cooperation requests from other national competent authorities, which may be refused on only limited grounds,[199] may extend to initiating on-site investigations in the country receiving the request.[200] Investigation requests assume that the requesting state is itself already knows or suspects some potential wrongdoing in its own jurisdiction and is seeking to investigate it, but knowledge of that wrongdoing might first emerge as a result of the activities of a competent authority in another Member State. The Member State with the knowledge must report the facts to the Member State where the activities appear to be located and to ESMA and both Member States are under an obligation to

---

[193] MAR arts 27 and 28.
[194] MAR art.32.
[195] Commission Implementing Directive (EU) 2015/2392.
[196] MAR art.32(4).
[197] MAR art.24.
[198] MAR art.25(1).
[199] MAR art.25(2).
[200] MAR art.25(6). That request may be given effect to in a variety of ways, ranging from the requested state carry it out itself to the requesting state doing so. ESMA may coordinate the cross-border investigation if one of the participating states so requests.

coordinate their subsequent actions.[201] What gives bite to these requirements is the role afforded to ESMA where a Member State's request for information or assistance is rejected by another Member State's competent authority or not accepted within a reasonable time. ESMA may either deal with the matter as an example of a disagreement between national authorities, as discussed above,[202] or, if it believes one of the competent authorities is acting in breach of EU law, take action against it on that basis. In either case ESMA may end up requiring the recalcitrant national authority to take specific action or to refrain from action or, if that fails, itself requiring market participants to take specific action or to refrain from action.[203]

Since financial activity is often a global matter, cooperation among EU regulators, although highly desirable, is unlikely to be enough. MAR therefore envisages cooperation agreements with the supervisory authorities of third countries. Reflecting prior practice, but somewhat out of tune with MAR's objectives, the conclusion of such agreements is a matter for national competent authorities. However, ESMA is inserted into the process. It is "where possible" to facilitate and coordinate the third-party agreements and is to draft regulatory technical standards, to be adopted by the Commission, aimed at producing a "template" for such agreements, which national competent authorities are to use, again "where possible".[204]

30–50

Under the pre-MAR rules the UK signed Memoranda of Understanding relating to co-operation with regulators from other leading countries in the financial services field, such as the US, Japan, Hong Kong, Switzerland and Australia. These international agreements and the pre-MAR EU obligations are underpinned by s.169 of FSMA, which authorises or, in the case of the EU obligation, requires the FCA to appoint investigators at the behest of a non-British regulator to investigate "any matter". The FCA may permit a representative of the overseas regulator to be present and ask questions, provided the information obtained is subject to the same confidentiality requirements in the hands of the overseas regulator as it would be under the FSMA.[205] Where assistance is not obligatory, the overseas regulator may be required to contribute to the costs of the investigation and the FCA considers, before granting the request, whether similar assistance would be forthcoming from the overseas regulator if it were requested by a British regulator, whether the breach of the law to be investigated has no close parallel in the UK, whether the matter is of importance to people in the UK and whether the public interest requires that the assistance be given.[206] In the case of insider dealing, it seems likely that these criteria could easily be satisfied, so that assistance should normally be given, even where there is no EU obligation to provide it, subject to the matter of cost. The Court of Appeal has interpreted the section liberally, notably by not requiring the FCA investigate the genuineness or validity of the foreign regulator's request

---

[201] MAR art.25(5).
[202] See para.30–42, above.
[203] MAR art.25(7) and arts 17 and 19 of Regulation (EU) No.1095/2010.
[204] MAR art.26.
[205] FSMA s.169(7) and (8).
[206] FSMA s.169(4).

and by permitting the investigators to require the production of any documents which are relevant to their investigation.[207]

Sanctions for market abuse

30–51 MAR requires a wide range of administrative sanctions to be available for breach of the prohibitions on market abuse.[208] These are expressly stated to be minimum requirements to which Member States may add, both by making sanctions available other than those listed in MAR and by making the listed sanctions more powerful.[209]

In relation to companies and individuals other than investment firms and their managers and employees, the sanctions required to be made available are:

- injunctions requiring the conduct constituting the market abuse to cease;
- disgorgement of profits made or losses avoided through the market abuse "insofar as they can be determined"[210];
- a maximum administrative penalty of 'at least' three times the profit made or loss avoided under the previous item[211];
- public warnings;
- financial penalties up to a maximum of €5,000,000 in the case of individuals and €15,000,000 or 15 per cent of annual turnover in the case of companies.[212]

In the case of investment firms and those employed within them there are additional sanctions consisting of temporary or permanent (i) withdrawal of the authorisation of the firm to carry on financial business; and (ii) bans on the individual from discharging managerial responsibilities within such a firm or dealing on their own account.

These sanctions are already available in principle to the FCA.

Penalties

30–52 The penalty provisions were another of the human rights battle grounds in the parliamentary debates preceding the passing of FSMA 2000 and a number of restrictions on the FCA's powers are the result. First, although there is no

---

[207] *R. (on the application of Amro International SA) v Financial Services Authority* [2010] 2 B.C.L.C. 40 CA.

[208] MAR art.30. A Member State may choose not to have administrative sanctions in an area where criminal sanctions are available, for example, in the UK under FSA 2012 Pt 7. The UK seems unlikely to take advantage of this provision since it traditionally has made both types of sanction available to the FCA in the area of market abuse. On the FCA's policy about the choice between criminal and administrative sanctions, see FCA, *Enforcement Guide*, paras 12.7–12.10.

[209] MAR art.30(3).

[210] On the potential difficulties with this remedy see para.26–28, above.

[211] In other words Member States may set the maximum penalty at a higher level but not at a lower level than three times the profit or loss. Although the actual penalty imposed will often be below the maximum, the thought is that the higher the maximum, the higher the range of penalties actually imposed.

[212] See previous note.

statutory restriction on the size of penalty the FCA may impose, the FCA is required to produce a statement of policy on the factors which will determine its approach to penalties.[213] That policy now appears in the Decision Procedure and Penalties Manual ("DEPP") which contains a list of the factors the FCA considers relevant to the decisions whether to seek a financial penalty, whether to substitute public censure for a monetary penalty and to determining the level of penalty. The FCA's views on the appropriate level of penalties were significantly strengthened as from March 2010, under the impact of the financial crisis.

Secondly, the FCA may not impose a penalty upon a person without sending him first a "warning notice" stating the level of penalty proposed or the terms of the proposed public statement.[214] Thirdly, if the FSA does impose a penalty or make a public statement, it must issue the person concerned with a decision notice to that effect,[215] which triggers the person's right to appeal to the Upper Tribunal.[216] That right must normally be exercised within 28 days.[217] The Tribunal, consisting of a legally qualified chair and one or more experienced lay persons, operates by way of a re-hearing of the case, and so can consider evidence not brought before the FCA, whether it was available at that time or not,[218] and must arrive at its own determination of the appropriate action to be taken in the case,[219] which, presumably, could be a tougher penalty than the one the FCA had proposed. There is a legal assistance scheme in operation for proceedings before the Tribunal, funded by the FCA, which recoups the cost from a levy on authorised persons.[220] Appeals lie on a point of law from the Tribunal to the Court of Appeal or Court of Session.[221]

Fourthly, a prohibition on the use of compelled testimony applies not only to subsequent criminal charges but also to proceedings for the imposition of a penalty, whether before the FCA or the Tribunal.[222]

Injunctions

The FCA may apply to the court under s.381 for an injunction to restrain future market abuse, whether such abuse has taken place already or not, and the court may grant an injunction where there is a "reasonable likelihood" that the abuse

30–53

---

[213] FSMA ss.124 and 125.

[214] FSMA s.126. Sections 392 and 393 extend the warning notice procedure to third parties, but only if the third party is identified in the FCA's decision notice: *Watts v Financial Services Authority* [2005] UKFSM FSM022.

[215] FSMA s.127. MAR art.34 requires decisions to impose sanctions normally to be published.

[216] FSMA s.126.

[217] FSMA s.133(1).

[218] FSMA s.133(4). Although the hearing function was transferred to the Upper Tribunal in 2010, the statutory provisions in FSMA, as amended, governing the appeal hearing continue to apply.

[219] FSMA s.133(4). The action must be one the FCA could have taken: s.133A.

[220] FSMA ss.134 and 135, even though in the case of market abuse appeals, the appellant may not be an authorised person. The details of the assistance scheme are set out in Financial Services and Markets Tribunal (Legal Assistance) Regulations 2001 (SI 2001/3632) and the Financial Services and Markets Tribunal (Legal Assistance—Costs) Regulations 2001 (SI 2001/3633).

[221] Now by virtue of the general provisions applying to appeals from the Upper Tribunal.

[222] FSMA s.174(2).

will occur or be repeated.[223] The court has two further and independent powers under s.381. If, on the application of the Authority, the court is satisfied that a person may be, or may have been, engaged in market abuse, it may order a freeze on all or any of that person's assets. This helps to ensure that any later restitution order has something to bite on. Secondly, if the court is satisfied that the person is or has been engaged in market abuse, it may, on the application of the Authority, order the person to take such steps to remedy the situation as the court may direct. Finally, in an injunction (or restitution) application the court may impose a penalty of such amount as it considers appropriate.[224]

Sanctions for breach of the criminal law

30–54   The Criminal Justice Act 1993 places exclusive reliance upon criminal sanctions for its enforcement. Section 63(2) states that no contract shall be "void or unenforceable" by reason only of an offence committed under the Act, a provision which was redrafted in 1993, it would seem, in order to close the loophole, as the Government saw it, identified in *Chase Manhattan Equities v Goodman*.[225] Although the Act does not deal expressly with the question of whether a civil action for breach of statutory duty could be built on its provisions, it seems unlikely that the Act would be held to fall within either of the categories identified for this purpose in the case law.[226]

The criminal sanctions imposed by the Act are, on summary conviction, a fine not exceeding the statutory maximum and/or a term of imprisonment not exceeding six months, and on conviction on indictment an unlimited fine and/or imprisonment for not more than seven years.[227] The power of the judge on conviction on indictment to impose an unlimited fine means that, in theory at least, the court could ensure that the insider made no profit out of the dealing.[228] Prosecutions in England and Wales may be brought only by or with the consent of the Secretary of State or the Director of Public Prosecutions. In England and Wales prosecutions may be brought by the FCA as well as by the usual prosecution bodies, the Crown Prosecution Service, the Serious Fraud Office and the relevant government department.[229] Indeed, the FCA has the prime responsibility for bringing criminal prosecutions for breach of the criminal laws

---

[223] FSMA s.381(1).

[224] FSMA s.129; *FCA v Da Vinci Invest Ltd* [2016] 1 B.C.L.C. 554, where Snowden J examines fully the scope of this power.

[225] *Chase Manhattan Equities v Goodman* [1991] B.C.L.C. 897 at 930–935, where the judge held that the previous legislative formulation did not prevent the court from holding a contract unenforceable when it had been concluded in breach of the 1985 Act's provisions.

[226] See especially *Lonrho Ltd v Shell Petroleum Co Ltd (No.2)* [1982] A.C. 173 HL.

[227] 1993 Act s.61.

[228] The Crown Court has power under the Criminal Justice Act 1988, as amended by the Proceeds of Crime Act 1995, to make an order confiscating the proceeds of crime, which could also be used to this end.

[229] FSMA s.402(1)(a). This implies that some cases which might previously have been dealt with through regulatory sanctions will now be subject to criminal prosecution, but the courts have refused to treat this change of policy as a ground for special leniency when sentencing offenders: *R. v McQuoid* [2010] 1 Cr. App. R. (S.) 43.

in the area of market abuse. As we have noted above, the number of criminal prosecutions brought by the FCA is small, but increasing.[230]

The FCA is also the lead prosecutor under Pt 7 of FSA 2012. This section is less used than the CJA provisions, but will be invoked in what the FCA regards as serious cases.[231]

Restitution orders and injunctions

On the application of the FCA or the Secretary of State, the court may impose a restitution order or an injunction where a breach has occurred or is threatened of Pt 7 of FSA 2012.[232] In practice, it is unlikely this adds anything significant to the court's and FCA's powers to seek restitution or an injunction on grounds of market abuse, since the criminal law is narrower than the civil penalty regime.

30–55

Disqualification

In addition to the traditional criminal penalties which may be visited upon those engaging in market abuse, the disqualification sanction is available against them in some cases, the effect of which is to disable the person disqualified from being involved in the running of companies in the future.[233] In *R. v Goodman*[234] the Court of Appeal upheld the Crown Court's decision to disqualify, for a period of 10 years, a managing director convicted of insider dealing. The Crown Court had invoked s.2 of the Company Directors Disqualification Act 1986 which enables a court to disqualify a person who has been convicted of an indictable offence in connection with the management of a company. The Court of Appeal took a liberal view of what could be said to be "in connection with the management of the company", so as to bring within the phrase the managing director's disposal of his shares in the company in advance of publication of bad news about its prospects. It would seem, too, that a disqualification order could be made on grounds of unfitness under s.8 of the 1986 Act upon an application by the Secretary of State in the public interest. In that case, conviction by a court of an indictable offence would not be a pre-condition to a disqualification order, but the court would have to be satisfied that the person's conduct in relation to the company made him unfit to be concerned in the management of a company and this section, unlike s.2, is capable of applying to market abuse only by directors and shadow directors.

30–56

---

[230] See para.30–30.

[231] See para.26–32.

[232] FSMA ss.382(9) and 380(6).

[233] See Ch.10, above. These powers are in addition to the powers of (probably more important) the FCA to disqualify persons from operating within the financial services industry.

[234] *R. v Goodman* [1993] 2 All E.R. 789 CA.

CONCLUSION

30–57   Regulation of market abuse has been an area of enormously rapid growth in recent years, to which the adoption of MAR has most recently added. Before 1980 insider dealing was tackled mainly through statutory disclosure requirements, whilst broader forms of market abuse received at best a shadowy control in the common law of crimes. Today, both insider dealing in particular and market abuse in general are the subject of detailed criminal and regulatory rules. Why should this have happened? It may well reflect a deterioration in standards of market conduct as a result of powerful financial incentives to "do the business". Probably, it also an example of the growth of shareholder (or, in this case, investor) power as financial markets have come to play a more important role in national and international business.[235] In general, the regulation discussed in this chapter aims to protect investors, individual and collective, against opportunistic behaviour by corporate and market insiders and thus make securities markets more attractive places in which to participate.

Of course, it is another question whether the law is as effective in practice as it could be. Research published by the FSA suggests there is still a high level of abnormal price movements ahead of takeover announcements, though in recent years there has been a decline in such movements ahead of trading statements.[236] Until recently, whilst the FCA's budget was not out of line with that of its US equivalent, the Securities Exchange Commission, when adjusted for market capitalisation, it seemed to devote a lower proportion of its budget to enforcement and to impose lower penalties when it did take action.[237] The FCA has up-graded the resources it devotes to enforcement and changed its view about the appropriate level of penalties since the financial crisis, but the effects of this policy re-orientation remain to be seen.

---

[235] cf. the increased importance of shareholder interests in corporate governance, above, Pt 3.

[236] FSA, *Updated Measurement of Market Cleanliness*, Occasional Paper 25, March 2007.

[237] J. Coffee Jr, "Law and the Market: The Impact of Enforcement" (2007) 156 University of Pennsylvania L.R. 229.

PART 7

DEBT FINANCE

At various points in this book we have referred to the comparative advantages of equity and debt finance for companies. Even more so than with the rights of shareholders, the rights of lenders to the company depend heavily on the terms upon which they contract with the company. Nevertheless, one can say that, in general, debt is both cheaper and more flexible, but is also more demanding as a form of finance for companies than equity shares. It is cheaper because insolvency priority[1] and contractual flexibility may reduce the risk to lenders, who can therefore be persuaded to lend on more advantageous terms; but it is more demanding because those terms create an entitlement (usually to payment of a fixed or narrowly fluctuating rate of interest, plus repayment of principal), whether the company is doing well or badly, whereas the declaration of a dividend on ordinary shares is usually a matter for the discretion of the directors. Clearly, the rate of interest a company has to pay for its debt depends to some considerable extent on the financial standing of the company and, if that is not enough, on whether it can offer a lender personal or proprietary security for its loan, and the quality of the security offered. Much of the law applicable here is the general law relating to lenders and borrowers, and does not have to be analysed in a book on company law. However, three aspects of the relevant law do deserve discussion in a company law text.

First, as part of its debt-raising activities, a company may issue debt securities and those securities may be traded on a public market, in the same way as equity securities are.[2] Indeed, the line between the two forms of investment in a company can be quite blurred, and—whether the debt securities are traded on the public market or not—debt-holders can play a significant role in the indirect governance of companies. We thus need to say something about the nature of a company's debt obligations. Secondly, although the issue of granting valid security is a general problem in the law of secured lending, Companies Acts have long included their own rules governing the registration of charges granted by companies. These rules have been the subject of attention of various review groups, including the Law Commission, and are examined here. Thirdly, in the

---

[1] On insolvency, a company's creditors are repaid before the shareholders: see Ch.33.
[2] Thus, some reference to such securities has already been made in Ch.25 (public offers).

creation of one form of security, company lawyers took the lead in the nineteenth century. This was with the floating charge, still a controversial mechanism because of the way it can operate to crowd out the interests of unsecured creditors, in terms both of the scope of the charge and the mechanisms for enforcing it. Thus, the floating charge is the third topic we need to look at in some detail.

CHAPTER 31

DEBTS AND DEBT SECURITIES

INTRODUCTION

A company will inevitably finance itself not only through issuing shares (of various classes) but also by taking loans or, alternatively, by making use of credit. Given that around 77 per cent of UK registered companies have an issued share capital of £100 or less,[1] the need for this sort of alternative funding is clear.[2] Of these options, taking loans, i.e. debt financing, including its more sophisticated

31–1

---

[1] BIS/Companies House, *Statistical Tables on Companies Registration Activities 2012/13*, Table A6.
[2] Apple is perhaps one of the few companies that may not need loans to fund its operations (although it chose to do so to maximise returns); it can rely on operating profits, especially as it has also had, until 2012, a policy of not paying dividends on shares.

variants, is the main source of non-equity finance for companies, and is the focus of this chapter. Nevertheless, most companies (small and large) will also make use of various forms of credit, including quite sophisticated forms of asset-based financing.[3]

One basic divide in all debt financing is between simple debts (not always so simple in their documentation, and including large syndicated loans) and marketable "debt securities"[4] (with their obvious parallels with equity securities, i.e. shares).[5] As with shares, debt securities may be issued and traded privately or on public markets, with the latter being more tightly regulated. With the terminology, context is important: the terms "debt" and "debt financing" can be used perfectly generally to embrace all the options open to a company; only as the terms become more specific, and "debt" and "debt securities" are contrasted, do they reveal anything of the nature of the underlying debt instrument.

Some elements of debt financing turn out to be especially important in the corporate context. We focus on these, especially the regulated use of marketable corporate debt contracts (i.e. debt securities), including the transfer of these interests; the protective creditor-imposed governance constraints common in all debt financing; and—at various points—the similarities and differences between debt and equity financing. But some introductory points are necessary before we can address that detail. We start with the basic differences between debt and equity, and the various structural choices in debt financing.

Difference between debt (loans), equity (shares) and hybrid instruments

31–2   Often the expected sharp differences between debt and equity are blurred or non-existent. Take the financing decision itself. The choice is for the directors, and is subject to all their general duties. At first blush the constraints on directors, and the controls given to members, seem greater with share issues than with debt: recall the decisions on "proper purposes" in share issues, and the statutory rules on pre-emption rights.[6] There are no direct general law parallels when the decision concerns debt, but in practice many lenders will impose even greater constraints in their own loan agreements, insisting on contractual terms prohibiting further corporate borrowing, or at least further secured borrowing (i.e. negative pledge clauses), unless the consent of the lender is first obtained.

---

[3] These forms of financing are not discussed here, but include, e.g. the familiar mechanisms of hire-purchase, retention of title, conditional sales, sale and leaseback, finance leases, supply-chain financing, debt/receivables factoring and "repos" (sale on terms providing for repurchase). These are all well-covered in specialist texts such as L. Gullifer and J. Payne, *Corporate Finance Law: Principles and Policy*, 2nd edn (Oxford: Hart Publishing, 2015). With all of these, proper characterisation can be problematic, raising the risk that the courts will instead characterise the arrangement as a charge, which may be void for want of registration: see below, paras 32–24 et seq.

[4] With these further subdivided into "bonds" and "stock", although with the use of global notes and intermediation, the modern differences between these have become rather slender.

[5] Or—looking at the transaction from the other end of the telescope—we might speak not of debts and debt securities, but "loans" and "marketable loans". The latter perhaps gives a clearer sense of the similarities and distinctions in issue.

[6] See paras 16–26 et seq. and 24–6 et seq. respectively.

DEBTS AND DEBT SECURITIES

The same blurring is true of the contrast between members and creditors: in law a member of the company has rights in it, while a creditor has rights against it. In reality, however, the difference between the debt-holder and the share-holder may not be anything like as clear-cut, for the debt instrument may give the holder contractual rights akin to those of a shareholder, e.g. to appoint a director; to receive a share of profits (whether or not available for dividend)[7]; to repayment at a premium; to attend and vote at general meetings.[8] Covenants in the loan instrument may also, as we shall see, give debt holders considerable influence over the way in which the company is managed.[9] Moreover, where the debt instrument is secured by a floating charge on all the assets and undertaking of the company, the holder will have a legal or equitable interest in the company's business, albeit of a different kind from that of its shareholders.

The line between the holder of a debt instrument and a share is particularly narrow if the contrast is made with a preference shareholder, who is a member of the company, but a member whose share rights may limit the shareholder's dividend to a fixed percentage of the nominal value of the share and give that shareholder no right to participate in surplus assets in a winding-up, and perhaps only limited voting rights.[10] The main difference between the two in such a case may then be that the dividend on a preference share is not payable unless profits are available for distribution,[11] whereas the debt holder's interest entitlement is not subject to this constraint; and that the debt holder will rank before the preference holder in a winding-up. Thus, the legal rules operate with a binary divide between debt and equity, but the accounting rules and general practice leads to the creation of securities whose classification in accordance with this divide is problematic.

These difficulties of classification are magnified in relation to securities which are "hybrid" in character, in that the terms of the issue provide for conversion, whether from a preference share convertible into debt, or a debt convertible into equity[12] at a later date and on fixed terms. A simple way of looking at such securities is to say that they are simply one form until conversion, at which point they become the other. However, where the bond is required to be converted into equity at a certain future date, for example, it may be possible to classify it as

31–3

---

[7] *Lemon v Austin Friars Investment Trust Ltd* [1926] Ch. 1 (instrument not prevented from being a debenture because interest payable only out of profit, which might or might not be earned in any particular year).

[8] But the debt-holder's vote should not be counted if the Act requires the resolution to be passed by "members".

[9] See below, para.31–26.

[10] On whether they should be treated as debt or equity, see W. Bratton and M. Wachter, "A Theory of Preferred Stock" (2013) 161 University of Pennsylvania L.R. 1815. The classification may be different for different purposes, e.g. accounting purposes, or tax purposes.

[11] See para.12–1. Whether the preference shareholder is entitled by contract to the dividend, even if the company cannot lawfully pay it, is a separate question. And a potentially important one, because non-payment of the contractually due dividend may trigger voting rights for the preference shareholders or affect the amount due to the preference shareholders when the company returns to profit or is wound up: *Re Bradford Investments Plc (No.1)* [1991] B.C.L.C. 224.

[12] An alternative to conversion is to issue debt securities with attached warrants which give the lender the option to subscribe for shares. The debt is then not swapped—it continues—but the lender has the added benefit of an equity interest in the company.

equity in the company's accounts from the beginning, whilst nevertheless treating the interest payable on the debt before conversion as deductible for tax purposes, so that the same security is equity for one purpose and debt for another.[13]

Notably, these hybrid securities do not provide a mechanism for avoiding the statutory rules regulating shares. They do not, for example, provide a way around the prohibition on issuing shares at a discount to their nominal value.[14] And in takeover situations, debts that are convertible to shares, or debts that have voting rights, are treated as if they were shares for the purposes of the squeeze-out and sell-out provisions in the Act.[15]

Should a company use debt or equity in its financing?

31–4   How does a company decide what mix of debt and equity is appropriate for its operations? Clearly its aim is to access the necessary funds at the least cost to the company. The options available will depend on the size of the company, the funding purpose, and the riskiness of the endeavour.[16] The choice can be difficult, since the similarities between corporate debts and shares are often strong, and can be made even stronger in "hybrid" securities, as we have seen. With both debts and shares, the investor has limited liability (limited to the sum invested by way of loan or share price); with both, the rate of return likely to be demanded is reduced if the security is highly liquid; and with both, the desire for some form of governance control is present, and increases with the risk of the investment. True, the return to the debt-holder is a binding and quantified commitment made in advance, and if not met according to its terms the company risks insolvency.

Despite this, financial economists have suggested that the cost of capital is unaffected by the debt to equity ratio: this is based on the Modigliani-Miller propositions that no combination of debt and equity is better than any other, and that a company's total market value is independent of its capital structure.[17] This, as with many economic theories, is based on an "ideal" market. When real market frictions are included, it seems that companies may add some debt without reducing the return to shareholders because the interest payable on debt is tax deductible for the company, whereas dividends payable to shareholders are not. But there is a tipping point: too much debt raises the risk of corporate default, and continuing default on debt obligations will, in the end, lead to corporate insolvency, whereas for shareholders it would simply lead to no payment of

---

[13] See generally P. Pope and A. Puxty, "What is Equity? New Financial Instruments in the Interstices between Law, Accounting and Economics" (1991) 54 M.L.R. 889.

[14] To issue at a discount debt instruments which can be immediately converted into shares of the full par value would be a colourable device to evade the prohibition on issuing shares at a discount (*Moseley v Koffyfontein Mines* [1904] 2 Ch. 108 CA) but appears to be unobjectionable if the instrument is convertible only when the debentures are due for repayment at par since the shares will then be paid up in cash "through the release of a liability of the company for a liquidated sum": s.583(3)(c). See also, above at para.11–15 on debt/equity swaps.

[15] See ss.989, 990 (but see ss.983(2)(b) and (3)(b) ignoring such debentures in calculating the 90 per cent threshold for the exercise of the sell-out right).

[16] See the summary in BIS, *Financing a Private Sector Recovery* (Cm 7923, July 2010), Ch.3.

[17] F. Modigliani and M.H. Miller, "The Cost of Capital, Corporation Finance and the Theory of Investment" (1958) 48 American Economic Review 433; and also see Miller, "The Modigliani-Miller Propositions After Thirty Years" (1988) 2 Journal of Economic Perspectives 99.

dividends. As well as the negative financial pressures of the debt-equity mix, there are however also advantageous pressures the mix puts on directors in their management of the company: managers can be over-inclined to prefer the interests of either themselves or their shareholders, and debt provides a disciplining effect because it requires directors to find the funds to make principal and interest repayments.

DIFFERENT STRUCTURES IN DEBT FINANCING

Terminology

The literature on debt financing quickly makes it plain that a wide variety of terms are used to describe different debt financing arrangements, although none constitute terms of art. Perhaps because the debt instrument is simply a creature of contract, and the relationship between debt-holder and company creates no particular conceptual puzzles—the relationship is simply the contractual relationship of debtor and creditor, coupled, if the debt is secured on some or all of the company's assets, with that of mortgagor and mortgagee or chargor and chargee—different terms have come to be used in commercial practice as a matter of fashion, and changing fashion at that. Many of the terms now in popular current usage emerge in the discussions which follow.

31–5

Defining a "debenture"

By contrast, instead of any of the modern terms in use in the market, the rather old-fashioned term "debenture" is the only one used in the Act. And even there it is not defined: s.738 merely says that the term "includes debenture stock, bonds and any other securities of a company,[18] whether or not constituting a charge on the assets of the company".[19] This is helpful in indicating that a debenture need not be secured on the company's assets, but not for much else; and indeed commercial practice rather contradicts this, typically using the word "debenture" to refer precisely to the proprietary security agreement which secures the debt owed by the company to its lender.[20]

31–6

This lack of clear definition is despite the fact that the Act contains a (short) Pt 19, headed "Debentures", as well as frequent references throughout the Act to debentures and debenture holders.[21] The question this raises is whether the term "debenture", as defined in s.738, is wide enough to include all debts (i.e. all loan agreements), or whether it is implicitly limited to "issues" of debt which have

---

[18] And, with unhelpful circularity, "securities" are then defined to "mean shares or debentures" (s.755(5)).

[19] See below, para.31–13, for more detail on debenture stock and bonds, neither of which are defined in the Act.

[20] See below, Ch.32. And unsecured loans are sometimes referred to as "loan stock", in contradistinction to "debenture stock".

[21] The courts have not done much better: *Levy v Abercorris Slate & Slab Co* (1887) 37 Ch. 260 at 264; *British India Steam Navigation Co v IRC* (1881) 7 Q.B.D. 165 at 172; *Lemon v Austin Friars Trust* [1926] Ch. 1 at 17 CA; *Knightsbridge Estates Co v Byrne* [1940] A.C. 613 HL.

parallels of some sort with issues of shares, noting of course that the latter embraces private issues as well as issues to the public.[22] The answer matters because of the particular statutory rules which then apply to "debentures".

Outside the statutory context, the term is certainly wide enough to include simple loans. In *Fons HK (In Liquidation) v Corporal Ltd, Pillar Securitisation Sàrl*,[23] the Court of Appeal had to decide whether an unsecured debt was a debenture, thus sweeping it into the assets subjected to a charge. The court reviewed and accepted earlier authorities which had held that simple loan agreements could be considered as debentures, and then held that, in the absence of other contractual terms or circumstances limiting the definition of debentures in the contract before them, the term simply meant an acknowledgement of debt recorded in a written document, whether or not secured. In doing so, the court rejected the approach of the lower court which had adopted a criterion of business common sense in contractual interpretation, and had held that, since an ordinary businessman would be surprised to hear a simple loan agreement described as a debenture, the contractual term did not cover unsecured debts.[24]

Although this case raised uncertainties in the market about similar breadth being assumed in the statutory definition, that seems misplaced. The case itself makes it clear that the necessary interpretation of agreements (and, by analogy, statutes) is contextual, and in the statutory context the term "debenture" is most often used in contexts where the analogy is with other issued securities.[25]

31–7 This is especially true of the statutory provisions requiring registration of "an allotment of debentures" (s.741), the keeping of a register of "debenture holders" (ss.743 et seq.), and the prohibition on private companies offering "securities" to the public, with "securities" meaning shares or debentures (s.755(5)).[26] These provisions are quite inapt for general application to all loan contracts.

The issue is perhaps less clear in two further contexts, where the statute overrides equity's traditional rules. First, s.740 provides that contracts to take up and pay for debentures may be specifically enforceable, thus overriding the normal contractual rule that the lender is liable only in damages.[27] The arguments for enforcing subscriptions and underwriting obligations when an "issue" of debt securities is made may be strong, but they do not seem to apply to a single creditor who, in breach of contract, fails to make an advance. Then, damages would seem a perfectly adequate remedy. The issue does not seem to have troubled modern courts,[28] but giving s.740 a more limited remit could be achieved either by defining "debentures" more narrowly, especially since s.740 refers to a contract to "take up and pay for" debentures (terminology which seems

---

[22] See above, Chs 24 and 25.

[23] *Fons HK (In Liquidation) v Corporal Ltd, Pillar Securitisation Sàrl* [2014] EWCA Civ 304 CA.

[24] *Fons HF (In Liquidation) v Corporal Ltd* [2013] EWHC 1801 (Ch).

[25] See Tijo, (2014) 73 C.L.J. 503; Roberts, [2014] J.I.B.F.L. 431.

[26] Where the difficult issue, if there is one, is usually whether there has been an offer to the public, rather than whether what is offered falls within the exceptionally wide and inclusive definition of a debenture.

[27] Thus overcoming the decision in *South African Territories Ltd v Wallington* [1898] A.C. 309 HL.

[28] Perhaps because the claim would in any event be regarded as one in debt, not damages; or perhaps that damages, assessed in context, would in any event give the company full recovery.

inapt for general loan agreements); or by relying on the use of "may" in s.740, and interpreting it as merely conferring a discretion on the court.

Secondly, s.739 specifically excludes irredeemable and long term debentures from the protective equitable doctrine prohibiting such "clogs on the equity". This, too, seems more appropriately applied to "issues" of debentures, but the statutory predecessor to s.739 was applied very generally, in 1940, in *Knightsbridge Estates Ltd v Byrne*.[29] The House of Lords held that an ordinary mortgage granted by a company was a debenture,[30] and so subject to the statutory provision disentitling the mortgagor from insisting on its equitable right to make early repayment. However, even a narrow application of the statutory provision, holding it inapplicable in this context, might not have prevented the same outcome on these facts: we might now simply say that a mortgagor has no right to early repayment unless the contract provides for it, and that a long but properly agreed maturity term is not itself sufficient to attract equitable relief.[31]

Despite these concerns, the absence of a precise statutory definition of "debenture" has given rise to surprisingly few problems, and to even fewer reported cases. In addition, modern financial markets regulation is typically directed at the product being issued rather than at the issuer or the investors, and it then defines its focus more clearly than by use of the broad term "debenture". Nevertheless, in what follows we have tried to avoid the use of the term "debenture" in favour of either more specific descriptions of the contracts in issue or, by contrast, when breadth is intended, the more generic term, "debt".

Small and large scale loans

Small and medium size companies tend to rely on loans from banks and, especially in very small companies, loans from directors and shareholders.[32] *Salomon*[33] is an old and typical illustration. Invariably the loan terms will be individually negotiated to reflect the risk, and, as we shall see, can be quite demanding in terms of the ongoing obligations imposed on the borrower, the potential consequences of any "event of default", and the various forms of security (proprietary and personal) required to support the company's primary obligation to repay the debt.

Large-scale debt financing for bigger companies is more varied. It comes in two main forms: from banks (perhaps by way of "indirect financing", so called

31–8

---

[29] *Knightsbridge Estates Ltd v Byrne* [1940] A.C. 613 HL.
[30] Whilst also accepting that the mortgage would not be a "debenture" for the purposes of some of the other sections of the Act: Viscount Maugham at 624. Clearly such a mortgage does not have to be registered in the company's register of debenture holders under s.743 in addition to registration of the mortgage under Pt 25.
[31] See *Hooper v Western Counties and South Wales Telephone Co Ltd* (1892) 68 L.T. 78; *Hyde Management Services (Pty) Ltd v FAI Insurances* (1979–80) 144 C.L.R. 541 Aust HC. And in the *Knightsbridge Estates* case, Viscount Maugham suggested as much, at least between competent and well-advised contracting parties: at 626.
[32] Care must be taken with these transactions. Often, it is true; the insiders provide loans on very favourable terms. But sometimes the terms are exploitative, and the risk is that they may then be held to amount to an unlawful return of capital: *Ridge Securities Ltd v IRC* [1964] 1 W.L.R. 479; *Progress Property Co Ltd v Moore* [2010] UKSC 55; [2011] 1 W.L.R. 1 SC.
[33] *Salomon v Salomon & Co Ltd* [1897] A.C. 22 HL. See above, para.2–1.

because the banks in turn need to seek investment funds from third parties) and from the capital markets ("direct financing", because the relationship is directly with the lender). Here, too, the terms of the debt security are individually negotiated, even if against industry models. Sizeable transactions may involve both types of debt. The initial debt finance for a major acquisition may, for example, be provided wholly by banks, often under a syndicated loan agreement[34] involving several banks and providing for a variety of types of senior and junior (or "mezzanine") debt, the terms "senior" and "junior" referring to the order in which the debt falls to be repaid (the ranking of their claims on the assets of the debtor).[35] The banks may, subsequently, offload that debt (in a wide variety of ways) to third parties so as to realise the value of the asset earlier than the debt's maturity date (i.e. capitalise the debt) or so as to shed some of the risk. On the company's side, sometimes this form of bank debt is too short-term and is provided on such financially unattractive terms that the company itself has a strong incentive to finance differently or to re-finance the bank loan as soon as possible.

Debts and "debt securities"

31–9 So far the distinction has been between small and large-scale loans, and single and multiple lenders. But lenders are likely to be persuaded to accept a lower rate of return if their loans are highly liquid. This is not to say that traditional loans cannot be transferred, as we shall see, but there is no organised secondary market for their transfer. Thus, as with shares, the company has an incentive to arrange for its debts, as "debt securities", to be traded on a secondary public market, so enabling a lender to liquidate its investment easily by selling it to a third party.[36] It follows that a company might make an offer of "debt securities" (analogous in many ways to "equity securities") on the public (retail or wholesale) markets, much like a company might offer a new issue of its equity securities (shares) so as to raise funds. It might also make similar issues privately. As with shares, public offers are strictly regulated; private offers less so. This is considered below, along with the different and rather more complicated structures used for different debt security issues, although otherwise many of the applicable rules are those which have already been dealt with in relation to shares.[37]

---

[34] With the various banks using either agency or trust structures to manage their relationship with each other: see below, paras 31–10 et seq.

[35] For a description of typical funding arrangements see FSA, *Private Equity: a discussion of risk and regulatory engagement*, DP 06/6, November 2006, paras 3.52 et seq.

[36] So, as with shares, the Stock Exchange can provide a primary market for the issuance of debt securities and a secondary market for trading in them.

[37] See above, Chs 24 and 25 and below, paras 31–17 et seq.

SINGLE AND MULTIPLE LENDERS

Single lenders

In the simplest of cases, the company borrows from a single lender. The loan contract between the parties will define their rights and obligations. As we will see later, their contract will undoubtedly include covenants restricting the company's power to act completely autonomously,[38] and may include terms providing for the debt to be secured against the company's assets, or for "equity-like" features (such as voting rights for the lender), or for conversion from debt to equity in defined circumstances.

31–10

The company may repeat this borrowing process as it grows, entering into sequential loans agreements with different lenders, with the general law then governing any competition between the lenders seeking to have their secured or unsecured loans repaid. The general law outcome is often varied by agreement between the lenders (a "subordination agreement"), although the limitations inherent in these subordination agreements should be noted: the borrower cannot agree with lenders that the general insolvency law rules will not apply to the distribution of its own assets, but that itself some other distribution will be effected; the lenders, by contrast, can agree amongst themselves to share their different insolvency entitlements in any way they wish. Thus a lender who might otherwise have had priority may agree with other lenders to be deferred; or a secured or unsecured lender may agree to take nothing until other lenders have been paid in full.[39] It may be wondered why lenders would agree to this, but it is relatively common for insiders (whether the company's directors or other members of the same corporate group) to agree to be subordinated so as to enable the company to attract further external financing, or at least to attract it on commercially acceptable terms.

This all works well for smaller scale financing needs, but if the company has more substantial needs, then it is likely to need to access a number of different lenders simultaneously. This can be achieved either by means of a syndicated loan or by the issue of marketable debt securities. The underlying contracts for such loans come in as many varieties as individual loans, with covenants and security interests as agreed by contract, but each must also of necessity be overlaid by some sort of organisational structure which enables the different lenders to co-ordinate their information and decision needs in relation to the borrower and, importantly, to control hold-out or independent-mover problems within the group. These problems are not unlike the various co-ordination problems which exist between shareholders.[40] As well, it will be in the interests of the lenders themselves that their chosen structure does not inhibit their rights to transfer their interests, although only debt securities are deliberately designed

---

[38] See below, paras 31–24 et seq.
[39] See below, para.32–12.
[40] See above, Ch.19.

as marketable securities. We discuss these transfer and governance features later, but first say a little more about the structures themselves.[41]

Syndicated loans

31–11   Syndicated loans are typically embodied in a single contract, signed by all parties, although usually put together by a lead bank or underwriter of the loan, known as the "arranger", "agent", or "lead lender".[42] This lender may put up a proportionally bigger share of the loan, or perform duties like dispersing cash flows amongst the other syndicate members, and other administrative tasks. But the syndicated lenders are explicitly not partners, and their interests are deliberately several, not joint, although, as perhaps one mark of the joint endeavour, their agreement is likely to provide for "no-action clauses" and for pari passu recovery should the borrower become insolvent,[43] thus denying any one lender a first-mover advantage if the debt looks risky.[44] As with all agreements involving multiple lenders, the lenders' own internal governance arrangements are often subject to decision by majority rule (as with shareholders), and to various exclusions of liability by the arranger: these are considered below.[45]

It can be seen even from this brief outline that syndicated loans are essentially scaled up versions of single bank loans (or loans from non-bank entities), and are likely to contain similar sorts of detailed protective covenants, although with the advantage that one lender is not required to carry the entire risk. As with single bank loans, it is also generally true that these transactions are not motivated by the lenders' desire to acquire marketable securities[46]; the lenders' interests may be transferable under general law provisions, and there is a good private market in such interests, but these lenders are quite likely to remain engaged in the deal for its full term.

Debt securities: distinguishing "bonds" and "stocks"

31–12   By contrast, where marketability of the underlying debt is a material consideration, the company usually attracts loans from multiple lenders, again typically financial institutions and specialist investors, by issuing either "bonds" (or "notes" or "commercial paper")[47] or "loan stock" (often labelled "debenture stock" if the loan is secured on a pool of assets, although neither term is a term of

---

[41] See L. Gullifer and J. Payne, *Corporate Finance Law: Principles and Policy*, 2nd edn (Oxford: Hart Publishing, 2015), Ch.8.

[42] On the related duties, see below, para.31–28.

[43] Assuming there is no pragmatic reason for some alternative explicit subordination agreement.

[44] See P. Rawlings, "The Management of Loan Syndicates and the Rights of Individual Lenders" (2009) 24 J.I.B.L.R. 179.

[45] See below, paras 31–28 and 31–30.

[46] And thus typically are not rated by credit rating agencies.

[47] The difference between the two used to be that bonds had longer maturities than notes or commercial paper, although it was never clear precisely where the line was drawn. Both terms are now used far more indiscriminately.

art, and both are often used more broadly).[48] Such issues are often tradeable on a public secondary market,[49] although this is not essential.[50] There was, historically, a fundamental structural difference between bonds and stock, although in modern practice both the structure and co-ordination problems turn out to be rather similar.

Bonds (or notes) are, in theory, individual debt obligations owed by the company to each of the bondholders, whether they are registered holders or holders of bearer bonds,[51] with the latter being far more common. Historically, each individual lender (bondholder) purchased a number of bonds from the company, denominated in appropriate amounts, much as shareholders purchase equity interests by buying different numbers of issued shares. In the same way, too, each bondholder became the legal owner of its own bonds.[52] Co-ordination problems between the bondholders were, and are still, typically resolved by appointing an appropriately authorised agent, or, more commonly, a trustee for the bondholders,[53] and also requiring, in certain circumstances, majority votes of the bondholders themselves.[54] However, as with shares, bonds are now typically held via an intermediary, whether or not they are traded on public markets. So a "global note" is issued by the company to the intermediary (representing the debt due from the company to the intermediary), and the intermediary, as legal owner (of either a registered or a bearer bond, again with the latter being more common, except when intended for the US market) holds its interest on trust for a number—often a large number—of account holders.[55] The intermediary can then perform a number of important services for the account holders, including holding any security for the bond, and, at least from a functional perspective, the resulting organisational structure ends up being similar to that operating with loan stock.[56]

Loan or debenture stock, by contrast, consists of a single debt obligation issued by the company and typically held by a trustee on behalf of the various stockholders.[57] If the loan is secured, the trustee will also hold the security on trust. The stockholders therefore have only an equitable interest in the debt

---

[48] As already noted, the definition of "debenture" in s.738 includes both "bonds" and "debenture stock".

[49] In the future, all traded securities will be obliged to be either dematerialised, or immobilised and held through intermediaries, in order to improve the efficiency and integrity of the market: Regulation (EU) No.909/2014, recital 11 and arts 3 and 79 (form 1 January 2023 for new issues after that date, and from 1 January 2025 for all transferable securities).

[50] Some would have the necessary characteristics, but nevertheless be traded "over the counter" ("OTC").

[51] See above, Ch.24, for the equivalent terminology in relation to shares.

[52] This was essential if the bond was a bearer bond, and thus intended to be a negotiable instrument.

[53] Although then there is the nice question of what, precisely, is the subject-matter of the trust: see L. Gullifer and J. Payne, *Corporate Finance Law: Principles and Policy*, 2nd edn (Oxford: Hart Publishing, 2015), pp.383–390.

[54] See below, para.31–30.

[55] For details of the transfer of intermediated securities, see Ch.27.

[56] See below, para.31–14.

[57] Alternatively, the company can create loan stock by deed poll, i.e. by unilaterally executing a deed which promises to pay those registered as stockholders, which is enforceable by anyone who is a stockholder. This structure is less common, usually confined to larger issues with few holders and no active market.

(secured or not), held as tenants in common in proportion to the amount of the debt they own (with no limit on how the fractions are denominated, in contrast to bonds). Even as beneficiaries under the trust, however, the stockholders are nevertheless entered on the company's register of debenture holders (in contrast to equitable owners of shares, who are not recognised in the company's register of shareholders[58]). These debenture holders receive a certificate (if the stock is certificated); if it is dematerialised, a similar register is kept in the CREST system.[59] It follows that, unlike the largely meaningless distinction between "shares" and "stock",[60] the similar distinction between "debentures" and "debenture stock" is far from meaningless and debenture stock has considerable practical advantages. Thus, in this structure, the stockholders have all the advantages of a protective trustee structure, but with the (relatively few) disadvantages of only having equitable interests in the underlying asset.[61]

31–13   One clear difference between bonds (and notes) and stock is that the former can be transferred only in complete units, whereas stock is expressed in terms of an amount of money and may be transferred in any fraction of that amount. This is an attribute of the transferable interest being merely a fractional equitable interest in a debt. Thus, if a public company wishes to raise £1 million, it could create £1 million of debenture stock, and then issue it[62] to subscribers in such amounts as each wants,[63] giving each a single certificate of an appropriate denomination,[64] and each subscriber can in turn sell and transfer any fraction of it. By contrast, the company could issue a series of bonds, say £1, £10, £100, or £1,000 bonds, each representing a separate debt totalling in aggregate £1 million. This would result in an enormous bundle of paper for the company to process and subscribers to handle. And, if a subscriber for a single bond wanted to sell half of it, that would not be possible at law, only in equity.

Debt securities: trustees for the bondholders or stockholders

31–14   As we have already noted, it is now almost invariable practice for an issue of marketable loans to interpose a trustee, normally a trust corporation,[65] between the company and the bondholders or stockholders. The loan contract is then

---

[58] 2006 Act s.126.

[59] See above, para.27–12.

[60] See above, para.23–11 where it is noted that conversion of shares into stock is no longer permitted.

[61] Made especially few because the competing interests are also typically equitable, e.g. sale of stock by a stockholder is sale of an equitable interest, so does not raise the spectre of competition with a bona fide purchaser for value. But also see *Re Dunderland Iron Ore Co* [1909] 1 Ch. 446, 452, and noted below, fn.67.

[62] Debenture stock can be created de novo; there is no need to create debentures and then to convert them to debenture stock as there is in relation to shares and stock.

[63] In practice there is likely to be a prescribed minimum amount which can be subscribed for or transferred. If this minimum amount is equal to the nominal value of any bonds which the company might otherwise issue, then, of course, this particular advantage of debenture stock disappears.

[64] A simple document of one sheet, similar to a share certificate, in contrast with a bond which will, unless there is a trust deed (see below, and now almost invariably the case), have to set out all the terms.

[65] Formerly it was common for banks to undertake this work but they have tended to fight shy of it since *Re Dorman Long & Co* [1934] Ch. 635 drew attention to the conflict of interest and duty which

between the company and the trustee, and any security over the company's assets can be made out in favour of the trustees, who hold it on trust for the benefit of the debt security holders. Such an arrangement has many advantages.

First, it greatly simplifies the security arrangements.[66] A legal mortgage can be vested in the trustees, on trust for the debt security holders, and the trustees retain custody of the title deeds; a charge can be granted in favour of the trustees, and the rights under the charge document exercised by the trustees for the benefit of the debt security holders. This is difficult, sometimes impossible, with multiple parties.

Secondly, the primary enforcement of the loan (and any security) will be between the company and the trustees, being the parties to the loan agreement.[67] A practical side-effect of this is to impose equality amongst the debt security holders, although their own governance arrangements generally reinforce that.[68]

Finally, it will provide a single trustee corporation or a small body of persons charged with the duty of monitoring the debt security holders' interests and of intervening if they are in jeopardy. This is obviously far more satisfactory than leaving it to a widely dispersed class of investors, each of whom may lack the skill, interest and financial resources required to take action alone.[69] It will also be possible, by the trust deed, to impose on the trustee company or its directors additional obligations, regarding the submission of information and the like, which might not otherwise be practicable.[70] Similarly, the trustees can be empowered to convene meetings of the holders in order to acquaint them with the position and to obtain their instructions.

ISSUE OF DEBT SECURITIES

Private issues

The act of issuing debt securities (assuming no public offer) is not much regulated by the Act. The one significant provision is to the effect that a contract with a company to "take up and pay for debentures" is specifically enforceable, as noted earlier.[71] Otherwise, in the absence of a public offer, the Act is notable

31–15

---

might arise when the bank was both a creditor in its own right and a trustee. Today, therefore, the duties are generally undertaken by other professional trust corporations.

[66] Such securities are, nevertheless, subject to all the rules considered in Ch.32. Note that it is uncommon for major publicly traded companies today to give security over their assets in public issues of debentures.

[67] *Re Uruguay Central and Hygueritas Railway Co of Monte Video* (1879) 11 Ch. D. 372; *Re Dunderland Iron Ore Co Ltd* [1909] 1 Ch. 446. Theoretically, although there are trustees, an individual security-holder could take steps to enforce the security (using the *Vandepitte* procedure: *Vandepitte v Preferred Accident Insurance Corp of New York* [1933] A.C. 70 PC), but trust deeds typically contain a "no action" clause. And, in other respects, the security-holder will not be regarded as a creditor of the borrowing company, so, for example, cannot petition for its winding up if there is default: *Re Dunderland Iron Ore Co* [1909] 1 Ch. 446, 452.

[68] See below, para.31–30.

[69] Although the governance arrangements typically prohibit this in any event: see below, para.31–30.

[70] See the facts which gave rise to the litigation in *New Zealand Guardian Trust Co Ltd v Brooks* [1995] 1 W.L.R. 96 PC.

[71] 2006 Act s.740. See above, para.31–7.

for the absence of regulation of the issuing process, assuming instead that debenture holders will themselves make appropriate provision for their own protection.[72]

In addition, and unlike the rule applying to shares,[73] there is no rule in the Act, even for public companies, requiring the authorisation of either the shareholders or the existing debt security holders for a new issue of debt, although this matter may well be one of the matters regulated in the trust deed of the existing debt securities.[74] In some ways this is surprising, since a large increase in the company's debt could have a significant impact—positive or negative depending on whether the venture in which the new funds are embarked is successful—on the prospects of the shareholders and debt holders.[75] Nor does the Act create pre-emption rights[76] on an issue of debt, probably because the rights of the existing debt holders are not affected by a new issue, although their value might be, since a company seen to be overburdening itself with debt would cause the market value of its existing debt instruments to fall. Again, however, this matter can be dealt with in the trust deed governing the existing debt.

Finally, since debt does not count as legal capital, the rules relating to issue at a discount and to the quality of the consideration received, which apply to shares,[77] are not extended to debt generally or debt securities in particular.[78] For the same reason, the distribution and capital maintenance rules[79] do not apply to loans, so that interest may (normally must) be paid on loans even though no profits have been earned, and debts may be freely repurchased by the company (subject to the loan terms themselves), assuming in both cases it has the cash to do so. The only specific statutory provision in this area in fact facilitates repurchases of debt by providing that redeemed debt securities may be reissued with their original priority, rather than cancelled, unless the company's articles contain provisions to the contrary or the company in some other way resolved to cancel them.[80]

31–16 Of course, the general duties of directors will still apply to their decisions relating to the issue of debt securities, even, perhaps especially, in the absence of specific statutory regulation in the area.

Although all this is left unregulated, the Act does contain a number of largely administrative provisions relating to the issue of debt securities. Section 741 requires companies to register an allotment of debentures with the Registrar of companies, as is required for shares, so that the existence of the debentures is public knowledge (unless the debentures are issued as bearer debentures). A

---

[72] See below, paras 31–24 et seq.

[73] See para.24–4.

[74] See below, at para.31–26.

[75] Even the "Class 1 transaction" rule of the Listing Rules, requiring shareholder consent, does not apply to an issue of securities, unless the transaction involves the acquisition or disposal of a fixed asset of the company or a subsidiary: LR 10.1.3.

[76] On pre-emption rights for shareholders see para.24–6.

[77] See Ch.11.

[78] *Re Anglo-Danubian Steam Navigation and Colliery Co* (1875) L.R. 20 Eq. 339.

[79] See Chs 12 and 13.

[80] 2006 Act s.752. On treasury shares, see para.13–24. Note also s.753 which is designed to remove the technical difficulties revealed in *Re Russian Petroleum Co* [1907] 2 Ch. 540 CA when a company secures its overdraft on current account by depositing with the bank a debenture for a fixed amount.

company is not obliged itself to keep a register of debenture holders, but, if it does, it must locate it and make it available for inspection by debenture holders and members of the public in the same way as the register of shareholders.[81] This includes the power, applicable also to the share register, to apply to the court for an order not to comply with the request for inspection.[82] Probably more important in practice is the provision which entitles a debenture-holder to be provided at any time (on payment of the appropriate fee) with a copy of the trust deed on which the debentures are secured, if, as is normal, there is such a trust.[83] This provision is perhaps the functional equivalent of the public availability of the articles in the case of shareholders.

Finally, as we shall see in Ch.32, where debentures are secured against the company's assets, it is often necessary to register those security instruments at Companies House, on pain of invalidity against the liquidator on the company's insolvency.

Public issues of debt securities

Matters change radically, however, if there is a public offer of debt securities. In that case, much of the law discussed in Ch.25 will be applicable. As with shares, this is to ensure that those buying debt securities on the primary or secondary markets have the appropriate information necessary to assess the risks. One difference, though, is that it might be thought that the risks are inherently smaller with debt securities, since the holder of a debt has the ultimate right to sue for the sum due under the debt, and is also commonly protected by powerful contractual and perhaps proprietary provisions to assist on that front, whereas the holder of the share has a mere expectation of benefit and therefore perhaps requires a wider range of information upon which assess the relevant risks. This is perhaps the explanation for the hierarchy of information requirements,[84] which puts equity securities ahead of debt securities issued to the retail market, and then debt securities issued to the wholesale market,[85] and leaves the private syndicated loan market completely unregulated by the Act.

31–17

The prohibition on private companies offering their shares to the public extends to a public offer of any securities, including debt securities.[86] If public companies do offer their debt securities to the public, the required disclosure varies depending upon whether the offer is general, or is, on the other hand, either explicitly directed only to sophisticated ("qualified") investors or is of such large denomination (i.e. at least €100,000) that it can be assumed to be addressed only

---

[81] 2006 Act ss.743–748. Less detail is required in the register of debentures, if there is one, than in the share register. On the share register, see para.24–21.

[82] 2006 Act s.745.

[83] 2006 Act s.749. Non-compliance is a criminal offence on the part of any officer of the company in default.

[84] See Commission Regulation (EC) No.809/2004 art.21(2).

[85] Compare Commission Regulation (EC) No.809/2004 Annexes I, IV and V.

[86] 2006 Act s.755. See para.24–2.

to such a sophisticated ("wholesale") market.[87] And if the issued securities are then to be traded on a secondary market, as would be typical for reasons already discussed,[88] the continuing disclosure rules again depend upon the sophistication of the market participants, with securities listed on the Professional Securities Market ("PSM") attracting a less onerous regime.[89]

It might be thought that if companies already have listed shares, then they would automatically opt for the more onerous regime, since it opens the debt issue to wider markets and the companies are already subject to onerous disclosure regimes in respect of their equity securities. However, the specific disclosure required for a new issue is substantial, and debt security issues are typically put together in quick order, so companies will make use of whatever exemptions are possible, while still ensuring they have access to the most fruitful markets.[90]

31–18   All this may change quite substantially in the near future, however, with the European Commission proposing to remove these heavy-weight debt exemptions, in the interest of opening up this exclusive market to smaller investors,[91] and achieving this by removing the incentive to create large-denomination debt securities, and at the same time putting in place an appropriate information regime for general investors.

Otherwise, many of the rules on public issues of shares also apply equally to public issues of debt securities, and for similar reasons. One notable difference however, is that there is no limitation on the payment of underwriting commissions, and an allotment may be made no matter how small a response there is to the offer.[92] This is no doubt because the rights of the debenture-holder are comprehensively specified in the debt contract, whereas with shares, the expected returns may depend very materially on these two features.

Finally, note that an issue may begin as a private issue to an underwriter or other financial institution, and those institutions may then themselves provide the necessary disclosure to enable the securities to be traded on either wholesale or retail markets.

---

[87] See Prospectus Directive art.3(2)(d) (no prospectus on a public offer of heavy-weight debt) and art.7(2)(b) (less detail in a prospectus if one is nevertheless needed on an introduction to trading). FSMA 2000 ss.102B, 86(1), (1A), (1B).

[88] Often bonds are traded over the counter ("OTC"), even though the bonds are listed. Many institutional investors are not permitted to invest in unlisted securities, so listing sometimes simply provides a necessary quality kitemark (as backed by the requirements of the LSE for listing).

[89] This is the exchange-regulated market, requiring only listing particulars (unless the securities are initially offered to the public generally). The LSE's regulated market for debt securities is the Gilt-Edged and Fixed Interest Market (sometimes also referred to as the Main Market, as is the analogous market for equity securities, although all debt security listings are "Standard", not "Premium"; for this market, a full Prospectus Directive prospectus is required: see above, para.25–17).

[90] This is unless the passporting of the prospectus to other EEA Member States is important: see Prospectus Directive 2003/71/EC art.17 and above, para.25–44.

[91] In November 2015, the European Commission proposed replacing the Prospectus Directive (an odd Directive in any event) with a Prospectus Regulation as part of its move to create a "capital markets union" within the EU: see above, para.25–10. The proposal is to remove the heavy-weight debt exemptions in PD arts 3(2)(d) and 7(2)(b), so that a prospectus is required for a public offer and more burdensome disclosure is required for an introduction to trading.

[92] i.e. for marketable loans, there is no equivalent of CA 2006 ss.552 and 578.

Special rules: covered bonds

A further means of regulation is focused not broadly on all public offers, but more **31–19** narrowly on specifically defined types of transactions. We see this in evidence in the regulatory regime which has been put in place relating to financial collateral,[93] and to the credit derivatives market.[94] Similarly, specific regulation has been implemented related to covered bonds, in the form of the Regulated Covered Bonds Regulations 2008.[95] A "covered" bond (sometimes called a "structured covered bond") is a particular form of bond which is payable by the issuer (typically a bank or building society[96]), but is also backed by a specific pool of high quality assets, in the UK held by a special purpose vehicle ("SPV"), so that the assets are ring-fenced with the result that, if the issuer becomes insolvent, the repayments on the bond can continue to be made by recourse to the those assets, and in priority to the issuer's general creditors.

The regulations are designed to ensure that the asset pool is high quality[97]; that its value is maintained throughout the life of the bond at a high enough figure to ensure that the bond is 8 per cent "over-collateralised",[98] thus guaranteeing sufficient resources to cover realisation costs and bondholder repayment in full; that there is regulated oversight of the collateral by the issuer and the "Asset Pool Monitor" (analogous to an external auditor)[99]; and that there is consistent and frequent reporting to investors. These additional reporting and oversight requirements aside, a covered bond differs from a normal securitisation principally in that the issuer of a covered bond remains liable to the bondholder, whereas a securitisation is typically non-recourse; and the pool of assets associated with a covered bond is regulated so that the issue is compulsorily "over-collateralised".

What has this structure achieved? From the company's point of view, it has turned (illiquid) mortgages into cash which it can use to expand its business. And, conversely, from the investors' point of view, they have made a loan to the company but of a highly secure type. Provided the SPV has been set up in such a way that the assets purchased by the SPV cannot be clawed back by the issuer in the latter's liquidation and provided the issuer is obliged to maintain the quality and value of the mortgages held by the SPV, the note-holders can remain unconcerned about such an event because their security will remain intact. This is

---

[93] For an informative description, see L. Gullifer, "What Should We Do About Financial Collateral?" (2012) C.L.P. 1.

[94] See S. Firth, *Derivatives Law and Practice* (London, Sweet & Maxwell, 2012); A. Hudson, *The Law on Financial Derivatives*, 5th edn (London, Sweet & Maxwell, 2012).

[95] SI 2008/346, as amended by SI 2008/1714, SI 2011/2859 and SI 2012/2977. Also see *Review of the UK's Regulatory Framework for Covered Bonds*—FSA and HM Treasury Consultation Paper, April 2011 (Consultation Paper).

[96] There are, in 2015, only 12 UK issuers registered to issue covered bonds.

[97] Public sector or residential or commercial mortgages, with the register indicating the class or the mixture, which cannot then be changed over the life of the bond. In order to maintain investor confidence, securitisations do not constitute eligible collateral.

[98] With the FCA having the right to impose over-collateralisation requirements on a case-by-case basis.

[99] 2008 Regulations reg.17A.

why the bond is "covered".[100] Overall, the issuer is incurring debt through the covered bond in order to further the business of itself making secured loans to others, its business model turning on its ability to borrow money through the bond at a lower rate of interest than it itself charges when lending to others.

31–20 It will be apparent that the above structure can be created by contract and so it may be wondered how the need for the Regulations arises. Such bonds were not brought into existence by the Regulations, though they are a relatively recent development in the UK. In fact, the purpose of the Regulations is to create a more ready market for covered bonds rather than to bring them into existence. The market for them is restricted, in the absence of the Regulations, by provisions in EU law and, equally, EU law indicates the way forward to the expansion of that market. In particular, the UCITS (undertakings for collective investment in transferable securities) Directive 2009/65/EC (as amended by Directive 2014/91/EU), which governs what are or used to be referred to in the UK as unit and investment trusts, contains the prudential rule that such a body may invest no more than 5 per cent of its assets in the securities issued by the same body.[101] However, this limit may be raised to 25 per cent in the case of bonds meeting certain quality standards, set out in the Directive.[102] A similar restriction on investment by insurance companies and relaxation of that restriction in the case of UCITS-compliant bonds are also to be found in EU law. Finally, UCITS-compliant bonds are less heavily weighted in banks' risk profiles than non-compliant bonds.[103]

However, producing a UCITS-compliant covered bond requires the use of legislation. Article 52(4) of the UCITS Directive requires (a) that the issuer (which may only be a "credit institution", i.e. a bank or similar deposit-taking body) be "subject by law to special public supervision designed to protect bond-holders"—presumably additional to the supervision to which it is already subject by virtue of being a bank—and (b) that the law control the assets in which the proceeds of the bond may be invested and ensure the priority of the investors' claims in the event of the insolvency of the issuer. It is perfectly lawful to continue to issue covered bonds which do not comply with the new regulations, but in this case they will not benefit from the additional market possibilities, noted above. The Regulations implement the above principles by creating

---

[100] The structure would be even simpler if the notes were issued by the SPV and the investors' money paid directly to it. However, investors may have good reasons for preferring the loans to be made to the issuer, so that the investors have the benefit of both the issuer's promise to repay and the claim on the asset pool held by the SPV. Where the note or bond is issued by the SPV itself, the arrangement is referred to as an "asset-backed" or "mortgage-backed" security, but is non-recourse and does not count as a covered bond. Equally, in the UK, if the issuer merely secures the bond against a ring-fenced pool of its own assets, without transferring them to a SPV, the arrangement is certainly a secured bond (assuming the security is properly registered), but it cannot be a covered bond in the UK (although other European jurisdictions have more relaxed rules in this regard, adopting what is called an "integrated model" covered bond), but the UK rules are designed to be as protective as possible to attract the greatest number of market participants.

[101] Directive 2009/65/EC, as amended, art.52(1)(a).

[102] 2009 Directive art.52(4).

[103] HM Treasury and FSA, *Proposals for a UK Recognised Covered Bonds regulatory framework*, July 2007, para.1.7. The third advantage, as with the other two, accrues, of course, to a bank which purchases the bonds, not to the issuer bank.

registers of "recognised" issuers and issues of covered bonds, access to which is controlled by the Financial Conduct Authority.[104] An applicant must have its registered office in the UK and be a body already authorised under the Financial Services and Markets Act to carry on activities as a deposit-taker and the FCA must also be satisfied that the applicant issuer and the owner of the asset pool (i.e. the SPV), will comply with the requirements imposed on them by the Regulations.[105] To claim to issue recognised covered bonds without issuer and issue being on the registers is a breach of the Regulations and makes the issuer liable at a minimum to monetary penalties imposed by the FCA.[106]

The proceeds of the issue may be used only to acquire "eligible assets" which term goes beyond mortgages on residential or commercial real property to include public sector loans, loans to a registered social landlord which may be secured on the income arising from letting of the properties as well as loans secured on the properties themselves, and loans to project companies under certain types of public-private partnerships. The property must be situated in any EEA State or in one of a limited number of other designated States.[107] Those assets must be transferred to an asset pool which must be capable throughout the life of the bond of covering the bond-holders' claims and the costs of administering the pool.[108] Priority is given to the claims of bond-holders in insolvency of the owner.[109]

TRANSFER OF DEBTS AND DEBT SECURITIES

Transfer of simple debts

Although the rules on legal capital do not stand in the way of re-purchase by a company of its debts, unlike its shares,[110] it may well be financially extremely inconvenient for the company to do so (or indeed it may be prohibited by the lender[111]). However, it is normally possible for the lender to find liquidity in other

31–21

---

[104] The Regulated Covered Bonds Regulations 2008/346 (as amended) Pts 2 and 3.

[105] 2008 Regulations reg.9. The owner is not an applicant for registration, though various obligations are laid on it by the Regulations. The proposals (above, fn.103) did not envisage a requirement for UK registration, but in this and in a number of other respects, the "credit crunch" of 2007 caused the Regulations to be more tightly drawn.

[106] The enforcement powers of the FCA are set out in Pt 7 of the Regulations and follow those normally available to it. See para.25–41.

[107] 2008 Regulations reg.2. Partly, this definition is achieved by cross-reference to art.129 Regulation (EU) 575/2013 (the requirements regulation), which determines which assets may be used to collateralise a covered bond, if a bank investing in such bonds is to benefit from a lower risk rating. However, a recognised covered bond is not limited to such collateral, though an issuer which uses the wider type of collateral will not be able to confer the benefit of the lower risk rating on banks which purchase the bonds.

[108] 2008 Regulations reg.17(2), imposing the obligation on the issuer; reg.23(1) imposing it on the owner of the asset pool.

[109] 2008 Regulations reg.27. The proposals (above, fn.103) envisaged an alternative model (the "integrated" model) in which the assets remained with the issuer but were ring-fenced. Insisting on a SPV made the priority issue somewhat simpler to deal with.

[110] See paras 13–2 et seq. The capital maintenance rules do not apply to debt because debt is not legal capital: above, para.11–1.

[111] *Knightsbridge Estates Ltd v Byrne* [1940] A.C. 613 HL.

ways. There may be a private market in the loans, and indeed many banks lending to private equity funds aim to have only a small, if any, proportion of the loans made on their books six months after the transaction completes.[112] These loans can be transferred by outright sales, such as invoice discounting to a financier (of distressed debt if the rating of the debt security is poor), or by securitisation transactions (real or synthetic),[113] or in other ways.

The ability to transfer debt in this way helps persuade lenders to agree to provide finance, but, on the other side, it may also tempt lenders to worry less about the repayment risks, knowing that they can shift those risks to third parties. The financial crisis in 2008 presents clear evidence of this. Where debt securities are traded on public markets, the compulsory disclosure rules are designed to minimise those risks for secondary purchasers, although their effectiveness in this regard might be questioned; otherwise, as elsewhere, the rule is, "buyer beware".

Transfer of debt securities

31-22 Turning from transfers of debt generally to transfers of debt securities, these can be absolute (whether at law or in equity) or by way of security interest (see Ch.32, below). We do not say a great deal about the legal rules here,[114] since the legislation clearly assumes that debt securities will be transferred in much the same way as shares, and so reference can simply be made to the discussion in Ch.27. Hence, initial allotments and subsequent transfers of registered debt securities must be registered (s.741, as s.554 for shares; and s.771 for transfers of both), and the register must be open for inspection with the right to obtain copies of it (ss.743, 744); as with shares, the bond documentation or certificates of debenture stock must be issued by the company to the holder within two months, unless the issue is to a clearing house or its nominee (ss.769, 776, 778, although

---

[112] FSA, above, fn.35, paras 3.67 et seq.

[113] The detail is not examined in this book, but the basic structure is that the bank sells the securities to a SPV, so that the bank obtains immediate cash (inevitably discounted) in return for the debts which were due for repayment in the future, and the sale also ensures that those debts are no longer on the bank's balance sheet. The SPV then in turn issues debt securities to third parties on the basis that their repayment is to come exclusively from the original assets (the debts) now held by the SPV (with the securities repayable on the basis of this non-recourse liability being, more positively, described as "asset-backed securities" ("ABS")). This basic structure has been developed in various ways. One of these is "synthetic securitisation", where the debts are not sold to the SPV, but the SPV instead makes a loan to the bank, secured on the pool of debts, and then the SPV, as before, issues securities to fund that loan. It is crucial to the success of this synthetic structure that the SPV can easily enforce its security against the pooled assets, and to that end the IA 1986 ss.72B–72D enables such floating charge security holders to continue to be able to appoint an administrative receiver provided the debt is over £50 million, and despite the abolition of administrative receivers generally in the Enterprise Act 2002 (see below, para.32–34). The credit rating of these bonds then depends upon the quality of the secured assets, not the overall credit rating of the company.

[114] Although there are some difficult conceptual problems, especially with transfer of intermediated securities: see L. Gullifer and J. Payne, *Corporate Finance Law: Principles and Policy*, 2nd edn (Oxford: Hart Publishing, 2015), Ch.9. As a result, the trust deeds of debenture stock issues or the documentation associated with bond issues typically provide explicitly that the holder takes free of all equities affecting the current and previous holders (including the account holder for bond issues). The effectiveness of these provisions is not guaranteed, and clear wording is essential: see *Re Kaupthing Singer and Friedlander Ltd; Newcastle Building Society v Mill* [2009] EWHC 740 (Ch).

for debt securities there is no equivalent of s.768 providing for the certificate to be evidence of title); and, as with shares, the transfer, unless by operation of law or by CREST, must be in writing using an appropriate instrument of transfer (s.770). Equally, the Uncertificated Securities Regulations 2001 (as amended) uses the word "securities", and so permits the transfer of title to debt securities held in uncertificated form.[115] And in relation to these debt securities held in uncertificated form, the Operator is now required to maintain in the UK a register of the names and addresses of those holding debt securities in this way, together with a statement of the size of the individual holdings.[116]

Transferees could also be faced with problems, similar to those in relation to shares, regarding equitable and legal ownership of debt securities and the priority of competing transferees. On general principles relating to assignments of choses in action, a transfer of legal title to a debt security should be an equitable assignment only, until it becomes a legal assignment when the company receives notice of it. But, as with shares, and given that registration is compulsory under the 2006 Act, it seems the legal title should pass from transferor to transferee only at the later date of actual registration. But it is now usually only the trustee for the debt security holders who has legal title to the debt. The question is different, of course, and can involve nice matters of law, where the transferor's interest is only ever equitable, as it invariably is with debenture stock (notwithstanding that the holders must be registered) and also with other intermediated securities, as is now common practice with most marketable debt securities.[117]

Other differences flow from the fact that, whereas the rights of shareholders depend mainly on the provision of the company's articles, which will have been drafted in the interests of the company, those of debt holders depend upon the terms of a contract between lender and borrower and its terms will have to be acceptable to the lender as well as the borrower. Some debt securities will, like shares, include non-assignability clauses, or clauses restricting assignment subject to conditions.[118] This might seem an odd clause to include in a debt, but it will protect the corporate debtor from losing potentially valuable post-assignment rights of set-off against the creditor, or protect against possible transfer of the debt to a third party who may not be quite so generous in deciding when and how to enforce the agreed debt covenants. The question then arises, precisely as with shares, whether a purported assignment in breach of the anti-assignment clause is effective to give the assignee any rights at all. The answer, as with shares, depends upon the precise terms of the clause, but the analysis can be difficult.[119]

---

[115] Reg.19 and the definition of "security" in reg.3(1). See generally Ch.27, above.

[116] Uncertificated Securities Regulations 2001 reg.22(3). If the terms of issue of the debentures require the company to maintain a register of holders in the UK, then this rule still applies but the company's register reflects that of the Operator: reg.22(1) and (2).

[117] The details are not discussed here, but the difficult issues of analysis are well described in L. Gullifer and J. Payne, *Corporate Finance Law: Principles and Policy*, 2nd edn (Oxford: Hart Publishing, 2015), Ch.9.

[118] In *Barbados Trust Co Ltd v Bank of Zambia* [2007] EWCA Civ 148, where consent of the debtor was required, such consent not to be unreasonably withheld.

[119] See *Barbados Trust Co Ltd v Bank of Zambia* [2007] EWCA Civ 148; *Linden Gardens Trust Ltd v Lenesta Sludge Disposal Ltd* [1994] 1 A.C. 85; *Morris v Royal Bank of Scotland Plc* unreported 3 July 2015 No. HC-2014-001910 Norris J; R. Goode, "Inalienable Rights?" (1979) 42 M.L.R. 553; M.

31-23 With marketable debt securities, by contrast, there will be no problems arising from restrictions on transferability or from a company's lien; debt securities will invariably provide that the money expressed to be secured will be paid, and that the debt securities are transferable, free from any equities or claims between the company and the original or any intermediate holder.[120] It is possible that the terms of issue of the debt securities will be inconsistent with their being held in uncertificated form, in which case they will need to be altered if the company wishes to make this form of holding debt securities available.[121] The Regulations do not provide a simple shortcut to the necessary amendments, as they do in the case of shares, but they do something to encourage trustees to agree to such amendments without holding a meeting of the debt security holders. A trustee for debt security holders is not to be chargeable with breach of trust by reason only of his assenting to changes in the trust deed necessary to enable the debt security holders to hold the debt securities in uncertificated form or to transfer them or exercise any rights attached to them electronically.[122]

The great contrast, however, between debt and equity securities is that debt securities secured by charges on the company's property throw up problems regarding the priority between conflicting charges. These problems are dealt with in the next chapter.

PROTECTIVE GOVERNANCE REGIMES IN DEBTS

General

31-24 The terms on which debt financing is agreed will depend upon the risk-reward calculations between the lender and borrower. Higher interest rates and greater restrictions on the debtor's autonomy, as well as proprietary security, are typical if the risk is high. As well, where there are multiple lenders, the lending parties need to put in place co-ordination rules. These aspects are considered briefly; they are not peculiar to companies.

Bridge, "The Nature of Assignment and Non-Assignment Clauses" (2016) 132 L.Q.R. 47; L. Gullifer and J. Payne, *Corporate Finance Law: Principles and Policy*, 2nd edn (Oxford: Hart Publishing, 2015), pp.434–443.

[120] Without this, debenture holders and their transferees would be in grave danger, for a debenture, unless in bearer form and thus a negotiable instrument (*Bechuanaland Exploration Co v London Trading Bank Ltd* [1898] 2 Q.B. 658), would, as a chose in action, be transferable only subject to the state of the account between the company and the transferor. As stressed in Ch.27, neither shares (unless in the form of share warrants to bearer) nor debentures (unless bearer bonds) are negotiable instruments like bills of exchange. Although CARD (above, para.25–15) requires listed shares and debt securities to be "freely negotiable" (arts 46 and 60) this is interpreted as "freely transferable" and not as prescribing that they must be "negotiable instruments" in full sense.

[121] See Ch.27, above.

[122] 2008 Regulations reg.40(2), provided notice is given to the holders at least 30 days before the changes become effective.

Defining repayment terms

A debt security issued by a company (or indeed any debt) is primarily a matter of **31–25** contract between lender and company. The legislature does not specify one, or even a number, of forms that the debt security must take, any more than it does with shares. Nor, however, does it even provide any equivalent of the model articles. It is thus difficult to describe a "typical" debt security. However, the security will normally have, unlike a share, an end-date, i.e. a point at which the amount still outstanding has to be repaid (its "maturity date")—though it is possible to make the loan totally irredeemable (s.739). That maturity date can be set as the parties wish, but may be quite long, for example, 40 years. The instrument also typically requires the amount lent to be repaid in regular instalments over the life of the loan (in which case it is called "amortising" debt), although it is also possible for the parties to provide that nothing needs to be repaid either until maturity (which is unlikely in the case of long maturities, unless the loan is backed by very high quality assets) or only after a considerable period of time has passed (say, eight to ten years), at which point the amount becomes repayable which would have been paid over this period through a normal amortisation arrangement. Such debt is sometimes called "bullet" debt, perhaps because of its likely impact on the borrower.[123]

The instrument will normally provide for the periodic payment of a fixed rate of interest at fixed points in time, but there is no reason why the interest rate so specified should not vary (provided there is a clear mechanism for working out what it is at any one time) nor, as we have seen, why interest should not be "rolled up" and be payable at a later date (sometimes on the maturity of the loan). In such a case the lender earns a return by buying the security at a discount to its face (or nominal or principal) value (i.e. the amount the company promises to repay) and takes the return as a capital gain rather than income, but only at maturity or, if the price of security in the market rises, upon sale to a third party.

The lender may have the right to recall or the borrower to repay the loan ahead of the repayment schedule,[124] or they may be specifically prohibited from so doing. Section 739 recognises that the security may be made irredeemable by the borrower, or redeemable only in certain circumstances, "any rule of equity to the contrary notwithstanding". This removes any doubt about the validity of such a restriction.[125]

---

[123] Where such debt is part of a private equity transaction, it is a strong candidate for early re-financing.

[124] And, for example, bank overdrafts are typically repayable on demand and regardless of breach (unless the facility agreement provides otherwise), with the bank not required to refrain from making a demand simply because it will tip the company into insolvency: *Williams and Glyn's Bank Ltd v Barnes* [1981] Com. L.R. 205.

[125] See above, para.31–7.

Protecting the debt holder against the borrower's possible default

31–26 None of the above clauses provide the lender with ongoing reassurance that the borrower remains able to repay the debt. Accordingly, it is common to insert a variety of covenants in the loan documentation with this objective in mind. Through such covenants, lenders become part of the corporate governance structure of the company, and may have a far more significant impact on management than the shareholders if the company is near to breaching its loan covenants.

Of course, the extent to which lenders are able to insert such covenants in their loans depends upon the level of competition in the market for such loans. For a period in the early 2000s up until the middle of 2007, competition among banks for the opportunity to fund private equity buy-outs was so great that "covenant-light" loans became common, i.e. bank loans with little by way of restrictive covenants inserted. In more normal circumstances, however, substantial loans are typically issued subject to important constraints on management.[126]

The best protection is proprietary security. That is discussed in the next chapter. If the lender does not have the bargaining power to insist on security, or if the company has no further assets over which security might be granted, then alternative contractual protections become increasingly important. They are, however, typically included even when security is taken.

31–27 Loan covenants typically require the borrowing company to provide the lender with periodic accounting information, perhaps including credit ratings, to conduct its operations so as to maintain pre-determined financial ratios between assets and liabilities, and to refrain from certain defined acts or activities, or at least refrain from them without the prior consent of the lender. The list of prohibitions typically includes disposing of substantial assets, changing the primary business activities of the company, taking on additional loans, granting further security, distributing dividends above a nominated level of return, or changing the management or ownership structure.[127] The list of possibilities does not end there, but their objective is clear. In addition, the debenture may provide for the lender to be part of the management of the company by giving it the right to appoint a director.[128]

If any of these covenants is breached, the debenture usually defines this as "an event of default" upon which the lender is given various rights, usually including the right to accelerate repayment, to take new security, to enforce existing security, to impose repayment penalties (drafted, of course, to avoid invalidity as a "penalty clause"[129]), and such like. From this list, the lender can elect the most

---

[126] Bratton, "Bond Covenants and Creditor Protection" (2006) 7 E.B.O.R. 39.

[127] However, since these are contractual restrictions, they will not bind third parties (in whose favour, for example, assets have been pledged in breach of covenant), unless equity will intervene (see above, para.16–134), or the ingredients of the tort of inducing breach of contract have been established, notably knowledge on the part of the third party of the contractual restrictions: *Swiss Bank Corp v Lloyds Bank Ltd* [1979] Ch. 548.

[128] Of course, such nominee directors owe their duties to the company, not the nominee: see the discussion above, para.16–63.

[129] *Lordsvale Finance Plc v Bank of Zambia* [1996] Q.B. 752; although now see *Cavendish Square Holding BV v Talal El Makdessi; ParkingEye Ltd v Beavis* [2015] UKSC 67.

appropriate course of action. It is not usual to make the consequences of default automatic, as undoing their automatic effect can be very difficult if the breach is, for example, merely technical and one which the lender is inclined to ignore.

It might be asked what consequences would follow if the company decided unilaterally to exercise its powers, either at board level or in general meeting, to subvert these covenants—for example by the general meeting dismissing the debenture holder's nominee director,[130] or effecting other significant changes to the articles. But this is hardly a live issue: the breach would invariably constitute an event of default, normally entitling the debenture-holder to require the debt to be repaid immediately and, if it was secured by a charge on the company's property, to enforce the security. This is a far more effective remedy—and disincentive—than a claim for damages for the breach. Thus, while the value of the lender's rights may depend on the continued prosperity of the company, particularly if the loan is unsecured, lenders (including debt security holders) are not normally subject, as is a shareholder, to any serious possibility that the agreed rights will be varied by the company by corporate action without the lender's consent.

Protecting multiple lenders from their lead intermediary

With both syndicated loans and debt securities, there is a "leader" in the collaboration between the multiple lenders, with the leader typically being the person to whom the corporate debtor is to make the necessary loan repayments, and who can enforce the debt, or implement acceleration provisions, or agree to modifications of the terms of the debenture. Thus, by contract, the parties provide for collective enforcement of their debt.[131]   **31–28**

But when things go wrong and the debt is not repaid according to its terms, or negotiations seem to go awry, these leaders are especially likely to come in for criticism. Different obligations are owed depending on the selected debt structure and the terms of the contractual engagement, but a brief outline gives the general features.

In syndicated loan agreements, the arranger, in putting the deal together, will clearly owe a duty of care to the other participants, although this duty can be expressly excluded in large measure,[132] especially in relation to misrepresentations as to the features of the loan and the standing of the debtor.[133] Whether, during the term of the loan, the arranger also owes the other lenders general fiduciary duties seems unlikely, unless the particular facts are such as to call into play such a relationship,[134] but otherwise the general rules of contract and tort apply, with no special statutory overlay.

---

[130] See above, para.19–25. It seems clear that an injunction could not be granted to restrain the general meeting from removing a nominated director under s.168.

[131] *Elektrim SA v Vivendi Holdings 1 Corp* [2008] EWCA Civ 1178.

[132] *IFE Fund SA v Goldman Sachs International* [2007] EWCA Civ 811 at [28]; *Raiffeisen Zentralbank Osterreich AG v Royal Bank of Scotland Plc* [2010] EWHC 1392 at [65].

[133] *Peekay Intermark v ANZ Banking Group* [2006] EWCA Civ 386.

[134] Although see the dicta in *UBAF Ltd v European American Banking Corp* [1984] Q.B. 713, 728.

31–29   By contrast, there is less flexibility with debt securities using trustees as intermediaries,[135] as is now the practice. The debt security holders are dependent on the trustees for the proper protection of their interests, and their remedies are primarily against the trustees, rather than the company. This is made all the more attractive since these trustees are likely to have deep pockets, although note that in modern structures with account holders and a string of sub-trusts, the beneficiary's only claim is against the immediate trustee—there is a "no look through" rule preventing access to trustees higher up the chain. The trustees are subject to all the general common law, equitable and statutory duties imposed on trustees, and the extent to which these can be relaxed by the trust deed is limited, not only by the common law,[136] but more importantly by what is now s.750, which invalidates provisions in trust deeds (or elsewhere) which purport to exempt a trustee from, or to indemnify him against, "liability for breach of trust where he fails to show the degree of care and diligence required of him as a trustee having regard to the provisions of the trust deed conferring on him any powers, authorities or discretions".[137] As a result, the powers and obligations of trustees are likely to be set out fairly fully in the trust deed, and to be supplemented, typically, by arrangements for debt holder voting on difficult issues, so as to protect the trustee against internal complaints and potential litigation concerning the exercise of its powers.[138]

Even so, trustees can be excessively cautious in fulfilling their obligations. In *Concord Trust v Law Debenture Trust Corp Plc*,[139] the House of Lords found that the debtor company had "terrified the trustee" into declining to implement a valid instruction given to it by the requisite majority of the bondholders unless the

---

[135] It is possible, although now less common, for the company to issue bonds directly to the bondholders, and for the bondholders then to appoint an agent to act as their point of contact. Such an appointed agent will have whatever powers are expressly agreed by the parties, and these may well be fewer than those typically enjoyed by a trustee for the bondholders in a structure where the trustee holds the global note and any associated security on trust for the bondholders. But such an agent is nevertheless subject to common law and equitable duties, providing the bondholders with fairly extensive protection.

[136] *Armitage v Nurse* [1998] 1 Ch. 241. Although see the pro-trustee approach to restrictive clauses in *Citibank NA v MBIA Assurance SA* [2006] EWHC 3215. Also see M. Bryan, "Contractual Modification of the Duties of a Trustee" in S. Worthington, (ed.), *Commercial Law and Commercial Practice* (Oxford, Hart Publishing, 2003), p.513.

[137] But note the exceptions and qualifications in subss.(2)–(4) permitting 75 per cent in value of the debenture holders present and voting to give a release from liability to the trustee in respect of prior specific acts or omissions of the trustee (or on the latter's death or ceasing to act). In addition, reg.40(2) of the Uncertificated Securities Regulations 2001 (above, Ch.27) exempts the trustees from liability simply for assenting to amendments of the trust deed to enable title to debentures to be held and transferred under the electronic system and for rights attached to debentures to be exercised in that way.

[138] Especially if the trustee's opinion differs: see *Citibank NA v MBIA Assurance SA* [2006] EWHC 3215 (Ch); [2007] EWCA Civ 11 (see "Issue 2" in the Court of Appeal); and *Law Debenture Trust Corp Plc v Concord Trust* [2007] EWHC 1380.

[139] *Concord Trust v Law Debenture Trust Corp Plc* [2006] 1 B.C.L.C. 616 HL. The event of default was a failure to maintain on the board of the borrowing company a nominee of the lenders, who had been placed there to protect the bond-holders' interests. Having accelerated the bond, as a consequence of the HL judgment, and secured substantial payments from the company, the trustee then took an overly cautious line about how much of the monies recovered it could distribute to the bond-holders: *Law Debenture Trust Corp Plc v Concord Trust* [2007] EWHC 1380 (Ch).

trustee was given an indemnity by the bondholders against what the court thought was a fanciful liability to the company on the part of the trustee should the trustee's action of declaring a default and accelerating the bond (i.e. requiring it to be repaid) turn out to be ill-founded.

Protecting multiple lenders from each other

As well as settling the boundaries for the relationship between the multiple lenders and their leader, the lenders need some protection from each other. Typical trust deeds therefore include "no action" and "pari passu" provisions, expressly prohibiting individual debt holders from seeking to enforce any rights against the debtor company, or to recover any more individually than would be recovered under collective action. In addition, in syndicated loans, there can be complicated subordination agreements between the different parties. All these, added to the formal collective action structure, are designed to prevent any one party gaining "first mover advantage".[140]

31–30

But these days the more difficult governance issue concerns the possible judicial review of voting at meetings of debt security holders. There has to be a decision-making process, but it must be such that it does not oppress minorities. The trust deed typically provides for the security holders to give directions, often by majority vote (perhaps a simple majority or some special majority, in number or in value or both, depending on the issue under review, or perhaps some other agreed regime that seems, at the time of the agreement, to afford the participants the necessary protection of their personal interests). This decision is commonly required to be reached at a meeting of the security holders, called in an agreed way, with specified notice, and typically allowing representation by proxies. The parallels between this contractually agreed regime for debt securities and the combined statutory and contractual regime for equity securities is obvious, and so too the legal issues in its resolution.[141]

In these circumstances the debt holders do not have the protection of the unfair prejudice provisions which apply only to "members".[142] The issues are left to the common law. The first requirement is that any decision must be fully informed. It is usually left to the trustee to ensure that proposals are fully and fairly explained in the circulars seeking the needed consents.[143] Further, the courts have applied to decisions of a majority of the debenture holders binding on the minority the same common law doctrine applied to decisions by shareholders to alter the articles,[144] i.e. the decision must be made bona fide[145] in the interests of the debenture

---

[140] The aim is to achieve, by contract between the multiple lenders alone, at least the level of protection that the IA 1986 attempts to deliver between all unsecured creditors, despite the fact that they are often strangers to each other. See below, Ch.33. See above, paras 31–24 et seq.

[141] See above, paras 19–4 et seq.

[142] See para.20–1. Nor, of course, will the class rights provisions afford protection as they too apply only to members. See para.19–13.

[143] The Listing Rules require that any circular must include an explanation of the effect of proposed amendments: LR 17.3.10.

[144] See the detailed discussion at paras 19–4 et seq., much of which is equally relevant here.

[145] *Goodfellow v Nelson Line (Liverpool) Ltd* [1912] 2 Ch. 324, 333.

holders,[146] and for the purposes for which the power is granted.[147] Taking each of these requirements in turn (although in older cases they are often regarded as comprehending a single test), the limits of the controls become readily apparent. It is usually impossible to prove absence of bona fides. Further, as we saw with shareholders, it is often equally difficult to prove that a decision is not "in the interests of the debenture holders", especially if—as with shareholders—this is taken to mean that the decision is one which the debenture holders themselves subjectively view as in their interests, subject only to a rationality test. Indeed, proof that a decision is not in their interests is generally even more difficult than with shareholders, since the voting requirement is often designed precisely to resolve issues where the different debtholders' interests may be in conflict. Faced with these facts, it is necessarily the final strand in the test—the proper purposes aspect—which is to the fore in determining whether the majority decision should stand.

31–31   However, even a "proper purposes" test does not give the courts much leverage to intervene, especially where the various interests of the debenture holders are in conflict, and the vote is designed (i.e. its purpose is) to resolve the outcome in favour of one or other side, and there is nothing in the facts which suggests more than a predictable difference of opinion.[148]

On the other hand, there are a small number of cases which show that the rule has some teeth.[149] Thus, in *British America Nickel Corp Ltd v O'Brien*[150] a decision of the majority of the bondholders, modifying their rights, was invalidated on the grounds that one of the bondholders, whose support was necessary for the passing of the resolution, was to receive under the scheme a block of ordinary shares, with that opportunity not available to the other bond-holders.[151] In the *O'Brien* case, Viscount Haldane said that the power of alteration "must be exercised for the purpose of benefiting the class as a whole", and the courts have often been quick to conclude that the purpose is self-interest, not class interest, where there are particular and exclusively personal benefits hanging on the voting outcome (beyond those, of course, which are inherently and necessarily delivered by the vote itself).

---

[146] *British America Nickel Corp Ltd v MJ O'Brien* [1927] A.C. 369, 371; *Redwood Master Fund Ltd v TD Bank Europe Ltd* [2002] EWHC 2703; [2006] 1 B.C.L.C. 149 at [84], a case concerning syndicated lenders, relying on the shareholder case of *Greenhalgh v Ardene Cinemas Ltd* [1951] Ch. 286, 291; and *Law Debenture Trust Corp Plc v Concord Trust* [2007] EWHC 1380 at [123]; *Assénagon Asset Management SA v Irish Bank Resolution Corp Ltd* [2012] EWHC 2090 (Ch).

[147] *Redwood Master Fund Ltd v TD Bank Europe Ltd* [2002] EWHC 2703; [2006] 1 B.C.L.C. 149 at [101]–[105]; *Assénagon Asset Management SA v Irish Bank Resolution Corp Ltd* [2012] EWHC 2090 (Ch) at [85]–[86].

[148] See the detailed analysis in *Redwood Master Fund Ltd v TD Bank Europe Ltd* [2002] EWHC 2703; [2006] 1 B.C.L.C. 149.

[149] R. Peel, "Assessing the Legality of Coercive Restructuring Tactics in UK Exchange Offers" (2015) 4 UCL Journal of Law and Jurisprudence 162.

[150] *British America Nickel Corp Ltd v O'Brien* [1927] A.C. 369 PC.

[151] There appears to be no problem if the opportunity to benefit by voting in a particular way is fully disclosed and available to all members of the class: *Azevedo v IMCOPA — Importacao, Exportaacao e Industria de Oleos Ltda* [2013] EWCA Civ 364.

This same approach was adopted by Briggs J in *Assénagon Asset Management SA v Irish Bank Resolution Corp Ltd*,[152] with more modern, and more explicit, reference to the equitable requirement of proper purposes in the exercise of power, and the need to ensure powers were not used to oppress minorities. This case involved a more complicated inducement from the debtor company to the debt holder to vote in a particular way,[153] adopting an apparently common technique of requesting "exit consents", which offered the debt holder a lower denomination bond in exchange for a commitment to vote in a way which would, effectively, destroy or extinguish the existing bond. Of course, the bondholders who did not accept this inducement before the pre-meeting deadline (thinking it priced their bonds too conservatively) ran the risk—the prisoner's dilemma—of the vote going against them, and being left with an old bond rendered almost worthless. Gamesmanship was clearly an essential part of the debtor company's strategy,[154] and its effectiveness was ensured because the timing went against effective co-ordination by the bondholders. But in legal terms, the real question is what distinguishes *Assénagon* from *Azevedo*.[155] In both cases there was an inducement offered to all bondholders, but accepted only by some; in both the vote reduced the value of the old bonds. The legal difference cannot, it seems, lie merely in the size of the inducement or the magnitude of the devaluation. But quite where it lies is not clear. These cases reinforce the conclusion that although this protection is important to debt security holders, and although the principles in play may be readily stated, they are anything but easy to apply with confidence.

Where there is some doubt as to the legitimacy of a decision taken in this way, the parties may feel more secure seeking the sanction of the court via a scheme of arrangement if the company is solvent,[156] or a company voluntary arrangement if the company is insolvent.[157]

CONCLUSION

From the above analysis it will be clear that the terms and structure of debt which **31–32** companies take on are left very much to be bargained out between lenders and borrowers. Consequently, most of the law in this area consists of the principles of the law of contract and the law of property, with relatively little in the way of special company law regulation, except where the company wishes to issue its debt securities to the public, or enable those securities to be traded on a secondary

---

[152] *Assénagon Asset Management SA v Irish Bank Resolution Corp Ltd* [2012] EWHC 2090 (Ch). Briggs J also held, as an alternative, that the vote belonged beneficially to, and was exercised by, the debtor company, in contravention of the trust deed, so the decision of the majority could not stand because the majority had no power to exercise, i.e. on these facts, the same result could be delivered by an analysis based on absence of power, or, alternatively (as discussed here), on abuse of power.

[153] As in *Azevedo v IMCOPA – Importacao, Exportaacao e Industria de Oleos Ltda* [2013] EWCA Civ 364.

[154] Otherwise the same outcome might have been achieved by a straightforward vote to devalue the old bond to the value of the offered inducement.

[155] See above, fnn.146 and 151.

[156] 2006 Act s.895; see above, paras 29–1 et seq. But note *Re Lehman Brothers International (Europe) (In Administration)* [2009] EWCA Civ 1161, indicating that beneficial owners (as opposed to creditors, even those with security) cannot avail themselves of these provisions.

[157] 2006 Act s.899; see below, para.29–24.

market (where the rules are similar to those applying to equity securities), or where the company agrees to give a charge over its property to secure the loan, which is the topic for the following chapter.

CHAPTER 32

COMPANY CHARGES

INTRODUCTION

Borrowers are often obliged to provide security for the repayment of their debts. In this respect a company is no different from any other borrower. However, there are sufficiently unique features associated with the granting of security by a company to justify it being treated here as a separate topic. In particular, one type of security (the floating charge) is practicable only if created by a body corporate,[1] there is a separate system for the registration of company charges,[2] there are distinct statutory procedures for the enforcement of the floating charge,[3] and certain provisions of the Insolvency Act 1986 affecting company charges apply on corporate insolvency. Coupled with these, the granting of security by a company is subject to the law relating to corporate capacity and directors' duties,[4] although compliance in that regard is assumed in what follows.

32–1

---

[1] See above at para.2–31.
[2] See paras 32–24 et seq., below.
[3] See paras 32–34 et seq., below.
[4] See Chs 7 and 16.

SECURITY INTERESTS

The legal nature of security interests

32–2 Some knowledge of this general topic is essential in order to understand the particular nature of the rights conferred on a secured charge holder, the priorities of charges, and the system for the registration of company charges.[5] Some understanding is also needed of nomenclature. Various forms of security are possible, as described below, but the most common form granted by a company is a charge. "Charge" has a restricted technical meaning in equity, although this technical distinction is not always maintained in the literature or in the Act,[6] and, unless the context indicates otherwise, the terms "charge", "security" or "security interest" are often used interchangeably.

Browne-Wilkinson VC, without claiming that it was comprehensive, accepted the following as a description of a security interest[7]:

> "Security is created where a person ('the creditor') to whom an obligation is owed by another ('the debtor') by statute or contract, in addition to the personal promise of the debtor to discharge the obligation, obtains rights exercisable against some property in which the debtor has an interest in order to enforce the discharge of the debtor's obligation to the creditor."

More recently in *Smith (Administrator of Cosslett (Contractors) Ltd) v Bridgend CBC*, Lord Scott remarked that[8]:

> "a contractual right enabling a creditor to sell his debtor's goods and apply the proceeds in or towards satisfaction of the debt is a right of a security character. [It is important to note that] the conclusion does not depend on the parties' intention to create a security. Their intention, objectively ascertained, is relevant to the construction of their contract. But once contractual rights have, by the process of construction, been ascertained, the question whether they constitute security rights is a question of law that is not dependent on their intentions."

These two statements highlight the essential features of a security interest. First, the classification of security interests is a matter of law, and depends upon the rights agreed between the parties, not on their intention to create one form of security rather than another, nor on the economic effect of their agreement. Secondly, every security interest ultimately gives the holder of the security a

---

[5] For more detail, see H.G. Beale, M. Bridge, L. Gullifer and E. Lomnicka, *The Law of Security and Title-Based Financing*, 2nd edn (Oxford: OUP, 2012); L. Gullifer, *Goode on Legal Problems of Credit and Security*, 5th edn (London: Sweet & Maxwell, 2015); E. McKendrick, *Goode on Commercial Law*, 4th edn (London: LexisNexis, 2010), Pt 4, especially Ch.25; P. Ali, *The Law of Secured Finance* (Oxford: OUP, 2002); F. Oditah, *Legal Aspects of Receivables Financing* (London: Sweet & Maxwell, 1991), Ch.1; and M. Bridge, L. Gullifer, G. McMeel and S. Worthington, *The Law of Personal Property* (London, Sweet & Maxwell, 2013), Ch.7.

[6] See s.859A(7), defining "charge" to include mortgage, and any other form of security.

[7] *Bristol Airport Plc v Powdrill* [1990] Ch. 744 at 760. Note that the property of a third party can also be made available by way of security, without any associated personal promise by the third party to meet the secured obligation: *Re Bank of Credit and Commerce International SA (No.8), Re* [1998] A.C. 214. See also *Re Curtain Dream Plc* [1990] B.C.L.C. 925 at 935–937; *Welsh Development Agency v Export Finance Co Ltd* [1992] B.C.L.C. 148; IA 1986 s.248. A charge can be created not only to secure the payment of a monetary obligation but also to secure other types of obligations: *Re Cosslett (Contractors) Ltd* [1998] Ch. 495.

[8] *Smith (Administrator of Cosslett (Contractors) Ltd) v Bridgend CBC* [2002] 1 A.C. 336, [53].

proprietary claim over assets, normally the debtor's, to secure payment of the debt. The position of a secured creditor is to be contrasted with that of an unsecured creditor who merely has a personal claim to sue for the payment of his debt and to invoke the available legal processes for the enforcement of any judgment that he may obtain.

Security interests can be divided broadly into consensual and non-consensual securities. We are interested in the former—i.e. securities agreed by companies to be granted in favour of their creditors. English law recognises only four types of security interest (mortgages, charges, pledges and common law liens[9]),[10] although these can be used in a wide variety of ways to give sophisticated protection to lenders.

It is not possible in a text of this nature to describe security interests in any great detail, but a number of questions typically arise with respect to the creation of such interests by a company: **32–3**

(i)   First, is the interest created by the security equitable or legal? This has a bearing on the priorities of different charges and of course an equitable charge holder can be defeated by a bona fide purchaser for value.[11]

(ii)   Secondly, is the security interest possessory in the sense that possession, either actual or constructive, of the property subject to the security is necessary in order to confer a security interest on the security holder? Obviously, if all security interests had to be possessory it would make secured borrowing virtually impossible since the debtor would be unable to use the secured assets in the course of business. The classic example of a possessory security is the pledge, which involves the pledgee (the security holder) taking possession of the goods of the debtor (the pledgor) until the debt is paid or the pledgee takes steps to enforce the pledge. The common law lien is also possessory. In the interests of commercial vitality, English law has thankfully long recognised non-possessory security interests, by way of mortgages and charges.

But it can be important to decide just what sort of arrangement the parties have entered into. "Stock lending", from its label, suggest a mere pledge of the underlying collateral: it is "on loan" from the borrower to the lender for the purposes of security, and recoverable on repayment of the loan; more importantly, should the lender become insolvent, the securities

---

[9] A *common law lien* arises when possession of goods is given to a creditor otherwise than for security—for example, so that the goods can be stored, repaired or transported—and the creditor is given, by custom, statute or contract, a right to retain the goods (and only that right, unless the parties expand upon it by contract) if the debt is not satisfied.

[10] *Re Cosslett (Contractors) Ltd* [1998] Ch. 495 at 508 (Millett LJ).

[11] Most securities created by companies are charges (using that term in its technical sense). A *legal mortgage* is created if the borrower transfers legal title to the property to the lender on the condition that it will be given back when the obligation is met. An *equitable mortgage* is created in the same way, but where the transfer is of equitable title rather than legal title; an equitable mortgage is also created by a specifically enforceable contract to create a legal mortgage. Note that a legal mortgage of land is no longer possible: these arrangements are now deemed by statute to create a *legal charge* (LPA 1925 ss.85(1) and 86(1)). All other charges, using "charge" in its technical sense, are *equitable charges*. These arise where, by contract, a specific item of property is appropriated to, or made answerable for, meeting the debtor's obligation.

belong to the borrower, not the lender. But typically these arrangements also give the lender the enormously valuable commercial advantage of being able to deal freely with the underlying securities, and an obligation to return to the borrower, when the time comes, not the precise securities lent, but simply equivalent securities.[12] The courts have held, perhaps unsurprisingly, that in these cases it is the lender who has title to the securities, not the borrower, with all the insolvency consequences that attracts.[13]

(iii)   Thirdly, what type of "proprietary" interest is vested in the chargee by the charge? This has a direct bearing on remedies. The remedies of charge holders will be dealt with later. But some brief comment is needed as to the remedies available to the holders of other types of security interests. First to be contrasted is the mortgage and the charge. Although the words are often used interchangeably, there is technically an essential difference between them: "a mortgage involves a conveyance of property subject to a right of redemption, whereas a charge conveys nothing and merely gives the chargee certain rights over the property as security for the loan".[14] This essential difference has an impact on remedies: unless the charge document expressly provides otherwise (which it now invariably does[15]), the remedy of a chargee is to apply to the court for an order for sale or for the appointment of a receiver; this is because a charge, unlike the mortgage, does not involve conveyance of title to the asset, so a chargee cannot automatically foreclose or take possession. The principal remedy of a pledgee is sale of the pledged goods; they can also be sub-pledged, with restrictions,[16] even before the right to sell arises. By contrast, a common law lien holder merely has the right to detain the goods subject to the lien until the debt has been paid.[17]

(iv)   Fourthly, is the security interest one that is created by the act of the parties or is it one created by operation of law? This is of critical importance with respect to the registration of company charges, since charges created by a

---

[12] "Repos", or sale and repurchase agreements, may equally be subjected to this analysis: on the surface they appear to be much like mortgages, but if the lender has the right to deal with the underlying securities and return only their equivalent, then the agreement is a true sale (plus an agreement the other way to sell equivalent securities), not a mortgage: *Lehman Bros International (Europe) (In Administration)* [2011] EWCA Civ 1544 CA.

[13] *Beconwood Securities Pty Ltd v ANZ Banking Group Ltd* [2008] FCA 594 Aust. Fed.Ct.; *Lehman Bros International (Europe) (In Administration)* [2011] EWCA Civ 1544 CA.

[14] *Re Bond Worth Ltd* [1980] Ch. 228 at 250. These rights are, however, proprietary, and protected as such. For some of the difficulties in distinguishing an equitable charge from a mortgage in terms of the quality of the security granted, see Oditah, above, fn.5, pp.94–96. Also see *Re Leyland Daf Ltd; Buchler v Talbot* [2004] 2 A.C. 298, where Lords Hoffmann (at [29]) and Millett (at [51]) used the language of mortgages, not charges, in describing the chargor of a crystallised charge as having only an equity of redemption.

[15] The usual provision is that, in the event of specified types of default by the chargor, the chargee is entitled to appoint a receiver to act as the agent of the chargor to sell the charged assets and use the proceeds to repay the outstanding debt to the chargee, after first paying those with statutory priorities, as discussed later.

[16] To ensure that the pledgee does not breach obligations to the pledgor.

[17] Although the right to sell is often expressly granted by contract. Subsequent security holders of course take subject to the lien: *George Barker (Transport) Ltd v Eynon* [1974] 1 W.L.R. 462.

company over its assets are registrable, whereas charges (or, more correctly, equitable liens) arising by operation of law are, of course, not.

(v)   Fifthly, if the charge has been created by the company, has it been registered as required by the Act? Registration is dealt with later.

(vi)   Finally, is the charge created by the company fixed or floating? This will have a significant impact on the rights and remedies available to the chargee, and to other third parties associated with the failing company. It too is dealt with later.

To complicate the picture further, there are a number of other devices which do not constitute legal security (because they do not involve the debtor granting an interest in *its* property to the secured creditor), but which nevertheless function in a similarly protective fashion, and so are referred to as quasi-security devices. Negative pledge clauses in unsecured lending, and retention of title by sellers of goods, are two common illustrations. The first involves an agreement by the debtor company and its unsecured creditor that the company will not create any securities which have priority to the creditor's claim. Although this does not vest a security interest in the creditor, it "behaves" like a security interest in that it precludes the debtor from using its assets freely and thus, as with a security interest, it provides the creditor with a measure of protection. In retention of title arrangements, the seller of goods simply retains title to the goods until the buyer has paid for them (or until some later time defined by the contract).[18] Some of the problems raised by this type of security are considered later in the discussion on registration.[19]

The benefits of taking security

There are a number of compelling reasons for a creditor to take security rather than rely solely on its personal claims against the debtor company. First, in the event of the debtor company's insolvency, a secured creditor will have priority over unsecured creditors (at least to the extent that the secured assets are of sufficient value to fund repayment of the secured debt), and may also, depending on the seniority of its claim, have priority over less senior security holders. This is a direct consequence of the fact that a security interest confers some type of proprietary interest on its holder. Priority on insolvency is one of the principal reasons for taking security.

32–4

Secondly, the secured creditor has the right to trace. If the debtor company wrongfully disposes of the charged property, the creditor is entitled to enforce its security against any identifiable proceeds of the disposition.[20]

---

[18] Functionally, but not legally, these arrangements operate much like a chattel mortgage (*Welsh Development Agency v Export Finance Co Ltd* [1991] B.C.L.C. 936 at 950; [1992] B.C.L.C. 148), and as a result, there have been several attempts to align their treatment at law with the treatment of other security interests, but so far unsuccessfully. See below, paras 32–33 et seq.

[19] See below, paras 32–26 et seq.

[20] The secured creditor is, alternatively, also be able to follow the original secured property into the hands of third parties, and assert its property rights against them, unless the property is acquired by a bona fide purchaser for value without notice of the earlier equitable interest.

Thirdly, a security interest gives its holder particular rights of enforcement depending on the nature of the security interest. Charge become enforceable in circumstances determined by the agreement itself, and the chargee may then take steps to enforce the charge. English law has traditionally placed few impediments in the way of enforcement of a charge: liberal rights are given by statute[21] and can be enhanced by contract. These rights allow the chargee to remain largely outside any concurrent insolvency proceedings and to enforce the charge independently of such proceedings,[22] although, as discussed later, this principle is substantially modified in the case of floating charges. Then various statutory rules give priority to preferential debts and to liquidation expenses,[23] and provide for a defined proportion of the floating charge realisations to be ring-fenced for the unsecured creditors.[24] Further rules operate in relation to the administration procedure (and its accompanying moratorium).[25]

Lastly, a charge affords a chargee a measure of control over the business of the debtor company. The terms of the security agreement may require the debtor company to report regularly to the chargee and, if the company gets into financial difficulties, the chargee may be made privy to management decisions.[26] In addition, the charge may be so all-embracing that there is no scope for the debtor company to obtain further secured credit.[27] In any event, a charge will obviously deter a second financier from providing funds where its charge would rank after a charge that the company has already created over its assets. Finally, unsecured creditors may see little advantage in seeking a winding-up where it appears that the secured creditors are entitled to all the company's assets.[28]

THE FLOATING CHARGE

The practical differences between fixed and floating charges

32–5   Subject to the issue of registration, discussed in the next section, the creation of a charge by a company is no different from the creation of a charge by any other debtor. And the creation of a floating charge, although devised for companies and still confined to them and to analogous vehicles, is no more difficult than the creation of a fixed charge.

A charge is an equitable proprietary security interest. It is created whenever parties agree that certain property belonging to the debtor (or some third-party

---

[21] IA 1986 s.42(1) and Sch.1, for example.

[22] *Sowman v Samuel (David) Trust Ltd* [1978] 1 W.L.R. 22; *Re Potters Oils Ltd* [1986] 1 W.L.R. 201.

[23] See paras 32–15 and 32–18, below.

[24] See para.32–17, below.

[25] See para.32–20, below.

[26] Although the chargee has to be careful not to become a shadow director and thus, e.g., potentially liable under the IA 1986 s.214. The chances of this are, on the whole, minimal: see *Re Hydrodam (Corby) Ltd* [1994] 2 B.C.L.C. 180.

[27] For an unsuccessful attempt to challenge a charge precluding the creation of charges in favour of third parties as being in violation of arts 85 and 86 of the EC Treaty, see *Oakdale Richmond Ltd v National Westminster Bank Plc* [1996] B.C.C. 919.

[28] Although see below, paras 32–15 to 32–17, for the rules on preferred creditors and on the prescribed fund to be dedicated to unsecured creditors from floating charge realisations.

guarantor) will be appropriated to the discharge of the debt or other obligation (e.g. the machinery in a factory may be charged in favour of repayment of the loan that funded its purchase, or, alternatively, a loan granted for an entirely separate purpose). The agreement is by contract, without any transfer of title. The proprietary interest created in this way is less than an ownership interest (either legal or equitable), but it allows the secured property to be appropriated and sold, with the proceeds of sale dedicated to the repayment of the outstanding secured obligation.[29] On the debtor's insolvency, this arrangement removes the secured property from any insolvency proceedings,[30] and so the secured creditor is more likely to be repaid in full when compared with the unsecured creditors who have to share pari passu in the proceeds derived from sale of the remaining unsecured assets.

All charges created in this way are either fixed or floating. A fixed (or "specific") charge expressly or impliedly restricts the debtor's power to dispose of, or otherwise deal with, the property without the creditor's consent. By contrast, a floating charge leaves the chargor free to deal with the charged property in the ordinary course of business without reference to the chargee. A floating charge thus has the very practical advantage that it allows a company to give security over assets which are continually turned over or used up and replaced as a matter of routine trading; a business can thus raise money on secured loans without removing any of its property from routine business activities.[31] The charge remains floating and the company is free to use the assets subject to the charge until the charge is converted into a fixed charge. This is referred to as "crystallisation" of the charge. The normal crystallising event is the taking of steps to enforce the charge, but there are others and these are dealt with later.[32]

No particular form of words is necessary to create a floating charge. From the earliest cases, it was recognised as sufficient if (a) the intention is shown to impose a charge on assets both present and future; (b) the assets are of such a nature that they would be changing in the ordinary course of the company's business; and (c) the company is free to continue to deal with the assets for its own benefit in the ordinary course of its business.[33] Recent authorities make it clear that only the last of these three attributes is crucial.[34]

32–6

---

[29] And if the proceeds are more than sufficient to repay all the secured debts (and other claims on the secured assets—see below, paras 32–13 to 32–19 (preferred creditors, etc.)), then the excess is returned to the debtor/chargor.

[30] Although see para.32–14, below, for particular rules relating to floating charges.

[31] See paras 2–16 and 2–31, above. For valuable analyses of the floating charge see J. Getzler and J. Payne, *Company Charges: Spectrum and Beyond* (Oxford: OUP, 2006); E. McKendrick, *Goode on Commercial Law*, 4th edn (London: Penguin, 2010), Ch.25; W.J. Gough, *Company Charges*, 2nd edn (London: LexisNexis, 1996), Ch.5. Floating charges and receivers in Scotland are dealt with by CA 2006 Pt 25 Ch.2, and IA 1986 Pt III Ch.II.

[32] See paras 32–8 et seq.

[33] *Re Yorkshire Woolcombers' Association Ltd* [1903] 2 Ch. 284 at 295 (Romer LJ); *Illingworth v Houldsworth* [1904] A.C. 355 HL. In practice, it is usual to state specifically that the charge is "by way of floating charge" but it suffices if it is expressed to be on the "undertaking" or the like: *Re Royal Mail Co* (1870) L.R. 5 Ch. App. 318; *Re Florence Land and Public Works Co* (1879) 10 Ch.D. 530 CA; *Re Colonial Trusts Corp* (1880) 15 Ch.D. 465.

[34] *Re Spectrum Plus Ltd* [2005] 2 A.C. 680 HL.

Interestingly, at the same time that courts in the UK were confirming the legitimacy of floating charges, courts in the US were moving in the opposite direction. According to US courts, allowing such freedom to the debtor/chargor was incompatible with the creation of a genuine security interest and was a fraud · on the creditors; if the creditor did not exercise reasonable dominion over the secured asset, then the security was illusory and void,[35] and any rights created could only be contractual, not proprietary.[36]

Despite this early judicial acceptance in the UK, the floating charge has always been treated by the legislature with something approaching suspicion, and successive Companies Acts and Insolvency Acts have adopted a variety of rules designed to restrict its full impact, which is potentially to sweep up *all* the company's resources (by securing "the undertaking" or "all the assets and undertaking" of the company) and dedicate them to securing the debt of *one* of the company's creditors,[37] leaving all the other creditors unprotected, able only to share pari passu in whatever remains of the proceeds from the secured assets (if anything) after the secured creditor has been paid in full.

32–7   Because of these various statutory incursions, floating charges (i.e. all charges *created* as floating charges[38]) are now subjected to more, and more onerous, invalidating provisions (including specific invalidity rules), and are also subjected to prior payment of administrator's and liquidator's costs and expenses, and then prior payment of claims from preferential creditors, and then compulsory distribution of a prescribed part to unsecured creditors. This differential treatment of floating charges, discussed in more detail below,[39] gives creditors an incentive to ensure their charges are classified as fixed, not floating.[40]

Given the vulnerability of floating charges, the question arises as to why a creditor should bother to obtain one. While obviously the fixed charge accords superior protection, there are sound reasons for taking a floating charge. First, where a subsequent holder of a registrable charge is deemed to have notice of the negative pledge clause which typically accompanies a floating charge,[41] then this accords priority to the floating charge holder. Secondly, the charge provides security against unsecured creditors. Thirdly, the floating charge holder will be able to take steps to enforce the charge and, as will be seen, this accords him considerable control over the company's affairs. Fourthly, the holder of a floating charge will have some measure of control over the company, even without taking

---

[35] *Geilfuss v Corrigan*, 95 Wis. 651, 70 N.W. 306 (1897); *Benedict v Ratner*, 268 U.S. 354, 45 S.Ct. 566, 69 L.Ed. 991 (1925).

[36] The commercial inconvenience of this judicial approach probably contributed to the early adoption of an alternative mechanism to achieve similar ends by way of the Uniform Commercial Code art.9.

[37] *Re Panama, New Zealand and Australian Royal Mail Co* (1870) 5 Ch. App. 318 CA, provided early confirmation that this is possible.

[38] IA 1986 s.251 provides that "floating charge" means "a charge which, *as created*, was a floating charge". See below, para.32–14.

[39] See paras 32–13 et seq.

[40] See paras 32–21 et seq. for the way the courts classify charges as fixed or floating.

[41] And this can be a fraught question given the current registration requirements. See below, para.32–11.

any steps to enforce its security.[42] Lastly, the holder of a floating charge may be able to block the appointment of an administrator, although now only in a limited range of cases.[43]

Crystallisation

As indicated above, a floating charge (unlike a fixed charge) leaves the debtor company free to use the secured assets in the ordinary course of its business until some point at which the charge is converted into a fixed charge. "Crystallisation" is the term used to describe this transition point.[44] Crystallisation is an important event, since it enables definition of the pool of assets available to the chargee as security for the obligation: a crystallised charge bites on all the assets that are presently in, or in the future come into, the hands of the chargor and are properly within the description of the charged assets.[45]

32–8

The effect of crystallisation is to deprive the company of the autonomy to deal with the assets subject to the charge in the normal course of business.[46] The events of crystallisation, on which there is general agreement, are: (i) the making of a winding-up order[47]; (ii) the appointment of an administrative receiver[48]; (iii) the company's ceasing to carry on business[49]; (iv) the taking of possession by the

---

[42] See para.32–4, above.

[43] See below, para.32–34.

[44] The language is often muddled: crystallisation is described as operating as an equitable assignment (by way of charge): *George Barker (Transport) Ltd v Enyon* [1974] 1 W.L.R. 462 at 467, 471, 475; or as conversion to a specific (fixed) charge: *Re Griffin Hotel Co Ltd* [1941] Ch. 129. And see the assertion that the company has an equity of redemption: *Ultraframe (UK) Ltd v Fielding* [2005] EWHC 1638 (Ch) at [1401].

[45] A floating charge agreement does not usually provide for crystallisation over part only of the assets to which it relates. There is no doctrinal reason for this. Partial crystallisation could, theoretically, be provided for by agreement, so long as the class of assets to be affected could be specified with certainty so as to define those which the chargor can and cannot deal with. This practicality creates the problem. It is submitted that *Robson v Smith* [1895] 2 Ch. 118 is not authority against partial crystallisation since the floating charge in that case did not confer any such right. In any event, such a provision is unlikely to be attractive in practice: it confers no significant benefit on the chargor, since the essence of security is that it only secures the outstanding debt, and any surplus (in cash or kind) is returned to the chargor; and it reduces the rights of the chargee in ways that may turn out to be unnecessarily detrimental when the event occurs.

[46] At the time the event of crystallisation occurs, there must be: (a) an outstanding obligation which the charge secures; (b) a valid and subsisting charge agreement; (c) identifiable charged assets in which the chargor has an interest or rights.

[47] *Wallace v Universal Automatic Machines* [1894] 2 Ch. 547 CA; *Re Victoria Steamboats Ltd* [1897] 1 Ch. 158. Even if the winding-up is for purposes of reconstruction: *Re Crompton & Co* [1914] 1 Ch. 954. It is the making of the order and not, for example, the presentation of the petition since there is always the chance that the court will decline to make the winding-up order. In Scotland the charge crystallises on the commencement of the winding-up of the company: Bankruptcy and Diligence etc. (Scotland) Act 2007 s.45 (not yet in force).

[48] *Evans v Rival Granite Quarries Ltd* [1910] 2 K.B. 979. The same applies to the appointment of a receiver by the court. See para.32–38 on administrative receivership.

[49] This occurs because the cessation removes the raison d'être of the floating charge, which is to permit the company to carry on business in the ordinary way insofar as the class of assets charged is concerned. *Re Woodroffes (Musical Instruments) Ltd* [1986] Ch. 366 (it is the cessation of business

debenture-holder[50]; and (v) the happening of an event expressly provided for in the debenture, often referred to as "automatic crystallisation". Events (i)–(iii) are implied as crystallising events in every floating charge agreement unless explicitly excluded.

Automatic crystallisation

32–9   Automatic crystallisation is not a term of art. It covers at least two situations which at first blush appear dissimilar. One is where the charge is made to crystallise on the happening of an event provided for in the charge agreement without there being any need for a further act by the chargee,[51] and the other is where the charge is made to crystallise on the serving of a notice of crystallisation on the company. However, these events have one important common feature, in that they will normally not be known to a person dealing with the company and therefore it seems appropriate to treat them together.

Initially there was some doubt about both the validity and the desirability of automatic crystallisation provisions. On validity, the matter is now settled beyond dispute, following acceptance of the judgment of Hoffmann J in *Re Brightlife Ltd*[52] upholding the validity of a provision enabling the floating charge holder to serve a notice of crystallisation on the company. Hoffmann J saw crystallisation as being a matter of agreement between the parties. On this reasoning there can be no objection to a charge being made to crystallise on the happening of a specified event. On the desirability of automatic crystallisation clauses, their acceptance as a matter of law indicates at least tacit approval that the benefits outweigh the detriments. The earlier arguments against such clauses focused on the disadvantages suffered by third parties. For example, insofar as insolvency law is committed to the principle that property within the apparent ownership of the company should be treated as the company's in the event of its insolvent liquidation, permitting party autonomy to effect automatic crystallisation clearly undermines this policy, but then English insolvency law is littered with similar exceptions.[53] Similarly, it has been argued that automatic crystallisation may prejudice subsequent purchasers and chargees who do not know, and indeed who may have no way of knowing, that the charge has crystallised.[54] Whether this is indeed the case is not clear cut. The matter is usually resolved as one of

---

and not ceasing to be a going concern assuming the latter is different). Express provisions for crystallisation will only exclude this implied provision for crystallisation if they expressly do so: *Re The Real Meat Co Ltd* [1996] B.C.C. 254.

[50] *Evans v Rival Granite Quarries Ltd* [1910] K.B. 979 at 997.

[51] The crystallising event could, for example, be the failure by the debtor to pay any monies due or to insure the charged property.

[52] *Re Brightlife Ltd* [1987] Ch. 200.

[53] English insolvency law achieves this policy to some extent by requiring registration of non-possessory securities. It does not, however, require registration of title retention clauses or trusts, and any assets in the possession (and apparent ownership) of the company but which are subject to these arrangements do not form part of the company's assets in a winding-up.

[54] It is common when taking a fixed charge or purchasing a substantial asset of the company to serve on it inquiries as to whether any floating charge has crystallised. This provides limited protection since the company can lie or, more likely, it may not appreciate that the charge has crystallised. In an early effort to overcome this problem, provisions were inserted into CA 1989 s.102, that empowered

priorities,[55] and subsequent purchasers or chargees will not necessarily be defeated by the earlier equitable charge.[56] In addition, Professor Goode has pointed out that the fact that the charge has crystallised will affect the relationship between the chargee and the company, but it does not necessarily affect a third party since, if the company is left free to deal with the assets in the normal course of its business, then the chargee (under the prior, now crystallised, floating charge) should be estopped from denying the company's authority to do so.[57]

The events implied as crystallising events in every floating charge agreement have already been mentioned. For the avoidance of doubt, there are no further implied terms defining events that cause crystallisation. In particular, default in the payment of interest or capital are not implied crystallising events,[58] nor (more controversially[59]) is the crystallisation of another floating charge, whether created earlier or later than the charge in question.[60] Of course, given the validity of automatic crystallisation clauses, these events could be nominated as crystallising events.

Note that even where default does not result in crystallisation, the company will be in breach of contract and the chargee will have appropriate contractual remedies. For example, the holder of an uncrystallised charge may apply for an injunction to prevent the company dealing with its assets otherwise than in the ordinary course of its business.[61]

Priority accorded to floating charges

Since a floating charge gives the debtor company management autonomy over the secured assets, the most serious risk facing the charge holder is that the assets will be dissipated, without replacement, leaving no security to support the outstanding obligation. Subject to any specific restrictions in the charge

32–10

the Secretary of State to pass regulations whereby events of crystallisation would have no effect until notified to the Registrar; however, these provisions were never brought into effect and have not been included in CA 2006.

[55] Where the subsequent interest-holder (purchaser or chargee) may have no actual or constructive notice that the earlier floating charge has crystallised. See E. McKendrick, *Goode on Commercial Law*, 4th edn (London: Penguin, 2010), pp.733–736.

[56] The interests that lose out to the crystallised floating charge are the subsequent equitable charge (provided the equities are equal), the common law lien over chattels and the interests of execution creditors: see W.J. Gough, "The Floating Charge: Traditional Themes and New Directions" in Finn (ed.), *Equity and Commercial Relationships* (Sydney, 1977), p.262.

[57] E. McKendrick, *Goode on Commercial Law*, 4th edn (London: Penguin, 2010), pp.734–735; a similar point is made by W.J. Gough, *Company Charges,* 2nd edn (London: LexisNexis, 1996), pp.255–256.

[58] *Government Stock and Other Securities Investment Co Ltd v Manila Railway Co Ltd* [1897] A.C. 81.

[59] See H.G. Beale, M. Bridge, L. Gullifer and E. Lomnicka, *The Law of Security and Title-Based Financing*, 2nd edn (Oxford: OUP, 2012).

[60] *Re Woodroffes (Musical Instruments) Ltd* [1986] Ch. 366.

[61] *Re Woodroffes (Musical Instruments) Ltd* [1986] Ch. 366 at 378: "it is a mistake to think that the chargee has no remedy while the charge is still floating. He can always intervene and obtain an injunction to prevent the company from dealing with its assets otherwise than in the ordinary course of its business. That no doubt is one reason why it is preferable to describe the charge as 'hovering', a word which can bear an undertone of menace, rather than as 'dormant'".

agreement, the debtor company is free to deal with the charged assets in the ordinary course of business. Of course this means that the chargor may sell the assets in the ordinary course of business, and purchasers take free of the security.

In addition, the company may grant subsequent security interests, and the earlier floating charge will be deferred to any subsequent fixed legal or equitable charge created by the company over its assets,[62] or any subsequent floating charges provided they are not over precisely the same assets,[63] but are over only part of the pool of assets[64] where the first charge contemplates the creation of the later charge.[65] In Scotland, however, it has been proposed that where the same property (or any part of the same property) is subject to two floating charges they rank according to the time of registration unless the instruments creating the charges otherwise provide.[66]

Similarly, if debts due to the company are subject to a floating charge, the interest of the floating charge holder will be subject to any lien or set off that the company creates with respect to the charged assets prior to crystallisation,[67] since a floating charge is not to be regarded as an immediate assignment of the chose in action,[68] but is subject to dealings in the ordinary course of business up until crystallisation.[69] In the same vein, if a creditor has levied and completed execution,[70] the debenture-holders cannot compel him to restore the money, nor, unless the charge has crystallised, can he be restrained from levying execution.[71] Put another way, the floating charge holder will take the company's property subject to the rights of anyone claiming by paramount title, and if the incursions into the secured asset arise in the ordinary course of business, then it matters not that they occur after the charge was created but before the charge crystallises.

---

[62] *Wheatley v Silkstone and Haigh Moor Coal Co* (1885) 29 Ch. D. 715; *Robson v Smith* [1895] 2 Ch. 118 at 124 (any dealing with the property subject to a floating charge "will be binding on the debenture holders, provided that the dealing be completed before the debentures cease to be merely a floating security"); *Re Castell and Brown Ltd* [1898] 1 Ch. 315. Although note that if B has *actual* notice that A's charge prohibits the creation of a later charge having priority, then A's charge will prevail: *Siebe Gorman & Co Ltd v Barclays Bank Ltd* [1979] 2 Lloyd's Rep. 142 (overruled by *Re Spectrum Plus Ltd* [2005] 2 A.C. 680, but not on this point): see below, para.32–11, on negative pledges.

[63] If the subsequent floating charge is over the same assets, then, the equities being equal, the first in time prevails: *Re Benjamin Cope & Sons Ltd* [1914] 1 Ch. 800.

[64] *Re Automatic Bottle Makers Ltd* [1926] Ch. 412 CA.

[65] *Re Automatic Bottle Makers Ltd* [1926] Ch. 412 CA, implies that this depends on the wording of the charge and of the express provision, if any, relating to the creation of further charges.

[66] Bankruptcy and Diligence etc. (Scotland) Act 2007 ss.40, 41 (not yet in force). But when the first chargee receives written notice of the registration of the later charge his priority is restricted to present advances and future advances which he is legally required to make plus interest and expenses: s.40(5) and (6).

[67] Even though, if *George Barker (Transport) Ltd v Eynon* [1974] 1 W.L.R. 462 CA is rightly decided, the lien or set off has not actually accrued.

[68] *Biggerstaff v Rowatt's Wharf* [1896] 2 Ch. 93 CA; *Rother Iron Works Ltd v Canterbury Precision Engineers Ltd* [1974] Q.B. 1 CA; *George Barker (Transport) Ltd v Eynon* [1974] 1 W.L.R. 462 CA.

[69] See *Cretanor Maritime Co Ltd v Irish Marine Management Ltd* [1978] 1 W.L.R. 966 CA, where the company's assets were subject to an injunction against their removal from the jurisdiction, obtained by an unsecured creditor. On the application of the holder of the debenture whose charge had crystallised, the court discharged the injunction. See also *Capital Cameras Ltd v Harold Lines Ltd* [1991] 1 W.L.R. 54 (successful application of a receiver to dismiss a *Mareva* injunction).

[70] Seizure alone does not suffice: *Norton v Yates* [1906] 1 K.B. 112 CA.

[71] *Evans v Rival Granite Quarries* [1910] 2 K.B. 979 CA.

However, once the floating charge crystallises,[72] this ability to deal with the charged assets in the ordinary course of business ceases, and the usual priority rules apply to determine whether the (now fixed) equitable charge has priority over any subsequently created legal or equitable interests.[73]

Negative pledge clauses

In an effort to enhance the security offered by a still floating charge as against subsequent security interests that would otherwise have priority, floating charge agreements almost invariably contain a provision that restricts the right of the company to create charges that have priority to or rank equally with the floating charge (called a negative pledge clause). Such restrictions are strictly construed,[74] but because they limit the company's actual authority to deal with its assets in the ordinary course of business, they remove the basis described above on which floating charges are automatically postponed to later charges. Instead, orthodox priority rules must be applied (e.g. an earlier equitable (floating charge) interest is deferred to a subsequent legal interest obtained bona fide and without notice of the earlier interest).

32–11

Notice (actual or constructive) of the terms of the floating charge and any negative pledge, is thus crucial in determining priority disputes.[75] Actual notice is easy enough. But constructive notice raises two problems: which matters are deemed noted, and who has such notice? The Act does not answer either question. On the first, the cases indicate that registration provides constructive notice only of those particulars which are required to be included on the register.[76] Since those particulars now include whether or not there is a negative pledge, it would seem that parties will be taken to have constructive notice of such clauses, thus doing away with a great deal of earlier uncertainty when the registration requirements were more limited.[77] But uncertainty remains over whether there will also be constructive notice of matters beyond the particulars, since the whole charge document must also be registered; and what will happen if the particulars do not accurately reflect the terms of the registered charge.[78]

On the second question, as to who will have such constructive notice, there is even less clarity. Registration might be taken to be notice to all the world, but the better view, consistent with the role of constructive notice elsewhere in the law, seems to be that registration is notice only to those who could reasonably be

---

[72] On crystallisation, see paras 32–8 et seq.

[73] *Re ELS Ltd* [1994] 1 B.C.L.C. 743.

[74] *Brunton v Electrical Engineering Corp* [1892] 1 Ch. 434; *Robson v Smith* [1895] 2 Ch. 118.

[75] *Re Portbase Clothing Ltd* [1993] Ch. 388 at 401. Contrast *Griffiths v Yorkshire Bank* [1994] 1 W.L.R. 1427, which must be doubted: see H.G. Beale, M. Bridge, L. Gullifer and E. Lomnicka, *The Law of Security and Title-Based Financing*, 2nd edn (Oxford: OUP, 2012), para.15.24.

[76] *English & Scottish Mercantile Investment Co Ltd v Brunton* [1892] 2 Q.B. 700 CA; *Wilson v Kelland* [1910] 2 Ch. 306.

[77] See, e.g. *English & Scottish Mercantile Investment Co Ltd v Brunton* [1892] 2 Q.B. 700 CA; *Re Castell & Brown Ltd* [1898] 1 Ch. 315; *Re Valletort Sanitary Steam Laundry Co Ltd* [1903] 2 Ch. 654.

[78] P. Graham, "Registration of Company Charges" [2014] J.B.L. 175, 191-192.

expected to search the register.[79] The boundaries of that rule are not certain, but it should include most lenders, especially secured lenders.

Finally, and despite the foregoing, subsequent interests that can be classed as purchase money security interests may have priority over an earlier floating charge which appears to cover the same assets, although that priority will only extend to the newly purchased assets. This follows, since the company's later purchase, secured by a mortgage, means that all that the company acquires from the purchase is an equity of redemption subject to the mortgage, so the later mortgagee will take priority, even if it has actual notice of the negative pledge.[80]

Subordination agreements

32–12 Finally, in *Cheah v Equiticorp Finance Group Ltd*,[81] Lord Browne-Wilkinson made it clear that where there were two charges over the same property, the chargees could agree between themselves to alter the priority of their security interests without the consent of the debtor. These types of subordination agreements do not affect the interests, even on insolvency, of either the debtor company or its other creditors; they merely redistribute what would otherwise be allocated to the chargees.[82]

Statutory limitations on the floating charge

32–13 Certain statutory provisions add further to the vulnerability of the floating charge. These provisions relate to (i) defective floating charges—which affects the validity of the charge; (ii) preferential creditors—which affects the priority of the charge; (iii) compulsory sharing of the security proceeds with other creditors—which diminishes the assets available for the floating charge holders; (iv) costs of the liquidation—which again diminishes the assets available for the floating charge holders; (v) the right of an administrator to override a floating charge—which affects the enforcement rights of the charge. These matters are dealt with in turn.

(i) Defective floating charges

32–14 An unsecured creditor with advance notice that insolvent liquidation is imminent may well be tempted to seek security to cover the outstanding obligation, thereby obtaining priority over the other unsecured creditors. Directors, perhaps more than most, are likely to have early warning of such danger in repayment of their

---

[79] See the discussion in L. Gullifer, *Goode on Legal Problems of Credit and Security*, 5th edn (London: Sweet & Maxwell, 2015), paras 2–25 to 2–31.

[80] *Re Connolly Bros Ltd (No.2)* [1912] 2 Ch. 25 CA; *Abbey National Building Society v Cann* [1991] 1 A.C. 56 HL. This of course presumes that the second security is properly registered, and thus enforceable on insolvency: see *Tatung (UK) Ltd v Galex Telesure Ltd* (1989) 5 B.C.C. 325 at 327; *Stroud Architectural Systems Ltd v John Laing Constructions Ltd* [1994] 2 B.C.L.C. 276.

[81] *Cheah v Equiticorp Finance Group Ltd* [1992] 1 A.C. 472.

[82] See above, para.31–10.

own unsecured loans.[83] And the only security likely to be available when the company is distressed is a floating charge security—the company's fixed assets will usually have been secured much earlier.

To prevent this, s.245 of the Insolvency Act 1986[84] provides that a floating charge created in favour of an unconnected person within 12 months[85] of the commencement of the winding-up or the making of an administration order[86] shall be invalid, except to a prescribed extent, unless it is proved that the company was solvent immediately after the creation of the charge.[87] If these conditions are not satisfied, the charge is valid only to the extent of any new value in the form of cash, goods or services supplied to the company,[88] or the discharge of any liability of the company, where these take place "at the same time as, or after, the creation of the charge".[89] It has been held that the phrase in quotations requires the new value to be provided contemporaneously with the creation of the charge.[90] Any delay, no matter how short, in the execution of the debenture after the advance has been made will result in the new value falling outside s.245.[91] Hence those who take a floating charge from a company which cannot be proved to be solvent,[92] and which does not survive for a further year, cannot thereby obtain protection in respect to their existing debts, but only to the extent that they provided the company with new value[93] and thus potentially increased the assets available for other creditors.

Where the floating charge is in favour of a "connected person", the rules are even more restrictive: the charge is vulnerable for two years after its creation,[94] and there is no need to show that at the time the charge was created the company

---

[83] In some cases the company has been deliberately floated with the intention of defrauding creditors by granting floating charges to the promoters and then winding the company up, with the charge attaching to goods which the company has purchased on credit: see Cohen Report, Cmnd. 6659, para.148.

[84] This applies to Scotland: IA 1986 s.245(1).

[85] The period was three months in the 1908 Act and six months in the 1929 Act: each was found to be inadequate in view of the ingenuity displayed in staving off liquidation.

[86] IA 1986 s.245(3)(b) and (5).

[87] The test of solvency is that laid down in s.123 of the 1986 Act: IA 1986 s.245(4).

[88] The value of the goods or services is their market value: IA 1986 s.245(6).

[89] IA 1986 s.245(2)(a) and (b).

[90] *Power v Sharpe Investments Ltd* [1994] 1 B.C.L.C. 111.

[91] *Power v Sharpe Investments Ltd* [1994] 1 B.C.L.C. 111 at 123a–b. If the delay is de minimis, for example, a coffee-break, it can be ignored: ibid. The inconvenience of this can be avoided by the parties creating a present equitable right to security rather than a promise to create security in the future: see *Re Jackson & Bassford* [1906] 2 Ch. 467.

[92] There is nothing in the section to displace the normal rule that he who asserts must prove, and thus the burden of proof would be on the liquidator or administrator. This should cause no great hardship as they will normally have sufficient information to found their action.

[93] For interesting illustrations of the way in which the rule in *Clayton*'s case ((1816) 1 Mer. 572) may protect a bank when the charge secures a current account, see *Re Thomas Mortimer Ltd* (1925) now reported at [1965] Ch. 186n; *Re Yeovil Glove Co Ltd* [1965] Ch. 148 CA. The Cork Committee recommended that *Re Yeovil Glove Co Ltd* be reversed by statute (paras 1561–1562) but why this should be so is far from clear since the bank by permitting the company to continue to draw on its overdrawn account is providing it with new value: see Goode, (1983) 4 Co.L. 81.

[94] IA 1986 s.245(3)(a).

was insolvent. The definition of connected person is complex, but includes a director, the director's relatives, and companies within a group.[95]

These provisions cannot be avoided by sleight of hand, for example by advancing further money on a floating charge on the understanding that this is to be used to repay existing loans specifically to the connected or unconnected person: a creditor cannot by use of the floating charge transmute an unsecured debt into a secured debt by manipulating the saving provisions of s.245.[96] In addition, it is important to note that not all value is "new value" for the purpose of s.245, as the latter is confined to money, goods or services and excluded are, for example, intellectual property rights and rights under a contract.[97]

These rules apply to floating charges and not to fixed charges. The policy justification for this has been questioned. The Cork Committee considered that these rules should not be extended to fixed charges since such charges would relate to the company's existing assets, whereas the floating charge could cover future assets.[98] This distinction is not in fact true,[99] but why it should make a critical difference in any event is far from clear. The exclusion of fixed charges from IA 1986 s.245 arguably reflects the favouritism shown to secured creditors in English company law. A fixed charge may of course be attacked as a preference where it is given to secure past value,[100] although not as a transaction at an undervalue since the assets of the company are not diminished by the creation of the charge.[101]

(ii)   Preferential creditors

32–15   The general rule on insolvency is that pre-insolvency rights are respected, and the company's unsecured creditors share the losses pari passu. However, this general rule has been varied by statute, giving certain classes of creditors added

---

[95] See ss.249 and 435 of the 1986 Act.

[96] *Re Destone Fabrics Ltd* [1941] Ch. 319 (this would now be a transaction with a connected person, on which see below); *Re GT Whyte & Co Ltd* [1983] B.C.L.C. 311. It is submitted that the transactions in these cases would not fall within s.245(2)(b) as there would be no discharge as a matter of substance of the debts at the time of the creation of the charge. Contrast *Re Matthew Ellis Ltd* [1933] Ch. 458 CA. The test seems to be whether the company receives what is genuinely new value.

[97] See E. McKendrick, *Goode on Commercial Law*, 4th edn (London: LexisNexis, 2010), p.919.

[98] Cmnd. 8558 at paras 1494 and 1553. The other reason given was that the extension of IA 1986 s.245 to fixed charges would compel creditors to seek repayment if fixed security could not be granted. This argument could also be applied to obtaining a floating charge.

[99] A company can create a fixed charge of accounts receivables, or a mortgage of future property, for example. The critical distinction between a fixed and a floating charge is that assets can be removed from the latter, and not from the former, without the specific consent of the chargee. Whether assets can be added (or not) is immaterial to the characterisation of the charge, and possible with both forms of charge: see below, paras 32–21 et seq.

[100] One important difference between the rules relating to preferences and to defective floating charges is that the time within which a preference in favour of an unconnected person can be challenged is six months (not 12 months). Also note that a preference will involve a diminution in the company's assets (giving one creditor a preference in repayment), whereas a floating charge constitutes a preferential claim on them.

[101] *Re MC Bacon Ltd* [1990] B.C.L.C. 324.

protection[102] by according them a statutory preference over some or all of the company's creditors. Perhaps surprisingly, the enforcement of a floating charge is to some extent treated as an insolvency proceeding whether or not the company is in the course of being wound up,[103] and these preferential creditors are given a similar priority out of the pool of floating charge assets (although only to the extent that the general assets of the company are insufficient to meet their claims).[104] To this extent, floating charge holders are treated a little like unsecured creditors (whose repayments are deferred in this way on the company's insolvency) rather than like other secured creditors with mortgages or fixed charges (who are entitled to realise the secured assets outside this insolvency regime).

There are various reasons supporting the adoption of this policy. It had been a strong criticism by the Cork Committee that banks, through a combination of fixed and floating charges, could scoop the asset pool and, in many cases, leave unsecured creditors with nothing in an insolvency. In addition, as already pointed out, some large-scale debt-financing arrangements are structured so that the ranks of debenture-holders (with floating charge security) closely resemble shareholders, forming a class that is interested in the company rather than merely one with claims against it. Consequently, it has been thought unjust that they should obtain priority over employees (one of the categories of preferential creditor) who have priority over the shareholders in the event of the company's liquidation.[105]

The preferential debts of the employees are set out in Sch.6 to IA 1986 and include four months' wages per employee up to a maximum prescribed by the Secretary of State and accrued holiday remuneration.[106] In the case of a floating charge, the relevant date for quantifying the preferential debts is the date of the appointment of the receiver by the debenture-holders.[107] Anyone who has advanced money for the payment of the employee debts which would have been preferential is subrogated to the rights of the employee.[108] It is important to note that the preferential creditors are given priority where a receiver is appointed with

---

[102] The same policy decisions have to be made with respect to bankruptcy: see, e.g. Insolvency Act 1986 s.336 dealing with the matrimonial home.

[103] e.g. the enforcement of the floating charge is dealt with in Pt III of IA 1986; administrative receivers have to be qualified insolvency practitioners (s.230(2)); and s.247(1) defines insolvency as including the appointment of an administrative receiver. IA 1986 ss.40, 175, 386–387 and Sch.6, and CA 2006 s.754 are the most relevant for the subordination of the floating charge. For the ability of these provisions to reach through earlier contractual engagements, see *Re Oval 1742 Ltd (in CVA) v Royal Bank of Scotland Plc* [2007] EWCA Civ 1262. Of course, if realisation of the security and application of the priority rules leaves the chargee carrying a loss, the floating chargee then ranks with the other unsecured creditors to the extent of any outstanding debts.

[104] IA 1986 s.175(2)(b).

[105] Another argument made in favour of employees is that they have no way of obtaining security for the payment of their salary which is normally made after the provision of the services. This is not strictly correct since money to pay employees could be placed in a trust account to be paid on the appropriate date. But this would be cumbersome and as a matter of practice does not happen.

[106] See IA 1986 Sch.6 paras 9 and 10. Para.8 brings in contributions to occupational pension schemes.

[107] IA 1986 s.387(4)(a). For the date of the appointment see IA 1986 s.33.

[108] IA 1986 Sch.6 para.11. This enables the company to be kept going where it is in financial difficulties but there is some chance that it can trade out of its difficulties. For case law on the previous statutory provisions see *Re Primrose (Builders) Ltd* [1950] Ch. 561; *Re Rutherford (James R) & Sons Ltd* [1964] 1 W.L.R. 1211; *Re Rampgill Mill Ltd* [1967] Ch. 1138.

respect to a charge "which, as created, was a floating charge"[109]; thus the fact that the charge has crystallised at the time a receiver is appointed does not result in preferential debts being denied their statutory priority.[110]

32–16 Employees have other protections. Where the company becomes insolvent, an alternative and speedier route for the employee to recover monies due is by way of application to the Secretary of State. Under Pt XII of the Employment Rights Act 1996, the Secretary of State is obliged to pay certain amounts due and then is subrogated to the employee's position in the employer's insolvency, including the employee's preferential rights, insofar as the debts discharged would have preferential status against the company.[111] This provision and its associated priority have remained, despite the more recent abolition of Crown priorities in the Enterprise Act 2002 (see below). In practice, the National Insurance Fund is probably the main beneficiary from this preference.

Prior to 2002, there were other preferential creditors on the statutory list, but these have now been all but eliminated by the Enterprise Act 2002 s.251, which abolished Crown preferences entirely, leaving only employee remuneration and contributions to pension schemes with a preference in insolvency, together with levies on coal and steel production, derived from EU law, which the UK is not free to repeal.

(iii)   Sharing with unsecured creditors—the "prescribed part"

32–17 Employees are not the only preferential creditors to eat into the assets available to the floating chargee, however. There is also now limited preferential treatment of general unsecured creditors. IA 1986 s.176A requires that when the assets of a company subject to a floating charge are realised, a certain proportion (the "prescribed part") must be set aside for the unsecured creditors.[112] The percentage is defined as follows[113]: (i) 50 per cent of the first £10,000; plus (ii) 20 per cent of the remainder; up to a maximum of £600,000.[114] The rule does not apply where (i) the company's net property is less than £10,000[115]; or (ii) the costs of distribution to unsecured creditors would be disproportionate and the court makes an order accordingly.[116]

This segregation of the prescribed part is made at the outset, and if what remains for the floating charge holder is insufficient to meet the debt due, the

---

[109] IA 1986 s.40(1).

[110] Under the old law the crystallisation of the charge prior to the appointment of a receiver resulted in the preferential creditors being denied their priority: see *Re Brightlife Ltd* [1987] Ch.200. This alteration of the old law has made automatic crystallisation clauses less attractive.

[111] Employment Rights Act 1996 s.189. The Pt XII rights of the employee as against the Secretary of State are in some respects wider and some respects narrower than the preferences accorded by the Insolvency Act against the company. Theoretically, the employee might want to pursue the preferential claim against the company in so far as it does not fall within Pt XII.

[112] Which category does not include the charge holder in relation to that part of the debt which has not been satisfied by the security, unless the unsecured debts have been fully met: IA 1986 s.176A(2).

[113] Insolvency (Prescribed Part) Order 2003 (SI 2003/2097).

[114] It is possible to vary this rule by means of a voluntary arrangement: IA 1986 s.176A(4).

[115] IA 1986 s.176A(3)(a); SI 2003/2097 art.2.

[116] IA 1986 s.176A(3)(b) and (5).

chargee is nevertheless not entitled to share in the prescribed part, notwithstanding that the outstanding debt is now unsecured: s.176A(2)(b).[117] This provision is interpreted as confining the prescribed part to the unsecured creditors until they are paid in full, and only returning any excess for the benefit of the floating chargeholder once that has happened, even though the debt secured by the floating charge may remain only partly paid.

These rules may affect companies other than those registered under the Act if, but only if, they are being wound up under it.[118]

(iv)   Costs of liquidation

None of these statutory incursions alters the fact that the first payments to come out of the floating charge realisations are the costs and expenses of liquidation (if the company goes into liquidation),[119] in priority even to the receivership expenses.[120] This can be a substantial drain on the funds eventually available to the floating chargee. Then come the costs and expenses of receivership,[121] and only then the preferential creditors, finally leaving a pool (if the parties are lucky) that is split between the floating chargee and the unsecured creditors according to the formula outlined above.

32–18

The position of fixed charge holders is quite different. Their asset pool is not subjected to claims from liquidators to fund liquidation expenses, nor from preferential or unsecured creditors. Any change to these rules would obviously affect both the terms of credit and the amount of credit available to chargors, but it is not clear that this adequately or rationally justifies the present position.

Chargees no doubt expect the expenses of their own receivership proceedings to be paid in priority to their secured debt, but the rather odd decision that liquidation expenses constitute a prior claim on floating charge receipts (but not on fixed charge receipts) was first reached by the Court of Appeal in *Re Barleycorn Enterprises Ltd*[122] on the basis that such receipts were assets *of the company*, and it is a principle of insolvency law that the expenses of a company's liquidation are payable out of the assets of the company[123] in priority to all other

---

[117] *Re Permacell Finesse Ltd* [2007] EWHC 3233 (Ch); *Re Airbase (UK) Ltd* [2008] EWHC 124 (Ch); [2008] 1 W.L.R. 1516.

[118] i.e. a floating chargee who appoints a receiver of a statutory or chartered company will not be subject to the claims of preferential creditors unless the company goes into compulsory liquidation under Pt V of the 1986 Act.

[119] Also see below, paras 33–24 et seq.

[120] And to the extent that the floating chargee is unable to recoup the outstanding debt from the floating charge proceeds, that shortfall becomes an unsecured debt, repayable pari passu with all the other unsecured debts owed by the company.

[121] Justifying the super-priority of receivership costs (but subject to what follows on the statutory priority, even over these, of liquidation costs), see *Batten v Wedgwood Coal and Iron Co* (1884) 28 Ch. D. 317. But a receiver has a duty not to incur expenses if to do so would lessen the amount otherwise available to pay the preferential creditors: *Woods v Winskill* [1913] 2 Ch. 303; *Westminster Corp v Haste* [1950] Ch. 442, both cases concerning the expenses in carrying on the company's business.

[122] *Re Barleycorn Enterprises Ltd* [1970] Ch. 465.

[123] The assets must, however, be the assets of the company and not, for example, assets held on trust. In certain limited circumstances, however, the court may order liquidation expenses to be paid out of assets the beneficial interest in which is not vested in the company: e.g. *Re Berkeley Applegate*

claims.[124] This decision was only overruled 35 years later by the House of Lords in *Buchler v Talbot* (also known as *Re Leyland Daf*),[125] which held that liquidation expenses are not payable out of floating charge assets, those being the property of the chargee and not the chargor. But the Government then almost immediately reversed this decision by inserting s.176ZA into IA 1986.[126]

32–19   So the current position, determined by statute, is that assets subject to a floating charge (i.e. assets subject to a charge that was created as a floating charge, even though it will have crystallised on liquidation) are available for payment of liquidation expenses. Where several charges have been granted over the same asset, this rule can lead to nice questions about the priority as between the various charges: if the charge with first priority is a floating charge, then the proceeds are subject to claims for liquidation expenses, but if the first charge (or equal ranking charge) is a fixed charge, the fixed chargee can realise the charged assets without making any such provision (either for the liquidation expenses or for the preferential creditors). This outcome advantages those many creditors who typically take a "fixed and floating charge" over all the company's assets: to the extent that a fixed charge is possible, it ranks equally with the floating charge and is protected from these expenses.[127] On the other hand, if the charge with priority is a floating charge, even if priority was gained by crystallisation, then the assets are subject to these rules relating to liquidation expenses and preferential debts.[128] These costs, combined with the claims of the preferential creditors, entail a substantial erosion of the entitlement of the floating charge holder.[129]

(Investment Consultants) Ltd (No.3) [1989] 5 B.C.C. 803, where the activities and efforts of the liquidator were essential in establishing and preserving the rights of the trust beneficiaries, and to that extent (only) his fees were payable out of the trust assets.

[124] For voluntary winding up see IA 1986 s.115; this section has been held to be a priority section and does not deal with the question of what constitute properly incurred expenses in a liquidation: see *Re MC Bacon Ltd* [1991] Ch.127. The position as regards court-ordered winding up is not so explicit but a combination of s.156 and Insolvency Rules 1986 rr.4.218 and 4.220 produces this effect.

[125] *Buchler v Talbot* [2004] 2 A.C. 298.

[126] See L.C. Ho, "Reversing *Buchler v Talbot*—The Doctrinal Dimension of Liquidation Expenses Priority" (2006) 3 J.I.B.F.L. 104. Note that IA 1986 s.176ZA(3) may allow these expenses to be restricted to expenses either approved by the chargee and preferential creditors, or by the court. See too *Re Premier Motor Auctions Leeds Ltd* [2015] EWHC 3568 (Ch) in which the effects of s.176Z were briefly discussed.

[127] *Re Lewis Merthyr Consolidated Collieries Ltd* [1929] 1 Ch. 498; *Re GL Saunders Ltd* [1986] 1 W.L.R. 215.

[128] *Re Portbase Clothing Ltd* [1993] Ch. 388 at 407–409. A more difficult problem arises where the two successive charges are floating charges, the second one crystallises first and so has priority over the first, but the receiver is not appointed under the second charge but under the first one. *Griffiths v Yorkshire Bank Plc* [1994] 1 W.L.R. 1427 may be technically correct in deciding that since no receiver is appointed under the second charge, the assets are not subject to the claims of preferential creditors. But this leaves the way open for floating chargees to avoid the operation of these provisions, and so the more strained analysis in *Re H and K (Medway) Ltd* [1997] 2 All E.R. 321, which concluded that the preferential debts had priority over both charges, may be preferable.

[129] Attempts to extend the *Portbase* principle decision have not been successful. In *Re MC Bacon Ltd* [1991] Ch. 127 the court held that the costs of the liquidator in bringing an action under s.214 of the 1986 Act and to challenge a transaction as a preference were not costs of realising the company's assets and thus did not enjoy the priority accorded to such expenses in a winding-up.

(v) Powers of the administrator

The final statutory limitation on the right of a floating charge holder is para.70 of Sch.B1 to the Insolvency Act 1986 which empowers an administrator to sell property subject to a charge which as created was a floating charge without the need to obtain a court order.[130] As protection, the floating charge holder is given the same priority with respect to any property representing directly or indirectly the property disposed of as he would have had with respect to the property subject to the floating charge.[131]

32–20

Distinguishing between fixed and floating charges

The previous sections (on priority, preference and invalidity rules) demonstrate why chargees prefer to have fixed rather than floating security over the assets of a corporate debtor. Prior to 1986, it was possible to achieve this status simply by showing that the charge had crystallised (and thereby become a *fixed* charge) before the commencement of the liquidation or other relevant statutory date.[132] This loophole was eliminated by IA 1986 s.251, which provides that "floating charge" means "a charge which, *as created*, was a floating charge". This means that lenders must now ensure that their security, as created, is categorised as a fixed charge, not a floating charge, if they are to avoid the disadvantages outlined earlier.

32–21

Given the consequences that follow the categorisation of a charge as fixed or floating, the courts do not simply accept the labels attached by the parties. The fact that a charge is called a "fixed" charge by the parties does not necessarily make it so. As Lord Millet indicated in the Privy Council decision, *Agnew v Commissioner for Inland Revenue* (also known as *Re Brumark*)[133]:

> "in deciding whether a charge is a fixed charge or a floating charge, the court is engaged in a two-stage process. At the first stage it must construe the instrument of charge and seek to gather the intentions of the parties from the language they have used….The object of this stage of the process…is to ascertain the nature of the rights and obligations which the parties intended to grant to each other in respect of the charged assets. Once these have been ascertained, the court can then embark on the second stage of the process, which is one of categorization, [which] is a matter of law."

In *Re Spectrum Plus Ltd*,[134] the House of Lords approved this approach and held that in characterising a charge as fixed or floating, the crucial element is the freedom of the company to use the assets in the ordinary course of its business,

---

[130] IA 1986 s.15(1) and (3).

[131] Where the charge has crystallised, the priority will be that of a fixed equitable charge.

[132] This was the case in *Re Brightlife Ltd* [1987] Ch. 200, where the debenture-holder had given the company a notice converting the floating charge into a fixed charge a week before a resolution for voluntary winding up was passed. The court held that the preferential creditors no longer had any right to be paid in priority to the charge.

[133] *Agnew v Commissioner for Inland Revenue* [2001] 2 A.C. 710 PC at [32].

[134] *Re Spectrum Plus Ltd* [2005] 2 A.C. 680. Also see *Re Armagh Shoes Ltd* [1984] B.C.L.C. 405 Ch. D. (NI).

not the nature of the assets charged.[135] The House of Lords had to consider a charge over book debts expressed in the same terms as that in *Siebe Gorman*[136] (which had been accepted as a fixed charge: see below). In a decision that overruled *Siebe Gorman* and reversed the Court of Appeal below, the House of Lords held that the charge was floating. This was so, despite the fact that the debenture prohibited the chargor from charging or assigning the debts, and required it to pay the proceeds of collection of the debts into an account with the lending bank (i.e. despite following the recipe prescribed in *Siebe Gorman*), because the debenture did not go on to specify any restrictions on the chargor's operation of the account. This very restrictive definition of a fixed charge removes the element of judgement permitted by earlier cases: a charge is fixed if and only if the chargor is legally obliged to preserve the charged assets, or their permitted substitutes, for the benefit of the chargee. In all other cases, the charge is floating and therefore subject to the disadvantageous statutory regime already described.[137]

32–22   The change effected by this approach can be seen most clearly by comparing earlier decisions.[138] The easy cases remain easy. Suppose the charge holder is a bank with a charge over a company's book debts: if use of the proceeds of the book debts is not controlled at all, then the charge is floating[139]; and if use of the proceeds is completely restricted, then the charge is fixed.[140] But if neither the freedom nor the control is absolute, then a judgement used to be required. In *Siebe Gorman & Co Ltd v Barclays Bank Ltd*,[141] Slade J (as he then was) held that a debenture over the borrower's book debts and its proceeds was correctly classified by the parties as a fixed charge. The charge agreement provided that the company could not assign or charge the secured book debts, and that the proceeds of the debts had to be paid into a designated bank account with the lending bank, although the chargor was then free to use the funds in the account.[142] On the basis of Slade J's decision, this form of debenture became a precedent and was widely used by most banks. The mere fact that the assets sought to be charged were a

---

[135] Thus clarifying the relevance of the description of a floating charge advanced by Romer LJ in *Re Yorkshire Woolcombers Association Ltd* [1903] 2 Ch. 284 at 295 (see above, para.32–6).

[136] *Siebe Gorman & Co Ltd v Barclays Bank Ltd* [1979] 2 Lloyd's Rep.142.

[137] S. Worthington, "An 'Unsatisfactory Area of the Law'—Fixed and Floating Charges Yet Again" (2004) 1 *International Corporate Rescue* 175–184 (adopted by the House of Lords in *Spectrum*); and "Floating Charges: Use and Abuse of Doctrinal Analysis", in J. Getzler and J. Payne, above, fn.31, p.28.

[138] Although also see *Gray v G-T-P Group Ltd* [2010] EWHC 1772, where the charge was held void as an unregistered floating charge, since the agreement between the parties entitled the chargor to draw on the relevant bank account proceeds effectively at will.

[139] *Re Brightlife Ltd* [1987] Ch. 200, although in this case the chargee was not itself a bank.

[140] *Re Keenan Bros Ltd* [1986] B.C.L.C. 242, where the chargee bank stipulated that the account could not be drawn against without the counter-signature of one of its officers.

[141] *Siebe Gorman & Co Ltd v Barclays Bank Ltd* [1979] 2 Lloyd's Rep.142.

[142] On this last point, Slade J may have interpreted the arrangement otherwise, assuming the bank was required to give permission for each release of funds; on that basis the decision was accepted in *Agnew*, but, on the contrary interpretation, was overruled in *Spectrum*.

fluctuating class of present and future assets was not by itself a fatal objection to the creation of a fixed charge.[143] This decision has now been overruled by *Spectrum*.

In *Re New Bullas Trading Ltd*,[144] the agreement provided for a fixed charge over the book debts while they remained uncollected, but, when collected and paid into a designated account (unless written instructions to the contrary were given by the chargee), the monies so received were released from the fixed charge and became subject to a floating charge. No directions were ever given. The Court of Appeal, reversing Knox J, held that the parties were contractually able to reach such an agreement, and the arrangement constituted a fixed charge over the (uncollected) book debts, and a floating charge over their (collected) proceeds in the bank account. This case, too, was overruled by the House of Lords in *Spectrum* on the basis that, since the chargor was free to deal with the charged assets (the book debts), for its own benefit and without the consent or interference of the chargee, by collecting the debts and using their proceeds at will, the charge over the book debts was therefore floating.

The restriction on the chargor's ability to deal with the assets must be legally binding. In *Royal Trust Bank v National Westminster Bank Plc*,[145] for example, an instrument creating a charge over book debts gave the chargee bank the right to demand that the company should open a dedicated account and pay all monies received on the collection of the debts into that account, but the bank never exercised this right, and in practice monies collected went into the company's ordinary trading account. The charge was held by Millett LJ to be floating.[146] Similarly, in *Re Double S Printers Ltd*,[147] the chargee, as a director of the company, had de facto control over the proceeds of the charged book debts since he had actual control of the bank account, but this was not backed by any contractual restraint on their disposal in the instrument itself. As in the *Royal Trust Bank* case, it was held that the company's freedom to deal (at least in law) led to the conclusion that the charge was floating. And a legally binding arrangement to create a fixed charge that is in fact ignored by the parties, who operate as if the charge is floating, will be treated by the courts as a sham.[148]

32–23

The *Spectrum* decision has substantially affected the rights of companies to grant fixed charge securities over what must remain, for good commercial reasons, their circulating assets, whether these are physical assets used or manufactured by the company or the company's book debts.[149] It remains to be

---

[143] Of course, in many cases, the fluctuating nature of the assets, especially of physical assets, means that managerial control of them can be given to the company only in a way which is inconsistent with a fixed charge: *Smith v Bridgend CBC* [2002] 1 A.C. 336.

[144] *Re New Bullas Trading Ltd* [1994] 1 B.C.L.C. 485 CA.

[145] *Royal Trust Bank v National Westminster Bank Plc* [1996] 2 B.C.L.C. 699 CA.

[146] All three members of the court concurred in the result; Nourse LJ on other grounds, and Swinford Thomas LJ without giving reasons.

[147] *Re Double S Printers Ltd* [1999] 1 B.C.L.C. 220.

[148] *Agnew v CIR* [2001] 2 A.C. 710.

[149] Although see *Russell Cooke Trust Co Ltd v Elliott* [2007] EWHC 1443 (Ch); [2007] 2 B.C.L.C. 637, where a charge described as floating was held to be fixed.

seen what techniques enterprising commercial parties will find to set up effective substitute security that attracts fewer of the disadvantages associated with floating charges.

REGISTRATION OF CHARGES

The purpose of a registration system

32–24   Part 25 of the Companies Act 2006 contains provisions relating to the registration of particular details in relation to certain charges with the Registrar of Companies. Following a major reform in 2013, the registration system has now changed from a mandatory one (and backed by criminal sanctions) to one which is optional and registration lies at the discretion of the Company.[150] The 2013 changes came about following multiple rounds of failed attempt to reform the system. To understand how we have come to where we are today, it may be helpful to understand the registration requirement, which has been a feature of the Companies Acts since 1900. What are the possible purposes of such a registration requirement?

First, and most obvious, the aim might be to give potential lenders to the company more accurate information about the company's apparent wealth by revealing the true extent of any earlier secured lending[151] that may rank ahead of their own contemplated advances. Such information may also be of interest to credit analysts, insolvency practitioners appointed upon the company's insolvency, shareholders and investors. Secondly (and for reasons aligned with the first objective), registration might be treated as an essential part of the process whereby a person obtains a security interest against the company. Without registration, the security interest would be void, and could not be relied upon as against the unsecured creditors of the company in the latter's insolvency.[152] The usual terminology is that registration is necessary for the "perfection" of the security. Thirdly, registration might determine priority among secured creditors. For example, priorities among secured creditors could be determined simply by the date of the registration of the security (and not, for example, by reference to the date of creation of the security, or by whether the later taker of a security knew of the earlier one): such a system is generally referred to as a system of "notice filing".

32–25   As the law stood before the 2013 changes, not one of these objectives was delivered. The first failed, since not all security interests needed to be registered, only those listed in the now-repealed s.860(7). The second failed for the same

---

[150] CA 2006 s.859A.

[151] Registration for this purpose is confined to registration of non-possessory securities. An obligation secured by a possessory security necessarily entails transfer of the secured asset into the possession of the security-holder, so that it does not remain on site as part of the "apparent wealth" of the borrowing company.

[152] This rule does not avoid the underlying obligation, and if the loan fell for repayment whilst the company was a going concern, for example, then it could simply be repaid by the company without any question of enforcement of a security arising. The problem arises on insolvency, when the protection of a security interest is most needed.

reason of limited application, although within that limited range any charges that ought to have been registered, but were not, were void as against the liquidator, administrator and any creditor.[153] And the third failed, as it was simply not part of the rules of the system: instead, if the security was valid (including properly registered, if it needed to be), then priority was judged according to the usual common law rules, generally based on the time of creation, the type of interest created, and the notice to subsequent security holders.

What is remarkable about this area of law is that proposals for radical change have been made by highly respected official bodies for over 40 years, but no change of either a radical or a tinkering kind was put in place until 2013 (and even that might be described as merely tinkering).[154] Radical change was proposed by the Crowther Committee in 1971,[155] endorsed by the Cork Committee in 1983,[156] and re-proposed by Professor Diamond in 1989.[157] The CLR began in tinkering mood,[158] partly because consultation on the previous radical proposals had not produced an enthusiastic response, but concluded by advocating radical reform.[159] In this positive spirit, the issue was handed over to the Law Commission,[160] which produced a consultation paper and a "consultative report", both favouring radical change, proposing a comprehensive scheme of notice-filing and associated priority rules that would extend to all securities and quasi-securities, whether granted by companies, unincorporated businesses or individuals.[161] Despite the early support, further consultation on this detailed proposal produced a more cautious response, and the Law Commission's final Report on Company Security Interests in 2005 recommended a less radical scheme, preserving its recommended notice-filing and priority rules for charges and outright sales of receivables, but not including quasi-securities nor, at least to start with, unincorporated debtors.[162]

In July 2005, the Department of Trade and Industry (the predecessor to the Department of Business, Innovation and Skills) considered these various recommendations and published a consultation document.[163] The results of all this effort can only be seen as disappointing. CA 2006 has now been amended, repealing the original Chs 1 and 2 of Pt 25 and replacing them with Ch.A1, but all to rather minimal effect.

---

[153] Companies Act 2006 s.874, and see the discussion below at paras 32–29.

[154] Some tinkering reform was included in the Companies Act 1989, but never brought into force.

[155] *The Report of the Committee on Consumer Credit*, Cmnd. 5427 (1971).

[156] *Insolvency Law and Practice*, Cmnd. 8558 (1982).

[157] *A Review of Security Interests in Property*, HMSO (1989).

[158] CLR, *Registration of Company Charges*, (October 2000) URN 00/1213.

[159] Final Report I, Ch.12.

[160] Reference was also made to the Scottish Law Commission, but in narrower terms: now see *Report on Registration of Rights in Security by Companies* (Scot Law Com No.197, 2004).

[161] Law Commission, *Registration of Security Interests: Company Charges and Property other than Land*, Consultation Paper 164 (2002); *Company Security Interests: A Consultative Report* (Law Com Consultation Paper No.176, August 2004).

[162] Law Commission, *Company Security Interests* (Law Com No.296, Cm 6654, August 2005), especially paras 1.31, 1.46–1.57, and 1.60–1.66.

[163] DTI, *The Registration of Companies' Security Interests (Company Charges): The Economic Impact of the Law Commissions' Proposals* Consultative Document (July 2005).

The reformed registration system

What has to be registered

32–26   As already mentioned, there is no longer any requirement to register security interests. But any charge created by the company[164] *may* be registered, save for four exceptions,[165] and s.859A(2) compels the registrar to register the charge if a statement pursuant to s.859D is submitted within the stipulated time period. In keeping with this general change of direction, the criminal sanction for non-registration is removed, although it remains the case that failure to register a registrable charge will render it void against the administrator, liquidator or any creditor of the company.[166] There is thus a very powerful practical sanction for non-registration.

It might be thought that the move away from a prescribed list of charges which were required to be registered (under the now repealed s.860(7)) would eliminate much of the argument about whether or not the charge was one that required registration. But given the invalidity consequences just noted, and in any event as was very largely the case under the previous rules, all the debate will simply be about whether the creditor's interest is a charge at all,[167] not whether it falls within or outside some prescribed list of charges.

The mechanics of registration

32–27   Registration may be effected by the company itself or by any person interested in the charge. The chargee is the person most motivated to register, so as to protect its security.

The period allowed for registration is 21 days beginning with the day after the date of creation of the charge (s.859A(4)), unless an order granting an extension can be obtained from the court, having regard to the restrictive requirements laid down in s.859F.[168] Section 859E defines the "date of creation of the charge", with ss.(1) stipulating the date of creation, in respect of three different types of charge, depending on whether it is a "standard security" and whether or not it is "created or evidenced by an instrument".

---

[164] Defined in s.859A(7).

[165] 2006 Act ss.859A(1) and (6).

[166] 2006 Act s .859H. It is the security which is void, not the underlying obligation (s.859(3) and (4)), and so for this purpose, creditor means secured creditor: *Re Teleomatic Ltd* [1994] 1 B.C.L.C. 90 at 95. Of course, if the company goes into liquidation or administration and the charge is unenforceable, this pro tanto protects the interests of the unsecured creditors: see *R. v Registrar of Companies, Ex p. Central Bank of India* [1986] Q.B. 1114 at 1161–1162. The previous provision, in similar terms, but applying only to the listed charges which required registration, was 2006 Act s.874 (now repealed).

[167] Or is, instead, e.g. a retention of title agreement or some other quasi-security. See, e.g. *Re Cosslett (Contractors) Ltd* [1997] Ch. 23; and [1998] Ch. 495 CA; and the failed retention of title cases, *Re Bond Worth* [1980] 1 Ch. 228; and *Borden (UK) Ltd v Scottish Timber Products Ltd* [1981] Ch. 25. The one exception to this is that, previously, not all fixed charges required registration, although all floating charges did, and so that particular characterisation could be especially important for validity (see paras 31–21 et seq. on the distinction), as well as for all the reasons discussed above at paras 31–29 et seq.

[168] See below para.32–30.

Where the debt is satisfied or the charged property or undertaking has been fully or partially released, a statement to that effect,[169] together with the relevant particulars,[170] should be submitted to the registrar. Upon receipt of such statement and particulars, the registrar must include in the register a statement of satisfaction or a statement recording the release of the charge.[171]

The register is accessible to the public. Reflecting concerns for confidentiality and privacy, certain personal information is not required to be included in the certified copy of the instrument delivered to the registrar.[172]

In addition to this registration at Companies House, the company is no longer required to keep a register of charges on its undertaking and property.[173] However, companies are still required to keep copies of instruments creating and amending charges available for inspection.[174]

Geographical reach of the registration provisions

The reformed system provides a single scheme for registration irrespective of the place of incorporation of the company within the UK (the previous scheme had one system for England, Wales and Northern Ireland, and a separate one for Scotland). The wide scope of s.859A means that a charge is registrable whether or not it is created in the UK, and whether or not the property being charged is located in the UK, with no special provisions or exceptions for these types of security.

32–28

Despite this, if the secured property is located outside the UK, then the effectiveness of any security is likely to depend upon the property law rules applying within that jurisdiction, and not simply on whether the charge should have been registered in the UK.[175]

If the debtor company is not one that is registered in England, Wales or Scotland, then special rules used to apply. The requirements under the Overseas Companies (Execution of Documents and Registration of Charges) Regulations 2009,[176] which effectively imposed the same registration requirements on registered overseas companies, are now repealed.

The effect of failure to register

As already noted, failure to register is no longer a criminal offence, although any registrable but unregistered charge created by the company will be void against the administrator, liquidator or any creditor of the company.[177] The person

32–29

---

[169] 2006 Act s.859L(1)–(3).
[170] 2006 Act s.859L(4).
[171] 2006 Act s.859L(5).
[172] 2006 Act s.859G.
[173] 2006 Act s.876(1)(b) (repealed).
[174] 2006 Act ss.859P and 859Q.
[175] H.G. Beale, M. Bridge, L. Gullifer and E. Lomnicka, *The Law of Security and Title-Based Financing*, 2nd edn (Oxford: OUP, 2012), paras 22–72 et seq.
[176] Overseas Companies (Execution of Documents and Registration of Charges) Regulations 2009 (SI 2009/1917) Pt 3.
[177] 2006 Act s.859H. See above, fn.166.

disadvantaged is the chargee, not the company; hence the rule allowing any person with an interest in the charge to register it. If the charge is not registered,[178] the chargee effectively loses its security. To reduce this hardship, the Act provides that if the charge is void to any extent for non-registration, then the whole of the sum thereby secured becomes immediately repayable on demand.[179] This, of course, also provides the company with an incentive to register. In addition, the unregistered charge is not void against the company (if still solvent), and there is nothing to prevent the chargee enforcing it (although often to little advantage if the company is solvent).[180] An unsecured creditor has no standing to prevent the holder of an unregistered but registrable charge from enforcing it.[181]

Late registration

32–30   Section 859F enables the company or a person interested in a charge that has not been registered within 21 days of its creation to apply to the court for an order extending the time for registration. This can be done if the court is satisfied that the failure to register was accidental or inadvertent and not likely to prejudice creditors or shareholders, or it is satisfied on other grounds that such relief is just and equitable.[182] This repeats earlier provisions, so older cases remain useful. The jurisdiction of the court is very wide,[183] but the court will not normally make an order once a winding-up has commenced.[184] This is because winding up is a procedure for the benefit of unsecured creditors, and registering a charge after the commencement of winding up would defeat their interests. The court may also refuse to exercise its discretion if the company is insolvent,[185] or if the company is in administration and it is inevitable that this will proceed to insolvent liquidation.[186]

If the court does exercise its discretion, the charge is normally registered on terms that do not prejudice the secured rights acquired by third parties prior to the actual date of registration.[187] Since a charge does not become ineffective until the normal time limit has expired, this standard proviso only protects third parties acting between the date when the charge ought to have been registered and its

---

[178] This happens surprisingly often; e.g. because of failure to realise that the charge is of the registrable class, or because both the company and the lender assume that the other will register.

[179] 2006 Act s.859H(4).

[180] If the chargee does so then the charge is spent and a liquidator or administrator cannot retrospectively challenge the enforcement of the charge.

[181] *Re Ehrmann Bros Ltd* [1906] 2 Ch. 697 CA.

[182] 2006 Act s.859F(2).

[183] 2006 Act s.859F(3). Once a failure to register is discovered, the charge must act expeditiously: the court will not exercise its discretion favourably where the chargee hangs back to see which way the wind blows: *Re Telomatic Ltd* [1994] 1 B.C.L.C. 90.

[184] *Re S Abrahams and Sons* [1902] 1 Ch. 695. In exceptional circumstances, however, the court may make such an order: *Re RM Arnold & Co Ltd* [1984] B.C.L.C. 535. See *Barclays Bank Plc v Stuart London Ltd* [2001] 2 B.C.L.C. 316 CA, for conditions imposed where liquidation was imminent.

[185] See *Re Ashpurton Estates Ltd* [1983] Ch. 110.

[186] *Re Barrow Borough Transport Ltd* [1990] Ch. 227.

[187] *Re IC Johnson and Co Ltd* [1902] 2 Ch. 101. The proviso will also preserve any agreements about priorities already made by the late-registering chargee with other creditors: ibid.

actual registration.[188] Unsecured creditors are not protected by such a proviso, and are not part of the court's considerations.[189]

Defective registration

Section 859M allows applications for rectification of omissions or misstatements in the registered particulars. The jurisdiction is defined in the same way as s.859F (see above). The particulars may, for example, fail to state accurately the property subject to the charge or the amount secured by the charge.[190] Note that the court's power is limited to correcting omissions or misstatements within an entry. The court cannot order the removal of an entry,[191] nor can it order the removal of information that the company would prefer not to be there,[192] and nor does the court's jurisdiction extend to particulars which are not required to be registered.[193]

32–31

Effect of registration

Where a charge is registered, the Registrar has to issue a certificate of registration and this is made conclusive evidence that the requirements of CA 2006 Pt 25 Ch.1A have been complied with.[194] This provides assurance to any transferees of the security that the validity of its registration cannot be challenged. The conclusiveness of the certificate means that the charge will be treated as validly registered even if it was not, but was registered by mistake[195]; and even if the registered particulars are inaccurate.[196] Note, however, that where there is such inaccuracy, registration validates the charge, but the operative terms are those agreed between the parties notwithstanding that third parties may have been

32–32

---

[188] *Watson v Duff Morgan and Vermont (Holdings) Ltd* [1974] 1 W.L.R. 450.

[189] *Re MIG Trust Ltd* [1933] Ch. 524 at 569–572 (Romer LJ).

[190] See generally, Prentice, "Defectively Registered Charges" (1970) 34 Conv. (N.S.) 410. The company's registered number is a detail required to be supplied but not a particular of the charge, so that an error in that regard cannot invalidate the charge: *Grove v Advantage Healthcare (TIO) Ltd* [2000] 1 B.C.L.C. 611.

[191] *Exeter Trust Ltd v Screenways Ltd* [1991] B.C.L.C. 888.

[192] *Igroup Ltd v Ocwen* [2004] 1 W.L.R. 451.

[193] *Igroup Ltd v Ocwen* [2004] 1 W.L.R. 451.

[194] 2006 Act s.859I.

[195] *Ali v Top Marques Car Rental Ltd* [2006] EWHC 109 (Ch).

[196] *National Provincial and Union Bank v Charnley* [1924] 1 K.B. 431 CA (where the property charged was incorrectly stated); *Re Mechanisations (Eaglescliffe) Ltd* [1966] Ch. 20 (amount secured misstated); *Re Eric Holmes (Property) Ltd* [1965] Ch. 1052; *Re CL Nye Ltd* [1971] Ch. 442 (date of creation misstated).

misled[197] by incorrect particulars.[198] Because the certificate is conclusive evidence of registration, there can be no judicial review of the Registrar's decision to register.[199]

On the other hand, registration does not cure any flaw in the charge itself as between the parties, so the validity of the charge remains challengeable by the company.[200] In addition, registration does not determine priority as between competing security interests (although failure to register renders the charge void, and therefore registration is a necessary, although not sufficient, condition to obtaining priority). Priority is determined by the usual common law and equitable rules of property. Indeed, the register does not necessarily provide accurate information to chargees about earlier charges that may rank ahead of any charge currently being negotiated. This is because of the "21 day invisibility problem", whereby if A registers a charge on 21 January, for example, there is no guarantee that the company has not created a charge shortly prior to this which may be registered within 21 days[201] and thus have priority. In applying the normal priority rules as between competing interests, any person taking a registrable charge over the company's property (and perhaps other persons[202]) will have constructive notice of any matter that requires registration and has been disclosed. To take an example, a person taking a contractual lien is probably not affected by constructive notice of the register, but a person taking a floating charge would be.

Reform proposals and registration systems elsewhere

32–33 The fate of recent and not so recent proposals for reform of the UK registration system has already been described.[203] Although some commentators doubt the need for a registration system at all,[204] most developed countries have one. Indeed, the major reform proposals most recently rejected in England and Wales had strong parallels with the systems already operating in the US (Uniform Commercial Code art.9), Canada, New Zealand and Australia, and under

---

[197] Given this feature, then, on those rare occasions where the mistake is that of the Registrar, it seems unlikely the Registrar would be liable to anyone suffering damages, despite *Ministry of Housing and Local Government v Sharp* [1970] 2 Q.B. 223: see *Davis v Radcliffe* [1990] 1 W.L.R. 821 HL and the cases cited therein; *Banque Keyser Ullmann SA v Skandia (UK) Insurance Co Ltd* [1990] 1 Q.B. 665 at 796–798 (on appeal [1991] 2 A.C. 449). But (in a quite different context) see *Serby v Companies House* [2015] 1 B.C.L.C. 670.

[198] See the illustrative cases cited above, fn.196.

[199] *R. v Registrar of Companies, Ex p. Central Bank of India* [1986] Q.B. 1114; followed in *Forthouse Development Ltd (In Administration), Re* [2013] NICh 6.

[200] Most usually on the grounds of capacity or authority, especially in dealings between the company and its directors.

[201] 2006 Act s.859A(4).

[202] See above, para.32–11.

[203] See above, paras 32–24 et seq.

[204] U. Drobnig, "Present and Future of Real and Personal Property" (2003) European Review of Private Law 623 at 660: "If all the information it [the register] offers is a notice that there may exist a security interest, so that intending creditors are put on notice but have to turn to the debtor in order to verify the true state of affairs is not nearly the same effect achieved in countries without a registration system where the courts proceed from a general presumption that business people must know that any major piece of equipment is bought on credit?"

consideration elsewhere. The most disappointing feature of the current position in England and Wales is not simply that the UK has been left with an outdated regime, but that it missed an opportunity to provide the first draft for a model European scheme. The work being done by the EBRD, UNCITRAL and UNIDROIT indicates the demand for sophisticated input on this front.[205] Older editions of this book provided some detail on the Law Commission's various 2002–2005 proposals, assuming that they had not quite been laid to rest,[206] but that detail is not repeated here.[207]

ENFORCEMENT OF FLOATING CHARGES

Receivers and administrators

The methods of enforcing a security interest depend upon the nature of the rights which it confers, and are often in no way peculiar to company law. However, company law has traditionally provided a distinct proceeding for the enforcement of a floating charge by the appointment of a receiver—termed, since the insolvency reforms of the 1980s, an "administrative receiver".[208] In this section, therefore, we return to our preoccupation with the floating charge. A major reform brought about by the Enterprise Act 2002 was substantially to restrict use of receivership in the future and to channel the enforcement of floating charges into the administration procedure, which is a general procedure for the handling of insolvent companies and thus not specific to the enforcement of the floating charge.

32–34

The main driver behind this reform was the desire to produce an enforcement mechanism for the floating charge in which the relevant insolvency practitioner owed duties to all the creditors of the company and not primarily to the floating charge holder.[209] Consistently with the case law origins of the floating charge in the nineteenth century, the receiver is a person appointed out of court by the charge holder under the provisions of the instrument creating the charge, and who takes management control of the company in order to realise sufficient assets to repay the appointor (the charge holder) and then hands the company back to its directors or to a liquidator,[210] depending on the financial state of the company at the end of the receivership.

---

[205] H.G. Beale, M. Bridge, L. Gullifer and E. Lomnicka, *The Law of Security and Title-Based Financing*, 2nd edn (Oxford: OUP, 2012), paras 23–22 et seq. Fundamental changes for UK in the longer term are being considered by the Secured Transactions Law Reform Project: see *http://securedtransactionslawreformproject.org/* [Accessed 27 February 2016].

[206] Also see above, paras 32–24 et seq.

[207] See the 9th edn, paras 32–53 to 32–56.

[208] The distinction is typically made between a person who has control of all, or substantially all, the assets of a company (an administrative receiver: IA 1986 s.29(2)) and a person who simply has control of a single asset or limited class of secured assets (a receiver). The former is in a position to manage the company as a going concern; the latter is not. Both hold their positions in order to realise the rights of the secured creditor (and other creditors, if the charge is floating—see above, paras 32–13 et seq.).

[209] Insolvency Service, White Paper, *Productivity and Enterprise: Insolvency—A Second Chance*, Cm. 5234 (July 2001), para.2.2.

[210] On winding up and liquidation, see Ch.33.

Compared with receivership, administration is a much more recent mechanism, introduced as a result of the recommendations of the Cork Committee.[211] Ironically, the statutory administration procedure was based on the common law receivership. Although the Cork Committee had criticisms to make of receivership, it took the view that it had one inestimable advantage over the then principal alternative way of dealing with an insolvent company, namely winding up. This was because the receivership was structured on the basis that the receiver would normally continue to run the company and in the process save the viable parts of its business (though often by selling them off to others). Such a "rescue culture" was thought to be more protective of the interests of all stakeholders in the business than a winding-up, and so the Committee recommended that the benefits of receivership be made available where there was no floating charge, so that the rescue culture could be extended to such cases.

32–35 Of course, the receivership rules could not simply be applied in total to a situation where there was no floating charge. In the absence of a charge holder to appoint the insolvency practitioner, that task was given to the court, on application by the company or its creditors. Further, the opportunity was taken of giving the statutory administrator the benefit of an institution which the receiver, as a product essentially of private law, had not had, namely, a moratorium during the administration on the enforcement of creditors' rights against the company. Finally, and in line with the notion of the administration as an extension of the receivership, the floating charge holder, if such had been created, was initially given, in effect, a veto over the appointment of an administrator.[212] This last feature was subsequently removed by the Enterprise Act 2002 and, going in the opposite direction, is supplanted by a prohibition in the normal case on the appointment by the floating charge holder of an administrative receiver.[213] Thus under the Enterprise Act 2002, it is not possible to appoint an administrative receiver under a floating charge created on or after 15 September 2003, except as in the cases specified in IA 1986 ss.72B–72H. Instead, the chargee is given the right to appoint an administrator: see IA 1986 Sch.B1 para.14(1). Chargees of charges created prior to this date may appoint an administrator, but retain the right to appoint an administrative receiver. The aim, stated in the White Paper preceding the Enterprise Act 2002, was that "administrative receivership should cease to be a major insolvency procedure".[214] The administrative receiver would instead be replaced by an administrator, who is an officer of the court, and must "perform his functions in the interests of the company's creditors as a whole".[215]

Note that a chargee whose charge does not cover the whole or substantially the whole of the assets of the company can still appoint a receiver (who will not be an administrative receiver), and cannot appoint an administrator.

---

[211] See above, fn.98, Ch.9. The Committee's proposals were not implemented precisely in the way the Committee had envisaged. See V. Finch, *Corporate Insolvency Law*, 2nd edn (Cambridge: CUP, 2009), pp.16–18.

[212] IA 1986 s.9(2) and (3), repealed by the Enterprise Act 2002.

[213] IA 1986 s.72A, introduced by the 2002 Act s.250. The prohibition does not apply to appointments under floating charges in existence before the date on which the new rules are brought into operation: s.72A(4).

[214] See above, fn.209, para.2.5.

[215] IA 1986 Sch.B1 para.3(2).

This policy of statutory patricide was subject, however, to two qualifications **32–36** which concern us. First, the White Paper recognised that the procedure for appointing a receiver had the advantages for the floating charge holder of being quick, cheap and entirely under the charge holder's control. It was further recognised that the earlier administration procedure would need to be reformed so as to reproduce those advantages, as far as possible, within the new structure. "Secured creditors," said the White Paper, "should not feel at any risk from our proposals".[216] Accordingly, the current administration procedure is not simply one that applies more generally, but is itself reformed, a new Pt II being inserted into the IA 1986 by the Enterprise Act 2002.[217]

Secondly, the common law administrative receivership system is retained in certain exceptional cases as mentioned above.[218] Most of these do not need to be discussed in a work of this nature, but one is of crucial importance to us. Under the new IA 1986 s.72B, as interpreted in the new Sch.2A,[219] a receiver may still be appointed where a company issues secured debentures[220] and where (a) the security is held by trustees on behalf of the debenture-holders[221]; (b) the amount to be raised is at least £50 million[222]; and (c) the debentures are to be listed or traded on a regulated market.[223] In terms of enforcement, therefore, an important distinction is drawn between two common forms of corporate finance. Where the debt is raised from the public by way of a large-scale offering of securities, the administrative receivership procedure will continue to be available. Where the debt is raised from a bank (or syndicate of banks), administration will be the enforcement procedure, unless one of the other exceptions contained in IA 1986 ss.72C–72G applies.[224] For this reason it is necessary to discuss briefly both the receivership and administration methods of enforcing the floating charge.[225] We begin with the older procedure.

Receivership

Appointment of an administrative receiver

Where an appointment of an administrative receiver remains possible, because **32–37** the case falls within one of the exceptions noted above and the necessary power is contained in an existing debenture, almost invariably the first step in the enforcement of a charge is for the debenture-holders or their trustee to obtain the

---

[216] See above, fn.209, para.2.6.

[217] Enterprise Act 2002 s.248. The operative provisions are contained mainly in a new Sch.B1 to the IA 1986, set out in Sch.16 to the 2002 Act.

[218] IA 1986 ss.72A–H.

[219] Set out in Sch.18 to the 2002 Act.

[220] IA 1986 s.72B(1)(b) and Sch.2A para.2(1)(a)—which makes a further reference to art.77 of the FSMA 2000 (Regulated Activities) Order 2001 (SI 2001/544), where the inclusion of debentures and debenture stock can be found.

[221] IA 1986 s.72B(1) and Sch.2A para.1(1)(a).

[222] IA 1986 s.72B(1)(a).

[223] IA 1986 Sch.2A para.2.

[224] Note *Feetum v Levy* [2006] Ch. 585: a right to appoint an administrative receiver does not amount to step-in rights.

[225] The use of administration generally is not discussed in this book.

appointment of a receiver.[226] This appointment will normally be made by the debenture-holder under an express or implied[227] power in the debenture, or by the court. Where the appointment is pursuant to a provision in the debenture then it must be clear that the conditions justifying the appointment have arisen, otherwise the receiver will be a trespasser and also liable for conversion.[228]

Once the conditions for the enforcement of a charge have arisen, English law places few constraints on the rights of the security holder to enforce the charge, and in this respect the regime is pro-security holder. For example, if the chargee is entitled to payment on demand, it is only necessary to give the company reasonable time to put into effect the mechanics of payment, not reasonable time in which to raise the funds to make payment.[229] Indeed, if the debtor makes it clear that funds are not available, this constitutes a sufficient act of default and there is no need to allow the debtor any time before treating it as being in default.[230] In addition, the chargee is not under any duty to the debtor company to refrain from exercising its rights merely because by doing so it could avoid loss to the company,[231] nor to exercise its rights promptly because the security is declining in value.[232]

If the security is not yet enforceable, but the debenture-holder's position is in jeopardy, the court may exercise its inherent discretion to appoint a receiver.[233] This is now very rare, but can be done by a debenture-holder's action, taken by one of the debenture-holders, on behalf of himself and all other holders.

---

[226] If the state of the company is so parlous that it is doubtful whether there will be enough to cover the receiver's remuneration it may be necessary for the trustees to take possession. If the "debenture" is just an ordinary mortgage of particular property, the debenture-holder may, of course, exercise its power of sale without the preliminary step of appointing a receiver.

[227] i.e. under LPA 1925 s.101 when applicable.

[228] Where the appointment is defective, the court can order the person making the appointment to indemnify the receiver: IA 1986 s.34. See also IA 1986 s.232, which deals with the validity of acts of a defectively appointed administrative receiver, and IA 1986 s.234 dealing with the seizure or disposal by an administrative receiver of property that does not belong to the company, and generally see *Re London Iron and Steel Co Ltd* [1990] B.C.L.C. 372; *Welsh Development Agency v Export Finance Co Ltd* [1992] B.C.L.C. 148.

[229] *Bank of Baroda v Panessar* [1987] Ch. 335; *Quah Su-Ling v Goldman Sachs International* [2015] EWHC 759 (Comm); this is normally a matter of hours during normal banking hours. In addition, the company may be estopped by its conduct from challenging the validity of the appointment of a receiver, and the appointment of a receiver on invalid grounds may be subsequently cured if grounds justifying the appointment are subsequently discovered: *Bank of Baroda* at 352–353 and *Byblos Bank SAL v Al-Khudairy* [1987] B.C.L.C. 232 respectively. There is no need for the debenture-holder to specify the exact sum due in any demand: see *NRG Vision Ltd v Churchfield Leasing Ltd* [1988] B.C.L.C. 624.

[230] *Sheppard & Cooper Ltd v TSB Bank Plc* [1996] 2 All E.R. 654; *Quah Su-Ling v Goldman Sachs International* [2015] EWHC 759 (Comm).

[231] *Re Potters Oils Ltd* [1986] 1 W.L.R. 201; *Standard Chartered Bank Ltd v Walker* [1982] 1 W.L.R. 1410. Also see *Alpstream AG v PK Airfinance Sarl* [2015] EWCA Civ 1318 CA.

[232] *China and South Sea Bank Ltd v Tan* [1990] 1 A.C. 536 PC; of course it will always be in the commercial interests of the chargee to exercise his rights if the security is declining in value. On other aspects of the receiver's duties to the company and others, see para.32–38, below.

[233] But the court will not normally have any power to appoint a receiver unless the debentures are secured by a charge: *Harris v Beauchamp Bros* [1894] 1 Q.B. 801 CA; *Re Swallow Footwear Ltd,* The Times, 23 October 1956. Also the court will not imply a term into a debenture empowering a chargee to appoint a receiver where his security is in jeopardy: see *Cryne v Barclays Bank Plc* [1987] B.C.L.C. 548 CA.

"Jeopardy" is established when, for example, execution is about to be levied against the company,[234] or when the company proposes to distribute to its members its one remaining asset.[235] "Jeopardy" is not assumed whenever the circumstances make it unreasonable, in the interests of the debenture-holder, that the company should retain power to dispose of the property subject to the charge. This is the statutory definition under Scottish law,[236] but the English decisions hardly go so far, and the fact that the assets on realisation would not repay the debentures in full has been held insufficient.[237]

Despite this option, appointment out of court is certainly preferable. The procedure in a debenture-holders' action is lamentably expensive and dilatory, since the receiver, as an officer of the court, will have to work under its closest supervision and constant applications will have to be made in chambers throughout the duration of the receivership, which may last years if a complicated realisation is involved. Since the 1986 Act allows a receiver, even though appointed out of court, to obtain the court's directions,[238] it is difficult to envisage circumstances in which an application to the court can be justified if the cheaper alternative is available, and the professional adviser who recommended it would be laying himself open to grave risk of criticism. In the discussion which follows, it will be assumed that what is being referred to is a receiver appointed out of court.

Function and status of the receiver and administrative receiver

The 1986 Insolvency Act views the appointment of an administrative receiver as being in some respects similar to insolvency proceedings and regulates it accordingly.[239] Thus administrative receivers must be qualified to act as insolvency practitioners[240] and can only be removed from office by the court.[241] Also, like the liquidator, the administrative receiver can compel those involved in the affairs of the company to provide him or her with information relating to the company's affairs,[242] and is also obliged to report to the Secretary of State if he or she forms the opinion that the conduct of the directors makes any of them unfit to act as director of a company.[243] The effect of the appointment of a receiver upon the company directors is that they no longer have any authority to deal with the company property. They do however officially remain in office and continue to be liable for the submission of documents to Companies House, and may still

32–38

---

[234] *McMahon v North Kent Co* [1891] 2 Ch. 148; *Edwards v Standard Rolling Stock* [1893] 1 Ch. 574; and see *Re Victoria Steamboats Co* [1897] 1 Ch. 158.

[235] *Re Tilt Cove Copper Co* [1913] 2 Ch. 588.

[236] IA 1986 s.52(2) (for the purpose of appointing a receiver), s.122(2) (for the purpose of making a winding-up order).

[237] *Re New York Taxicab Co* [1913] 1 Ch. 1.

[238] IA 1986 s.35.

[239] See IA 1986 s.247(1) for the definition of "insolvency".

[240] IA 1986 s.388(1). A body corporate, an undischarged bankrupt, or a person disqualified to act as a director may not act as an insolvency practitioner: see IA 1986 s.390(1) and (4).

[241] IA 1986 s.45(1); they can resign, ibid.

[242] IA 1986 ss.47 and 236; *Re Aveling Barford Ltd* [1989] 1 W.L.R. 360; *Cloverbay Ltd (Joint Administrators) v BCCI SA* [1991] Ch. 90.

[243] Company Directors Disqualification Act 1986 s.7(3)(d).

institute proceedings in the company's name. In other ways, too, the appointment of a receiver must not be equated with that of a liquidator: (i) where a receiver is appointed, the company need not go into liquidation,[244] and if it does, the same person who acted as receiver will normally not be appointed liquidator; (ii) liquidation is a class action designed to protect the interests of the unsecured creditors, whereas, as we shall see, receivership is designed to protect the interests of the security holders who appointed the receiver and it is for this reason that a receiver can be appointed even where the company is in liquidation[245]; (iii) liquidation terminates the trading power of the company,[246] whereas this is not the case with receivership; (iv) a liquidator has power to disclaim onerous property,[247] something not possible in the case of receivership; (v) a liquidator in a compulsory winding-up is an officer of the court,[248] whereas this is not the case with a receiver unless appointed by the court[249]; (vi) lastly, it is easier to obtain recognition of liquidation as opposed to receivership in proceedings in foreign courts.[250] These are the most important differences but there are others, particularly with respect to liability on contracts.[251]

An administrative receiver might be assumed to be the agent of those who appointed him but this is not the case; IA 1986 s.44 makes him the agent of the company.[252] The reason for this is to avoid those who appointed the administrative receiver being treated as mortgagees in possession[253] or being held liable for the receiver's acts, which would be the case were the receiver to be treated as their agent.[254] As many have pointed out, the receiver's agency is a peculiar form of agency. This is because the primary responsibility of the receiver is to protect the interests of the security holders and to realise the charged assets for their benefit.[255] Nevertheless, the way the receiver carries out these

---

[244] See IA 1986 s.247(2). Although generally a receiver should not be seen as a doctor but rather as an undertaker.

[245] *Re Potters Oils Ltd* [1986] 1 W.L.R. 201.

[246] Also without the leave of the court legal proceedings cannot be brought against the company: see IA 1986 s.130.

[247] See IA 1986 s.178.

[248] *Parsons v Sovereign Bank of Canada* [1913] A.C. 160.

[249] It is contempt of court to interfere with the exercise of power by a court-appointed receiver without the leave of the court.

[250] IA 1986 s.72 permits an English or Scottish receiver to act throughout Great Britain provided local law permits this. The White Paper (above, fn.209 at para.23) suggested that an advantage of greater use of administration was that it would receive easier international recognition.

[251] See paras 32–40 et seq.

[252] Also the debenture will invariably provide that irrespective of the type of receiver appointed by the charge holder he is to be the agent of the company. A receiver appointed by the court is not an agent of anyone but an officer of the court: see *Moss SS Co v Whinney* [1912] A.C. 254 HL.

[253] The duties of a mortgagee in possession are onerous: see H.G. Beale, M. Bridge, L. Gullifer and E. Lomnicka, *The Law of Security and Title-Based Financing*, 2nd edn (Oxford: OUP, 2012), para.18.39.

[254] If the chargee interferes with the receiver's discharge of his duties this could, provided the interference is sufficiently pervasive, result in the receiver being treated as the agent of the chargee: see *American Express International Banking Corp v Hurley* [1985] 3 All E.R. 564.

[255] The receiver would not, for example, be considered to be participating in the management of the company since he is not managing the company but the assets of the company: *Re B Johnson & Co (Builders) Ltd* [1955] Ch. 634; *Re North Development Pty Ltd* (1990) 8 A.C.L.C. 1004. Although contrast the analysis in *Buchler v Talbot* [2004] 2 A.C. 298, above, para.32–18.

responsibilities will profoundly affect parties other than the chargee. If the secured assets are not realised for their full value and there is a shortfall in paying the secured debt, the shortfall may become payable by a guarantor who might feel aggrieved to be called upon if the shortfall seemed unnecessary. Equally, the company—and, if it is insolvent, its creditors—will feel aggrieved if the value of secured asset has been in some way wasted on meeting only the secured creditor's claims when a more careful exercise might have generated a surplus for the benefit of the company. For these reasons, there are a number of parties interested in the various duties the receiver owes in the exercise of his or her role.

This has been a fraught question. The powers of administrative receivers are extensive and they will have complete control over the assets subject to the charge under which the appointment was made.[256] In addition they may apply to the court for an order empowering them to dispose of property subject to a prior charge.[257] In the exercise of these extensive powers, the courts have struggled with the standards that ought to be imposed. The low water mark was probably the decision of the Privy Council in *Downsview Nominees Ltd v First City Corp*,[258] of course much welcomed by insolvency practitioners. Lord Templeman in that case held that the receiver owed no general common law duty of care to interested parties; his duties lay exclusively in equity, which required him merely to act in good faith, although if he did decide to sell the property (as he invariably would), then he was required to take reasonable care to obtain a proper price. Nevertheless, and predictably, the receiver's role could not withstand the onslaught in the development of common law principles of the duty of care. The position now is that receivers are under a duty to the debtor company to take reasonable care to obtain the best price reasonably possible at the time of sale[259]; this duty is also owed to a guarantor of the company's debts.[260] However, as the receiver in exercising a power of sale is in a position analogous to that of a mortgagee, receivers are not obliged to postpone sale in order to obtain a better price or to adopt a piecemeal method of sale.[261] If they delay the sale, they are also under a duty, while they manage the property, to manage it with reasonable care and due diligence.[262]

---

[256] IA 1986 s.42 confers on an administrative receiver the powers set out in Sch.1 to the Act in so far as they are not inconsistent with the terms of the debenture. There are 23 powers enumerated and they are very wide; for example, number 14 confers on an administrative receiver "Power to carry on the business of the company".

[257] IA 1986 s.43. The rights of the security holder are protected in the same way as they are in the case of administration: see para.32–20, above.

[258] *Downsview Nominees Ltd v First City Corp* [1993] A.C. 295 PC.

[259] *Cuckmere Brick Co Ltd v Mutual Finance Ltd* [1971] Ch. 949 CA; *Bishop v Bonham* [1988] 1 W.L.R. 742; *AIB Group (UK) Plc v Personal Representative of James Aiken (Deceased)* [2012] N.I.Q.B. 51.

[260] *Standard Chartered Bank Ltd v Walker* [1982] 1 W.L.R. 1410; *American Express International Banking Corp v Hurley* [1985] 3 All E.R. 564; *AIB Group (UK) Plc v Personal Representative of James Aiken (Deceased)* [2012] N.I.Q.B. 51.

[261] *Cuckmere Brick Co Ltd v Mutual Finance Ltd* [1971] Ch. 949 CA; *Alpstream AG v PK Airfinance Sarl* [2015] EWCA Civ 1318 CA. And if the receiver does wait, he is not liable if the market declines: *Tse Kwong Lam v Wong Chit Sen* [1983] 1 W.L.R. 1349.

[262] *Medforth v Blake* [2000] Ch. 86.

32–39   The basis of the receiver's duty set out above was initially considered to involve a controversial extension of the common law of negligence to supplement equity,[263] but the courts now tend to treat it as something which flows directly from the special nature of the relationship between the chargee and chargor.[264] The result is that the receiver must act in good faith, and not for improper purposes, and must have regard to the chargor's interests while at the same time allowing that the chargee's interests are paramount. The most recent significant English authority, *Medforth v Blake*,[265] treats the standard of care required in equity as the same as that required at common law, and in that case held the receivers, who negligently conducted the business of which they had taken control, to be liable to the mortgagor, who suffered loss when (after the secured debt had been discharged) the business was handed back to him in a less good state than if it had been properly run by the receivers. Although this decision goes some way towards protecting debtor companies, and, by extension, their unsecured creditors, from the incompetence of receivers, the Court of Appeal made it clear that it was not purporting to overturn the principle that the primary duty of the receiver is to bring about the repayment of the debt owed to the secured creditor. In this particular case, there was no conflict of interest between the mortgagor and mortgagee, since both potentially suffered harm as a result of the receivers' incompetence.[266] The case, thus, is not authority for the proposition that it is negligent for the receivers to give primacy to the appointor's interests as against those of the mortgagor (or the company and its unsecured creditors).

A person dealing with an administrative receiver in good faith and for value is not bound to enquire if the receiver is acting within his or her powers.[267] Unlike a winding-up, the board of directors is not discharged on the appointment of a receiver, but the directors' powers are substantially superseded since they cannot act so as to interfere with the discharge by the receiver of his or her responsibilities and accordingly their powers are suspended "so far as is requisite to enable a receiver to discharge his functions".[268] Given the extent of the powers of the administrative receiver, the directors will have a miniscule aperture within which they are free to exercise their powers. However, they do possess certain residual powers and, for example, it has been held that they can bring

---

[263] See G. Lightman and G. Moss, *The Law of Administrators and Receivers of Companies*, 5th edn (London: Sweet & Maxwell, 2011), Ch.7.

[264] *Parker-Tweedale v Dunbar Bank Plc* [1991] Ch. 12 CA (mortgagee owes no duty to beneficiary of mortgaged property); *Downsview Nominees Ltd v First City Corp* [1993] A.C. 295 PC; *Cukurova Finance International Ltd v Alfa Telecom Turkey Ltd* [2013] UKPC 2; [2015] 2 W.L.R. 875.

[265] *Medforth v Blake* [2000] Ch. 86 CA; thus somewhat back-tracking on the decision of the Privy Council in *Downsview Nominees Ltd v First City Corp* [1993] A.C. 295. See also *Knight v Lawrence* [1993] B.C.L.C. 215; and, recently, *Purewal v Countrywide Residential Lettings Ltd* [2015] EWCA Civ 1122 CA.

[266] On the facts, the appointor suffered no loss because the business, even in its damaged state, generated enough profit to satisfy the appointor's claims.

[267] IA 1986 s.42(3). If an administrative receiver is seen as being an organ of the company, then this provision is arguably not in compliance with art.9(2) of the First Directive. See Ch.7, above.

[268] *Re Emmadart Ltd* [1979] Ch. 540 at 544; see also *Gomba Holdings UK Ltd v Homan* [1986] 1 W.L.R. 1301.

proceedings in the company's name.[269] This authority has been doubted because of the conflict that would arise were the receiver and the directors to have different views on whether an action should be brought, and also on the handling of any counterclaim.[270] Whatever the status of the *Newhart* decision,[271] it is clear that it will be confined to very narrow limits, since to allow every such action would interfere with the primary duties of the receiver to protect the interests of the security holder.[272] On the other hand, the directors can certainly take proceedings to challenge the validity of the receiver's appointment,[273] or sue the receiver for breach of duty,[274] or oppose a petition to wind up the company.[275]

Finally, as the directors remain in office, the receiver is under an obligation to provide the directors with the information that they request to enable them to comply with their reporting obligations under the Companies Act.[276] The receiver is also obliged at the end of his receivership to hand over to the company any documents belonging to the company other than those brought into existence for the discharge of his own professional duties or his duties to the chargee.[277]

The receiver's liability with respect to contracts

An administrative receiver taking over the management of a company will need to manage the company's existing (partly performed) contracts, and will need to enter into new contracts on behalf of the company. These raise separate issues.

32–40

Consider first the contracts already in existence when the receiver is appointed. As an administrative receiver is the agent of the company, the

---

[269] *Newhart Developments Ltd v Co-operative Commercial Bank Ltd* [1978] Q.B. 814 CA (it is important to note that in that case the company was indemnified for any costs that it might incur and the receiver had decided not to bring any action against his appointor).

[270] *Tudor Grange Holdings Ltd v Citibank NA* [1992] Ch. 53. As Browne-Wilkinson VC pointed out in that case, it would be more appropriate for receivers or their appointor to use IA 1986 s.35. *Tudor Grange* has itself come in for criticism: see *Re Geneva Finance Ltd* (1992) 7 A.C.S.L.R. 415 at 426–432.

[271] It could be argued that the right to bring an action against the debenture-holder could not be an asset covered by the charge. This, however, proves too much since it would mean that the directors would always be in a position to bring an action against the debenture-holder even when the special factors in *Newhart* were not present. And while this argument rightly emphasises the scope of the receiver's authority it fails to give effect to his functions. Also the agency of the receiver may have sufficient content to impose on him a duty to seek redress against a debenture-holder in appropriate cases.

[272] See also *Gomba Holdings UK Ltd v Homan* [1986] 1 W.L.R. 1301; *Watts v Midland Bank Plc* [1986] B.C.L.C. 15 (a case which illustrates that since the power to use the corporate name in litigation is normally vested in the directors, a shareholder will normally be precluded from bringing a derivative action against a receiver, none of the usual reasons for the exceptions applying on these facts).

[273] *Hawkesbury Development Co Ltd v Landmark Finance Pty Ltd* (1969) 92 WN (NSW) 199.

[274] *Watts v Midland Bank Plc* [1986] B.C.L.C. 15.

[275] *Re Reprographic Exports (Euromat) Ltd* (1978) 122 SJ 400.

[276] *Gomba Holdings UK Ltd v Homan* [1986] 1 W.L.R. 1301; see also at 1305–1306 where Hoffmann J points out that equity may impose on a receiver a duty to account which is wider than his statutory obligations.

[277] *Gomba Holdings UK Ltd v Minories Finance Ltd* [1988] 1 W.L.R. 1231 CA. Once a receiver has sufficient funds to pay off the debt and his own expenses he should cease managing the company's assets: *Rottenberg v Monjack* [1993] B.C.L.C. 374.

appointment does not of itself affect existing contracts. If, in the interests of the chargee, the receiver causes the company to repudiate these contracts, the injured parties will be left to their normal contractual remedies in damages, but with the company unlikely to be left with the funds to pay such claims.[278] Since, in doing this, the receiver acts as an agent of the company, he cannot be liable for the tort of inducing a breach of contract.[279] The only exceptions to this general rule are the normal exceptions applying with contracts that are specifically enforceable[280] or subject to injunctions: the appointment of an administrative receiver makes no difference to the court's response in these cases. On the other hand, if the receiver does not repudiate the contract, he is said to "adopt" it.[281] This is rather misleading terminology: the contract is not a new contract at all; it remains the contract entered into by the company on the terms agreed by the company. Indeed, this itself can cause problems for receivers where adoption brings into play contractual liens[282] or set-offs.[283]

As a matter of policy, it seems desirable to impose a limited duty on the receiver to continue to trade or otherwise act positively where this would not jeopardise the chargee's interests and a failure to do so would impose gratuitous damage on the company.[284] Not to extend his duty in this way would stretch the pro-creditor bias of receivership to ridiculous lengths. But, as described below, this obligation is limited: the primary purpose of receivership is to realise the assets for the benefit of the secured creditor.

32–41 Special mention should be made of contracts of employment. These contracts are not automatically terminated by the receiver's appointment unless the receiver does something which is inconsistent with the continuation of the contract,[285] for example by selling the company's business.[286] If the receiver sees no hope of selling the business as a going concern, then he is likely to dismiss the employees forthwith. Such dismissal will likely be because of redundancy, and will almost certainly not be unfair dismissal (provided there is no unfair selection of the persons to be dismissed). The receiver may take some time to decide what to do. Nothing that is done or omitted to be done in the first 14 days of the receiver's appointment is taken as showing that the receiver has adopted a contract of

---

[278] *Airline Airspares Ltd v Handley Page Ltd* [1970] Ch. 193.

[279] *Said v Butt* [1920] 3 K.B. 497; *Welsh Development Agency v Export Finance Co Ltd* [1992] B.C.L.C. 148; *Belcher v Heaney* [2013] EWHC 4353 (Ch).

[280] *Freevale Ltd v Metrostore (Holdings) Ltd* [1984] Ch. 199; *AMEC Properties Ltd v Planning Research and Systems Plc* [1992] B.C.L.C. 1149; and cf. *Ash & Newman Ltd v Creative Devices Research Ltd* [1991] B.C.L.C. 403.

[281] *Powdrill v Watson* [1995] 2 A.C. 394.

[282] *George Barker (Transport) Ltd v Eynon* [1974] 1 W.L.R. 462 CA.

[283] *Rother Iron Works Ltd v Canterbury Precision Engineers Ltd* [1974] Q.B. 1.

[284] *Knight v Lawrence* [1991] B.C.C. 411; *Medforth v Blake* [2000] Ch. 86. See below, para.32–47. Contrast the two *obiter* comments that a receiver does (*R. v Board of Trade, Ex p. St Martins Preserving Co Ltd* [1965] 1 Q.B. 603) and does not (*Re B Johnson and Co (Builders) Ltd* [1955] Ch. 364) have a duty to preserve the goodwill of the company. Also see *Purewal v Countrywide Residential Lettings Ltd* [2015] EWCA Civ 1122 CA.

[285] *Griffiths v Secretary of State for Social Services* [1974] Q.B. 468. The appointment of the receiver by the court does terminate contracts of service: *Reid v Explosives Co Ltd* (1887) 19 Q.B.D. 264; cf. *Sipad Holding v Popovic* (1995) 19 A.C.S.R. 108.

[286] *Re Foster Clark's Ltd's Indenture Trusts* [1966] 1 W.L.R. 125.

employment.[287] After that, if nothing is done, the receiver will be taken to have impliedly adopted these contracts.[288] Once adopted, the administrative receiver is, by statute, personally liable for the company's liability for wages or salary, contributions to an occupational pension scheme, holiday and sick pay, and deductions for income tax and national insurance,[289] from the date of adoption of the contract.[290] The administrative receiver cannot contract out of this liability for adopted employment contracts,[291] but is entitled to an indemnity out of the assets of the company.[292]

Where the receiver enters into new contracts, this is done as agent for the company, and the contracts will therefore be binding on the company. More importantly, however, the receiver is also personally liable by statute on any contract entered into on behalf of the company unless the contract provides otherwise.[293] Exclusion of liability may be express or implied. Administrative receivers will invariably try to contract out of liability. They will in any event have a statutory indemnity out of the company's assets[294] and will usually also have an indemnity from the chargee.

Publicity of appointment and reports

Where a receiver or manager is appointed then this must be stated in various business documents relating to the company.[295] All receivers also have to make prescribed returns to the Registrar,[296] and the administrative receiver has to report to creditors, including unsecured creditors, but will not have to report to those who have opted out of receiving notices.[297] A receiver who fails to comply with his reporting obligations can be ordered to do so[298] and, more importantly, can be disqualified from acting as a receiver or manager.[299] There is no similar obligation to report where a debenture-holder enters into possession and it has been recommended that this omission be corrected.[300]

32–42

---

[287] IA 1986 s.44(2).
[288] *Powdrill v Watson* [1995] 2 A.C. 394.
[289] *Re FJL Realisations Ltd* [2001] I.C.R. 424.
[290] IA 1986 s.44.
[291] But contrast newly negotiated contracts, below.
[292] IA 1986 s.44(1)(c).
[293] IA 1986 s.44(1)(b) as amended by the Insolvency Act 1994 s.2. He is entitled to indemnification out of the assets of the company (s.44(1)(c)), and can also contract for indemnification by those who appointed him (s.44(3)).
[294] IA 1986 s.44(1)(c).
[295] IA 1986 s.39.
[296] IA 1986 s.38 (receivers) and s.48 (administrative receivers).
[297] IA 1986 s.48.
[298] IA 1986 s.41. Also of relevance are the Insolvency Rules 1986 Pt 3.
[299] Company Directors Disqualification Act 1986 ss.1(1)(a), 3 and 22(7); see *Re Artic Engineering Ltd (No.2)* [1986] 1 W.L.R. 686.
[300] Jenkins Committee, para.306(k).

Administration[301]

Function

32–43 The "rescue" goals of the revised administration procedure are clearly displayed in the current definition of the objectives of administration, set out in Sch.B1 to the IA 1986. Three objectives are listed but are put into a clear hierarchy. Priority is given to "rescuing the company as a going concern",[302] which is the objective which the administrator must pursue unless he or she thinks it is not practicable to achieve it or that the second objective would better serve the creditors' needs.[303] That second objective is "achieving a better result for the company's creditors as a whole than would be likely if the company were wound up".[304] Thus, preservation of the company as a going concern, to the benefit, for example, of employees, is not essential if the creditors would be worse off as a result. The third objective is "realising property in order to make a distribution to one or more secured or preferential creditors".[305] The administrator may pursue this objective only if it is not reasonably practicable to achieve the other two objectives, and it must be pursued in such a way that it will "not unnecessarily harm the interests of the other creditors of the company as a whole".[306] Subject to the qualification implied where the administrator legitimately pursues the third objective, the administrator must act "in the interests of the company's creditors as a whole".[307]

Although on an application to the court, the purpose of the proposed administration has to be stated, that purpose does not have to be confined to a single goal. It is more likely, therefore, that the statutory purposes will simply control the way in which the administrator, after appointment, exercises his or her powers. The floating charge holder may read these provisions with some gloom, for the priority given to the second objective over the third appears to mean that if the creditors as a whole would be better off than in a winding-up, the administrator should pursue that course of action, even if the charge holder will be worse off.[308]

Appointment

32–44 As is now generally required in the insolvency area, only a qualified insolvency practitioner may be appointed as an administrator.[309] An administrator may be appointed by the court, on application by the company, its directors or one or

---

[301] This discussion will concentrate on the appointment of an administrator where the company has granted a floating charge, though, as we have seen (above, para.32–34) administration is not confined to such situations.

[302] IA 1986 Sch.B1 para.3(1)(a).

[303] IA 1986 Sch.B1 para.3(3).

[304] IA 1986 Sch.B1 para.3(1)(b).

[305] IA 1986 Sch.B1 para.3(1)(c).

[306] IA 1986 Sch.B1 para.3(4).

[307] IA 1986 Sch.B1 para.3(2).

[308] This is subject to the "unfair harm" protection discussed below.

[309] IA 1986 Sch.B1 para.5.

more creditors,[310] where the company is or is likely to become unable to pay its debts[311] and the appointment is "reasonably likely" to achieve one of the specified purposes.[312] This seems to put into statutory form the position at which the courts had arrived under the old law, which used a different form of wording, namely, that there must be a "real prospect" that the purpose or purposes will be achieved.[313] The change is important, for a higher hurdle materially increases the costs (as well as decreasing the chances) of securing an administration order, especially by encouraging applicants to commission an extensive report by an independent person in support of the application.[314]

An administrator may also be appointed out of court, and this now is the preferred route in the interest of saving costs. The ability to do this[315] was one of the important changes introduced by the Enterprise Act 2002, to reduce opposition to the proposals from banks.[316] The holder of a "qualifying floating charge",[317] being a charge or charges which relate to the whole or substantially the whole of the company's property, may appoint an administrator out of court where the instrument creating the charge gives the holder the power to do so.[318] Such an administrator will still be an officer of the court,[319] and what has been said above about the objectives of the administration still applies. Notice and other documents have to be filed with the court after the appointment.[320] If it turns out that the appointment was invalid (for example, because the appointor did not hold a valid floating charge),[321] the court may order the appointor to indemnify the person appointed against liability arising (for example, to the company in trespass or conversion).[322]

---

[310] IA 1986 Sch.B1 para.12 (or by the chief executive of a magistrates court in the case of fines imposed on companies).

[311] In one context (see IA 1986 Sch.B1 para.35) this is not a requirement: this is where the application is made to the court by a floating charge holder who has the power to make an appointment out of court (see below). As we have seen above (para.31–26), the terms of debentures may give charge holders the power to appoint even though the company is able to pay its debts.

[312] IA 1986 Sch.B1 para.11.

[313] *Re Harris Simmons Ltd* [1989] 1 W.L.R. 368; *Re Primlaks (UK) Ltd* [1989] B.C.L.C. 734; cf. *Re Consumer & Industrial Press Ltd* [1988] B.C.L.C. 177.

[314] Provision is made for such reports by r.2.2 but they are not mandatory and the Chancery Division judges have sought to encourage concise reports not based on protracted and expensive investigation: Practice Note [1994] 1 W.L.R. 160.

[315] Though, as we have seen (above, para.32–34), the floating charge holder is not excluded from applying to the court for an appointment.

[316] Banks feared not only the cost of court applications, but, more so, the delay involved, during which desperate directors might spirit assets out of the company, once they knew of the petition.

[317] A floating charge over a company's property is a qualifying floating charge if it alone, or in conjunction with other floating or fixed charges, covers the whole, or substantially the whole of the company's property and the contract creating the floating charge states that the chargee may so appoint an administrator (IA 1986 s.72A and Sch.B1 para.14).

[318] IA 1986 Sch.B1 para.14. He or she must give two days' notice of the intention to appoint to the holder of any prior floating charge (so that that person may take action, if desired), but the intention does not have to be advertised generally, which would defeat one of the objectives of this power.

[319] IA 1986 Sch.B1 para.5.

[320] IA 1986 Sch.B1 para.46.

[321] This means that the charge must be enforceable when the notice of appointment is filed under para.18, as that is when the appointment is made: *Fliptex Ltd v Hogg* [2004] EWHC 1280 (Ch); [2004] B.C.C. 870.

[322] IA 1986 Sch.B1 para.21.

The company or the directors may also appoint an administrator out of court,[323] but not if a receiver is in office,[324] and five days' notice of the intention to appoint has to be given to any floating charge holder, whose consent to the appointment is required.[325] This has two consequences. First, it gives the floating charge holder the opportunity to act first and appoint an administrator of its own choosing.[326] Secondly, in those cases where the charge holder still has the right to appoint an administrative receiver,[327] such an appointment may be made instead. Alternatively, the floating charge holder could simply block the appointment proposed by the company or its directors by not giving consent. In such a case the company or its directors would presumably apply to the court for an appointment. Indeed, it appears that the court can appoint an administrator even though a receiver has already been appointed,[328] but the situations in which the court may exercise this power are limited.[329] Thus, where the appointment of an administrative receiver is still allowed under the new regime, it is logically given priority over the appointment of an administrator.

Powers and duties

32–45 The first task of the administrator is to produce a set of proposals for the future of the company's business, which are put before its creditors for their approval. This must be done within eight weeks of appointment, and sooner if possible.[330] The time limit may be extended by the court on application by the administrator.[331] Notice of the proposals has to be given to members as well as creditors who have not opted out of receiving notice,[332] since in some cases the members may have a financial interest in the success of the rescue. A wide range of outcomes is possible in the case of an administration. They do not need to be examined in detail here. They may be successful, as in acceptance by the creditors of proposals for a restructuring of their rights under a scheme of arrangement[333] that enables the company to come out of administration and be returned to its previous management, although perhaps with the former creditors now owning a majority of the shares. They may be unsuccessful, as in rejection of the administrator's plans by the creditors and the company being put into liquidation. And there are many variations in between. Whatever the decision reached, the administrator must report the outcome to the court and to the Registrar. Failure to

---

[323] IA 1986 Sch.B1 para.22.

[324] IA 1986 Sch.B1 para.25(c).

[325] IA 1986 Sch.B1 para.28.

[326] In addition, on an application to the court by a non-floating charge holder, the charge holder has a presumptive right to have its nominee for administrator appointed in place of the applicant's: para.36.

[327] See above, para.32–37.

[328] IA 1986 Sch.B1 para.12(1)(a) clearly contemplates that a receiver may be in place when the application to the court for an administrator is made, as does para.41, which provides for an administrative receiver to vacate office when an administrator is appointed.

[329] IA 1986 Sch.B1 para.39—essentially where the charge holder consents or the charge is thought to be subject to challenge, for example under s.245 (above, para.32–14).

[330] IA 1986 Sch.B1 para.49(5).

[331] IA 1986 Sch.B1 paras 49(8) and 107.

[332] IA 1986 Sch.B1 para.49(4).

[333] See above, Ch.29.

do so attracts a fine.[334] It is worth noting that amendments brought about by the Small Business, Enterprise and Employment Act 2015 has simplified the insolvency procedure by removing the need for creditors' meetings as the default means of decision making.

Between appointment and approval of the proposals, the administrator may exercise all the powers conferred by IA 1986 Sch.B1 para.59 and Sch.1, and this includes the power to dispose of the company's property if an attractive offer is made.[335]

During the administration process, the company benefits from a moratorium on both winding up[336] and legal proceedings for the enforcement of claims against it, except, in the latter case, with the consent of the administrator or the court.[337] A somewhat more limited moratorium also applies from the moment any formal step is taken to seek an administration order.[338] The administrator has general authority to manage the company's business, acting as its agent,[339] as well as the powers specified in Sch.1 to the Act[340]; may appoint and remove directors[341]; and, as we have noted,[342] may dispose of property subject to the floating charge[343] and, with the consent of the court, even property subject to a fixed charge.[344] However, the court may so order only if the court thinks the disposal would be likely to promote the purposes of the administration and there is applied to discharging the security the net proceeds of the disposal and any additional amount needed to bring that amount up to the market value of the asset. Since the moratorium will prevent the charge holders (fixed or floating) from enforcing their security, the position may be that charge holders not only cannot repossess their property but that the administrator has disposed of it. However, the floating charge holder will have his or her security transferred to the proceeds of the sale,[345] whilst the conditions attached to the court's power to sanction a sale over property in relation to which a fixed charge obtains mean the only detriment to the fixed charge holder is that he cannot control the timing of the realisation of his security, which will be undertaken by the administrator, probably as part of a larger disposal, instead of by the security holder as a single transaction.

---

[334] IA 1986 Sch.B1 para.53(2) and (3).

[335] Re Transbus International Ltd [2004] 1 W.L.R. 2654 at [12]–[14].

[336] But not winding up under IA 1986 s.124A on public interest grounds: see para.18–13. See para.42(4)(a).

[337] IA 1986 Sch.B1 paras 42 and 43. Paragraph 43(4) includes the landlord's right of forfeiture by peaceable re-entry, which had been an issue disputed in the pre-2002 case-law. This extension was made initially by the Insolvency Act 2000 s.9. However, intervention by regulators appears to remain outside the moratorium. See *Air Ecosse Ltd v Civil Aviation Authority* (1987) 3 B.C.C. 492; *Re Railtrack Plc* [2002] 2 B.C.L.C. 755.

[338] IA 1986 Sch.B1 para.44.

[339] IA 1986 Sch.B1 para.69, so that the company, not the appointor, is liable for unlawful acts of the administrator.

[340] IA 1986 Sch.B1 para.59.

[341] IA 1986 Sch.B1 para.61.

[342] See above, para.32–20.

[343] IA 1986 Sch.B1 para.70.

[344] IA 1986 Sch.B1 para.71.

[345] IA 1986 Sch.B1 para.70(2), thus in effect putting the charge holder in the position which obtained before the charge crystallised.

32–46   Overall, the administrator has all the powers normally vested in the board of directors,[346] now supplemented by some of those given to liquidators, specifically the power to bring actions against directors claiming compensation on behalf of the company for fraudulent or wrongful trading.[347] In contrast with an administrative receiver,[348] he or she is not personally liable on contracts entered into on the company's behalf. However, the Act contains an alternative mechanism for ensuring that the administrator secures the discharge of the obligations he or she causes the company to incur. When the administrator relinquishes office, undischarged liabilities are charged on the company's assets and rank ahead of any floating charge or the administrator's own remuneration.[349]

The moratorium, which, as we have noted, was not available to the administrative receiver, may prove an important means of reconciling the banks to the use of the administration. Although it prevents them from enforcing their security, it also keeps unsecured creditors at bay and may promote the sale of the company's business at a higher price, from which those with security will be the first to benefit financially. However, the impact of the moratorium depends in part on how willing the courts are to grant leave. Some guidance on this was given by the Court of Appeal in *Re Atlantic Computer Systems (No.1)*[350] of which the following is a summary. Since the prohibitions in s.11 are intended to assist the administrator to achieve the purpose of the administration, it is for the person who seeks leave (or consent) to make out a case for being granted it. If leave is unlikely to impede the achievement of that purpose, leave should normally be given. In other cases it is necessary to carry out a balancing exercise, weighing the legitimate interests of the applicant and those of the other creditors of the company. In carrying out that exercise the underlying principle is that an administration should not be conducted at the expense of those who have proprietary rights which they are seeking to exercise, except to the extent that this may be inevitable if the purpose of the administration is to succeed and even then only to a limited extent. Thus, it will normally be a sufficient ground for granting leave if significant loss would otherwise be suffered by the applicant, unless the loss to others would be significantly greater. In assessing the respective losses all the circumstances relating to the administration should be taken into account and regard paid to how probable they are likely to be. The conduct of the respective parties may sometimes also be relevant. Similar considerations apply to decisions regarding imposing terms.

Of course, an unpaid creditor of a company in administration does not have an obligation to continue with supplies or to make further advances unless

---

[346] The directors, although still in place, may not exercise management power without the consent of the administrator: para.64.

[347] IA 1986 ss.246ZA–246ZC, added by SBEEA 2015. See discussion of the parallel provisions for liquidators, in IA 1986 ss.213–215, at paras 9–4 et seq.

[348] Who, despite the fact that he too acts as an agent is personally liable on contracts he enters into unless they provide to the contrary. See above, para.32–40.

[349] IA 1986 Sch.B1 para.99(4). For the application of this rule in relation to adopted employment contracts, see *Powdrill v Watson* [1995] 2 A.C. 394 HL; partially reversed by the Insolvency Act 1994; and Pollard, (1995) 24 I.L.J. 141.

[350] *Re Atlantic Computer Systems (No.1)* [1992] Ch. 505. See also *Bristol Airport Plc v Powdrill* [1990] Ch. 744 CA.

contractually or statutorily required to do so.[351] Thus, the moratorium may protect the company in administration from pressure from its existing creditors, but it falls far short of guaranteeing that the administrator will be able to carry on the business effectively during the administration. That is likely to require fresh funding and the availability (or not) of such funding is one of the matters the court needs to consider when deciding whether to appoint an administrator.

Protections for creditors and members as against the administrator

It is clear that an administration may give rise to many of the same agency problems which we have examined in previous chapters in relation to companies that are going concerns. There may be conflicts between majority and minority creditors, and administrators may exercise their wide powers unfairly or incompetently. The Schedule provides some remedies aimed at such conduct. First, administrator proposals to the creditors may not involve downgrading the rights of secured or preferential creditors, without their consent or use of a scheme of arrangement or a company voluntary arrangement (which contain mechanisms for the protection of minorities).[352] Thus, although the secured creditor is put into a collective insolvency procedure, it is given specific protection that the administrator may not propose action which "affects the right of a secured creditor to enforce his security".[353] Secondly, and more generally, protection against unfair prejudice[354] is extended to actions of the administrator, so that any member or creditor of the company can apply to the court for relief[355] on the grounds that the administrator is acting, has acted or proposes to act in a way which is "unfairly harms" the interests of the applicant.[356] It is not clear whether the substitution of the phrase "unfairly harms" for the phrase "unfairly prejudicial", which is used in the equivalent CA provision[357] and was used in the original version of the IA 1986[358] is intended to produce a substantive change. Thirdly, an application can also be made on the grounds that the administrator "is not performing his functions as quickly or efficiently as is reasonably practicable",[359] thus giving members and creditors an uncomplicated route to

32–47

---

[351] *Leyland DAF Ltd v Automotive Products Plc* [1994] 1 B.C.L.C. 245 CA.

[352] IA 1986 Sch.B1 para.73. Thus, in creditor meetings to approve a scheme secured and unsecured creditors would be put in separate classes: above, paras 29–8 et seq.

[353] It is important not to overestimate the extent of this specific protection. It applies only to the right to enforce the security; it would not apply to action which fails to maximise the value of the assets to which the security attaches.

[354] See above, Ch.20.

[355] The court has broad relief powers (para.74(3) and (4)), but there is no specific mention of a power to order litigation in the name of the company (though presumably the court could do so under its general authority to "grant relief") or the compulsory purchase of shares (hardly likely to be an appropriate order in an administration).

[356] IA 1986 Sch.B1 para.74. This applies whilst the company is "in administration". If it is not, the creditor may no longer petition; if it is, this paragraph effectively replaces CA 2006 s.994 as far as members are concerned, for the administrator's or court's consent would be needed under the moratorium provisions for a s.994 petition to be launched.

[357] Now CA 2006 s.994.

[358] IA 1986 s.27, now repealed.

[359] IA 1986 Sch.B1 para.74(2).

complain about negligence on the part of the administrator.[360] Fourthly, the misfeasance provisions from IA 1986 s.212[361] are elaborated in their application to administrators.[362] Together, these last three provisions lay down standards by which the creditors and members can challenge conduct of the administrator which either falls below the standard of competence they are entitled to expect or which does not give appropriate weight to their interests.[363]

Publication of appointment

32–48   A newly appointed administrator must notify the company, the Registrar, and the company's creditors of the appointment.[364] While the company is in administration, every business document must state that fact and name the administrator.[365]

Administration expenses

32–49   Debts or liabilities arising out of contracts entered into by the administrator have priority (often called "super-priority") over the administrator's own remuneration and expenses.[366] This can amount to a hefty liability. The expenses of administration, including the administrator's remuneration, then have priority over a debt secured by a floating charge.[367] After this, the normal priority rules apply.[368]

End of administration

32–50   Under IA 1986 s.76, the appointment of an administrator ceases to have effect at the end of the period of one year beginning with the date on which the

---

[360] cf. the uncertainties surrounding the use of CA 2006 s.994 (previously CA 1985 s.459) against negligence, above, paras 20–14 et seq.

[361] See above, Ch.17.

[362] IA 1986 Sch.B1 para.75.

[363] The risk that these provisions will be used by particular creditors or members opportunistically to block a resolution of the company's problems is somewhat reduced by para.74(6) which says that no order by way of relief may be made by the court if it would "impede or prevent the implementation of a scheme agreed under the CA or a company voluntary arrangement agreed under Pt I of the IA or administrator proposals approved by creditors, unless, in the last case, the application is made within 28 days. However, a fixed charge holder can use this procedure even when the court has authorised the administrator to dispose of the property (see para.74(5)(b)), presumably lest the administrator carry out the disposal in an unfair or negligent way".

[364] IA 1986 Sch.B1 para.46.

[365] IA 1986 Sch.B1 para.45.

[366] IA 1986 Sch.B1 para.99. But the provisions are strictly construed, and damages for wrongful dismissal or other payments in lieu are not entitled to super-priority: *Re Leeds United Association Football Club Ltd (In Administration)* [2007] I.C.R. 1688 at 1761 (Ch).

[367] IA 1986 Sch.B1 para.99.

[368] See above, paras 32–15 et seq.

appointment took effect, unless the term of office is extended by the court or with the consent of the creditors. The term may be extended by consent only once[369] and by no more than one year.[370]

Alternatively, on the application of the administrator, the court may provide for the appointment of the administrator to cease to have effect, if the purpose of the administration has been sufficiently achieved in relation to the company.[371] Administrators are often keen for these provisions to be interpreted pragmatically in order to enable them to escape accruing business liabilities; the courts have generally complied.[372] The administrator may now also be obliged to make such an application if the company's creditors decide that he must do so.[373]

CONCLUSION

A company must be able to raise debt finance, and so it must be able to grant effective security to lenders. It is possible to conceive of a legal regime in which the position of companies giving security is in essence no different from that of any other borrower. There would inevitably be some company law aspects to security transactions—for example, are the directors authorised to enter into the particular transaction contemplated?—but those company law aspects would not be unique to security transactions. As we saw in Ch.7, the issue of directors' authority can easily arise in relation to transactions that do not involve a grant of security.

32–51

In fact, however, as this chapter has shown, the current law on the granting of security does have two features that are specific to the corporate nature of the debtor. These are the availability of the floating charge and the system of registration of charges granted by companies. We have also seen, however, that the modern tendency is to whittle away these uniquely corporate features. Thus, the unique enforcement mechanism for the floating charge by means of the appointment of an administrative receiver has been substantially replaced by the general insolvency mechanism of the appointment of an administrator, as introduced by the Enterprise Act 2002. Going further, the Law Commission has queried the justification for retaining the provisions in the Bills of Sales Acts which prevent non-corporate businesses granting floating charges (as have other bodies before them).[374] Equally, in its proposals for radical reform of the companies charges system, the Law Commission clearly regards the optimal solution as being a registration system applying to charges (and quasi-securities) granted by all debtors,[375] although its proposals were not adopted. Could it be that, like corporate insolvency and public offers of corporate securities before

---

[369] IA 1986 Sch.B1 para.78(4).
[370] IA 1986 Sch.B1 para.76(2)(b), as amended by s.127 of the Small Business, Enterprise and Employment Act 2015.
[371] IA 1986 Sch.B1 para.79(3)(b).
[372] *Re TM Kingdom Ltd* [2007] B.C.C. 480; *Re GHE Realisations Ltd* [2006] B.C.C. 139.
[373] IA 1986 Sch.B1 para.79(2)(c).
[374] See above, Law Commission CP 164 (2002), fn.161, Pt IX. In one limited area, that of farmers, the problem was addressed as long ago as 1928 in the Agricultural Credits Act of that year.
[375] See each of the Law Commission documents noted above in fnn.160 and 161.

them, security interests granted by companies is a topic which is on its way out of core company law, in order to join up with the rules that apply where a company is not involved?

PART 8

INSOLVENCY AND ITS CONSEQUENCES

CHAPTER 33

WINDING UP, DISSOLUTION AND RESTORATION

INTRODUCTION

Where a company no longer has the funds to function, or its members no longer wish it to function, then there needs to be a process for bringing the existence of the legal entity to an end. This is achieved by winding up, or liquidation (the two terms can be used interchangeably).[1] The process of winding up, or liquidation, is designed to ensure that, before the company ceases to exist, all its outstanding obligations are met (so far as they can be) and any surplus assets (if there are any) are distributed to the members according to their agreed entitlement.[2] For reasons which might be obvious, especially given the competing interests which may need to be balanced, this process is not undertaken by the company's own directors, but by independent appointees who are qualified insolvency practitioners and who act professionally as company liquidators (alternatively, in some circumstances, the process is carried out by the Official Receiver). When this process is completed, the company is removed from the register: it is "dissolved".

33–1

---

[1] And, more rarely, simply by striking the company off the register: see below, paras 33–29 and 33–30 et seq.

[2] See Ch.23, above.

Clearly this is a dramatic step, and, as we have seen already, there are less terminal alternatives which may provide avenues for the successful rescue of failing companies: recall the use of administration, administrative receivership and company voluntary arrangements and reconstructions, often also making use of professional outsiders.[3]

The provisions relating to winding up and dissolution are now to be found almost exclusively[4] in the Insolvency Act 1986 and Pt IV of the Insolvency Rules,[5] and not in the Companies Act: and rightly so where the company is insolvent. But, although insolvency is the most common reason for winding up, it is far from being the only one and, when the company is fully solvent, it seems, on the face of it, somewhat illogical to treat the process as part of insolvency law rather than company law. The reason why the legislation relating to liquidation of solvent companies is in the Insolvency Act is probably to avoid duplicating those many provisions that apply whether or not the company is insolvent—to repeat them in the Companies Act would have added substantially to the length of the combined legislation. But it can also be justified as realistic. Once a company goes into liquidation, the distinction between shareholders and creditors becomes more than usually difficult to draw: the members' interests will, in effect, have become purely financial interests deferred to those of the creditors.

TYPES OF WINDING UP

33–2   The basic distinction is between voluntary winding up and compulsory winding up by the court.[6] But voluntary winding up is subdivided into two types—members' voluntary winding up and creditors' voluntary winding up. In relation

---

[3] See above, Chs 29, 32.

[4] But see Pt 31 of CA 2006, noted below, paras 33–29 and 33–30.

[5] Insolvency Rules 1986 (SI 1986/1925), amended on numerous occasions, and with the Insolvency Service planning a revised and consolidated version for 2016, to take effect from 1 October 2016. The details of these new Rules can be found at *https://www.gov.uk/government/news/draft-insolvency-rules-sent-to-the-insolvency-rules-committee-for-statutory-consultation* [Accessed 27 February 2016]. The Explanatory Notes indicate that the new Rules (i) consolidate existing rules; (ii) modernise and simplify the language; and (iii) incorporate various changes in the law intended to reduce the burden of red tape (especially in relation to creditors' meetings, which will become the exception, rather than the default rule). To the extent that the rules are consolidated and recast, this is not intended to change the law. Both IA 1986 and the Rules eschew the use of the word "members" and substitute "contributories", thus perhaps giving the misleading impression that it means only members who are called upon to contribute because their shares are partly paid (or in the case of guarantee companies because of the minimal amounts that they have agreed to contribute on a winding up). To avoid this impression, here "members" has been substituted; but this too is not wholly accurate, for "contributories" also includes past members unless they ceased to be members more than 12 months before the commencement of the winding up: see IA 1986 ss.74 and 76; and *Re Anglesea Collieries* (1866) L.R. 1 Ch. 555 CA; and *Re Consolidated Goldfields of New Zealand* [1953] Ch. 689. On the other hand, the benefits of participating as a contributory are denied to those whose obligation to contribute arises from a misfeasance to the company: see IA 1986 s.79(2) in respect of liability under IA 1986 ss.213, 214 (fraudulent and wrongful trading respectively); and *Re AMF International Ltd* [1996] 1 W.L.R. 77 in respect of liability under IA 1986 s.212.

[6] In relation to the winding up of "unregistered companies" (on which see paras 1–31 et seq., above) winding up by the court is the only method allowed: see IA 1986 Pt V. A company incorporated

to companies registered under the Companies Acts which are dealt with in Pt IV of the Insolvency Act, Chs I and VII–X of that Part relate to all three types, except where it is otherwise stated; Chs II and V relate to both types of voluntary winding up; Ch.III relates only to members' voluntary winding up; Ch.IV only to creditors' voluntary winding up; and Ch.VI only to winding up by the court. This arrangement of the sections is not exactly "user friendly" for it means that, to grasp which sections apply to the type of winding up with which one is concerned, it is necessary to refer to various chapters of Pt IV. Nor is life made easier because other Parts of the Act may also be relevant: for example Pt VI on "miscellaneous provisions" and Pt VII on "interpretation for first group of Parts".

As their names imply, an essential difference between compulsory winding up by the court and voluntary winding up is that the former does not necessarily involve action taken by any organ of the company itself, whereas voluntary winding up does. The essential difference between members' and creditors' winding up is that the former is possible only if the company is solvent, in which event the company's members appoint the liquidator, whereas, if it is not, its creditors have the whip hand in deciding who the liquidator shall be. In all three cases, the winding up process is not exclusively directed towards realising the assets and distributing the net proceeds to the creditors and, if anything is left, to the members, according to their respective priorities; it also enables an examination of the conduct of the company's management to be undertaken. This may result in civil and criminal proceedings being taken against those who have engaged in any malpractices thus revealed[7] and in the adjustment or avoidance of various transactions.[8]

Winding up by the court

Grounds for winding up

Under s.122 of the Insolvency Act, a company may be wound up by the court[9] on one or more of eight specified grounds. Of these grounds, by far the most important is ground (f), that the company is unable to pay its debts, and the next most important is ground (g), that the court is of the opinion that it is just and equitable that the company should be wound up. The latter has been dealt with in Ch.20 (where we saw that it may be used as a remedy in cases where members are being unfairly prejudiced or there is a deadlocked management) and in Ch.18 (where we saw that it may be invoked by the Secretary of State following the exercise of his or her investigatory powers). The presence of a minority protection remedy in the Insolvency Act is, in fact, something of an anomaly.

33–3

---

outside Great Britain which has been carrying on business in Britain may be wound up as an unregistered company notwithstanding that it has ceased to exist under the law of the country of incorporation: IA 1986 s.225.

[7] See IA 1986 Pt IV Ch.X.

[8] See IA 1986 Pt VI ss.238–246.

[9] Normally the High Court, but the county court of the district in which the company has its registered office has concurrent jurisdiction if the company's paid-up capital is small and if that county court has jurisdiction in relation to bankruptcy of individuals: IA 1986 s.117.

Who may petition for a court ordered winding up?

33–4   It should be noted that the company itself can opt for winding up by the court, since ground (a) is that the company has by special resolution resolved that the company be so wound up. But normally that is the last thing that those controlling the company will want: winding up by the court is the most expensive type of winding up and the one in which their conduct is likely to be investigated most thoroughly.[10] Alternatively, s.124 makes it clear that a wide range of people may, in different and sometimes specifically limited circumstances, petition for the winding up of a company by the court; the list includes the company's directors, its members,[11] its creditors (including prospective and contingent creditors), and various parties with official public status.[12]

Proof that a company is unable to pay its debts

33–5   Creditors are among those who may petition for a winding up[13] and this they are likely to do once it becomes widely known that the company is in financial difficulties[14]; like a petition for the bankruptcy of an individual, a petition for winding up is the creditors' ultimate remedy. Indeed, about 95 per cent of petitions for court ordered winding ups are by creditors. And although the company itself or its directors[15] or members[16] may petition, the court will be reluctant to grant it on ground (f) if it is opposed by a majority of the creditors.

   The Insolvency Act s.123 affords creditors owed more than £750 a simple means of establishing ground (f), that the company is unable to pay its debts, by serving a "statutory demand".[17] Because of the presumption of insolvency inherent in this, the courts are astute to prevent creditors relying on the sub-section if the debt itself is disputed,[18] or if the sum is disputed so that £750 may not be owed,[19] or if the statutory demand has not been properly put together

---

[10] But it might be used if the court is already involved because the liquidation of the company is part of a scheme requiring its sanction in accordance with the provisions discussed in Ch.29, above.

[11] Notwithstanding anything to the contrary in the articles: *Re Pervil Gold Mines Ltd* [1898] 1 Ch. 122 CA.

[12] And, as we have noted earlier, the Secretary of State (also see ss.124A, 124B), the FCA (also see s.124C), the Regulator of Community Interest Companies, the Official Receiver of the court, and designated officers of the magistrates court, each in specified circumstances.

[13] IA 1986 s.124.

[14] Until then each may try to obtain judgment and levy execution thus getting ahead of the pack.

[15] Prior to the 1985/86 statutory reforms, it was held, somewhat surprisingly, that directors could not apply: *Re Emmerdart Ltd* [1979] Ch. 540. Now they can. For the interpretation of "the directors" see *Re Equiticorp International Plc* [1989] 1 W.L.R. 1010.

[16] But unless the membership has been reduced below two, a member cannot apply unless his (or her) shares were originally allotted to him or have been held and registered in his name for at least 6 months during the 18 months prior to the commencement of the winding up (on which see below) or have devolved on him through the death of a former holder: IA 1986 s.124(2). This is designed to prevent a disgruntled person (e.g. an ex-employee) from buying a share and then bringing a winding up petition (or threatening to do so).

[17] In accordance with IA 1986 s.123(1)(a).

[18] Indeed, a creditor whose debt is bona fide disputed cannot petition at all: *Stonegate Securities Ltd v Gregory* [1980] Ch. 576 CA; *Re Selectmove Ltd* [1995] 1 W.L.R. 474.

[19] *Re A company (No.003729 of 1982)* [1984] 1 W.L.R. 1090.

or properly served.[20] Otherwise, it is usually necessary for the creditor to prove "to the satisfaction of the court that the company is unable to pay its debts as they fall due".[21]

The court's discretion

The court has a statutory discretion to refuse to order a winding up on a contributor's petition if some other remedy is available and it seems that the petitioners are acting unreasonably in seeking this rather drastic option.[22] In addition, the court has an inherent jurisdiction to refuse to make the order if it considers the petition to have been brought for improper or extraneous purposes,[23] and may simply strike out as an abuse of process any petition which is bound to fail.[24]

33–6

Liquidators, provisional liquidators and official receivers

If a winding up order is made, the first step needing to be taken will be to appoint a liquidator to whom, as in all types of winding up, the administration of the company's affairs and property will pass. In contrast with an individual's trustee in bankruptcy, the company's property does not vest in the liquidator[25]; but the control and management of it and of the company's affairs do, and the board of directors, in effect, becomes functus officio.[26] A liquidator may, indeed, be appointed before a final order for winding up is made, for at any time after the presentation of a winding up petition the court may appoint a provisional liquidator, normally the official receiver attached to the court.[27]

33–7

The important role played by official receivers in compulsory liquidations in England and Wales[28] is perhaps the major difference between compulsory and

---

[20] *Re A company (No.008790 of 1990)* [1991] B.C.L.C. 561; *Stylo Shoes Ltd v Prices Tailors Ltd* [1960] Ch. 396.

[21] IA 1986 s.123(1)(e). See *BNY Corporate Trustee Services Ltd v Eurosail-UK 2007-3BL Plc* [2013] UKSC 28; [2013] 1 W.L.R. 1408 SC. While discrediting the "point of no return" test, the Supreme Court affirmed the decision of the Court of Appeal that the ability of a company to meet its liabilities, both prospective and contingent, was to be determined on the balance of probabilities with the burden of proof on the party asserting "balance-sheet insolvency".

[22] IA 1986 s.125(2). This is typically relied on to resist orders made on the "just and equitable" ground, where the unfair prejudice alternative may seem preferable.

[23] *Re Surrey Garden Village Trust Ltd* [1995] 1 W.L.R. 974 Ch; *Re JE Cade & Sons Ltd* [1992] B.C.L.C. 213. On the other hand, if the purpose of the petition is legitimate, it does not matter if the petitioner's motive is malicious: *Bryanston Finance Ltd v De Vries (No.2)* [1976] Ch. 63 CA.

[24] *Charles Forte Investments Ltd v Amanda* [1964] Ch. 240 CA.

[25] Unless the court so orders, as it may: IA 1986 s.145(1).

[26] By common law, even though not made explicit in the IA 1986 for compulsory winding ups: *Re Farrow's Bank Ltd* [1921] 2 Ch. 164 CA (contrast the statutory provision in voluntary winding up (s.90(2)).

[27] IA 1986 s.135.

[28] Scotland manages without them but when the Government, in a desire to reduce civil service manpower and public expenditure, proposed to remove their role in individual bankruptcy there was bitter opposition (not least from the Cork Committee: see Cmnd. 8558, Ch.14) and the proposal was dropped.

voluntary liquidations.[29] Official receivers are officers of the Insolvency Service, an Executive Agency of BIS, attached to courts having bankruptcy jurisdiction.[30] Not only will an OR normally be the provisional liquidator (if one is appointed) but he or she will generally be the initial liquidator and often will remain the liquidator throughout in a court ordered winding up. On the making of a winding up order[31] the OR automatically becomes liquidator by virtue of his or her office and will remain so unless and until another liquidator is appointed.[32] The OR may succeed in getting rid of the office by summoning separate meetings of the creditors and of the members for the purpose of appointing another liquidator.[33] And if that does not succeed,[34] the OR may decide to refer the need to appoint another liquidator to the Secretary of State who may appoint.[35] But, whenever any vacancy occurs, the OR again becomes the liquidator until another is appointed.[36]

The liquidator, provisional liquidator and official receiver are all officers of the court, required to behave as such, if they have been appointed by the court to execute a court ordered compulsory liquidation.

Whether or not the official receiver becomes the liquidator, the OR has important investigatory powers and duties. When the court has made a winding up order, the OR may require officers, employees and those who have taken part in the formation of the company to submit a statement as to the affairs of the company verified by affidavit.[37] It is the duty of the OR to investigate the causes of the failure, and to make such report, if any, to the court as he or she thinks fit.[38] The OR may apply to the court for the public examination of anyone who is or has been an officer, liquidator, administrator, receiver or manager of the company, or anyone else who has taken part in its promotion, formation or management, and must do so, unless the court otherwise orders, if requested by one-half in value of the creditors or three-quarters in value of the members.[39] And

---

[29] In the latter, their role is principally in relation to disqualification of directors under the Directors Disqualification Act (on which see Ch.10, above).

[30] Official receivers have the unique distinction of being entitled to act as liquidators notwithstanding that they are not licensed insolvency practitioners under Pt XIII of the IA 1986: ss.388(5) and 389(2).

[31] Except when it is made immediately upon the discharge of an administration order or when there is a supervisor of a voluntary arrangement under Pt I of the Act, when the former administrator or the supervisor of the arrangement may be appointed by the court as liquidator: IA 1986 s.140.

[32] IA s.136(1) and (2).

[33] See IA 1986 s.136(4) and (5). The nominee of the creditors prevails unless, on application to the court, it otherwise orders (s.139) which it is unlikely to do if the company is insolvent.

[34] Which it may not since both creditors and members may be happy to leave the liquidation to the official receiver since that may prove less expensive.

[35] IA 1986 s.137.

[36] IA 1986 s.136(3).

[37] IA 1986 s.131. See also ss.235 and 236. See *Re Chesterfield United Inc* [2012] EWHC 244 (Ch); [2013] 1 B.C.L.C. 709; *Re Comet Group Ltd* [2014] EWHC 3477 (Ch); *Re Corporate Jet Realisations Ltd* [2015] EWHC 221 (Ch).

[38] IA 1986 s.132.

[39] IA 1986 ss.133 and 134. It is this public examination that is the most dreaded ordeal, particularly if the company is sufficiently well known to attract the attention of the general public and the Press.

if the OR is not the liquidator, the person who is must give the OR all the information and assistance reasonably required for the exercise of these functions.[40]

Once a liquidator is appointed, the process of the winding up proceeds very much as it would in the case of a voluntary liquidation since the objective is identical and the liquidator's functions are the same as those in voluntary windings up, namely "to secure that the assets of the company are got in, realised, and distributed to the company's creditors[41] and, if there is a surplus, to the persons entitled to it".[42] The main difference is that, in a winding up by the court, the liquidator in the exercise of powers given under Sch.4 to the Insolvency Act will more often be required to obtain the sanction of the court before entering into transactions, and that throughout the liquidation process the liquidator will be subject to the surveillance of the OR, acting, in effect, as an officer of the court.

In a court-ordered winding up where the liquidator is not the OR, the creditors may appoint a "liquidation committee", so that they have some formal voice in the liquidation proceedings.[43]

Timing of commencement of winding up

On the making of a winding up order the winding up is deemed to have commenced as from the date of the presentation of the petition (or, indeed, if the order is made in respect of a company already in voluntary winding up, as from the date of the resolution to wind up voluntarily).[44] This dating back is important since it can have the effect of invalidating property dispositions[45] and executions of judgments[46] lawfully undertaken during the period between the presentation of the petition and the order,[47] and of affecting the duration of the periods prior to "the onset of insolvency" in which, if certain transactions are undertaken, they are liable to adjustment or avoidance in the event of winding up or administration.[48]

33–8

Voluntary winding up—general

Instigation of winding up

In contrast with winding up by the court, voluntary winding up always starts with a resolution of the company. In the unlikely event of the articles fixing a period for the duration of the company[49] or specifying an event on the occurrence of

33–9

---

[40] IA 1986 s.143.

[41] Giving priority, of course, to preferred creditors as set out in Sch.6 to IA 1986.

[42] IA 1986 s.143(1). Normally the members (except in the case of non-profit-making or charitable companies) in accordance with their class rights on a winding up.

[43] See below, para.33–15.

[44] IA 1986 s.129.

[45] IA 1986 s.127.

[46] IA 1986 s.128.

[47] Which may be considerable if hearings are adjourned, as is not infrequent.

[48] See IA 1986 ss.238–245.

[49] This is rare but charters of incorporation of limited duration are not uncommon.

which it is to be dissolved,[50] all that is required is an ordinary resolution in general meeting.[51] Otherwise, what is required is a special resolution that the company be wound up voluntarily.[52] In either case the resolution is subject to the requirement that a copy of it has to be sent to the Registrar within 15 days[53] and the company must give notice of the resolution by advertisement in the *Gazette* within 14 days of its passing.[54]

Timing of commencement of winding up

33–10   A voluntary winding up is deemed to commence on the passing of the resolution[55]; there is no "relating back" as there is in the case of winding up by the court. As from the commencement of the winding up, the company must cease to carry on its business, except so far as may be required for its beneficial winding up,[56] and any transfer of shares, unless made with the sanction of the liquidator, is void, as is any alteration in the status of the members.[57]

Members' voluntary winding up

Declaration of solvency

33–11   The most important question which the directors of the company will have had to consider prior to the passing of the resolution is whether they can, in good conscience and without dire consequences to themselves, allow the voluntary winding up to proceed as a members', as opposed to a creditors', winding up. In order for that to occur they, or if there are more than two of them, the majority of them, must, in accordance with IA 1986 s.89, make at a directors' meeting[58] a statutory declaration (the "declaration of solvency") to the effect that they have made a full inquiry into the company's affairs and that, having done so, they have formed the opinion that the company will be able to pay its debts in full, together with interest at the "official rate",[59] within such period, not exceeding 12 months

---

[50] It is possible to conceive of circumstances in which this might be done: e.g. when a partnership converts to an incorporated company because its solicitors and accountants advise that this would be advantageous tax-wise, the partners might wish to ensure that it could be dissolved by a simple majority if they were later advised that it would be better to revert to a partnership.

[51] IA 1986 s.84(1)(a).

[52] IA 1986 s.84(1)(b).

[53] IA 1986 s.84(3).

[54] IA 1986 s.85(1).

[55] IA 1986 s.86. And CA 2006 s.332, which provides that a resolution passed at an adjourned meeting is treated as passed on the day it was in fact passed, prevents companies backdating the commencement of winding up.

[56] IA 1986 s.87(1).

[57] IA 1986 s.88. Contrast the wording of the comparable IA 1986 s.127, above, in relation to winding up by the court: that avoids also any disposition of the company's property (unless the court otherwise orders) which IA 1986 s.88 does not.

[58] This, on the face of it rather curious, use of a board meeting as a venue for the making of statutory declarations ensures that all the directors know what is going on.

[59] i.e. whichever is the greater of the interest payable on judgment debts or that applicable to the particular debt apart from the winding up: IA 1986 ss.189(4) and 251.

from the commencement of the winding up, as may be specified in the declaration.[60] This was the origin of the declaration of solvency now used in the out-of-court procedure for a reduction of capital[61] and in respect of an acquisition of shares out of capital.[62]

The declaration is ineffective unless:

(a)   it is made within five weeks preceding the date of the passing of the resolution; and

(b)   it embodies a statement of the company's assets and liabilities as at the latest practicable date before the making of the declaration.[63]

If a director makes the declaration without having reasonable grounds for believing that the company will be able to pay its debts with interest within the period specified in the declaration, he or she is liable to a fine and imprisonment,[64] and if the debts are not so paid it is presumed, unless the contrary is shown, that the director did not have reasonable grounds for that opinion.[65] It therefore behoves the directors to take the utmost care and to seek professional advice before they make the declaration. Especially is this so because, even if the winding up is a members' one, a licensed insolvency practitioner will have to be appointed as liquidator and the liquidator is likely to detect whether the declaration was over-optimistic long before the expiration of the 12 months. Formerly, small private companies could, and often did, appoint as liquidator one of the directors and, in effect, continued to proceed much as they would have when a partnership was being dissolved. This is no longer possible[66]: despite the efforts begun by the 1989 Act to reduce the burdens on private companies, the Insolvency Act has increased their burdens as regards winding up even if they are quasi-partnerships.

If the professional liquidator, appointed as described below, forms the opinion that the company will not be able to pay its debts within the stated period, he or she must summon a meeting of the creditors and supply them with full information in accordance with IA 1986 s.95 and, as from the date when the meeting is held, the winding up is converted under s.96 from a (solvent) members' to a (insolvent) creditors' voluntary winding up.[67] So long, however, as the liquidator shares the view of the directors (and if they are wise they will have

---

[60] IA 1986 s.89(1). In practice the declaration will play safe and not specify a shorter period than 12 months even if the directors expect that it will be shorter.

[61] See above, para.13–39 et seq.

[62] See above, para.13–4.

[63] IA 1986 s.89(2). The declaration must be delivered to the Registrar within 15 days immediately following the passing of the resolution: IA 1986 s.89(3) and (4).

[64] IA 1986 s.89(4).

[65] IA 1986 s.89(5).

[66] But see below at paras 33–30 et seq. for the possible resort to s.1003 of the Companies Act.

[67] Indeed, it may become a winding up by the court, for a winding up order may be made notwithstanding that the company is already in voluntary winding up and an official receiver, as well as the other persons entitled under IA 1986 s.124, may present a petition: IA 1986 s.124(5). But unless the court, on proof of fraud or mistake, directs otherwise, all proceedings already taken in the voluntary winding up are deemed to have been validly taken: IA 1986 s.129(1).

consulted him, as their proposed nominee, before they made the declaration) all should proceed smoothly as a members' winding up.

Appointment and obligations of liquidator

33–12
The company in general meeting will appoint one or more liquidators for the purpose of winding up the company's affairs and distributing its assets[68] whereupon "all the powers of the directors cease except so far as a general meeting or the liquidator sanctions their continuance".[69] If a vacancy in the office of liquidator "occurs by death, resignation or otherwise" the company in general meeting may fill the vacancy,[70] subject to any arrangement with the creditors.[71] If the winding up continues for more than a year,[72] the liquidator must summon a general meeting at the end of the first and any subsequent year, or at the first convenient date within three months from the end of the year or such longer period as the Secretary of State may allow.[73] The liquidator must lay before the meeting an account of his or her acts and dealings, and of the conduct of the winding up during the year.[74]

When the company's affairs are fully wound up the liquidator must draw up an account of the winding up, showing how it has been conducted and the company's property disposed of, and must call a final meeting of the company for the purpose of laying before it the account and giving an explanation of it.[75] The fact that this meeting is being called is something which is of wider interest than to members alone for, as we shall see,[76] it will lead to the final dissolution of the company. The Insolvency Act provides that it shall be called by advertisement in the *Gazette*, specifying its time, place and object and published at least one month before the meeting.[77] Within one week after the meeting the liquidator must also send the Registrar a copy of the account and make a return of the holding of the meeting.[78]

---

[68] IA 1986 s.91(1).

[69] IA 1986 s.91(2).

[70] IA 1986 s.92(1). The meeting to do so may be convened by any continuing liquidators if there was more than one or by a member: IA 1986 s.92(2).

[71] This reference to "creditors" is presumably to cover the case where the members' voluntary winding up forms part of a reorganisation of one of the types dealt with in Ch.29, above, in which creditors are involved.

[72] Which it may, because although the creditors should be paid within 12 months the subsequent distribution of the remaining assets or their proceeds does not have to be completed within any prescribed time.

[73] IA 1986 s.93(1).

[74] IA 1986 s.93(2).

[75] IA 1986 s.94(1).

[76] See below, paras 33–27 et seq.

[77] What is surprising is that neither the IA 1986 nor the Insolvency Rules seem to require the liquidator to give written notice to the members. If this is not done, it is not surprising that the final meeting is frequently inquorate.

[78] IA 1986 s.94(3) and (4). If a quorum is not present the liquidator must send instead a return that the meeting was duly summoned and that no quorum was present.

Creditors' voluntary winding up

Instigation of winding up

Here, in contrast with members' winding up, the company is assumed to be insolvent and it is the creditors in whose interests the winding up is undertaken and they who have the whip hand. If no declaration of solvency has been made, the company must cause a meeting of its creditors to be summoned for a day not later than the 14th day after the resolution for voluntary winding up is to be proposed. It must cause notices to be sent by post to the creditors not less than seven days before the date of the meeting and must advertise it once in the *Gazette* and once at least in two newspapers circulating in the locality in which the company's principal place of business in Great Britain was situated during the previous six months.[79] This must state either (a) the name of a qualified insolvency practitioner[80] who, before the meeting, will furnish creditors with such information as they may reasonably require; or (b) a place where, on the two business days before the meeting, a list of the company's creditors will be available for inspection free of charge.[81] Further, the directors must prepare a statement of the company's affairs verified by affidavit and cause it to be laid before the creditors' meeting. The directors must also nominate one of their number to preside at the creditors' meeting—an unenviable task which it is the nominee's duty to perform.[82]

33–13

Appointment of liquidator

At their respective meetings, the creditors and the members may nominate a liquidator, and if the creditors do so their nominee becomes the liquidator, unless, on application to the court by a director, creditor or member, the court directs that the company's nominee shall be liquidator instead of, or jointly with, the creditors' nominee, or it appoints some other person instead of the creditors' nominee.[83] Provisions, similar in effect, apply when a members' winding up is converted to a creditors' winding up because the liquidator concludes that the company's debts will not be paid in full within the 12 months, except that the obligations of the directors have to be undertaken by the incumbent liquidator.[84]

33–14

"Liquidation committee"

In a creditors' voluntary winding up,[85] or in a winding up by the court,[86] the creditors may decide at their initial or a subsequent meeting to establish what

33–15

---

[79] IA 1986 s.98(1).
[80] In practice he or she will probably be the person that the directors intend to propose to the company meeting for appointment as liquidator.
[81] IA 1986 s.98(2).
[82] IA 1986 s.99.
[83] IA 1986 s.100.
[84] IA 1986 ss.95 and 96.
[85] IA 1986 s.101, and, when a members' is converted to a creditors' winding up, IA 1986 s.102.
[86] IA 1986 s.141.

used to be called a "committee of inspection" but which the Insolvency Act now calls a "liquidation committee", and, in the case of a creditors' winding up, may appoint not more than five members of it.[87] If they do so, the company in general meeting may also appoint members not exceeding five in number.[88] However, if the creditors resolve that all or any of those appointed by the general meeting ought not to be members of the committee, the persons concerned will not be qualified to act unless the court otherwise directs.[89]

The functions of a liquidation committee are to be found in the Insolvency Rules rather than the Insolvency Act, and for present purposes can be summarised by saying that they give the liquidator the opportunity of consulting the creditors and the members without having to convene formal creditors' and company meetings, and indeed the committee has substantial powers to agree to matters on behalf of the creditors or the company.[90] They also provide additional means whereby the creditors and members can keep an eye on the liquidator. In the latter respect, liquidation committees are, perhaps, likely to be more valuable in creditors' voluntary windings-up (rather than in windings-up by the court) owing to the lesser role played by official receivers.

It may be thought somewhat anomalous that, when the company is insolvent, the members should have equal (or any) representation on the liquidation committee. But the Cork Committee rejected the argument that they should not, because "it is rarely possible to assess the interest of shareholders at the outset of proceedings".[91] This is certainly true. What at the commencement of the winding up would seem to be a clear case of the company's liabilities greatly exceeding its assets (so that the shareholders have no prospective stake in the outcome of the winding up) may turn out otherwise if the winding up is prolonged.[92]

In other respects a creditors' winding up proceeds up to and including the final meeting in much the same way as in a members' winding up, although notably SBEEA 2015 and the proposed new Insolvency Rules 2016 now much reduce the requirements for, and formalities of, any creditors' meeting, including the largely pointless final meeting.[93]

If the required procedures are not followed, the court can give directions under IA 1986 s.166. This was done in *Re WeSellCNC.Com Ltd*,[94] where it was discovered by the appointed liquidator that no declaration of solvency had been

---

[87] IA 1986 s.101(1). In the case of windings-up by the court the position under IA 1986 s.141 and Ch.12 of Pt IV of the Rules is somewhat different and is designed to ensure that, when the official receiver is the liquidator, the committee's functions are performed instead by the Insolvency Service and that, if the liquidator is some other person, it is left to that person to decide whether to convene a meeting of creditors to establish a liquidation committee (unless one-tenth in value of the creditors require him to do so).

[88] IA 1986 s.101(2).

[89] IA 1986 s.101(3).

[90] See, e.g. IA 1986 ss.103, 110, 165(2)(b) and (6), and the Insolvency Regulations 1986 (SI 1986/1994), reg.27(2), and Insolvency Rules 1986 (as amended), r.4.151ff.

[91] Cmnd. 8558, para.939.

[92] But, unless it is, the reverse is at present likely to be the case, resulting in members' windings-up having to be converted into creditors' (or to winding up by the court).

[93] See IA 1986 ss.246ZE and 246ZF, and Insolvency Rules 2016 Explanatory Notes (*https://www. gov.uk/government/news/draft-insolvency-rules-sent-to-the-insolvency-rules-committee-for-statutory- consultation* [Accessed 27 February 2016]).

[94] *Re WeSellCNC.Com Ltd* [2013] EWHC 4577 (Ch).

made; this was therefore necessarily a "creditors' voluntary winding up" pursuant to IA 1986 s.89, but no creditors' meeting had been summoned (and no statement of affairs prepared). Accepting that the company was in fact well and truly solvent with a considerable surplus, and with all creditors having been paid and distributions made to shareholders, the judge declared that the liquidation was a creditors' voluntary winding up, but dispensed with the requirement of a creditors' meeting (and the laying before it of a statement of affairs).

POWERS AND DUTIES OF THE LIQUIDATOR

In order to make possible the orderly winding up the company, the Insolvency Act confers a wide range of powers on the liquidator (ss.165 et seq.), and Sch.4 sets out an extensive list of specific powers, including the power to carry on the company's business, to borrow and grant security over the company's property, and to bring and defend proceedings. Importantly, ss.178 et seq. empowers the liquidator to "disclaim any onerous property", meaning that the liquidator can terminate the company's obligations under any unprofitable contracts, and the contracting counterparty is then left to claim damages as a creditor in the company's insolvency. This power is typically used to terminate the company's leases of premises and other property, on the basis that otherwise the company's available assets would be disproportionately appropriated to the creditor holding the onerous right.[95]

33–16

In exercising these powers, the liquidator typically acts in the company's name[96] (the company retains its separate legal personality until the winding up is completed and the company is dissolved).[97]

The liquidator's duties are owed to the company,[98] not to individual creditors or members, and the liquidator may therefore be sued in misfeasance proceedings under IA 1986 s.212 and held personally liable for misapplication of the company's assets,[99] negligence[100] or breach of fiduciary duties (conflicts and profits rules) owed to the company.

---

[95] *Re Celtic Extraction Ltd* [1999] 2 B.C.L.C. 555 at 568 CA.

[96] With the exception of the exercise of certain statutory powers given specifically to the liquidator: e.g. IA 1986 ss.212, 213 and 214.

[97] But the liquidator may nevertheless sometimes incur personal liability if costs exceed the company's assets: *Re Wilson Lovatt & Sons Ltd* [1977] 1 All E.R. 274.

[98] *Knowles v Scott* [1891] 1 Ch. 717.

[99] *Re Home and Colonial Insurance Co Ltd* [1930] 1 Ch. 12; *Pulsford v Devenish* [1903] 2 Ch. 625.

[100] *Re Windsor Steam Coal Co (1901) Ltd* [1928] Ch. 609.

COLLECTION, REALISATION AND DISTRIBUTION OF THE COMPANY'S ASSETS

Maximising the assets available for distribution

33–17   The task of the liquidator in winding up the company is to finalise the company's affairs, and to get in the company's assets so as to maximise the return to those entitled to the assets on a winding up.[101] In getting in the assets, the liquidator will take control of all the assets owned beneficially[102] by the company and, crucially, will seek to "claw back" assets which the company should not have disposed of (or should not have disposed of on the terms actually agreed) and will also pursue claims against any officers or third parties who may be liable to the company for breach of their duties or for other wrongs.[103] In this way, the asset pool available for distribution will be maximised, to the benefit of those entitled to share in it.

In all of this, a word ought to be said about the position of secured creditors in order to draw attention to the difference between their position and that of general creditors on a winding up, and also the different between their position on a winding up compared with that during an administration. As we saw, so far as the latter is concerned, unless the secured creditors have taken steps to enforce their security prior to the administration, they may be in difficulties in doing so while it lasts.[104] In contrast, on a winding up, a secured creditor is in the enviable position of having the choice of realising its security and, if this does not raise sufficient to pay what is due in full, to prove for the balance, or to surrender its security for the benefit of the general body of creditors and prove for the whole debt.[105] Normally, of course, the former option will be adopted.[106]

Statutory "claw back" and avoidance provisions

33–18   From the date of commencement of the winding up,[107] transfers of shares are avoided,[108] and, for compulsory liquidations, dispositions of the property by the

---

[101] This will be the creditors only, and perhaps not even all of them, if the company is insolvent; and both creditors and members if the company is solvent. Special rules govern the order of distribution, as described below.

[102] Thus excluding assets in the company's possession but, e.g. held on hire purchase, or subject to retention of title agreements; or assets which the company does own, but which are held on trust for the benefit of third parties or are subject to valid security interests in favour of third party creditors.

[103] This latter option for enhancing the asset pool has largely been examined already in earlier chapters: see Ch.9 on fraudulent and wrongful trading.

[104] See paras 32–44 et seq., above.

[105] Insolvency Rules 1986 (as amended) r.4.88. If the winding up follows an administration in which the administrator has exercised his or her powers under Sch.B1, paras 70 and 71 (para.32–45, above) it would seem that the effect of paras 70(2) and 71(3) will be to preserve the security holder's rights by treating the sums mentioned in those subsections as the security in the winding up.

[106] Unless the secured creditor is unusually altruistic or wants to maximise his or her votes at a creditors' meeting.

[107] i.e. presentation of the petition (compulsory winding up, s.129) or passing of the resolution (voluntary winding up, s.86).

[108] IA 1986 ss.88, 127.

company (unless the court otherwise orders)[109] and attachments, distress and execution which have not been completed[110] are void. This can prove awkward, unless the court is minded to approve what has happened. For example, in *Re Gray's Inn Construction Co Ltd*,[111] the company continued to trade unprofitably after the date the winding up petition had been presented; counsel conceded that both sums credited and debited to the company's bank account were "dispositions" which, in the exercise of its discretion, the court mostly declined to validate in the interests of preserving rateable distributions to all creditors rather than enabling some to be paid in full. The banking community has, however, since been reassured that its potential exposure to restitutionary liability of this sort is rather less, with the important Court of Appeal decision in *Hollicourt (Contracts) Ltd v Bank of Ireland*,[112] to the effect that where a bank meets a cheque drawn by the company as its customer (whether the account is in credit or overdrawn), it does so merely as the company's agent; as a result, while there is clearly a disposition in favour of the payee, there is no disposition to the bank itself. Where, on the other hand, the company merely pays sums into its bank account, if the account is overdrawn, then the payment is a disposition to the bank,[113] whereas if the account is in credit then it has been held that the payment is not a disposition,[114] which is perhaps a pragmatic conclusion since the transaction simply converts the company's cash receipts into an equivalent claim against the bank.

Far more significantly, however, the liquidator is also given the right to look backwards, and unwind transactions entered into within prescribed periods before the commencement of an insolvent winding up. We have seen this already in relation to avoiding floating charges created within 12 months (or, in the case of connected persons, two years) of that date.[115] Similar rules enable the liquidator to unwind transactions entered into at an undervalue (s.238) within two years of the onset of insolvency, at a time where the company was already insolvent[116] or became so as a result of the transaction.[117] The court has wide powers in framing its orders to effect restitution of the company's estate.[118] Another provision with the same timing restrictions avoids transactions motivated by the desire to prefer one creditor over other (s.239).

A leading case on both these provisions remains *Re MC Bacon*,[119] the first decided case on s.239. The company, a bacon importer and wholesaler, went into liquidation some time after losing its principal customer. The liquidator challenged a debenture granted to the company's bank during the period where

---

[109] IA 1986 s.127.

[110] IA 1986 s.128, and see ss.183–184 for all winding ups.

[111] *Re Gray's Inn Construction Co Ltd* [1980] 1 W.L.R. 711 CA.

[112] *Hollicourt (Contracts) Ltd v Bank of Ireland* [2001] Ch. 555 CA.

[113] On this point it seems *Re Gray's Inn Construction Co Ltd* [1980] 1 W.L.R. 711 CA, is still good authority.

[114] *Re Barn Crown Ltd* [1995] 1 W.L.R. 147.

[115] IA 1986 s.245, and see above, para.32–14.

[116] On the s.123 test.

[117] IA 1986 s.240(2). There is a rebuttable presumption that this is the case if the transaction is with a connected person.

[118] IA 1986 s.241.

[119] *Re MC Bacon* [1990] B.C.L.C. 324 Ch.

the company was attempting to stay afloat, and when it was probably insolvent or almost so, and could not have continued without the support of its bank. Millett J declined to strike down the debenture, holding that it was not a voidable preference, since the company had not been motivated by a desire to prefer the bank but merely by a desire to avoid their overdraft being recalled; and it was not a transaction at an undervalue,[120] since the granting of security had neither depleted the company's assets nor diminished their value (although the unsecured creditors may well have taken a rather different view of this).

This outcome, although clearly defended in the judgment, raises starkly the substantial practical shortcomings of these claw back provisions. The fact that a preference is only voidable if motivated by the insolvent debtor's desire to prefer creates the rather odd result that if the creditor aggressively demands early repayment under threat of refusing further supplies or services, the payment is unlikely to be caught, to the distinct advantage of the creditor who has now been paid in full and the corresponding disadvantage of the remaining unsecured creditors. By contrast, in both the US and Australia, a disposition is voidable if it has the *effect* of preferring one creditor, whatever the debtor's motivation. And the practical consequences for unsecured creditors where valid late security is granted (presumably security not otherwise caught by the floating charge provisions in s.245) is obvious on the face of it. Interestingly, this odd outcome has been the subject of some attention, obiter only, with Arden LJ suggesting that the grant of a legal mortgage could in the right circumstances be classified a transaction at an undervalue[121]; this then raises the nice question of whether the property disposition required to effect a legal mortgage merits a different treatment from the granting of a security interest by way of charge.

Whatever their shortcomings, however, these claw-back provisions can provide vital additional reserves for creditors, and occasionally for members, but, in conclusion, it might also be noted that their backdated effect sits uneasily with the aims of the protective notice rules which require notice of the winding up to be published in the *Gazette*.[122]

Statutory provisions requiring wrongdoers to make contributions

33–19   We have in earlier chapters already considered the provisions in the Insolvency Act which enable the liquidator to pursue the directors, and sometimes others, making them liable to account or pay compensation or contribute to the assets of the company by way of remedy for their breach of duty (s.212, a purely procedural provision, but one which does give the court a discretion to require compensation to be paid in full or in part "as the court thinks just", although the wrong being pursued is necessarily a general law wrong, either statutory or common law), fraudulent trading (s.213), or wrongful trading (s.214, also allowing the court a discretion to order "such contribution (if any) as the court thinks proper").[123]

---

[120]   Also see *Phillips v Brewin Dolphin Bell Lawrie Ltd* [2001] 1 W.L.R. 143 HL.
[121]   *Hill v Spread Trustee Co Ltd* [2006] EWCA Civ 542 (a case on IA 1986 s.423).
[122]   Companies Act 2006 s.1079.
[123]   See above, Ch.9.

The common law "anti-deprivation principle"

When a company is insolvent, the widely accepted objective of regulated **33–20** insolvency distribution, and the clear goal of the statutory rules just considered, is to ensure that the company's assets are preserved for distribution, and that the distribution, when effected, is for the collective benefit of the company's creditors. Put another way, although it is accepted that some businesses will inevitably fail, even when run without fault,[124] and that innocent parties will then have to bear the resulting losses, the general consensus is that the losses should then be borne rateably.[125]

This then raises the question of whether there is common law support for this endeavour, or whether the task falls entirely to statute. A number of old cases and one House of Lords authority suggest the common law has a role. In *British Eagle International Airlines Ltd v Cie Nationale Air France*,[126] the House of Lords, by a 3:2 majority, overruled both the Court of Appeal and the trial judge to hold that a contractual netting-out agreement between international airline companies could not operate on Air France's insolvency so as to prevent Air France from collecting in full the sums owed to it by certain airlines, even though sums which it owed to different airlines would obviously not be met in full.[127]

Perhaps predictably, the 2008 financial crisis generated litigation which tested the breadth of this common law restriction. The difficult case of *Belmont Park Investments Pty Ltd v BNY Corporate Trustee Services Ltd and Lehman Brothers Special Financing Inc*[128] is the only case to reach the Supreme Court to date. The clause under review was not a *British Eagle* "contracting out" provision (operating against the pari passu rule),[129] but a clause which effected an insolvency-triggered deprivation to the pool of assets available for distribution (as outlawed in *Ex p. Mackay*[130]).[131] The Supreme Court did not follow the analysis in *Mackay*, but gave powerful backing to freedom of contract, and unanimously upheld these "flawed asset" depletion provisions, denying that they offended the common law anti-deprivation principle. The derivatives markets, and perhaps financial markets more generally, applauded the outcome and the freedom it provides to parties to organise their affairs at will, although the result stands in stark contrast to the strict approach still favoured in *British Eagle* type

---

[124] But where there is fault, the defaulters should contribute to the insolvent company's assets, as we have already seen.

[125] With some minor exceptions for identified vulnerable creditors (see below, at para.33–24), and of course the major exception accorded to secured creditors who often escape the burden of shared loses entirely, and in doing so disproportionately reduce the assets available for those who are unsecured (see above, Ch.32).

[126] *British Eagle International Airlines Ltd v Cie Nationale Air France* [1975] 1 W.L.R. 758 HL.

[127] By contrast, had the issue been mutual debits and credits been between Air France and a single third party airline, insolvency set off would have allowed offsetting.

[128] *Belmont Park Investments Pty Ltd v BNY Corporate Trustee Services Ltd and Lehman Brothers Special Financing Inc* [2011] UKSC 38. Commented on in Worthington, "Good faith, flawed assets and the emasculation of the UK anti-deprivation rule" (2012) 75 M.L.R. 112.

[129] The existing approach to which the Supreme Court supported.

[130] *Ex p. Mackay* (1873) L.R. 8 Ch. App. 643.

[131] It achieved this by clauses which altered net liability and flipped non-recourse security arrangements so that third parties were preferred, not the insolvent company (and therefore its general creditors).

arrangements, and also to the broader approach to protecting creditors against flawed asset provisions that is favoured in US bankruptcy legislation.

Benefit of the statutory claw backs and wrongdoer contributions

33–21 Money that is ordered to be paid under most of the sections just discussed (ss.238, 239, 213 and 214, but not s.212) typically goes into the general assets of the company in the hands of the liquidator, not to individual victims of the wrongs, and not, importantly, into the clutches of floating charge holders. This is because the right to sue belongs exclusively to the liquidator, not the company. Receipts from s.212 actions, by contrast, are regarded as the products of a chose in action which belonged to the company before liquidation, and so will be caught by an appropriately worded floating charge.[132]

Proof of debts and mandatory insolvency set off

33–22 The liquidator will only pay those debts which are provable in the insolvency, and proved. The rules specifying which debts these are and how they are proved are contained in the Insolvency Rules 1986.[133] All claims by creditors are provable, whether the debts are present or future, certain or contingent, ascertained or sounding only in damages,[134] provided the company was, on that basis, subject to the claim at the time the winding up commenced.[135] The liquidator has the power to estimate the value of contingent or uncertain debts,[136] and may if necessary apply to the court for assistance.[137]

In a compulsory winding up, the creditors must submit written "proof" or their debts, and in a voluntary winding up the liquidator usually elects to impose the same requirement. The liquidator then examines the proofs and decides whether to admit all or part of the debt or reject it; aggrieved creditors may apply to the court for review.[138] This all sounds eminently simple and sensible, and generally it is, although more complicated facts can throw up conceptually difficult problems. One rule which helps solve some of these problems is the "rule against double proof", which prevents more than one creditor suing the insolvent company for the same debt. This is not as unlikely as it might at first seem. For example, consider the situation where A guarantees a debt which B owes to C. Although this looks like a problem where there are two debtors, not two creditors, looked at the other way it is also true that the primary creditor (C) has a right to sue B on the debt, and the guarantor (A) has a contingent right to sue B to enforce its indemnity rights under the guarantee. If B is insolvent, can A and C both prove in the insolvency? The answer is no, and the rule against double proof prevents

---

[132] *Re Anglo-Austrian Printing & Publishing Union* [1895] 2 Ch. 891. Also see *Re Oasis Merchandising Services Ltd* [1998] Ch. 170.
[133] Insolvency Rules 1986 rr.4.73–4.94.
[134] Insolvency Rules 1986 r.12.3(1).
[135] Insolvency Rules 1986 r.13.12(1).
[136] Insolvency Rules 1986 r.4.86.
[137] IA 1986 s.168(3),(5).
[138] Insolvency Rules 1986 rr.4.73, 4.82, 4.83.

this, denying creditors whose rights relate to the same underlying debt the possibility to prove together. Were it otherwise, it would follow that if a debt were guaranteed by several parties, they could all prove in the liquidation; this makes it clear that the logic delivering this conclusion is flawed. So held the Supreme Court in *Kaupthing Singer & Friedlander Ltd (In Administration); sub nom Mills v HSBC Trustee (CI) Ltd.*[139]

As already noted, secured creditors often elect to stand outside this process.[140]

A further limitation on the amount for which creditors may prove is imposed by **33–23** the mandatory insolvency set off rules,[141] which require the sums due from the creditor to be set off against the sums due from the company where those sums arise from mutual credits, mutual debts or other mutual dealings between the company and the creditor proving in the liquidation. In practice, this arrangement invariably benefits the creditor, because at least some part of the debt due to the creditor from the company is effectively paid off in full by virtue of the set off, and the creditor only has to prove for the remaining balance (which balance will constitute a claim against the insolvency pool, with the inevitable risk of being paid very little, as we shall see).

It is quite hard to find a compelling justification for this rather generous exception to the strict pari passu rule of insolvency distribution, which generally insists that losses are shared rateably, and that all unsecured creditors are only paid pro rata. True, the rule is longstanding,[142] and perhaps it simplifies the work required to be done by the liquidator in accepting proof of debts,[143] and perhaps it reduces exposure and therefore total risk in the financial markets,[144] but it is quite hard to find reasons of fairness[145] which explain why creditors with mutual dealings with the insolvency debtor should effectively be preferred in the sharing of losses by all the debtor's unsecured creditors.[146]

Whatever the justifications for the rule, because it is so advantageous to creditors, they will be keen to classify their dealings as mutual. Often this can be relatively easy to prove. The 1990s litigation surrounding the collapse of the Bank of Credit and Commerce International[147] illustrated that customers who both saved with and borrowed from the bank came within the rules, and so were protected from having to repay their loans in full while only recovering a fraction of their savings as unsecured creditors in the insolvency. The same was true of companies who had borrowed on the security of their own deposits with the

---

[139] *Kaupthing Singer & Friedlander Ltd (In Administration); sub nom Mills v HSBC Trustee (CI) Ltd* [2011] UKSC 48; [2011] 3 W.L.R. 939 SC.

[140] See above, fn.125.

[141] Insolvency Rules 1986 r.4.90.

[142] *Stein v Blake* [1996] 1 A.C. 243 at 251 (Lord Hoffmann).

[143] *National Westminster Bank Ltd v Halesowen Presswork and Assemblies Ltd* [1972] A.C. 785 at 809 (Lord Scarman), although the extent is surely not great.

[144] P. Wood, *Set-off and Netting, Derivatives and Clearing Systems*, (London: Sweet & Maxwell, 2007), para.1–012.

[145] Although, to the contrary, see the claims for fairness in *National Westminster Bank Ltd v Halesowen Presswork and Assemblies Ltd* [1972] A.C. 785 at 813 (Lord Cross); *Stein v Blake* [1996] 1 A.C. 243 at 251 (Lord Hoffmann); *Forster v Wilson* (1843) 12 M. & W. 191 at 204 (Parke B).

[146] Contrast this outcome with that where the debts are not mutual, as in *British Eagle*: see above, para.33–20.

[147] *Re Bank of Credit and Commerce International SA (No.8)* [1998] A.C. 214 HL.

Bank. But where these types of corporate loans were secured not on the borrowing company's own Bank deposits, but on deposits belonging to third parties, typically those of the borrowing company's director, the outcome was different. The directors, so it was held, had not undertaken any personal liability to the Bank; they had merely allowed their assets to be used as security; there was therefore no debt owed by the director to the Bank which could be set off against the debt owed by the Bank to the director in relation to the director's deposit.[148] The net result was that the borrowing companies would have to repay their loans in full (the Bank could not be forced to rely on the director's secured guarantee), and the directors by contrast would recover only minimal sums in the Bank's insolvency. The seeming injustice of the outcome did not escape Lord Hoffmann.

And of course, no set off is possible if the creditor's claims against the company arose after the commencement of winding up,[149] or if the creditor's obligations to the company arose by way of liability for misfeasance (that not being a mutual "dealing" with the company).[150]

Distribution of the company's assets

33–24   Once the liquidator has gathered in the company's assets, they must be distributed in an orderly fashion to those entitled to them. The basic rules are clear. The funds are devoted first, to paying the expenses of liquidation; then to the preferred creditors; then the general unsecured creditors; then the deferred creditors; then, if there is anything left, the members, according to the entitlements associated with their class rights. If the funds are not sufficient to pay all of a particular class in this hierarchy in full, then they share pro rata. It then follows, necessarily, that the classes below that class will receive nothing. It is common knowledge that the unsecured creditors often secure almost nothing in an insolvent liquidation; the banks take the lion's share, as secured creditors, and the preferential creditors take most of the little that remains.

In examining in more detail the order of distribution of the company's assets, recall, first, that the pool of assets includes only assets owned beneficially by the company.[151] Moreover, the claims of secured creditors to the assets specifically secured rank ahead of any claim in the winding up to those secured assets, including even the costs of liquidation,[152] but with the significant exception noted in Ch.32 in relation to floating charge holders, who must cede priority to quite an astonishing number of preferred claims.[153]

The first call for payment from the company's assets are the proper expenses of liquidation, as defined authoritatively by the classes of debts set out in the IR 1986 r.4.218, which also defines the priorities as between these classes of

---

[148] Contrast the outcome in *MS Fashions Ltd v BCCI SA (No.2)* [1993] Ch. 425, where the guaranteeing director had expressly agreed to accept liability as principal debtor for the borrowing company's loan.

[149] Insolvency Rules 1986 r.4.90(3).

[150] *Manson v Smith* [1997] 2 B.C.L.C. 161 CA.

[151] See above, para.33–17.

[152] But if the security is more than adequate to enable full repayment of the outstanding secured debt, then the extra is added to the insolvency pool to be distributed in the same way as the rest.

[153] See above, paras 32–15 et seq.

expenses.[154] There is no additional implicit requirement that to be classed as an expense, the expenditure must also have been, or have been intended to be, for the benefit of the company.[155] These liquidation expenses include the liquidator's remuneration (without which guarantee no liquidator would be persuaded to act), post-liquidation debts and certain pre-liquidation debts.[156] The total size of these claims can be enormous, but perhaps the greatest recent surprise was delivered by *Re Nortel GmbH and Lehman Bros International (Europe) Ltd*,[157] which held that a Financial Support Direction (an order to pay) issued by the Pensions Regulator to a holding company after the commencement of that company's liquidation, was a liquidation expense, and therefore, with the other liquidation expenses, had to be paid in priority to all the company's other unsecured claims. This would clearly have had a dramatic impact on the likely payout to claimants further down the chain, and so it came as some relief when the Supreme Court overturned this decision, in *Bloom v Pensions Regulator*,[158] to hold that the debt was simply one of the company's general unsecured debts, provable and payable in the ordinary course.

Costs of litigation can also be recovered as an expense. After several contrary judicial determinations, the statutory rules have now been changed to make it clear that a liquidator who is sanctioned to bring proceedings directed at clawing back assets or pursuing wrongdoers to compel them to make contributions to the company's assets will be able to recover the costs of such litigation as a proper expense of the liquidation.[159]

33–25

Finally, in the context of expenses, the 1986 Insolvency Act introduced protective provisions to prevent public utilities from putting pressure on liquidators to pay their outstanding pre-commencement debts as a condition of further supply,[160] which effectively enabled such companies to extract preferential repayment of their pre-winding up debts. Any supply which comes after the commencement of winding up will normally rank as a liquidation expense, and so is likely to be paid in full, but suppliers are nevertheless permitted to require the liquidator personally to guarantee payment.[161]

The second call on the pool is to pay the preferential creditors, as defined in IA 1986 s.386 and Sch.6.[162]

---

[154] *Re Toshuku Finance UK Plc, Kahn v IRC* [2002] UKHL 6 (on the relevant corporations tax being such an expense). Also see IA 1986 s.156 and IR 1986 r.4.220(1) which gives the court a discretion in a compulsory winding up to change this order of priority between expenses. But once something is determined to *be* a liquidation expense, the court has no discretion to deny it priority over other creditors' claims which are *not* liquidation expenses.

[155] *Re Toshuku Finance UK Plc, Kahn v IRC* [2002] UKHL 6.

[156] IA 1986 s.156 (compulsory liquidation) and s.115 (voluntary liquidation).

[157] *Re Nortel GmbH and Lehman Bros International (Europe) Ltd* [2011] EWCA Civ 1124 CA.

[158] *Bloom v Pensions Regulator* [2013] UKSC 52; [2014] A.C. 209.

[159] IA 1986 1986 Sch.4 and IR 1986 r.4.218(a) as amended, effectively reversing the outcome in *Re MC Bacon Ltd (No.2)* [1990] B.C.L.C. 607 (Millett J); *Re RS&M Engineering Ltd, Mond v Studdards* [1999] 2 B.C.L.C. 485 CA; and *Re Floor Fourteen Ltd, Lewis v IRC* [2001] 2 B.C.L.C. 392 CA.

[160] IA 1986 s.233(2)(b).

[161] IA 1986 s.233(2)(a).

[162] See the earlier discussion in relation to floating charges, above, para.32–15.

33–26   The third call on the funds is to pay the general unsecured creditors, unless their debts are deferred, as described next below. Recall that the unsecured creditors may also receive a boost to the pool dedicated to them as a result of compulsory contributions of a "prescribed part" from floating charge realisations.[163]

The fourth call on the funds is to pay deferred debts to creditors. There are three classes of such deferred debts. First, interest on all debts payable in the winding up, calculated from the date of commencement of the winding up until the date of payment of the interest, with all relevant debts treated as ranking equally for this purpose.[164] Secondly, money due to a member on a contract to redeem or repurchase shares which was not completed before the winding up.[165] And, thirdly, debts due to members in their character as members, whether by way of dividends, profits or otherwise.[166] The House of Lords had cause to consider the scope of this last category in *Soden v British and Commonwealth Holdings Plc*,[167] and held that it embraced only claims by members based on the statutory contract between the company and its members, and that debts due to members in other capacities, such as lenders to or trade creditors of the company, are not deferred in the same way, but are typically general unsecured debts. In the case in question, the member was claiming damages for misrepresentations which allegedly induced the member to acquire shares in the company. The House of Lords held this was a claim arising outside the context of what is now the Companies Act 2006 s.33 contract, so would not be a deferred debt.

And, finally, whatever remains then goes to the members. Typically the class rights as between shareholders will ensure that the preferential shareholders get preferential rights to the return of their capital, then capital is returned to the ordinary shareholders, and then any surplus after that is usually only for the ordinary members (the preferential shareholders often not being entitled to share in any surplus on a winding up).

It is tolerably clear that the objective behind these distribution rules, so far as they apply on insolvency, is for the company's creditors and members to share the inevitable losses roughly according to pari passu rules, whilst marginally adjusting those rules to specially favour those who have contractually pre-agreed security rights[168] or who are non-adjusting creditors with little wherewithal to negotiate for their own priority (e.g. employees), and, by contrast, to disfavour those with debts that are truly of second order importance (e.g. interest only on all provable debts) or with debts that reflect the claims of members to the company's capital (at least as the position appears on insolvency), which claims should, in the natural order of things, be deferred to the claims of the company's creditors.

---

[163] See above, para.32–17.

[164] IA 1986 s.189.

[165] Companies Act 2006 s.735.

[166] IA 1986 s.74(2)(f).

[167] *Soden v British and Commonwealth Holdings Plc* [1997] 2 B.C.L.C. 501 HL.

[168] The justifications for this are various, not all equally compelling, but the gist is that assets that are owned and worked produce more wealth, which is good for all, and the availability of credit provides liquidity, enabling capital to be used profitably.

DISSOLUTION

After winding up

The normal process

In contrast with the formalities attendant on the birth of a company,[169] its death **33–27** takes place with a singular absence of ceremony. In the case of voluntary liquidations, once the liquidator has sent to the Registrar the liquidator's final account and return,[170] and on the expiration of three months from their registration, the company is deemed to be dissolved,[171] unless the court, on the application of the liquidator or any other person who appears to the court to be interested, makes an order deferring the date of dissolution.[172]

Normally, the position is much the same where the winding up is by the court. Once it appears that the winding up is for all practical purposes complete, the liquidator must currently summon a final meeting of creditors[173] (although this is expected to be abolished in late 2016[174]) which receives the liquidator's report on the winding up and determines whether the liquidator shall be released.[175] The liquidator then gives notice to the court and to the Registrar that the meeting has been held and of the decisions (if any) of the meeting. When the Registrar receives the notice, it is registered and, unless the Secretary of State, on the application of the official receiver or anyone else who appears to be interested, directs a deferment,[176] the company is dissolved at the end of three months from that registration.[177]

If the official receiver is the liquidator, the procedure is the same except that registration is of a notice from the official receiver that the winding up is complete.[178]

---

[169] See Ch.4.

[170] In accordance with IA 1986 s.94 (members' voluntary) or IA 1986 s.106 (creditors' voluntary).

[171] IA 1986 s.201(1) and (2).

[172] IA 1986 s.201(3). It is then the duty of the applicant to deliver a copy of the order to the Registrar for registration: IA 1986 s.201(4).

[173] The relevant statutory provisions appear to apply to windings-up by the court on any ground and whether or not the company is insolvent and not to require any final meeting of the company (as in a voluntary liquidation). If this is correct, it is very curious. In a winding up on the petition of a member on the ground that it is just and equitable, if the company's creditors have been fully paid it is only the members who will have any interest in the result of the winding up.

[174] See the draft Insolvency Regulations 2016: *https://www.gov.uk/government/news/draft-insolvency-rules-sent-to-the-insolvency-rules-committee-for-statutory-consultation* [Accessed 27 February 2016].

[175] IA 1986 ss.146 and 172(8).

[176] IA 1986 s.205(3). An appeal to the court lies from any such decision of the Secretary of State: IA 1986 s.205(4).

[177] IA 1986 s.205(1) and (2).

[178] IA 1986 s.205(1)(b).

Early dissolution

33–28   However, there is a sensible procedure whereby the OR may bring about an early dissolution if it appears that the realisable assets are insufficient to cover the costs of the winding up[179] and that the affairs of the company do not require any further investigation.[180] Before doing so, the OR must give at least 28 days' notice of the proposal to the company's creditors and members and to an administrative receiver if there is one,[181] and, with the giving of that notice, the OR ceases to be required to undertake any duties other than to apply to the Registrar for the early dissolution of the company.[182] On the registration of that application, the company becomes dissolved at the end of three months[183] unless the Secretary of State, on the application of the official receiver or any creditor, member or administrative receiver,[184] gives directions to the contrary before the end of that period.

The grounds upon which the application to the Secretary of State may be made are (a) that the realisable assets are in fact sufficient to cover the expenses of the winding up; or (b) that the affairs of the company do require further investigation[185]; or (c) that for any other reason the early dissolution of the company is inappropriate.[186] And the directions that may be given may make provision for enabling the winding up to proceed as if the official receiver had not invoked the procedure or may include a deferment of the date of dissolution.[187]

There are no similar provisions for early dissolution on a voluntary winding up; once the company has resolved on voluntary winding up it is expected to go through with it. But if there is a vacancy in the liquidatorship and no one can be found who is willing to accept the office because there is clearly not enough left to pay the expenses of continuing it (no insolvency practitioner will accept office in such circumstances unless someone is prepared to pay the costs), it is difficult to see how the Registrar could do other than to strike the company off the register as a defunct company (see below)—as, indeed, that section specifically recognises.

---

[179] In Scotland (lacking official receivers) there is a procedure for early dissolution on this ground alone but it involves an application to the court: IA 1986 s.204.

[180] IA 1986 s.202(1) and (2).

[181] IA 1986 s.202(3).

[182] IA 1986 s.202(4).

[183] IA 1986 s.202(5).

[184] There is an apparent inconsistency between IA 1986 s.202(5) which says that the application can be made by the official receiver "or any other person who appears to the Secretary of State to be interested" and IA 1986 s.203(1) which says that it must be by one of the persons mentioned in the text above. Presumably the Secretary of State will not regard any other person as "interested".

[185] Neither of which is likely to be accepted by the Secretary of State if the official receiver has concluded the contrary.

[186] IA 1986 s.203(2).

[187] IA 1986 s.203(3). There can be an appeal to the court against the Secretary of State's decision: IA 1986 s.203(4).

Striking off of defunct companies

The striking off of defunct companies affords a method whereby a small **33–29** company can, in practice, often be inexpensively dissolved without the expense of any formal winding up. Although the rules are contained in Pt 31 of the Companies Act, rather than in the Insolvency Act, they are an integral part of the machinery by which companies cease to exist.

Under s.1000 of the Companies Act 2006, if the Registrar has reasonable cause to believe that a company is not carrying on business or is not in operation, the Registrar may send to the company a letter inquiring whether that is so. If within a month of sending the letter a reply is not received, the Registrar shall, within 14 days thereafter, send a registered letter referring to the first letter and stating that no answer to it has been received and that, if an answer to the second letter is not received within one month from its date, a notice will be published in the *Gazette* with a view to striking the company's name off the register.[188] If the Registrar receives a reply to the effect that the company is not carrying on business or is not in operation, or if, within one month of sending the second letter, no reply is received, the Registrar may publish in the *Gazette* and send to the company by post a notice that at the expiration of three months from the date of the notice the name of the company will, unless cause to the contrary is shown, be struck off the register and the company will be dissolved.[189] At the expiration of the time mentioned in the notice, the Registrar may, unless cause to the contrary is shown, strike the company off the register and publish notice of this in the *Gazette*, whereupon the company is dissolved.[190]

This section is most commonly used when what has afforded the Registrar reasonable cause to believe that the company is not carrying on business or in operation is the fact that it is in arrears with the lodging of its annual returns and accounts.[191] When so used by the Registrar, it is both a method of inducing those companies that are operating in breach of their filing obligations to mend their ways, as well as a method of clearing the register of companies which are indeed defunct.

A problem discovered by the CLR arises out of the fact that the section requires the Registrar to communicate with the company at its registered address[192] which, for a variety of good and not-so-good reasons, might be an ineffective form of communication. The CLR encouraged the Registrar to experiment with writing also to the directors of the company at their last known residential address, where correspondence to the company's address was returned, before striking the company off, and it appears that this measure has had some success and is now part of the Registrar's administrative practice.[193] The advantage is that it may avoid striking off companies which are in fact still operational, and thus avoid the expense of seeking to restore them to the register

---

[188] CA 2006 s.1000(2). From hereon references to "the Act" are to the Companies Act 2006 unless the context otherwise requires.
[189] CA 2006 s.1000(3).
[190] CA 2006 s.1000(4)–(6).
[191] See para.21–34.
[192] See CA 2006 s.1002 for the methods of communication with the company.
[193] Final Report I, para.11.20.

when they discover they have been struck off (see below). From 11 July 2014 onwards, the Registrar may now send communications electronically, as opposed to communicating via letters by post.[194]

However, the above procedure can also be used to deal with the situation referred to above when winding up proceedings have been started but insufficient resources are available to complete them.[195] If the Registrar has reasonable cause to believe either that no liquidator is acting or that the affairs of the company are fully wound up and, in either case, that the returns required to be made by the liquidator have not been made for a period of six consecutive months, the Registrar shall publish in the *Gazette* and send to the company or the liquidator (if any) a like notice which causes the company to be dissolved.[196]

Voluntary striking off

33–30   Further, the predecessor to the above sections used to provide companies with a method of dissolving without the expense of a formal winding up and especially without the appointment of an insolvency practitioner to oversee the process: the directors of a company which had ceased trading would simply write to the Registrar inviting the Registrar to exercise the statutory power to strike it off. Under the Deregulation and Contracting Out Act 1994,[197] perhaps somewhat ironically, this practice was formalised in the statute and it is understood that the Registrar discontinued the old practice and will now only entertain formal applications for striking off under the new procedure. The new sections in large part replicated the old practice, so the change helped to make this course of action more transparent.

The statutory procedure enables a company,[198] which has not traded or carried on business[199] during the previous three months, to apply by its directors (or a majority of them)[200] to the Registrar for the company to be struck off. The directors must ensure that notice of the application is given to a list of persons, who include, notably, its creditors (contingent and prospective creditors being embraced within the term),[201] its employees, the managers and trustees of any pension fund and its members.[202] On receipt of the application the Registrar publishes a notice in the *Gazette* stating that the company may be struck off and inviting any person to show cause why it should not be.[203] Not less than three

---

[194] Companies (Striking Off) (Electronic Communications) Order 2014; ss.1000 and 1002 as amended.
[195] CA 2006 s.1001.
[196] CA 2006 s.1001(1)–(4).
[197] CA 2006 s.13 and Sch.5.
[198] Under s.652A of the 1985 Act the provision applied only to private companies, but s.1003 of the 2006 Act applies to public companies as well.
[199] What this involves (or rather does not involve) is set out in some detail in s.1004. A change of name during the period will bar an application even if there has been no trading: s.1004(1)(a).
[200] CA 2006 s.1003(2).
[201] CA 2006 s.1011.
[202] CA 2006 s.1006(1).
[203] CA 2006 s.1003(3).

months later the Registrar may strike the company off and, on publication of a notice to this effect in the *Gazette*, the company is dissolved.[204]

The purpose of requiring notice to be given by the directors is obviously to see if the people most likely to object to the striking-off in fact oppose this course of action, but the legislation lays down no particular procedure which the Registrar must follow in dealing with objections. The fact that the company has creditors clearly does not debar it from using this procedure (otherwise the Act would not require notice to be given to creditors) but it is not intended to be used in place of liquidation where the company has substantial assets or liabilities outstanding at the time of application.[205] Nor may an application be made for striking off where the company is currently the subject of an application to the court for consent to a compromise or arrangement under the Companies Act[206] or other procedures for handling insolvent companies contained in the Insolvency Act 1986.[207]

The range of matters which the Registrar must keep in mind upon an application under s.1003 is much reduced by the provision that dissolution under the procedure does not inhibit the enforcement of any liability of the erstwhile company's directors, managing officers or members, so that these people cannot escape their common law or statutory duties by causing their company to be dissolved.[208] Moreover, a company dissolved under the new procedure, like companies dissolved in other ways, may be restored to the register in certain circumstances, a topic to which we now turn.

RESURRECTION OF DISSOLVED COMPANIES

A contrast between the death of an individual and that of a company is that, without divine intervention, a dissolved company can be resurrected. Following the CLR,[209] the Act made two innovations in this area. First, it introduced a limited form of administrative restoration to the register, a result which had previously required a court order. Secondly, a single method of court restoration replaced the formerly existing two methods, which the courts had found some difficulty in making sense of and which overlapped to a considerable extent.

33–31

---

[204] CA 2006 s.1003(4),(5).

[205] If the company has assets and the application is successful, these will become bona vacantia upon the dissolution of the company and so pass to the Crown or one of its emanations: s.1012. Chapter 2 of Pt 31 contains provisions dealing with the methods and consequences of disclaimer by the Crown of bona vacantia, which are not dealt with here.

[206] See Ch.29, above.

[207] CA 2006 s.1005—or the Insolvency (Northern Ireland) Order 1989. If an application for striking off has been made and any of these events occurs or the company does any of the acts mentioned in s.1004 (see fn.199, above), the then directors of the company are under a duty to withdraw the application: s.1009.

[208] CA 2006 s.1003(6)(a). The same provision applies to a striking off under the Registrar's own motion: s.1000(7)(a).

[209] Final Report I, paras 11.17–11.19.

Administrative restoration

33–32   The new form of administrative restoration applies only where the company was dissolved by the Registrar under the provisions relating to defunct companies.[210] Thus, it does not apply to either dissolution after winding up or to voluntary striking off. The conditions for administrative restoration to the register confine it to situations where the company was carrying on business or in operation at the time it was struck off.[211] Thus, the main purpose of administrative restoration is to deal more cheaply with reversing a striking off which, ideally, should not have occurred in the first place. For probably the same reason, the application for restoration may be made only by a former director or former member of the company,[212] but no application for restoration may be made more than six years after its dissolution.[213] If any of the company's property is vested in the Crown as bona vacantia,[214] the Crown's representative must consent and the applicant must offer to pay any costs of the Crown in relation to the application and, more importantly, dealing with the property during the period of dissolution.[215] Finally, the applicant must deliver to the Registrar such documents as are necessary to bring the company's public records up-to-date and to pay any penalties outstanding at the time the company was dissolved.[216]

If these conditions are met, the Registrar is under a duty to restore the company to the register.[217] Notice of the decision must be given to the applicant and the restoration takes effect when that notice is sent.[218] Public notice must be given of the restoration.[219] The effect of restoration is that the company is deemed to have continued in existence as if it had not been struck off.[220] However, any consequential directions, if necessary, for placing the company and all other persons in the position (as nearly as possible) as they would have been in, had the company not been struck off, are to be given, not by the Registrar, but by a court, to which application may be made within three years of the restoration.[221]

---

[210] CA 2006 s.1024(1).

[211] CA 2006 s.1025(2). See *Re Priceland Ltd* [1997] 1 B.C.L.C. 467.

[212] CA 2006 s.1024(3)—who must provide a certificate that he or she has the necessary standing: s.1026.

[213] CA 2006 s.1024(4). By that time, it may be thought, those involved with running the former company will have accepted its striking off.

[214] See fn.205, above.

[215] CA 2006 s.1025(3),(4).

[216] CA 2006 s.1025(5).

[217] CA 2006 s.1025(1). There is no formal right of appeal if the Registrar refuses to restore, but (a) presumably judicial review is available; and (b) the disappointed applicant could re-apply under the court-based procedure (see below) and is given 28 days to do so, even if the six-year time limit for that procedure has expired: s.1030(5).

[218] CA 2006 s.1027(2).

[219] CA 2006 s.1027(3),(4).

[220] CA 2006 s.1028(1)—but not so as to make the company liable for failing to file reports and accounts during the period of dissolution (s.1028(2))! Section 1033 deals with the situation where the company cannot be restored under its former name without a breach of s.66 because another company now has that name. See Ch.4.

[221] CA 2006 s.1028(3), (4). The statute appears not to undermine the distinction drawn by the courts between dissolution after winding up and administrative striking off (of either type) in terms of the

Restoration by the court

The two court-based restoration methods previously provided were contained in ss.651 and 653 of the 1985 Act. The current provisions are based on those of s.653, the somewhat simpler procedure. The court-based procedure applies to all forms of dissolution[222] and a much wider range of persons may apply for restoration. These include not just former directors or members, but any creditor of the company at the time of its dissolution, anyone who but for the dissolution would have been in a contractual relationship with it, any person with a potential legal claim against the company, any manager or trustee of an employee pension fund, any person interested in land in which the company had an interest, and the Secretary of State.[223] This caters for a much wider range of reasons for wanting to have the company restored to the register, a common one being in order to sue or assert a right against it. Normally, such persons must act within six years of the date of dissolution,[224] but a claim for restoration in order to bring a claim for damages for personal injury against the company may be made at any time.[225]

33–33

The court has power to order restoration if (a) in the case of striking off of a defunct company, it was carrying on business or in operation at the time; (b) in the case of voluntary striking off, the conditions for such a striking off were not complied with; and (c) in any other case the court thinks it just to do so.[226] Restoration, if ordered, takes effect from the time the court's order is delivered to the Registrar and the Registrar must give publicity to the order in the usual way.[227] The effect of restoration by the court is the same as with administrative restoration,[228] and the court may give the necessary directions to effect the principle that the company should be treated as if never dissolved.[229]

---

impact of restoration on action purportedly taken by the company in litigation during the period of dissolution. In the latter case subsequent restoration automatically validates action during the period of dissolution: *Top Creative Ltd v St Albans DC* [2000] 2 B.C.L.C. 379 CA.

[222] CA 2006 s.1029(1).

[223] CA 2006 s.1029(2).

[224] CA 2006 s.1030(4). Under the 1985 Act the limitation period for s.651 claims was two years and for s.653 claims 20 years. Six years is the period in England and Wales after which many claims against the company will be time-barred.

[225] CA 2006 s.1030(1)—though if the claim against the company appears to the court to be time-barred, it may not order the restoration of the company: s.1030(2), (3). However, the court may order under s.1032(3) that the period of dissolution should not count for limitation purposes in respect of the personal injury claim. See *Smith v White Knight Laundry Ltd* [2002] 1 W.L.R. 616 CA.

[226] CA 2006 s.1031(1). The wording of the section suggests that the third ground applies as well to a defunct company and voluntary striking off where the particular ground set out in (a) or (b) is not available. On the exercise of the court's discretion see *Re Priceland Ltd* [1997] 1 B.C.L.C. 467; *Re Blenheim Leisure (Restaurants) Ltd (No.2)* [2000] B.C.C. 821; *Re Blue Note Enterprises Ltd* [2001] 2 B.C.L.C. 427.

[227] CA 2006 s.1031(2),(3).

[228] CA 2006 s.1032(1),(2).

[229] CA 2006 s.1032(3). See *Joddrell v Peaktone Ltd* [2012] EWCA Civ 1035; [2013] 1 W.L.R. 784 CA at [40]–[49] (Munby LJ) for a description of the retrospective effect of s.1032. Note, too, *County Leasing Asset Management Ltd v Hawkes* [2015] EWCA Civ 1251, where a limitation direction preventing time running granted in favour of a restored company.

CONCLUSION

33–34   This final chapter has considered the means by which the lives of companies are deliberately brought to an end, against their natural characteristic of perpetual succession. The overview has been brief, especially given the great complexities and doctrinal and policy difficulties in the current structure. The source of those difficulties is, at root, the result of a simple problem: mostly when companies are wound up, they are insolvent; their liabilities exceed their assets. In such circumstances, innocent parties will inevitably face losses, whatever efforts are made to protect them (and we have seen the lengths to which the winding up regime goes in that regard). Perhaps then the best the law can do is try to minimise obvious unfairness and ensure the rules, even if not perfect, are at least certain. Given the entrepreneurial imagination of commercial parties and our flexible and sophisticated mix of statute, contract and property law rules, this is a challenge, but one against which the current winding up regime might be judged to be doing tolerably well.

INDEX

This index has been prepared using Sweet and Maxwell's Legal Taxonomy. Main index entries conform to keywords provided by the Legal Taxonomy except where references to specific documents or non-standard terms (denoted by quotation marks) have been included. These keywords provide a means of identifying similar concepts in other Sweet and Maxwell publications and online services to which keywords from the Legal Taxonomy have been applied. Readers may find some minor differences between terms used in the text and those which appear in the index. Suggestions to *sweetandmaxwell.taxonomy@thomson.com*.

All references are to paragraph number

Gower's Principles of Modern

Tenth Edition